Fashion Sourcebook 1920s

Published by Fiell Publishing
www.fiell.com

A catalogue record for this book is available from the British Library

Project concept: Charlotte Fiell
Editorial: Charlotte Fiell & Emmanuelle Dirix
Preface text: Charlotte Fiell
Introductory text: Emmanuelle Dirix
Captions & Biographies: Emmanuelle Dirix & Charlotte Fiell
Picture Sourcing: Charlotte Fiell & Clementine Fiell
Indexing: Isabel Wilkinson
Design: Guy Jackson
Proofing & copy-editing: Rosanna Negrotti
Reprographics & imaging: DL Imaging & Jane Brodie
Production: Zoë Fawcett

Printed in Italy
ISBN 978-1-906863-48-7

Fashion Sourcebook 1920s

Edited by Charlotte Fiell & Emmanuelle Dirix

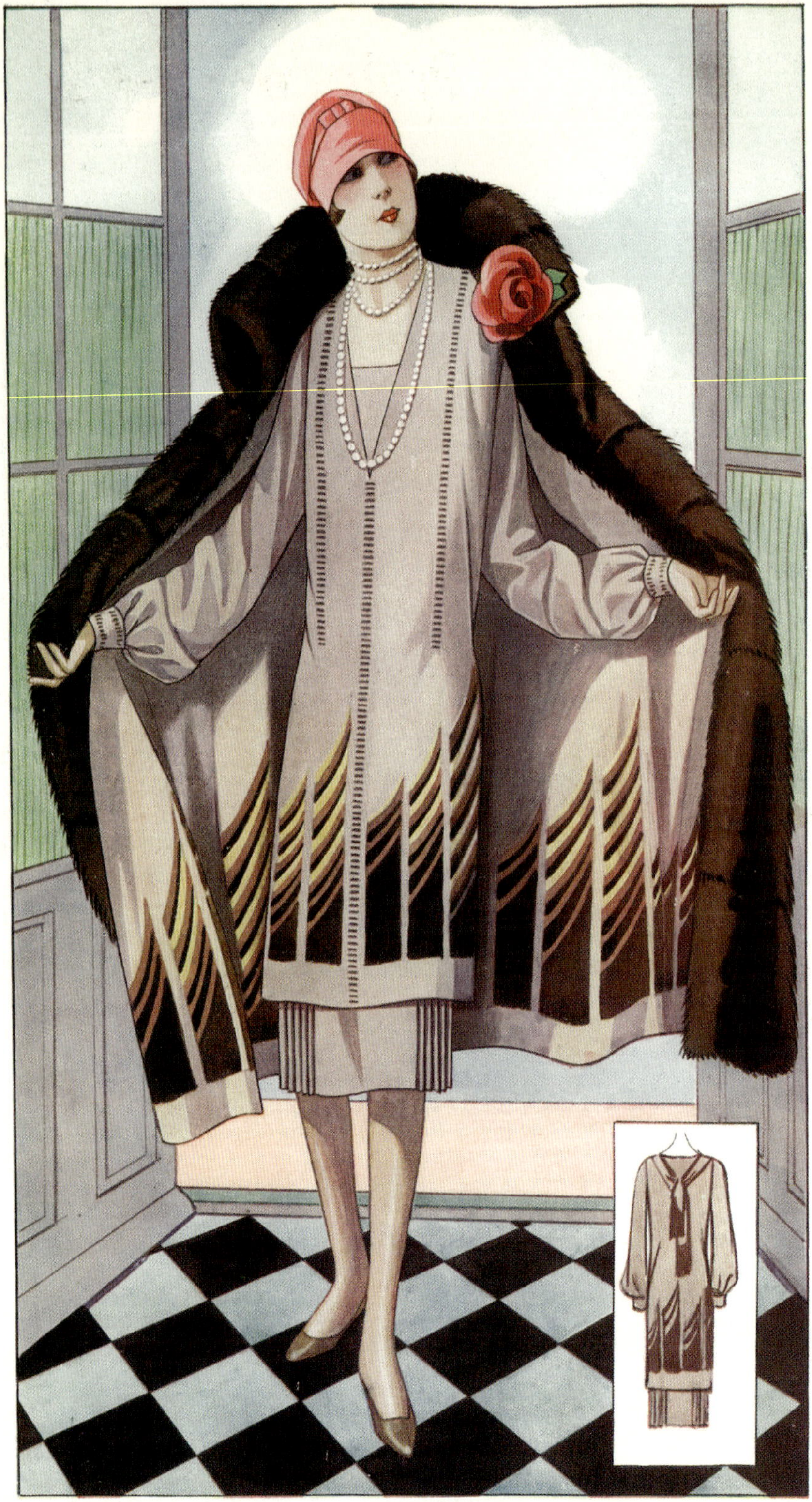

ENSEMBLE CONFORTABLE POUR LES JOURS FROIDS
ÉXÉCUTÉ AVEC LES " PIQUES ZIBLIKASHA "

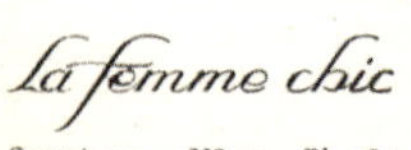

Supplément - N° 190. Pl. 154.

Preface

The 1920s were a period of unbridled optimism with people looking to the future and putting their trust in technological progress. The First World War had changed the very fabric of society, and in its wake had brought women unprecedented freedoms and, of course, this was reflected in the fashions they chose to wear. From silk sack dresses and T-bar shoes to tight-fitting cloche hats and elegantly casual sportswear, the fashionable flappers and 'bright young things' of this era sought youthful clothes that were in accord with their more liberated lives. In so doing, they helped to democratise fashion for the first time in its history.

This unique publication seeks to explore this phenomenon by showcasing over 600 original photographs and skillfully drawn illustrations that reveal the extraordinary diversity of styles that were offered by not only the well-known Parisian haute couture houses but also by department stores and mail-order catalogues. In addition, the introductory essay seeks to contextualise and explains the driving socio-economic and political forces of this period in relation to its fashions. It is hoped, therefore, that this publication will not only allow the rediscovery of many fashion designers and fashion illustrators, whose undeniable talents have until now been lost in the mists of time, but that it will also help bring a wider understanding of Art Deco fashion.

By comprehensively documenting the elegant silhouettes, exquisite detailing and masterful tailoring of 1920s fashions this book should prove to be an invaluable source of information for fashion historians, whilst also providing a rich font of inspiration for fashion designers, vintage collectors and, of course, all self-respecting fashionistas.

Left
'Comfortable' dress and coat ensemble for 'cold days' with 'Piques Ziblikasha' motifs. *La Femme Chic*, 1926

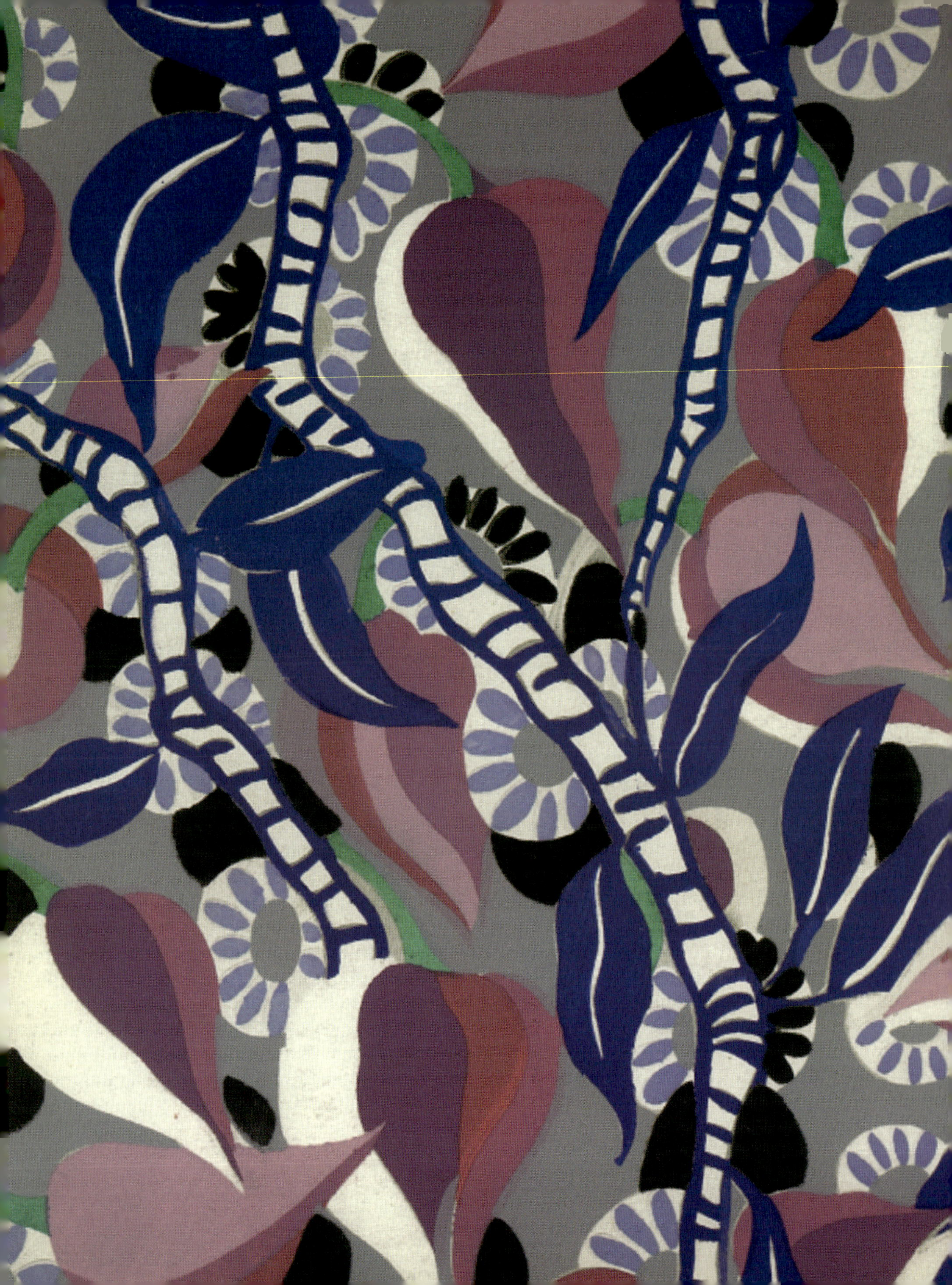

Contents

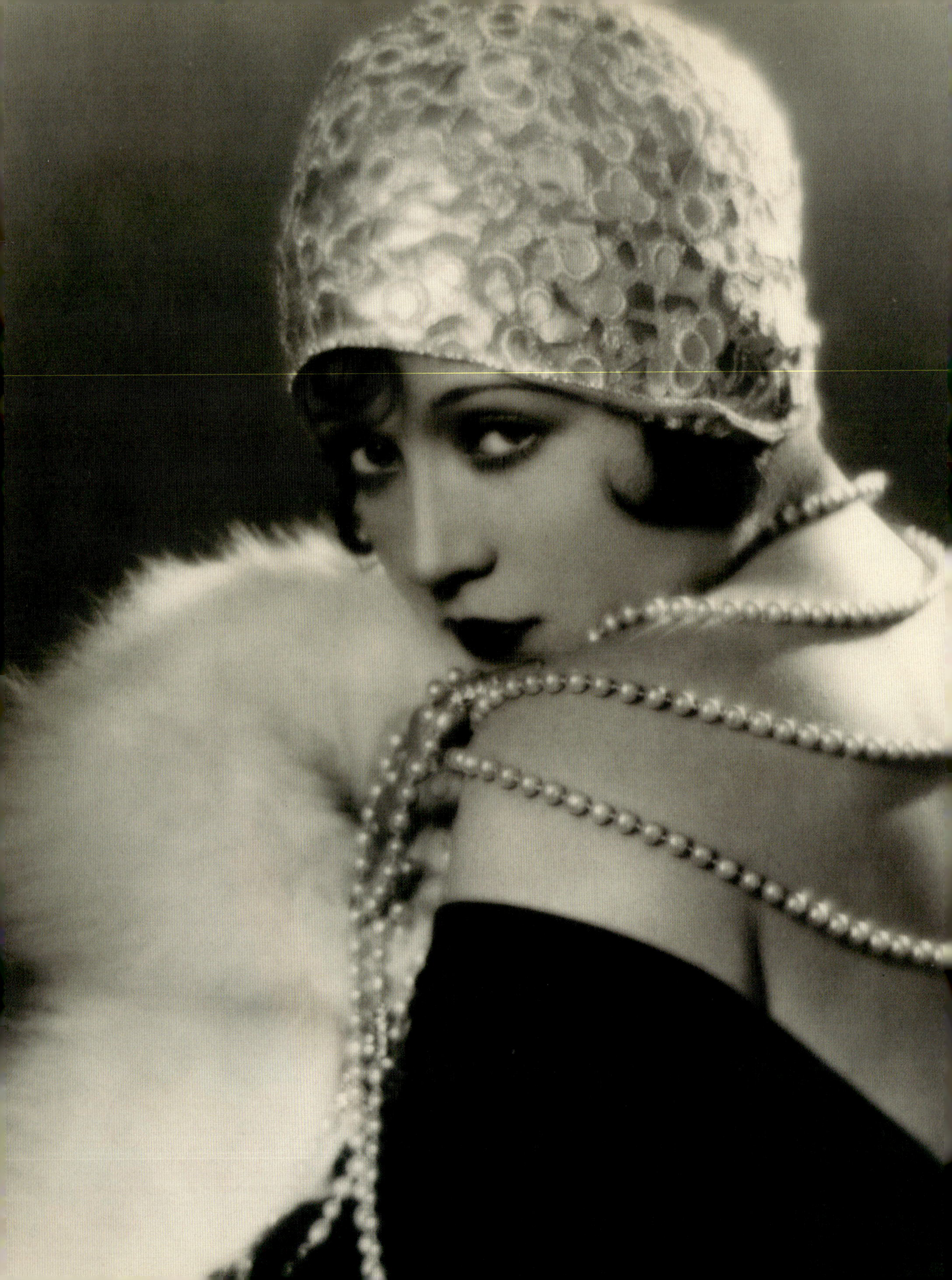

Twenties Fashion

Fashionable Timing

This sourcebook looks in detail at fashion in a single decade, between the years 1920 and 1929. It's a common historical technique to parcel time up into the ten-year periods that fall between years ending with a nought, naming the decades (the 1920s, '30s, '40s and so on) accordingly. It is as if the passing of time can be organised into unique and distinctive eras. Unfortunately, the reality is somewhat different – the events that form both our culture and history don't always follow the calendar: things happen, often before or after a decade begins. In fashion terms, the Twenties is no exception to this, and many of the ideas, developments and designs we associate with that period of time actually took root much earlier. The story of fashion in the 1920s starts, in fact, a good few years before the decade began.

This is not to say that the 1920s did not offer anything new; indeed quite the contrary, and each page of this book tells a story of the new and the modern. But the novelty and modernity of the looks presented here needs to be seen in a much wider context if we are to understand quite how radical and exciting these fashions were for women.

This should come as no surprise; common sense alone tells us that fashion is rarely revolutionary in the way that the fashion press and popular histories would have us believe. In the same way that rarely one designer is responsible for changing the entire look of a woman's wardrobe, so no one simple set of dates can be stuck on such a process either. Thus for example the straighter silhouettes that would later become the boyish shapes we associate with flappers had been introduced as early as 1907; the bright colours and exoticism so synonymous with 1920s evening wear, had equally been introduced into high fashion via various other broader cultural influences, as well as through the work of progressive fashion designers in previous decades. But it would take the 1920s to synthesise all these elements in the jubilant post-war zeitgeist, which provided such a fertile breeding ground for the magnificent and varied fashions we associate with the age.

In this way, it's not the fact that many of the characteristics of 1920s fashion make their debut in earlier years that is important, but the fact that they all come together in that period. The Twenties was a time of significant social and cultural shifts, and as such is an exciting and unique era to study through the lens of fashion.

The story of fashion is never just a story of fashion. Fashion is part of culture, and it's not created in an ivory tower. It is a visual language, full of clues we can read about the morals and values of the society that produced it. By examining fashion, we can study the very fabric of society, and this book allows for exactly such a study. A rich collection of fashion images from the 1920s is contained within these pages, including some photographs but predominantly fashion illustration (photography had yet to supersede illustration – colour stocks had still to be invented, and it was impossible to capture fine detailing on film). However, this is not a limitation, indeed quite the opposite; for the style of illustration and imaginary backdrops that were used to show off the garments, all contribute to a much wider picture. Indeed, because the illustrations are taken from such a broad spectrum of publications – from the high-end, hand-tinted Parisian *Gazette du Bon Ton* featuring the most luxurious offerings from the haute couturiers, to the ready-to-wear fashions in the Printemps department store catalogue – it paints a realistic picture of what women from different echelons of society wore and allows us to make a visual comparison of how elite fashions came to influence cheaper ready-made garments.

Previous page and below
Silent film starlet, Sally O'Neil wearing a lame cloche hat and strings of pearls, c.1925

A mauve crepe Georgette evening dress embroidered with large silver pearls, draped at the side held by ribbons in different shades. *Dernières Creations*, c.1923

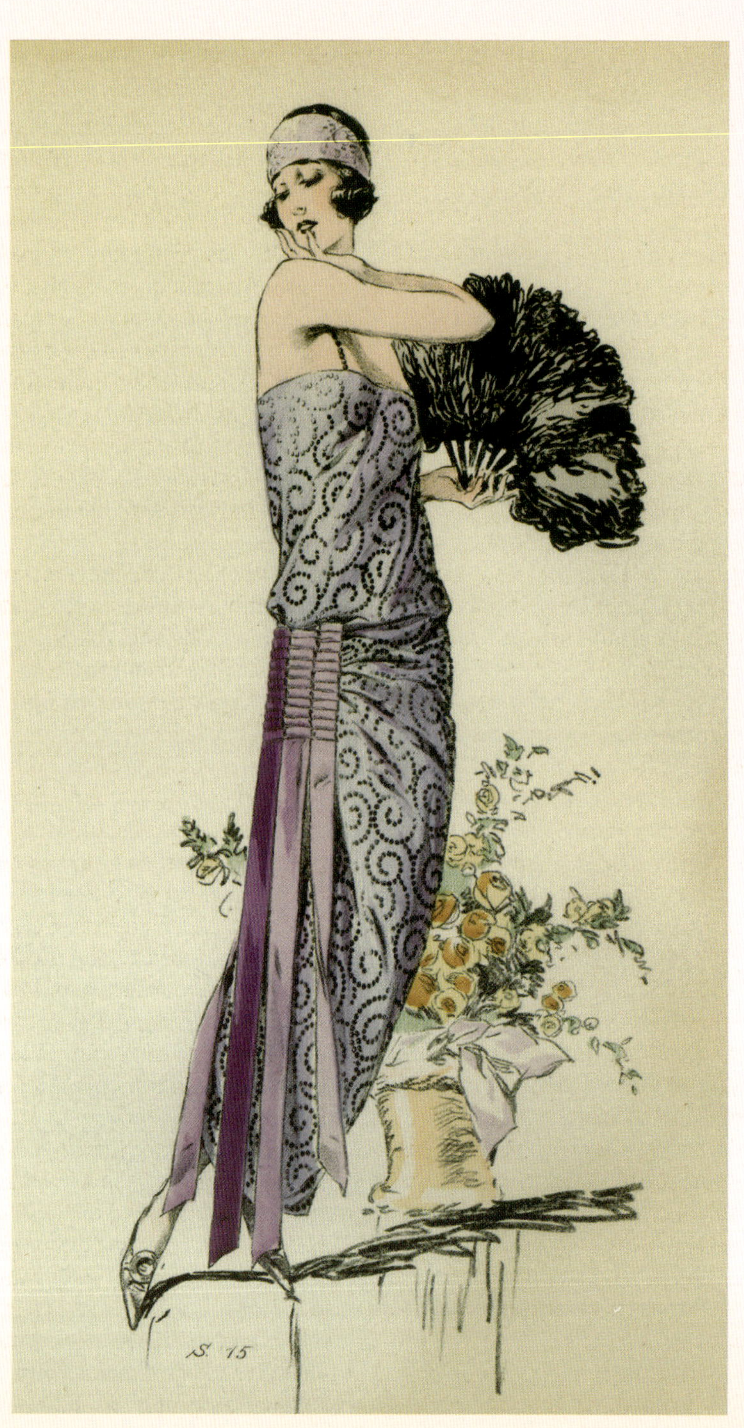

The Flapper & 1920s Style

No other decade is quite so alive and vivid in popular consciousness as the 1920s; Art Deco, the Jazz Age, *les années folles,* the Roaring Twenties. Numerous films, TV shows, exhibitions and books have been dedicated to the era and the various movements within it, and fashion plays a pivotal role in all of these. It would be impossible to picture the Twenties without imagining young flappers in beaded dresses, with short hair and boyish silhouettes dancing the night away. Puffing on cigarettes and flashing their knees as they danced, their genteel, Edwardian mothers would have been appalled.

However, this new female brazenness is only part of a larger, more complex and more varied picture of women, their fashions and their bodies. So to focus only on the flapper would be to miss, and misinterpret so many other important developments at the time. The emphasis placed on the flapper as the key female and fashion figure of the age is largely due to the fact that our conception of the Twenties has been heavily influenced and shaped by the moving image, by both the films made at the time and later cinematic interpretations.

In terms of film, the 1920s opened with Olive Thomas starring in 'The Flapper' as a naughty schoolgirl who falls from grace. The film cemented the link between the name, the look and the shocking identity of the flapper; a concept that was disseminated throughout the decade by amongst others Clara Bow in 'The Plastic Age' and 'It'; Louise Brooks in 'Pandora's Box' and 'Diary of a Lost Girl'; and Joan Crawford in 'Our Dancing Daughters'. The flapper was young, boyish, had buckets of sex appeal, paraded around in shift dresses and fur coats, and wore cloche hats over her bobbed hair. It's that same flapper we're still having projected at us decades later in films such as 'Thoroughly Modern Millie', 'Bugsy Malone', and in endless television episodes of 'Agatha Christie's Poirot'.

It is because she was so shocking and distinctive in comparison to her mother and grandmother, and because she represented the extremes of the new, more liberal post-First World War society, that she has become the predominant focus of so many studies of the 1920s. Too often any Twenties woman in a cloche hat, bobbed hair and make-up is labelled a flapper, and indeed many of the women in the photographs and drawings in this book have the look we associate with these temptress sirens – but one should not confuse a look with an attitude.

It's as much a cultural misunderstanding to think that all women in the 1920s dressed in close-fitting hats and bold, colourful beaded dresses, as it is to imagine that all women who did dress this way were flappers. For many, the wearing of these sack dresses and cloche hats and the adoption of a cropped hairstyle was simply and only an act of fashion.

It's important to acknowledge that what we see on the pages of this book are without exception the young dressed in the latest fashions. Just as today's fashion magazines do not represent accurately what the majority of the population looks like and how they dress, neither did magazines then. By definition fashion is only interested in the new, the luxurious and the beautiful. What we see on the pages of magazines then as now is an ideal. A mature woman in the 1920s was as unlikely to dress in a short beaded dress, as a mature woman now would indulge in the latest hot-pants craze. Nevertheless, these images give us not only an idea of what the young were wearing, but they also provide an insight into the looks and beauty ideals women aspired to, and how these trickled down into mainstream fashions.

However, what is different about the Twenties

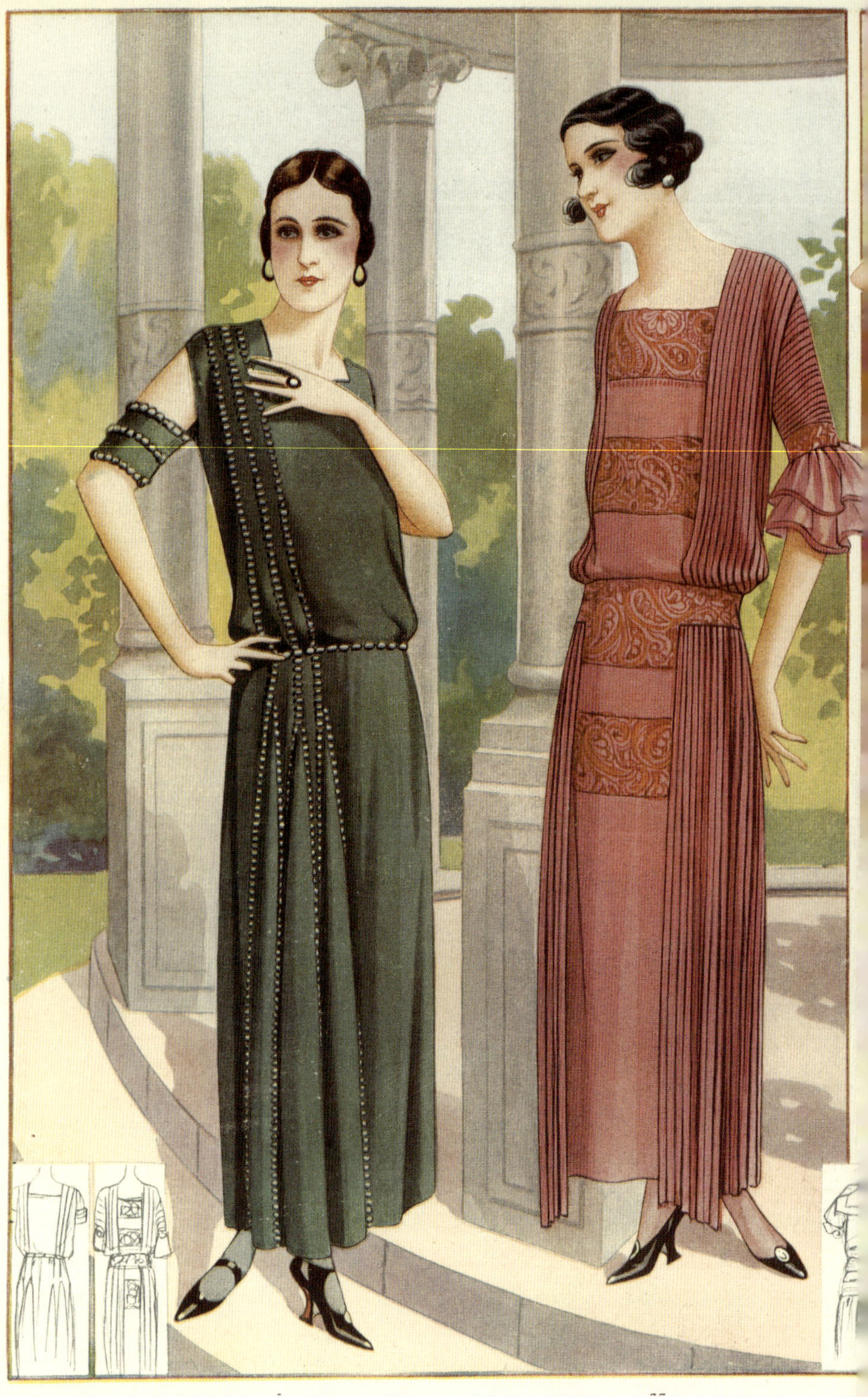

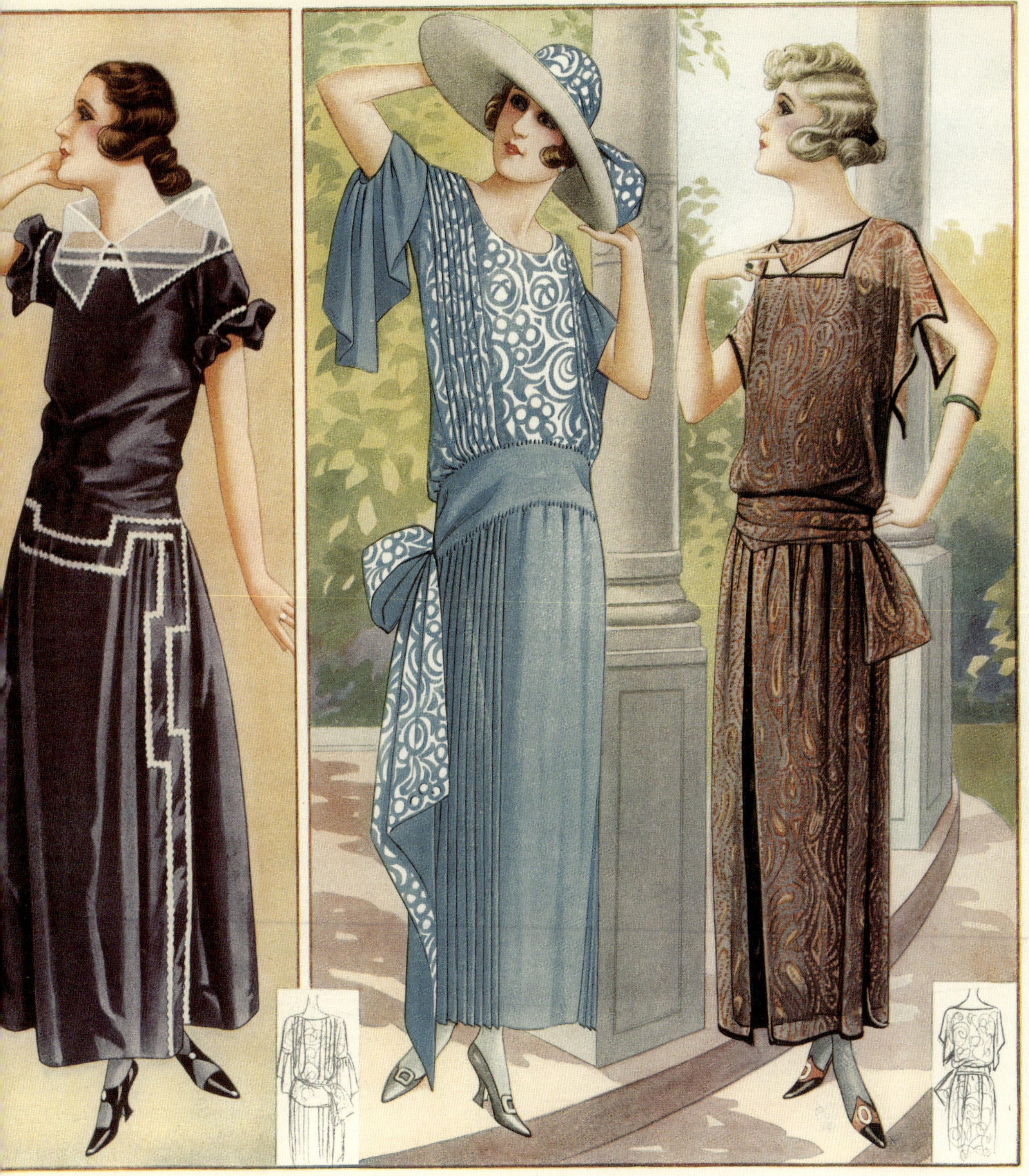

Previous page
Green day dress, black dress with gauze collar and chiffon dress with paisley patterning – all by Berthe Hermance, together with a pink dress with pleating and a blue and white dress with matching hat.
La Femme Chic, 1923

is that it represents the first time in history when the printed press constitutes a more or less accurate representation and recording of what 'ordinary' young women wore – unlike in previous decades and centuries when representations were limited to the elite. High-end luxury fashion publications reserved for the wealthy were joined by hosts of cheaper women's magazines and fashion-oriented newspaper supplements aimed at lower income groups. Advances in printing techniques and a lowering of printing and publishing costs played an important part in this process.

More importantly, though, the 1920s saw the rise of what could be termed the 'democratisation' of fashion. For the first time in history, women who had been previously excluded from partaking in fashion for economic and practical reasons, were now allowed to indulge and incorporate fashionable dressing into their lives.

In terms of cause and effect, more women could afford fashion, so publications to 'aid' them in their purchasing choices appeared in droves. This desire for fashion at the lower levels of the market is also clearly noticeable in the much-expanded fashion sections of the 1920s mail-order catalogues of companies such as Sears, Roebuck & Co. and McCall's in the USA, and in the catalogues of the London-based department stores in the United Kingdom.

New Wardrobes for New Women

The main reason for this wider participation and interest in fashion can be attributed largely to the fact that the style of clothing women aspired to wear had simplified significantly from the elaborate pre-war haute couture gowns into fashions that were looser, more comfortable and, crucially, easier to make and copy. It would however be too restrictive to look at this democratisation only from a design point of view. The Great War, which ended only two years before the decade began, did precipitate changes and simplification in design due to material shortages; but all of these shifts were only really possible and acceptable because the idea of what a woman should be was also shifting concurrently.

The war introduced many changes into the lives of women of all classes. Working-class women not only found themselves often solely in charge of the household, they were also catapulted from the kitchen sink to employment outside the home, and so were now often the principal breadwinners. Employment opportunities varied from posts in heavy industry, to driving ambulances or buses, to working in soup kitchens or taking on clerical roles. Of course, many women had worked prior to the war but their employment opportunities, such as domestic service, were very limited and more often than not gave them little responsibility or autonomy.

Many middle-class women experienced a similar change in experience and opportunity, and contrary to popular belief even upper-class women took on work – although this tended to be more genteel than the types of work their social inferiors were involved in. Not only did women perform vital tasks during the war, for the first time many experienced both social and financial freedom. Needless to say, in the post-war period women were not particularly inclined to meekly return to their previous domestic duties of baking and childrearing once their men came home.

This active employment of women also had wider social repercussions. Not only did they have more freedom in terms of finances and employment, social shifts were taking place both out of necessity and from changes in public attitude, which had a positive and liberating impact on women's lives.

By the 1920s the city was no longer the exclusive domain of men, largely because the war had put an end to the chaperoning system. Previously, ladies of a certain class never did anything so disreputable as venture into a city alone; post-1918, etiquette and social mores had to be relaxed as women needed to be able to travel to work. The simple visibility of women in cities effected a change in attitude towards them from men – they were no longer the invisible domestic angels of earlier times, they were the women who had gone to work and kept the country going in times of crisis.

It also needs to be remembered that prior to the war, the suffragette movement had already gained momentum and that the end of the war saw women over the age of 30 granted the vote in Britain – with the USA following a year later. The 1920s, however, would see a revival of women's demands for equal status culminating in the 'Flapper Vote' of 1928 that granted suffrage to all British women over the age of 21, giving them full equality with male voters. These changes were not only legislatively important, socially they granted women more recognition and gave them freedoms they had not previously experienced. The press termed this newly liberated creature 'The New Woman'.

This 'New Woman' was heavily discussed in the contemporary press, indicating quite how much had changed. She was 'New' because she was able to take on new roles and responsibilities, because she was no longer stuck at home, and because she was not simply going to shut up and return to her former life. This 'New' liberated woman needed and got a wardrobe to match– one of simpler, more comfortable elegance to correspond with her freer life.

The Fashionable Silhouette

By the start of the 1920s the fashionable female silhouette lacked structure, to the extent that dresses were often referred to as 'sacks', 'chemises', 'slips' or 'slip-overs', indicating the absence of a defined shape and the ease with which one put them on and took them off.

This silhouette, which was radically different from the more traditional pre-war heavily corseted Edwardian fashions, had developed out of the changes introduced by haute couturier, Paul Poiret. As early as 1907 he created a vogue for neo-classical empire line garments, which instead of accentuating and enhancing curves favoured a vertical silhouette. His designs abandoned the S-line corset; he himself hailed this as his triumph, however it needs to be noted that for the majority of women, save those with boyish narrow figures, this was simply replaced with straighter elasticated corsets that flattened curves and were not necessarily any more comfortable. By 1912 this straighter shape triumphed and could be seen in nearly all the Parisian couturiers' collections, and only the very old or old-fashioned had not adopted this modern, straighter look.

The change in garment length was also a process that started prior to the Twenties. Hemlines had started creeping up during the war in response to shortages and rationing; the straighter silhouette remained popular and developed into more architectural proportions for the same reason. By 1913 women were showing a little ankle; by 1918 fashionable dresses and coats had made their way up to calf length, which is where with some minor variations they would remain until around 1921 or 1922.

Whilst Poiret's pre-war creations introduced simplicity of silhouette, they were ultimately still very intricate, elaborate and extremely luxurious in regards to construction, materials and embellishment. Nevertheless his idea of

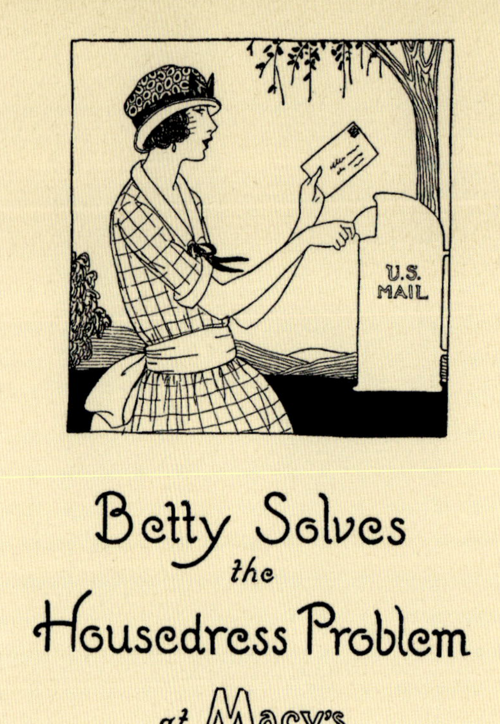

Left and right
Cover of Macy's mail order catalogue, 1923

A postcard of a young woman working behind her Singer sewing machine. A beaded dancing dress is displayed on a dressmaker's dummy to her side. c.1925.

simplifying female attire was taken up and taken to new levels by Gabrielle 'Coco' Chanel. She was a visionary designer in her own right but she also understood the new ideas and needs brought about by the war and translated these into dress.

Chanel grasped that the leisure classes who escaped to Biarritz and Deauville to sit out the war in style now had a greater need for comfortable yet elegant clothes as they discovered the joys of outdoor activities. For this reason, Chanel opened her first fashion boutique in Biarritz in 1915, presenting elegant leisurewear in jersey, a material formerly only used for workwear and undergarments. Chanel openly acknowledged her designs drew inspiration from servant girls, fishermen and ordinary workfolk. Her *pauvre chic* or 'poverty chic' fashions were a great success but one should not be fooled: her garments were anything but pauvre; they were exquisitely made and often lined in more luxurious material such as silk. Nevertheless, the changes she introduced to the silhouette were paramount to establishing the 1920s fashionable shapes.

Another factor that contributed to the acceptance and popularity of more comfortable and simpler fashions was the fact women had to take on men's roles during the war: working in factories, driving buses and ambulances, and most importantly coming to the aid of the war industries. At work they were required to wear practical clothing that would not endanger them, so for many factory girls full knickers, a variation on bloomers, became their working uniform. These aptly named 'slack girls' would never have dreamt of wearing their workgear in public as it was purely utilitarian and therefore not only un-ladylike but also unfashionable. However the comfort introduced by these slacks was something that held great appeal, and indeed something women were not about to abandon after the war.

What more and more of these young women were doing after work hours also had its impact on the need for comfort: dancing. The years just before, during and after WWI saw a growing interest and enthusiasm for dancing, but a far more energetic style of dancing than that of previous generations. Whilst traditional dances did not disappear, they were joined and later superseded by new exotic styles such as the Tango, which had originated in the brothels of Buenos Aires and which required garments that allowed for higher and wider leg movements.

Another less credited yet no less important factor that influenced the development of freer

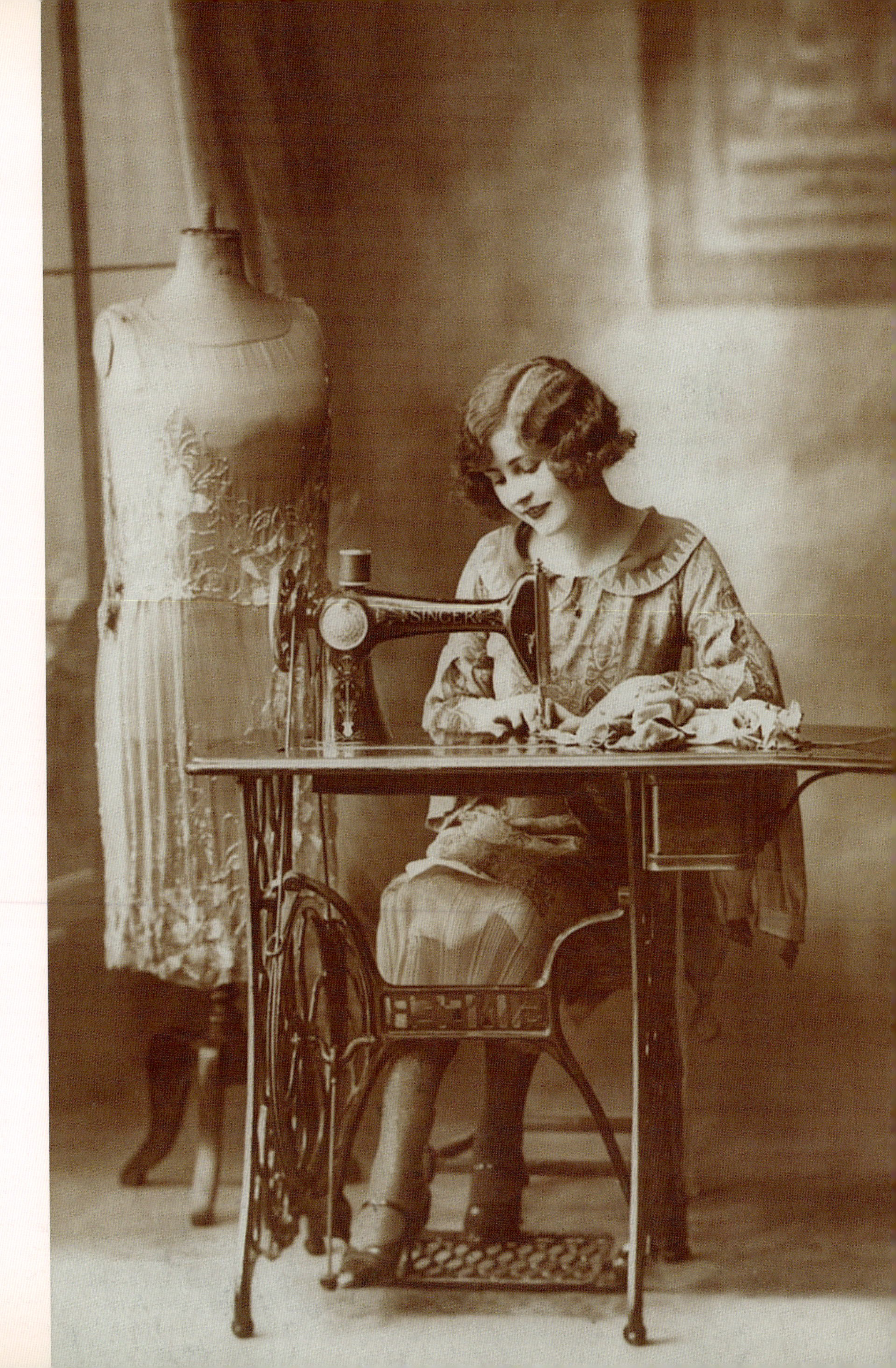
SINGER

styles was the growing impact and importance of avant-garde art movements. Artists frequently collaborated with fashion designers as fashion illustrators, textile designers and on actual fashion designs, but it was the ideas of these new and exciting art movements that really infused fashion with renewed dynamism and alternative approaches and aesthetics; the Wiener Werkstätte, Russian Constructivism, Fauvism, Futurism, Cubism… in varying capacities all contributed to a rethinking of various aspects of fashion design including the simplified female silhouette.

The Futurists, Constructivists and Cubists were the most influential in this context. Both the Russian and Italian avant-garde saw its involvement with fashion as an ideological engagement: fashion was part of a bigger social revolution and needed therefore to be rethought. Even though their ideology differed considerably in political terms, both Constructivist and Futurist artists conceptualised and designed garments for workers which were utilitarian yet original, and functional yet beautiful. The use of bold blocks of colour characterised designs of both movements and was derived from Cubist art; by using these blocks of contrasting colour, a need for a simpler cut was paramount as the body effectively became a canvas. Even though these utopian 'art' designs were rarely put into commercial production, they nevertheless functioned as a catalyst for debate about appropriate female attire. More importantly they also served as inspiration for designers who took on board the notion of 'the body as canvas', and went on to incorporate and popularise straighter female silhouettes into fashion.

So by the time we reach the Twenties, ideas of liberation, simplification and practicality were firmly established as the dominant fashion trend. Furthermore, thanks to the popularisation of Chanel's leisurewear designs, comfort was no longer the antithesis of luxury, elegance and high fashion.

Stylish Participation

This simplification of garment structure had two clear consequences, which directly impacted on the spread of fashionable clothing. Firstly, there was an exponential rise in home dressmaking, as women with little or even no experience could now tackle a dress project with relative ease and produce simple garments. Women's magazines aimed at the lower middle and upper working classes featured droves of adverts for dressmaking courses organised by a variety of private and public institutions.

These adverts often featured illustrations of fashionable ladies carrying armfuls of garments accompanied with taglines such as, 'I made all these clothes myself quite easily and they cost me less than half the usual price'. The adverts not only played on women's desire to be part of fashion, but also the novelty of their ability to now be part of it. The use of slogans and articles explaining that home dressmaking was in fact a money-saving activity clearly shows that there was still anxiety and trepidation on the part of many women that fashion was frivolous and wasteful; something for the elite only and not for the likes of them. For that reason, the reassurance that being fashionable was morally acceptable had to be sold to women as a responsible domestic and economic act.

The second consequence of the silhouette simplification was the easier, high-volume production of ready-to-wear clothing. The war had greatly advanced production techniques as large volumes of quality uniforms had to be produced in small spaces of time. This

Below
A green silk evening dress with pointed skirt panels. *How to make Dresses the Modern Singer Way*, The Singer Company, c.1924

Below
An orange and blue patterned tunic dress, draped at the back and worn over an orange wide-sleeved underslip. *Short Cuts to Home Sewing*, The Singer Sewing Company, c.1923

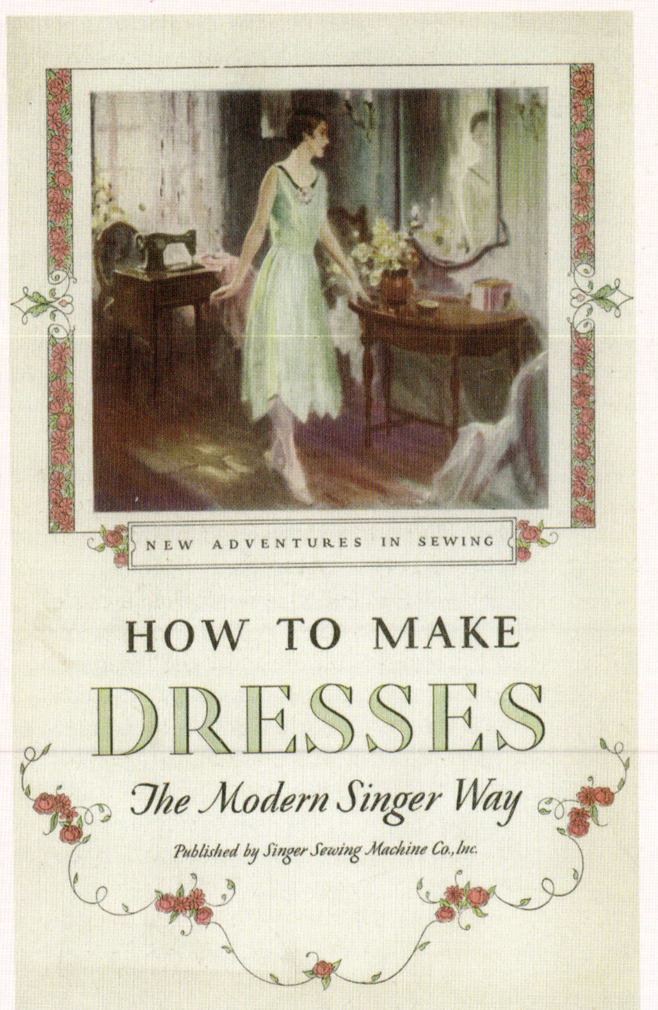

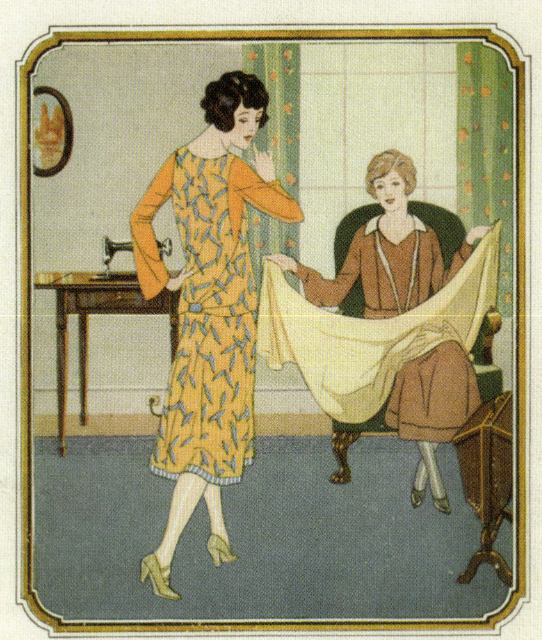

Short Cuts
to
Home Sewing

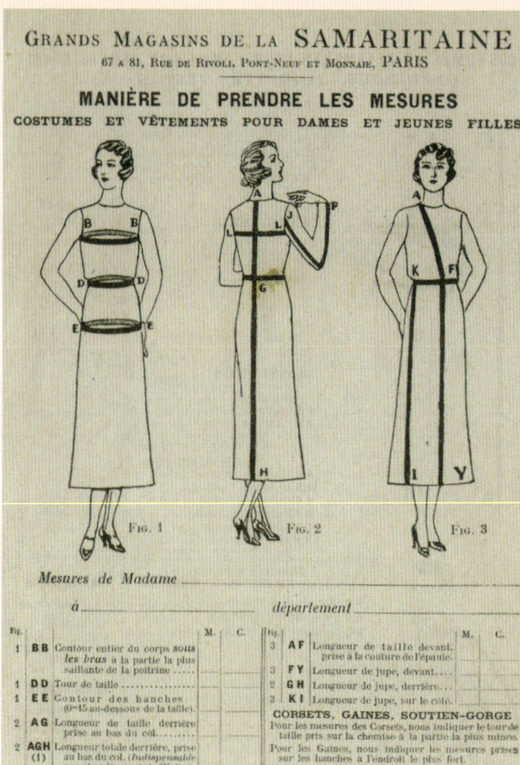

Grands Magasins de la SAMARITAINE
67 à 81, Rue de Rivoli, Pont-Neuf et Monnaie, PARIS

MANIÈRE DE PRENDRE LES MESURES
COSTUMES ET VÊTEMENTS POUR DAMES ET JEUNES FILLES

Mesures de Madame ____________

à ____________ *département* ____________

Fig.			M.	C.
1	BB	Contour entier du corps ***sous les bras*** à la partie la plus saillante de la poitrine		
1	DD	Tour de taille		
1	EE	Contour des hanches (0m15 au-dessous de la taille).		
2	AG	Longueur de taille derrière prise au bas du col.........		
2	AGH (1)	Longueur totale derrière, prise au bas du col. (*Indispensable pour les vêtements de fillettes*).		
3	AF	Longueur de taille devant, prise à la couture de l'épaule.		
3	FY	Longueur de jupe, devant....		
2	GH	Longueur de jupe, derrière...		
3	KI	Longueur de jupe, sur le côté.		

CORSETS, GAINES, SOUTIEN-GORGE

Pour les mesures des Corsets, nous indiquer le tour de taille pris sur la chemise à la partie la plus mince.

Pour les Gaines, nous indiquer les mesures prises sur les hanches à l'endroit le plus fort.

Pour les Soutien-gorge, nous donner contour de

Left
Sizing guide. Grand Magasins de la Samaritaine, c.1928

knowledge and experience would be applied to the growing ready-to-wear industry of the 1920s.

Sizing had also got somewhat better, although there was still no such thing as standard dress sizes and most manufacturers made up their own sizing system which was often based on little, inaccurate or no body data at all. However as fashions at the start of the Twenties were rather vertical and voluminous this was not an immediate problem – only later in the decade when dresses became more closely fitted to the torso did these inadequate sizing systems cause problems and endless home alterations. Correct sizing and perfect tailoring remained the premise of haute couture, and whilst fashionable styles were now easier to copy, the perfect fit remained a marker of distinction

Production & Consumption

The ready-to-wear industry flourished in the Twenties, especially in America through the development of national markets accessed through chain stores and mail-order catalogues, and the impact of these cheaper, fashionable clothes was clearly felt.

In addition to these production developments the spread of new low-cost man-made fibres resembling satins and silks, allowed more women to consume the latest fashionable styles at a relatively low cost. In particular rayon, which had been developed and improved since the late 19th century and was known as art-silk (artificial silk) allowed the mimicking of a luxury fabric at low cost. This meant that both the handy housewife and ready-to-wear manufacturers could now copy silk garments previously reserved for the elite at a fraction of the cost.

Art-silk may not have felt like the real deal, but it looked sufficiently like silk to achieve a look of luxury and fashionability. Contemporary sources complained it was always a little too much on the wrong side of shiny, in particular when used for stockings, but the practical and fashionable young lady solved this problem by powdering her stockings with face or talcum powder. This not only shows ingenuity but also points to women's increasing engagement with and knowledge and understanding of fashion.

Despite the huge growth in the ready-to-wear market, the 1920s did not see the disappearance of the middle-market's vogue for custom-made dresses. This section of the trade catered to ladies who wanted garments made to their size and specification, but who could not necessarily afford haute couture. Within the custom-made or couture business there were great differences in pricing bands. Those operating at the cheaper end of the scale mostly provided copies of Parisian models only, whilst at the top end of this market these copies were complemented with ranges of own in-house designs.

Only the elite could afford haute couture and, until the 1920s, even they mostly only relied on it for luscious evening wear; for everyday clothes such as street dresses, tea frocks and sportswear these women employed their local dressmaker. After the War there was little demand for luxurious evening wear, and so couturiers set out to supplant these seamstresses by designing women's entire wardrobes – from the overcoat down to the negligee. These wearable, everyday designs were less expensive than their previous offerings, and brought haute couture into the wealthy clientele's everyday dress. So even within the lofty world of haute couture, we see some sort of democratisation taking place.

However, the majority of women remained almost entirely reliant on home dressmaking – only buying new and ready-made items such as accessories, stockings and jewellery to finish off their outfits.

Paris – Capital of Fashion

Even though London and New York had a booming fashion industry, fashions with a capital 'F' were set if not dictated by Paris. If a garment did not come from the French capital, it had, at the very least, to be inspired by a creation from the haute couture salons of Paris – otherwise, it simply wasn't fashion. The city was the epicentre of elegance and taste and had been the proprietor of all things luxurious and *de rigueur* since the court of Louis XVI.

This reputation was cemented in the 19th century by the establishment of haute couture as a creative industry by Charles Frederick Worth, who introduced seasonality and fashion collections and firmly linked art to commerce.

As true fashion could only originate in Paris, the elite travelled twice a year from all over the globe to marvel at and purchase the latest fashions by their favoured haute couturiers. This fashionable set was joined by department store owners and ready-to-wear manufacturers, who also travelled far and wide to find out what their clients back home in Buenos Aires, Havana or New York would be clambering for in the coming season. Copying had been a part of the haute couture industry from its beginnings, and fully aware that imitation would happen no matter what, Parisian maisons sold official models for duplication in an attempt to regulate and capitalise on this common practice. Bonded models were original couture garments, and were sold to manufacturers and retailers who used them as a source for line-for-line copies; toiles which were muslin models sold for similar purposes. The former were aimed at the upmarket department stores such as Harrods and Macy's, which advertised their lines as official Chanel, Patou and Lanvin models and copied the garment as closely as possible; the latter were aimed at the middle-market ready-to-wear industry, which used them as inspiration for cheaper copies produced in high volume. The salons even offered paper patterns produced for the lower end of the same market, demonstrating that Parisian fashion was as much about artistry and design excellence as it was a well organised and profitable industry – an industry capitalising on its position and reputation.

The very word 'Parisian' was synonymous with all things luxurious, elegant and of good taste, and advertisers exploited this in every way possible. The emerging beauty and cosmetics industry relied heavily on its links – either real or imagined – with Paris, but equally products as banal as chocolate mints or diet pills could be turned into something exotic and special merely by adding the word Parisian into the advertising copy.

In this way, through a simplification in silhouette, an organised ready-to-wear industry and new materials, Parisian couture, which had previously been exclusive to the upper classes and the ultra wealthy, now trickled down to a much wider section of society.

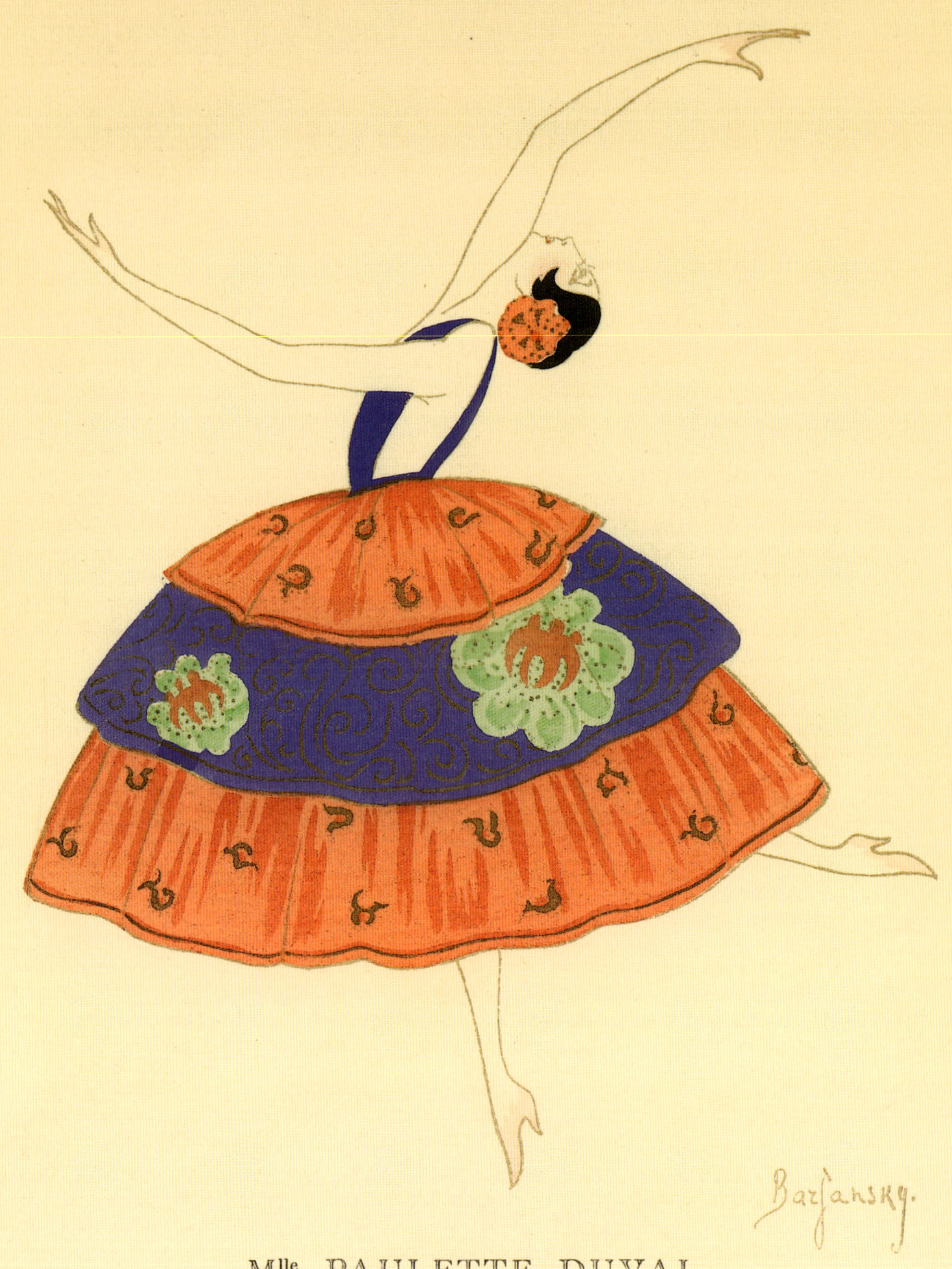

Mlle PAULETTE DUVAL

Costume de Dœuillet

Left
The famous dancer and actress Paulette Duval in a costume by Doeuillet. Illustration by Vladimir Barjansky. *Gazette du Bon Ton*, 1920

Design & Decoration

If the change in silhouette was radical, the actual variety in designs – especially in decoration – was even more so. These new modes of dressing were not just looser, freer, more functional and thoroughly modern, but also revealed a range of influences and inspiration that drew on a wide variety of sources.

The opening decade of the 20th century saw the reintroduction of a vivid colour palette into fashion. Paul Poiret is credited as the first designer to embrace bright colours and present haute couture creations in jonquil yellows, electric blues, bright pinks and vivid greens. His inspiration for these brightly multicolored creations came from the arts: the Fauvist painters had caused a stir at the 1905 Salon d'Automne with their non-naturalist colour palettes and quasi-expressionist style, and in 1909 the Ballets Russes had taken Paris by storm with their Oriental fantasies. Colour was in the arts and, as an avid art collector, Poiret wanted to elevate fashion to the same status by translating these contemporary artistic expressions into his creations. The resulting garments were bright, innovative and most of all luxurious.

The Ballets Russes' influence was not limited to colour but also crossed over into the stylistic development of fashion. Its style of Orientalism, best described as an imaginary mix of exotic influences from far-off times and places, could be clearly seen in Poiret's collections. The Orient in this context is not so much a geographical location as an imaginary idea. It encompassed areas of influence as diverse as South America, Africa and Asia, and did not limit itself to reality of time and place; rather it drew on ancient and often mythical histories and peoples to achieve its wide fantastical spectrum. The result of this Orientalist influence was that items such as harem trousers, kimono capes, turbans and tunics entered the fashionable Western wardrobe.

Whilst other couturiers quickly followed suit in abandoning the Edwardian pastel palette and outdated corseted styles in favour of these exotic, voluptuous and more fluid garments, Parisian haute couture initially continued to promote elitist and luxurious fashions. Consequently, this first shift had little impact on what the average woman wore. It was a reinterpretation of this Orientalism in the 1920s that trickled down to the woman in the street, and had a veritable and universal impact on women's style.

During the war, Poiret's fantastical 'One Thousand and One Nights' gowns went out of fashion, but the exotic element in these creations re-emerged in a more wearable and practical format: embellishment. So by the start of the 1920s, the eastern and exotic shapes explored by Poiret had shifted to the aforementioned altogether more flat, square and straight dresses, but with an abundance of Oriental detailing ranging from Chinese and Russian folk embroideries, African- and South American-inspired motifs, kimono-style sleeves and coats, opulent beading and tassels of imagined slave dresses, Oriental-inspired jewelled turbans and headbands, marabou feather fans and capes, compacts and cigarette holders in bold colours and motifs…

Africa, or at least an imagined Eurocentric version of it, provided a rich source of inspiration in the form of tribal prints, slave bracelets and chunky costume jewellery. A driving force behind contemporary art movements, the continent also made its appearance in fashion. Paris was entranced by Josephine Baker's antics in her banana skirt, while Chez Bricktop, a nightclub owned by African-American vaudevillian star, Ada 'Bricktop' Smith, was the hottest ticket

Below and right

Four hat designs by Parisian milliner Jeanne Vivet. *Trés Parisien*, 1926

Advertisement for Madeleine Vionnet. *L'Illustration des Modes*, 1920

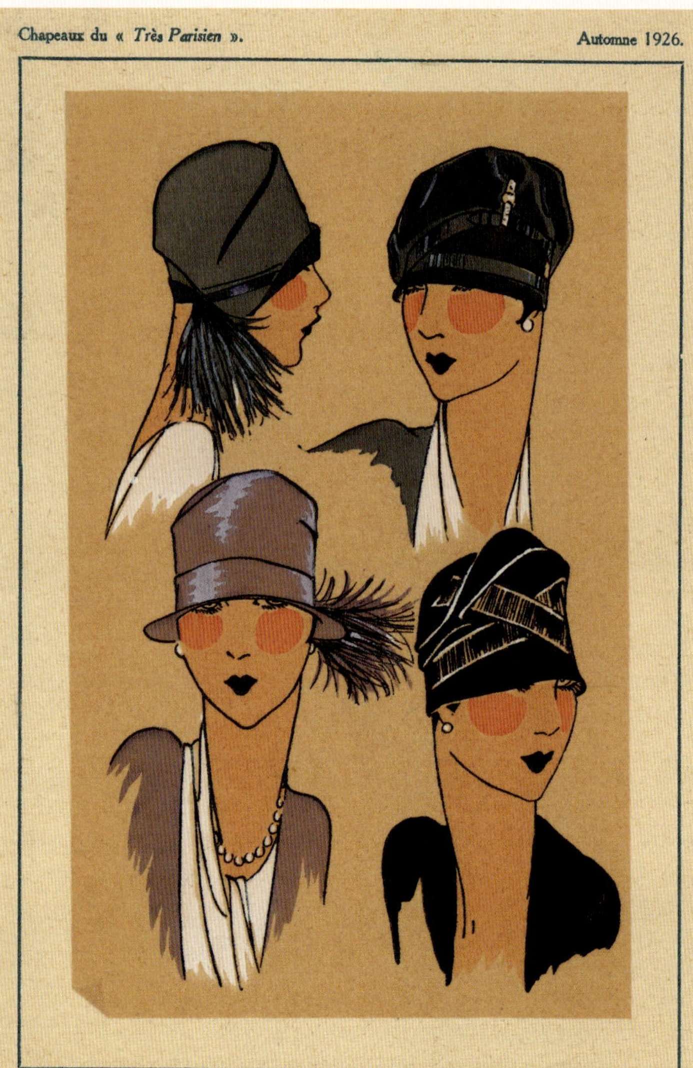

Créations JEANNE VIVET

I. — BLUETS. - Ce feutre bleu drapé de côté s'accompagne d'un pouf d'aigrettes. Un joli béret de velours saphir, entouré de ruban plissé, est piqué d'une broche de diamants.
Un canotier à bords un peu larges entouré de gros grain et garni de héron.
Une jolie toque de velours noir, ornée de gros grain.

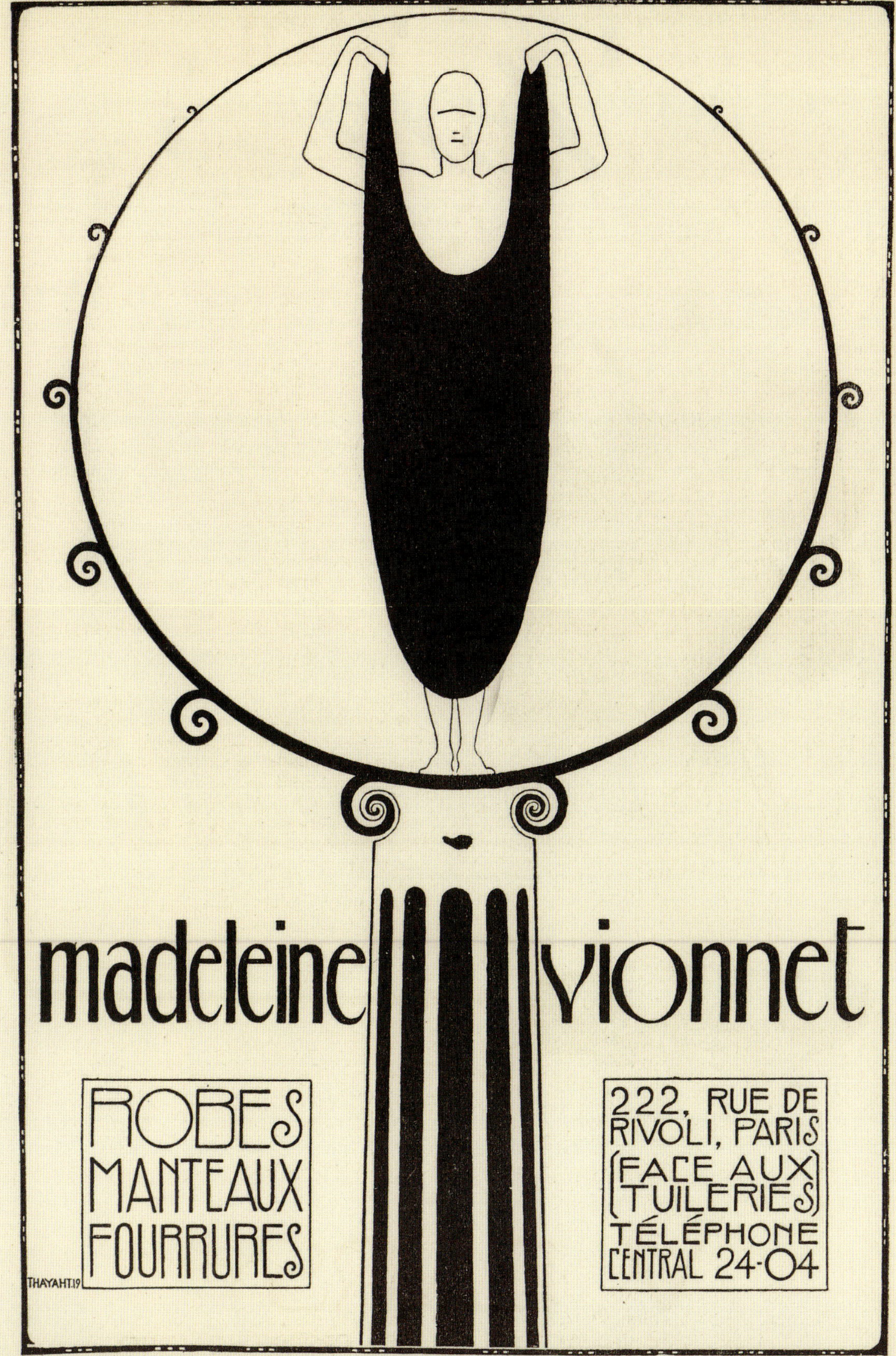

Madeleine VIONNET montre sa nouvelle collection de Robes, Manteaux, Fourrures, depuis le *1er Octobre.*

Below
A postcard of the Hollywood actress Pola Negri wearing a fur-trimmed Russian inspired coat with peasant-style embroidery, c.1921

in town. Jazz and 'black' dances such as the Lindy Hop and Charleston were considered the height of modernity...Paris was under the spell of 'negrophilia' as it was known at the time, and naturally fashion followed suit.

Another African source of inspiration came in the form of Ancient Egypt. It had been a source of inspiration prior to the Twenties, but after Howard Carter's 1922 discovery of Tutankhamen's tomb the world was caught up in Egyptomania. Cinemas built to resemble Ancient Pharaonic temples, Singer sewing machines decorated with lotus and sphinx motifs, fashions with hieroglyphic patterns, over-the-top costume jewellery 'resembling' the spoils discovered in the death chamber, lotus flower embroideries, bicorne and tricorne Egyptian hats with an albeit vague resemblance to Pharaonic headdress... the Egyptian obsession can also be seen in a stylistic shift in fashion illustration, as several high-end publications temporarily adopted an Egyptian perspective by depicting models in profile against a flat background.

The vogue for Russian embroideries was also rooted in a cultural development. The result of the 1917 Russian Revolution was the arrival of over 150,000 Russian émigrés in Paris, many of whom would end up either setting up their own couture houses or working for established Parisian houses. Many of the women had learnt embroidery in their childhood, and soon a fashion for these vivid embellishments was established – not least as they offered a substitute for luxurious fabrics in the immediate post-war years. But the Russian influence could be seen in other developments too. Taking their cue from the *kosovorotka*, a traditional embroidered men's tunic, the Russian houses such as Kitmir, Irfe and Yteb created a distinctive garment for women that became extremely sought after. The Russians also introduced Paris to their traditional fur and fabric combinations that would become a classic on blouses, dresses and coats in the Twenties. Their most lasting impact, however, would be on headgear through the *kokoshnik*, a traditional Russian headdress, which together with the cloche hat would come to epitomise Twenties fashions.

Historic styles continued to inspire designers too, though our view of the decade has been shaped by the modernity and innovation of the racier creations. The most important and popular example is the 'picture dress', a long dress with a wide, hooped infanta skirt, attached to a fitted bodice. The dress first made its appearance in the previous decade but remained a favourite of older women, and was seen as a more feminine alternative to the younger, straighter styles.

In terms of the colours used by designers, it is nearly impossible to speak of a single colour that defines the decade. A clear distinction between day and evening wear is possible; the latter saw a wide variety from the brightest pinks, yellows, greens and blues, whilst the former favoured more conservative colours such as dark browns, greys, blues and black. That said, bright red, green and orange daywear also existed. A class distinction can also be observed: a working woman's wardrobe, whilst featuring fashionable styles, came in safer neutral and darker colours as her clothes had to last longer and could not fall victim to the whims of fashion. Brighter colours were nevertheless introduced in the form of accessories such as hats, gloves, bags and scarves, items that could be updated to fall in line with the fashions of the day at a relatively low cost. There was, of course, also a seasonal divide with summer clothes being lighter in colours and materials.

A Twenties fashion colour that deserves closer attention is black. Whilst often the popularity for black is attributed to Chanel's Little Black Dress of 1926, the picture is somewhat

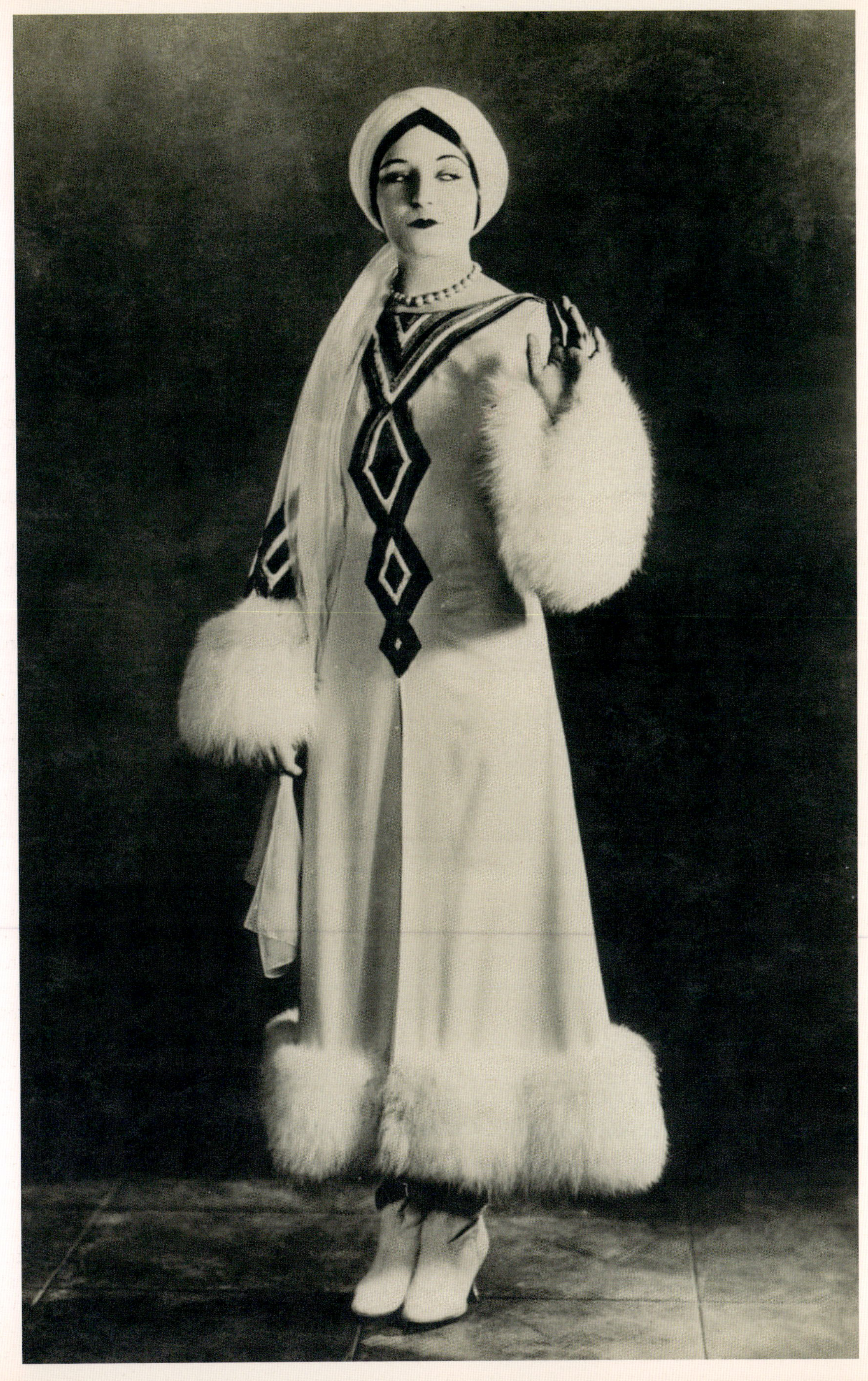

Below

Four golfing outfits, France. *La Mode-Sport*, 1929 – a two-piece jersey ensemble with appliqué initials, a beige Kasha dress, a dress of dark blue crepe with a printed scarf, and a black skirt worn with a yellow jersey jumper.

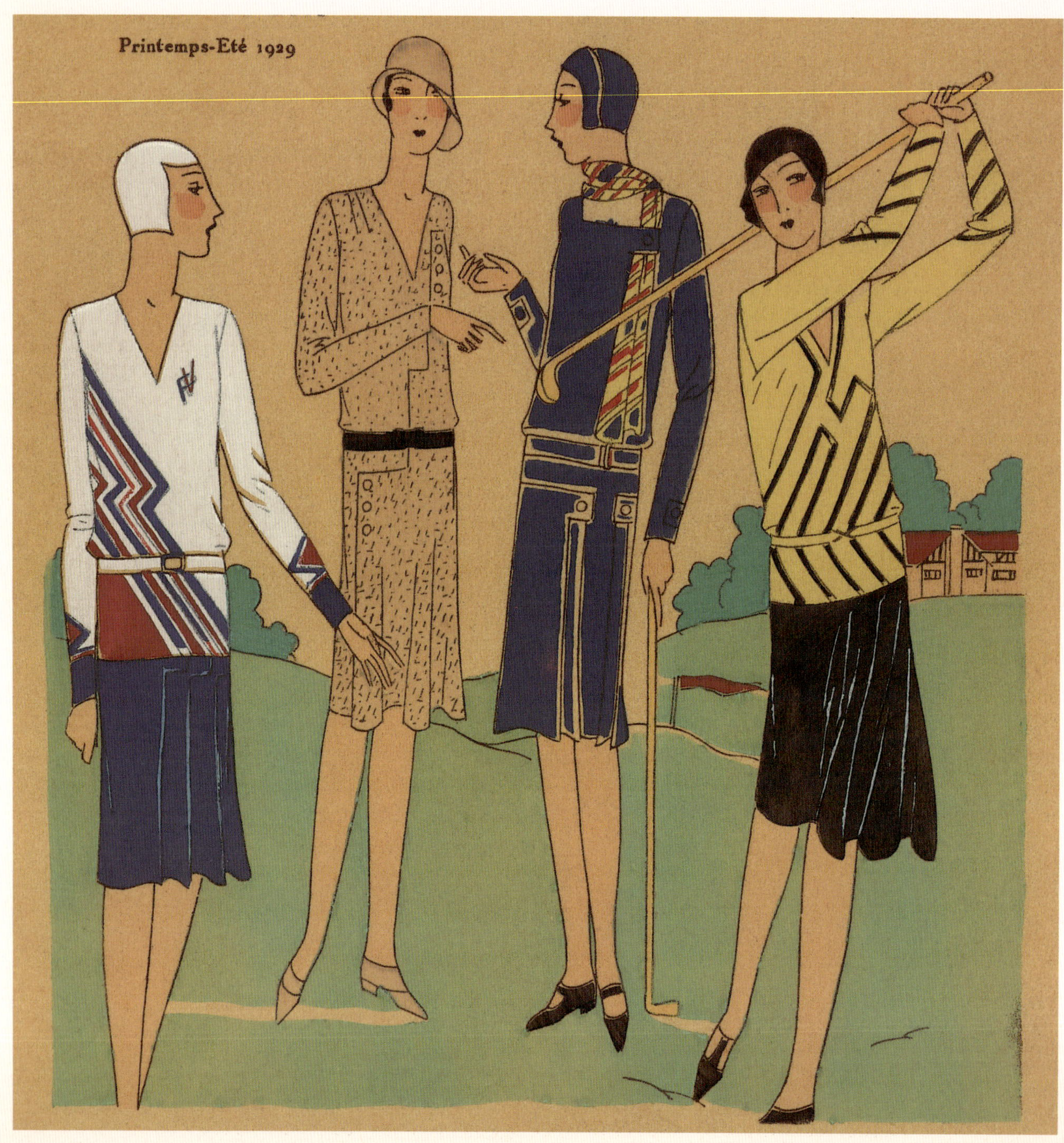

more complex. American Vogue in 1926 described her LBD as the 'Chanel Model T', predicting it would become a universal uniform for women. However, black was fashionable before the 1920s – especially for daywear. It was still the mourning colour but not exclusively. And as the images in this book demonstrate, the widespread enthusiasm for simple black dresses in both upper- and middle-market publications dispels the myth that only after Chanel launched her LBD was it possible for women of all classes to copy it and turn it into a universal uniform. In fact, evidence hints very clearly that black was more than likely a staple of working and lower middle class wardrobes, both as work and fashionable wear before the elite adopted it. As *The New Republic: A Journal of Opinion* observed as early as July 1921, 'So for street wear especially, we have throngs of females black from head to foot.'

Favoured fabrics still included rich silks, velvets, embroidered nets, and woven gold and silver lamé at the top end of the market; these were mostly reserved for eveningwear. This list was however joined by other more comfortable and practical fabrics such as jersey, mohair, gabardine, crepe, kasha and rayon, which directly reflects the freer urban lifestyle enjoyed by women.

Sportswear

Women also saw the introduction of various 'new' garments, best described as sportswear, into their wardrobes. Initially only for members of the elite, the influence of these types of clothes nevertheless trickled down to less well-off consumers. Sportswear is by far the most important type of attire to impact on women's lives in the Twenties. This is true in two distinct yet related ways. As already stated, the privileged echelons of society had discovered the joys of outdoor pursuits during the war, and new garments had been developed to cater to these new hobbies. This was particularly true for women; their new and more liberated social status allowed their increased engagement in athletic pursuits. Prior to this, sports such as golfing, skating, hunting, skiing and riding had not excluded female participation, but women had always undertaken these activities in clothes that were in keeping with the feminine ideal of the time. Not only did this mean they had to wear uncomfortable and restrictive gowns, they actually wore corsets underneath these 'sports' ensembles.

The late 1910s but more so the 1920s saw a host of new, more comfortable interpretations of female sportswear. Indebted to Chanel's introduction of jersey and her use of male tailoring, and in cultural terms to the social shifts which had 'freed' women from some of the more restrictive regulations of pre-war times, these changes were now clearly reflected in the new style and comfort of women's general attire – but most particularly in their sports wardrobes.

The modern sportswear wardrobe saw the introduction of altogether new garments such as motoring and even flying fashions, as the modernity of cars and airplanes was reflected in emerging styles. High-end fashion publications featured women descending from cars in long woollen and leather coats, accessorised with the latest in glove and headgear design. Indeed the motor industry particularly targeted the modern women and there appeared endless adverts of women driving cars, at once affirming their 'new' status and propagating the modernity of the female body.

These sports fashions, whilst often being just fashions, nevertheless reveal that the post-war years saw an increasing interest in matters of health for both men and women. Physical education in schools was becoming a more important part of the curriculum, while local and national sports clubs grew in membership. Even though there was still a clear gender difference in terms of which sports were taught and marketed to men and women, the overriding health discourse meant women were actively encouraged to partake in a much wider variety of physical activities than in previous decades.

Health had been pushed onto the agenda by medical advances but the shocking figures that in 1917 only 36% of the men examined were suitable for full military duties and that 40% were entirely unfit or classified as unable to undergo physical exertion, probably had a much greater impact on this drive for health. A need for a healthy nation was paramount especially as the '20s wore on, and the early signs that WWI may not have been 'the war to end all wars' were starting to appear. Indeed this renewed cult of the body beautiful would take on extremely sinister connotations in Germany in the following decade. It would appear that the interest in sports and its accompanying new fashions has to been seen in a much wider social and political context to grasp its full importance.

Another sport that became incredibly popular, particularly with women, was swimming. Women had been allowed to swim in the Olympic Games of 1912, and from there on the sport grew in popularity – especially during the second half of the 1920s after Miss Gertrude Ederle's 1926 swim across the Channel beat the record by two hours. Even more impressive, when you consider that at the time, the record was held by a man

This official Olympic seal of approval for swimming as a female-friendly sport was a catalyst for the development of a more modern and practical women's swimming costume. The Edwardian culottes and skirt combination was replaced in the 1920s with woollen jersey sleeveless tank suits, reminiscent of earlier male swimming costumes. These semi-elasticated garments came in a wide variety of colours and patterns, and were infinitely more suited to water pursuits than their historic counterparts. As the swimwear company Jantzen declared in its advertising slogan of 1929, this was 'the suit that changed bathing into swimming'.

This dramatic redesign of women's swimwear was only possible because ideas about women and modesty had shifted considerably in line with the other cultural developments previously highlighted. This more liberal attitude by society to women and their bodies was also reflected in a related cultural phenomenon – the exponential rise in the number of outdoor public swimming pools in the inter-war years.

Public pools had become features of most larger cities in the 19th century due to increasing health and hygiene concerns. Initially these were reserved for men only, and even when they opened their doors to women, pools for both sexes were segregated to the extent that each even had a separate entrance to the pool buildings. Mixed bathing was introduced in several locations as early as 1901, but did not become acceptable practice until much later – indeed, certain ponds and pools did not allow it until the 1930s. It is the lidos which proliferated in the 1920s that both propagated and affirmed the positive shifts in gender division, as the majority allowed mixed bathing and were marketed as family spaces. The modern women in her modern swimming costume became an icon of the era – the "Bathing Belle", who could be found anywhere from travel posters advertising seaside resorts to Hollywood films, was hailed as an aspirational figure and the popularity of her look only increased that of swimming.

Below
Jantzen swimwear advertisement – the suit that changed bathing to swimming. *Liberty*, 1929

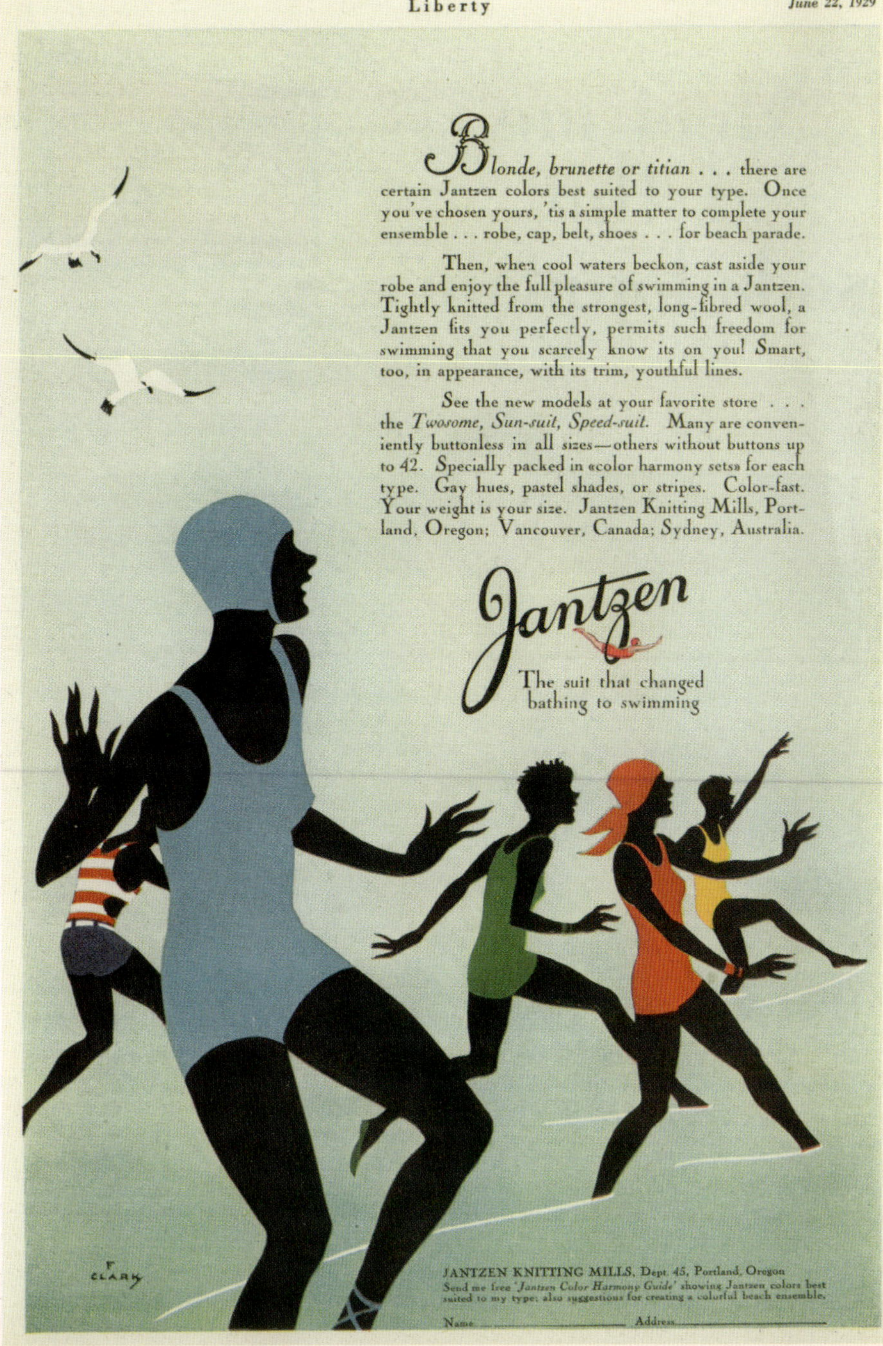

Below
Portrait of Hon. Mrs. Richard Norton reputed to be 'The Most Beautiful Woman in Britain', 1926

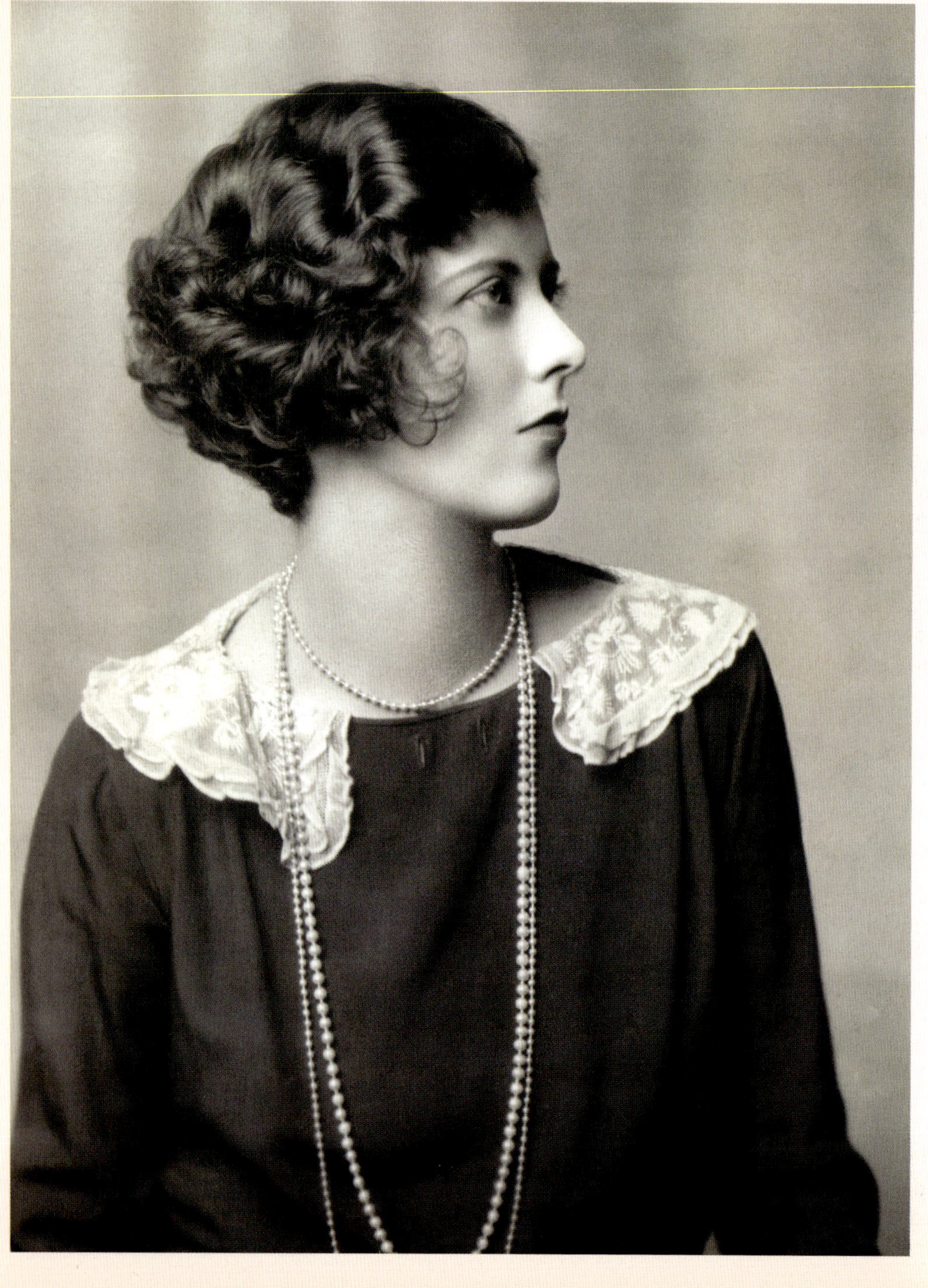

Beauty Ideals

Another factor that contributed to the vogue for outdoor bathing locales and the need for less restrictive and modest swimming costumes was the vogue for sunbathing. Whilst for centuries tanned skin had been shunned by the elite as a sign of poverty and low status, the new interest outdoor pursuits saw a major shift in this, and suntans came to be considered not only a sign of good health, but also a fashionable look. The mode for tans can also be linked to the appearance of dresses with plunging backs, sleeveless gowns and the rising of hemlines. The more the body was on display, the more it had to be groomed and disciplined.

Another body discipline that is linked to the vogue for athletic participation and health awareness was the rise of dieting. Whilst as late as 1917 adverts for 'stoutening' pills and creams can be found in ladies magazines, the '20s silhouette was slender and virtually curve-less. Whilst some younger women naturally possessed this boyish shape, for the majority elasticated de-emphasising corsets and dieting had to lend a helping hand. Fashion is never just about clothes; they need a body to animate them. In this way, to explore fashion is to explore the intimate relationship between body and fabric. By examining the design and style of clothes we can read the beauty ideals of any given time, as clothing is always designed with the ideal body in mind. In the 1920s, it's clearly apparent only a slender frame would do: the lack of tailoring around the waist, later the dropped waist, the flat dresses that hid the breasts...the ideal body of the period was definitely slender and boyish.

This boyish frame was set off with the boyish haircut that has come to symbolise the era – the cropped bob. Women had cut their hair short at various points in history but these had always been short-lived trends rather than prolonged general fashions. Long hair is seen as a marker of femininity; its cutting off therefore is often interpreted as political. It is not clear who started the fashion, but what is certain is that it was not an overnight change, but a slower process. It started with a softer waved cut in the opening decade of the century and transmuted into, at its most extreme, an angular short bob closely cut to the skull in the mid 1920s. Furthermore, there was no single defining 'bobbed' haircut – many women cut their hair short, but the variety of bobs was wide. Initially men and older generations were horrified by this trend, but very quickly it became the accepted beauty ideal featured in both upmarket and cheap fashion publications – although it is worth noting that the images produced for the lower end of the market mostly featured the softer, less shocking variety of the haircut.

Both at the time and in retrospective histories, this fashion is seen as women adopting male traits. In the contemporary press the issue was heavily discussed and was seen as a quasi-assault on masculinity and a loss of femininity. More conservative papers saw this as such a threat and a symbol of doom that they proclaimed this would be the end of women cooking and looking after their men. For some this may have been a political statement; for others it was a haircut that suited their new freer lifestyles. For most it was just fashion.

The bob was the perfect cut for the cloche, or indeed the cloche was the perfect hat for the bob. The cloche, with its deep crown and small brim, was worn pulled down very low over the eyes and has become, like the bob, a defining characteristic of the era. Contrary to popular belief, though, it was not a Twenties 'invention' but had been worn since the mid-teens. Equally it was far from the only 'type' of headgear donned by fashionable woman. In fact, the opening years of the decade saw a plethora of different styles

Next page
Drawing of various ensembles by Jean Patou. *L'Illustration des Modes*, 1922

including bicorne and tricorne hats, turbans, Chinese toques, the Russian kokoshnik and a whole host of fantastical Oriental creations often combining two different types of headgear into one – such as turbans embroidered with kokoshniks, or cloches with bicornes. The only linking feature was that most were, like the cloche, worn very low over the head. Throughout the decade hats took on semi-sculptural proportions, and the existing variety was joined by new creations. These include the tightly fitted casque, which was derived from racing helmets, and the beret. Previously reserved for children and the working classes, the beret saw itself transformed into a fashion item – often accessorised with a flechette brooch.

Bobs and deep hats framed the face and turned it into a canvas. To accentuate and indeed complete the modern look, another new trend needs to be considered: visible make-up. Whilst previous generations had experimented with make-up, they had used it to bring out their natural beauty – that is to say to hide flaws – chic make-up was soft, pale and natural. The fashionable Twenties girl however wore a rather different face. Lips were coated in brightly coloured lipstick; eyes made up with dark eyeshadows and cheeks powdered with rouge. Prior to this, visible make-up had been the province of chorus girls and prostitutes; it was considered vulgar and its wearer of low status. This changed dramatically with the growing popularity of Hollywood films. Early lighting was so bright that stars had to wear make up to accentuate their features so their faces could be clearly seen on screen. This was exceptionally important before the arrival of the talkies in the late 1920s as facial expressions had to convey emotion and narrative in lieu of dialogue. As film developed from short 'stories' to full-blown features with more complex storylines, the stars of the silver screen became aspirational icons whose looks were copied worldwide. Max Factor, a Polish cosmetician, chemist and wigmaker soon developed a business empire, which not only provided the film industry but women worldwide with his cosmetics. Fancy powder compacts and lipstick holders in abstract deco designs appeared on the market and were a must-have in the fashionable woman's purse.

Other accessories that could be procured quite cheaply included bracelets, clips, necklaces and earrings in coloured Bakelite or paste and diamanté. These cheap accessories were the perfect way of adding a touch of glamour to a home-made dress. Shoes also came in a wide and exciting variety of colour, cut and embellishment. Rising hemlines meant legs and feet were now on display and so shoes became a focal point. The majority of shoes were high heeled and styles included T-bars and crossover straps. Leather, brocades, silks, gold and silver kid and a host of embellishments including embroideries in silks, beading, painted designs and diamanté clips and straps turned footwear into 'foot jewellery'. Like hats and other accessories, a pair of fashionable shoes was the perfect way to update an outfit. So from head to toe women could incorporate new and exciting shapes, colours, patterns and designs into what they were wearing.

Whilst often highly mythologised and at times misinterpreted, 1920s fashions have earned their right to be remembered and celebrated, not least because of their spectacular nature, beauty, variety and novelty. They are the sartorial embodiment of a society in change; a change that greatly benefitted women and saw significant steps in their social, economic and political liberation. This 'New Woman' deserved nothing less than a 'New' wardrobe to accompany and represent her 'New' life.

The different motifs of the new-found freedoms are all contained within the pages of this stylish book, which presents a record of the plethora of choices on offer to her in arguably the most iconic decade of the 20th century. The Twenties were about so, so much more than flappers and cloche hats.

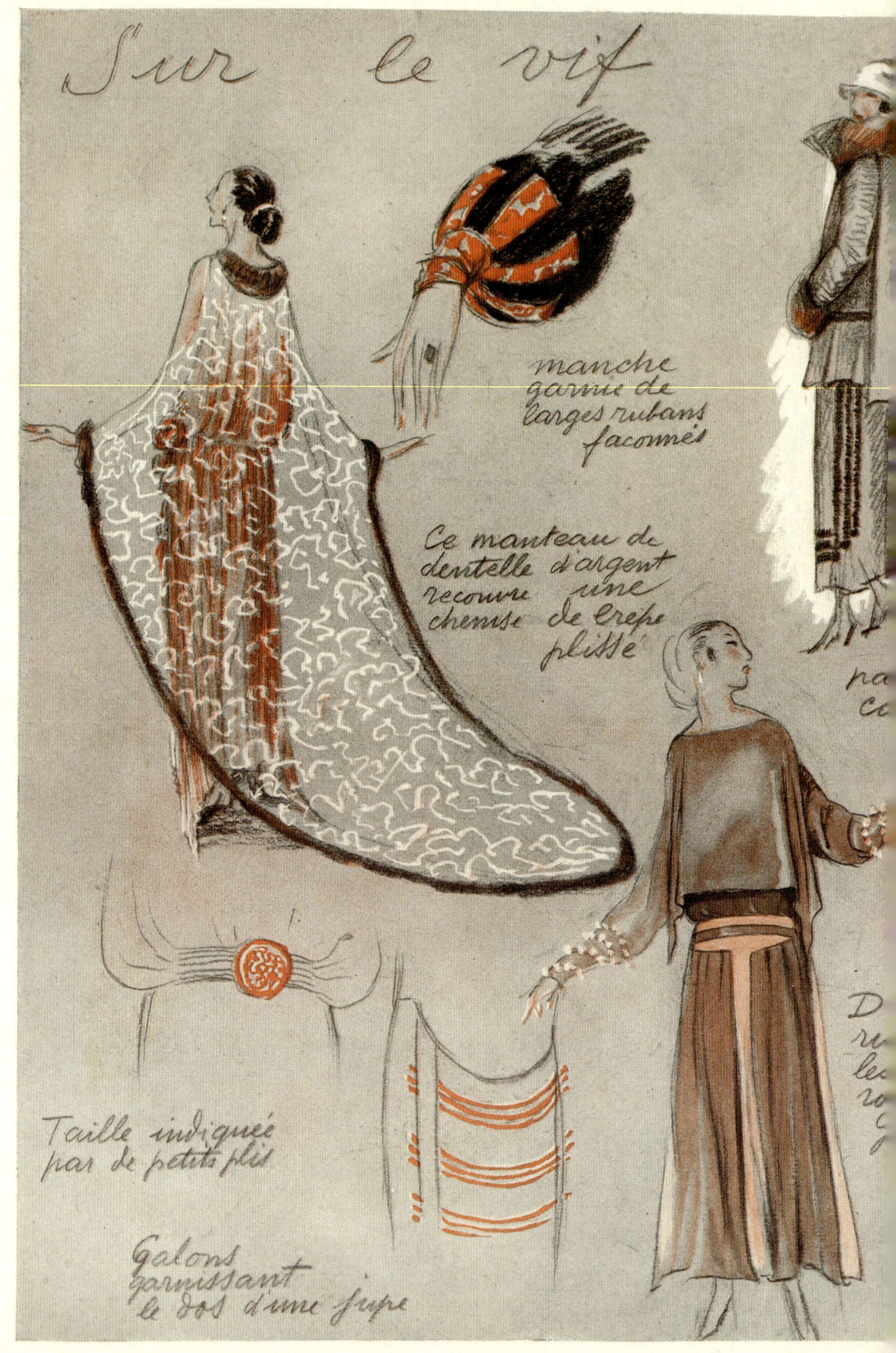
Sur le vif
manche garnie de larges rubans façonnés
Ce manteau de dentelle d'argent recouvre une chemise de crêpe plissé
Taille indiquée par de petits plis
Galons garnissant le dos d'une jupe

chez Jean Patou

décolleté en crêpe froncé et uni —

Pour l'auto: manteau de peau de daim marron

...leur de
...n nègre
et
...nt de
—

Robe de crêpe Georgette blanc brodée de perles — Ruban à la Taille

...clettes de
garnissent
...hes de cette
crêpe
...tte 2 tons

Grande robe du soir en satin noir et broché d'argent

Un amusant bas de manche

Pinces lisérées d'agneau assortie au col

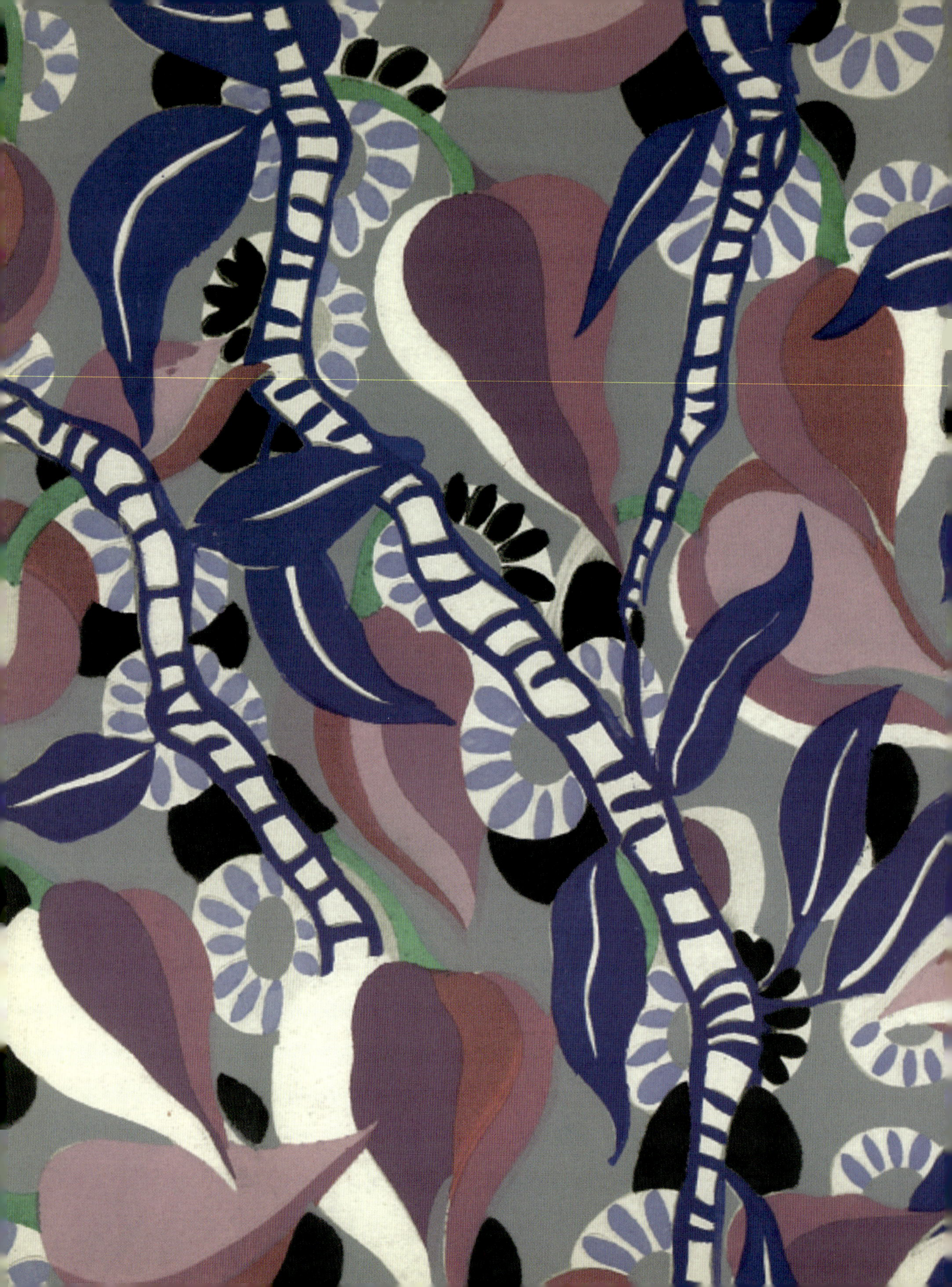

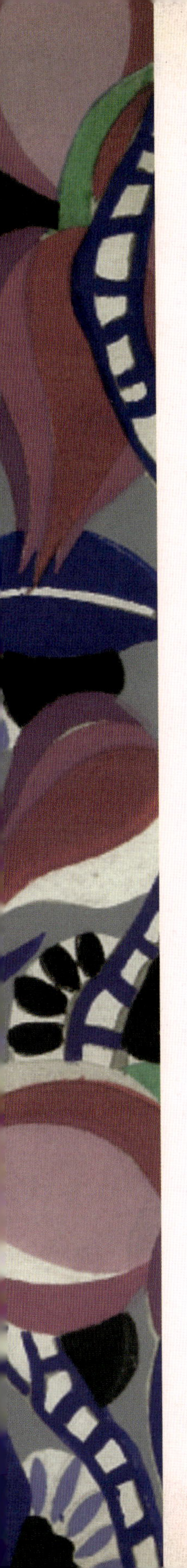

Daywear

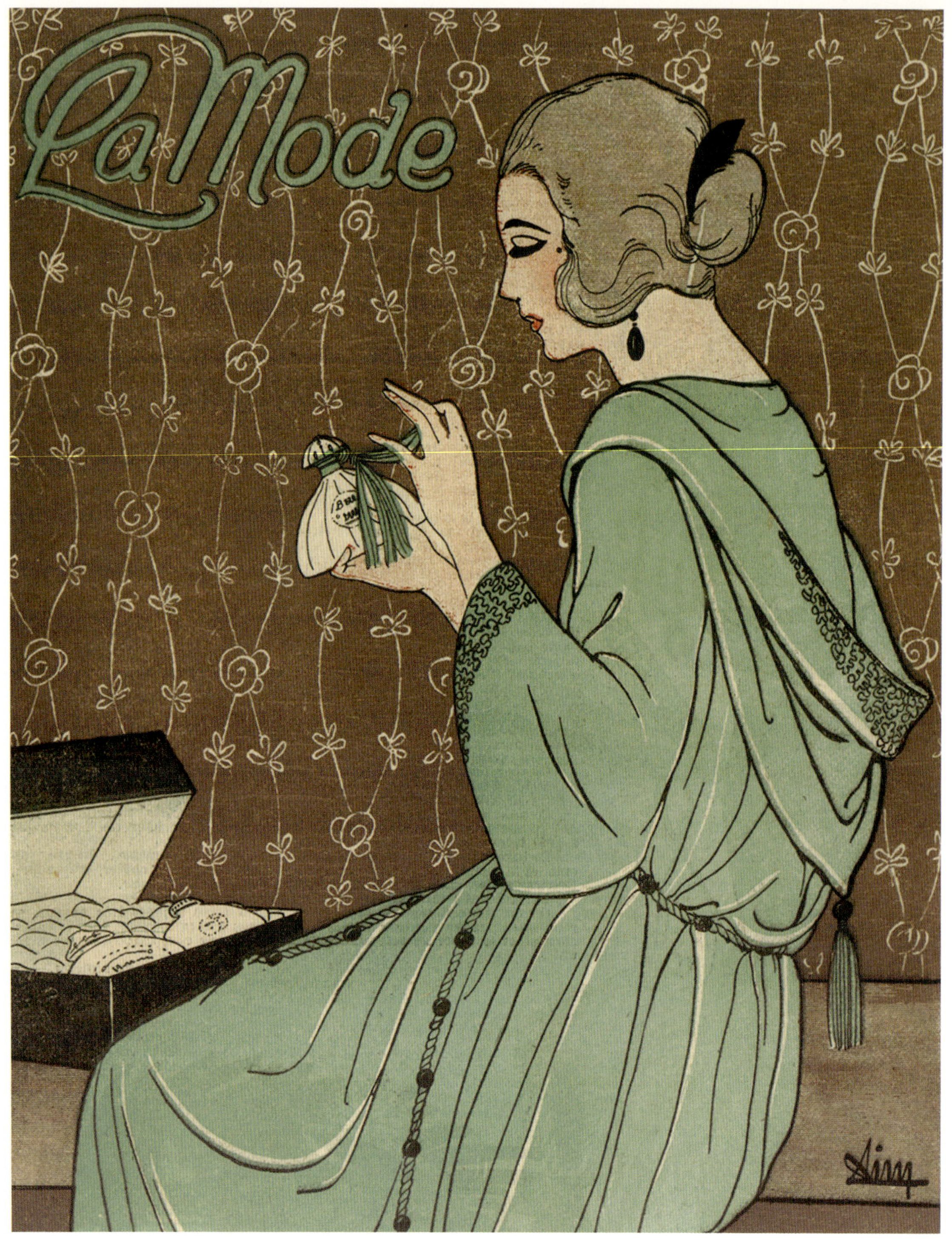

Above
Woman in a green housecoat with a draped hood, and rope and tassel detail. *La Mode*, 1920

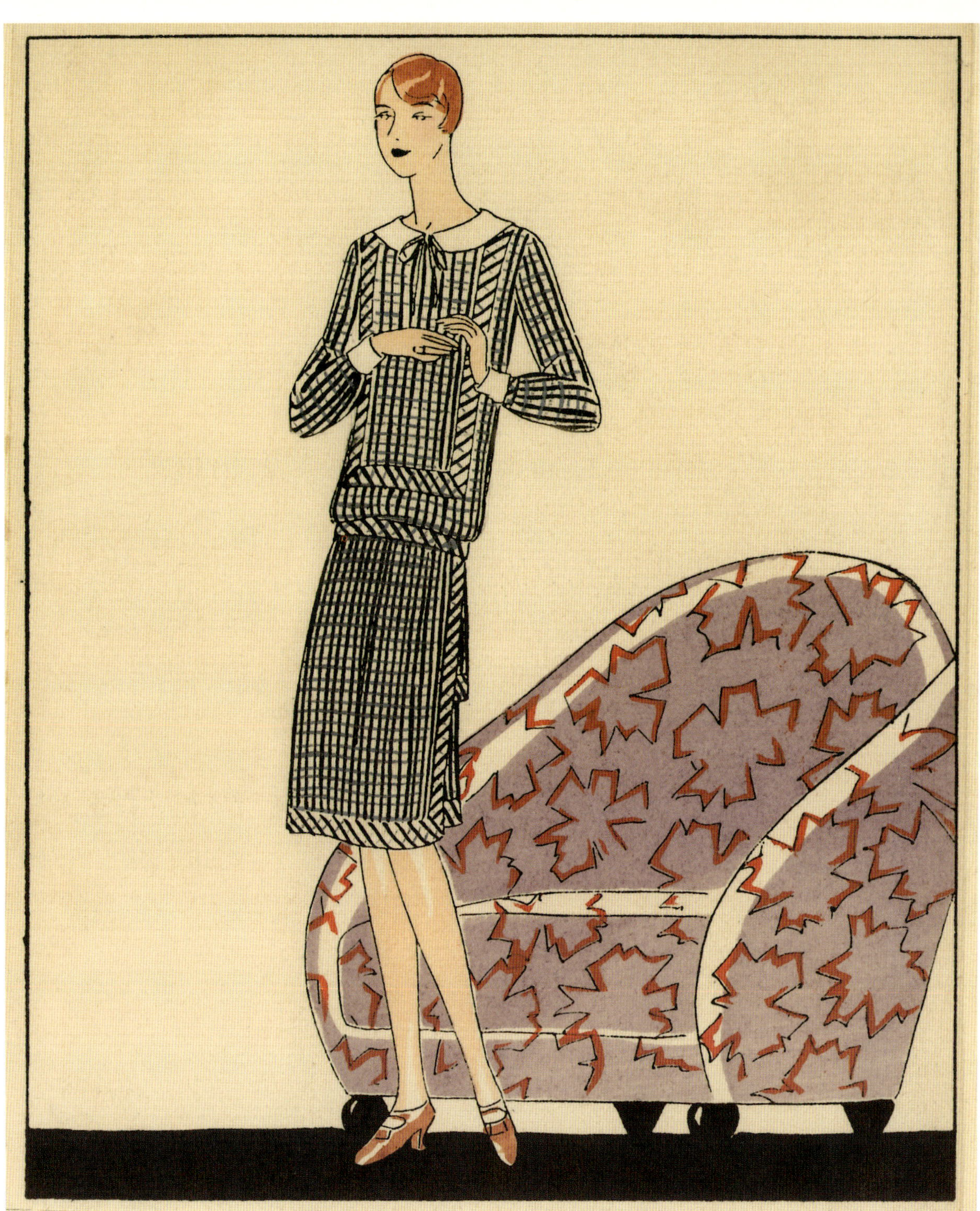

Above
Black and white checked dress
with drop waist by Martial et Armand.
Le Style Parisien, 1926

Below
Two women in winter dresses.
Le Petit Echo de La Mode, 1922

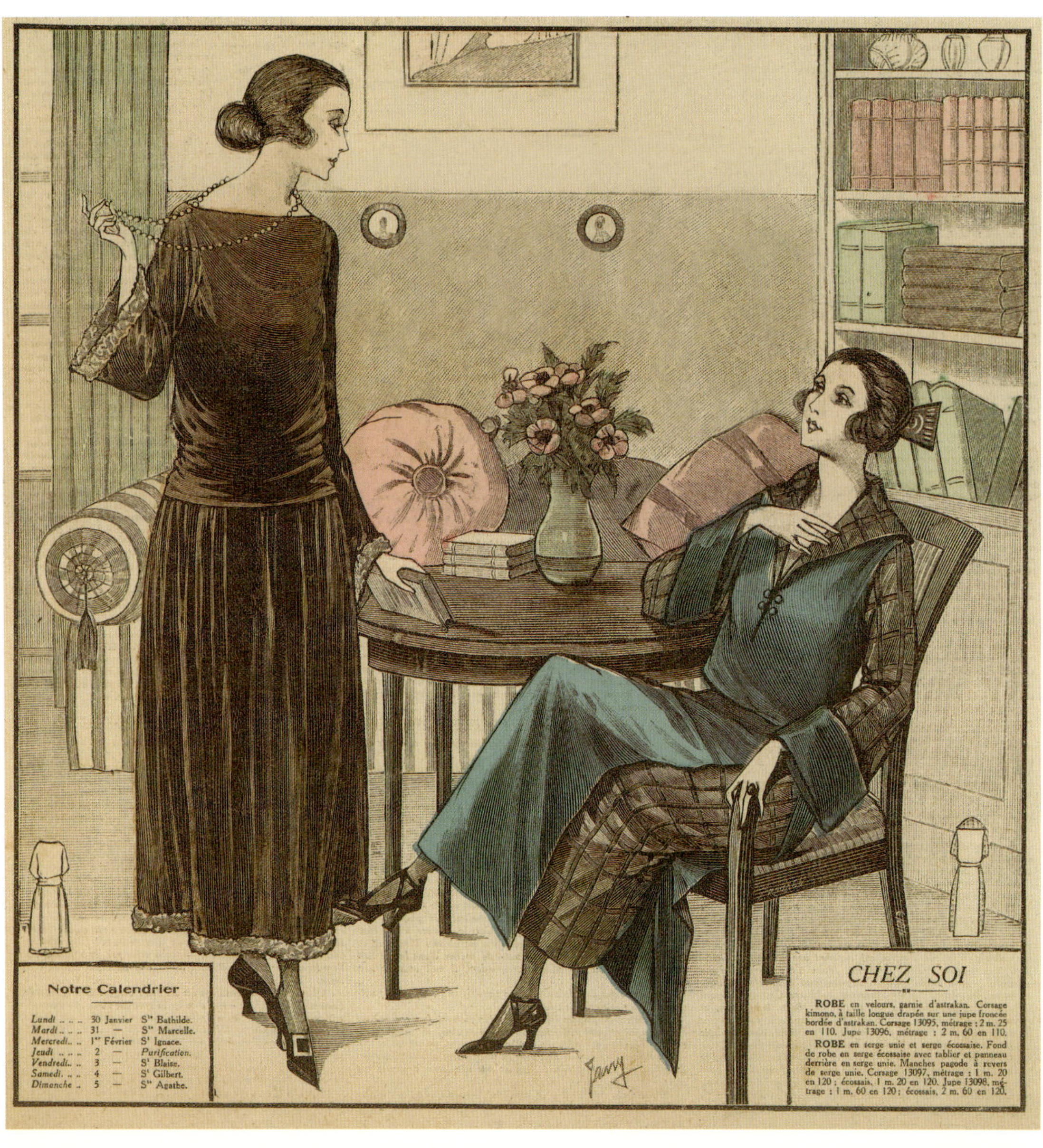

Below
Three women in long day dresses.
Le Petit Echo de la Mode, 1924

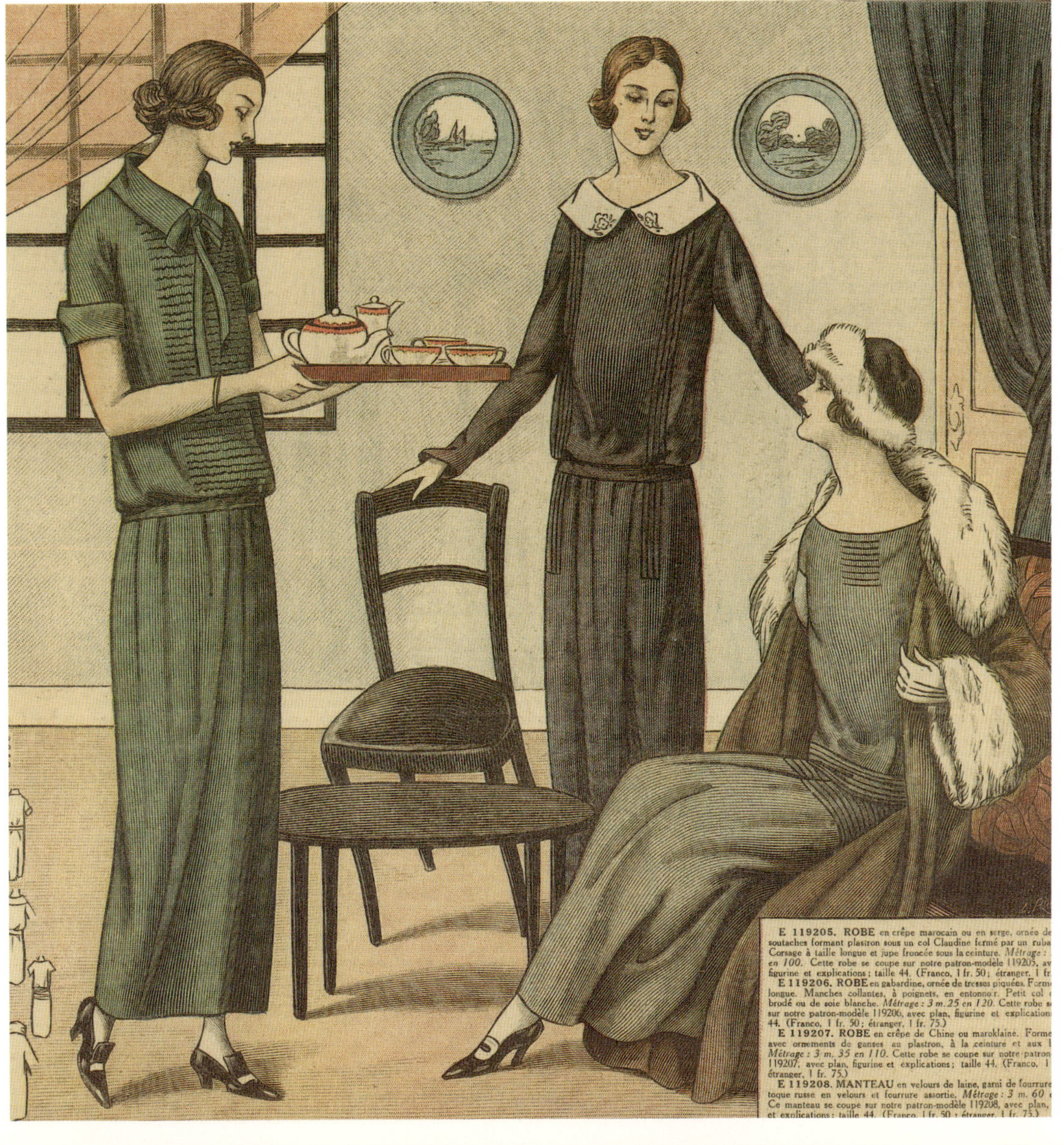

Right

Grey crepe de Chine dress by Chéruit, navy blue and black dress by Jeanne Lanvin, and orange and white dress by Worth. Illustration by Pierre Brissaud, *L'Illustration des Modes*, 1920

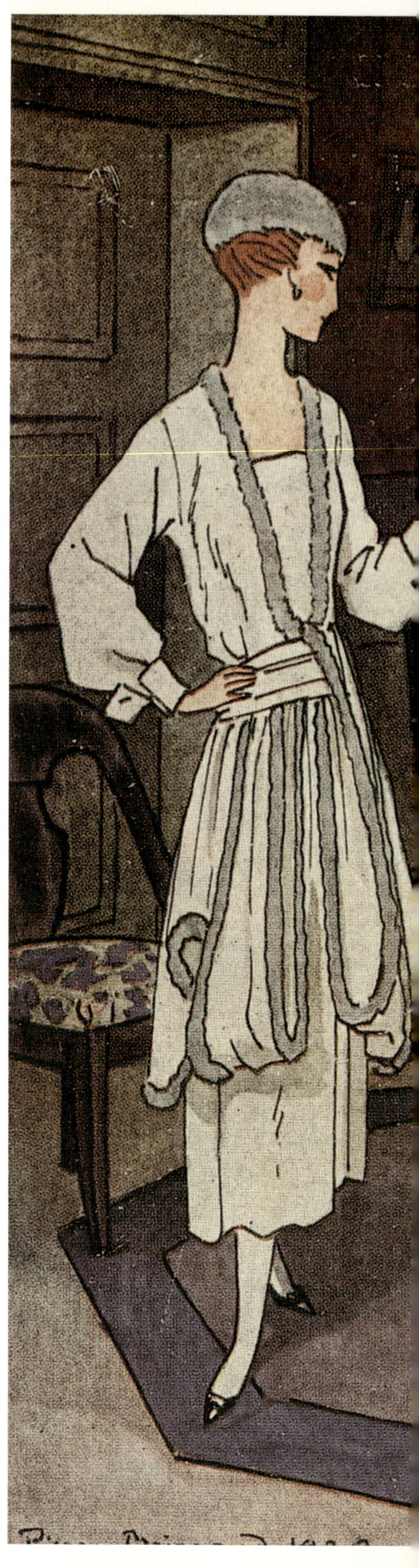

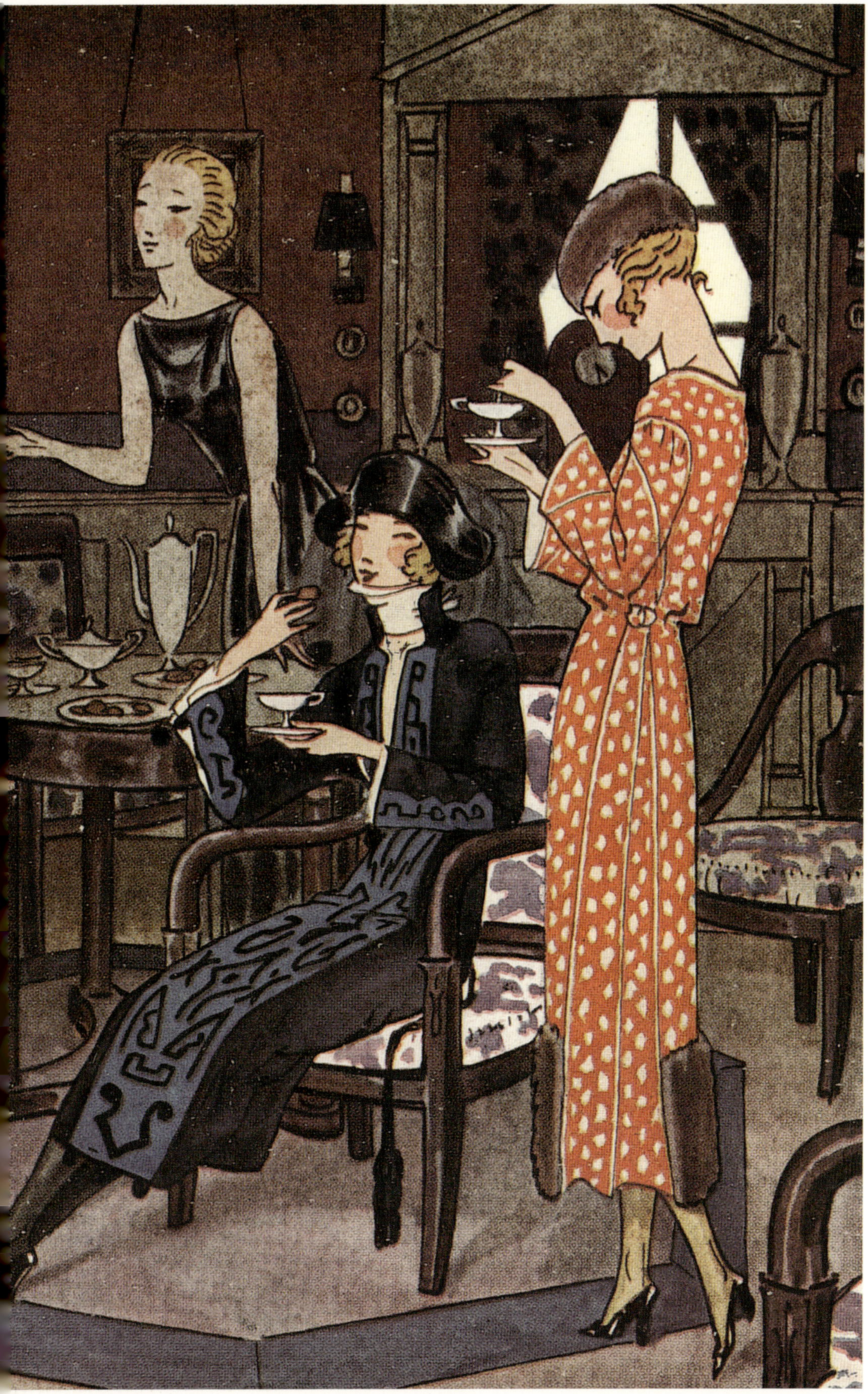

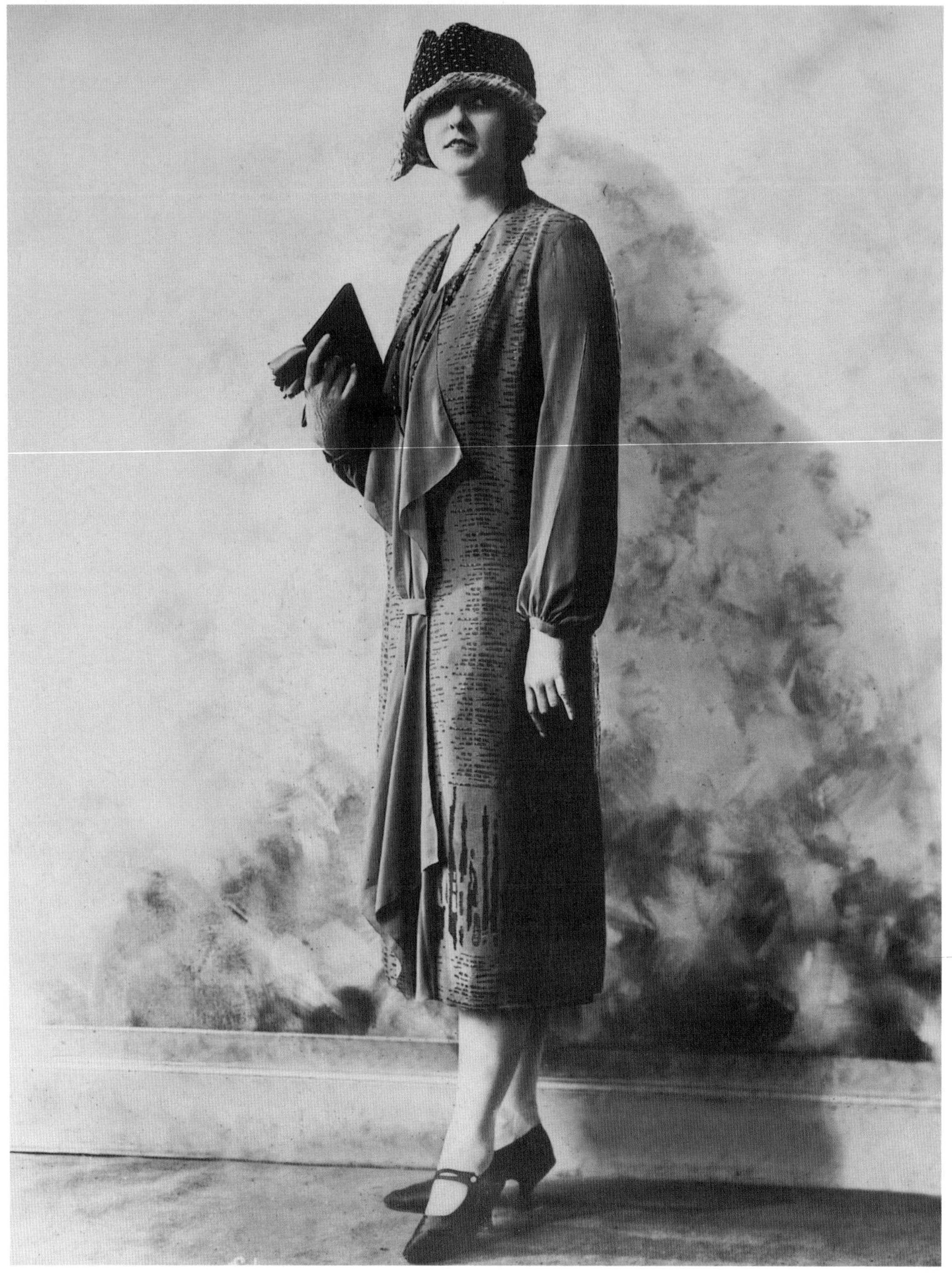

Above
Tan silk afternoon dress with a gathered lapel detail at the waist, c.1924

Right
Actress Jacqueline Gadsden who starred alongside Clara Bow in "It", modelling a morning dress of blue flat crepe trimmed with silver braid that forms a vestee and is also used to edge the patch pocket, c.1926

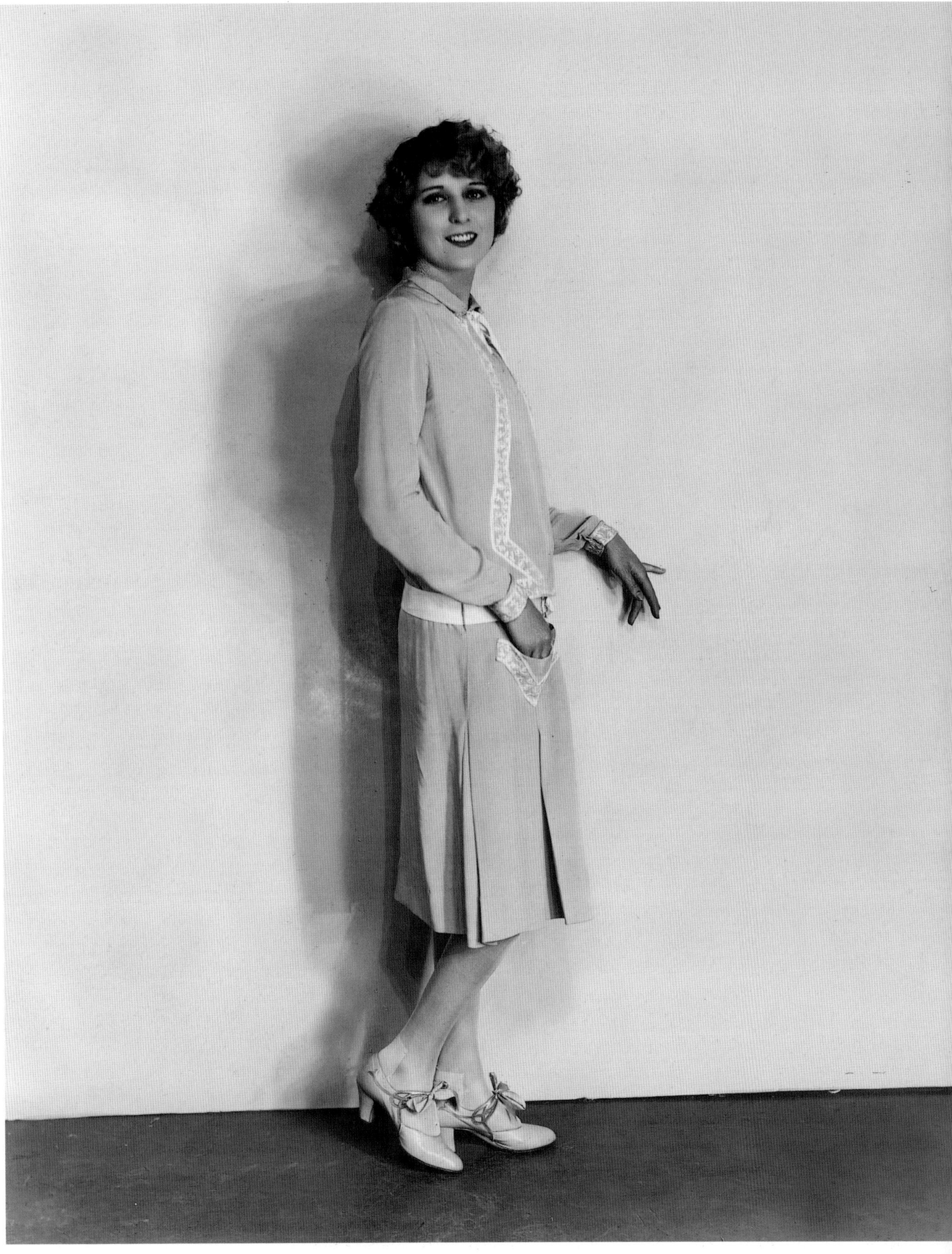

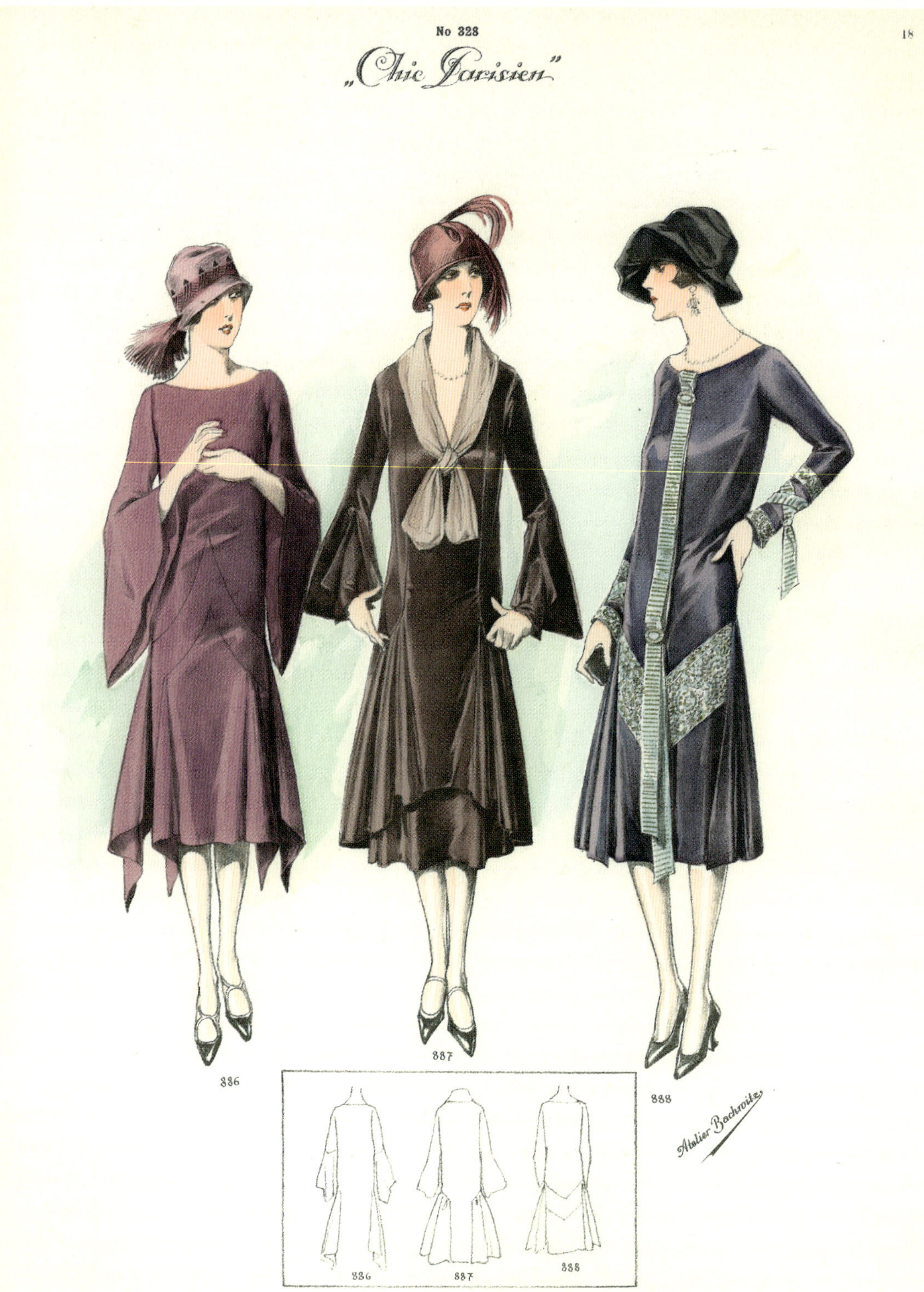

Above

An afternoon dress of crepe satin with bell pleats, a satin afternoon dress with slashed front and bell shaped tunic, and a satin princess robe with faille ribbon cravats by Atelier Bachroitz. *Chic Parisien Beaux-Arts des Modes*, 1925

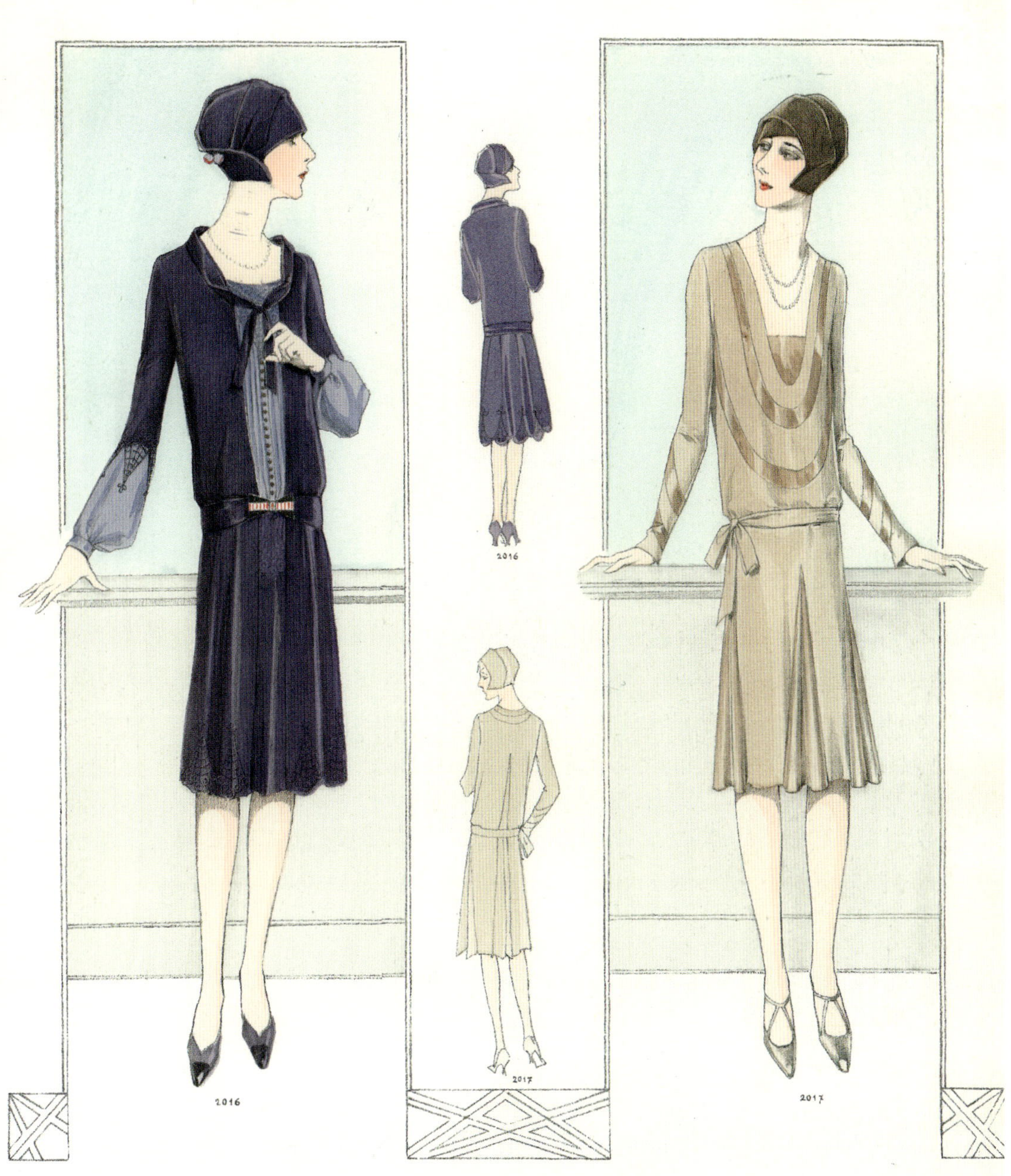

Above

Crepe afternoon dress with front tie collar, and a crepe bridge dress with circular bands on the bodice and sleeves by Atelier Bachroitz. *Chic Parisien Beaux-Arts des Modes*, 1927

Right
Street robe with inset front tunic with godet flounces, a street robe in Kasha with ruche pleats, and a street dress with a narrow plastron and inserted skirt panels by Atelier Bachroitz.
Grande Mode Parisienne, 1926

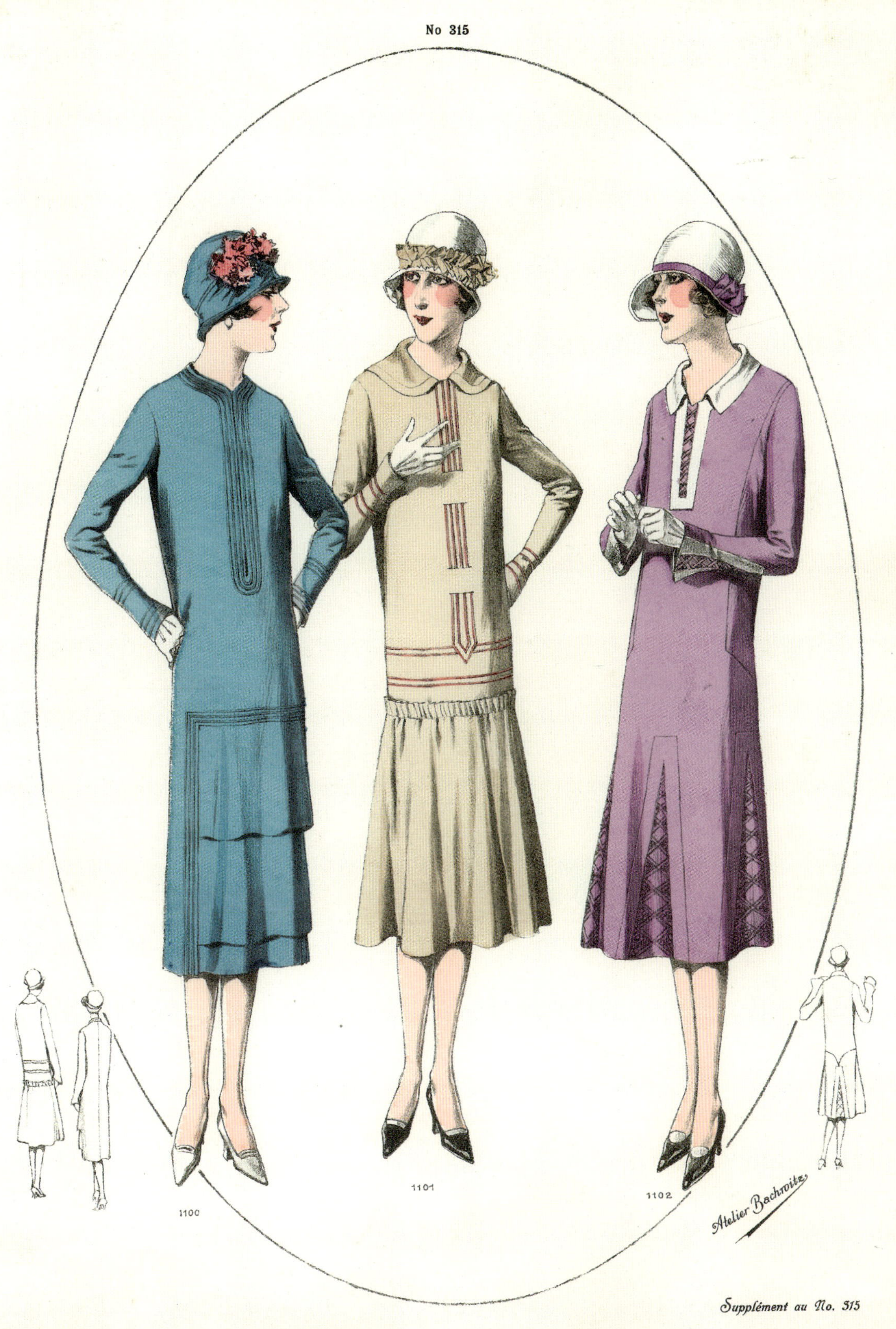
No 315
1100
1101
1102
Atelier Bachwitz
Supplément au No. 315

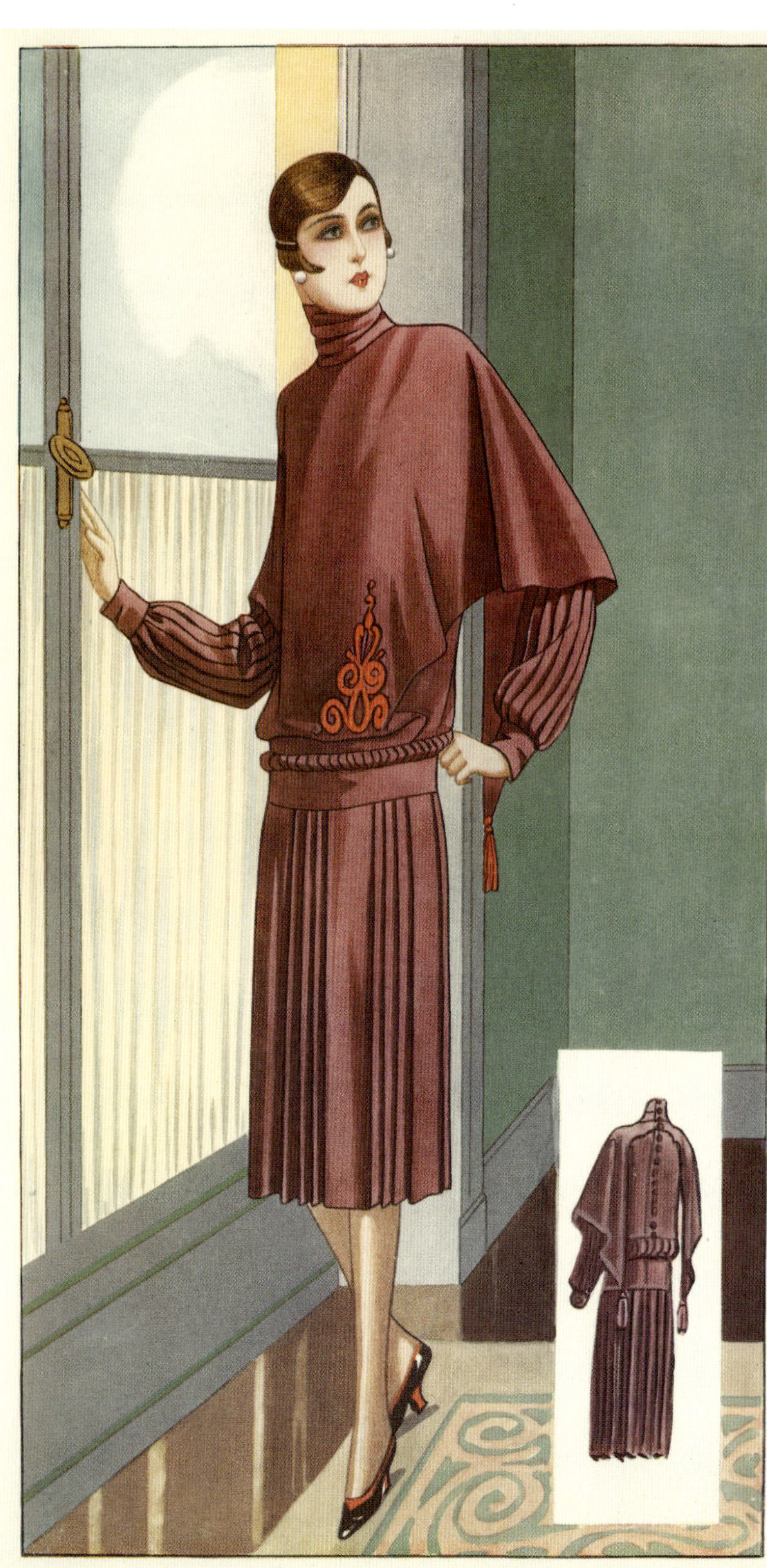

Left and right
Afternoon ensemble with pleated skirt and sleeves and a tasselled scarf blouse by Alice Bernard. *La Femme Chic*, 1926

Designs for blouses and sweaters. *La Femme Chic*, c.1925

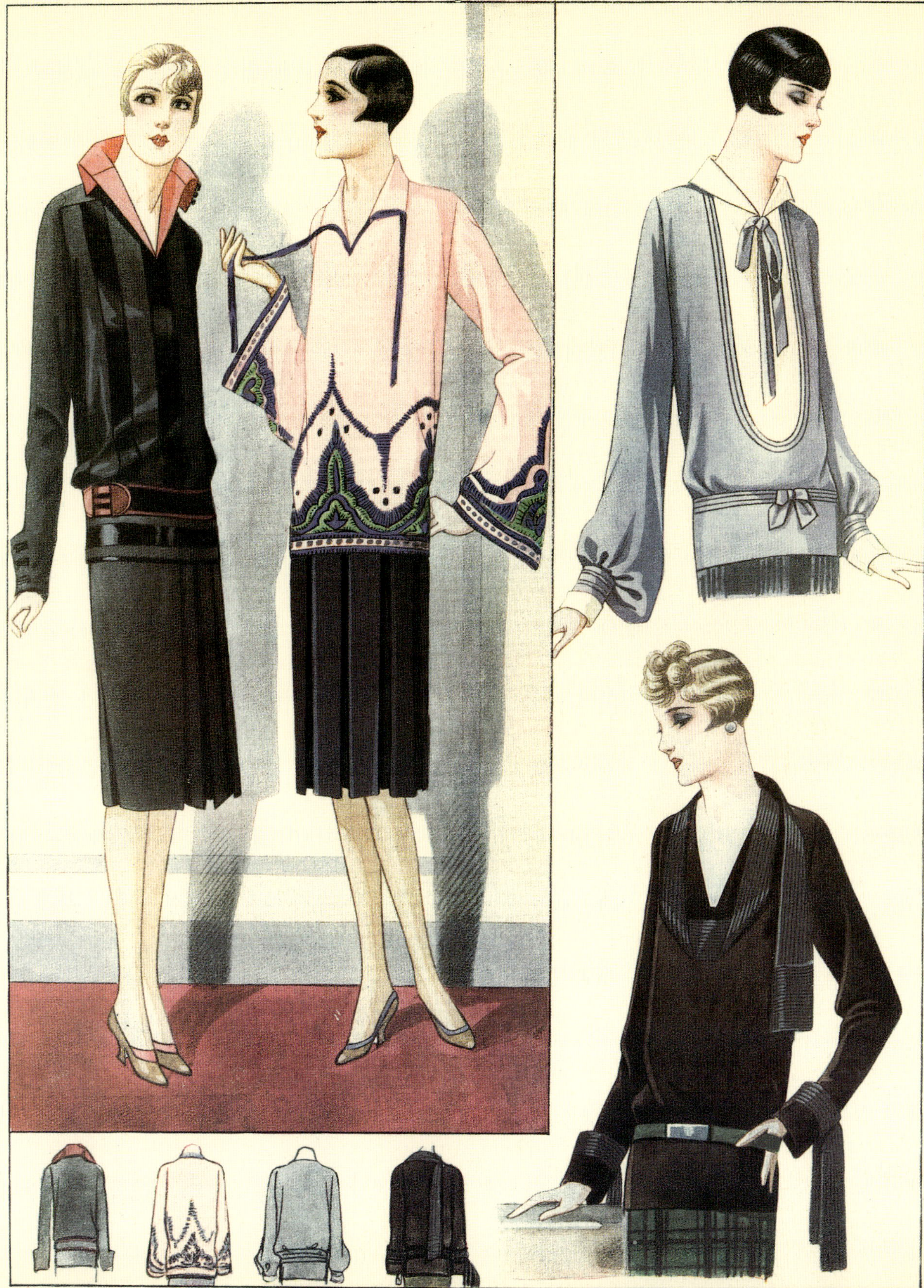

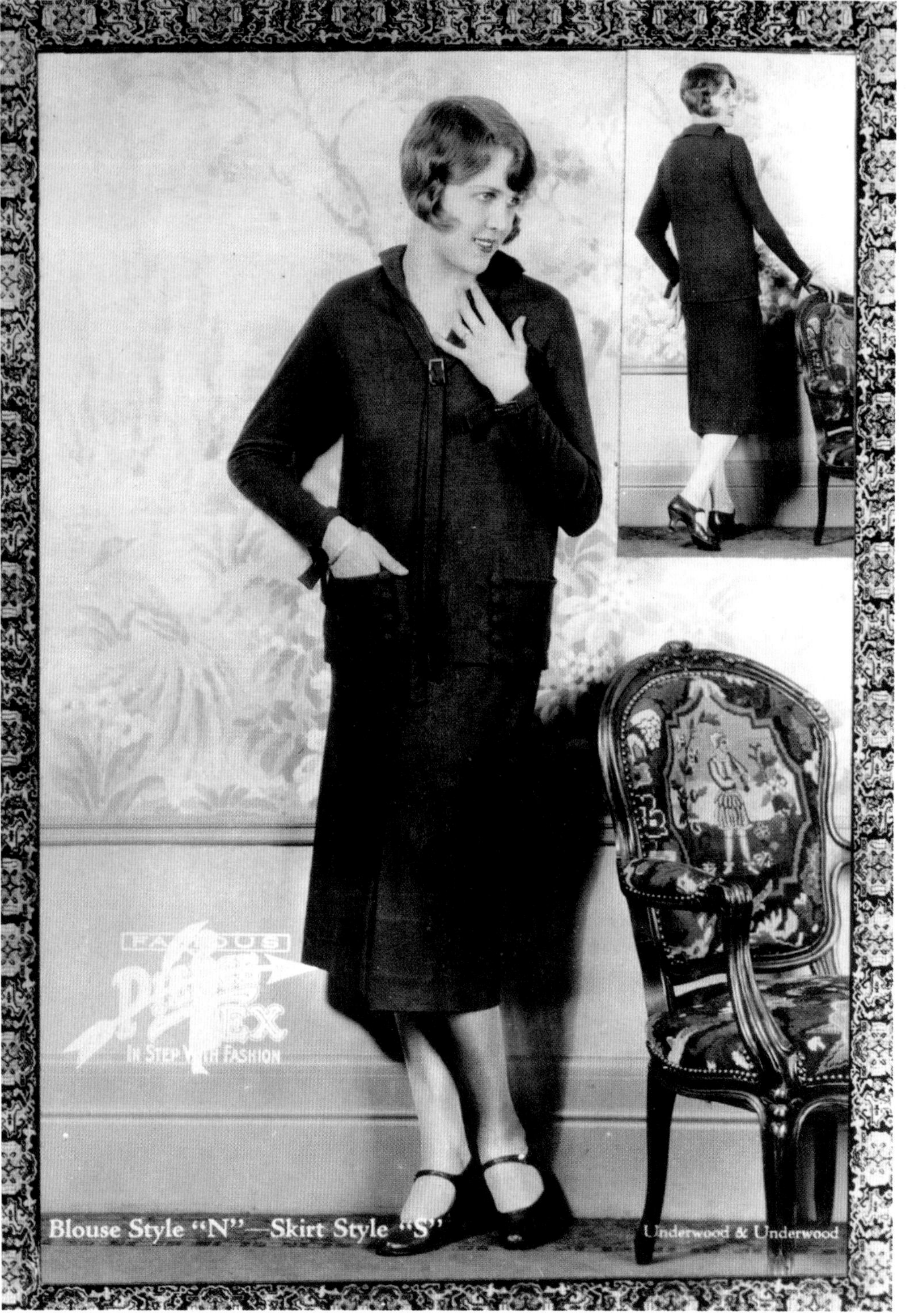

Above and right

Matching blouse and skirt ensemble by Pierce Tex. Underwood and Underwood, c.1922

Day dress with lace collar by Bernard et Cie. *La Femme Elégant à Paris*, 1926

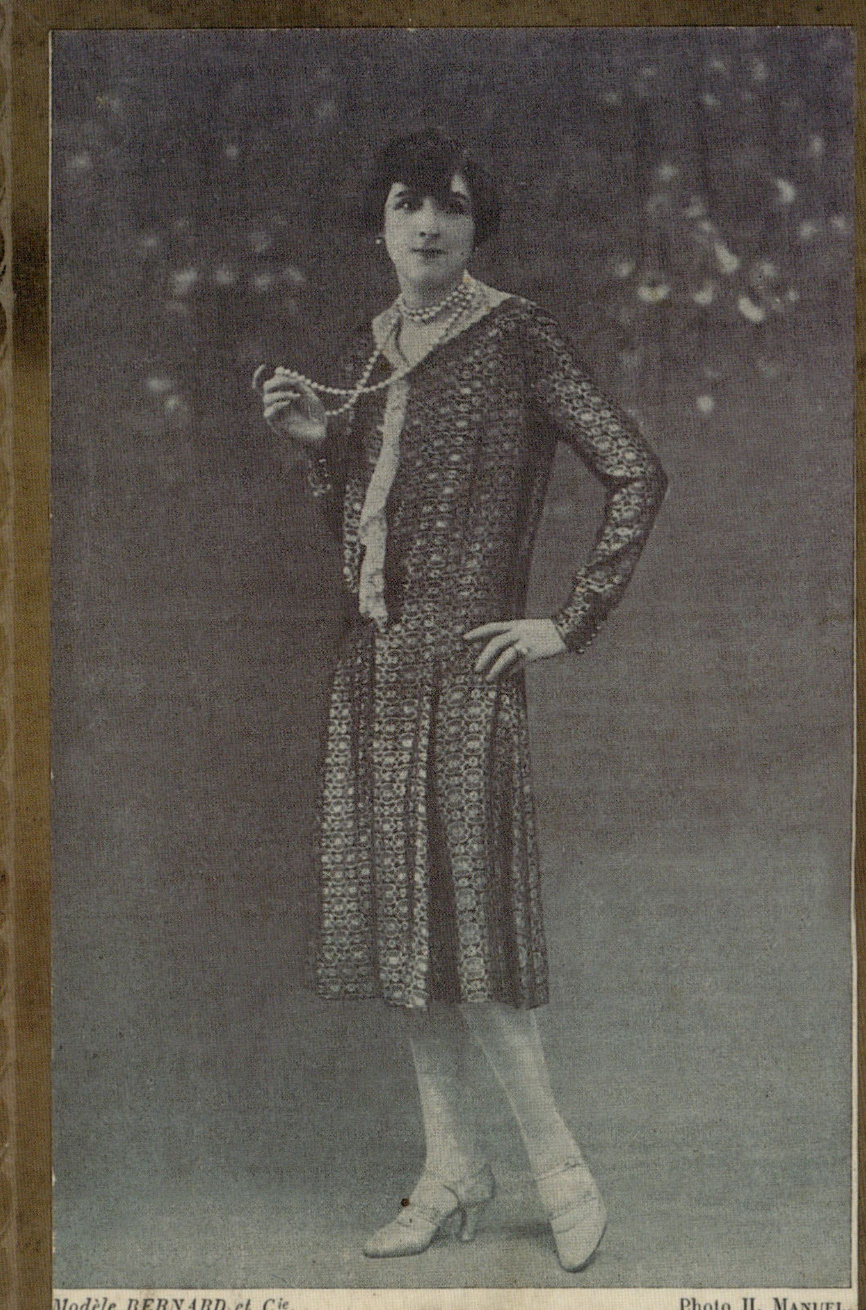

Modèle BERNARD et Cie. Photo H. MANUEL.

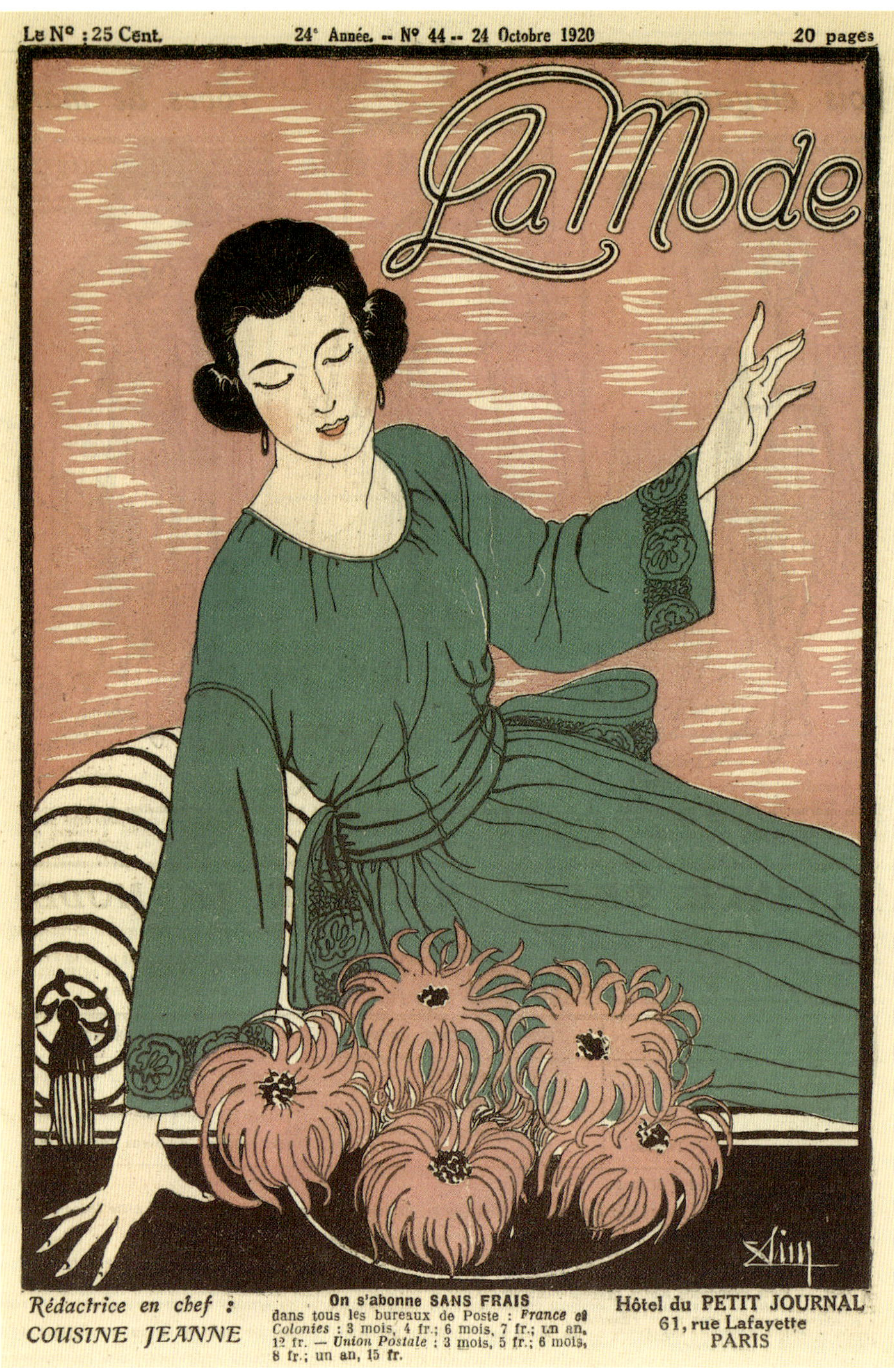

Above
Woman in a green day dress.
La Mode, 1920

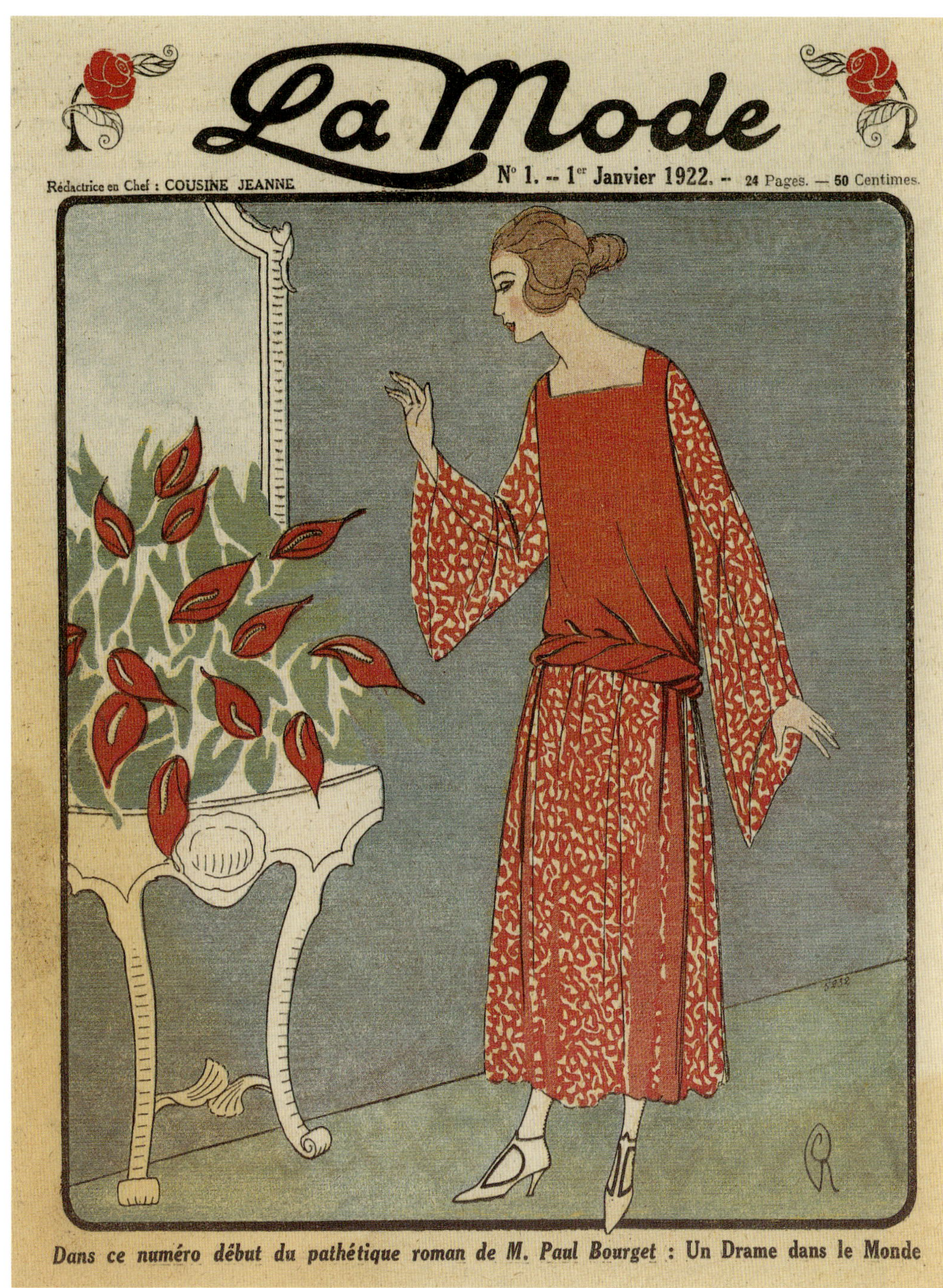

Above
A woman wearing a red patterned dress with bell sleeves and a twisted belt. *La Mode*, 1922

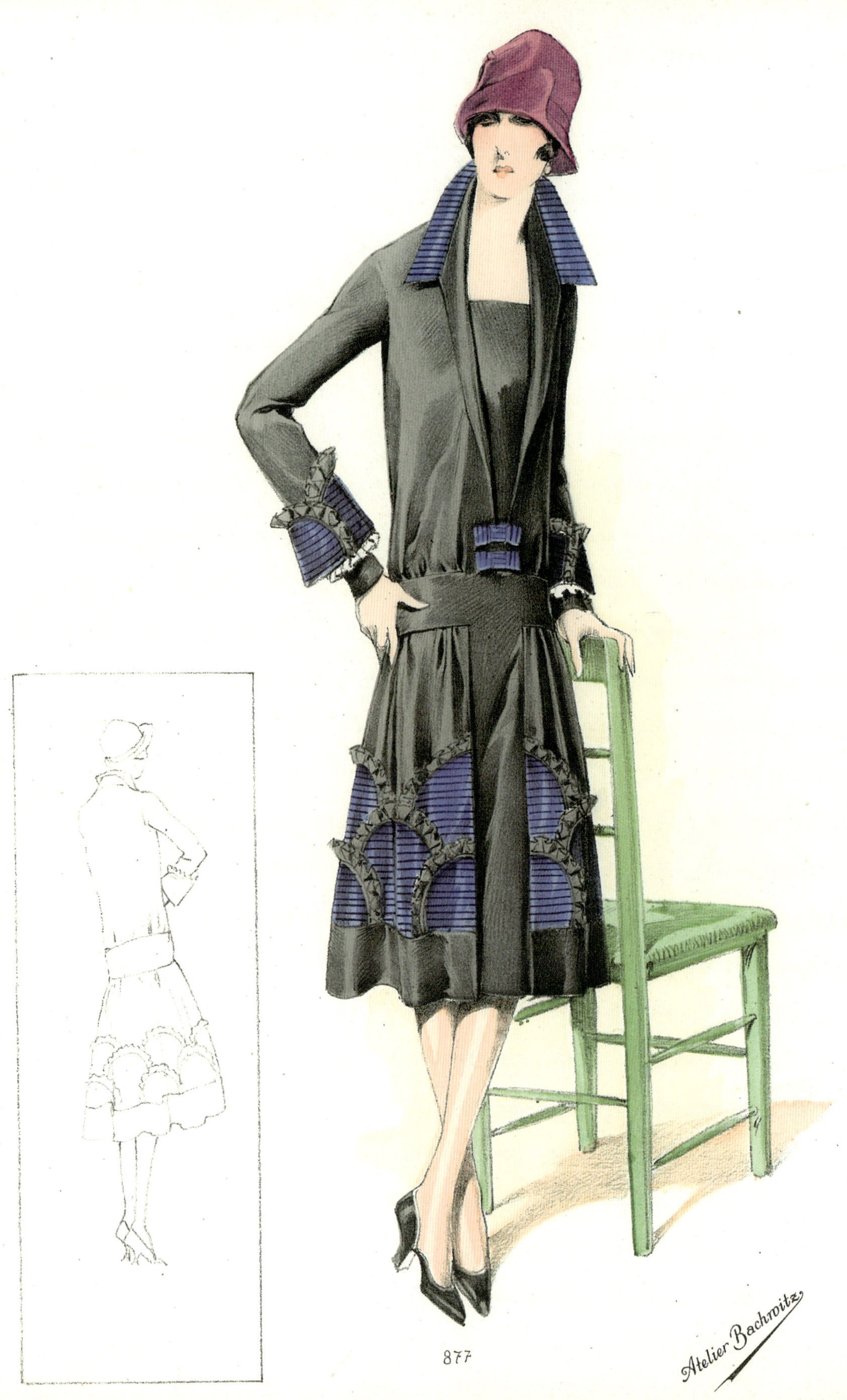
877
Atelier Bachwitz

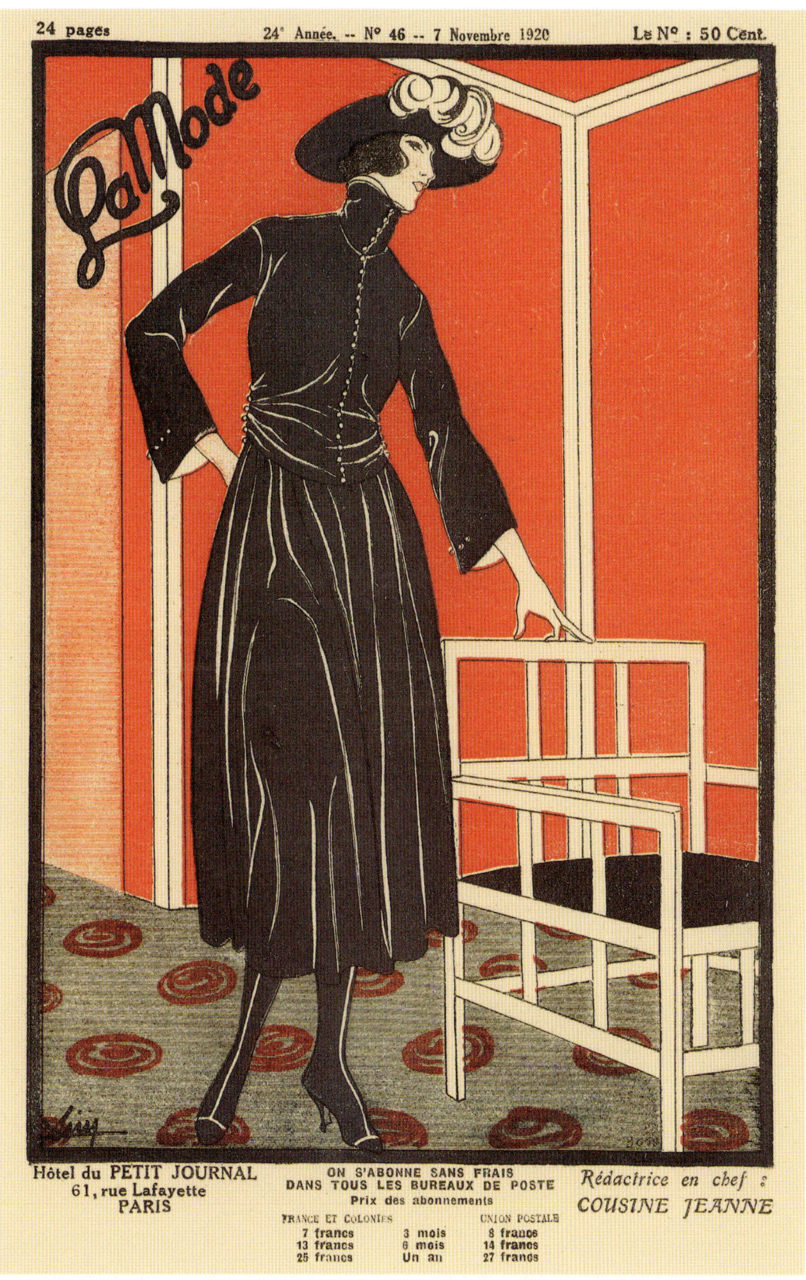

Left and above

Afternoon dress of black faille with coloured velvet application bordered with pleated silver galloons by Atelier Bachroitz. *Chic Parisien Beaux-arts des Modes*, 1925

Woman in a black coat with a high-buttoned collar. *La Mode*, 1920

Below
Rayon jersey sportswear ensemble by Van Ultra. Underwood and Underwood Photography, c.1923

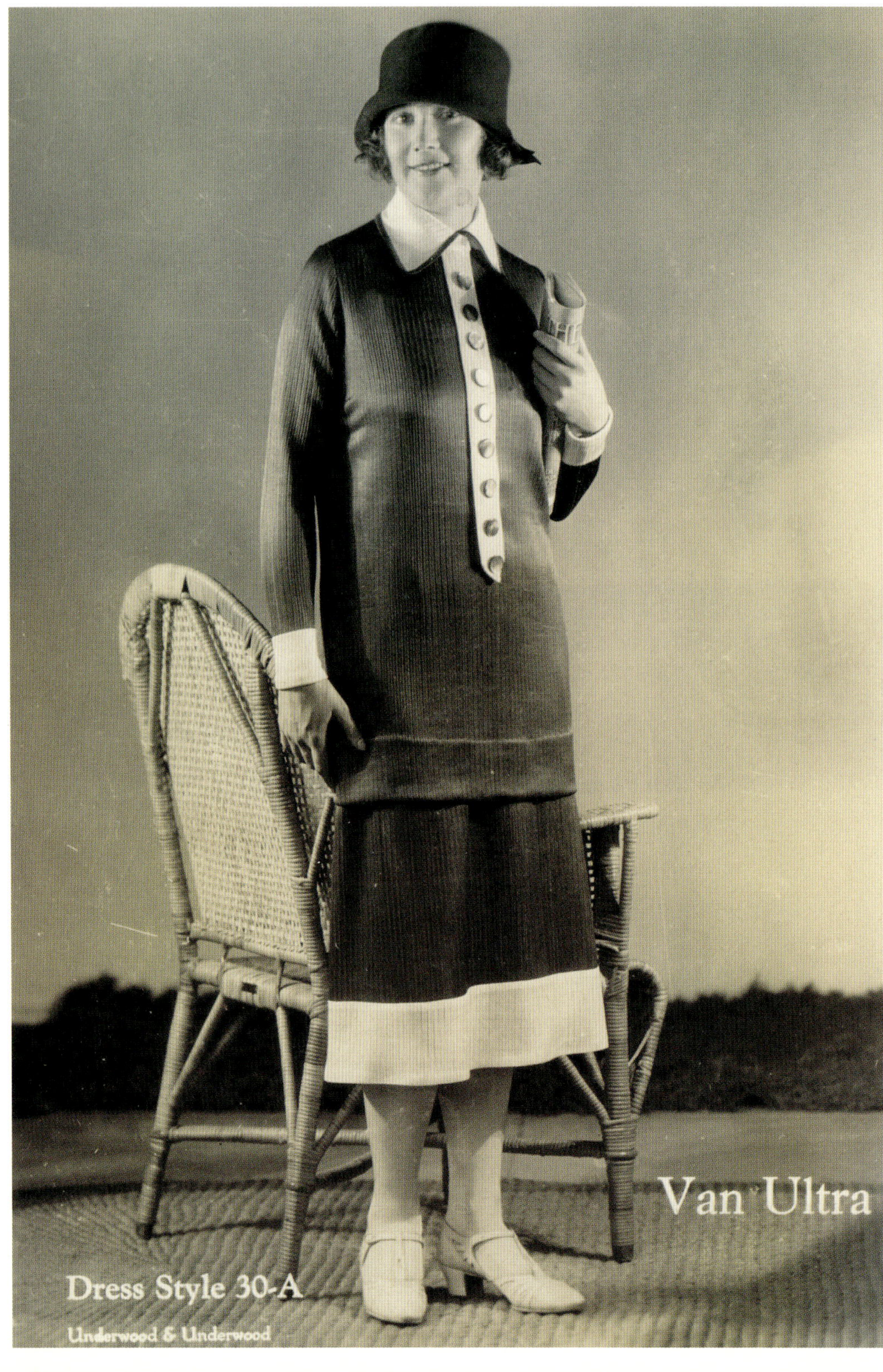

Below
Rayon jersey dress with sailor collar by Van Ultra. Underwood and Underwood Photography, c.1923

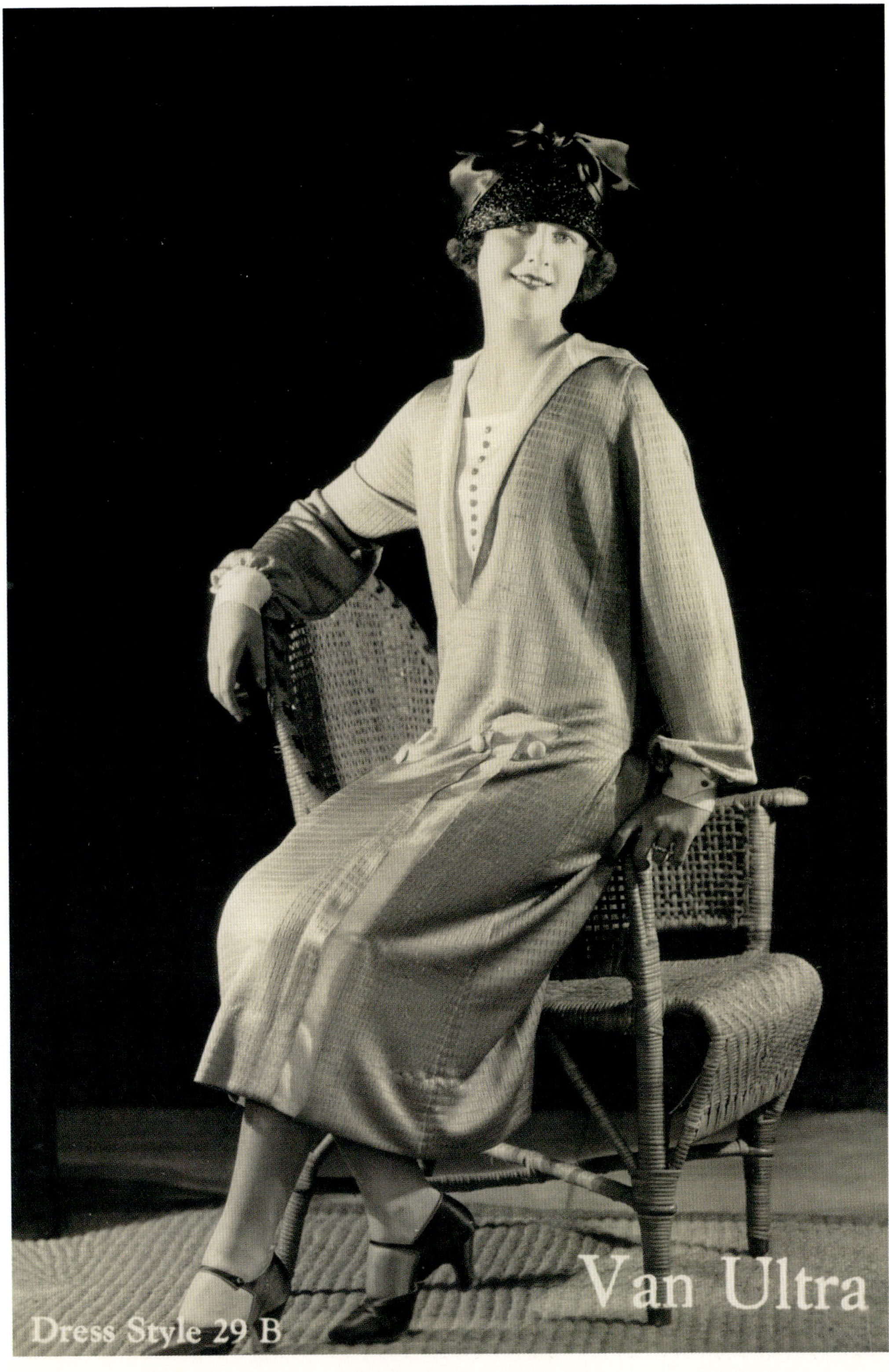

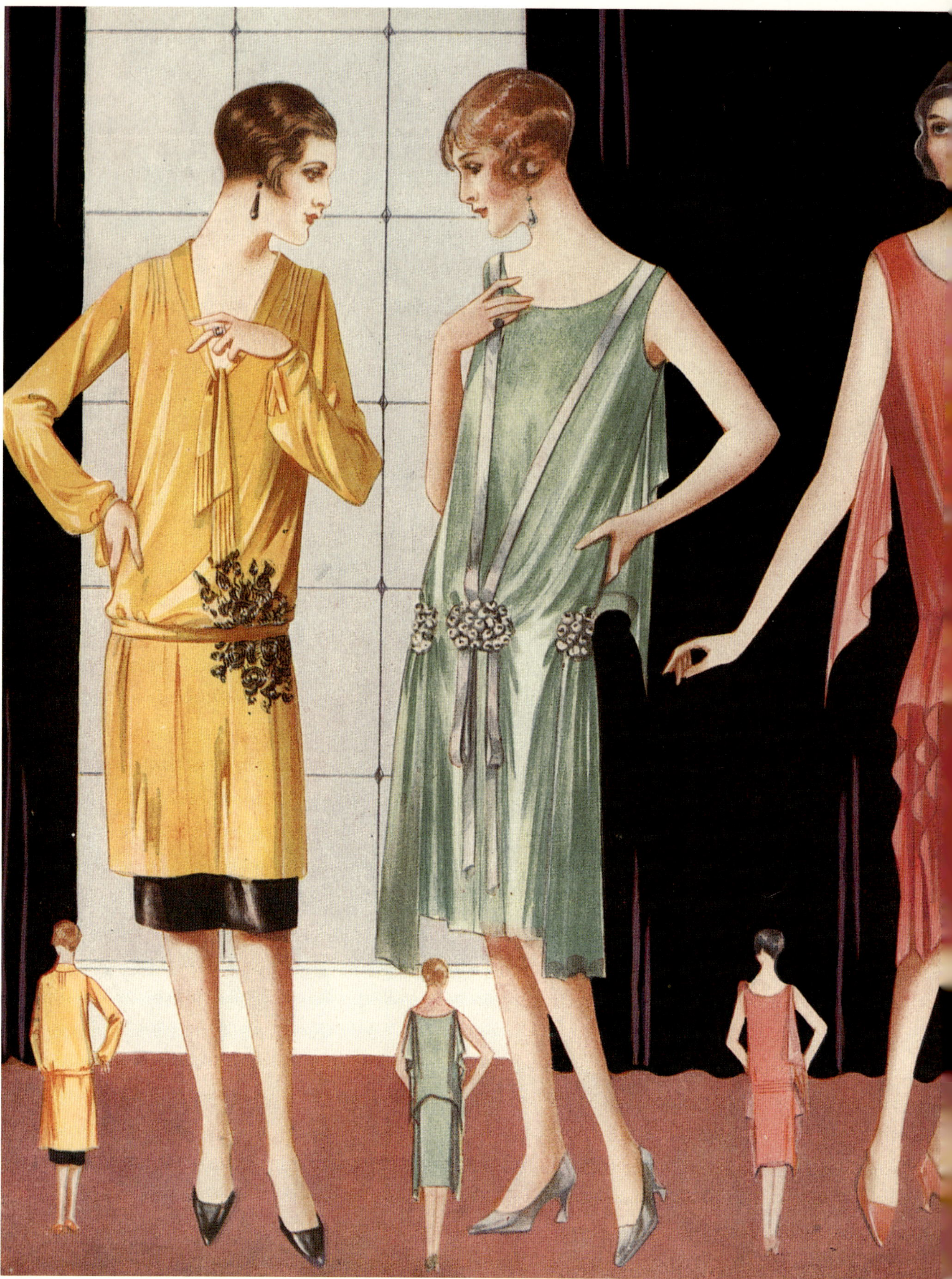

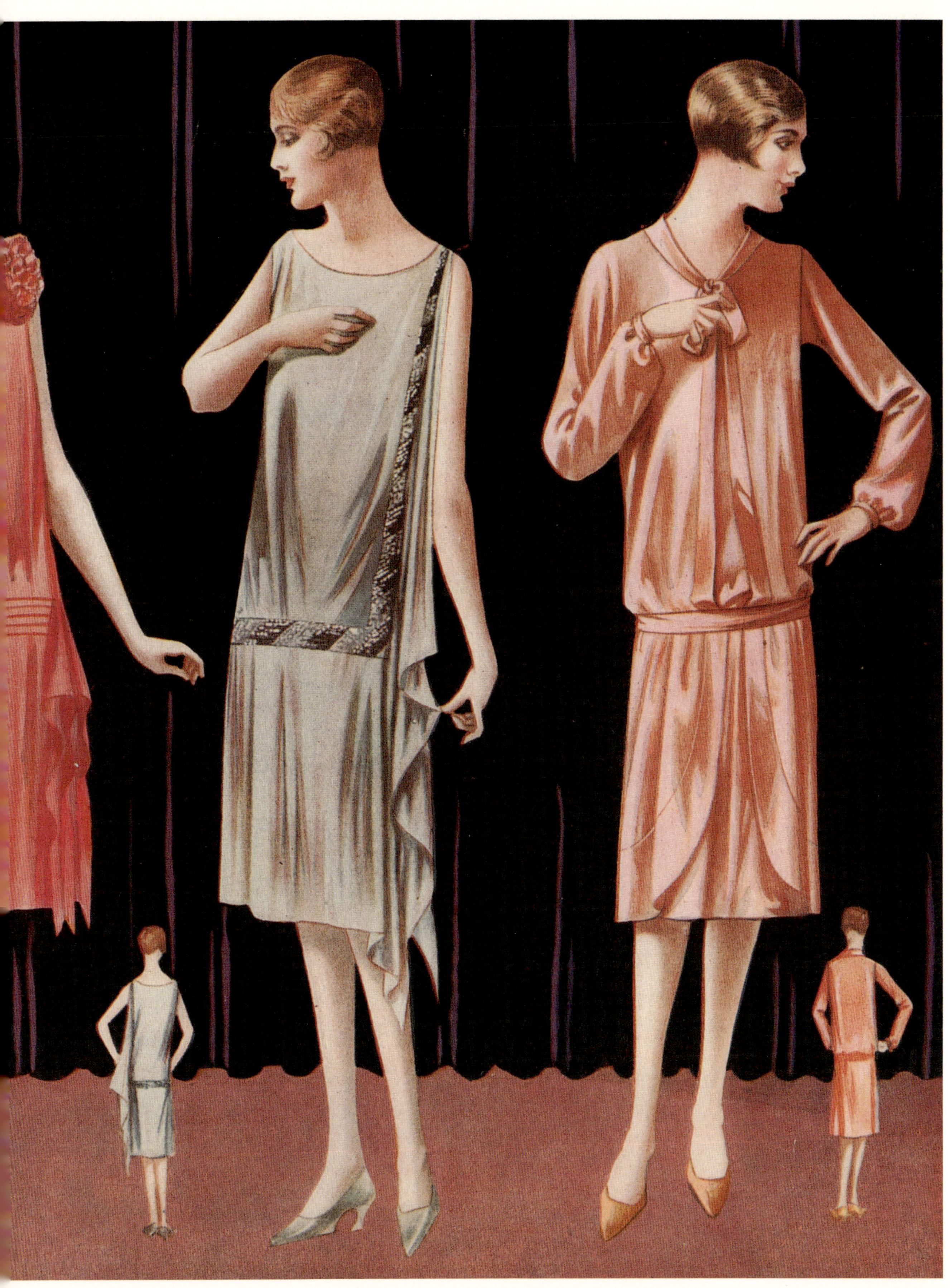

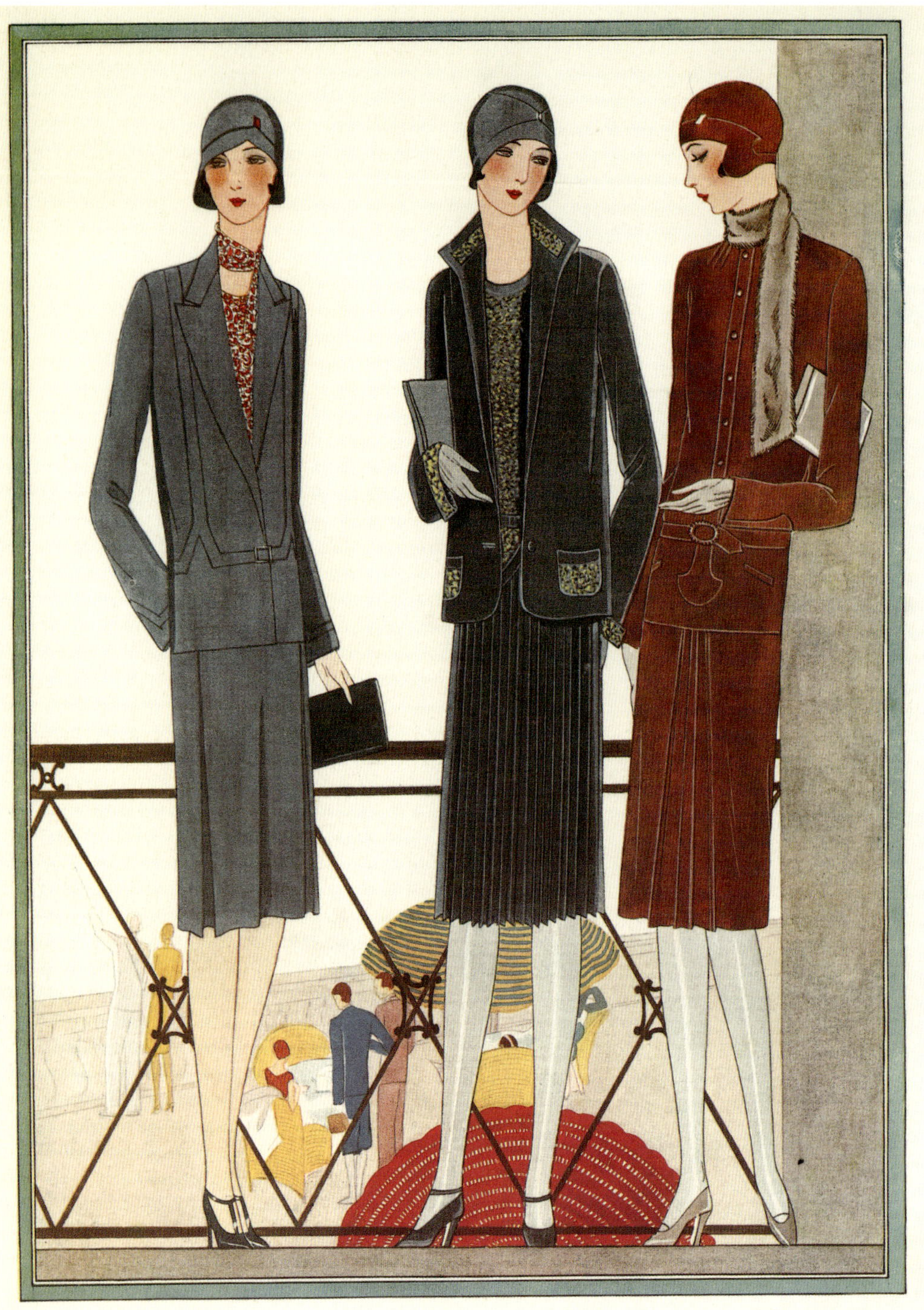

Previous page and above
Five afternoon dresses.
Fashion for All, 1927

Three skirt suits with matching cloche hats. *Sélection*, c.1927

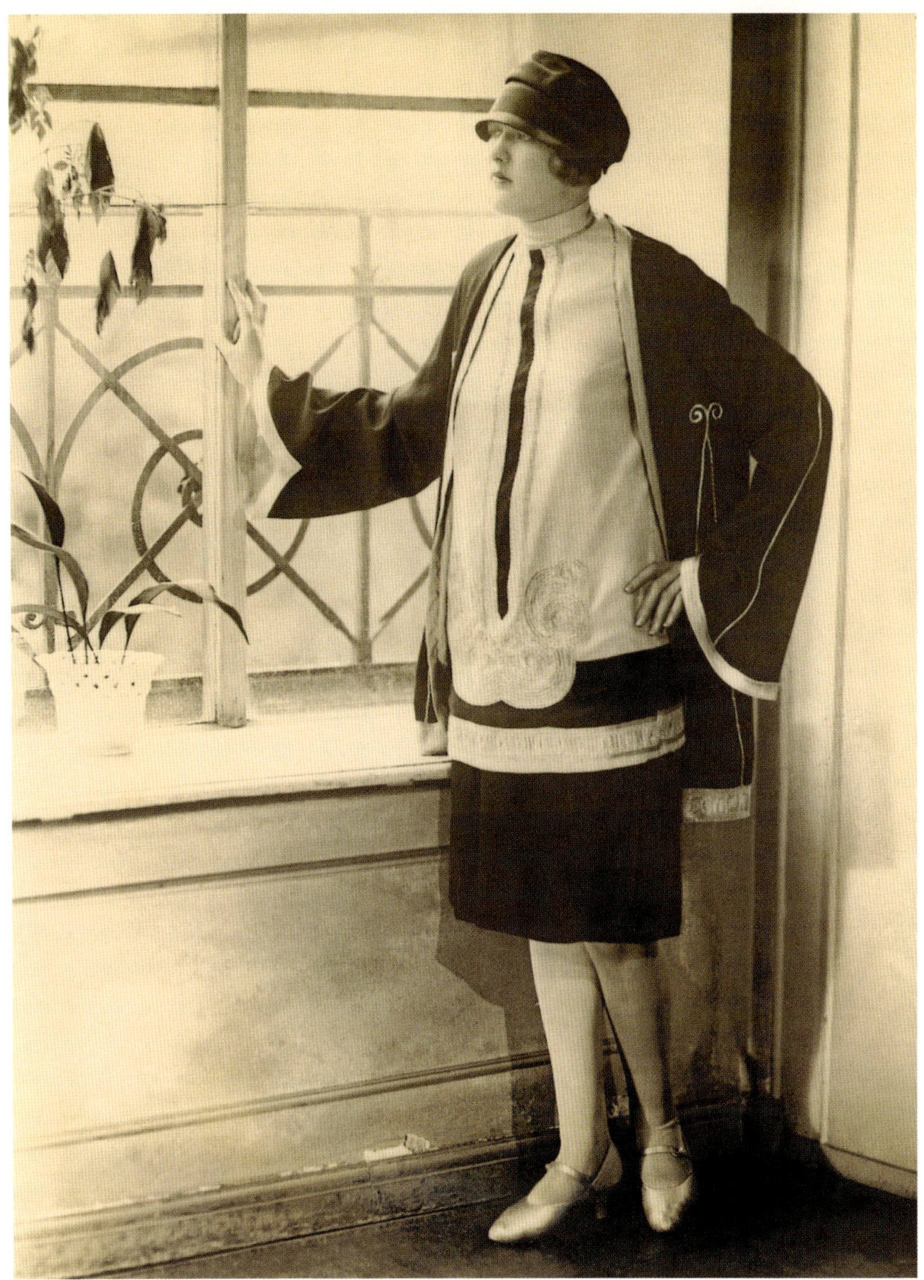

Above

Two-piece afternoon outfit of blue and white crepe de Chine, c.1925. The jumper is elaborately encrusted with tiny seed pearls in rich stylised wave designs, while the loose fitting blue coat is piped and embroidered to match the jumper design. A tight fitting cloche hat completes the outfit. The wave design is probably inspired by Katsushika Hokusai's "Great Wave off Kanagawa" woodblock print from c.1829.

Right

Studio fashion photograph of the 'Canada' creation by Groult, c.1925. The design on the dress is described as 'Indian', which in this instance refers to Canadian First Nations and it incorporates stylised traditional First Nations' designs. This type of stylistic appropriation is an example of less obvious Orientalism in fashion.

Next page

Five silhouettes for a 'reception at the villa'. Dresses and coats are calf length and long handkerchief sleeves are favoured although as the Soeurs Boue model reveals shorter lace sleeves were also fashionable. The black coat and dress dispel the myth that black at this stage was still only worn whilst in mourning, and instead show that black was a fashion colour well before Coco Chanel introduced her "Little Black Dress" in 1926. *La Femme Chic*, c.1922

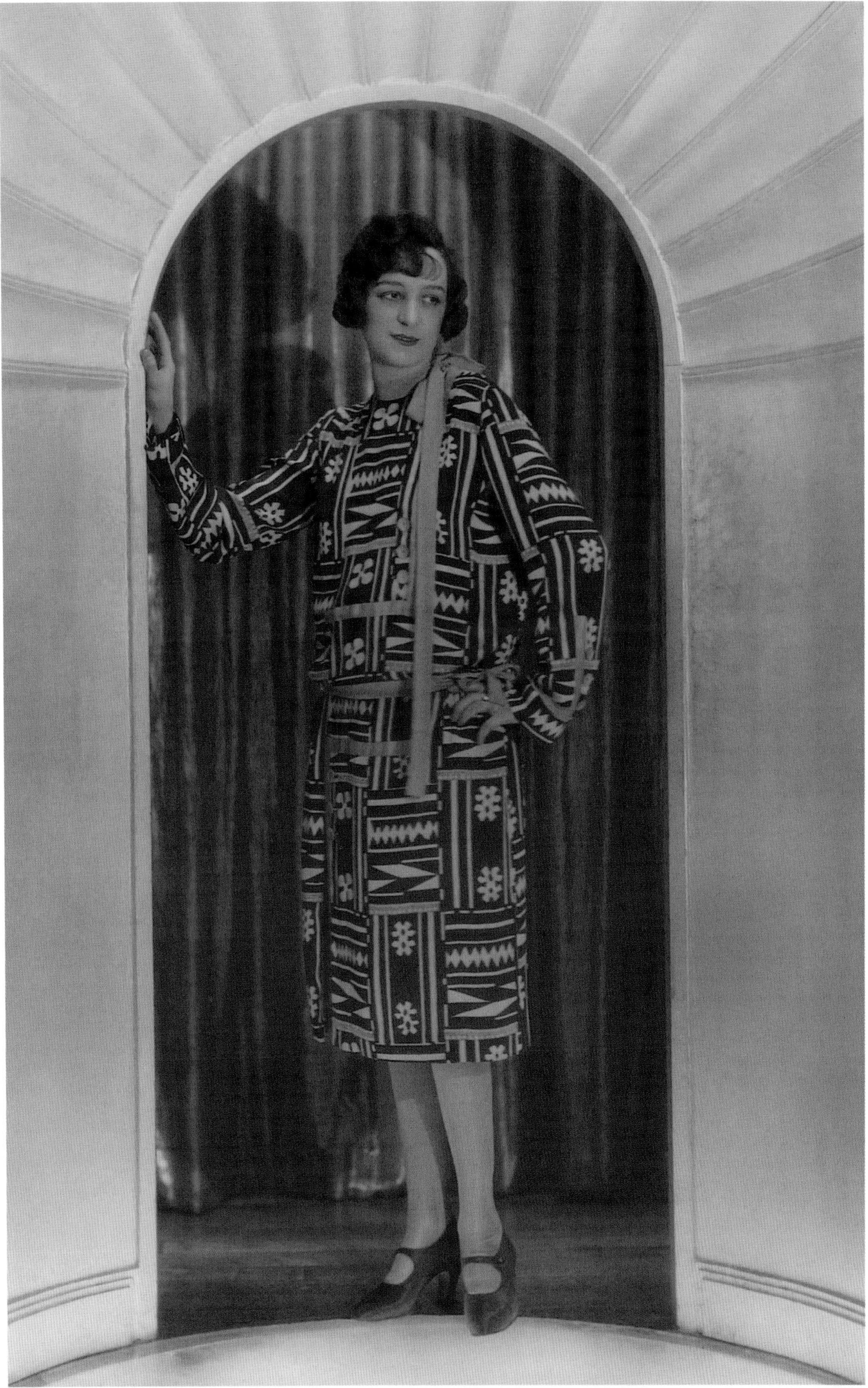

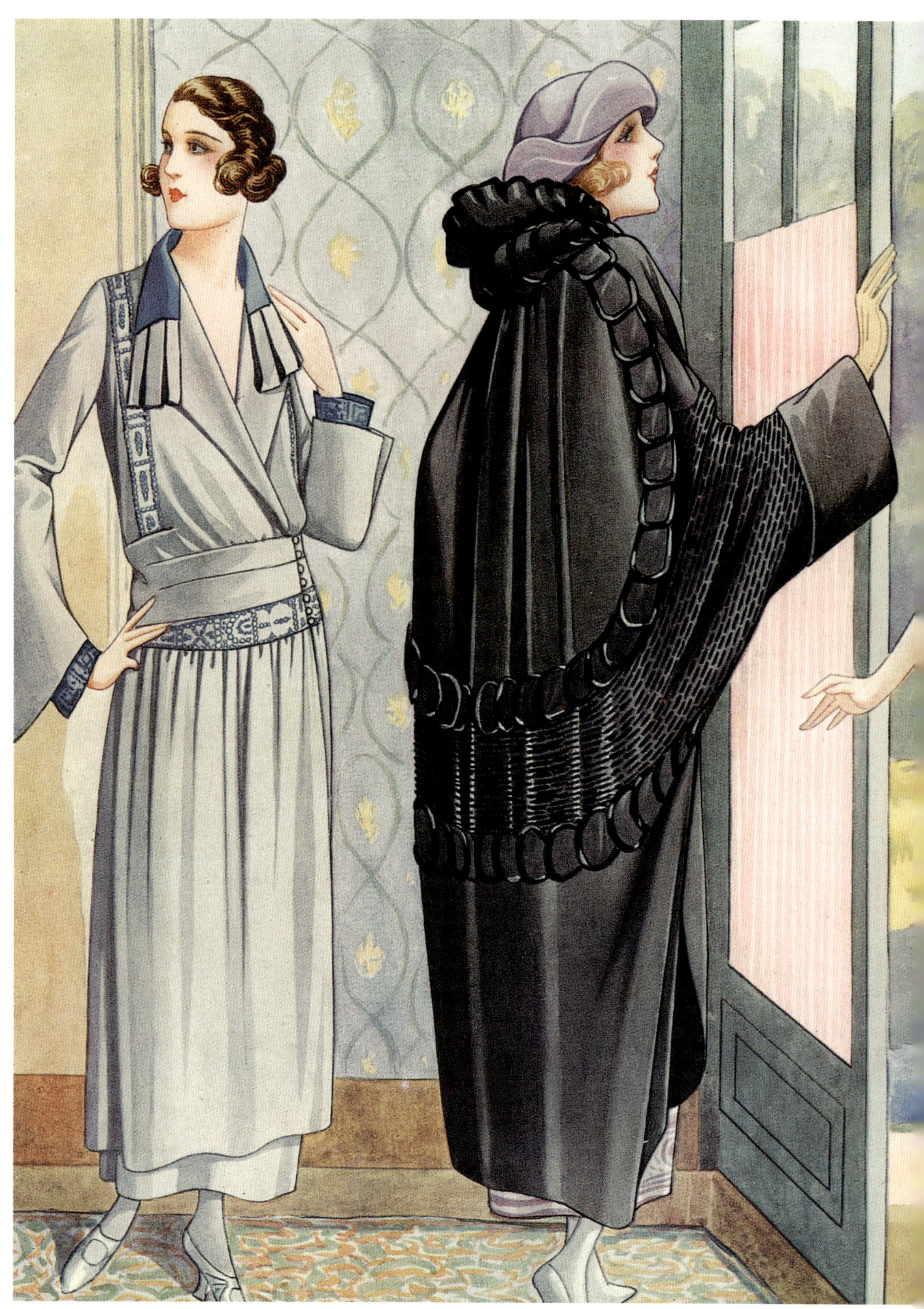

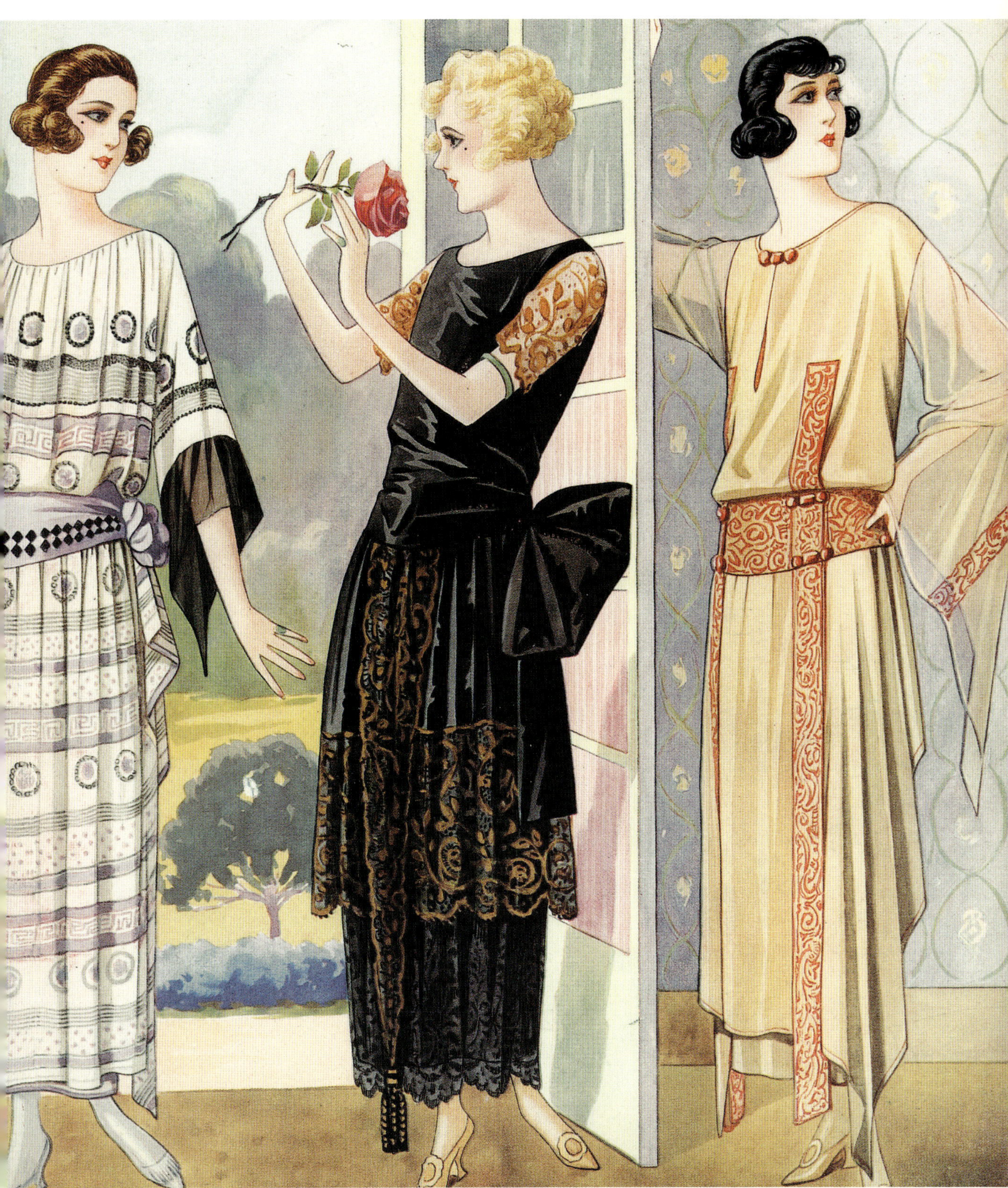

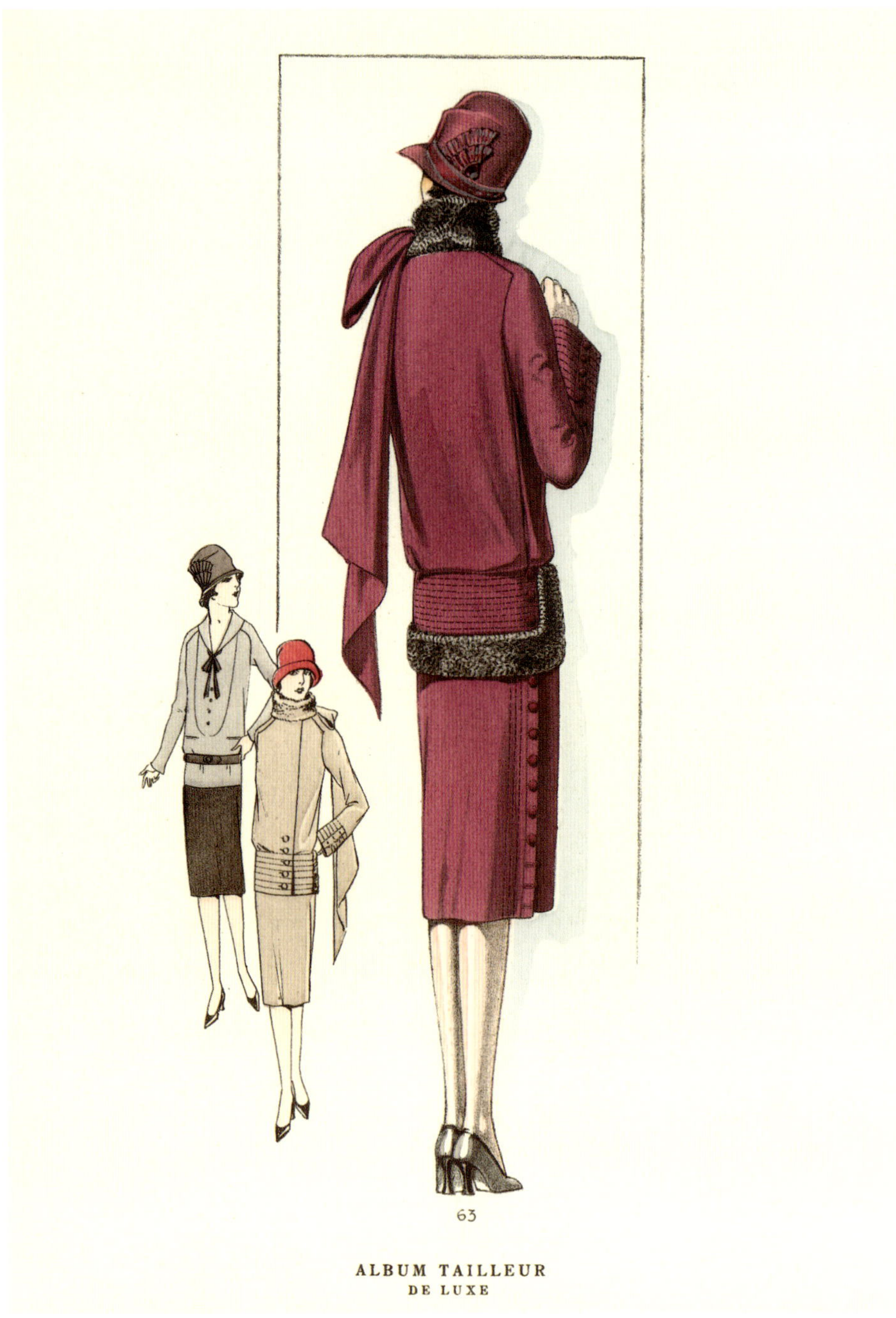

Above and right

Burgundy skirt suit, the jacket trimmed with fur. *Album Tailleur de Luxe*, c.1925

Two day dresses. *Sélection*, c.1927. The black dress is very similar to Coco Chanel's "Little Black Dress" of 1926

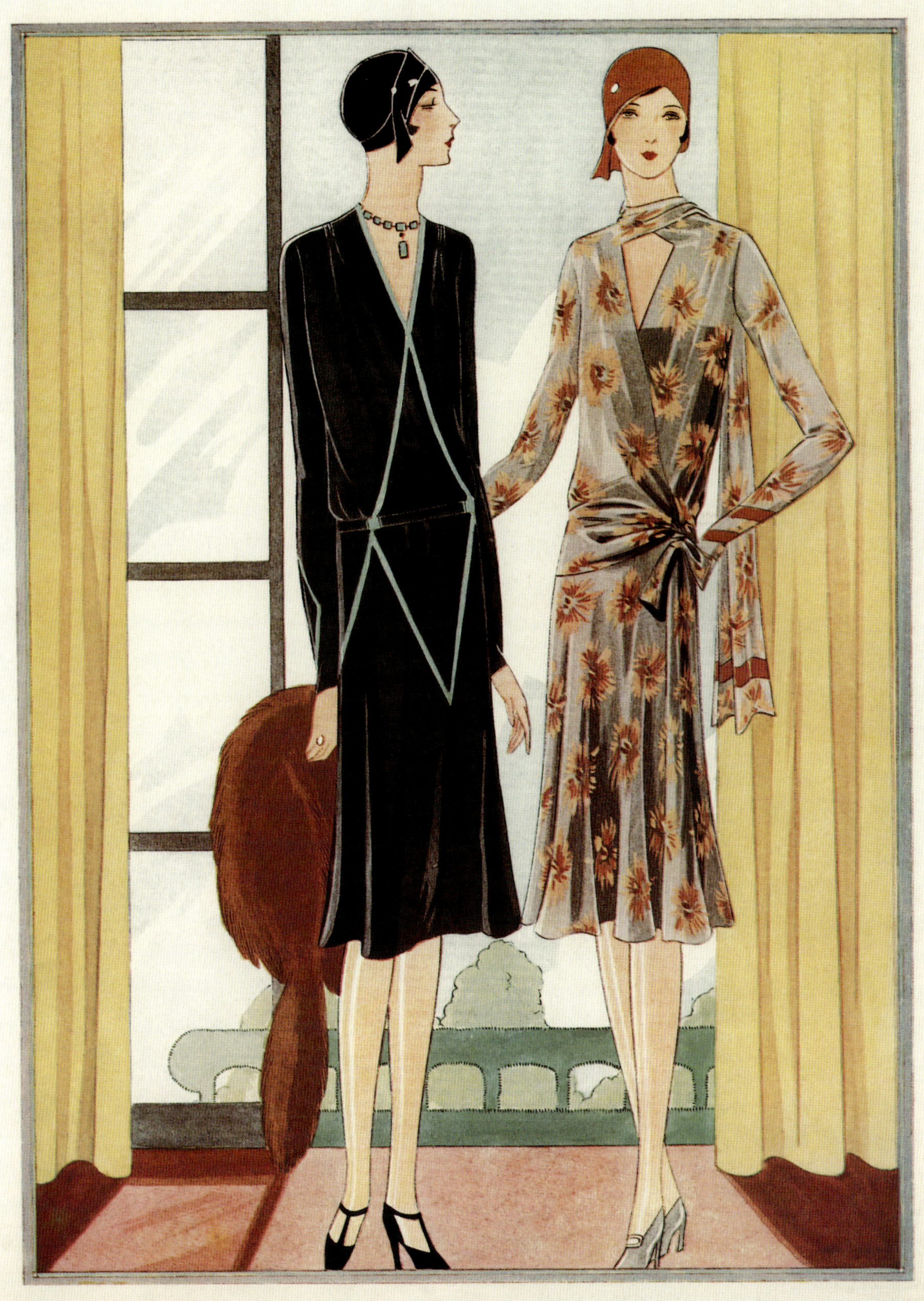

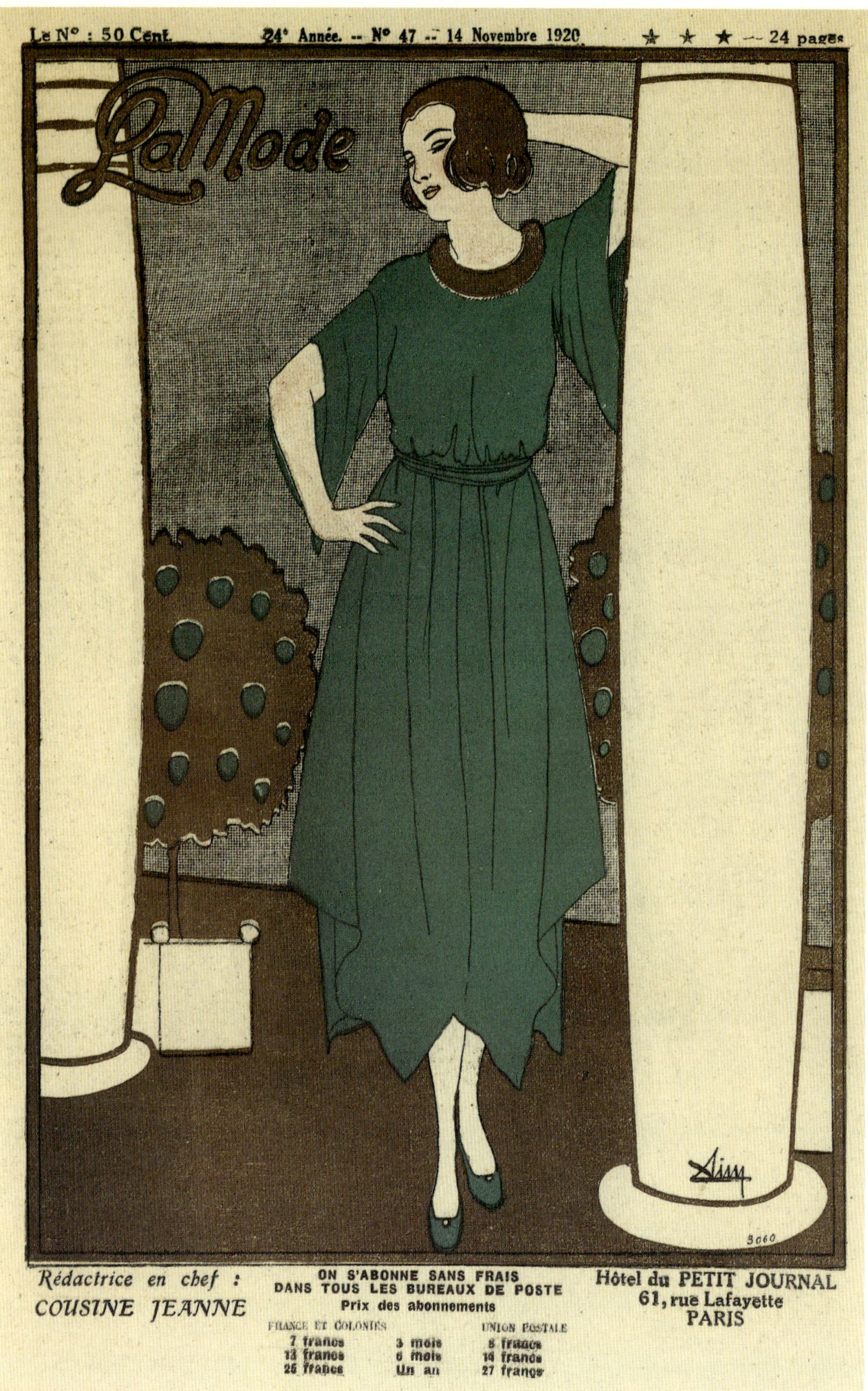

Above and right

A woman in a green dress with short bell sleeves and a fur collar. *La Mode*, 1920

A Parisian ensemble, c.1924. The model wears a beige cape draped off the shoulders with a light silk dress that has a knife-pleated skirt in beige and red.

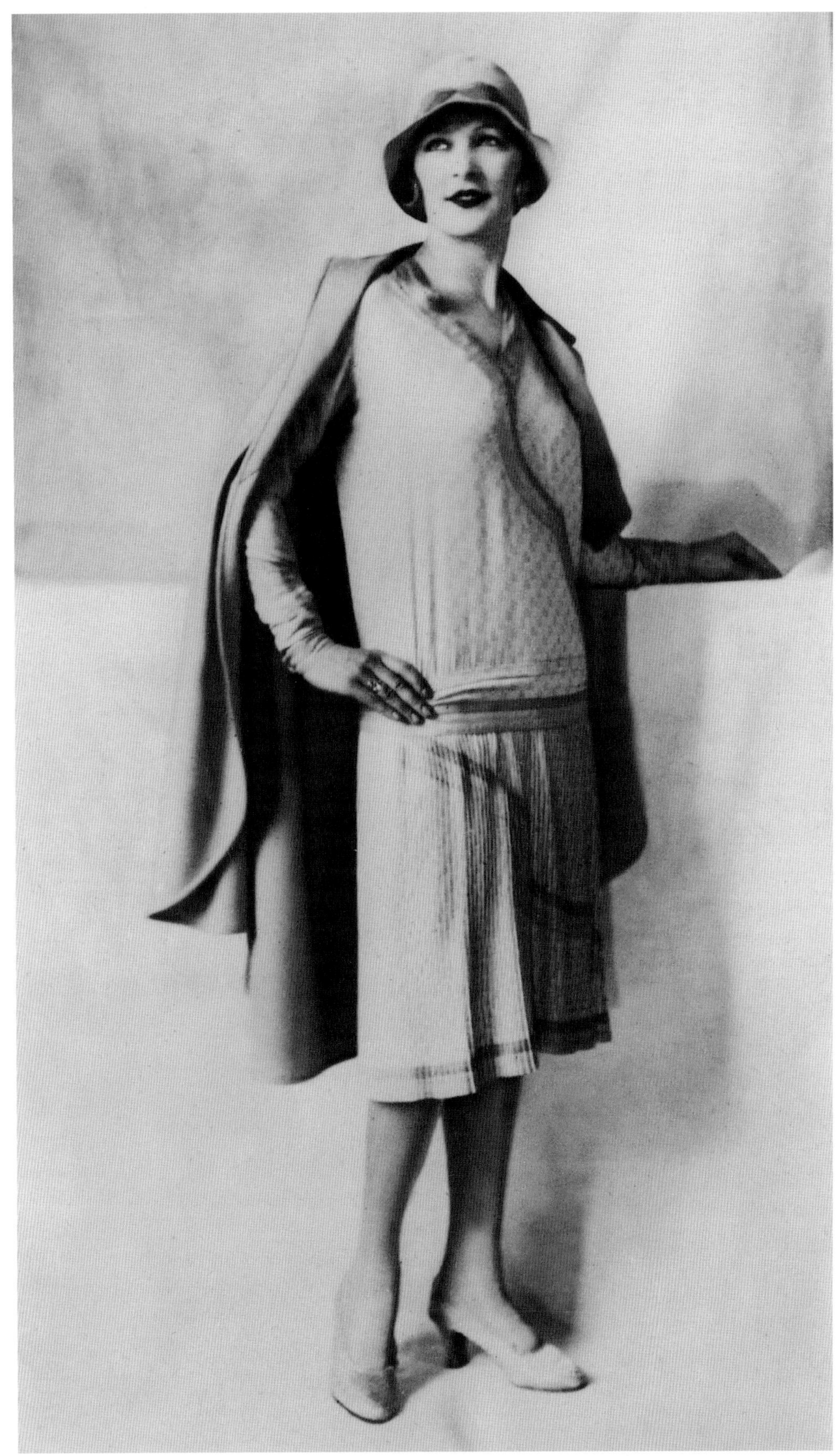

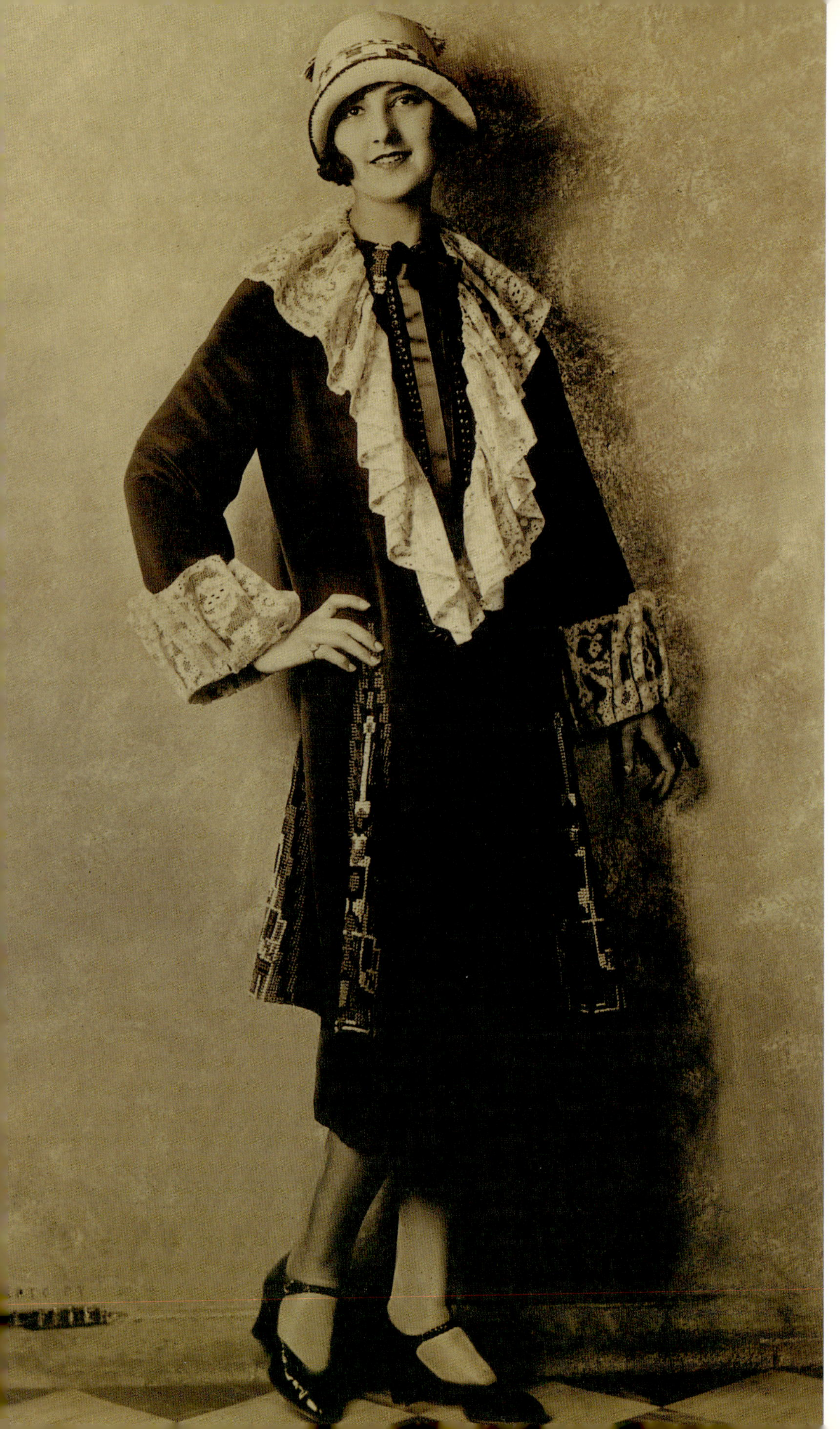

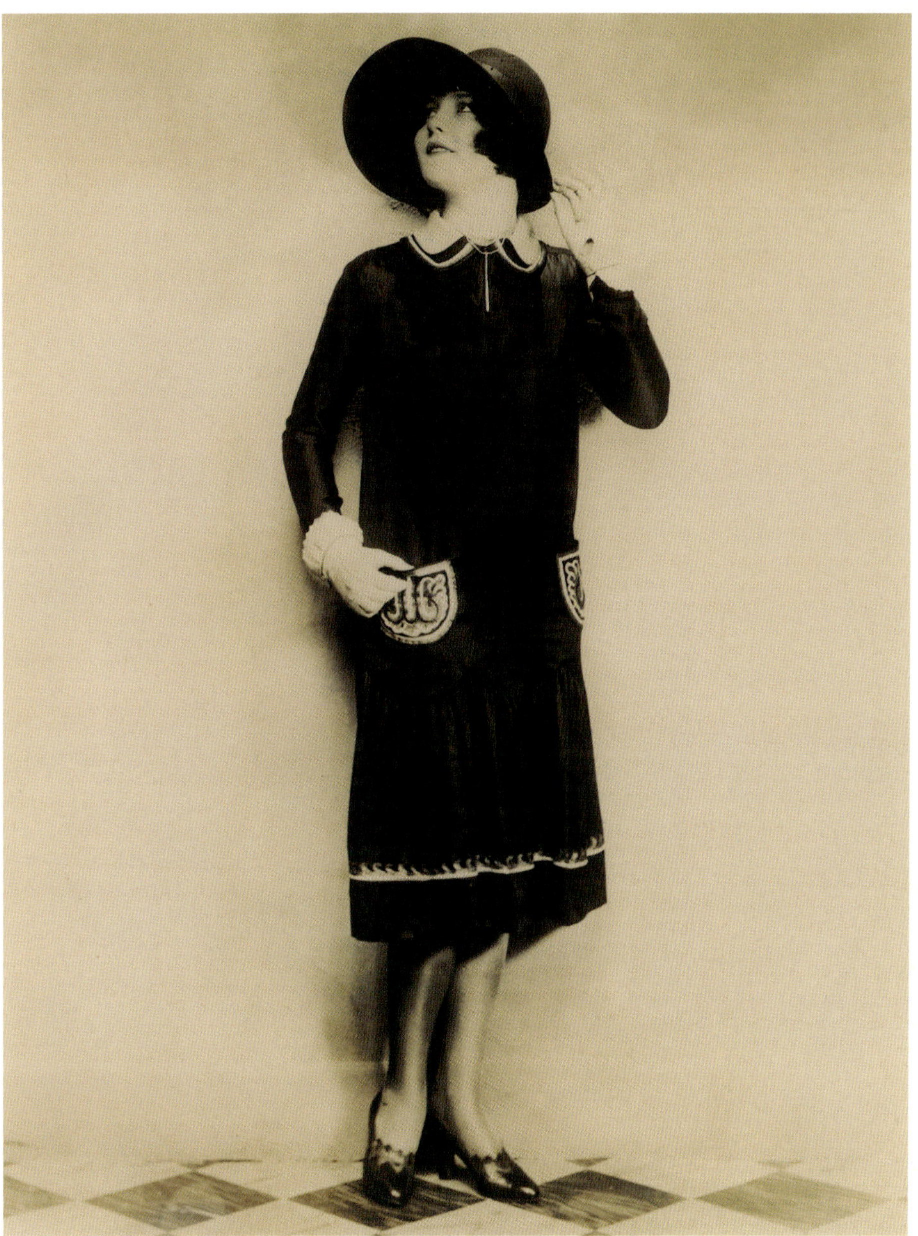

Left and above

A model in a bengaline creation – a woven ribbed man-made fibre ensemble, heavily embroidered with peasant inspired motifs and trimmed with fine lace around the collar and cuffs, c.1923

Black satin day dress embroidered in yellow on the pockets and around the hem, while the shoes are of black kid and the hat is a black wide-brimmed cloche. USA, c.1923

Below and right

"Jouerai-je?" (Should I play?), dress for the races by Beer. Illustration by Pierre Brissaud. *Gazette du Bon Ton*, 1920

White skirt and blouse ensemble. The blouse has lace inserts and is decorated with a diamante clip, while the calf length skirt is finely pleated. The model wears a slave bracelet on her upper arm. USA, c.1923

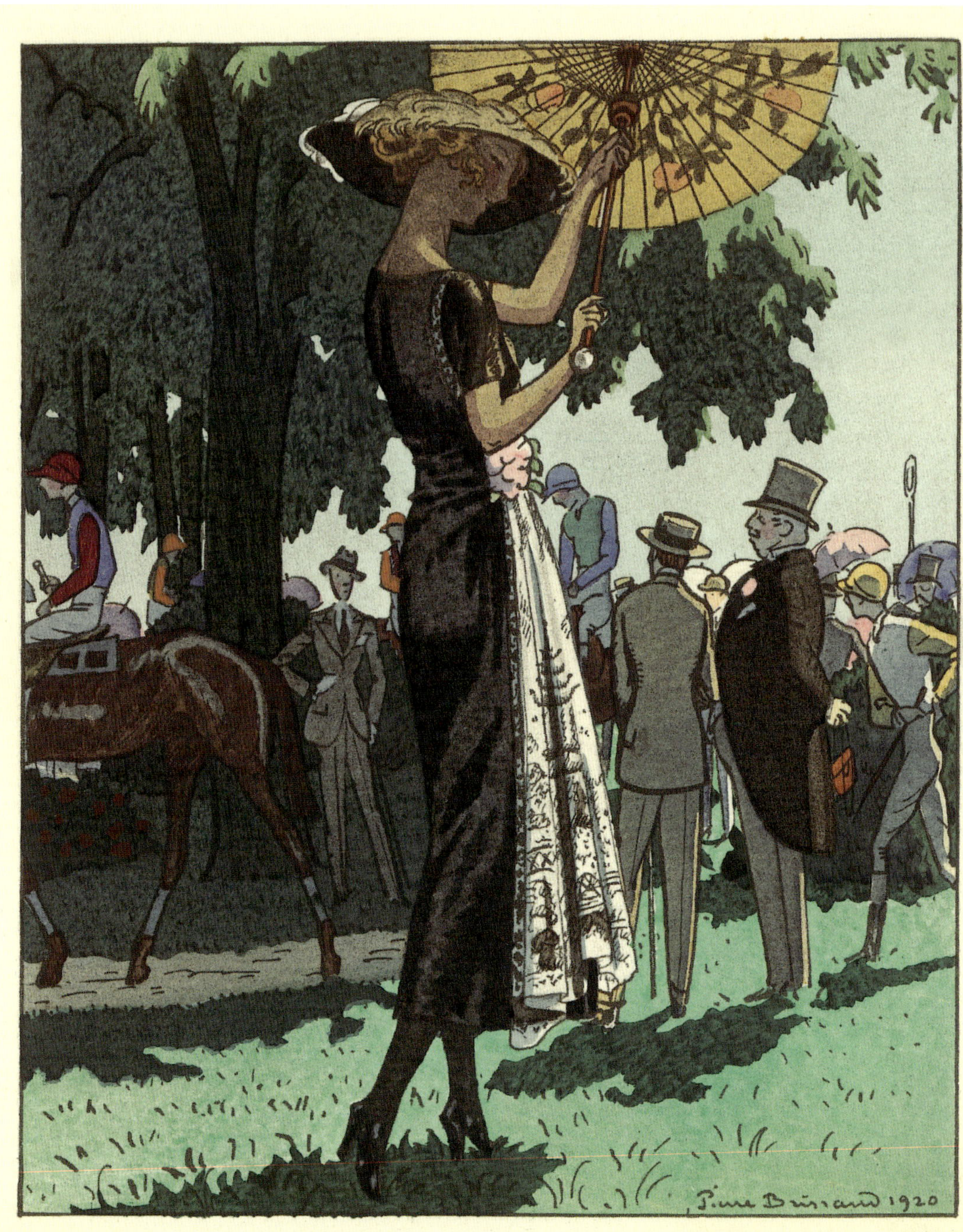

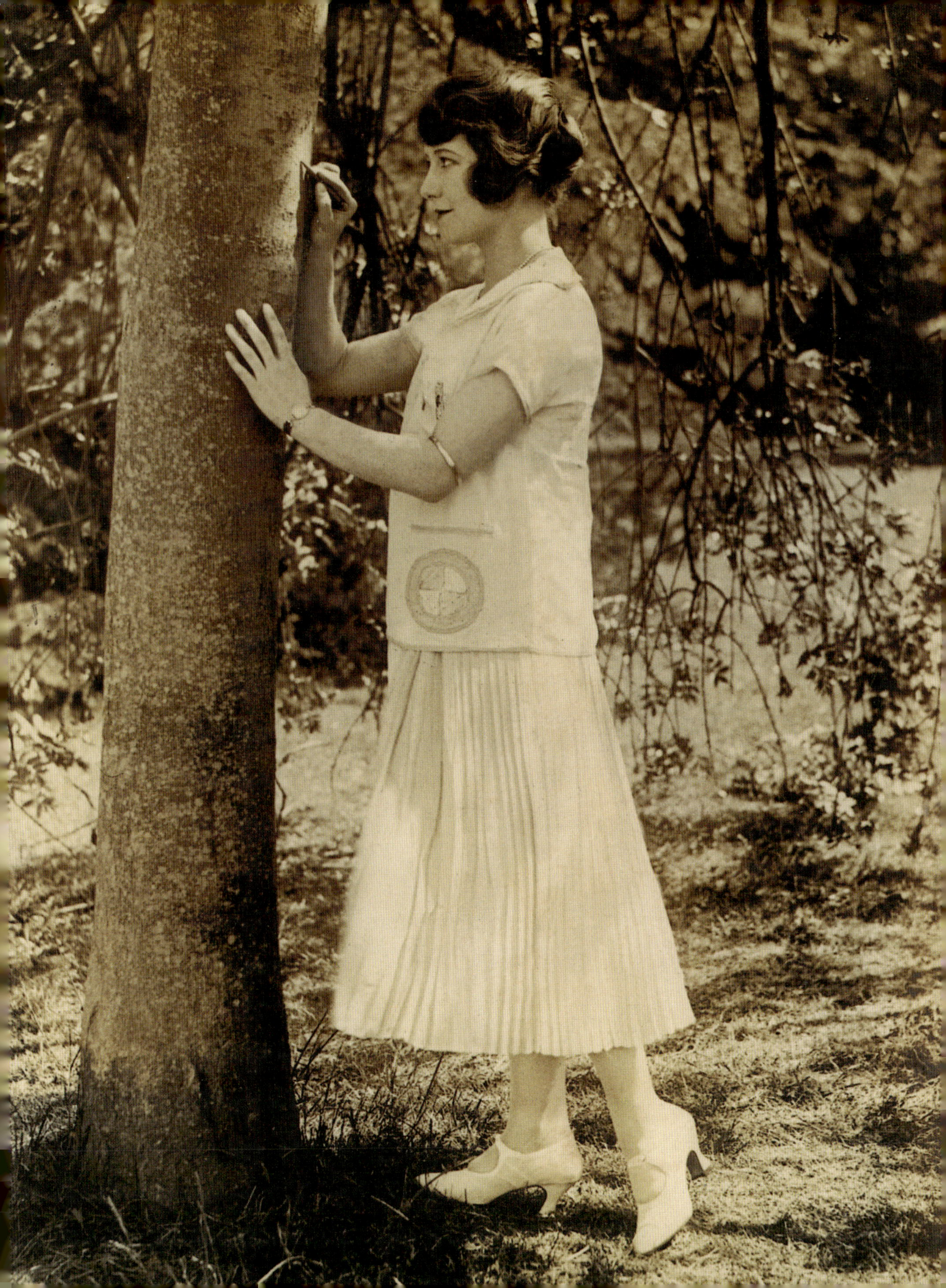

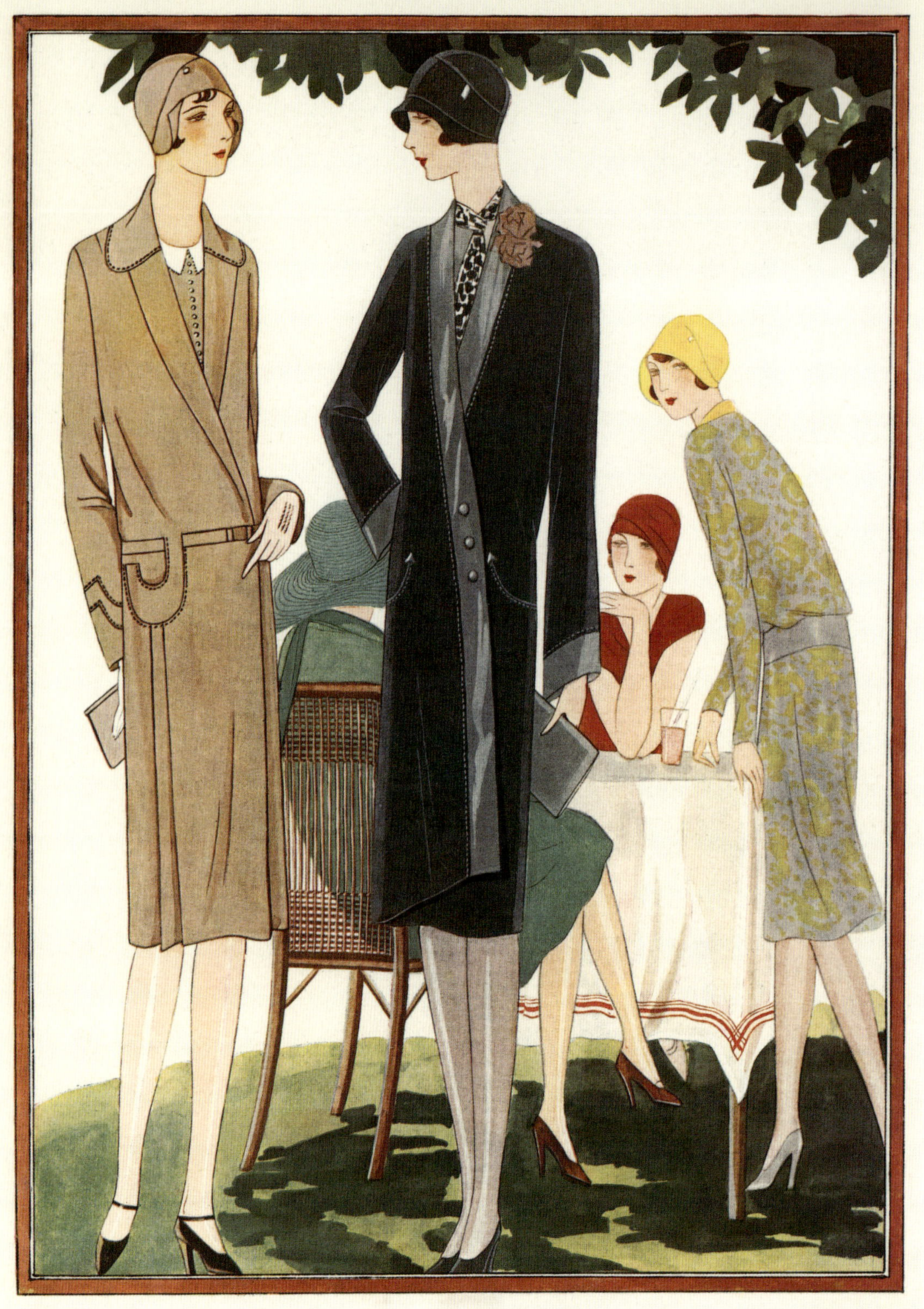

Above and right
Two day coats accessorized with tight fitting cloche hats. *Sélection*, c.1927

Selection of summer dresses, Printemps catalogue, 1924

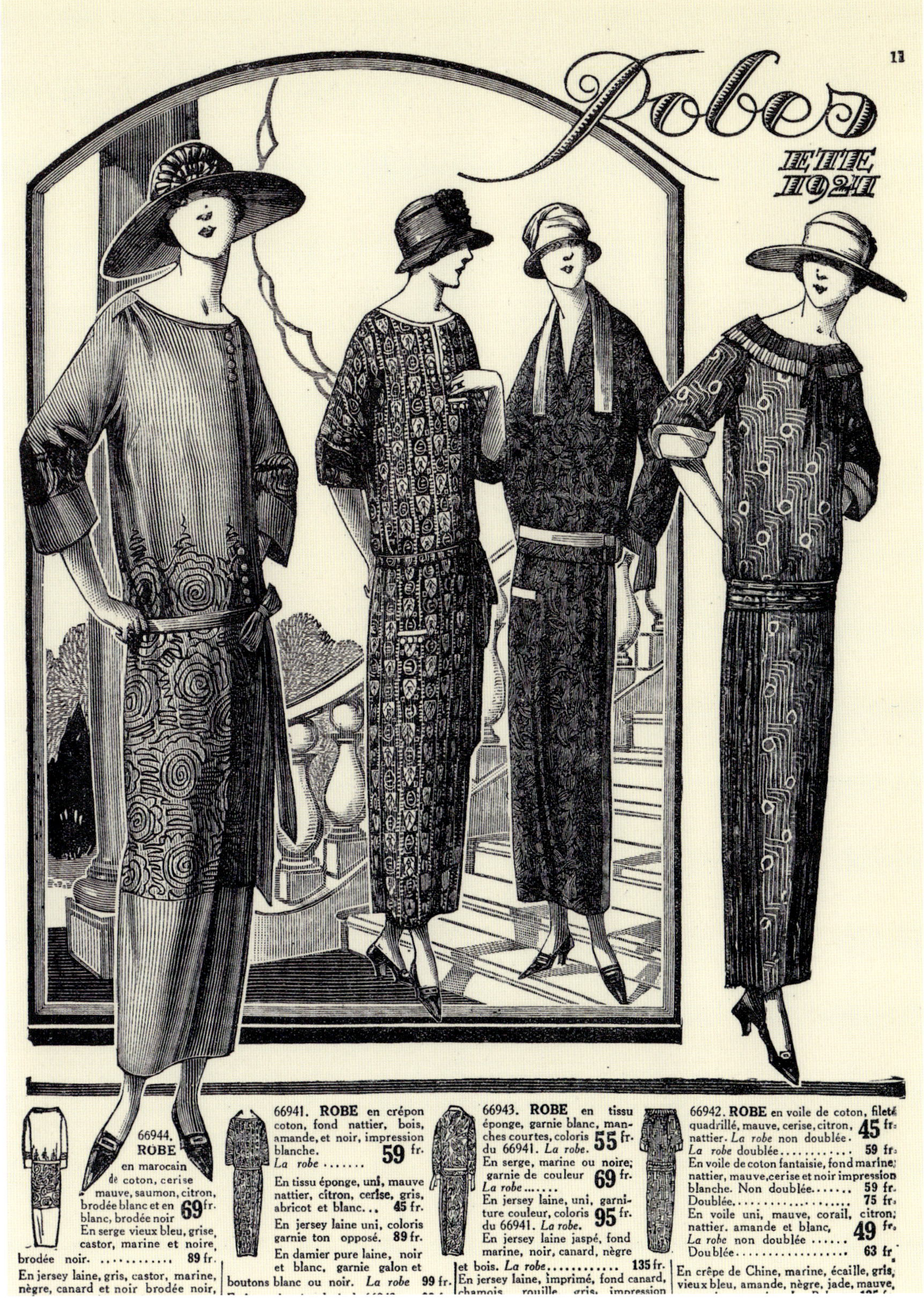

Next page
Selection of summer dresses, Printemps catalogue, 1924

12

Robes

Au Printemps
paris

66945. ROBE en crépon fin, fond blanc brodé mauve, cerise, citron, nattier, noir, ou tout blanc, garniture couleur. *La robe* **69** fr.
En voile de coton fond écru, cerise, gris, impression couleur ou blanc, impression noire. *La robe non doublée* **69** f.
La robe doublée .... 85 fr.
En foulard marine ou noir, dessins blancs. **110** fr.
En jersey soie fond beige, blanc, crème imprimé noir, ou marine imprimé gris.
La robe, non doublée. **135** fr.
— *doublée*. 185 fr.

66946. ROBE en marocain coton, broderie blanche coloris du 66944.
La robe .... **79** fr.
En serge coloris du 66944 broderie couleur ou assortie.
La robe ...... **115** fr.
En jersey laine uni, coloris du 66941
Prix .... **125** fr.
En marocain de laine, amande rouille castor, gris marine ou noir. *La robe*. **135** f.

36924. **Petit CHAPEAU** en laize de crin noir ou nègre, garniture assortie. 75 f.

36925. **CLOCHE** en paille fantaisie blanche ou mordoré garnie roses roses .... 80 fr.

66948 **ROBE** en popeline marine ou noire, broderie couleur ou assortie.
La robe **145** fr.
En marocain de laine, coloris du 66946.
La robe .... **155** fr.
En crêpe marocain gros grain, acaiou, castor, nègre, amande, gris, vieux bleu, marine ou noir. **195** fr.

36926. **Petit CHAPEAU** en laize brillante marron, garni gland effilé soie assorti .... 59 fr.

66947.
ROBE-MANTEAU en serge pure laine, marine ou noire broderie lacet . assorti. *La robe*. **210** fr.
En popeline belle qualité marine ou noire.
La robe .... **225** fr.

13927. **CAPELINE** en crêpe de Chine noir, calotte en tagal, garnie motif de perles, tons écossais, 95 fr.

66949
ROBE en crêpe de Chine, nœud de même tissu avec boucle, mêmes coloris que le 66 942. *La robe* **150** fr.
En marocain gros grain, coloris du 66948.
La robe.. 175 fr.
En marocain gros grain, fond amande, rouille, bleu, noir imprimé couleur, ou fond blanc imprimé noir. *La robe*. 135

36928. **PETITE CLOCHE** satin noir garni broderie paille cerise 79

Pour nous permettre de répondre mieux et plus rapidement aux désirs de notre Clientèle, nous la prions de bien vouloir se conformer autant que possible aux prescriptions indiquées aux pages suivantes.

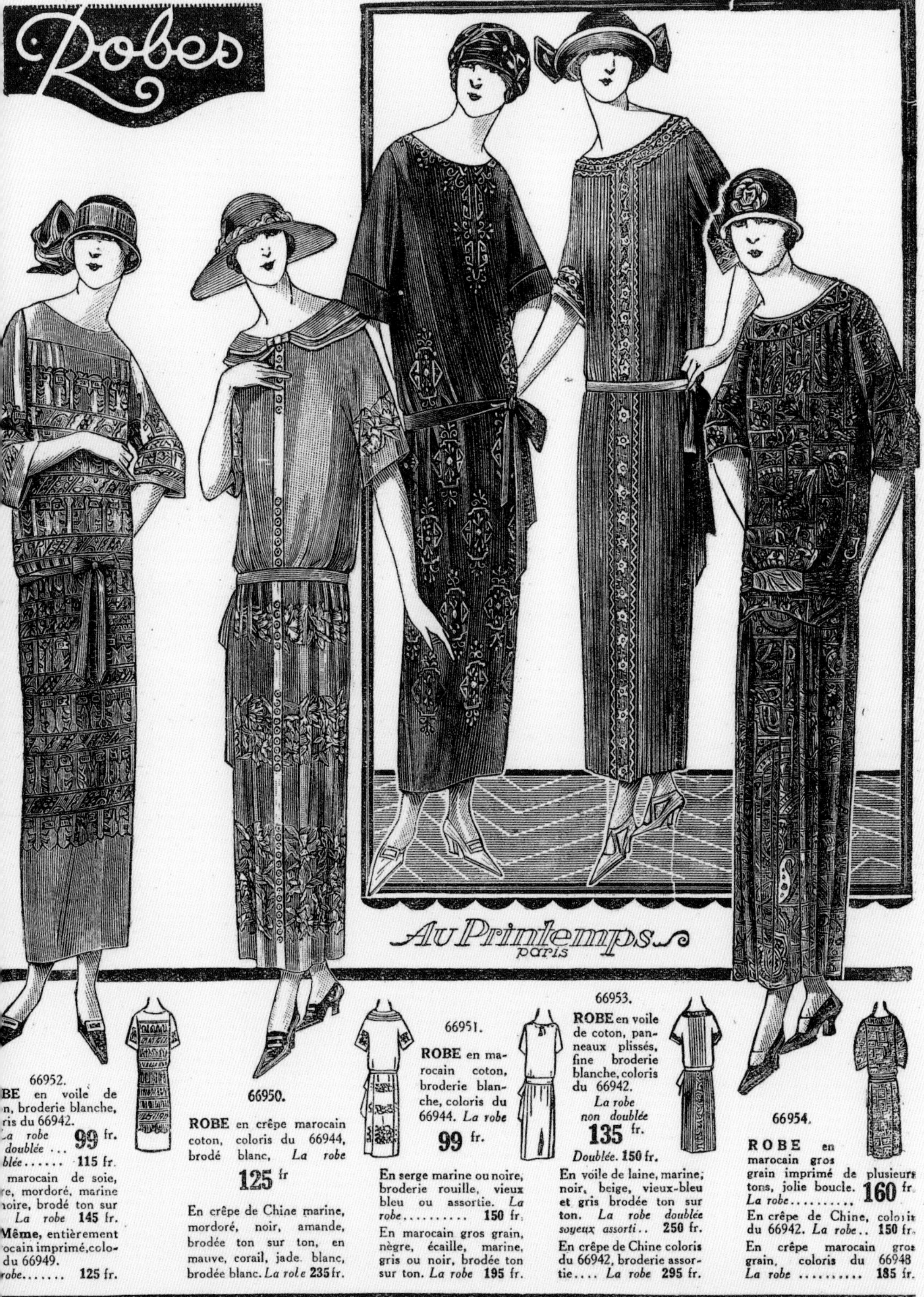
13

Robes

66952.
BE en voile de
n, broderie blanche,
ris du 66942.
La robe 99 fr.
doublée ...
blée ...... 115 fr.
marocain de soie,
e, mordoré, marine
noire, brodé ton sur
La robe 145 fr.
Même, entièrement
ocain imprimé, colo-
du 66949.
robe ...... 125 fr.

66950.
ROBE en crêpe marocain coton, coloris du 66944, brodé blanc, *La robe* 125 fr

En crêpe de Chine marine, mordoré, noir, amande, brodée ton sur ton, en mauve, corail, jade. blanc, brodée blanc. *La robe* 235 fr.

66951.
ROBE en marocain coton, broderie blanche, coloris du 66944. *La robe* 99 fr.

En serge marine ou noire, broderie rouille, vieux bleu ou assortie. *La robe*.......... 150 fr.

En marocain gros grain, nègre, écaille, marine, gris ou noir, brodée ton sur ton. *La robe* 195 fr.

66953.
ROBE en voile de coton, panneaux plissés, fine broderie blanche, coloris du 66942. *La robe non doublée* 135 fr.
Doublée. 150 fr.

En voile de laine, marine, noir, beige, vieux-bleu et gris brodée ton sur ton. *La robe doublée soyeux assorti*.. 250 fr.

En crêpe de Chine coloris du 66942, broderie assortie.... *La robe* 295 fr.

66954.
ROBE en marocain gros grain imprimé de plusieurs tons, jolie boucle. *La robe*.......... 160 fr.

En crêpe de Chine, coloris du 66942. *La robe*.. 150 fr.

En crêpe marocain gros grain, coloris du 66948 *La robe* .... 185 fr.

N'OUBLIEZ PAS DE NOUS INDIQUER : LA TEINTE

Below
Designs for summer dresses.
The Delineator, 1922

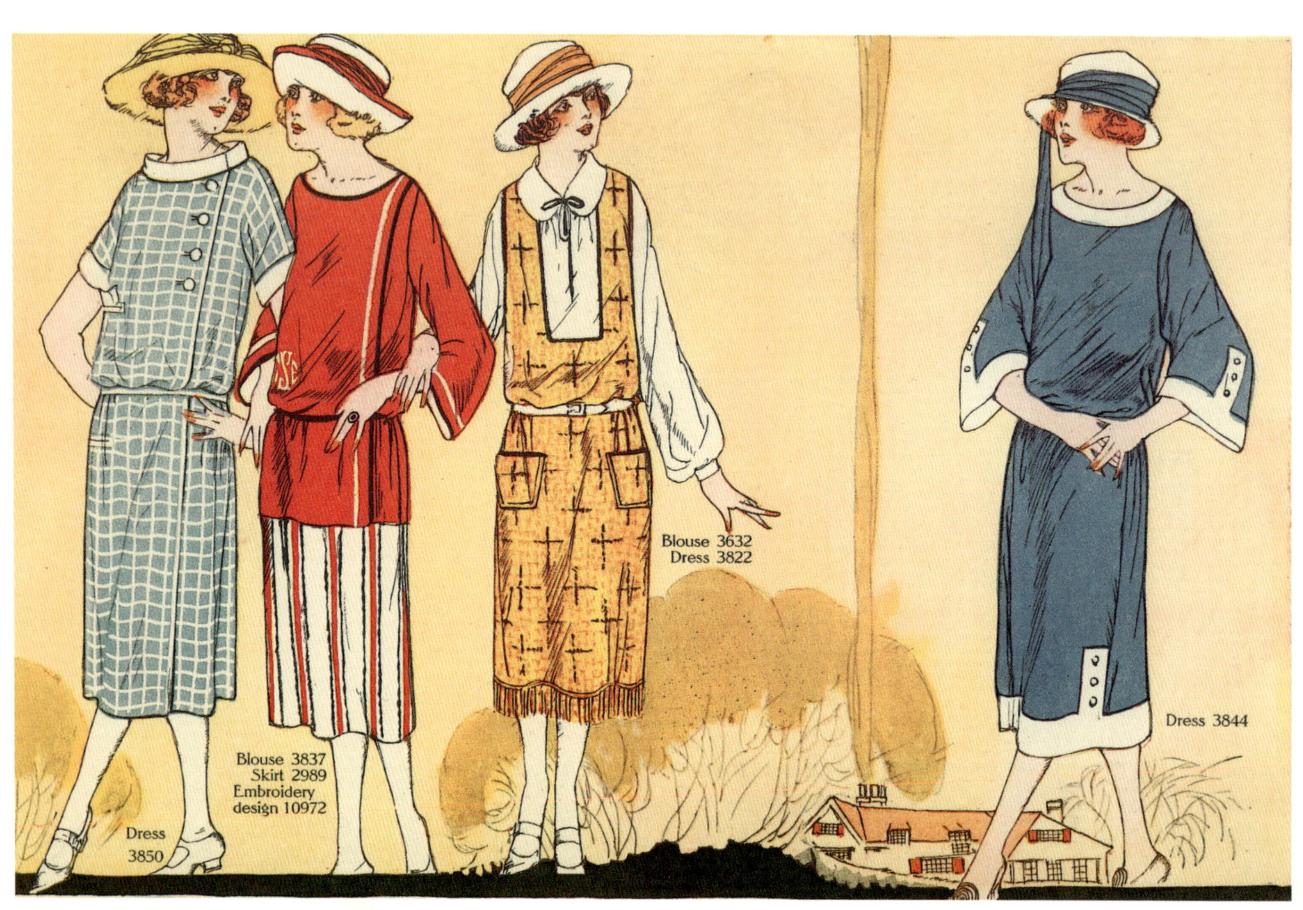

Below
Designs for summer dresses.
The Delineator, 1922

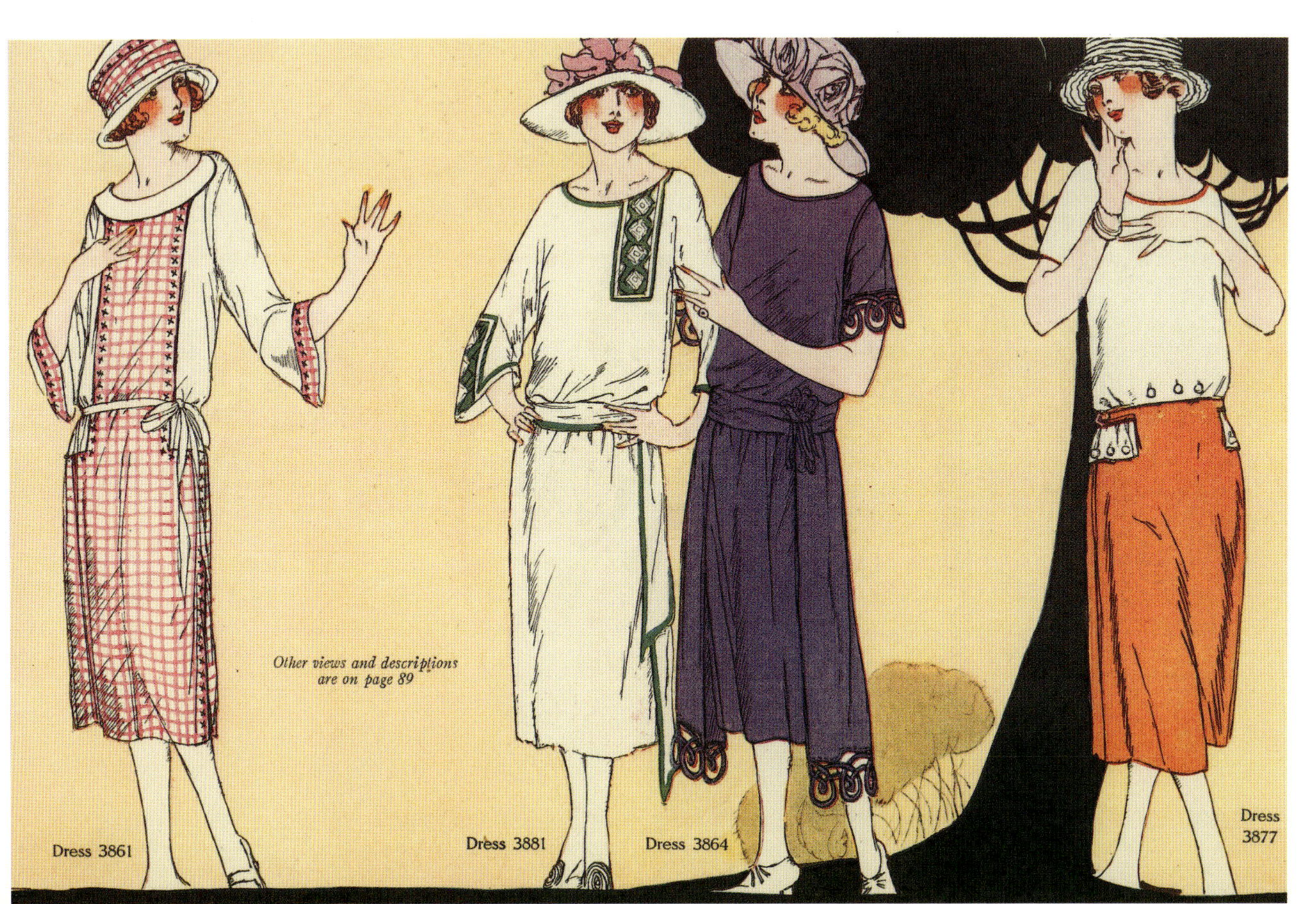

Below
"Un Peu Beaucoup" (A little, a lot), two day dresses. Illustration by Fernand Simeon. *Gazette du Bon Ton*, 1920

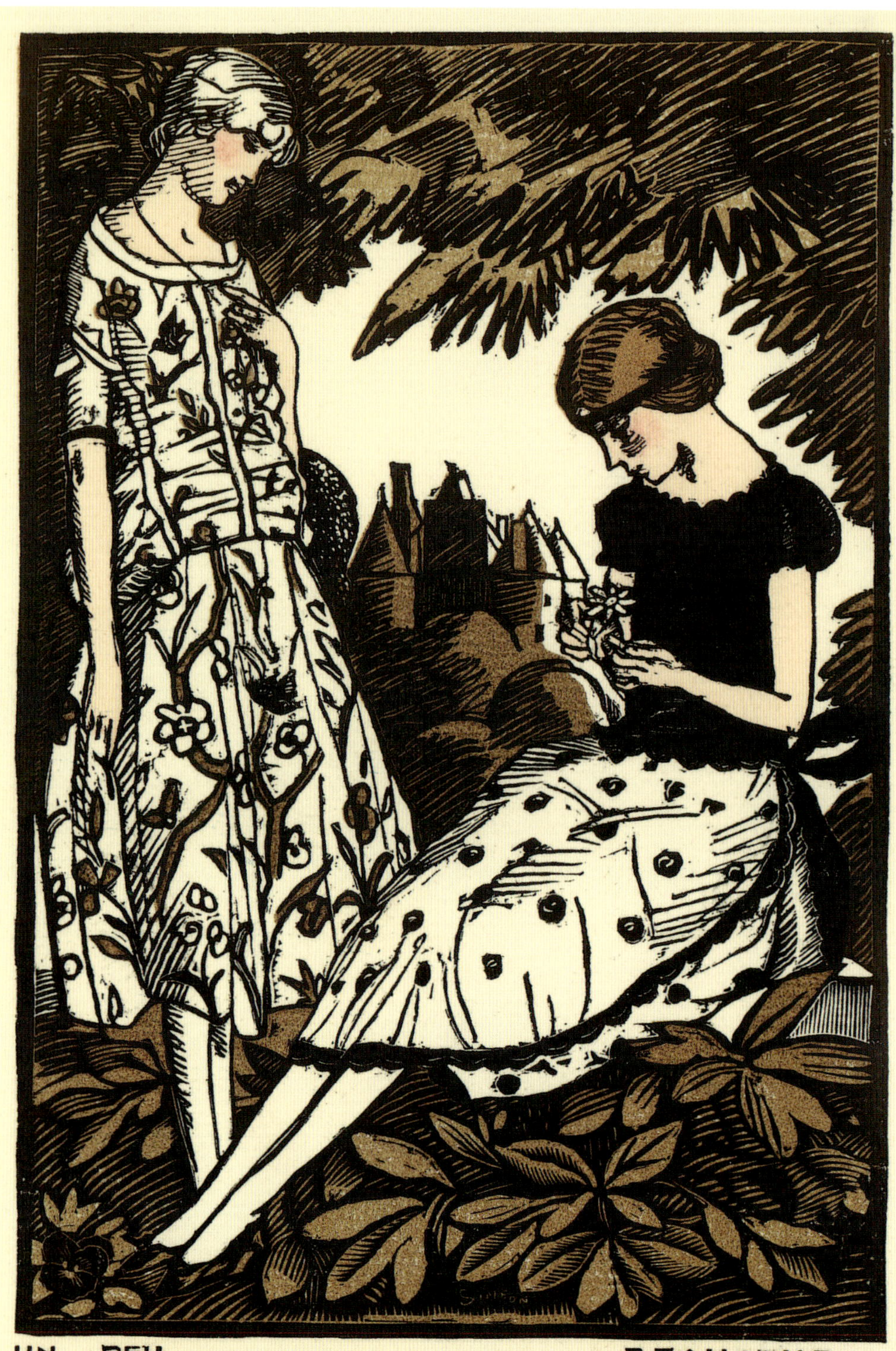

Below
A beach dress in cream washed silk with a pleated skirt and a openwork lace detailed blouse-style top, 1927

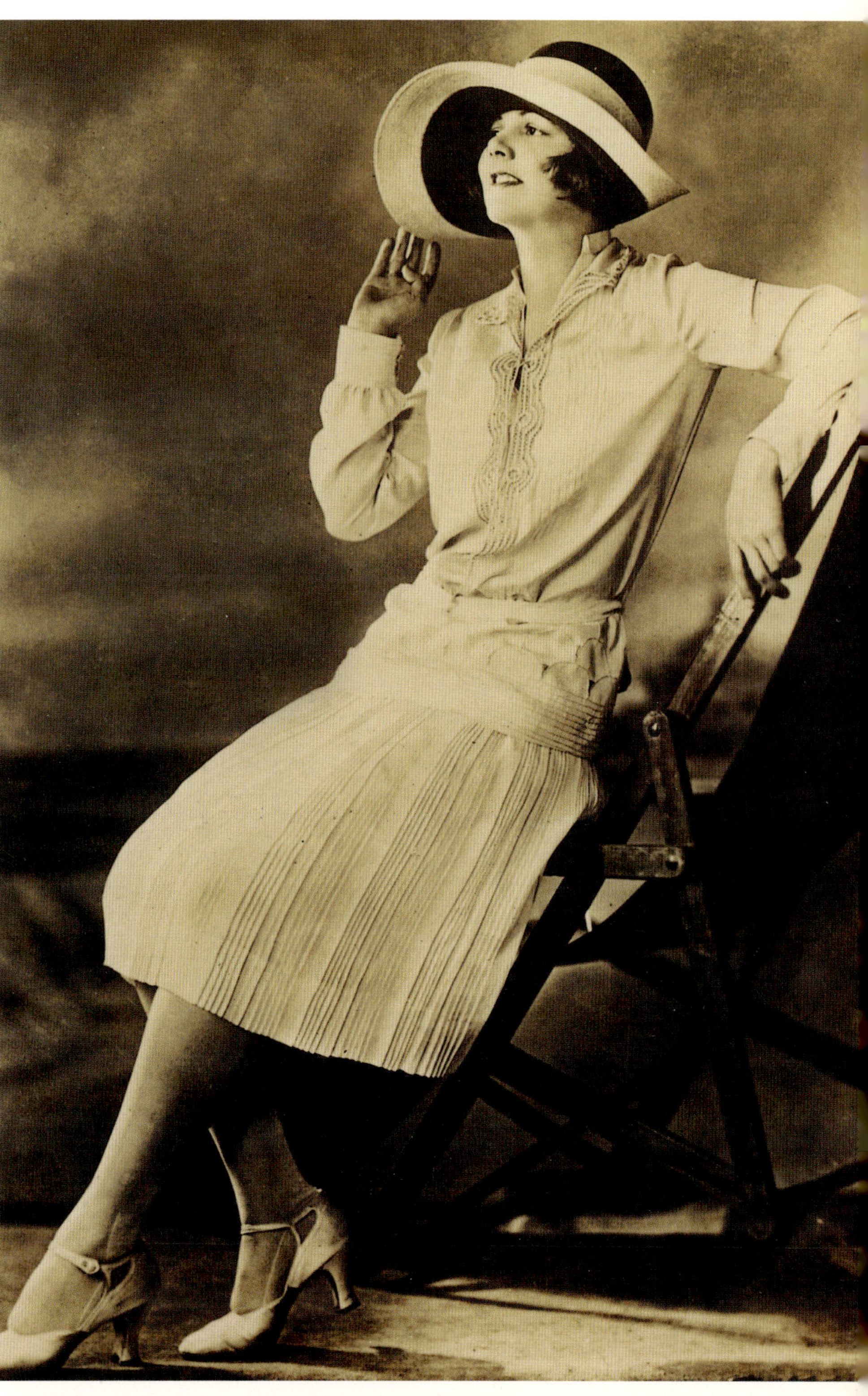

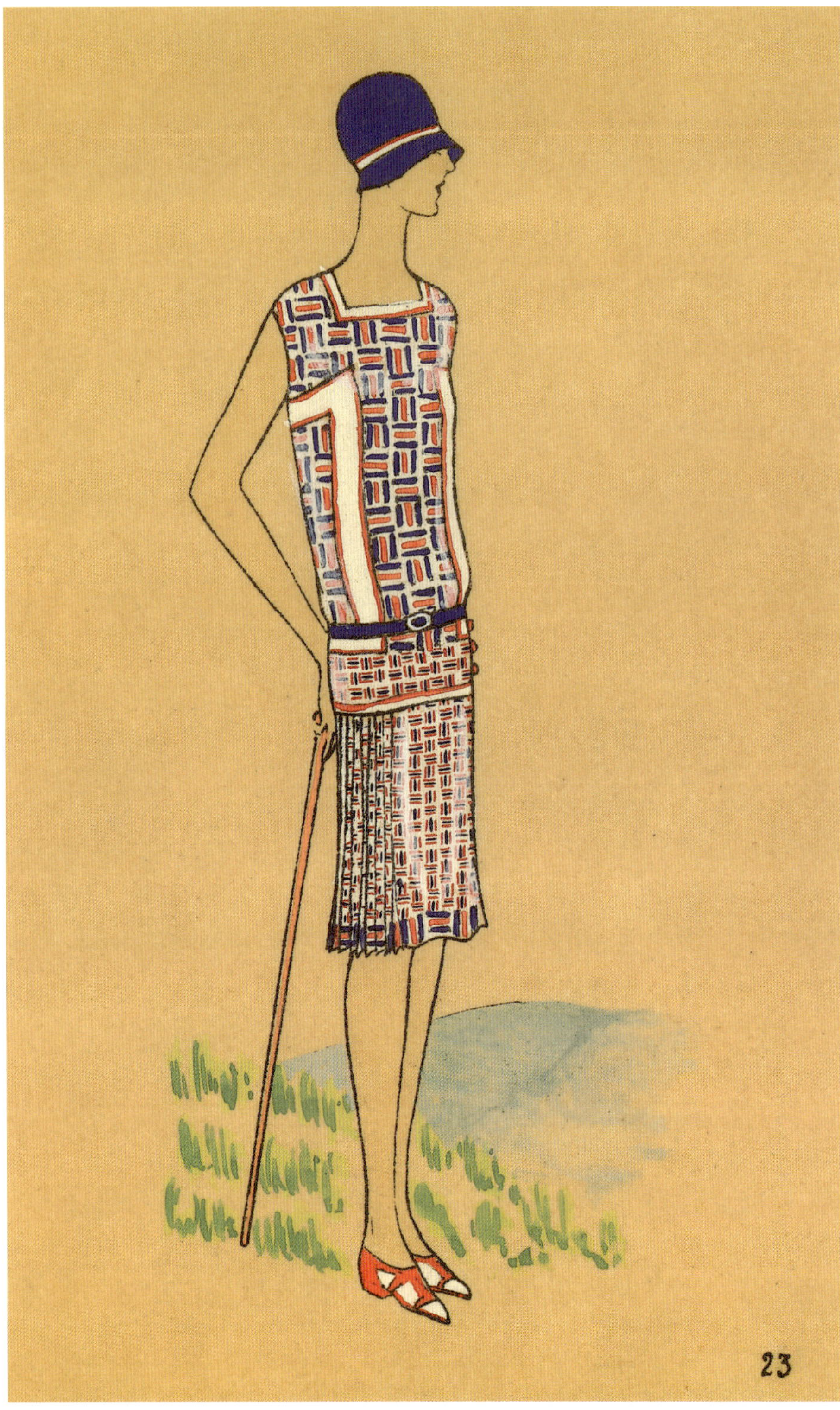

Above
A sleeveless walking ensemble in blue, white and red with a blue belt and tri-colour cloche hat. France, c.1925

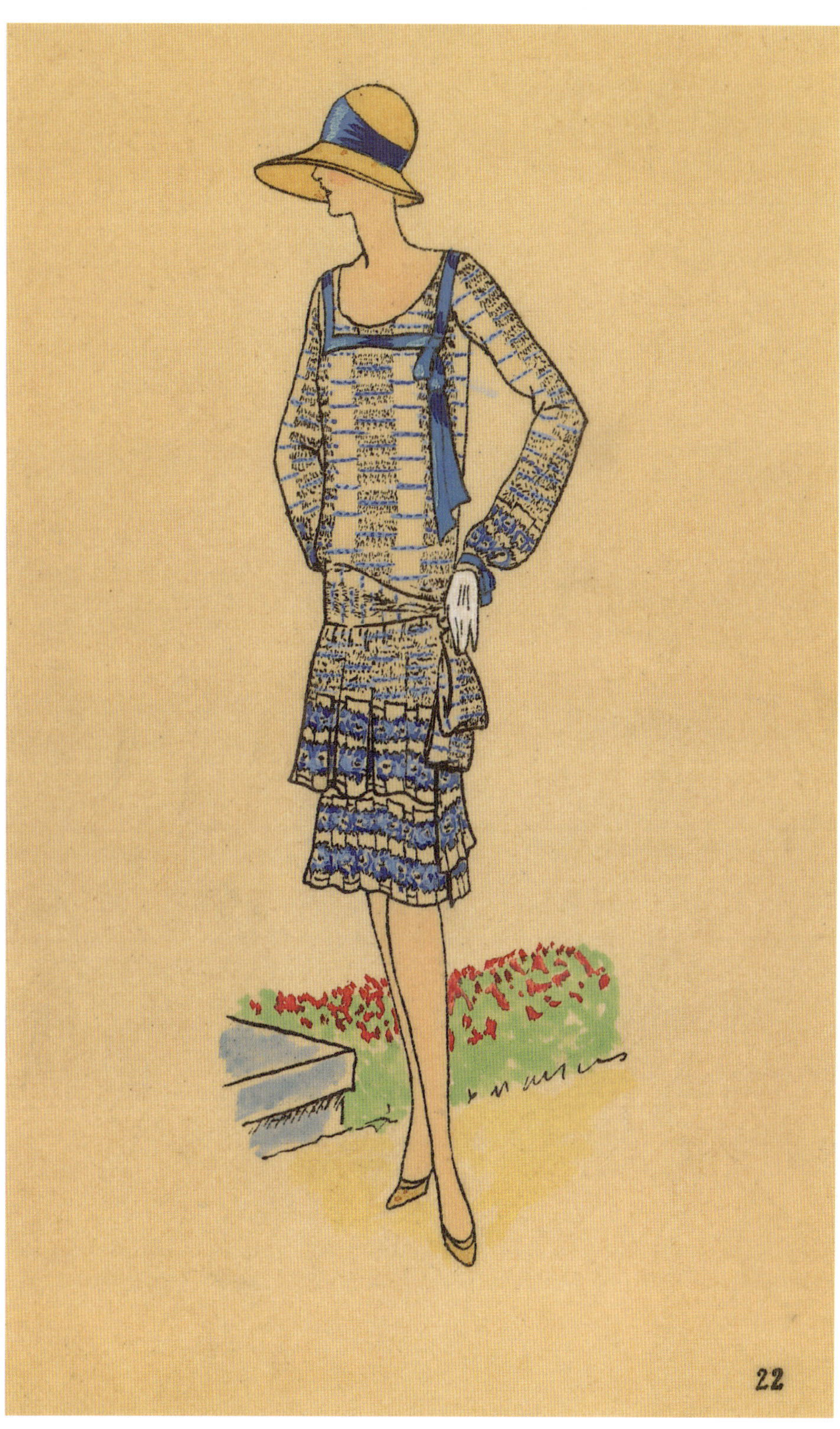

Above
A tiered afternoon summer day dress worn with a straw hat and white gloves. France, c.1925

Right
A long sleeved blue, white and red day dress, accessorised with a large yellow artificial flower on the shoulder, and a blue cloche hat with smaller yellow flowers. France, c.1925

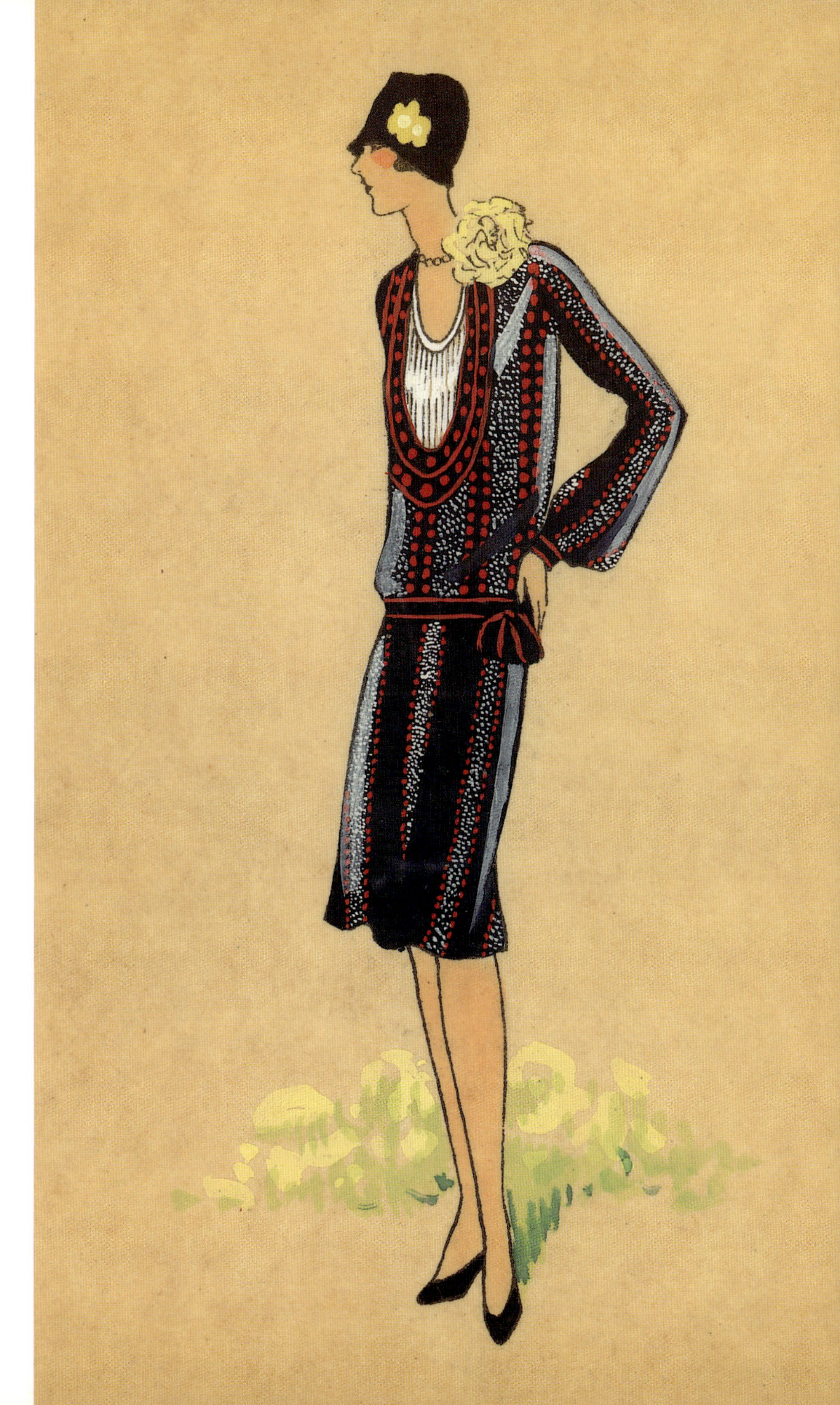

Below
An in-between dress with a straight collar overlaid with lace and fancy openwork underlaid with coloured silk, a dress with Medici collar and box pleat skirt, and a street dress of plain silk with horizontal wool panels by Atelier Bachroitz. *Grande Mode Parisienne*, 1926

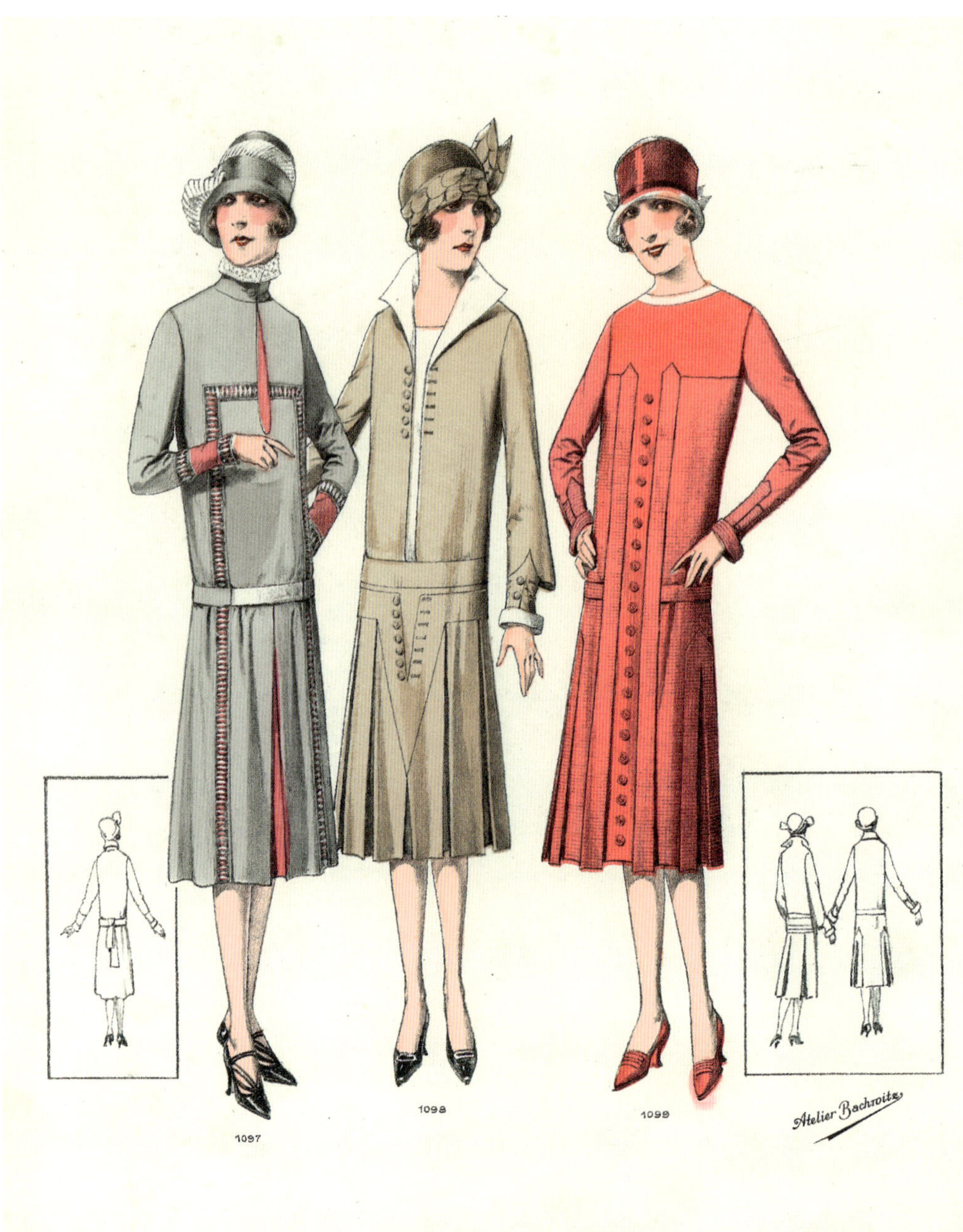

Below
Sweater dress in Kasha with pleated skirt, a spring dress with embroidered collar and material straps trimmed with buttons, and a cashmere sweater dress with an inverted pleats skirt by Atelier Bachroitz. *Grande Mode Parisienne*, 1926

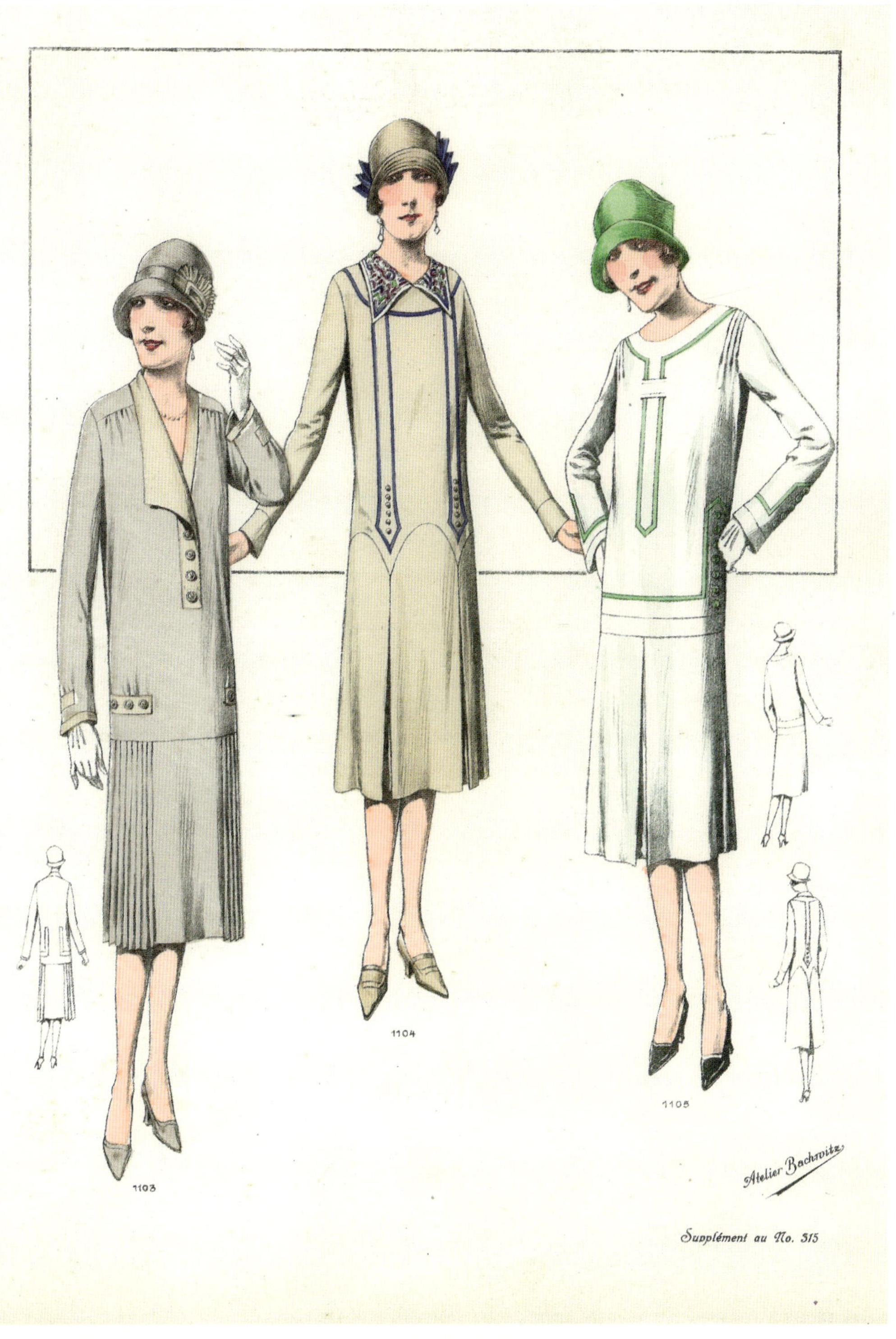

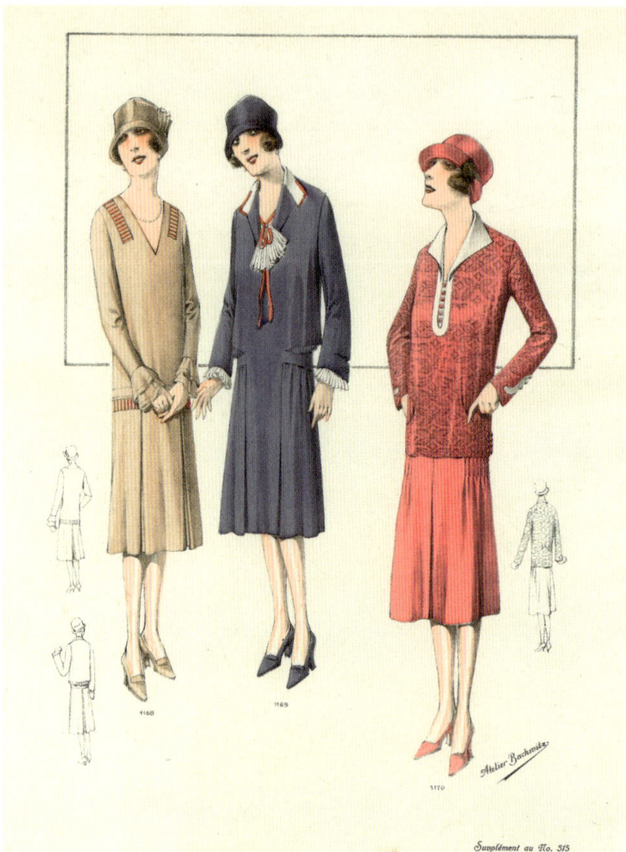

Left
Sweater dress with silk belt and shoulder straps, a woollen dress with bolero gathered at the sides, and a silk sweater dress with a top of patterned silk and a plain silk skirt drawn in pleats at the side by Atelier Bachroitz. *Grande Mode Parisienne*, 1926

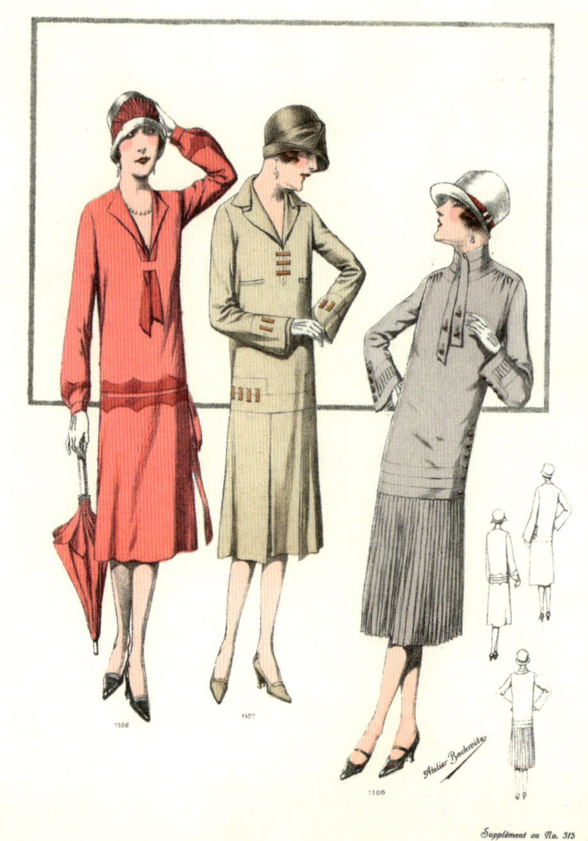

Right
Bright pink walking dress with a run-through tie, a walking dress with narrow strap details of deer skin, and a crepe sweater dress with cravette and pleated skirt by Atelier Bachroitz. *Grande Mode Parisienne*, 1926

Right
Street dress with triangular pockets and embroidered belt, an ensemble in charmelaine with a bolero and ruches of crepe, and a day dress with a straight collar, gathered skirt and a tight neck plastron by Atelier Bachroitz. *Grande Mode Parisienne*, 1926

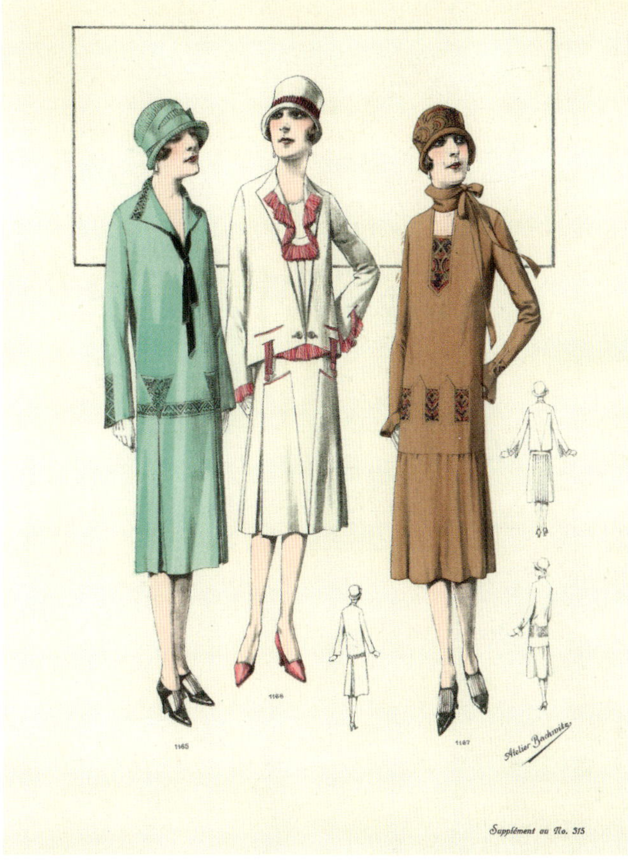

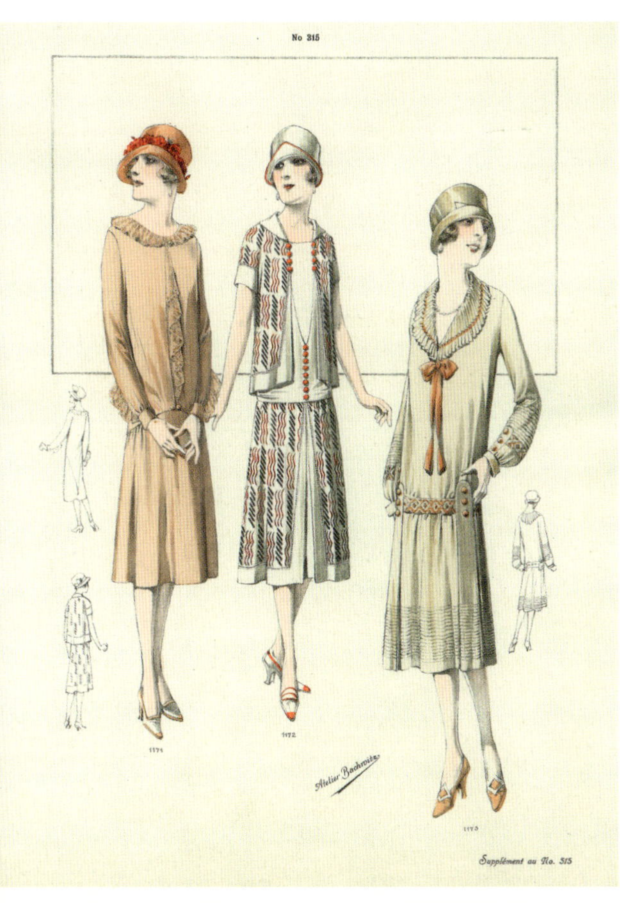

Left
Silk crepe afternoon dress with lace jabot and sleeve ruches, an ensemble in plain and patterned silk with a short sleeved bolero, and a silk poplin afternoon dress with a pleated collar by Atelier Bachroitz. *Grande Mode Parisienne*, 1926

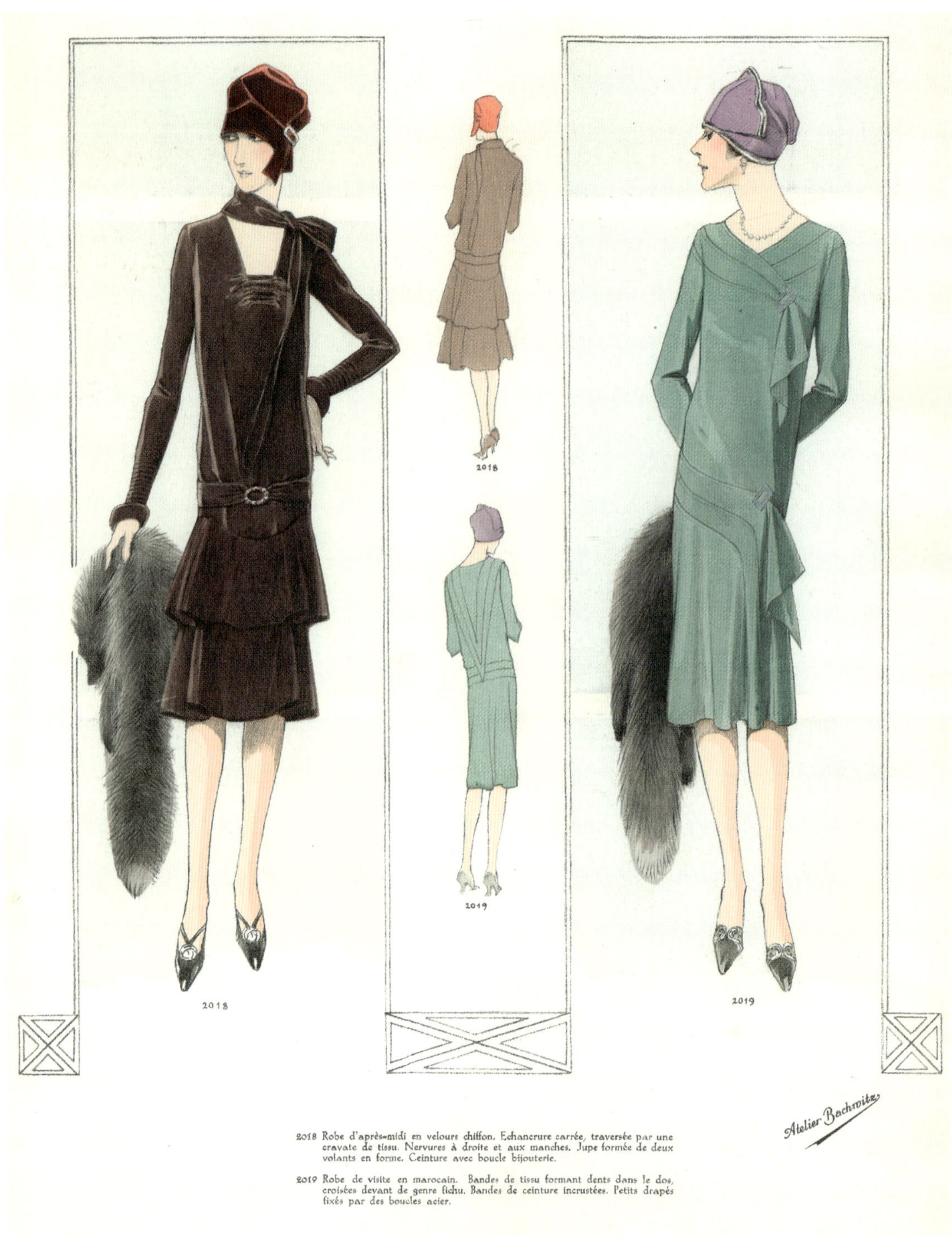

Above

Chiffon velvet afternoon dress, and a silk afternoon dress with draped panels fixed with buckles by Atelier Bachroitz. *Chic Parisien Beaux-Arts des Modes*, 1927

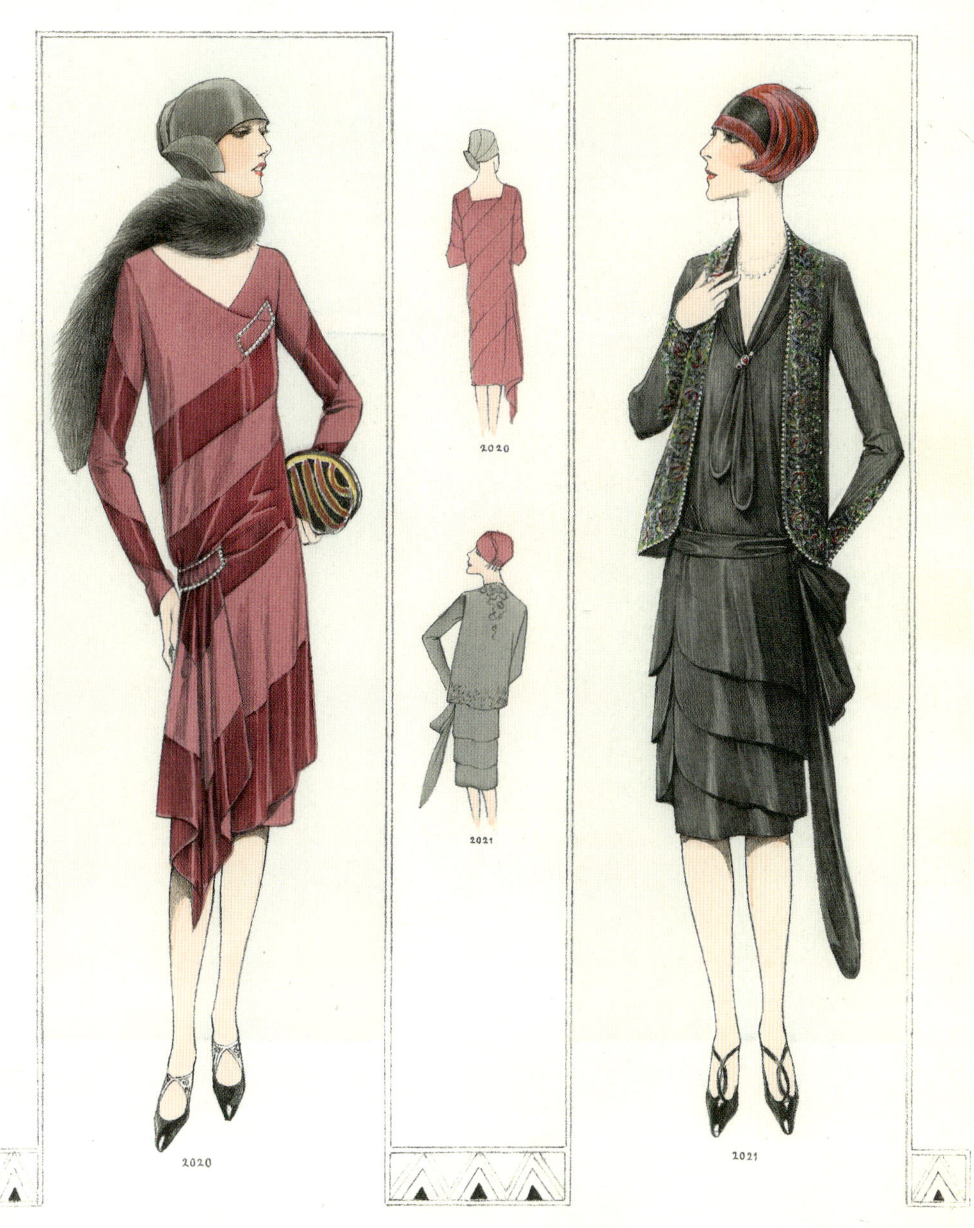

2020 Robe princesse en crêpe satin. Echancrure carrée dans le dos, en cœur devant et terminée par une boucle bijouterie. Lé de côté formant pan et drapé par une boucle pareille. Incrustations disposées en biais du côté brillant du tissu.

2021 Robe de thé en satin. Boléro brodé soie de couleur et métal, petits boutons de métal. Col avec cravate. Volants de jupe divisés à droite. Ceinture écharpe de tissu avec long pan.

Atelier Bachroitz

Above

Crepe satin princess dress with two jeweled buckles, and a satin afternoon dress with a metal and silk bolero jacket and cravat collar by Atelier Bachroitz. *Chic Parisien Beaux-Arts des Modes*, 1927

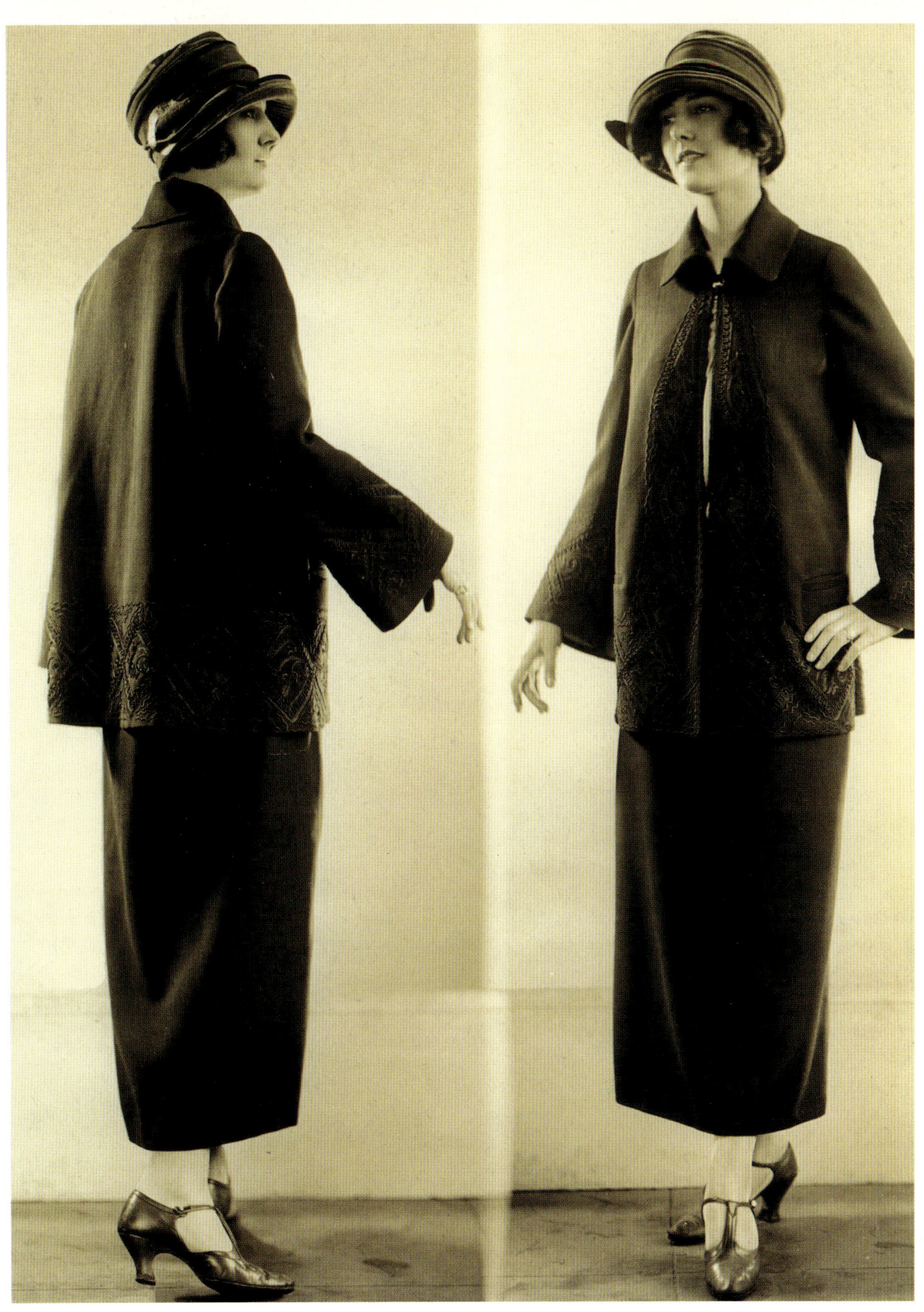

Above
A skirt suit with a richly embellished jacket in primitive folk-style decorations, c.1921

Dress 3627

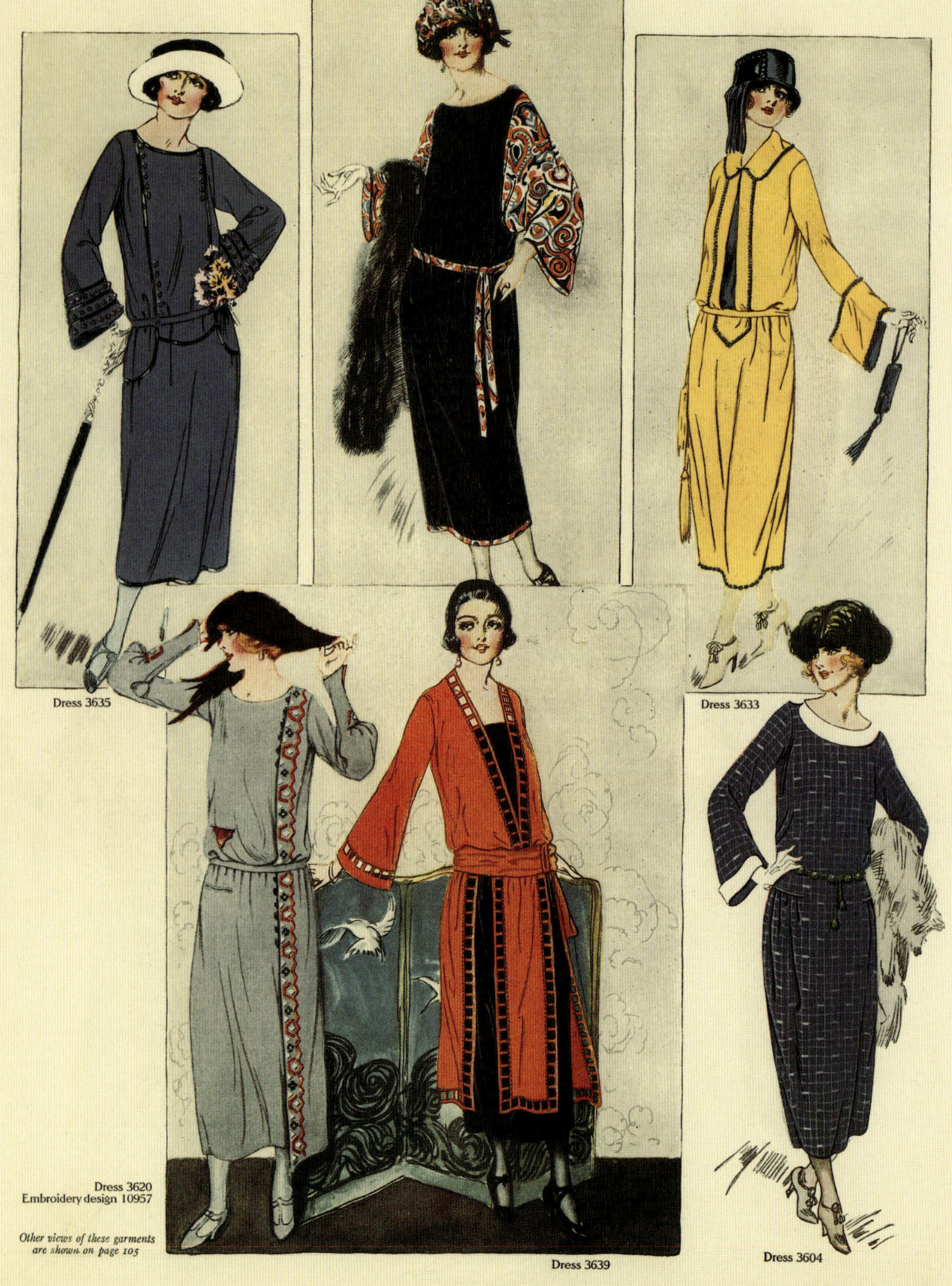

Dress 3635

Dress 3633

Dress 3620
Embroidery design 10957

Other views of these garments are shown on page 105

Dress 3639

Dress 3604

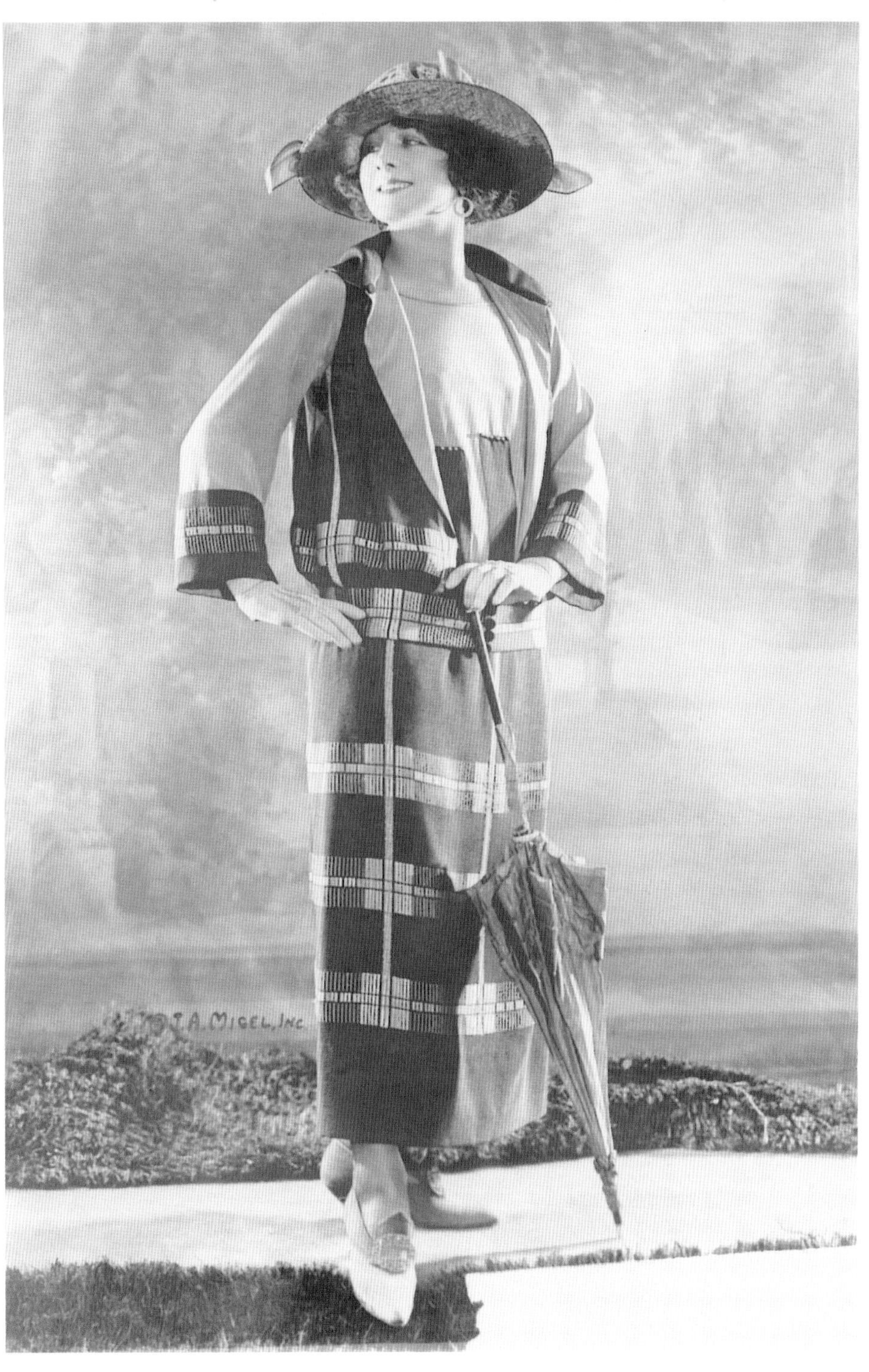

Left and above
Designs for day dresses.
The Delineator, 1922

The actress Norma Shearer wearing a three-piece spring suit made of "Spiral Spun" and "Moon-Glo" crepe, c.1920

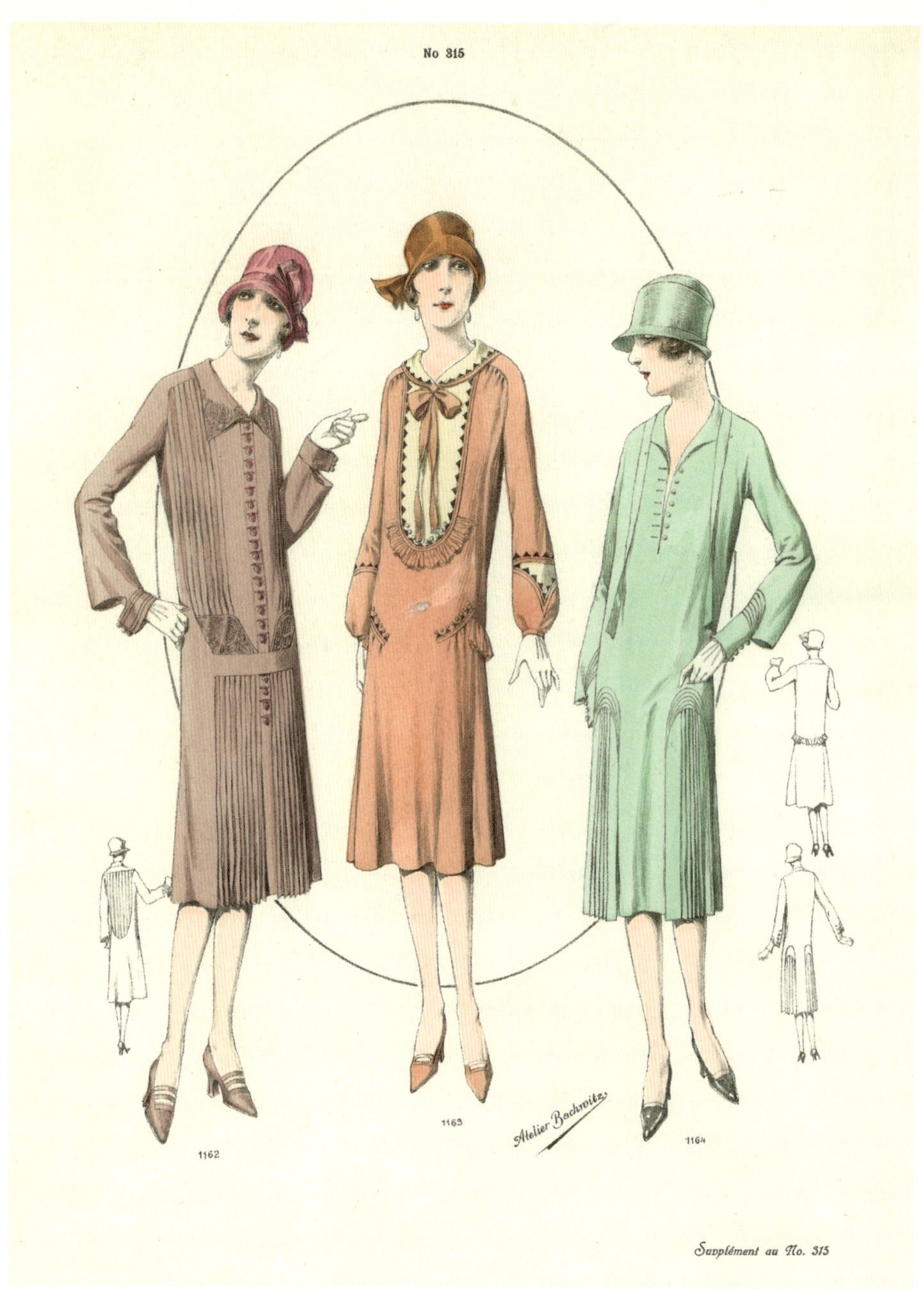

Above

Poplin dress with inserted pleated panels, a silk princess robe with a cravat, puffed sleeves and pleated ruching, and a silk princess robe with curved skirt panels drawn in opposite pleats by Atelier Bachroitz. *Grande Mode Parisienne*, 1926

Right

Crepe de Chine afternoon dress with a tunic decorated with hole embroidery and trimmed with beads over a chiffon slip hemmed with satin, and an afternoon dress of crepe band laid diagonally by Atelier Bachroitz. *Chic Parisien Beaux-Arts des Modes*, 1927

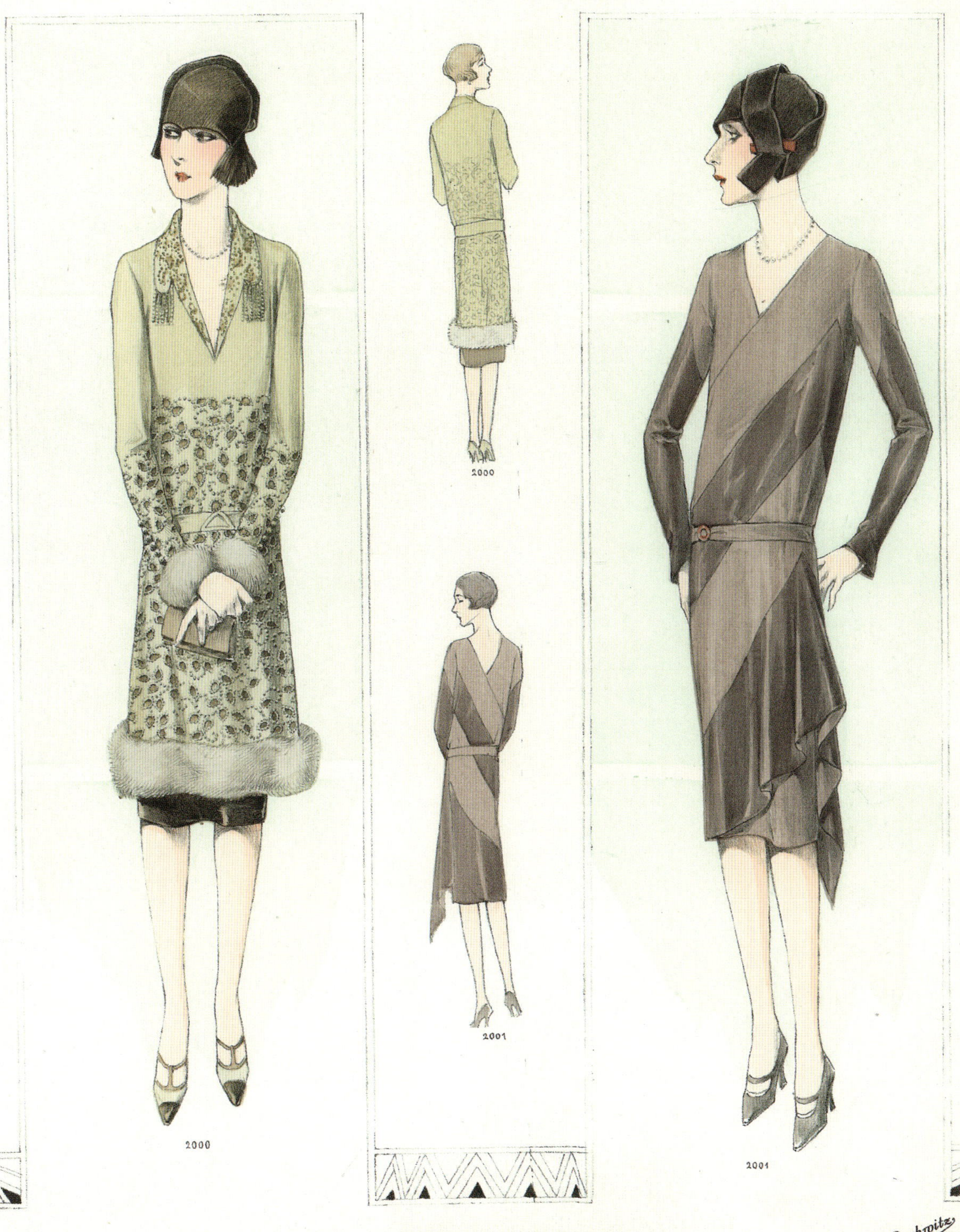

2000 Toilette de thé en crêpe de Chine clair. Longue casaque. Broderie anglaise sont cernée de perles. Manches garnies de séries de perles. Poignets et bordure de renard. Fourreau de mousseline bordé de satin foncé.

2001 Toilette d'après-midi en crêpe satin. Haut croisé. Incrustation et volant en forme du côté brillant du tissu. Manches pareilles rapportées en dent. Ceinture de tissu.

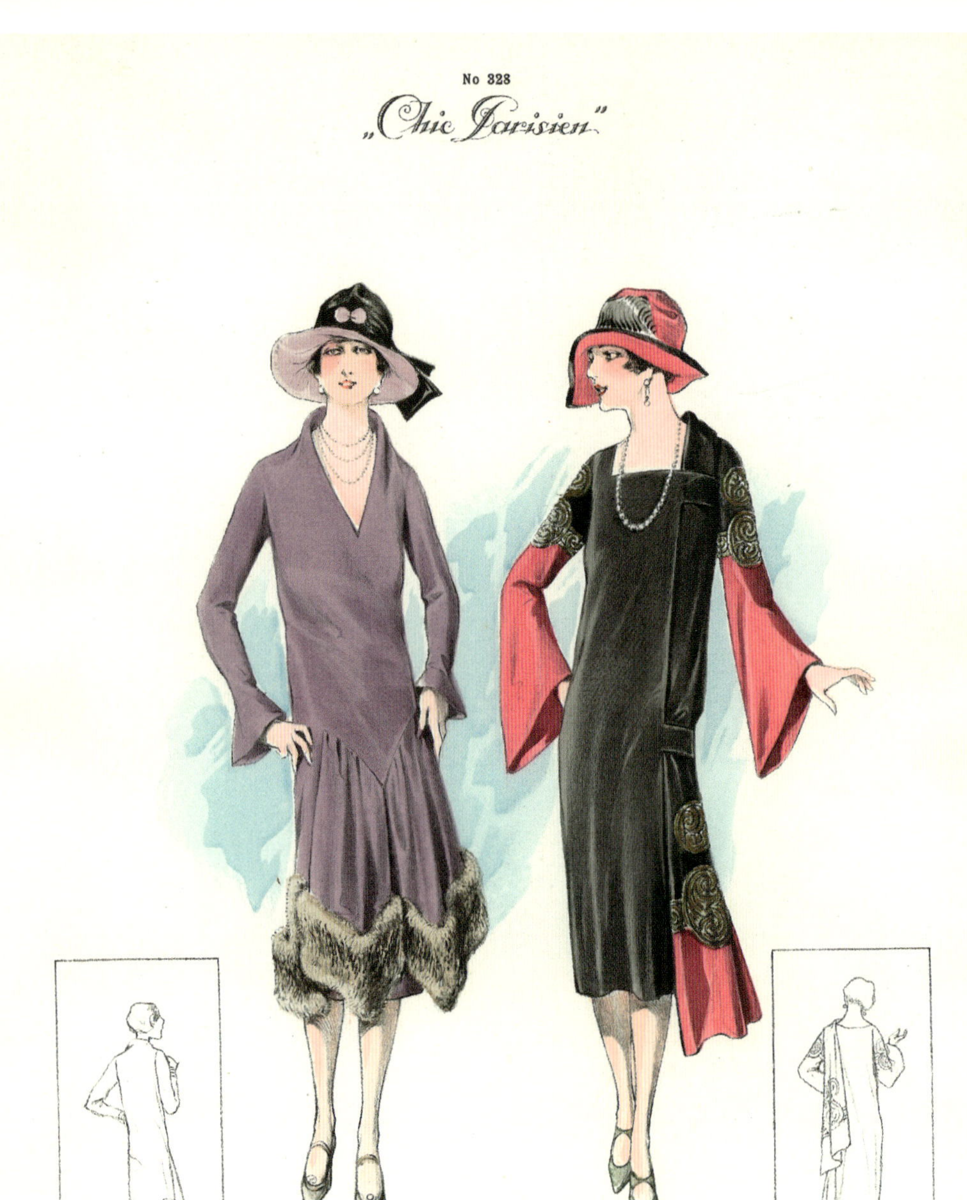

Above
Silk velvet afternoon robe banded with chinchilla fur and an afternoon velvet dress with silk and gold embroidery by Atelier Bachroitz. *Chic Parisien Beaux-Arts des Modes*, 1925

Right
Sweater frock of wool velour with ocelot fur collar and cuffs by Atelier Bachroitz. *Chic Parisien Beaux-arts des Modes*, 1925

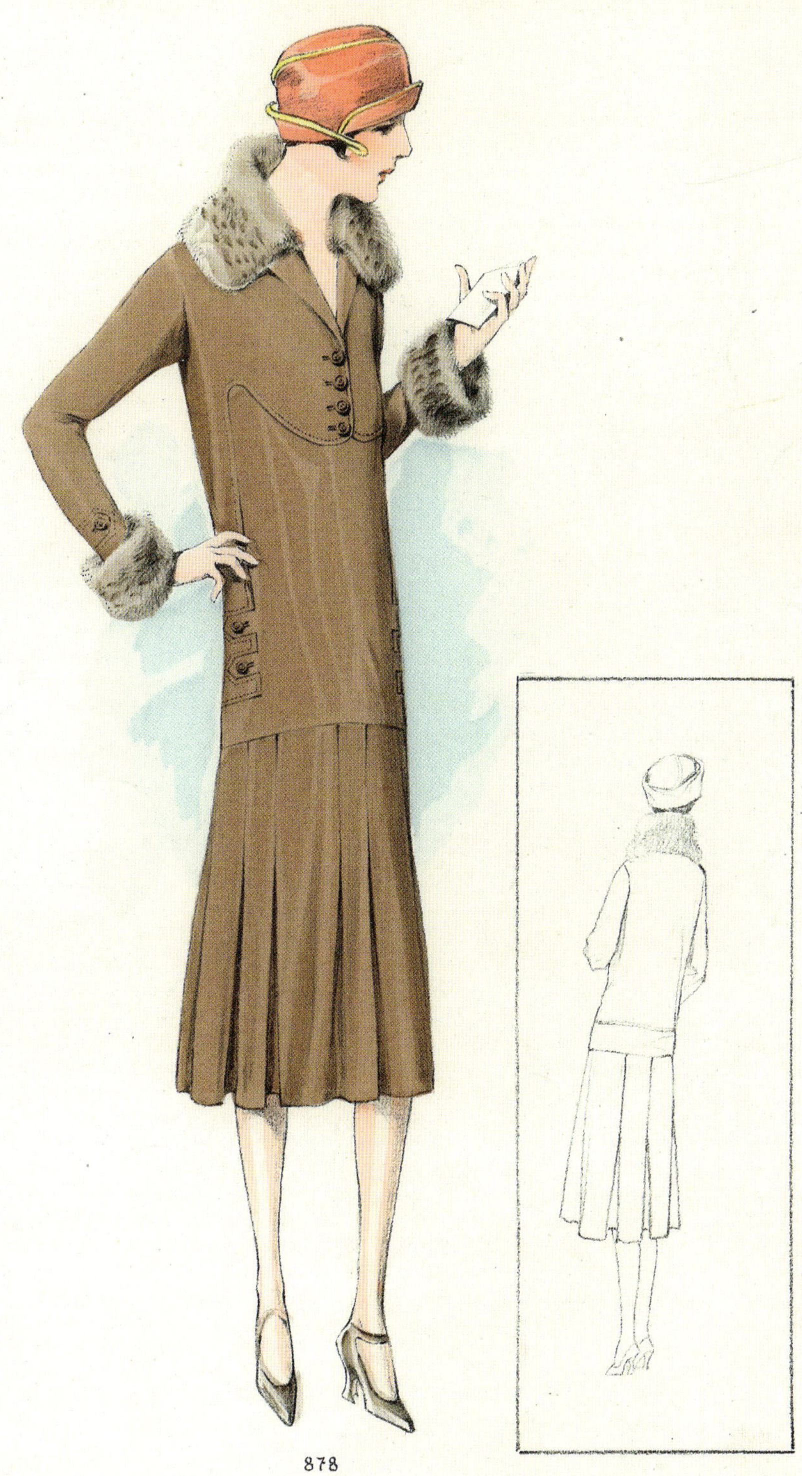

878

Atelier Bachwitz

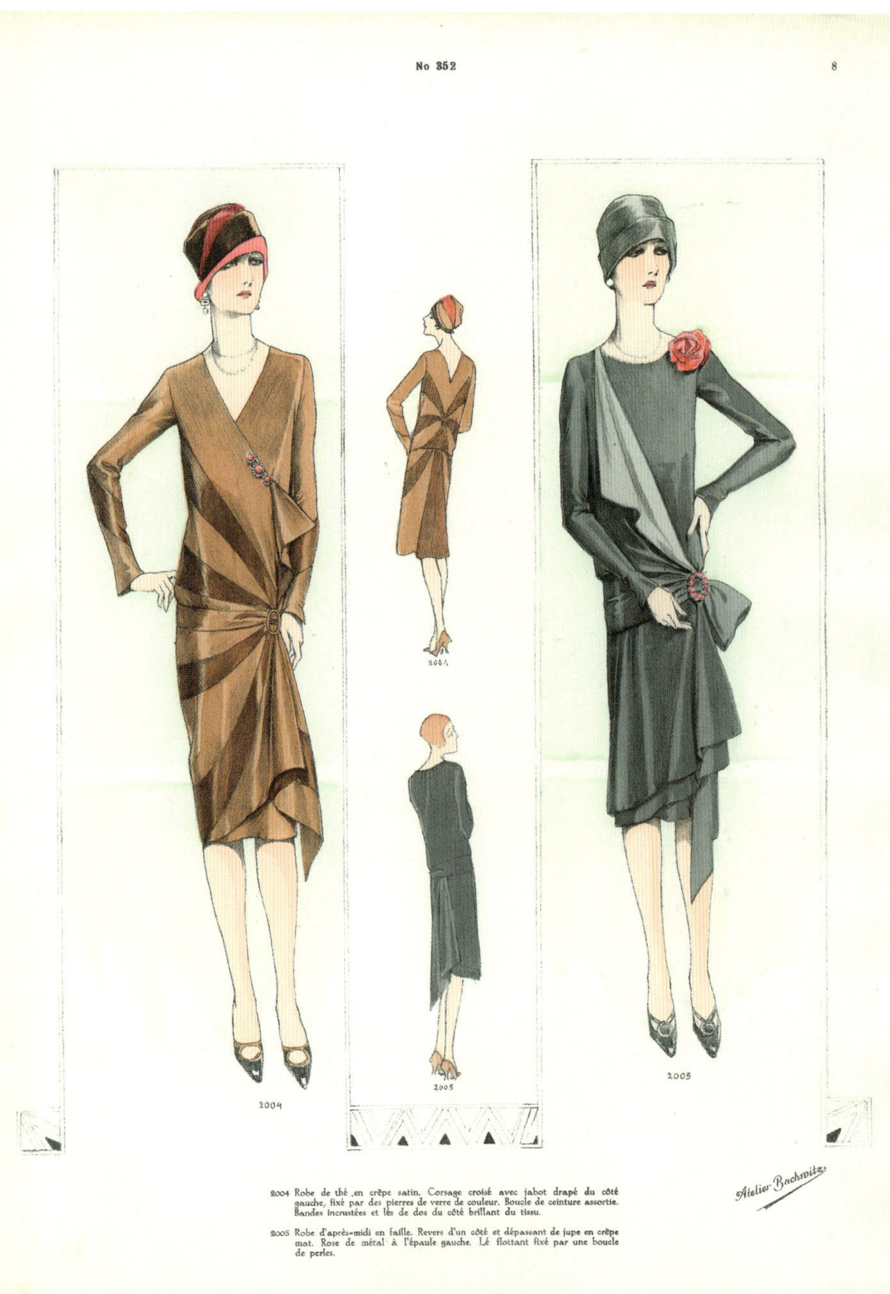

Above

Crepe satin afternoon dress with a crossed waist and draped left panel kept in place with a large brooch, and an afternoon dress of faille with a crossed waist and a flaring underskirt kept in place with a large bead buckle by Atelier Bachroitz. *Chic Parisien Beaux-Arts des Modes*, 1927

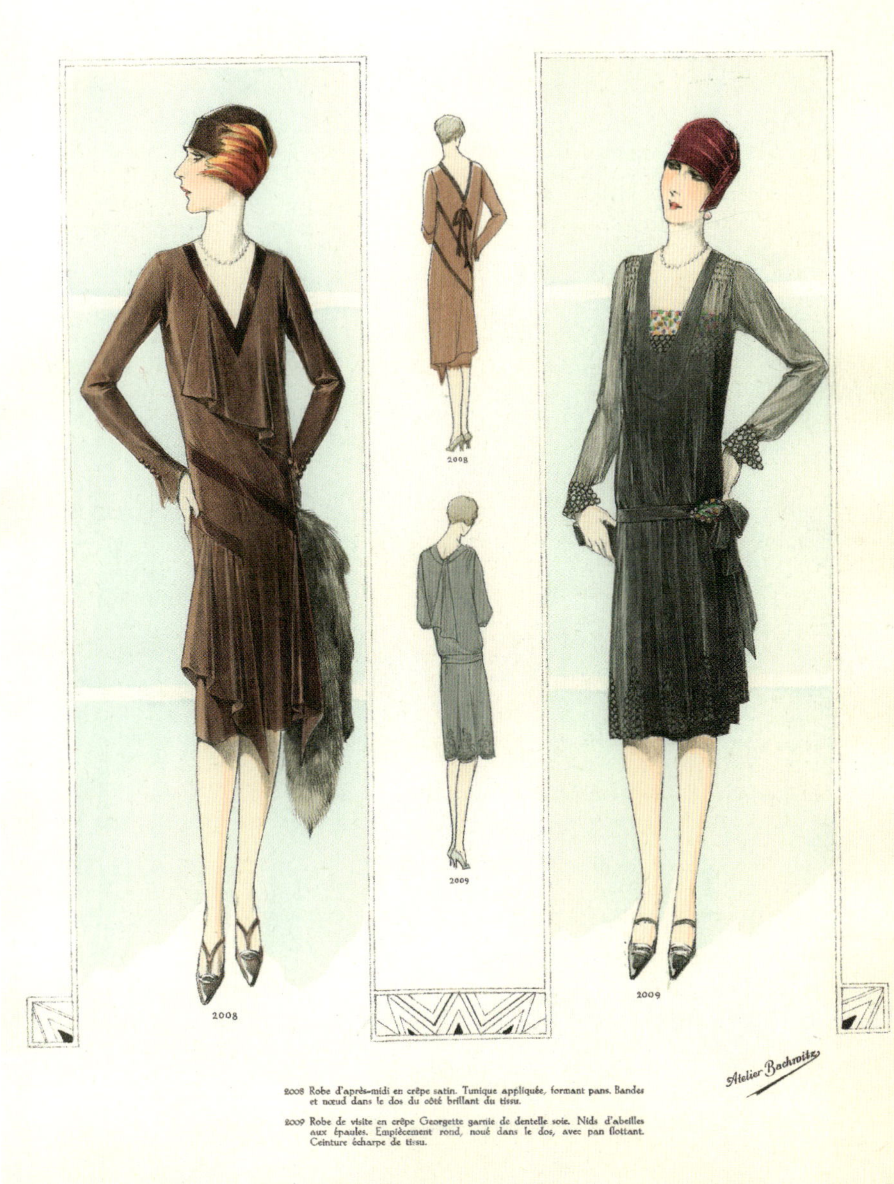

Above and next page

Satin crepe afternoon dress with diagonal bands, and an afternoon dress of Georgette trimmed with silk lace by Atelier Bachroitz. *Chic Parisien Beaux-Arts des Modes*, 1927

Six afternoon dresses by Atelier Bachroitz. *Grande Mode Parisienne*, 1926

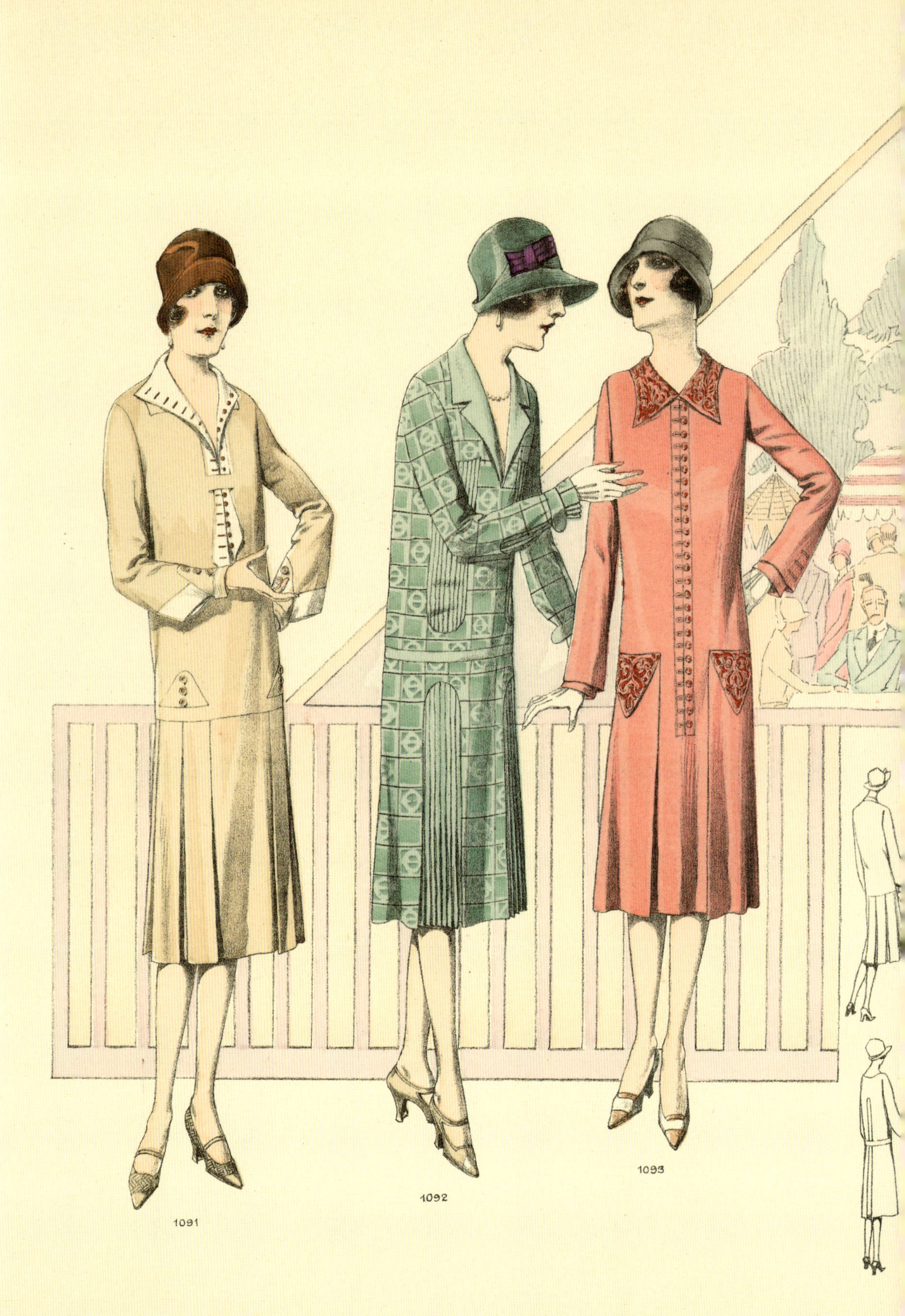
1091
1092
1093

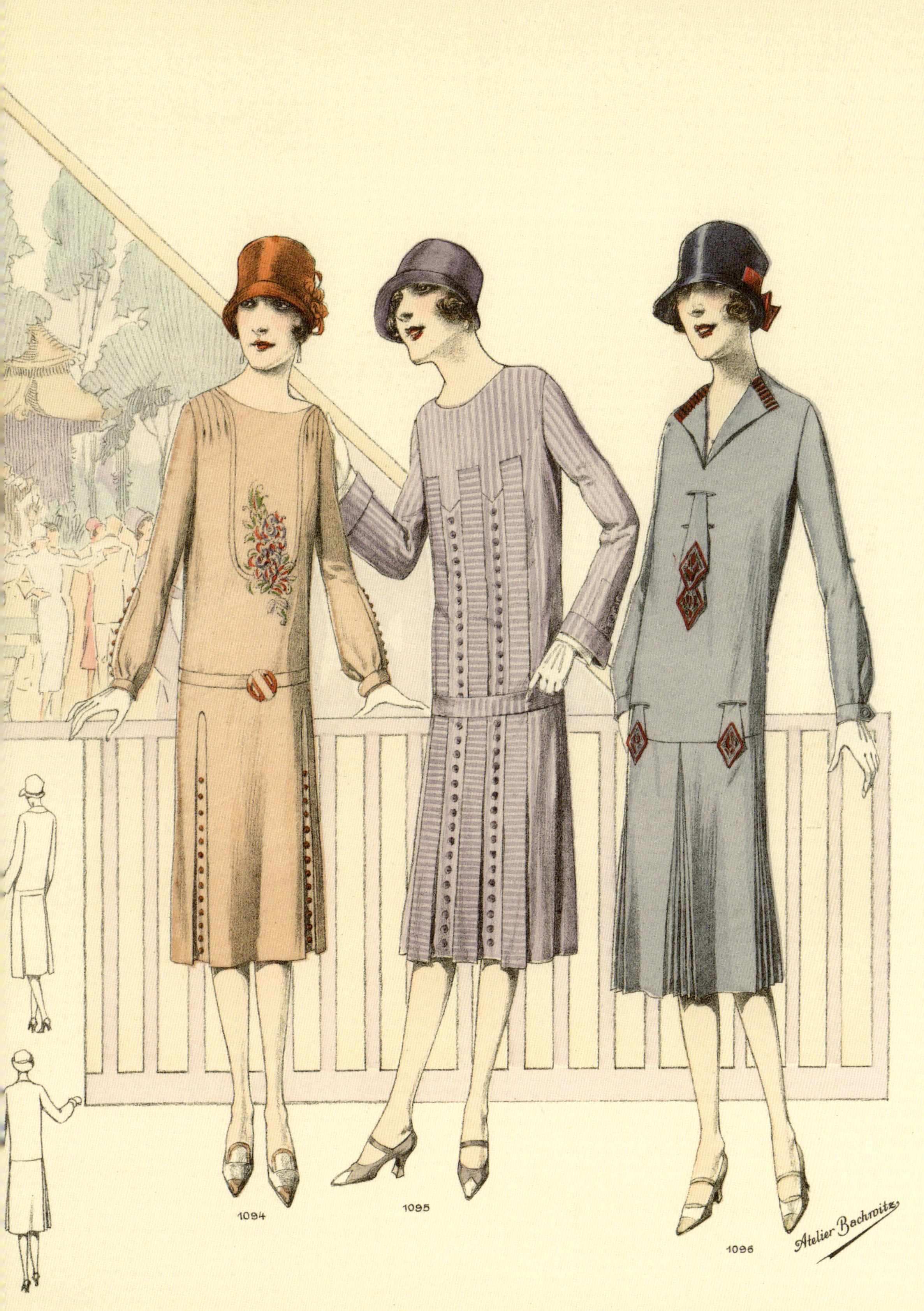

Supplément au No. 315

Right
"Le fruit vert" (The green fruit), coat. Illustration by Benito. *Gazette du Bon Ton*, 1920

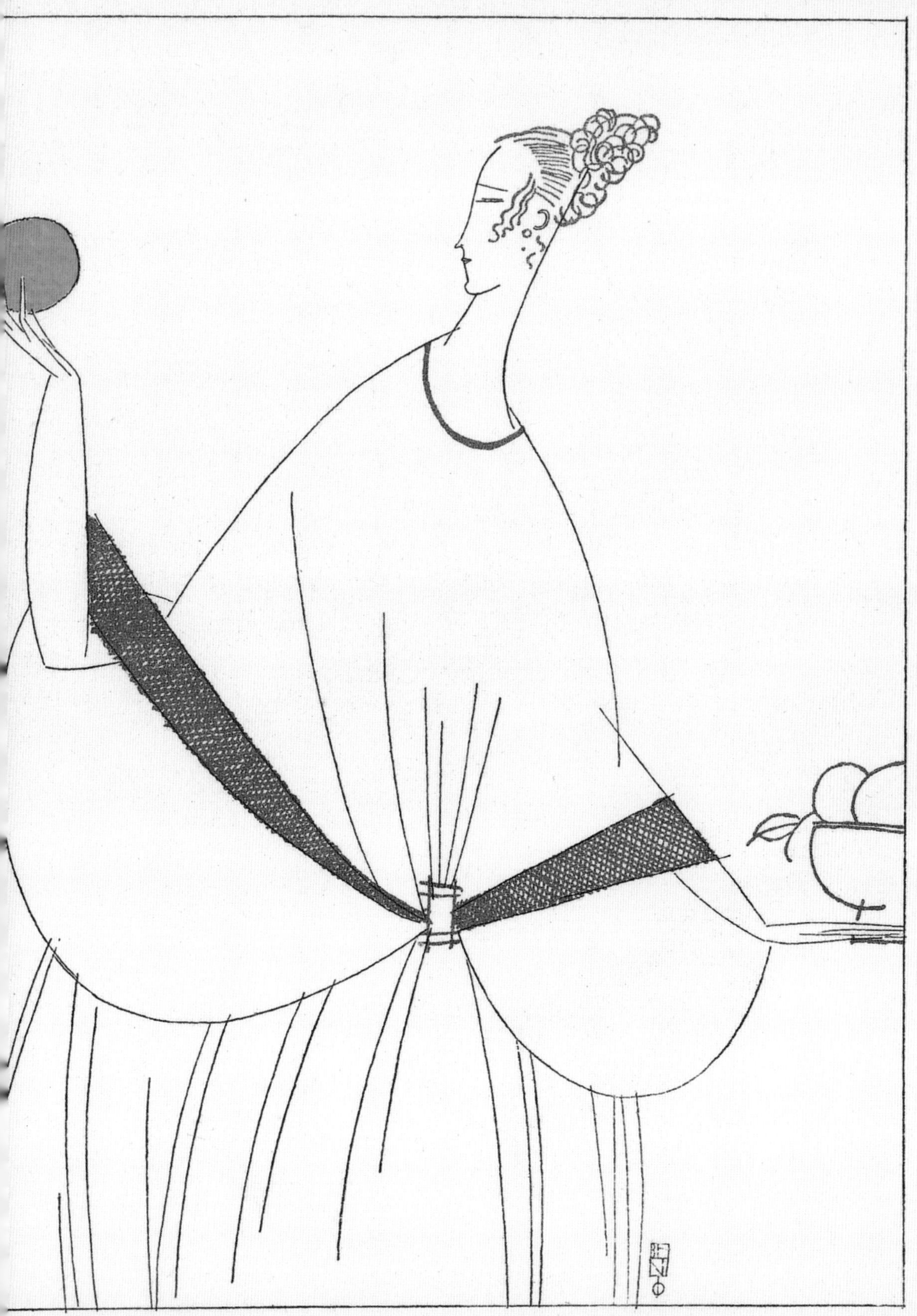

Below and right

Two day dresses with side and back flounces and panels by Atelier Bachroitz. *Chic Parisien, Beaux-Arts des Modes*, c.1928

Four spring dresses for young women. *Paris Mode*, c.1924

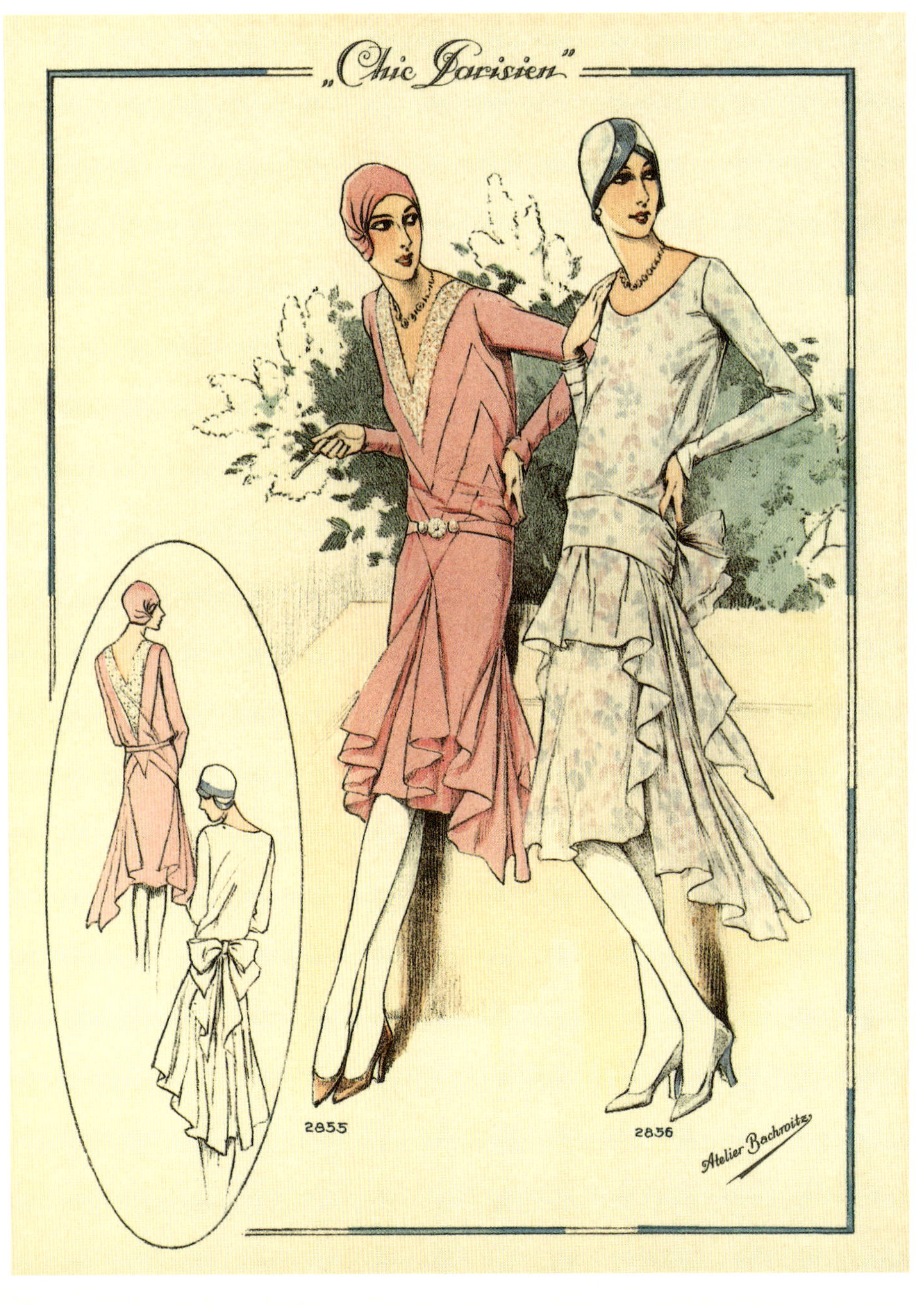

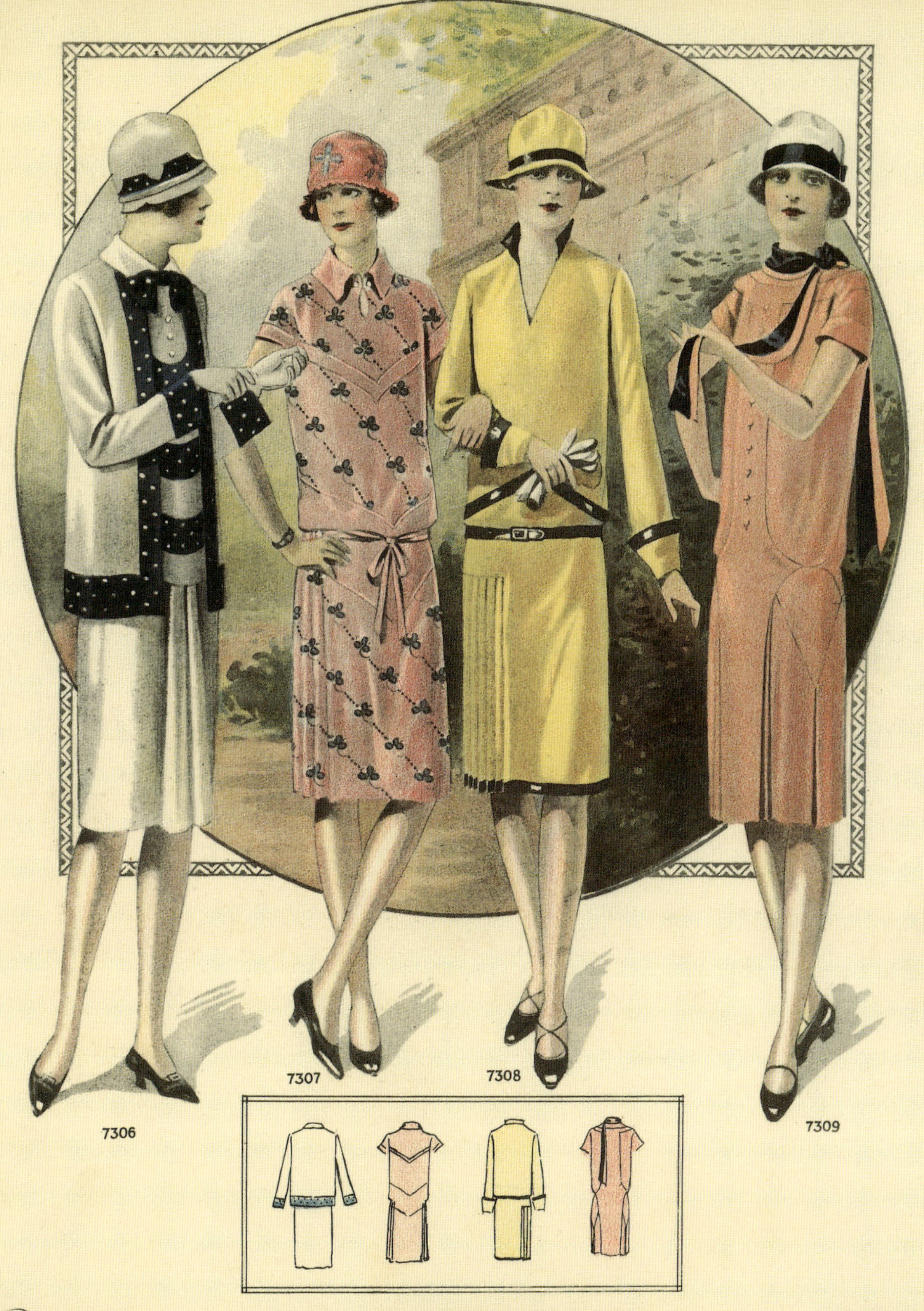

Les fraiches toilettes juvéniles

Paris-Mode
29, Rue de la Sourdière
PARIS (1er arrt)

SUPPLÉMENT
No 227 Pl. 477

Right
"L'oiseau Mort" (The Dead Bird), Czechoslovakian-inspired dress. Illustration by L'Hom. *Gazette du Bon Ton*, 1920

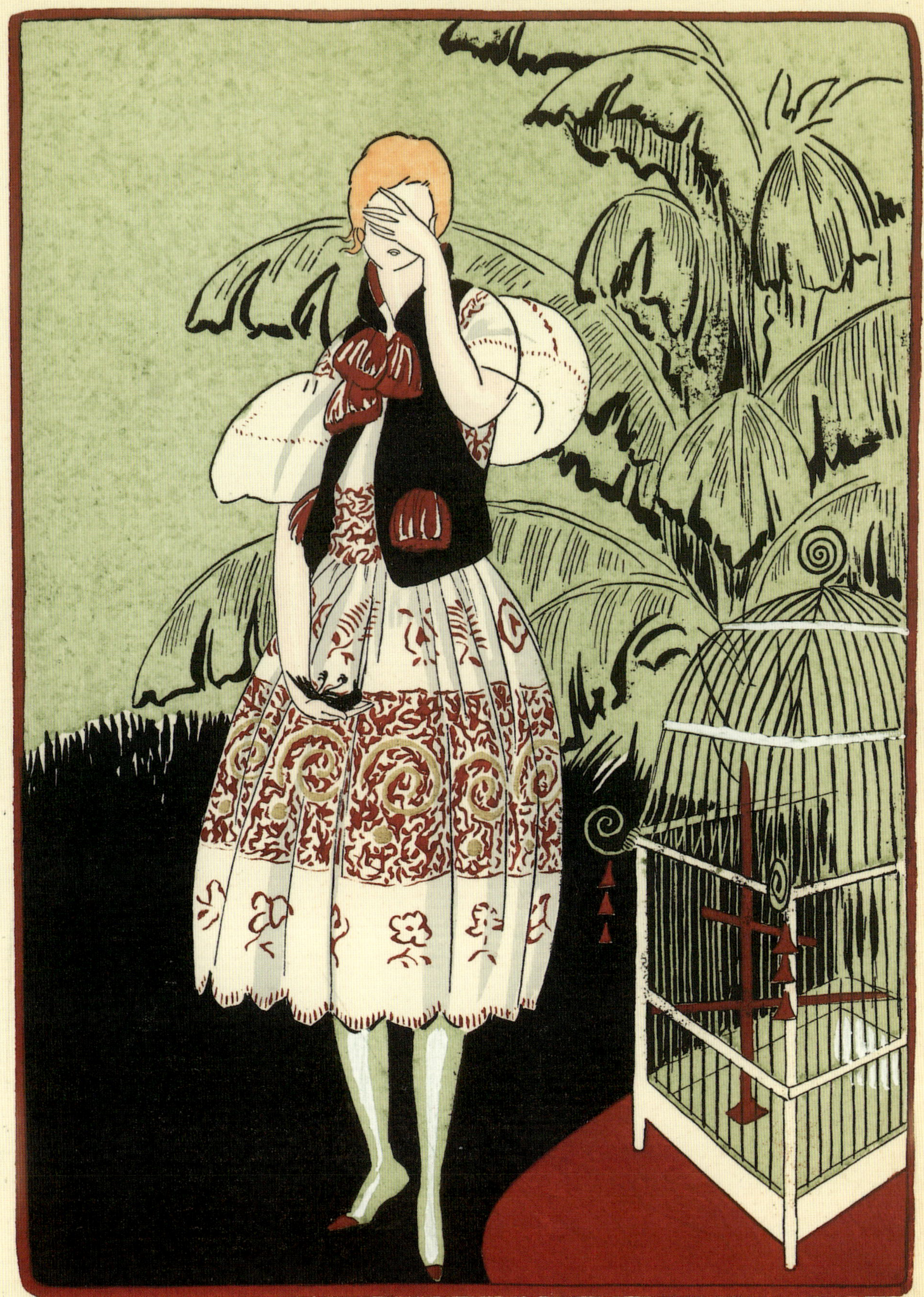

Right
"La belle Journée" (The glorious day), summer dress by Paul Poiret. Illustration by George Lepape. *Gazette du Bon Ton*, 1920

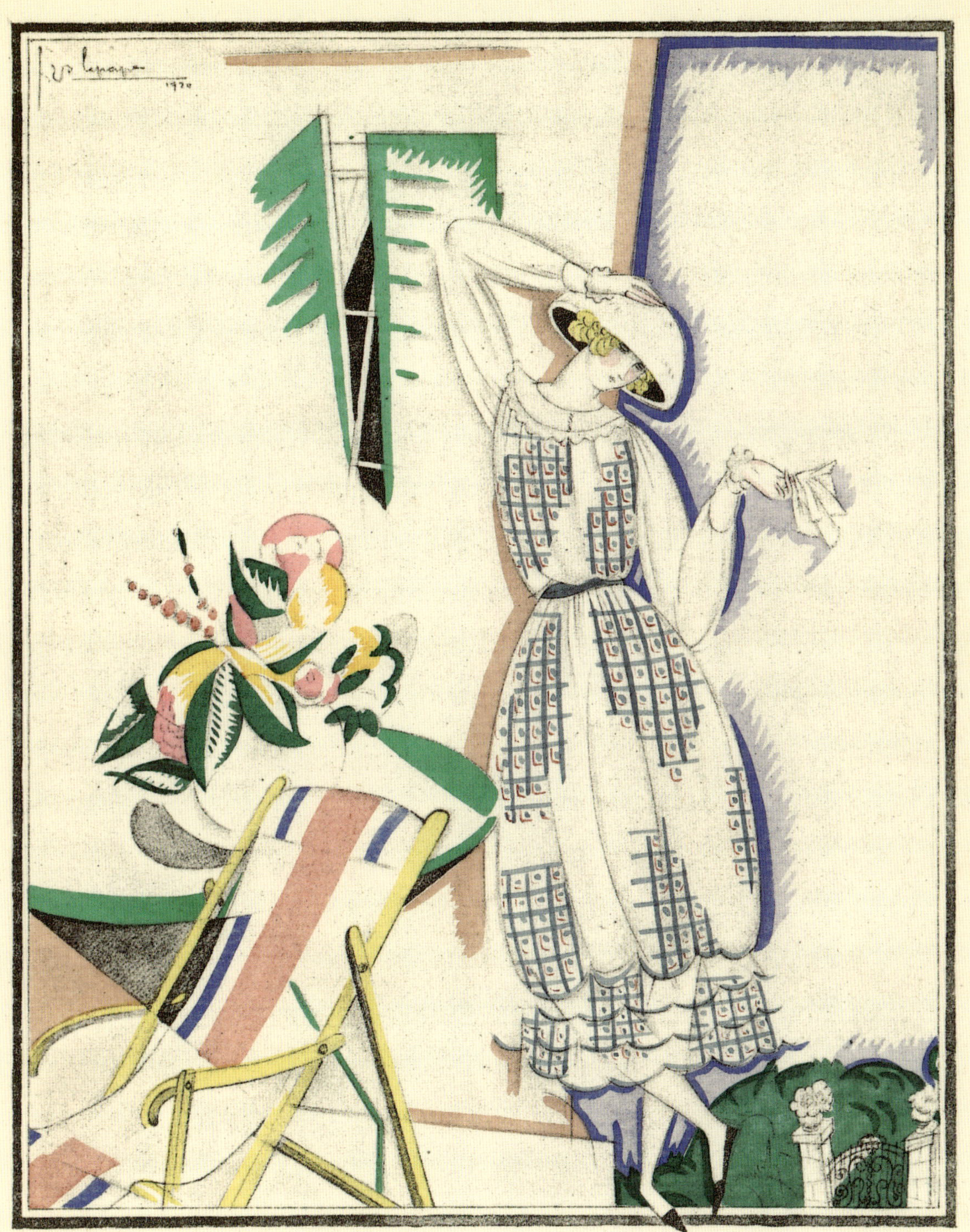

LA BELLE JOURNÉE

Robe d'été, de Paul Poiret

Below

Designs for evening and day dresses.
McCall's, 1922

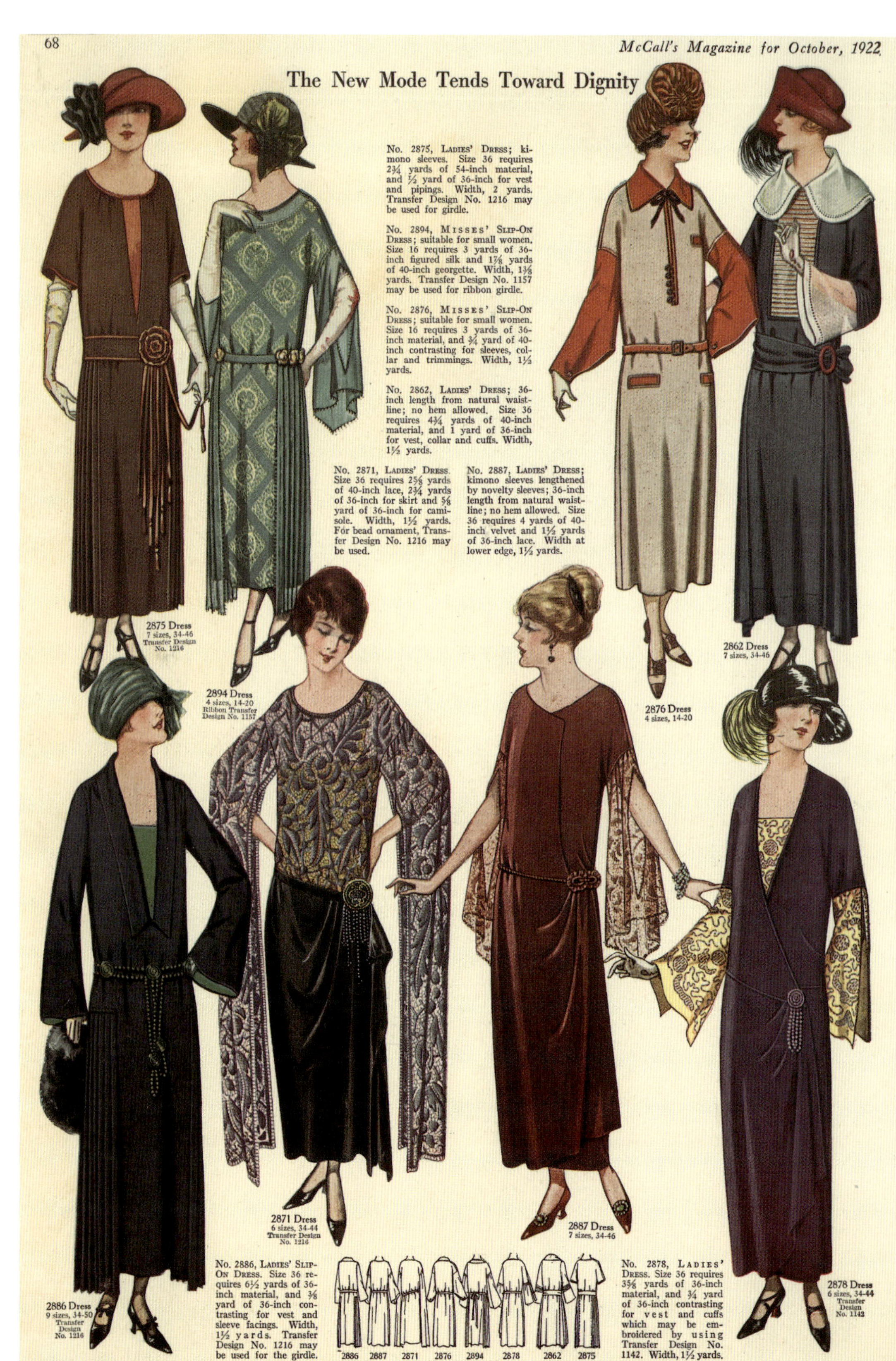

68 McCall's Magazine for October, 1922

The New Mode Tends Toward Dignity

No. 2875, Ladies' Dress; kimono sleeves. Size 36 requires 2¾ yards of 54-inch material, and ½ yard of 36-inch for vest and pipings. Width, 2 yards. Transfer Design No. 1216 may be used for girdle.

No. 2894, Misses' Slip-On Dress; suitable for small women. Size 16 requires 3 yards of 36-inch figured silk and 1⅞ yards of 40-inch georgette. Width, 1⅜ yards. Transfer Design No. 1157 may be used for ribbon girdle.

No. 2876, Misses' Slip-On Dress; suitable for small women. Size 16 requires 3 yards of 36-inch material, and ¾ yard of 40-inch contrasting for sleeves, collar and trimmings. Width, 1½ yards.

No. 2862, Ladies' Dress; 36-inch length from natural waistline; no hem allowed. Size 36 requires 4¾ yards of 40-inch material, and 1 yard of 36-inch for vest, collar and cuffs. Width, 1½ yards.

No. 2871, Ladies' Dress. Size 36 requires 2⅝ yards of 40-inch lace, 2¾ yards of 36-inch for skirt and ⅝ yard of 36-inch for camisole. Width, 1½ yards. For bead ornament, Transfer Design No. 1216 may be used.

No. 2887, Ladies' Dress; kimono sleeves lengthened by novelty sleeves; 36-inch length from natural waistline; no hem allowed. Size 36 requires 4 yards of 40-inch velvet and 1½ yards of 36-inch lace. Width at lower edge, 1½ yards.

2875 Dress
7 sizes, 34-46
Transfer Design
No. 1216

2894 Dress
4 sizes, 14-20
Ribbon Transfer
Design No. 1157

2876 Dress
4 sizes, 14-20

2862 Dress
7 sizes, 34-46

2871 Dress
6 sizes, 34-44
Transfer Design
No. 1216

2887 Dress
7 sizes, 34-46

2886 Dress
9 sizes, 34-50
Transfer
Design
No. 1216

No. 2886, Ladies' Slip-On Dress. Size 36 requires 6½ yards of 36-inch material, and ⅜ yard of 36-inch contrasting for vest and sleeve facings. Width, 1½ yards. Transfer Design No. 1216 may be used for the girdle.

2886 2887 2871 2876 2894 2878 2862 2875

No. 2878, Ladies' Dress. Size 36 requires 3⅝ yards of 36-inch material, and ¾ yard of 36-inch contrasting for vest and cuffs which may be embroidered by using Transfer Design No. 1142. Width, 1½ yards.

2878 Dress
6 sizes, 34-44
Transfer
Design
No. 1142

Below
Designs for day dresses.
The Delineator, 1922

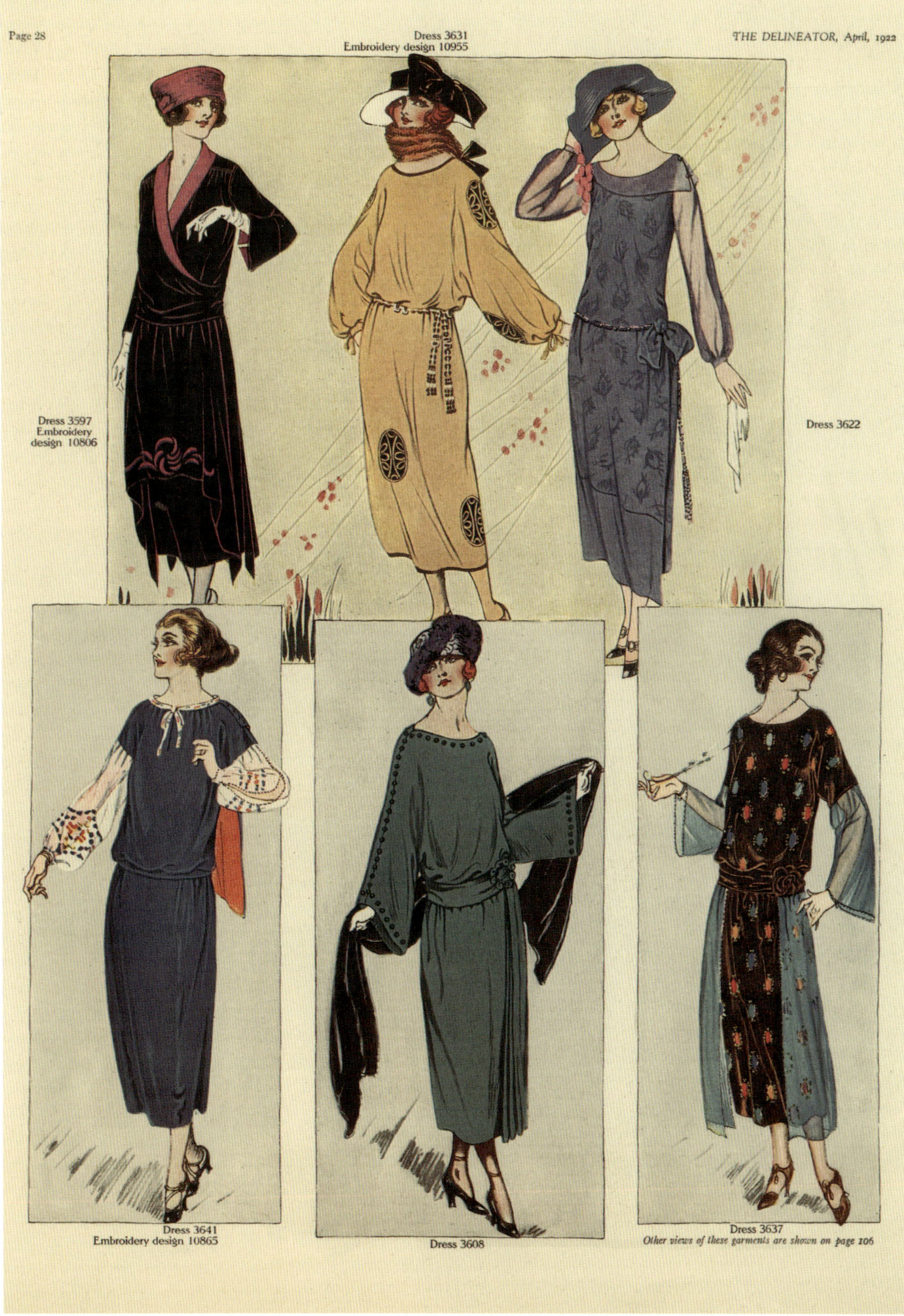

Page 28 THE DELINEATOR, April, 1922

Dress 3631
Embroidery design 10955

Dress 3597
Embroidery design 10806

Dress 3622

Dress 3641
Embroidery design 10865

Dress 3608

Dress 3637
Other views of these garments are shown on page 106

Right
Day dress with wide black silk sleeves worn with wide-brimmed hat and buckled shoes. *Journal des Demoiselles*, 1921

JOURNAL
DES DEMOISELLES

15 Octobre 1921

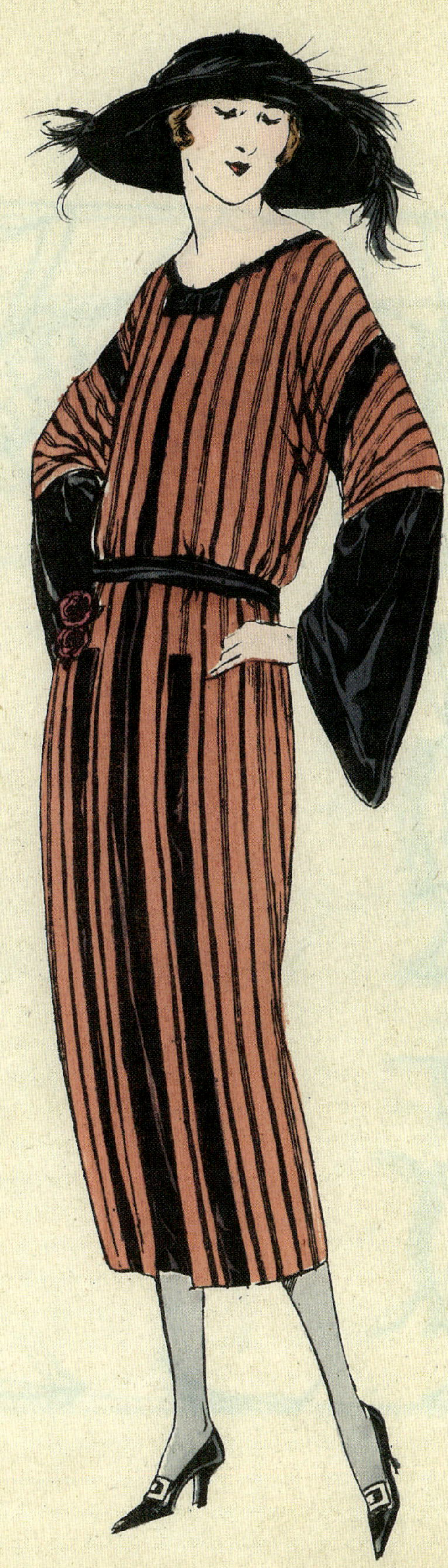

A. THIÉRY, DIRECTEUR
79, Boulev. Saint-Germain, PARIS

Extrait des « Élégances Parisiennes »

Supplément au n° 20

Le Gérant : Baeurlé

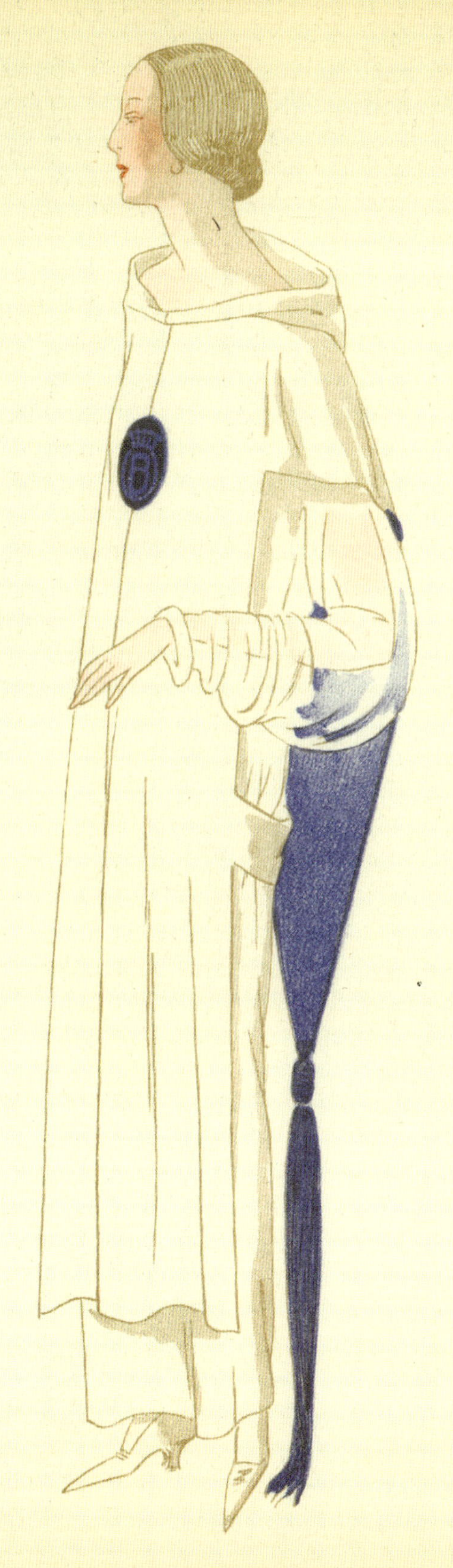

N° 10 de La Gazette

Année 1922. — Croquis N° VIII

CHARTRE
ROBE DE MAIS

Left
Chartreux (Carthusian) "House" day dress. The name of the dress refers to the similarities with the white hooded habit worn by monks of the Carthusian order. Illustration by David. *Gazette du Bon Ton*, 1922

Below
Dress Immaculée Conception (Immaculate Conception). The model is wearing a Russian inspired headdress and the blue flowers sash refers to the colour of the Virgin Mary. *Gazette du Bon Ton*, 1922

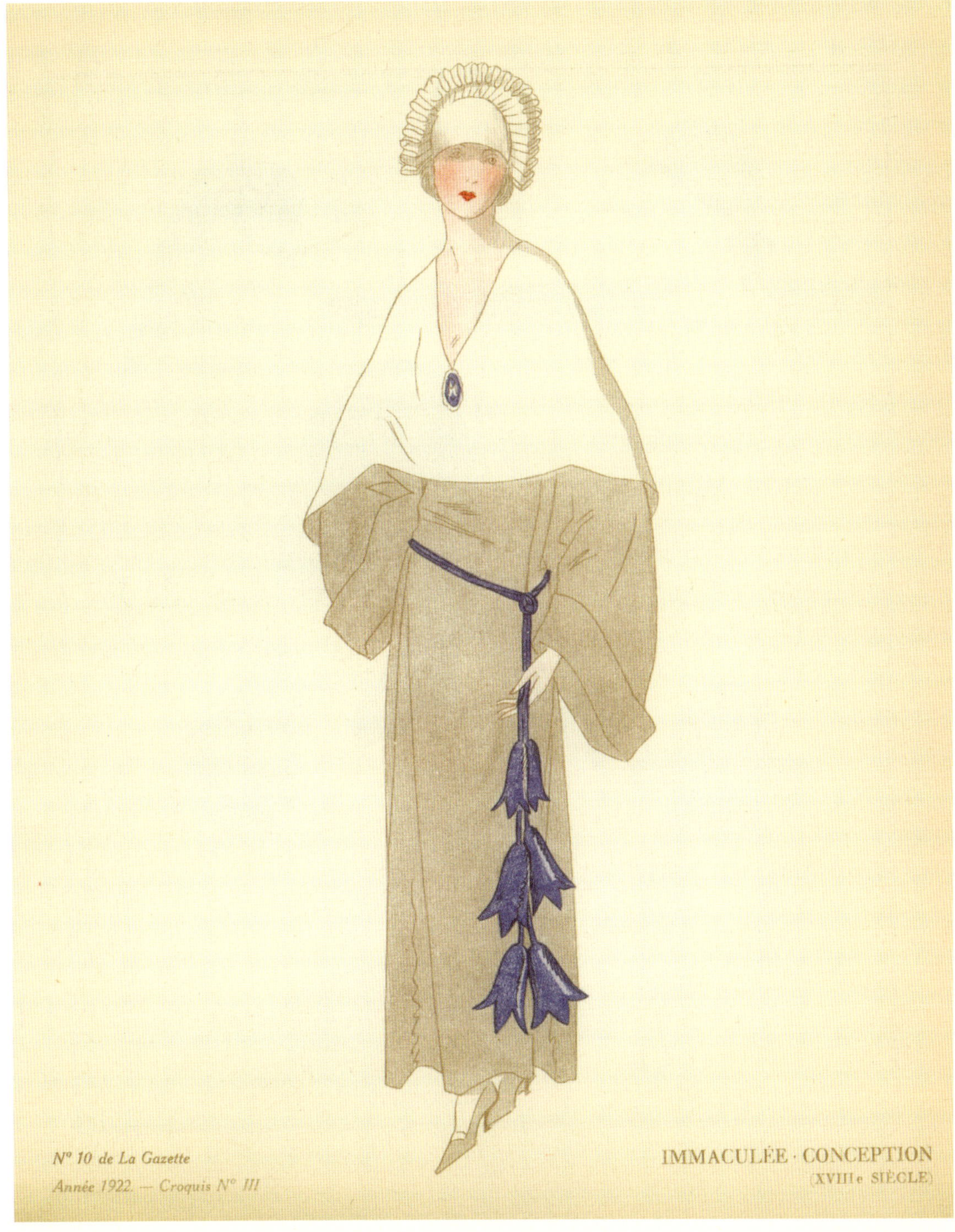

Below and right

Day dress with matching hat by Germaine. *L'Illustration des Modes*, 1922

Abbé (Abbot) walking dress. Illustration by David. *Gazette du Bon Ton*, 1922

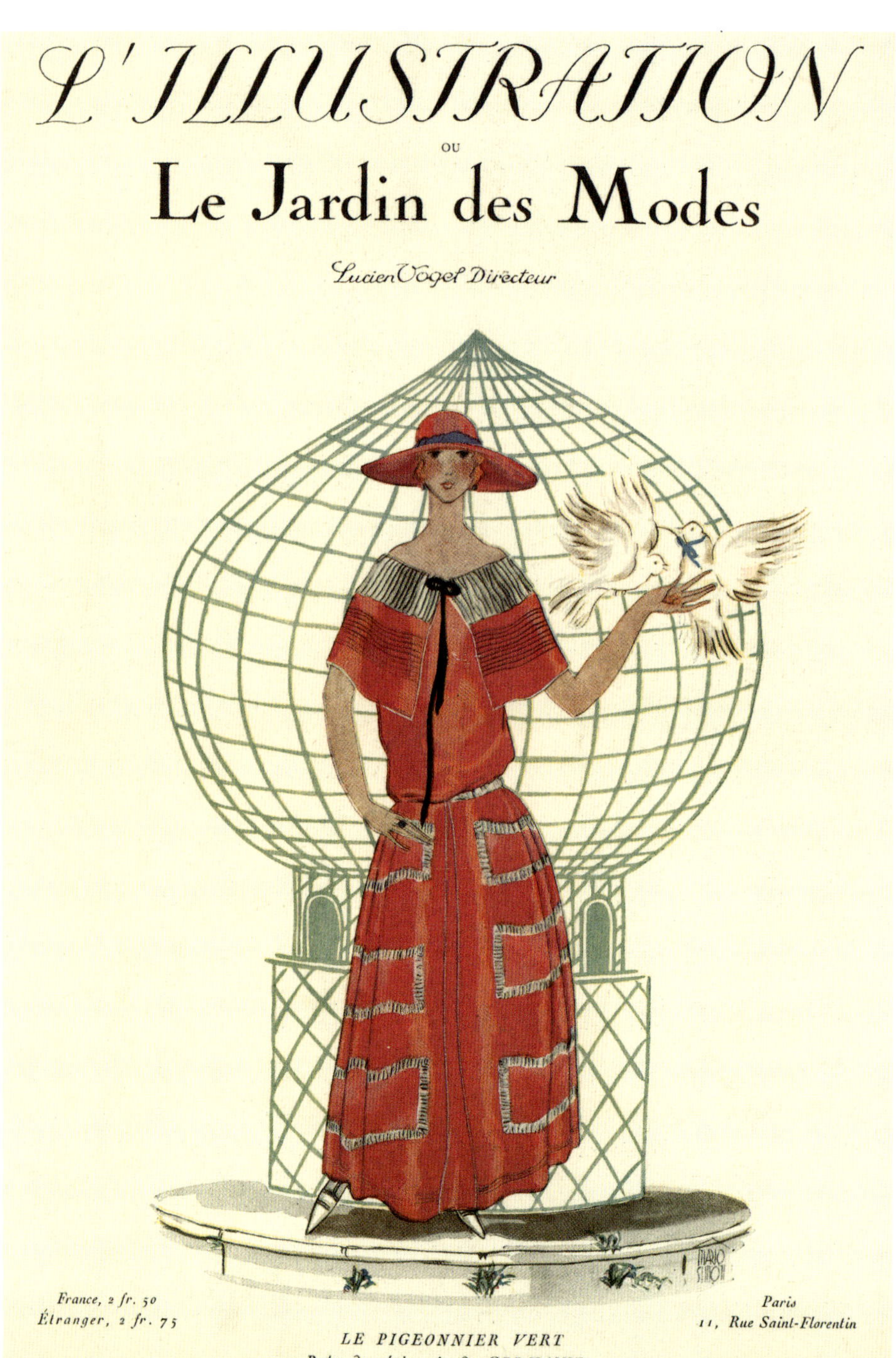

L'ILLUSTRATION

OU

Le Jardin des Modes

Lucien Vogel Directeur

France, 2 fr. 50
Étranger, 2 fr. 75

Paris
11, Rue Saint-Florentin

LE PIGEONNIER VERT
Robe de plein air de GERMAINE

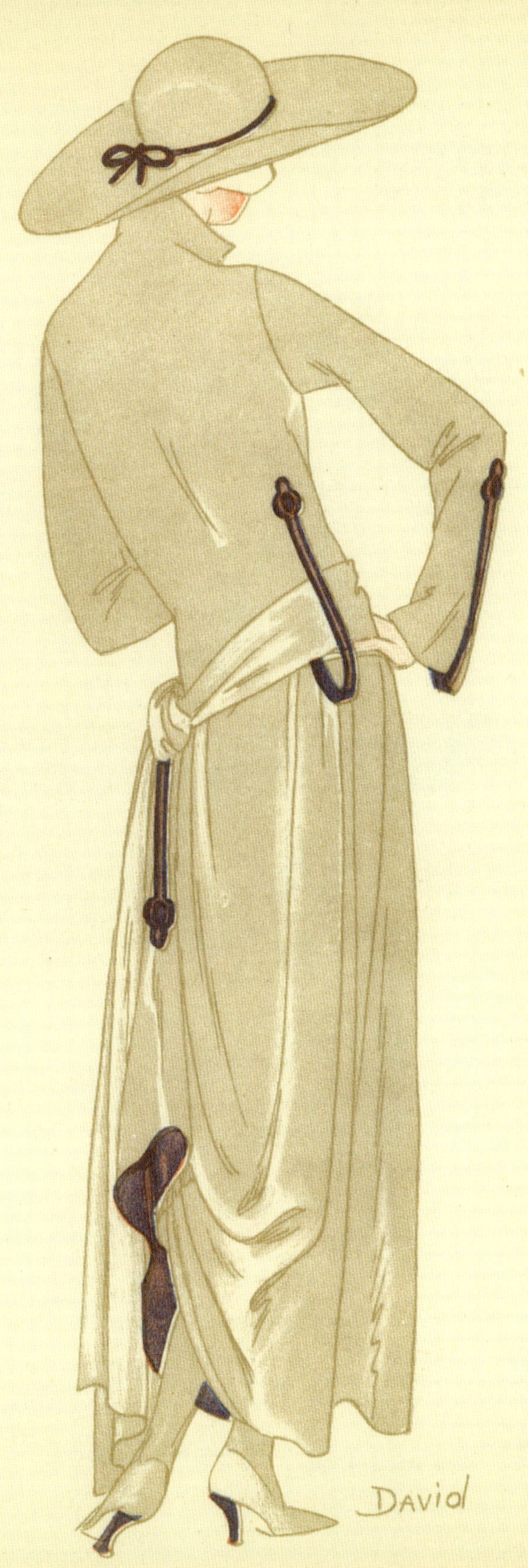

10 de La Gazette
ée 1922. — Croquis N° IV

ABBÉ

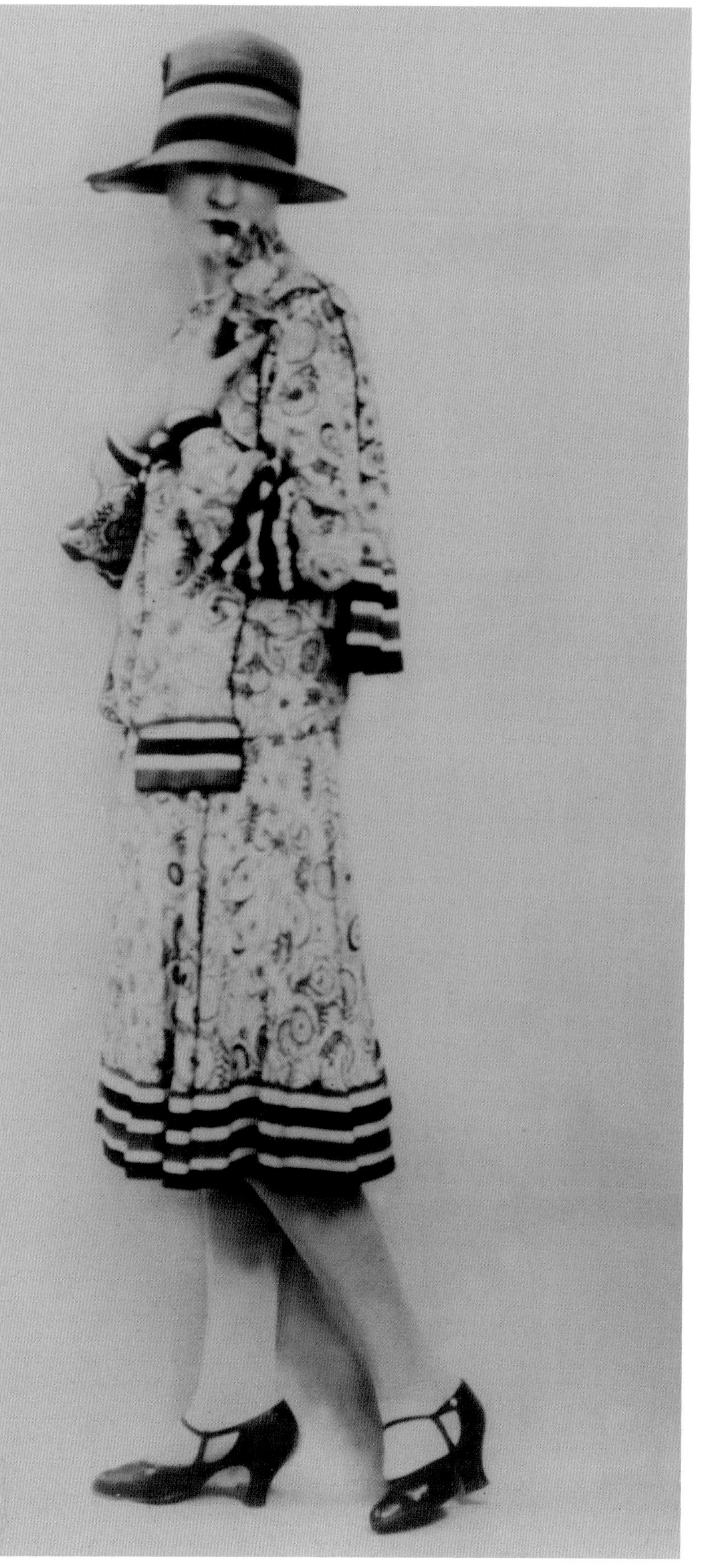

Left and right

Photograph of a model wearing a Parisian floral crepe de Chine gown. Berlin, c.1923

A transparent embroidered gold brocade dress worn over a black crepe slip, accessorised with a large crinoline hat trimmed with a large fabric rose, c.1924

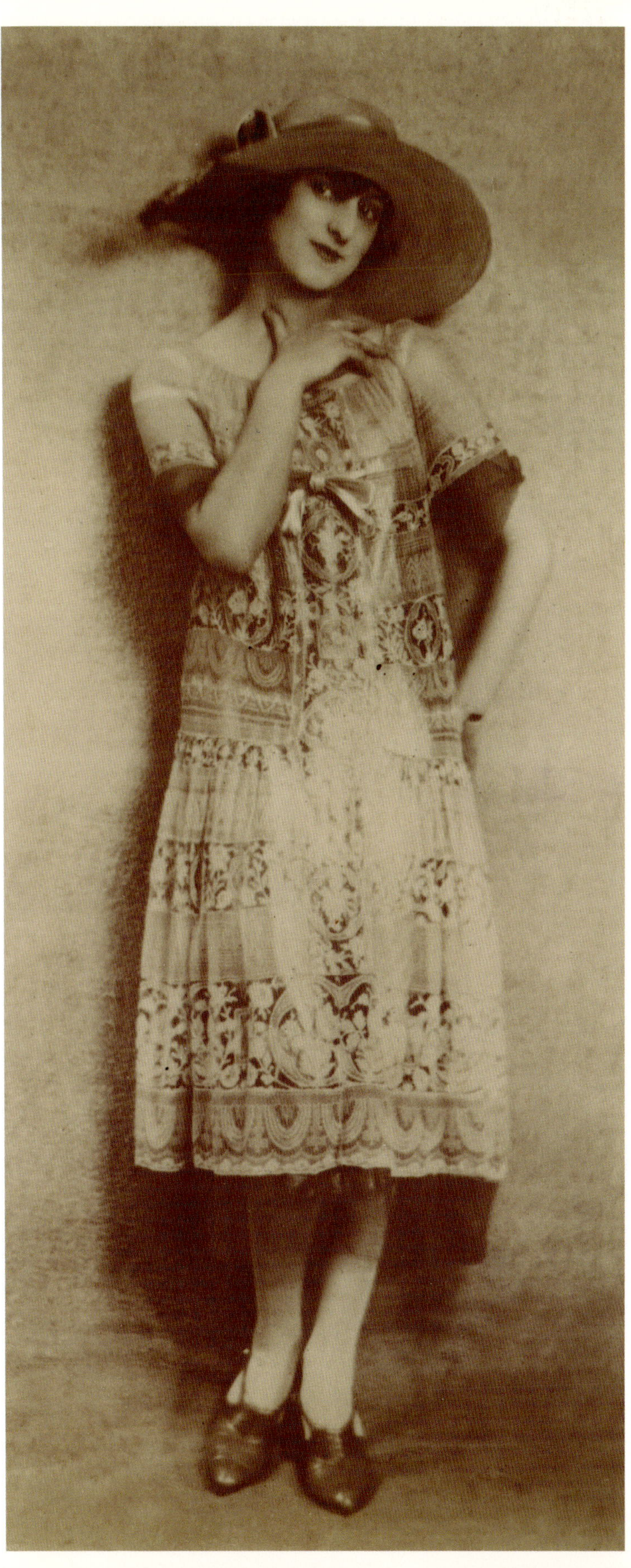

Modèles Originaux

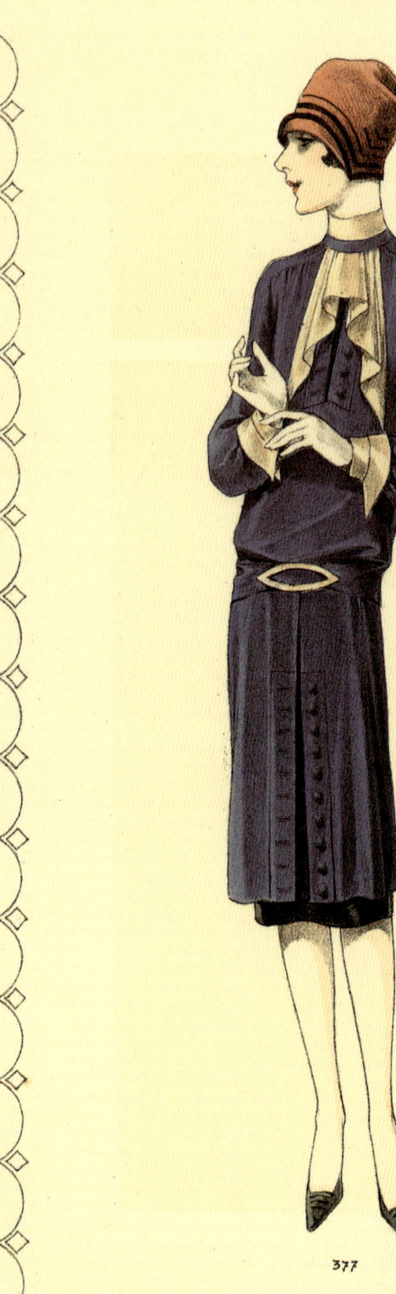

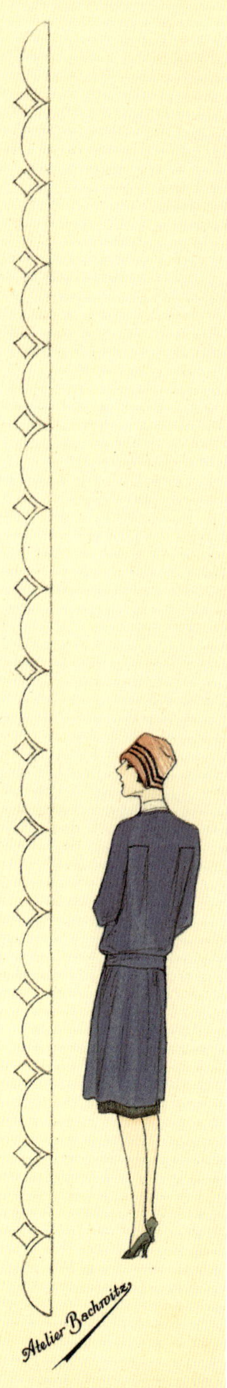

377

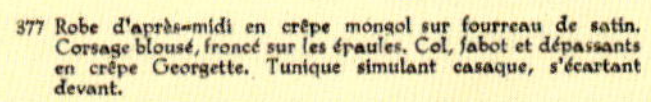

377 Robe d'après-midi en crêpe mongol sur fourreau de satin. Corsage blousé, froncé sur les épaules. Col, jabot et dépassants en crêpe Georgette. Tunique simulant casaque, s'écartant devant.

Atelier Bachwitz

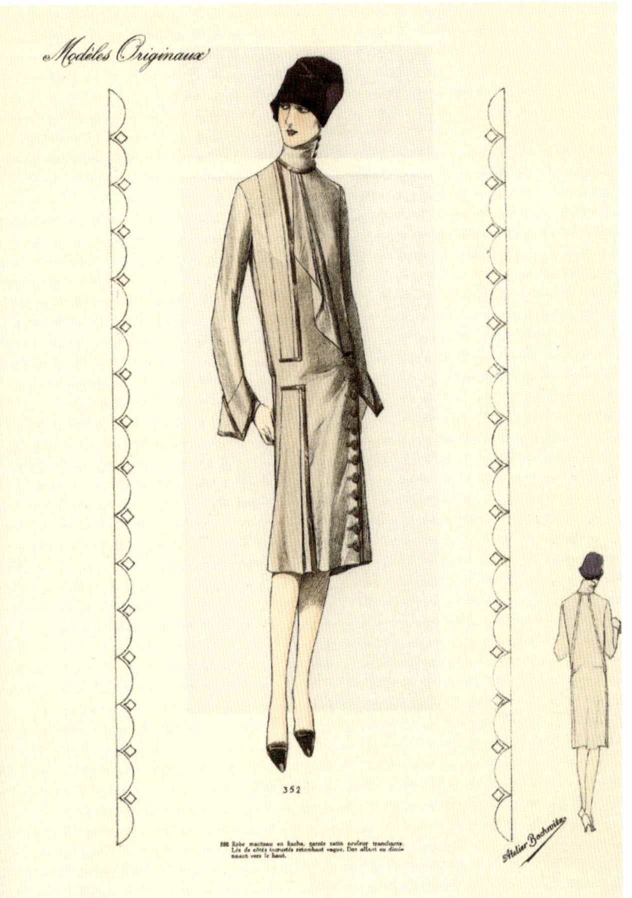

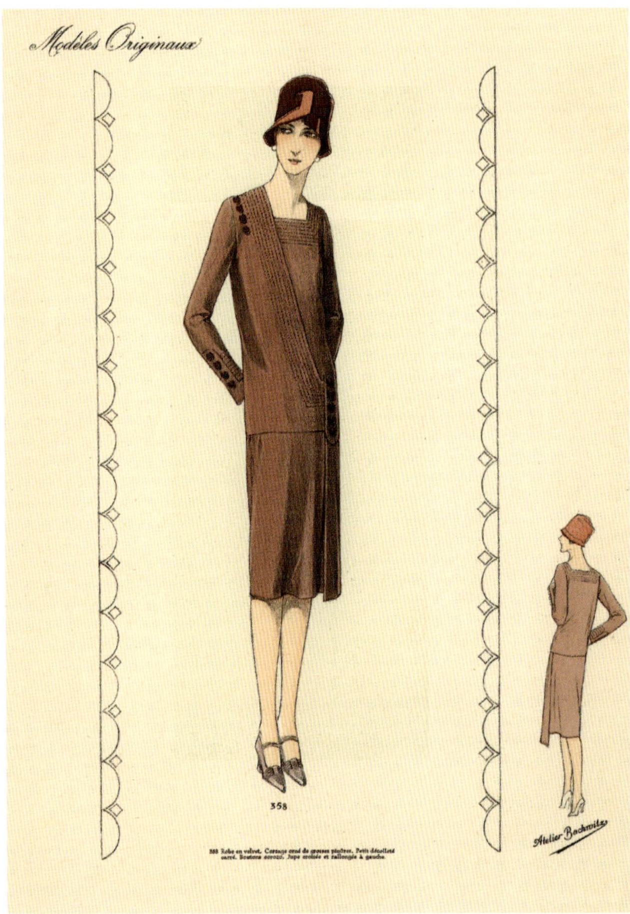

Left and right above

A coat dress in pale brown Kasha edged in matching silk by Atelier Bachroitz *Modèles Originaux*, c.1926

A brown velvet dress with a square neckline, ornamental stitching and large buttons by Atelier Bachroitz *Modèles Originaux*, c.1926

Left image

Blue tunic dress in Mongolian crepe with satin flounced collar and cuffs by Atelier Bachroitz *Modèles Originaux*, c.1926

Right
Velvet afternoon dress with scalloped tiering, and a faille afternoon dress with a slashed bolero top and two bell-shaped skirt flounces by Atelier Bachroitz. *Chic Parisien Beaux-Arts des Modes*, 1927

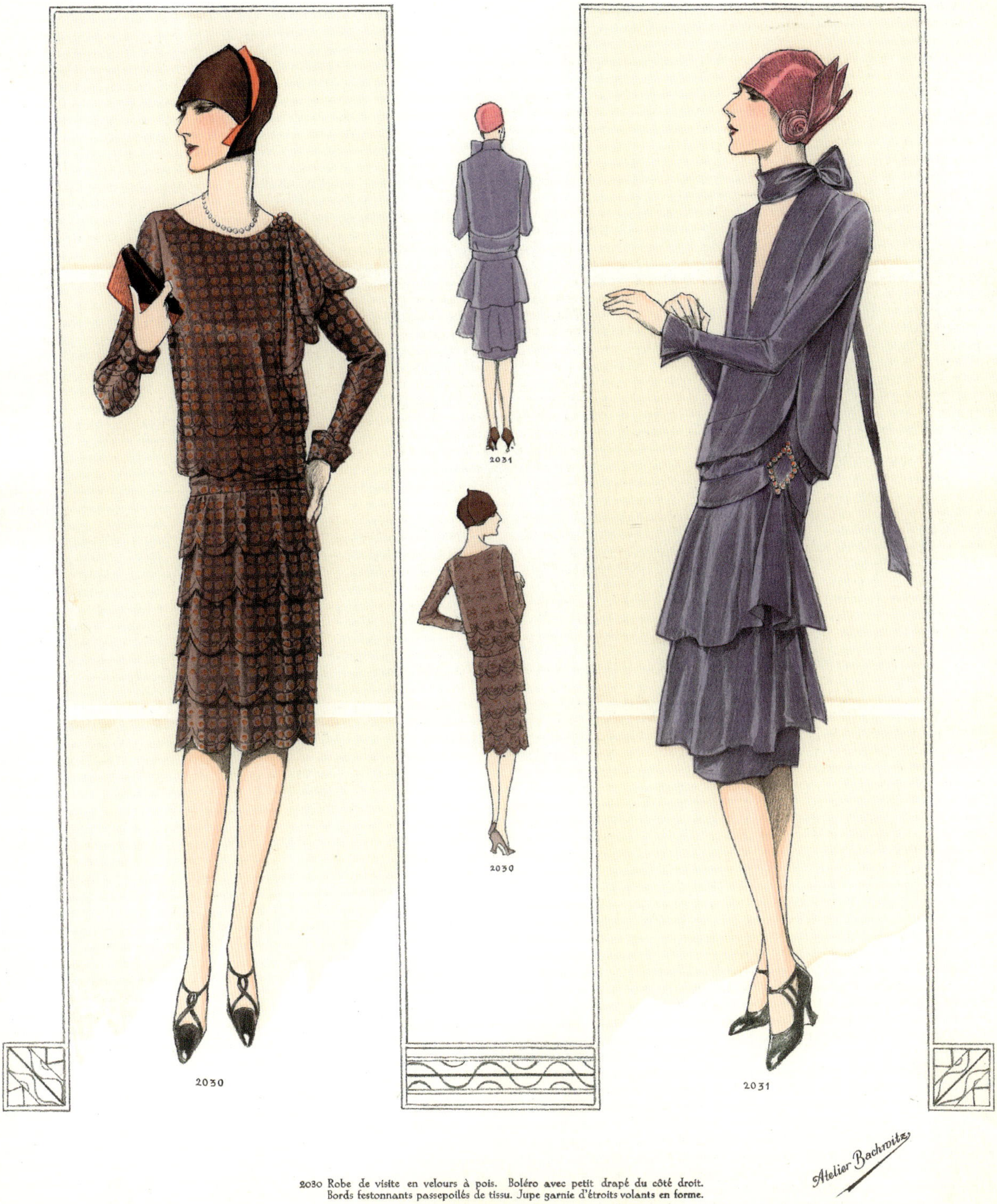

2031

2030

2030

2031

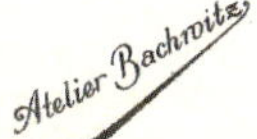

2030 Robe de visite en velours à pois. Boléro avec petit drapé du côté droit. Bords festonnants passepoilés de tissu. Jupe garnie d'étroits volants en forme.

2031 Robe de thé en faille. Boléro ouvert des deux côtés. Echarpe nouée avec long pan flottant. Ceinture de tissu avec boucle perlée. Jupe à deux volants en forme.

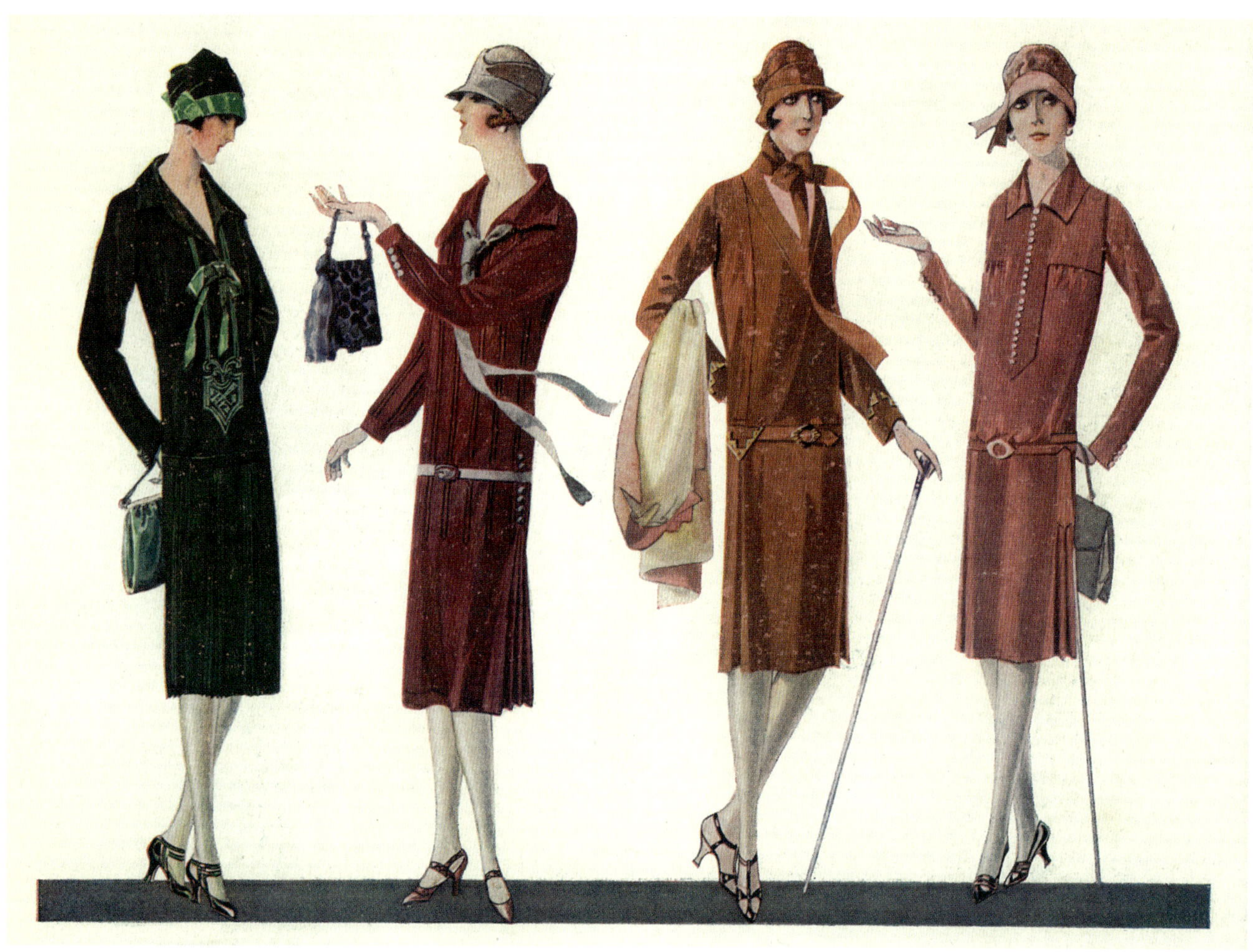

Above
Four day dresses by Maison Gerda.
Maison Gerda catalogue, c.1925

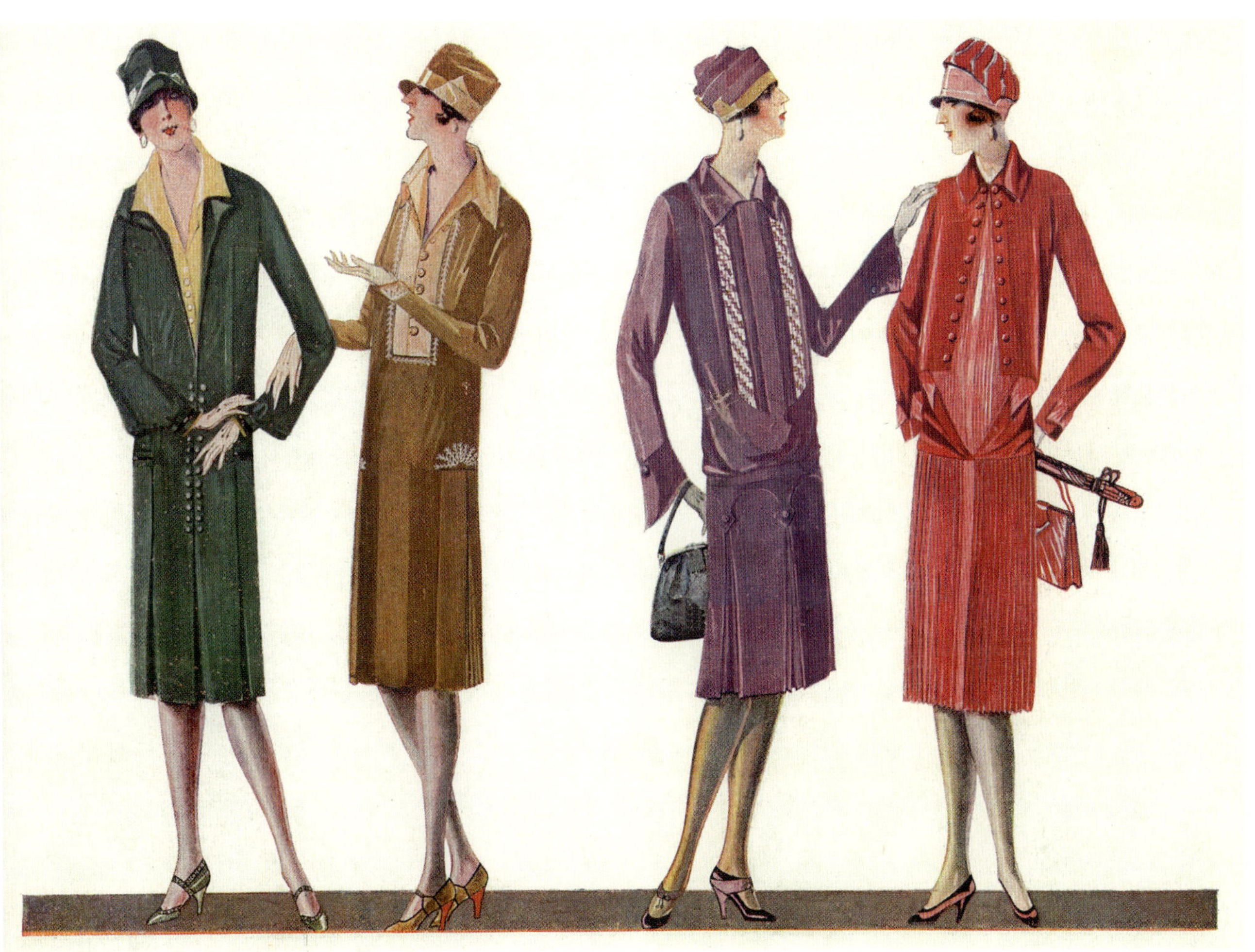

Above
Four day dresses by Maison Gerda.
Maison Gerda catalogue, c.1925

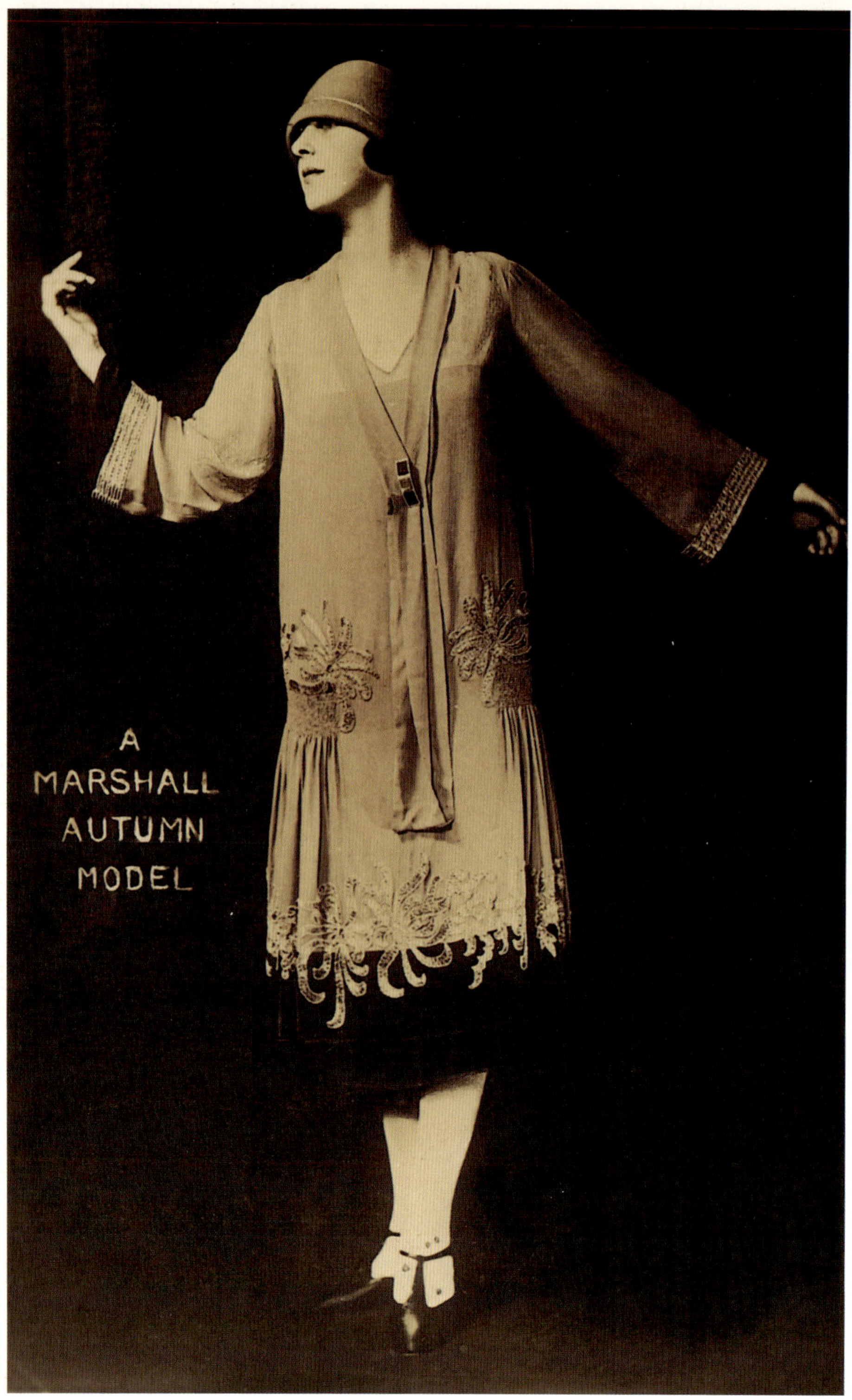

Above
Postcard of a Marshall autumn model showing an embellished silk crepe dress with sash-tie. USA, c.1925

Right
A Parisian model in red and white printed crepe, with long sleeves and jabot flounces, c.1924

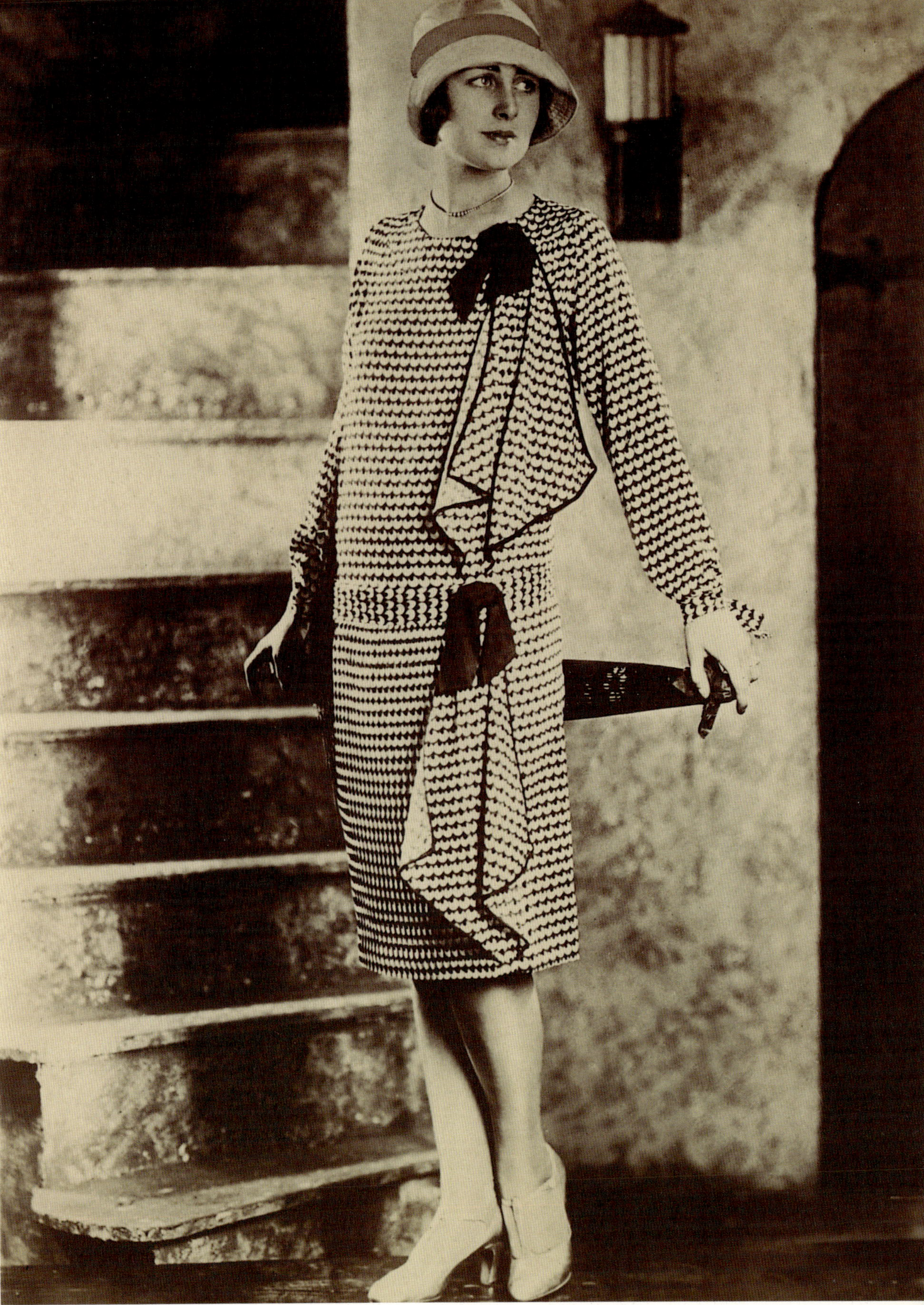

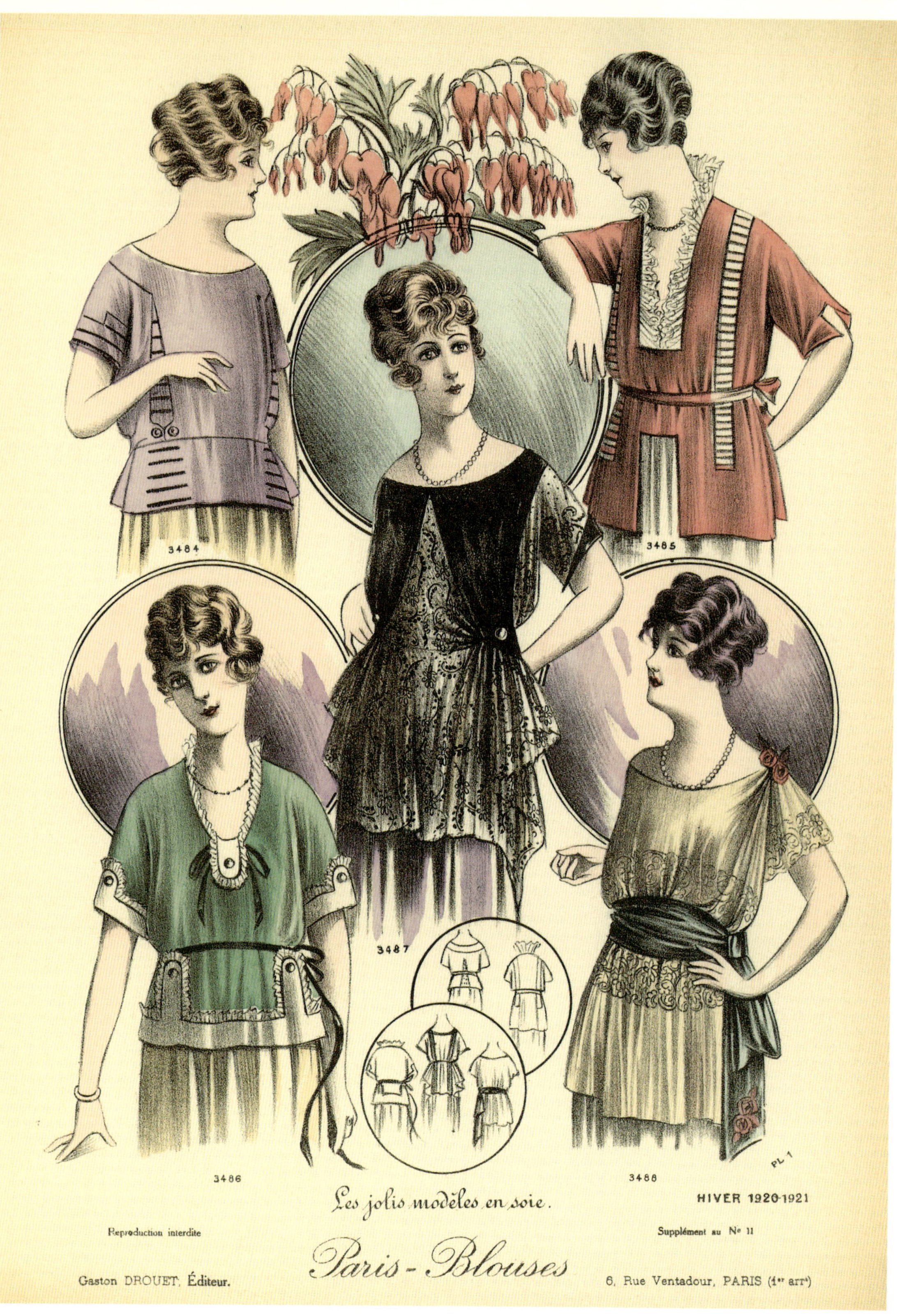

Above
Selection of belted silk blouses.
Paris-Blouses, 1920

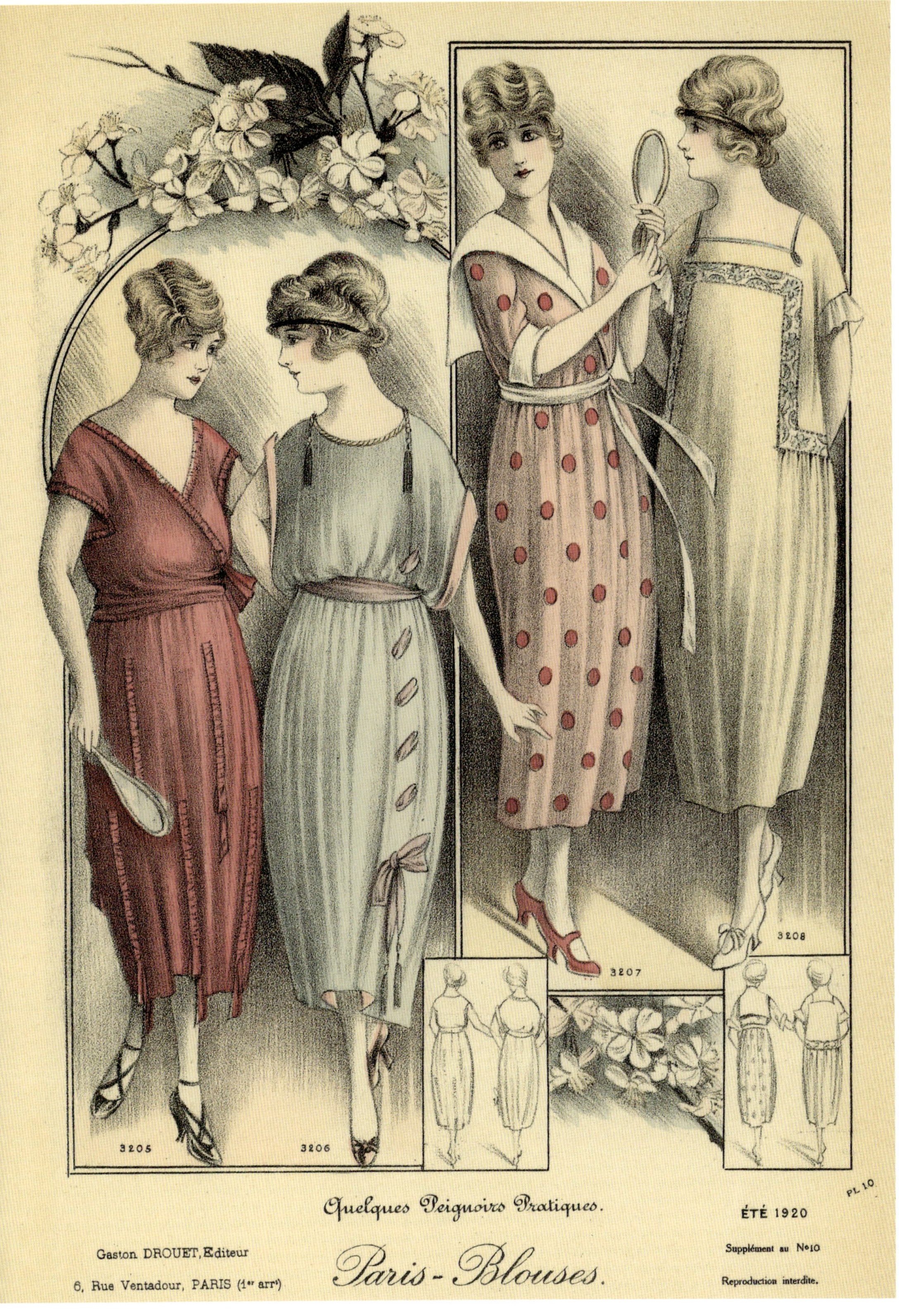

Above
Four 'practical housecoats'.
Paris-Blouses, 1920

Right
Selection of belted silk blouses.
Paris-Blouses, 1920

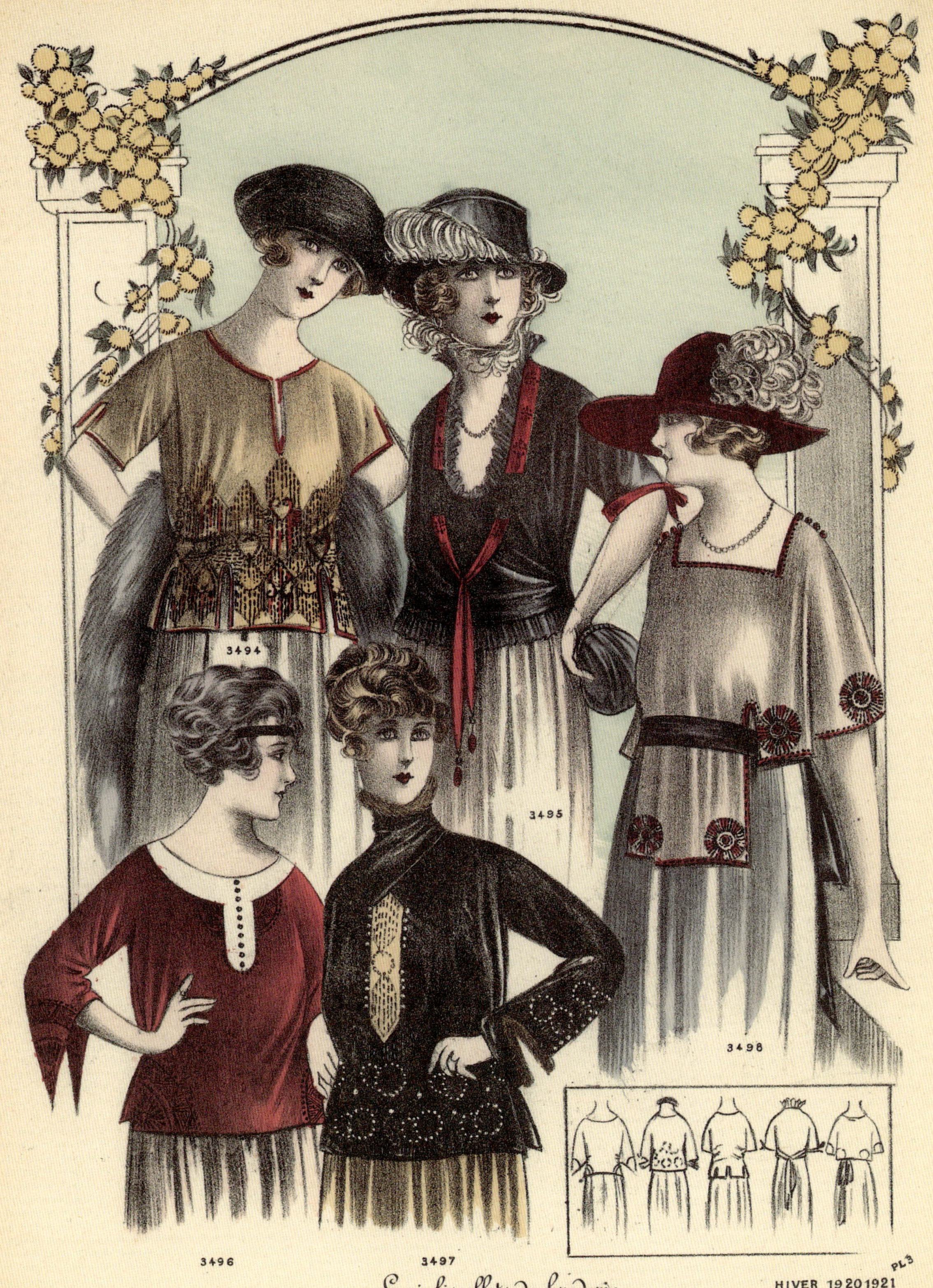

Les jolis effets de broderie.

HIVER 1920 1921

Supplément au No 11

Paris-Blouses.

Gaston DROUET Éditeur.

6, Rue Ventadour, PARIS (1er arr)

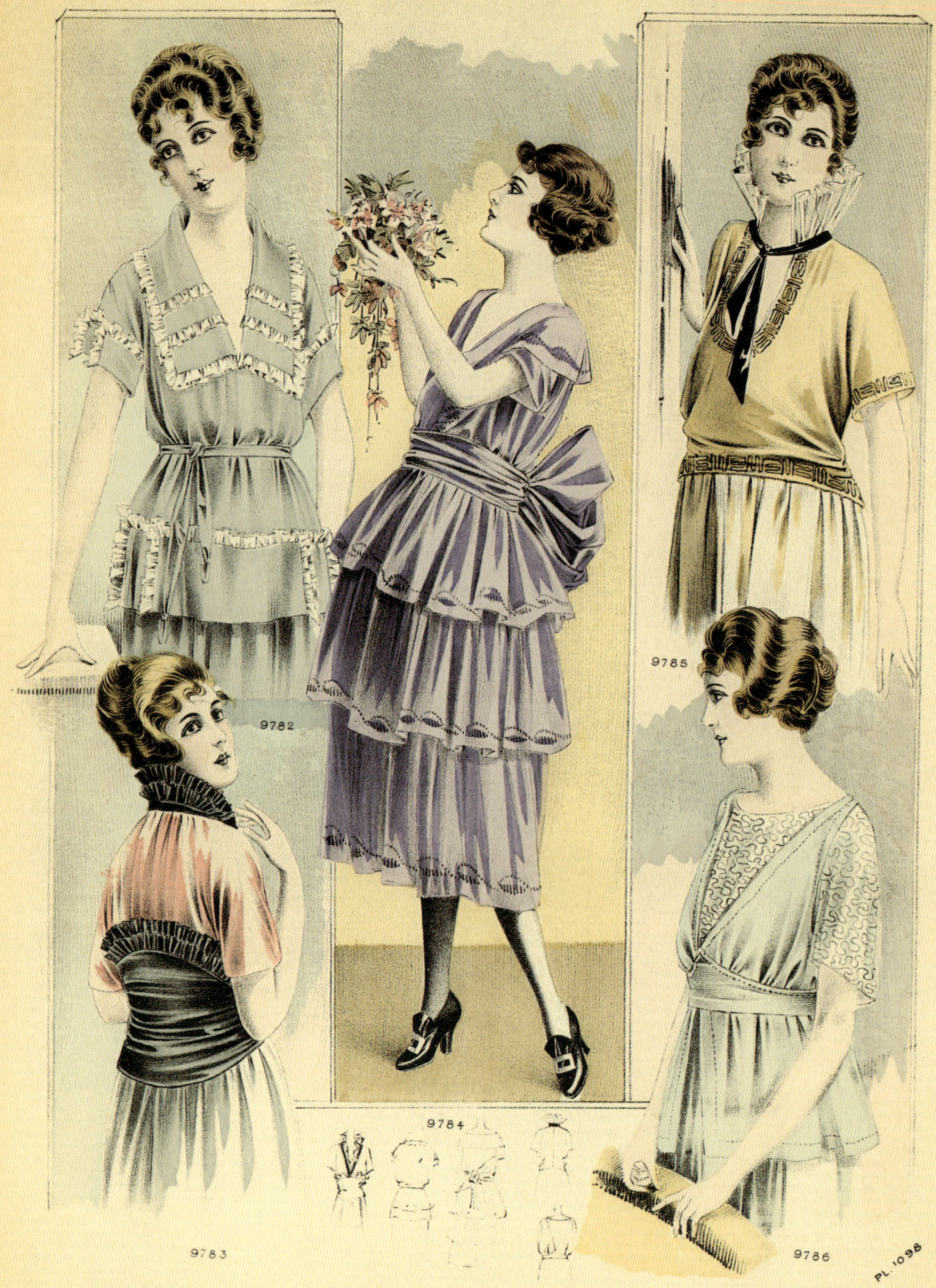

GASTON DROUET, Editeur
6 Rue Ventadour, PARIS

Robe et blouses légères pour l'Été.

Paris Elégant

Supplément au N° 130-1920

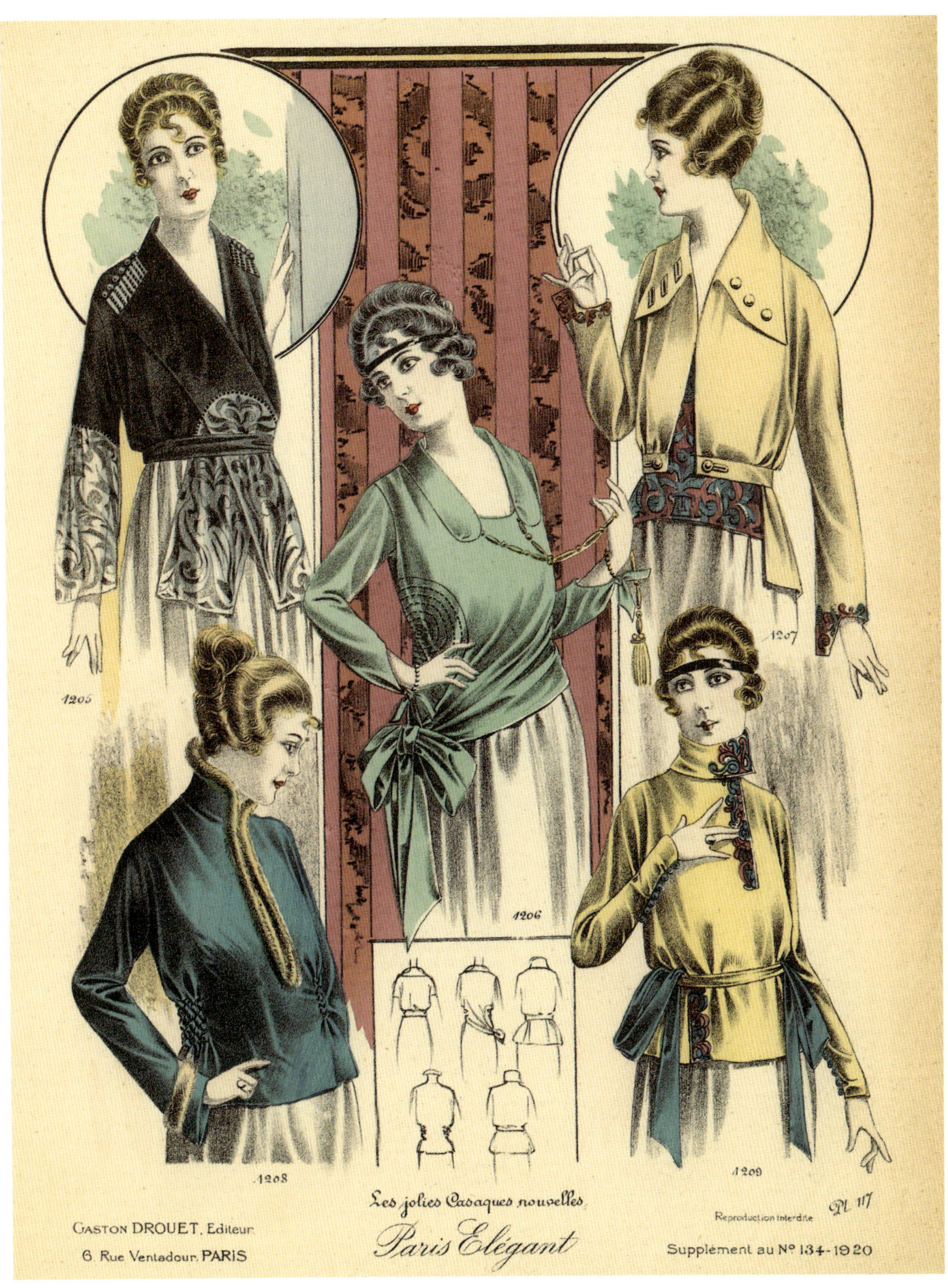

Left and above

Selection of light summer dresses and blouses in pastel hues. *Paris Élégant*, 1920

Five casaque designs. *Paris Élégant*, 1920

Below
Ensemble for the countryside by Margaine Lacroix consisting of a sailor's collar blouse and a pleated skirt. *La Femme Chic*, c.1923

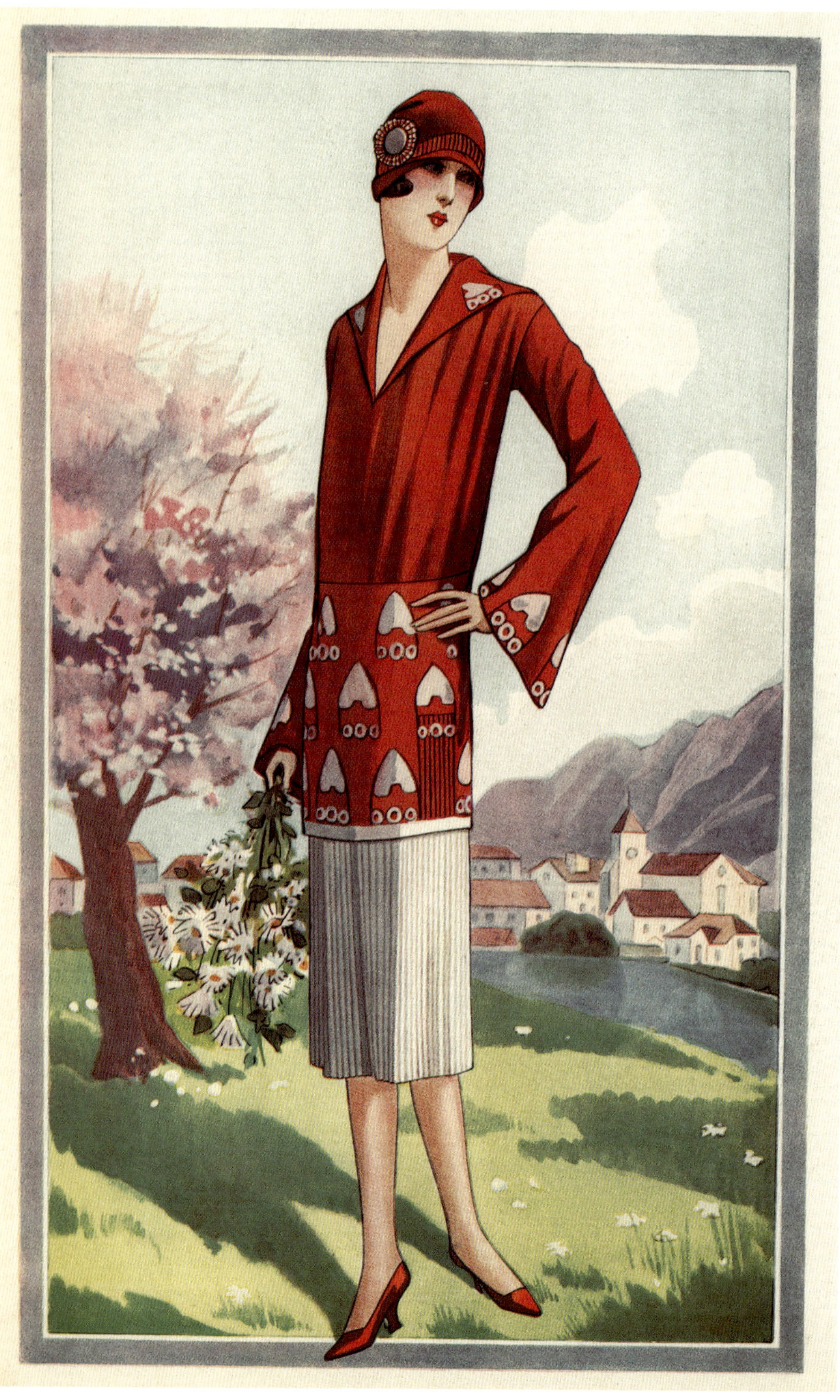

Below
Four "fashionable" sweaters.
La Femme Chic 1926

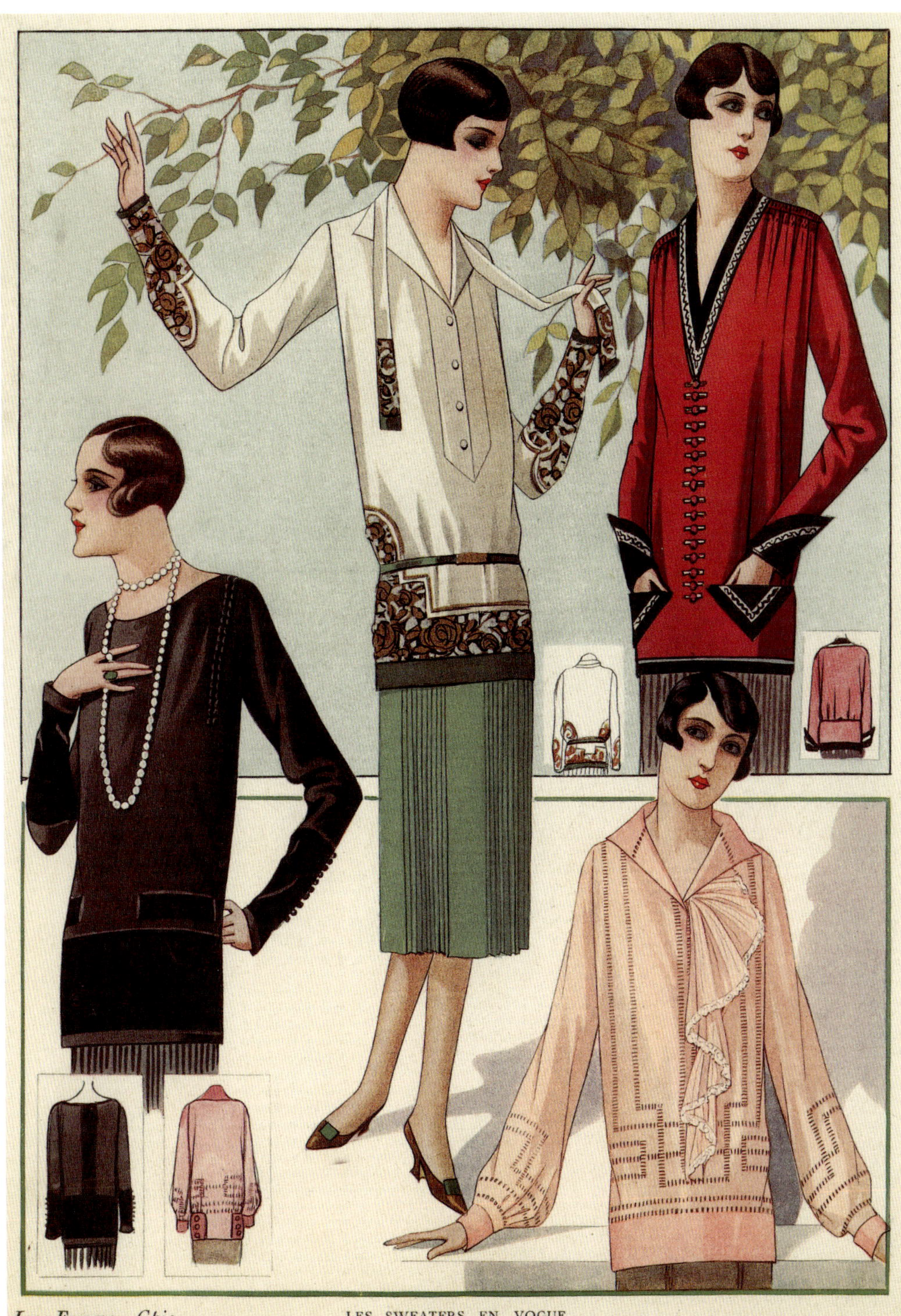

Right
Four long blouses. *La Femme Chic*, 1926

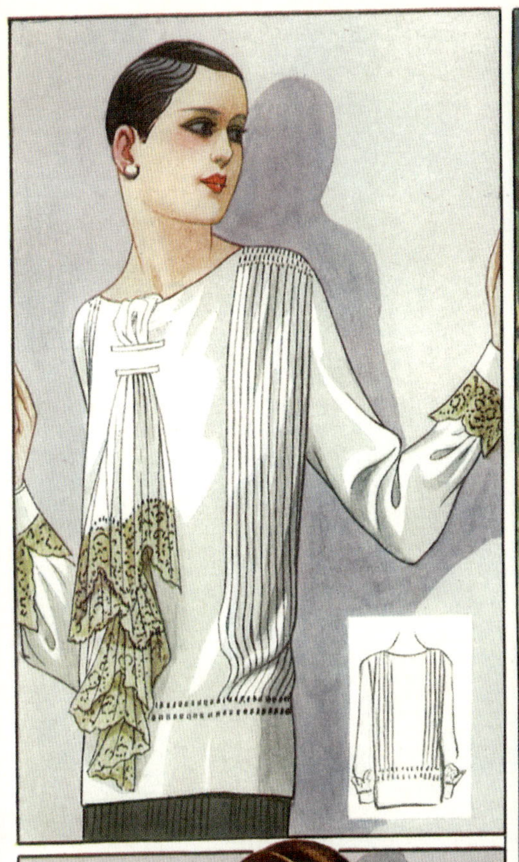

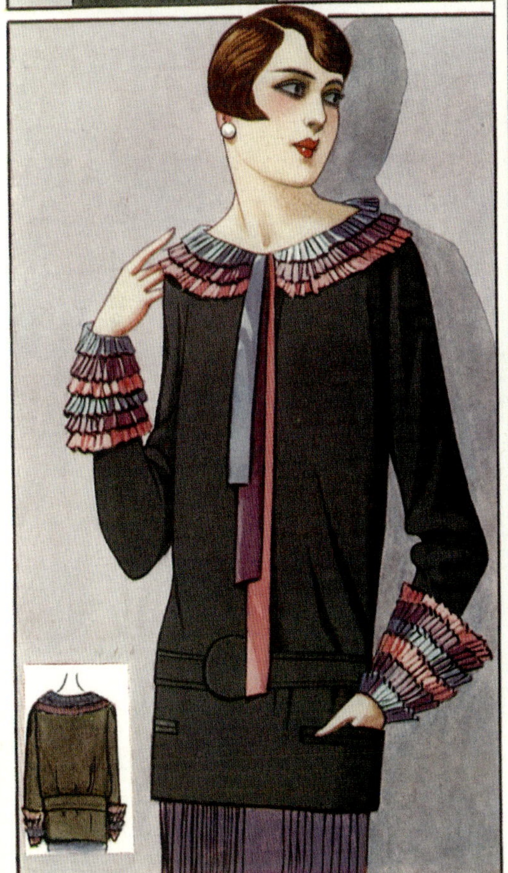

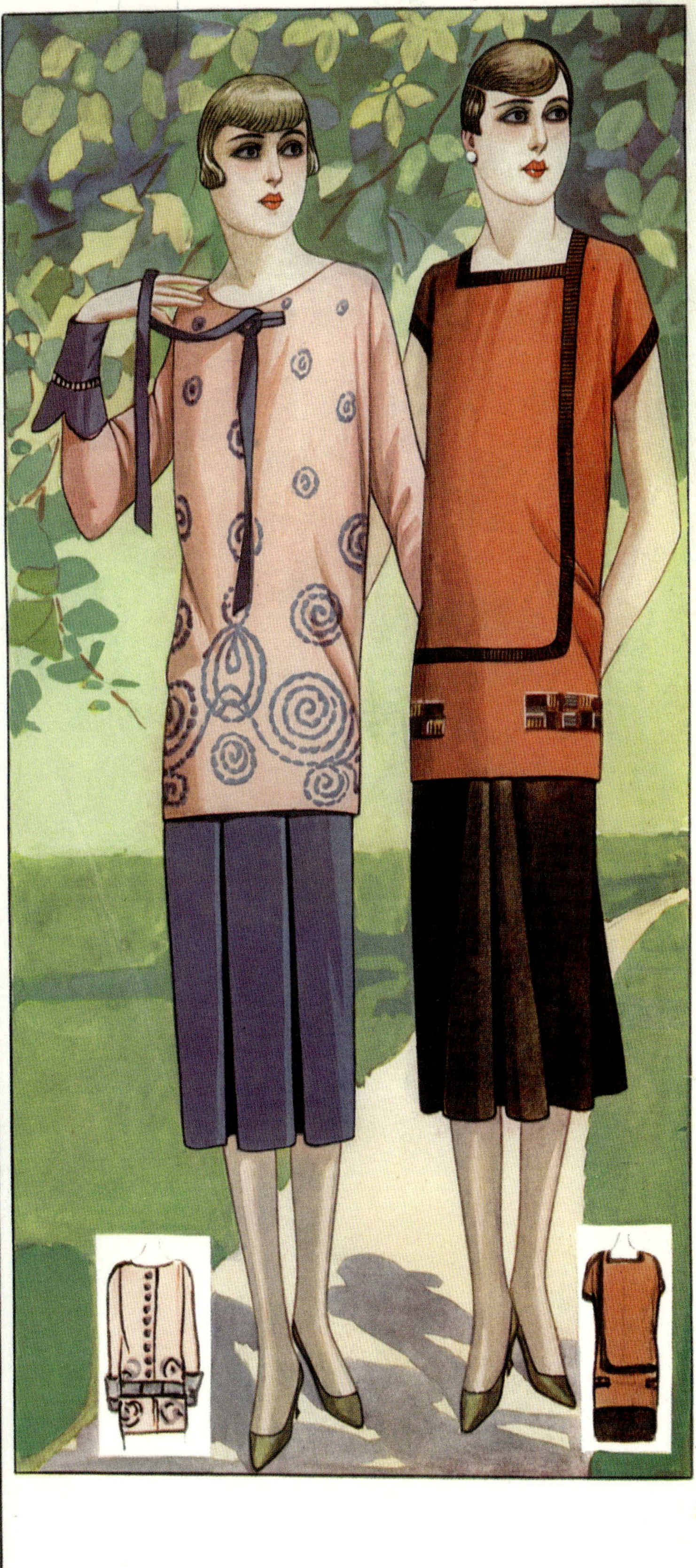

Below

Blouses by Ruffie. The Venetian backdrop of the images lends an air of luxury and travel to the fashions. The top right blouse is adorned with traditional inspired 'Russian' embroideries whilst the top left model takes it inspiration from ancient South American motifs. All examples have kimono-like sleeves. *La Femme Chic*, c.1922

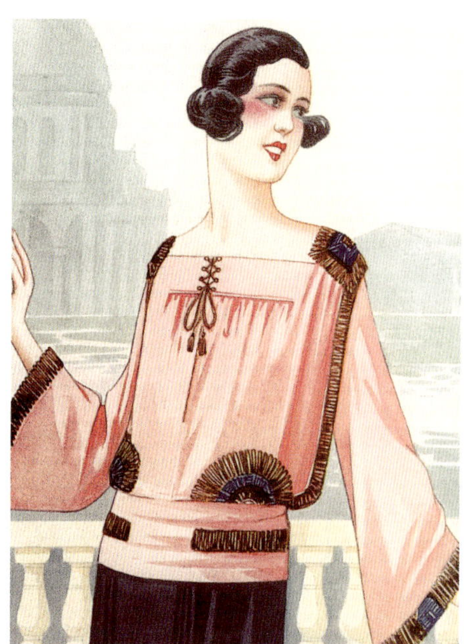

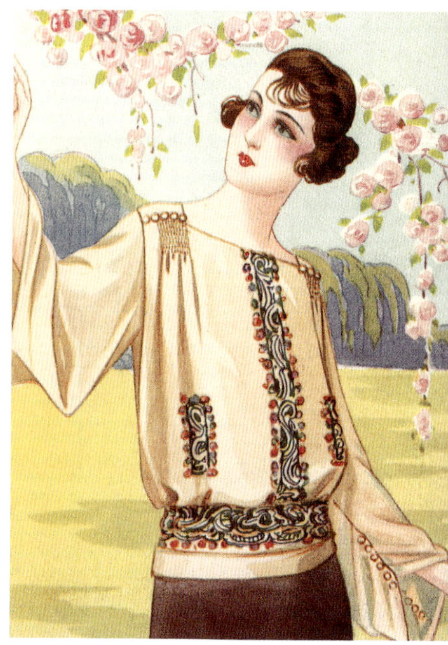

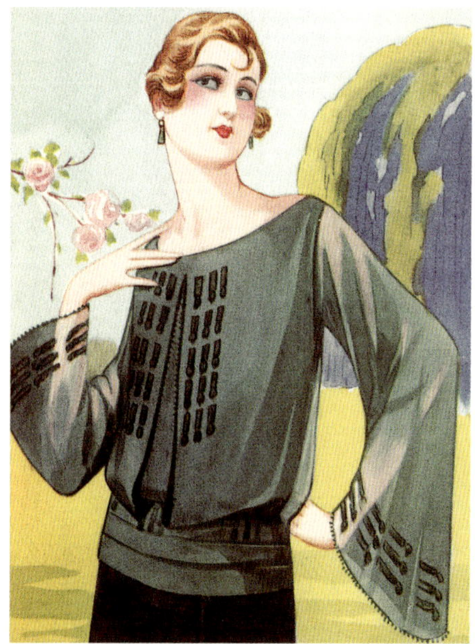

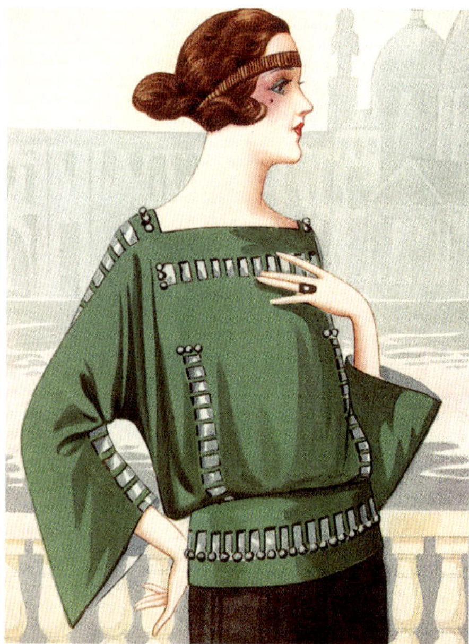

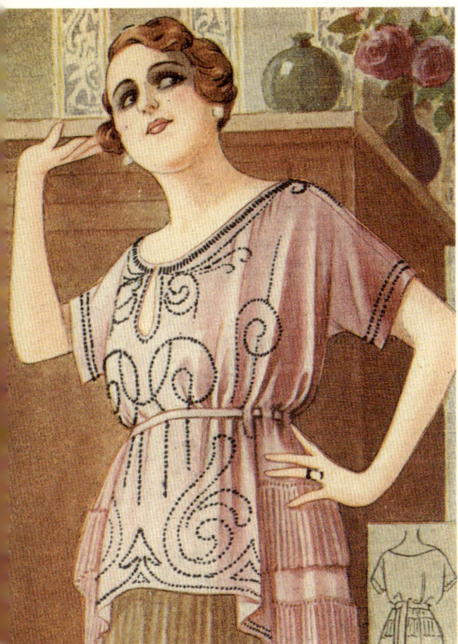

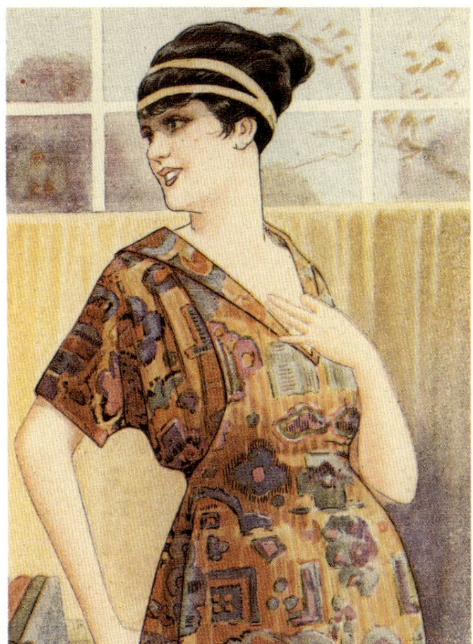

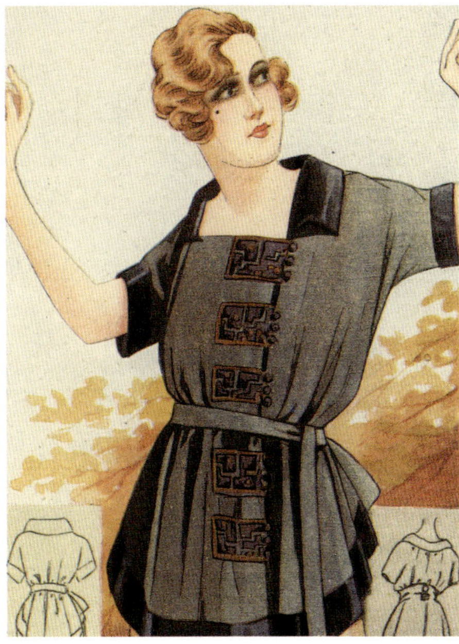

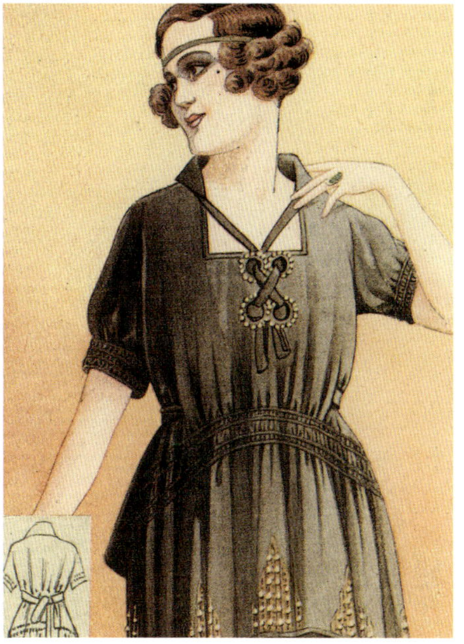

Above
Four blouses by Liberty.
La Femme Chic, c.1923

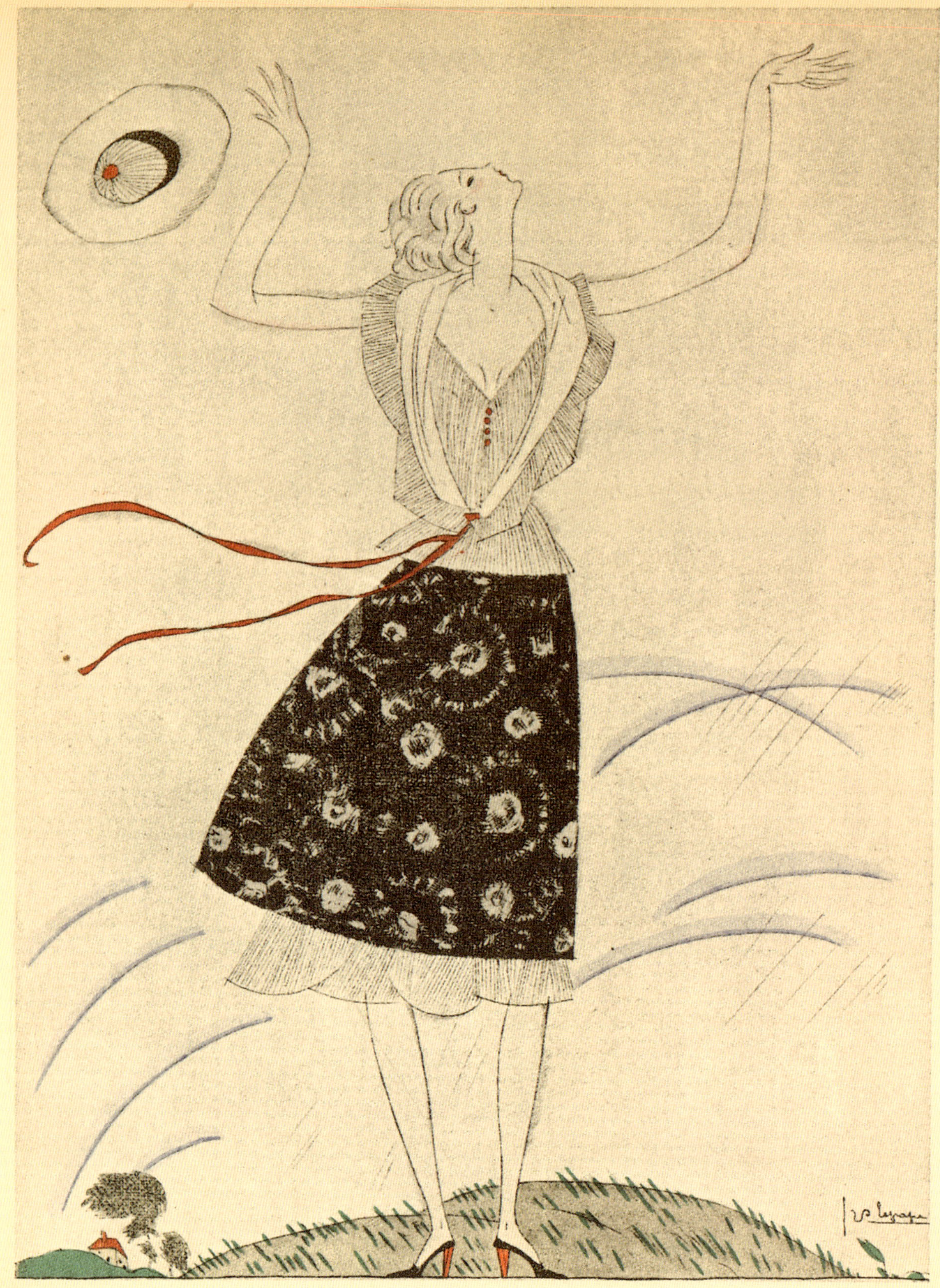

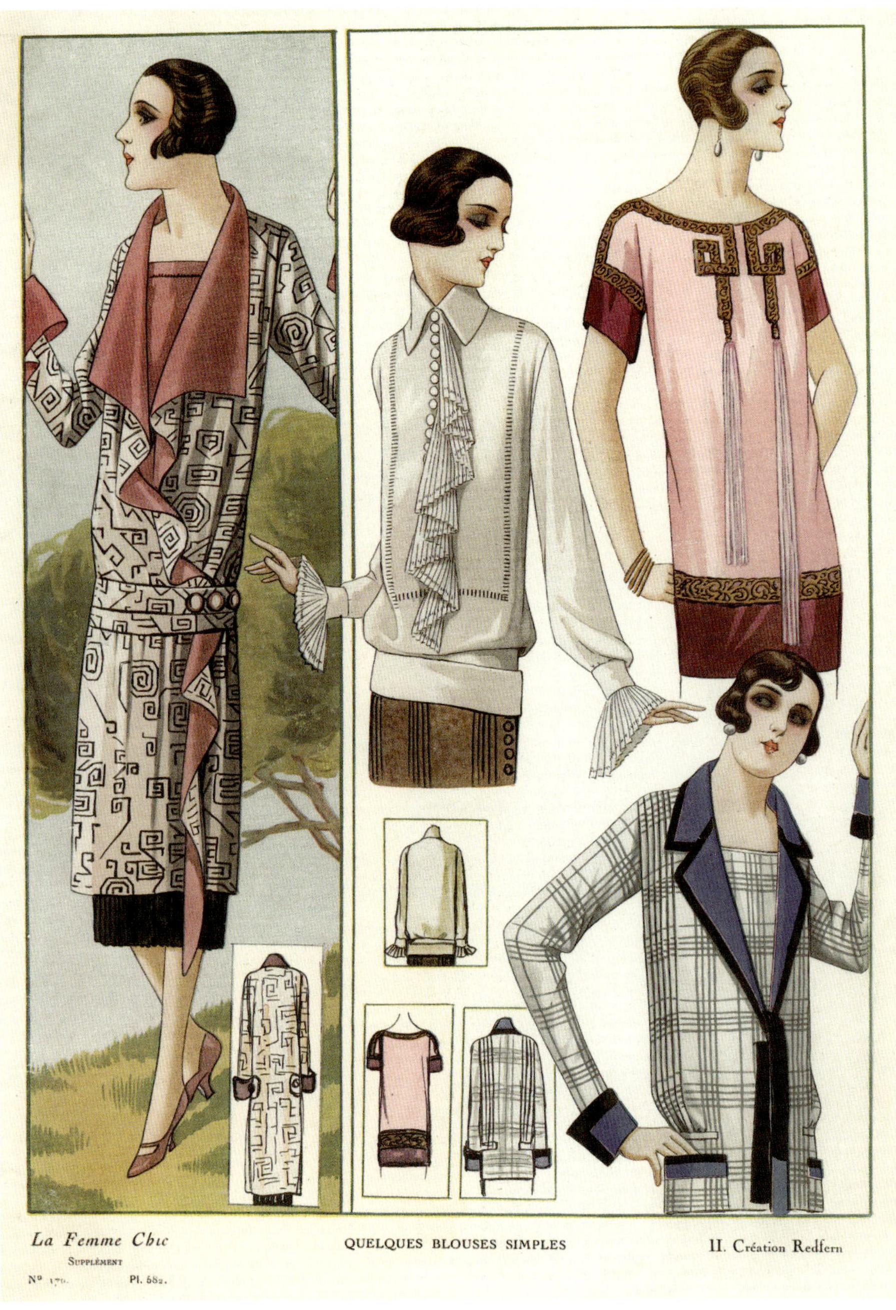

Left and above

"Voici L'orage" (Here comes the storm), afternoon dress by Paul Poiret. Illustration by George Lepape. *Gazette du Bon Ton*, 1920

Designs for a coat and simple blouses, including a checked design by Redfern. *La Femme Chic*, c.1925

Below and right

A young woman in a summer ensemble of a pink pleated skirt and a red belted blouse. *La Mode*, 1921

Designs for summer dresses. *The Delineator*, 1922

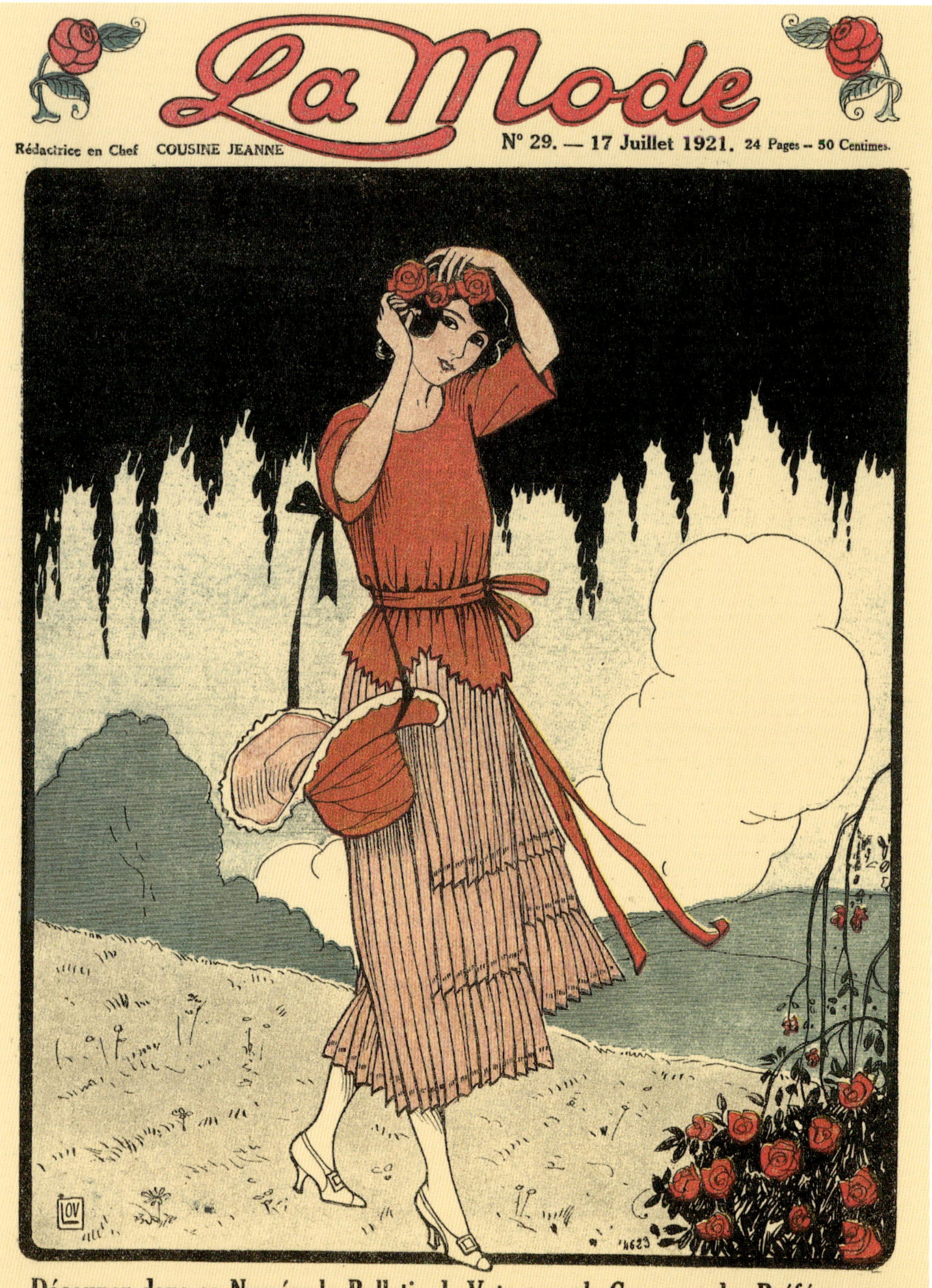

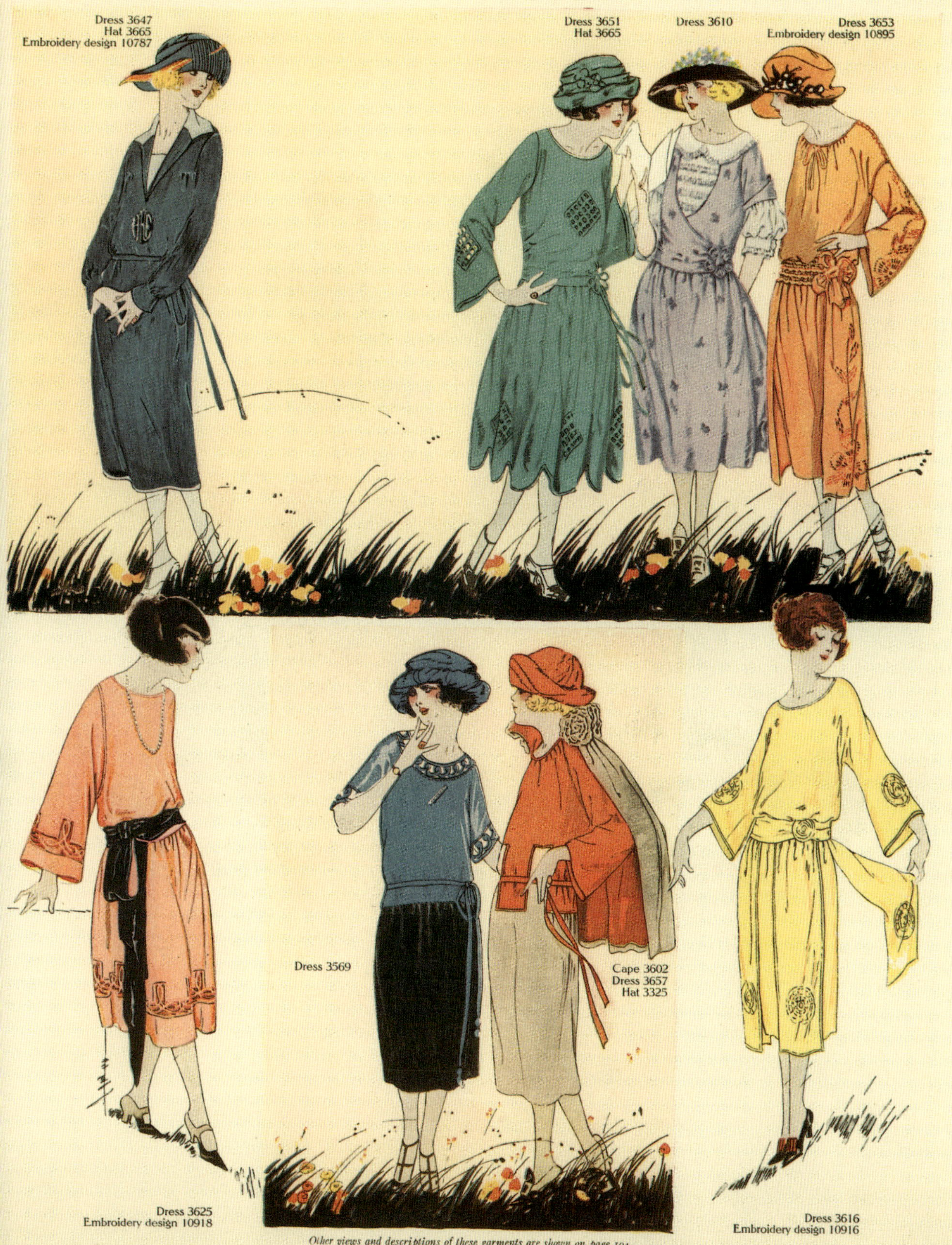

Other views and descriptions of these garments are shown on page 104

Below

Four blouse designs with embroidered detailing by Maison Caro. *La Femme Chic*, c.1923

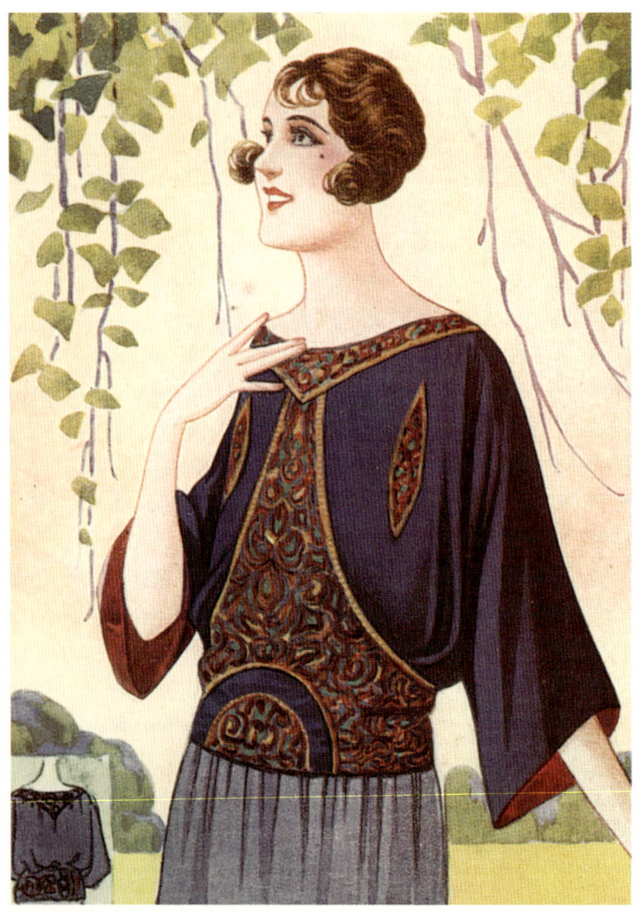

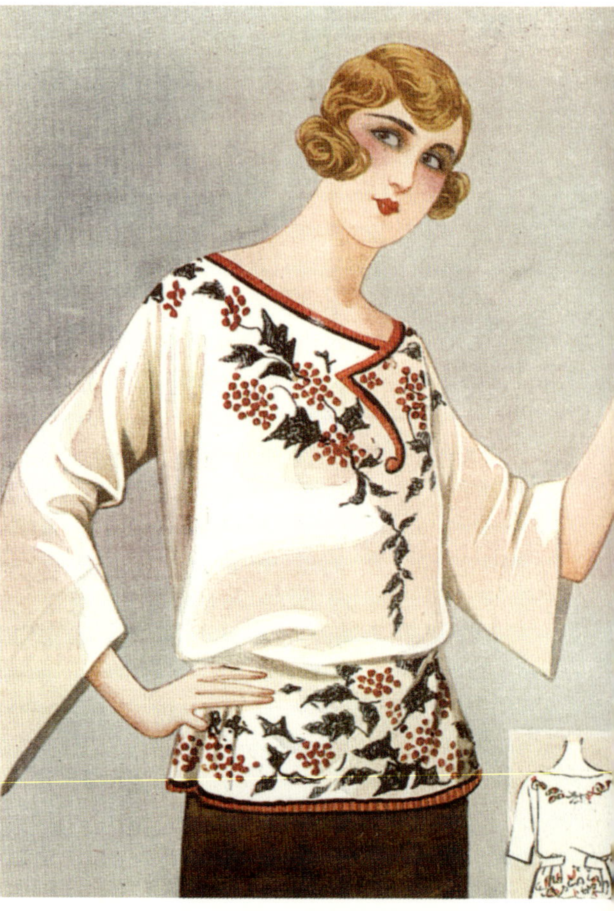

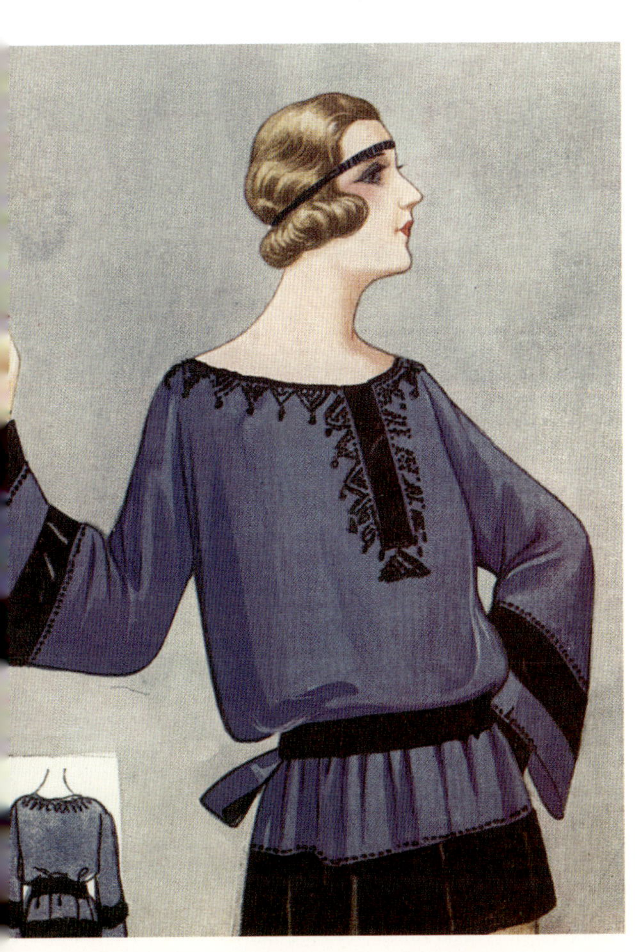

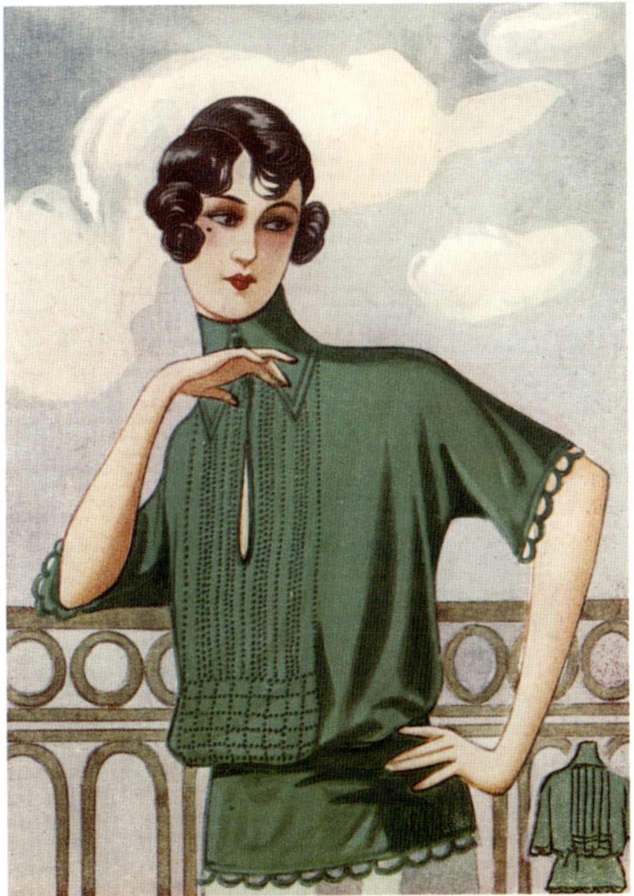

Right
"Les Voila!" (There they are!), two summer dresses by Doeuillet. Illustration by André Edouard Marty, 1920

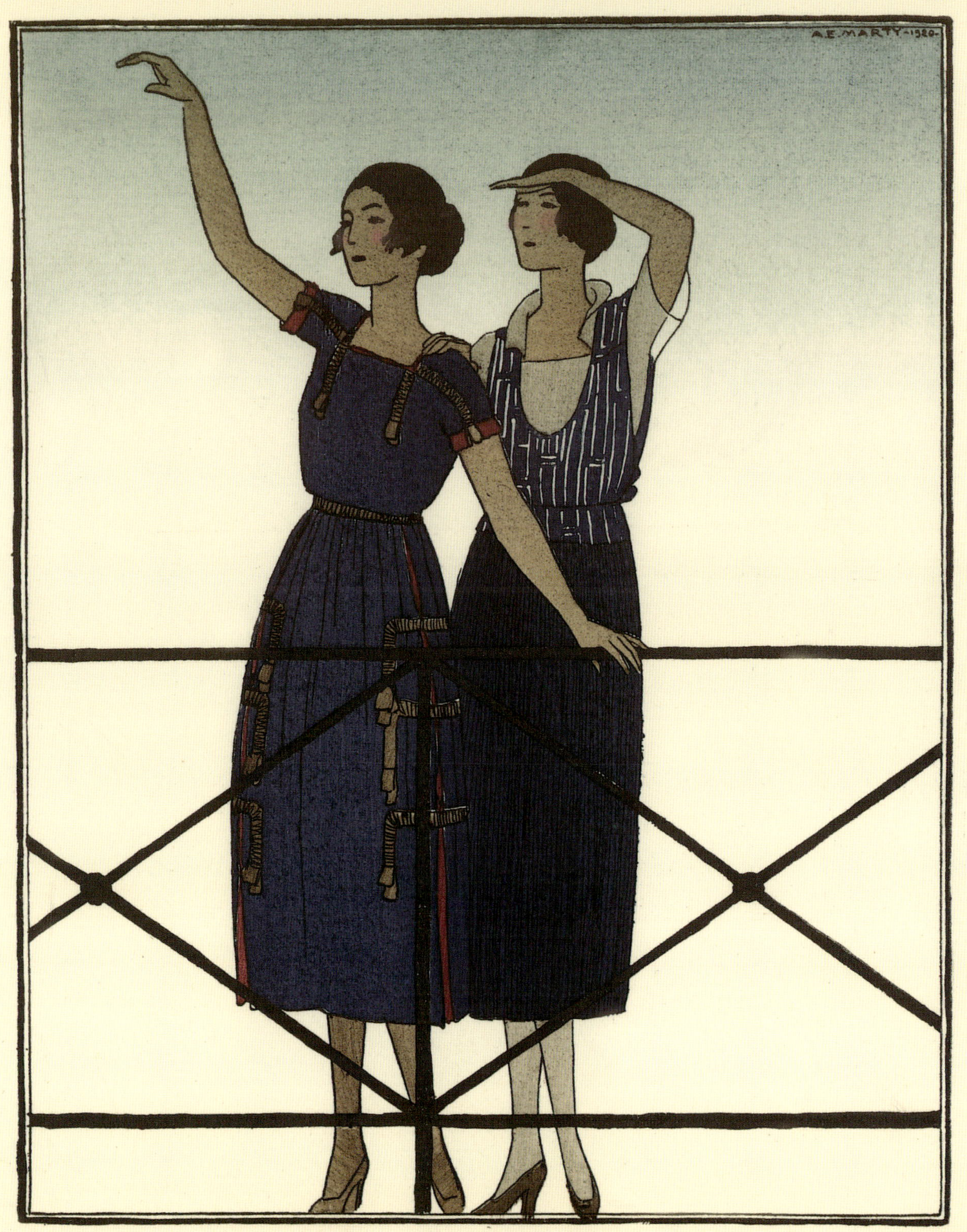

LES VOILA !

Robes d'Été, de Dœuillet

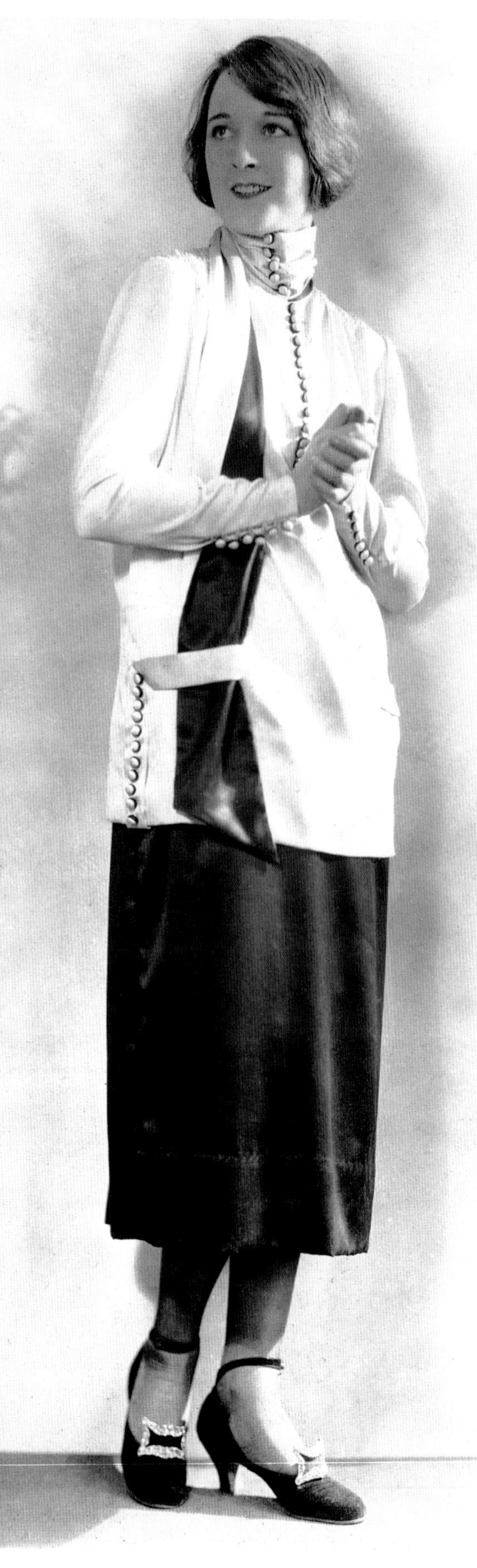
APEDA
N.Y.

Left and below

White and black satin frock worn by Hollywood actress Eleanor Boardman, c.1922

Selection of casaquins and blouses. *Le Petit Echo de la Mode*, 1922

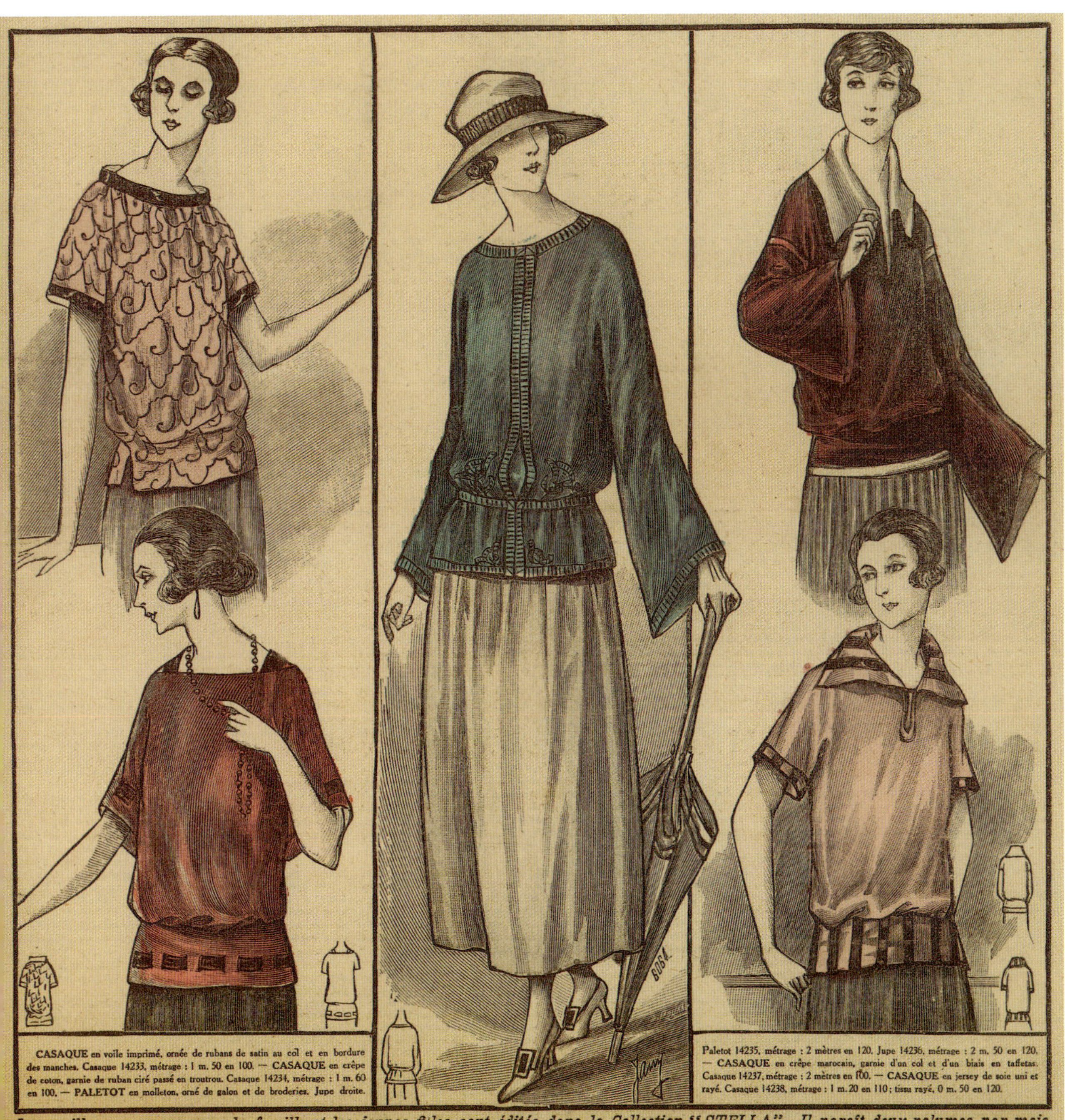

CASAQUE en voile imprimé, ornée de rubans de satin au col et en bordure des manches. Casaque 14233, métrage : 1 m. 50 en 100. — **CASAQUE** en crêpe de coton, garnie de ruban ciré passé en troutrou. Casaque 14234, métrage : 1 m. 60 en 100. — **PALETOT** en molleton, orné de galon et de broderies. Jupe droite.

Paletot 14235, métrage : 2 mètres en 120. Jupe 14236, métrage : 2 m. 50 en 120. — **CASAQUE** en crêpe marocain, garnie d'un col et d'un biais en taffetas. Casaque 14237, métrage : 2 mètres en 100. — **CASAQUE** en jersey de soie uni et rayé. Casaque 14238, métrage : 1 m. 20 en 110 ; tissu rayé, 0 m. 50 en 120.

Les meilleurs romans pour la famille et les jeunes filles sont édités dans la Collection "STELLA". Il paraît deux volumes par mois.

"GERDA" 20 boul^d MONTM

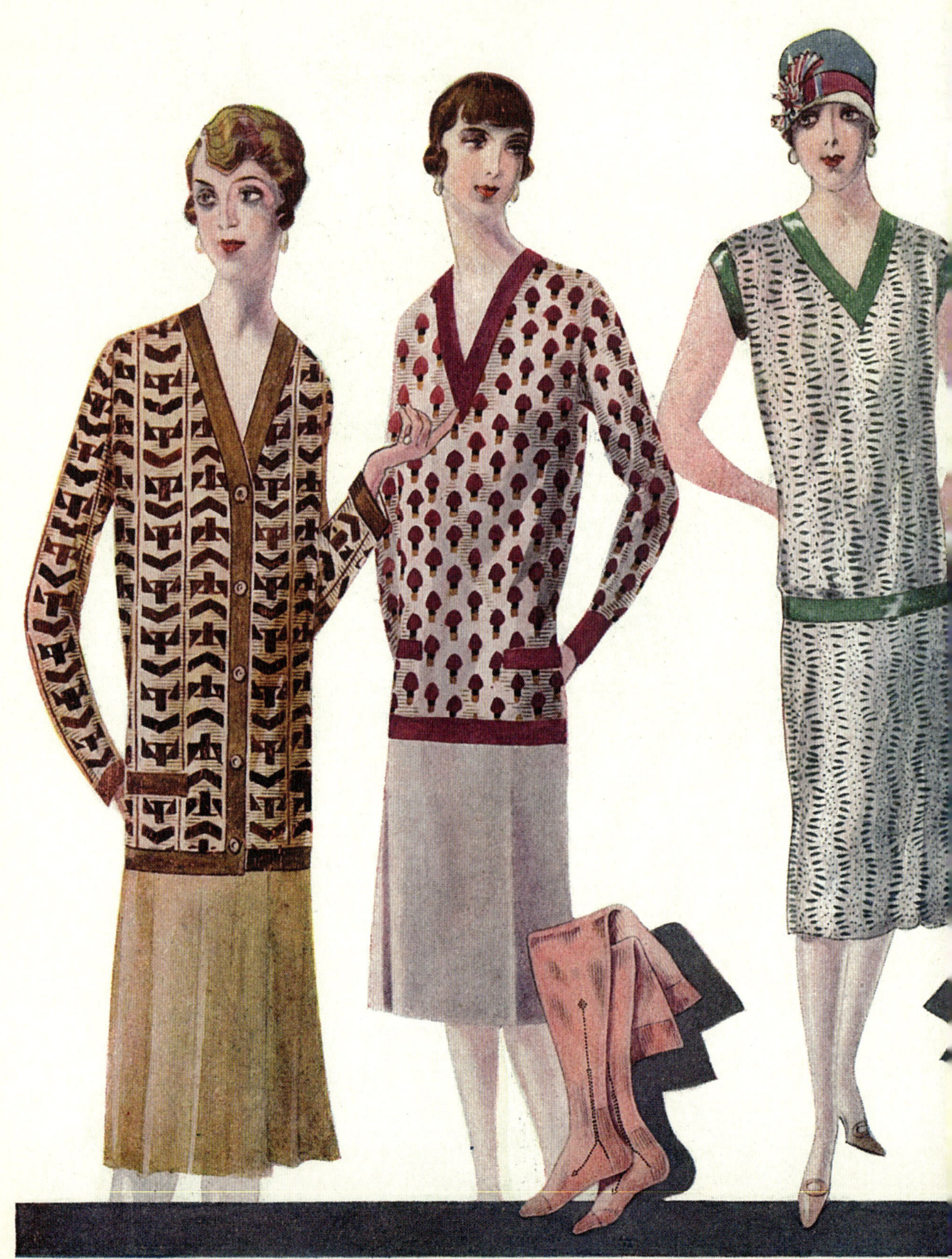

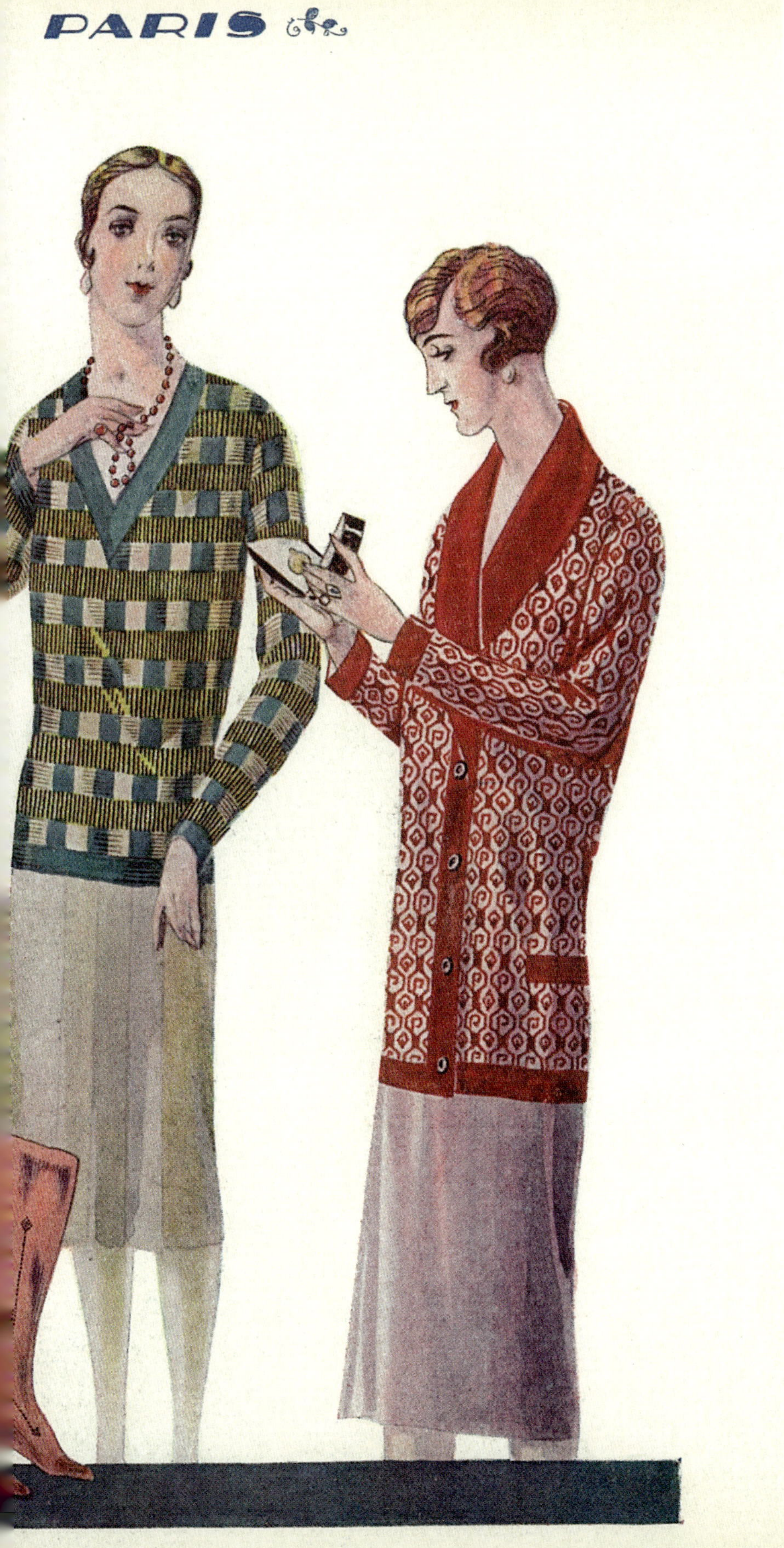

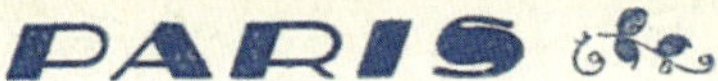
PARIS

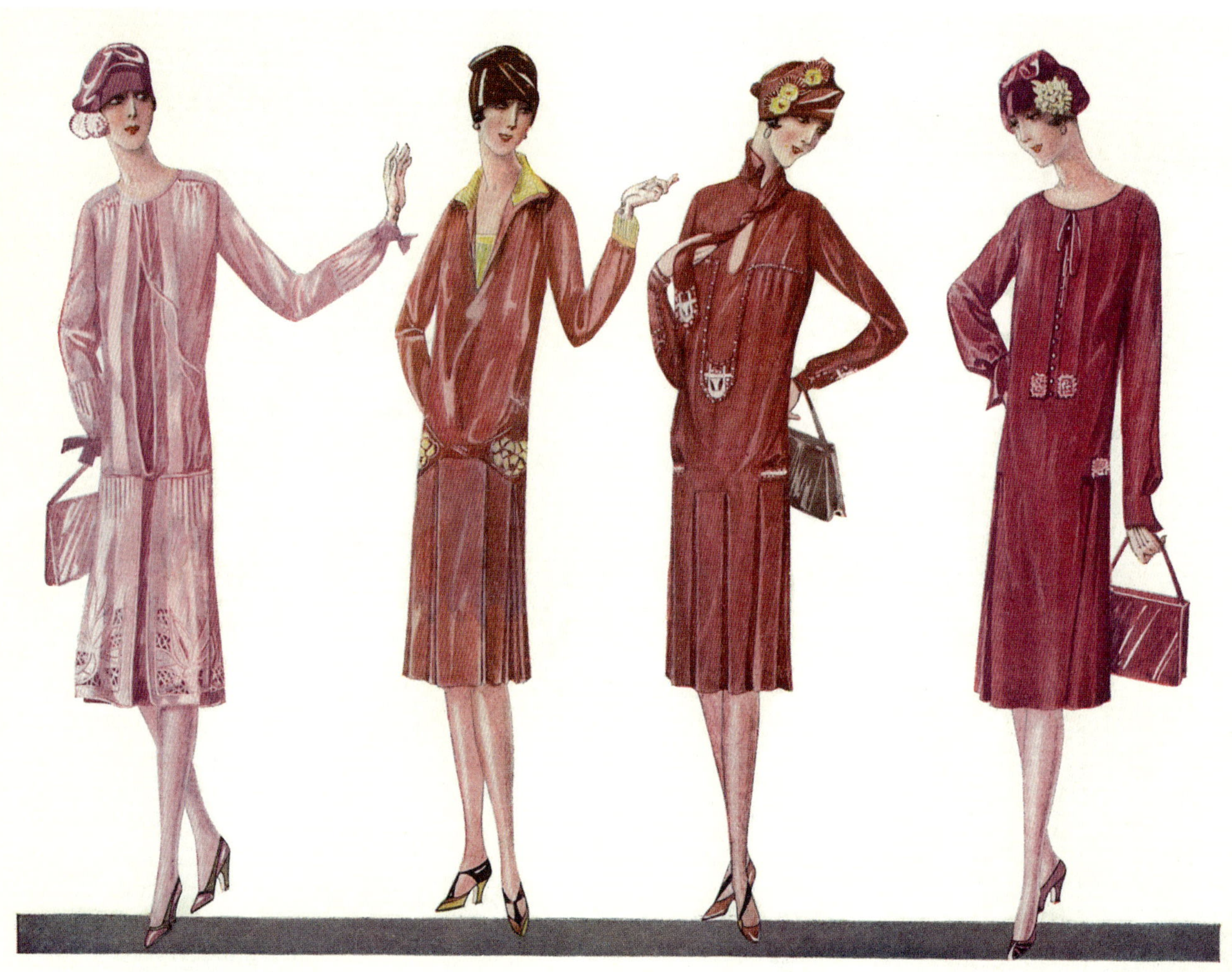

Previous page
Five knitwear designs by Maison Gerda.
Maison Gerda catalogue, c.1925

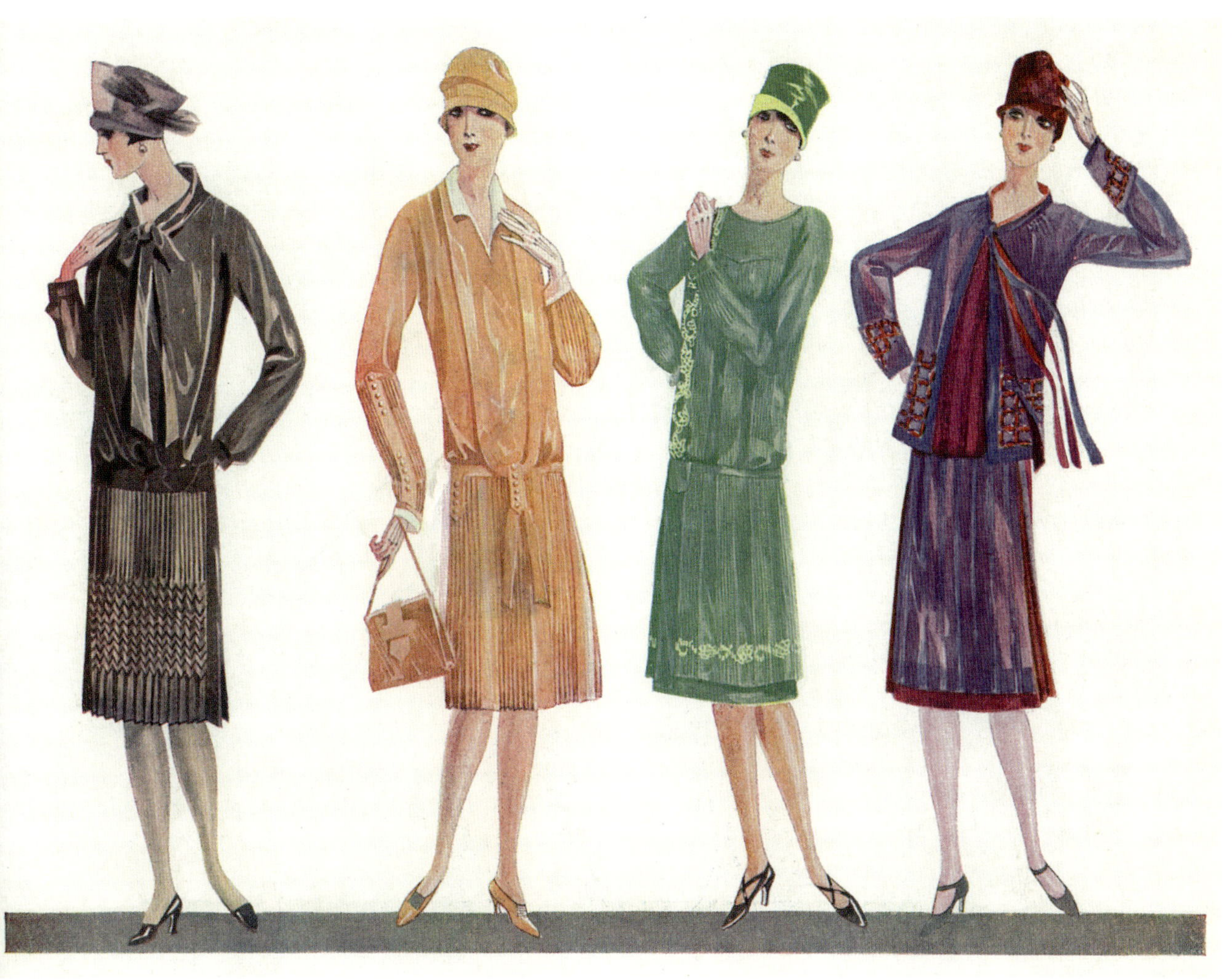

Above left and right
Four day dresses by Maison Gerda.
Maison Gerda catalogue, c.1925

Four day dresses by Maison Gerda.
Maison Gerda catalogue, c.1925

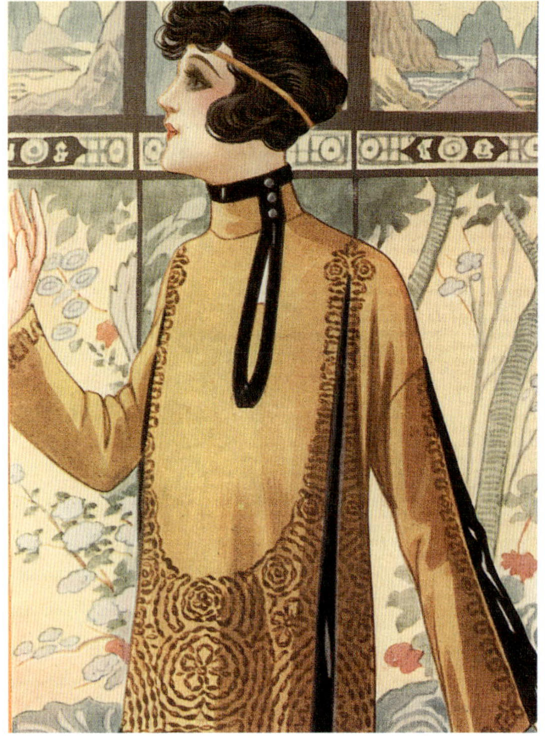

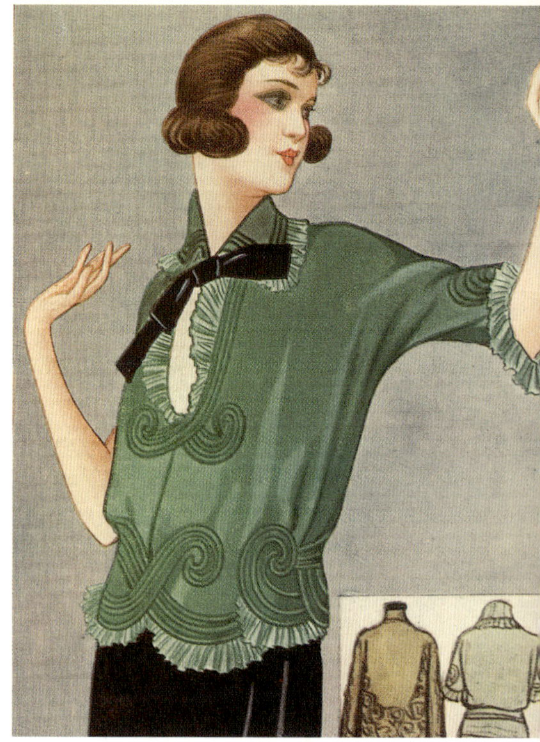

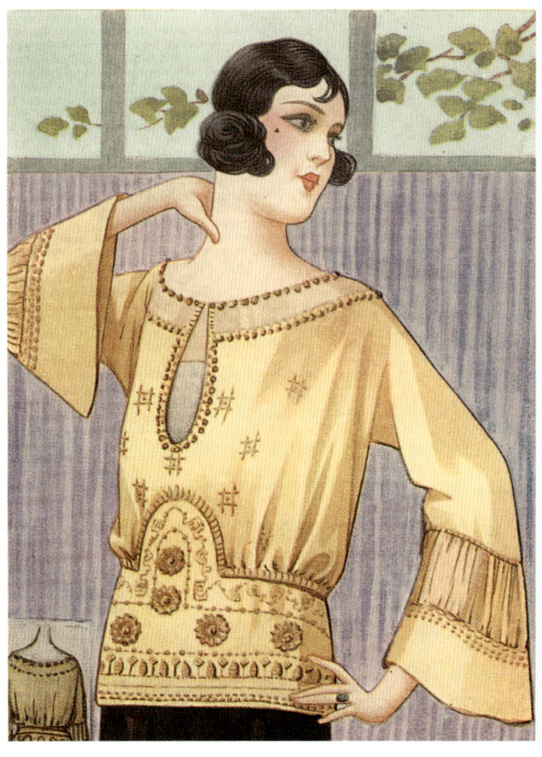

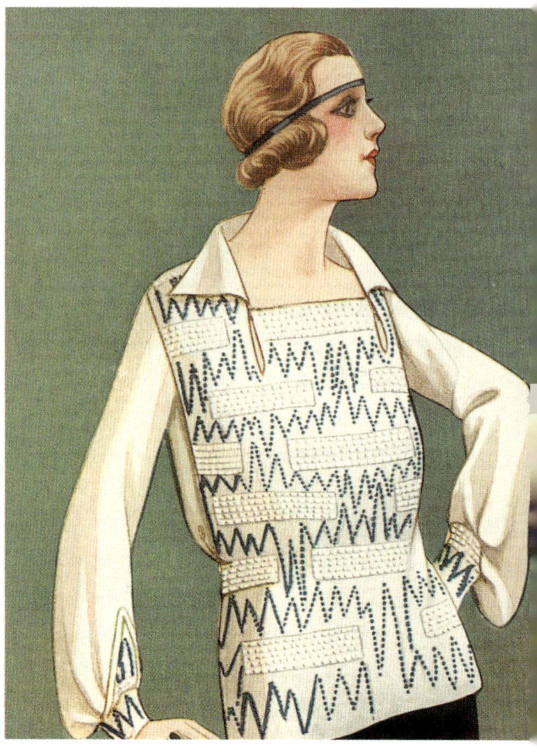

Above
Four blouses by André Schwab, all with extensive embroidered detailing. *La Femme Chic*, c.1923

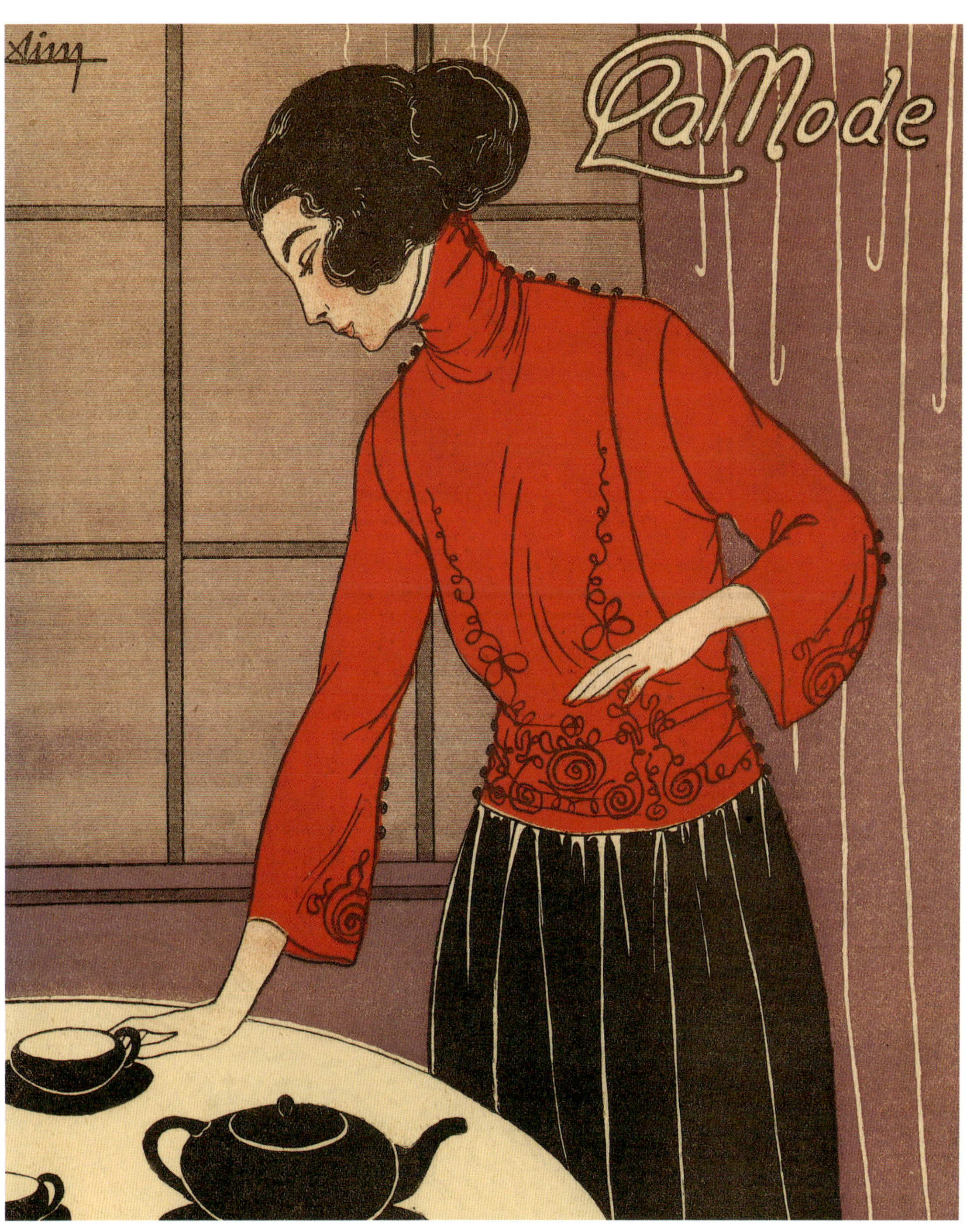

Above
A woman in a black skirt and a red Russian blouse with a high neck and ornamental buttons. *La Mode*, 1920

Below
A two-piece black satin costume by French designer Marthe Dion with a jumper of white Georgette and satin giving the effect of a waistcoat, c.1923

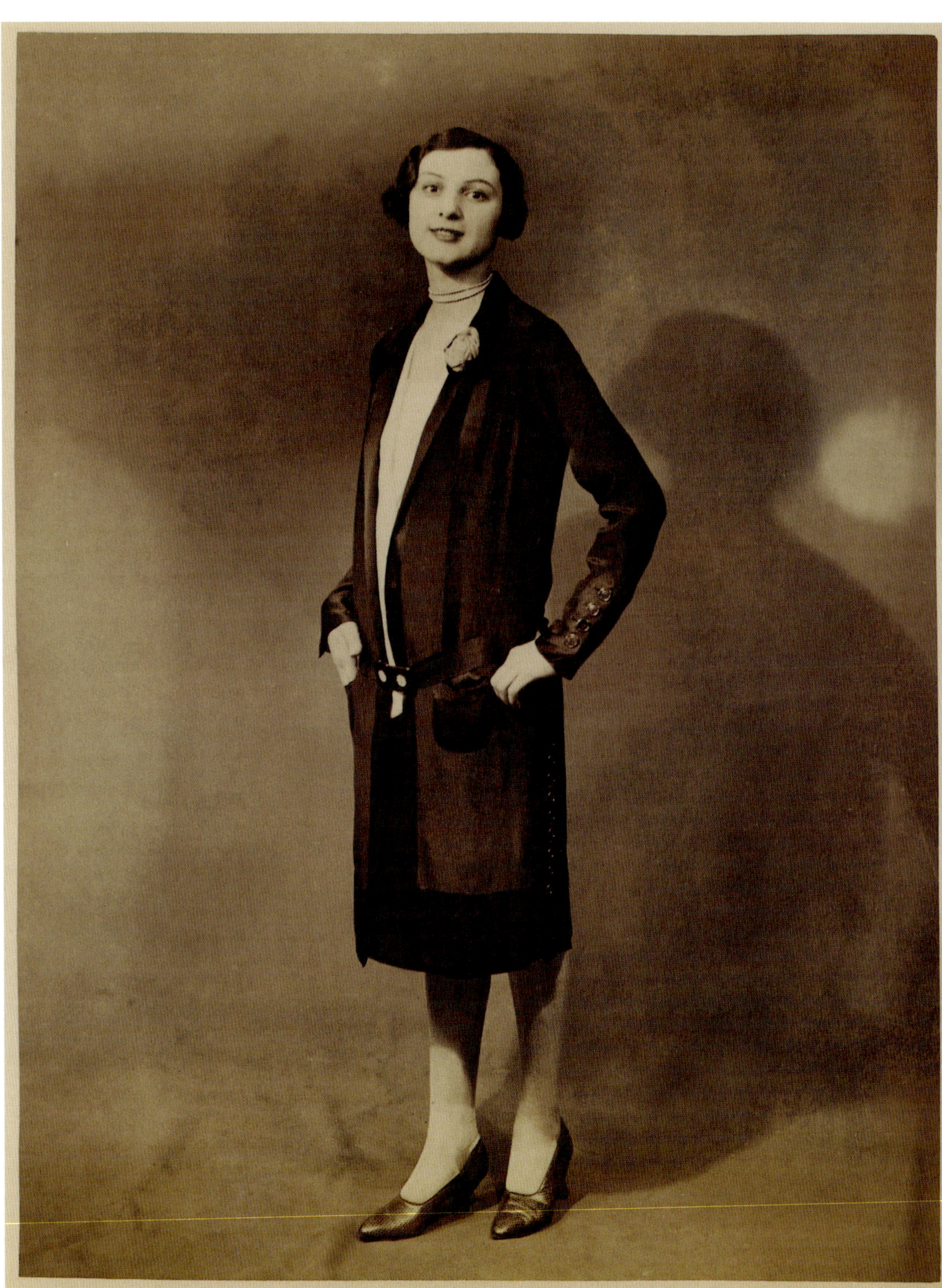

Below
A knitted jumper and pleated skirt ensemble, c.1926

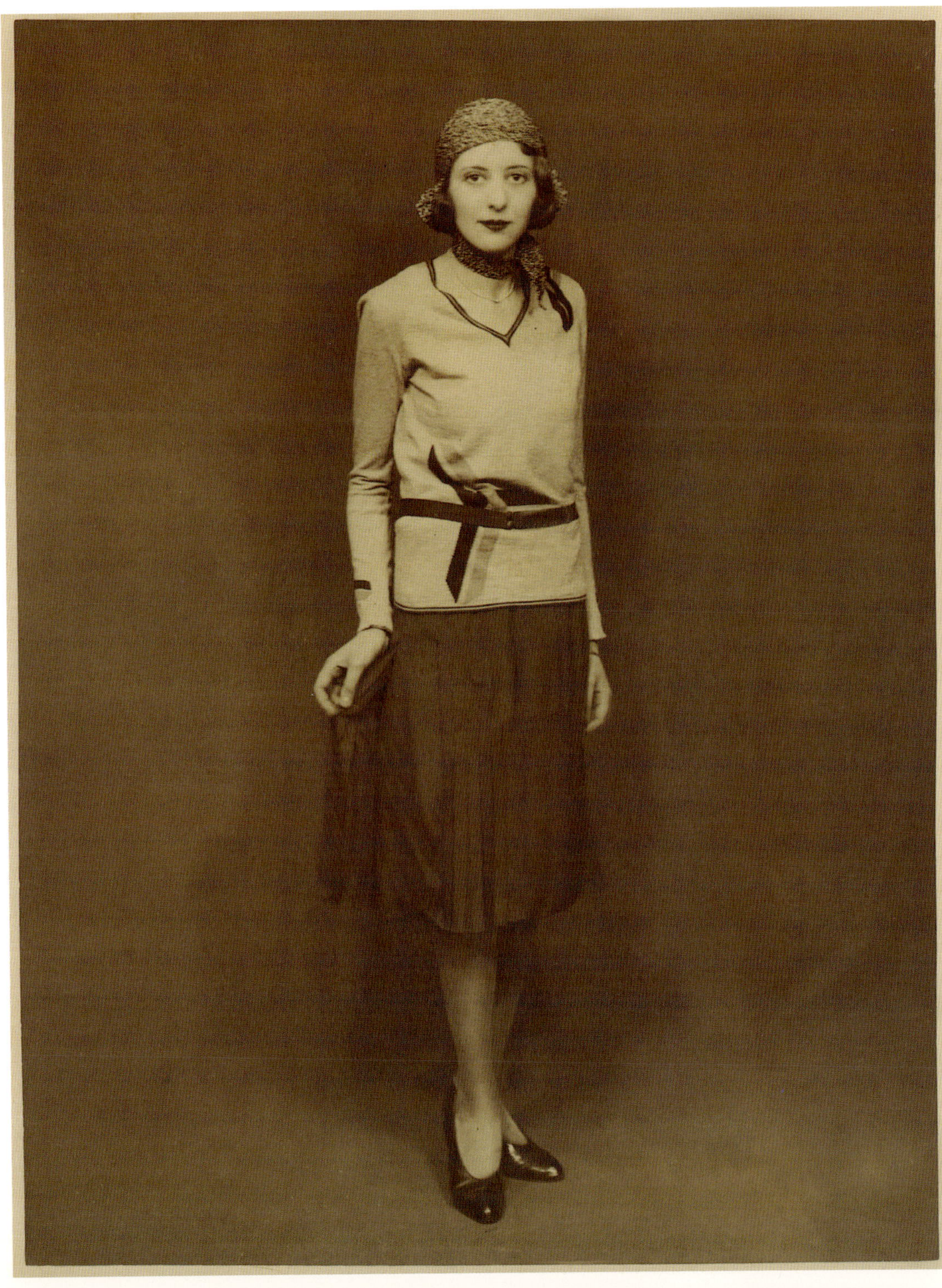

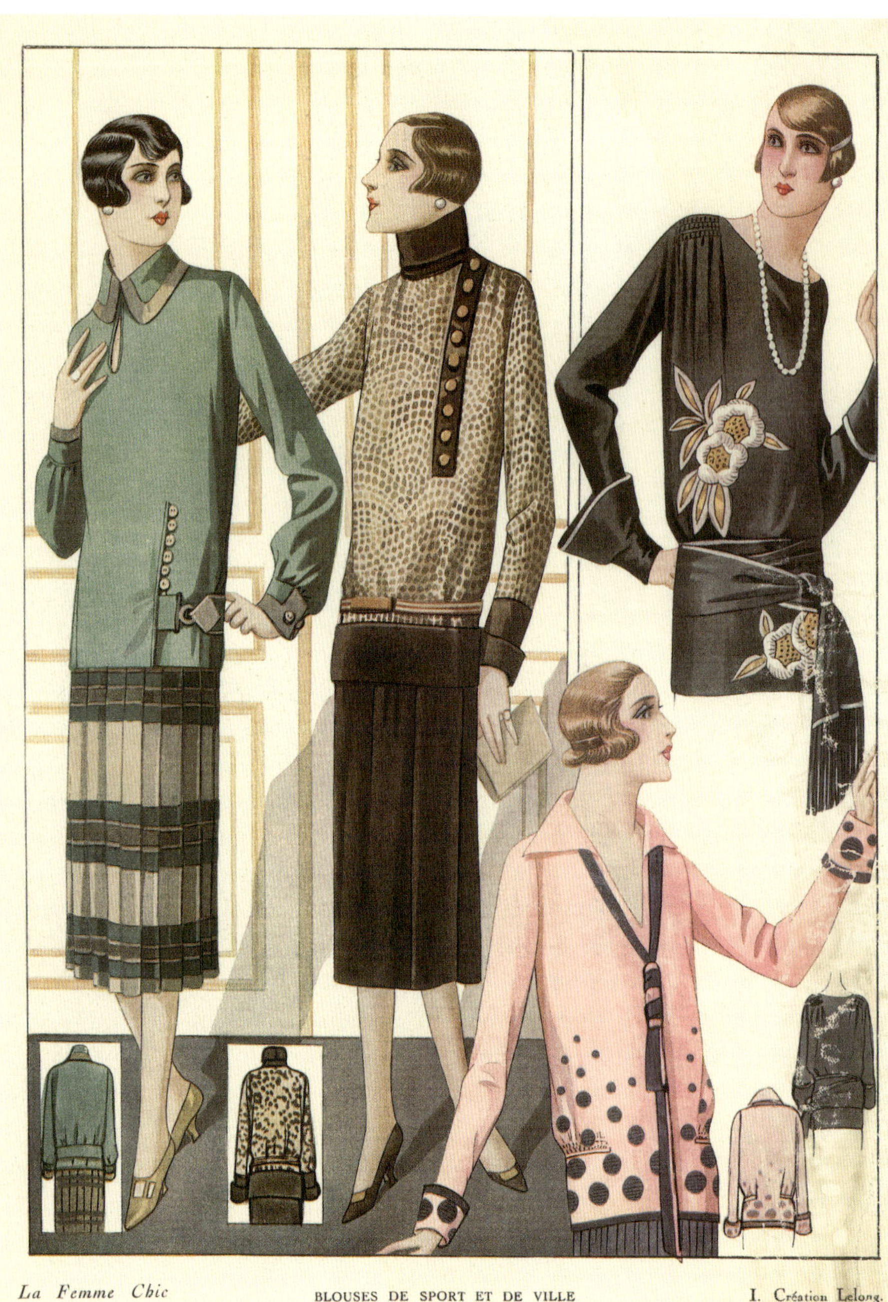

Above
Designs for sports and city blouses including two pink and black embroidered designs by Lucien Lelong. *La Femme Chic*, c.1925

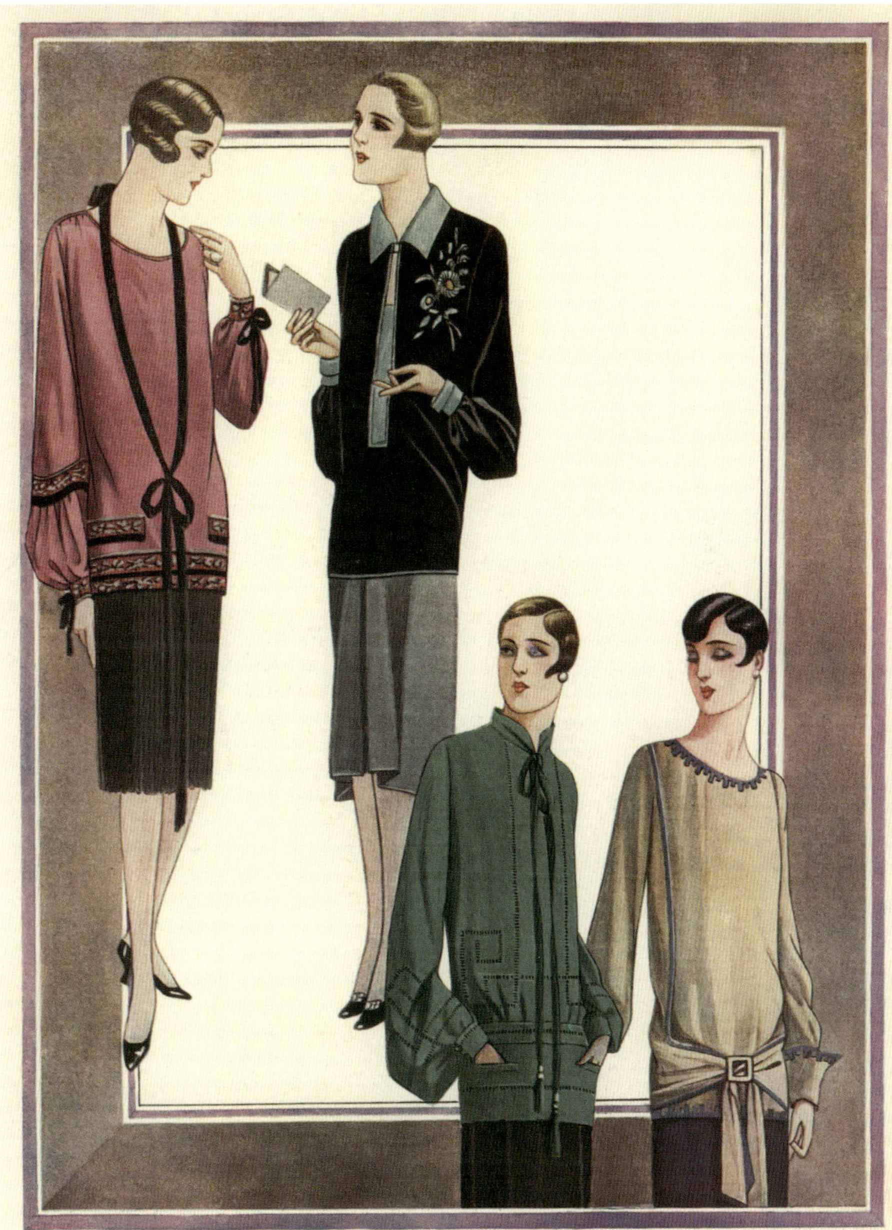

Above
Designs for blouses.
La Femme Chic, c.1926

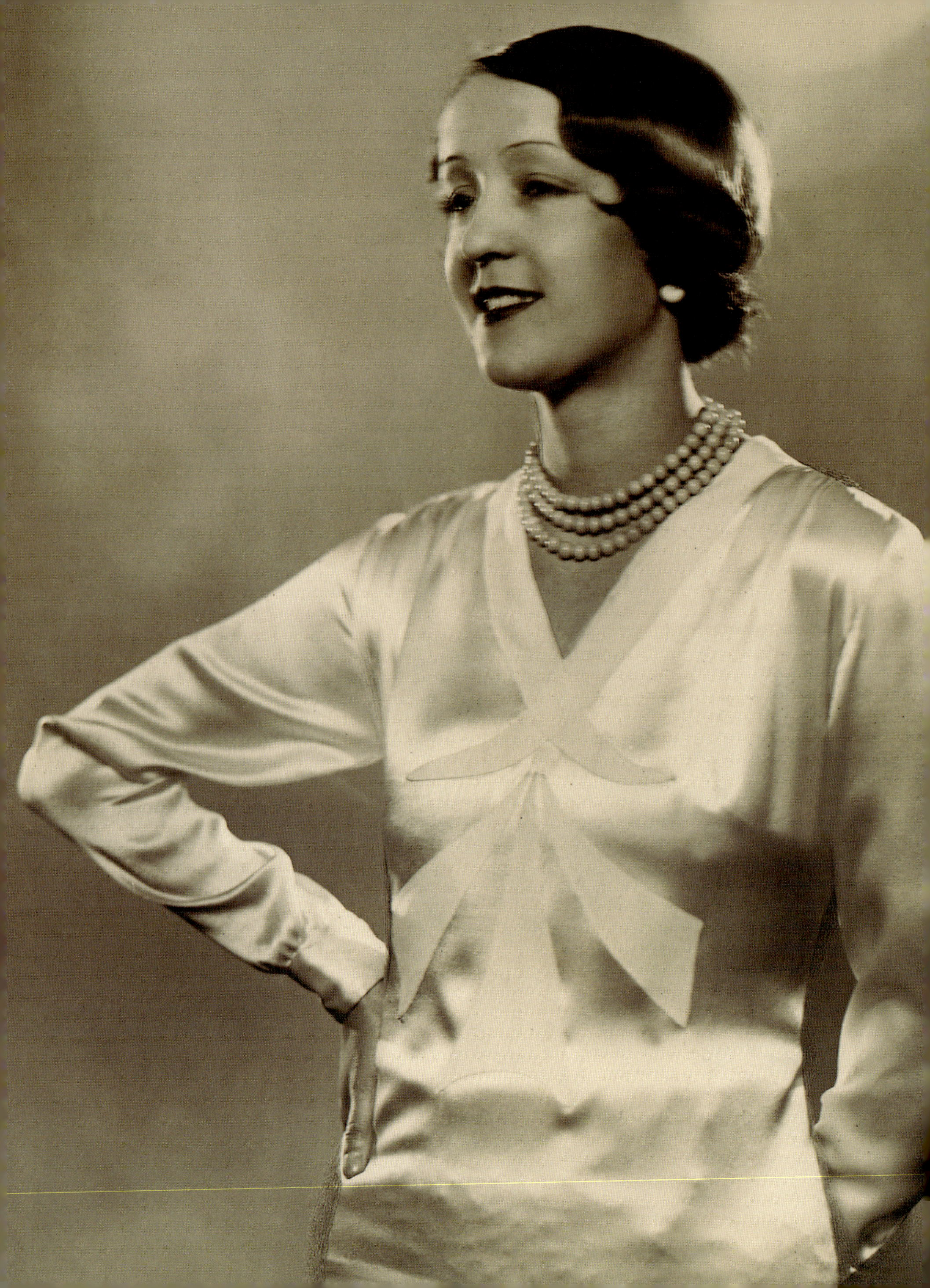

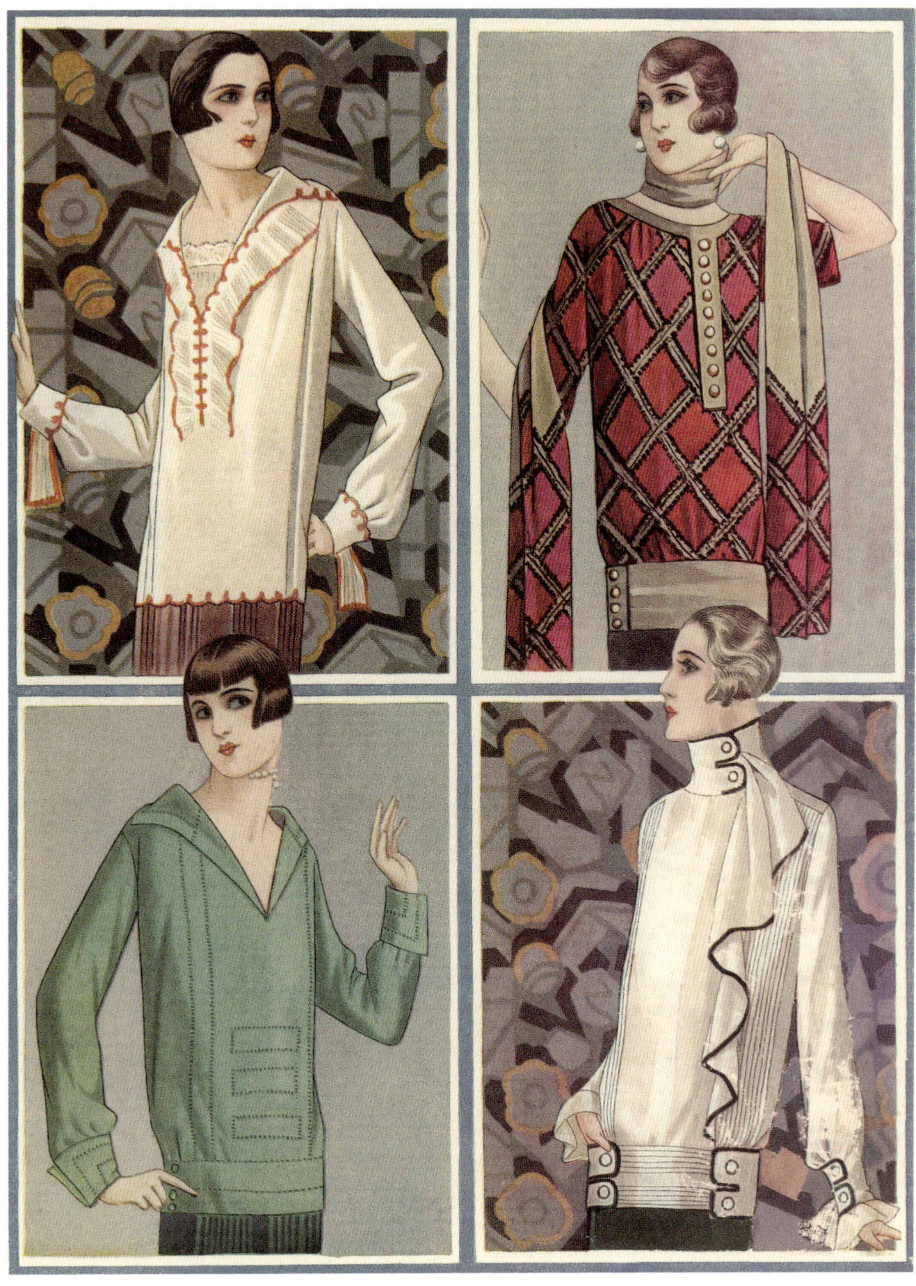

Left and above

Model posing in a white satin jumper blouse with a trompe l'oeil pattern by La Maison David, c.1925

Designs for blouses including designs by Bernard and Lucien Lelong. *La Femme Chic*, c.1925

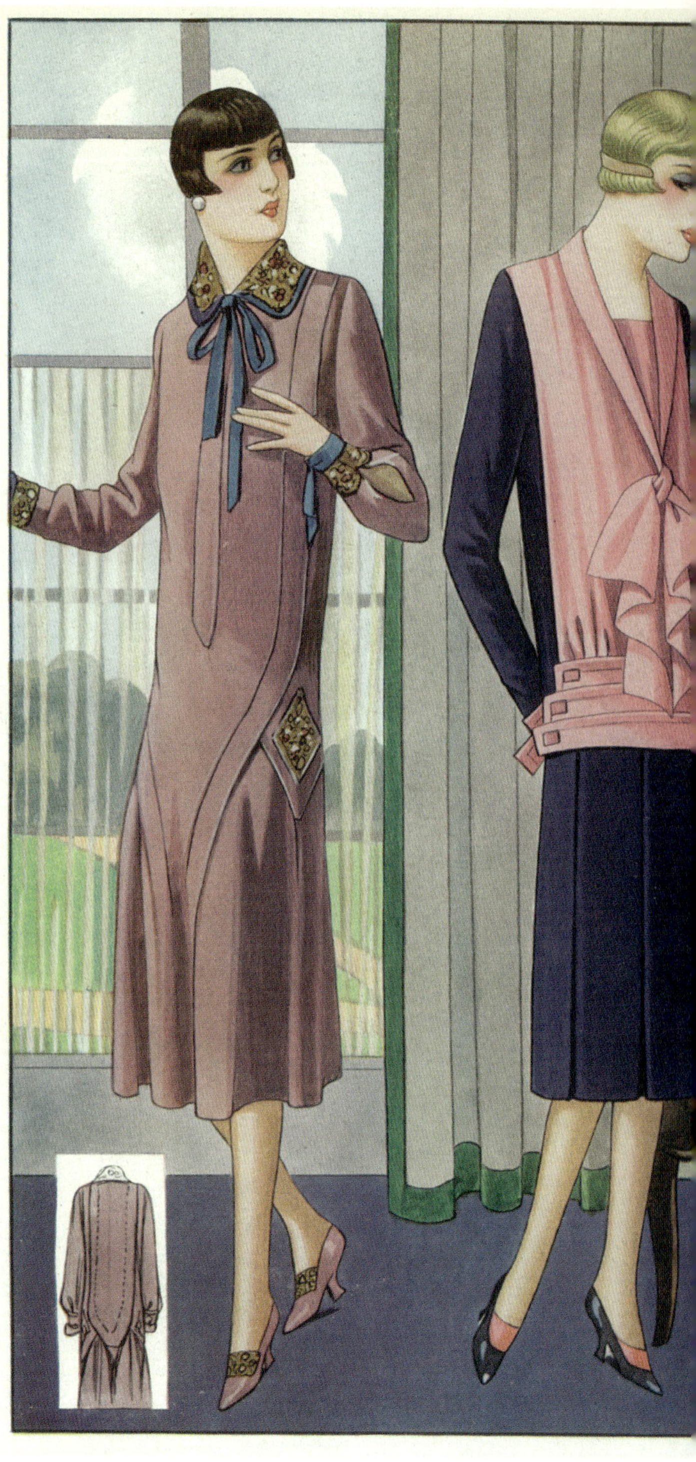

Above
Several dresses for the spring by Magdeleine des Hayes.
La Femme Chic, 1926

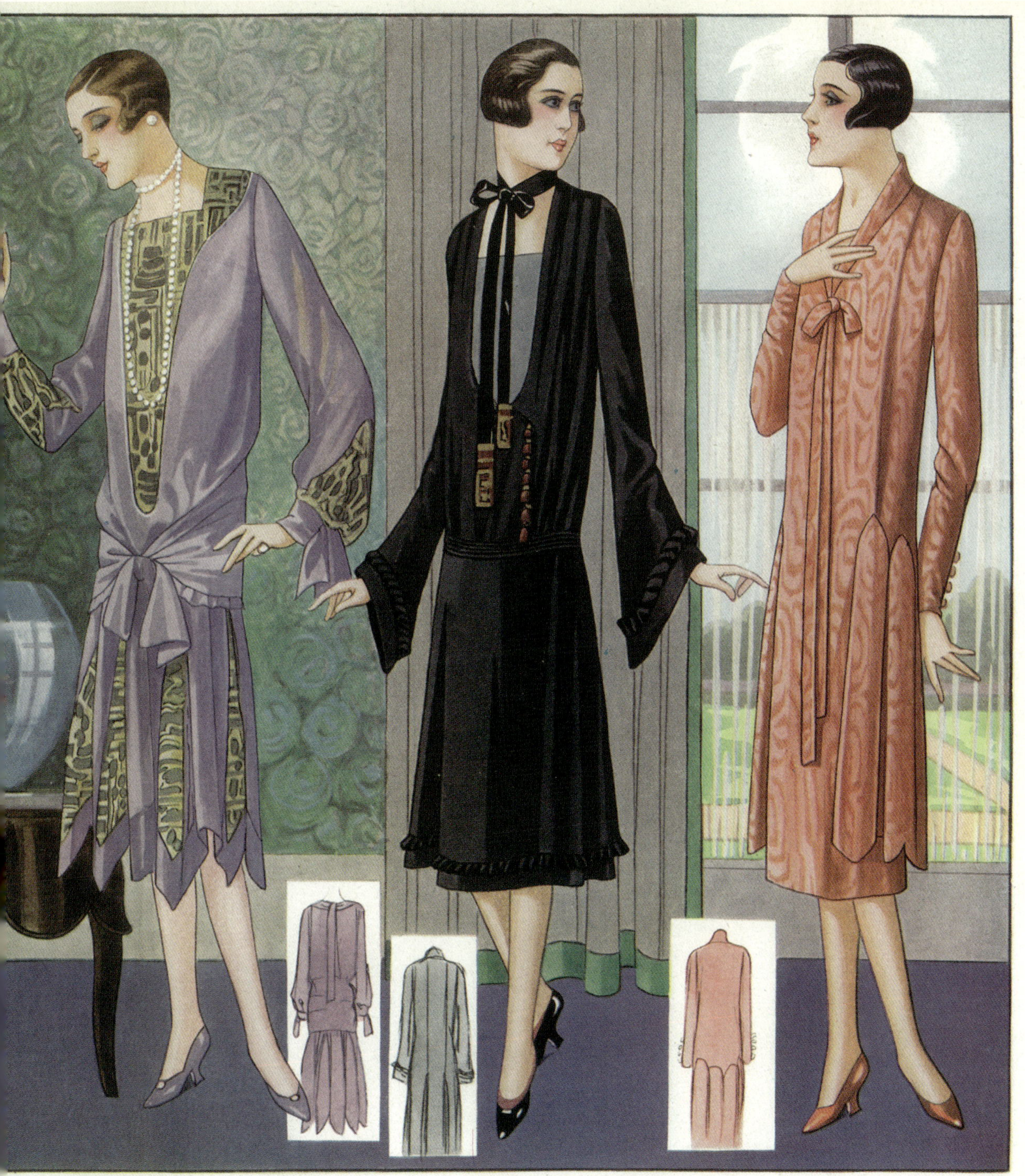

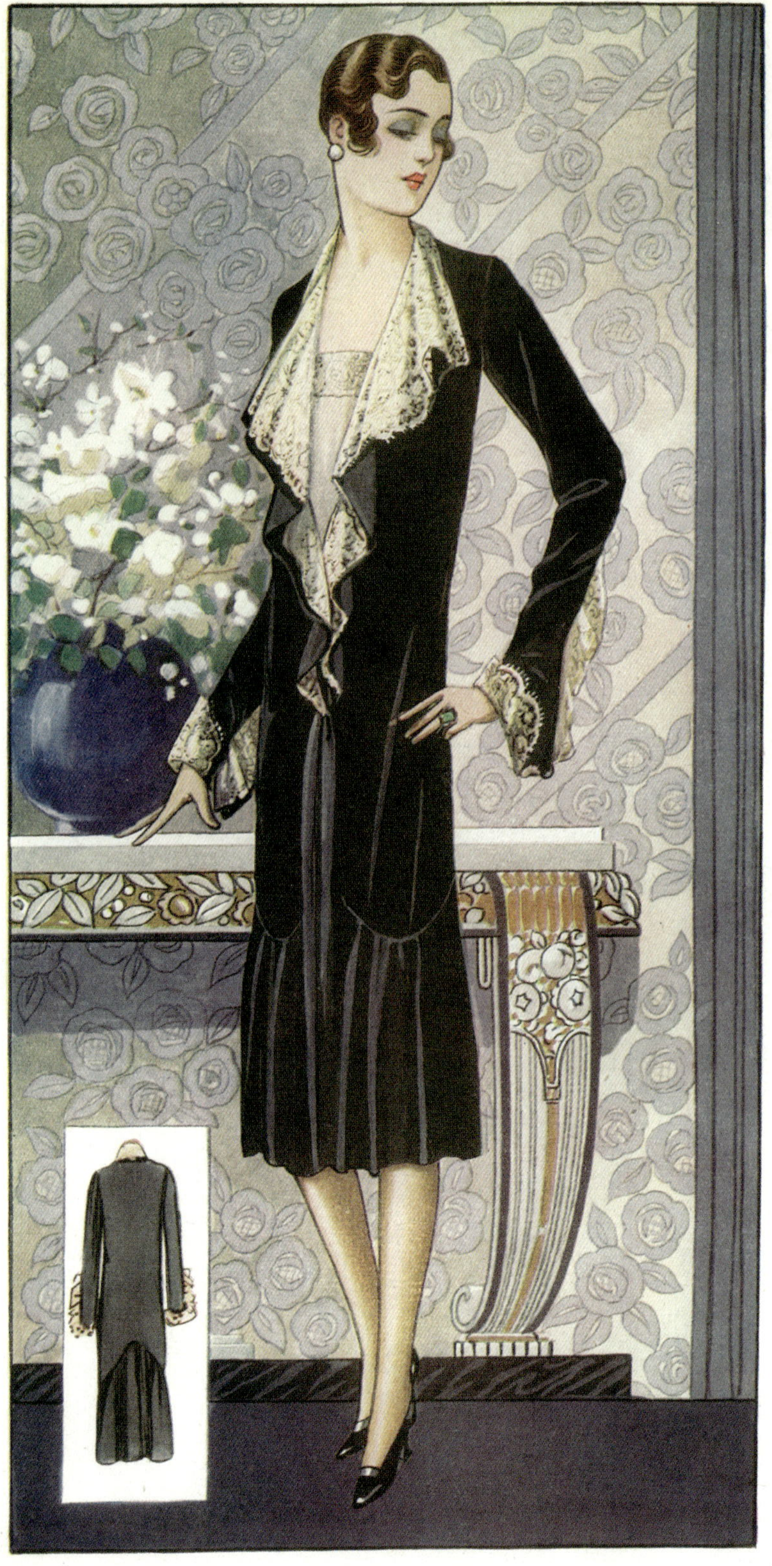

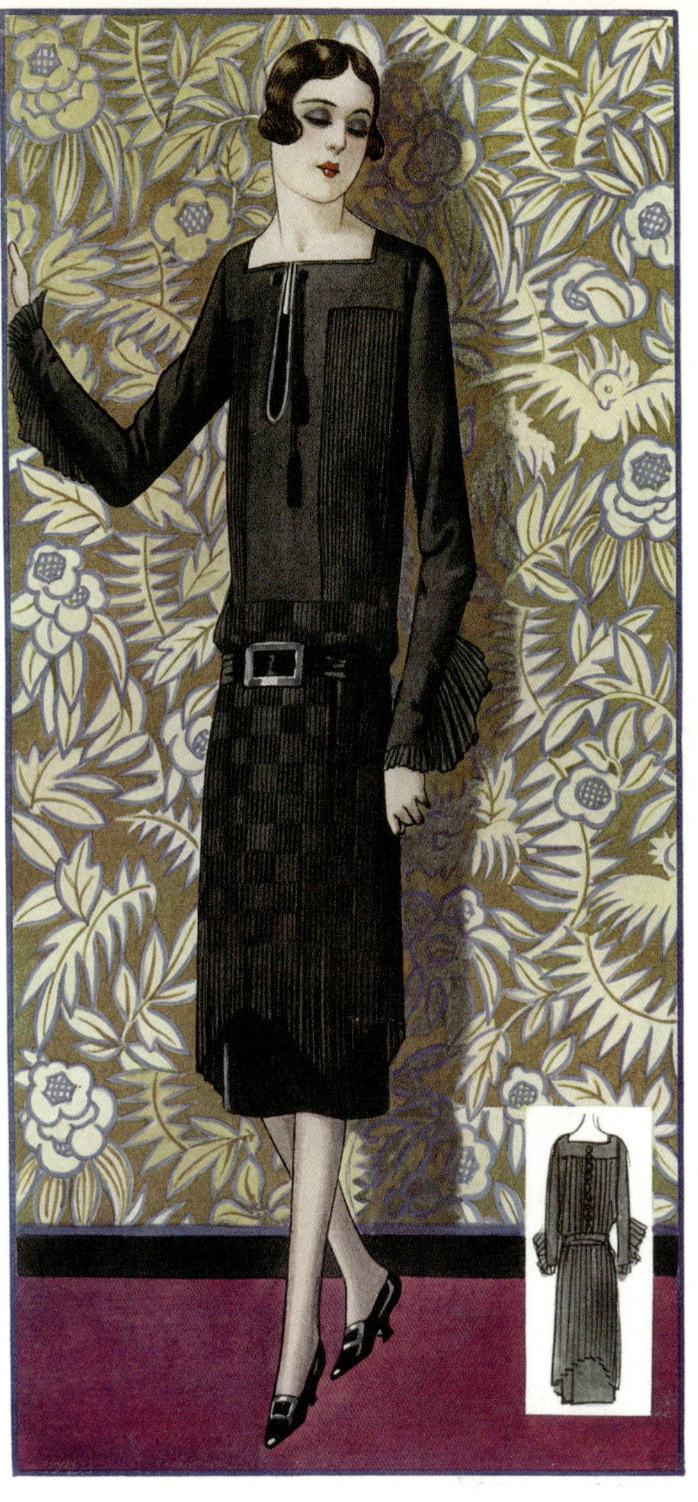

Left and above

"Le Chic du Noir" (stylish black) dress with a flounced lace collar and cuffs by Magdeleine des Hayes, *La Femme Chic*, 1926

Black pleated afternoon dress. *La Femme Chic*, 1926

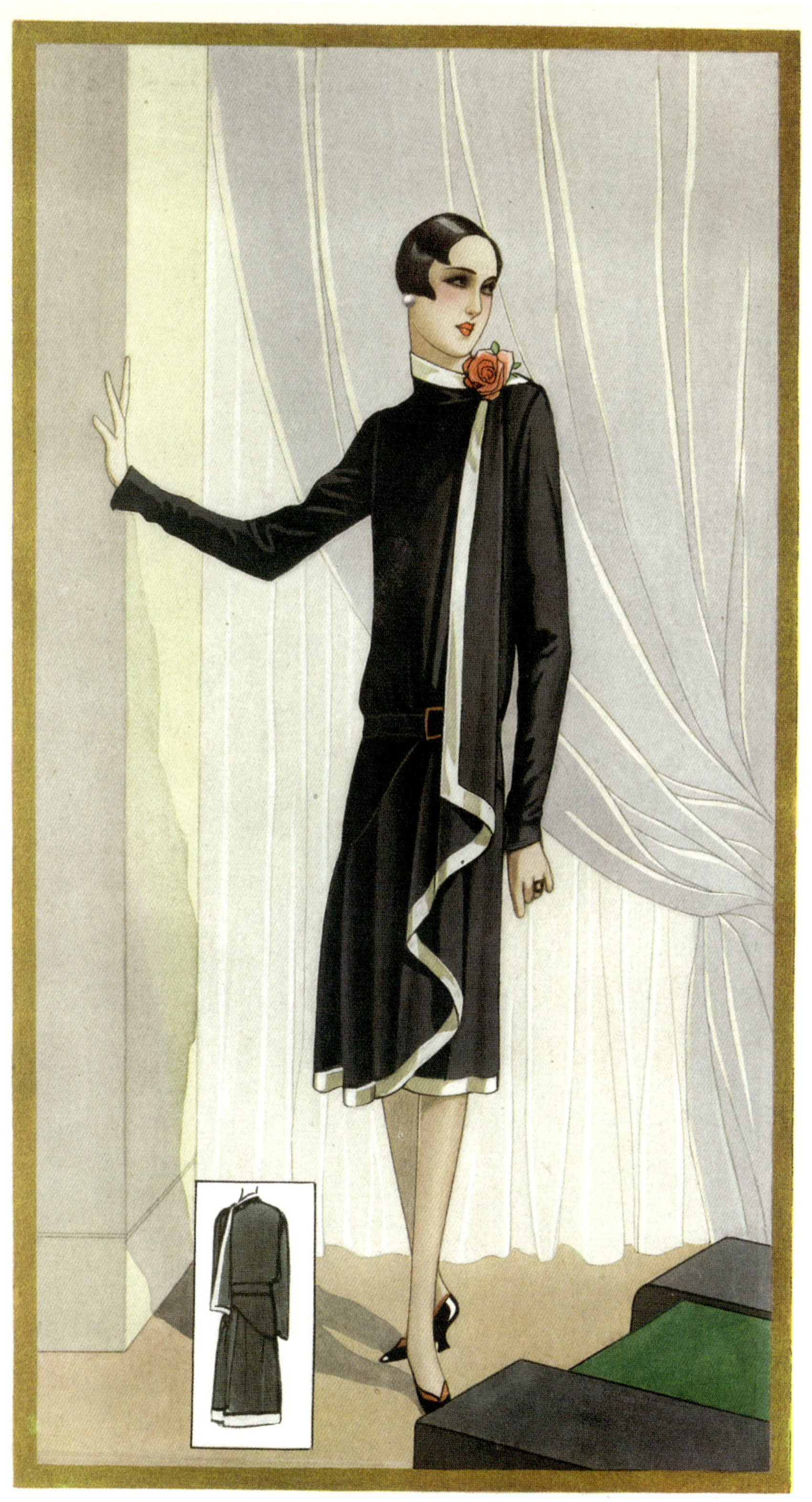

Above

Black dress in crepe de Chine with a full length flounce and a silk rose by Premet. *La Femme Chic*, 1927

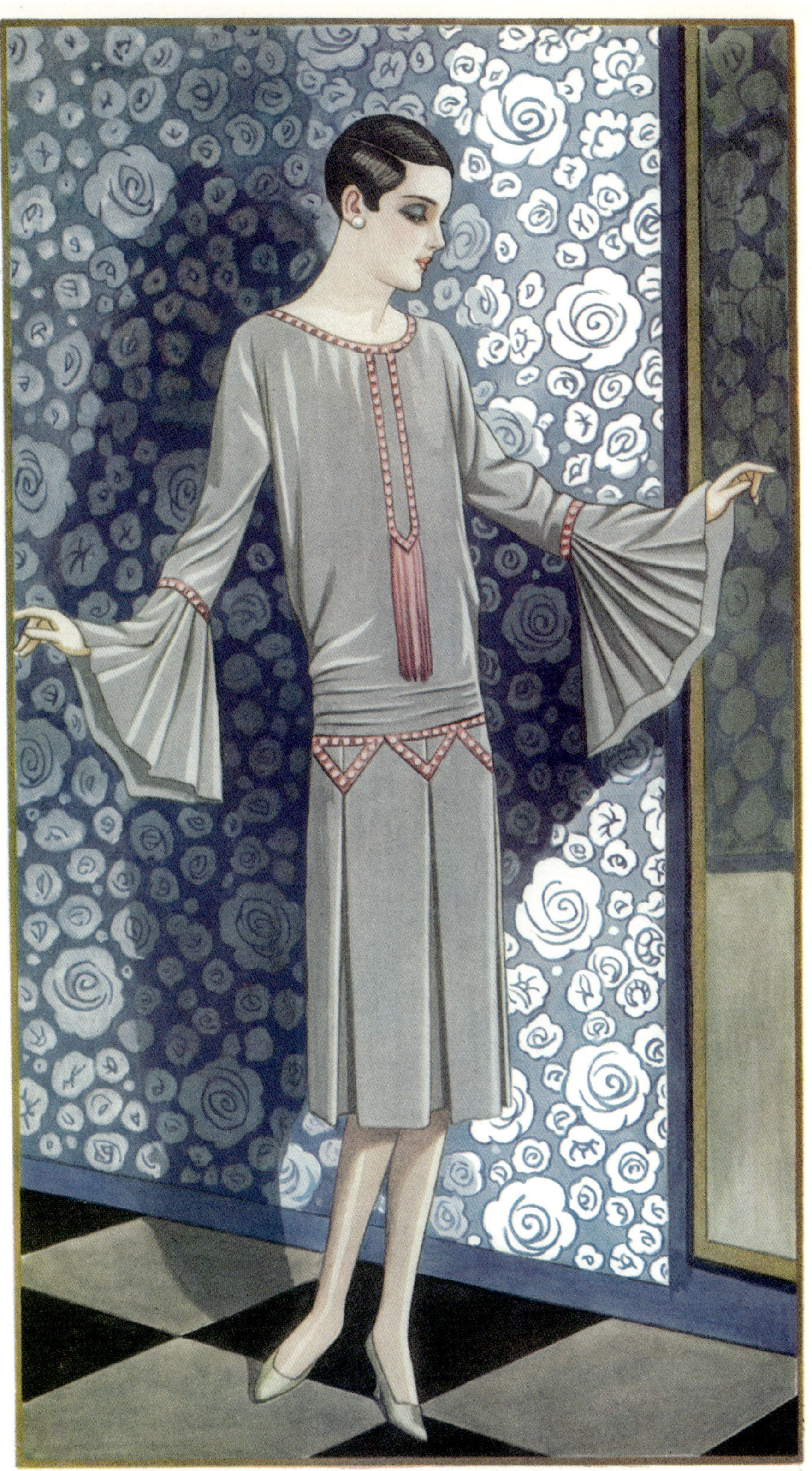

Above
Afternoon dress with flaring pleated sleeves by Alice Bernard.
La Femme Chic, 1926

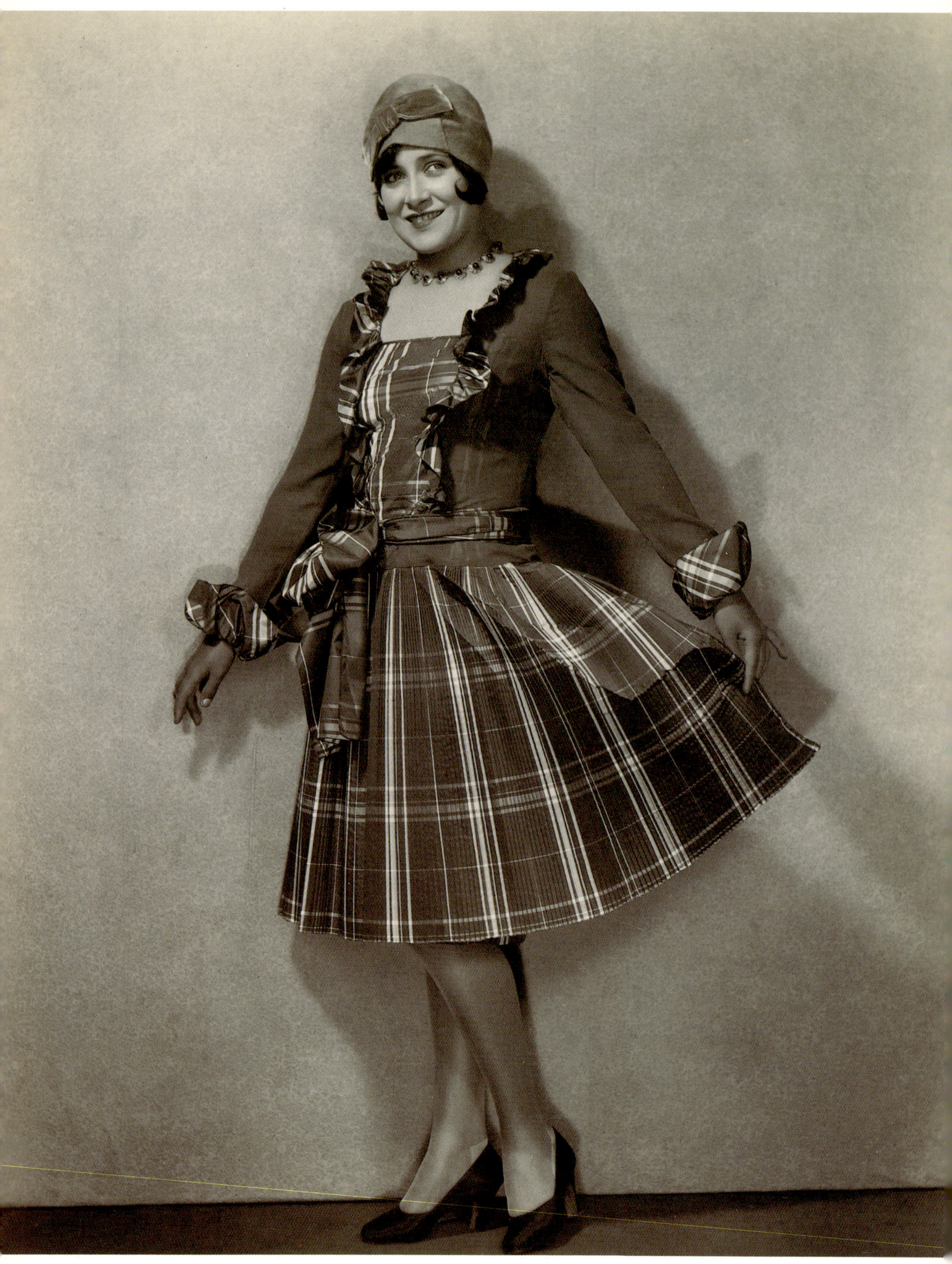

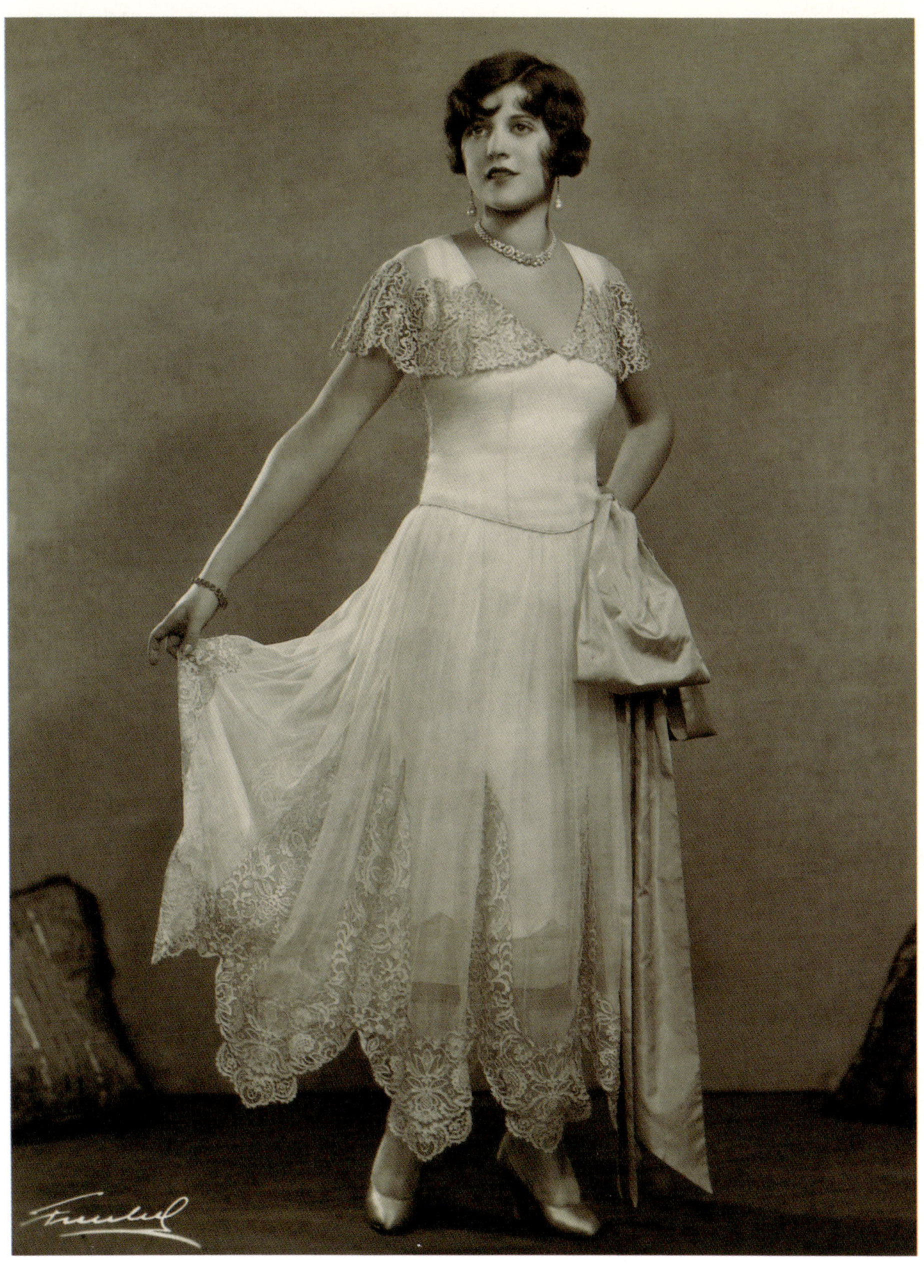

Left and above

Actress Kathryn Crawford in a blue and white plaid taffeta and navy blue Georgette crepe ensemble with an accordion pleated skirt and tight bodice, 1928

Actress Dorothy Gulliver in a white silk mull afternoon dress trimmed with lace, and a sash of rose coloured ribbon is fastened at the side of the waist with long loops hanging almost to the floor, 1928

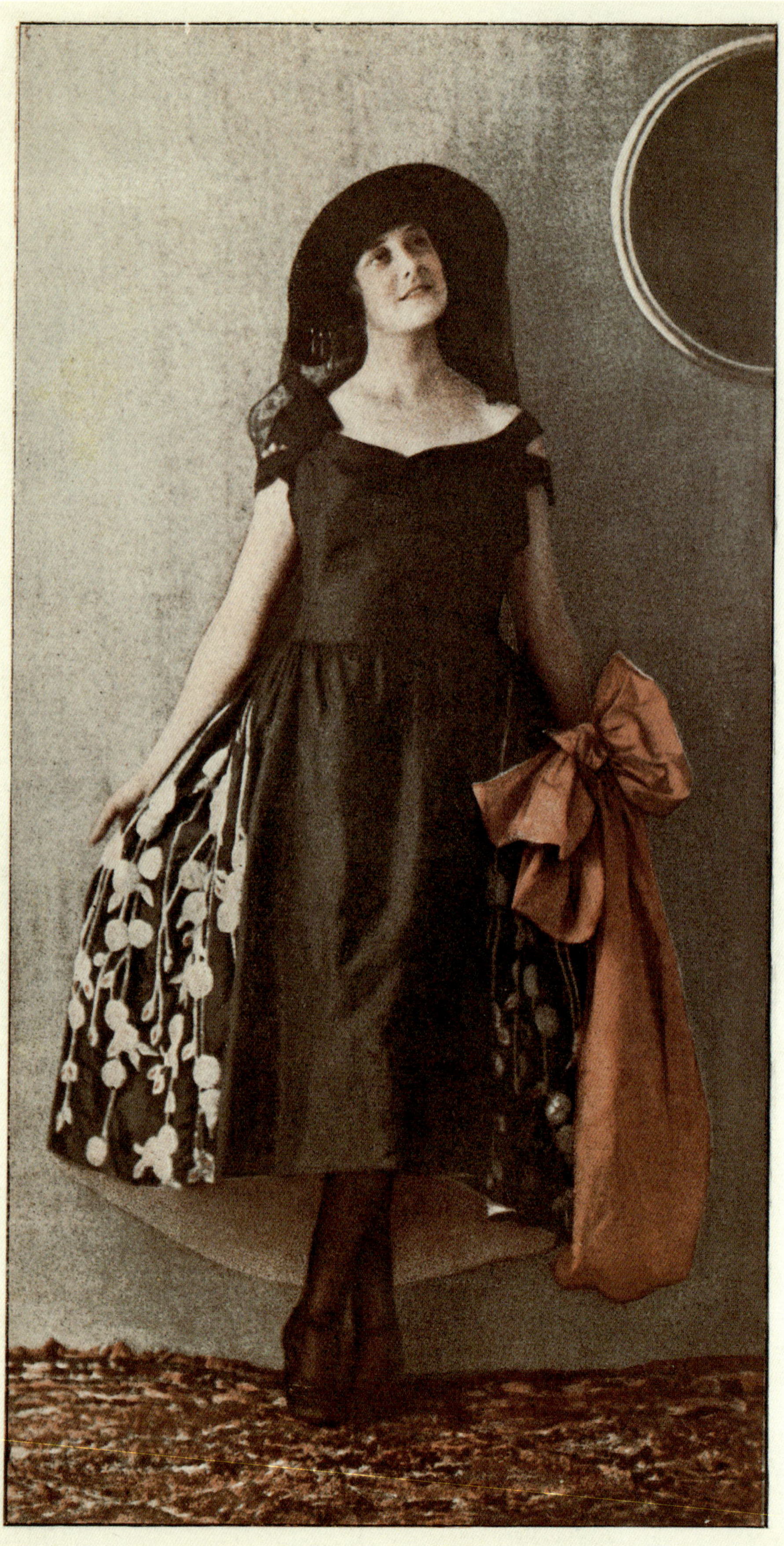

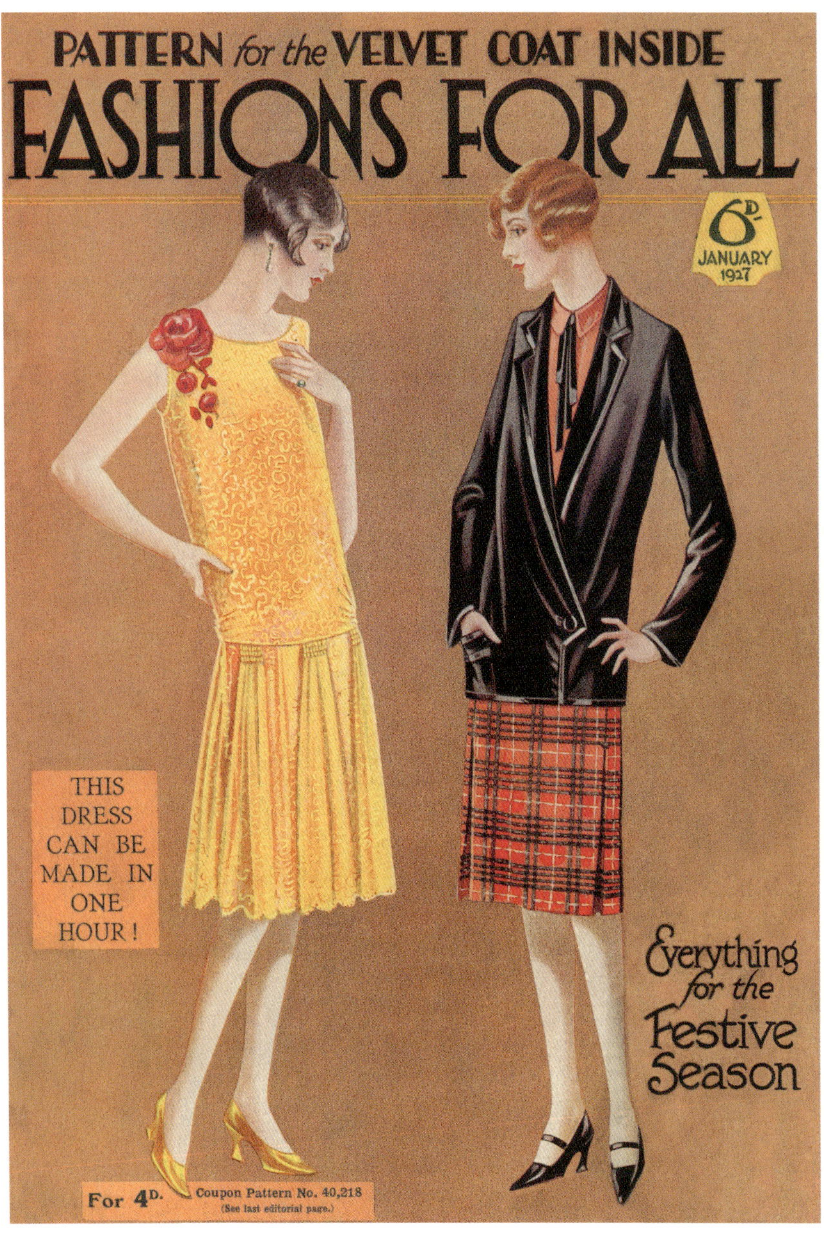

Left and above

Embroidered taffeta dress with red bow by Jeanne Lanvin. *L'Illustration des Modes*, 1920

Evening dress and skirt suit with tuxedo-style jacket. *Fashion for All*, 1927

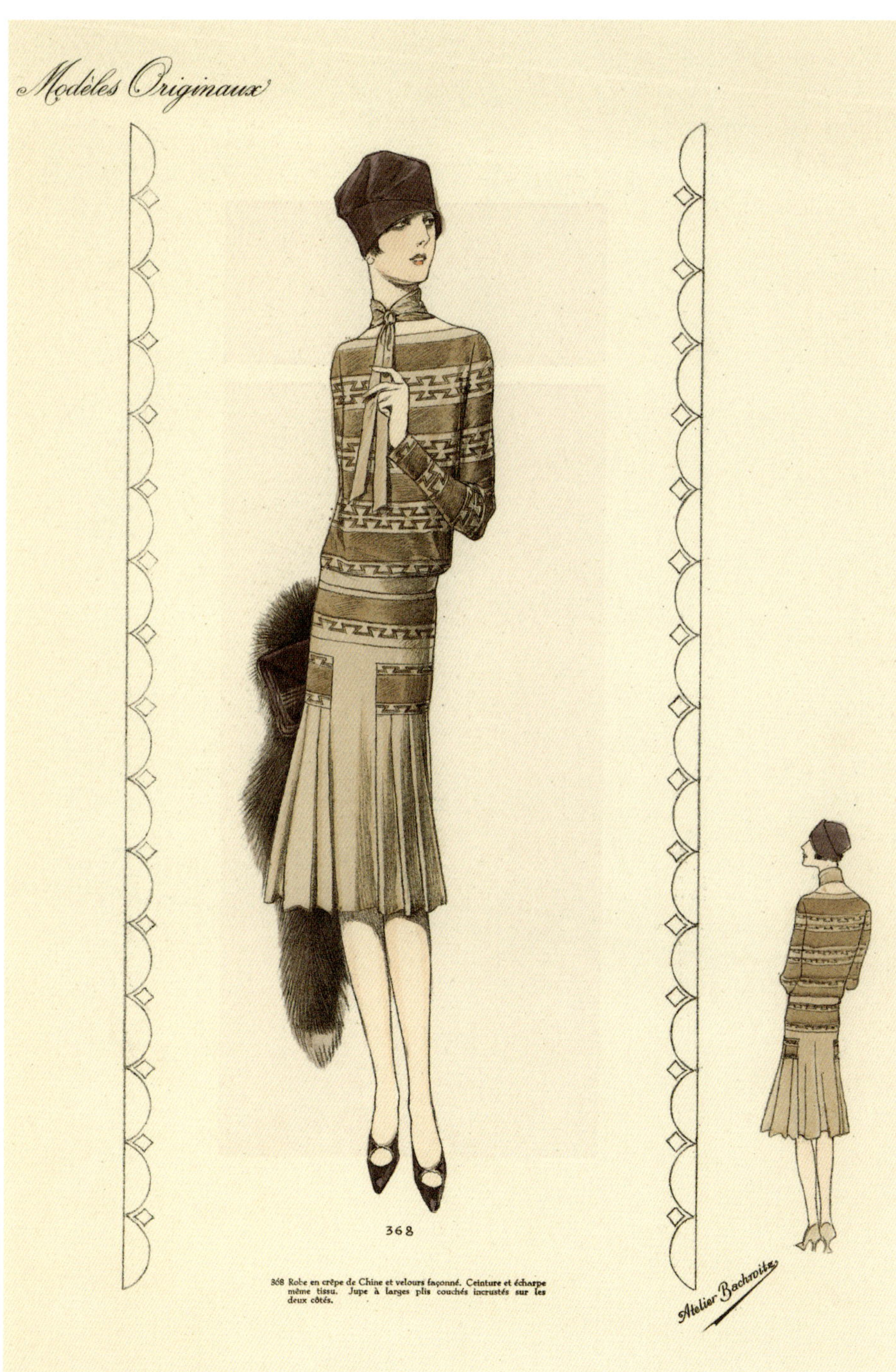

Above

Beige day dress in crepe de Chine and jacquard velvet with pleated side panels and a matching scarf by Atelier Bachroitz. *Modèles Originaux* c.1926

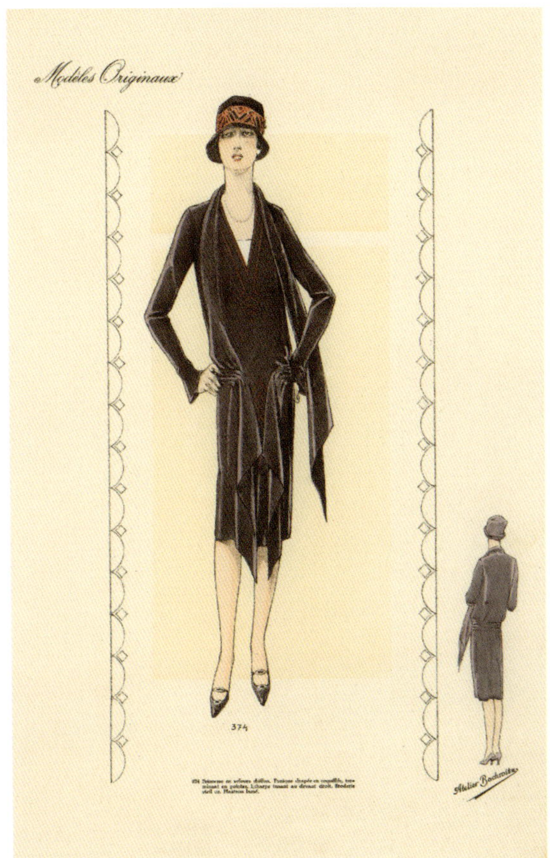

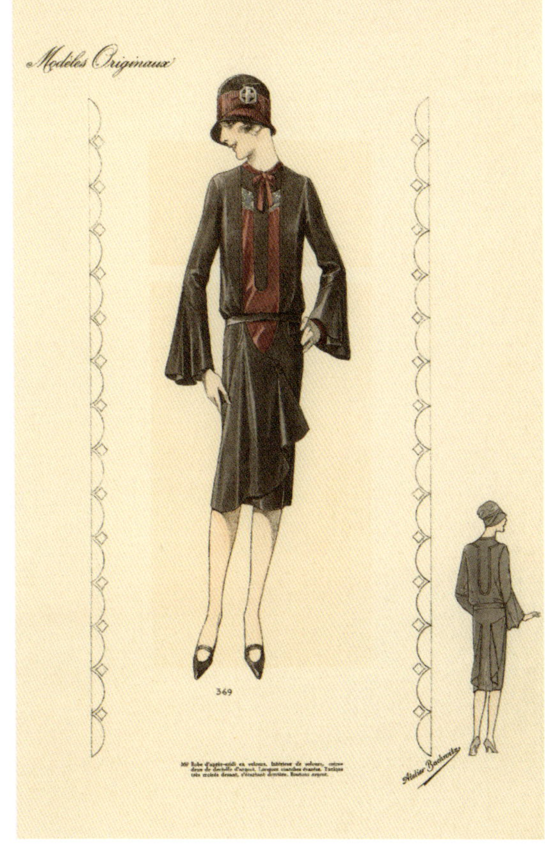

Above left and right

Black day dress in chiffon velvet with old gold embroidered motifs, draped at the front and terminating in points and accessorised with a lamé scarf by Atelier Bachroitz. *Modèles Originaux*, c.1927

Velvet afternoon dress with silver lace and burgundy velvet panels gathered at the back and with a crossover flounce at the front by Atelier Bachroitz. *Modèles Originaux*, c.1927

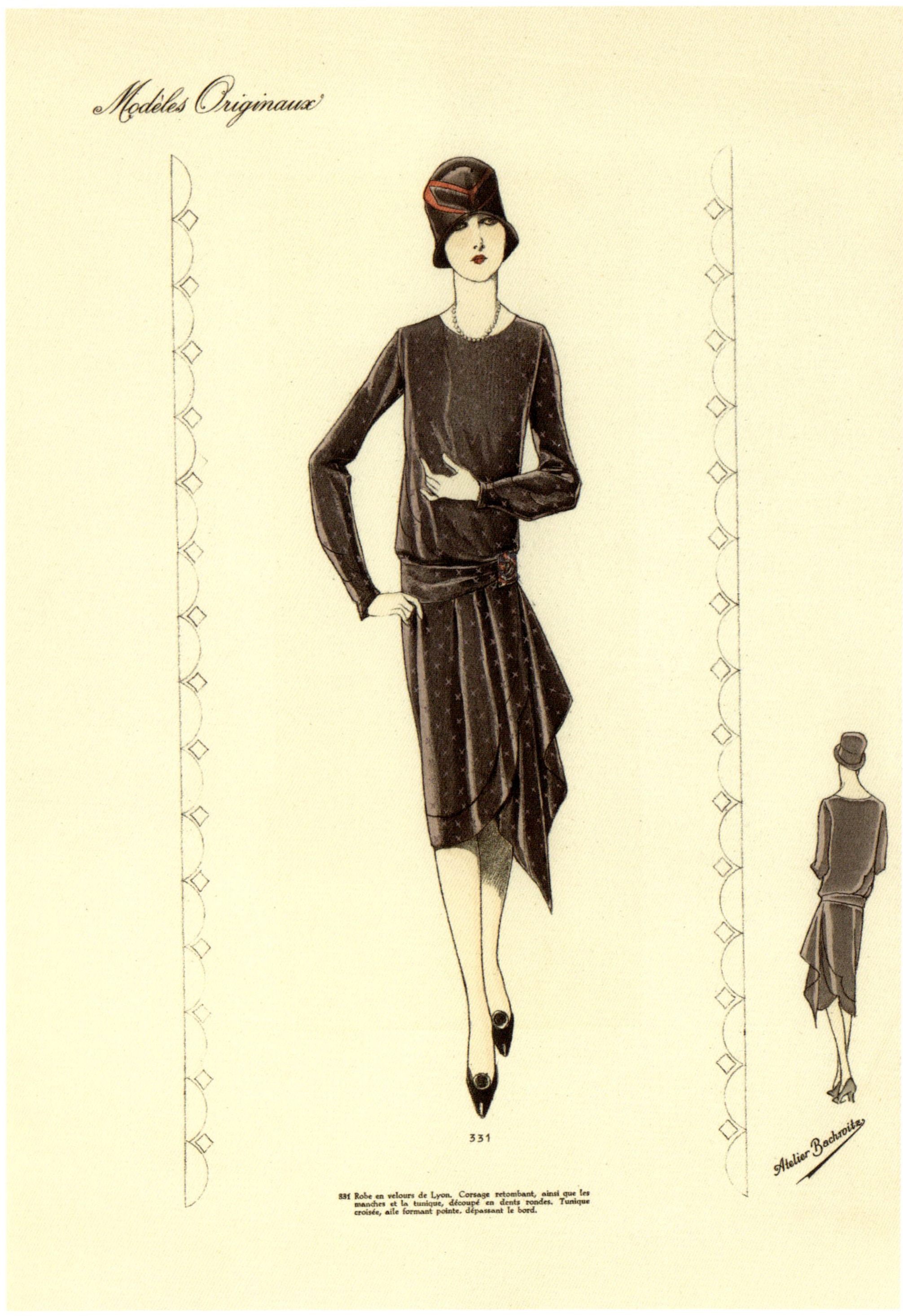

Above

Day dress in brown patterned velvet by Atelier Bachroitz. *Modèles Originaux*, c.1926

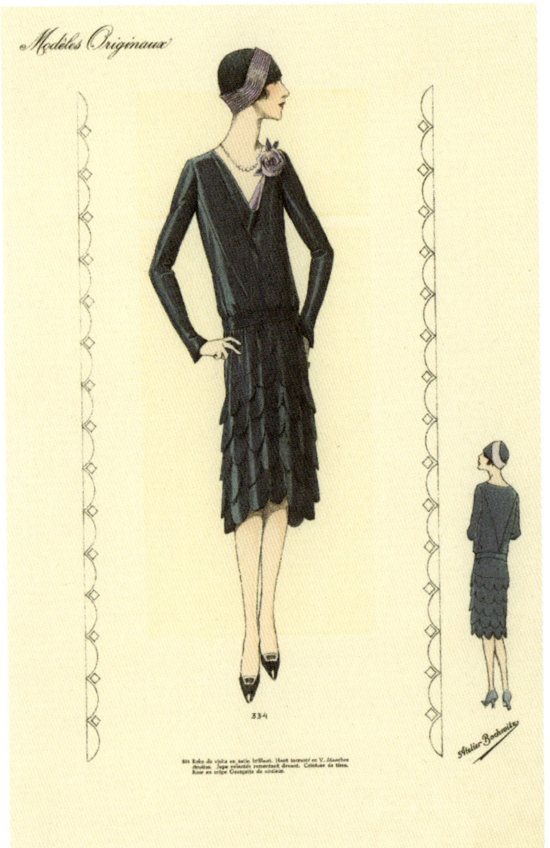

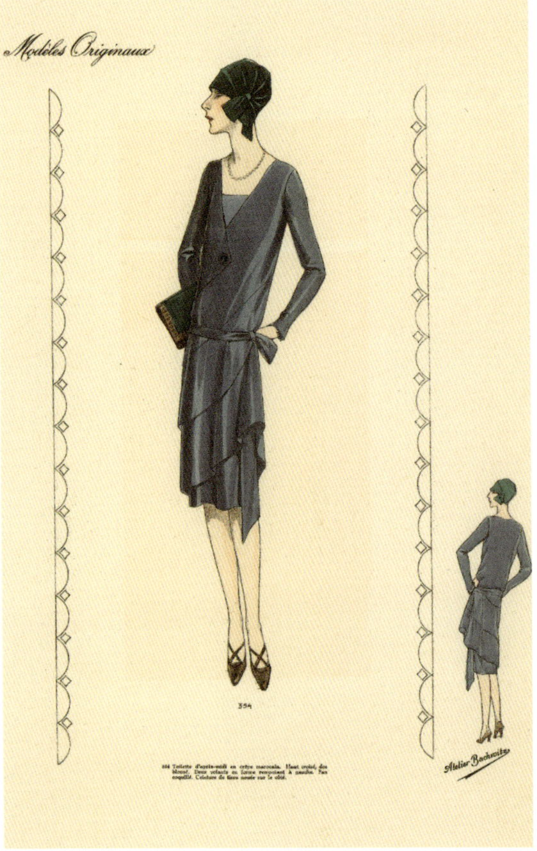

Above Left and right

Petrol blue afternoon dress in shiny satin with a v-neckline and a petalled skirt by Atelier Bachroitz. *Modèles Originaux*, c.1926

Blue day dress in ribbed crepe with diagonal panels for the skirt by Atelier Bachroitz. *Modèles Originaux*, c.1926

Right
Cover of *La Femme Chic*, April 1926

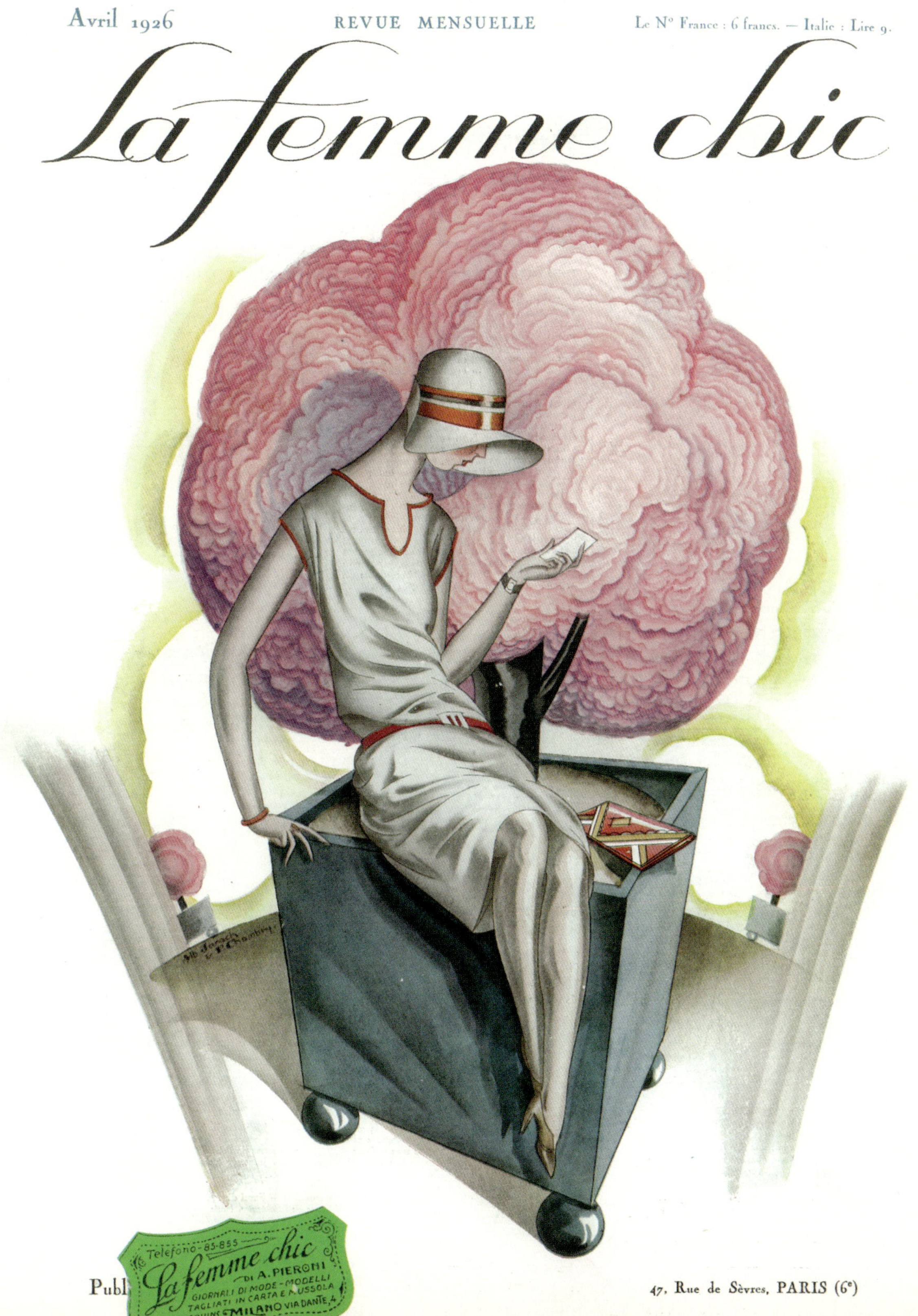
Avril 1926
REVUE MENSUELLE
Le N° France : 6 francs. — Italie : Lire 9.
La femme chic
Publ
Telefono-85-855
La femme chic
DI A. PIERONI
GIORNALI DI MODE - MODELLI
TAGLIATI IN CARTA E MUSSOLA
MANNEQUINS MILANO VIA DANTE, 4
47, Rue de Sèvres, PARIS (6e)

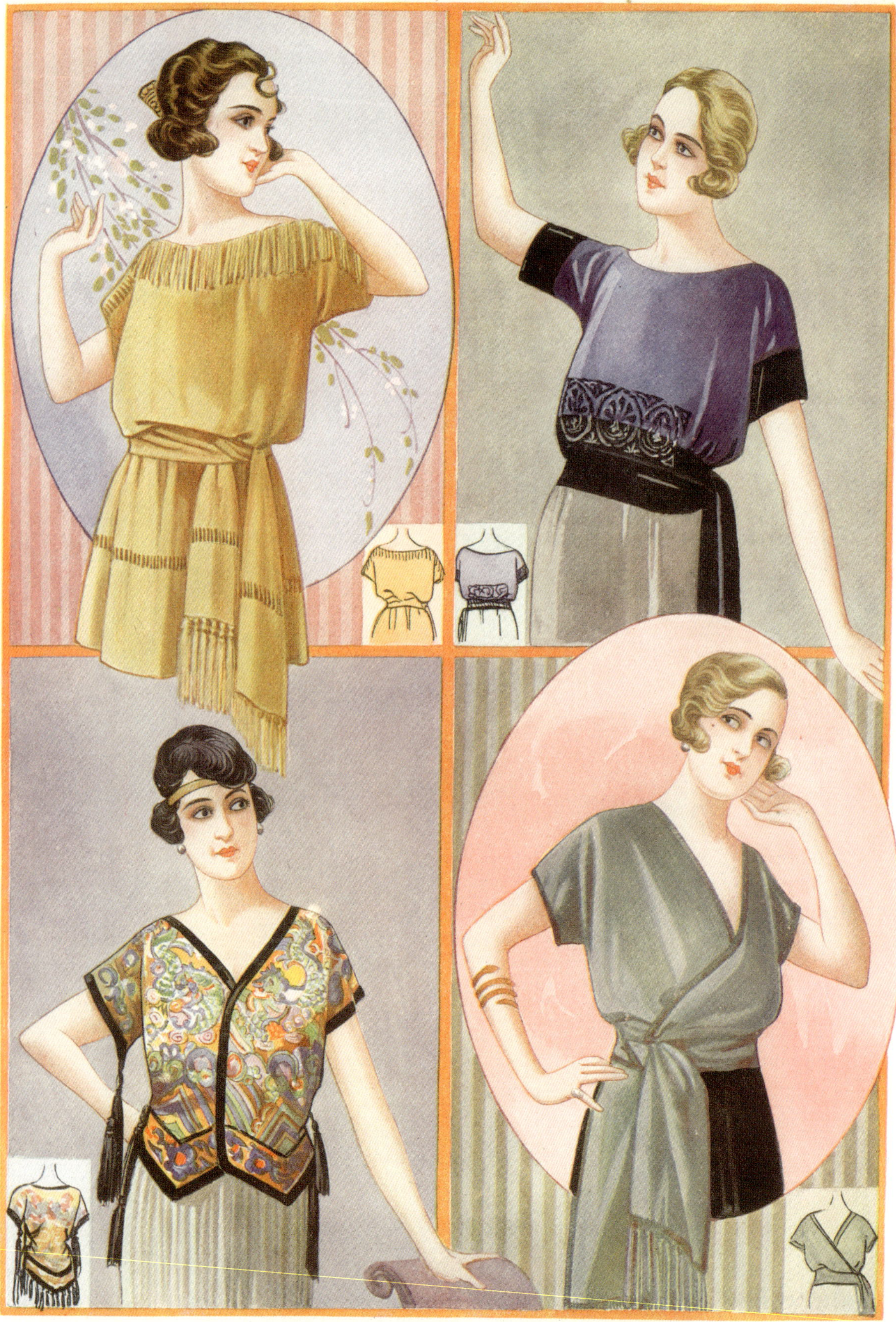

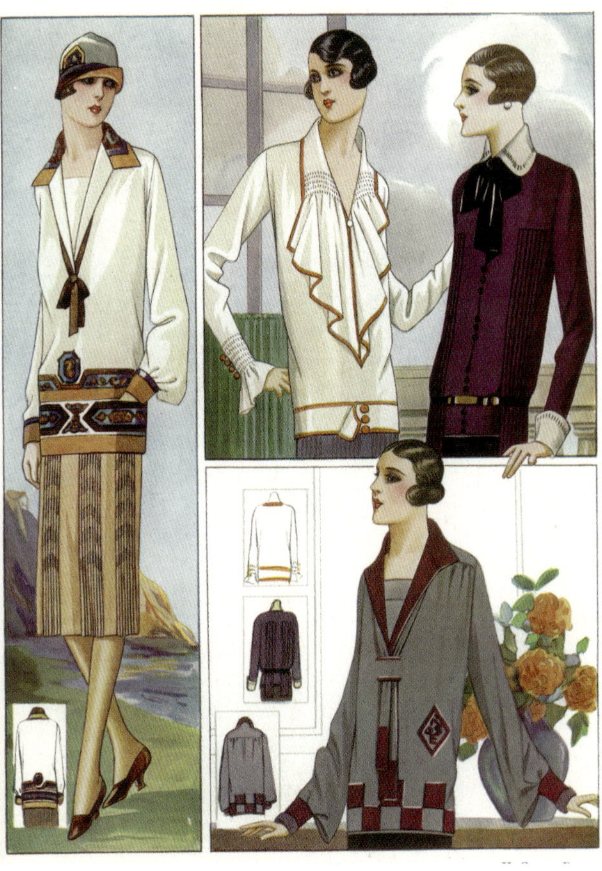

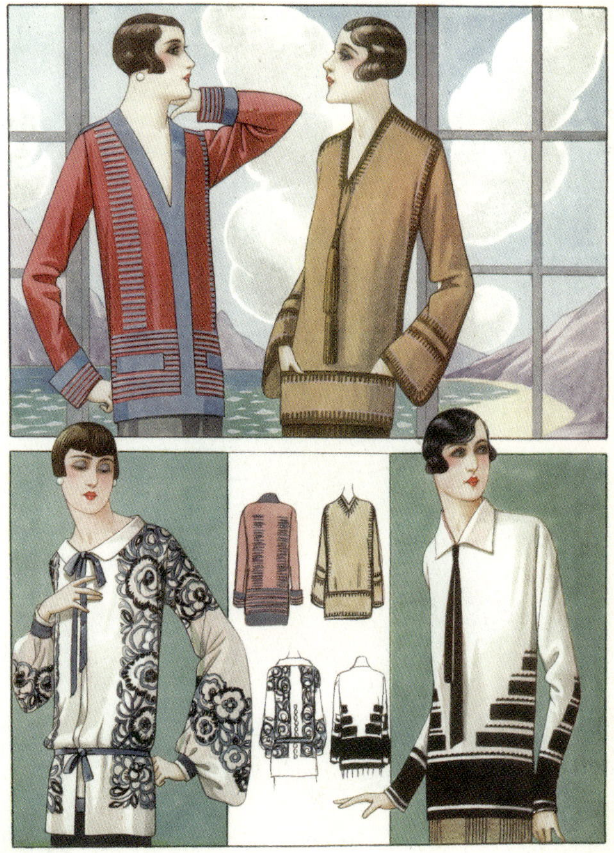

Left
Four designs for blouses by the Princesse Baratoff. *La Femme Chic*, 1921

Above left and right
Four "sportswear" blouses by Dupony. La Femme Chic, 1926

Four "sportswear" blouses. La Femme Chic, 1926

Below and right

Afternoon dress with large buckle and trumpet sleeves by Alice Bernard. *La Femme Chic*, 1926

Simple blouses and a velour sweater, *La Femme Chic*, 1926

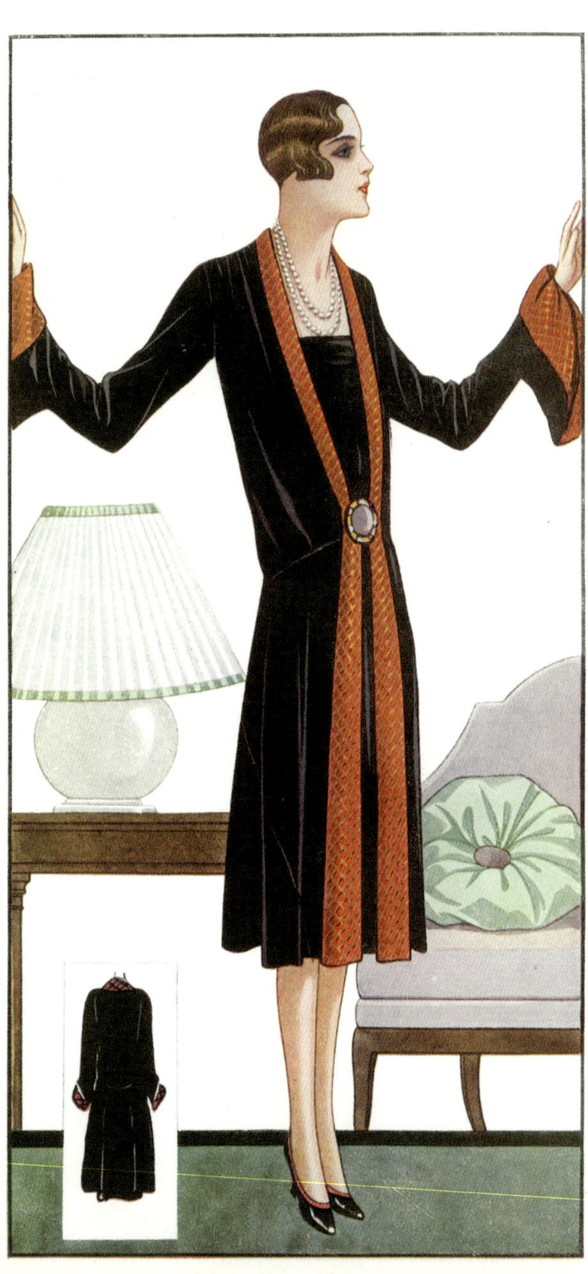

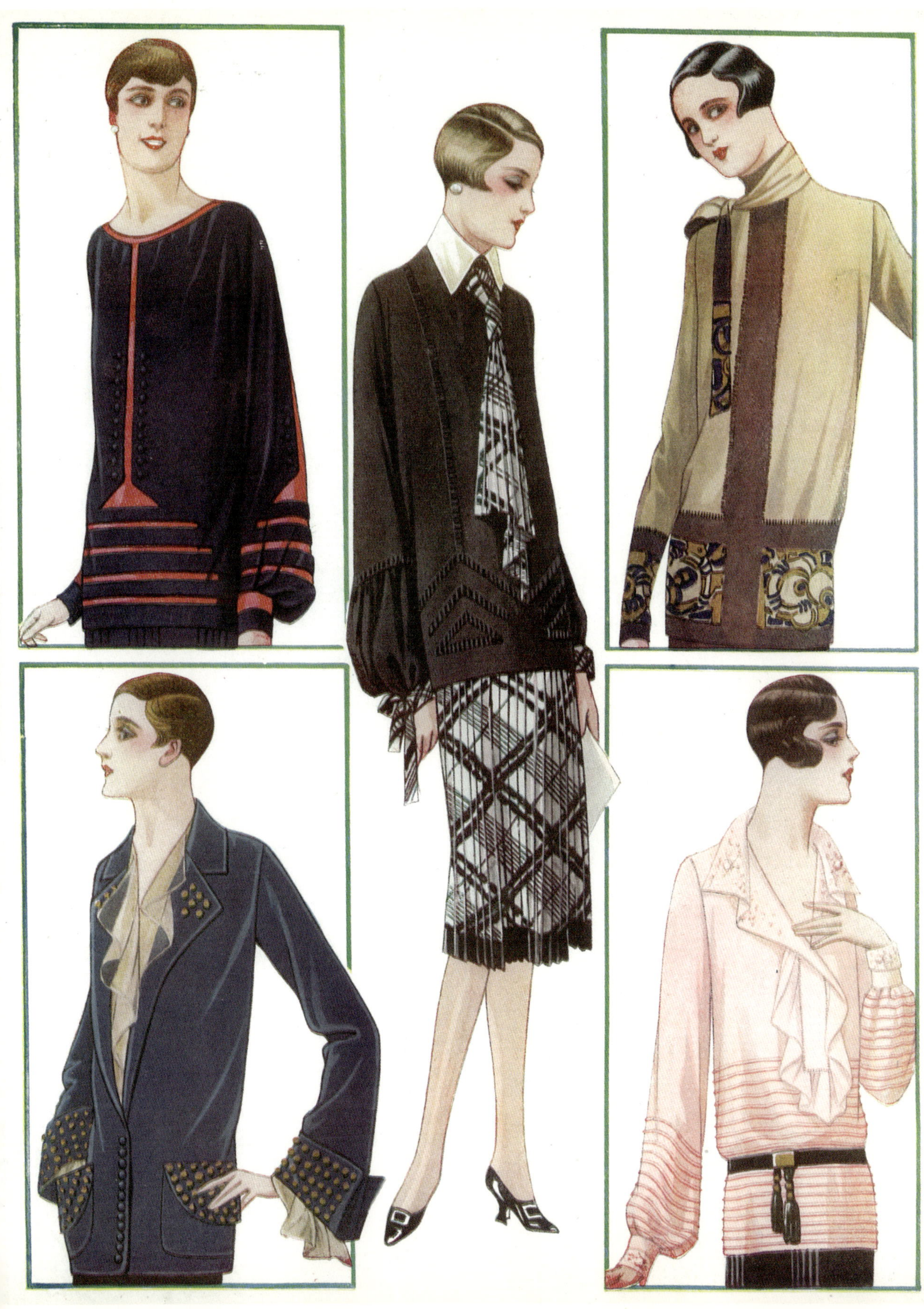

Right
A cream tunic dress with black embroidery worn over a green underdress with wide embellished sleeves. *Les Modèles Chics*, c.1920

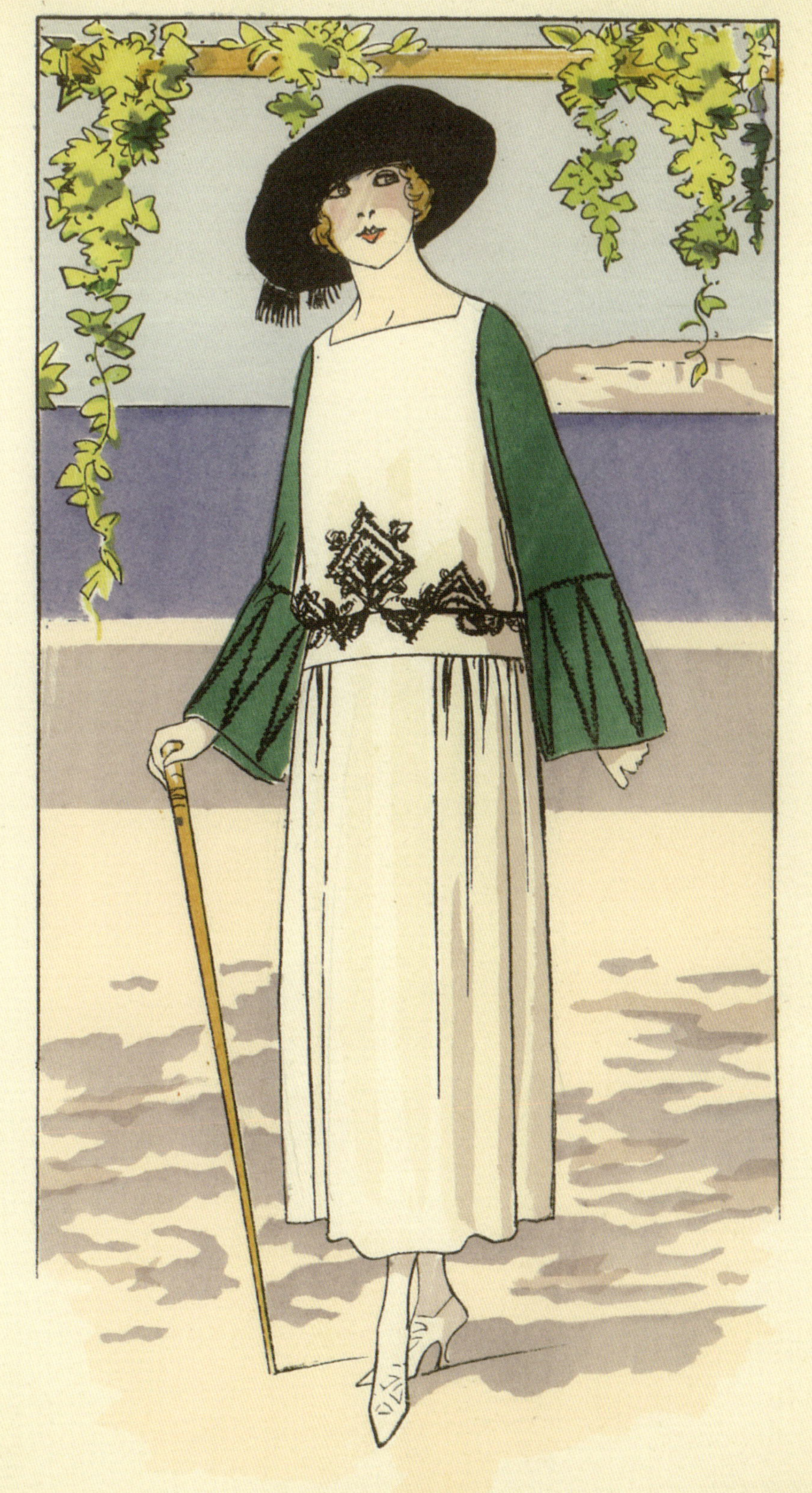

Below
"For the Easter Vacation", grey ensemble by Alice Bernard, red ensemble with oriental motifs by Lina Mouton, turquoise ensemble and black tunic dress by Alice Bernard, floral patterned dress with flounced tiered skirt, pink dress with lace panels and collar by Francis, and dress made from "Les Fleurs de Thuya" fabric by Francis. *La Femme Chic*, 1926

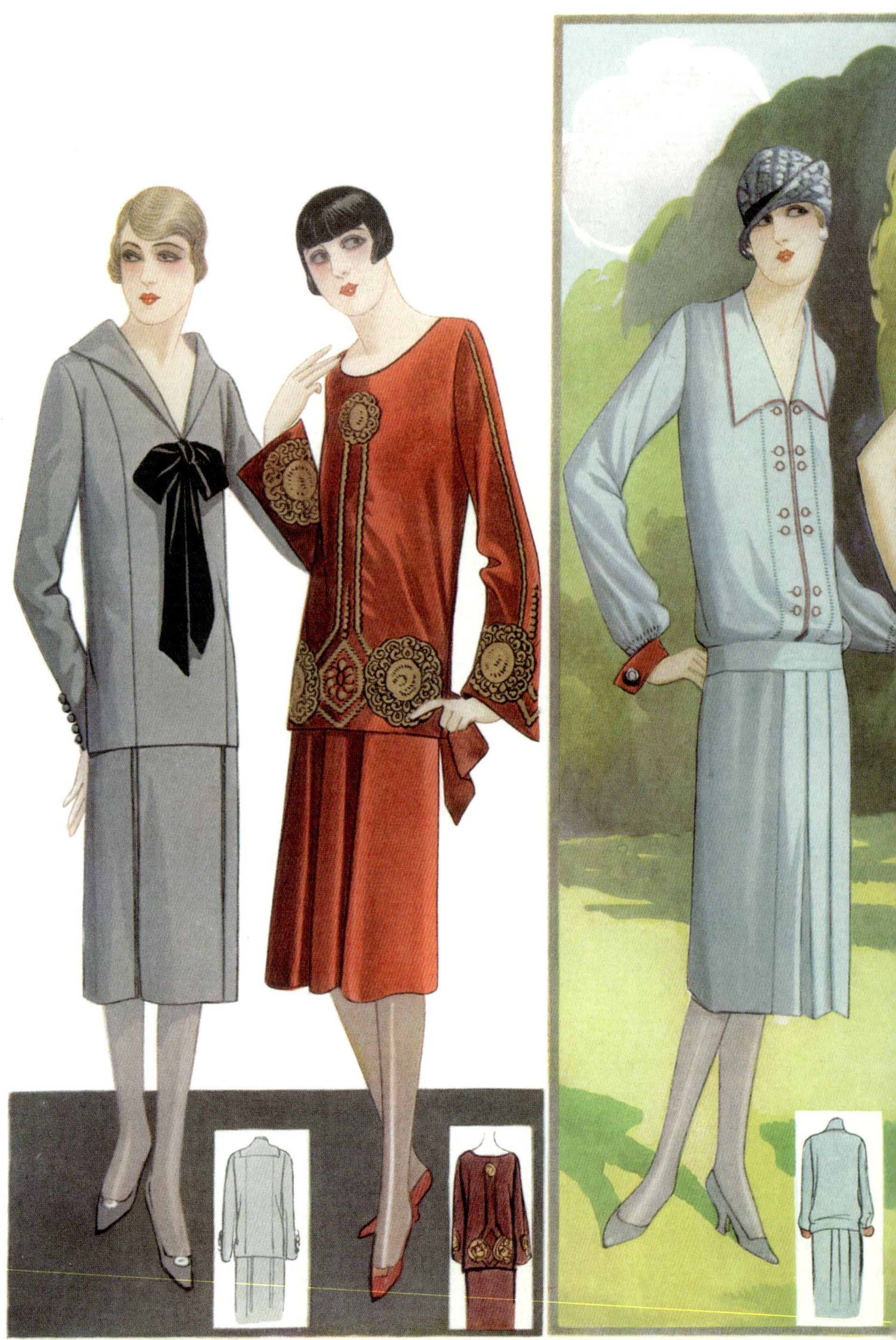

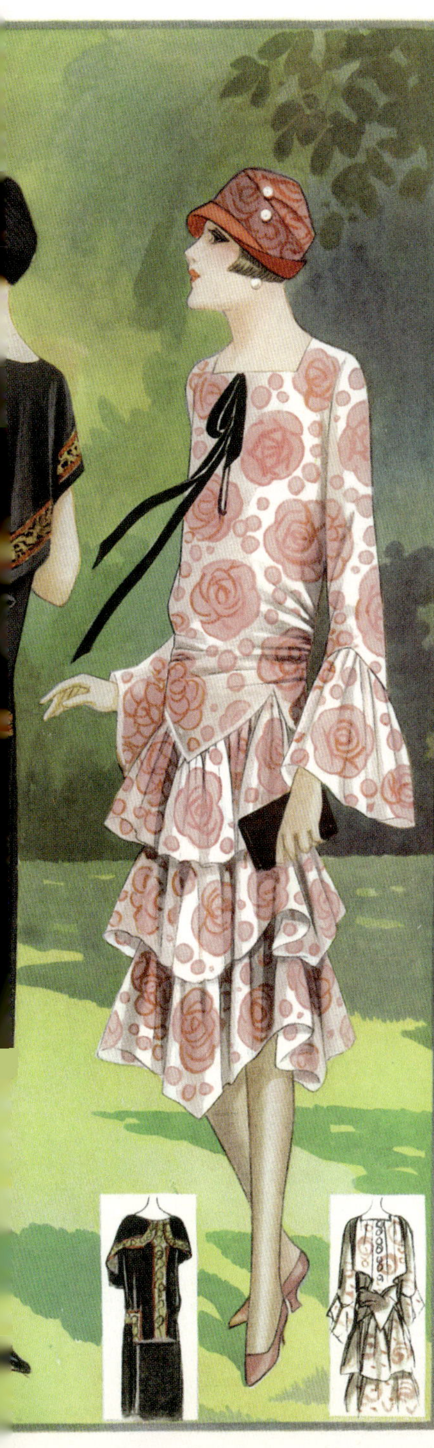

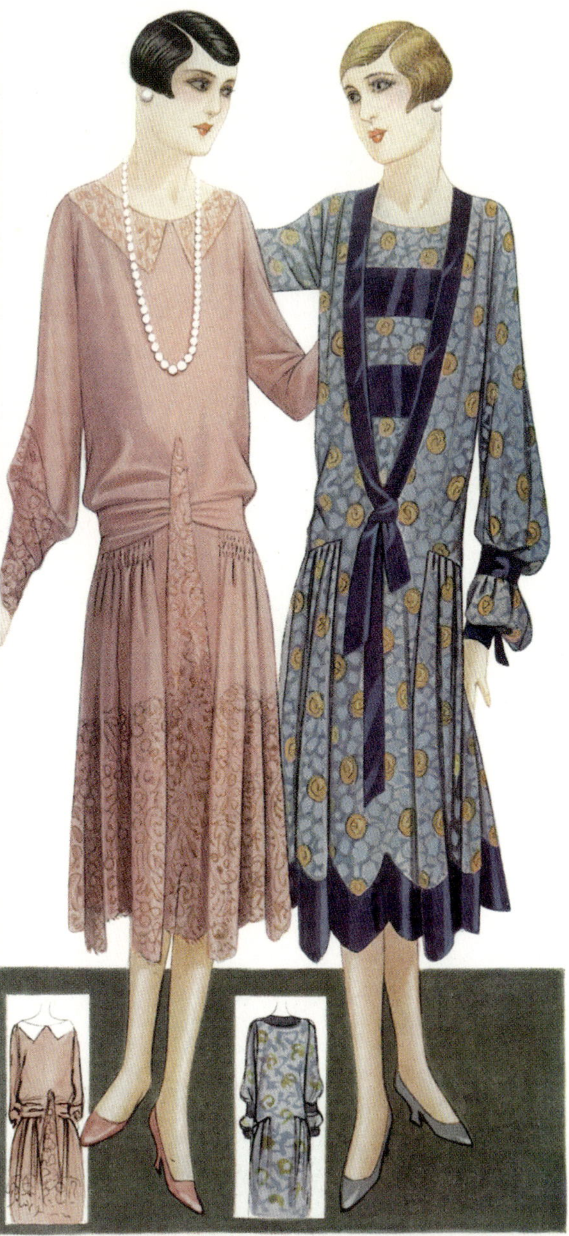

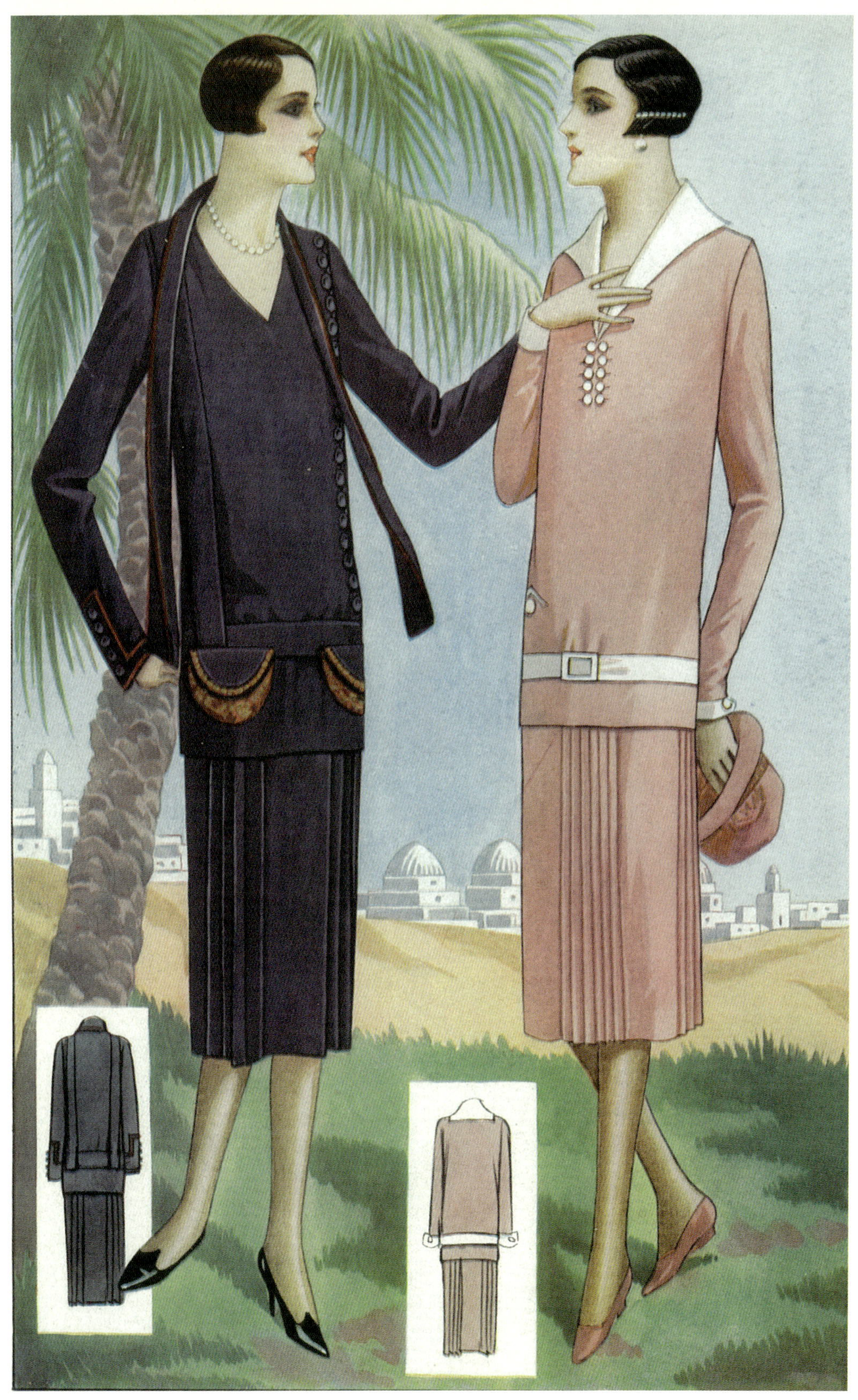

Above
Two travelling dresses by Zimmermann.
La Femme Chic, 1926

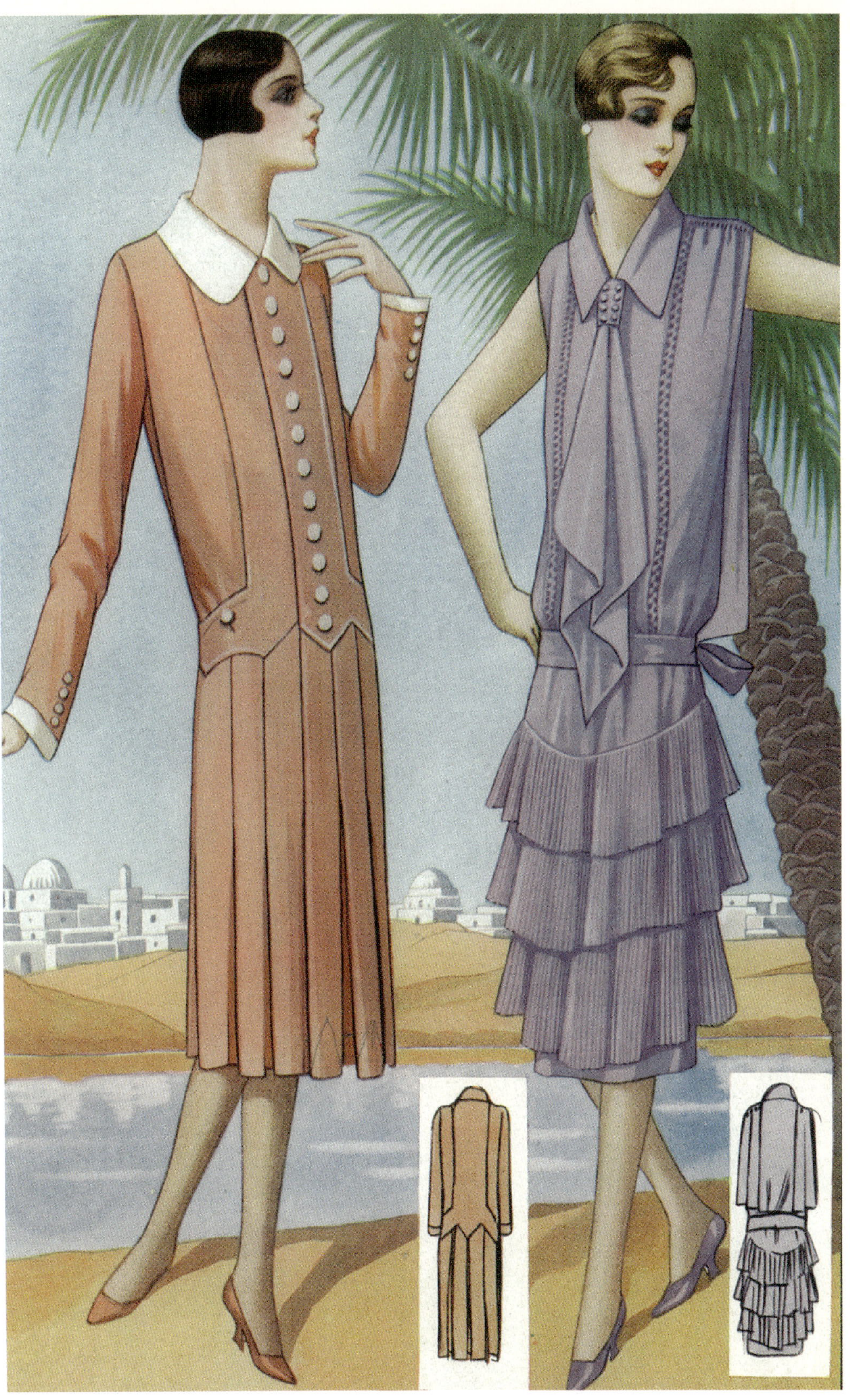

Above
Travelling dress by Bernard and lilac travelling dress by Zimmermann. *La Femme Chic*, 1926

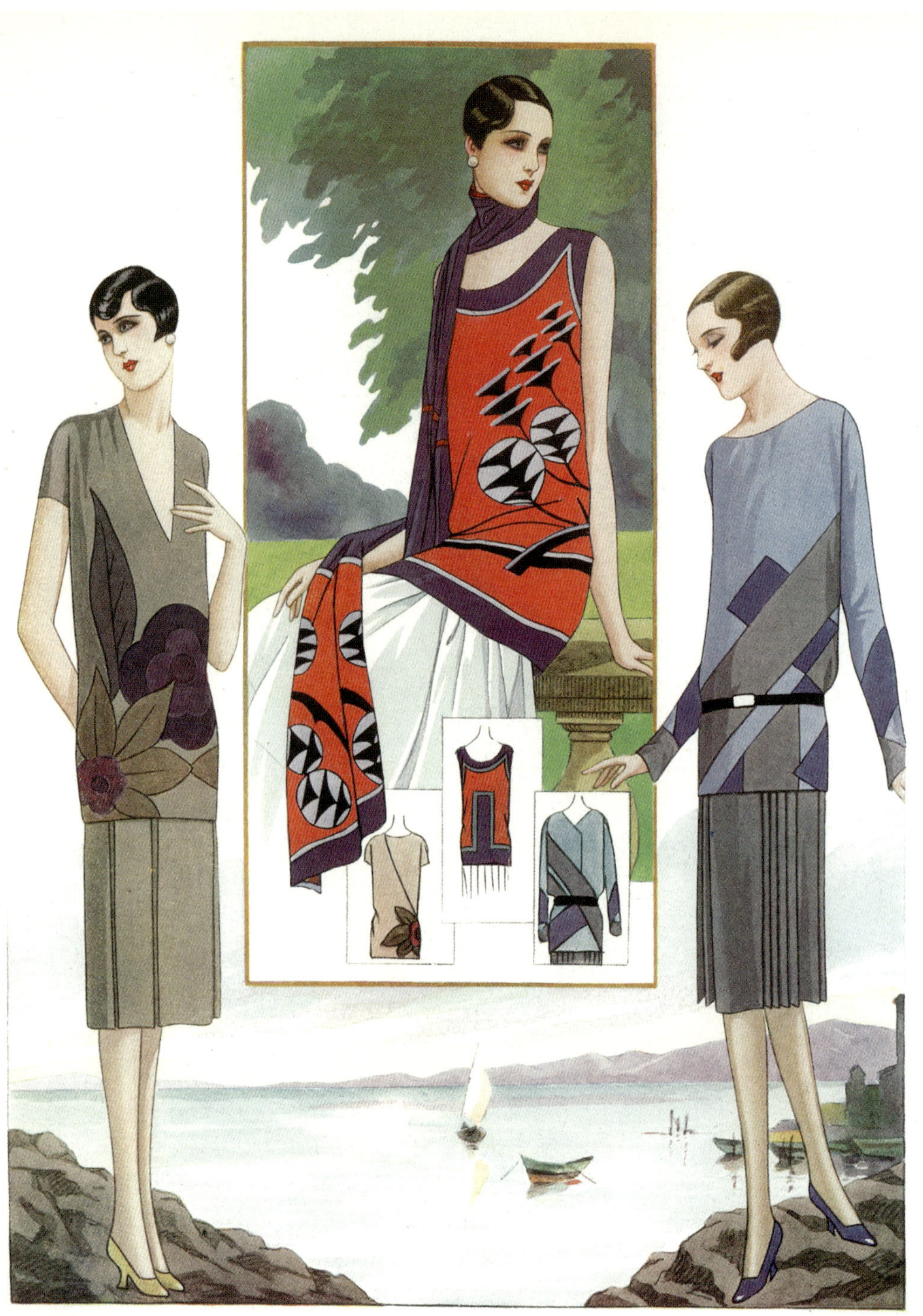

Above and right

Three blouses with stylised floral and geometric motifs. *La Femme Chic*, 1927

Cover of *La Femme Chic à Paris*, March 1926

Mars 1926 REVUE MENSUELLE Le N° France : 7 francs. — Italie : Lire 1

La femme chic à Paris

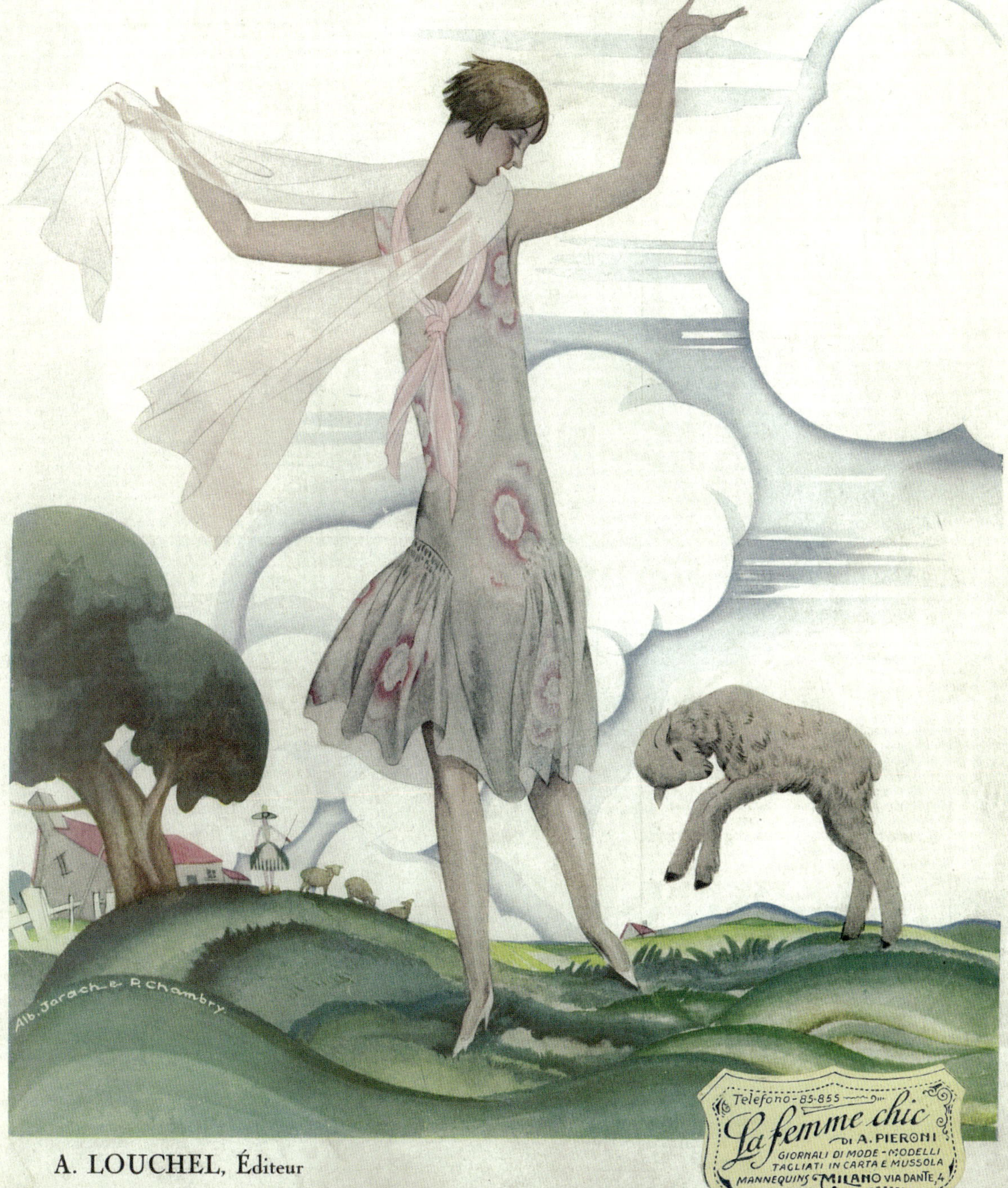

A. LOUCHEL, Éditeur

NUMÉRO SPÉCIAL DES MODES DE PRINTEMPS

Below
"Light dresses for Spa Towns", pink and black dress, red dress and blue and lilac dress with sprig motif by Zimmermann; navy dress and beige dress by Premet; dress with "Le Tourbillon de fleurs champêtres" fabric; "sports" dress in "DjersaKasha" fabric by Zimmermann. *La Femme Chic*, 1927

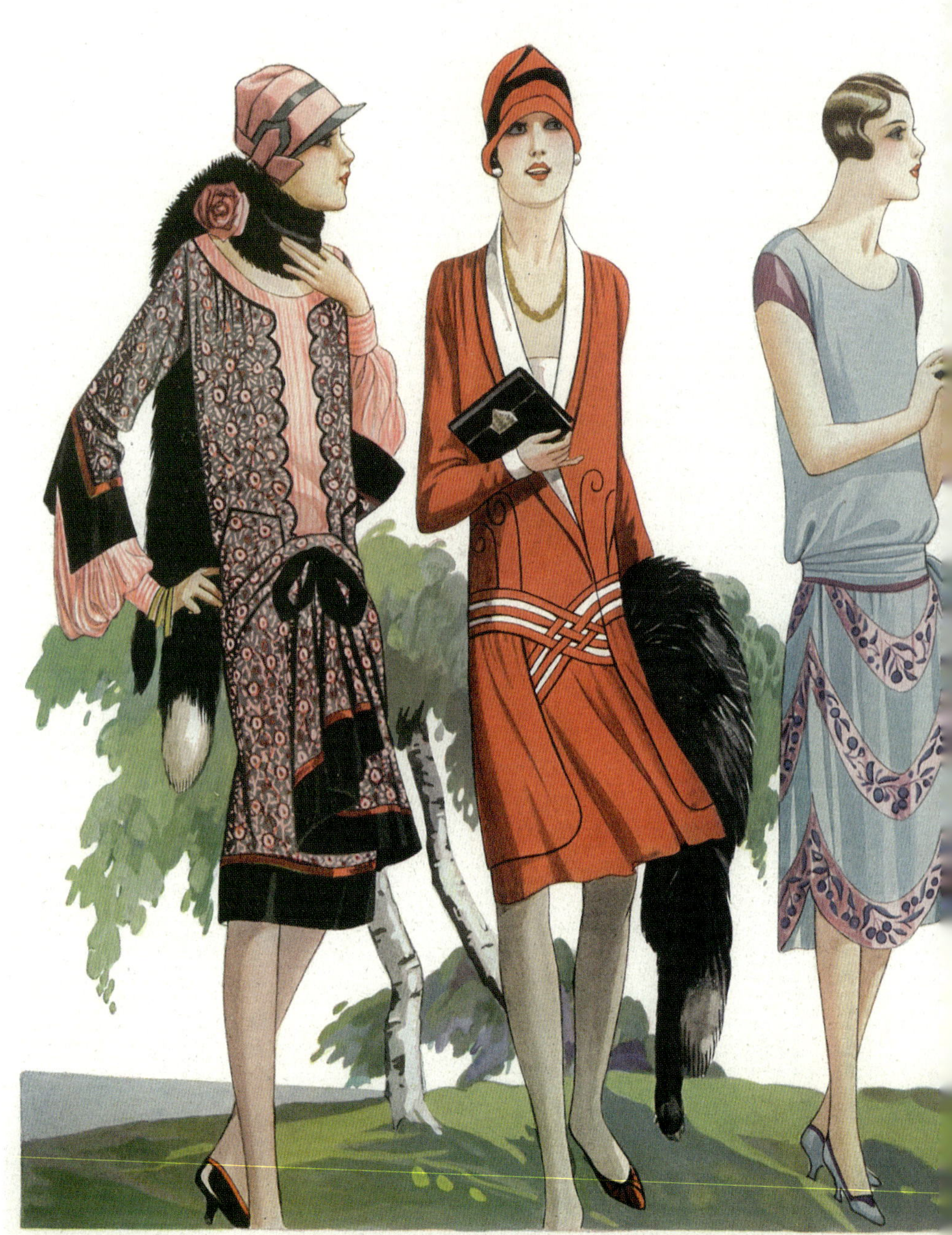

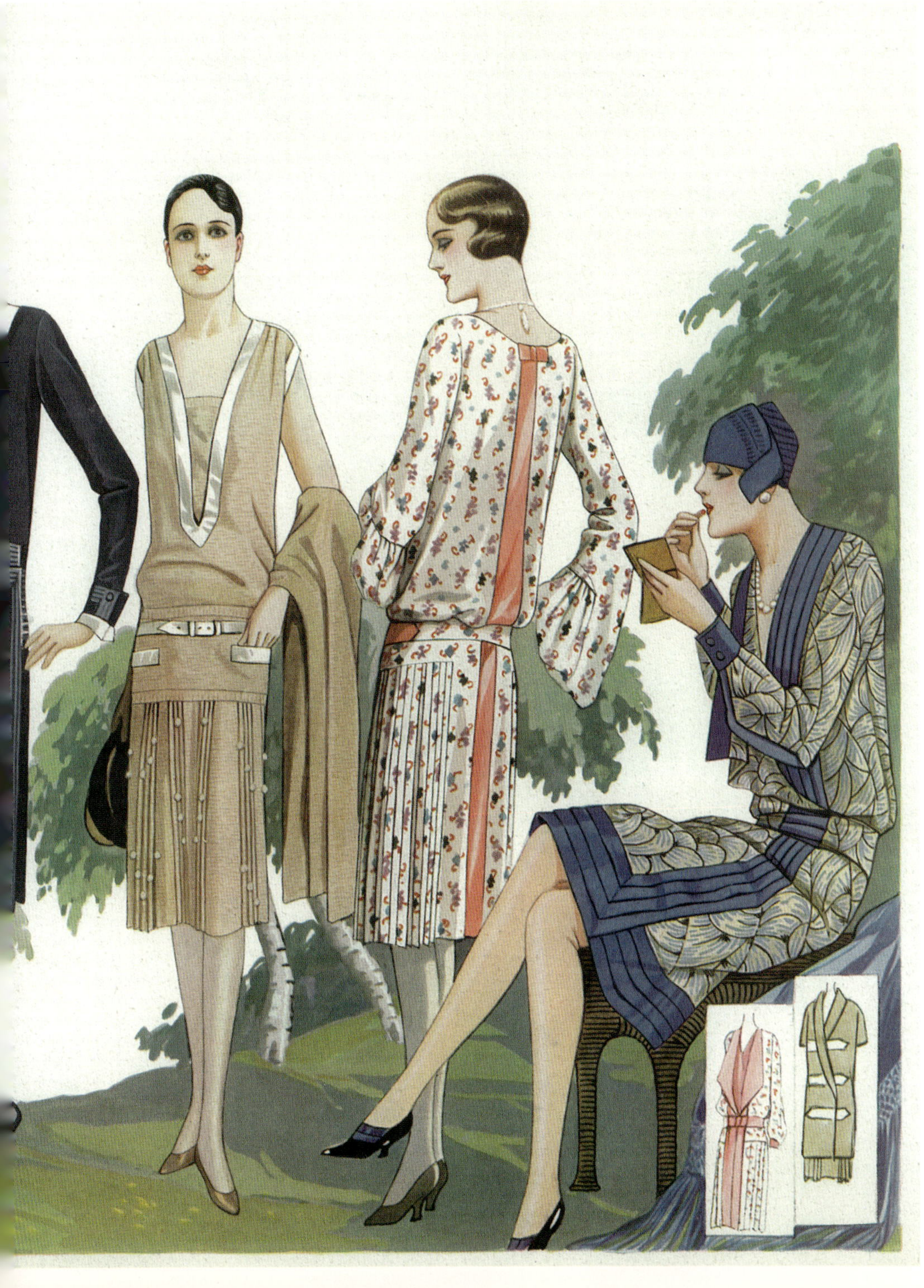

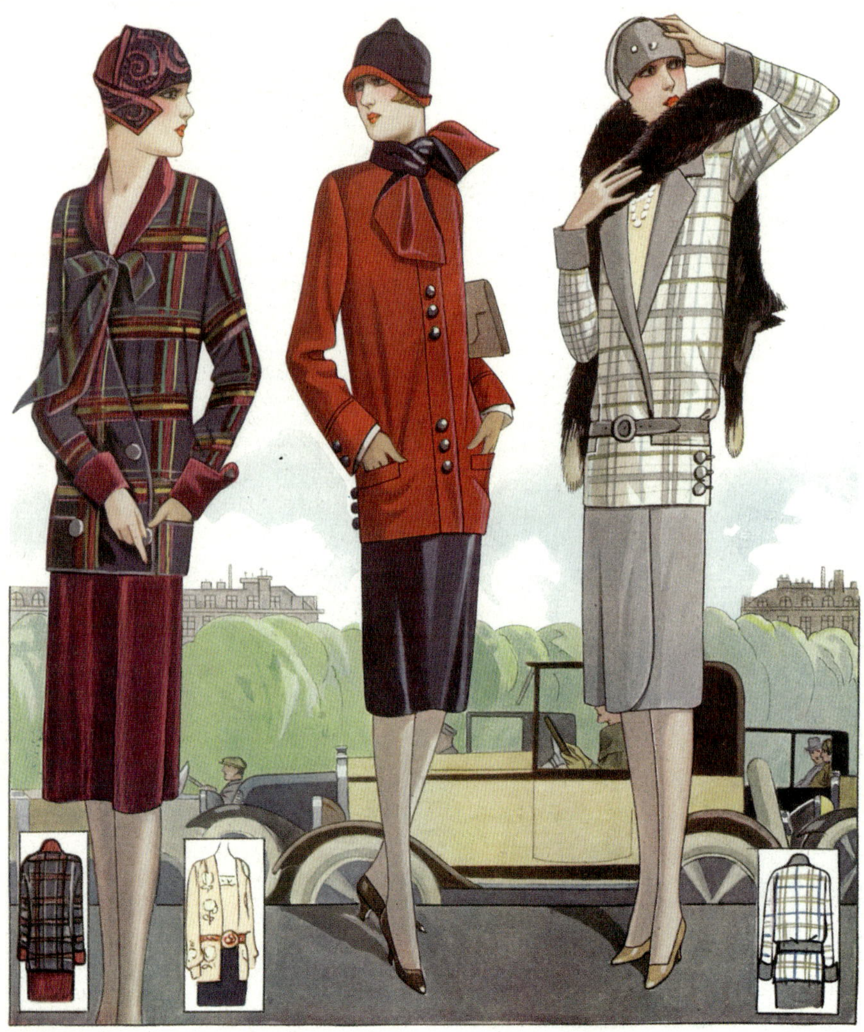

Above and right

Two day suits by Martial et Armand and a grey checked suit by Paul Poiret. *Le Femme Chic*, 1927

Two outfits for country receptions by Paul Poiret. *La Femme Chic*, 1927

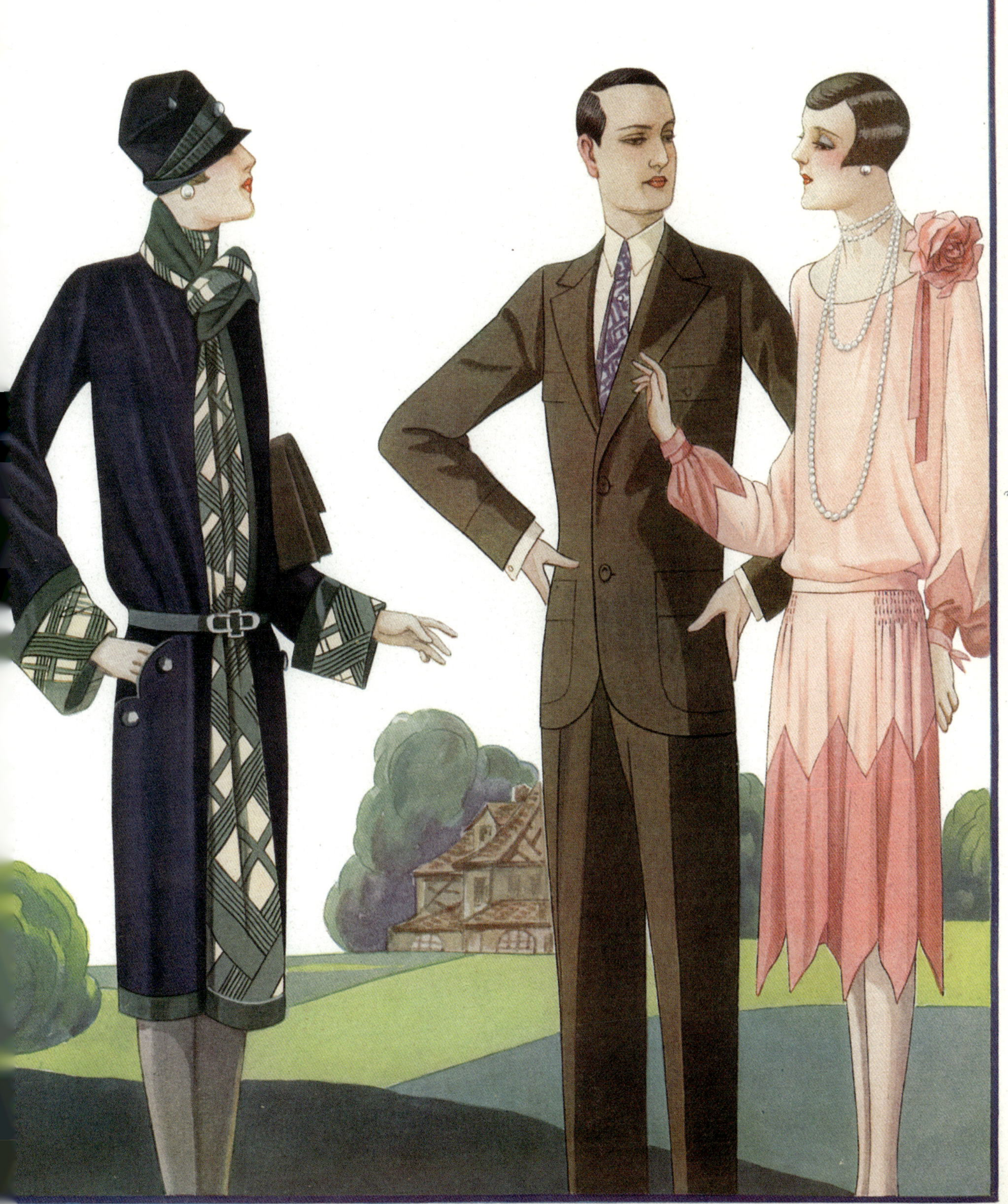

Below left and right

Two designs for sportswear outfits.
La Femme Élégante à Paris, 1926

Two day suits.
La Femme Élégante à Paris, 1926

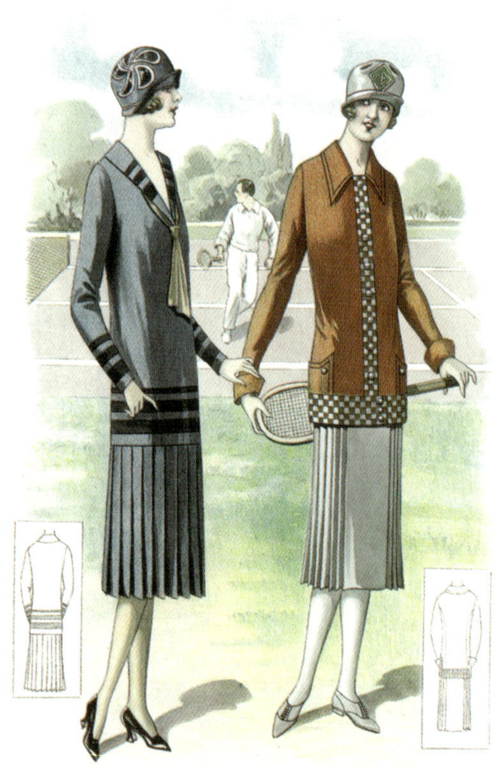

1288 1289

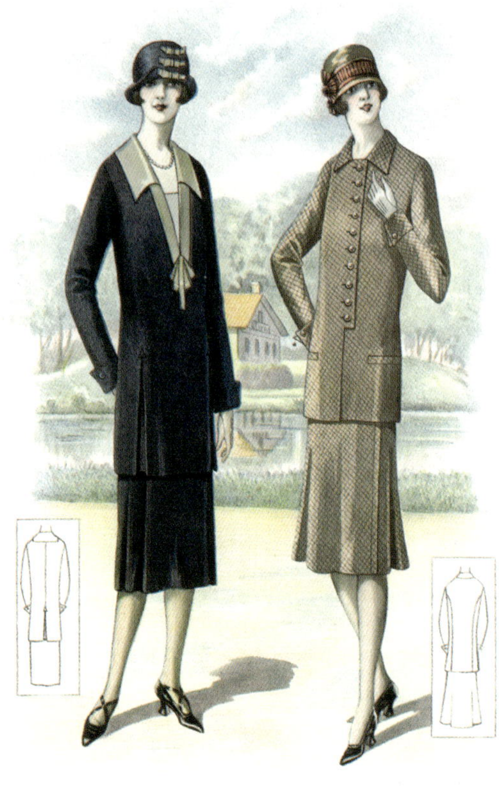

1284 1285

Below
Two designs for skirt suits.
La Femme Élégante à Paris, 1926

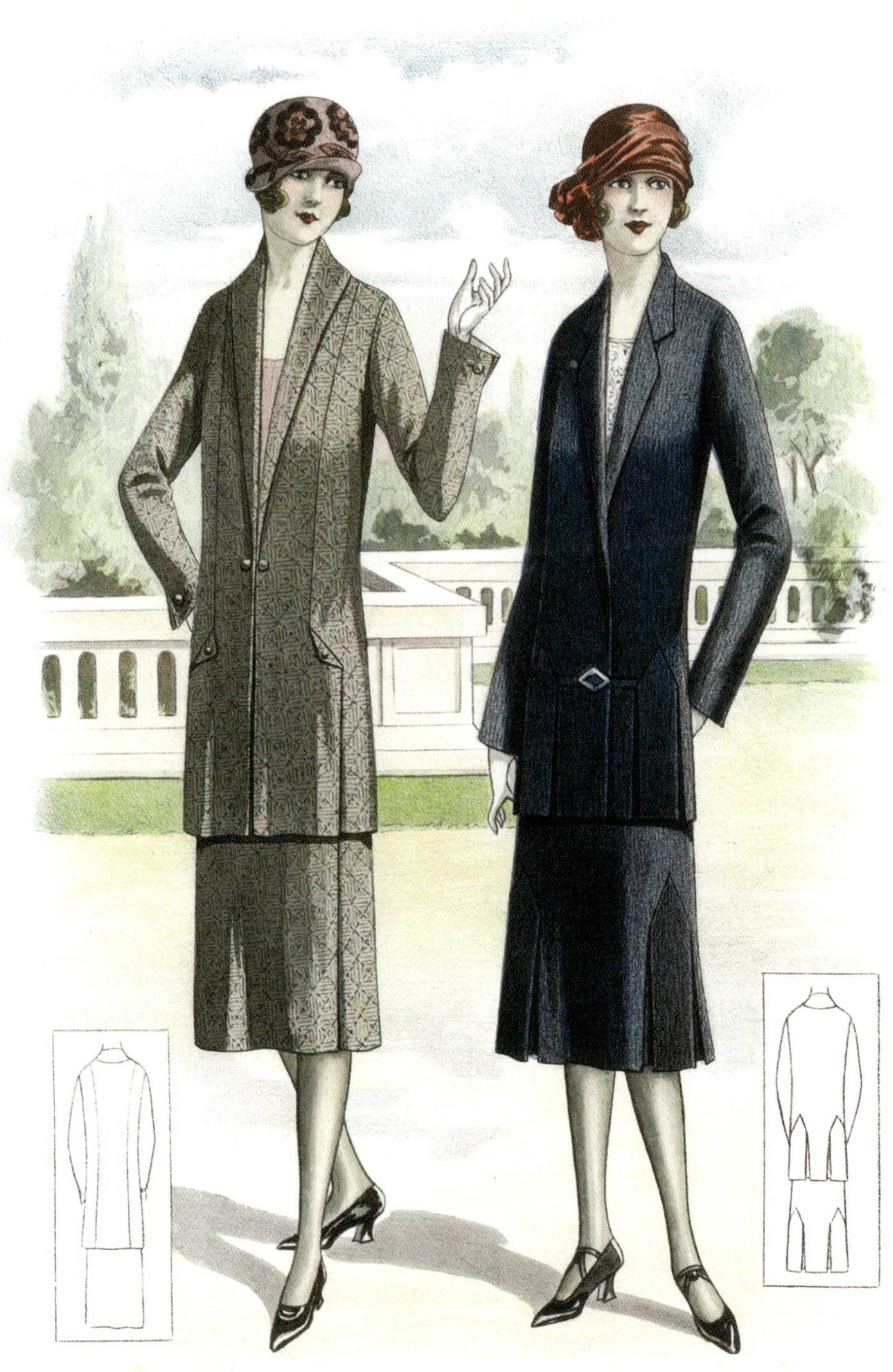

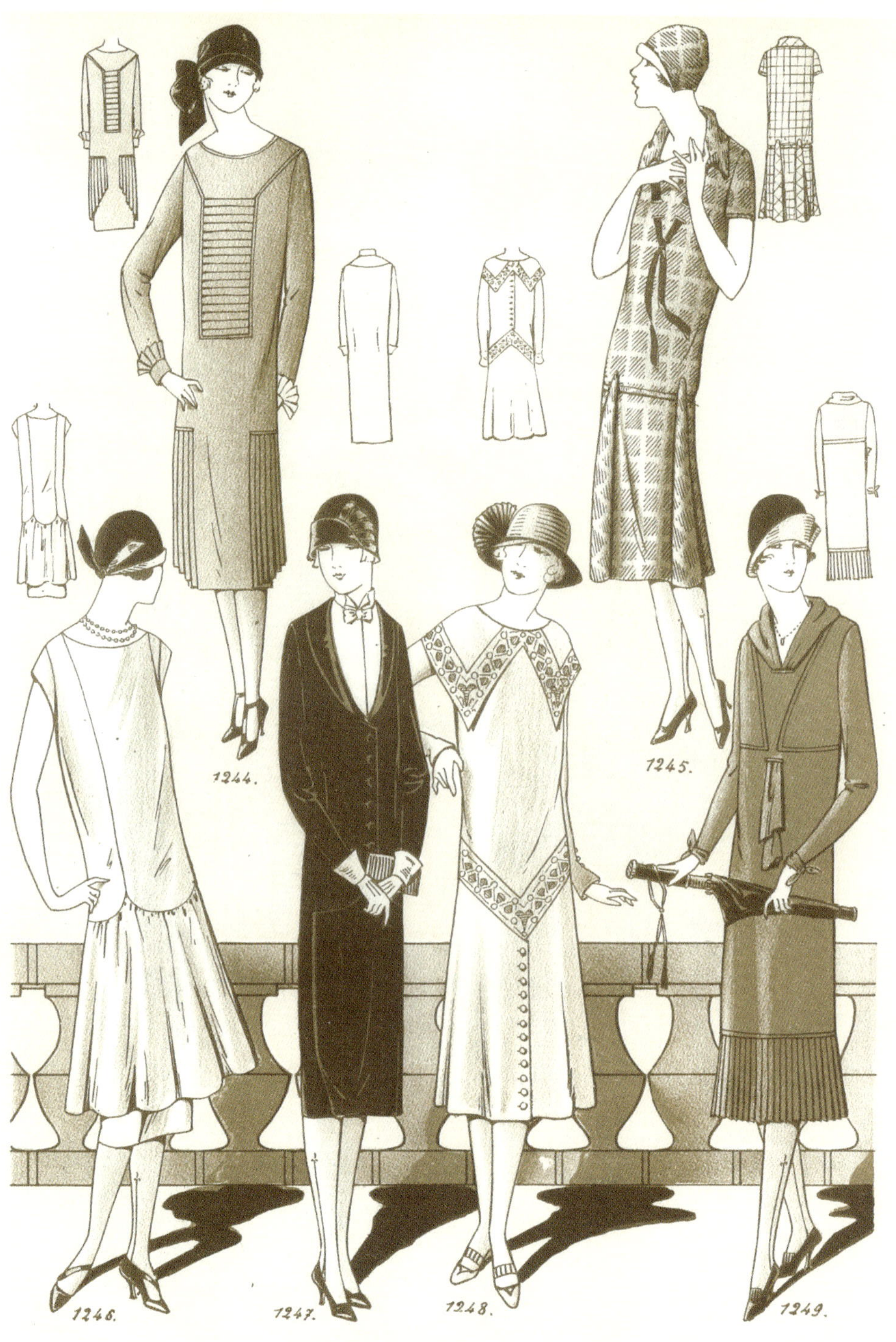

Above
Selection of day dresses.
La Femme Élégante à Paris, 1926

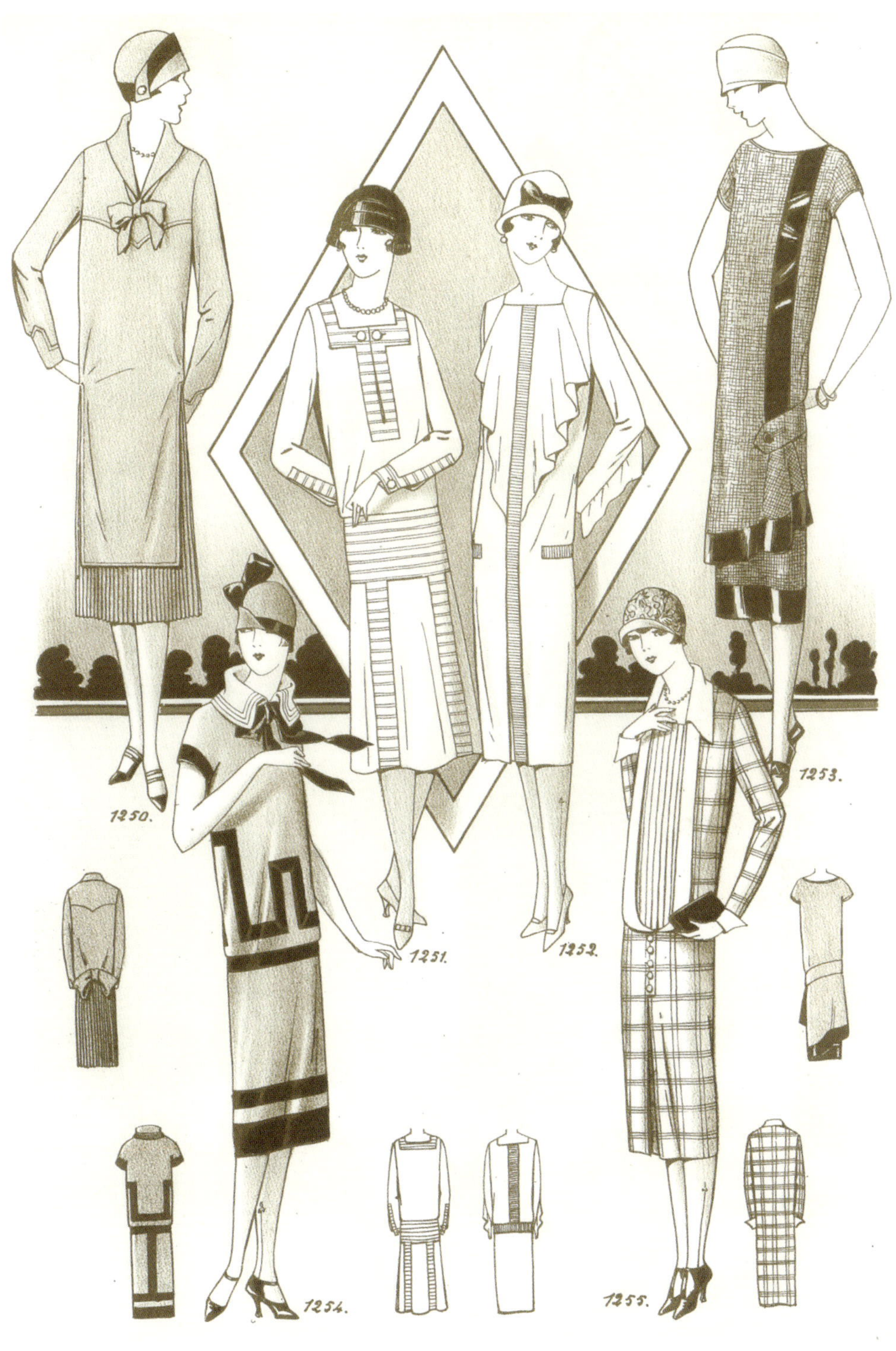

Above
Selection of day dresses.
La Femme Élégante à Paris, 1926

Spring Lines in Midseason Frocks for Matrons

For general daytime wear brown oxfords with matching woolen hose, or black oxfords with gray or beige, are very smart. Suède is good for afternoon slippers, gold and silver brocade for evening, and straps are still essential.

3411

An interesting departure from the conventional sports suit for Southern wear is this combination of gray-and-yellow-wool plaid skirt and cape with a blouse of yellow silk Jersey. Pattern sizes, small, medium, large.

(Continued from Page 73)

seaming. Pin this bias strip around a circle of the satin seven and a half inches in diameter, sew the two together on the wrong side with a fine running stitch and make a sloping seam where the ends of the bias pieces join. To join the crown and the brim, pin the seam of the crown to the center back of the brim, at the base, and sew it with long, fairly loose stitches, back-stitching now and then for greater security.

The lining may be of taffeta, China silk or the silk and cotton material much used for dress linings, and is made in exactly the same way as the crown. Last of all, soft folds should be tacked in the sides of the crown; and these can be arranged best when the hat is on.

The average woman considers the large black hat an essential part of her wardrobe. If such a hat, by the interchanging of a satin band appliquéd with flowers and a bow of lace insertion, can be worn for both sports and dress, so much the better. The photographs on page 73 prove that this transformation is possible.

Buy a buckram frame with a brim about three and a half inches wide in front and two and a half inches in back, and sides five inches wide. In order to have the lines of the hat soft and graceful, the frame should be covered with thinnest outing flannel. Double a yard of the flannel and pin it on the underside of the frame to the outer edge of

(Continued on Page 87)

3453

The popularity of the coat dress shows no sign of waning, and it is particularly good for early spring. The dress above is of navy tricotine or twill with a colorful brocade facing the collar and a belt of fancy steel plaques. Pattern comes in sizes 36 to 44.

3433

The frock above is good-looking in cloth or silk crêpe for early spring or may be made of white cotton brocade with collar and plaited sides of lawn for summer wear. The pattern may be had in sizes 16, 36 to 44.

3427

A coat dress of black tricotine trimmed with an odd bit of fur may be worn without a wrap during the early spring; and later, brocade may replace the fur. Another possibility, since Worth sponsors soft silks for coat dresses, is to use Canton crêpe or a heavy crêpe de Chine and trim it with old-fashioned inch-wide ruchings in ladders or circles. The pattern shown at the left is furnished in sizes 36 to 44.

Patterns may be secured from any store selling Home Patterns; or by mail, postage prepaid, from the Home Pattern Company, 18 East 18th Street, New York City. Dresses, 35 cents; Coats, 35 cents; Blouses or Skirts, 30 cents; Children's Patterns, 25 cents.

Left and right

"Spring Lines in Midseason Frocks for Matrons" – four spring ensembles for the more mature woman. *The Ladies' Home Journal*, 1922

Lane Bryant advertisement for "Modish Clothes with Slenderizing Lines" – the model is wearing a black beaded dress and a bicorne hat, c. 1922

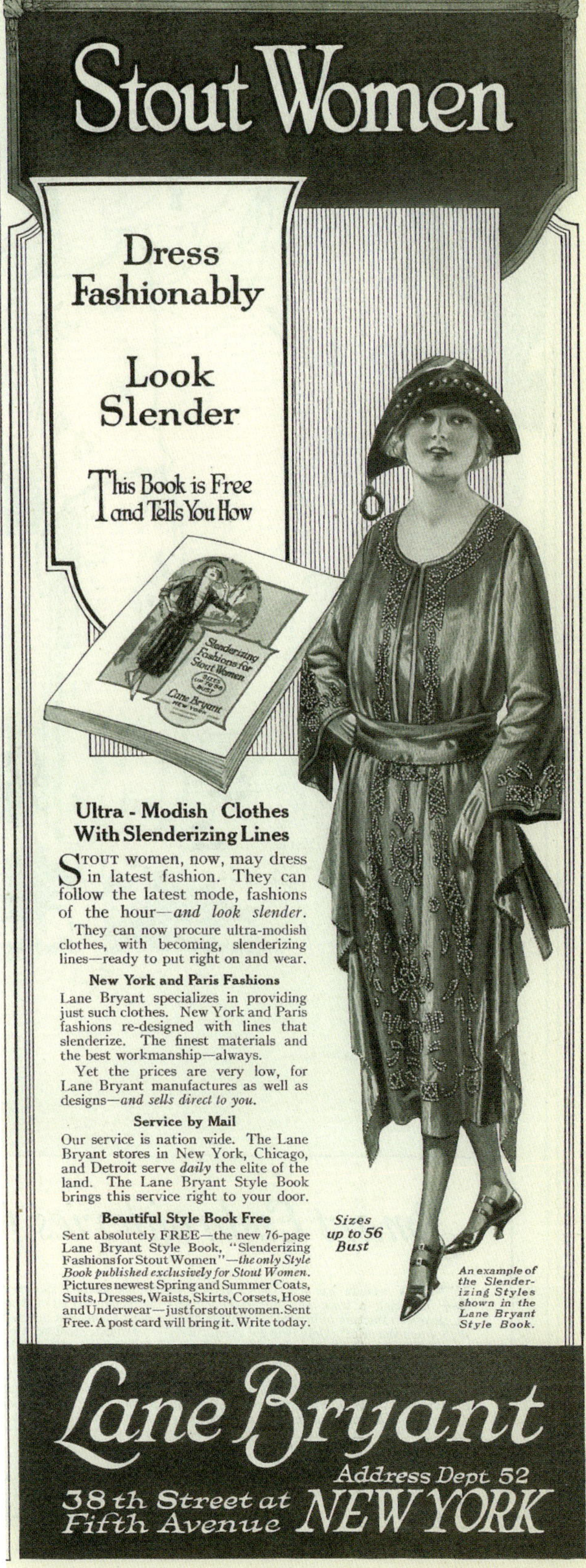

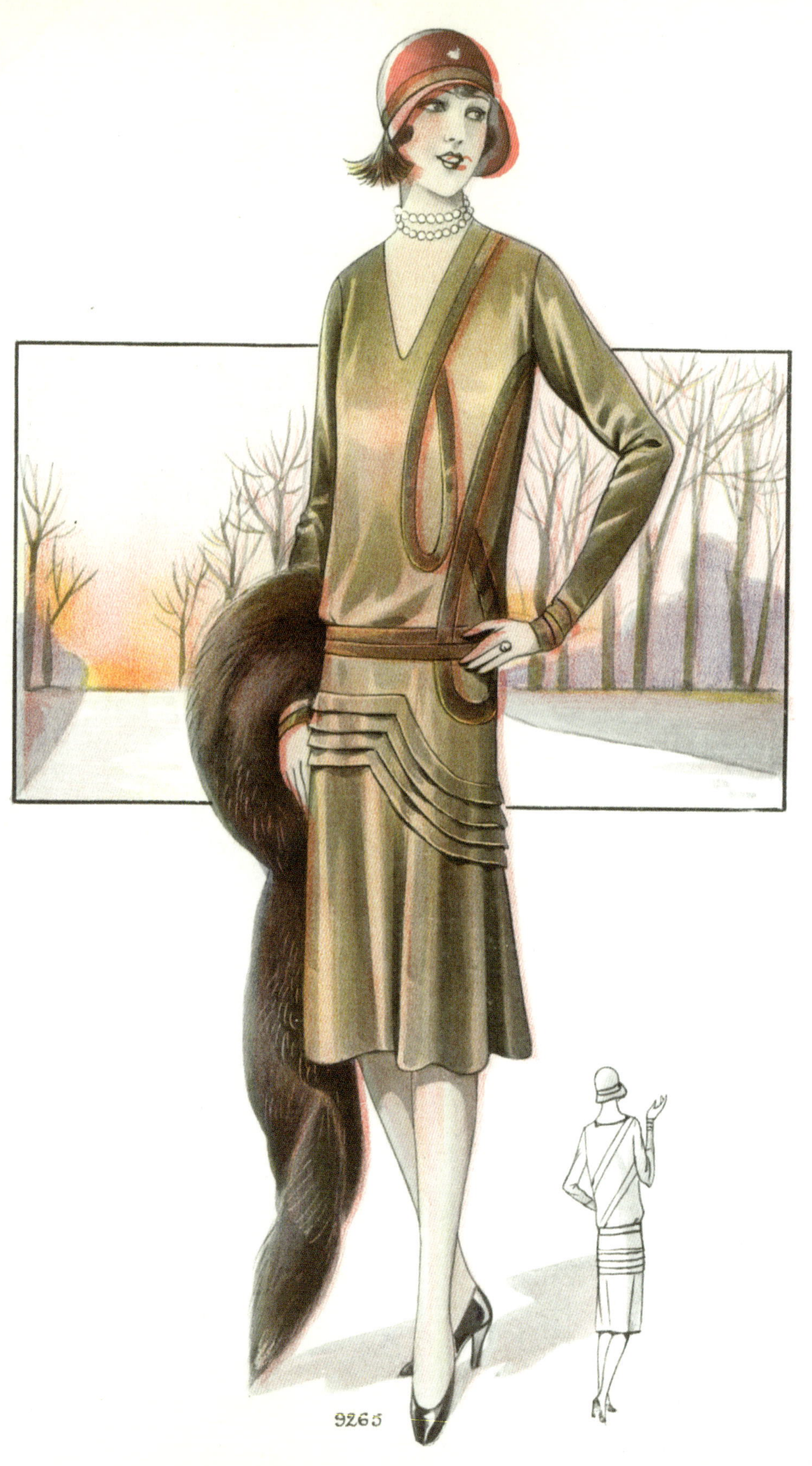
9265

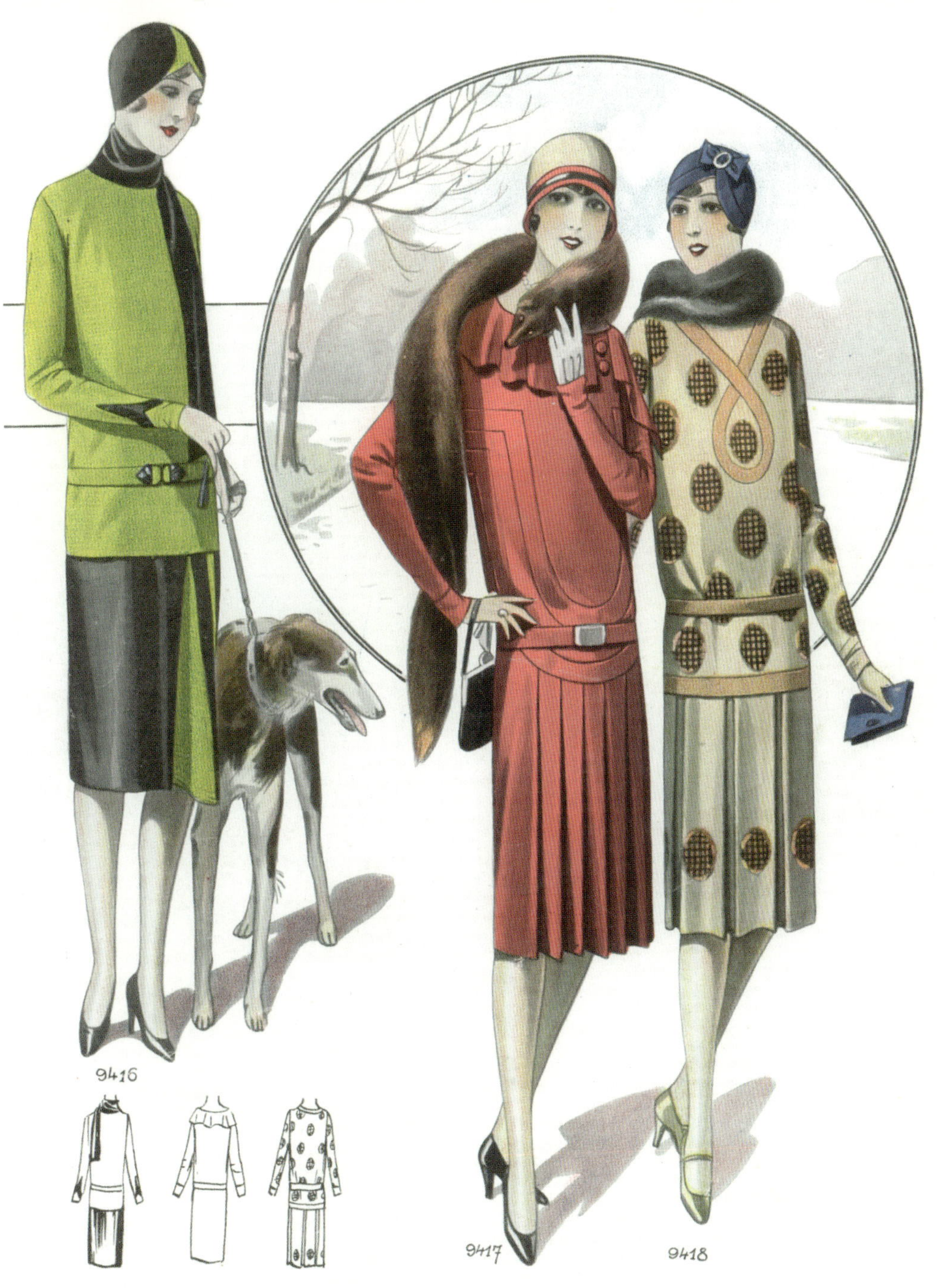

Left and above

A rust-coloured afternoon dress with tiered skirt panels accessorized with a large fox fur stole. *Paris Élégant*, c.1925

Three sportswear style ensembles. *Paris Élégant*, c.1925

Right
Mademoiselle 'Coco' Chanel wearing a jersey suit in Biarritz, France, 1928

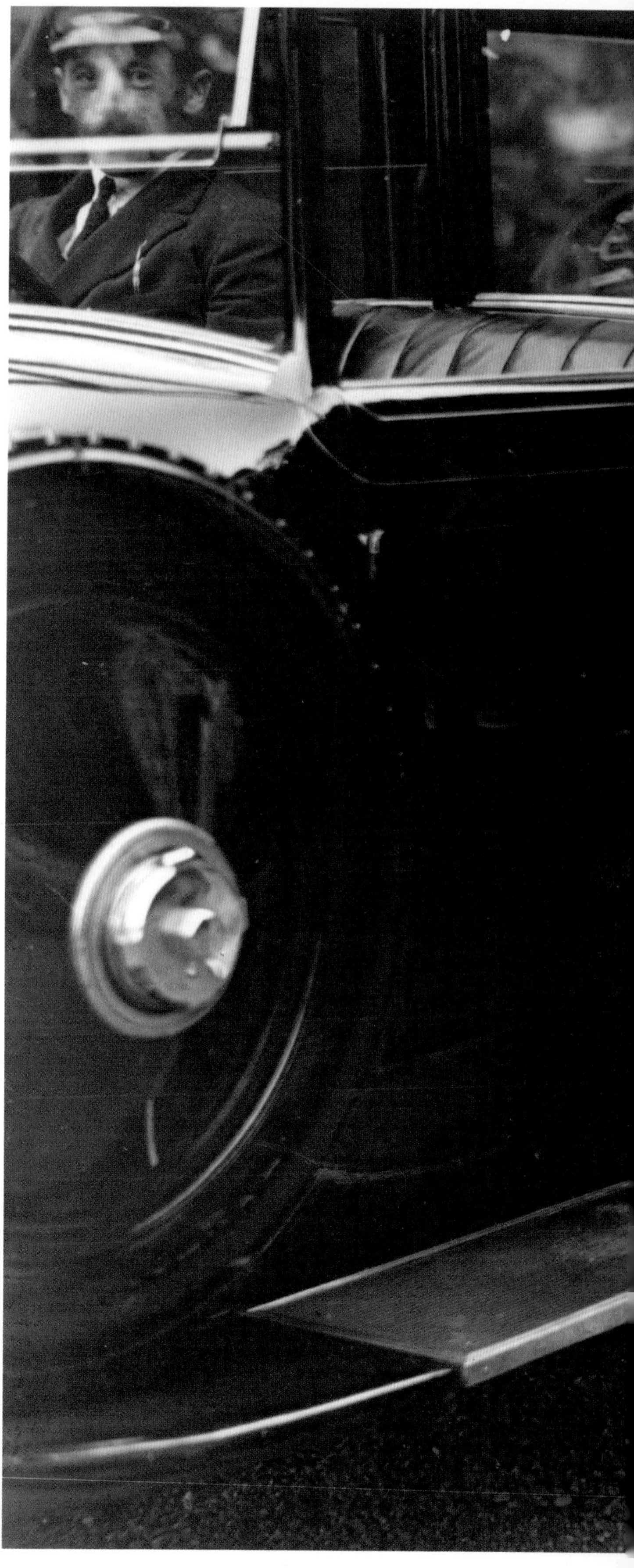

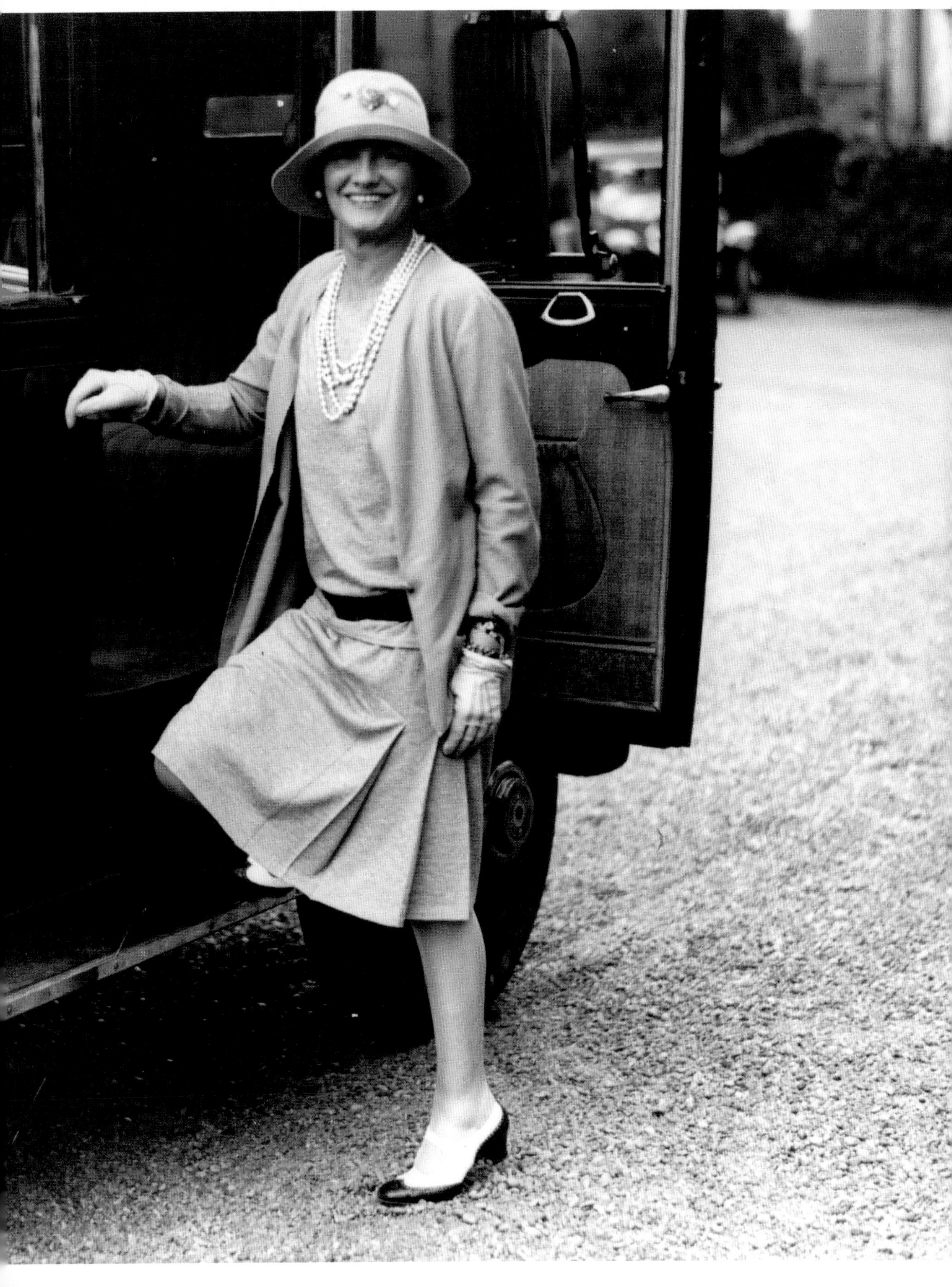

Right
A taffeta dress with pleated side panel and extensive satin and lace trimmings. Shown at the Auteuil races. 1923

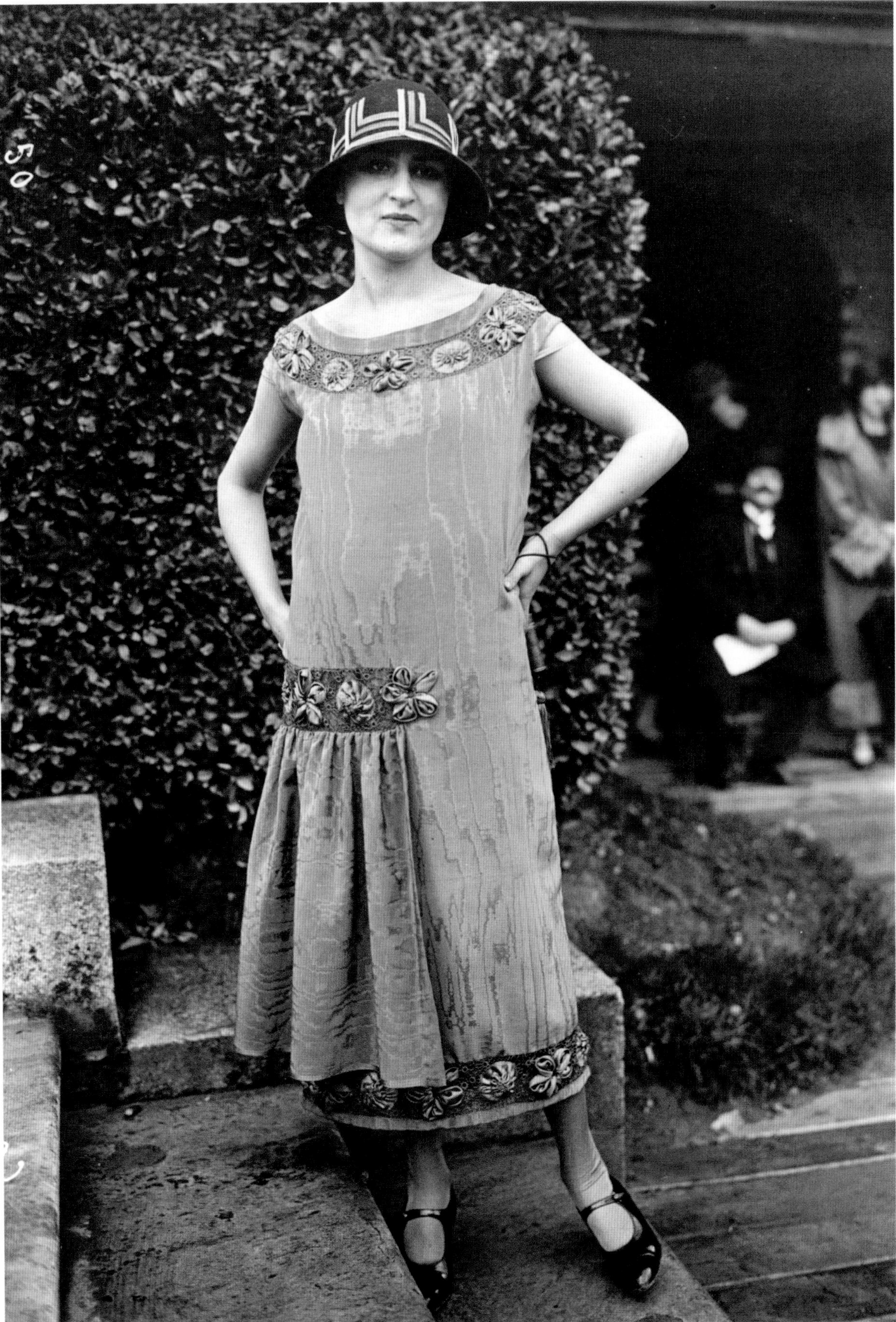

Below

Five afternoon dresses by Drecoll, Elise Poret and Martial et Armand. *La Femme Chic*, c.1921

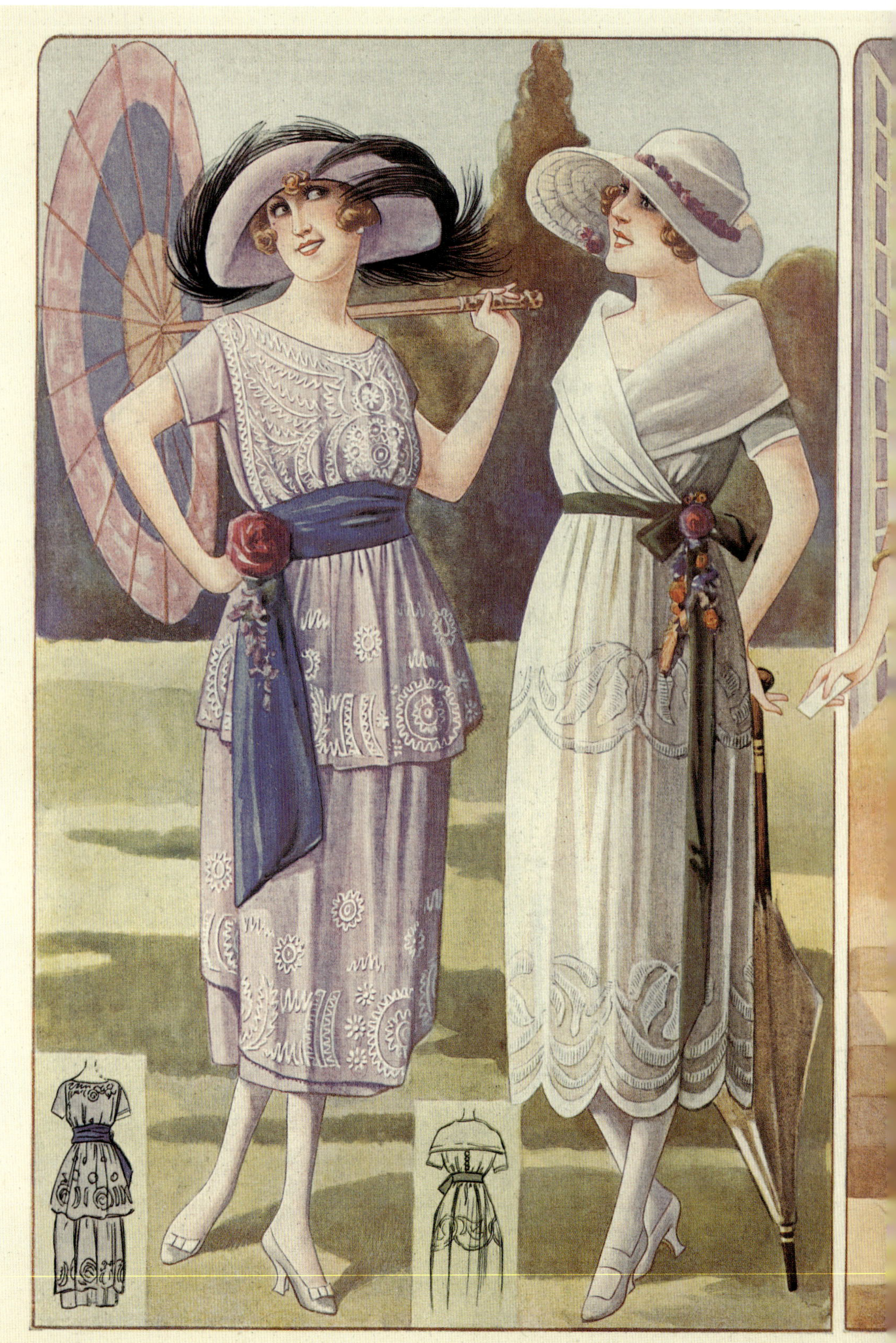

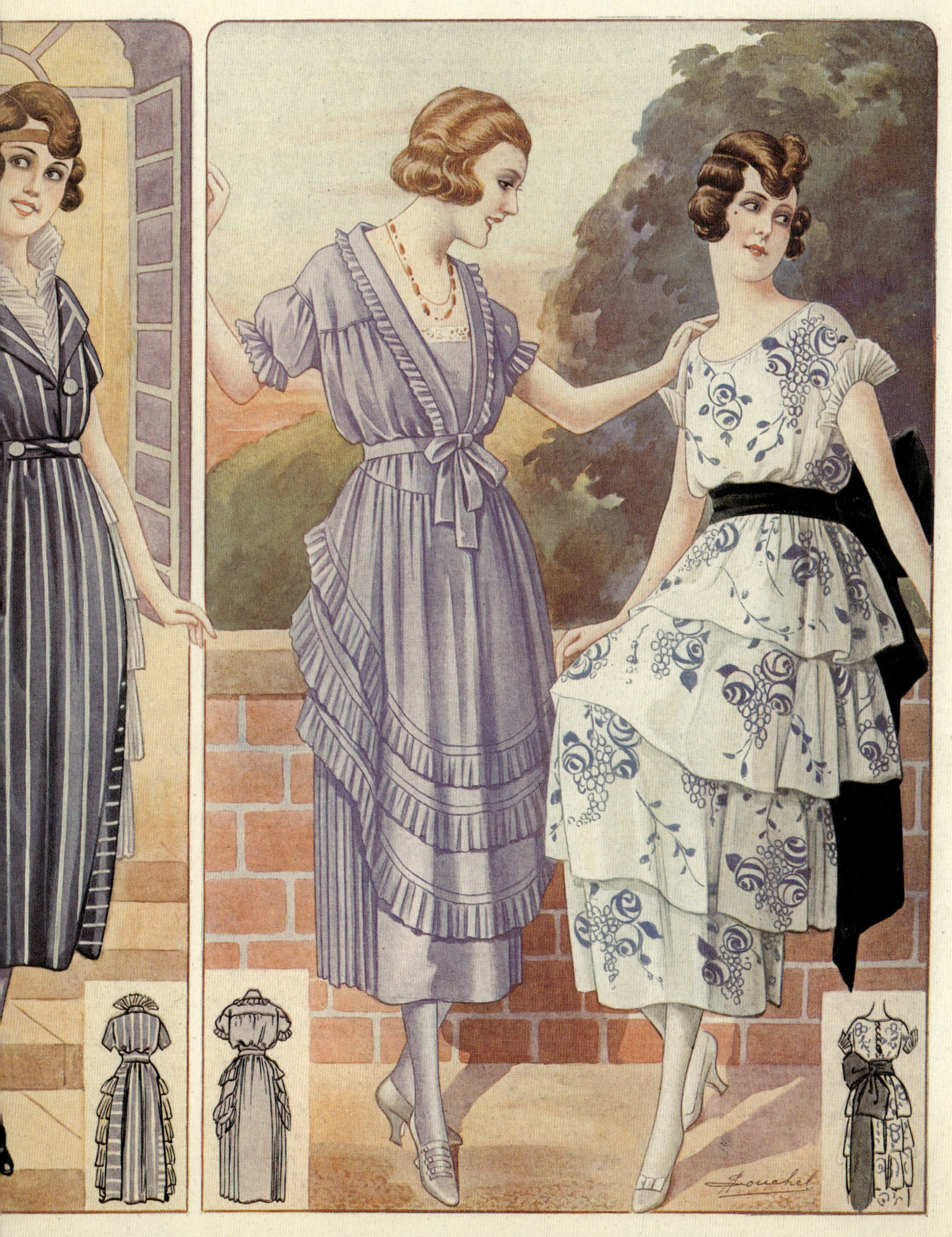

Right

Two walking outfits and an afternoon dress. Au Louvre catalogue, 1925

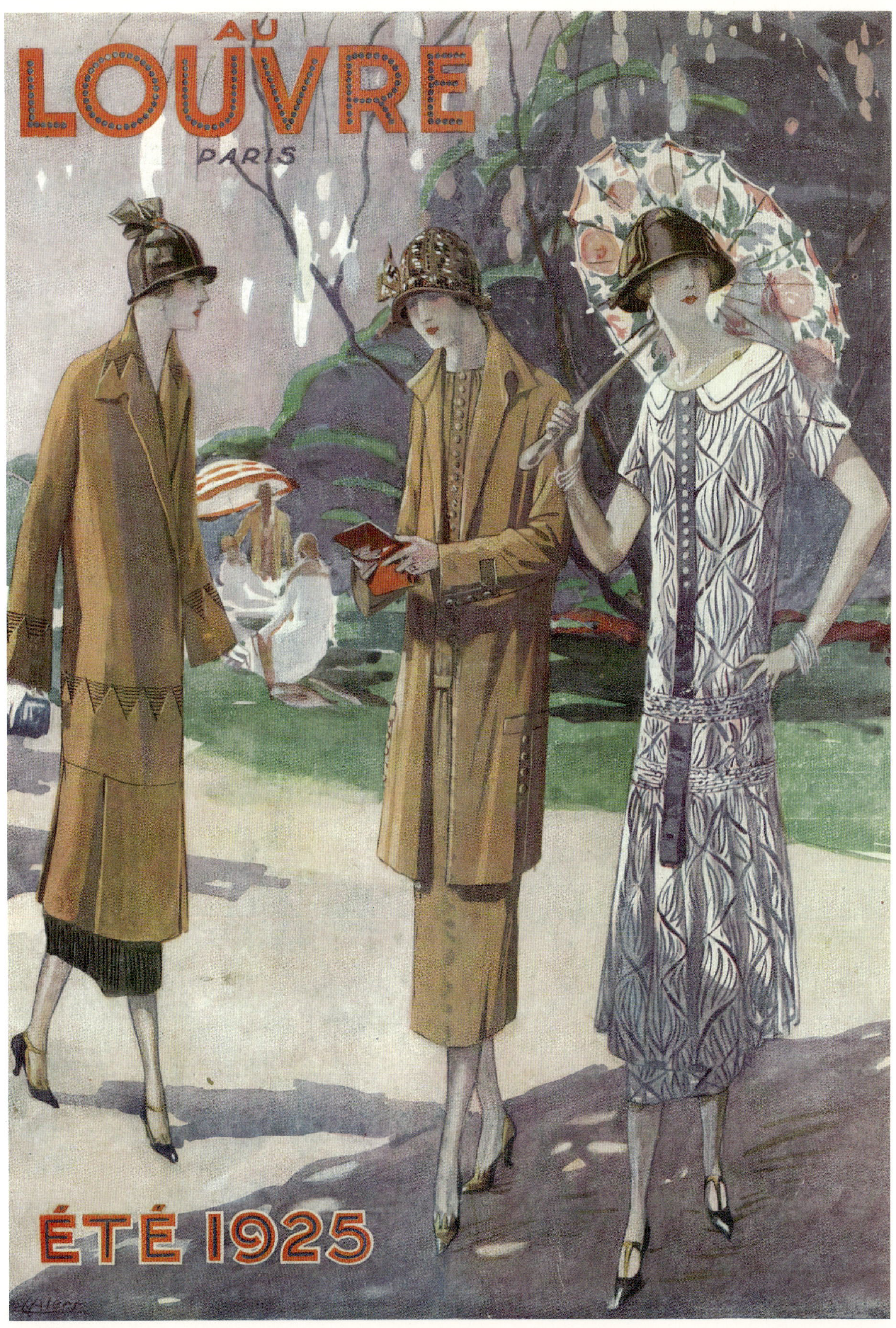
AU
LOUVRE
PARIS
ÉTÉ 1925

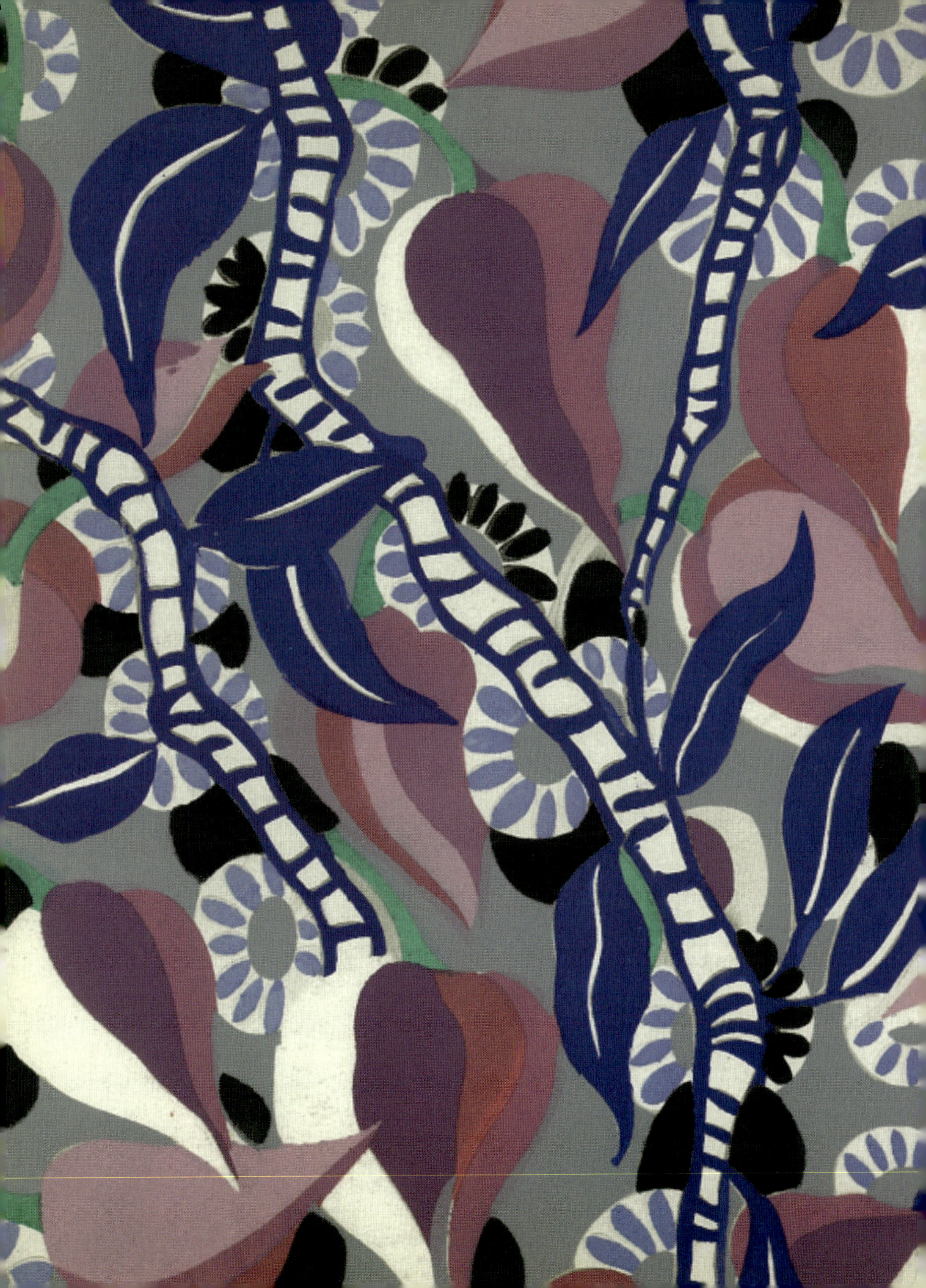

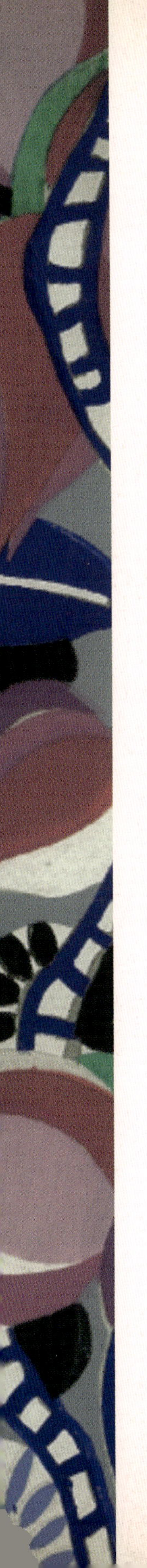

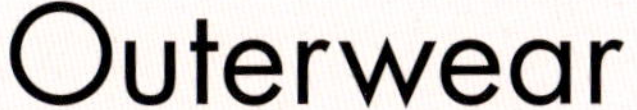

Outerwear

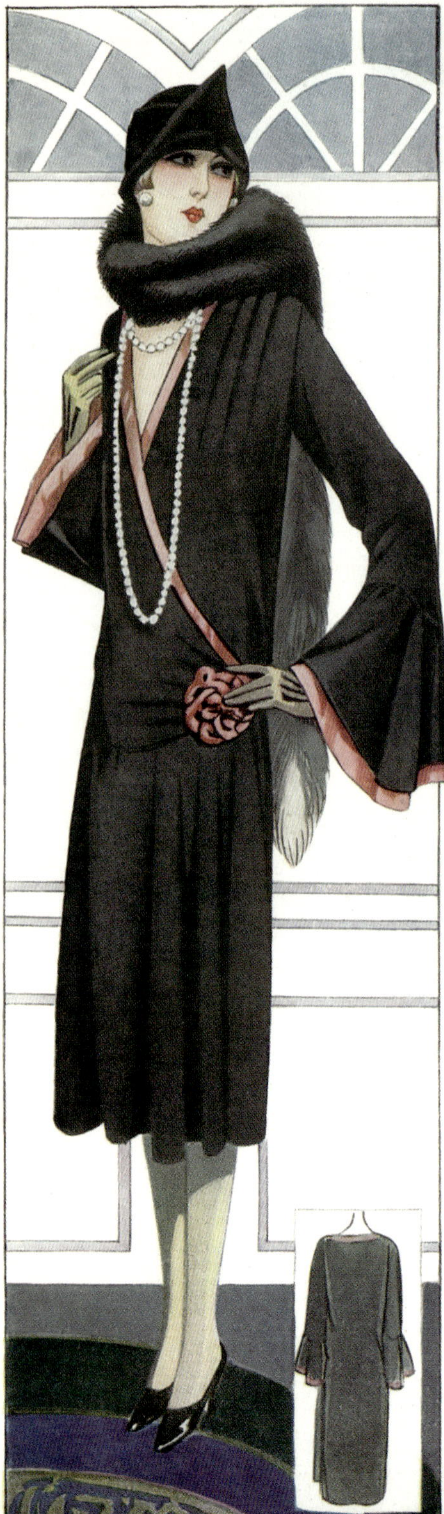

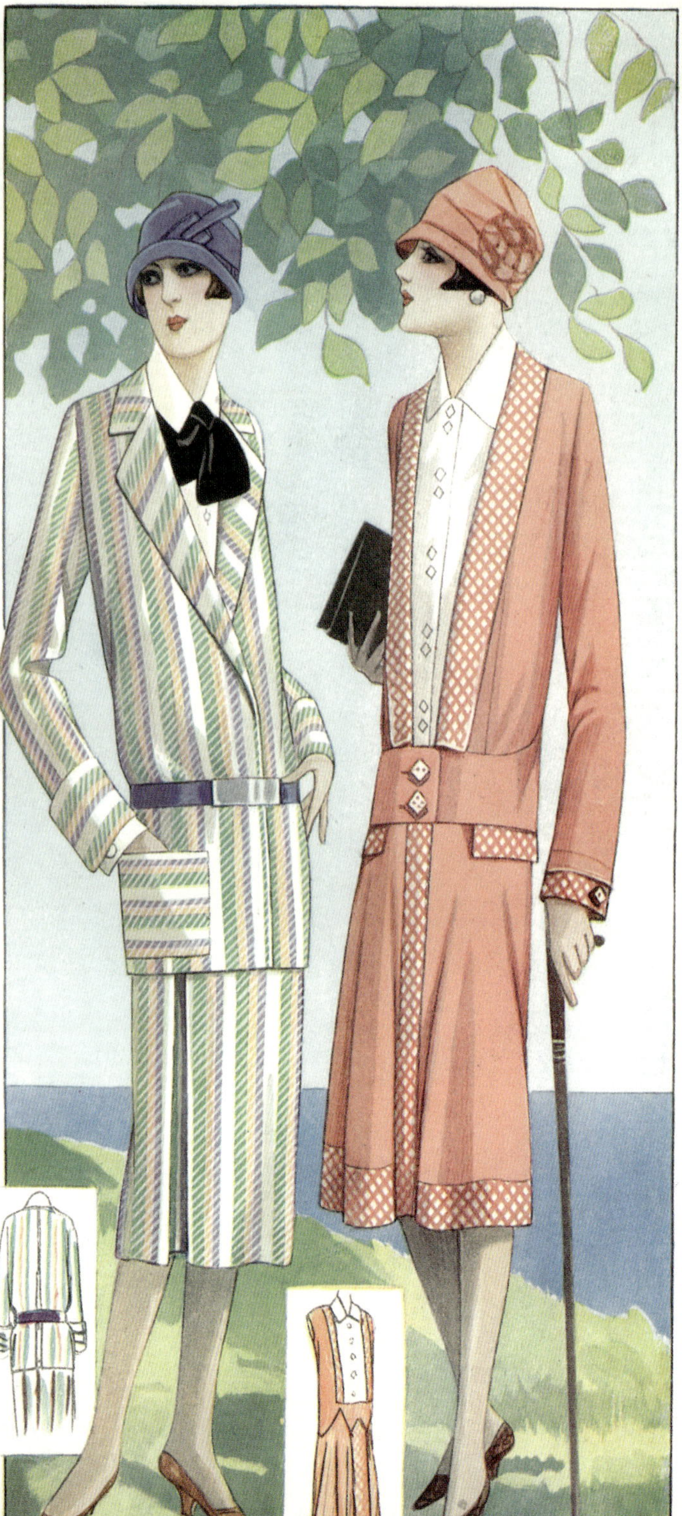

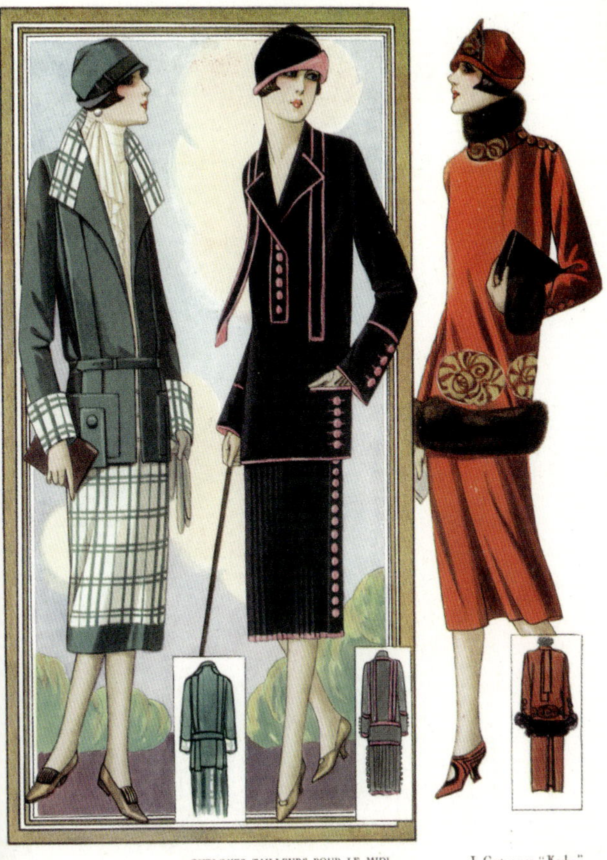

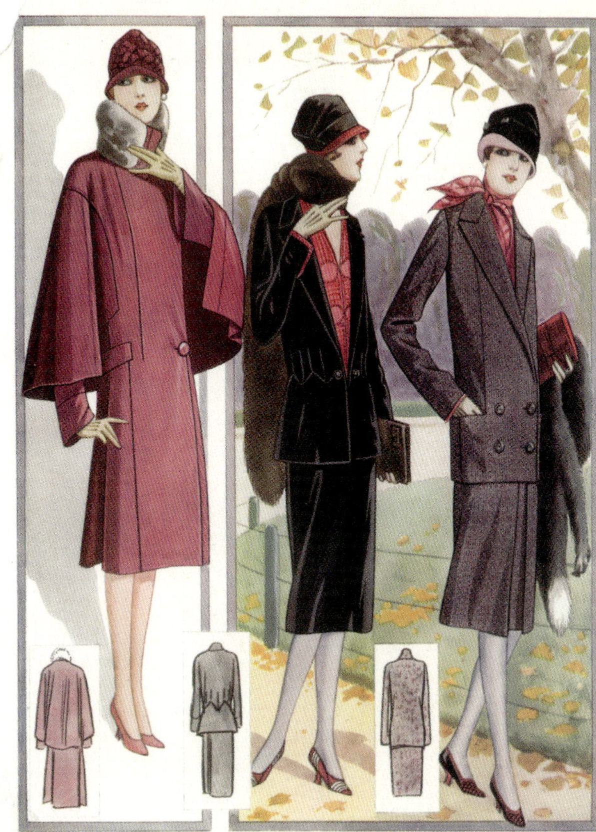

Left

Wrap dress by Alice Bernard, a striped summer suit in "Pékins Buranic" fabric, and a coral summer suit by Francis. *La Femme Chic*, 1926

Above Left and right

Two day ensembles and a Kasha ensemble trimmed with fur. *La Femme Chic*, 1926

Coat and matching hat in "Crêpelliver" by Francis and two skirt suits by Alice Bernard. *La Femme Chic*, 1926

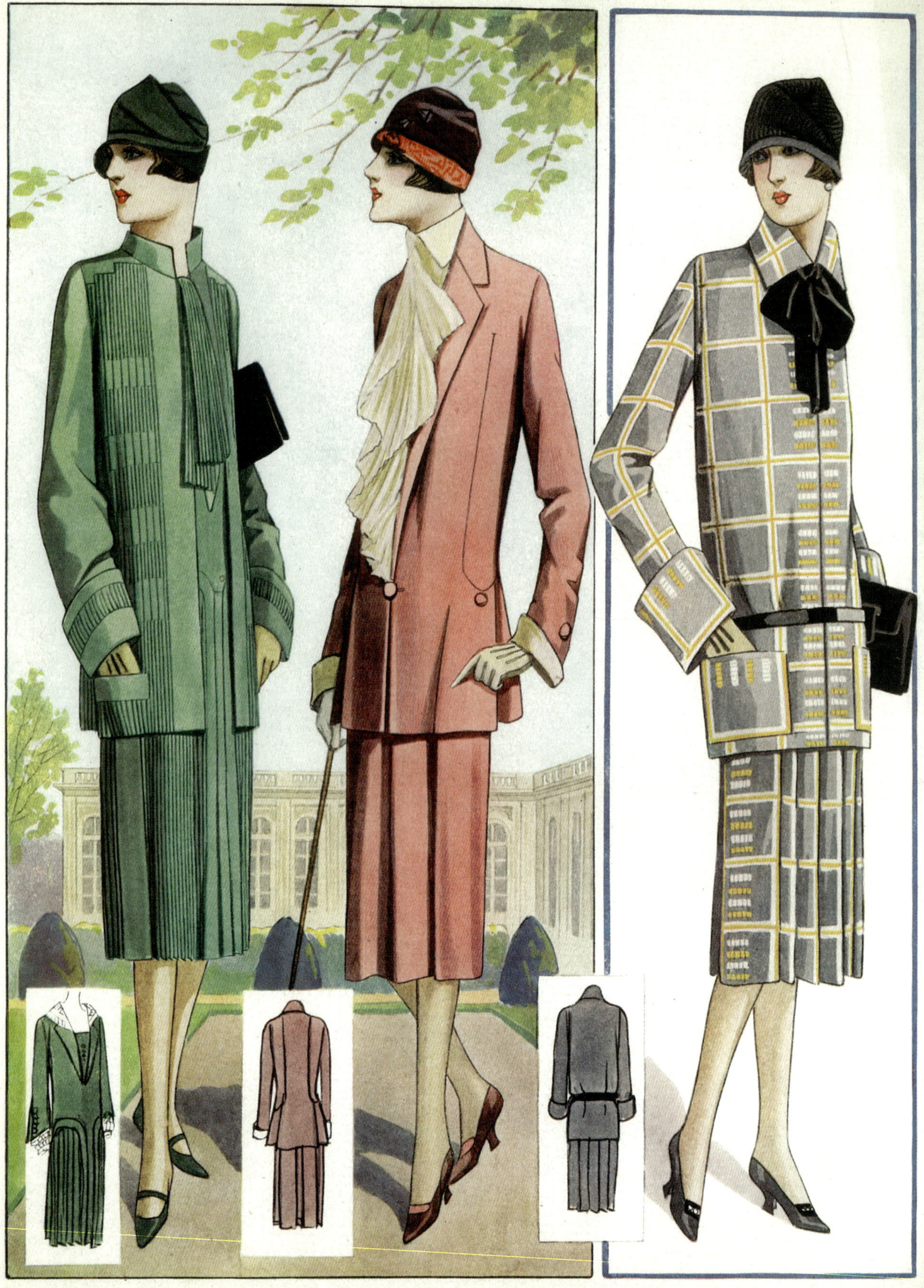

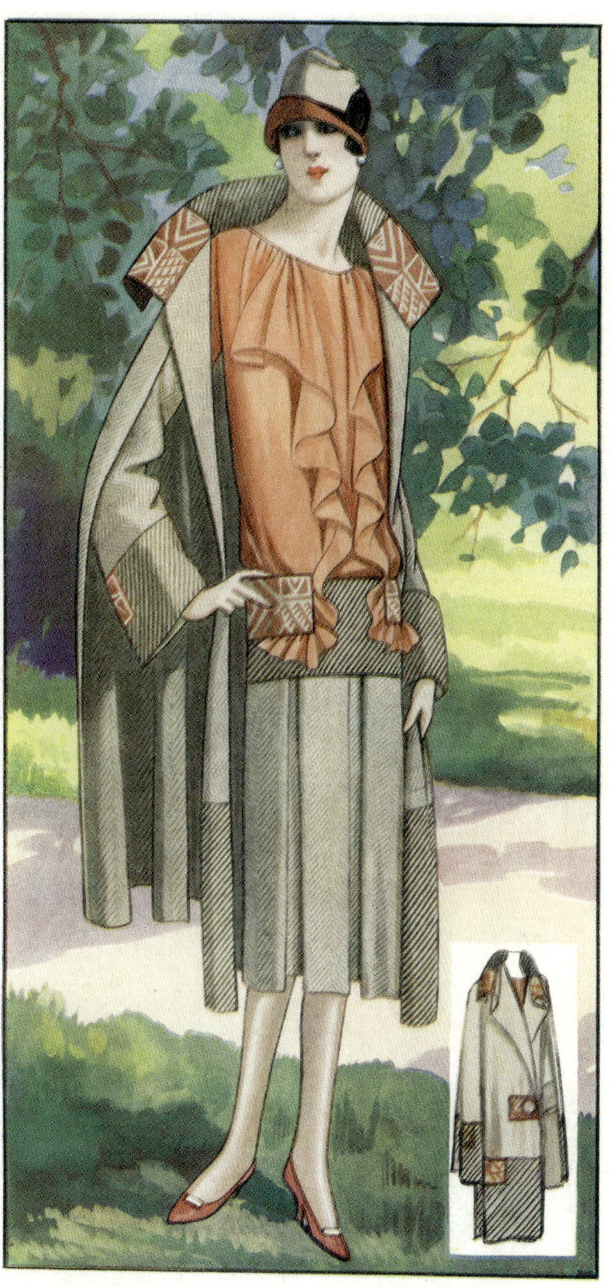

Left and above

Two summer ensembles by Bernard and an ensemble in checked Kasha. *La Femme Chic*, 1926

Driving ensemble in "Diafil Crauté". *La Femme Chic*, 1926

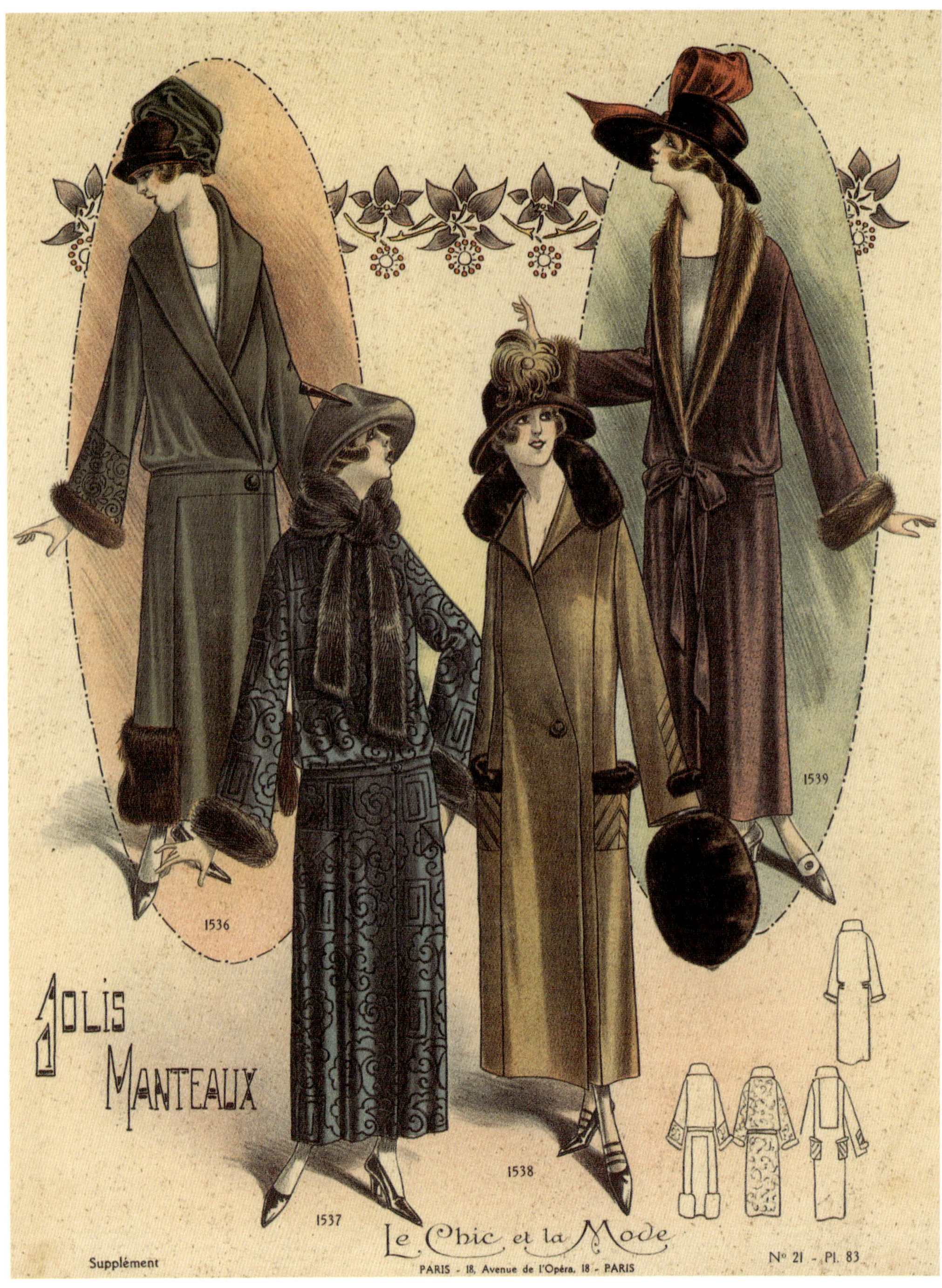

Above and right

Four fur-trimmed coats. *Le Chic et la Mode*, c.1923

Four afternoon coats with wide collars. *Le Chic et la Mode*, 1923

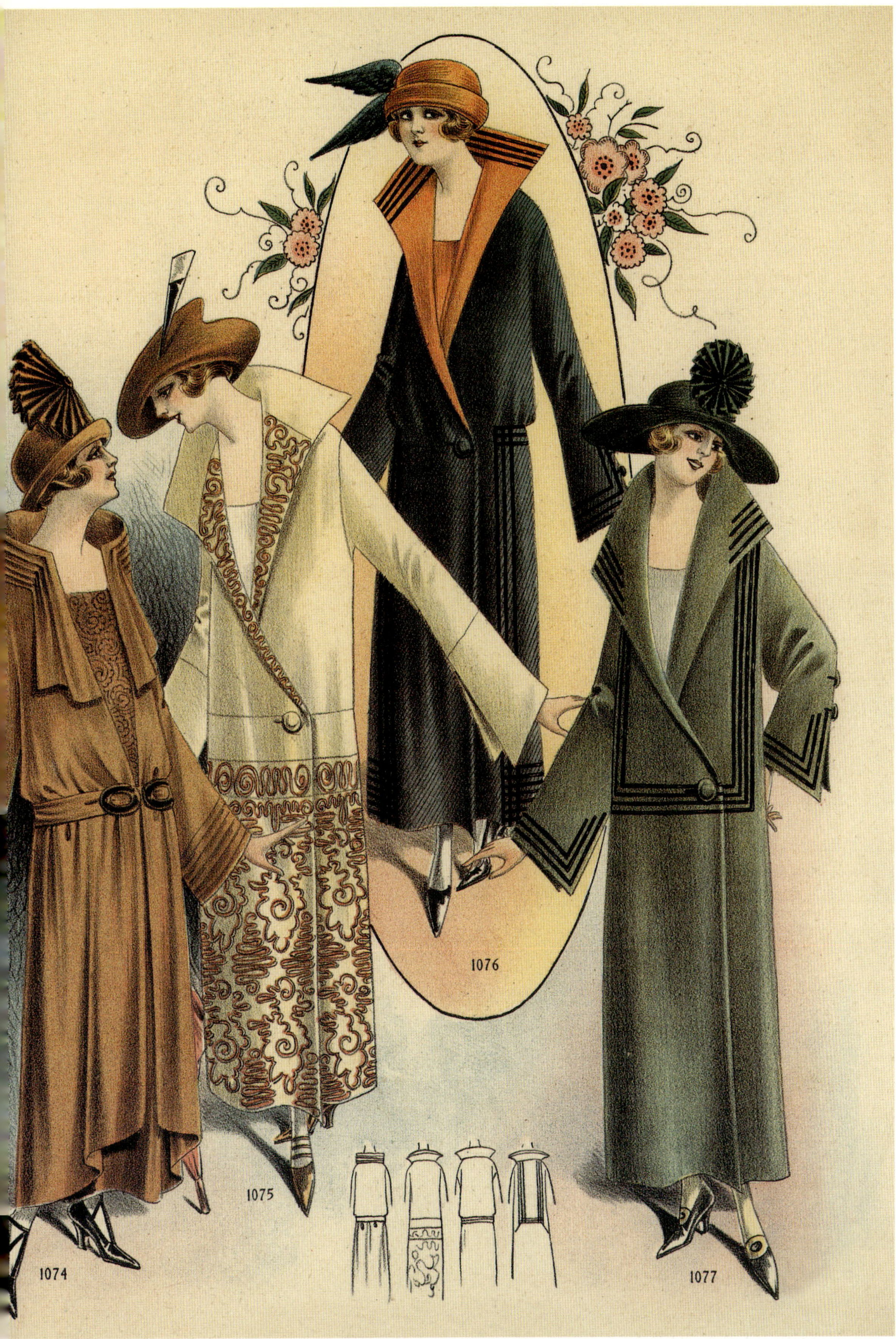
1076
1075
1074
1077

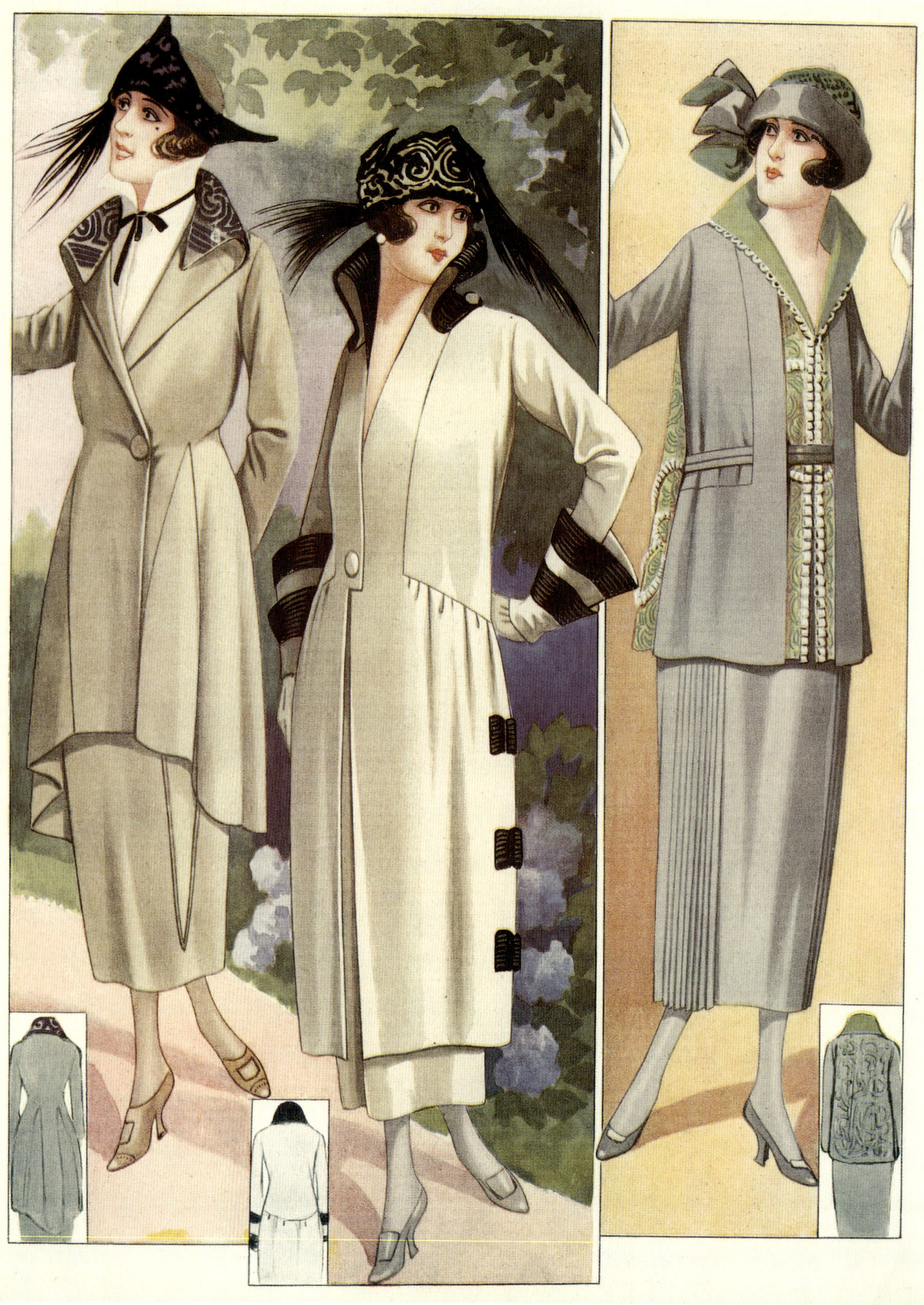

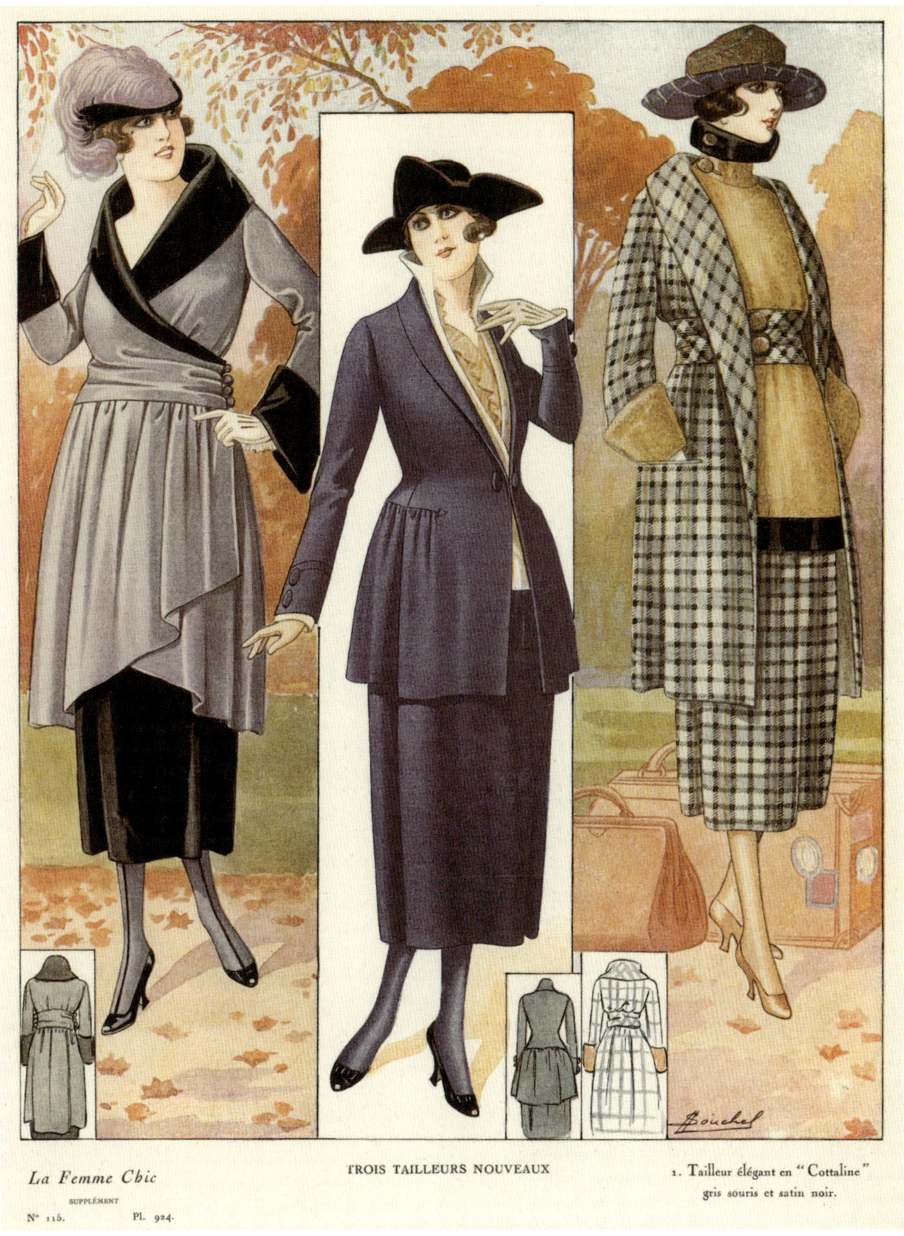

Left and above

Three elegant skirt suits. *La Femme Chic*, c.1923

Mouse grey "cottaline" and black satin skirt suit and two other tailored skirt suits. *La Femme Chic*, c.1923

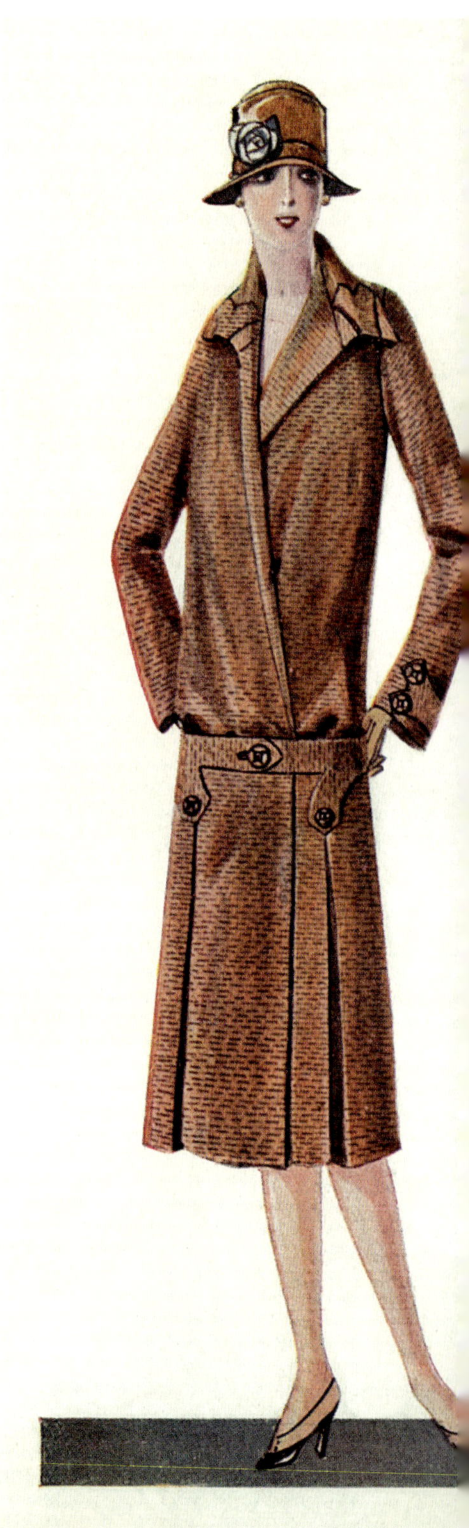

Right
Four city coats by Maison Gerda.
Maison Gerda catalogue, c.1925

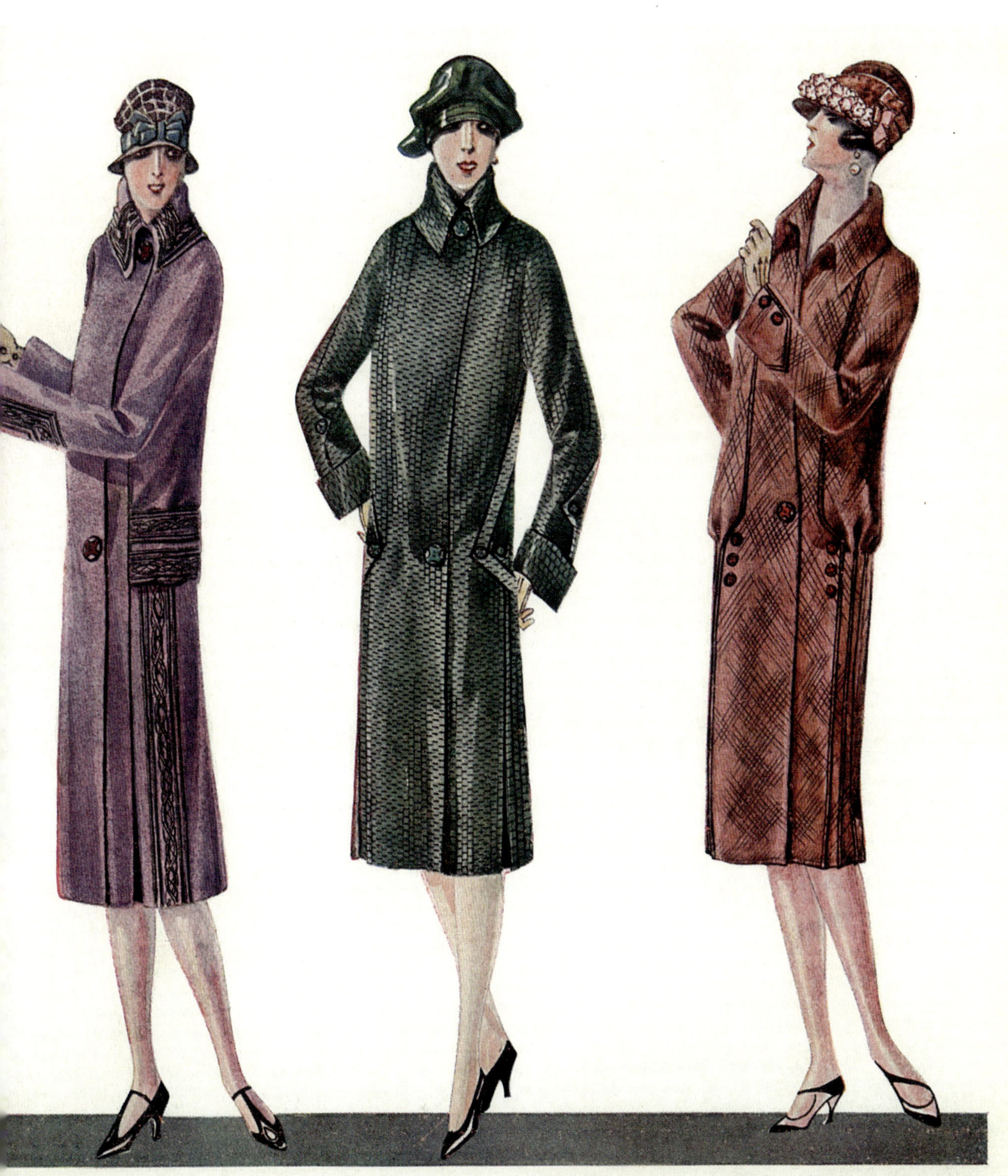

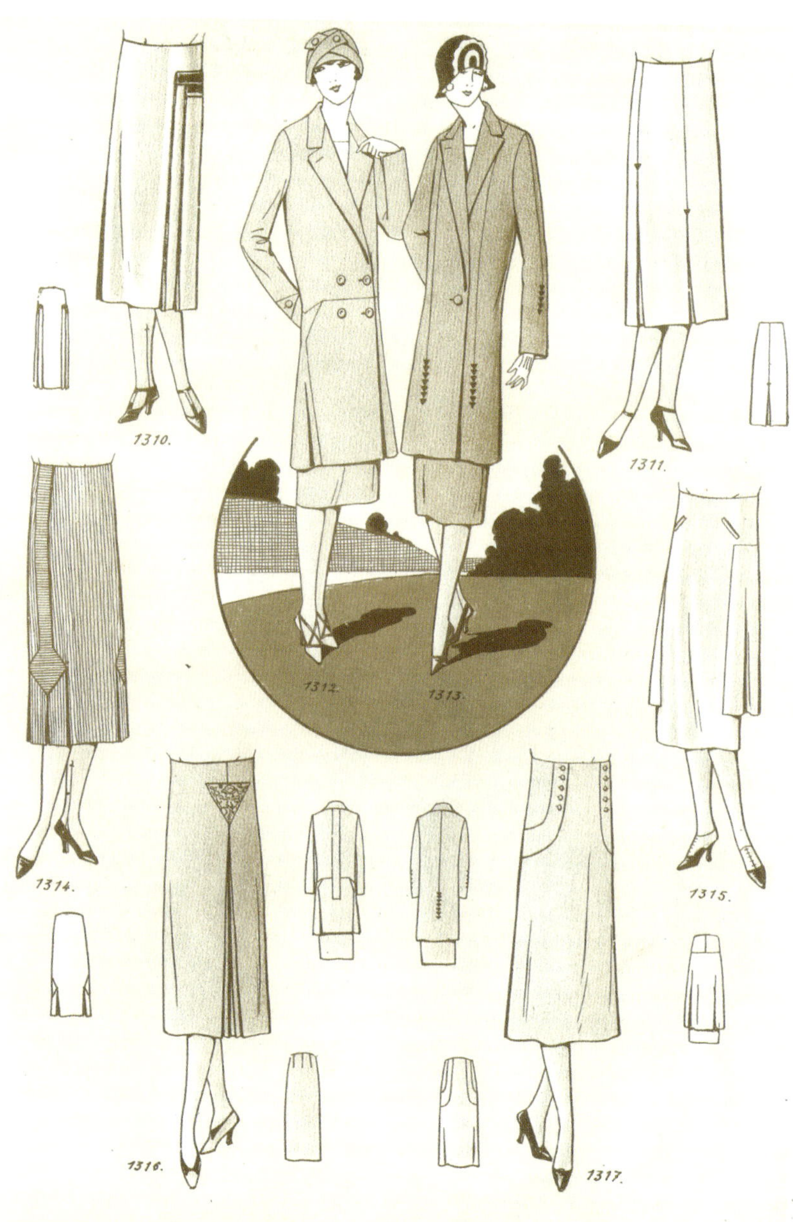

Above and right
Various designs for skirts.
La Femme Élégante à Paris, 1926

Various designs for skirts.
La Femme Élégante à Paris, 1926

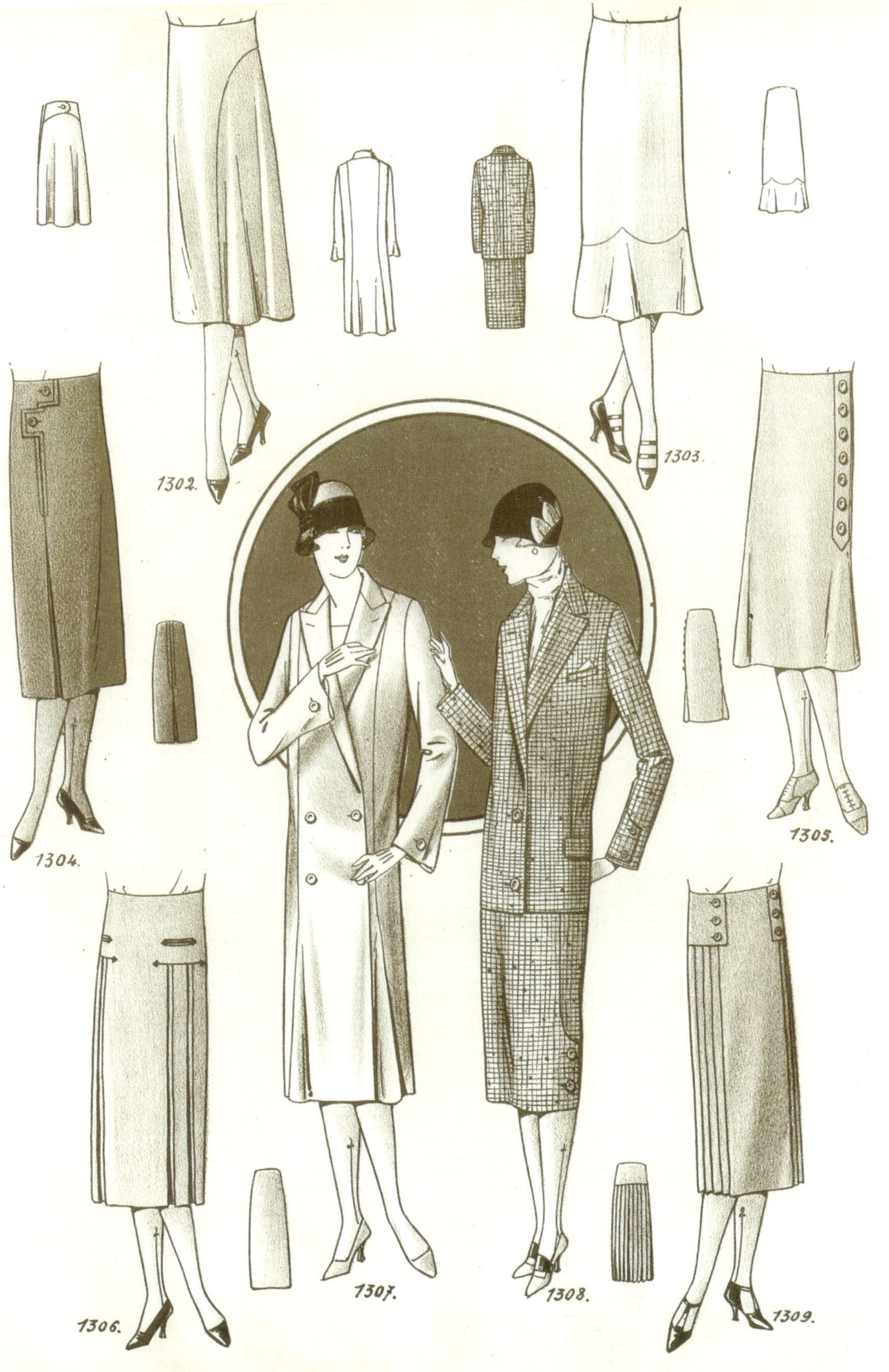
1302.
1303.
1304.
1305.
1306.
1307.
1308.
1309.

Below
Two designs for skirt suits.
La Femme Élégante à Paris, 1926

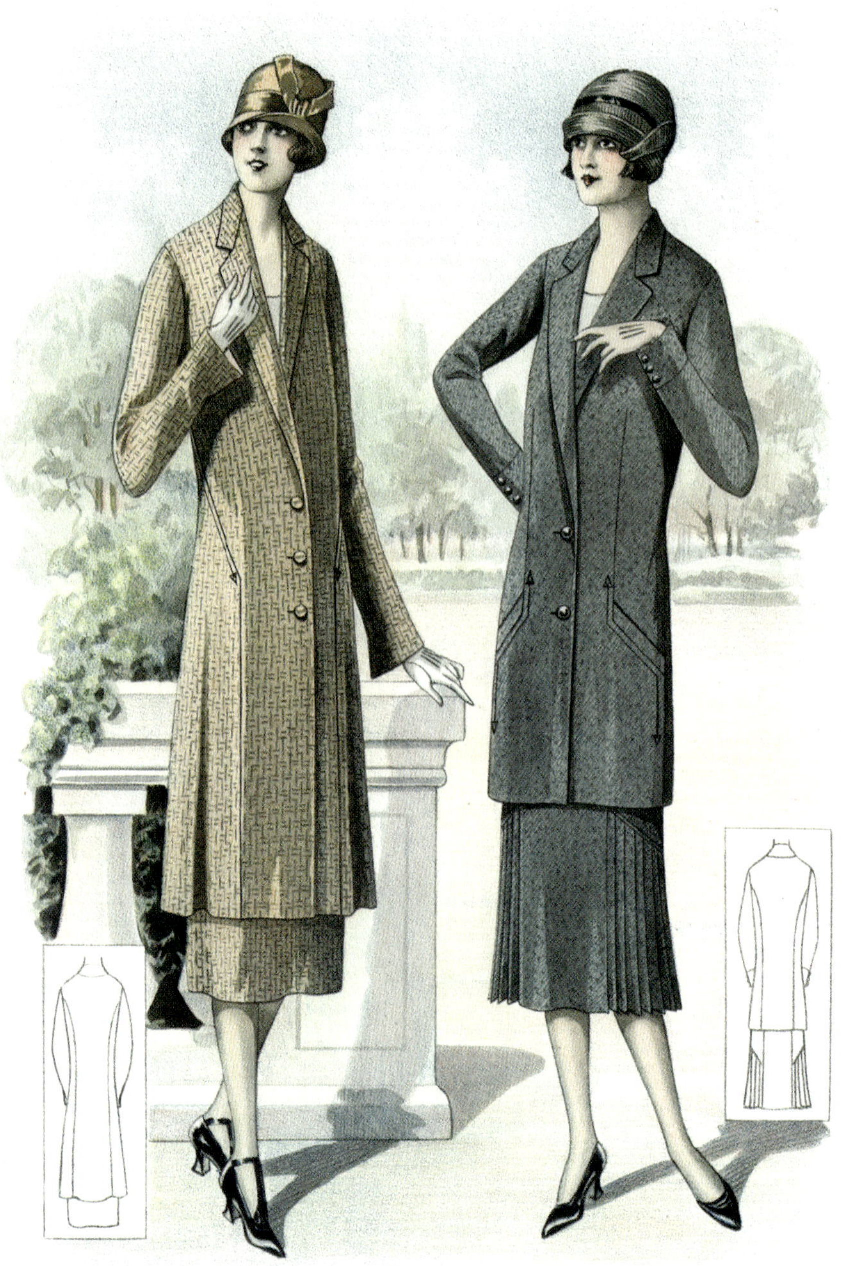

Below
Two designs for skirt suits. The right-hand model is a tuxedo suit worn with a bow tie. *La Femme Élégante à Paris*, 1926

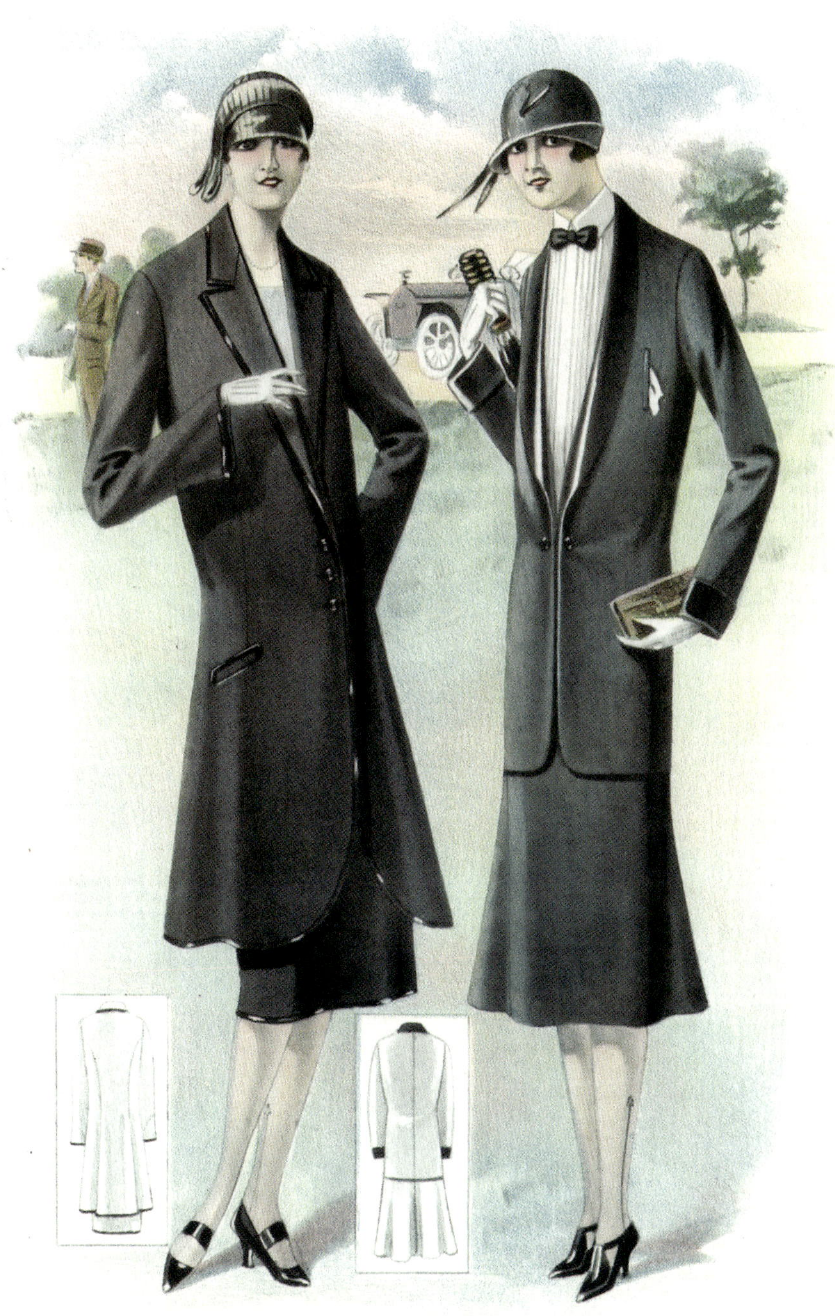

1276 1277

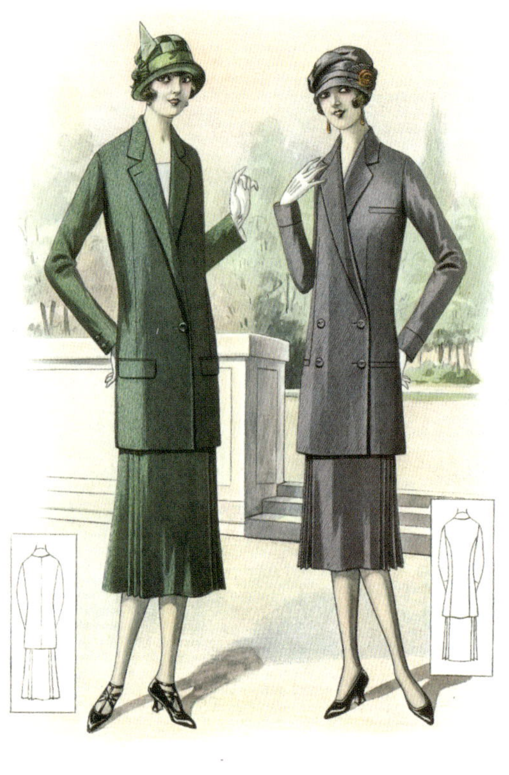

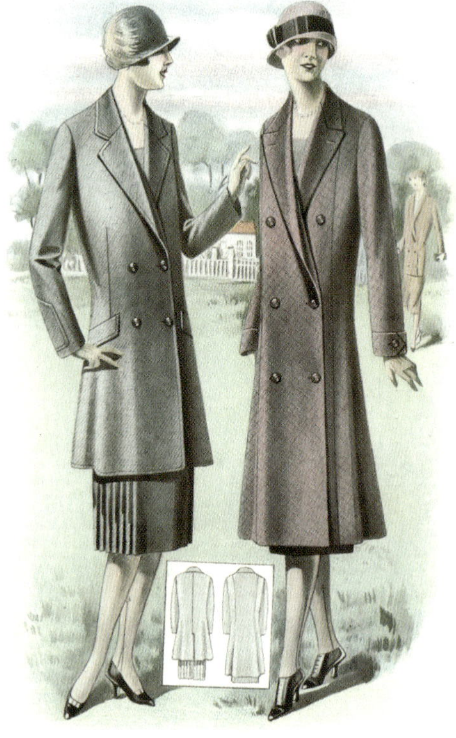

Above left and right
Two designs for skirt suits.
La Femme Élégante à Paris, 1926

Two designs for skirt suits.
La Femme Élégante à Paris, 1926

Right
Two woollen walking suits with masculine-style jackets. *La Femme Élégante à Paris*, 1926

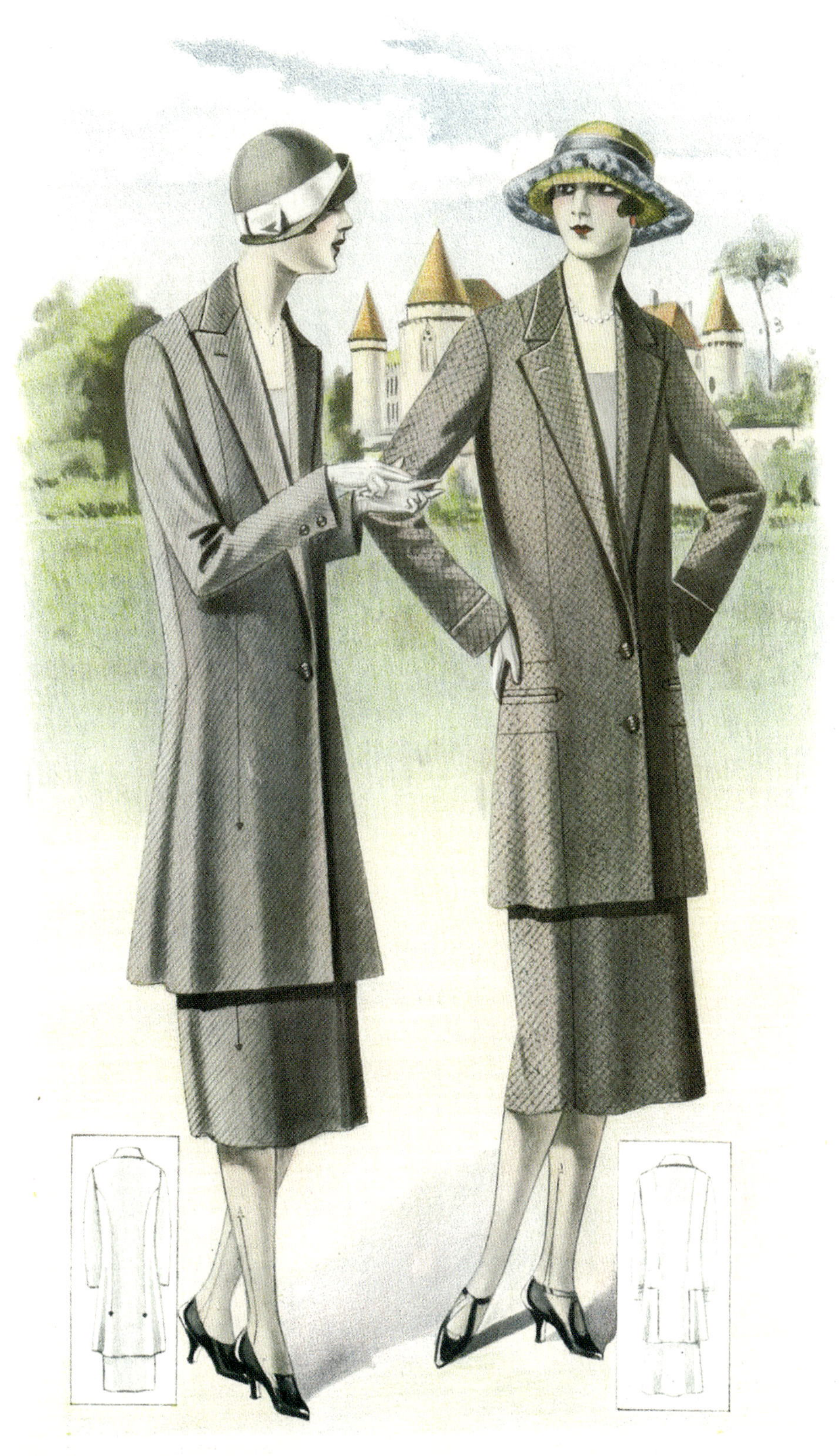

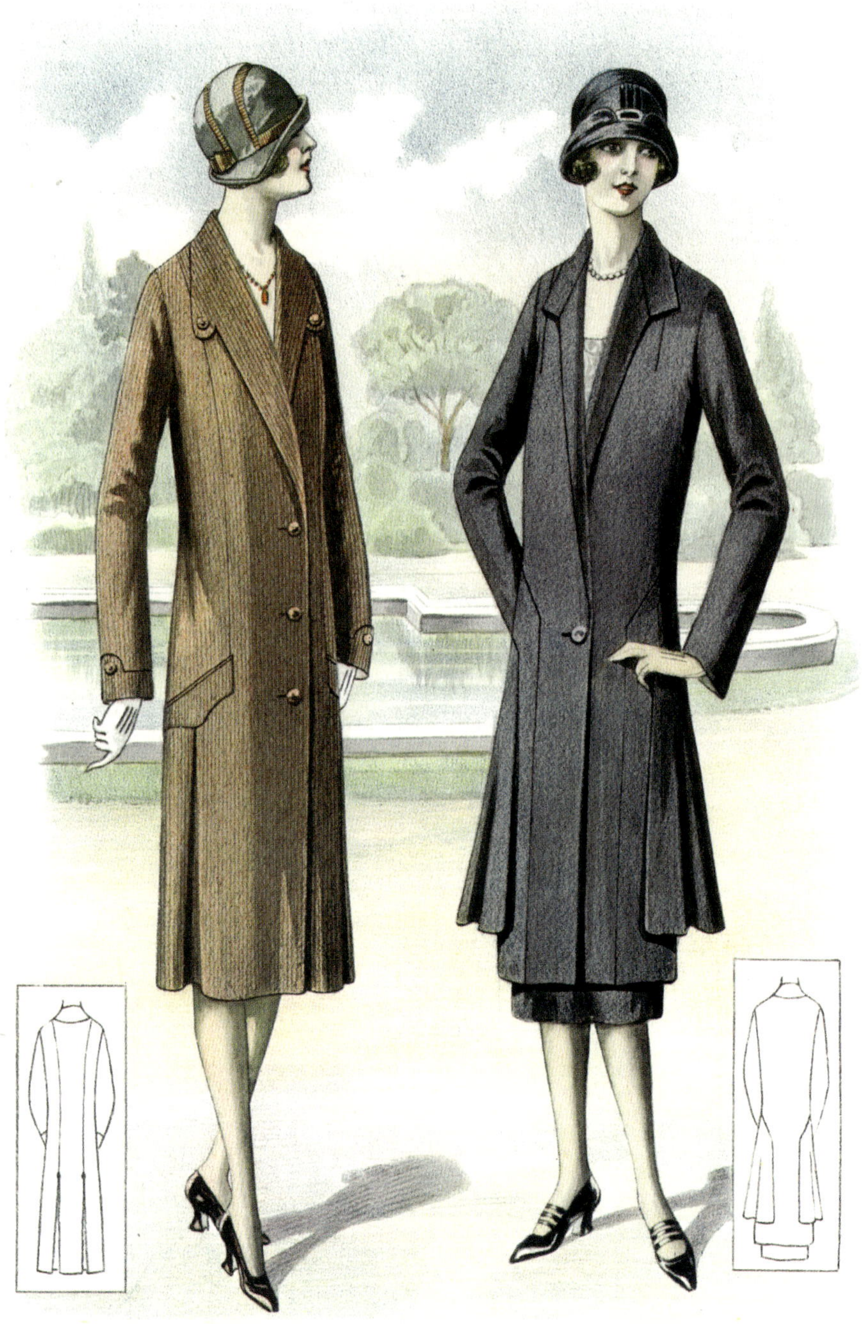

1286 1287

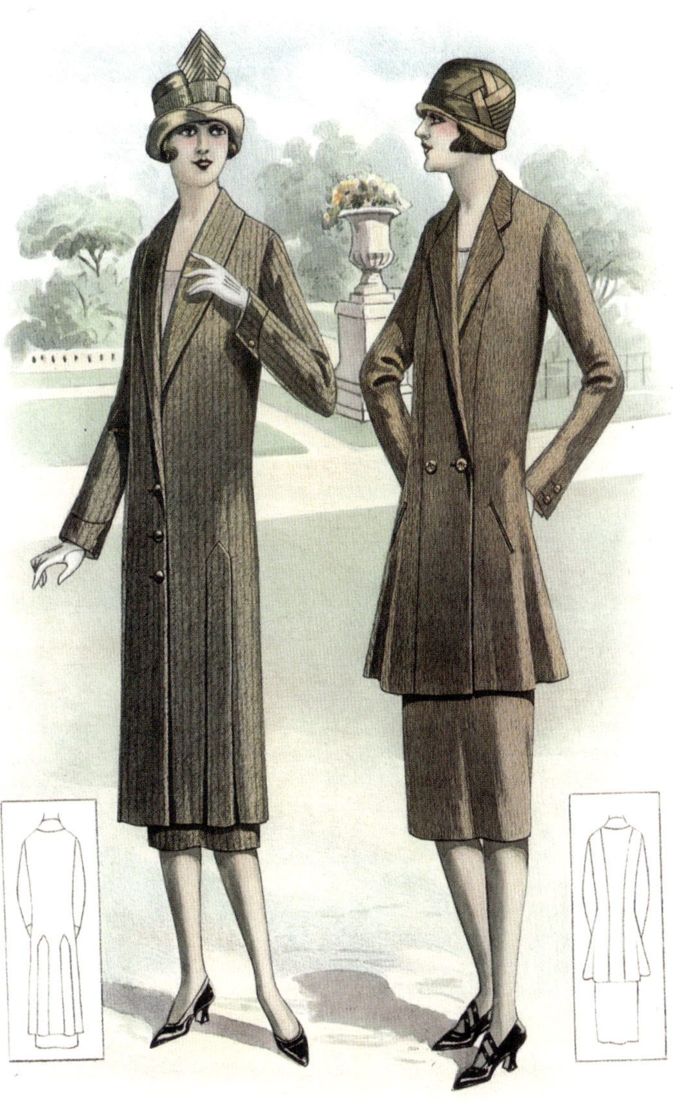

1282 1283

Left and above

A design for a coat and a skirt suit.
La Femme Élégante à Paris, 1926

Two designs for skirt suits.
La Femme Élégante à Paris, 1926

Below

Two designs for skirt suits.
La Femme Élégante à Paris, 1926

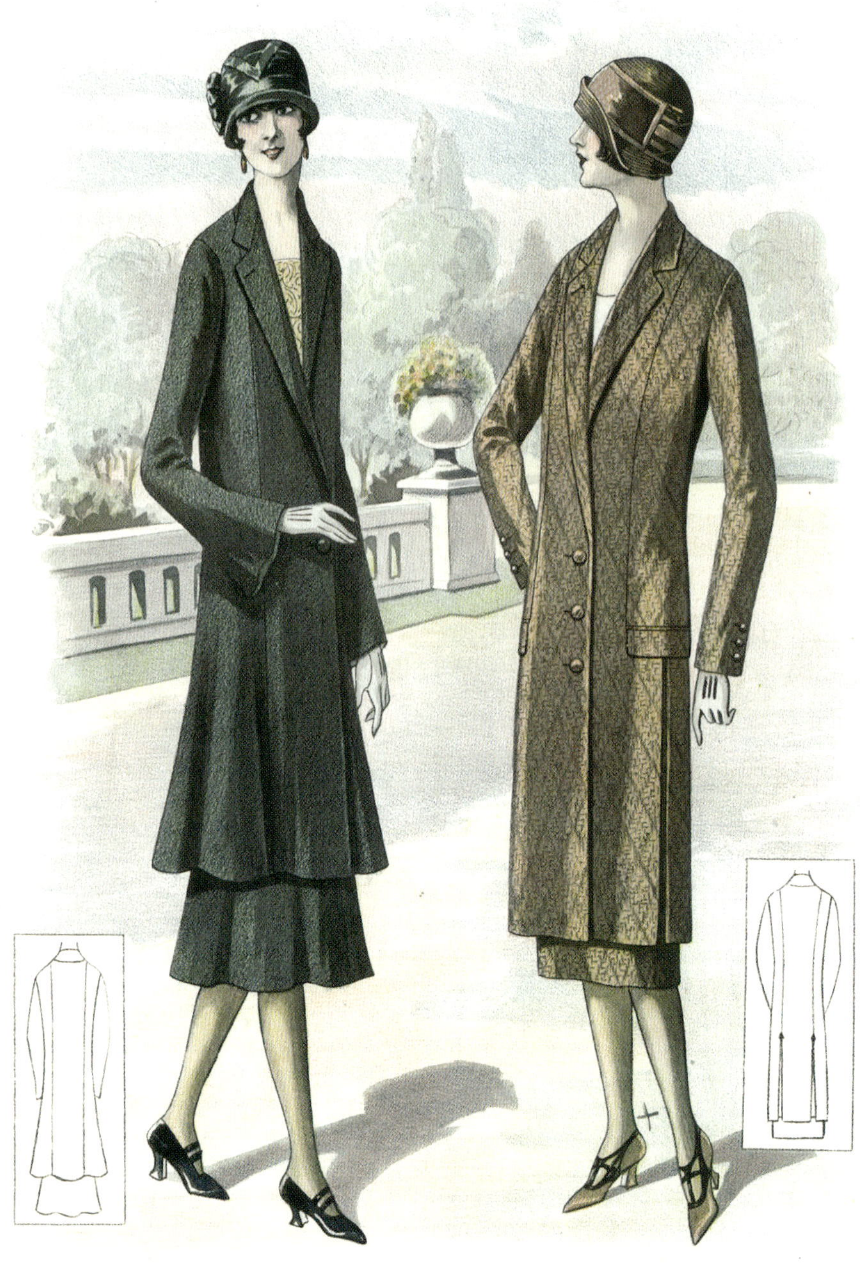

1270 1271

Below
A checked walking suit and a green walking suit with diamond shaped button detailing. *La Femme Élégante à Paris*, 1926

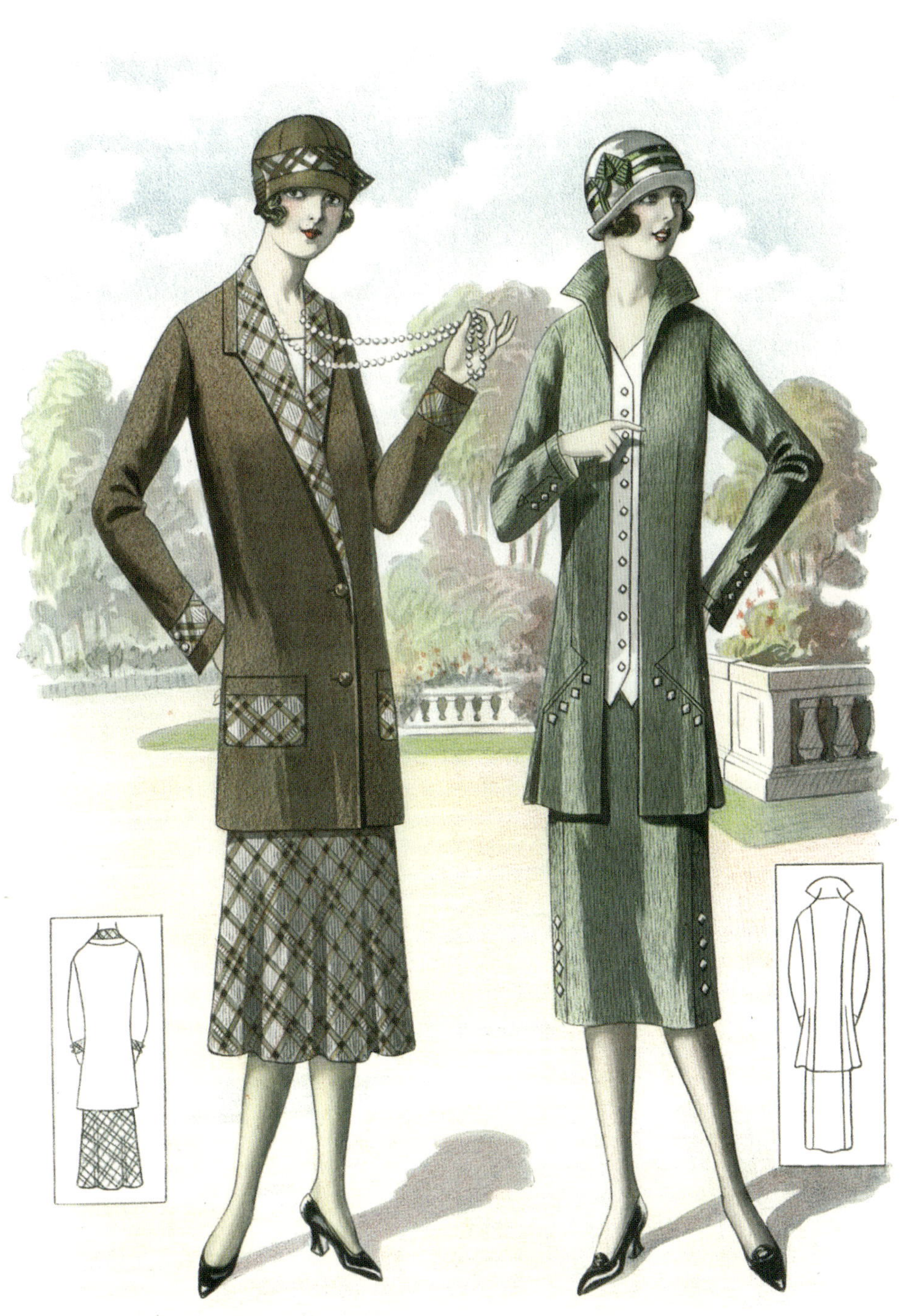

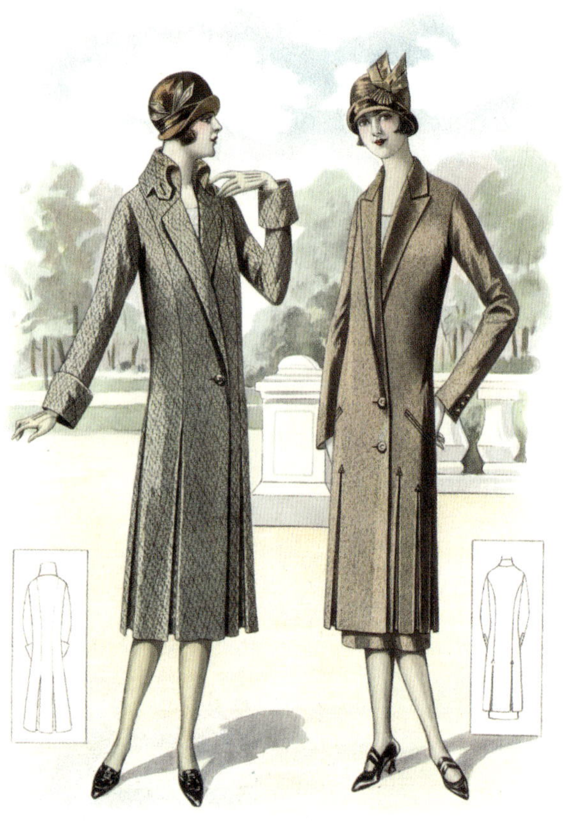

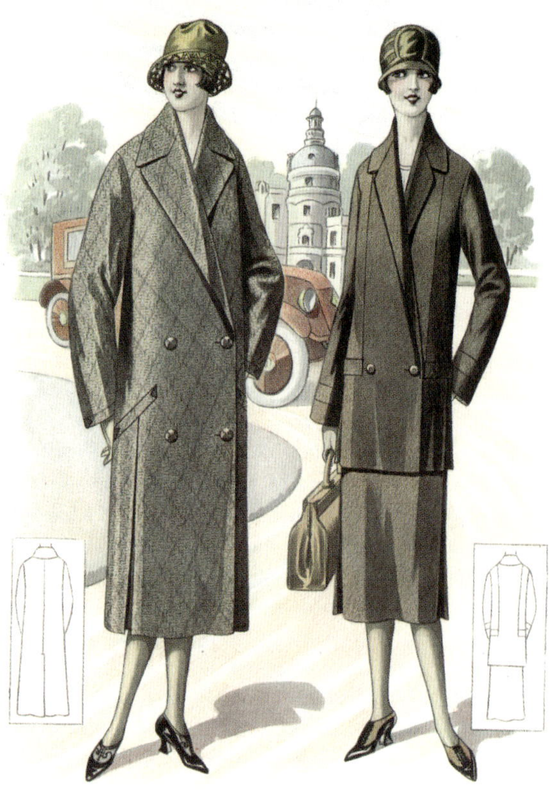

Above left and right

Two coats with pleats.
La Femme Élégante à Paris, 1926

Motoring coat and skirt suit.
La Femme Élégante à Paris, 1926

Right

Two walking suits.
La Femme Élégante à Paris, 1926

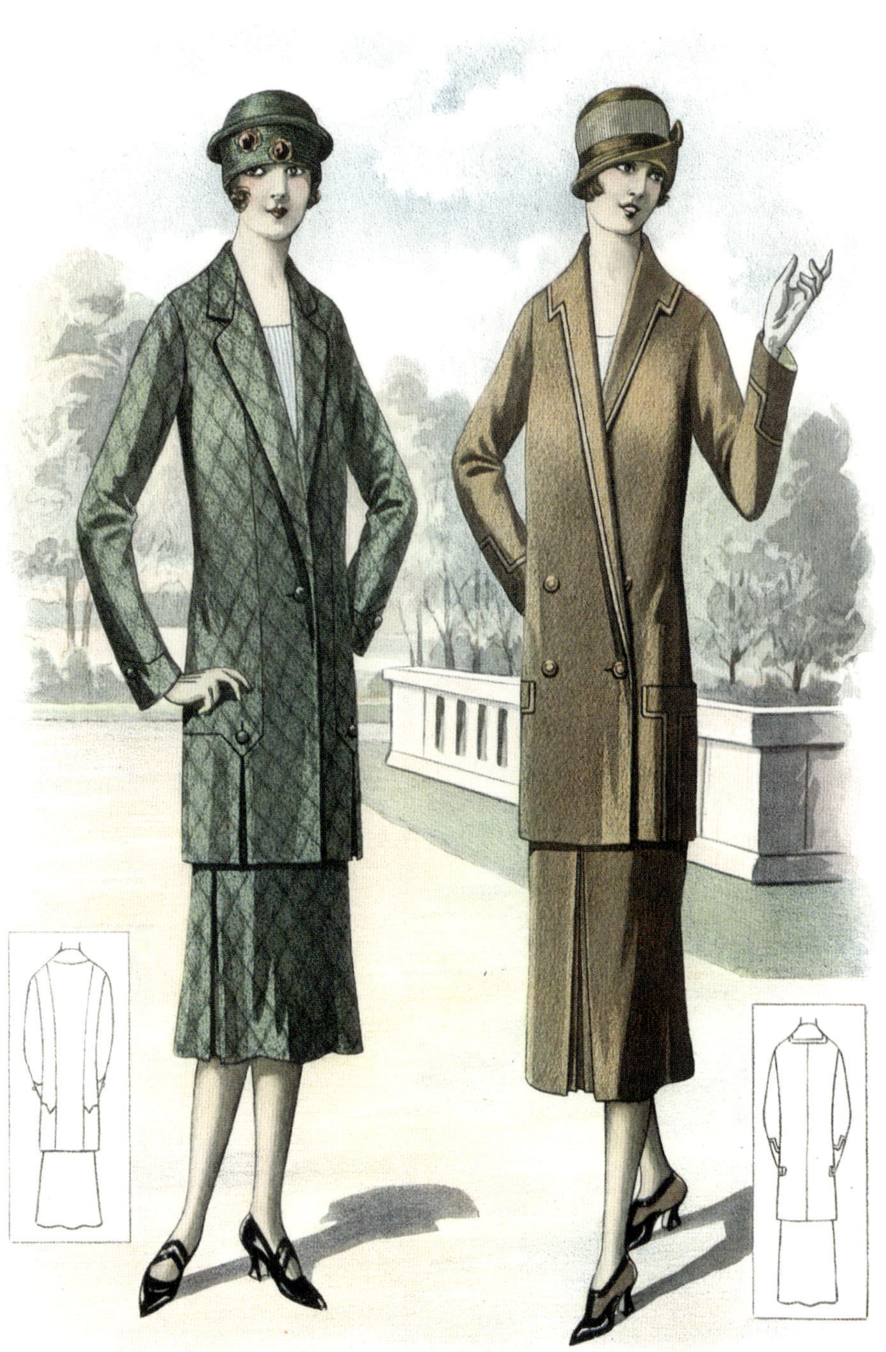

1274 1275

Below

Various summer coat and skirt suit designs. *La Femme Élégante à Paris*, 1926

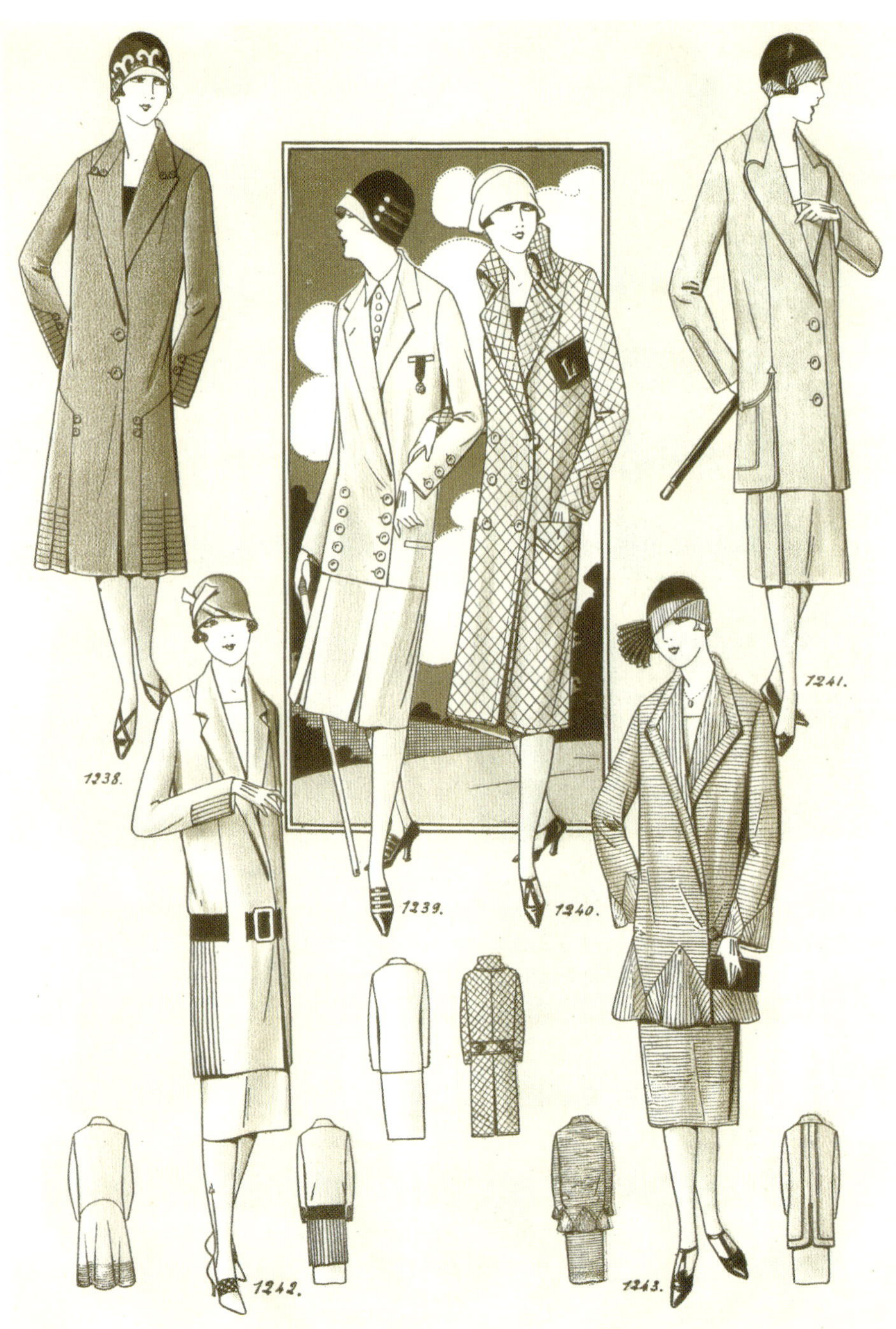

Below

Various summer coat and skirt suit designs. *La Femme Élégante à Paris*, 1926

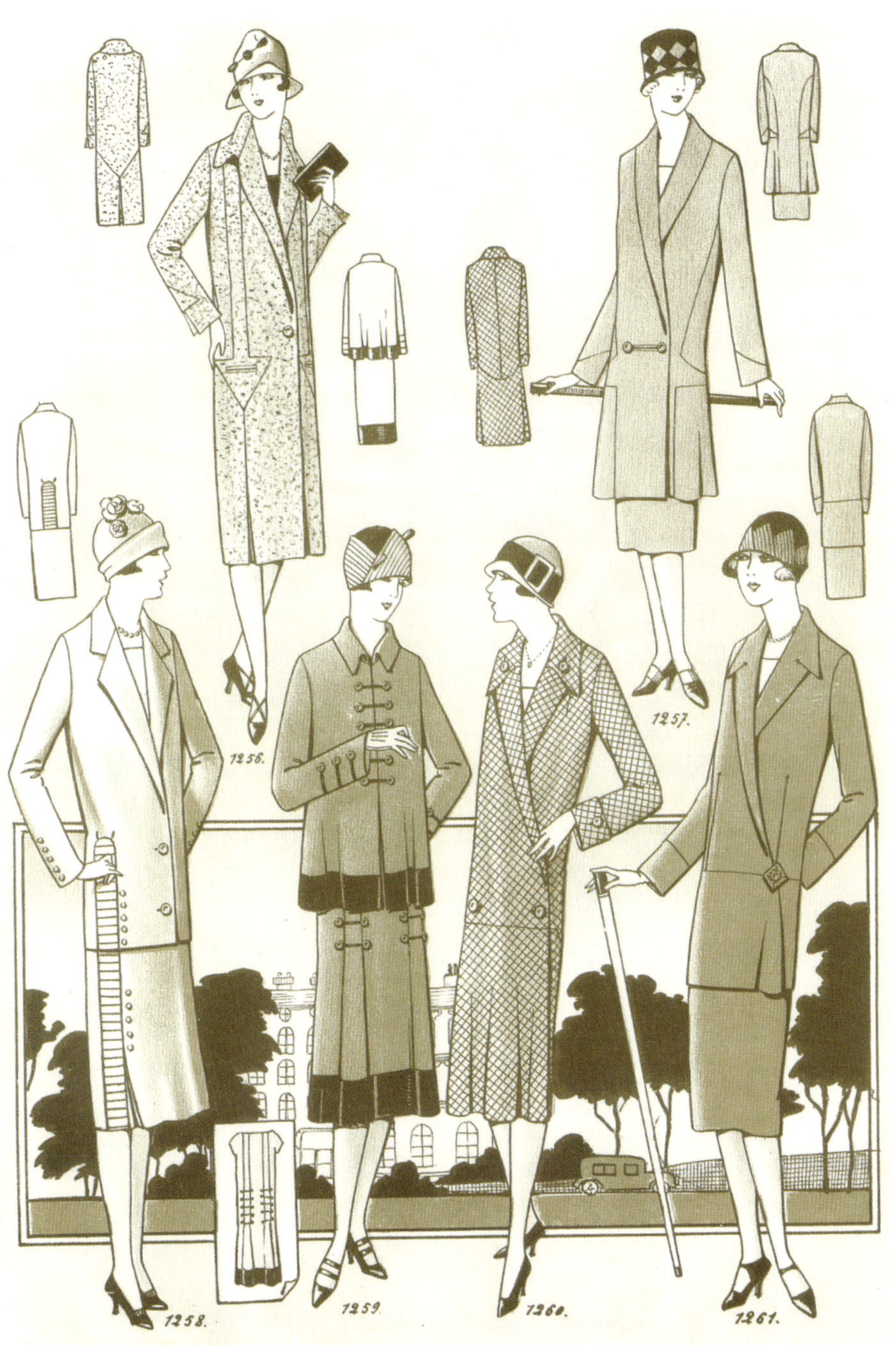

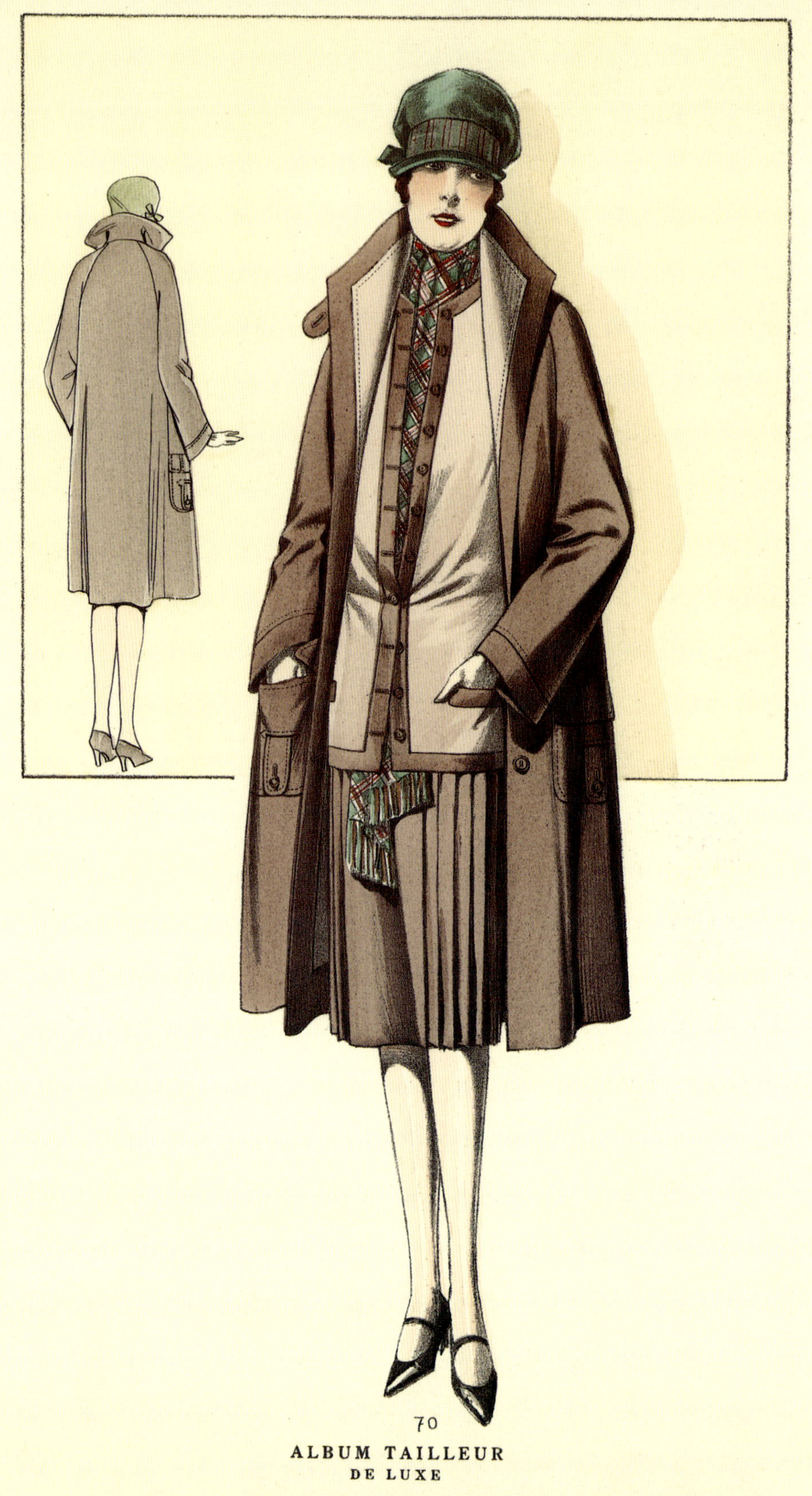
70
ALBUM TAILLEUR
DE LUXE

Left and below
Autumn ensemble of a two-tone brown coat, skirt and jacket accessorised with a checked scarf. *Album Tailleur de Luxe*, c.1925

Pink spring coat in Kashalyne and a blue Kashafyl dress with pink scallops by Atelier Bachroitz. *Grande Mode Parisienne*, 1926

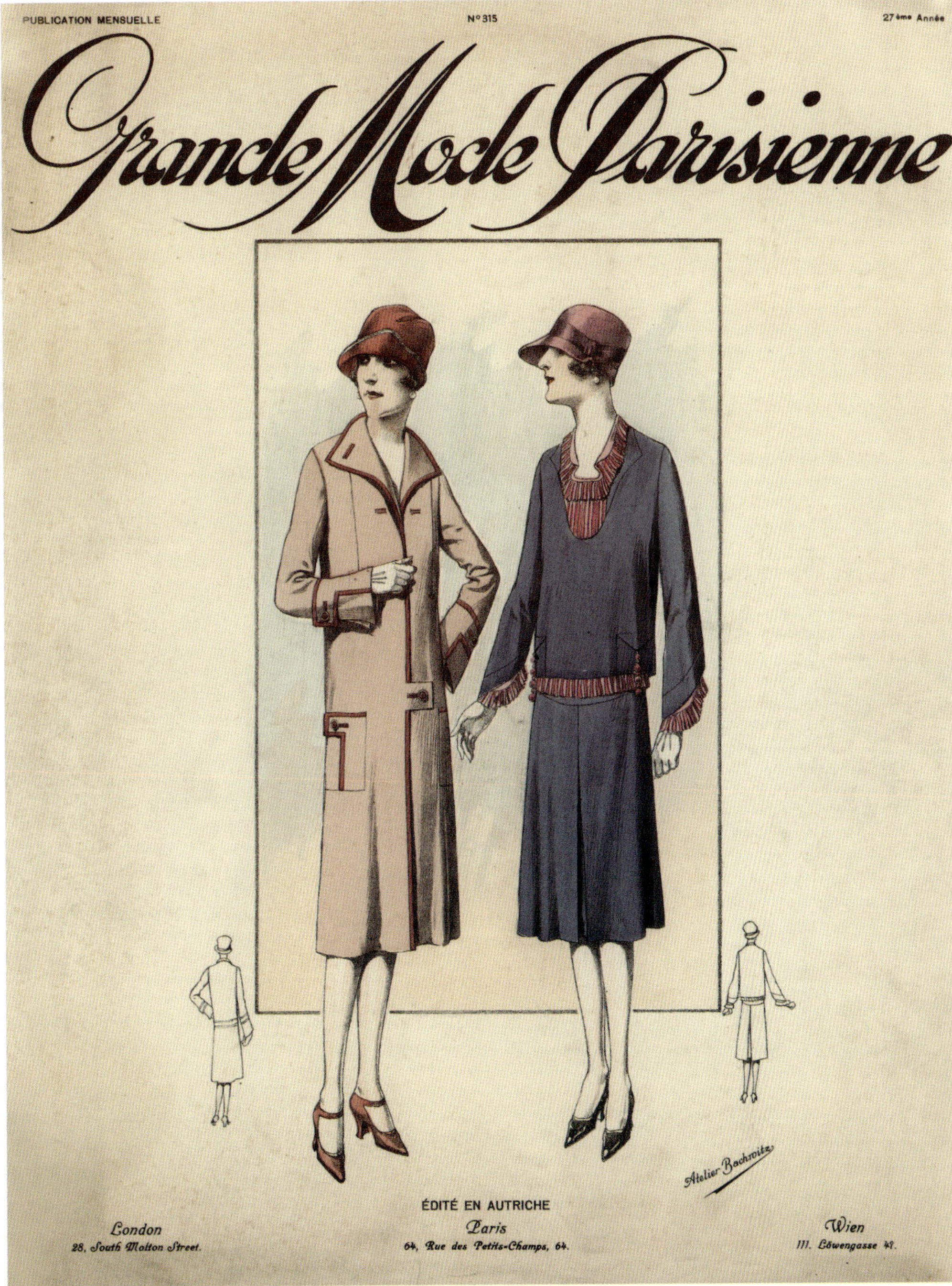

Below left and right

Selection of day coats, Printemps catalogue, 1924

Selection of knitted suits, Printemps catalogue, 1924

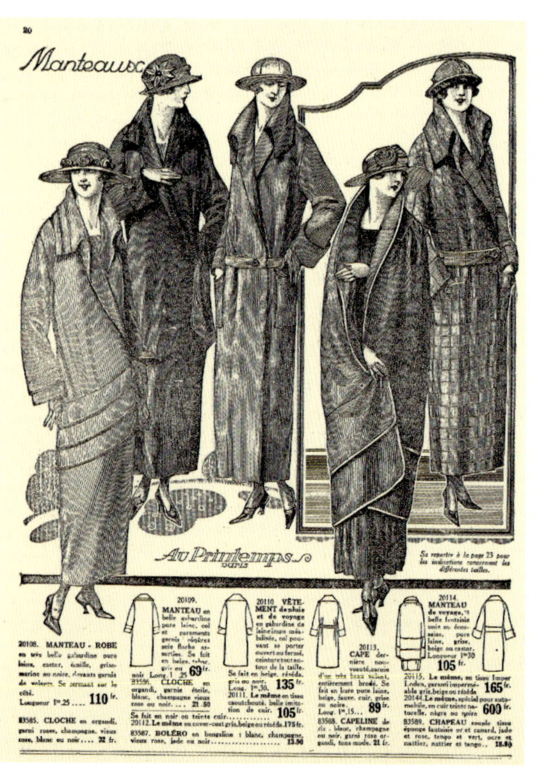

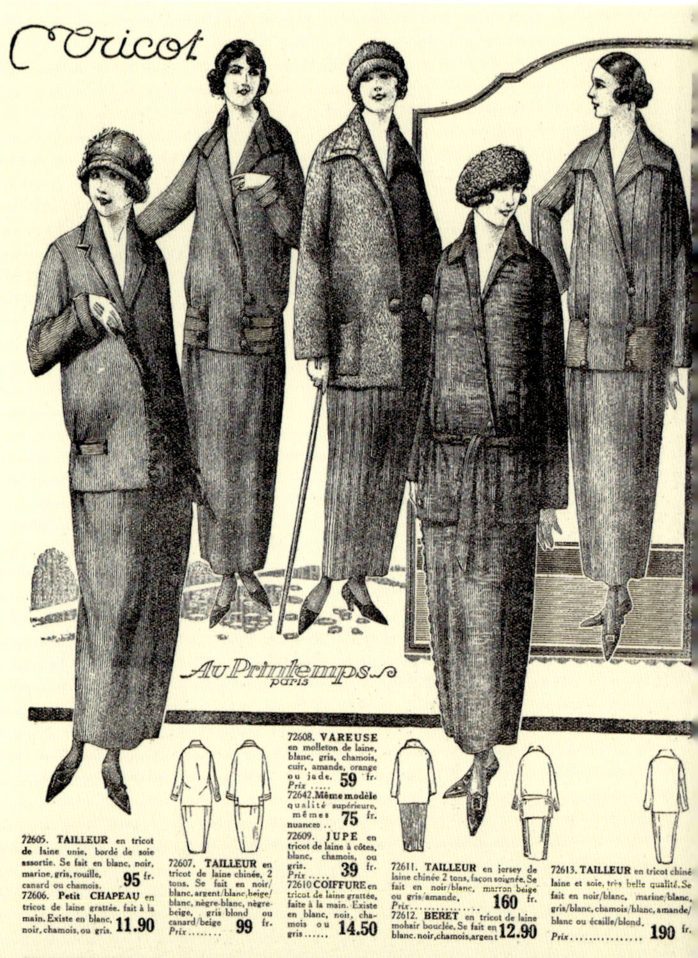

Brown left and right

Selection of day and evening coats and capes, Printemps catalogue, 1924

Selection of skirt suits, Printemps catalogue, 1924

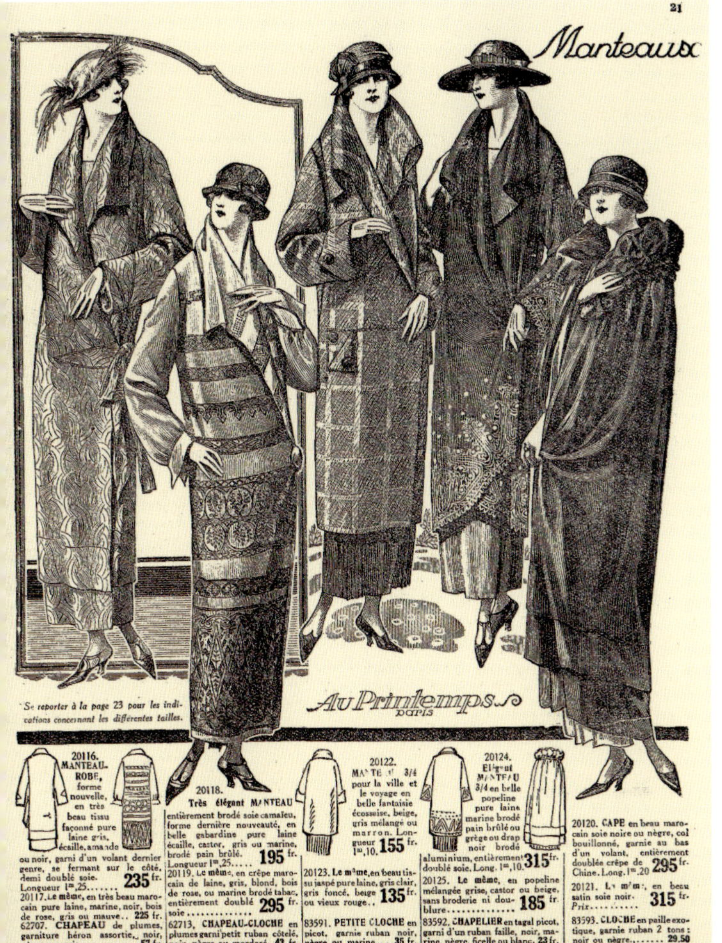

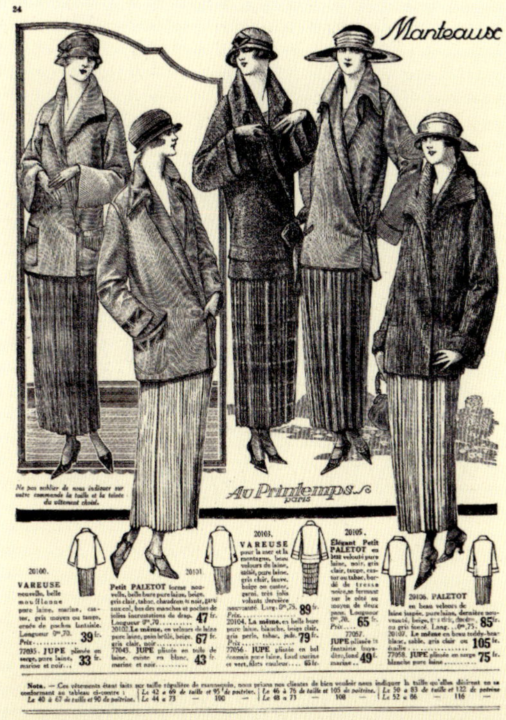

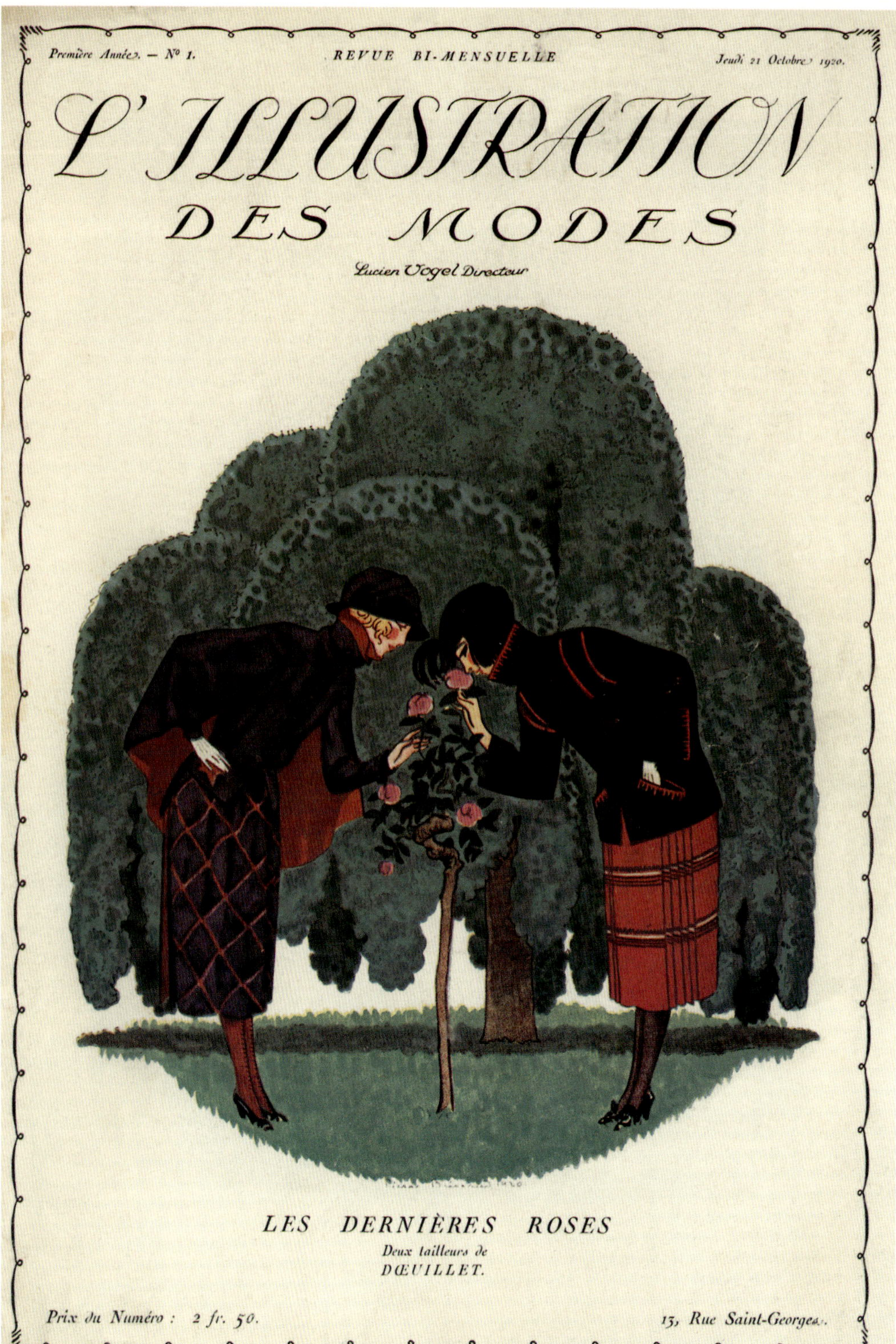

Above

Two tailored suits by Doeuillet.
L'Illustration des Modes, 1920

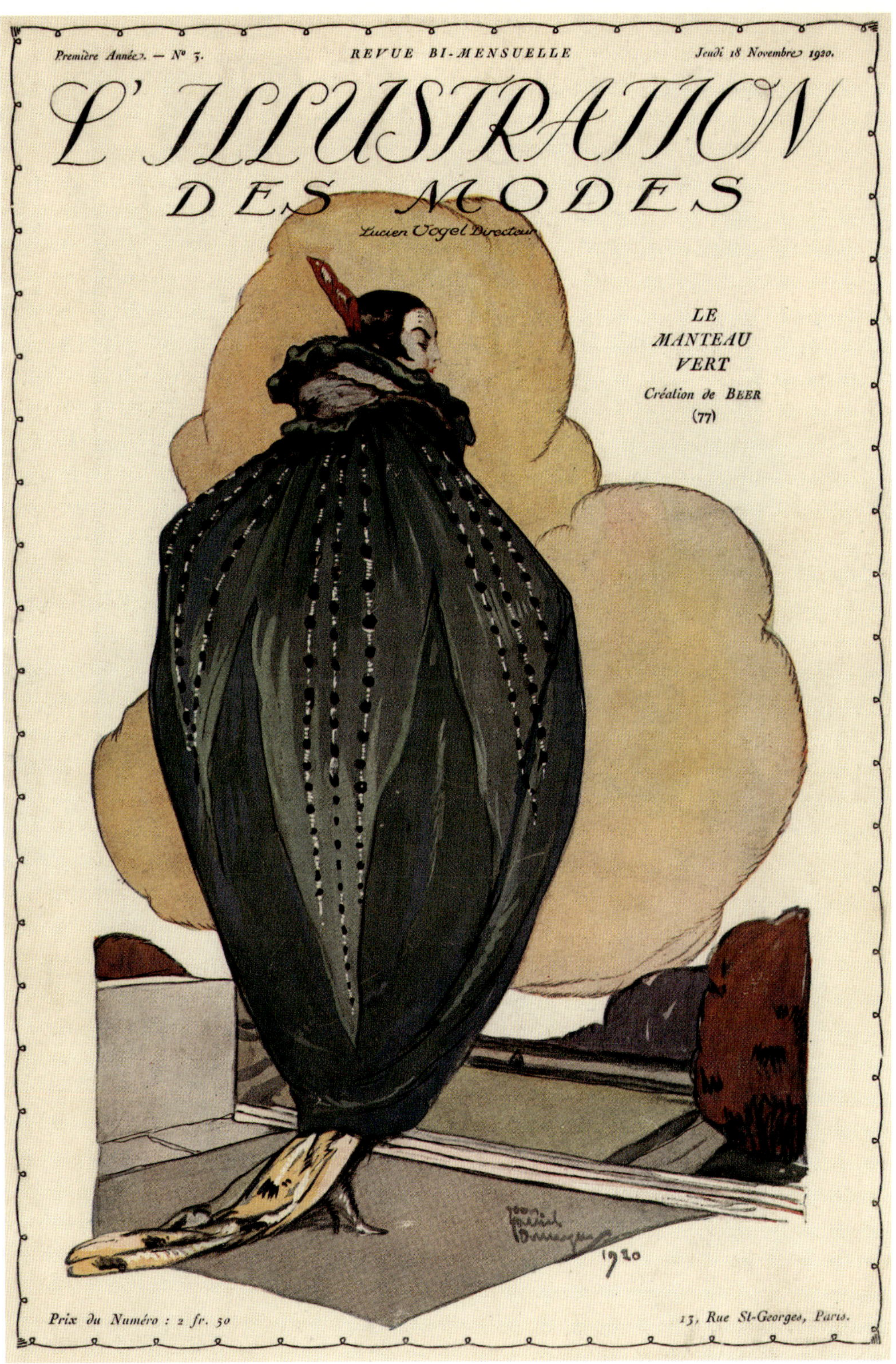

Above
Green evening coat by Beer.
L'Illustration des Modes, 1920

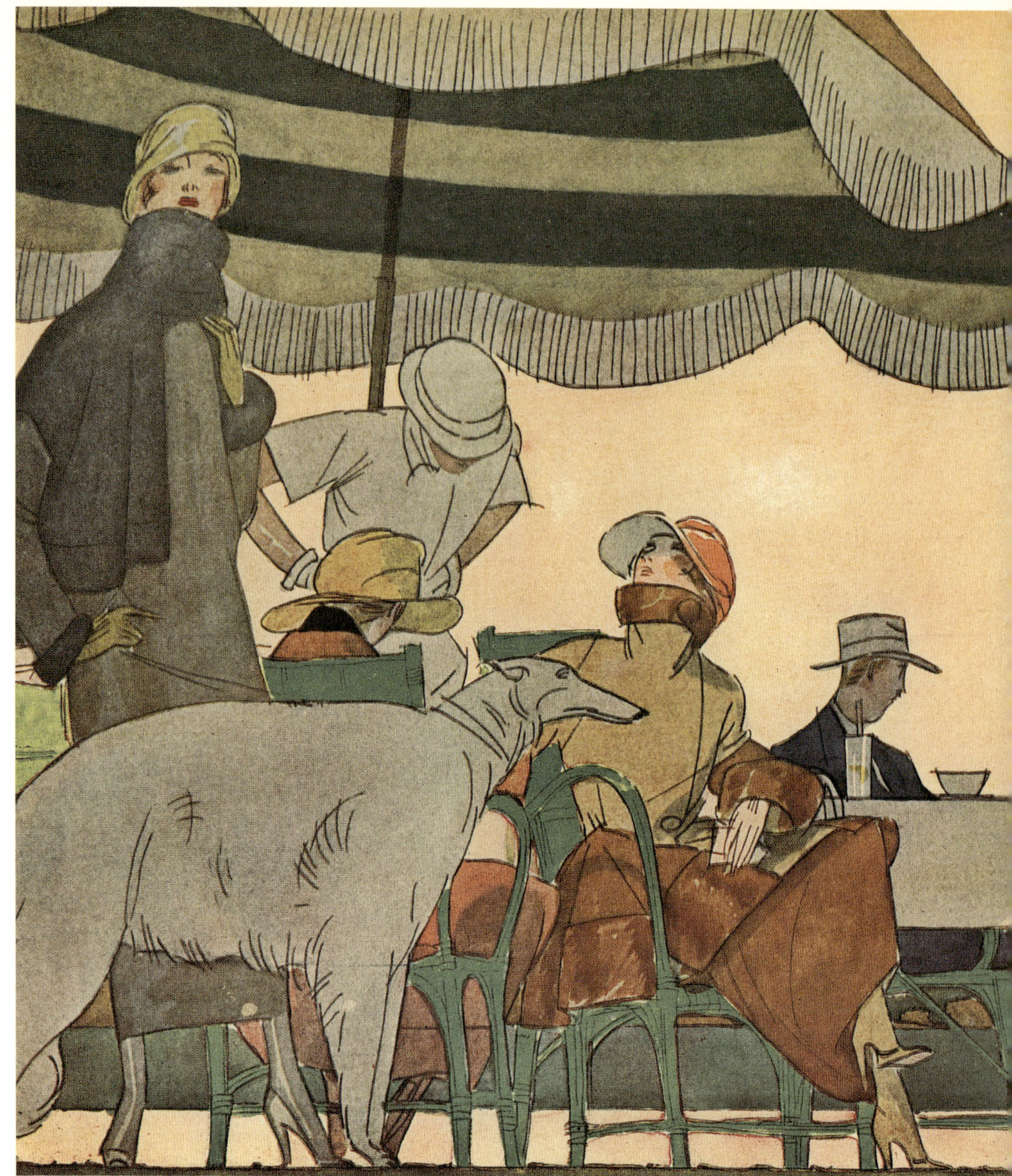

Above

"Au Polo" (At Polo) – grey woollen coat by Paquin, brown tailored ensemble by Worth, red and blue skirt suit by Jenny, beige and brown tailored ensemble by Beer, black ensemble with green vest by Lanvin, and brown jacket and skirt with Morrocan-style motif by Poiret. *L'Illustration des Modes*, 1920

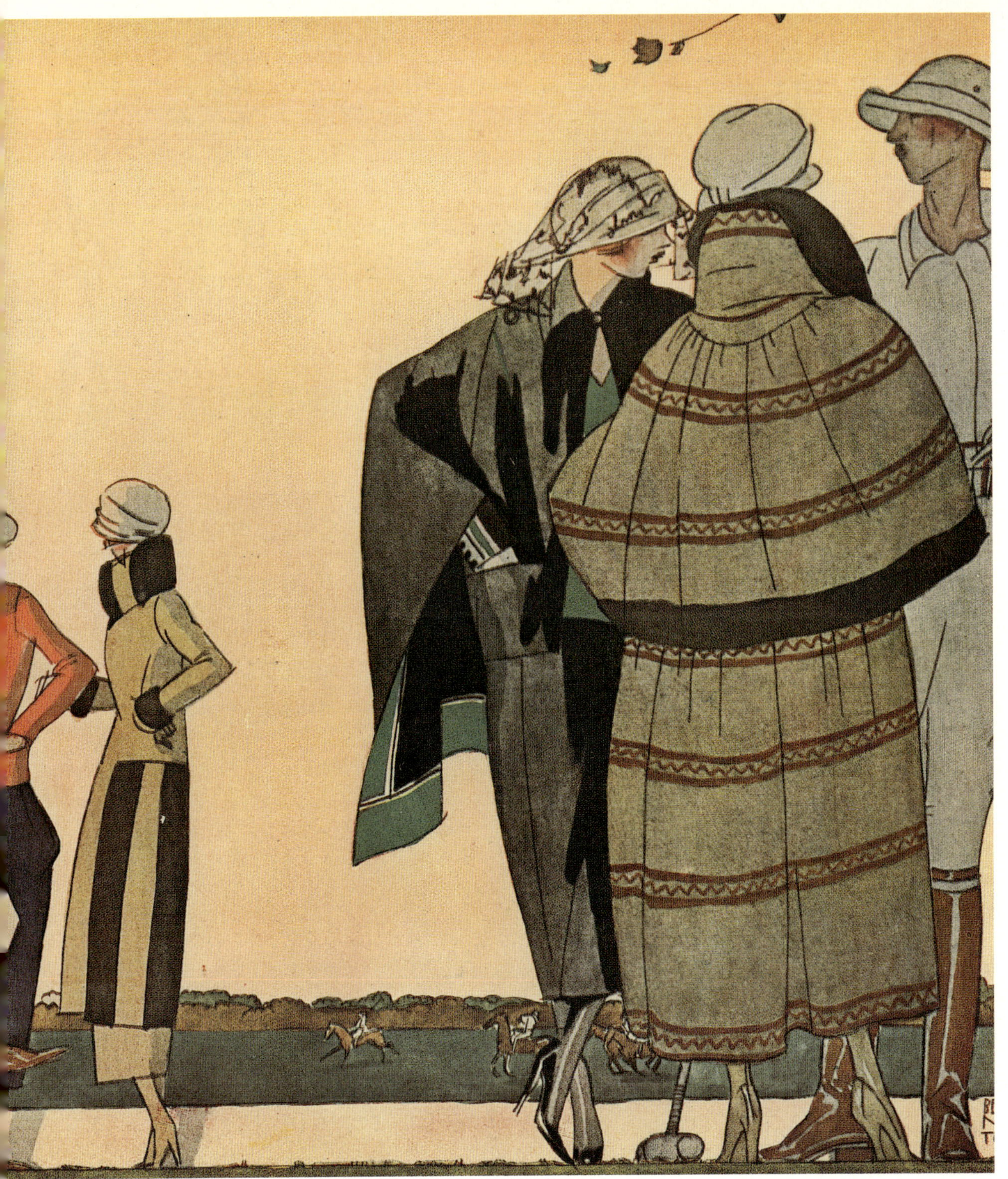

Below and right

Three winter day suits described as "comfortable models". *La Femme Chic*, c.1925

Ira Richards at a horse show wearing a knitted jumper with abstract motif and a woollen skirt suit, accessorized with a mink stole and a large floral corsage, 1929

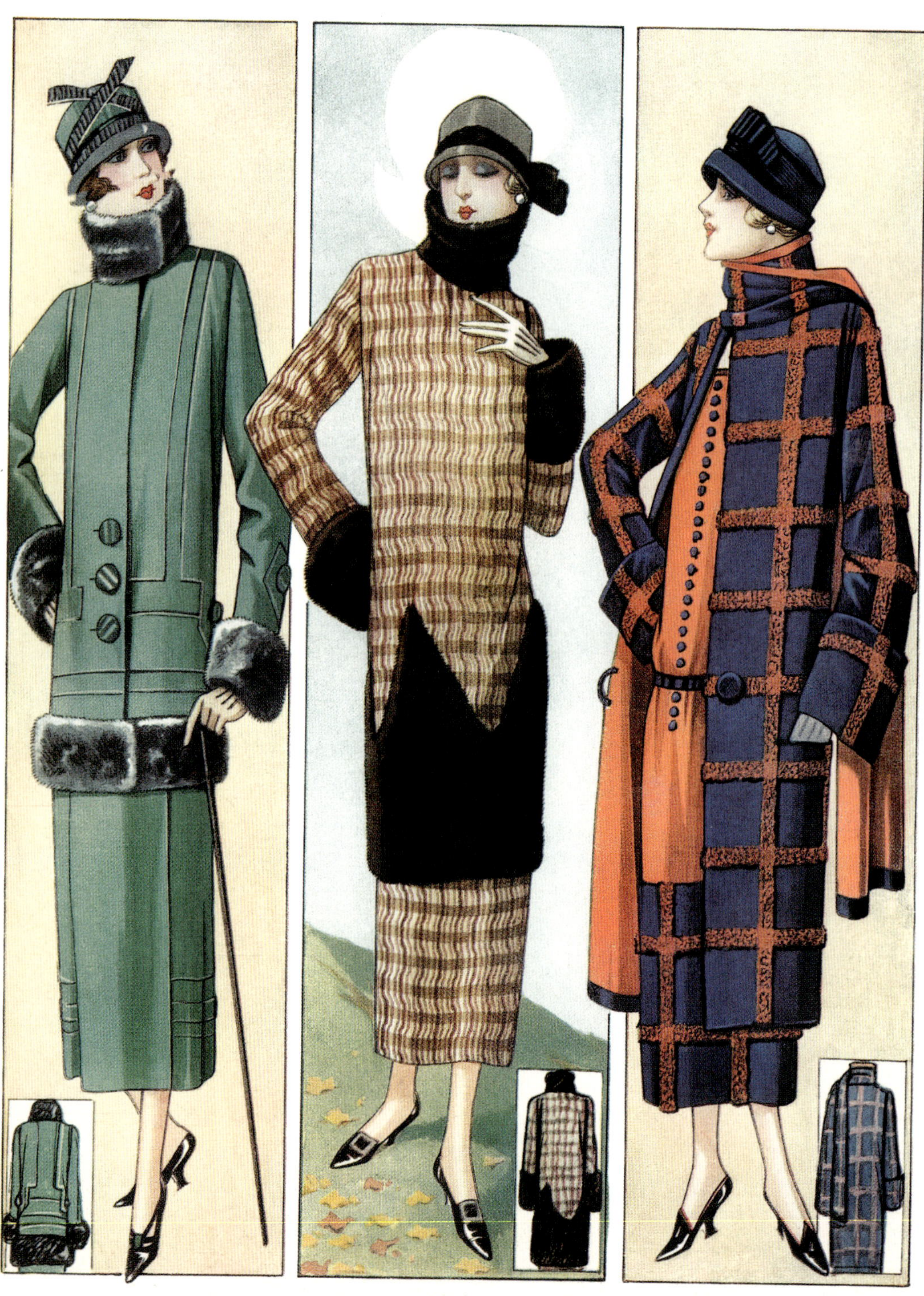

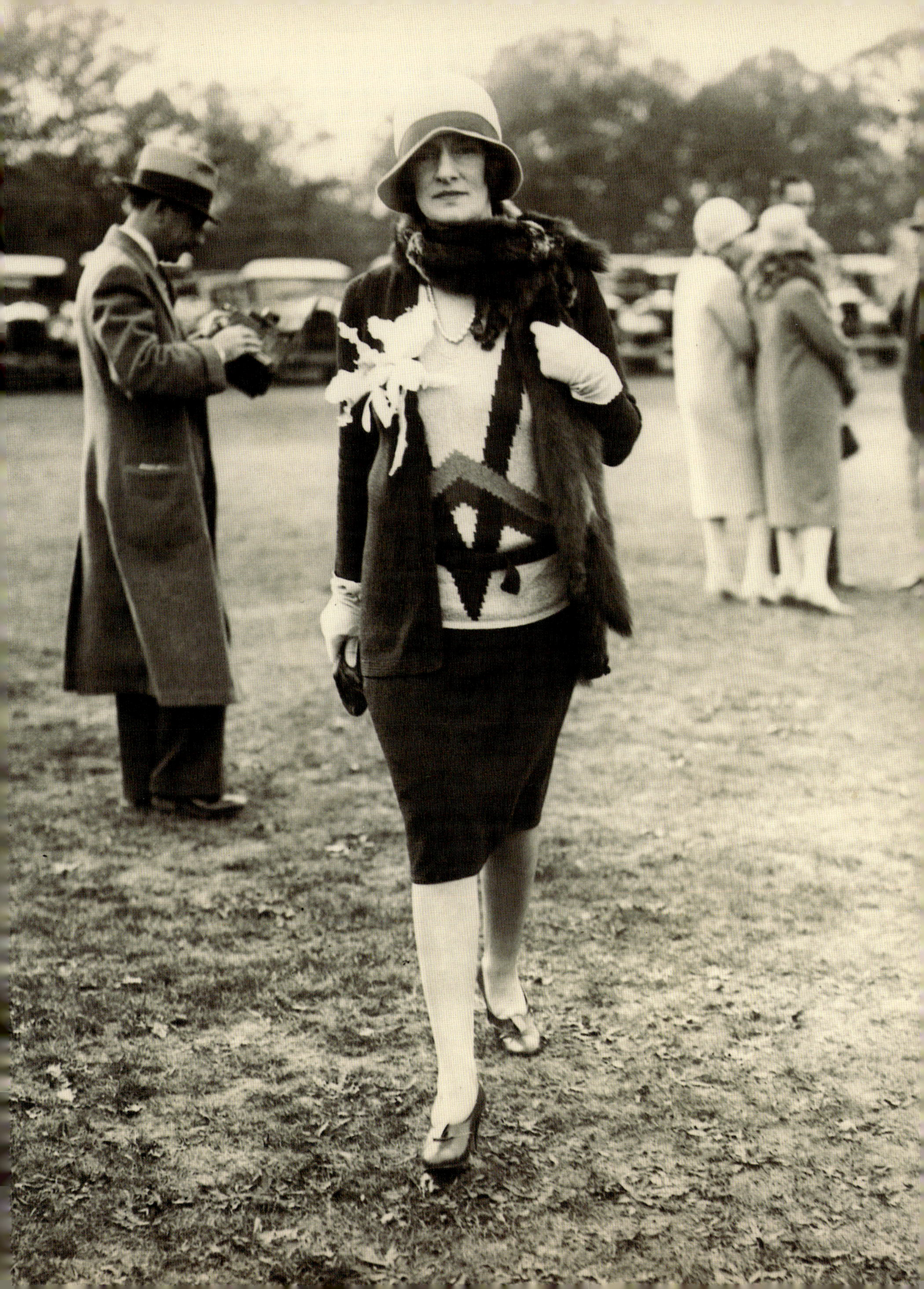

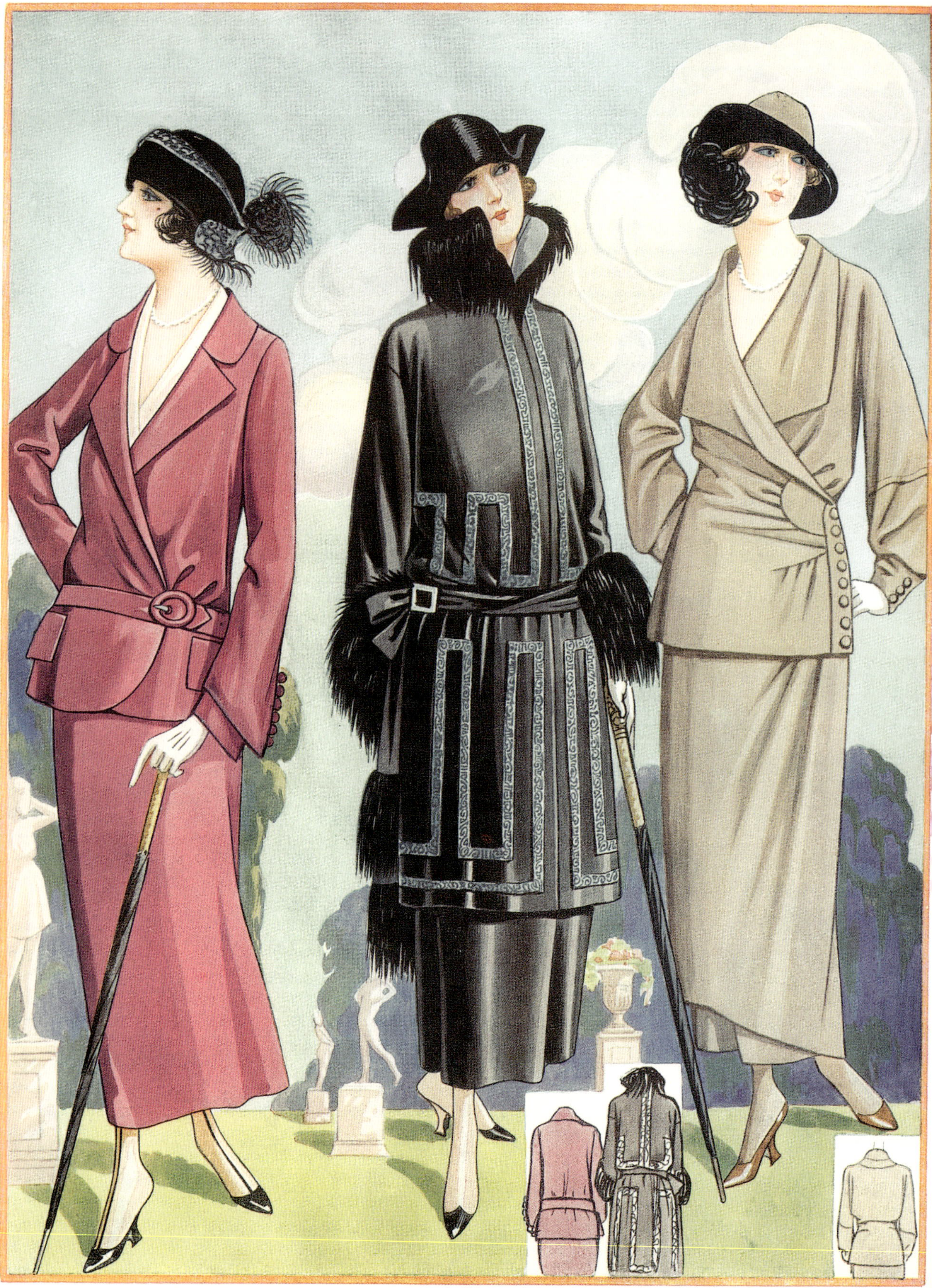

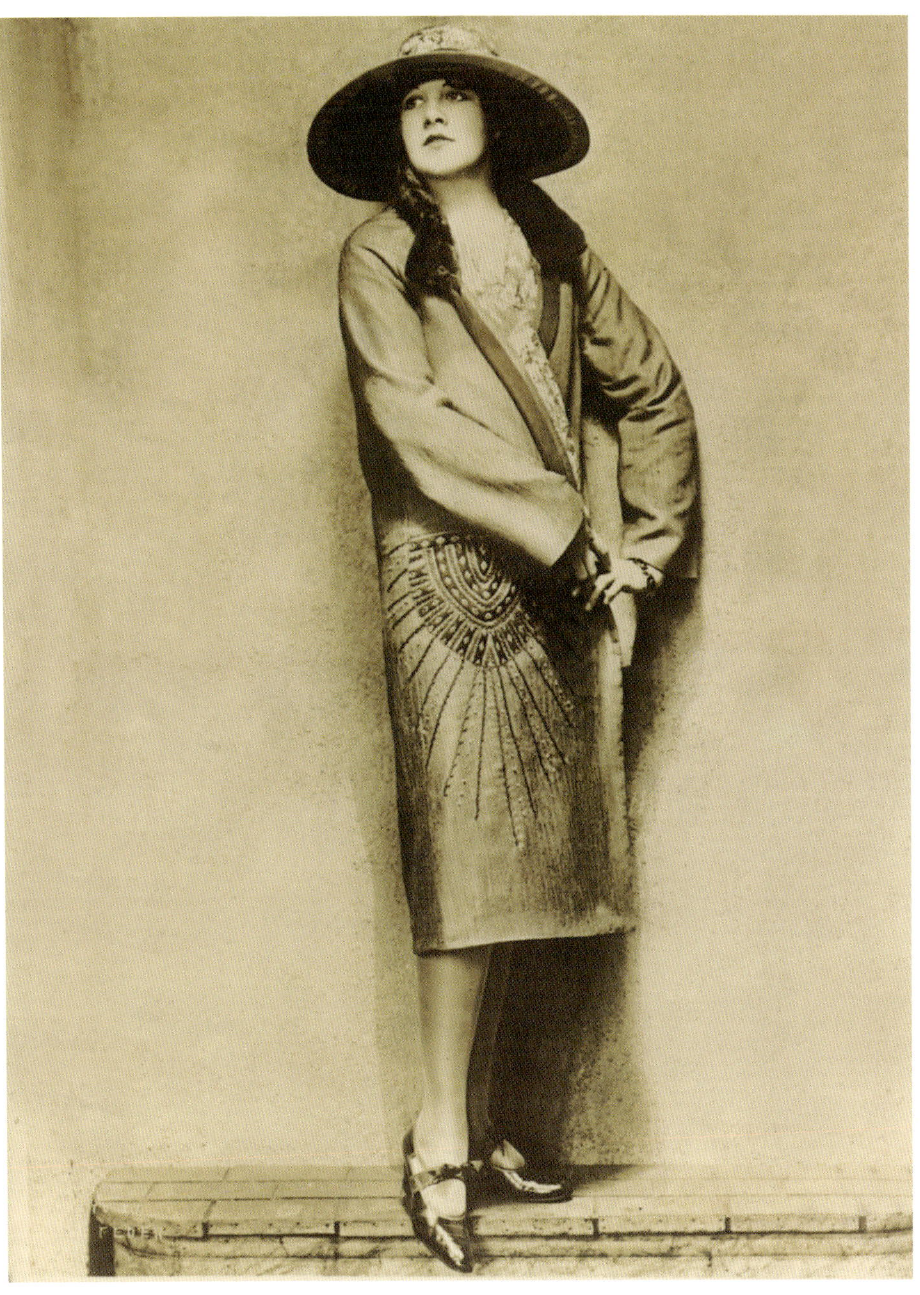

Left and above
Three spring suits. The landscaped gardens lend the outfits an air of high class and sophistication. *La Femme Chic*, c.1924

A heavily embroidered spring coat worn with a wide-brimmed hat, 1927

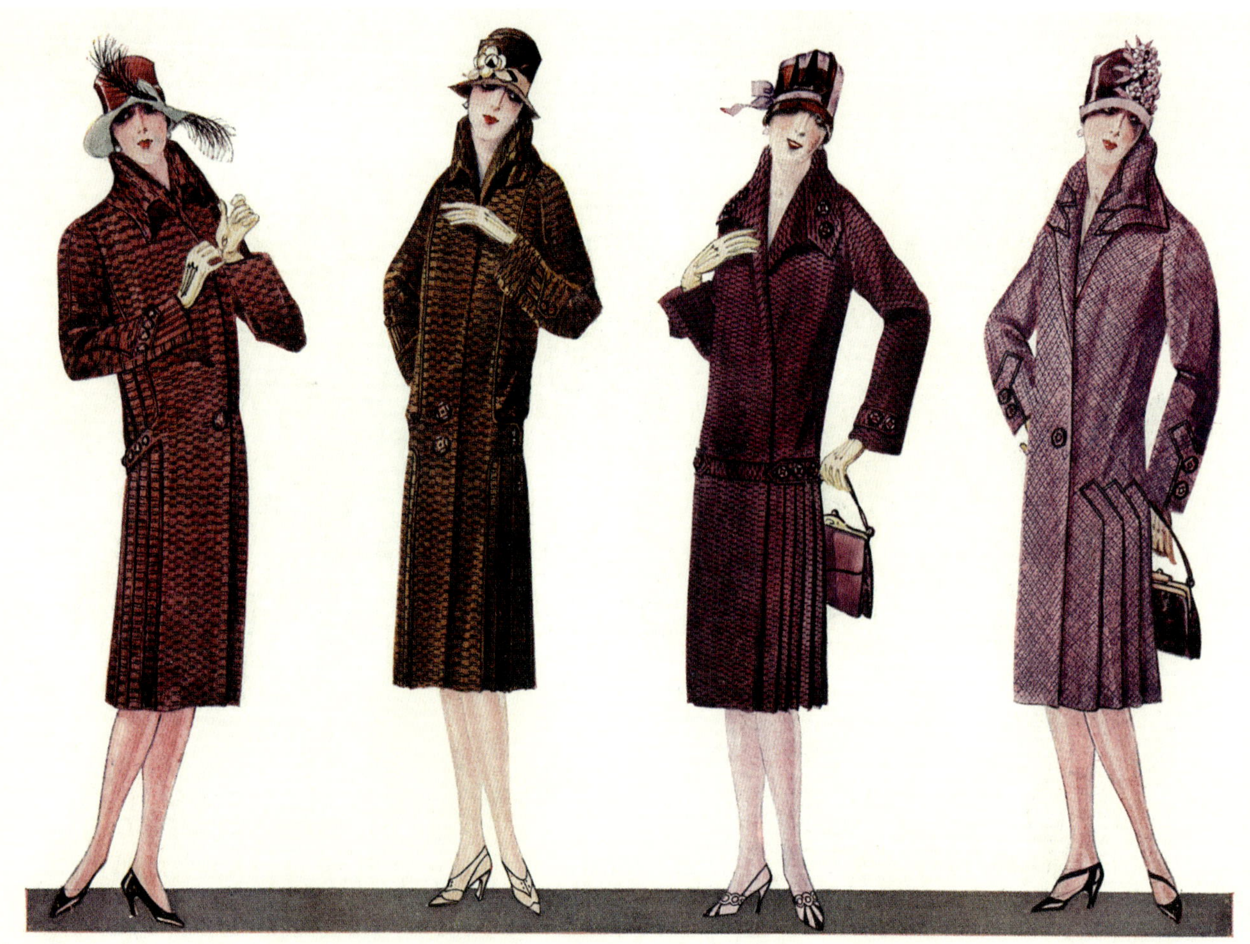

Above
Four city coats by Maison Gerda.
Maison Gerda catalogue, c.1925

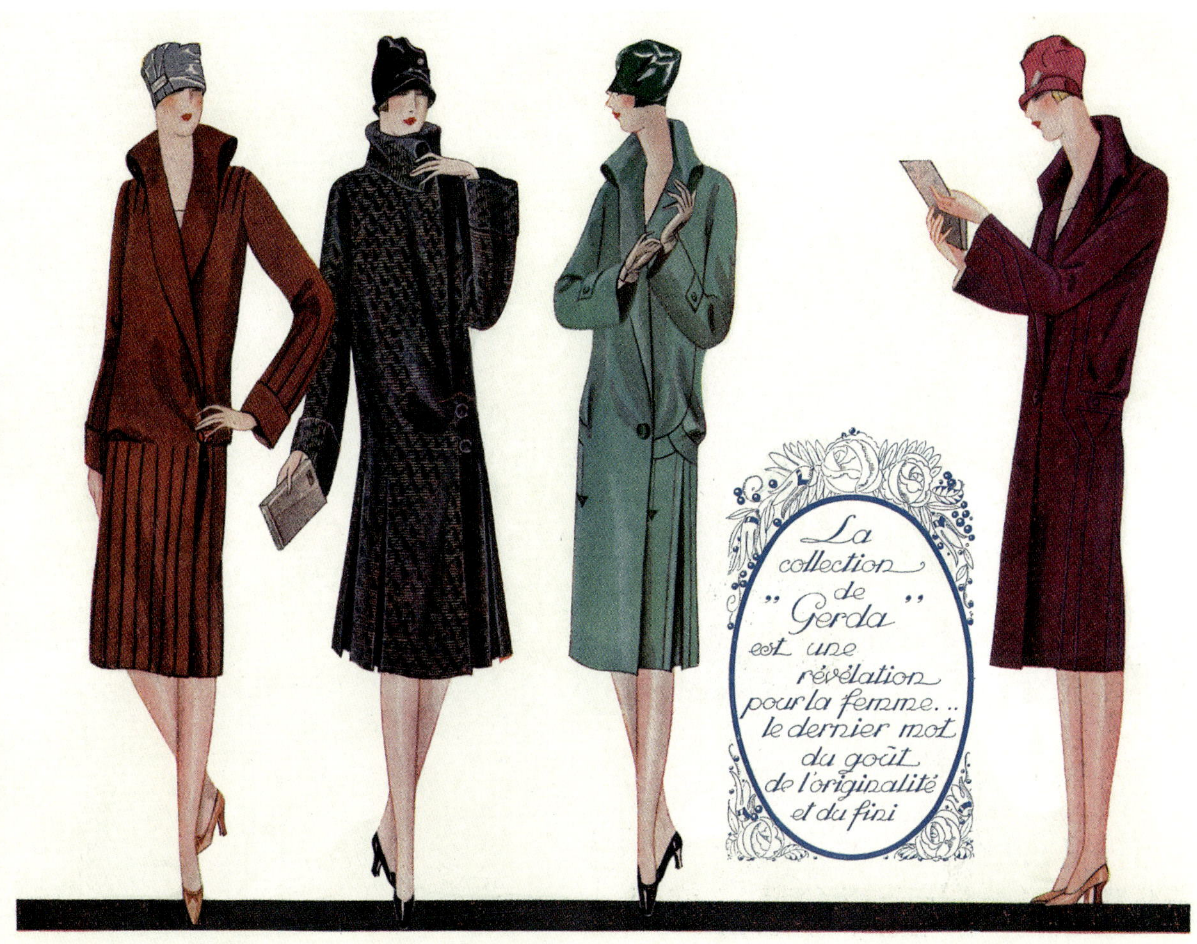

Above
Four city coats by Maison Gerda.
Maison Gerda catalogue, c.1925

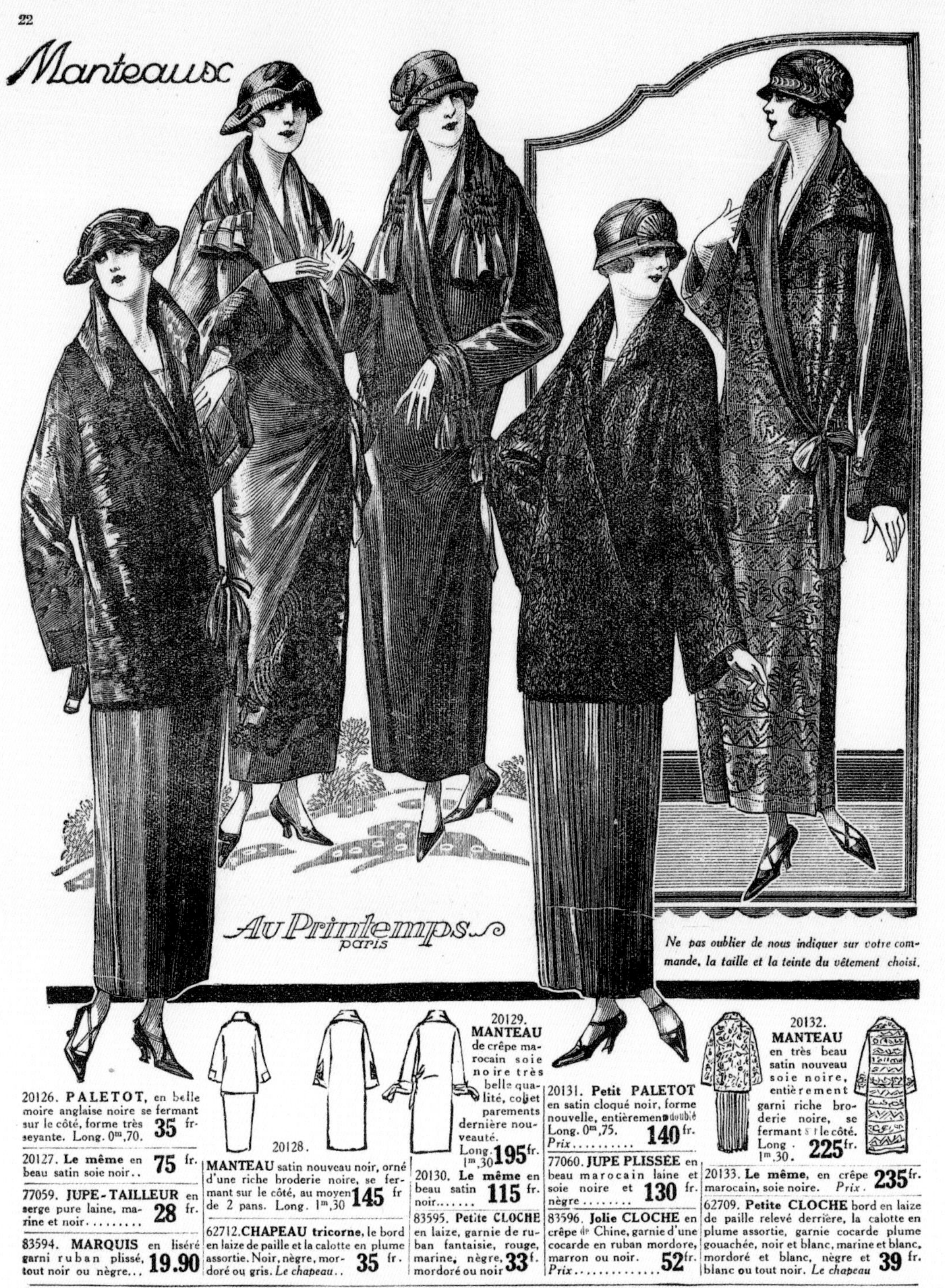

Above
Selection of evening coats and jackets, Printemps catalogue, 1924

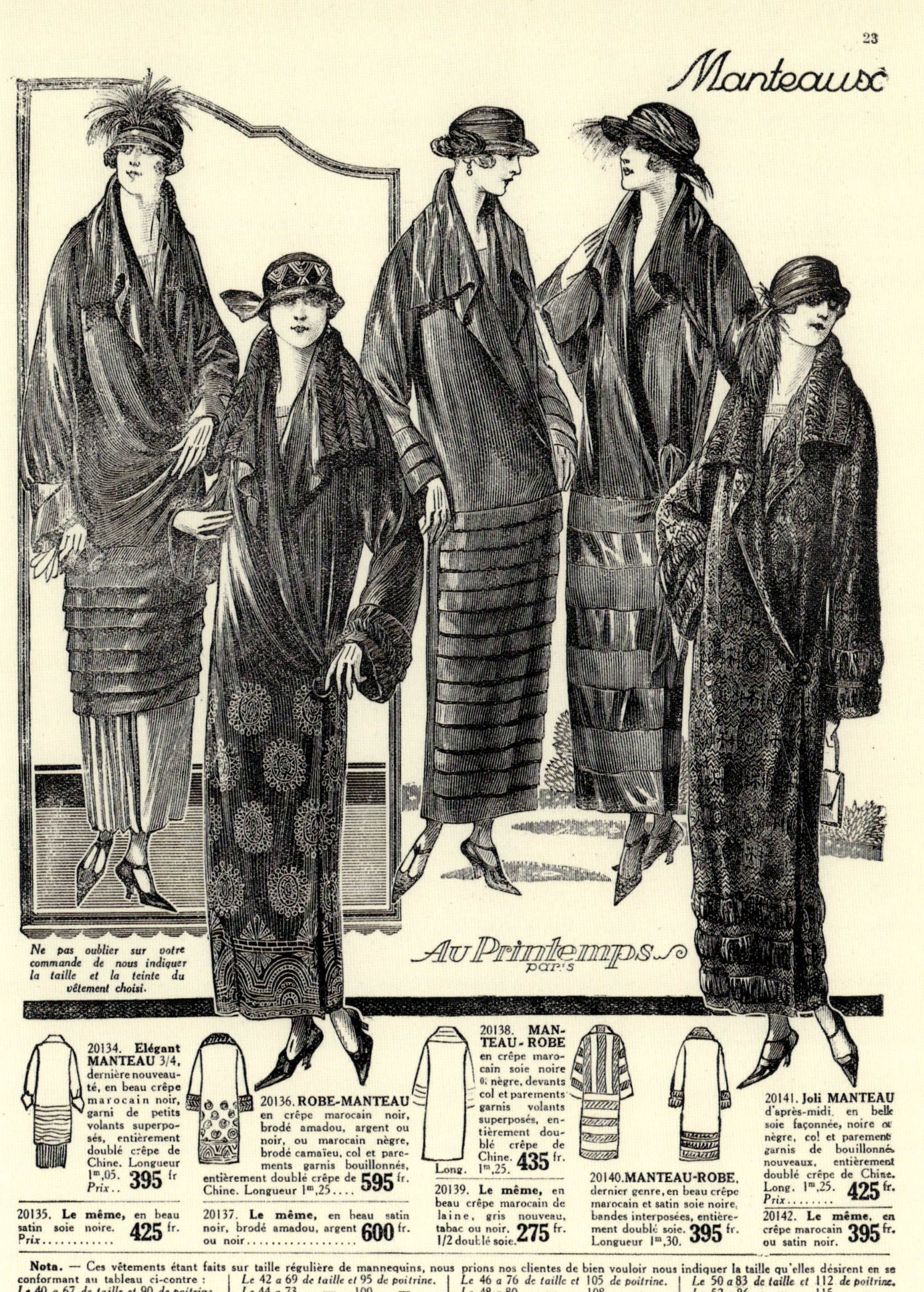

23

Manteaux

Ne pas oublier sur votre commande de nous indiquer la taille et la teinte du vêtement choisi.

Au Printemps paris

20134. **Elégant MANTEAU 3/4,** dernière nouveauté, en beau crêpe marocain noir, garni de petits volants superposés, entièrement doublé crêpe de Chine. Longueur 1m,05. *Prix*.. **395** fr.

20135. **Le même,** en beau satin soie noire. *Prix*............ **425** fr.

20136. **ROBE-MANTEAU** en crêpe marocain noir, brodé amadou, argent ou noir, ou marocain nègre, brodé camaïeu, col et parements garnis bouillonnés, entièrement doublé crêpe de Chine. Longueur 1m,25.... **595** fr.

20137. **Le même,** en beau satin noir, brodé amadou, argent ou noir.................. **600** fr.

20138. **MANTEAU-ROBE** en crêpe marocain soie noire ou nègre, devants col et parements garnis volants superposés, entièrement doublé crêpe de Chine. Long. 1m,25. **435** fr.

20139. **Le même,** en beau crêpe marocain de laine, gris nouveau, tabac ou noir. 1/2 doublé soie. **275** fr.

20140. **MANTEAU-ROBE,** dernier genre, en beau crêpe marocain et satin soie noire, bandes interposées, entièrement doublé soie. Longueur 1m,30. **395** fr.

20141. **Joli MANTEAU** d'après-midi, en belle soie façonnée, noire ou nègre, col et parements garnis de bouillonnés nouveaux, entièrement doublé crêpe de Chine. Long. 1m,25. *Prix*........ **425** fr.

20142. **Le même,** en crêpe marocain ou satin noir. **395** fr.

Nota. — Ces vêtements étant faits sur taille régulière de mannequins, nous prions nos clientes de bien vouloir nous indiquer la taille qu'elles désirent en se conformant au tableau ci-contre :

Le 40 a 67 de taille et 90 de poitrine. | *Le 42 a 69 de taille et 95 de poitrine.* | *Le 44 a 73* — 100 — | *Le 46 a 76 de taille et 105 de poitrine.* | *Le 48 a 80* — 108 — | *Le 50 a 83 de taille et 112 de poitrine.* | *Le 52 a 86* — 115 —

Above

Selection of evening coats, Printemps catalogue, 1924

Below and right
"A las Baleares" (To the Balearics), skirt suit by Beer. Illustration by Benito. *Gazette du Bon Ton*, 1921

A French postcard featuring a model in a hieroglyph design coat, 1923. Egyptian motifs became immensely popular in fashion after Howard Carter's discovery of Tutankhamen's tomb in 1922.

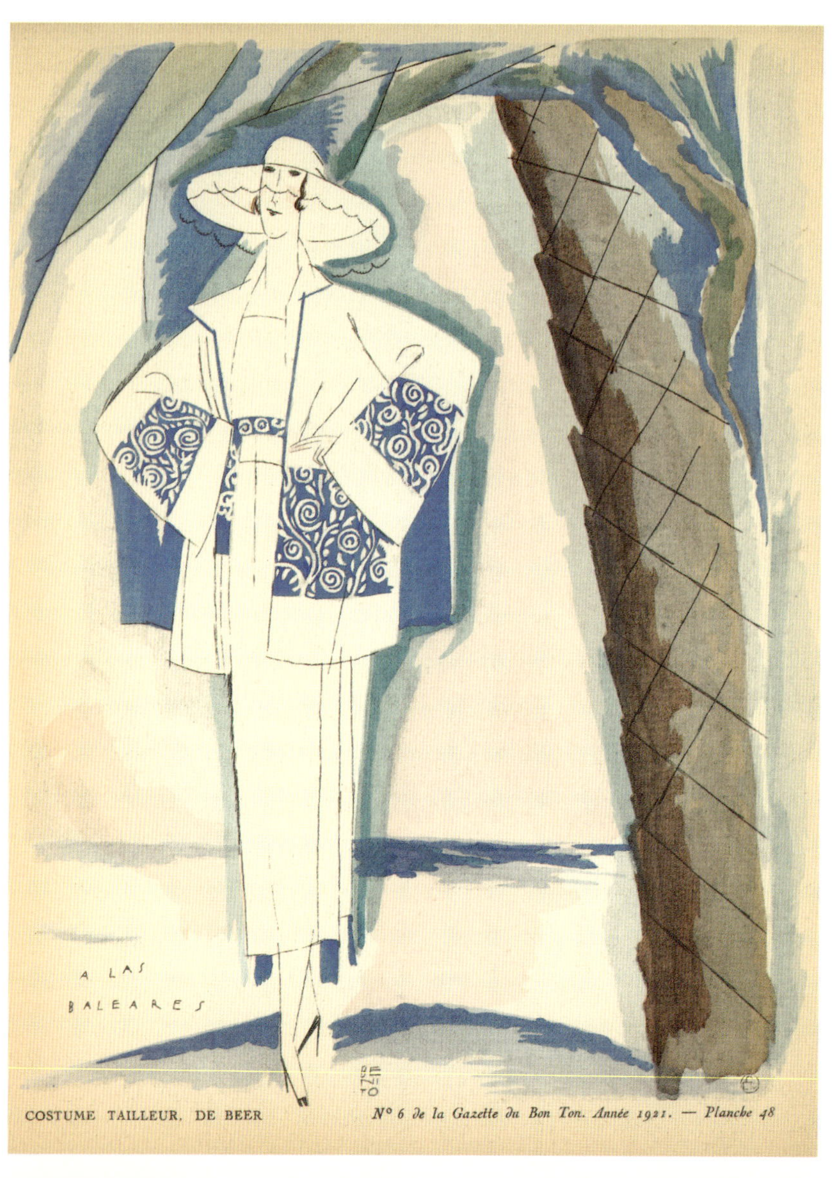

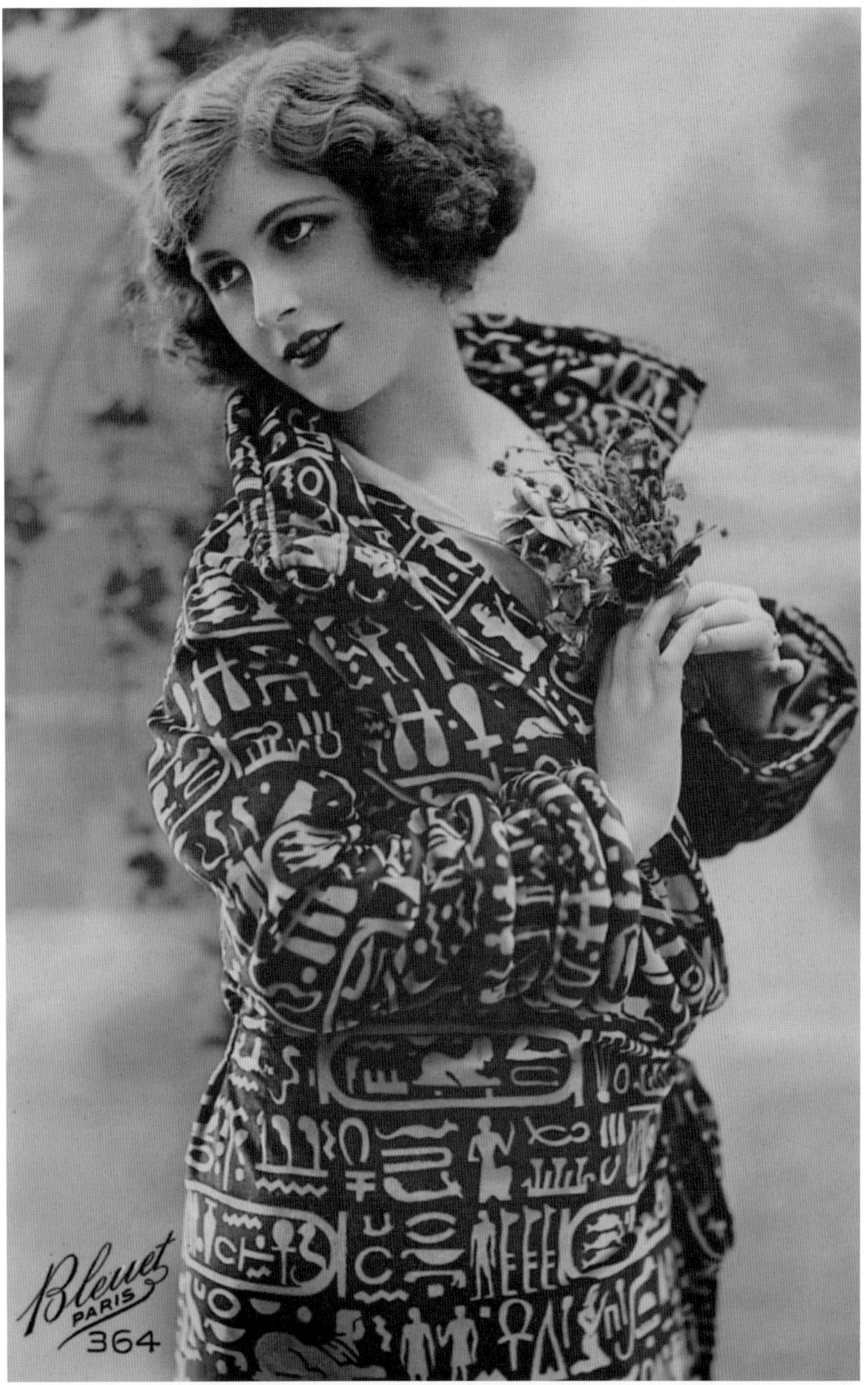
Bleuet
PARIS
364

Right
Grey and black silk walking dress and blue coat suit with sheepskin fur trim, hat and muffler. *Journal des Demoiselles*, 1921

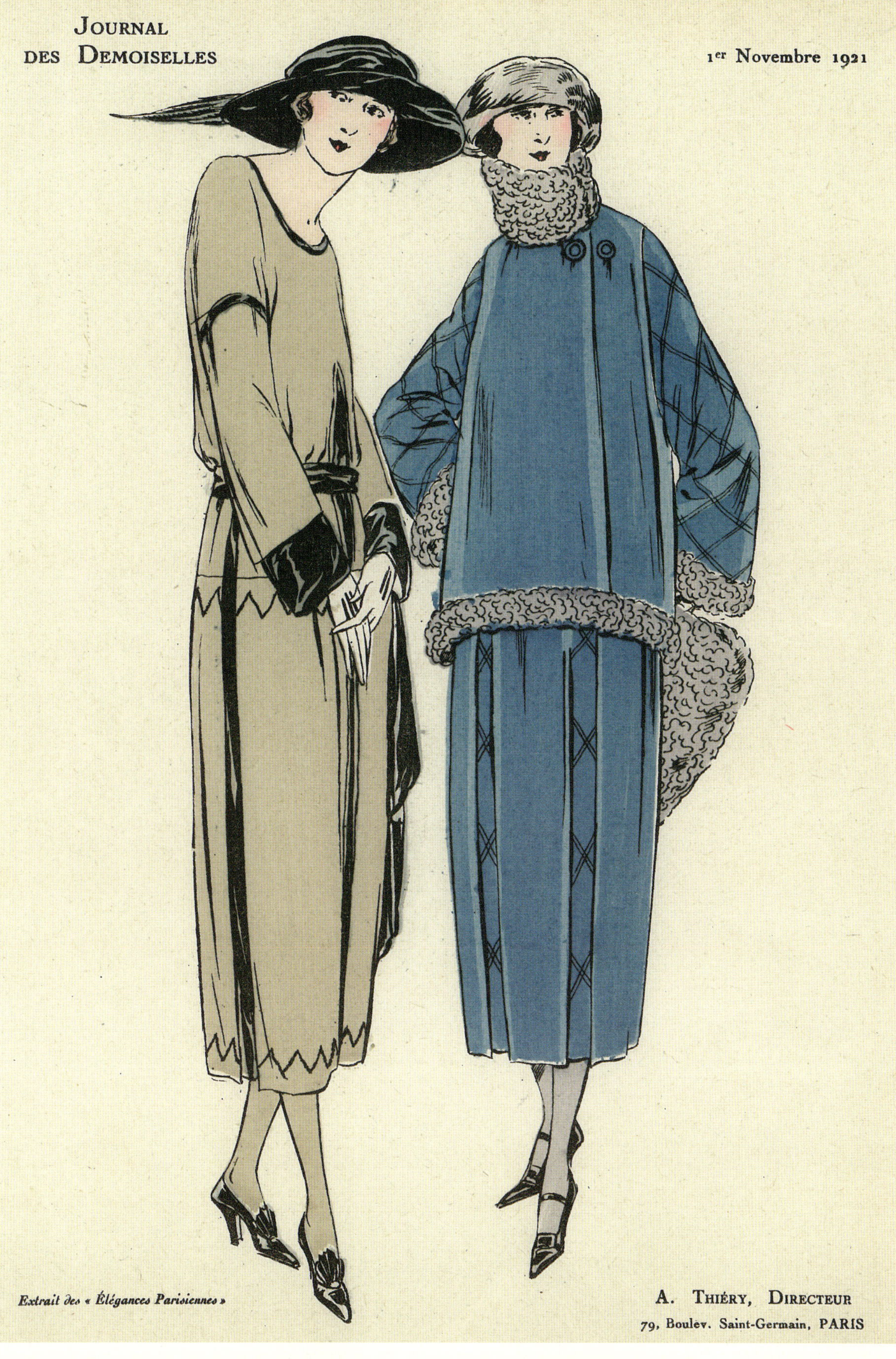
JOURNAL
DES DEMOISELLES
1er Novembre 1921
Extrait des « Élégances Parisiennes »
A. THIÉRY, DIRECTEUR
79, Boulev. Saint-Germain, PARIS

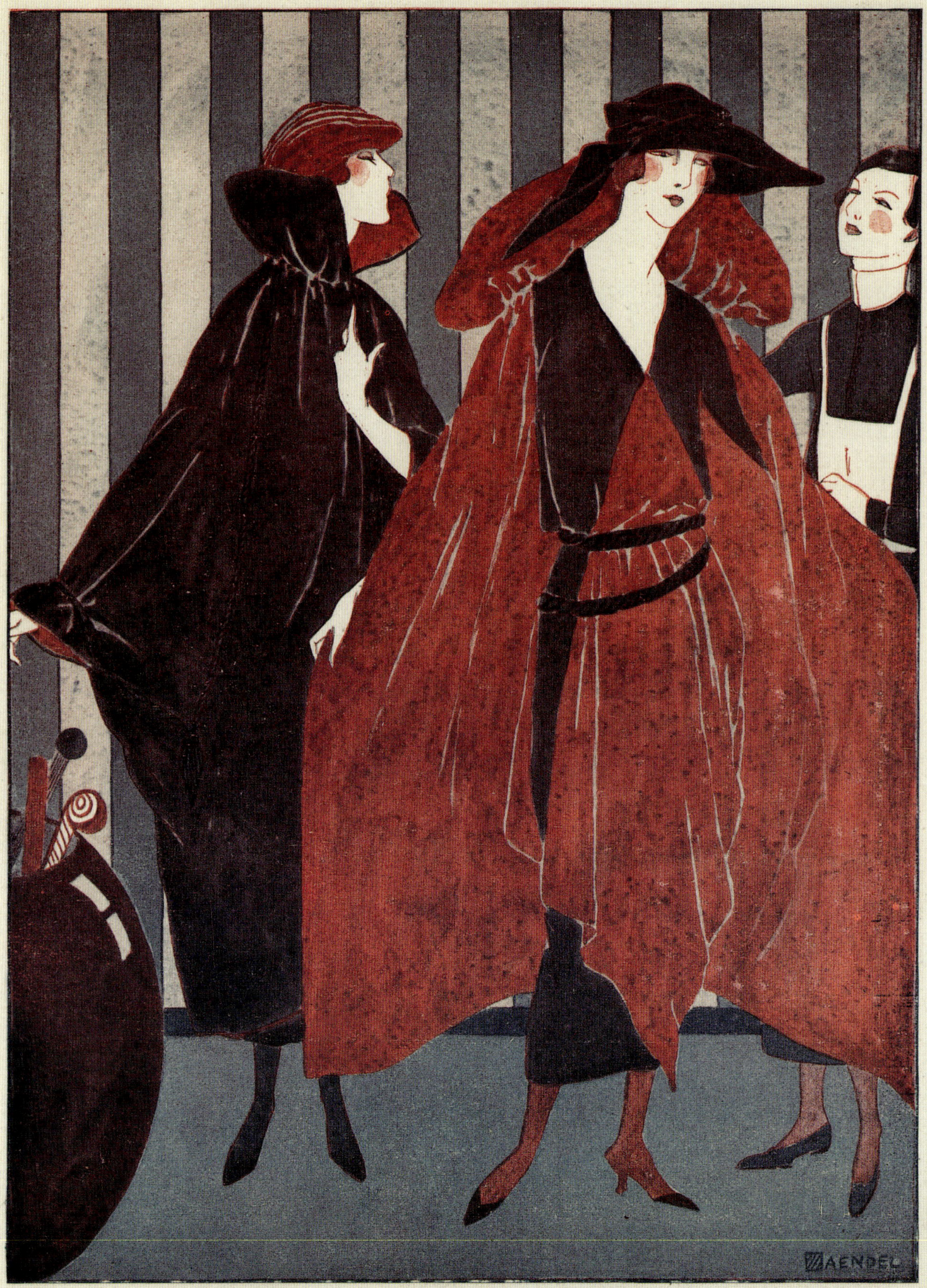
AENDEL

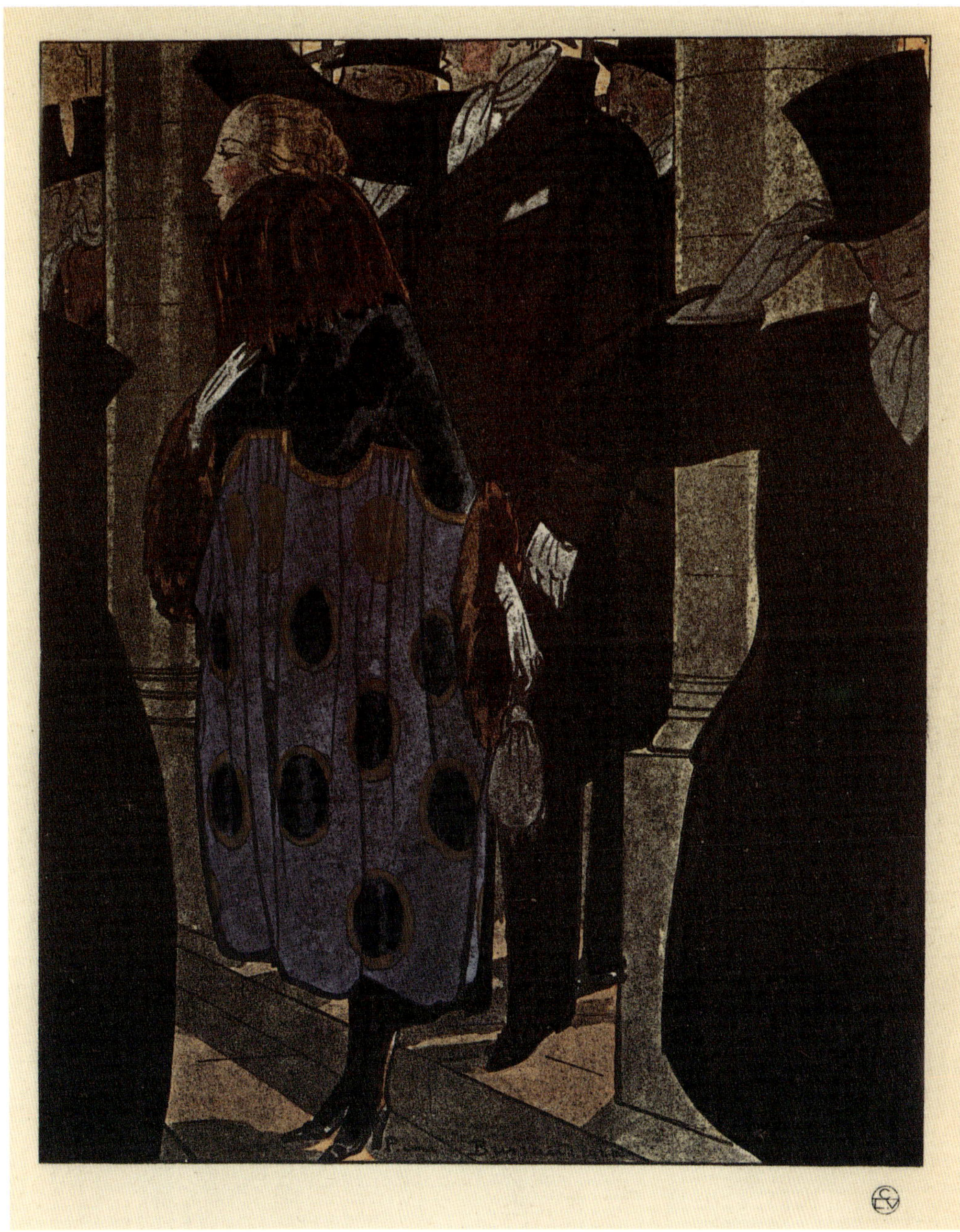

Left and above

"Sommes-nous les dernières?" (Are we the last?) – two ensembles in velour with chenille belts by Redfern. *L'Illustration des Modes*, 1920

"Appelez Urbain de L'avenue du Bois", evening coat by Beer. Illustration By Pierre Brissaud. *Gazette du Bon Ton*, 1920

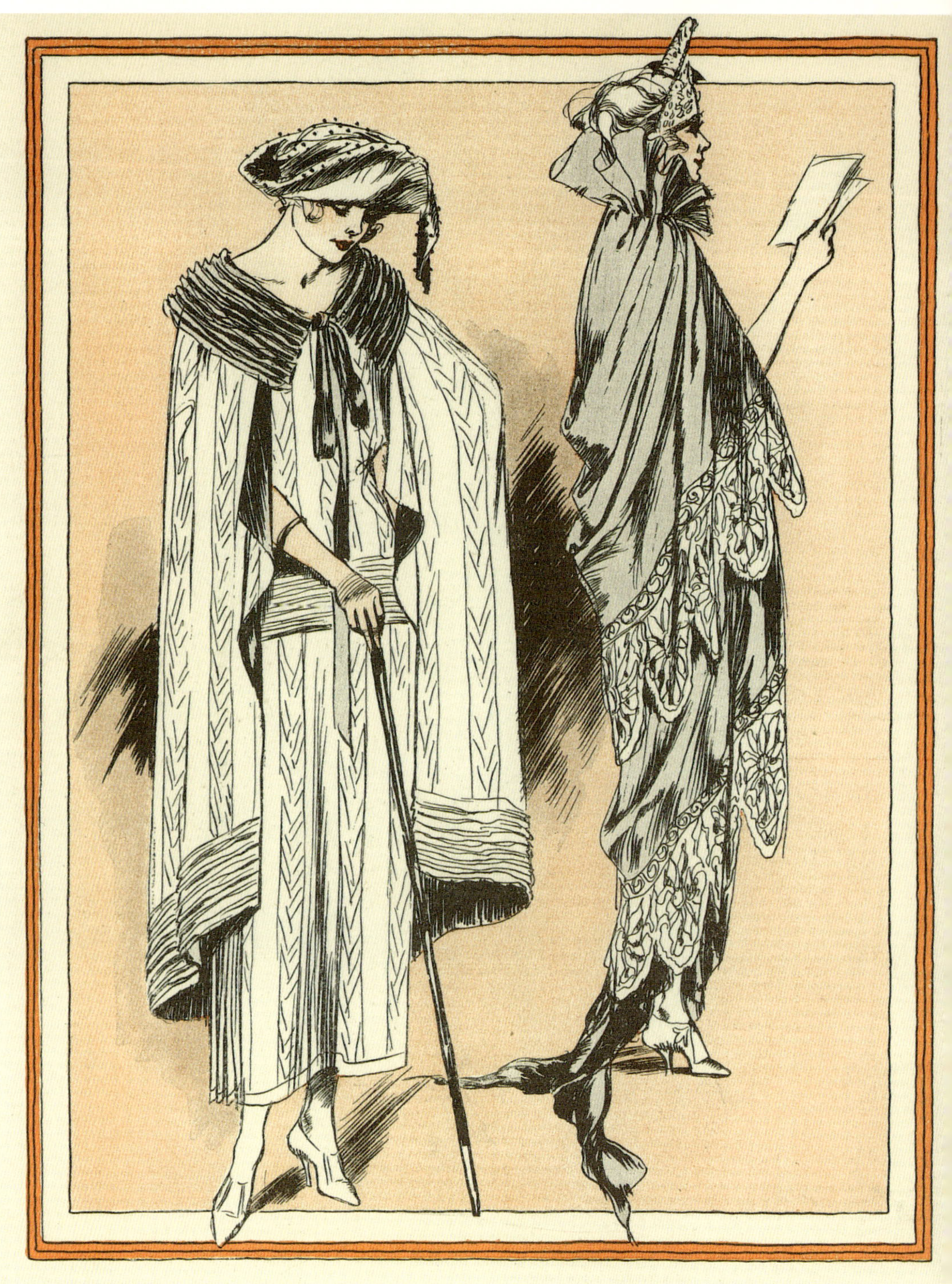

Above
Two cape and dress designs by Paul Carat. *The Delineator*, 1922

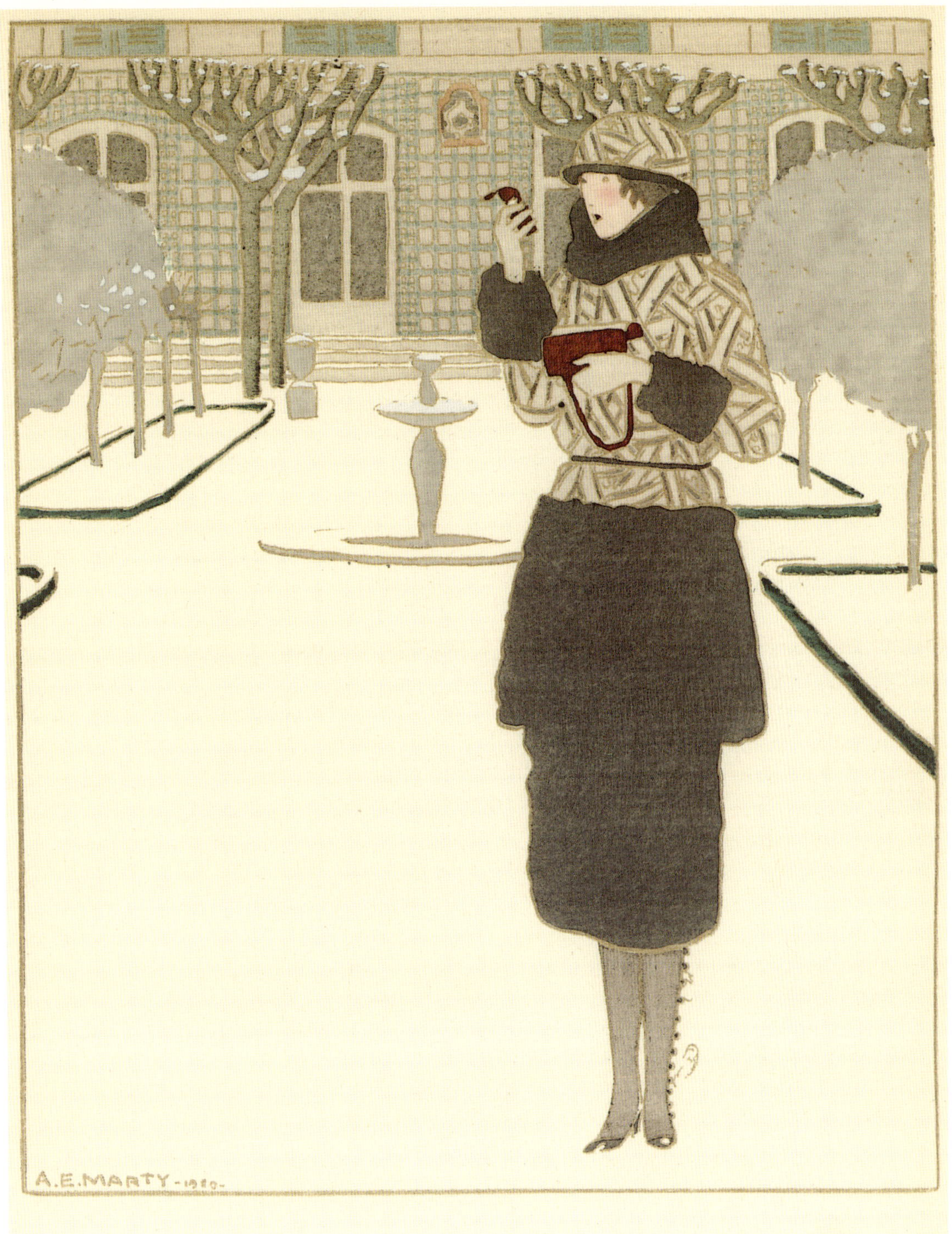

Above
"J'ai le bout du nez Rouge ou Un malheur vite repare" (The tip of my nose is red or an easily fixed misfortune), winter ensemble by Worth. Illustration By André Edouard Marty. *Gazette du Bon Ton*, 1920

Right
Postcard of a model in a brown day suit and patterned blouse with a matching cloche hat, 1922

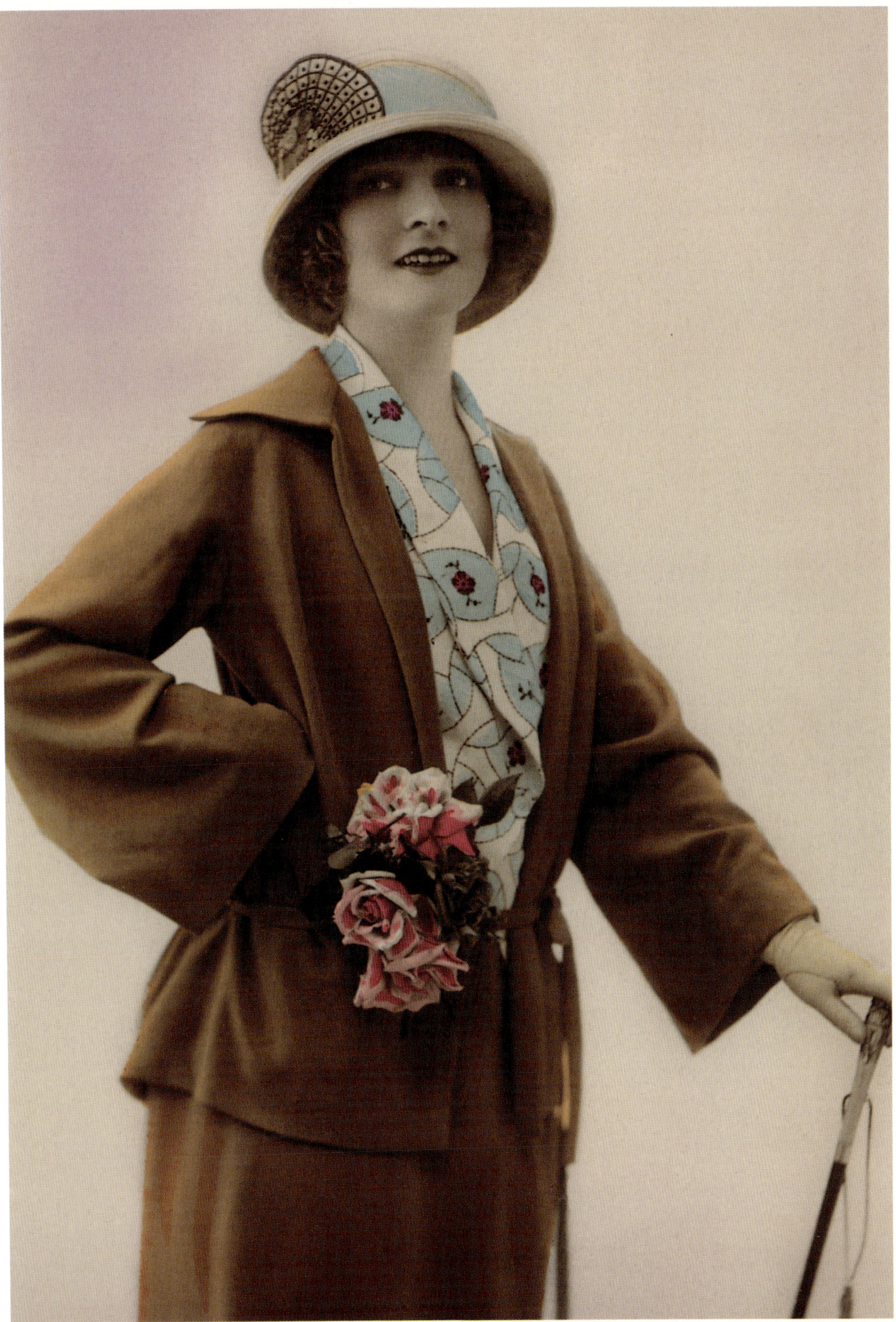

Right
Two wool crepe walking suits.
La Femme Élégante à Paris, 1926

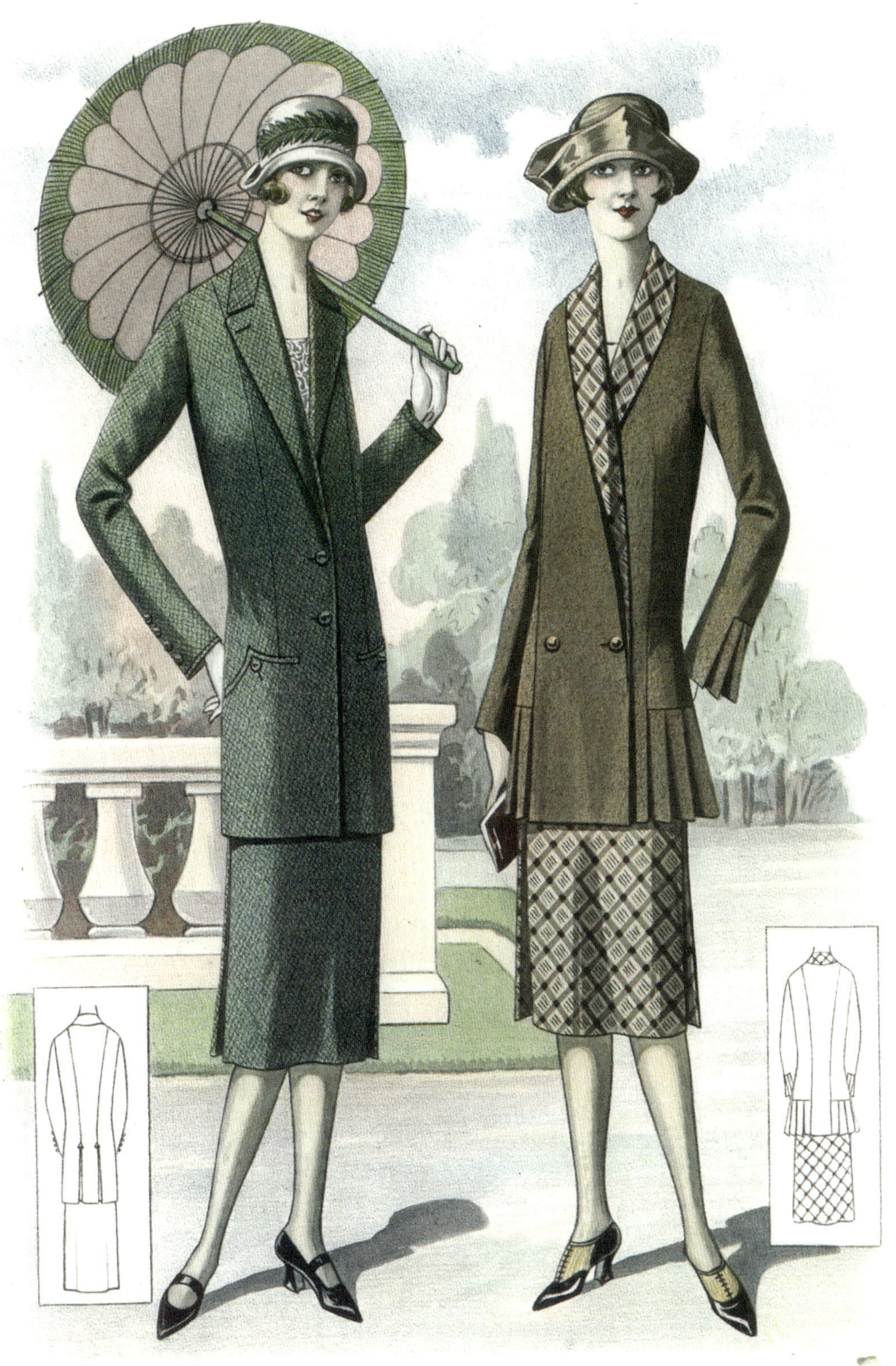

1268 1269

Right
Two walking outfits.
Les Dernières Modes de Paris, 1920

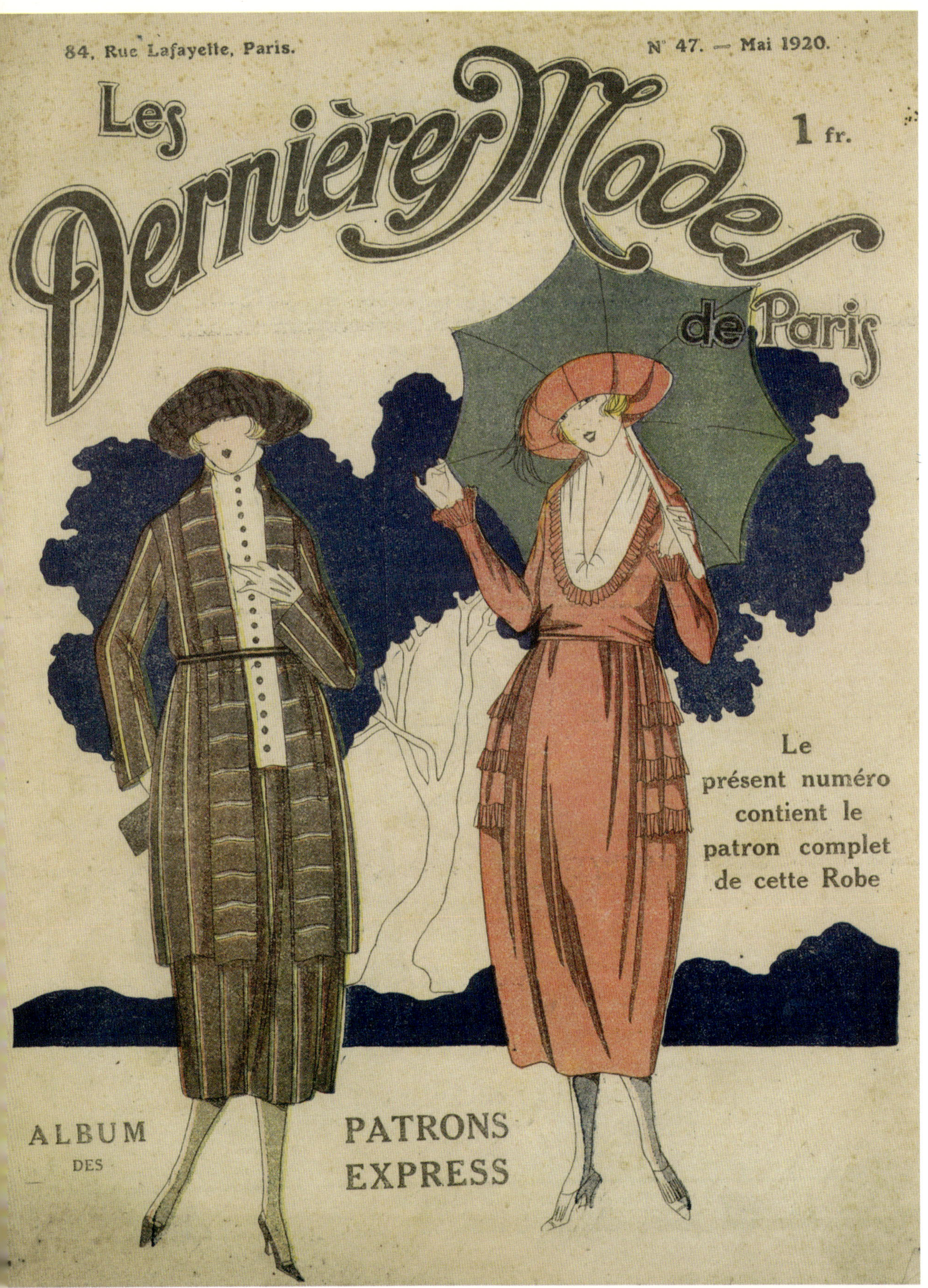
84, Rue Lafayette, Paris.
N° 47. — Mai 1920.
Les Dernières Modes de Paris
1 fr.
Le présent numéro contient le patron complet de cette Robe
ALBUM DES
PATRONS EXPRESS

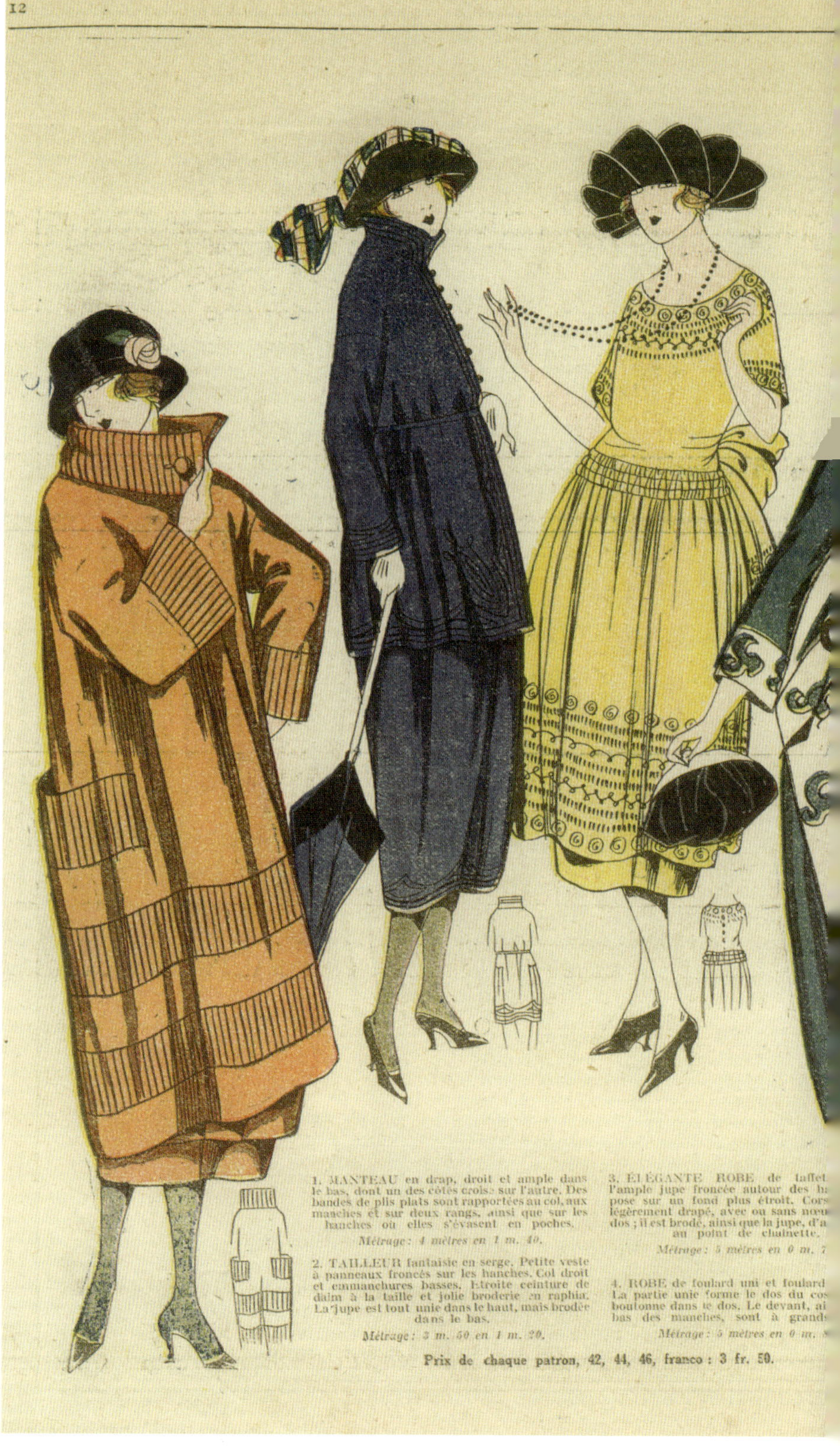

12

1. MANTEAU en drap, droit et ample dans le bas, dont un des côtés croise sur l'autre. Des bandes de plis plats sont rapportées au col, aux manches et sur deux rangs, ainsi que sur les hanches où elles s'évasent en poches.

Métrage : 4 mètres en 1 m. 40.

2. TAILLEUR fantaisie en serge. Petite veste à panneaux froncés sur les hanches. Col droit et emmanchures basses. Etroite ceinture de daim à la taille et jolie broderie en raphia. La jupe est tout unie dans le haut, mais brodée dans le bas.

Métrage : 3 m. 50 en 1 m. 20.

3. ÉLÉGANTE ROBE de taffet
l'ample jupe froncée autour des h
pose sur un fond plus étroit. Cors
légèrement drapé, avec ou sans nœu
dos ; il est brodé, ainsi que la jupe, d'a
au point de chaînette.

Métrage : 5 mètres en 0 m. 7

4. ROBE de foulard uni et foulard
La partie unie forme le dos du co
boutonne dans le dos. Le devant, ai
bas des manches, sont à grand

Métrage : 5 mètres en 0 m.

Prix de chaque patron, 42, 44, 46, franco : 3 fr. 50.

Above
Various coats, dresses and skirt suits.
Les Dernières Modes de Paris, 1920

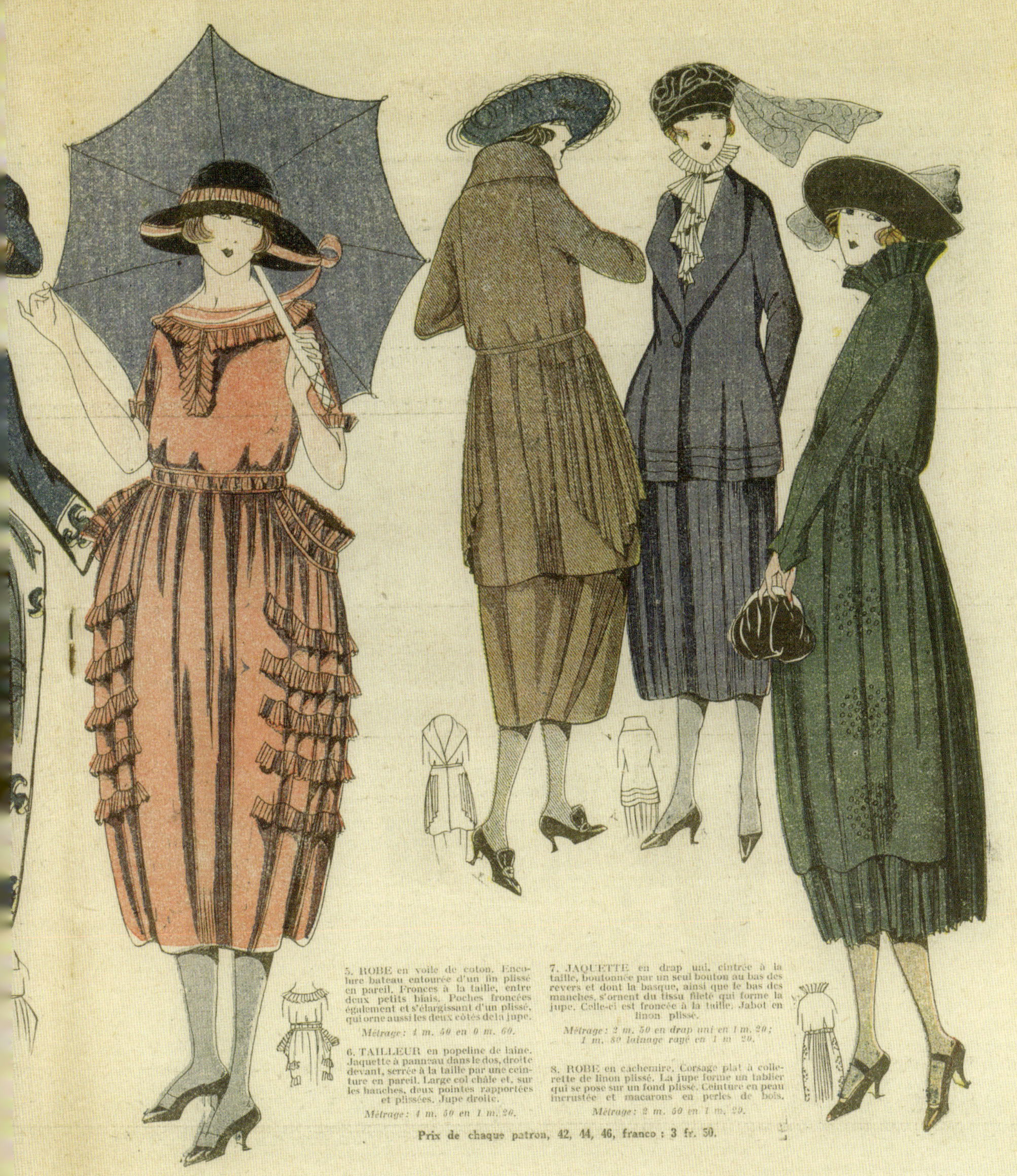

5. ROBE en voile de coton. Encolure bateau entourée d'un fin plissé en pareil. Fronces à la taille, entre deux petits biais. Poches froncées également et s'élargissant d'un plissé, qui orne aussi les deux côtés de la jupe.

Métrage : 4 m. 50 en 0 m. 60.

6. TAILLEUR en popeline de laine. Jaquette à panneau dans le dos, droite devant, serrée à la taille par une ceinture en pareil. Large col châle et, sur les hanches, deux pointes rapportées et plissées. Jupe droite.

Métrage : 4 m. 50 en 1 m. 20.

7. JAQUETTE en drap uni, cintrée à la taille, boutonnée par un seul bouton au bas des revers et dont la basque, ainsi que le bas des manches, s'ornent du tissu fileté qui forme la jupe. Celle-ci est froncée à la taille. Jabot en linon plissé.

Métrage : 2 m. 50 en drap uni en 1 m. 20 ; 1 m. 80 lainage rayé en 1 m. 20.

8. ROBE en cachemire. Corsage plat à collerette de linon plissé. La jupe forme un tablier qui se pose sur un fond plissé. Ceinture en peau incrustée et macarons en perles de bois.

Métrage : 2 m. 50 en 1 m. 20.

Prix de chaque patron, 42, 44, 46, franco : 3 fr. 50.

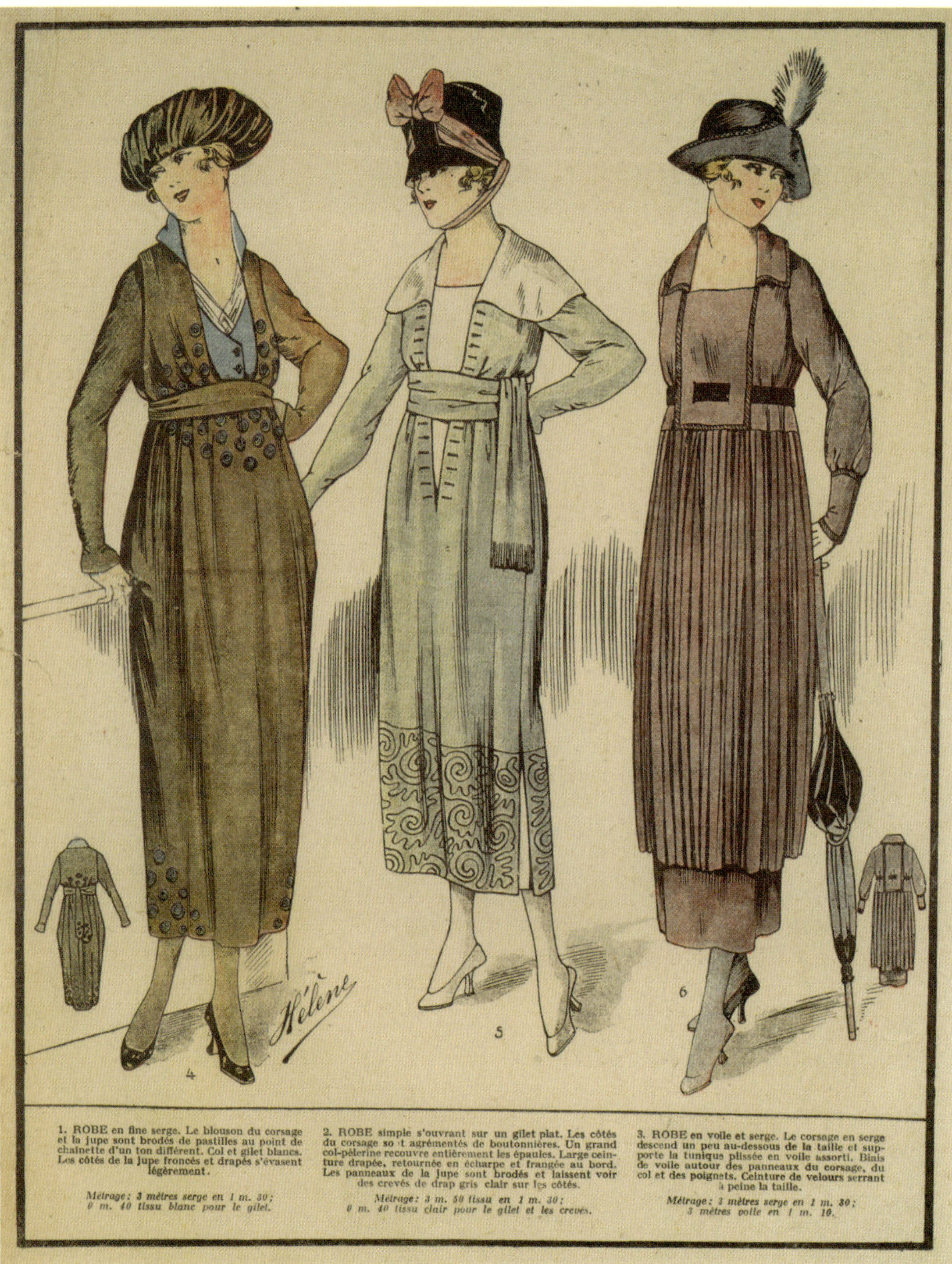

Above

Three walking dresses with waist sashes. *Les Dernières Modes de Paris*, 1920

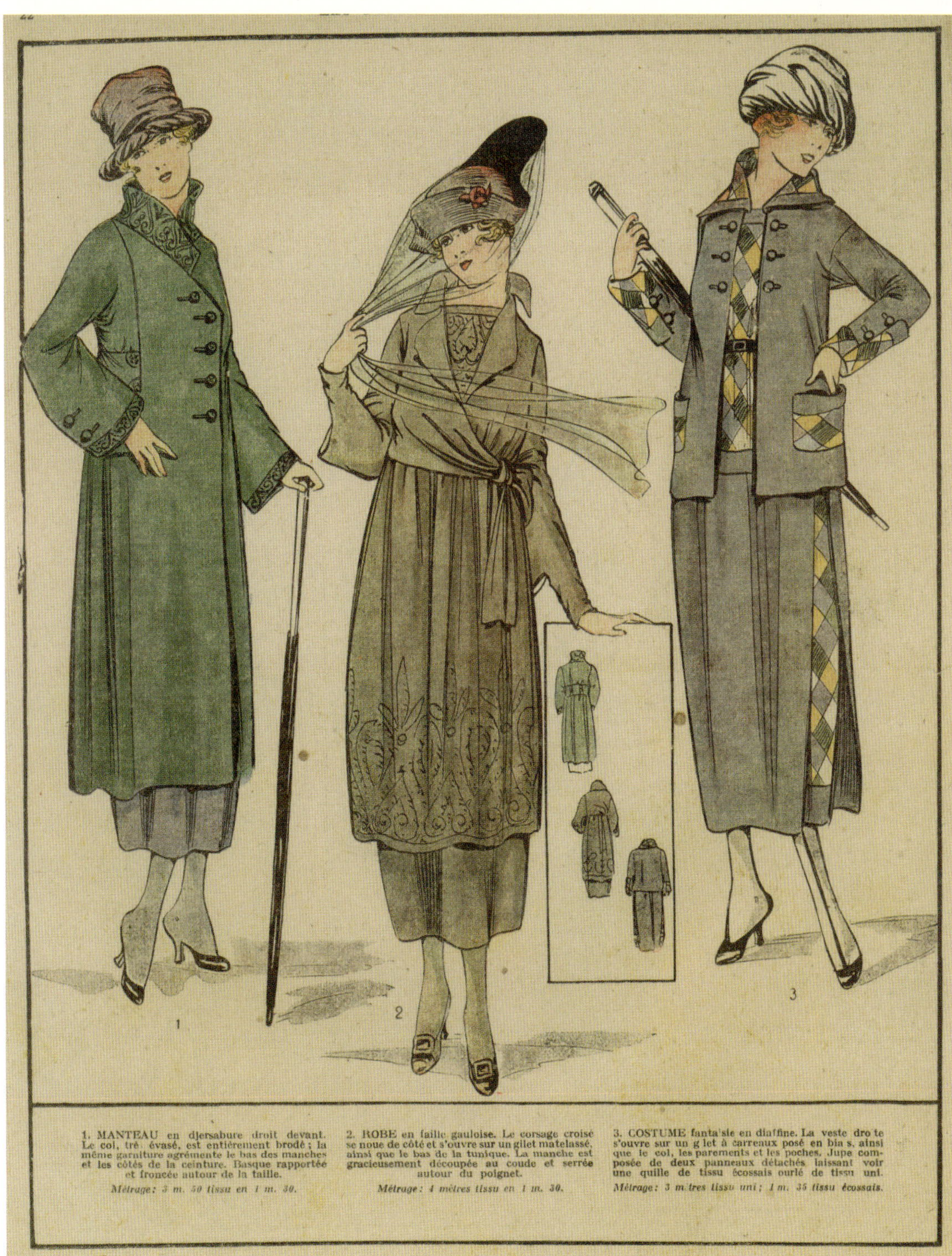

1. MANTEAU en djersabure droit devant. Le col, trè. évasé, est entièrement brodé ; la même garniture agrémente le bas des manches et les côtés de la ceinture. Basque rapportée et froncée autour de la taille.

Métrage: 3 m. 50 tissu en 1 m. 30.

2. ROBE en faille gauloise. Le corsage croisé se noue de côté et s'ouvre sur un gilet matelassé, ainsi que le bas de la tunique. La manche est gracieusement découpée au coude et serrée autour du poignet.

Métrage: 4 mètres tissu en 1 m. 30.

3. COSTUME fanta'sie en diaffine. La veste dro te s'ouvre sur un g let à carreaux posé en bia s, ainsi que le col, les parements et les poches. Jupe composée de deux panneaux détachés laissant voir une quille de tissu écossais ourlé de tissu uni.

Métrage: 3 m tres tissu uni; 1 m. 35 tissu écossais.

Above

Three walking outfits.

Les Dernières Modes de Paris, 1920

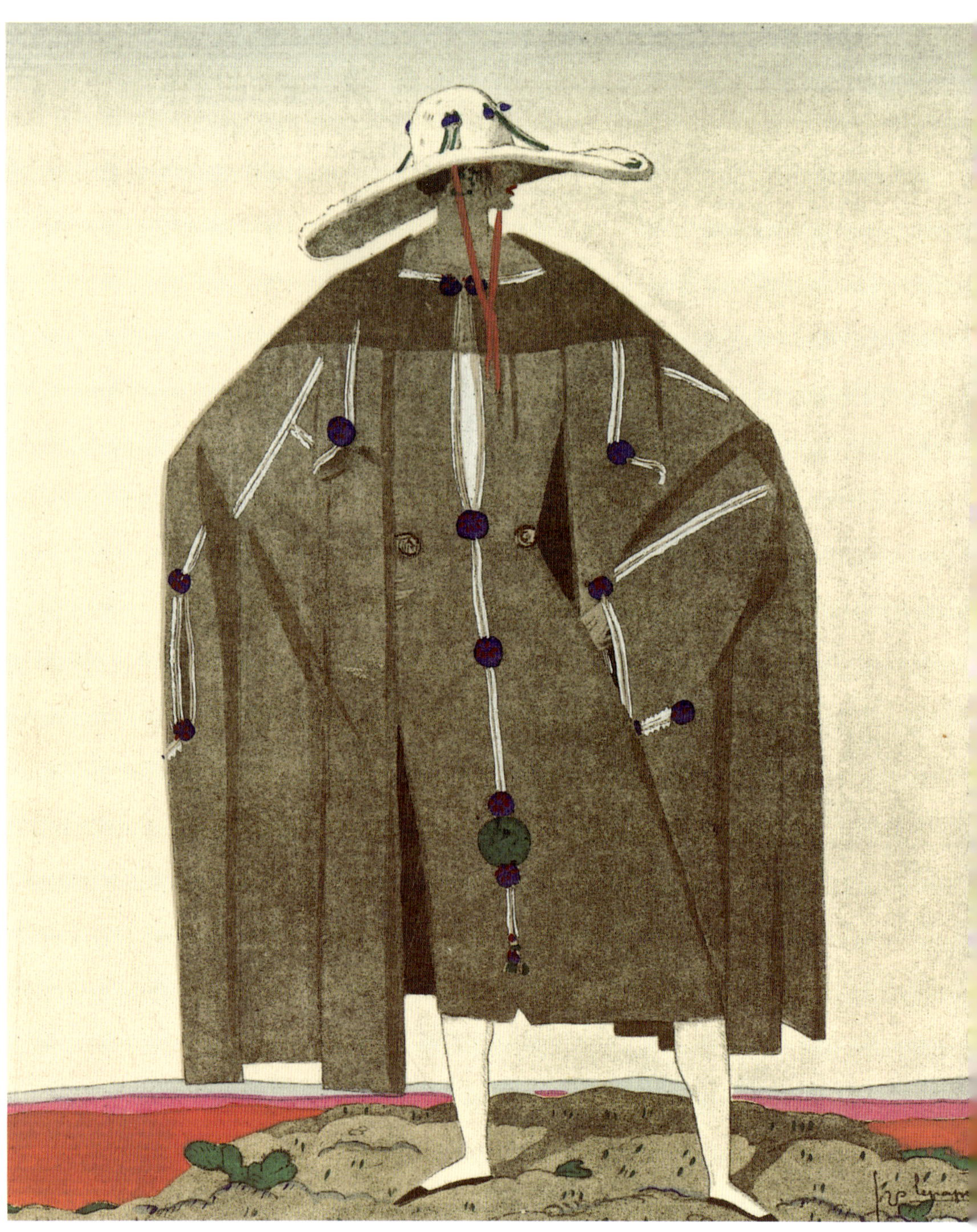

Above
"Tanger ou Les charmes de l'exil" (Tangiers or the charm of being in exile), afternoon dress and cape by Paul Poiret. Illustration by George Lepape. *Gazette du Bon Ton*, 1920

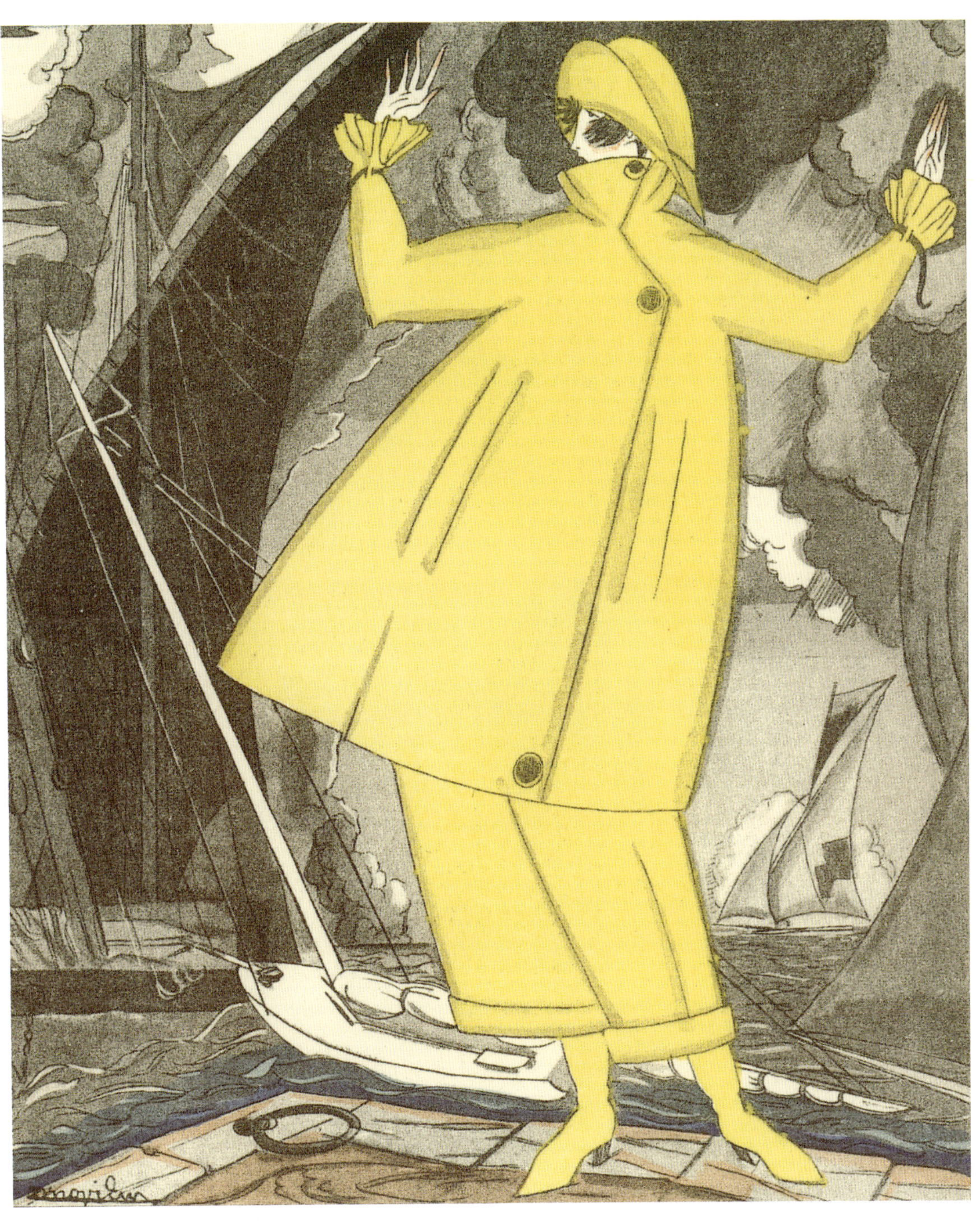

Above
"Gros temps" (Stormy weather), yachting outfit. *Gazette du Bon Ton*, 1920

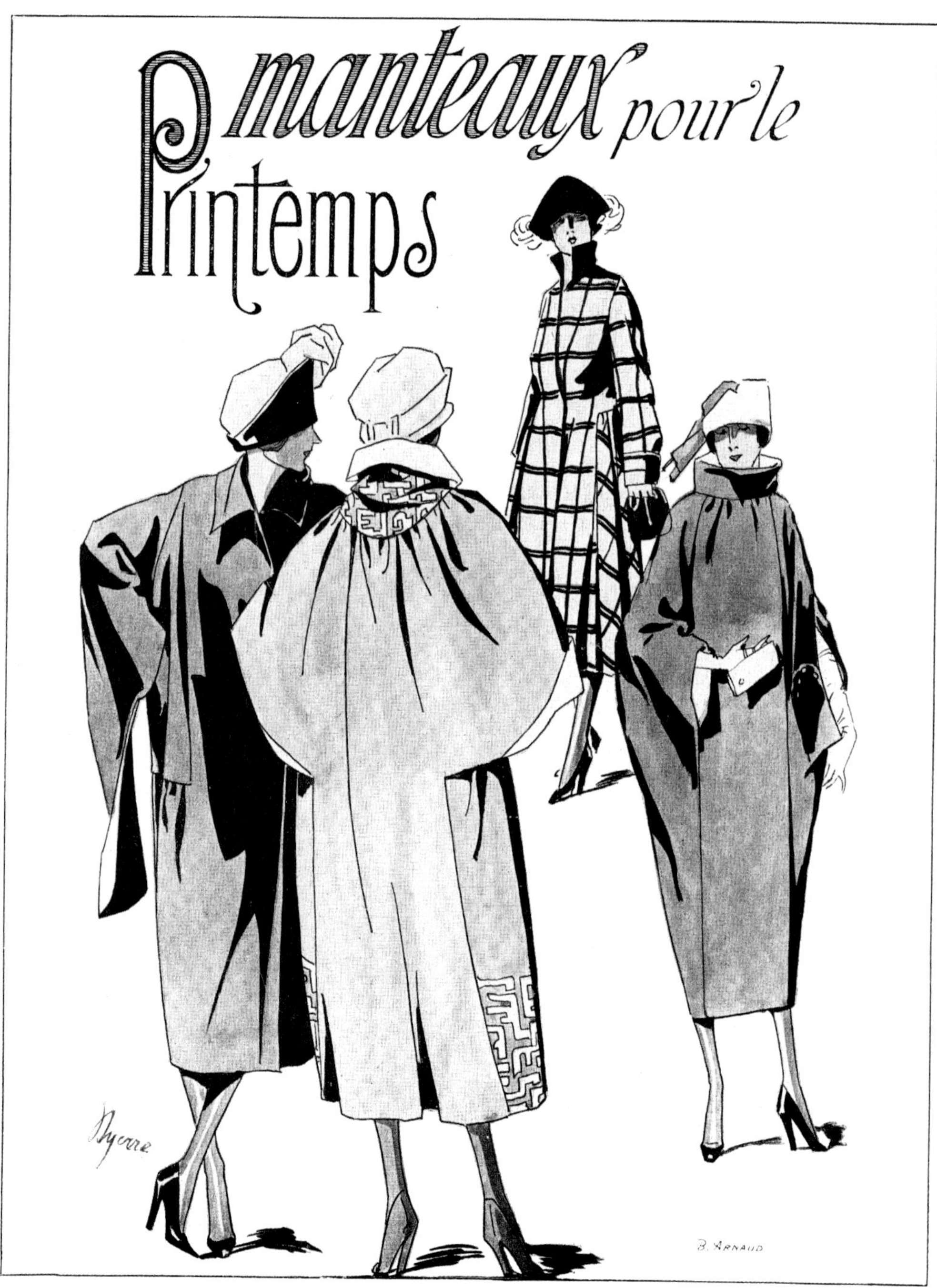

Above

Four coat models for spring.
La Nouveauté Francaise, 1921

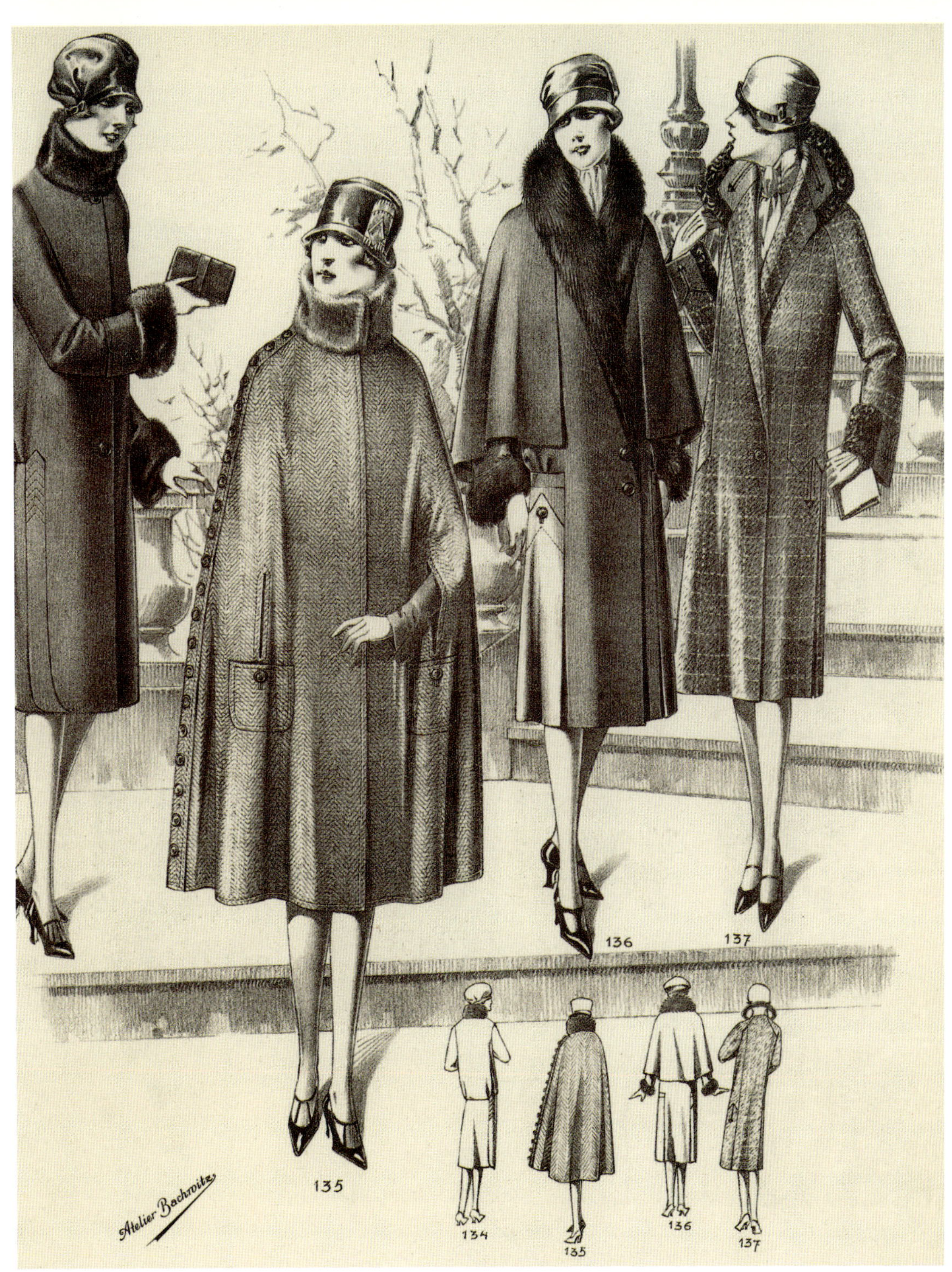

Above
Three coats and a cape by Atelier Bachroitz, c.1924

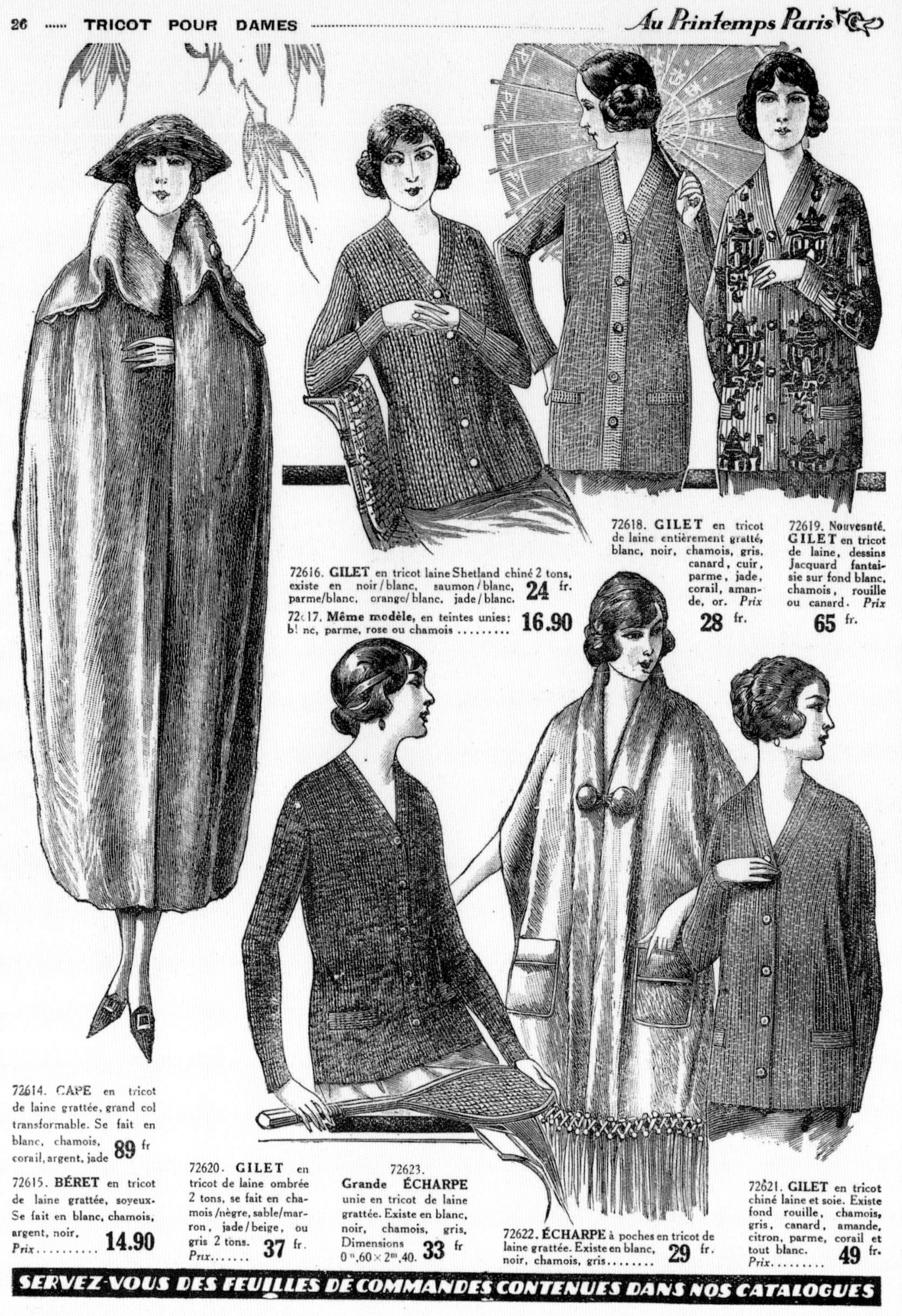

26 ...... TRICOT POUR DAMES .... *Au Printemps Paris*

72616. **GILET** en tricot laine Shetland chiné 2 tons, existe en noir/blanc, saumon/blanc, parme/blanc, orange/blanc, jade/blanc. **24** fr.

72617. **Même modèle,** en teintes unies: blanc, parme, rose ou chamois **16.90**

72618. **GILET** en tricot de laine entièrement gratté, blanc, noir, chamois, gris, canard, cuir, parme, jade, corail, amande, or. *Prix* **28** fr.

72619. Nouveauté. **GILET** en tricot de laine, dessins Jacquard fantaisie sur fond blanc, chamois, rouille ou canard. *Prix* **65** fr.

72614. **CAPE** en tricot de laine grattée, grand col transformable. Se fait en blanc, chamois, corail, argent, jade **89** fr

72615. **BÉRET** en tricot de laine grattée, soyeux. Se fait en blanc, chamois, argent, noir. *Prix* **14.90**

72620. **GILET** en tricot de laine ombrée 2 tons, se fait en chamois/nègre, sable/marron, jade/beige, ou gris 2 tons. *Prix* ...... **37** fr.

72623. Grande **ÉCHARPE** unie en tricot de laine grattée. Existe en blanc, noir, chamois, gris. Dimensions 0m,60 × 2m,40. **33** fr

72622. **ÉCHARPE** à poches en tricot de laine grattée. Existe en blanc, noir, chamois, gris .... **29** fr.

72621. **GILET** en tricot chiné laine et soie. Existe fond rouille, chamois, gris, canard, amande, citron, parme, corail et tout blanc. *Prix* .... **49** fr.

SERVEZ-VOUS DES FEUILLES DE COMMANDES CONTENUES DANS NOS CATALOGUES

Above

Selection of knitwear including capes and cardigans, Printemps catalogue, 1924

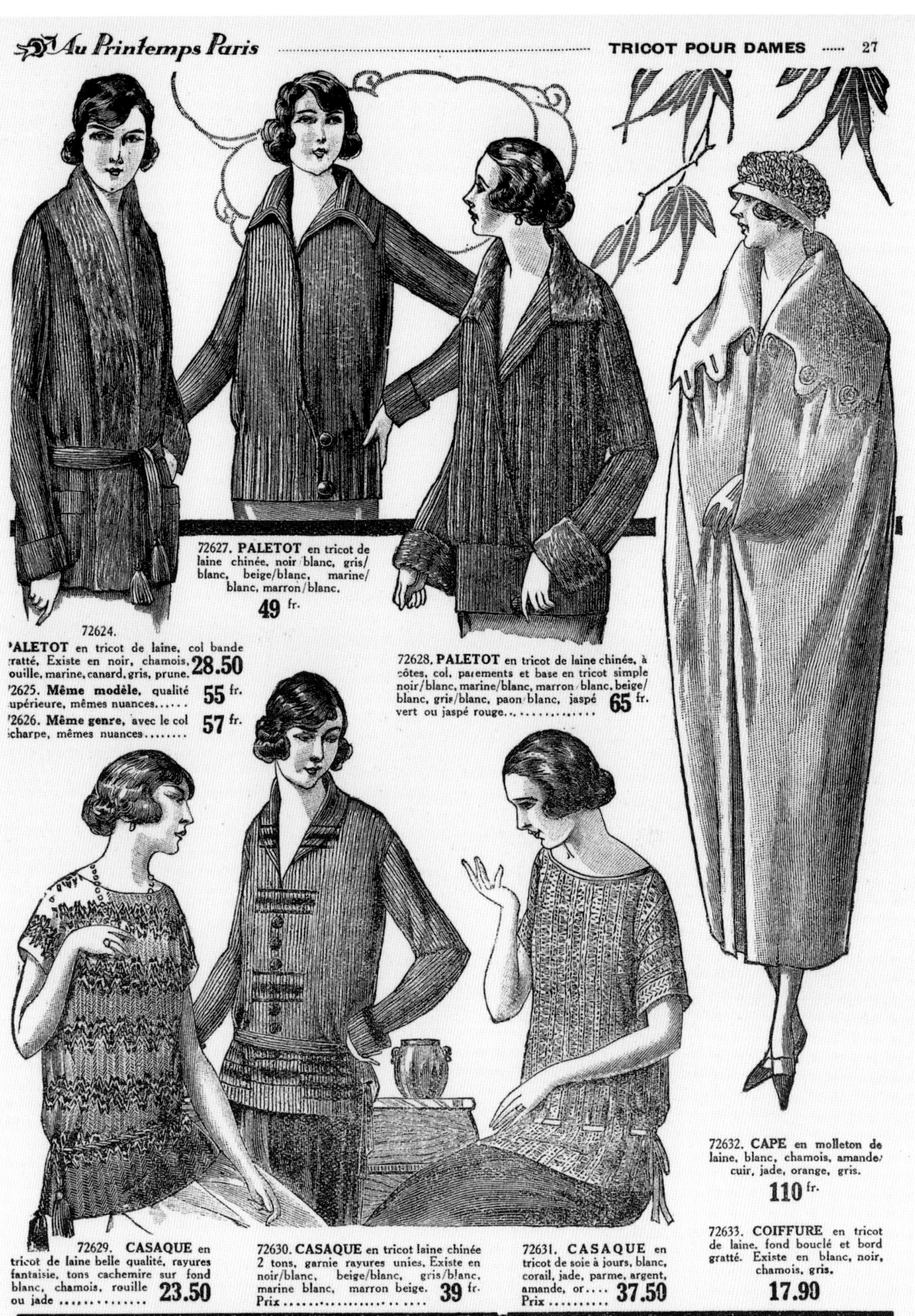

Above
Selection of knitwear including capes, cardigans and jumpers, Printemps catalogue, 1924

Below

An ensemble of a red-brown satin with a matching jacket of velvet trimmed with light-coloured fur by Atelier Bachroitz
Modèles Originaux, c.1926

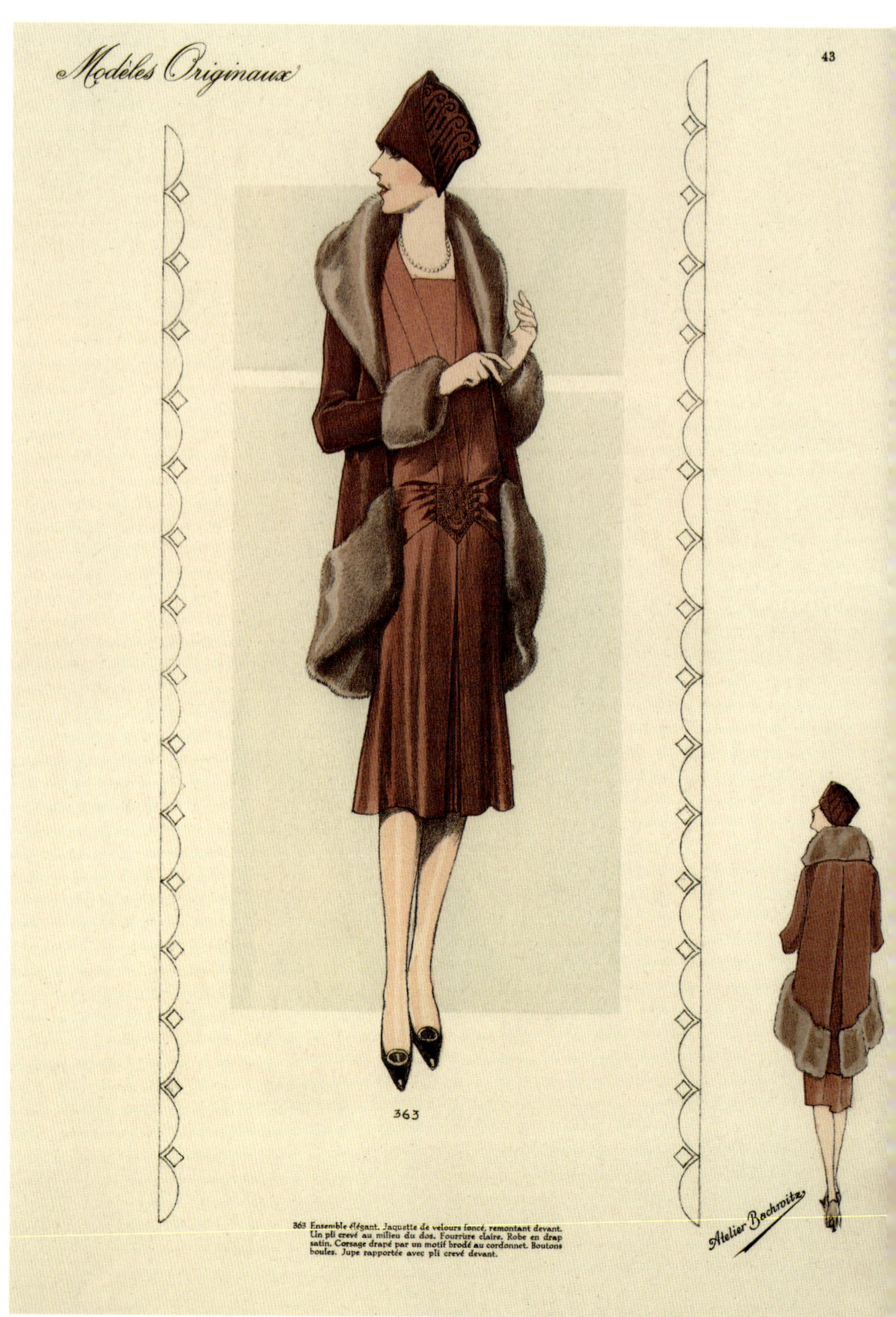

Below
Three suits and jackets. *La Femme Chic*, c.1923. All the coats are trimmed with fur showing a Russian influence.

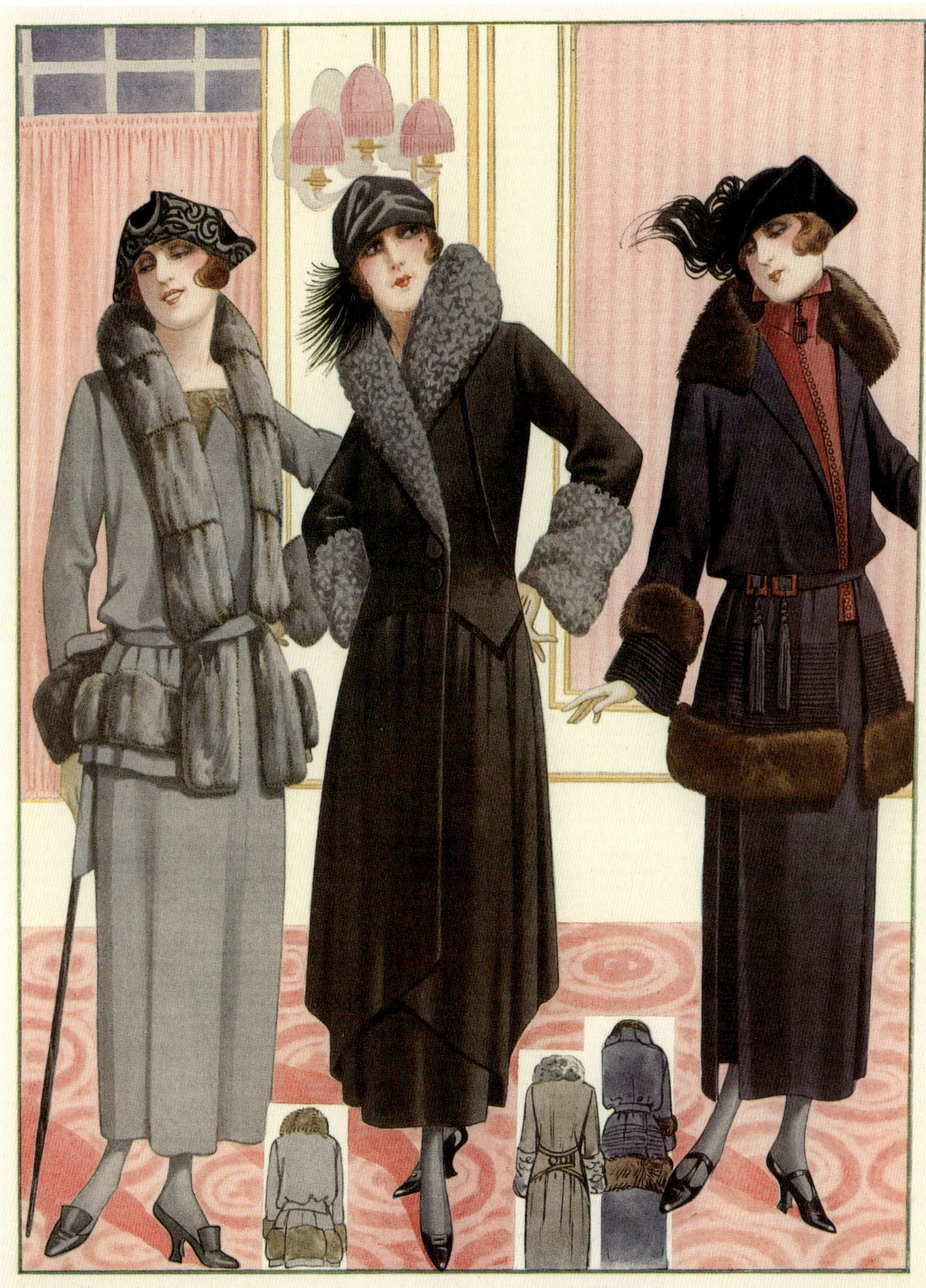

Right
Hollywood actress Mae Bush wearing a suit of Mesange blue Kasha combined with the same shade of crepe de Chine. The coat is trimmed with silver fox and the dress is made with an uneven skirt. The hat is flesh coloured horse hair trimmed with a pearl ornament and blue ribbon. This press photograph announces that Miss Mae will be wearing this outfit in her upcoming Metro-Goldwyn-Mayer production "Time, The Comedian". The outfit is attributed to Érte. 1925

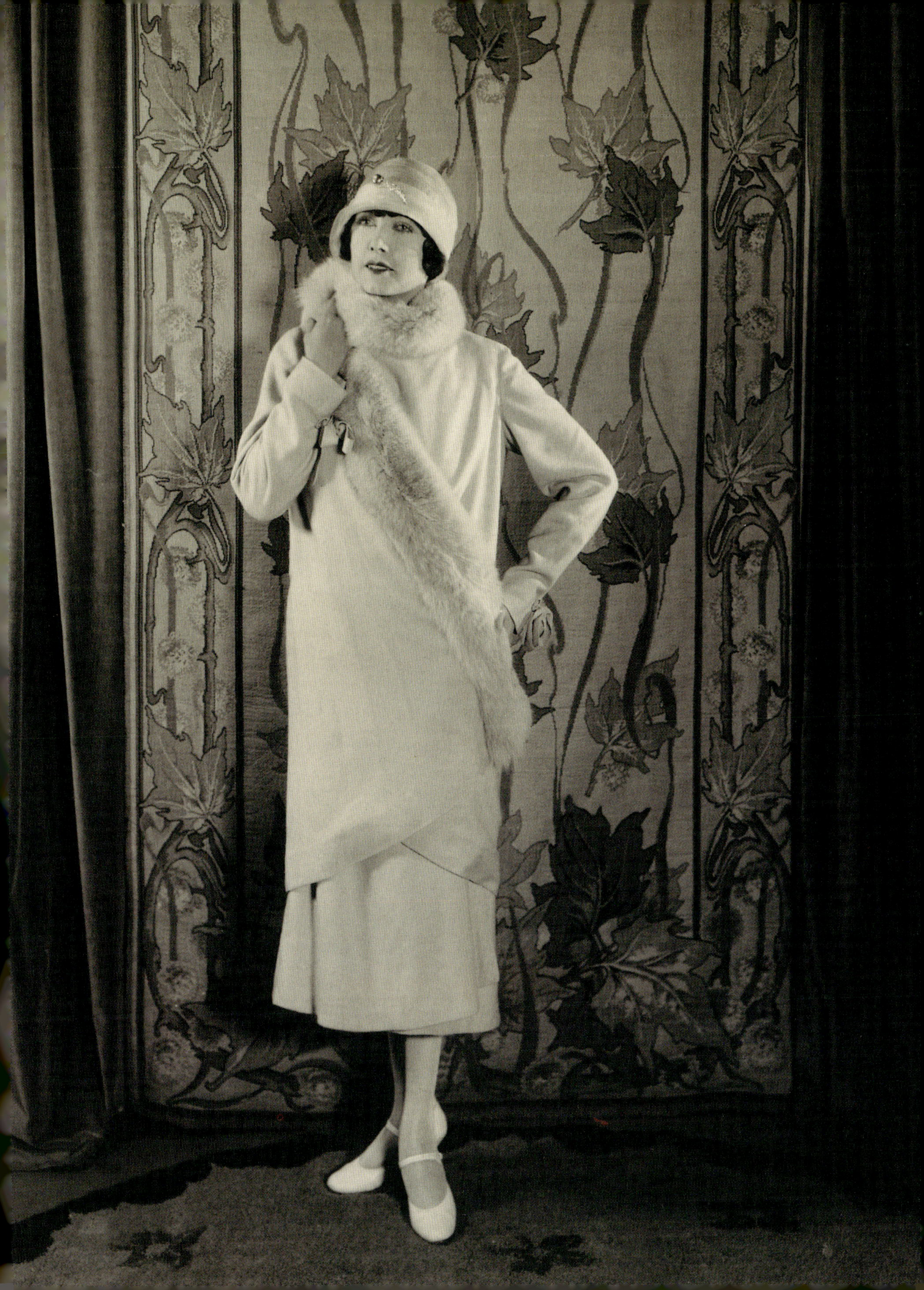

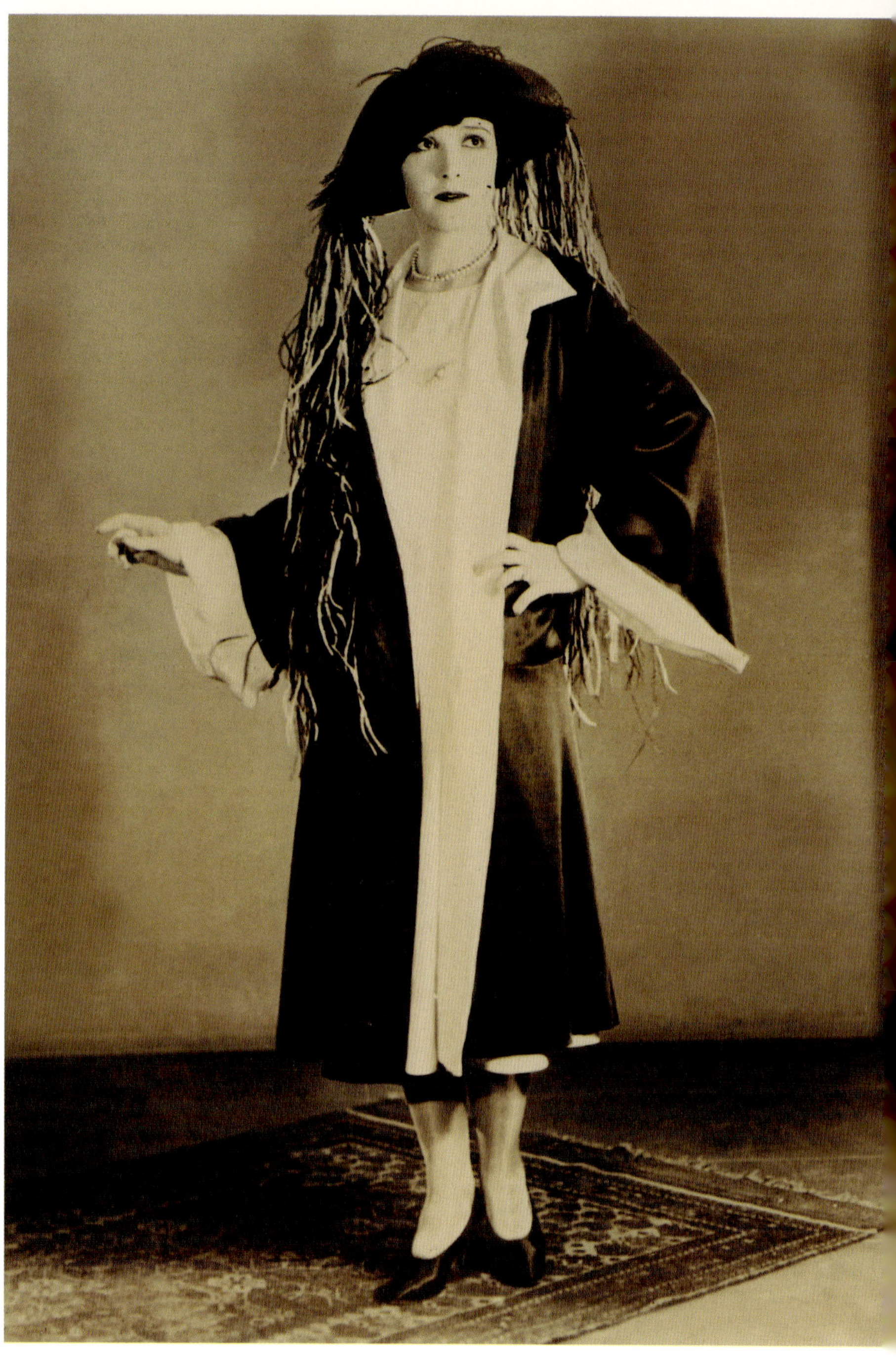

Above and right
Black and white costume over a straight crepe dress, c.1923. The black satin coat is lined with white satin and boasts a circular hem, while the hat is adorned with long drooping feathers.

Fall suit of flat "American broadtail" fur with a matching hat and handbag, c.1925

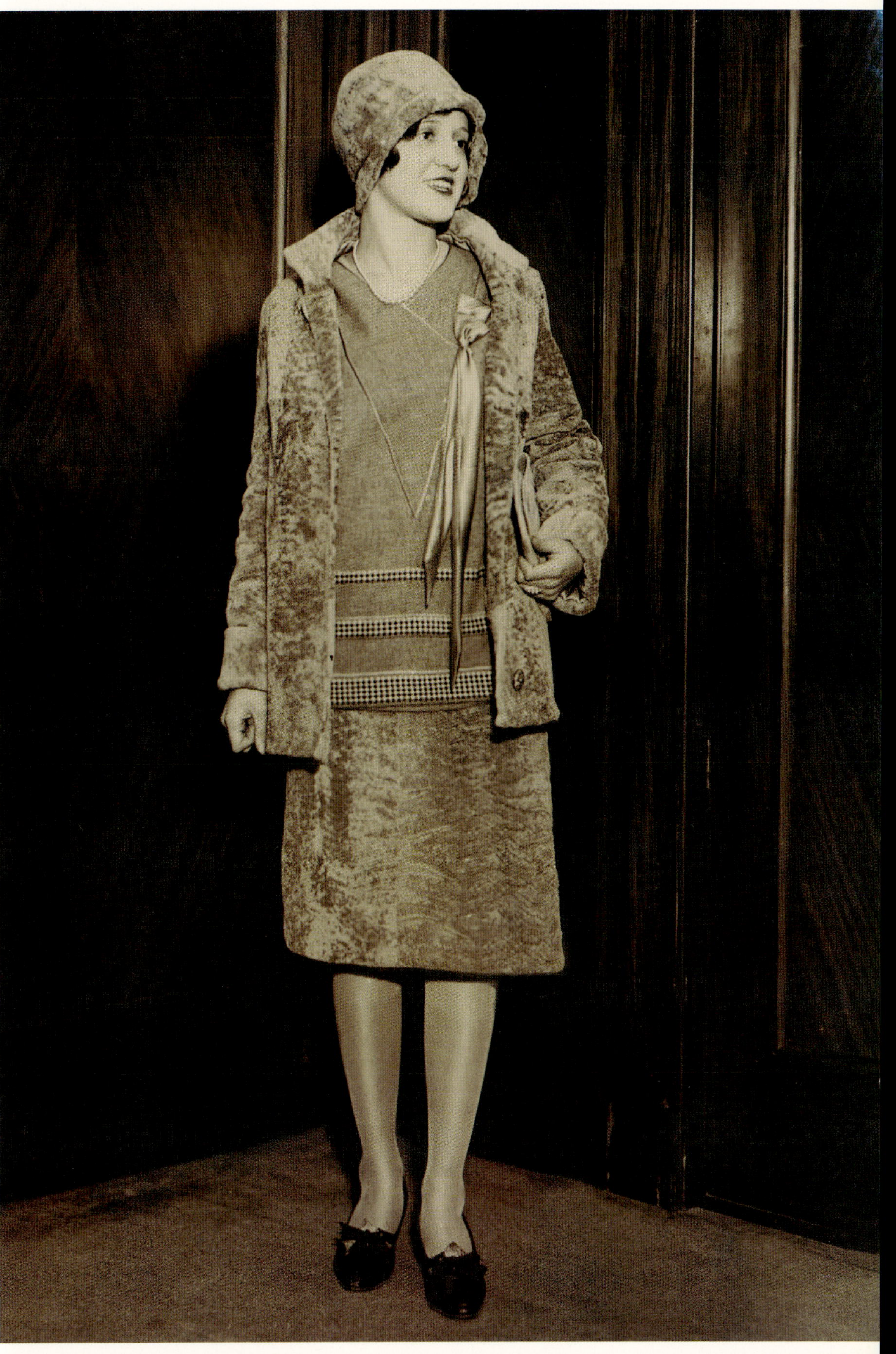

Right
Knitted day coat by Pierce Tex, possibly a golfing coat. USA, c.1926

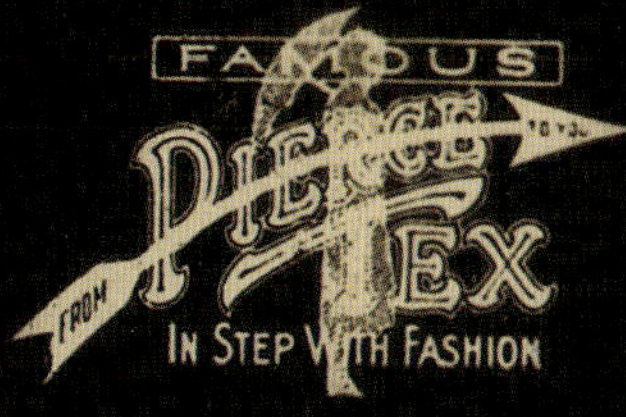

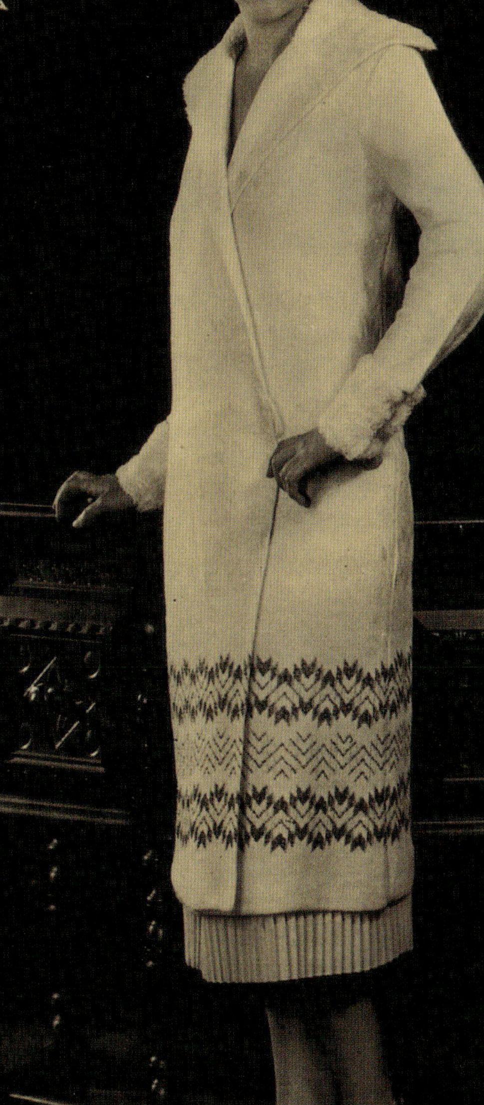

Coat Style 10

Underwood & Underwood

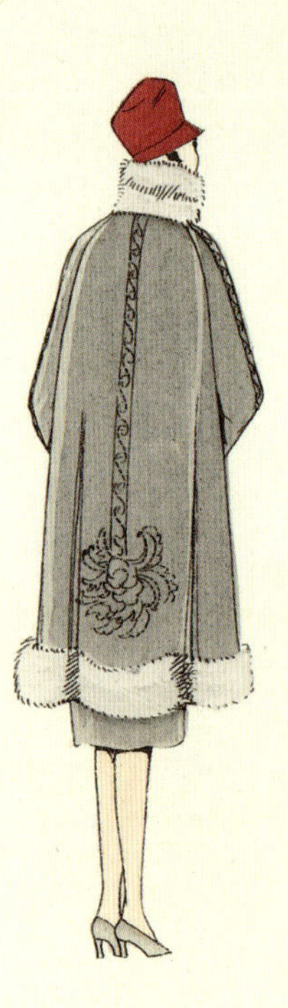

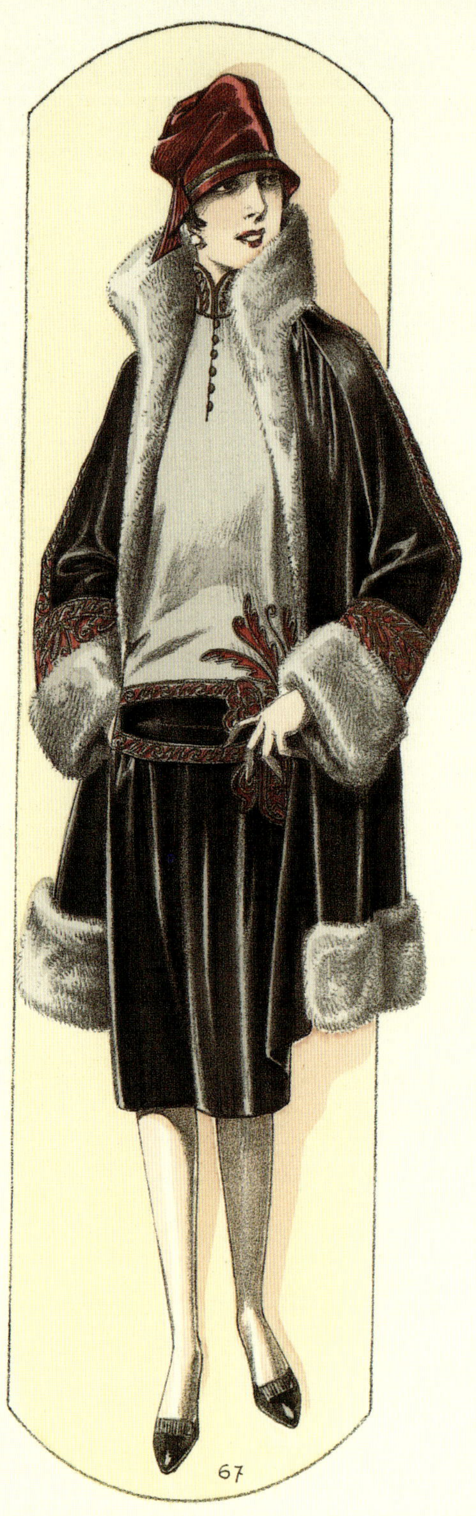

ALBUM TAILLEUR
DE LUXE

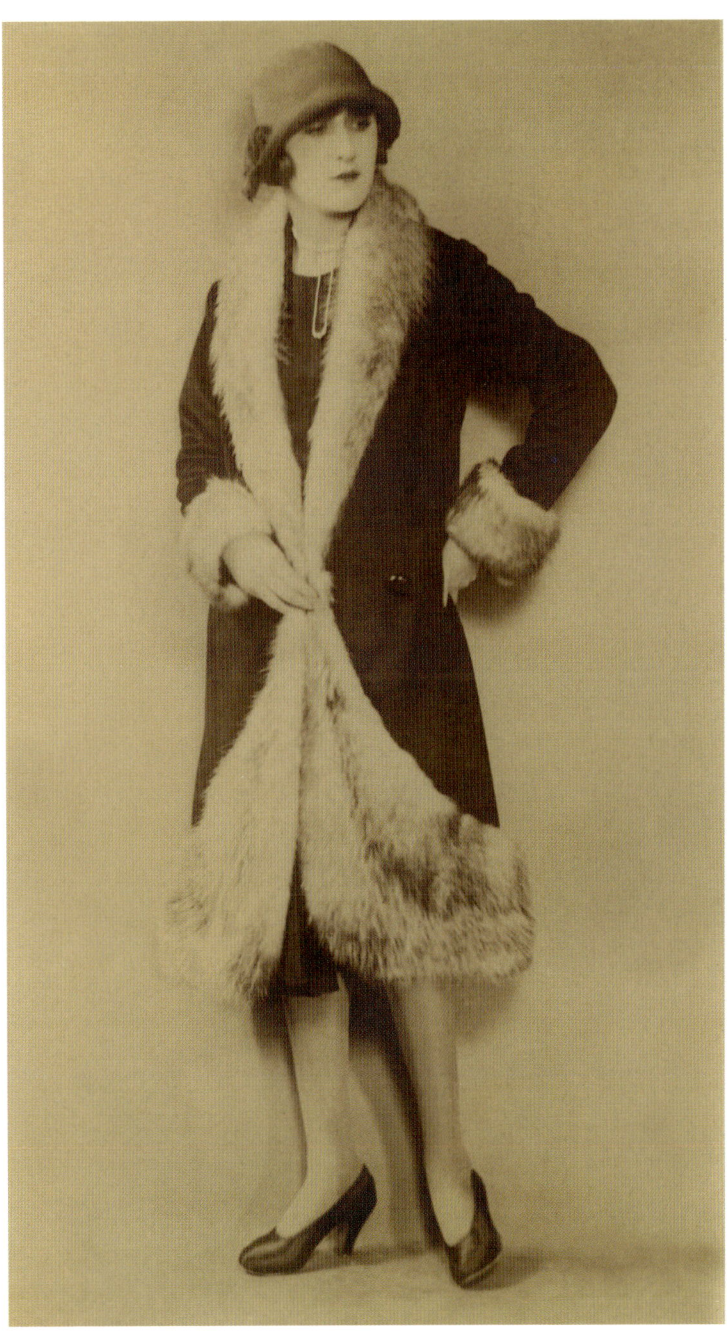

Left and above

Winter ensemble of a grey and black dress with elaborate red and silver embroidery, and a black cape coat with matching embroidery and trimmed in grey fur. *Album Tailleur de Luxe*, c.1925

A black velour winter coat trimmed with fur, which instead of doing up is supposed to be held together by the wearer, c.1925

Right

Two summer ensembles; the model on the left is wearing a grey Georgette and lace two-piece suit trimmed with grey fox fur, the model on the right is wearing a black and biscuit net dress with three-tier frill effect and accordion pleats. The collar is made of foxaline, a cheaper pelt dyed to resemble fox fur, c.1926

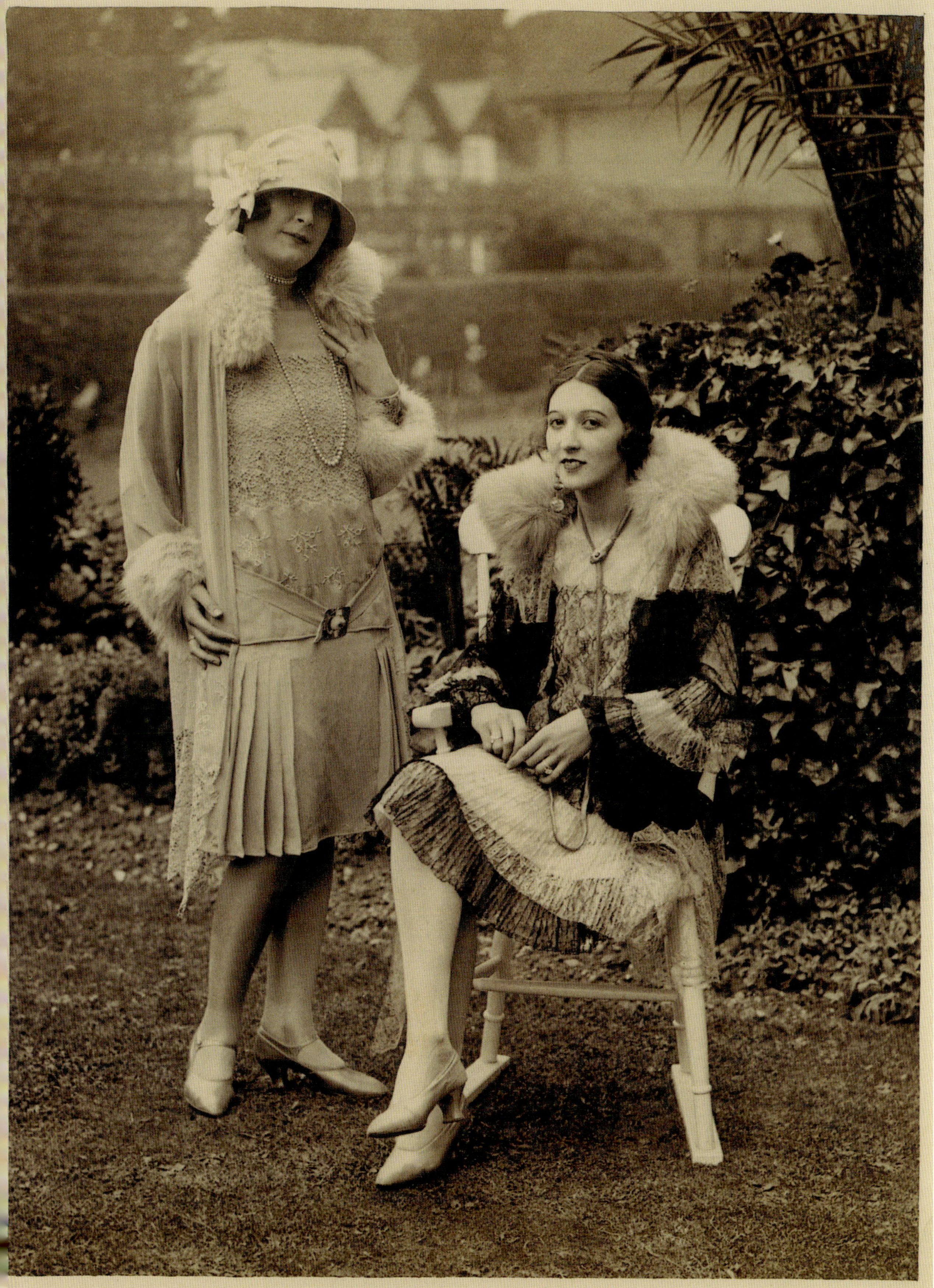

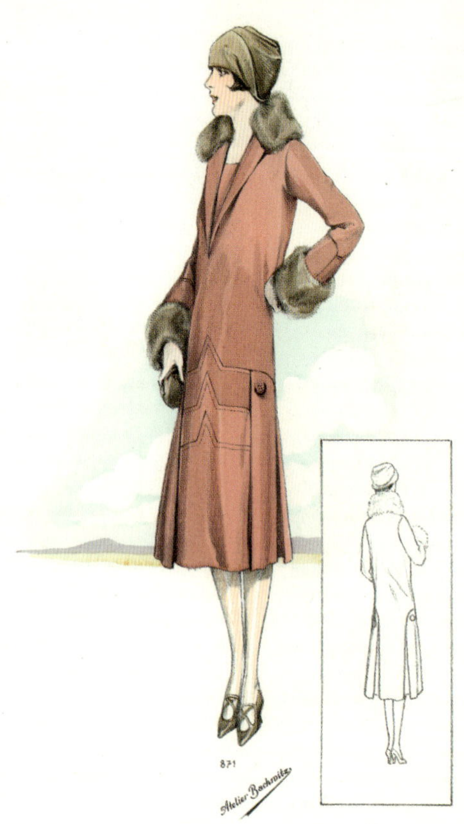

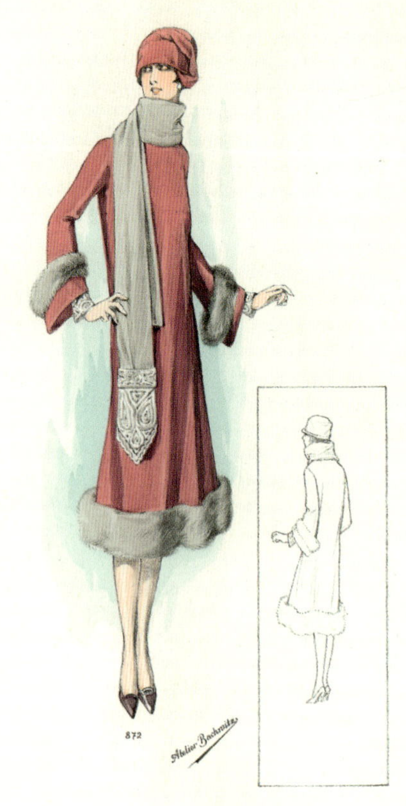

Above left and right

Street robe cut in scallops at the front with pale fur collar and cuffs by Atelier Bachroitz, *Chic Parisien Beaux-arts des Modes*, 1925

Velvet street dress with tight sleeves and wide cuffs by Atelier Bachroitz – both scarf and cuffs are embroidered in wool. *Chic Parisien Beaux-arts des Modes*, 1925

Right

An ensemble costume of Kasha and silk crepe with metal embroidered belt motif, a full length coat with fur collar and cuffs, an ensemble costume of checked wool faced with silk crepe and a wool velour coat with fur collar, cuffs and banding by Atelier Bachroitz. *Chic Parisien Beaux-Arts des Modes*, 1925

„Chic Parisien"

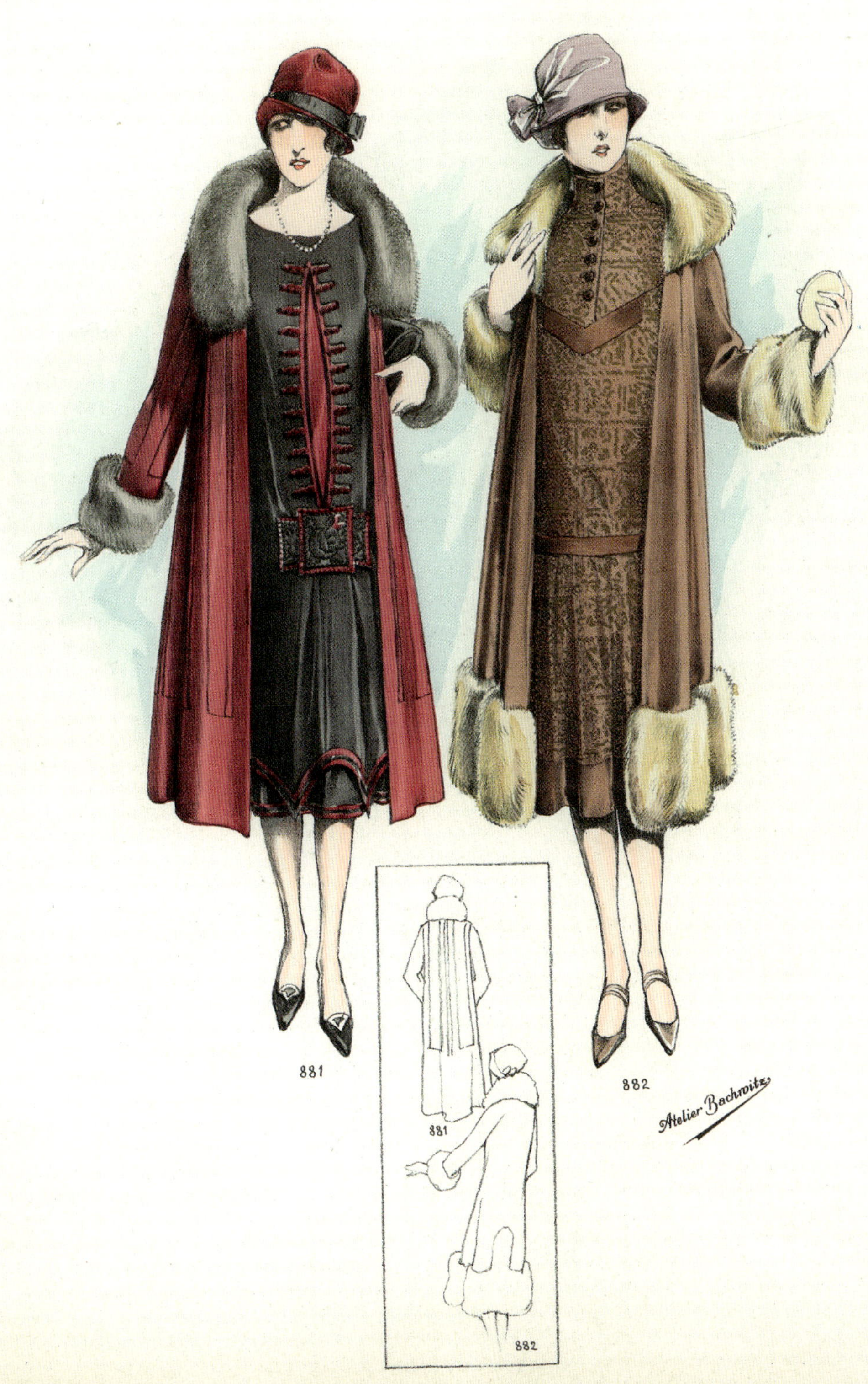

Right
Four designs for coats
by Atelier Bachroitz, c.1924

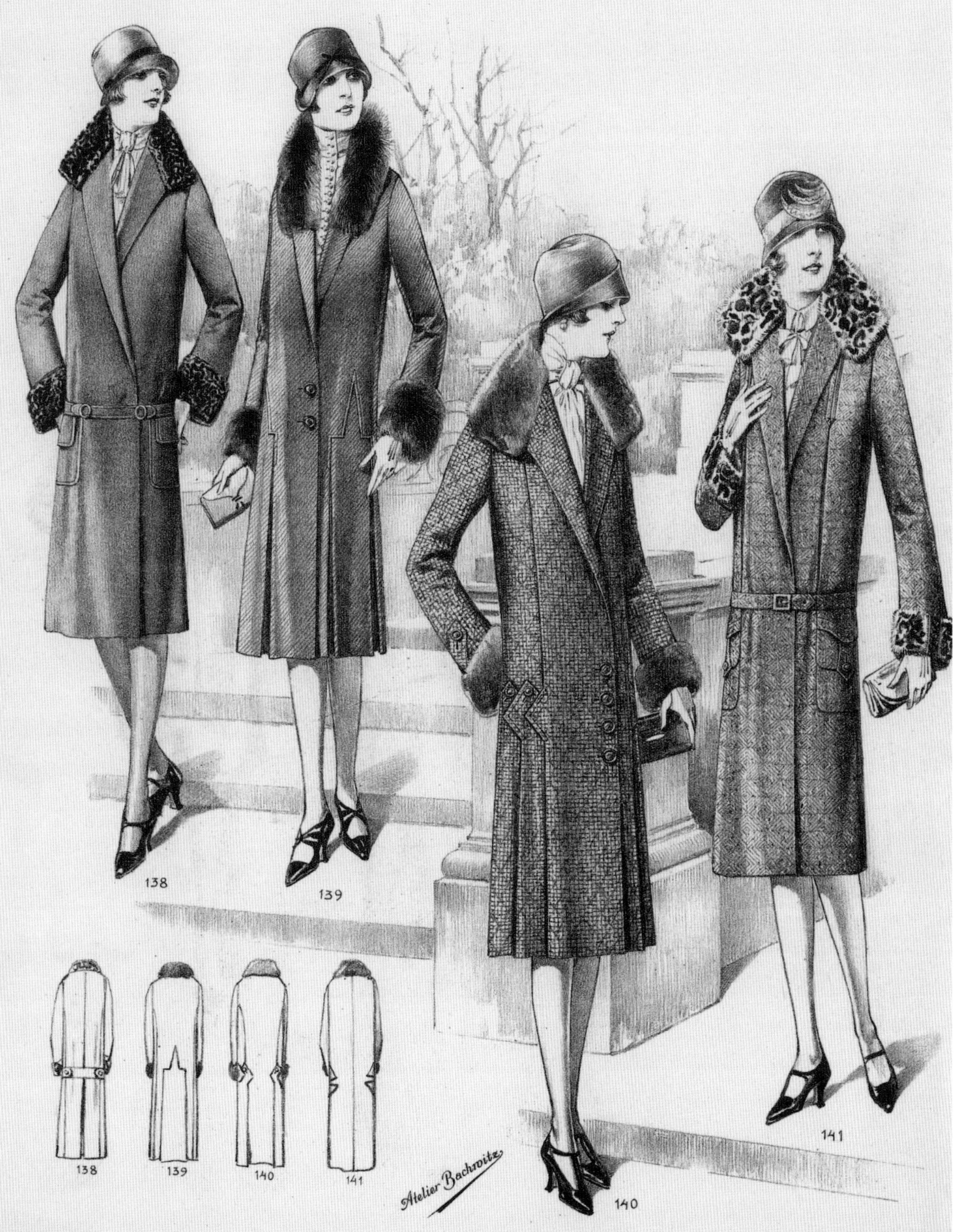

138 Manteau d'hiver en burafyl. Col et parements d'astrakan. Ceinture de tissu. Poches appliquées.

138 Winter coat of burafyl. Collar and cuffs of Persian lamb. Material belt. Back seam, large pocket flaps.

139 Manteau d'hiver en diagonal. Col et parements de renard. Incrustations dentelées, formant plis crevés.

139 Single breasted winter coat of diagonal. Fox collar and cuffs. Panels incrusted in scallops and drawn in inverted pleats.

140 Manteau trotteur en lainage quadrillé. Col et parements de fourrure. Lés plissés rapportés en dents.

140 Trotteur coat of checked woollen. Fur collar and cuffs. Panels attached in scallops and drawn in pleats..

141 Manteau en mêlé. Col et parements en cha tigré. Coutures à plis crevés. Doubles poche aves pattes.

141 Coat of mixing. Collar and cuffs of tige cat. Front seams opening out in inverted pleats. Double pockets with tabs.

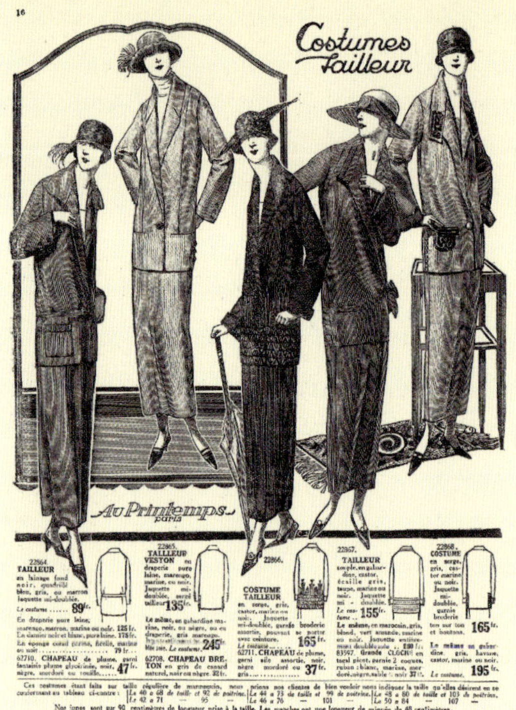

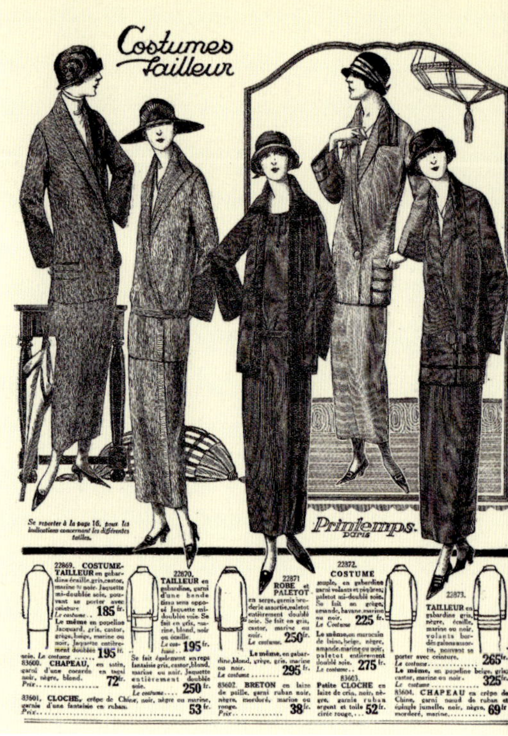

Above left and right

Selection of tailored skirt suits,
Printemps catalogue, 1924

Selection of tailored skirt suits,
Printemps catalogue, 1924

Below left and right

Selection of tailored skirt suits, Printemps catalogue, 1924

Selection of mourning outfits, the accompanying text points out that all mourning orders are fulfilled as quickly as possible. Printemps catalogue, 1924

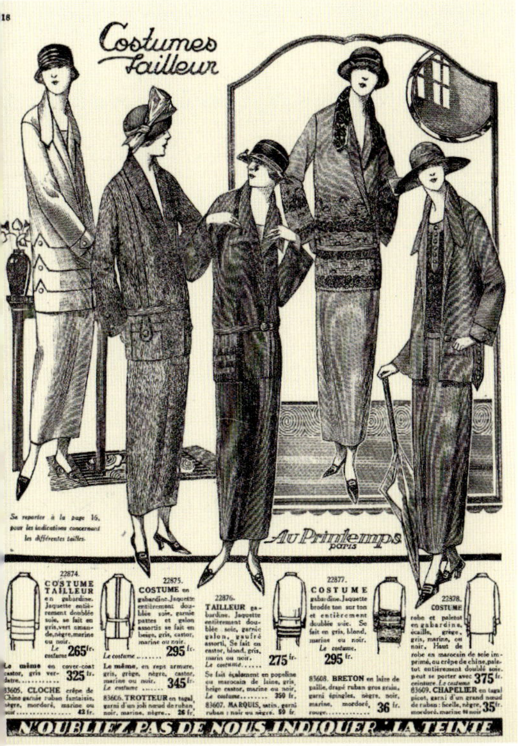

18

Costumes Tailleur

Se reporter à la page 16, pour les indications concernant les différentes tailles.

Au Printemps
paris

22874. COSTUME TAILLEUR en gabardine. Jaquette entièrement doublée soie, se fait en gris, vert amande, nègre, marine ou noir. Le costume 265 fr.

Le même en cover-coat castor, gris verdâtre........... 325 fr.

83605. CLOCHE crêpe de Chine garnie ruban fantaisie, nègre, mordoré, marine ou noir................ 43 fr.

22875. COSTUME en gabardine. Jaquette entièrement doublée soie, garnie pattes et galon assortis se fait en beige, gris, castor, marine ou noir. Le costume .... 295 fr.

Le même, en reps armure, gris, grège, nègre, castor, marine ou noir. Le costume .... 345 fr.

83606. TROTTEUR en tagal, garni d'un joli nœud de ruban, noir, marine, nègre.. 26 fr.

22876. TAILLEUR gabardine. Jaquette entièrement doublée soie, garnie galon, gaufré assorti. Se fait en castor, blond, gris, marin ou noir. Le costume..... 275 fr.

Se fait également en popeline ou marocain de laine, gris, beige castor, marine ou noir. Le costume........ 350 fr.

83607. MARQUIS, satin, garni ruban : noir ou nègre. 59 fr.

22877. COSTUME gabardine. Jaquette brodée ton sur ton et entièrement doublée soie. Se fait en gris, blond, marine ou noir. Le costume. 295 fr.

83608. BRETON en laize de paille, drapé ruban gros grain, garni épingles, nègre, noir, marine, mordoré, rouge............. 36 fr.

22878. COSTUME robe et paletot en gabardine, écaille, grège, gris, marine, ou noir. Haut de robe en marocain de soie imprimé, ou crêpe de chine, paletot entièrement doublé soie, peut se porter avec ceinture. Le costume 375 fr.

83609. CHAPELIER en tagal picot, garni d'un grand nœud de ruban : ficelle, nègre, mordoré, marine ou noir 35 fr.

N'OUBLIEZ PAS DE NOUS INDIQUER · LA TEINTE

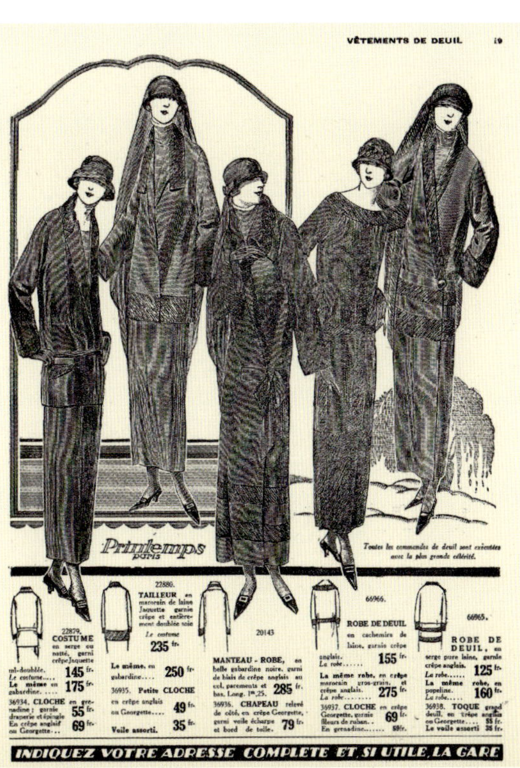

VÊTEMENTS DE DEUIL 19

Toutes les commandes de deuil sont exécutées avec la plus grande célérité.

Printemps
paris

22879. COSTUME en serge ou natté, garni crêpe Jaquette mi-doublée. Le costume..... 145 fr.

Le même en gabardine. .... 175 fr.

36934. CLOCHE en grenadine ; garnie draperie et épingle 55 fr.

En crêpe anglais ou Georgette... 69 fr.

22880. TAILLEUR en marocain de laine Jaquette garnie crêpe et entièrement doublée soie Le costume 235 fr.

Le même, en gabardine.... 250 fr.

36935. Petite CLOCHE en crêpe anglais ou Georgette.... 49 fr.

Voile assorti. 35 fr.

20143 MANTEAU - ROBE, en belle gabardine noire, garni de biais de crêpe anglais au col, parements et bas. Long. 1m,25. 285 fr.

36936. CHAPEAU relevé de côté, en crêpe Georgette, garni voile écharpe et bord de tulle. 79 fr.

66966. ROBE DE DEUIL en cachemire de laine, garnie crêpe anglais. La robe...... 155 fr.

La même robe, en crêpe marocain gros-grain, et crêpe anglais. La robe........ 275 fr.

36937. CLOCHE en crêpe Georgette, garnie fleurs de ruban.. 69 fr.

En grenadine...... 59 fr.

66965. ROBE DE DEUIL, en serge pure laine, garnie crêpe anglais. La robe..... 125 fr.

La même robe, en popeline. La robe.... 160 fr.

36938. TOQUE grand deuil, en crêpe anglais ou Georgette.... 55 fr.

Le voile assorti 35 fr.

INDIQUEZ VOTRE ADRESSE COMPLETE ET, SI UTILE, LA GARE

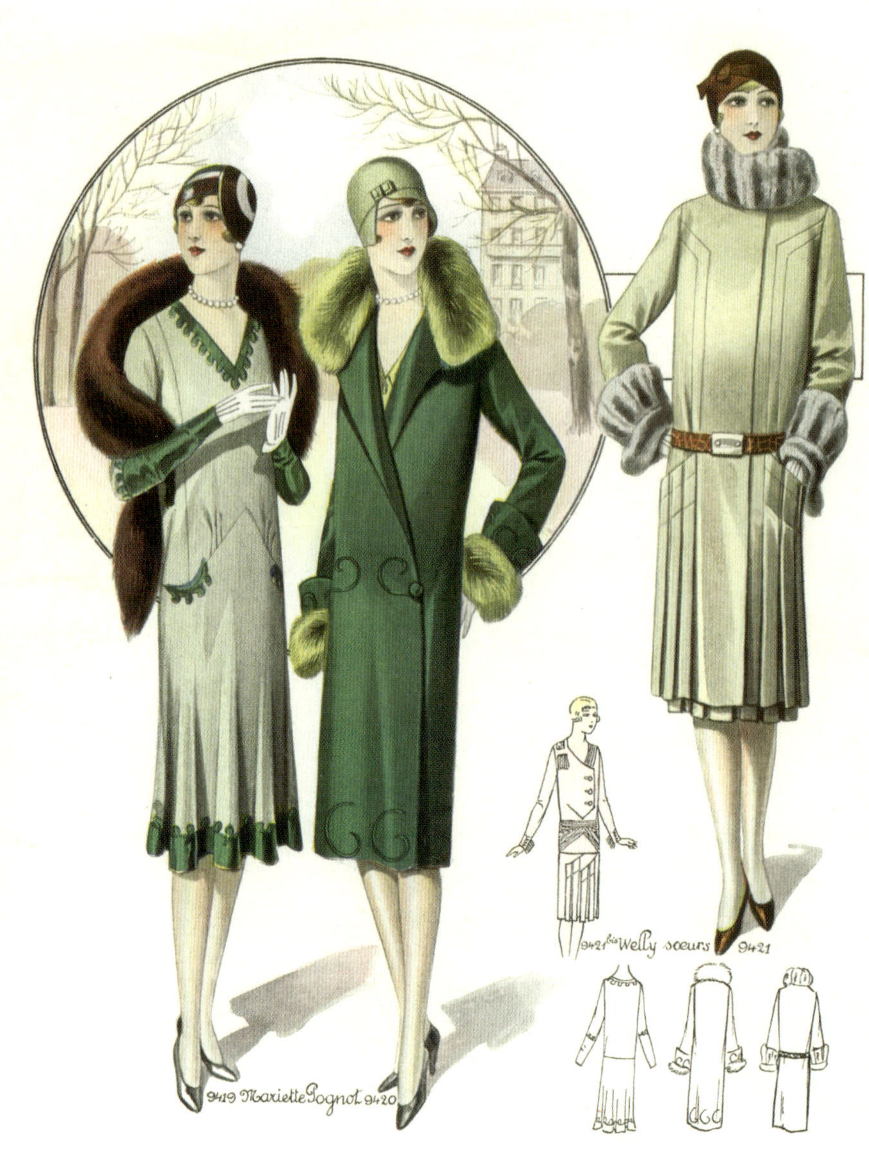

Above and right

Three walking ensembles by Mariette Pognot and the Welly Soeurs. *Paris Élégante*, c.1925

A day dress with a pleated skirt and matching skirt borders, waist panels and cravat, and a dark orange coat with a fur trim cuff and collar by Mariette Pognot. *Paris Élégante*, c.1925

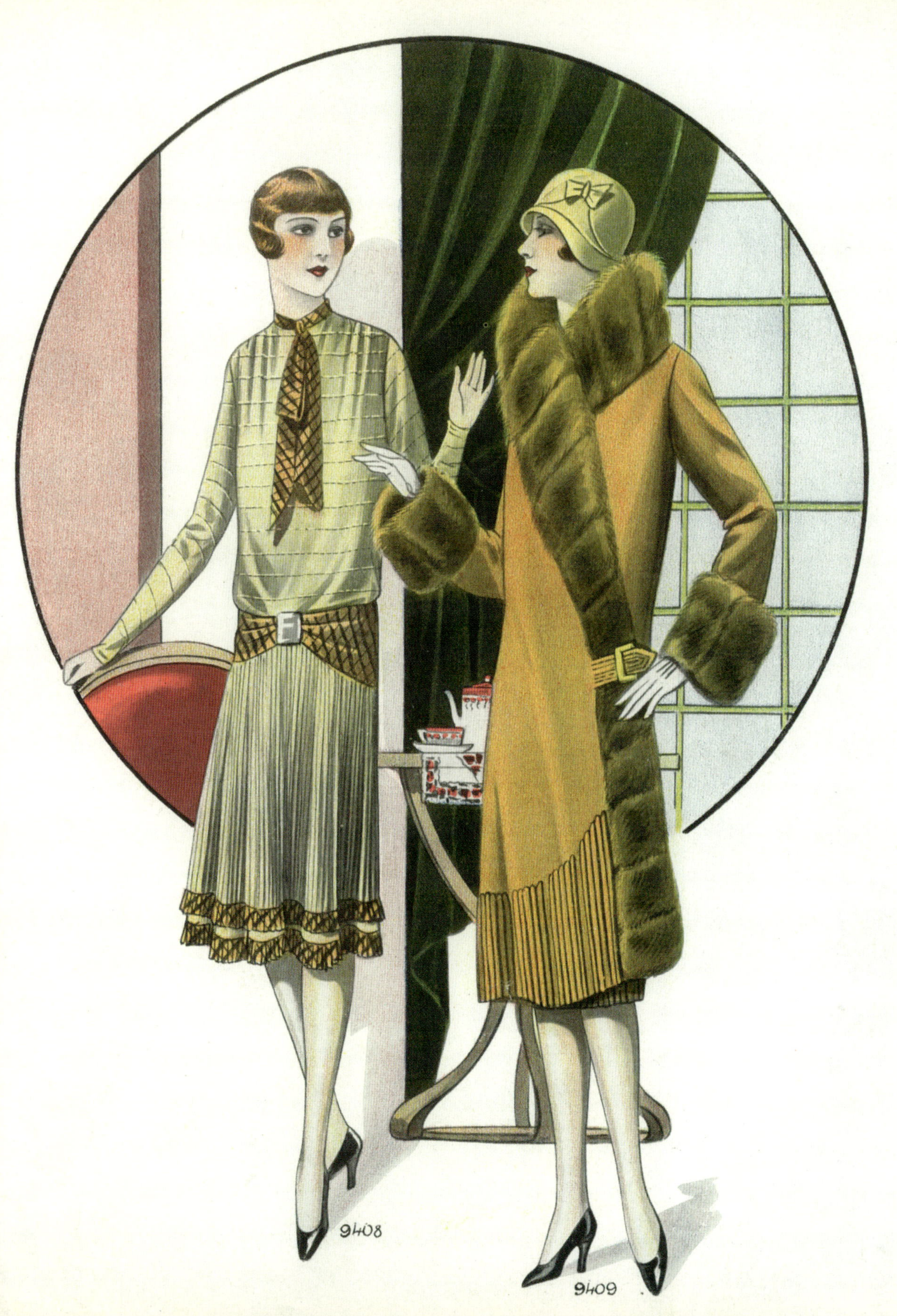
9408
9409

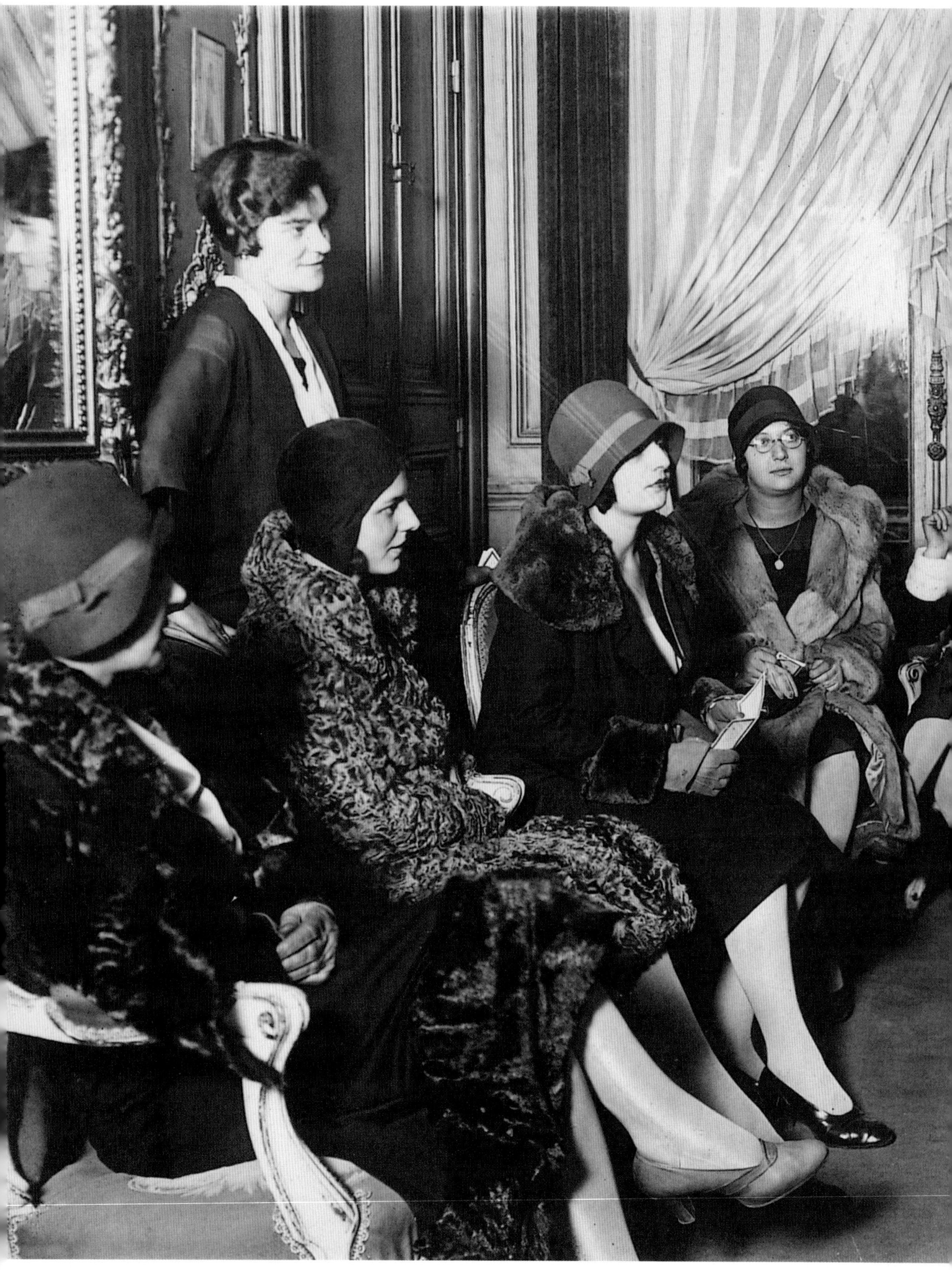

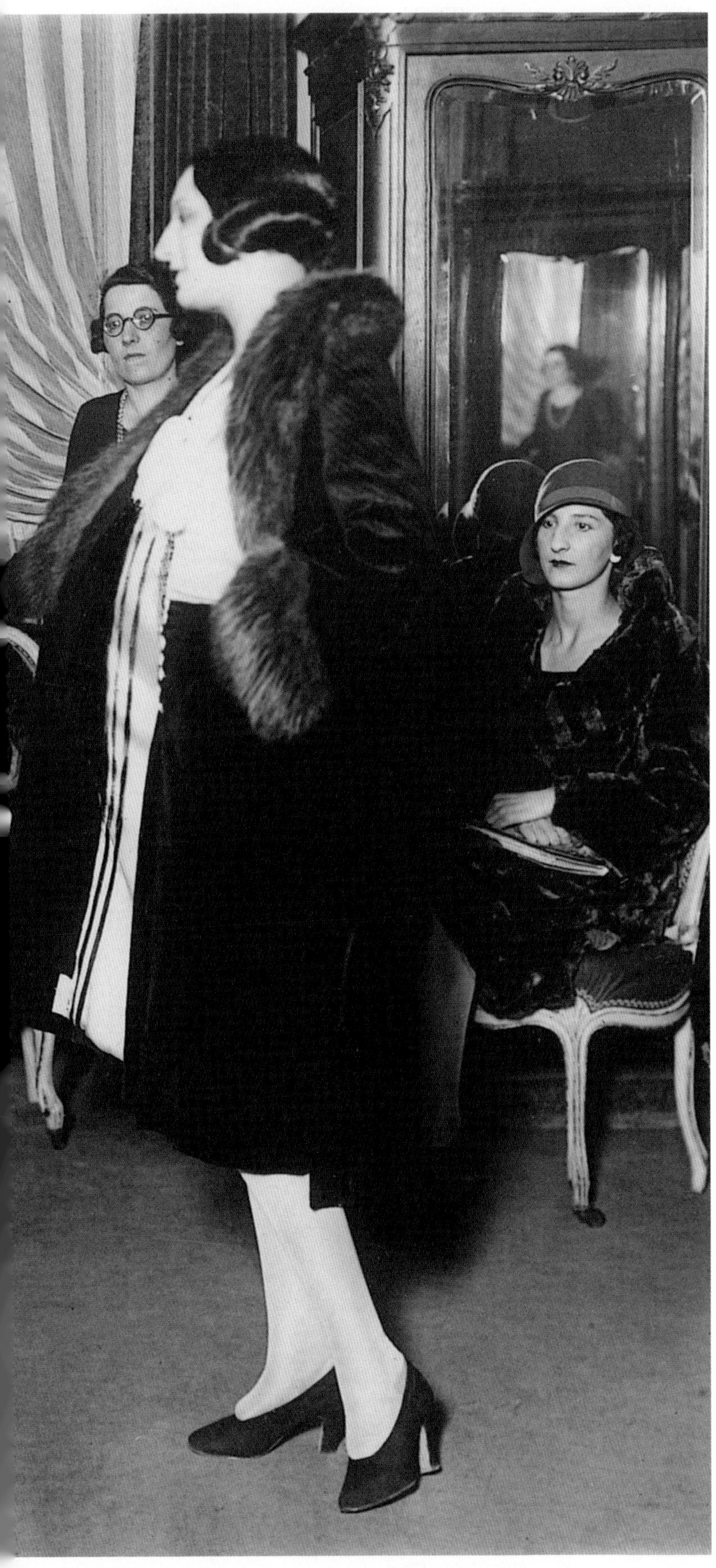

Previous page
Photograph of a fashion display in a Parisian Couture salon, c.1924

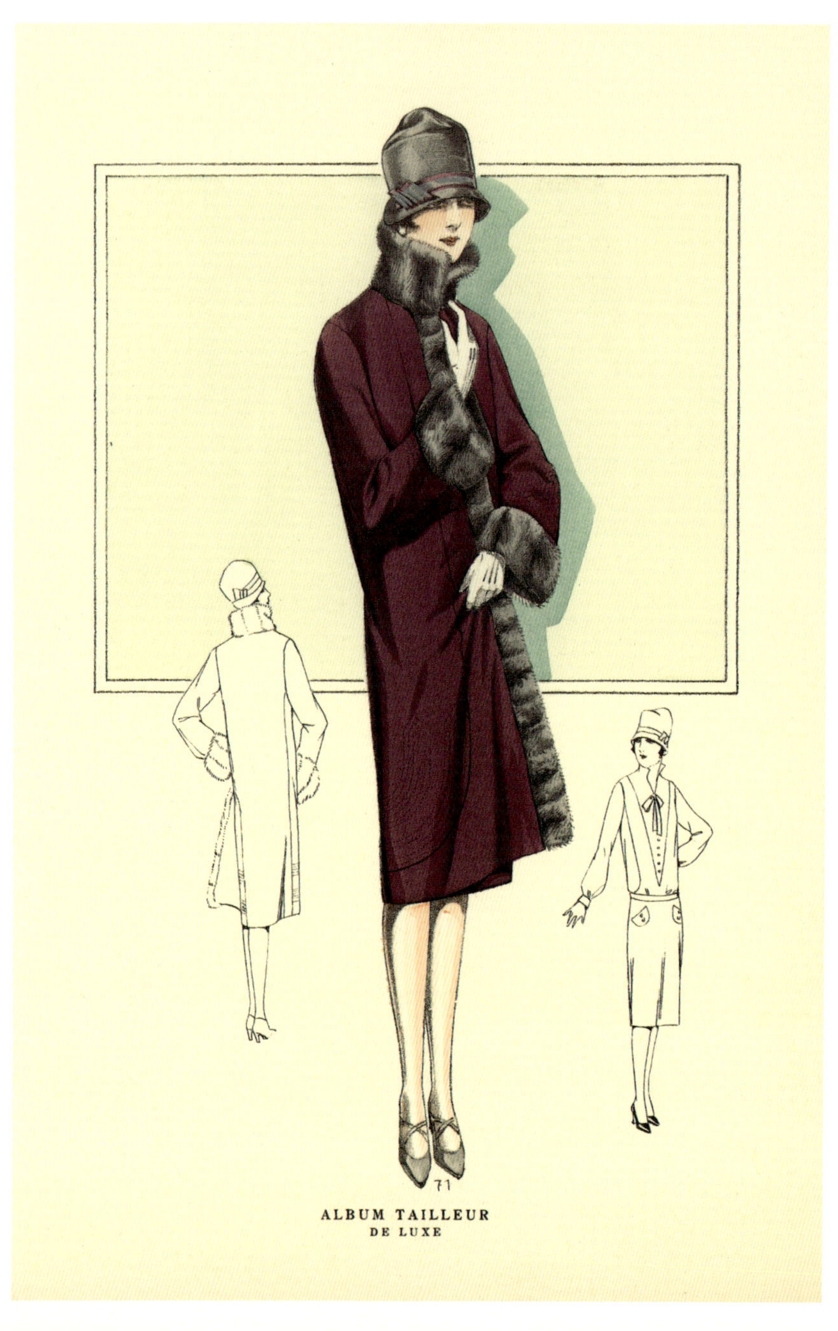

Below left to right

Burgundy coat with ornamental stitching and trimmed in fur. *Album Tailleur de Luxe*, c.1925

Burgundy ribbed velvet coat trimmed with fur. *Album Tailleur de Luxe*, c.1925

Burgundy patterned velvet coat trimmed with fur. *Album Tailleur de Luxe*, c.1925

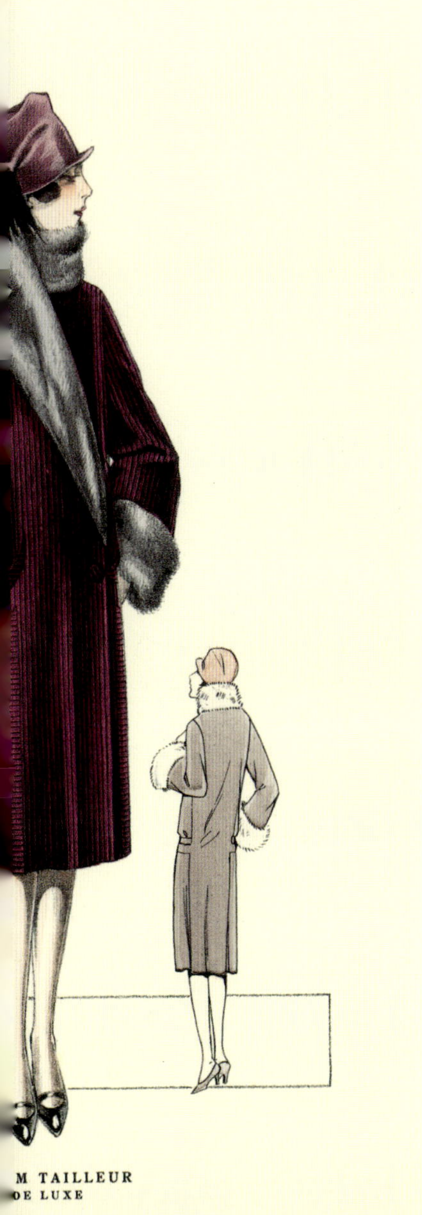

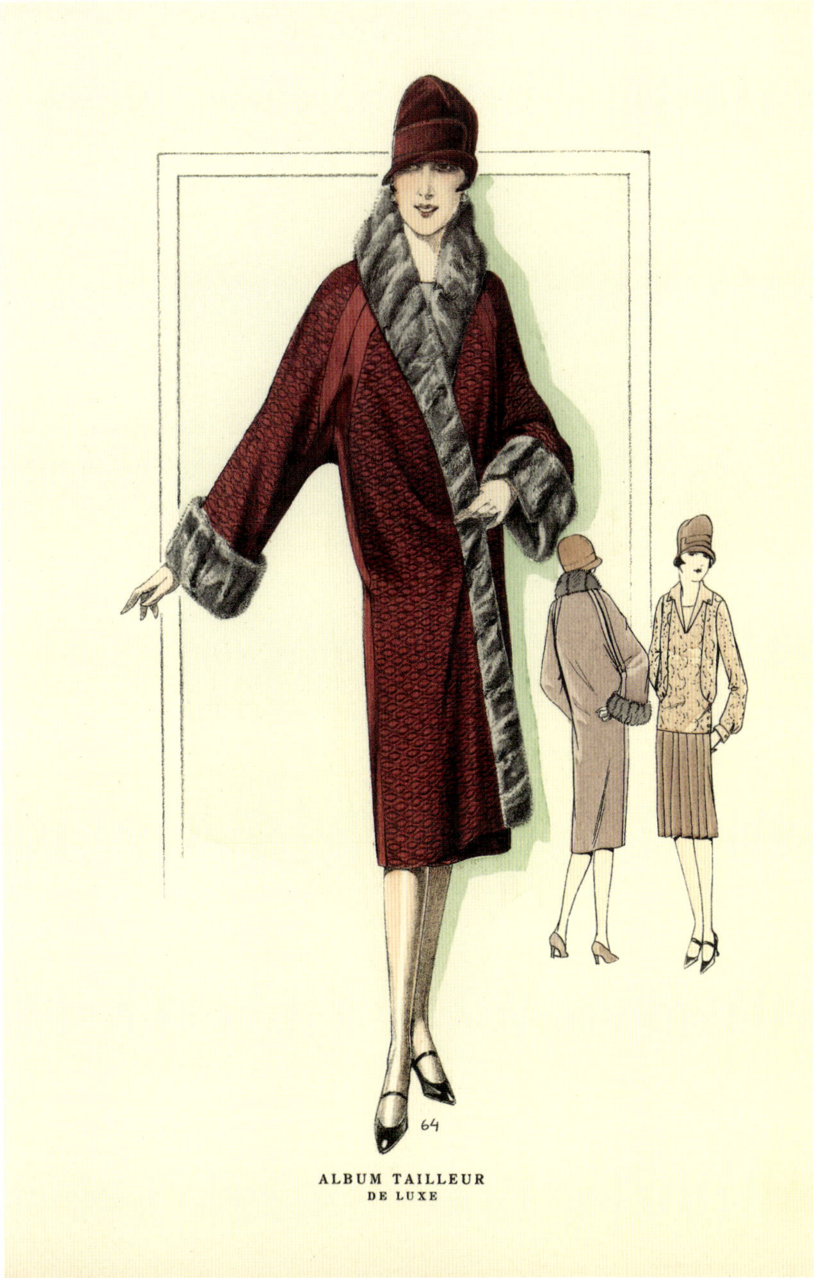

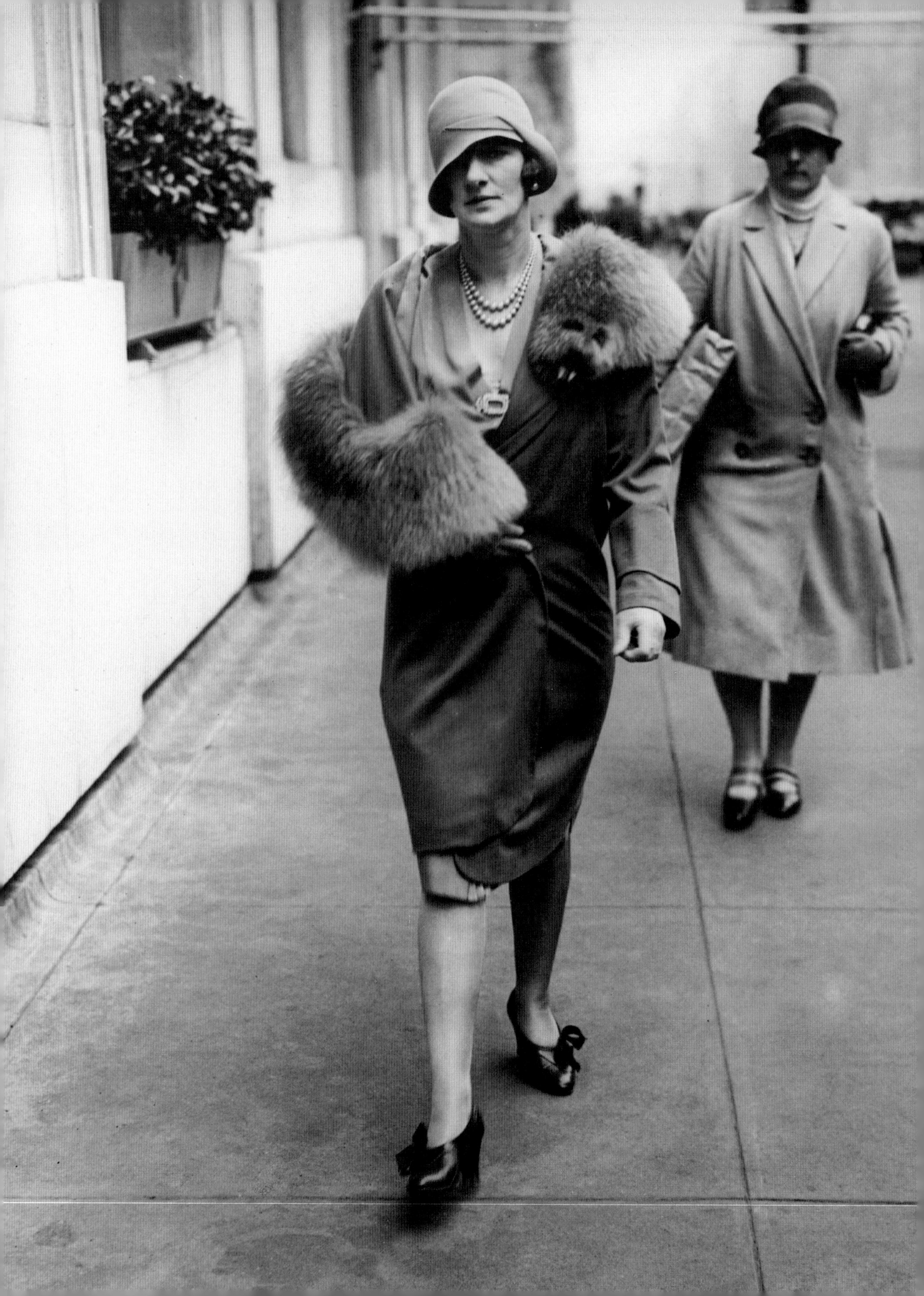

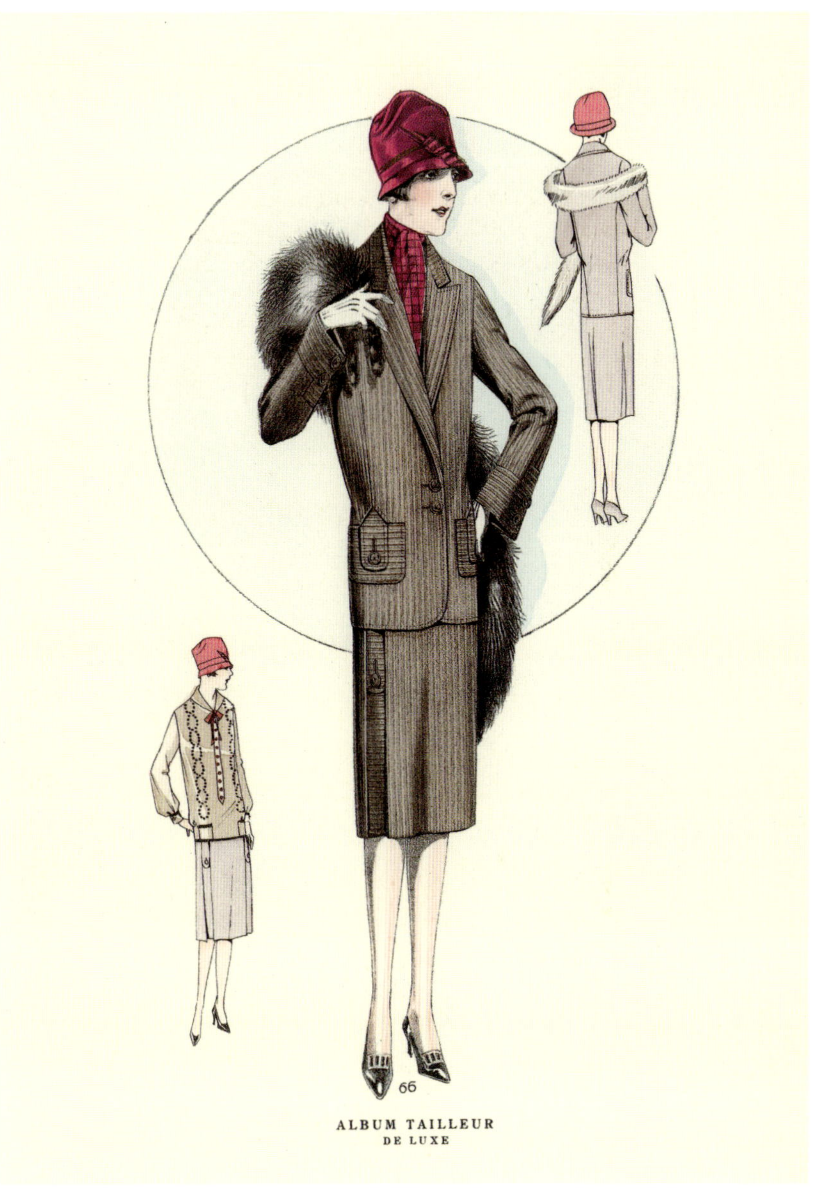

Left and above

New York socialite Ira Richards wearing a beaver shrug, cloche hat and pearls, 1928

Brown ribbed velvet skirt suit worn with a fur stole and matching red cloche and scarf. *Album Tailleur de Luxe*, c.1925

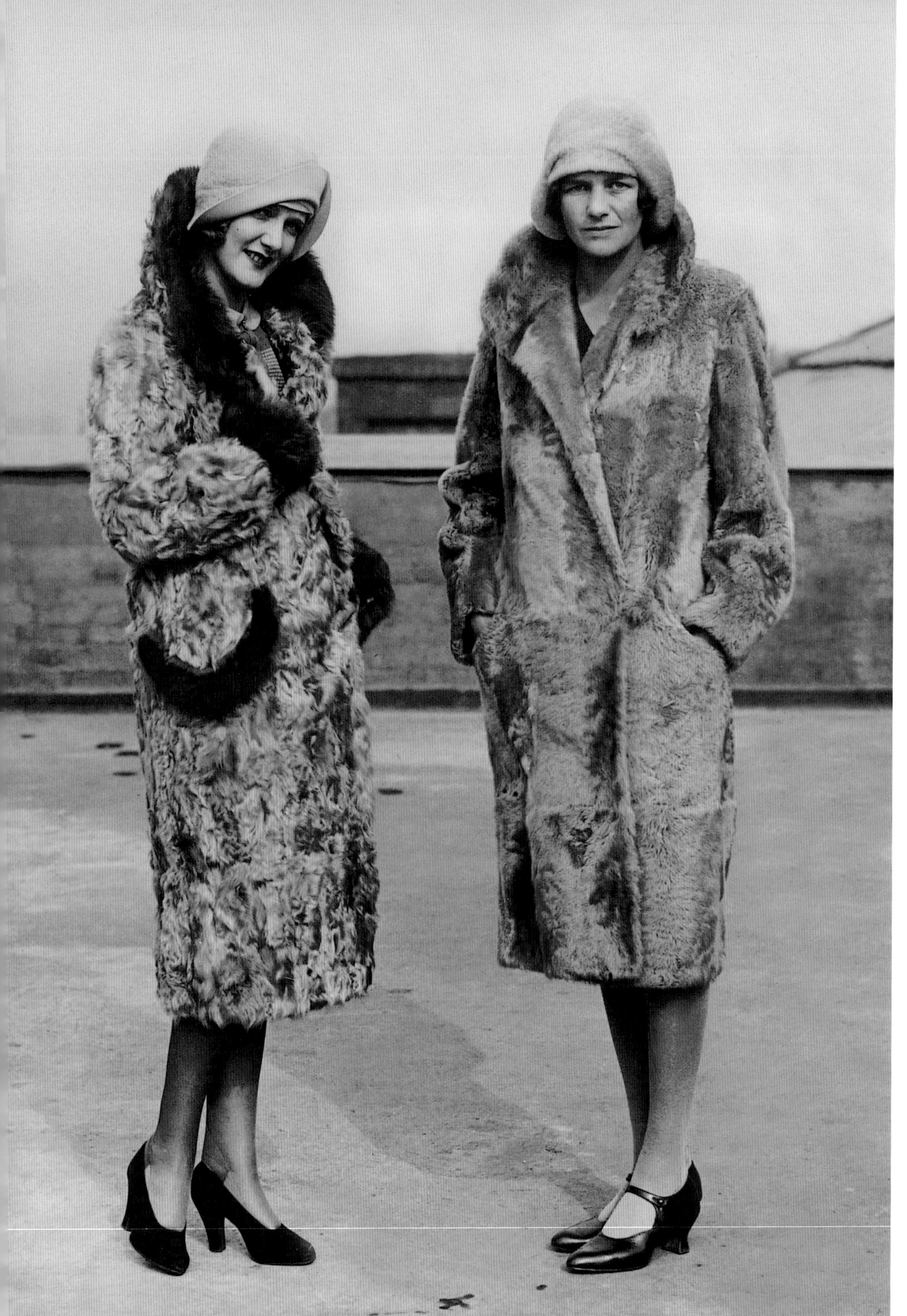

Left and below

Two models in fur coats, the left is made of lambskin, while the right is made of dyed rabbit-skin, c.1924

A model showing off over-the-knee gaiters at the British Industry Fair, c.1926

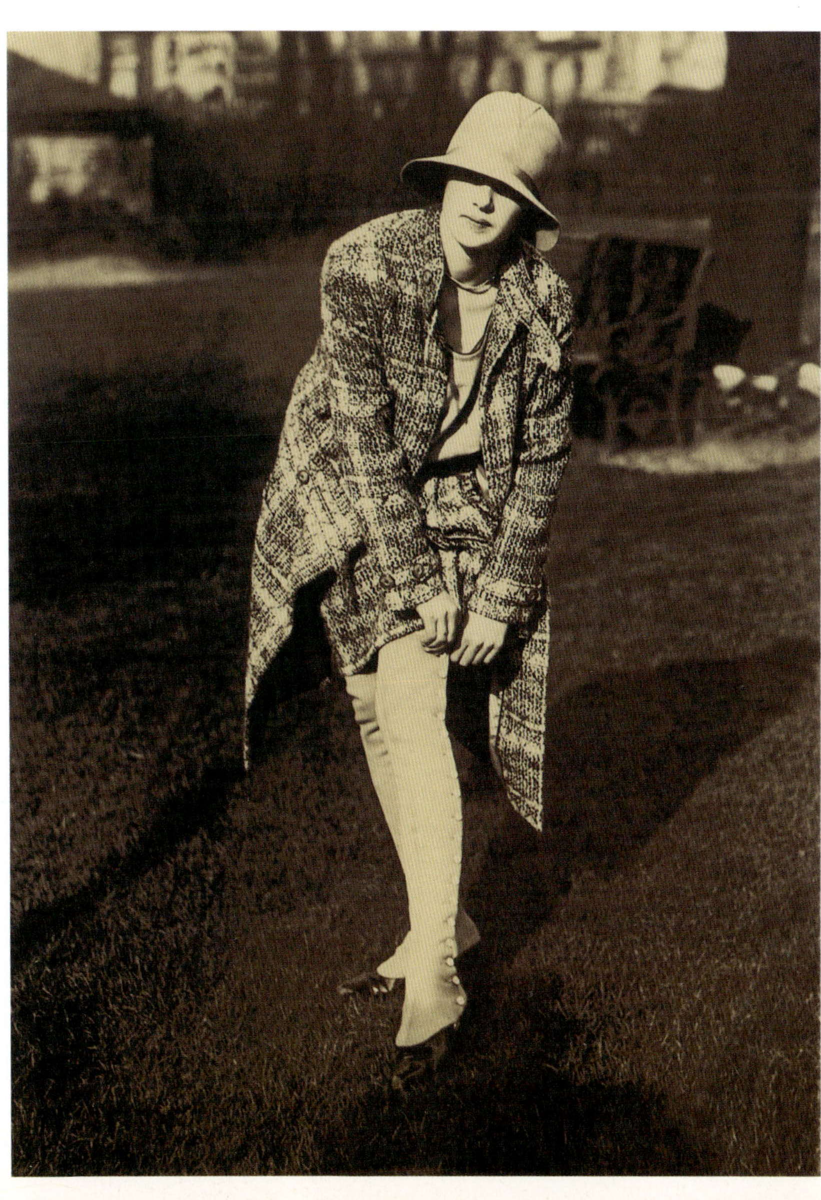

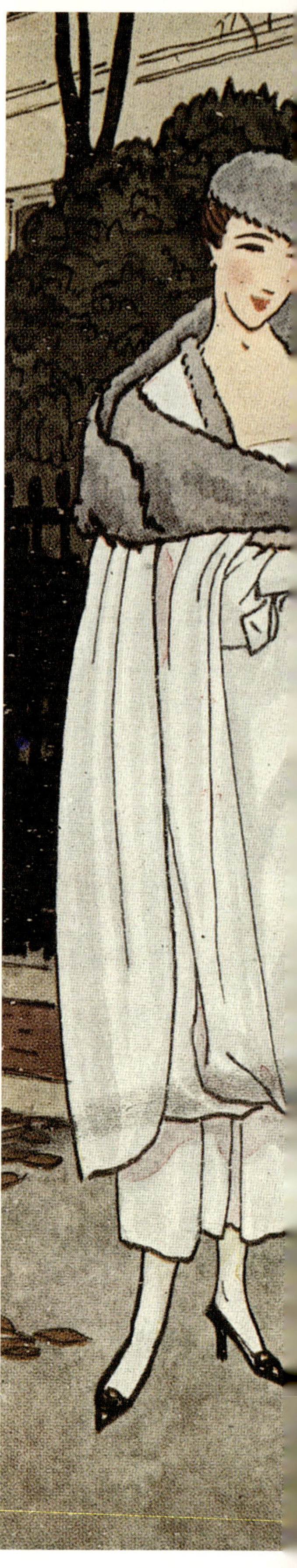

Right
Grey cape with fur trim by Chéruit, brown coat with V-shape back by Worth, and black buttoned cape by Lanvin, Illustration by Pierre Brissaud, *L'Illustration des Modes*, 1920

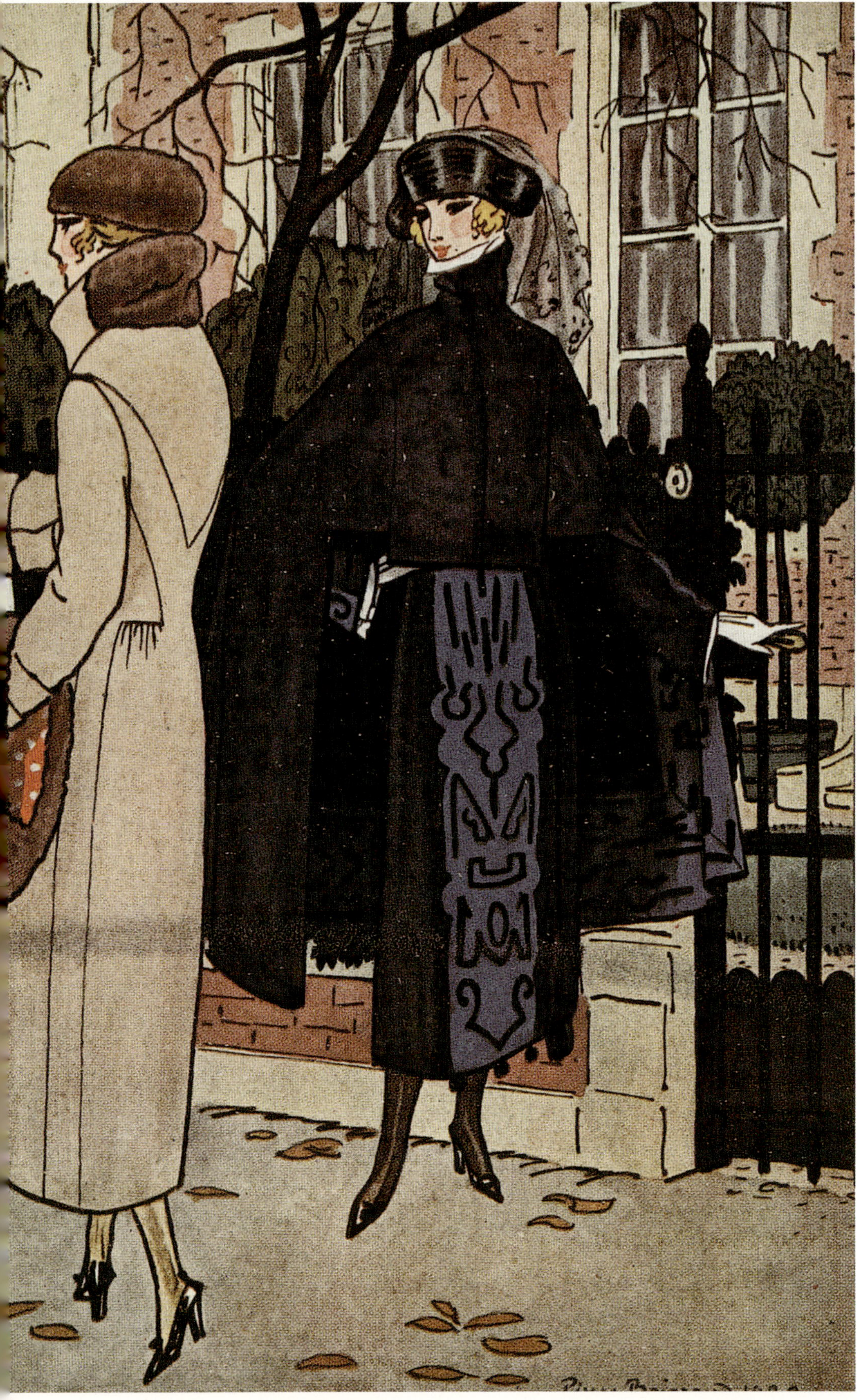

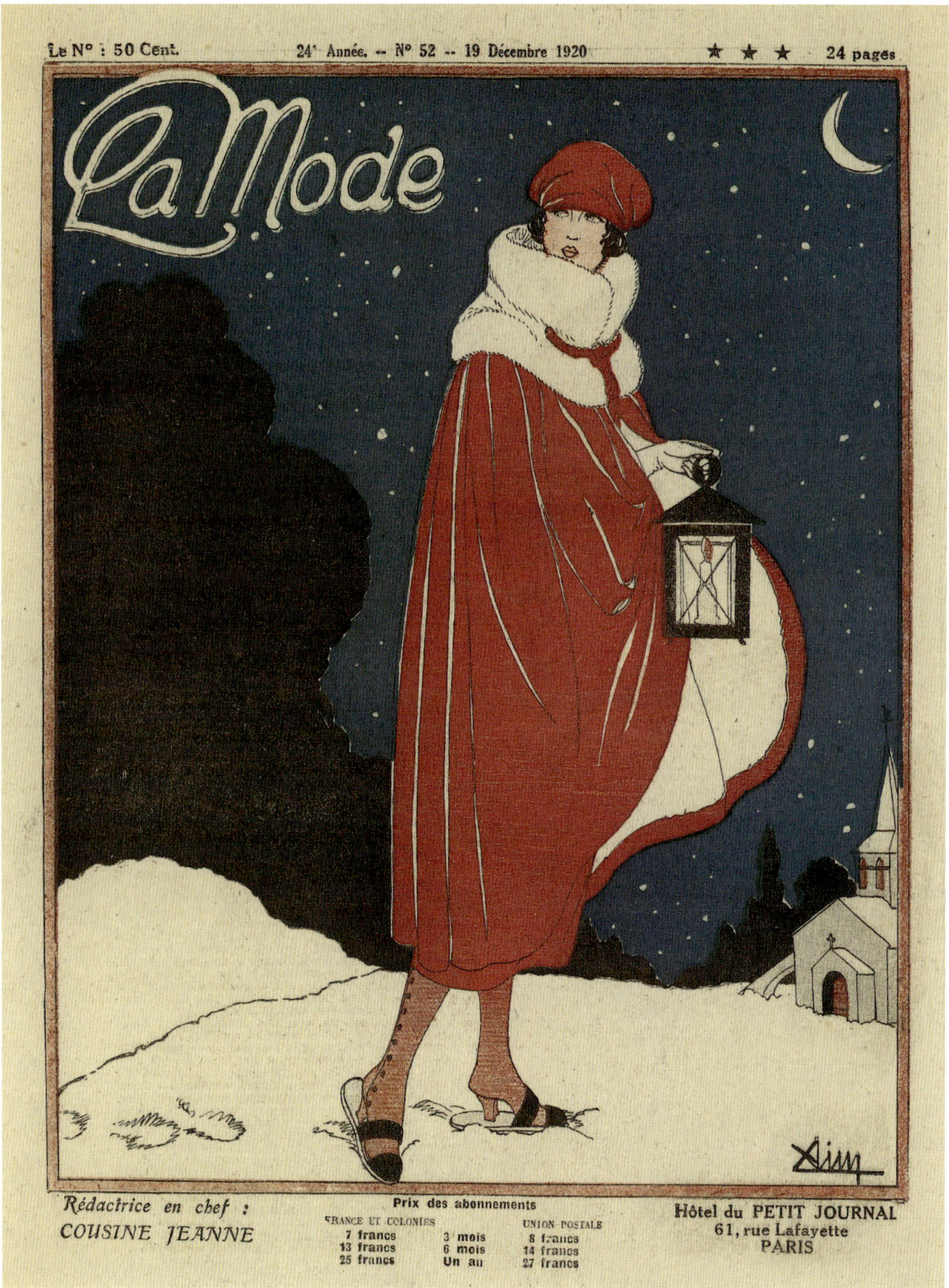

Above and right

A woman in a red cape coat trimmed with white fur. The red boots are protected with snow shoes. *La Mode*, 1920

Three winter suits. *La Femme Chic*, c.1923

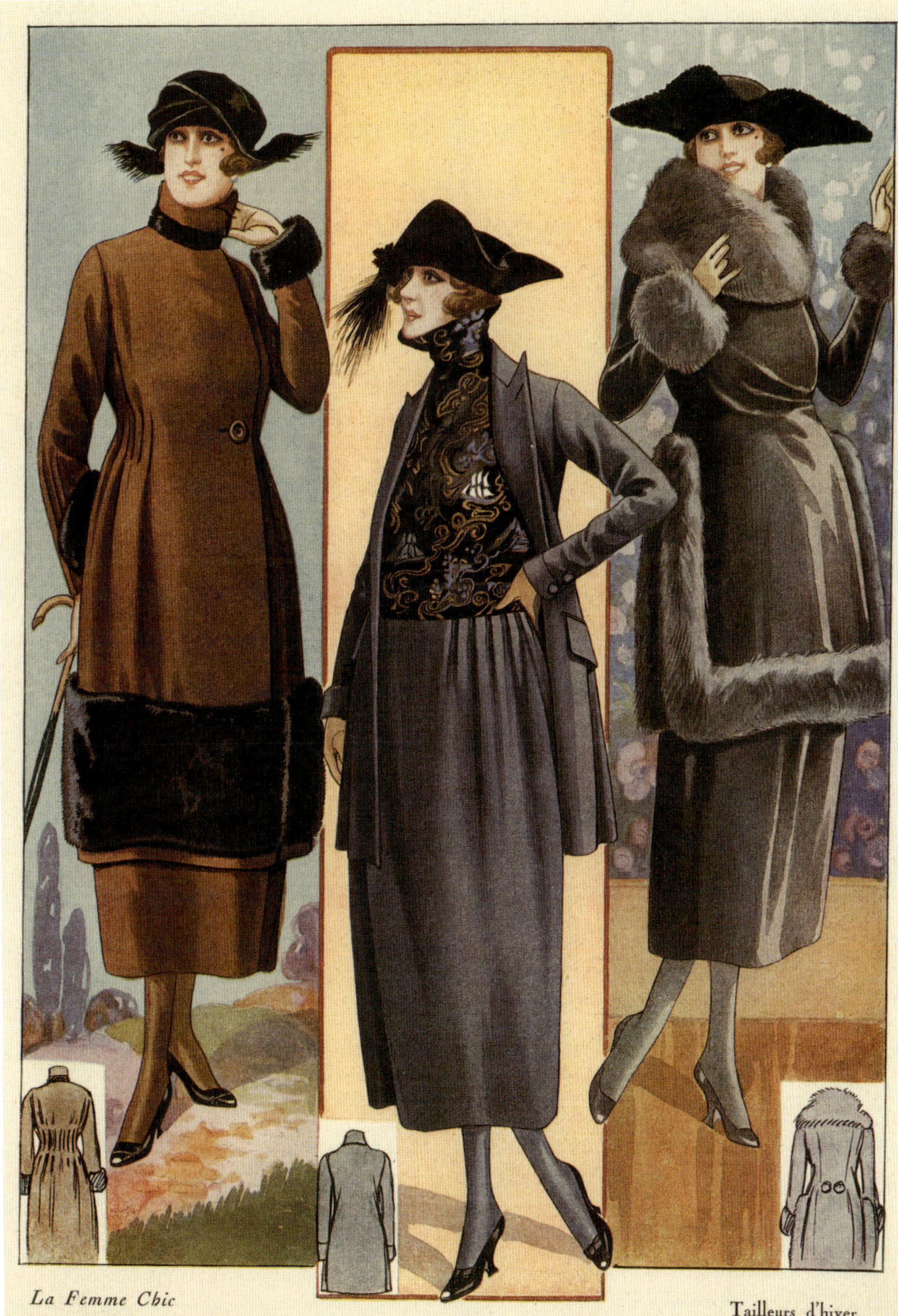
La Femme Chic
SUPPLÉMENT
Nº 118.
Pl. 961.
Tailleurs d'hiver.
I. Création de Pitoëff.

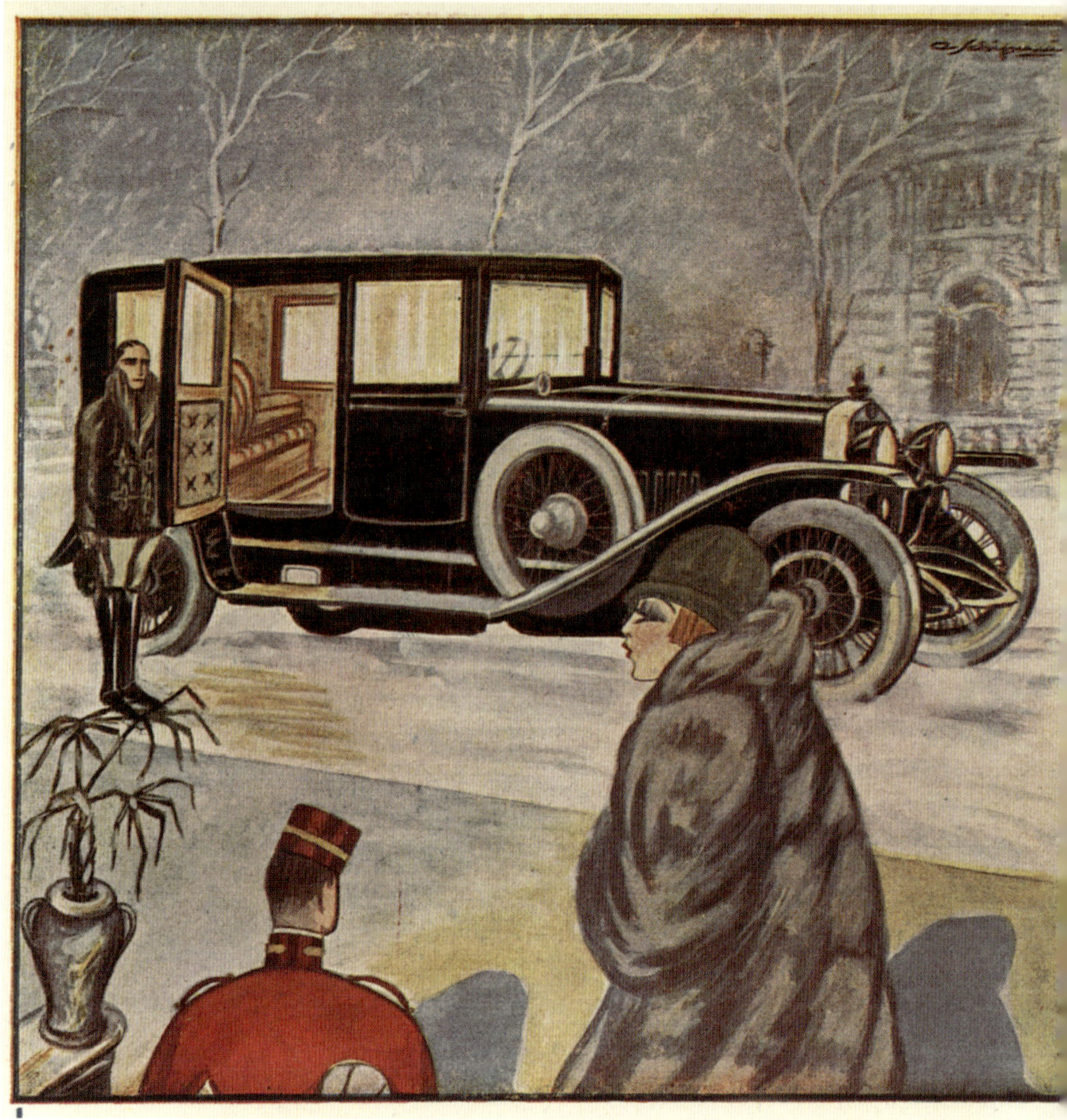

Above and right

Italian advertisement for Alfa Romeo featuring a woman in a lush fur coat and a cloche hat, c.1926

New York socialite Ira Richards attending a cancer charity benefit wearing a black day ensemble, a fox fur stole, a cloche hat, diamante buckled shoes and white gloves, 1927

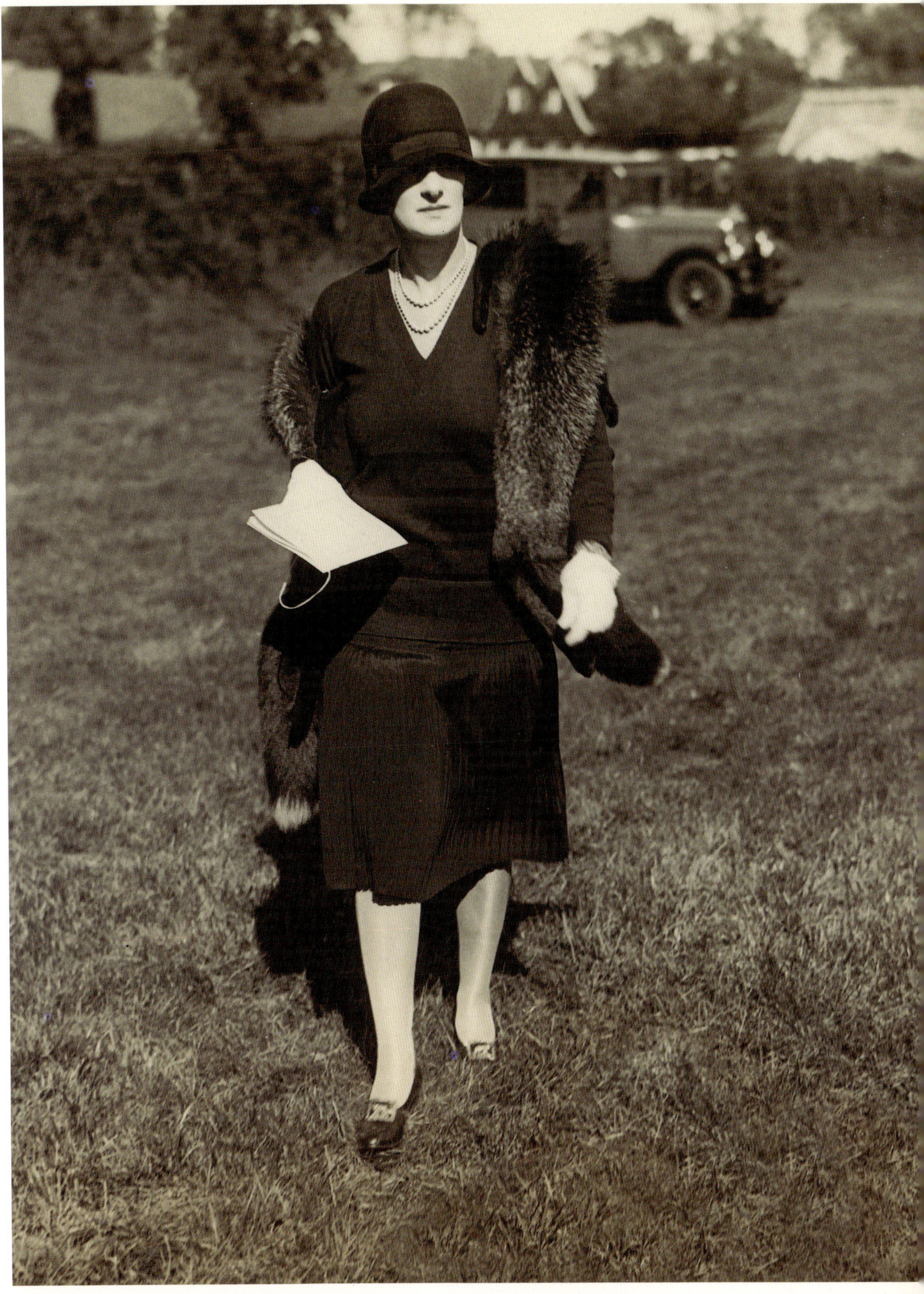

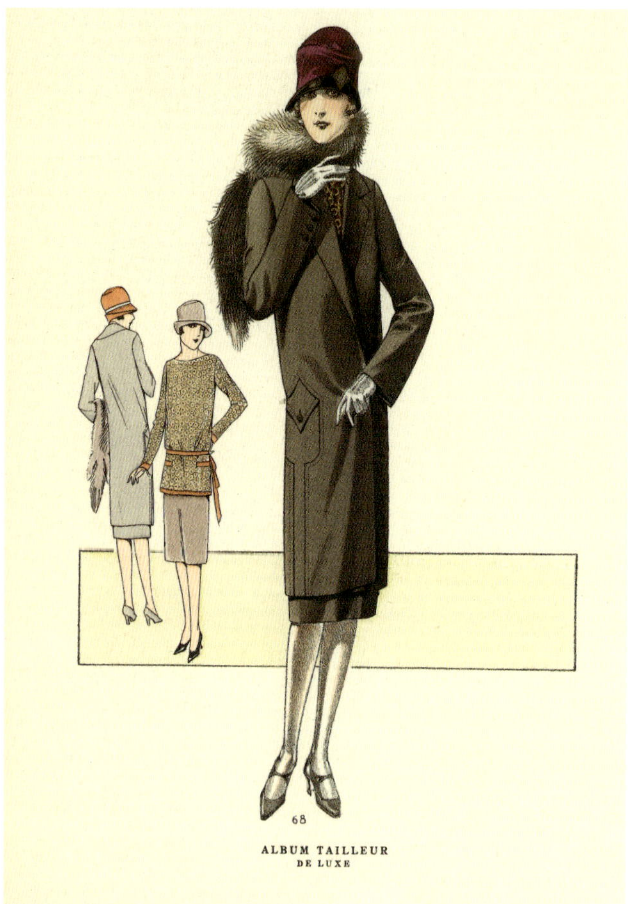

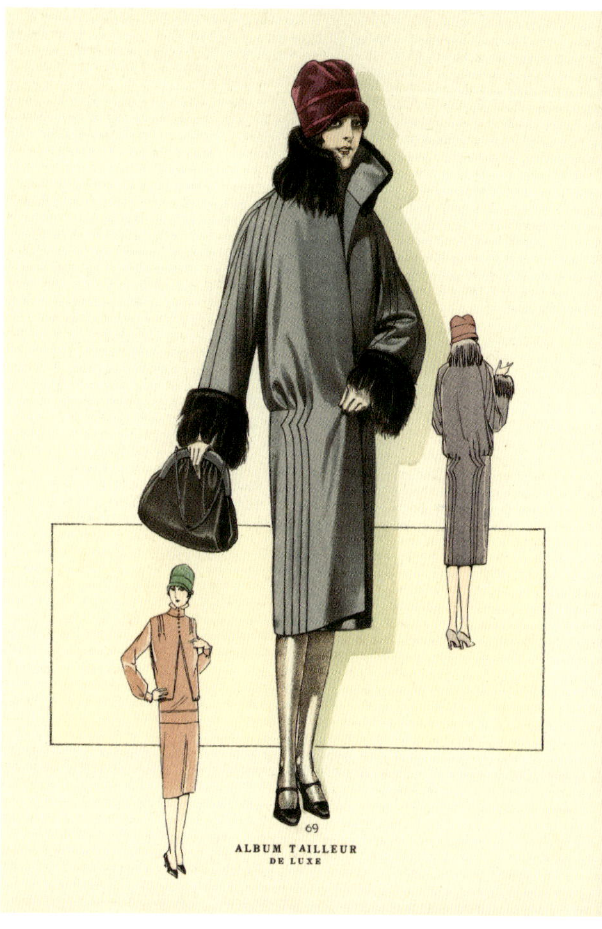

Above left and right

Single-breasted dark brown autumn coat worn with a fur stole. *Album Tailleur de Luxe*, c. 1925

Dark grey winter coat with ornamental stitching and trimmed with black monkey fur. *Album Tailleur de Luxe*, c.1925

Right

A dark green coat with pleated side panels and trimmed with moleskin fur. *Album Tailleur de Luxe*, c.1925

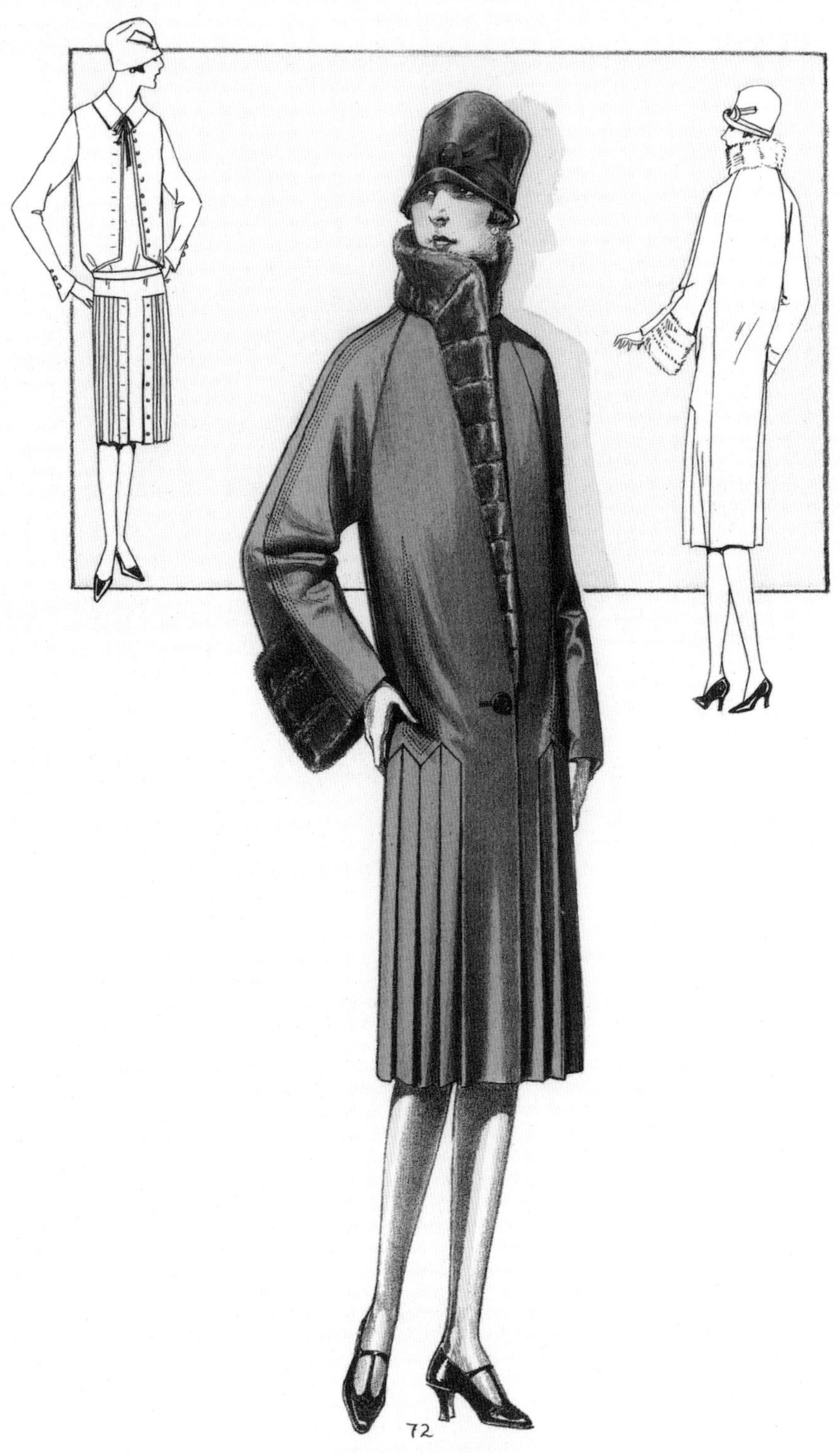
72
ALBUM TAILLEUR
DE LUXE

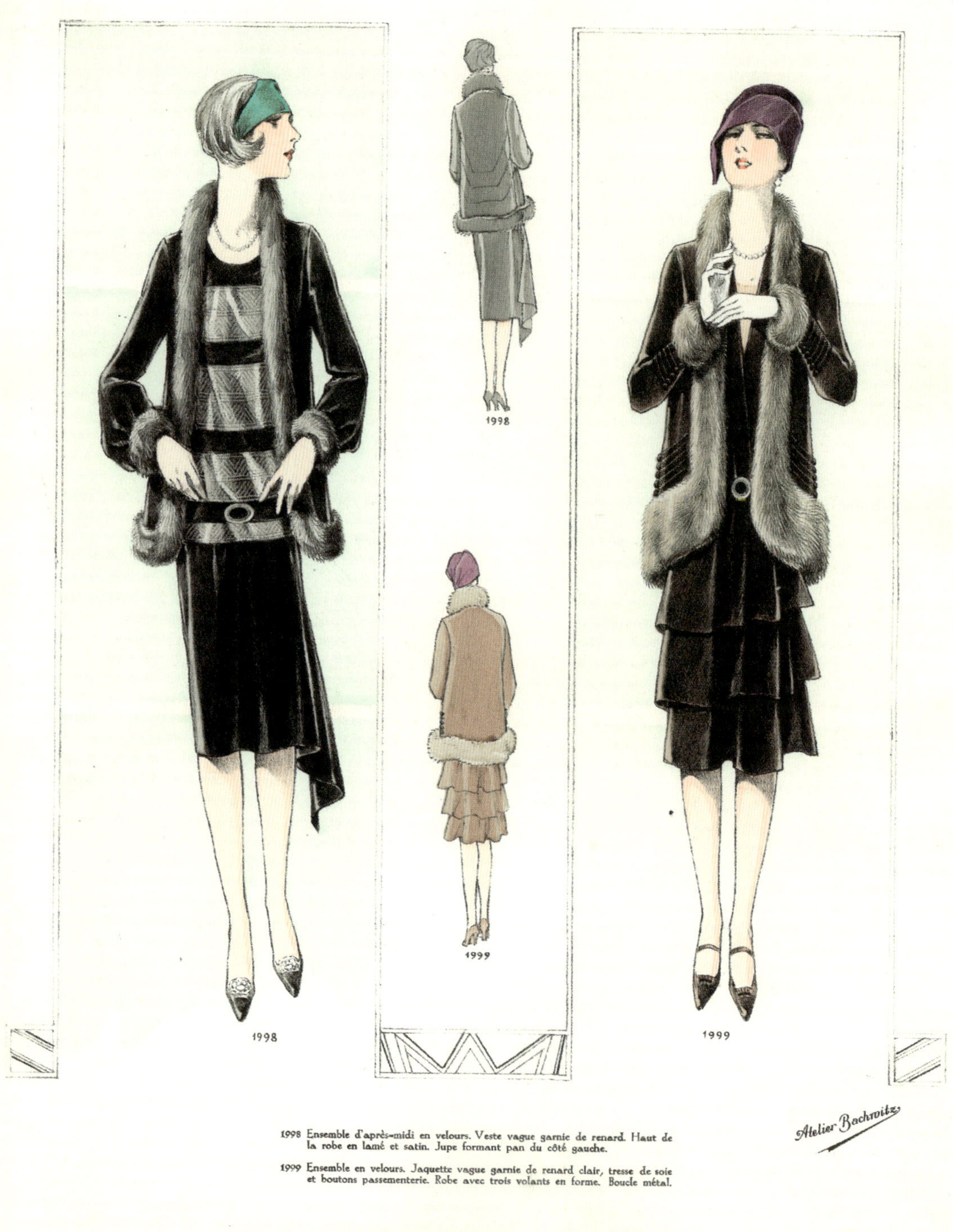

Above

Velvet afternoon suit with a short coat faced with fox fur, a dress with metal lamé top and dark satin strips, a velvet ensemble with an open jacket faced with fox fur and a tiered dress by Atelier Bachroitz. *Chic Parisien Beaux-Arts des Modes*, 1927

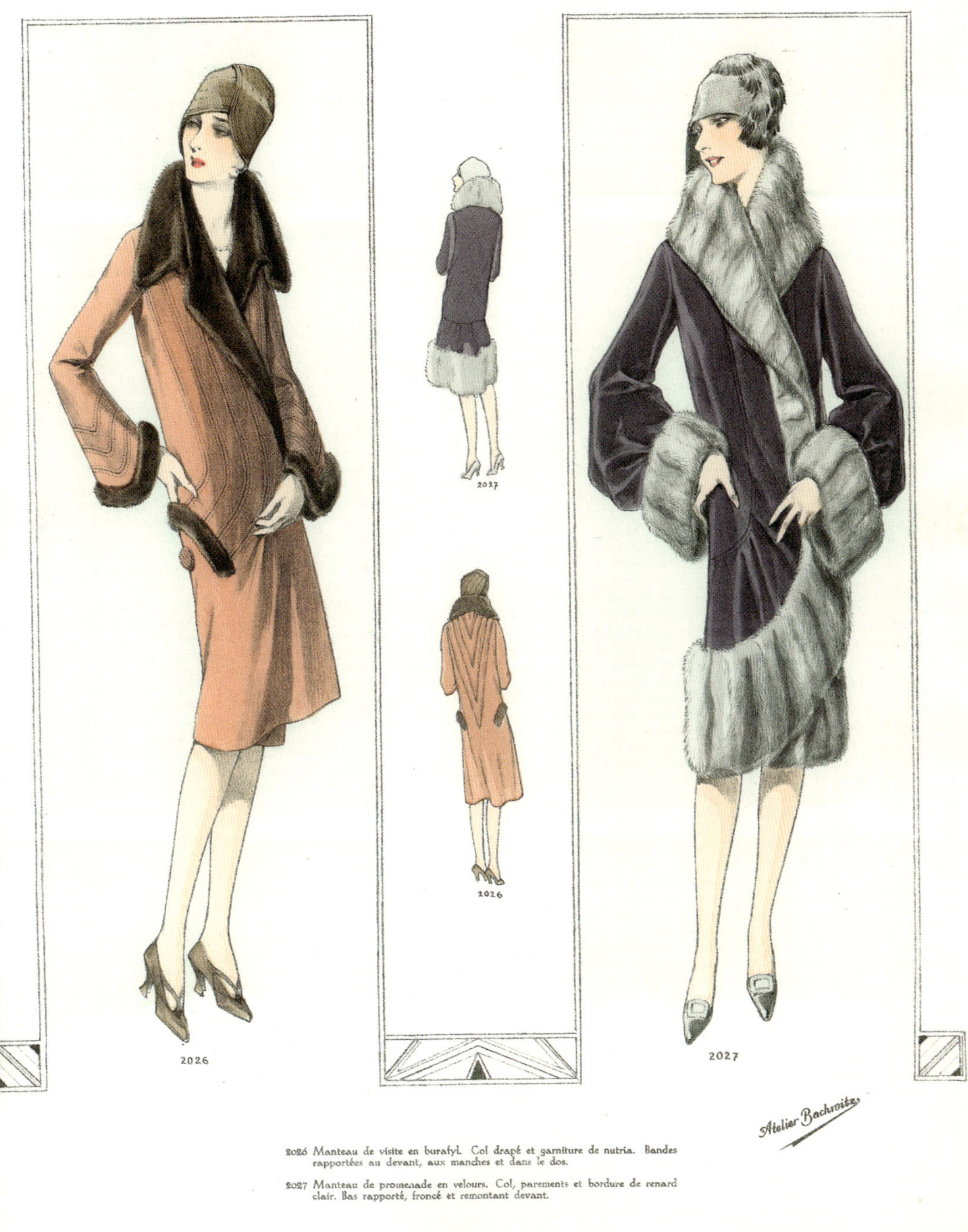

Above
Afternoon coat edged with fur, and a velvet promenade coat edged with fox fur by Atelier Bachroitz. *Chic Parisien Beaux-Arts des Modes*, 1927

Right
Black velvet coat with large fox fur panels and collar by Atelier Bachroitz, *Chic Parisien Beaux-Arts des Modes*, c.1926

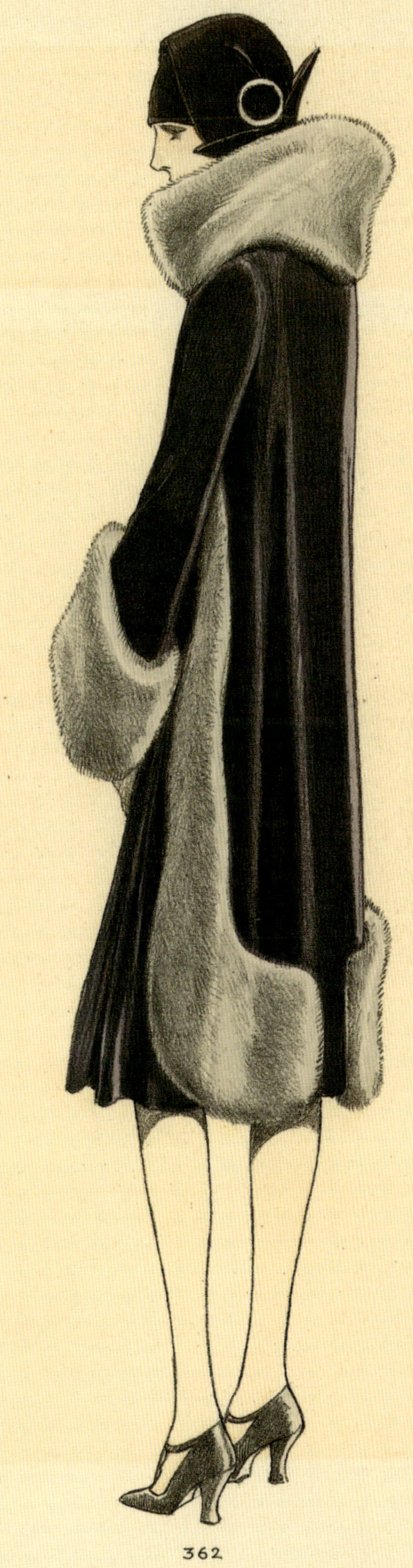

362

362 Manteau inédit de velours noir, garni de renard. Devants droits, formant godets.

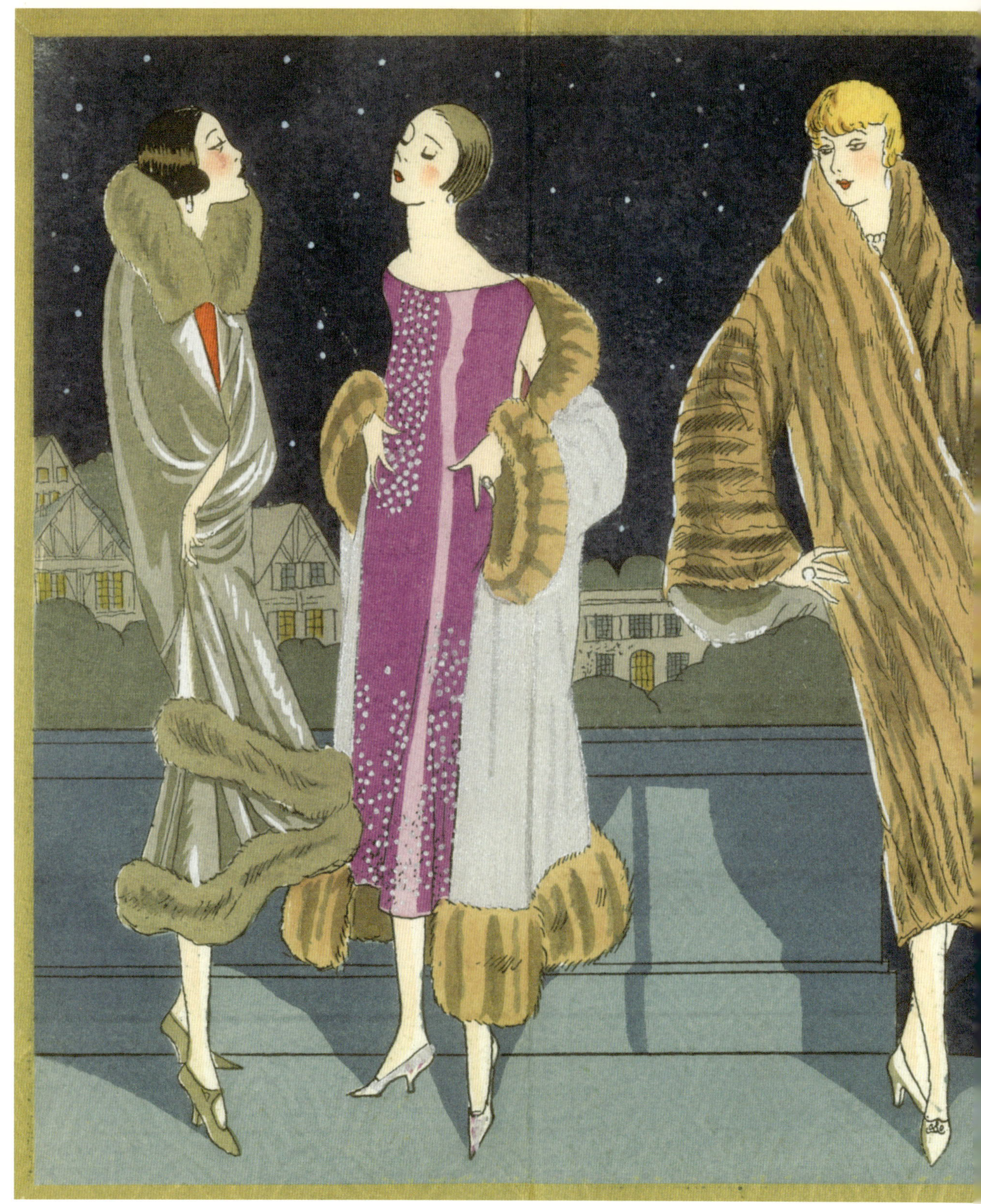

Above
Four luxurious fur or fur-trimmed coats, c.1922

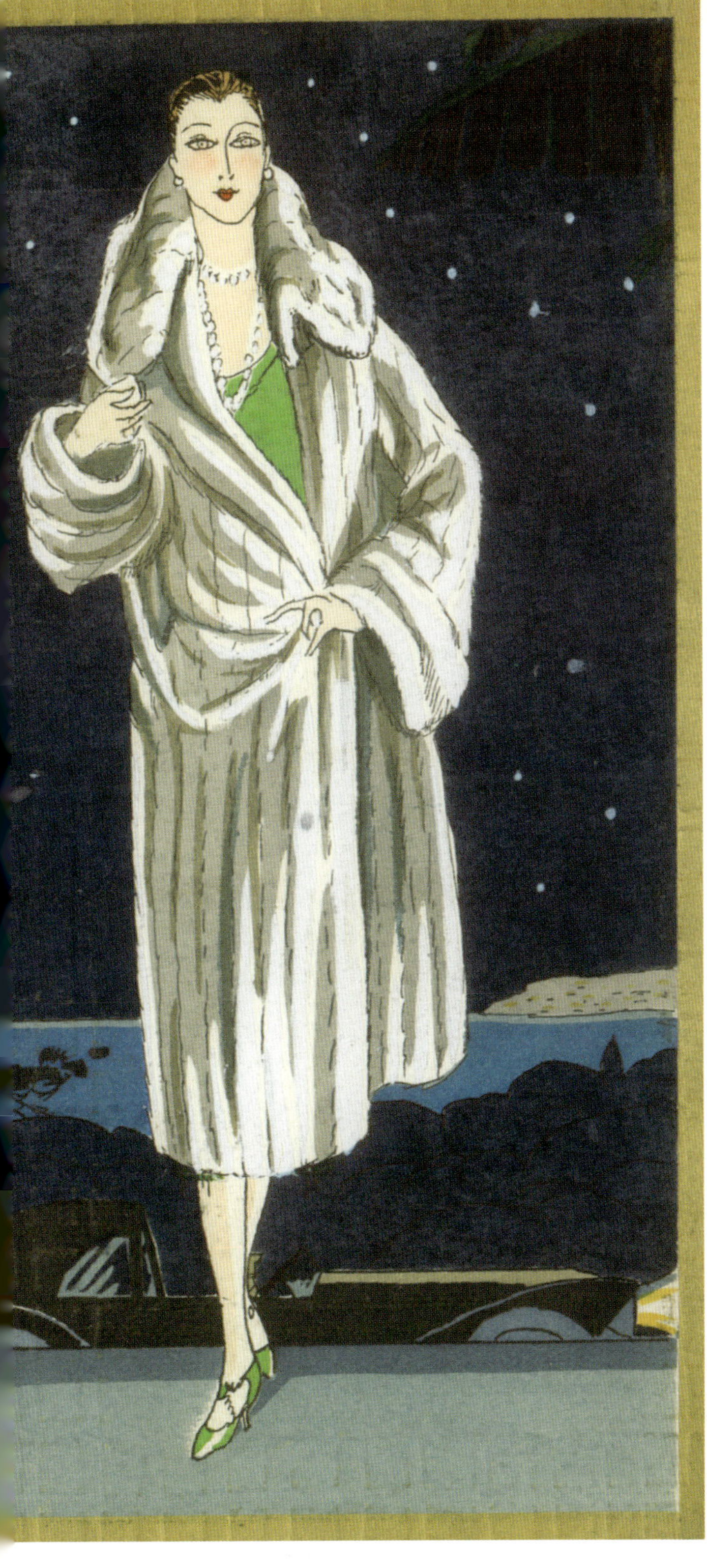

Novembre 1926 REVUE MENSUELLE Le N° France : 8 francs. — Italie : Lire 10.

La femme chic

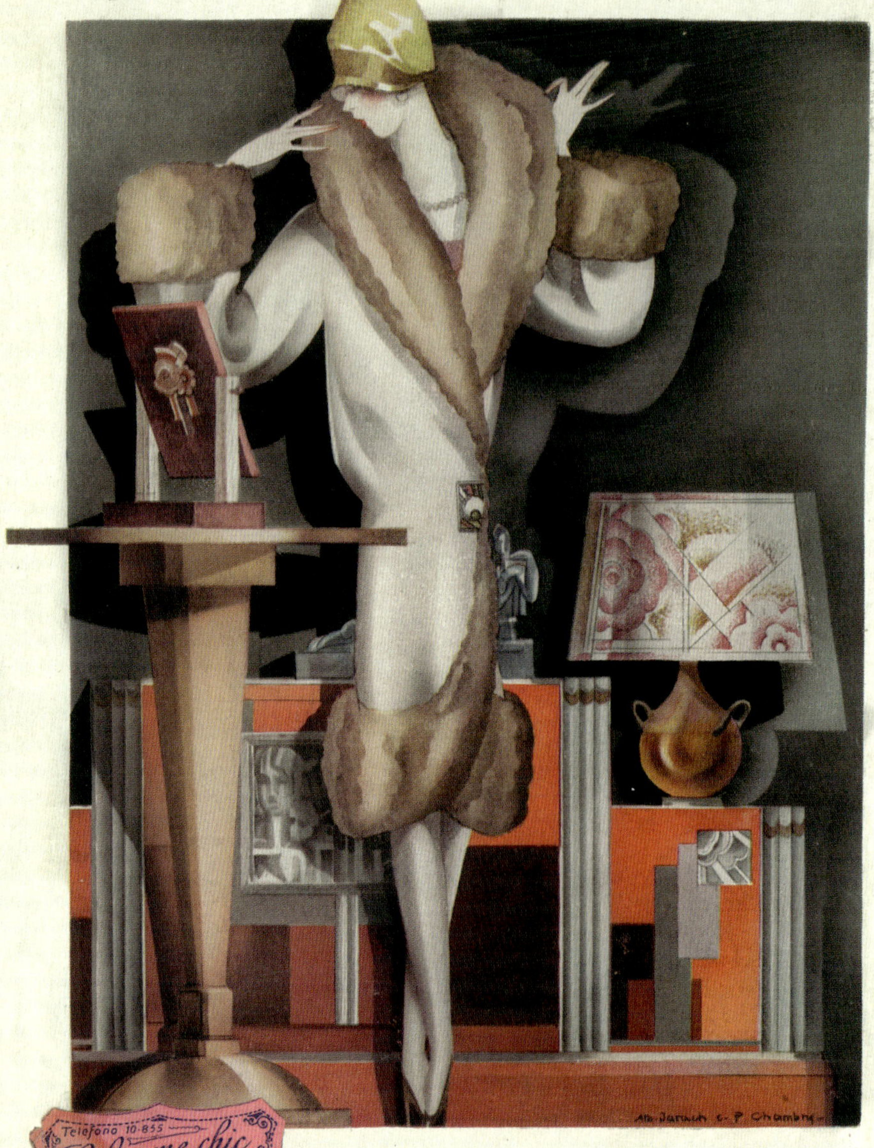

Pu[illegible] 47. Rue de Sèvres, PARIS (6e)

Above

Cover of *La Femme Chic* à Paris, November 1926

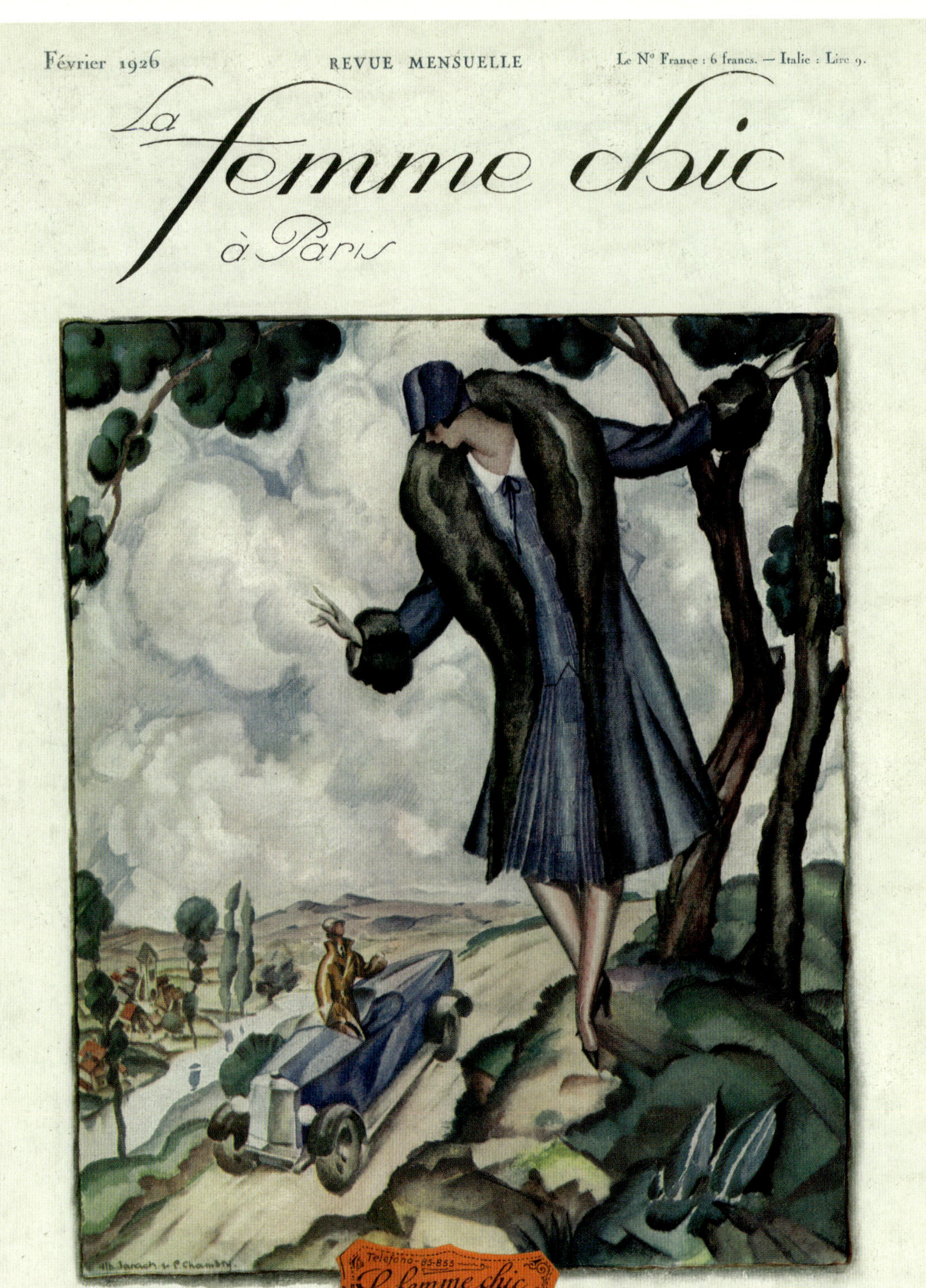

Above
Cover of *La Femme Chic* à Paris, February 1926

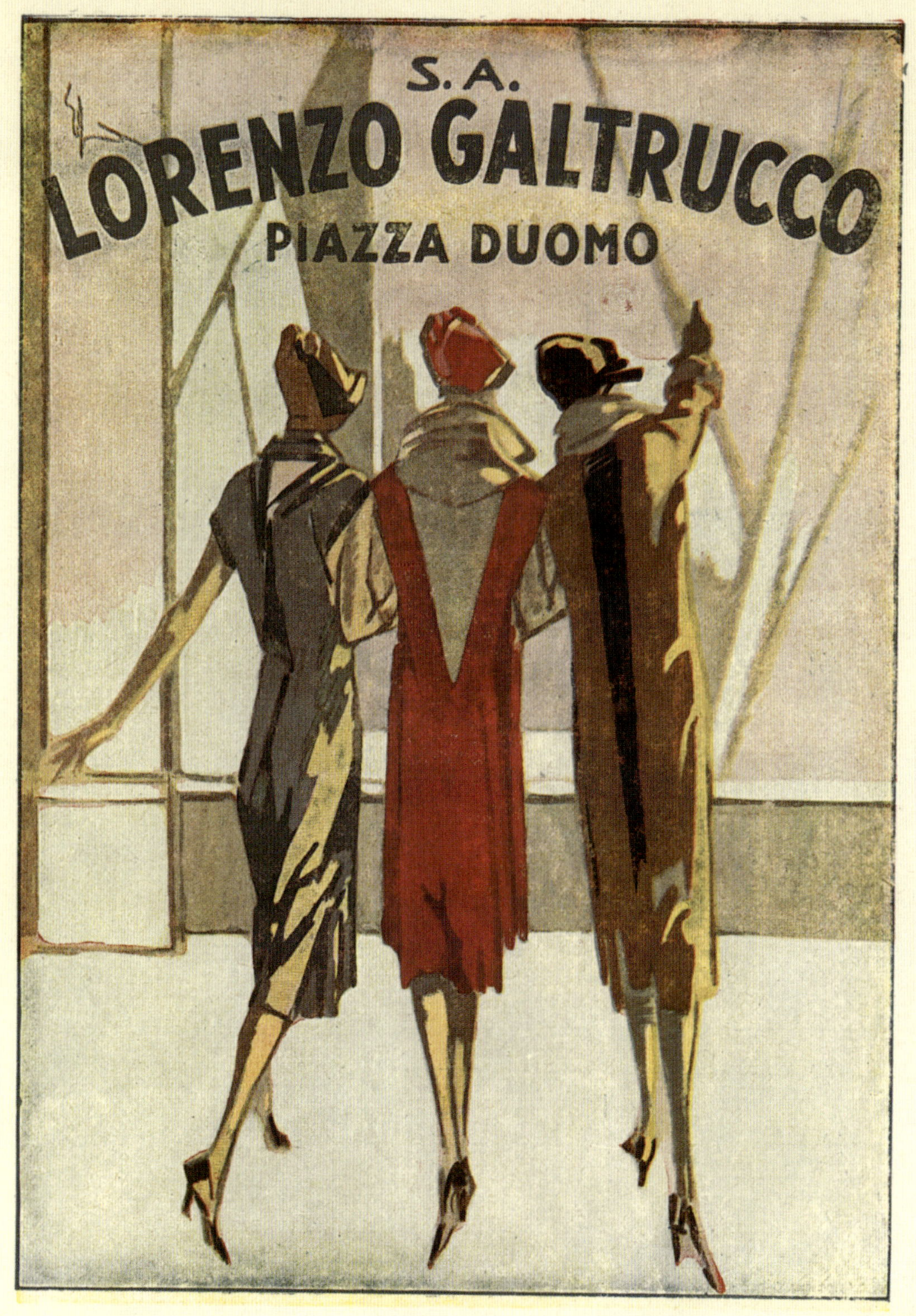

Le migliori stoffe
I prezzi più convenienti

Left and below
Italian advertisement for Lorenzo Galtrucco fabrics featuring three women in fashionable day dress, c.1926

A fur-trimmed coat with scalloped panels and a day dress with a scarf capelet, cravat and a pointed skirt. *The New Silhouette from Paris,* Hamilton Garment Co. New York catalogue, c.1929

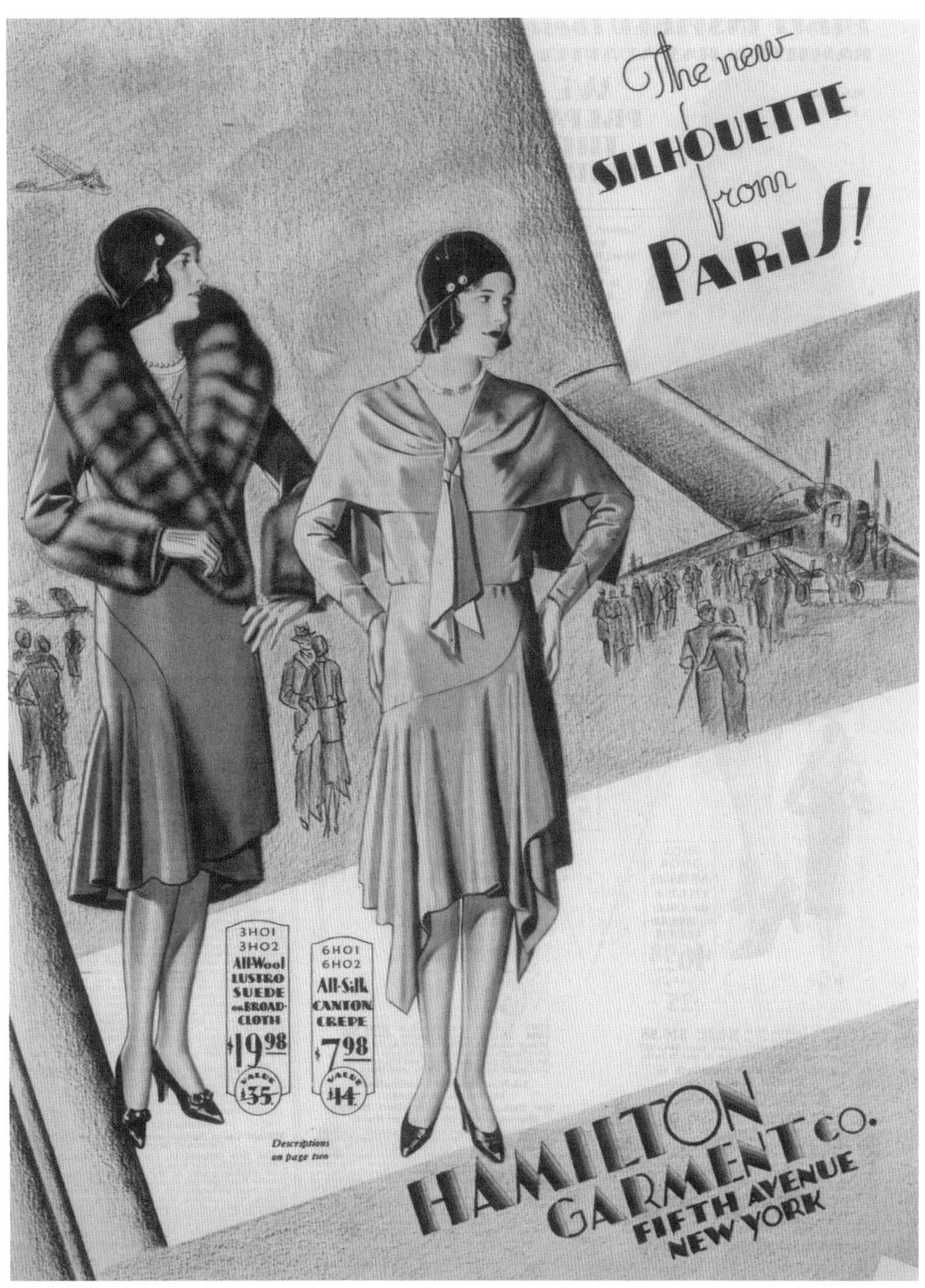

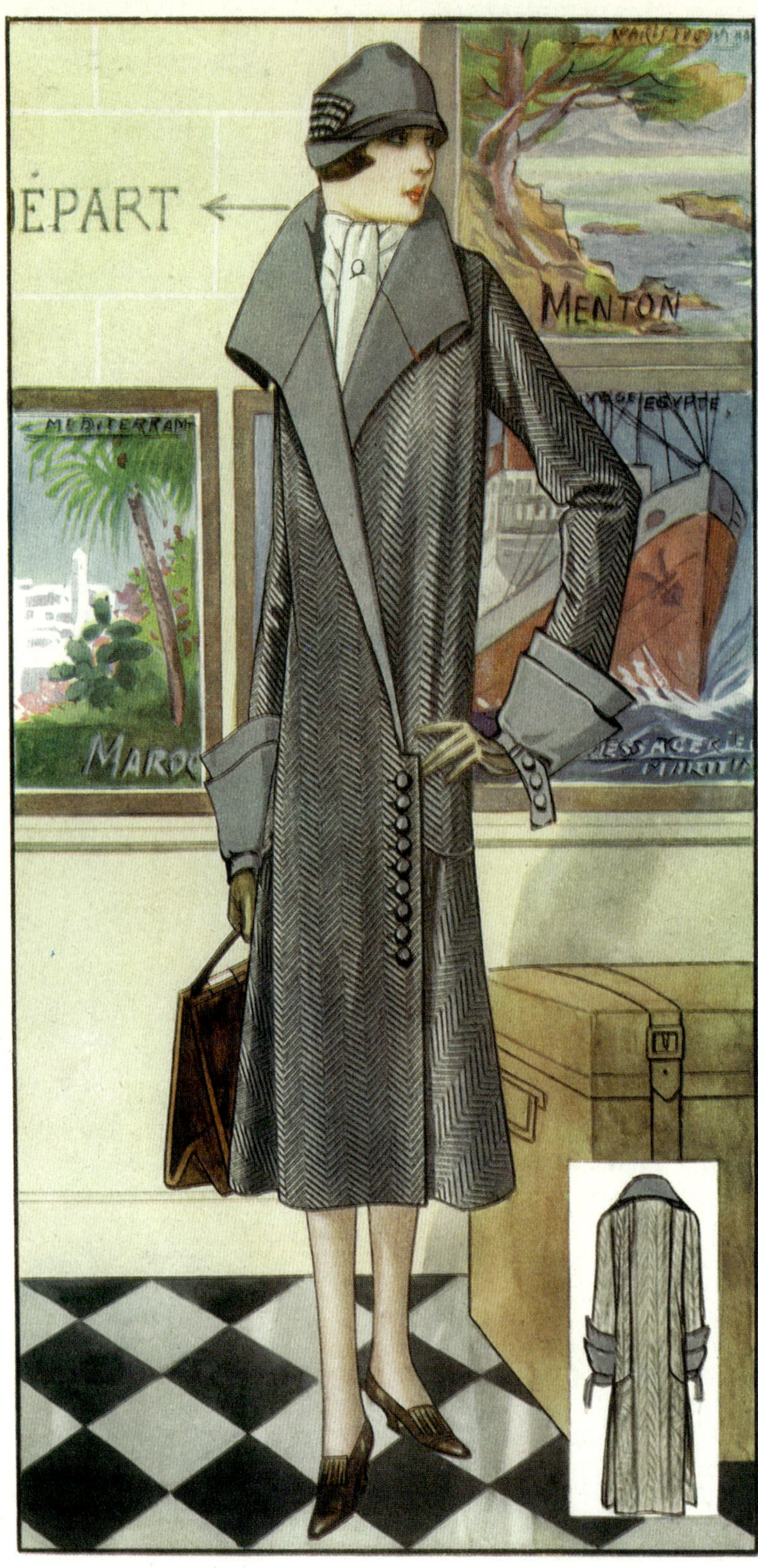

Left and right

Travelling coat in herringbone tweed. *La Femme Chic*, 1926

Fur-trimmed ensemble with crepe de Chine dress by Redfern. *La Femme Chic*, 1926

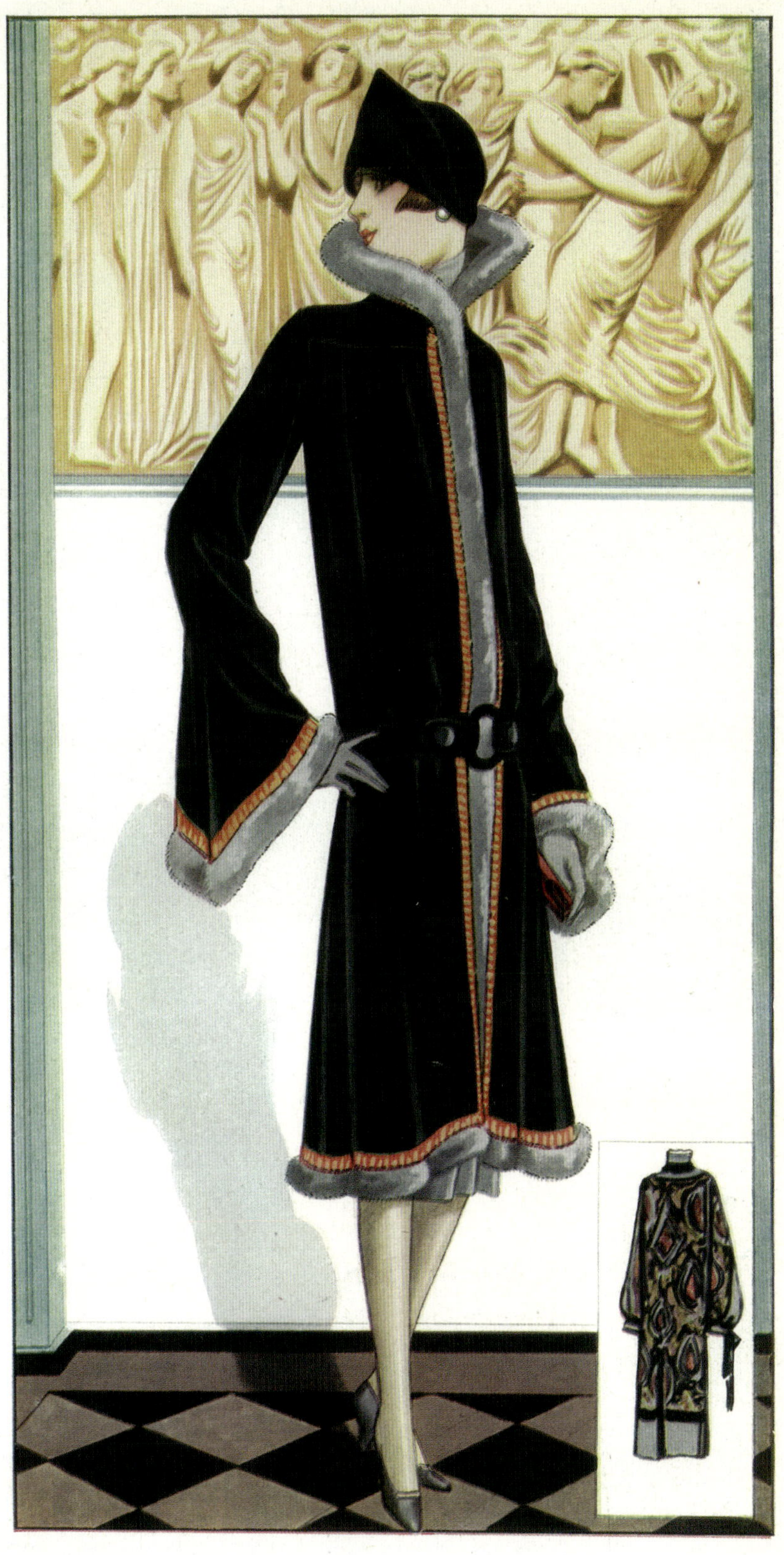

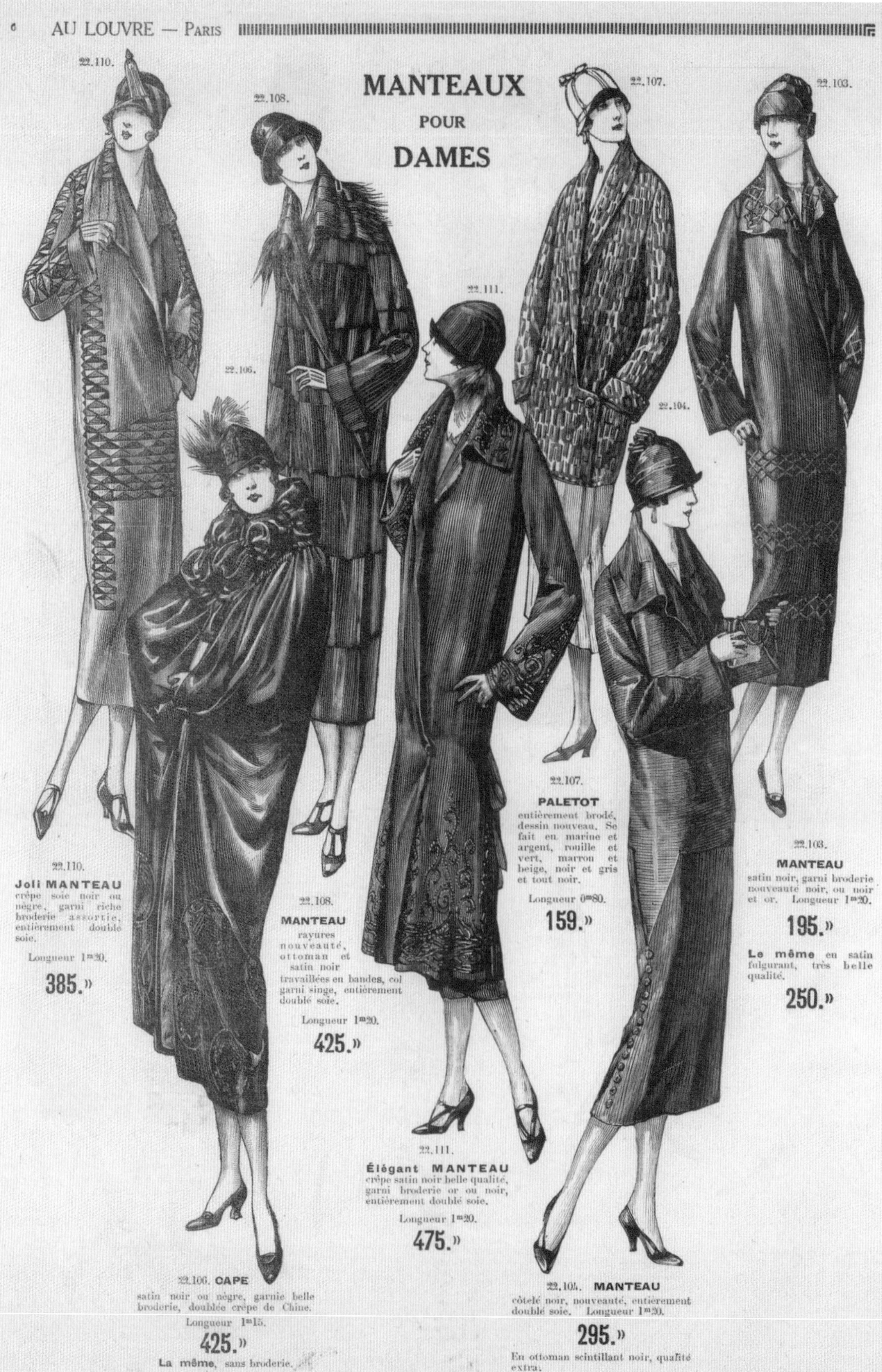

MANTEAUX POUR DAMES

22.110.

Joli MANTEAU
crêpe soie noir ou nègre, garni riche broderie assortie, entièrement doublé soie.

Longueur 1m20.

385.»

22.108.

MANTEAU
rayures nouveauté, ottoman et satin noir travaillées en bandes, col garni singe, entièrement doublé soie.

Longueur 1m20.

425.»

22.107.

PALETOT
entièrement brodé, dessin nouveau. Se fait en marine et argent, rouille et vert, marron et beige, noir et gris et tout noir.

Longueur 0m80.

159.»

22.103.

MANTEAU
satin noir, garni broderie nouveauté noir, ou noir et or. Longueur 1m20.

195.»

Le même en satin fulgurant, très belle qualité.

250.»

22.111.

Élégant MANTEAU
crêpe satin noir belle qualité, garni broderie or ou noir, entièrement doublé soie.

Longueur 1m20.

475.»

22.106. **CAPE**
satin noir ou nègre, garnie belle broderie, doublée crêpe de Chine.

Longueur 1m15.

425.»

La même, sans broderie.

22.104. **MANTEAU**
côtelé noir, nouveauté, entièrement doublé soie. Longueur 1m20.

295.»

En ottoman scintillant noir, qualité extra.

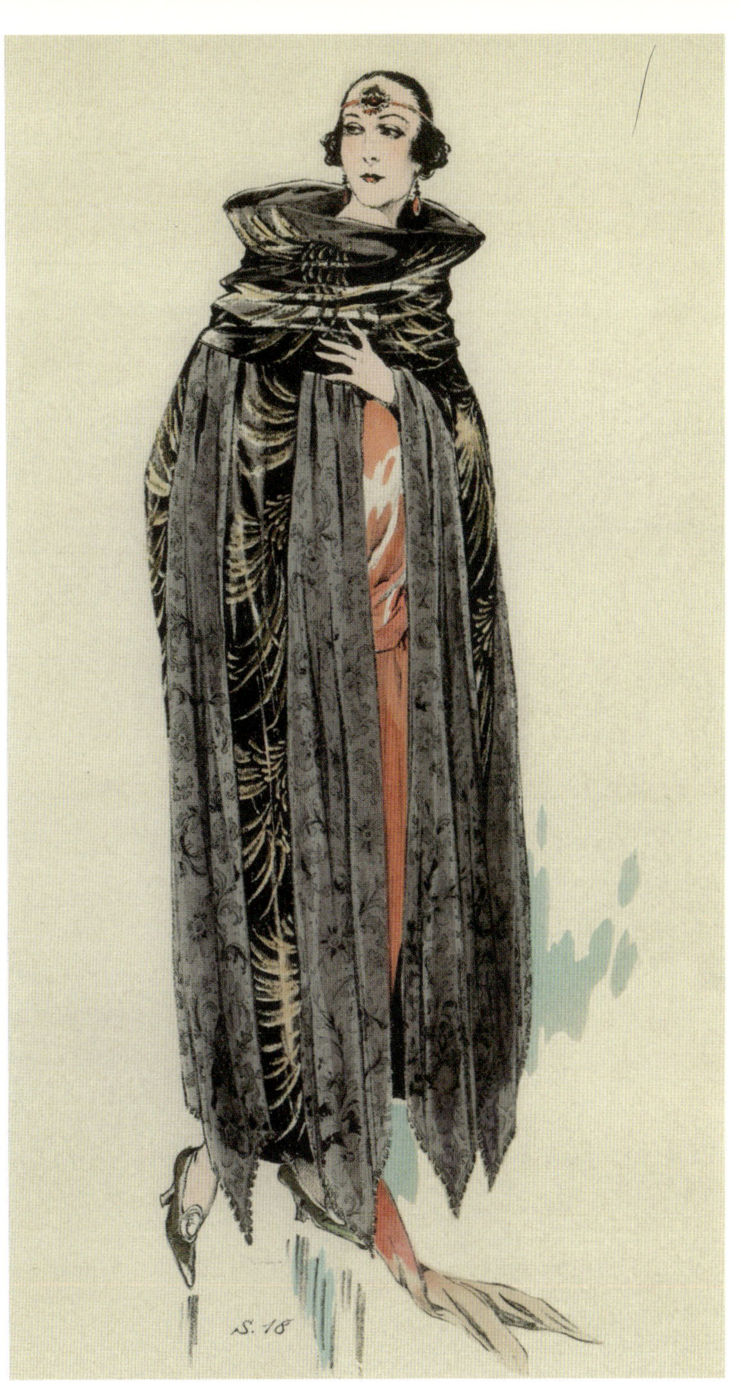

Left and above

Selection of day and evening coats and capes. Au Louvre catalogue, 1925

A gold and silver brocade and black lace evening cape. *Dernières Creations*, c.1923

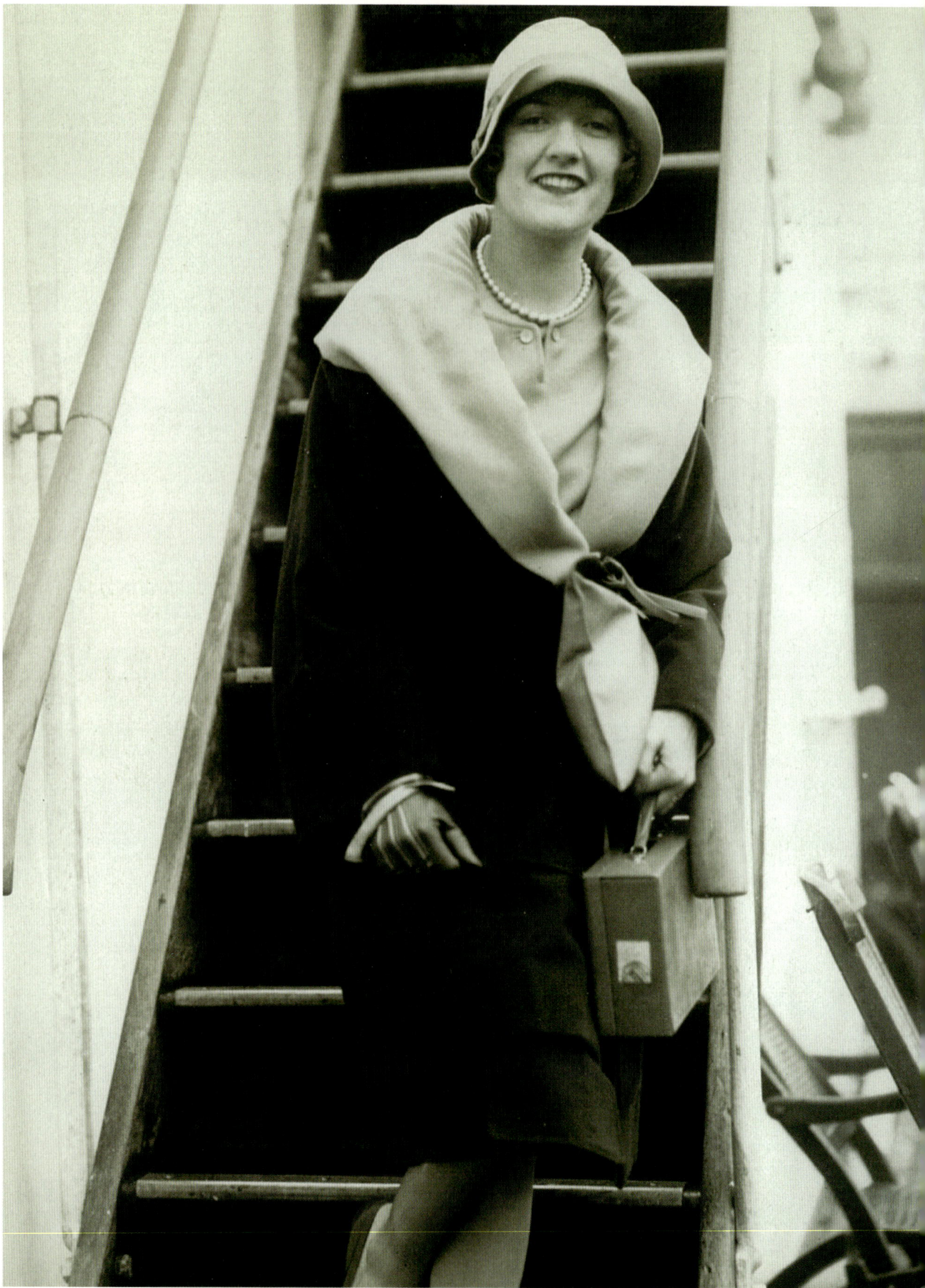

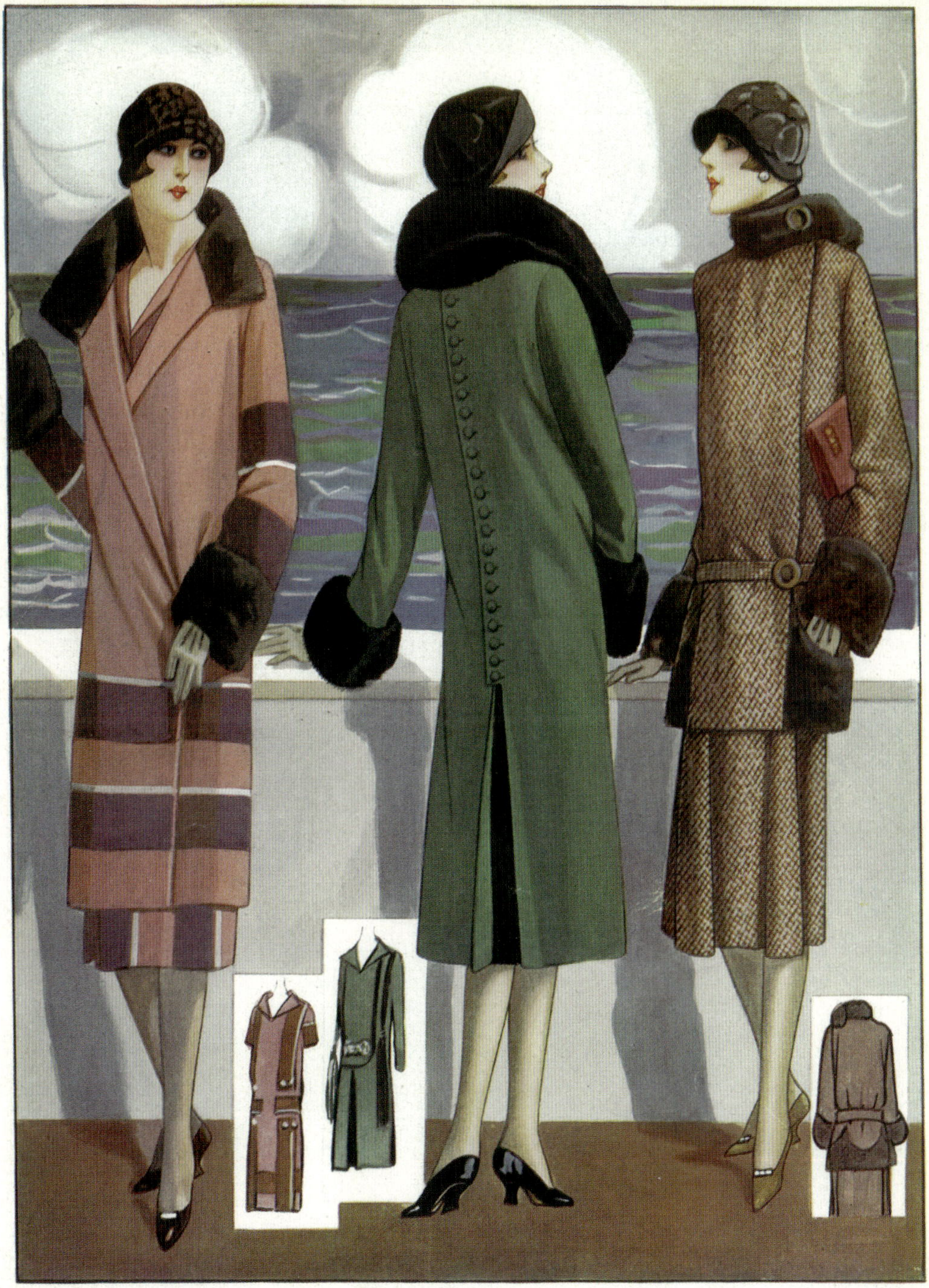

Left and above

Actress Constance Talmadge wearing a satin-collared coat and cloche hat, 1927

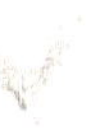

Three travelling ensembles by Berthe Hermance. *La Femme Chic*, 1926

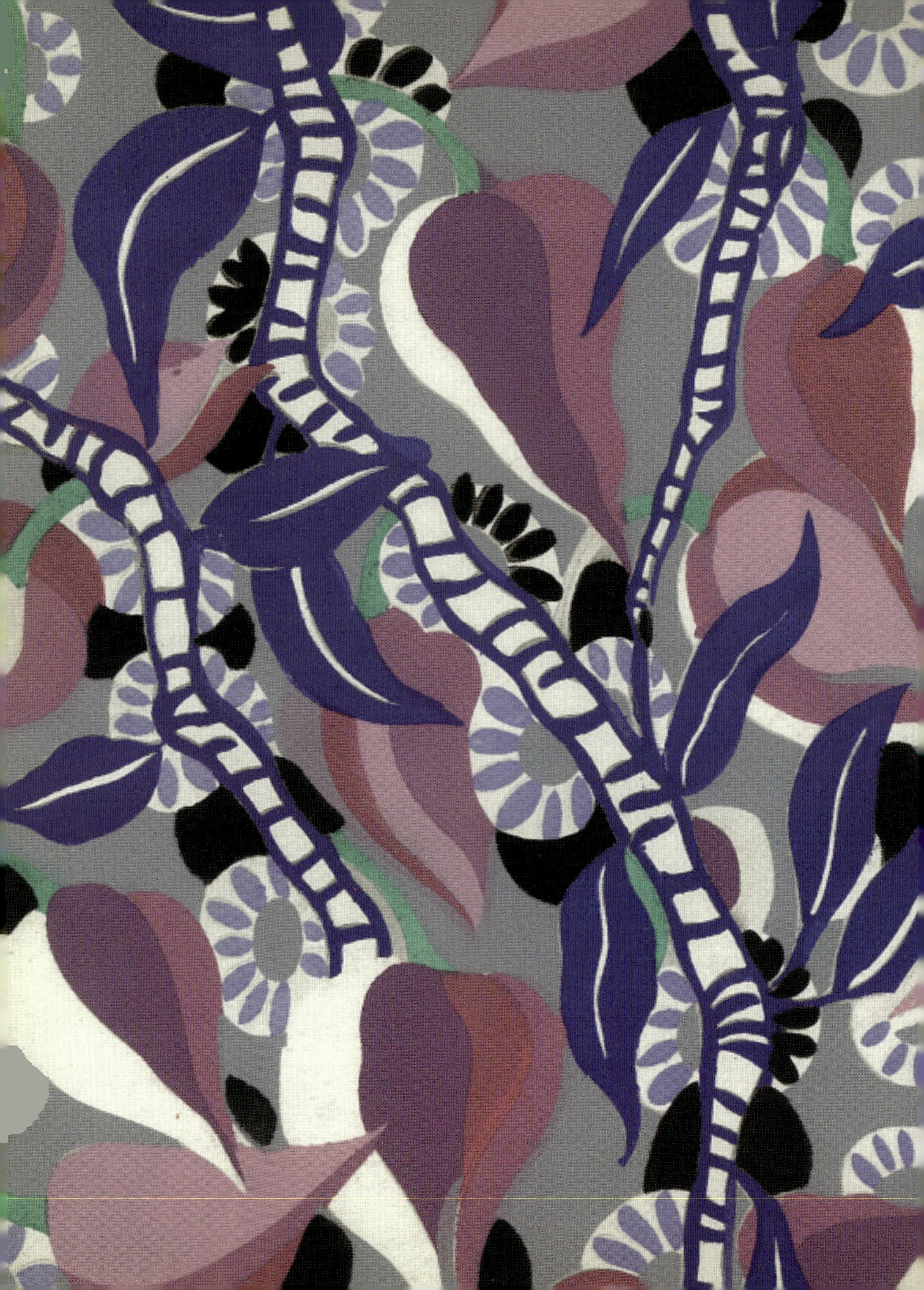

Eveningwear

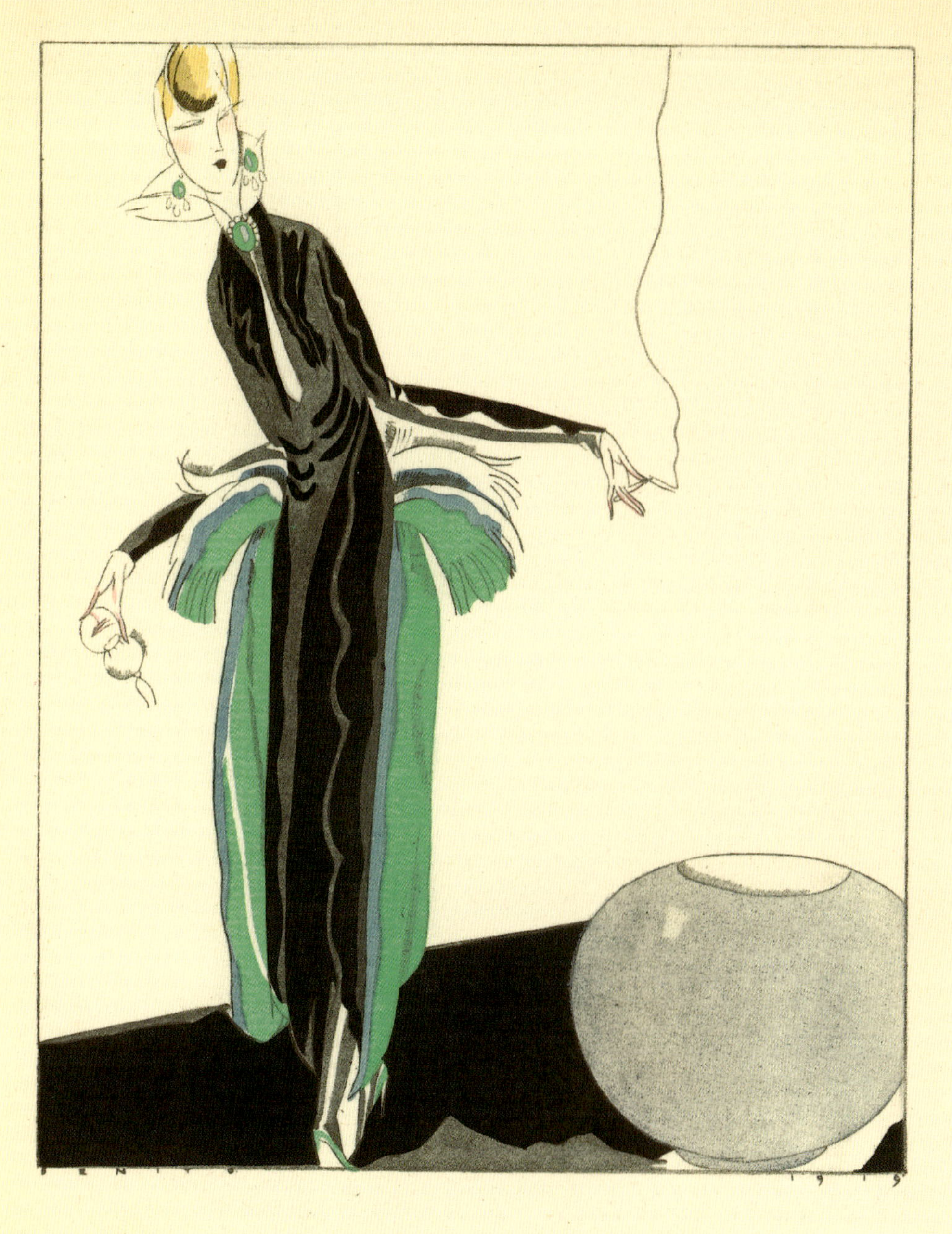

Above
"Le Bassin D'argent" (The Silver Basin), dinner dress. Illustration by Benito. *Gazette du Bon Ton*, 1920

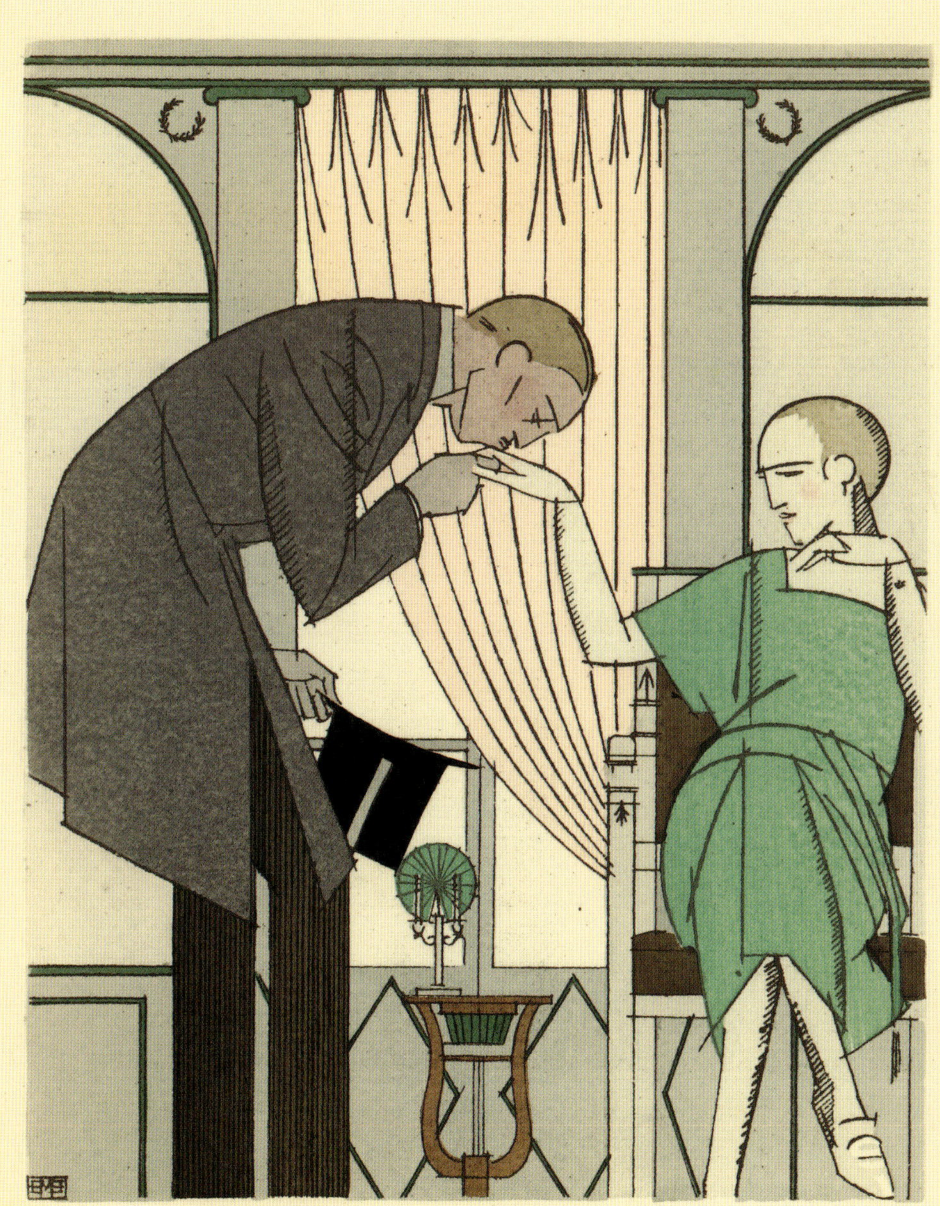

Above
"La Redingote ou le retour aux traditions" (The frockcoat or the return to tradition), illustration by Bernard Boutet De Monvel. *Gazette du Bon Ton*, 1920

Below
"La Lettre Surprise" (The Surprise Letter), illustration by Fernand Simeon. *Gazette du Bon Ton*, 1920

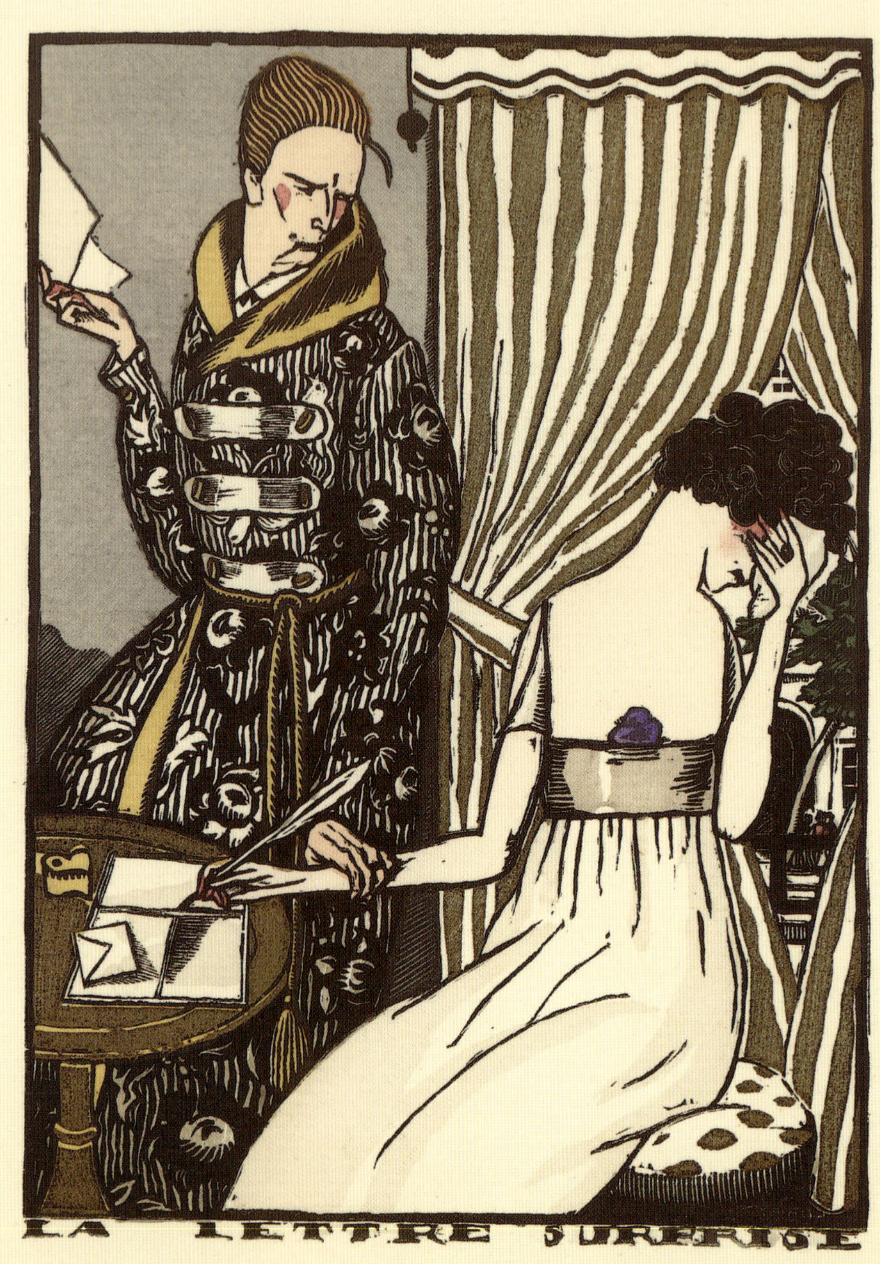

Below
"Que vas-tu faire!" (What are you going to do!), evening dress by Worth. Illustration by Etienne Drian. *Gazette du Bon Ton*, 1920

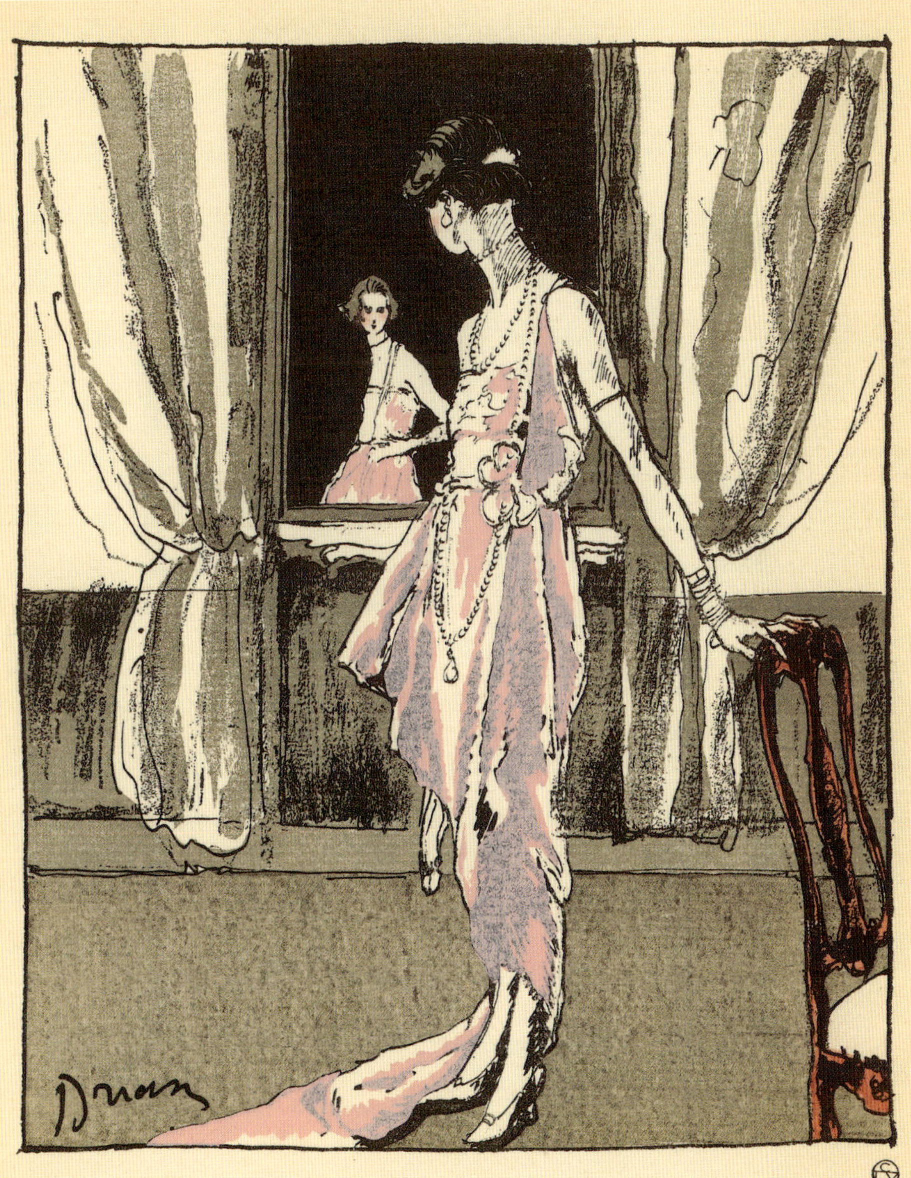

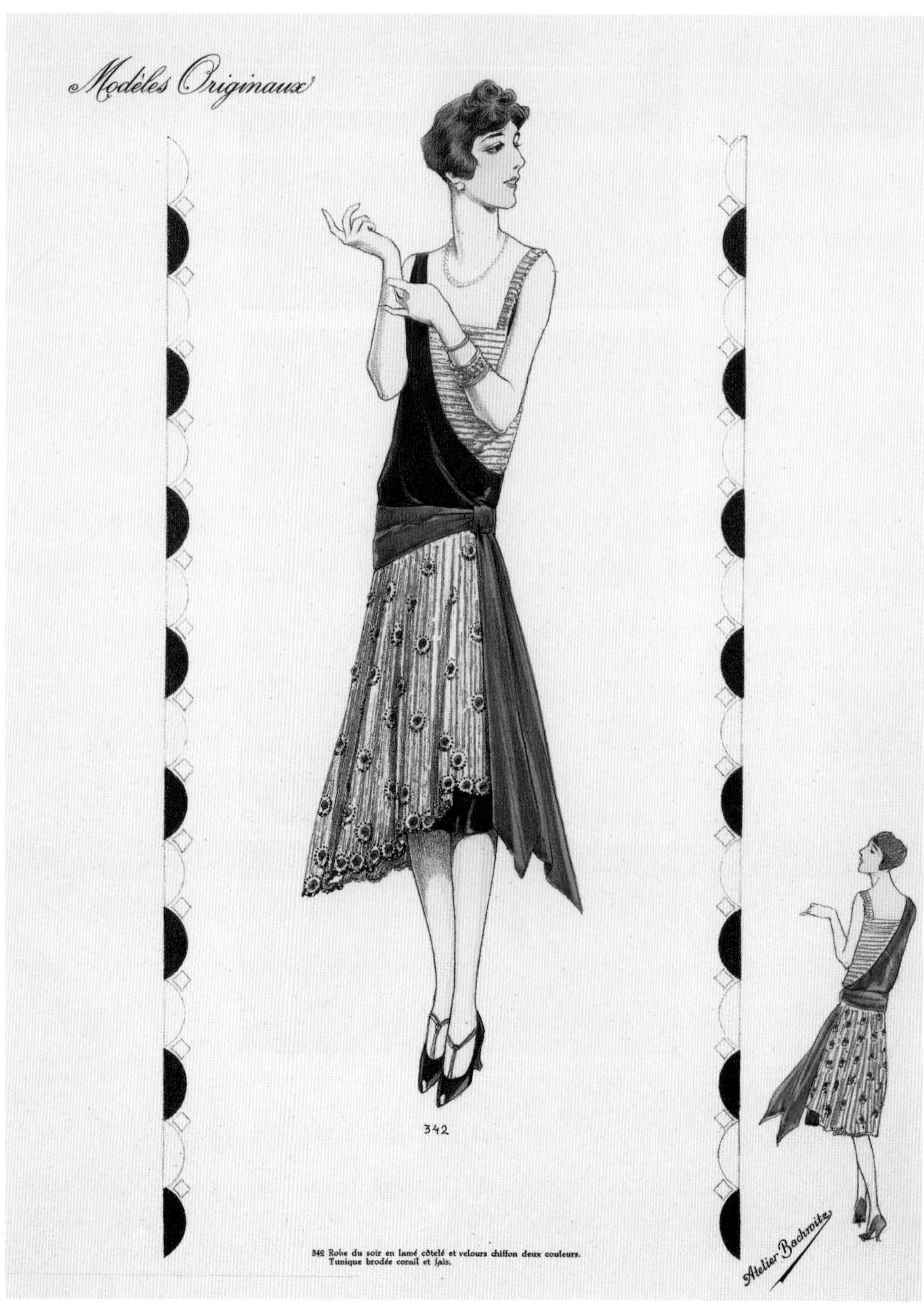

Above

Evening dress of ribbed silver lamé and chiffon velvet in blue and black by Atelier Bachroitz. *Modèles Originaux*, c.1926

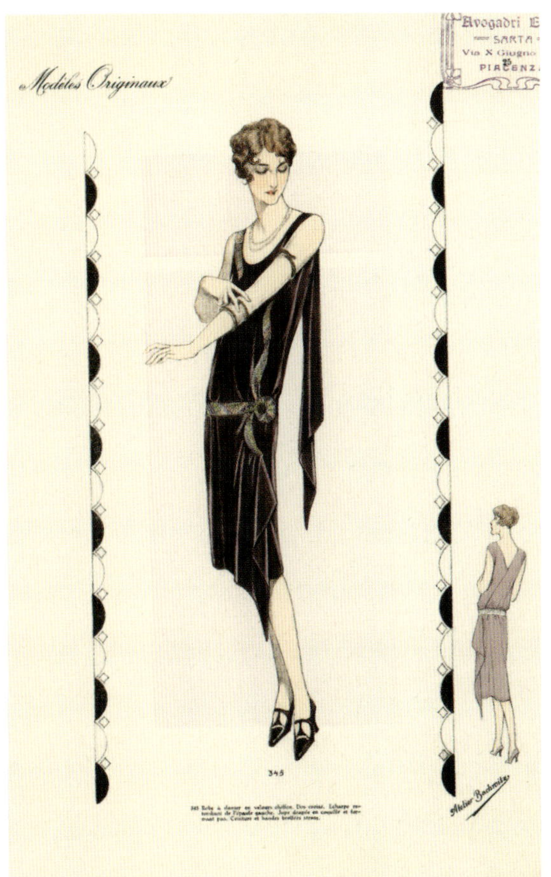

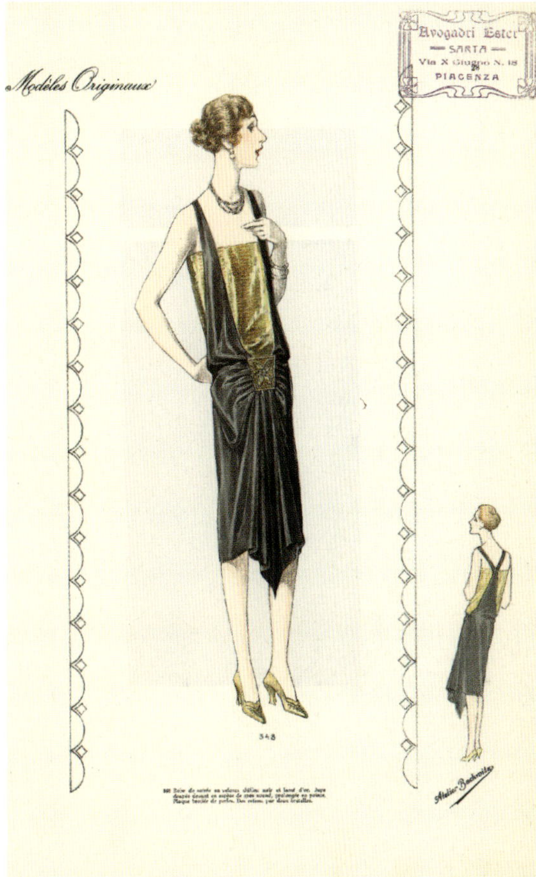

Above left and right

Black dancing dress in chiffon velvet with crossed back and sash by Atelier Bachroitz. *Modèles Originaux*, c.1926. The belt and detailing are of paste embroidery and the model is wearing slave bracelets on one arm, a fashion in keeping with exotic influences, which moved from all-over dress designs to detailing by the middle of the decade.

Black chiffon velvet and gold lamé evening dress with a design for breeches in the background by Atelier Bachroitz. *Modèles Originaux*, c.1926. The dress is draped in a knot-like manner at the front to create the pointed silhouette, while the central part of the knot is embroidered with pearls.

Right
Black evening dress of muslin and lace worn over a silver slip by Atelier Bachroitz. *Modèles Originaux* c.1926

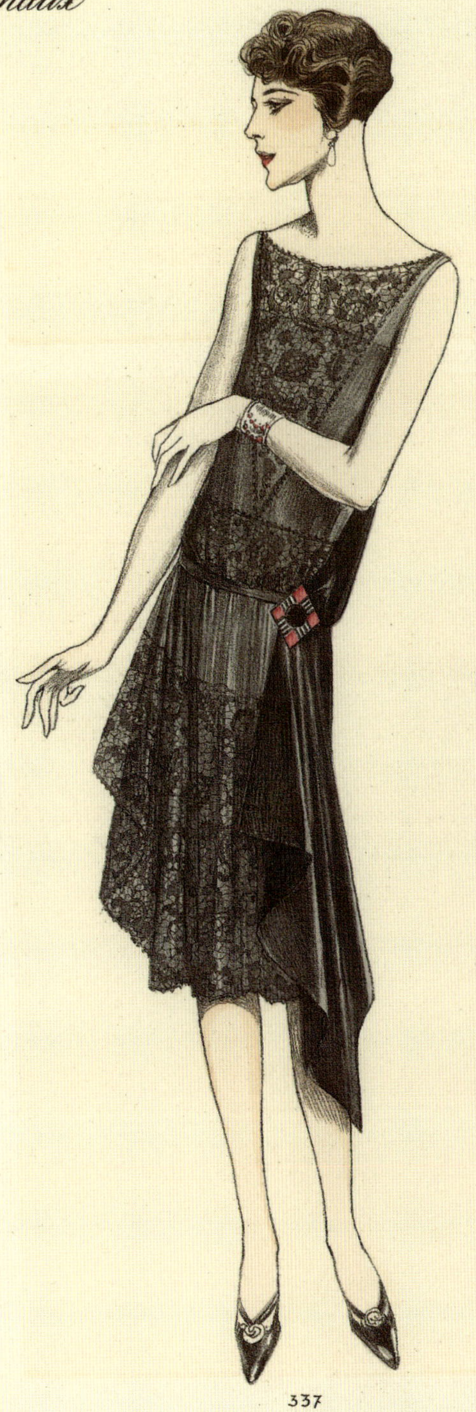

337

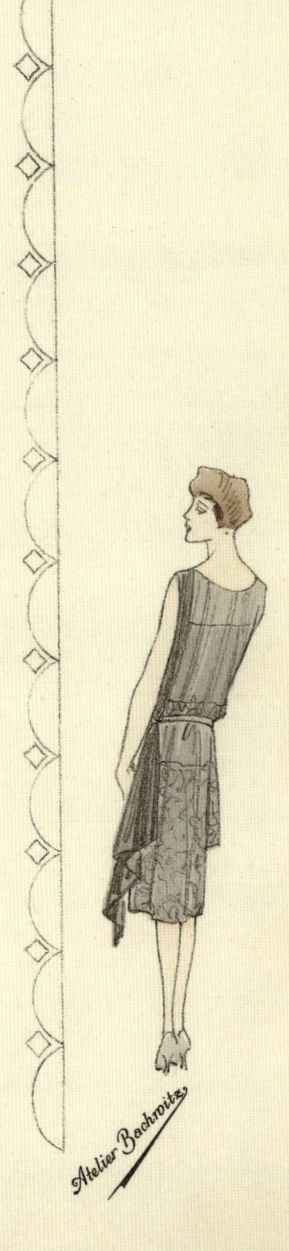

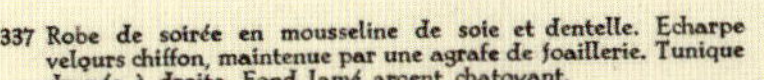

337 Robe de soirée en mousseline de soie et dentelle. Echarpe velours chiffon, maintenue par une agrafe de joaillerie. Tunique drapée à droite. Fond lamé argent chatoyant.

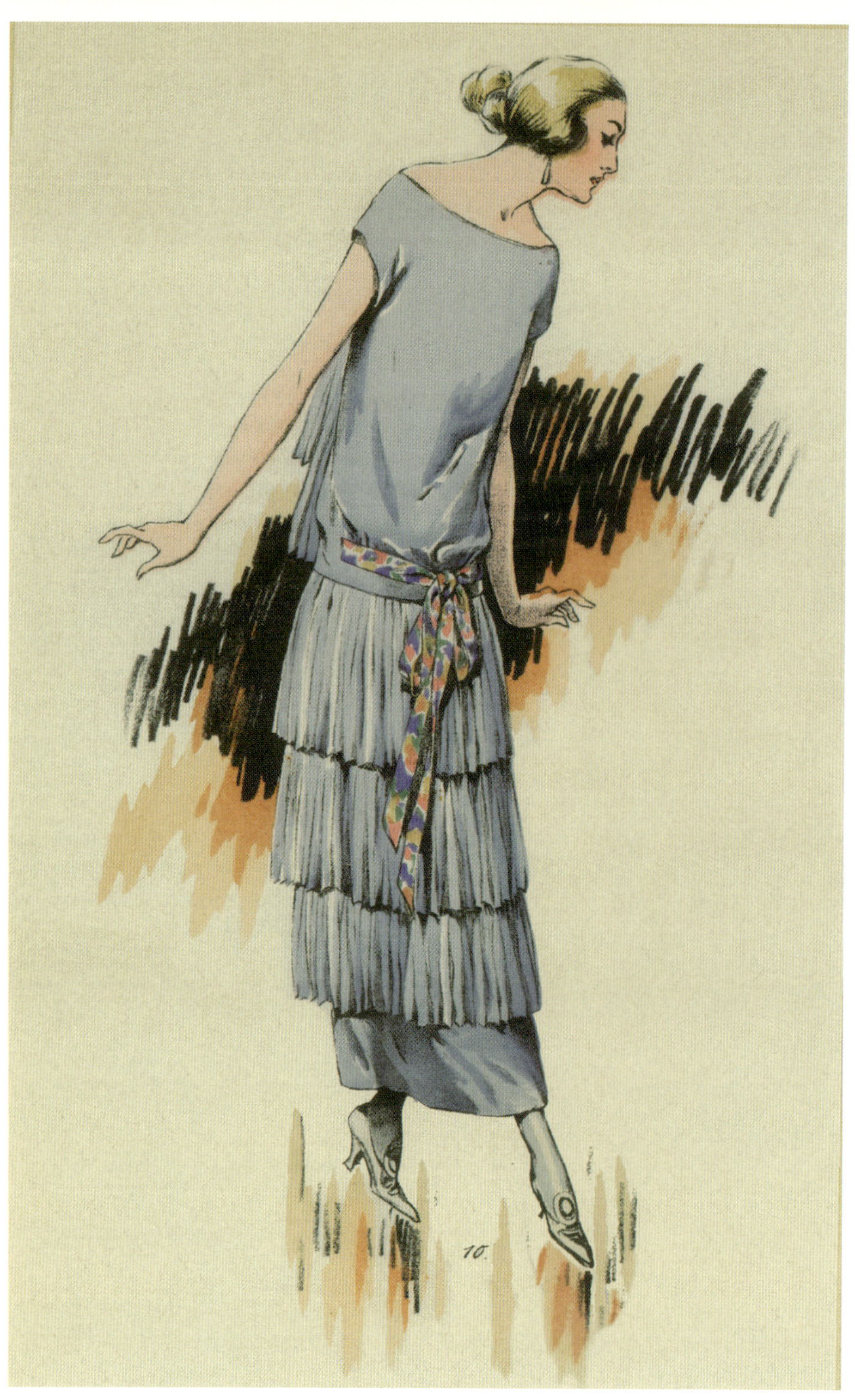

Above
A lavender blue crepe de Chine ball dress with a pleated flounced skirt.
Dernières Créations, c.1923

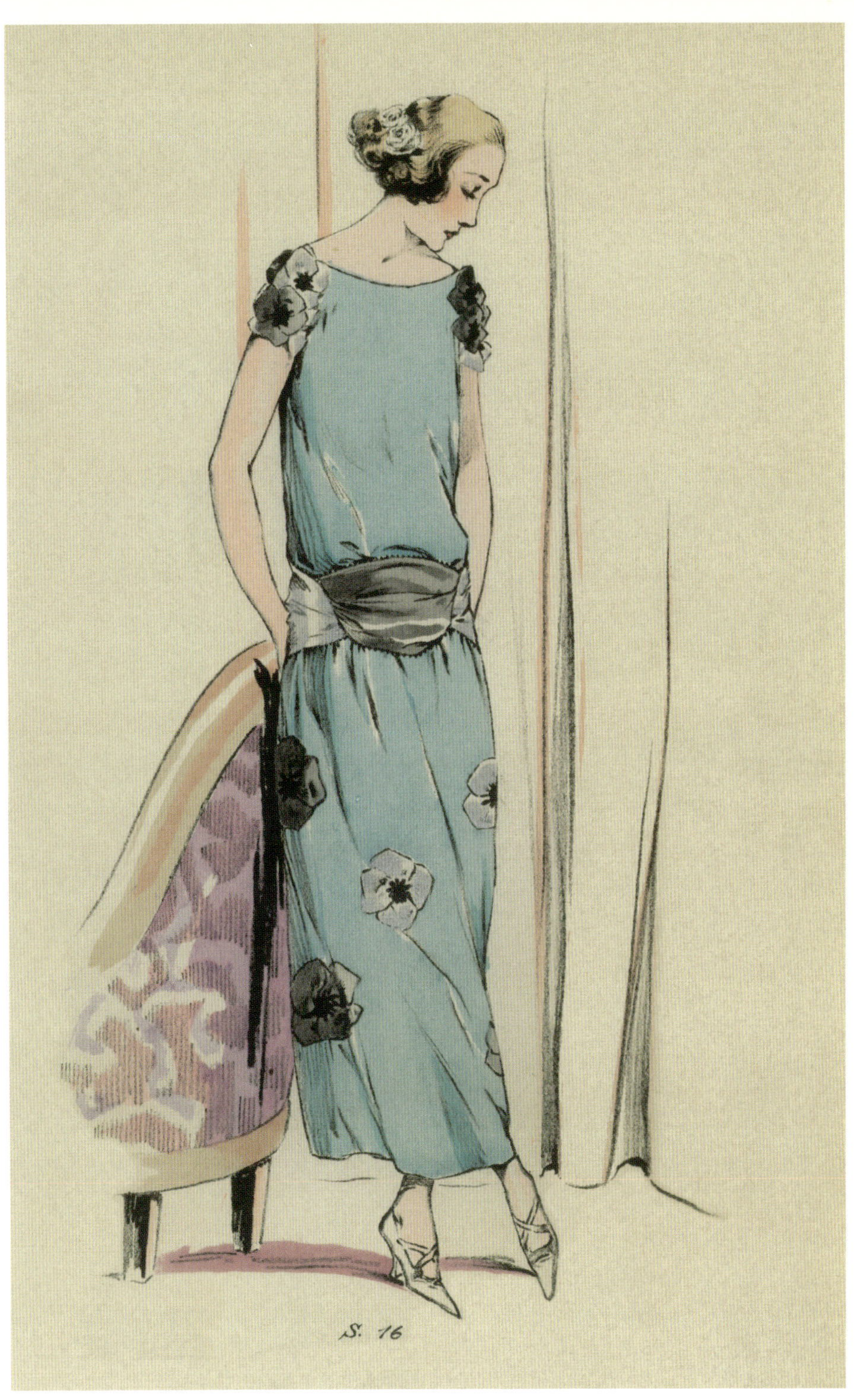

Above

A blue crepe de Chine evening dress finished with grey velvet flowers and a worsted girdle of grey and silver ribbon. *Dernières Créations*, c.1923

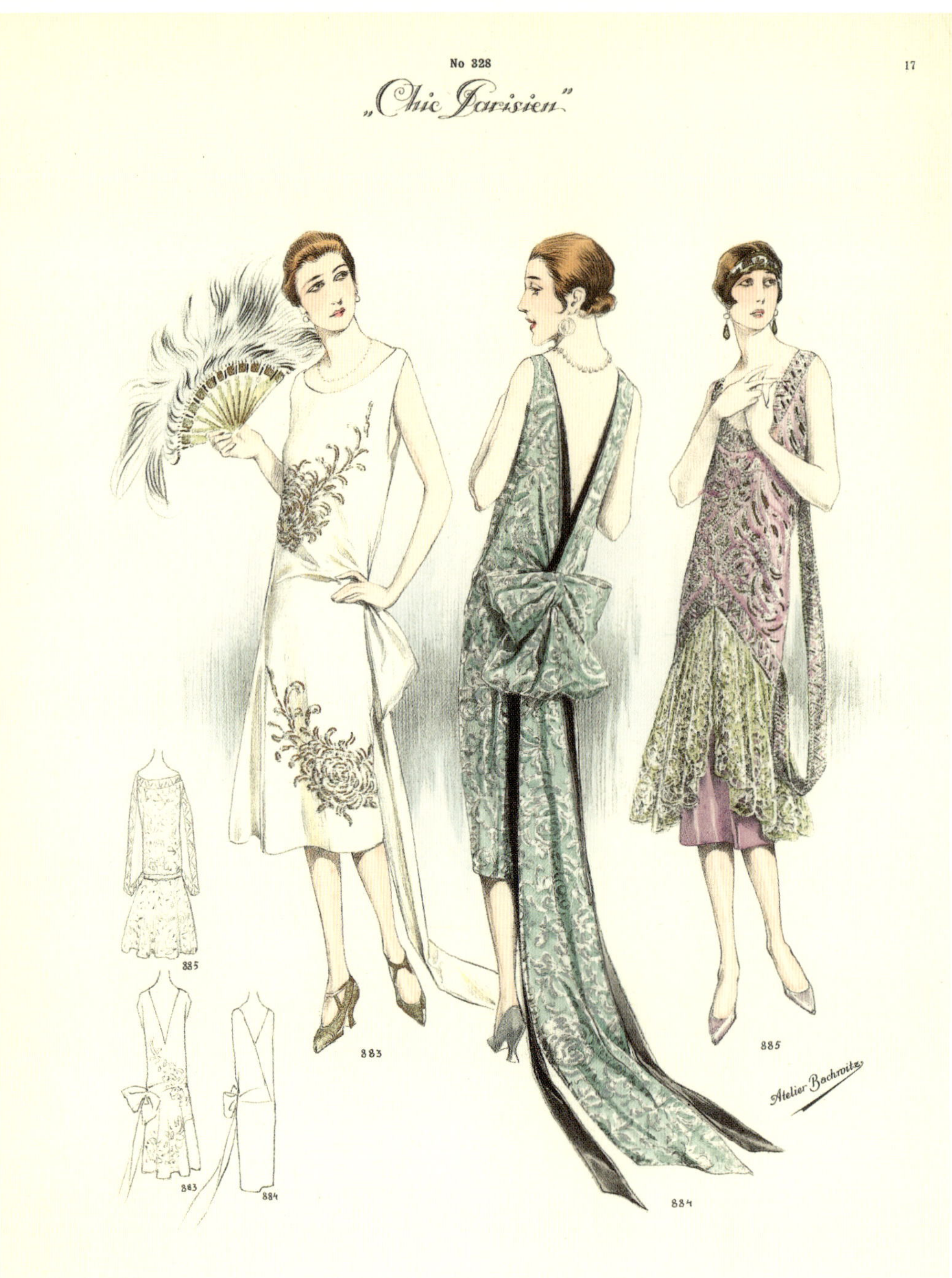

Above
Three evening dresses by Atelier Bachroitz. *Chic Parisien Beaux-Arts des Modes*, c.1927. The marabou feather fan was a popular accessory and its gold detailing matches the floral embellishment of the dress. The middle dress has a long train affixed with a large bow. This style of dress became popular in the second half of the decade.

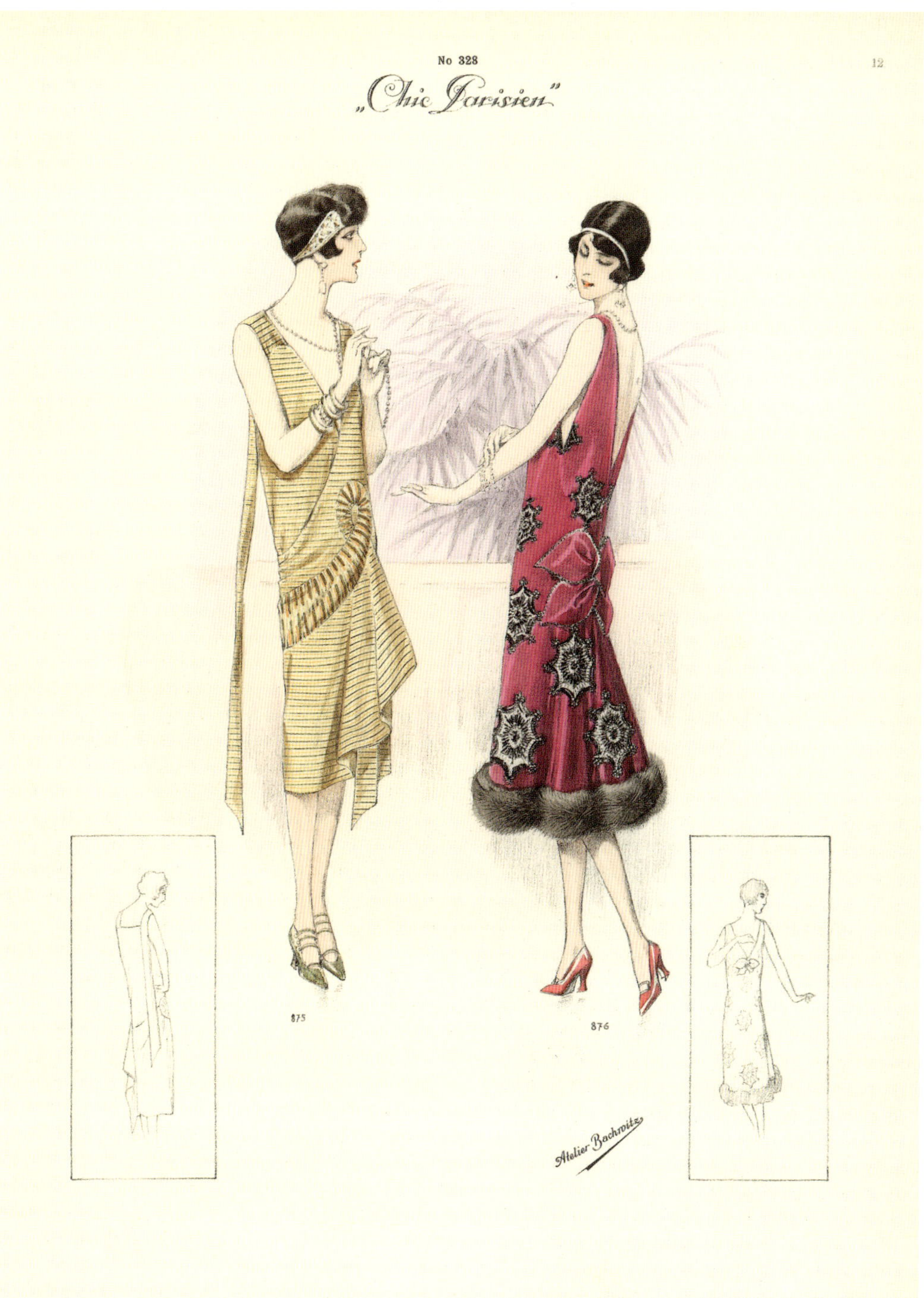

Above
Two Atelier Bachroitz evening dresses. *Chic Parisien Beaux-Arts des Modes*, c.1927. The model on the left is a wrap-over design which affixes at the waist and the right model has a deep cut v-shaped back and is embellished with snowflake designs, a large embellished bow and trimmed in fur.

Right
A woman in a white evening dress embellished with black beaded fringes.
La Mode, 1921

Next page
Five dresses for holidays on the Côte d'Azur. Several of the dresses show classic Greek influences which are enforced by the models poses and the backdrop of a classical colonnade.
La Femme Chic, c.1922

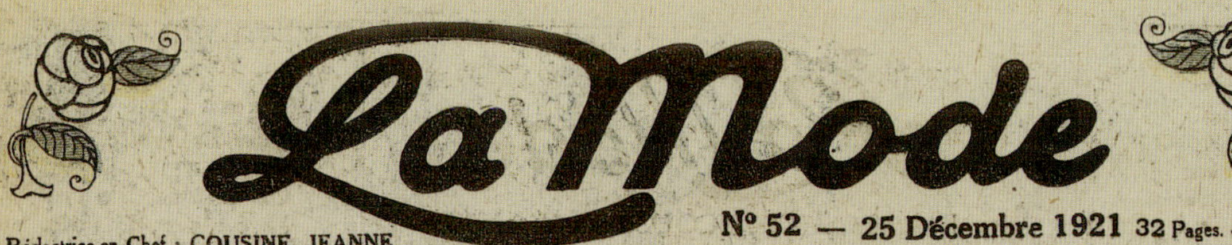

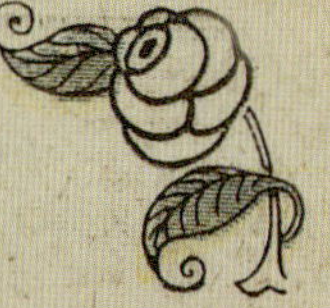

Rédactrice en Chef : COUSINE JEANNE.

N° 52 — 25 Décembre 1921 32 Pages. -- 50 Centimes

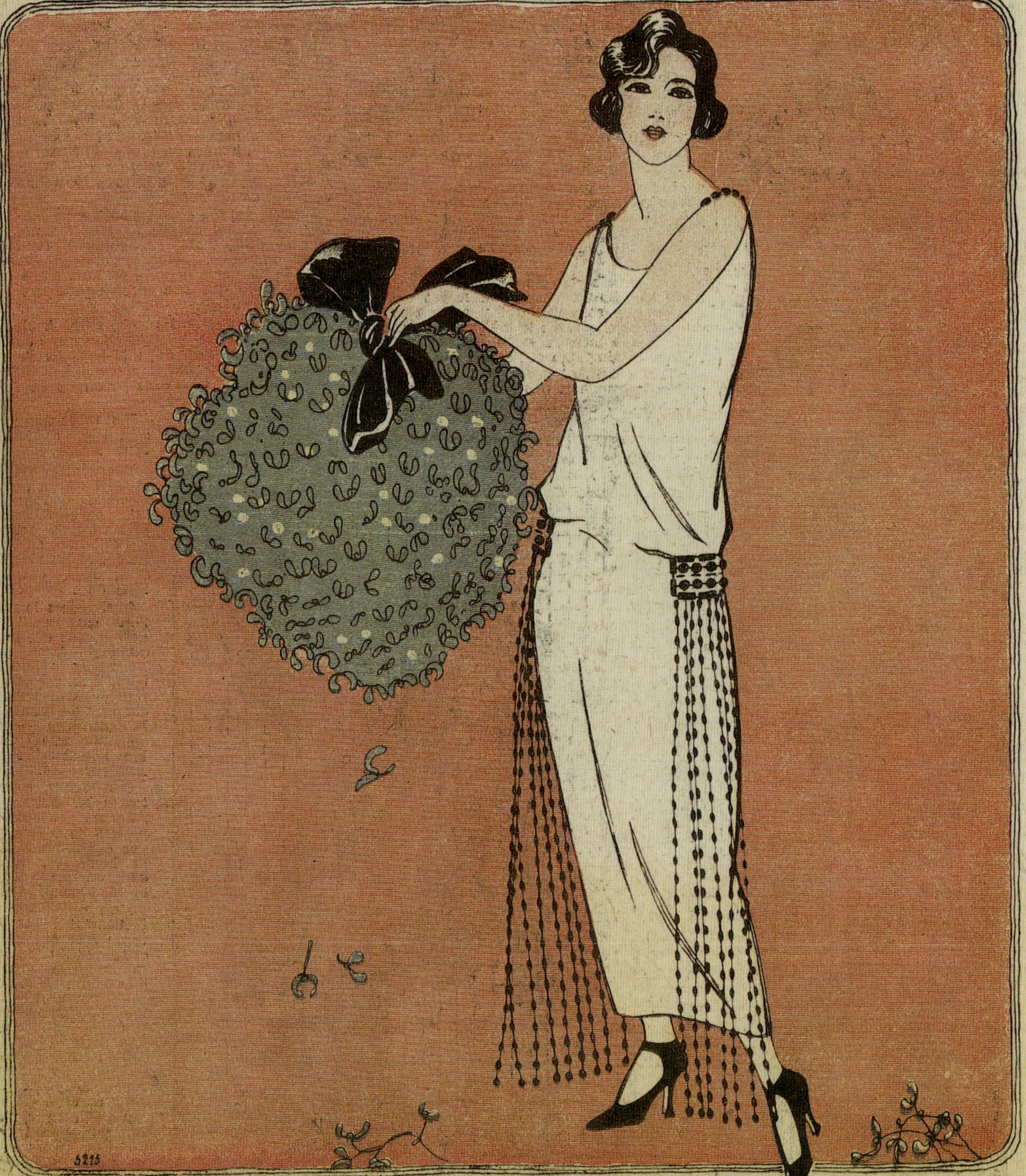

Numéro de Noël : 8 pages de plus, 50 centimes. -- Attention ! ne pas couper la planche de travaux

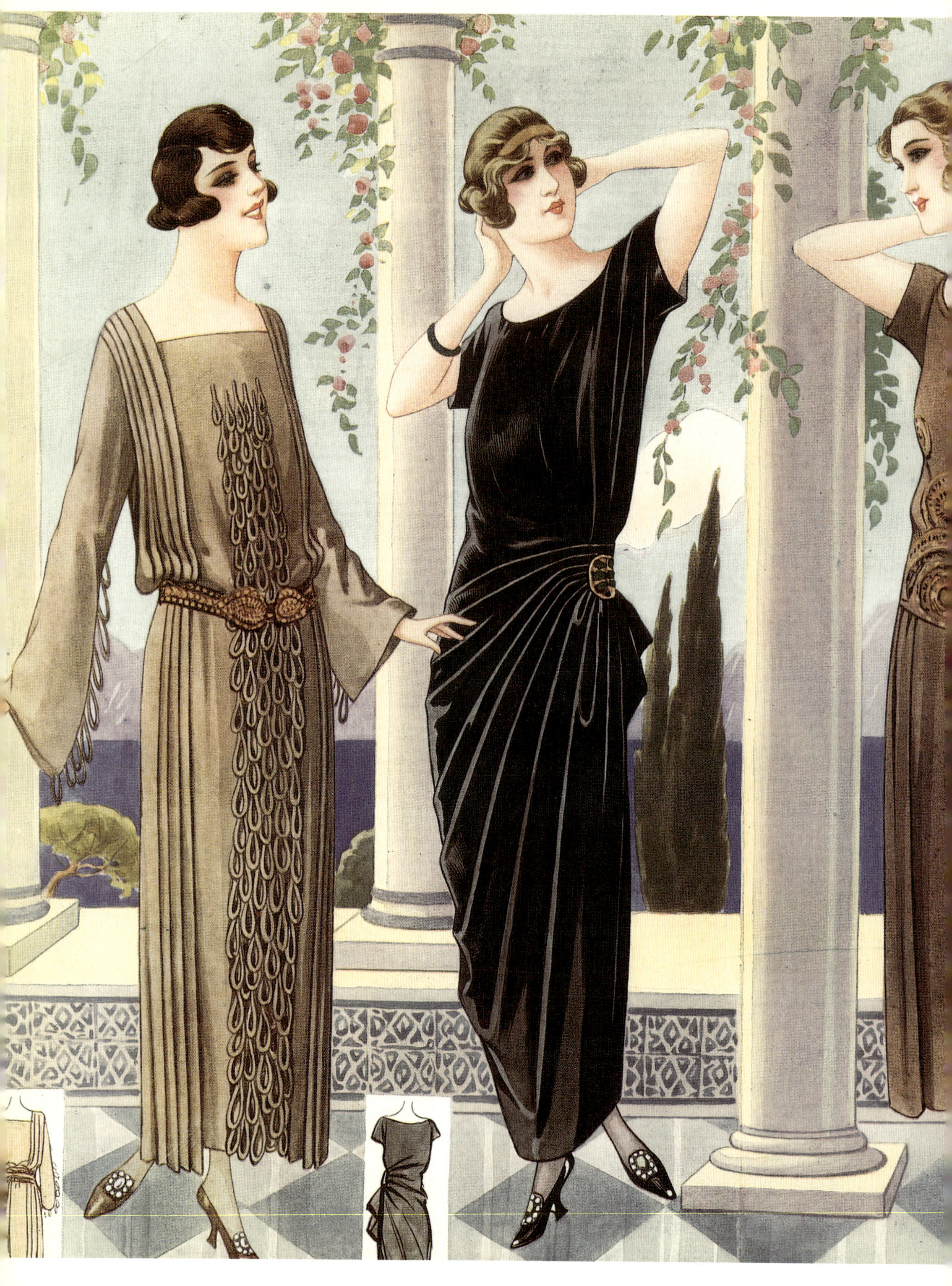

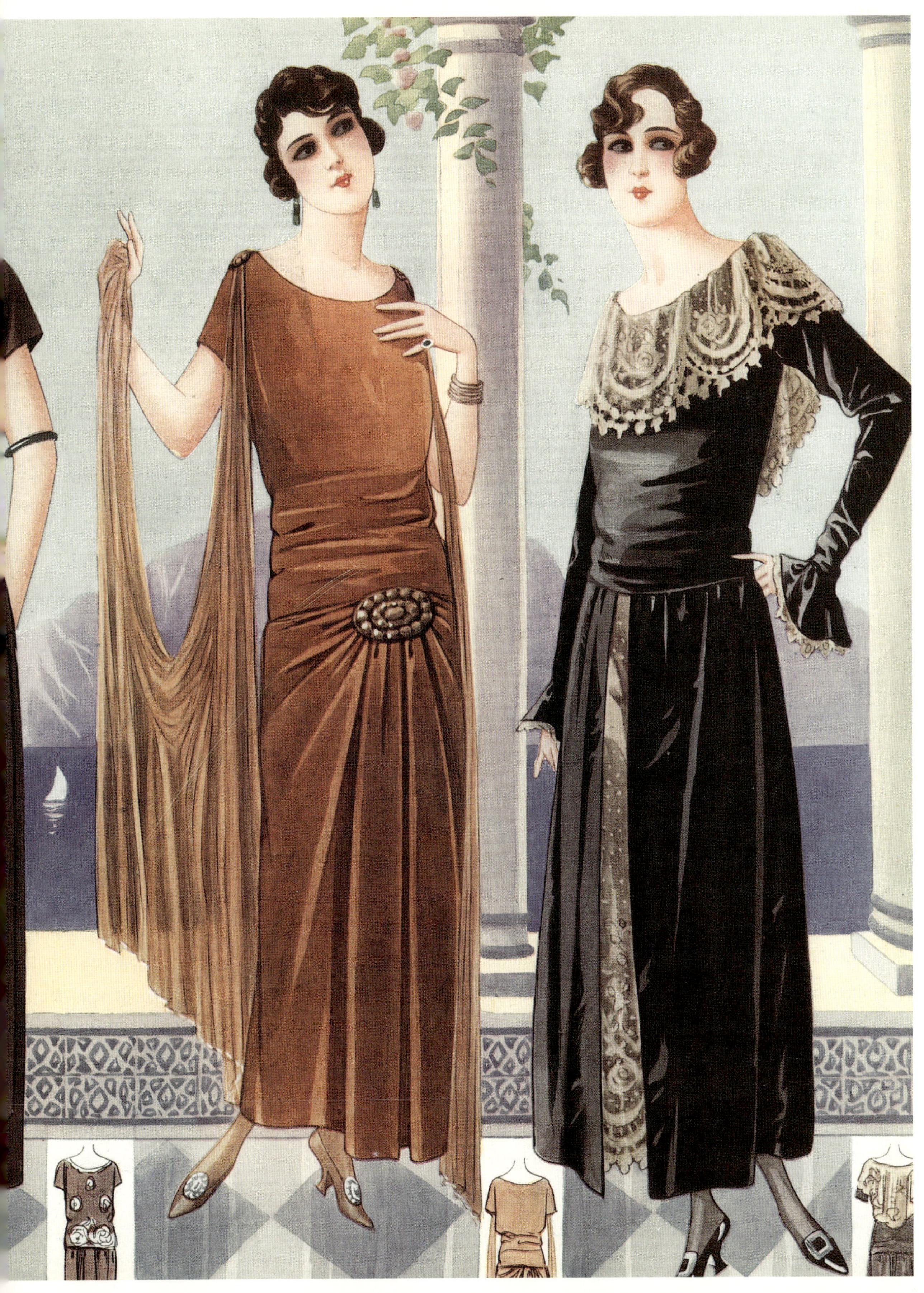

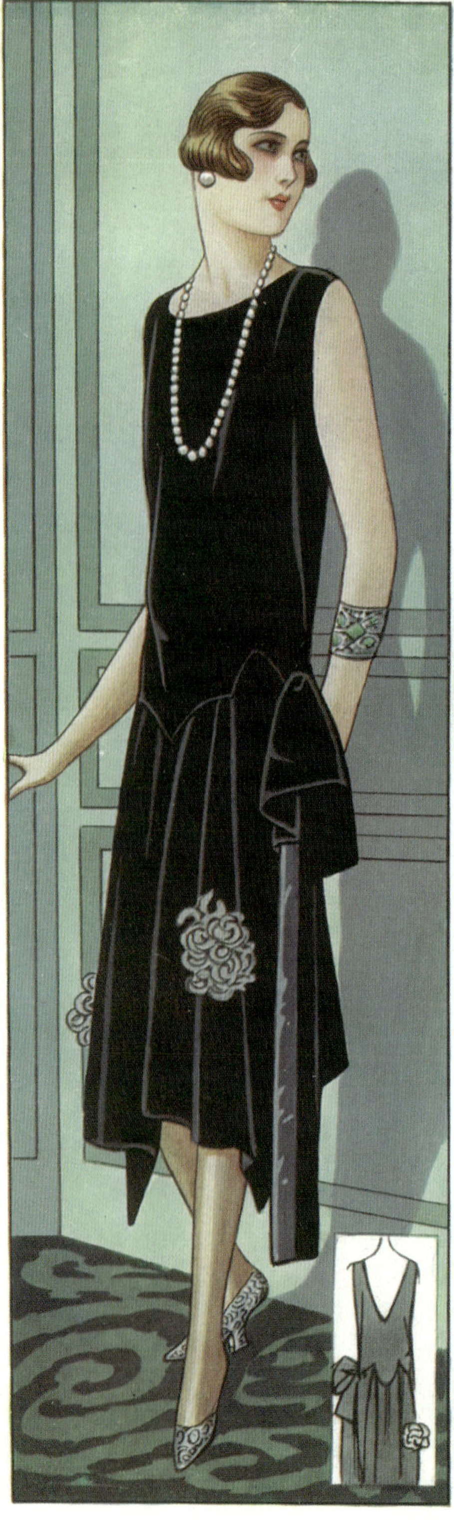

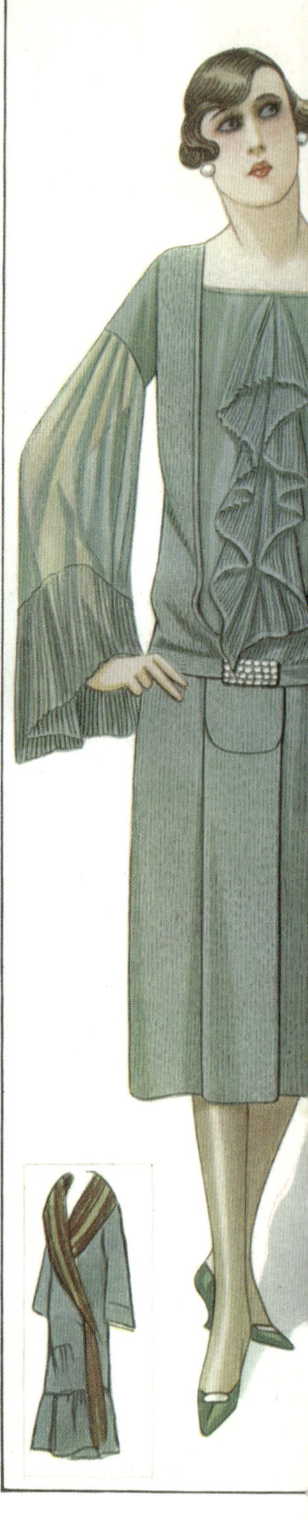

Above
Four dresses by Georgette and a navy dress with mustard trim by Dupony.
La Femme Chic, 1926

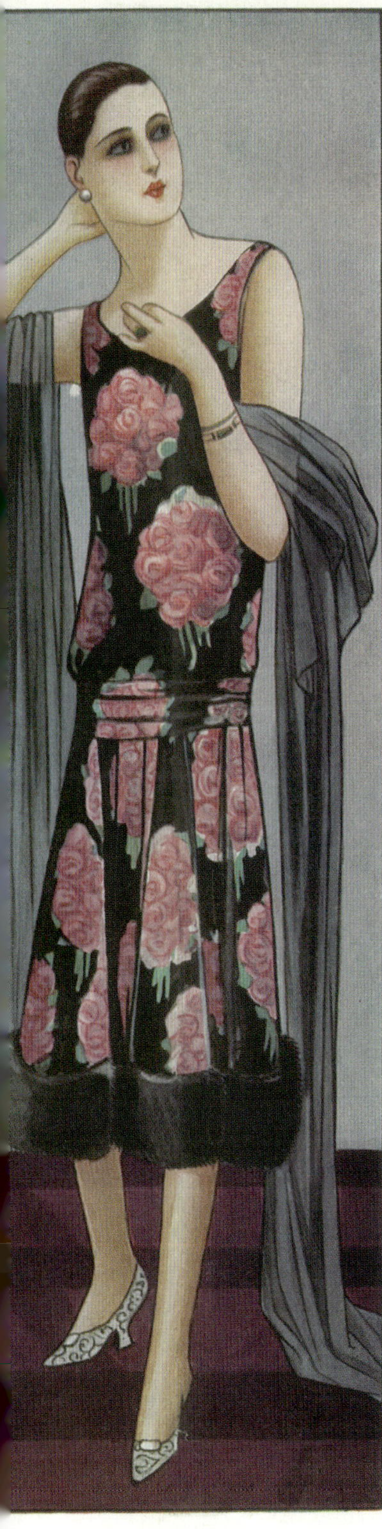

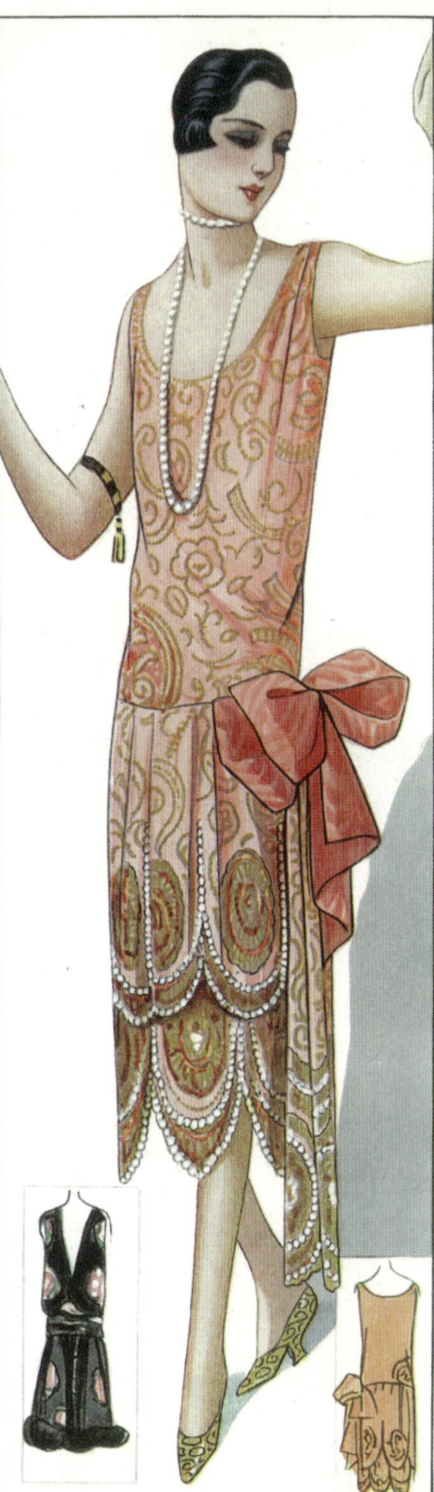

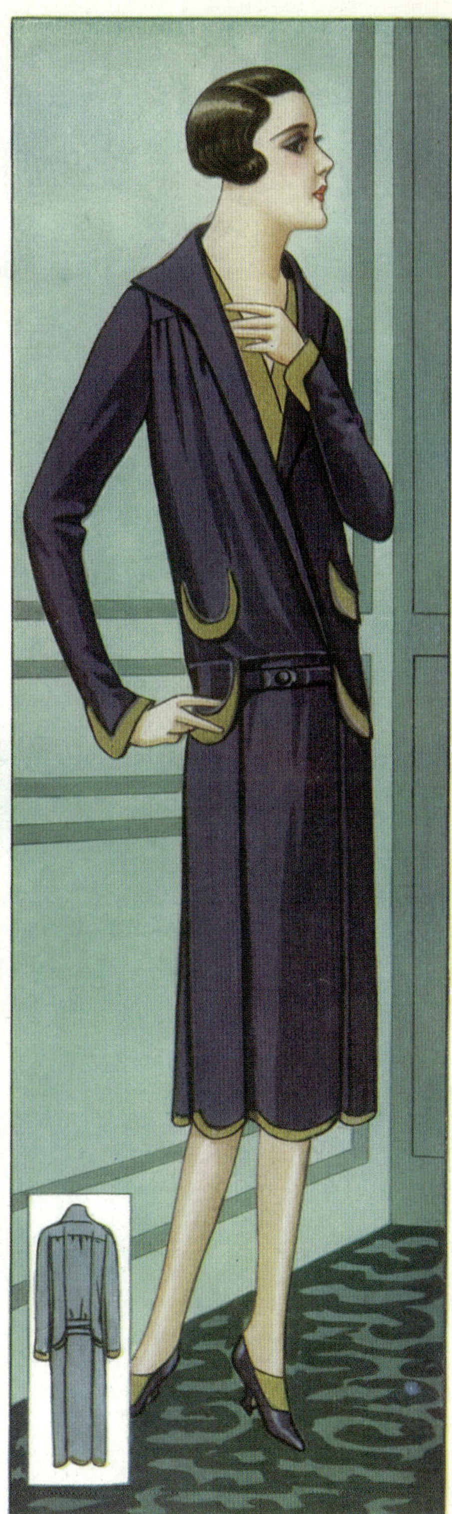

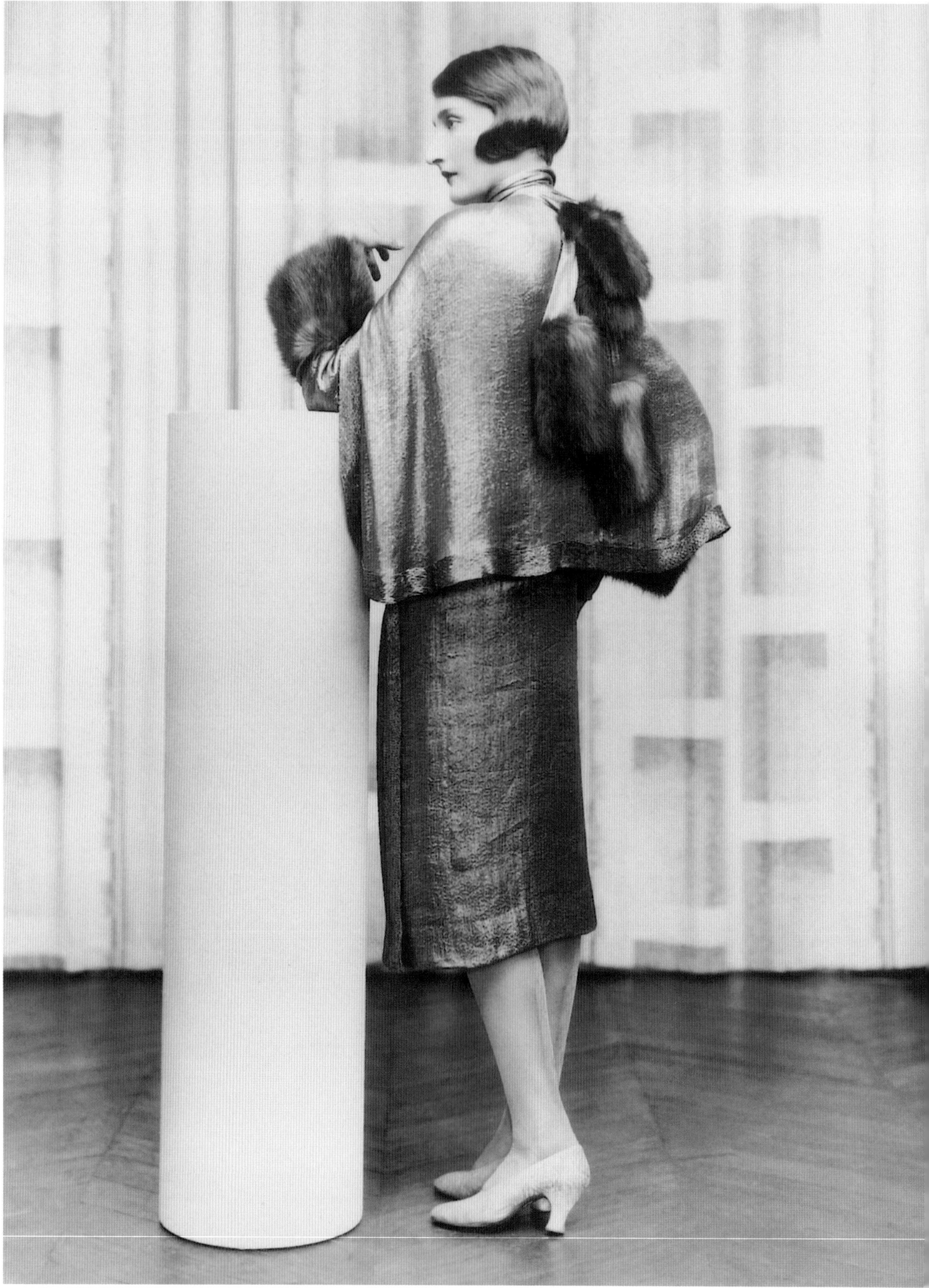

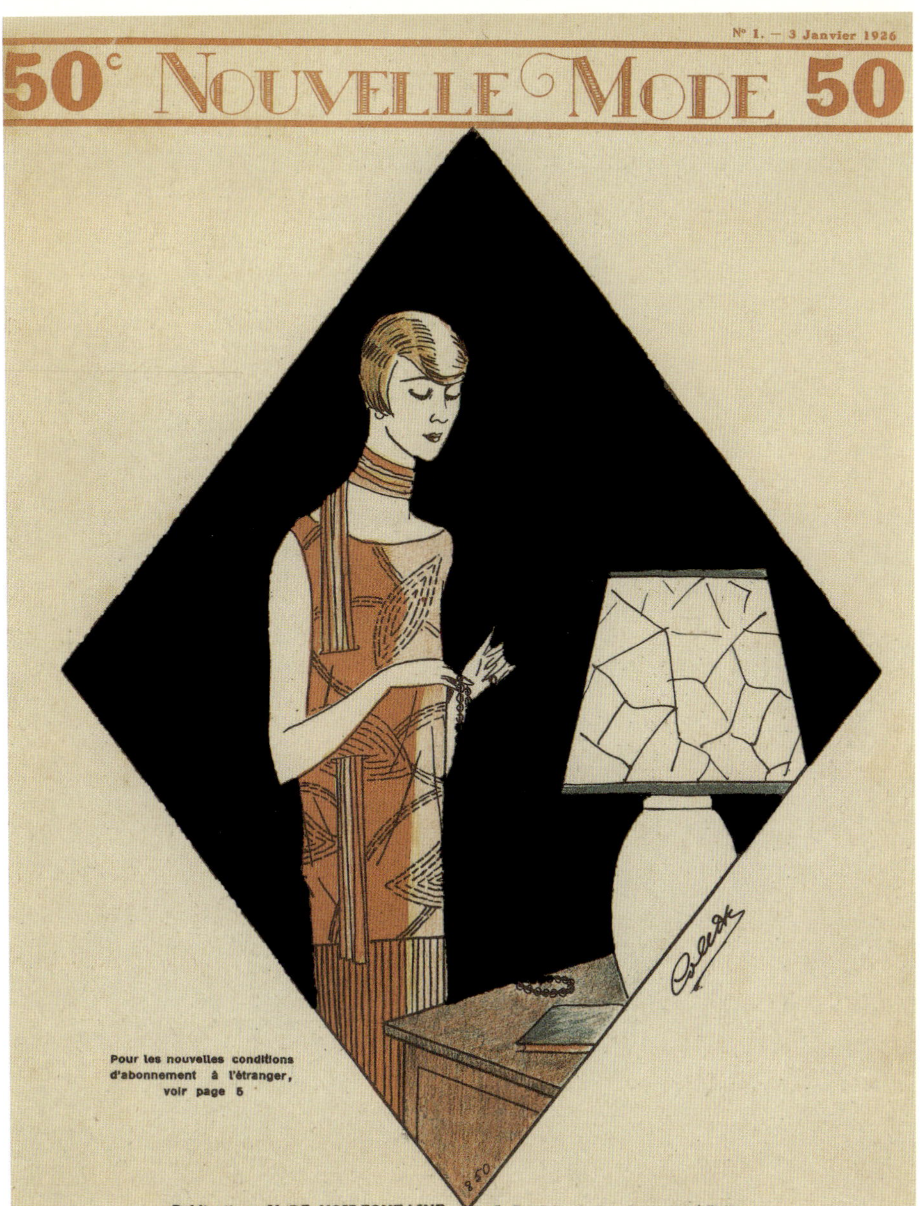

Left and above

"Golconde" gold lamé cape coat with skunk-trimmed sleeves and scarf, c.1925. The name of the dress probably refers to the Indian city of Golconda which was once famed for its diamond mines. By the late 19th Century, the word Golconda had come to signify 'something associated with great wealth', and so the name fits perfectly with the idea of a gold outfit.

Woman in an evening dress with a run-through neck scarf and pleated skirt. *Nouvelle Mode*, 1926

Below

Five designs for the first cold days – a voluminous grey coat by Morand, a "cache coeur" evening dress, a black panelled dress by Martial et Armand, a black dress with an ornate Russian-style jacket, and a fur-trimmed brown coat by Morand. *La Femme Chic*, c.1921

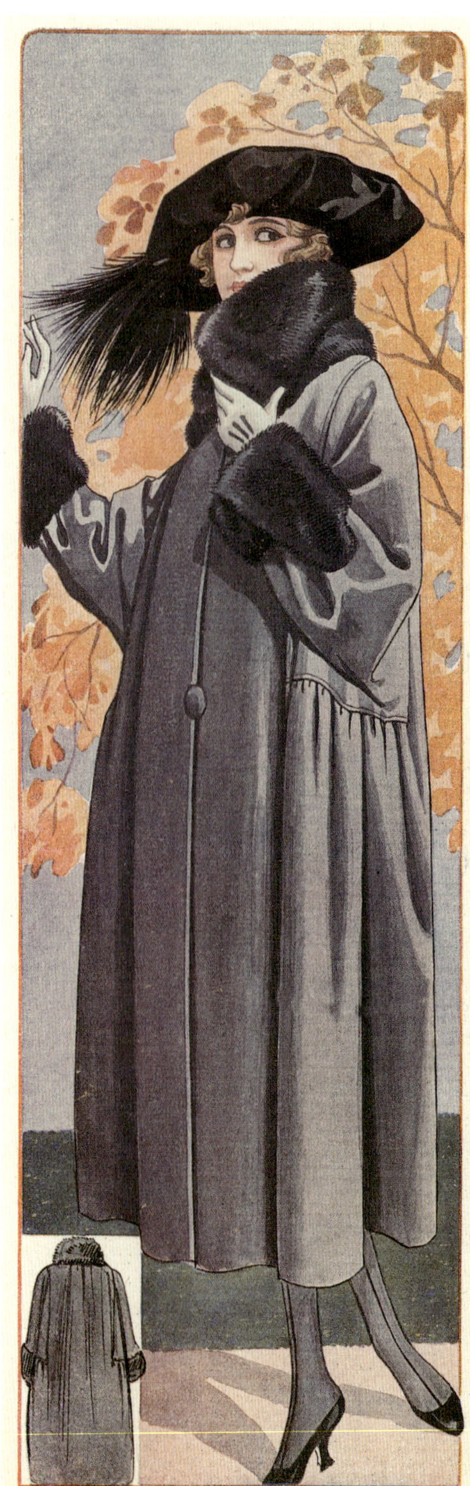

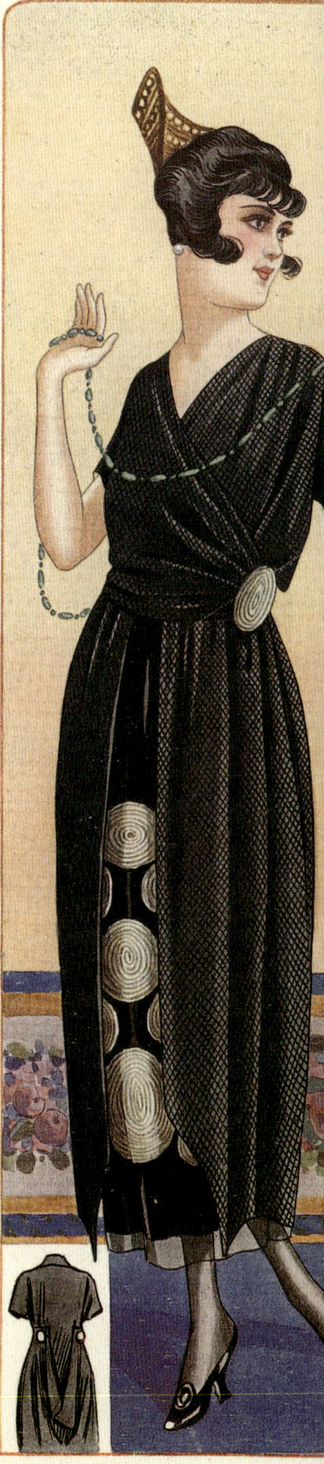

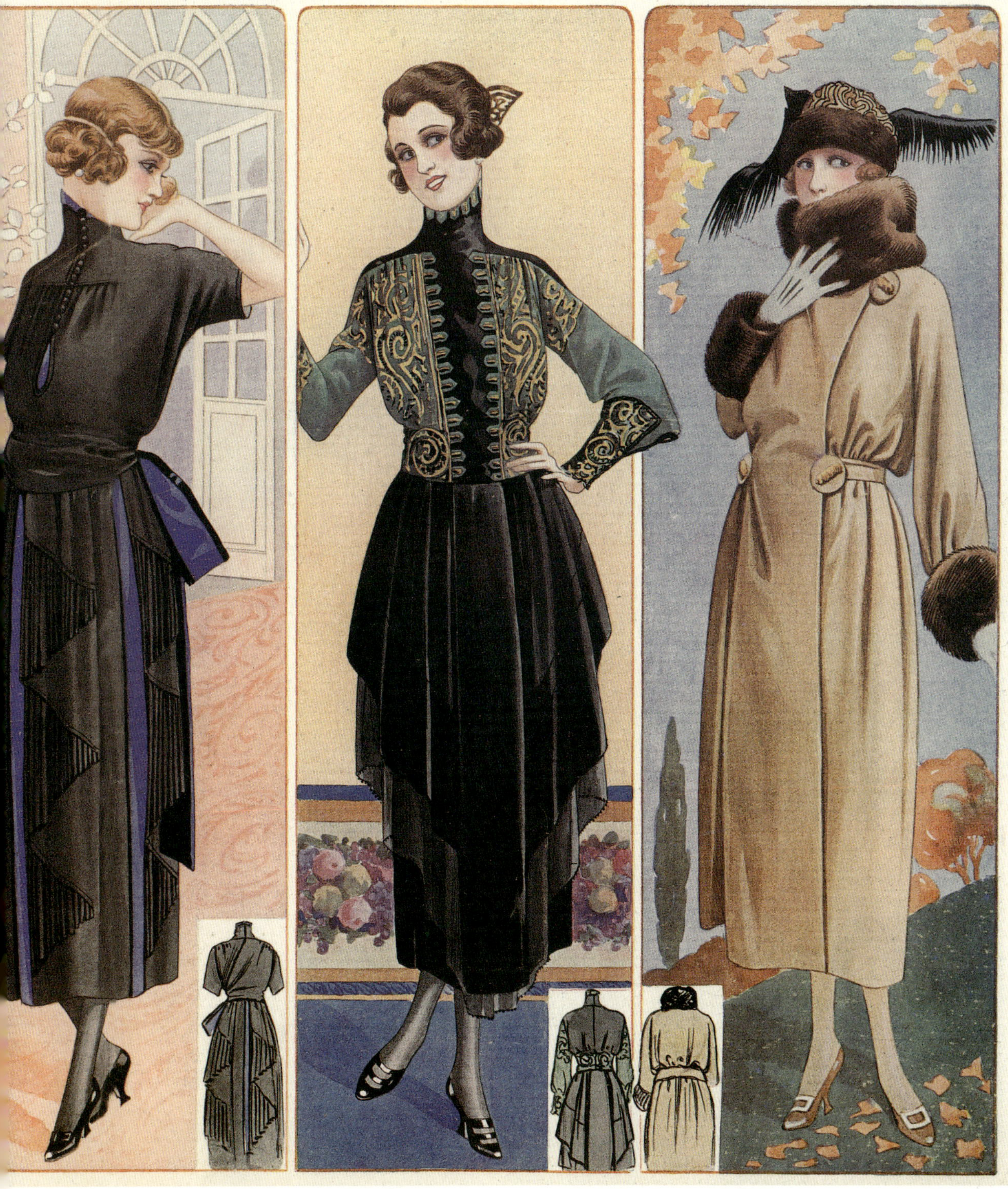

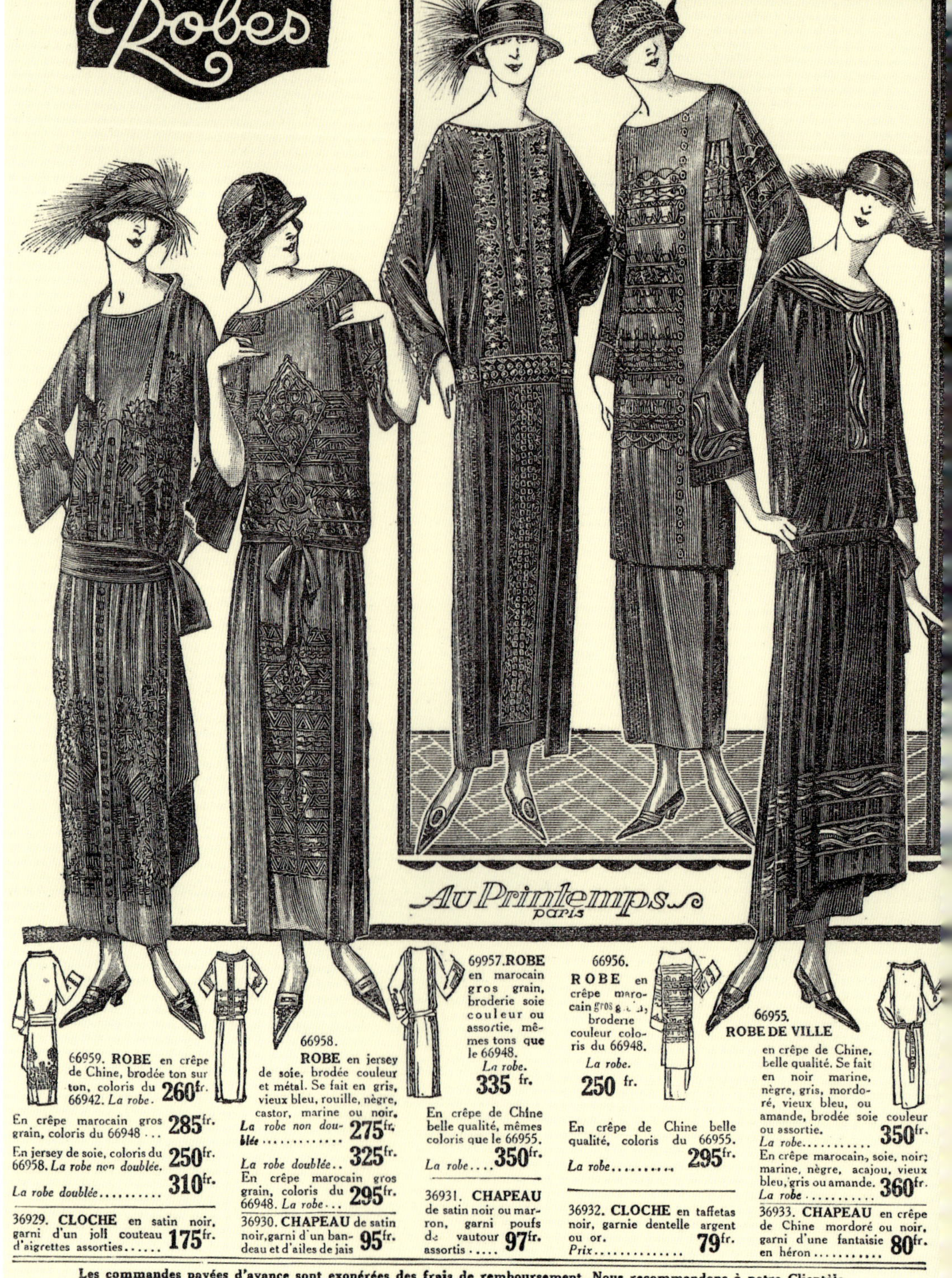

Above
Selection of day and evening dresses, Printemps catalogue, 1924. Note the Russian-inspired embroideries on several of the gowns.

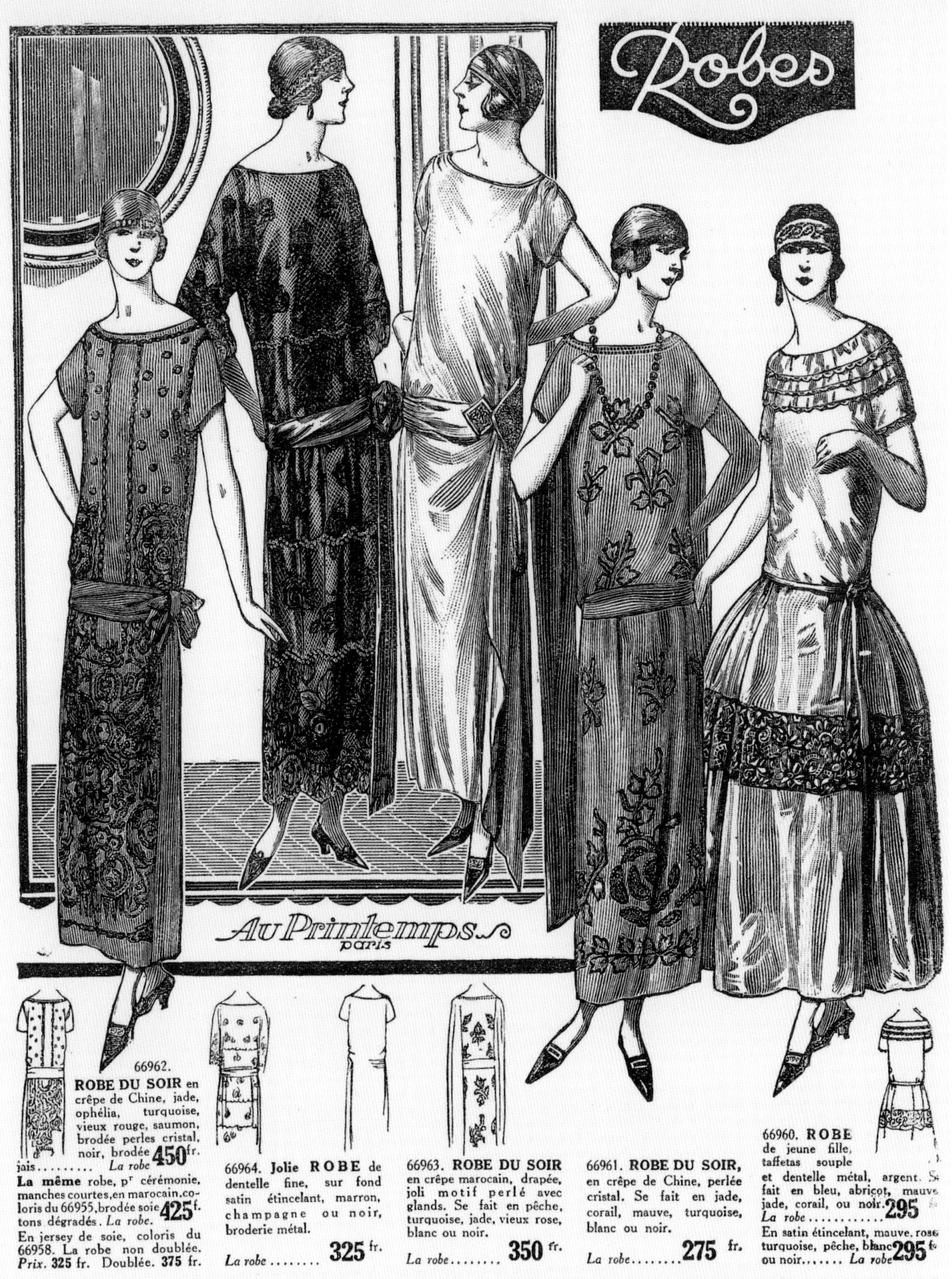

Above
Selection of day and evening dresses, Printemps catalogue, 1924.

Right

Four evening dresses "to see in the New Year" by Agnès, Rolf and Berthe Hermance. *Le Femme Chic*, c.1920. The evening coat trimmed in fur and accessorized with a fur muff is by Agnès. The dresses have clear Oriental and exotic influences, with the pink and yellow models having harem and slave girl references in their design, embellishment and accessories. The fringes and sashes are very Mata Hari-esque, revealing that the famed performer and exotic dancer remained a figure of fascination even after her execution in 1917 for alleged spying.

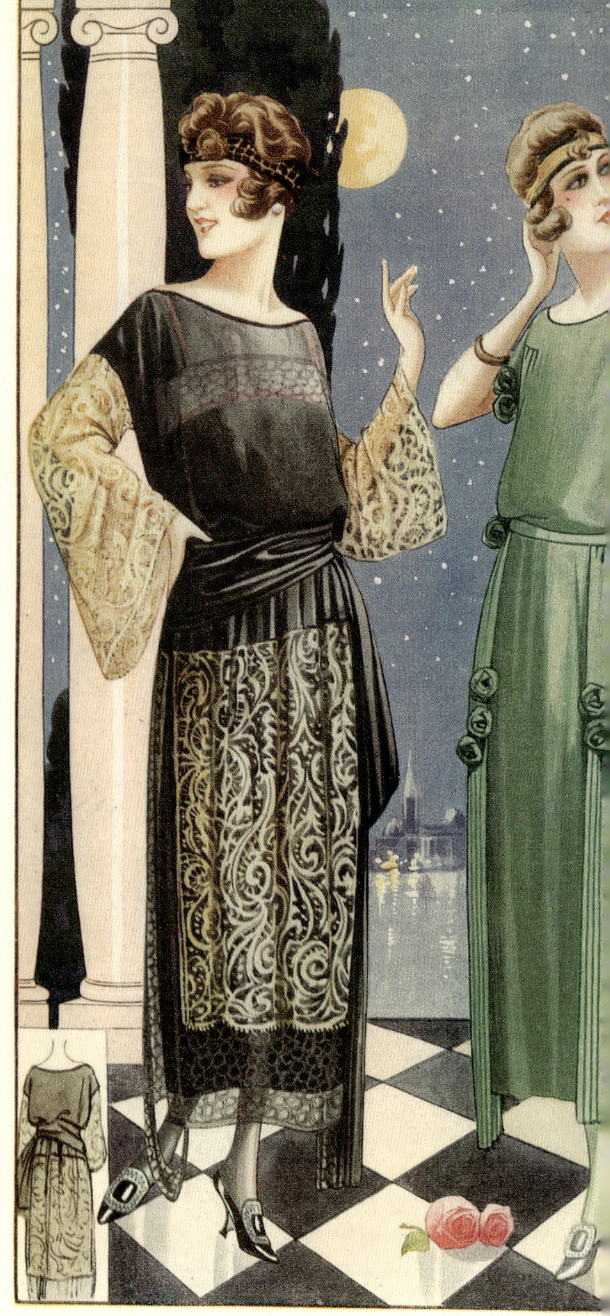

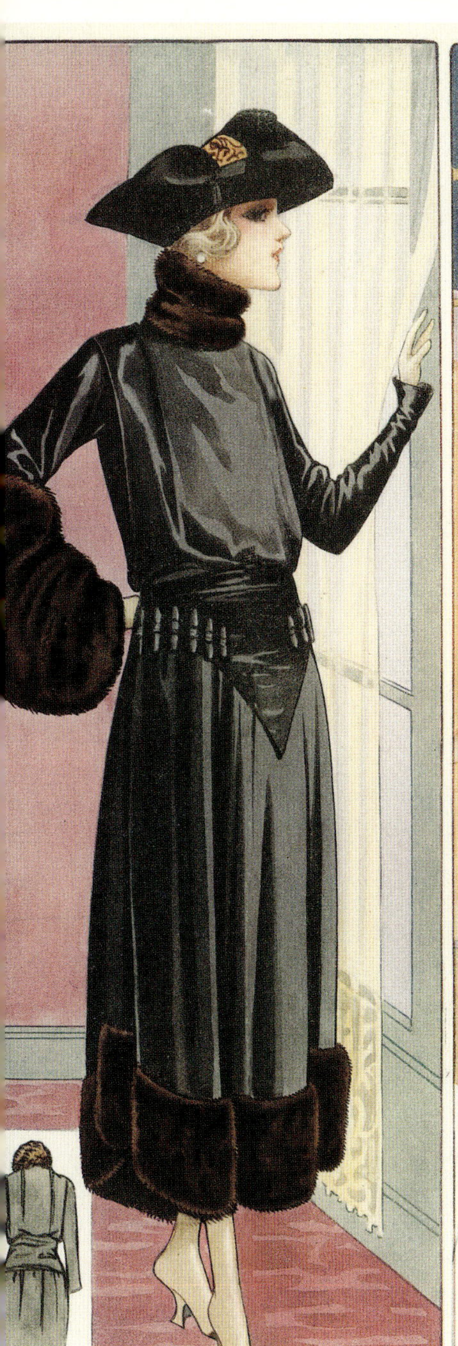

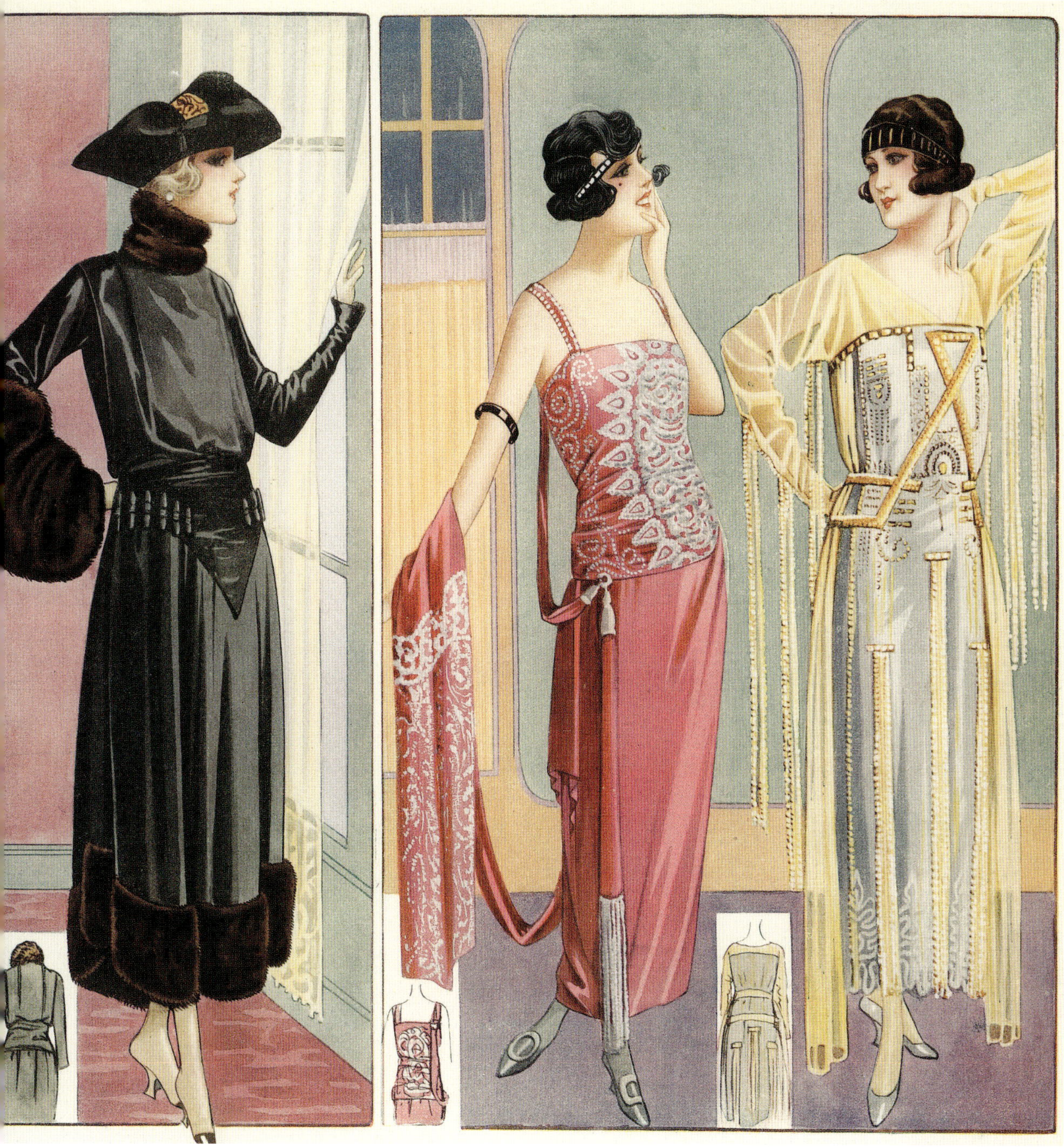

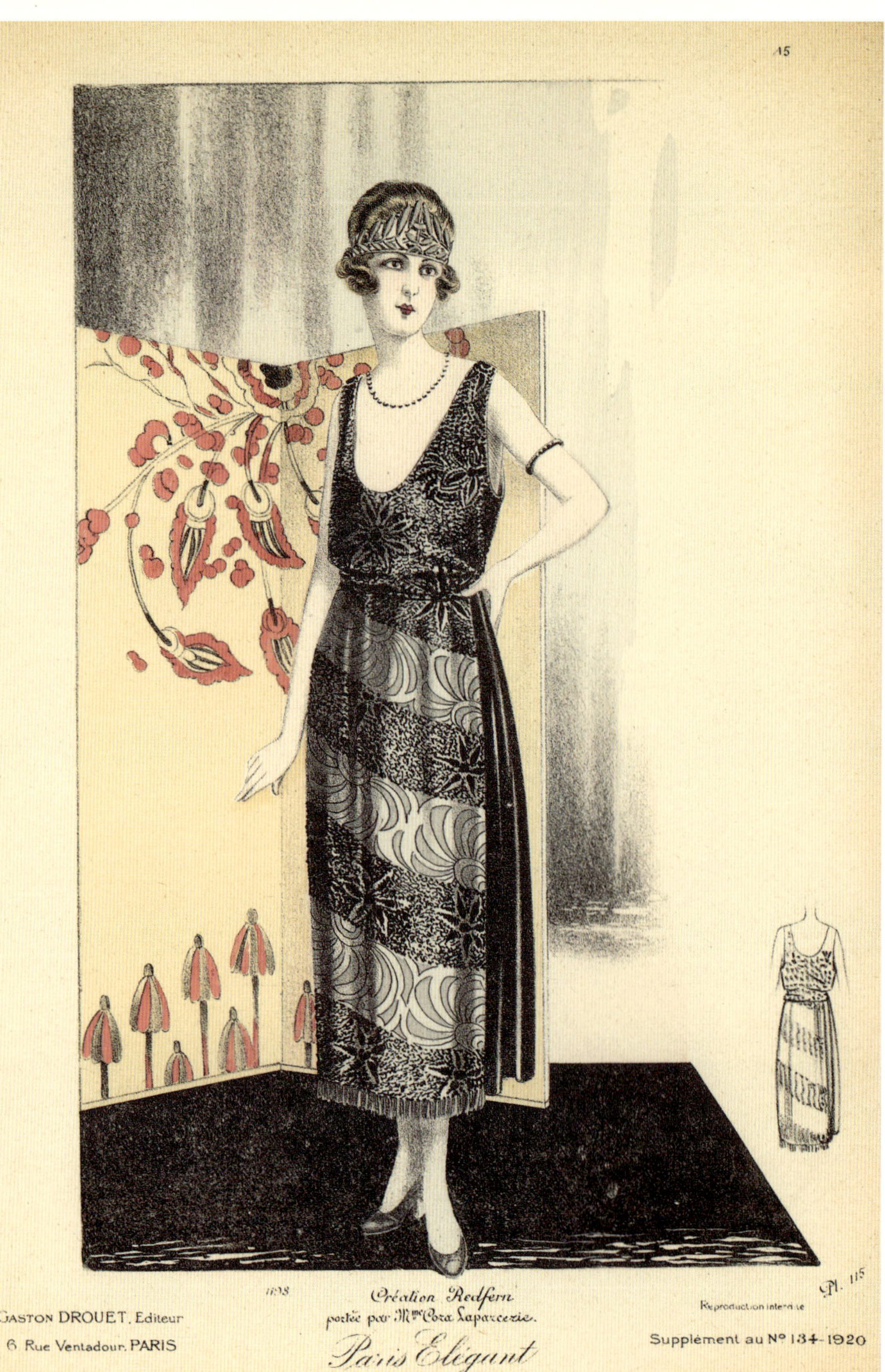

Above

An evening dress of black and grey patterned silk with a sash of black silk by Redfern. *Paris Élégant*, 1920

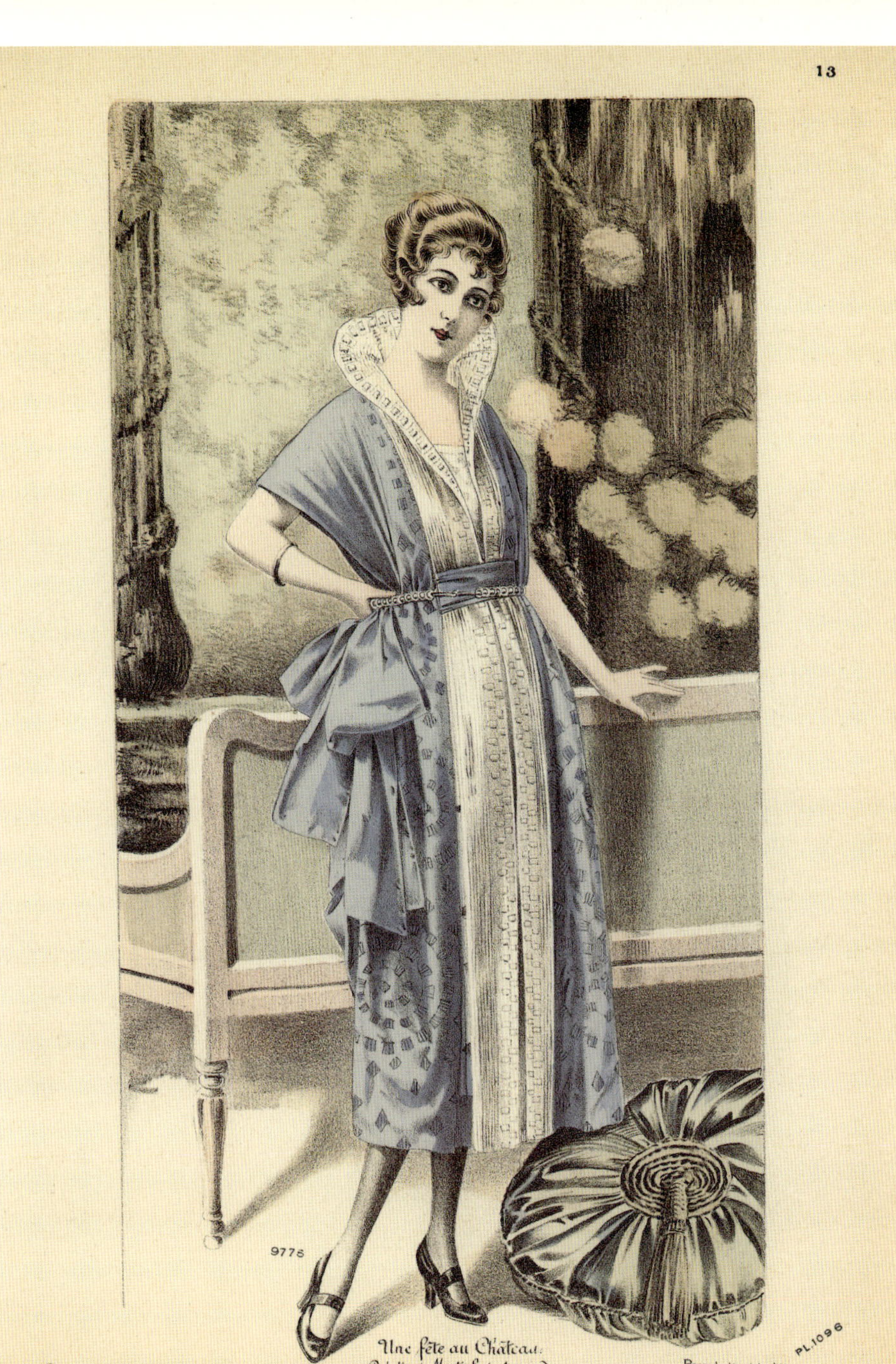

Above
A luxurious evening dress with draped ruches and "Elizabeth" collar by Martial et Armand. *Paris Élégant*, 1920

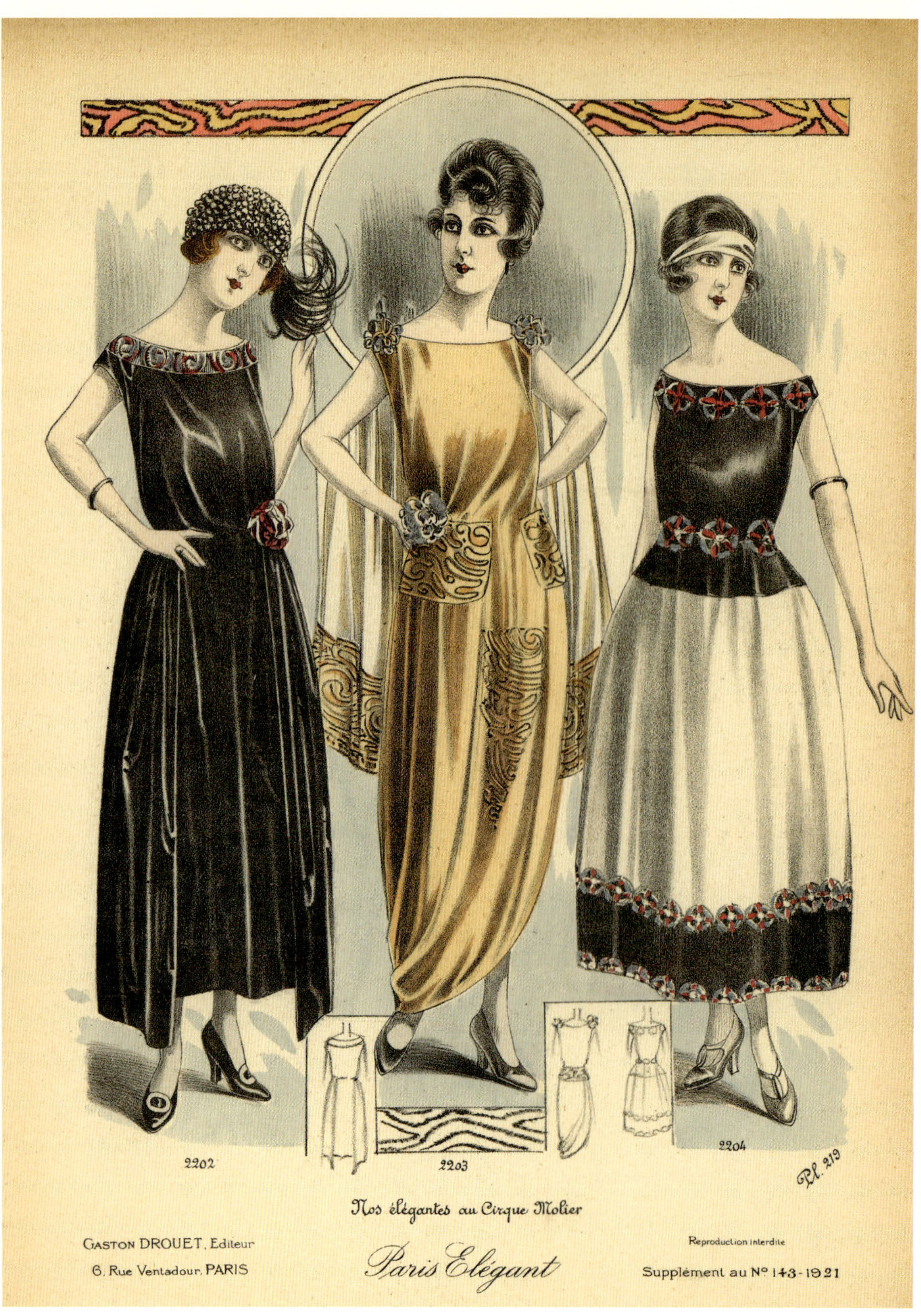

Above

Three evening dresses modeled at the private Cirque Molier, a highlight in the Parisian social calendar. *Paris Élégant*, 1921

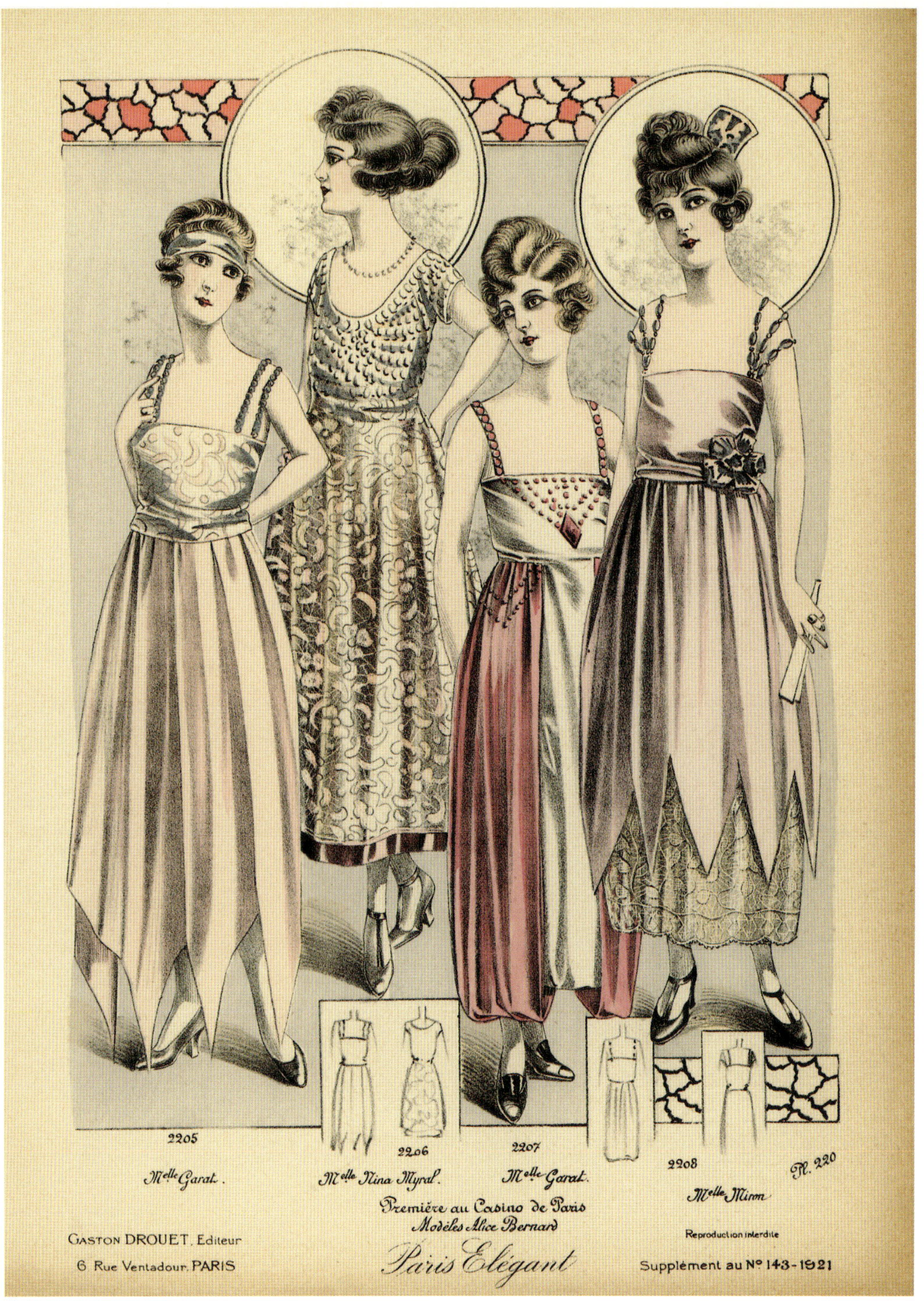

Above
Four evening dresses by Alice Bernard represented on contemporary actresses and models who premiered the gowns at the Casino de Paris. *Paris Élégant*, 1921

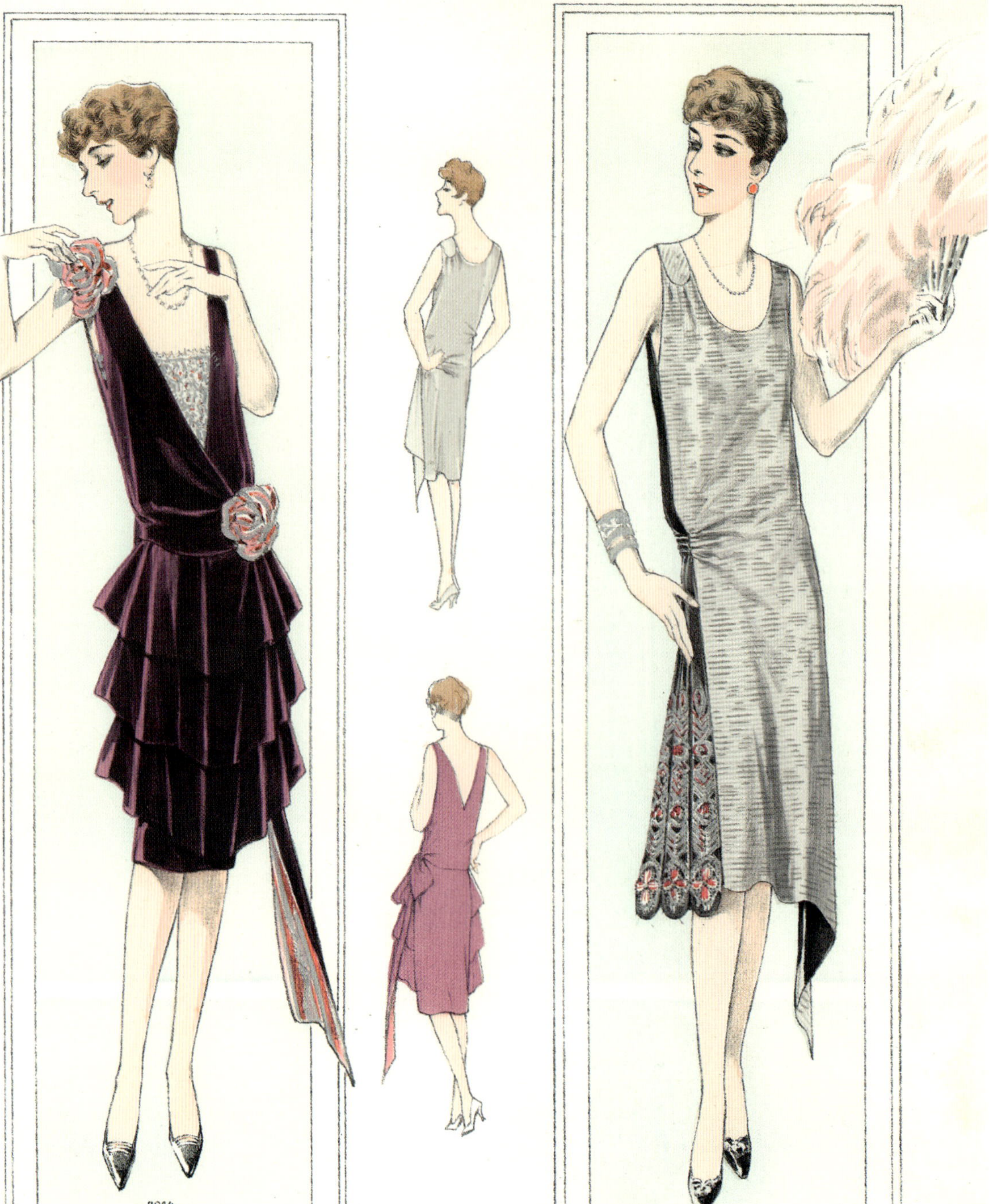

2014

2015

2014 Robe à danser en velours souple. Corsage très croisé. Plastron de dentelle métal. Roses de lamé. Pan doublé de même. Trois volants en forme.

2015 Princesse en fulgurante claire. A droite un lé de satin foncé, se terminant en trois pans arrondis brodés bijoux et perles. Du côté gauche un drapé doublé de satin noir.

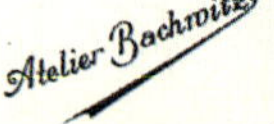

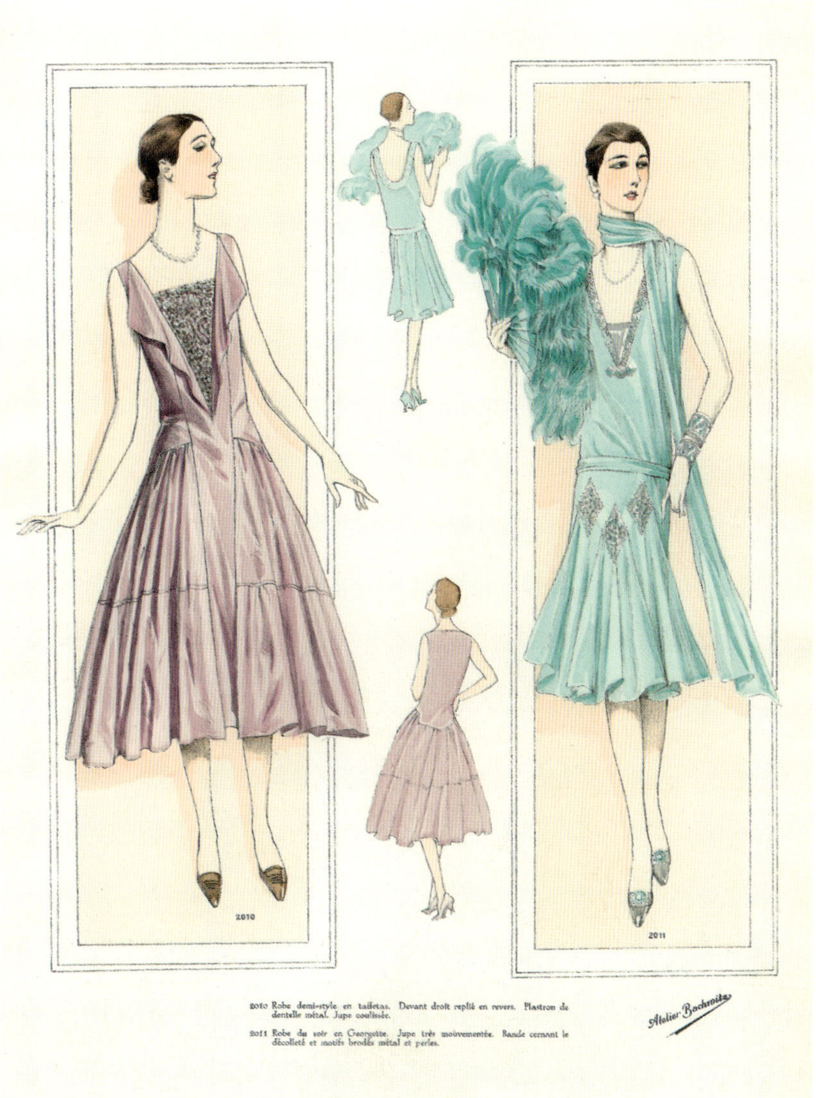

Left and above

Velour dancing dress with a crossed bodice and metal vestee, and a princess evening robe of fulgurante with dark satin scallops trimmed with beading and rhinestone embroidery by Atelier Bachroitz. *Chic Parisien Beaux-Arts des Modes*, 1927

Demi-style taffeta dress with metal lace, and a Georgette evening dress embroidered with metal and pearls by Atelier Bachroitz. *Chic Parisien Beaux-Arts des Modes*, 1927

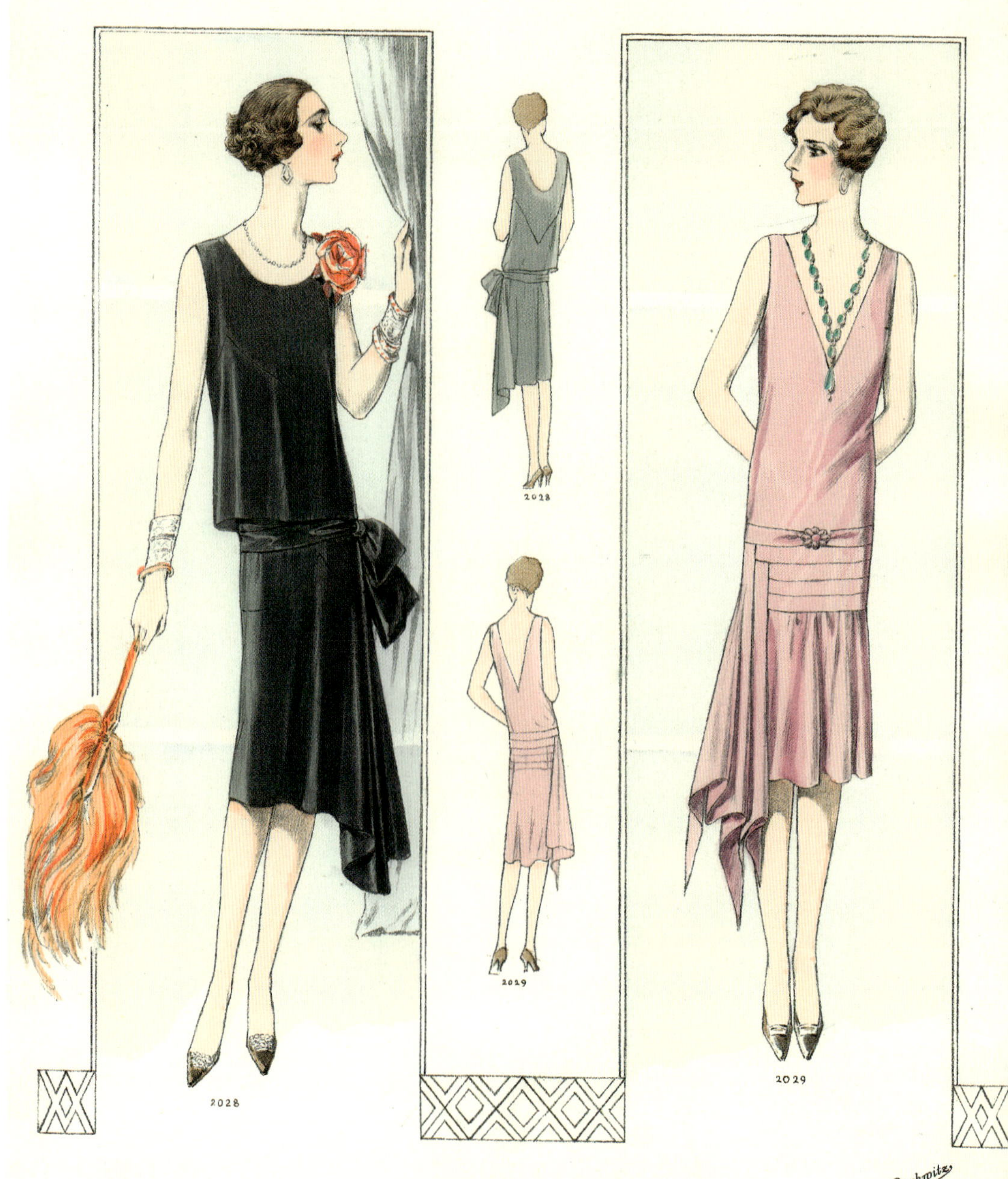

Above
Black satin evening dress, and a pale crepe de Chine dancing frock by Atelier Bachroitz. *Chic Parisien Beaux-Arts des Modes*, 1927

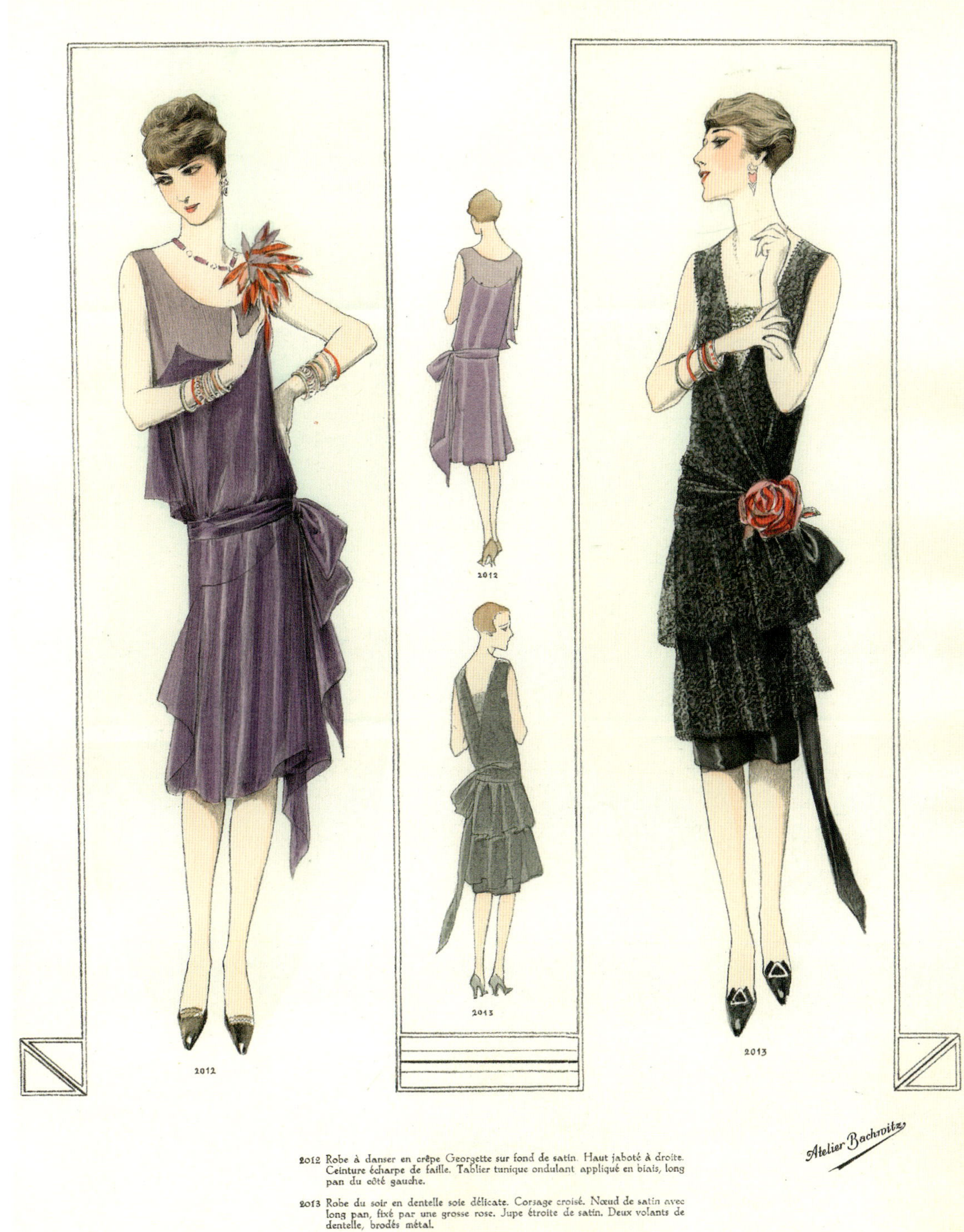

Above

Georgette dancing frock worn over a satin slip, and a silk lace evening dress with a crossed bodice and a tight fitting skirt covered with lace flounces by Atelier Bachroitz. *Chic Parisien Beaux-Arts des Modes*, 1927

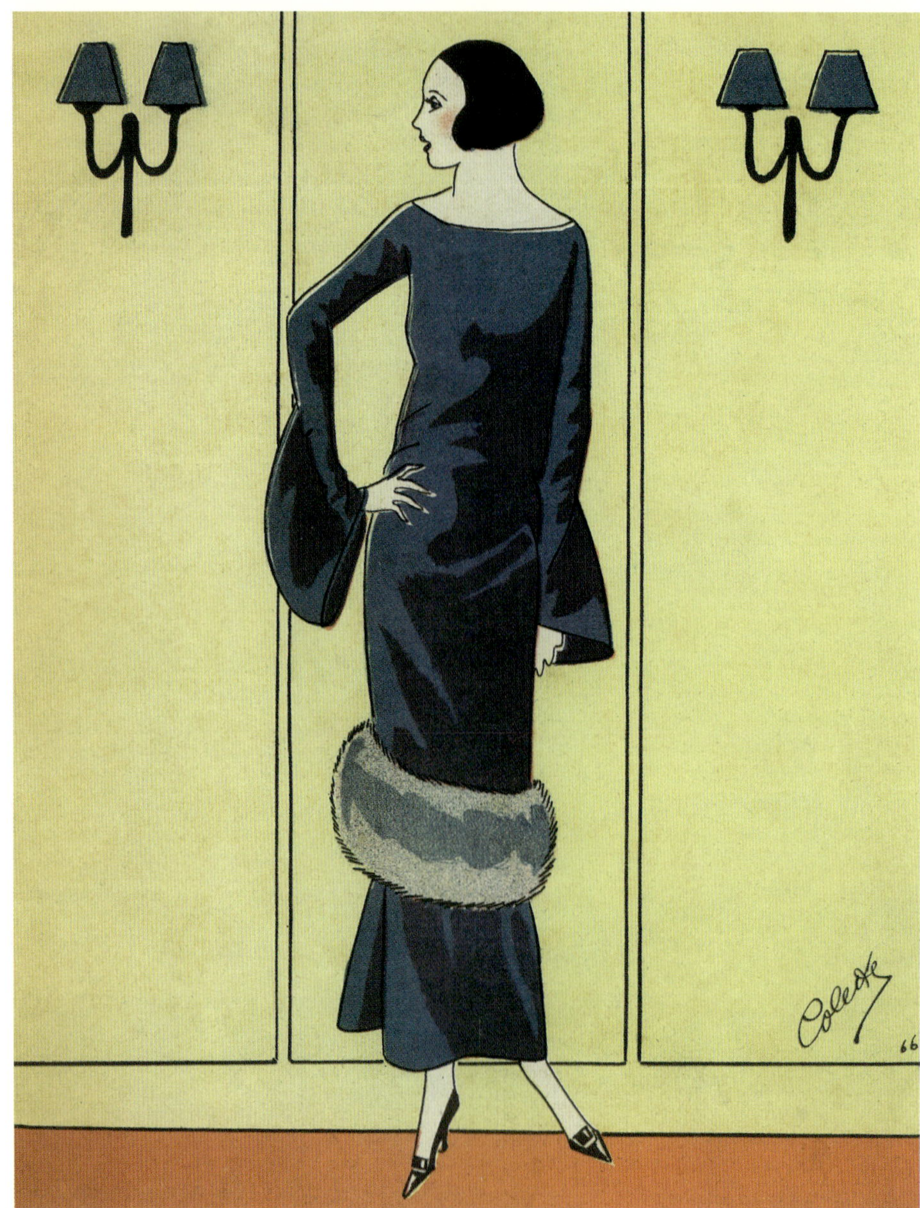

Above and right

Woman wearing a blue evening dress with bell sleeves and a large white fur trim. *Nouvelle Mode*, 1923

A woman in a low-waisted green dress with a deep v-neckline. *Nouvelle Mode*, 1926

NOUVELLE MODE

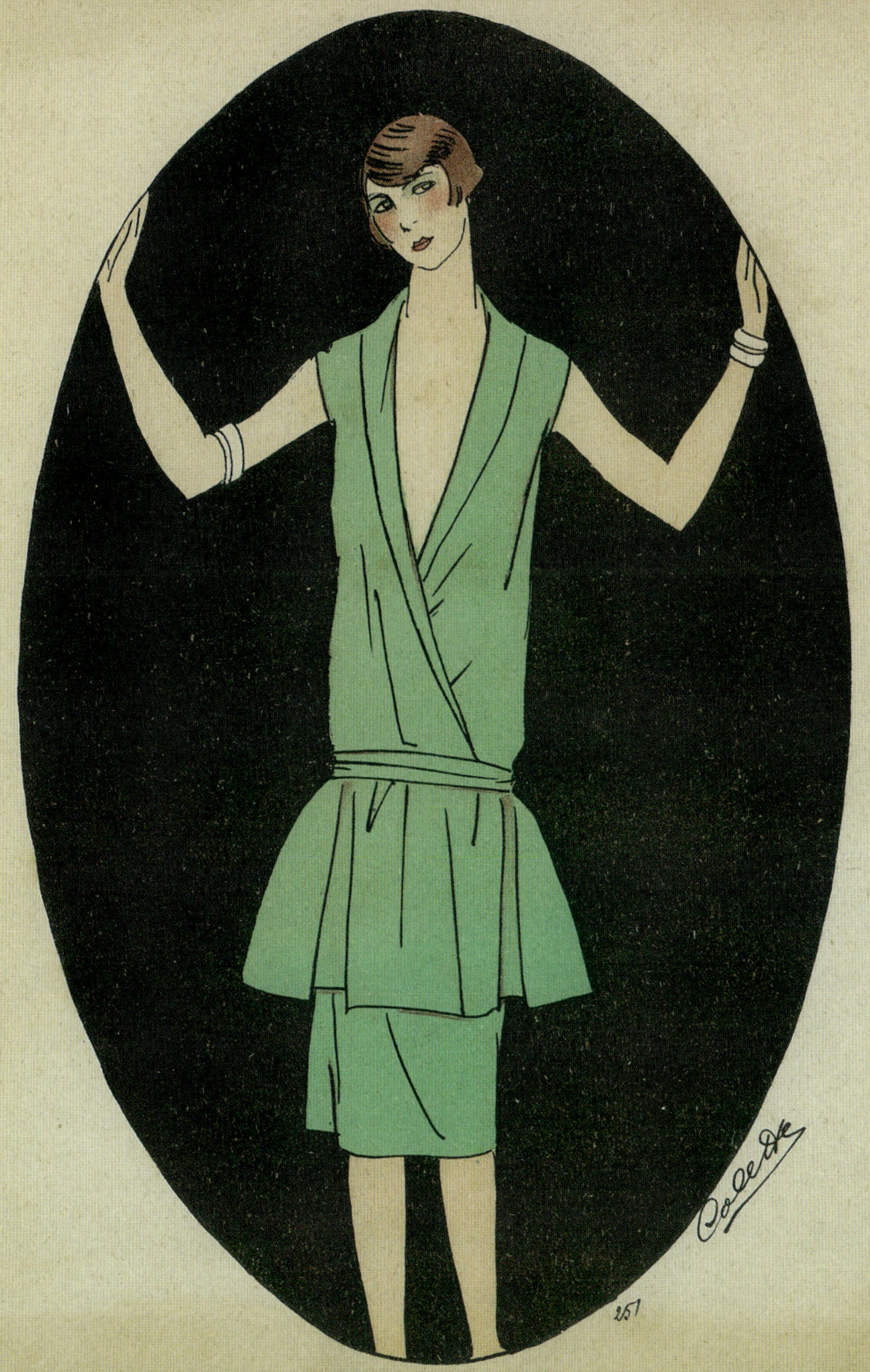

Publications V. DE NOIRFONTAINE, 5. Boulevard des Capucines Paris.

Right
Hollywood actress Agnes Ayres in a white chiffon dress trimmed with black and white paillettes by Lambert. The dress was a costume she wore in the 1927 comedy, 'Eve's Love Letters'. 1927

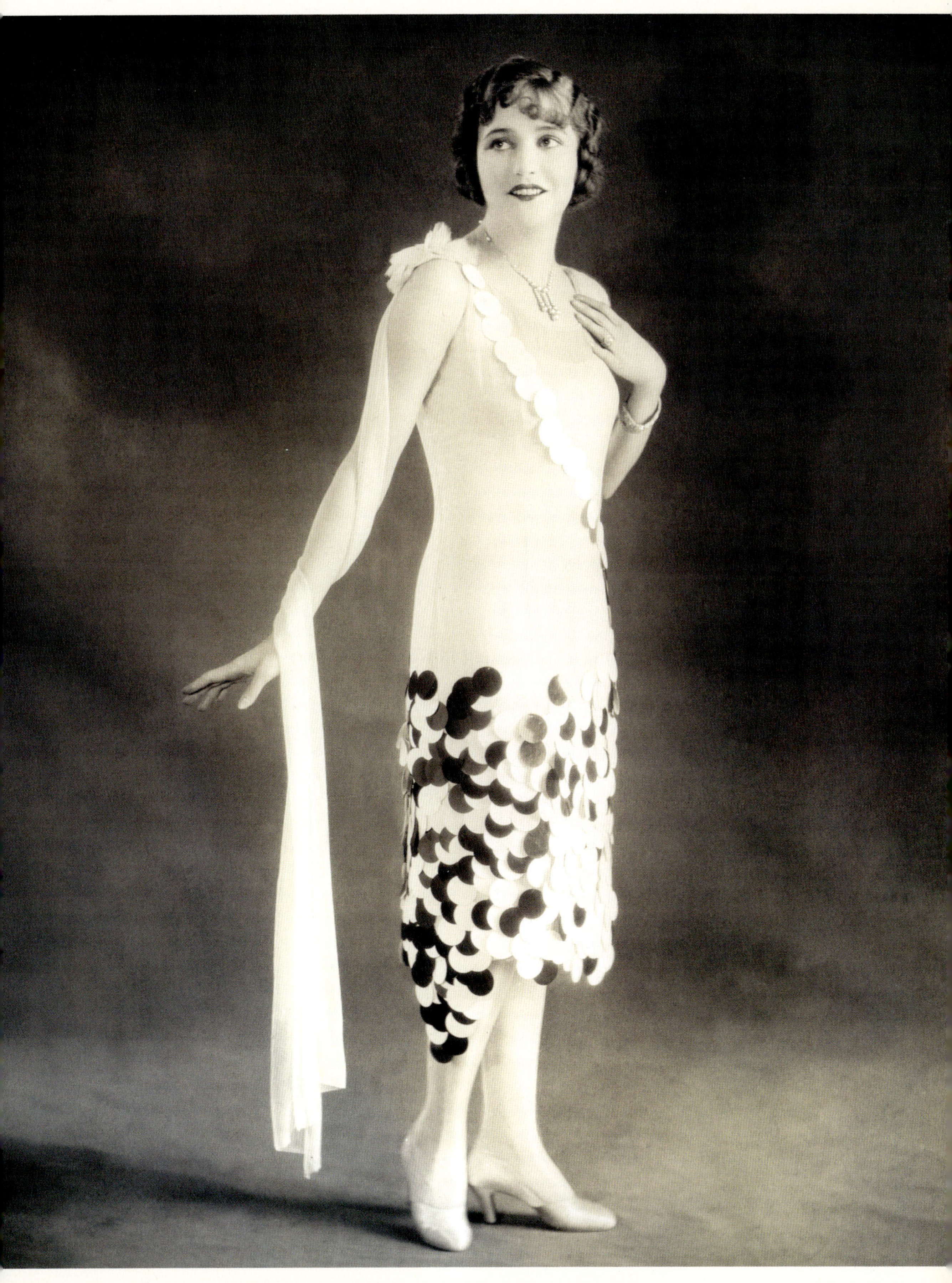

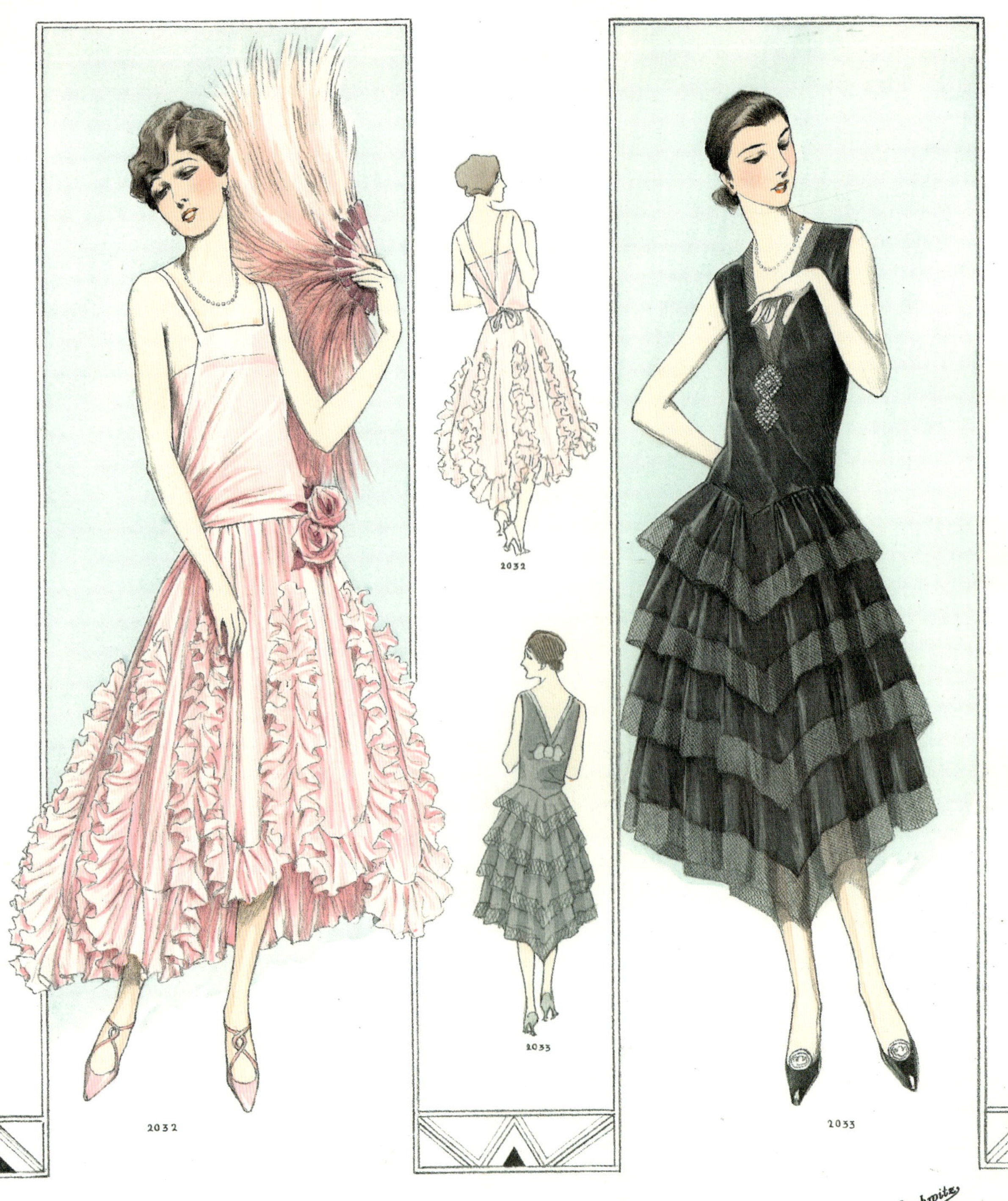

2032 Robe de style en tulle soie ou mousseline sur fond de taffetas. Corsage très échancré dans le dos, retenu par quatre bretelles. Ample jupe plus longue dans le dos que devant et garnie de ruches de tissu. Deux roses de soie à la hanche gauche.

2033 Robe de style en taffetas fleur. Corsage en pointe avec petit décolleté. Jupe étagée, bords de tulle. Plaques bijouterie

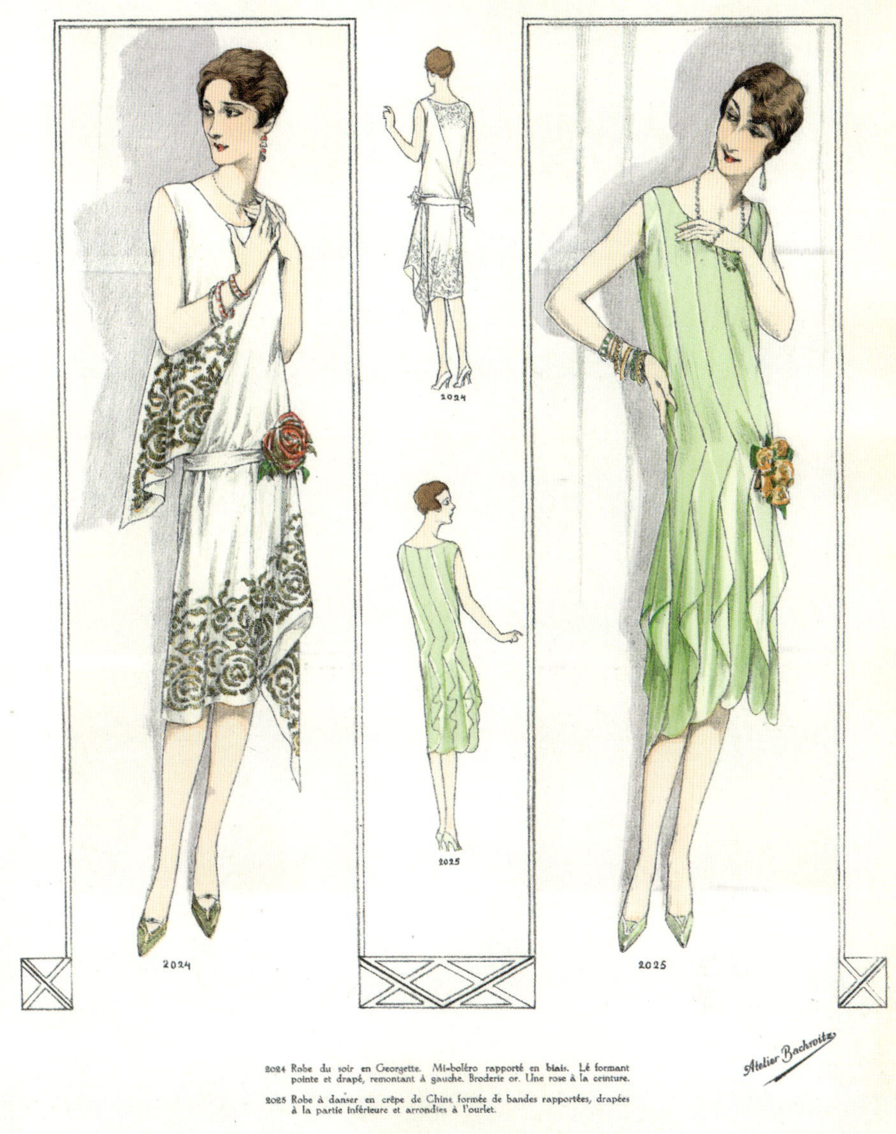

Left and above

Pink frock in silk net bolstered by a foundation of taffetas, and a black taffeta frock bordered with net by Atelier Bachroitz. *Chic Parisien Beaux-Arts des Modes*, 1927

Georgette dancing dress with gold embroidery, and a dancing frock with bands of crepe de Chine joined together by Atelier Bachroitz. *Chic Parisien Beaux-Arts des Modes*, 1927

Next page

Georgette evening dress with a pleated skirt and curved edges, a chiffon velour and lace evening gown, a crepe princess dress with bead embroidered bolero, a crepe dancing frock with draped side wings, a taffeta evening dress with draped side wings, a taffeta evening dress with lace vestee and strass embroidery, a demi-style dress in black net, and a Georgette dancing frock with a bolero of metal lace by Atelier Bachroitz. *Chic Parisien Beaux-Arts des Modes*, 1927

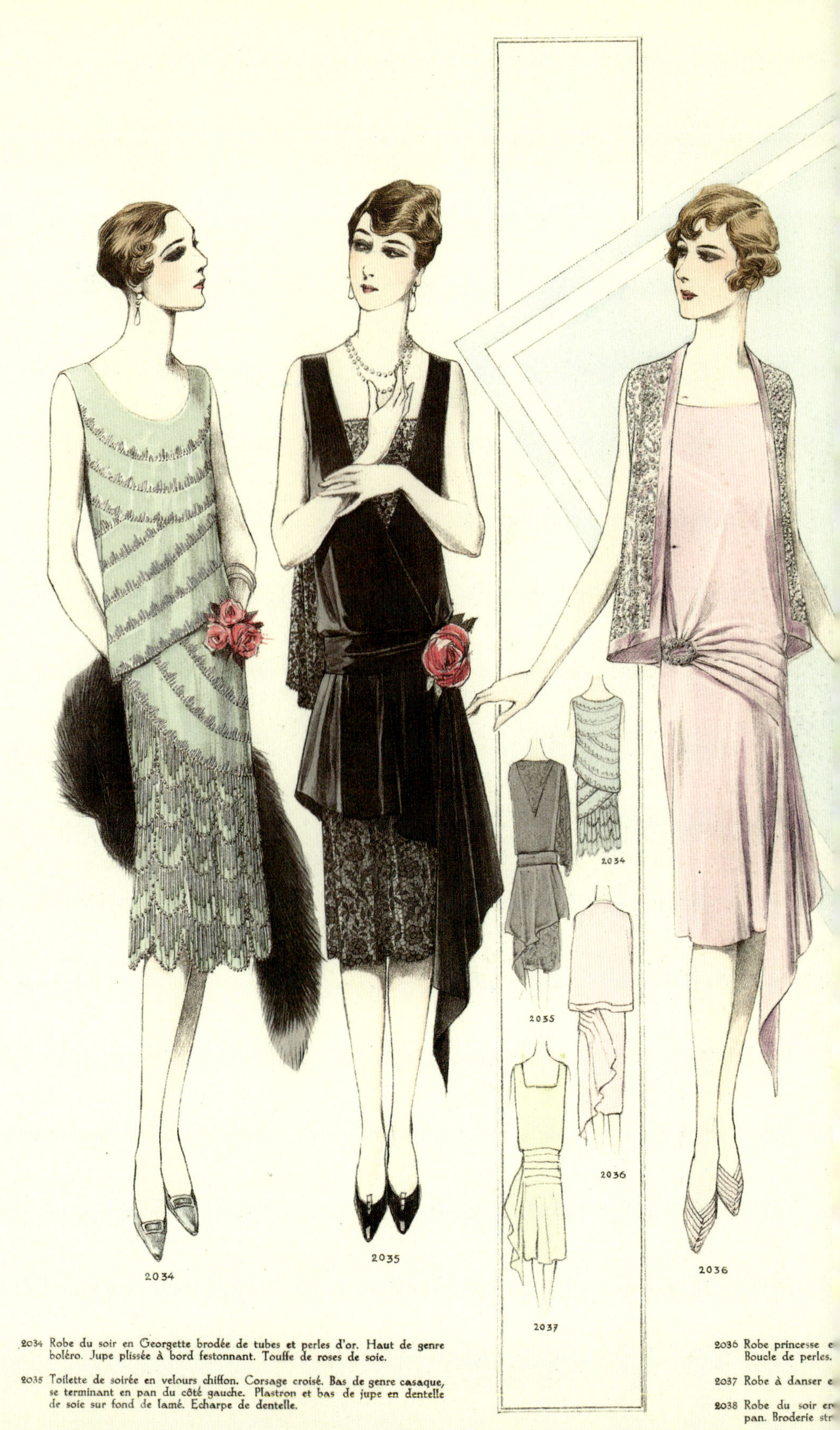
2034
2035
2036
2034
2035
2036
2037
2034 Robe du soir en Georgette brodée de tubes et perles d'or. Haut de genre boléro. Jupe plissée à bord festonnant. Touffe de roses de soie.
2035 Toilette de soirée en velours chiffon. Corsage croisé. Bas de genre casaque, se terminant en pan du côté gauche. Plastron et bas de jupe en dentelle de soie sur fond de lamé. Echarpe de dentelle.
2036 Robe princesse e
Boucle de perles.
2037 Robe à danser e
2038 Robe du soir e
pan. Broderie str

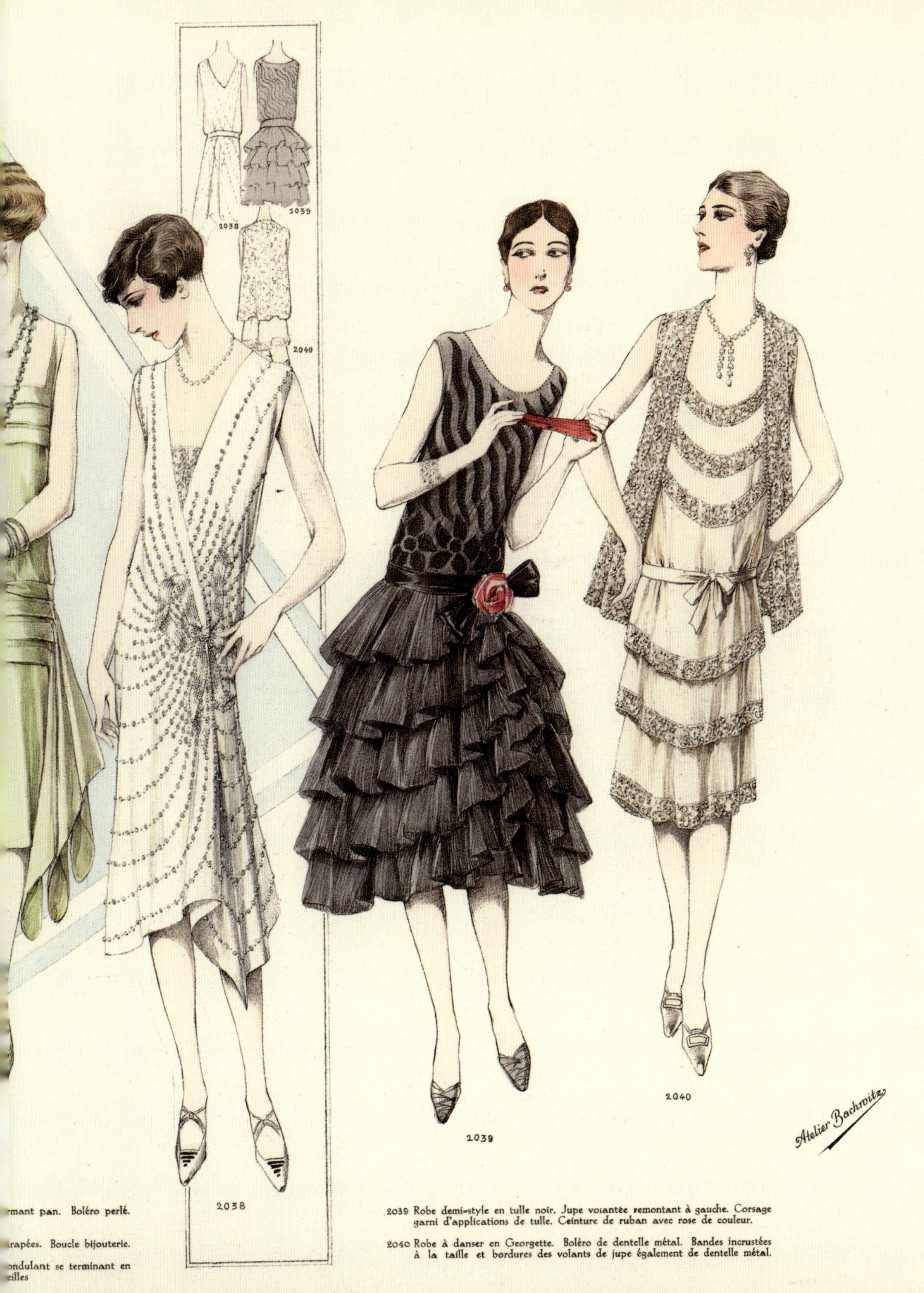

rmant pan. Boléro perlé.

rapées. Boucle bijouterie.

ondulant se terminant en
eilles

2039 Robe demi-style en tulle noir. Jupe volantée remontant à gauche. Corsage garni d'applications de tulle. Ceinture de ruban avec rose de couleur.

2040 Robe à danser en Georgette. Boléro de dentelle métal. Bandes incrustées à la taille et bordures des volants de jupe également de dentelle métal.

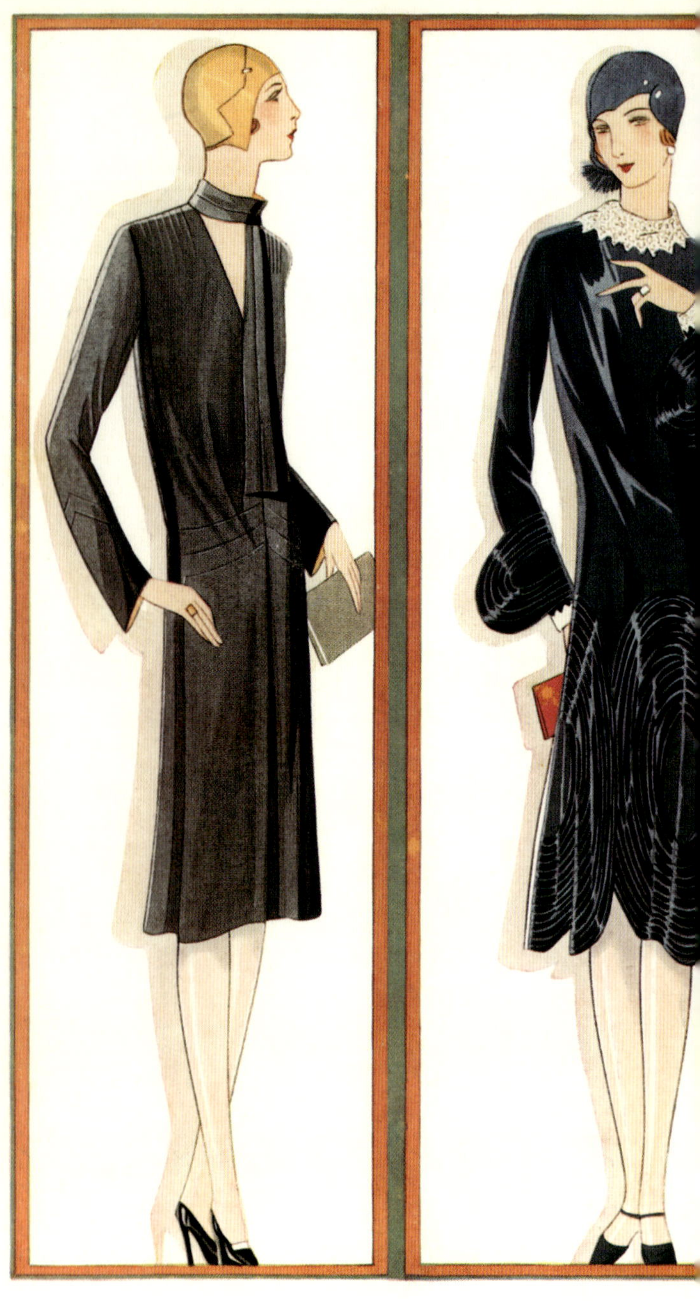

Above
Five dresses by Parisian couturiers Jane Regny, Jenny, Bernard et Cie, Redfern and Suzanne Talbot. *Sélection*, c.1927

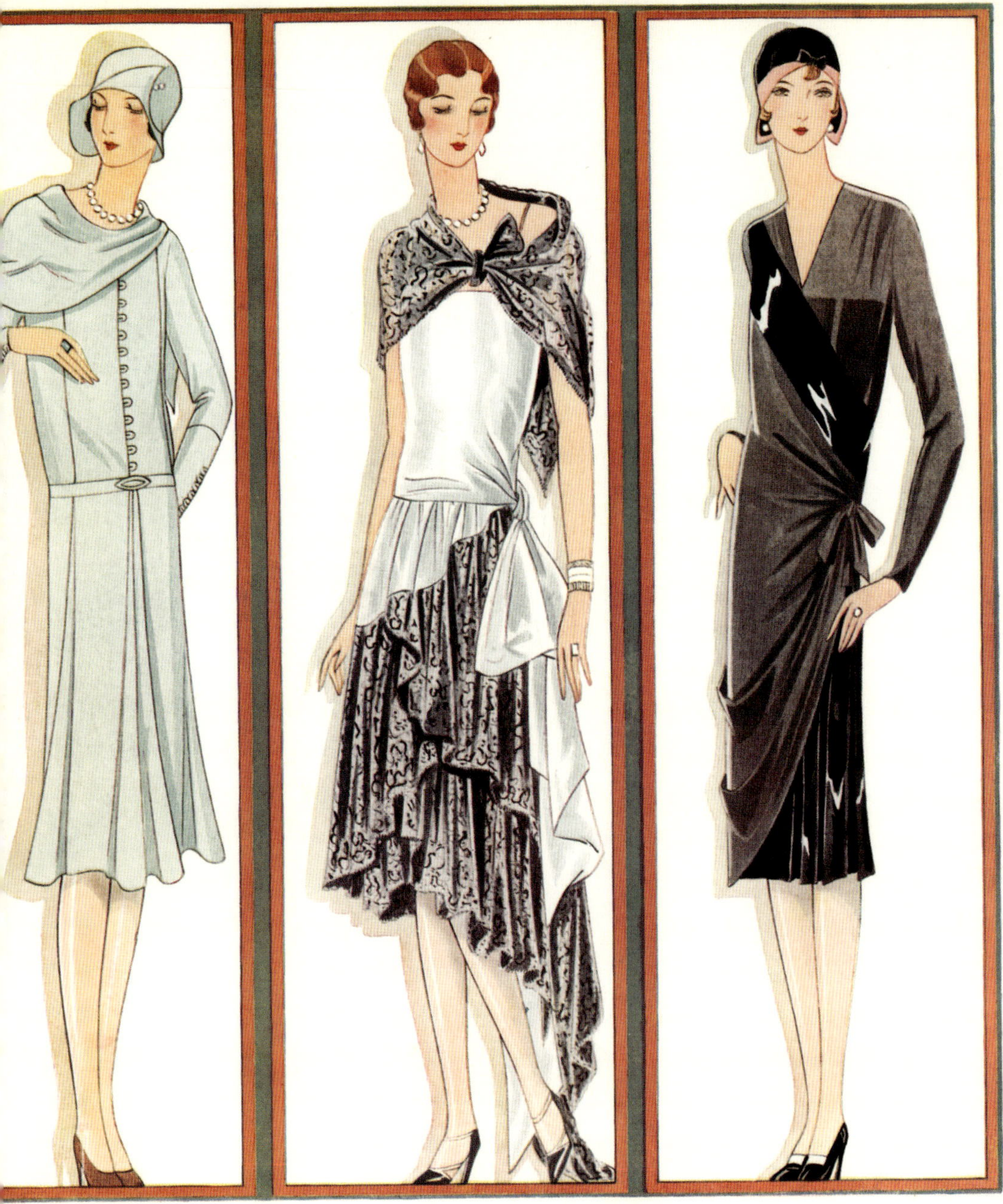

Right

Beaded evening dress and black velvet dress. *Fashion for All*, 1927

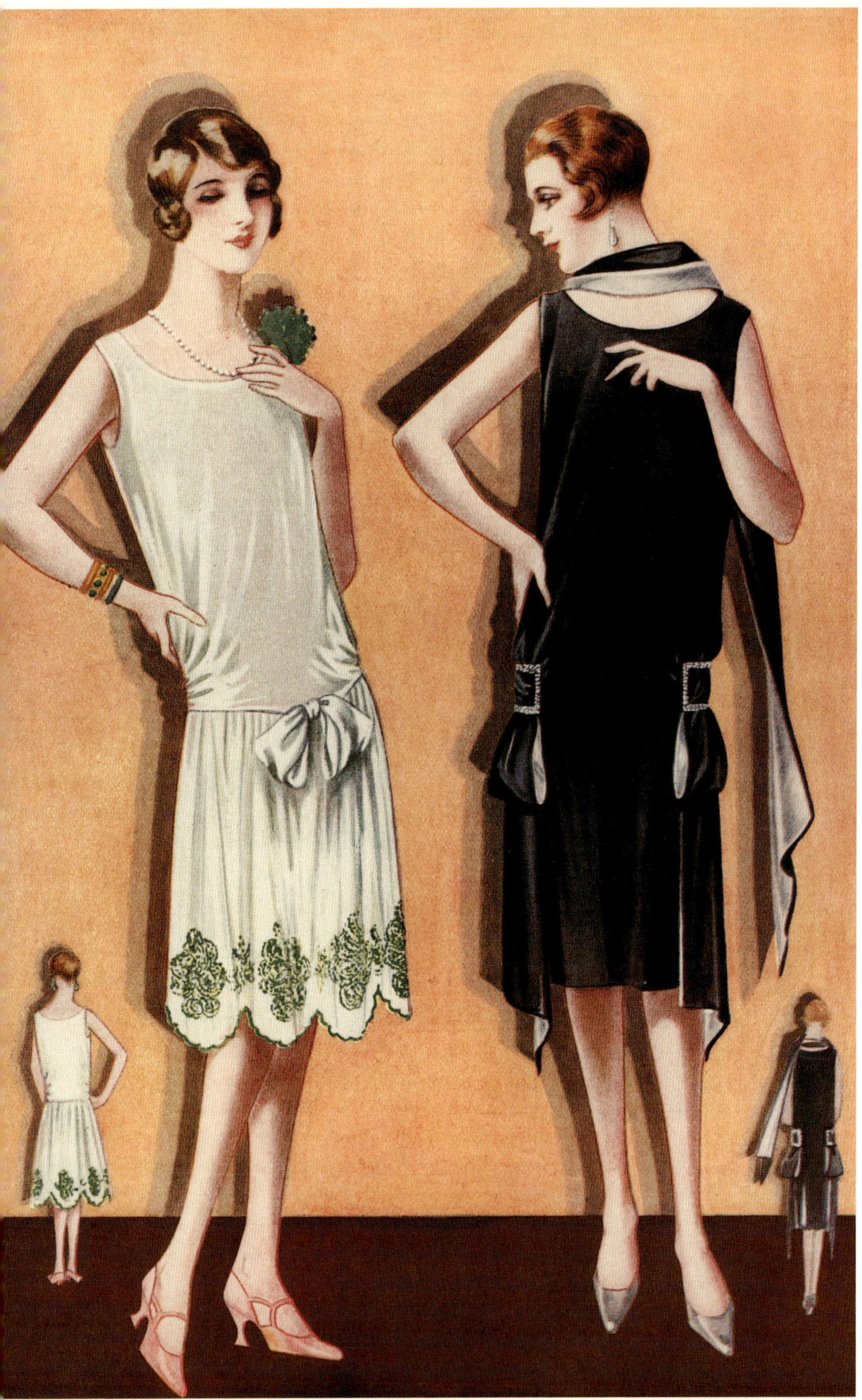

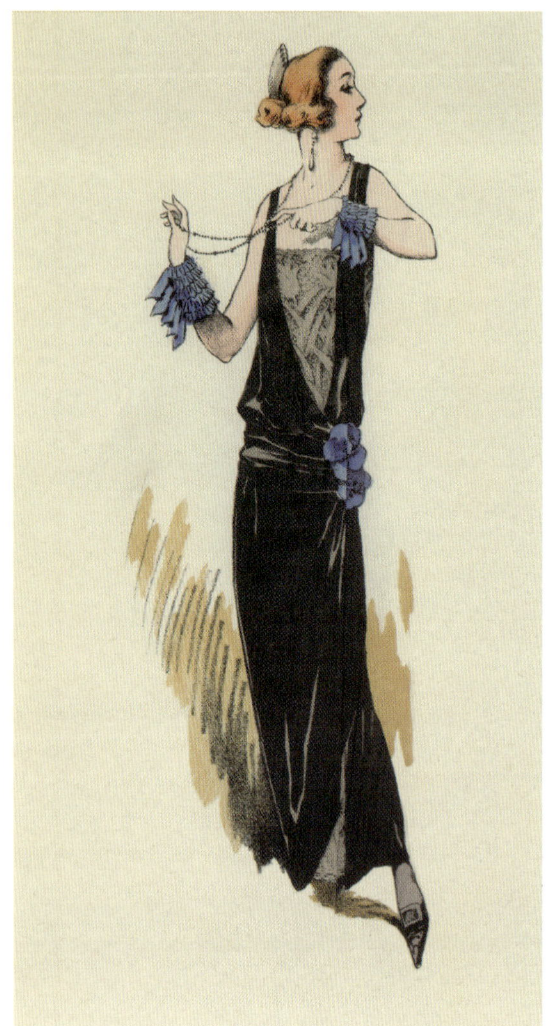

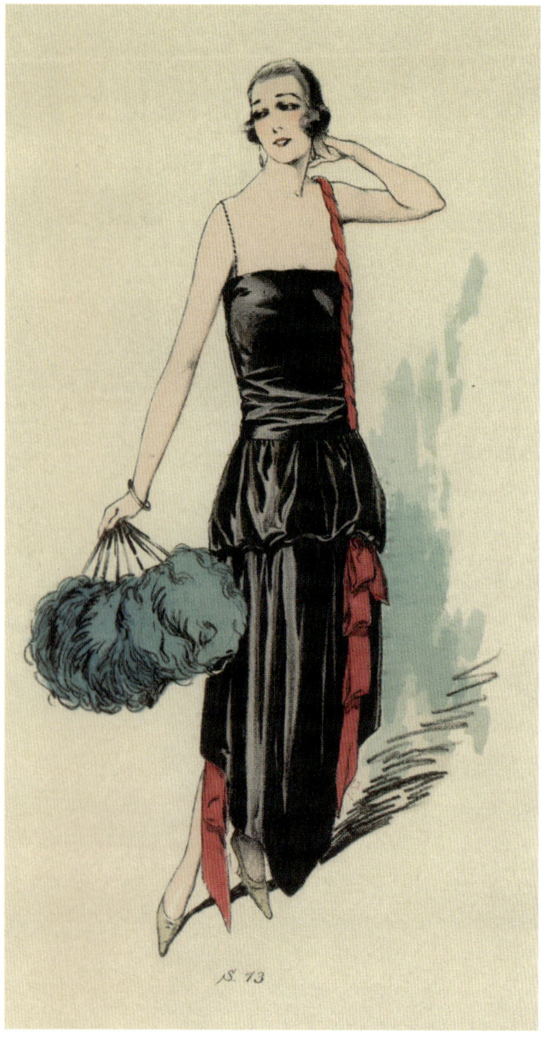

Above left and right

A black moiré evening dress with a large blue floral corsage at the waist and matching ruffed cuffs. *Dernières Créations*, c.1923

A gold and black lamé evening dress with a pointed skirt draped on the hips. *Dernières Créations*, c.1923

Right

A black and gold broched silk theatre wrap with an ape skin collar. *Dernières Créations*, c.1923

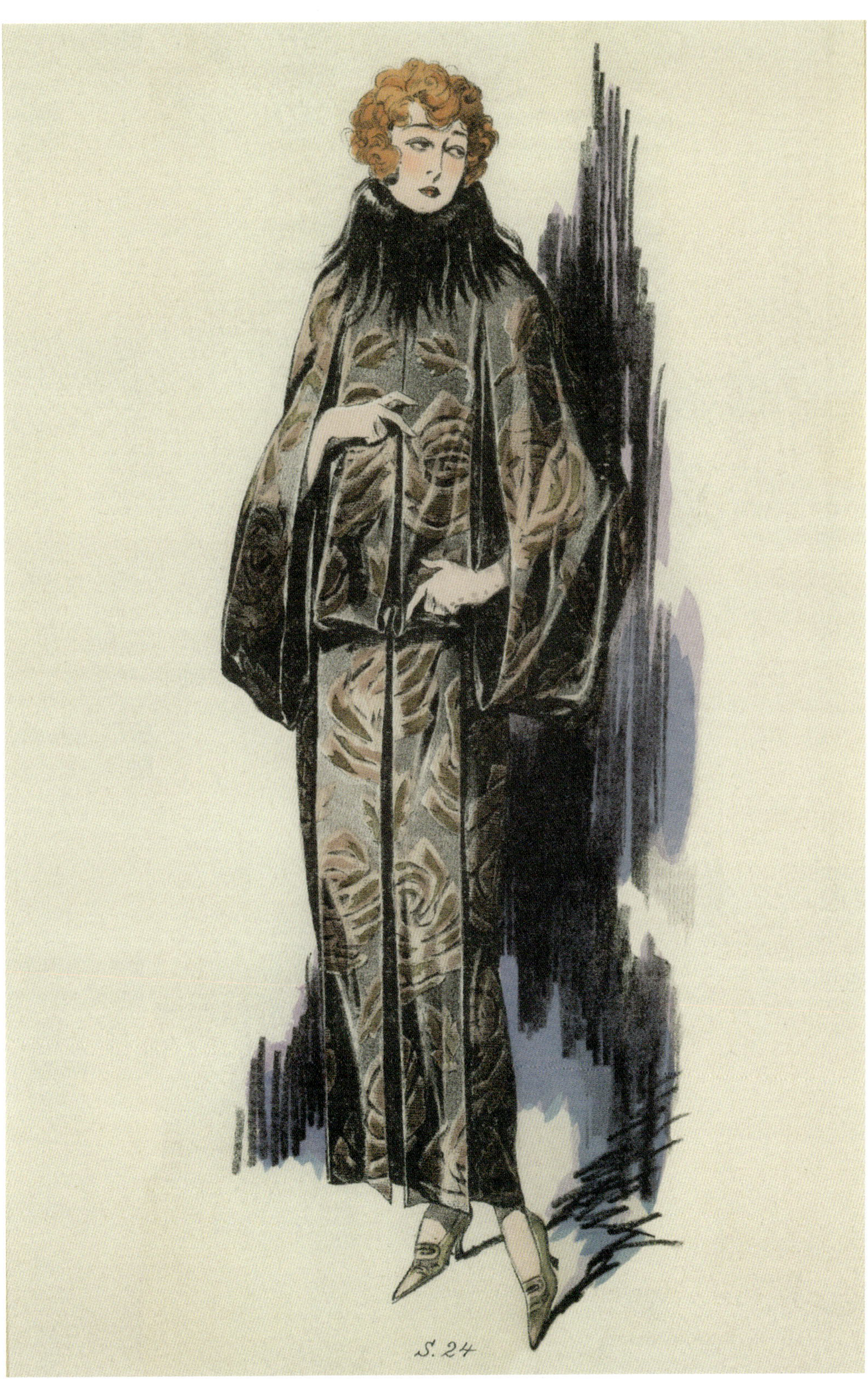
S. 24

Below
A lilac silk evening dress draped at the front and held by a darker bow worn over a silver lace underslip. *Dernières Créations*, c.1923

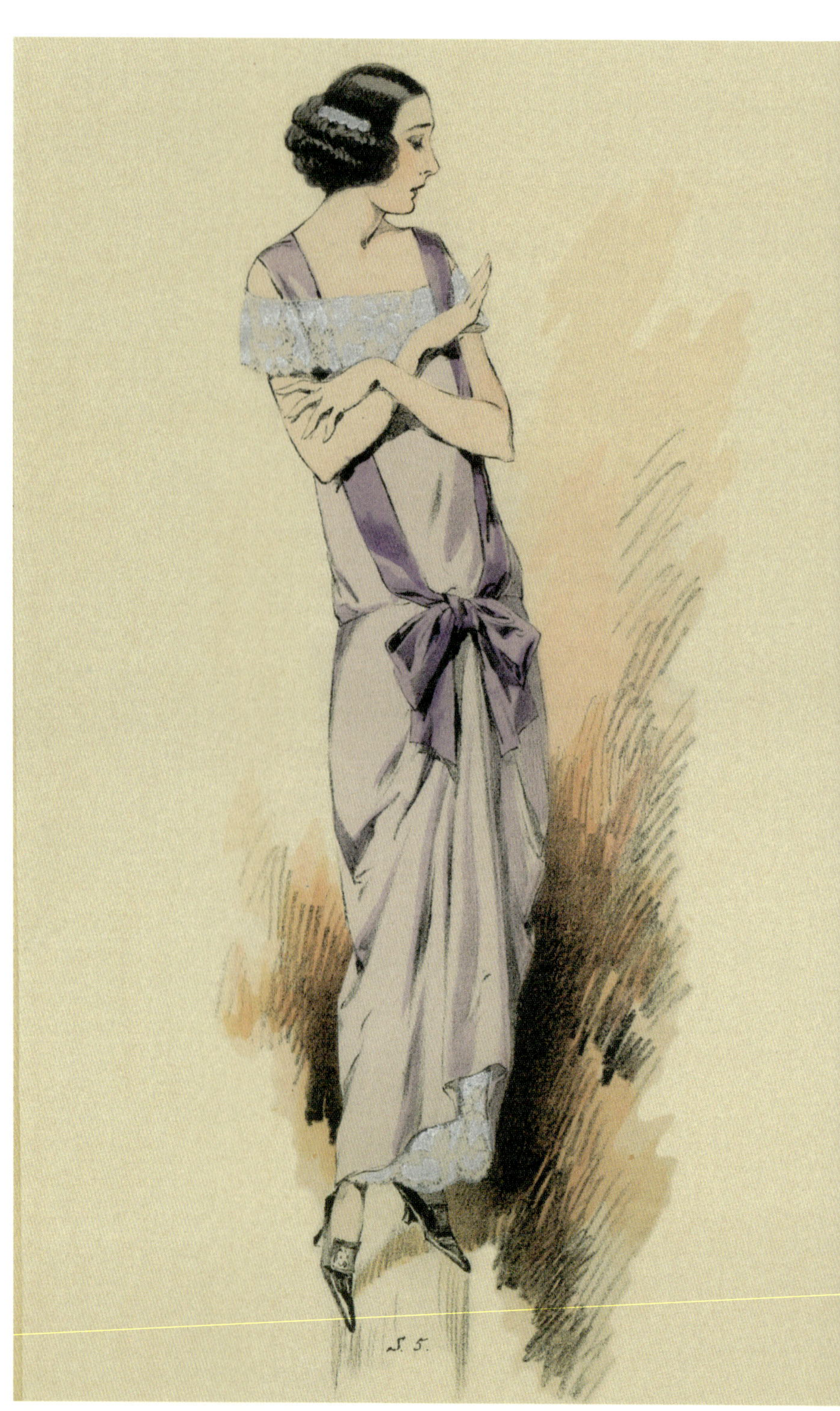

Below
A silver lace evening dress with a large embroidered front panel with pearls and a silk tassel. *Dernières Créations*, c.1923

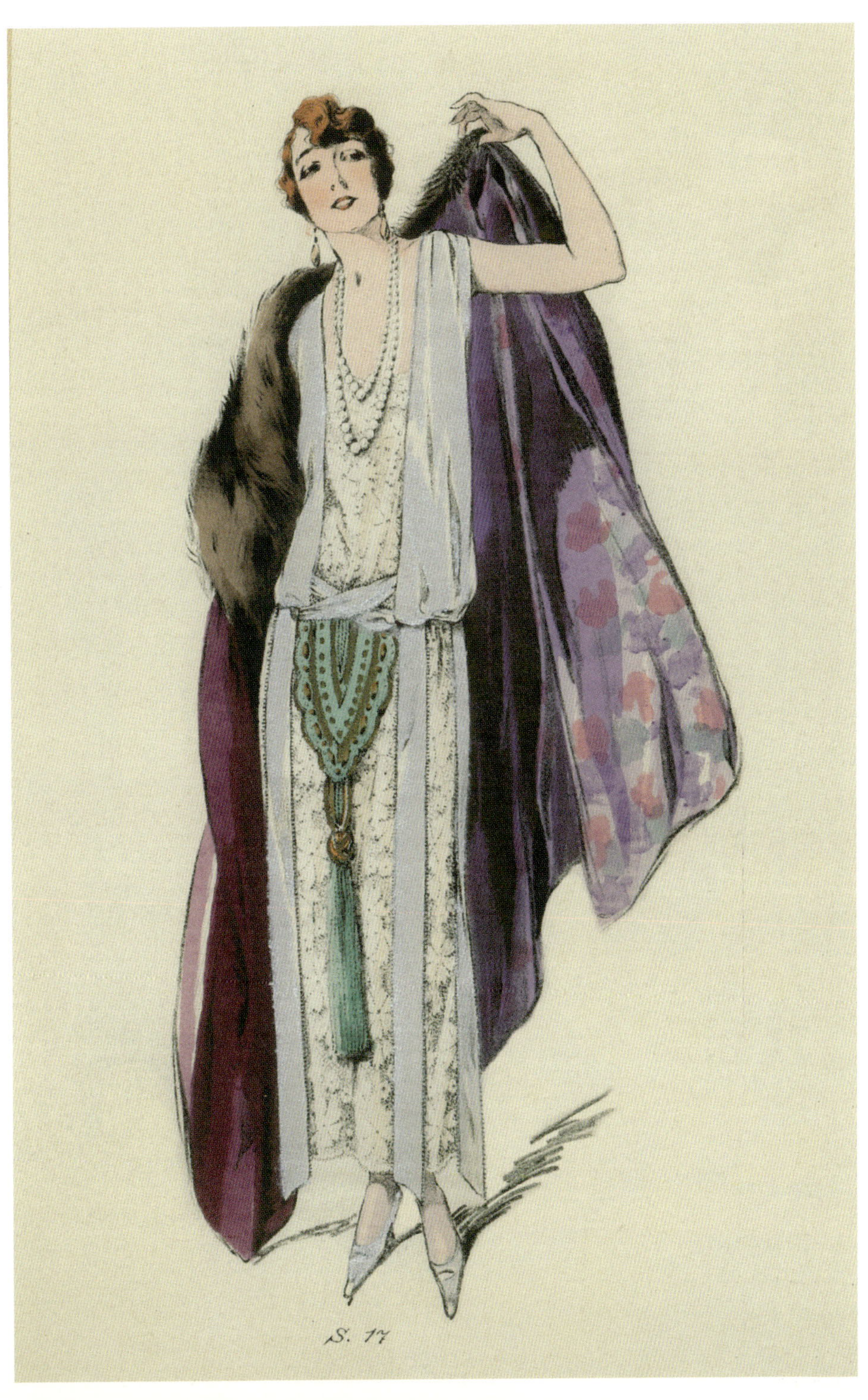

Right
A red silk cashmere party dress with a large skirt sash tied at the back as a large loop. *Dernières Créations*, c.1923

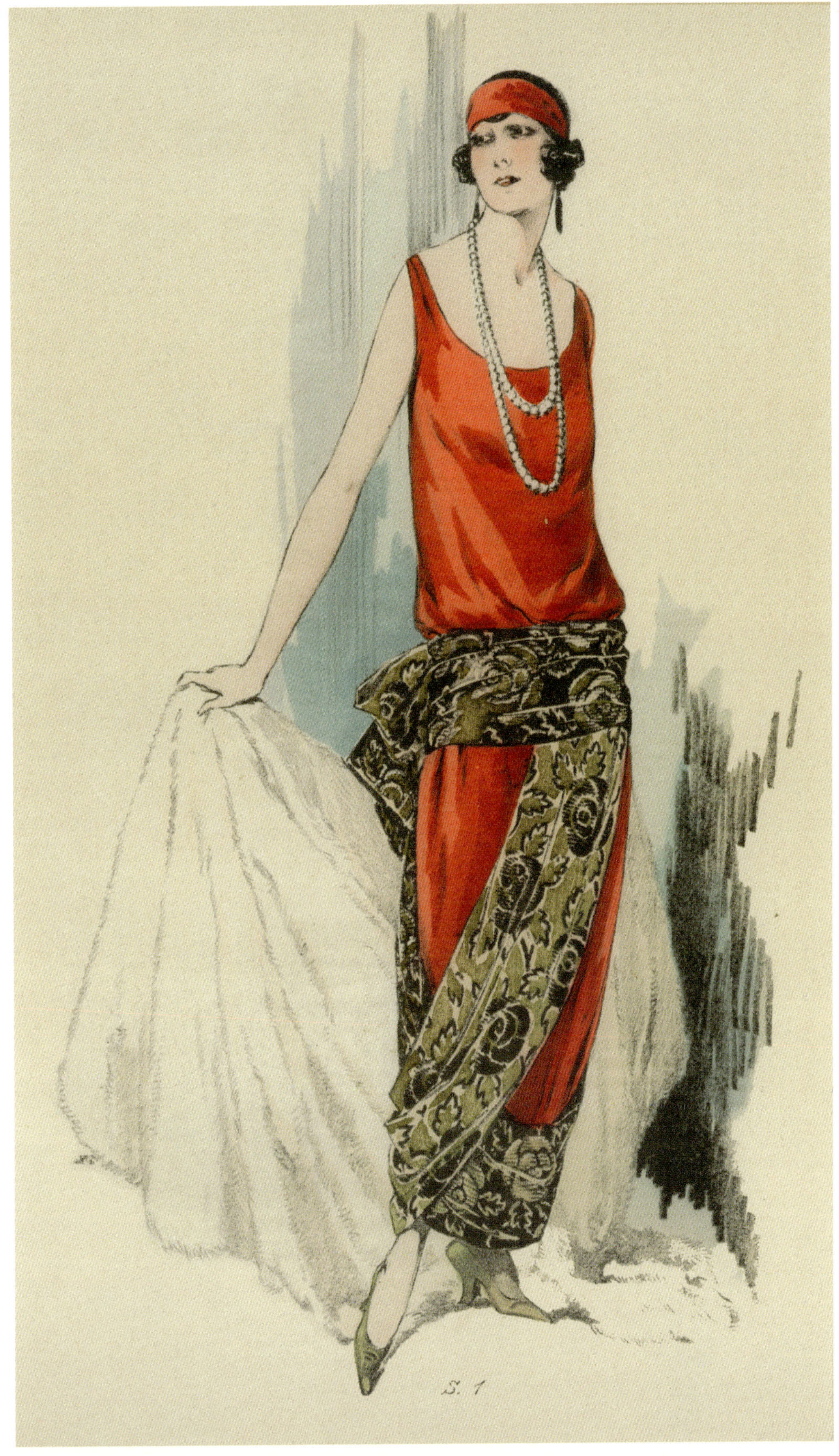
S. 1

Below left and right

A maize yellow Marocain crepe evening dress with wide velvet orange waist ribbons. *Dernières Créations*, c.1923

A silk cashmere evening dress with a pleated skirt held on the hips. *Dernières Créations*, c.1923

Right

A crepe Georgette evening dress with a fox fur skirt border. *Dernières Créations*, c.1923

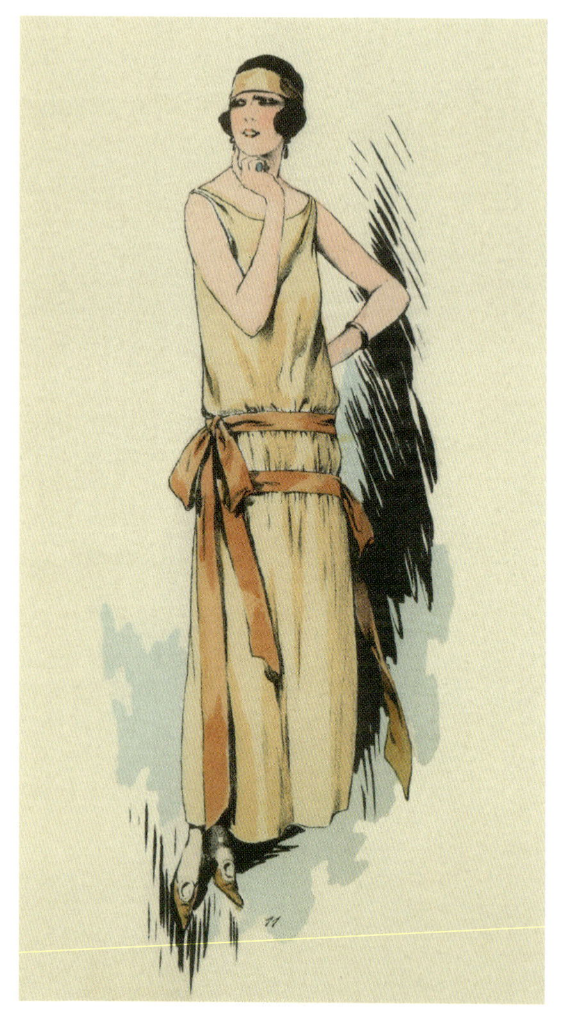

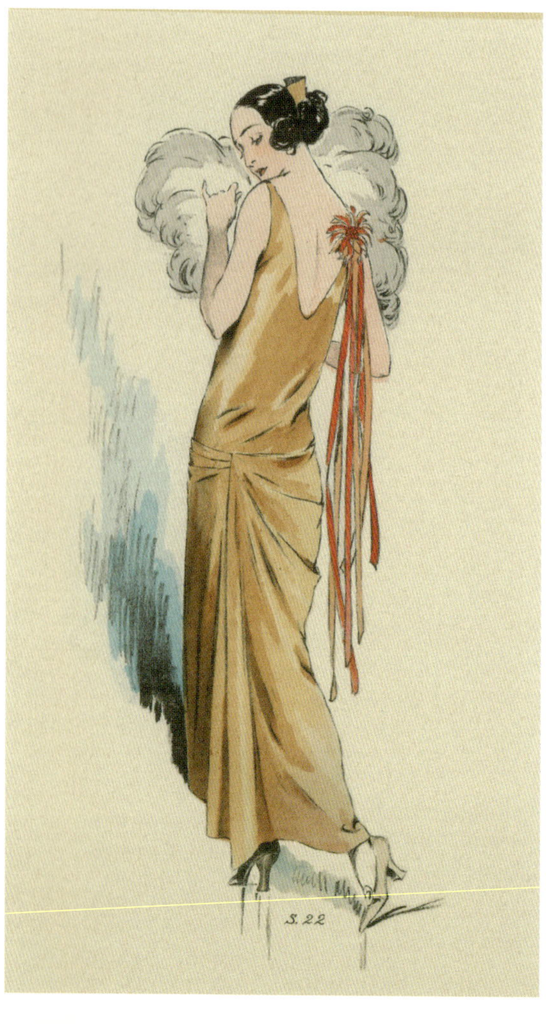

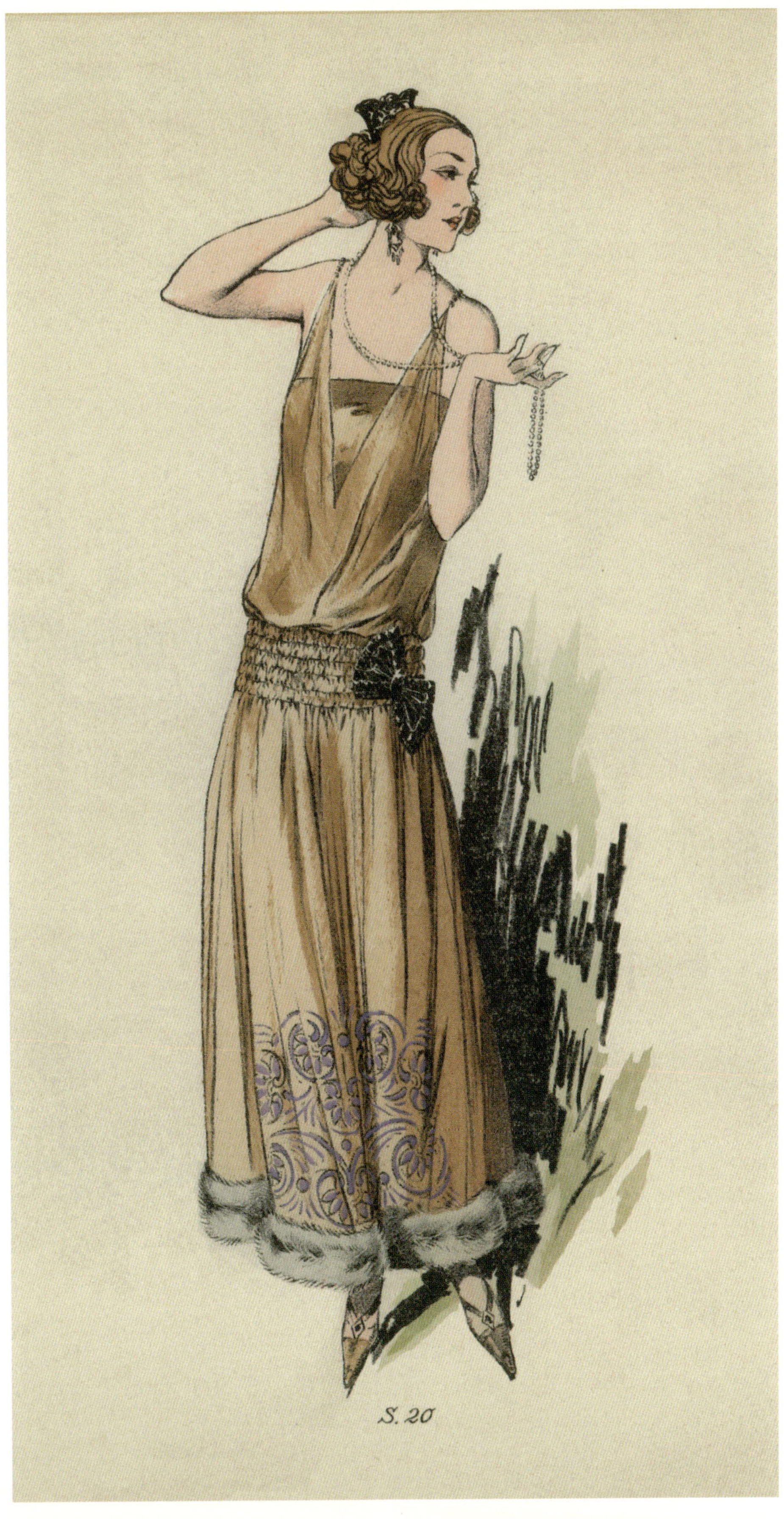
S. 20

Below left and right

A light silk ball dress with lace flounce and bow and two sloping flounces on the skirt. *Dernières Créations*, c.1923

A rose 'picture' dress with an appliqued lace skirt. *Dernières Créations*, c.1923

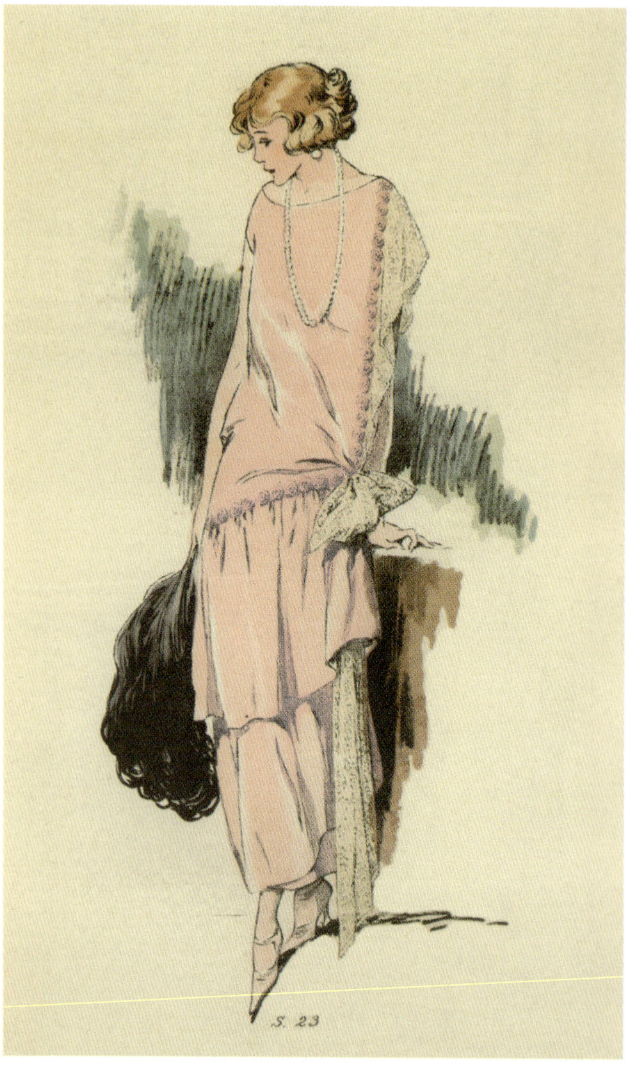

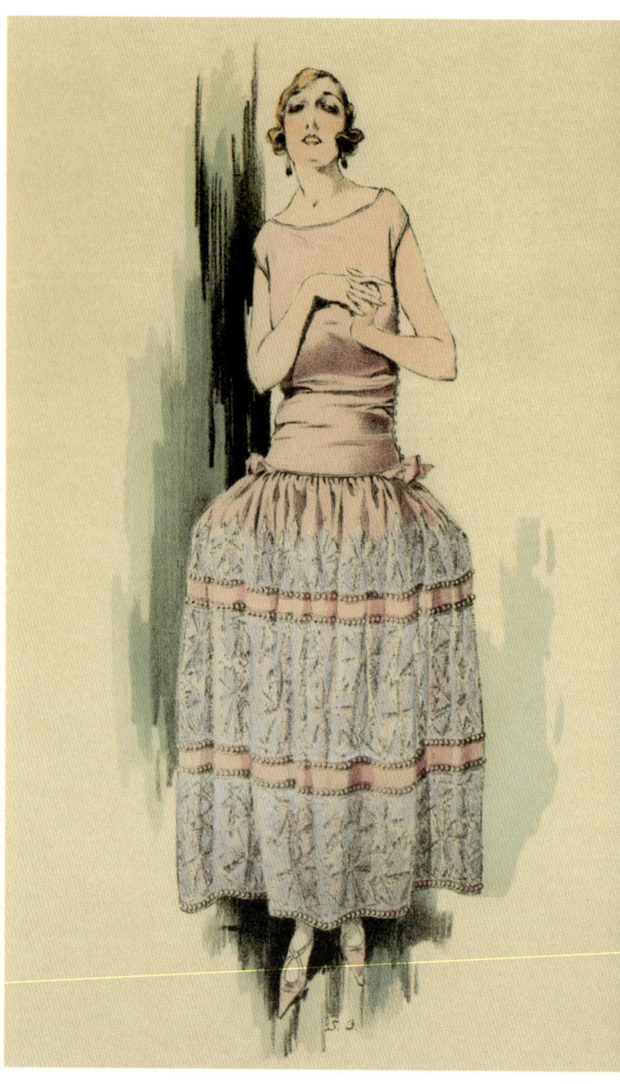

Below left and right

A crepe de Chine dancing dress with side lace panels. *Dernières Créations*, c.1923

A rose silk and crepe Georgette dancing dress with a flounced collar and skirt. *Dernières Créations*, c.1923

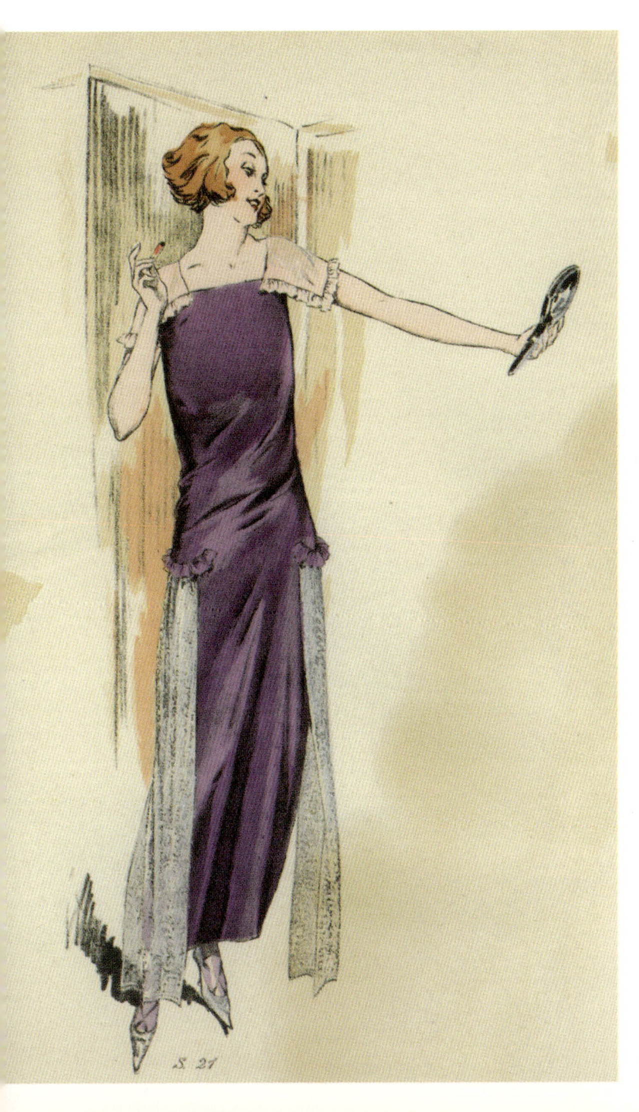

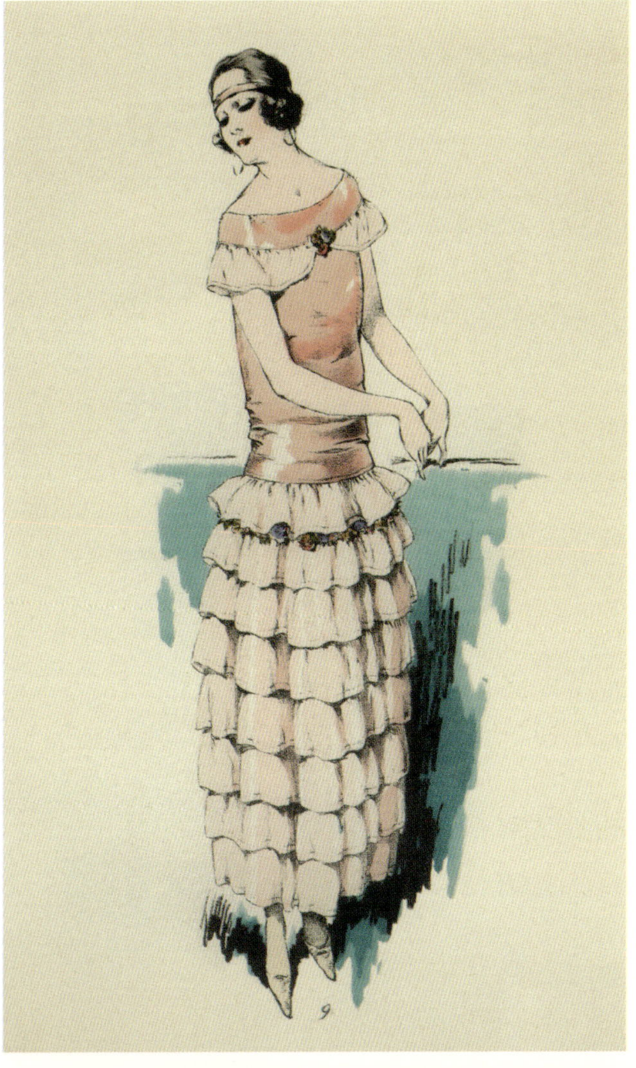

Below
A green moiré dress with fur-trimmed skirt flounces and a shoulder shawl tied at the back. *Dernières Créations*, c.1923

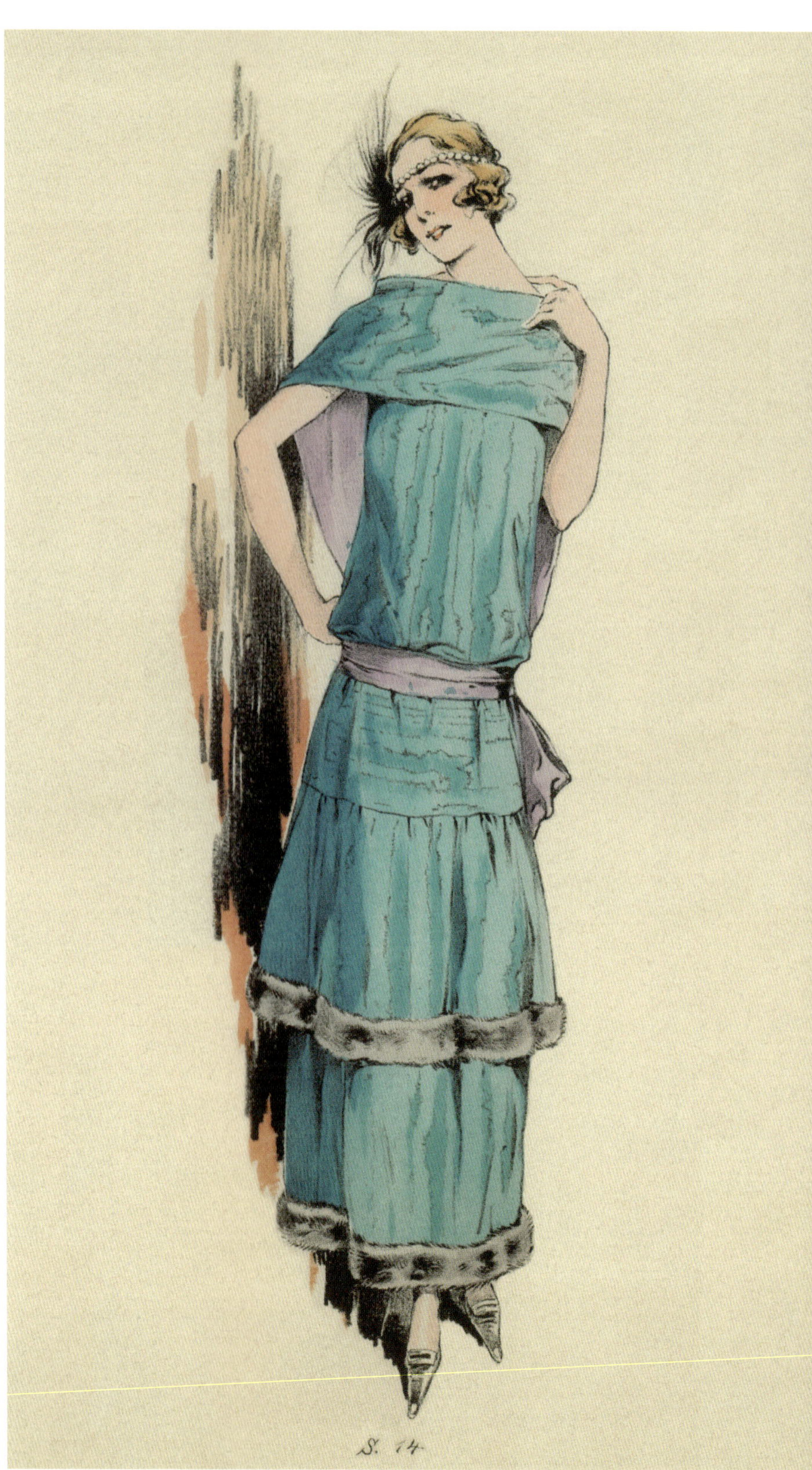

Below

A turquoise silk ball dress with a black silk overskirt. *Dernières Créations*, c.1923

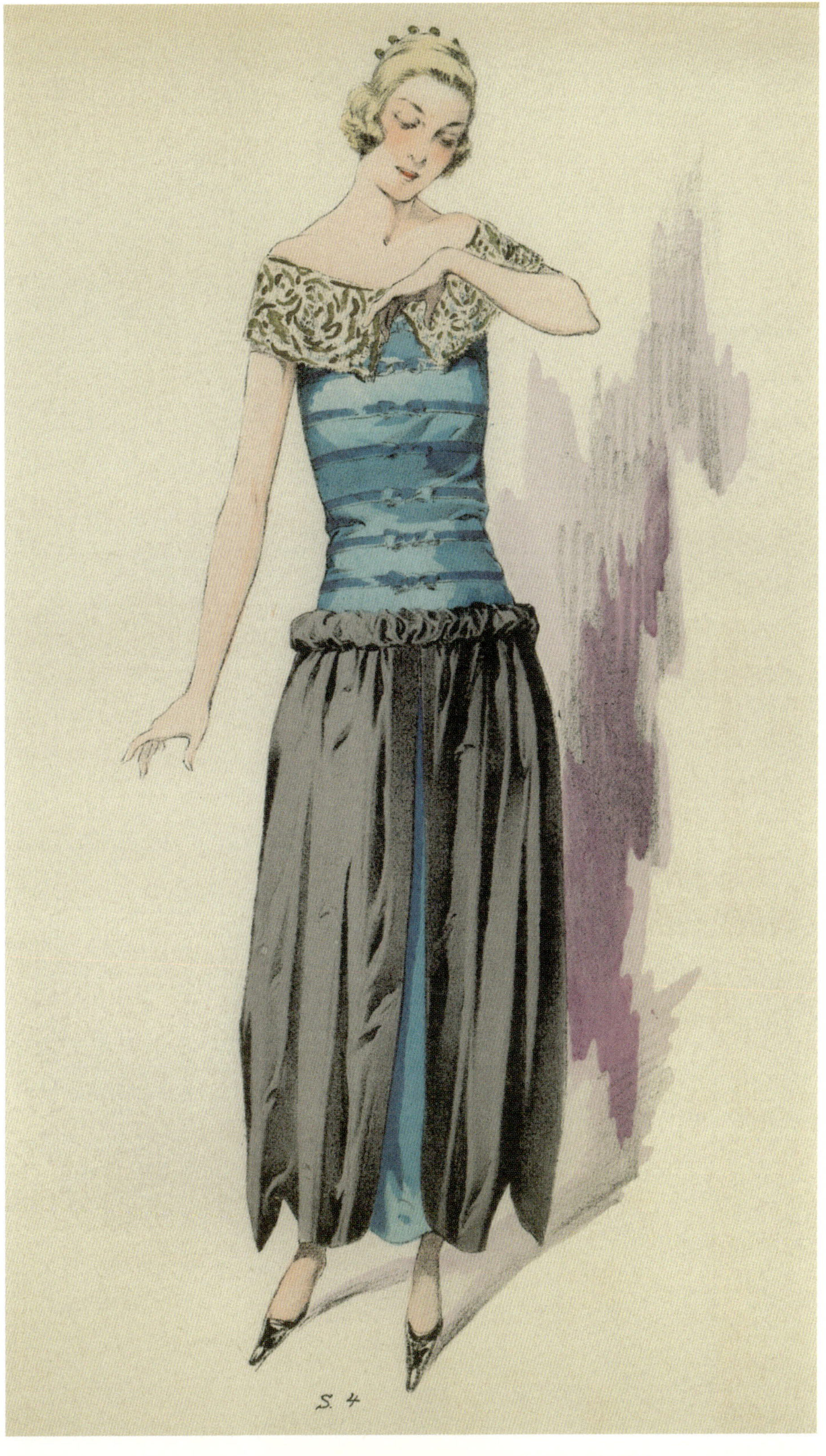

Below
A Parisian evening dress of blue and white crepe de Chine with a figured pattern worked on the waistline and the skirt. A narrow scarf of blue crepe with an artificial large rose is worn around the neck, c.1923

Right
Pink picture-style evening gown with large bow and lacing at the back, c.1923

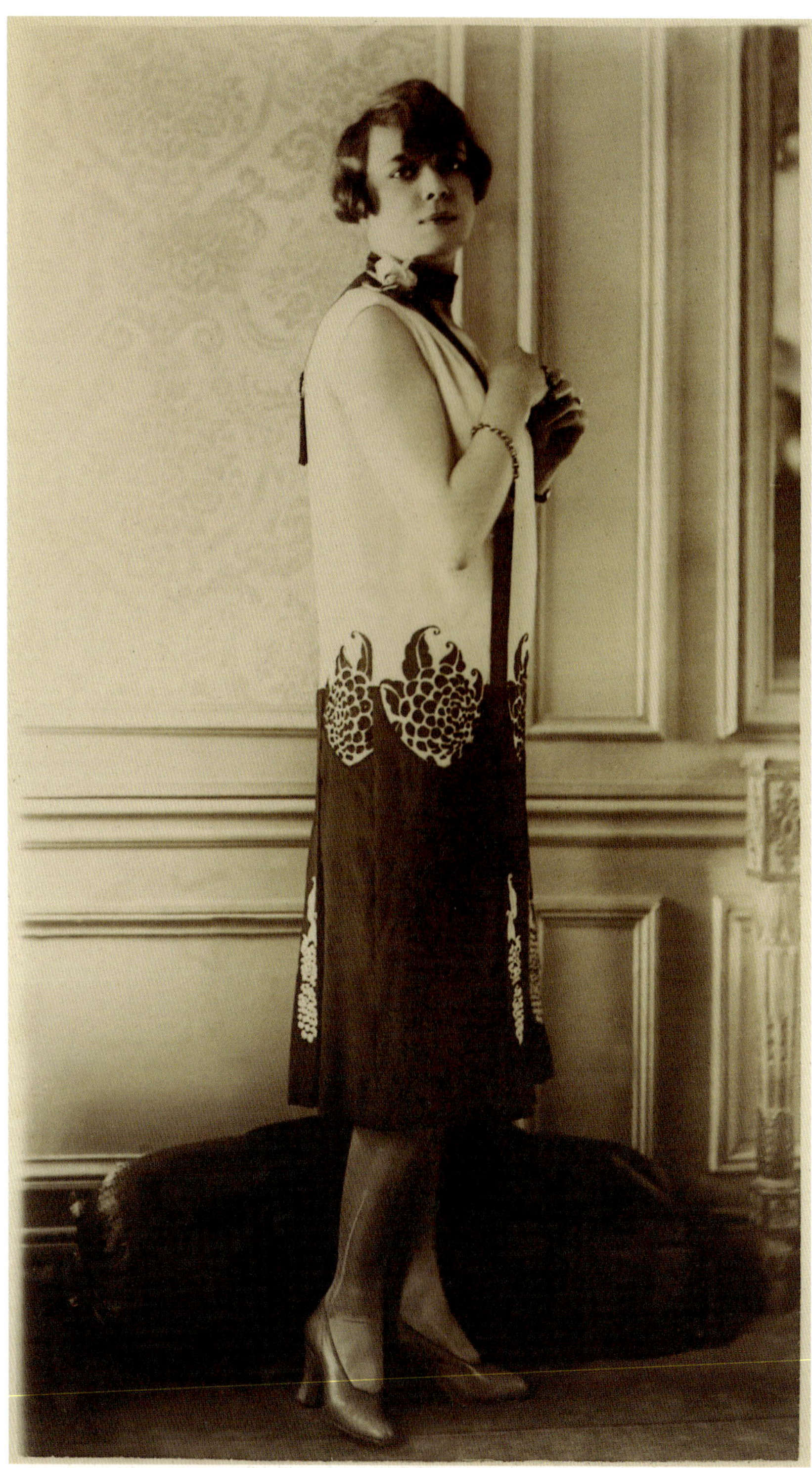

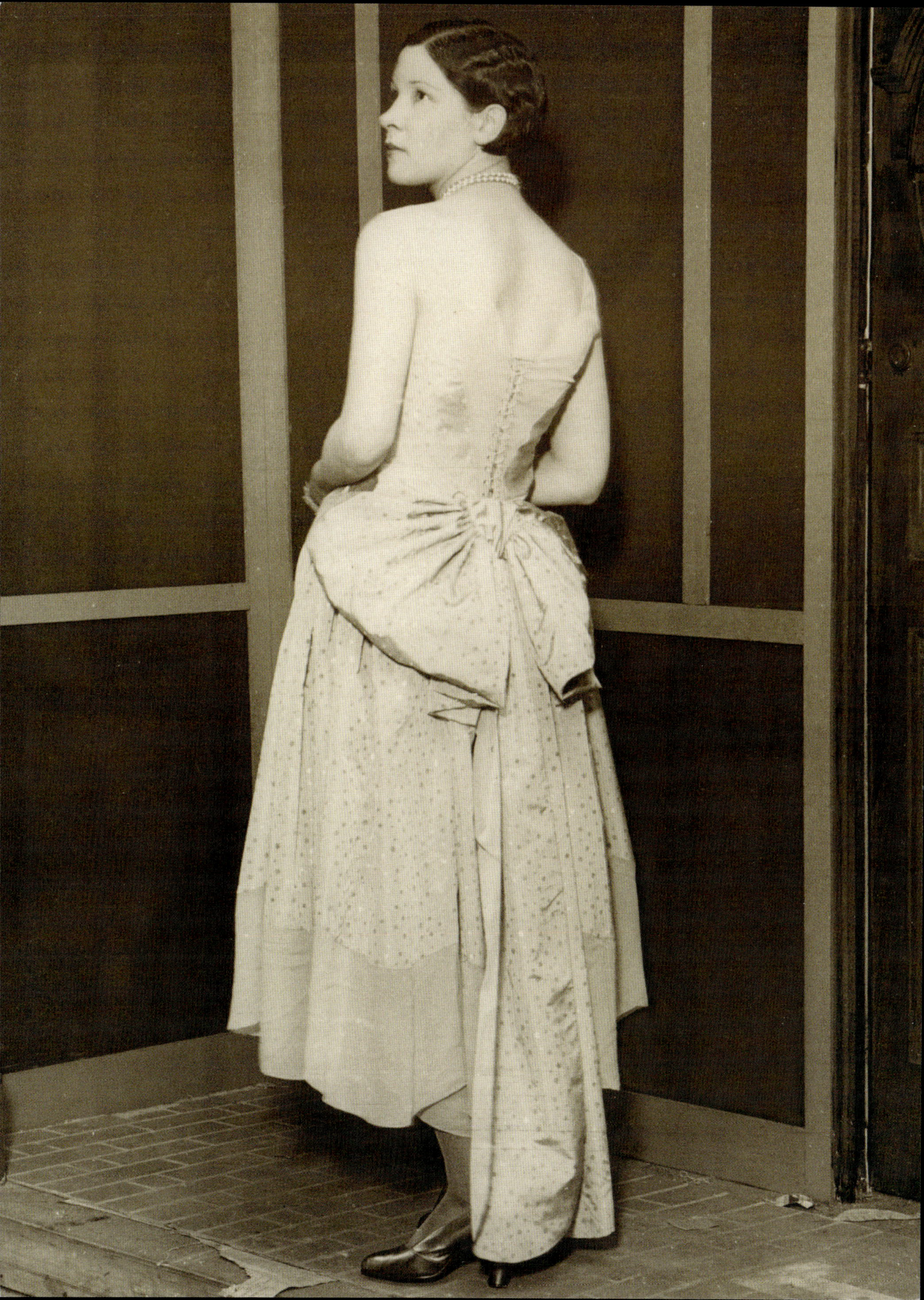

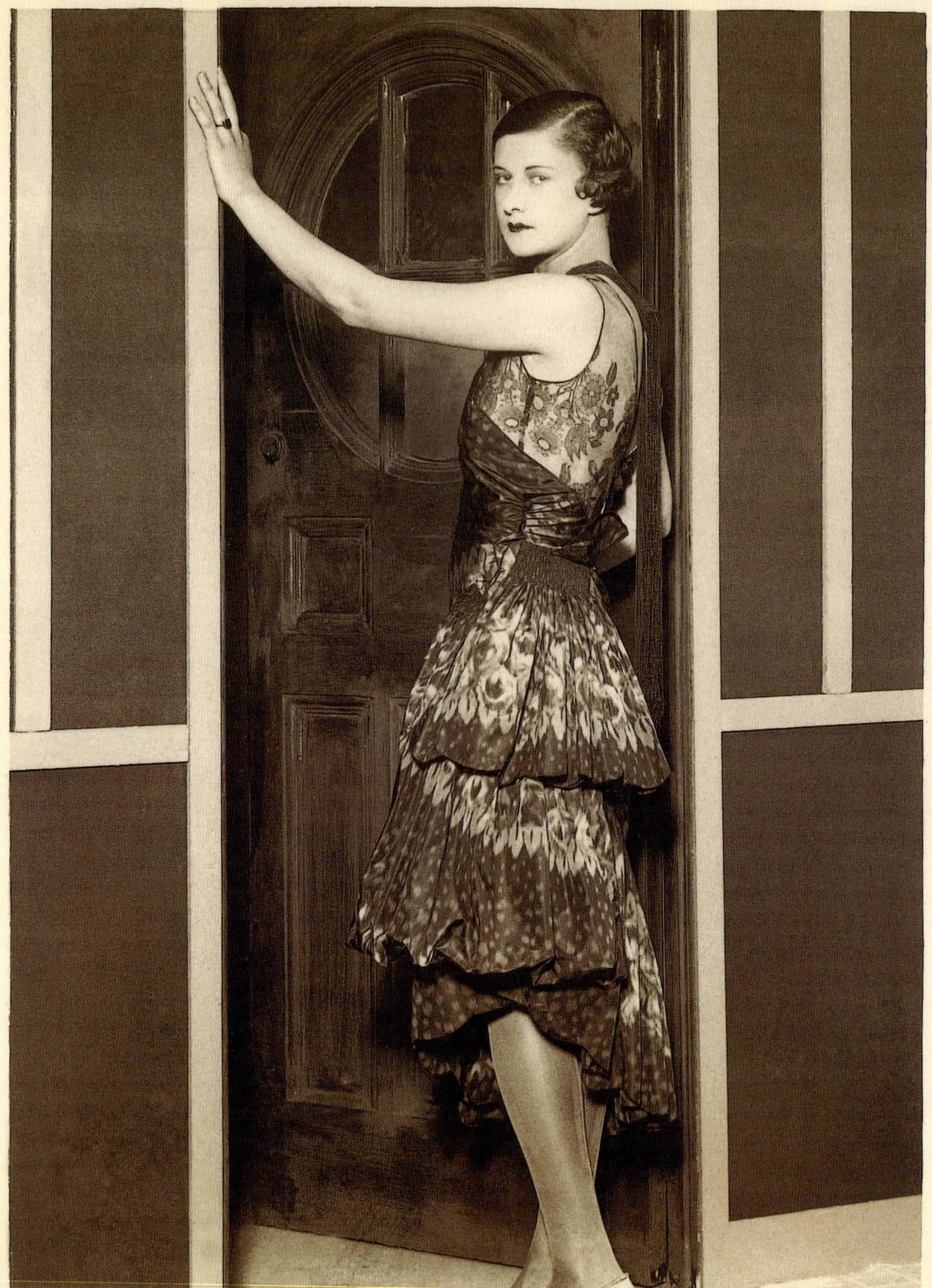

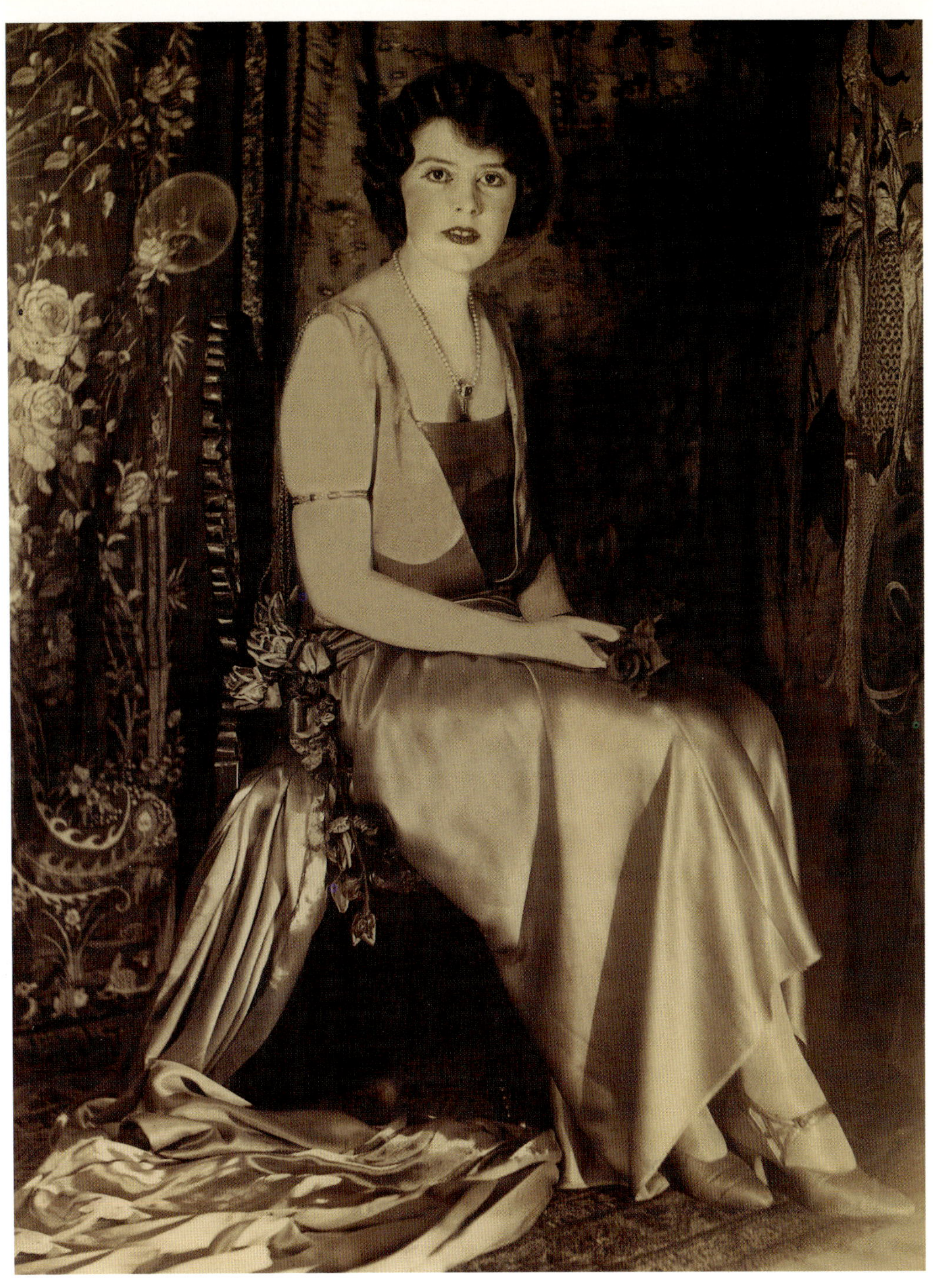

Left
A tiered printed taffeta evening gown with a beaded and fringed scarf, c.1925

Above
Photograph of a model posing at a fashion fair in a Richard Hickson gown of jade green silk accessorized with silk sash, artificial flowers and a slave bracelet around her arm. The model is said to have received more marriage proposals than any other girl in America. c.1921

Right
Extravagant stage costume, lavishly embellished with pearl and bead embroideries and complimented with a wraparound opera coat equally richly decorated. The headdress is made of pheasant feathers, while long multiple strands of pearls and a variety of diamante bracelets complete the look. Paramount Pictures, c.1924

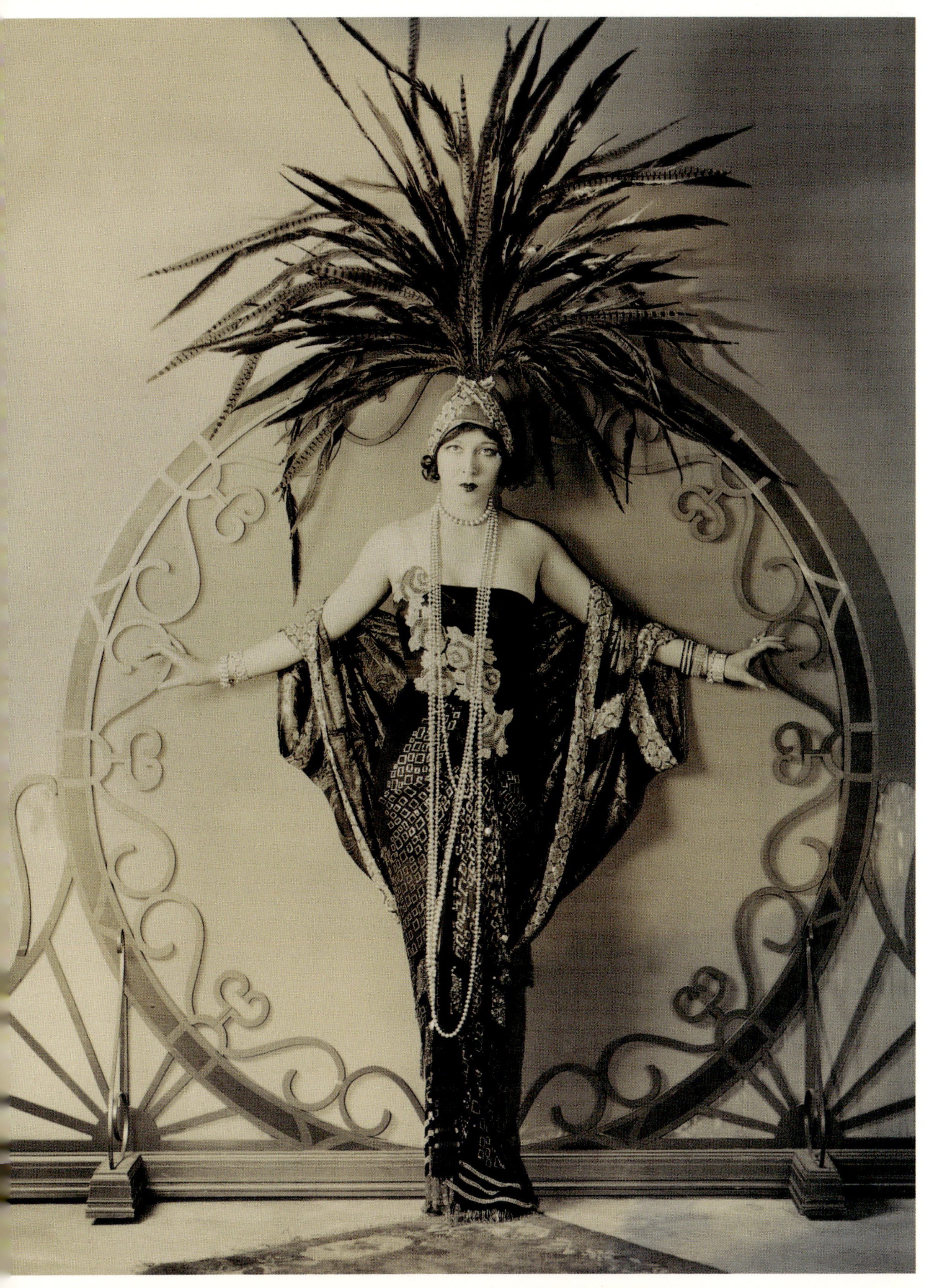

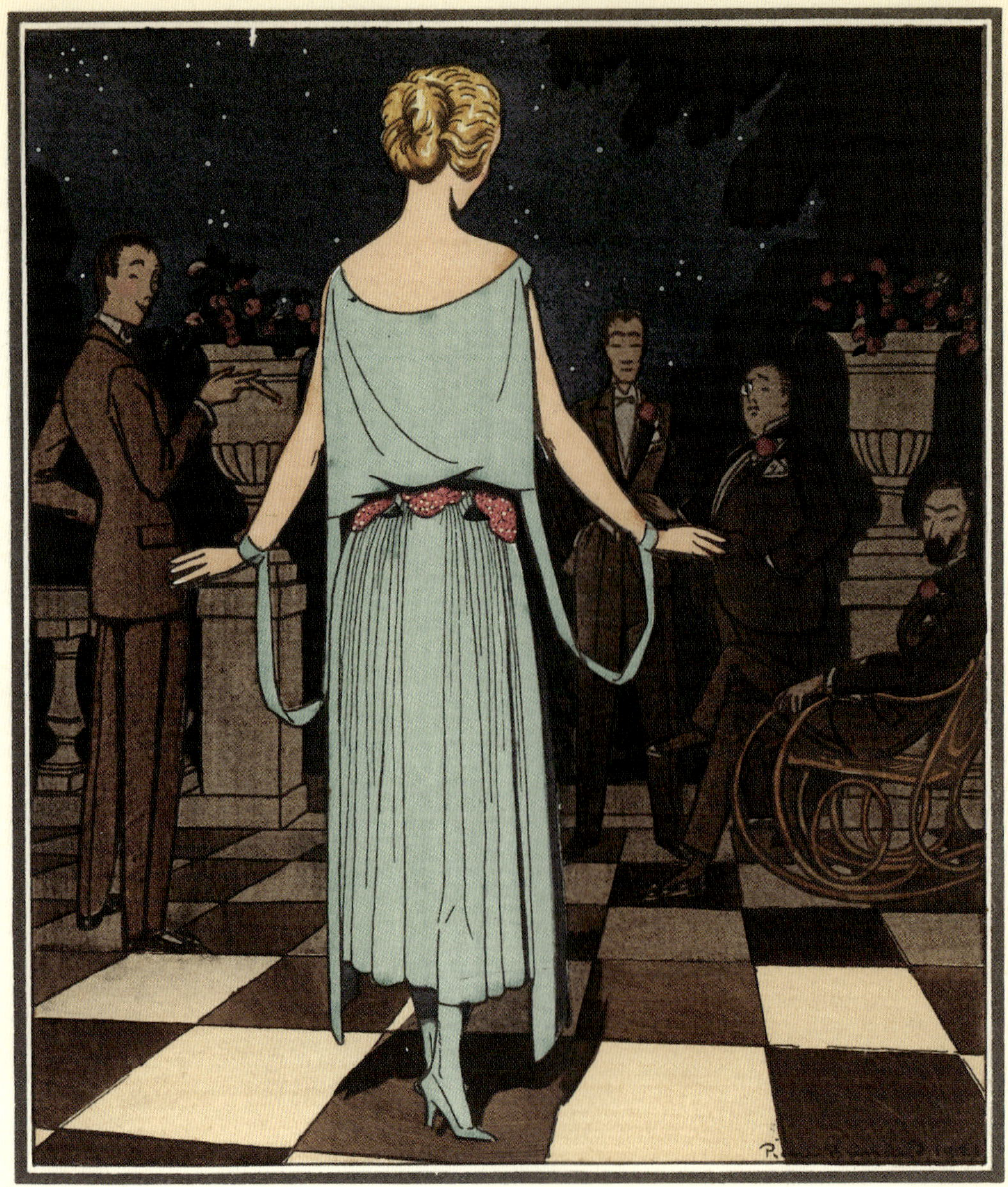

Above
"Venez Danser" (Come Dancing), evening dress by Jeanne Lanvin, illustration by Pierre Brissaud. Both the design and the name of the dress refer to the 1920s craze for new dances such as the Charleston, Foxtrot and Black Bottom which were far more energetic than dances from previous generations and so required looser flowing gowns. *Gazette du Bon Ton*, 1921

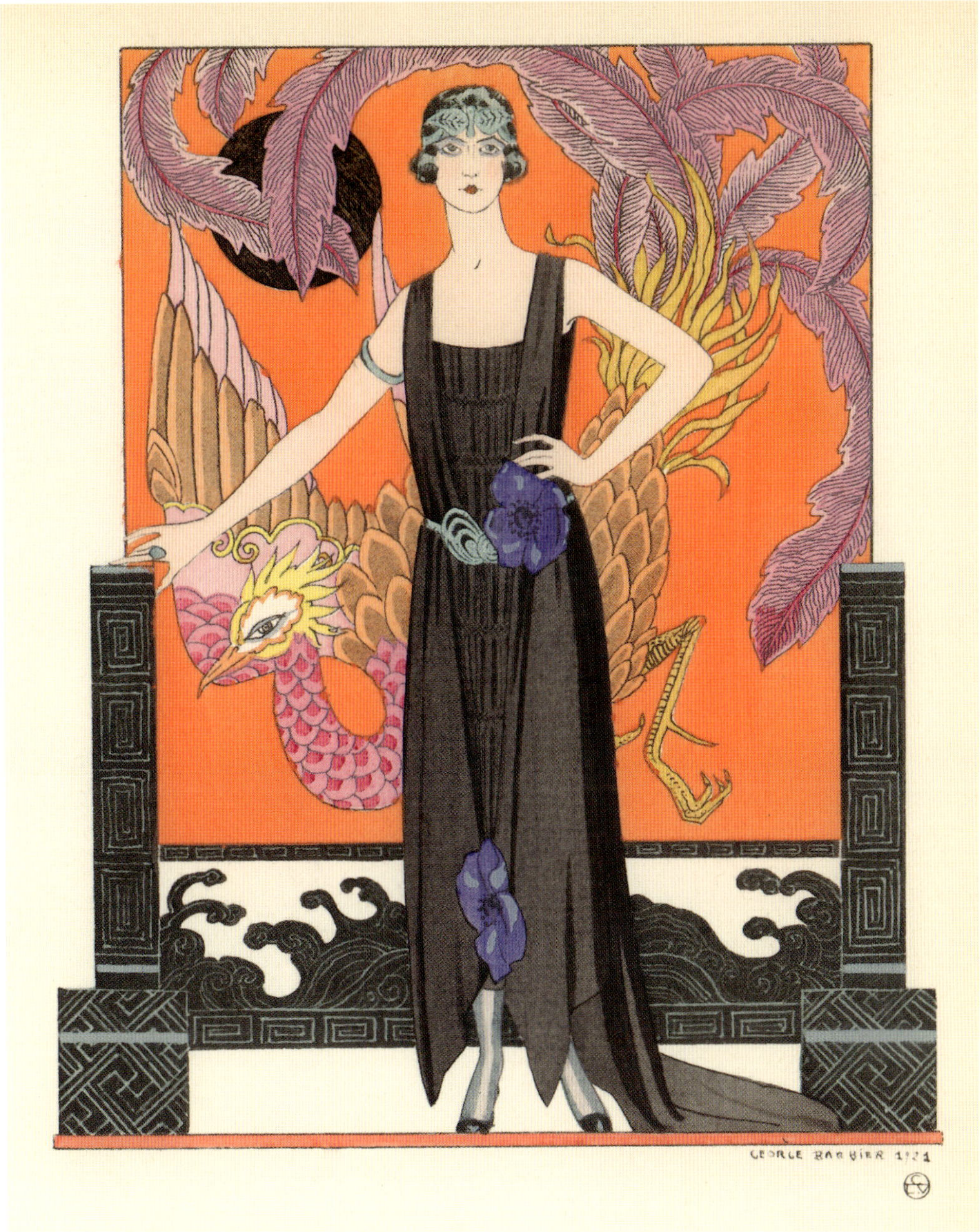

Above

"La Belle Dame sans Merci" (The Beautiful Lady without Mercy), evening dress by Worth. Illustration by George Barbier. The mythical Belle Dame sans Merci derives her name from a 15th century poem. She went on to inspire poets such as John Keats as well as Pre-Raphaelite artists and by 1921 was an established term for a femme fatale. *Gazette du Bon Ton*, 1921

Right
An evening dress by Worth.
Gazette du Bon Ton, 1920

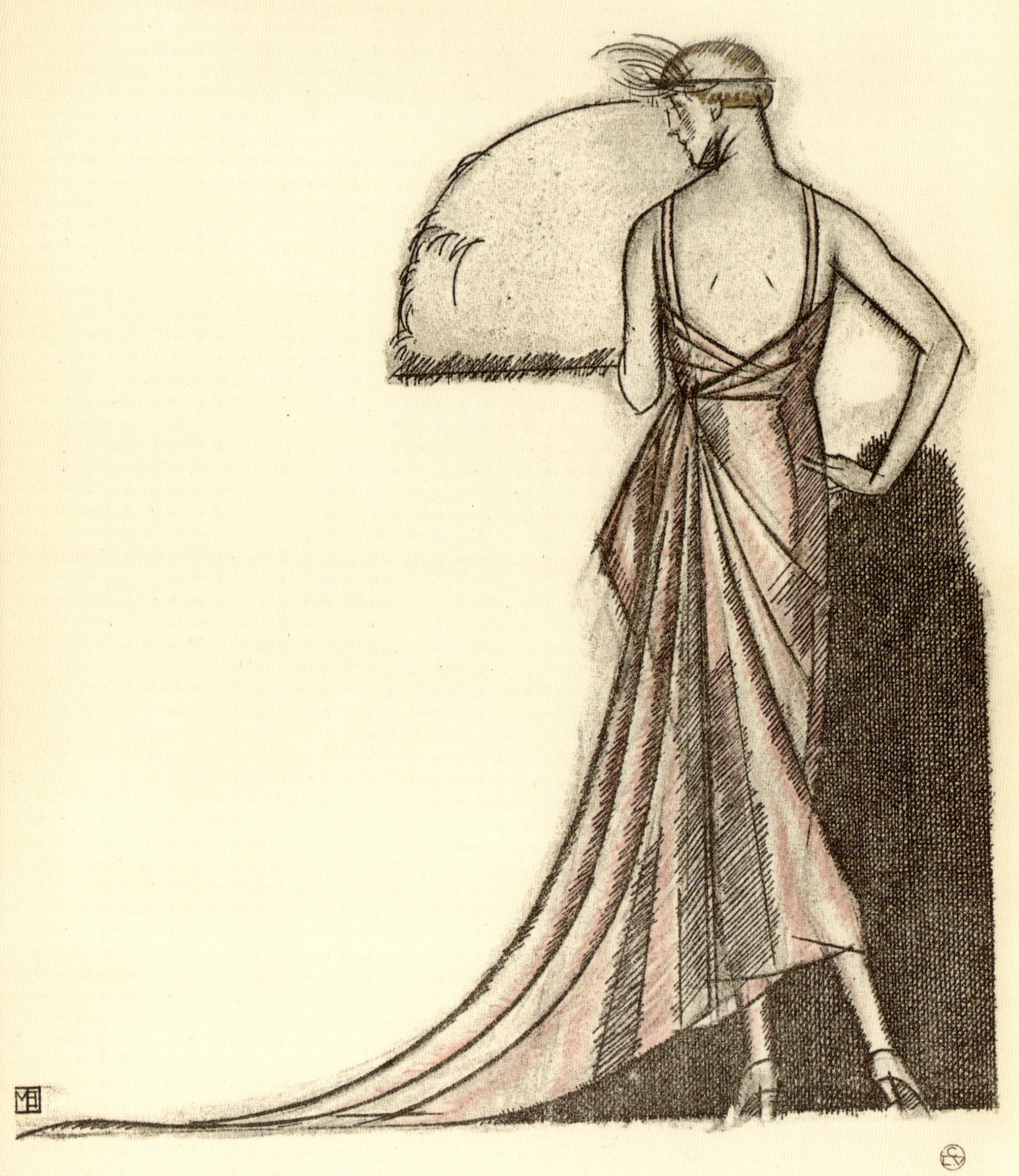

UNE ROBE DU SOIR DE WORTH

Below
"La Soubrette Annamite" (The Ladies' Maid from Indochina), evening dress with sash by Doeuillet. Illustration By André Edouard Marty. *Gazette du Bon Ton*, 1920

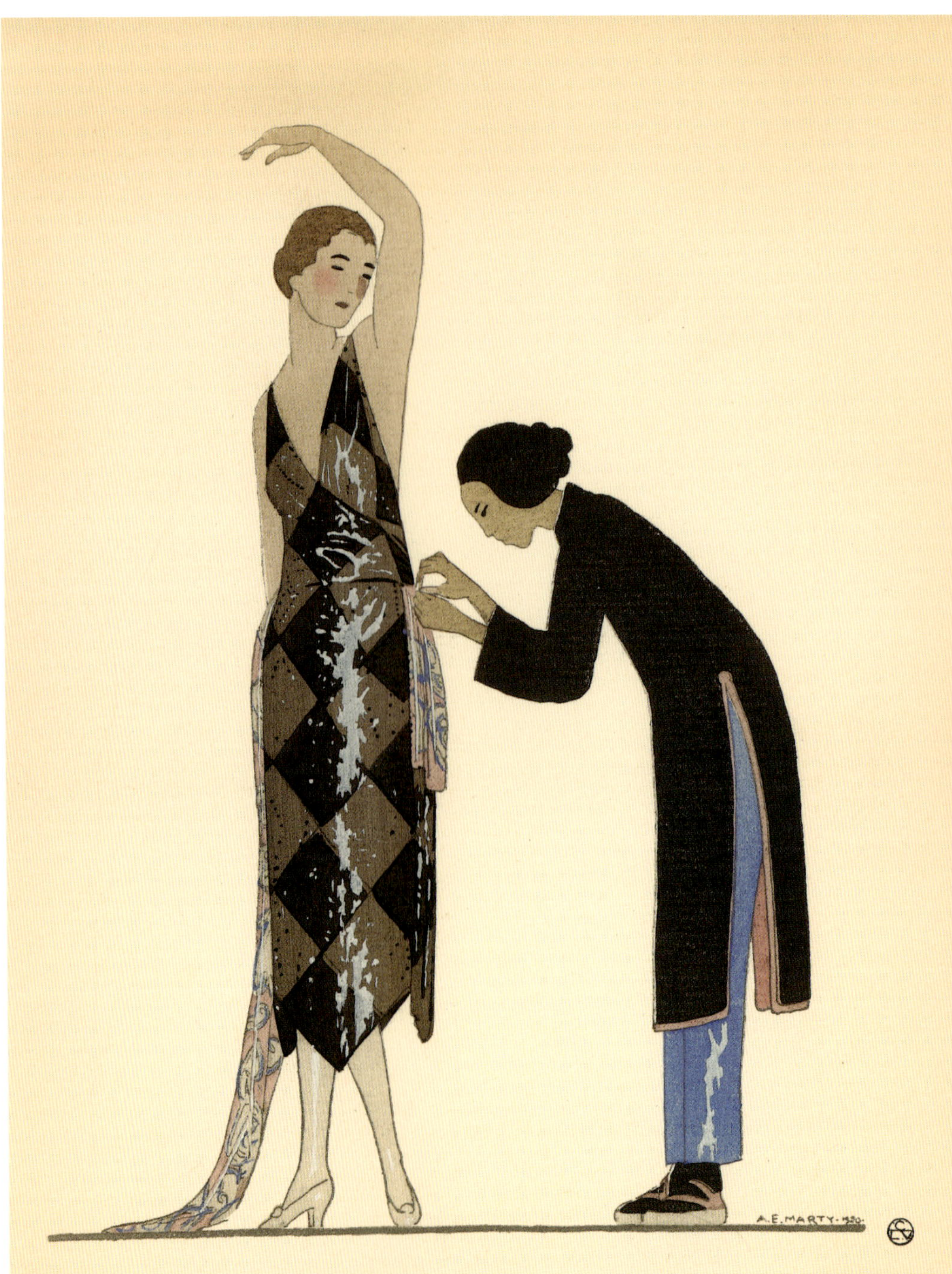

Below
"En plein coeur" (Shot through the Heart), evening dress by Paul Poiret. Illustration by André Edouard Marty. *Gazette du Bon Ton*, 1922

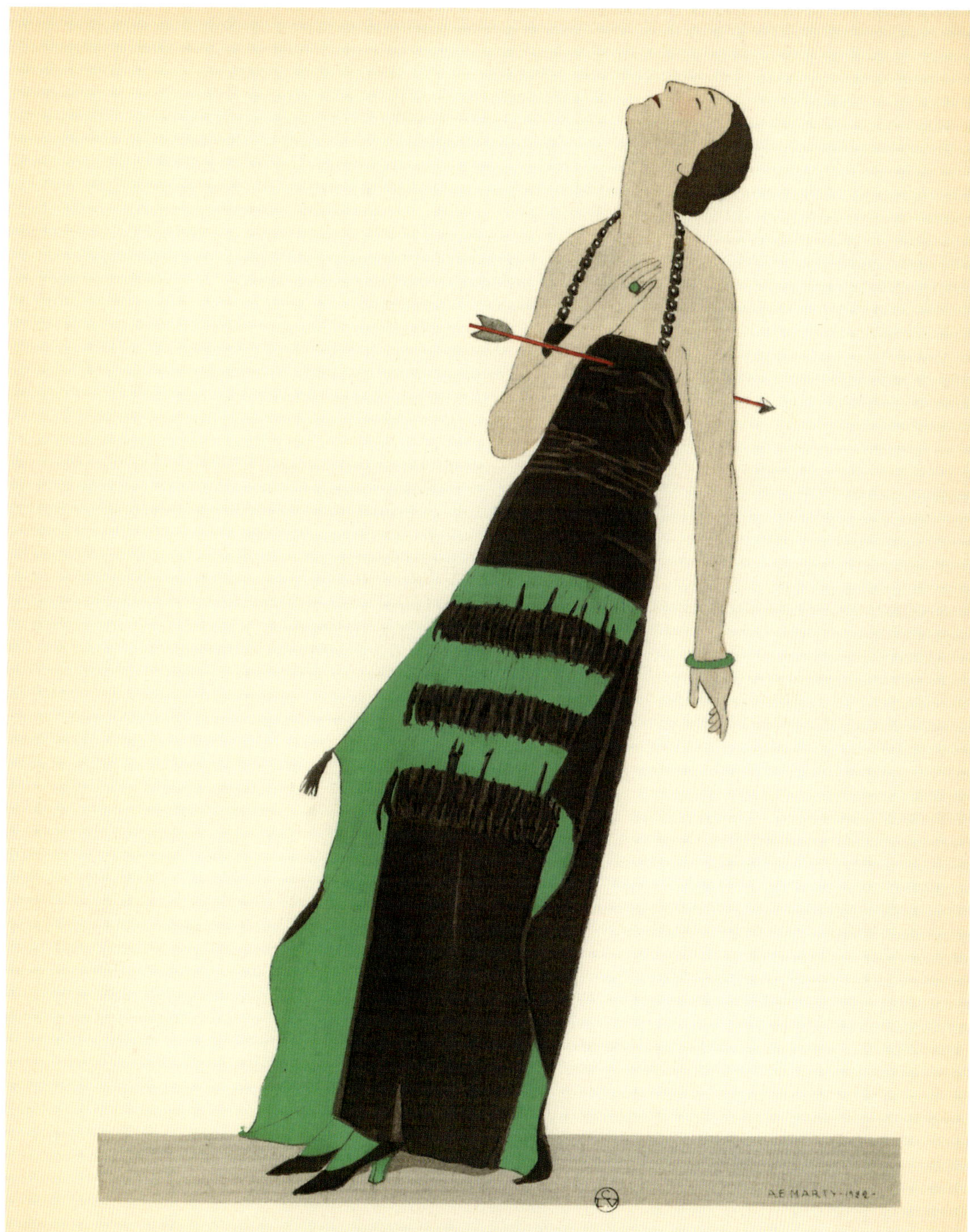

Right
French film actress Arlette Marchal dressed in a chiffon negligee dress worn with a metallic lace coat and an ostrich feather boa accesorised with a tight-fitting turban hat and satin silk shoes with diamante clasps, c.1924

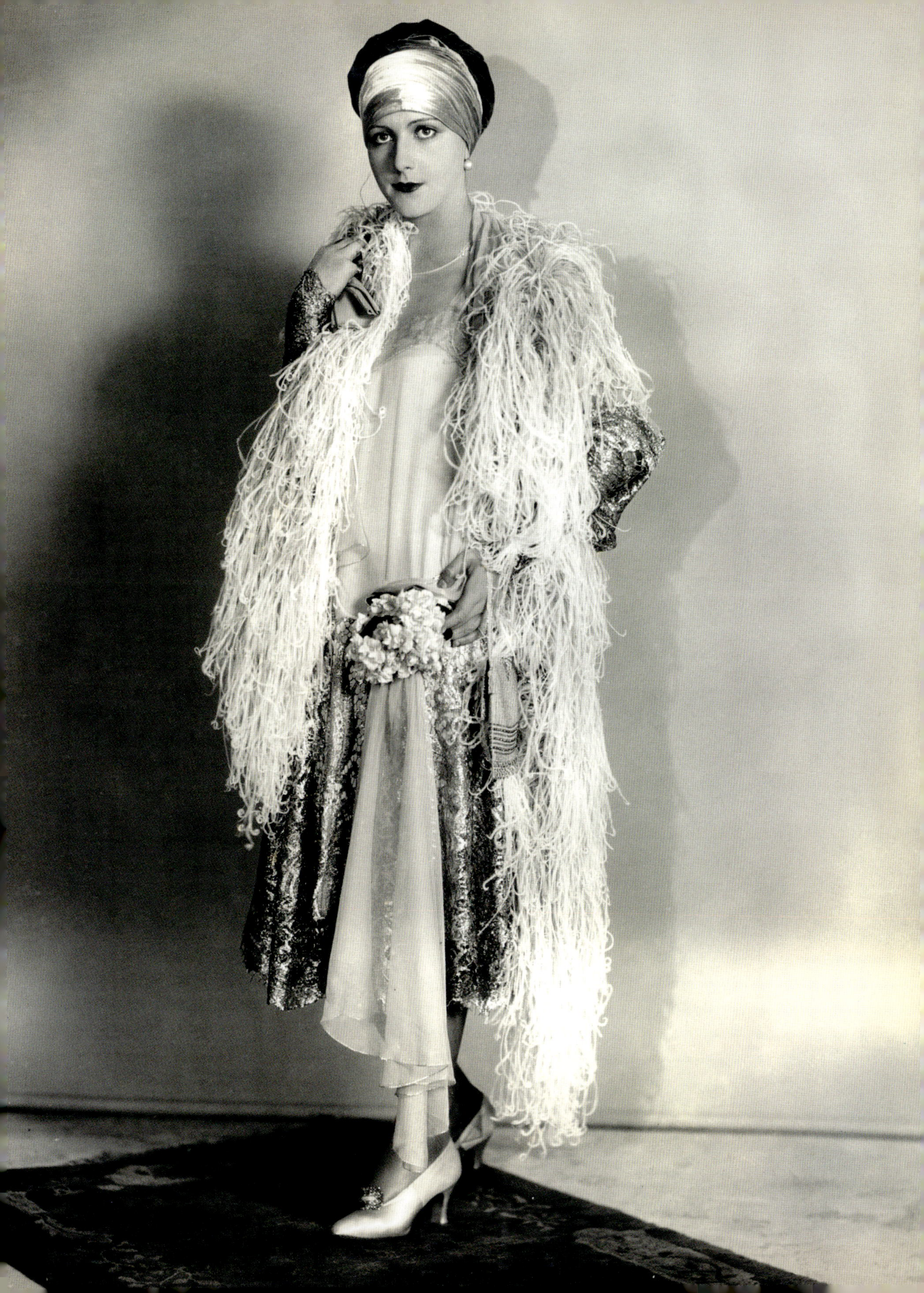

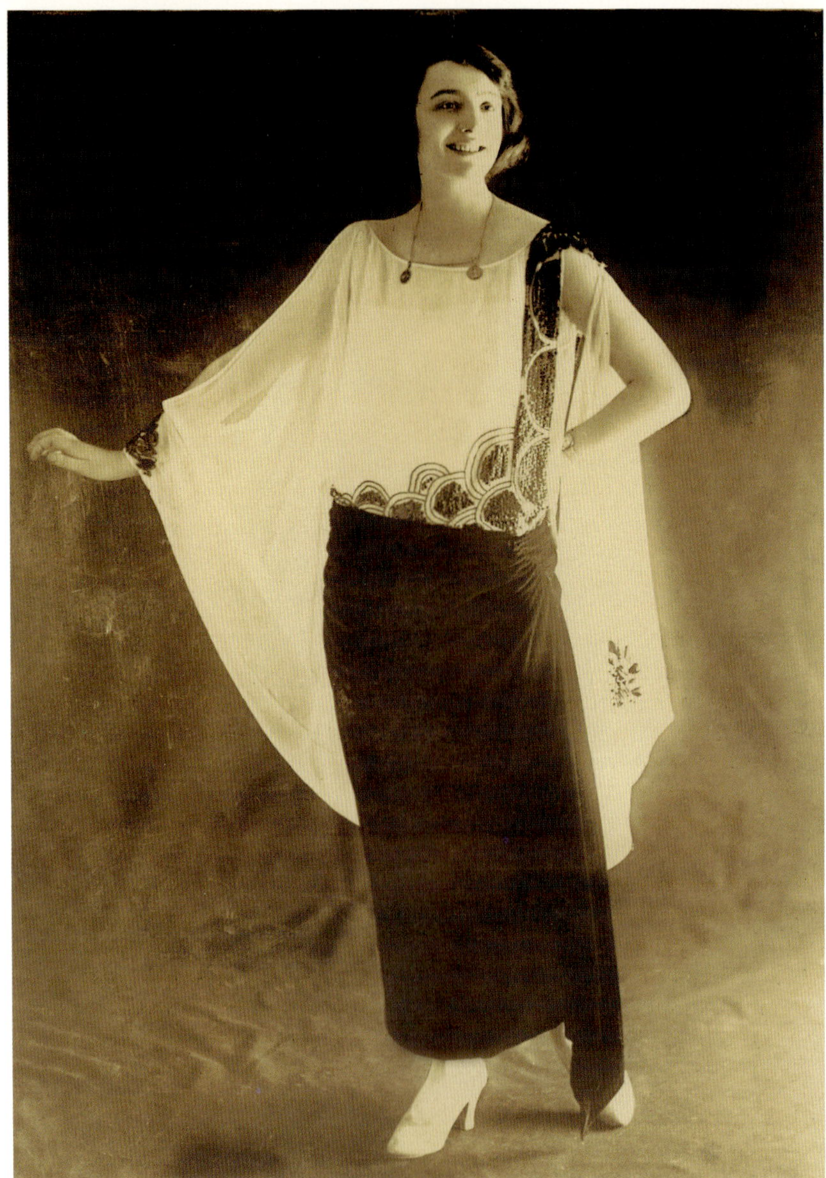

Above and right
Photograph of a fashionable Grecian-inspired creation by the Paris designer Elise Poret, who became famous for her lingerie designs. The white blouse is made of crepe de Chine and is embroidered in black beads at the waist and sleeves. The skirt is a simple draped model in black silk velvet with a panel extending to the ground, c.1921

Actress Helena D'Algy in one of her costumes from "Confessions of a Queen", 1925

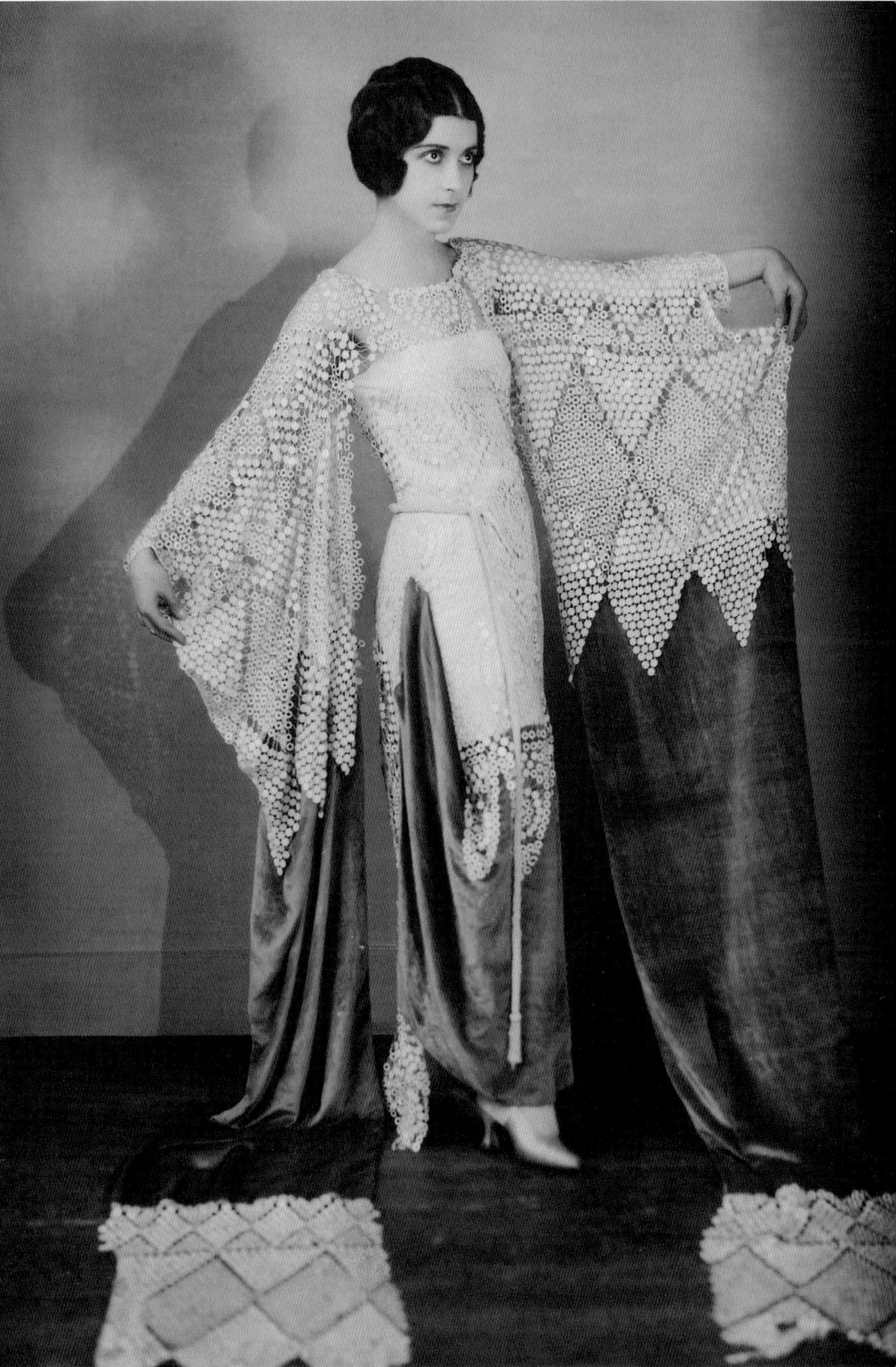

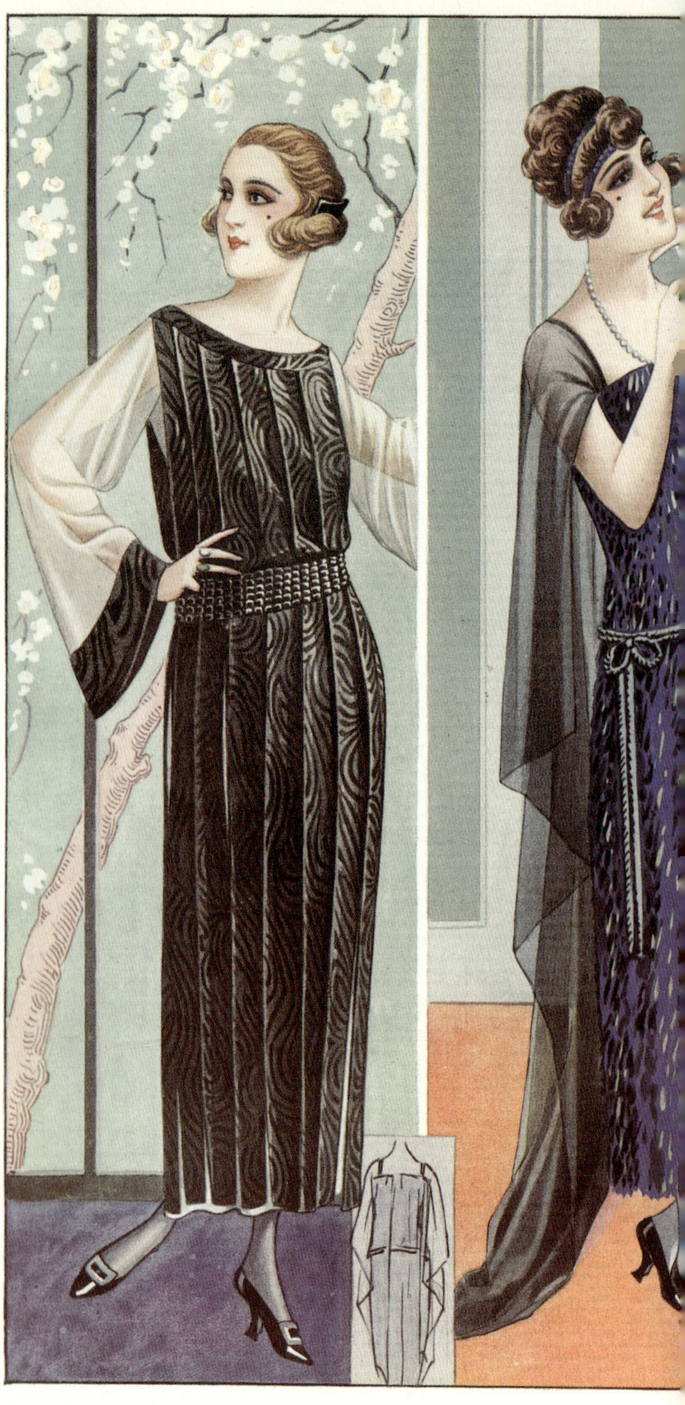

Above
A black pleated dress with voile sleeves by Dorat, a blue petalled evening gown with a voile train, a mustard yellow dress with black embellished voile panels and sleeves, a black fan dress by Premet and a dark blue woollen coat and skirt by Beer. *La Femme Chic*, c.1920

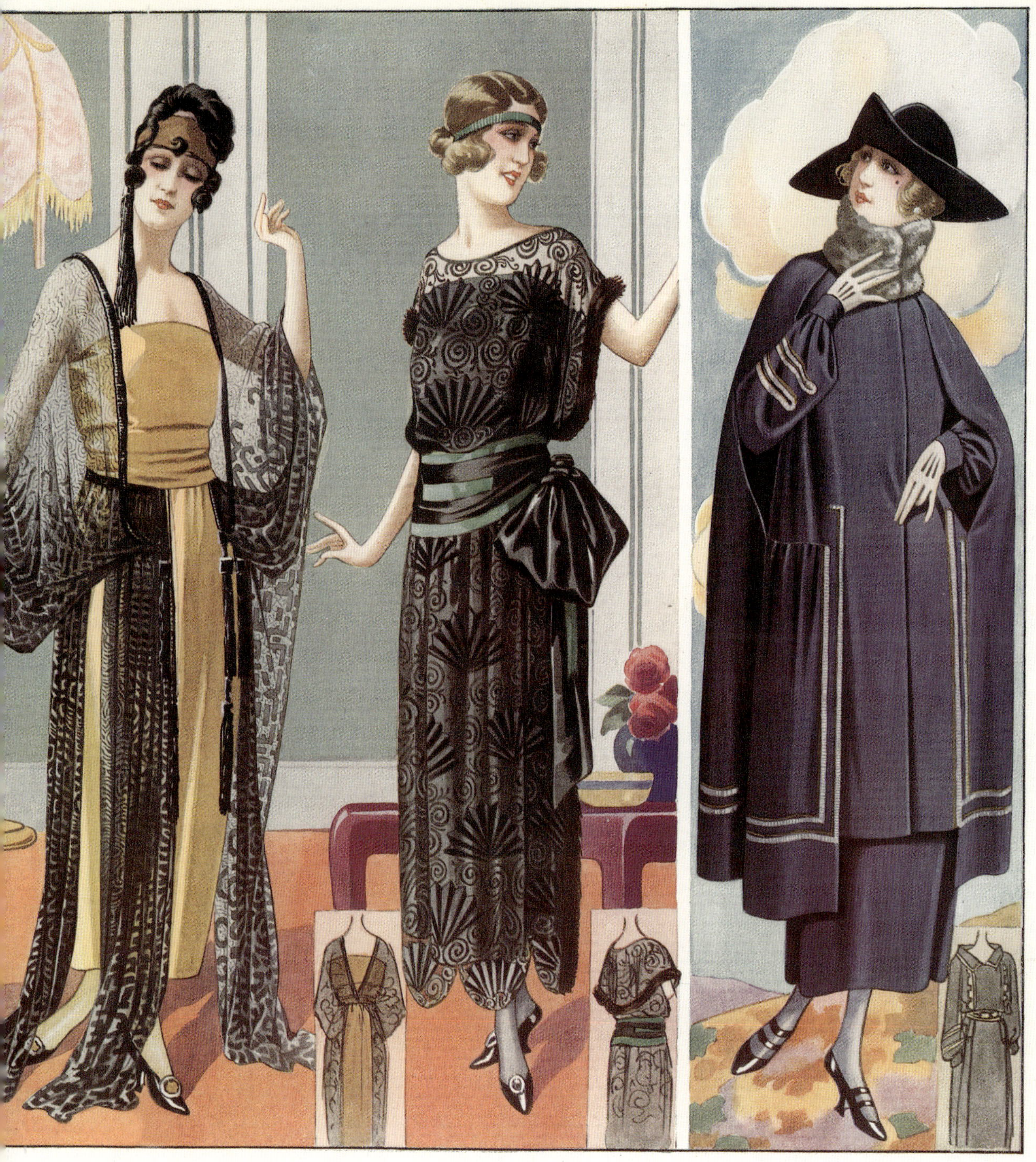

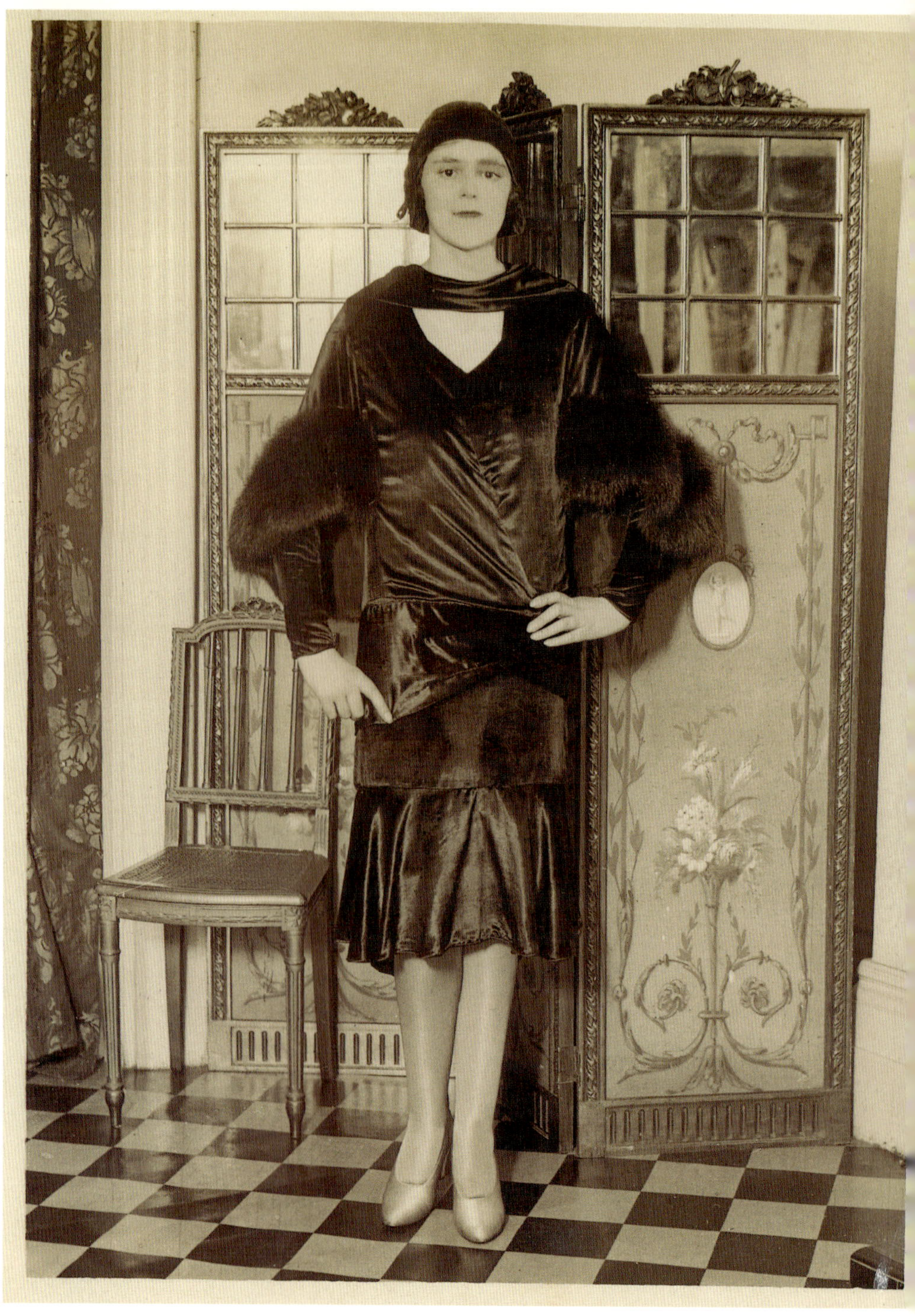

Above
A model wearing a black Panne velvet dress and cape trimmed with black fox fur, c.1925

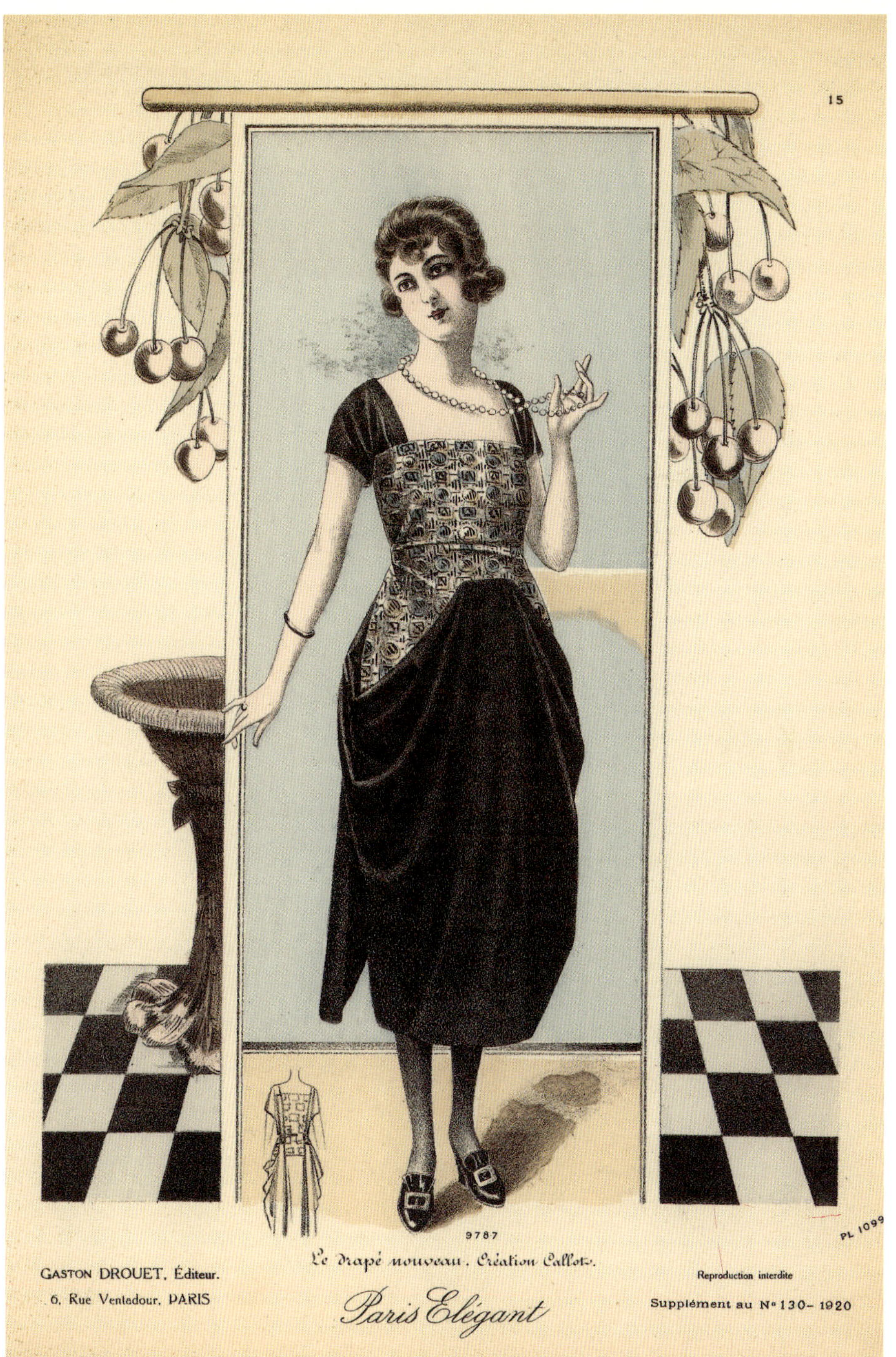

Above

A black evening dress with a fitted bodice and draped skirt by the Soeurs Callot. *Paris Élégant*, 1920

Right
Tiered green silk and lace evening dress with matching hat. *Paris Élégant*, 1921

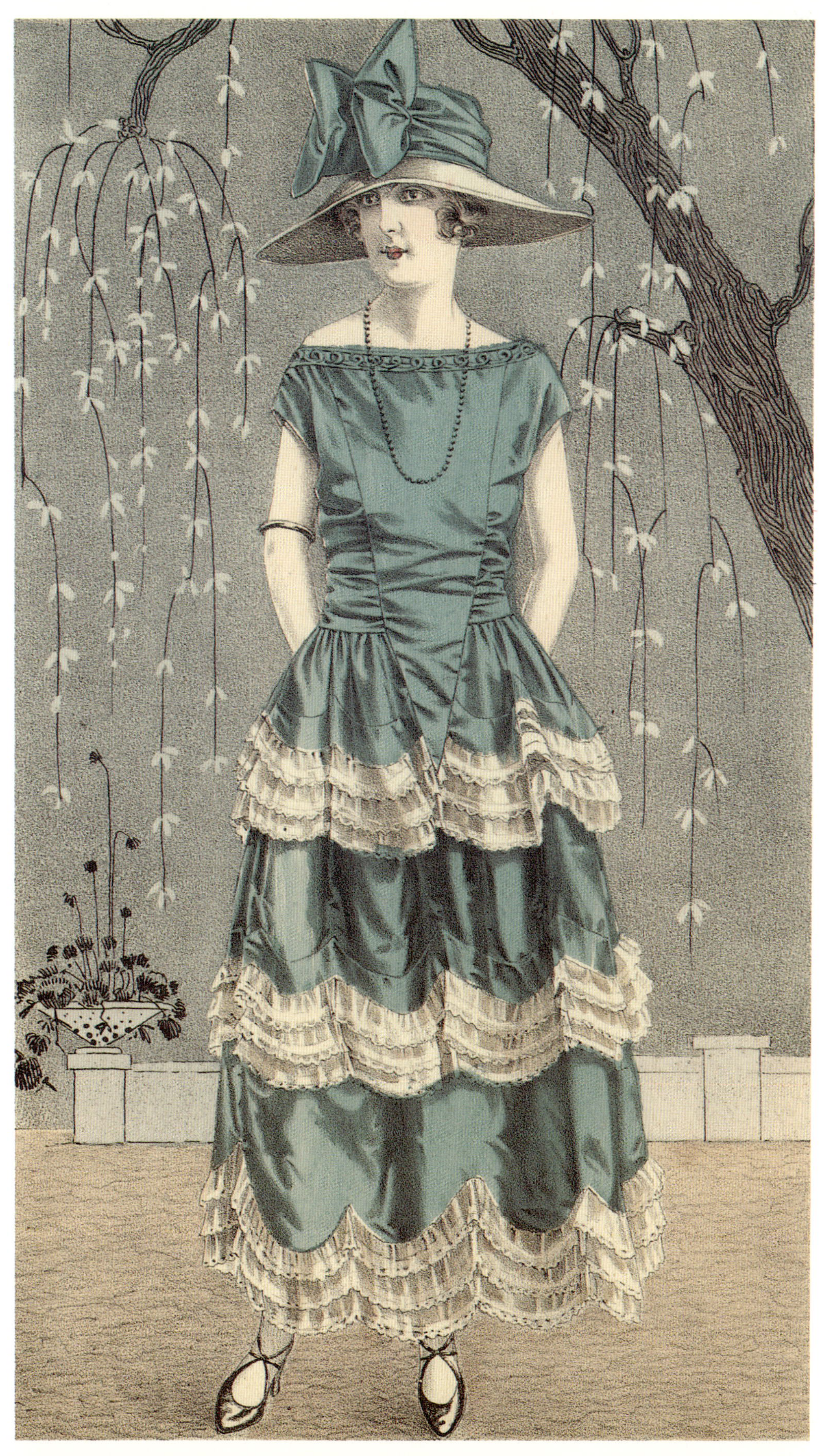

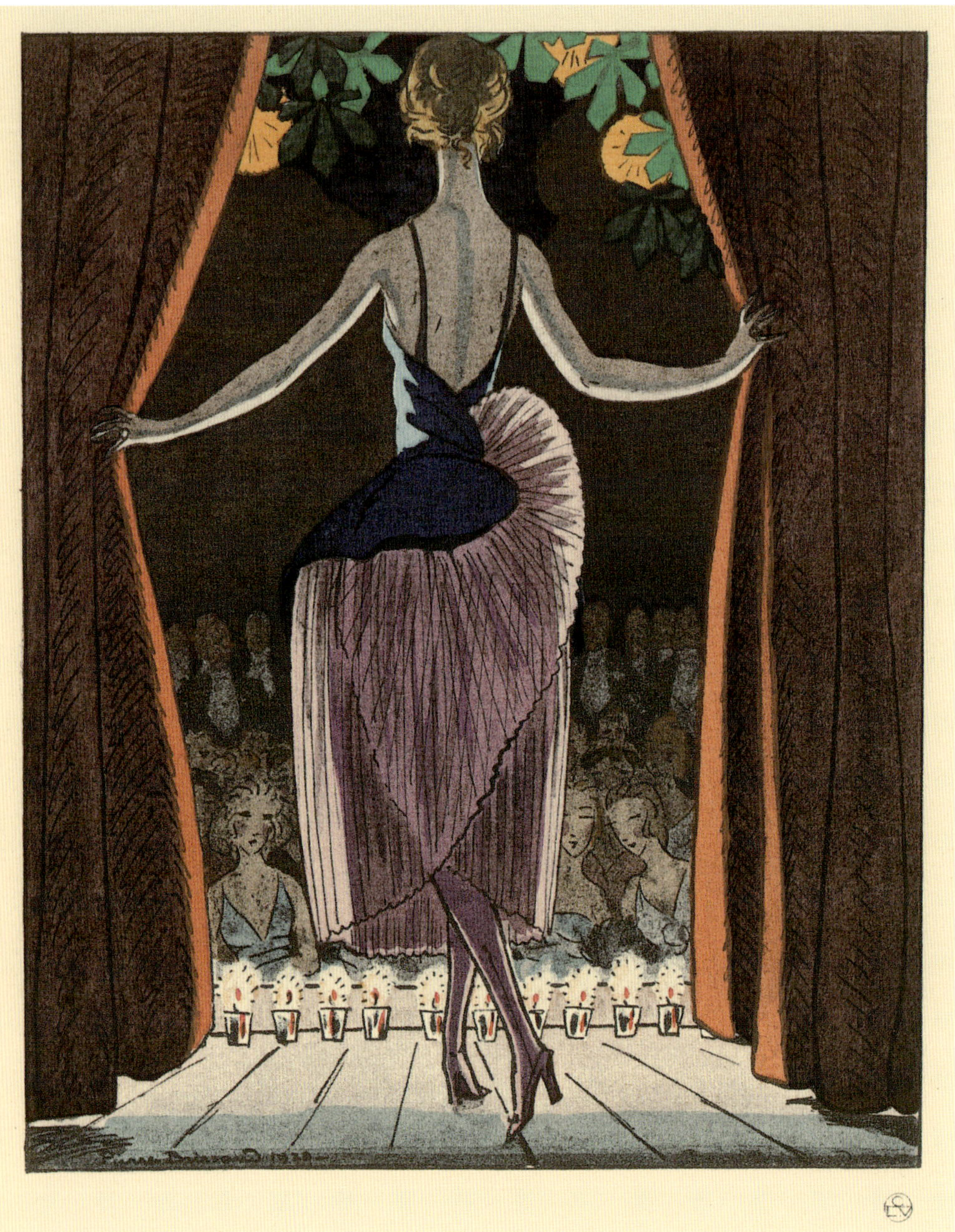

Above and right
"Le Prologue ou La Comedie au Chateau" (The Grand Opening), design for a stage dress. Illustration by Pierre Brissaud. *Gazette du Bon Ton*, 1920

A collection of silk blouses. The designs on various of the blouses shows the exotic influences so popular in the previous decade. *Paris-Blouses*, 1920.

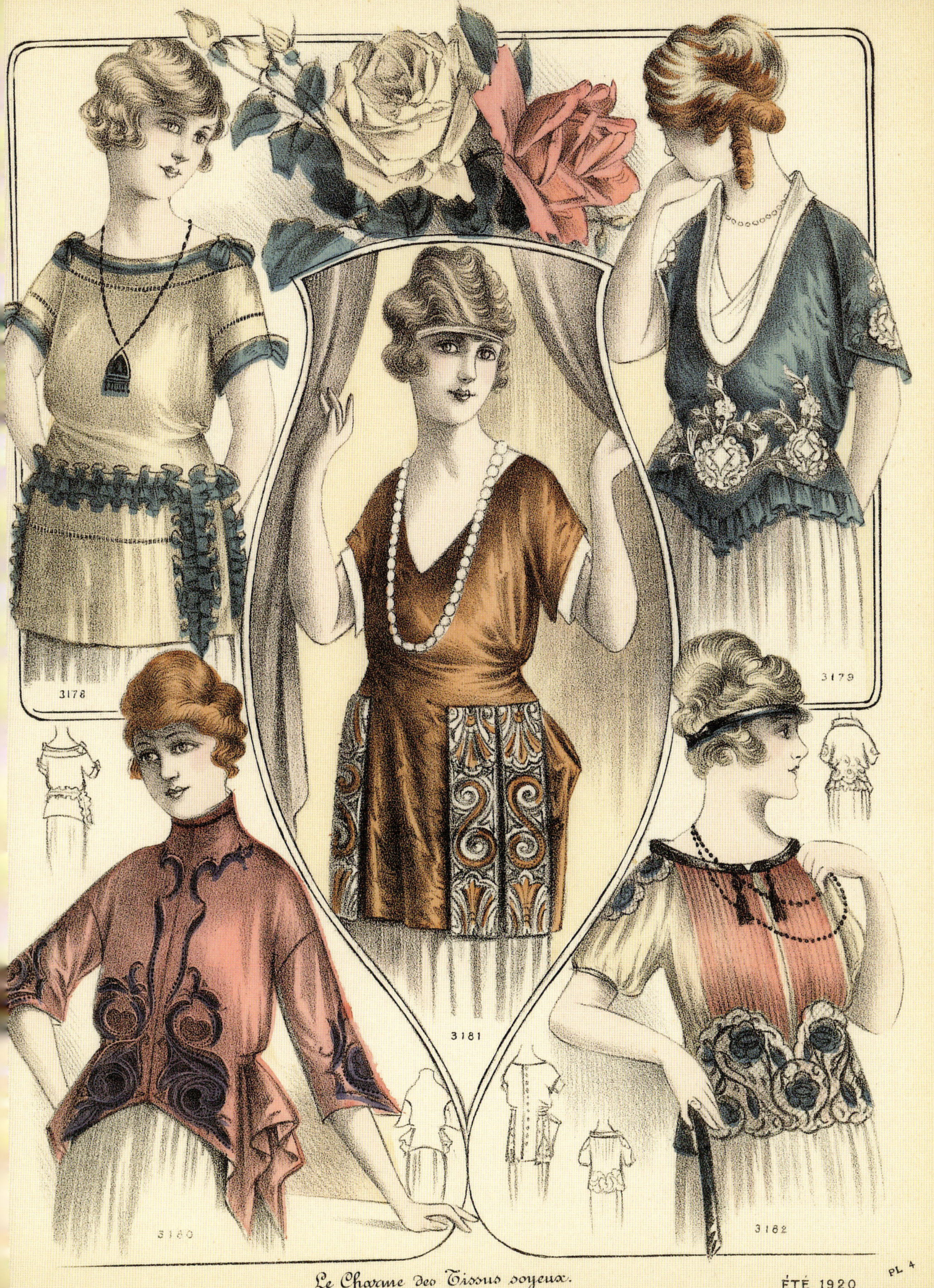
3178
3179
3181
3180
3182
Le Charme des Tissus soyeux.
ÉTÉ 1920
PL 4

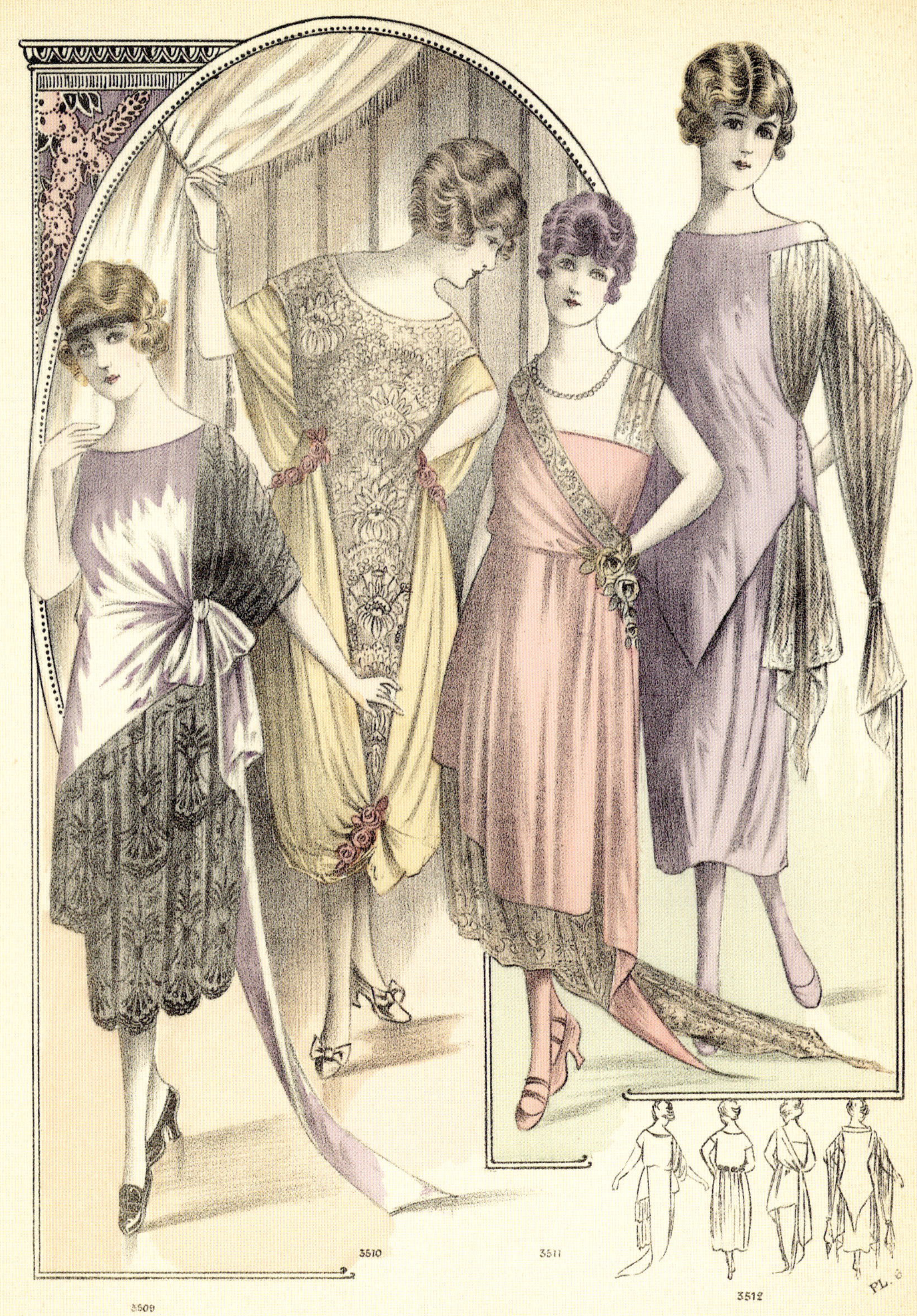
3509
3510
3511
3512
PL. 8
Les jolis Tea Gowns
Paris-Blouses.
HIVER 1920-1921
Reproduction interdite
Supplément au N° 11
Gaston DROUET, Éditeur.
6, Rue Ventadour, PARIS (1er arr^t)

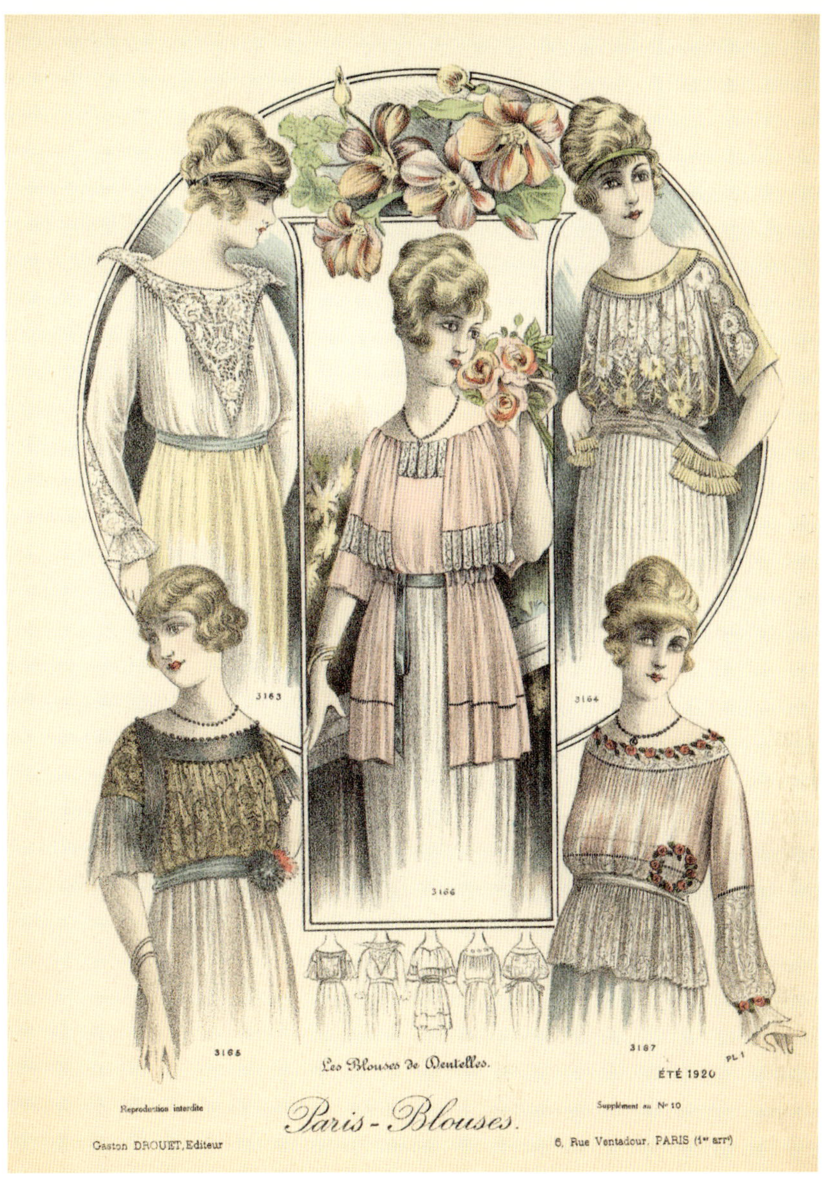

Left and above

Four French 'pretty' tea gowns in pink, yellow and purple, some with lace panelling and artificial flower detailing. Tea gowns were a late 19th century English invention, but the vogue for comfortable un-corseted afternoon dresses, initially only worn in the intimacy of one's own home, was quickly taken up by the French. By the 1920s the tea gown had moved out of the boudoir and the drawing room into more public spheres. *Paris-Blouses*, 1920-21

A collection of lace blouses. *Paris-Blouses*, 1920.

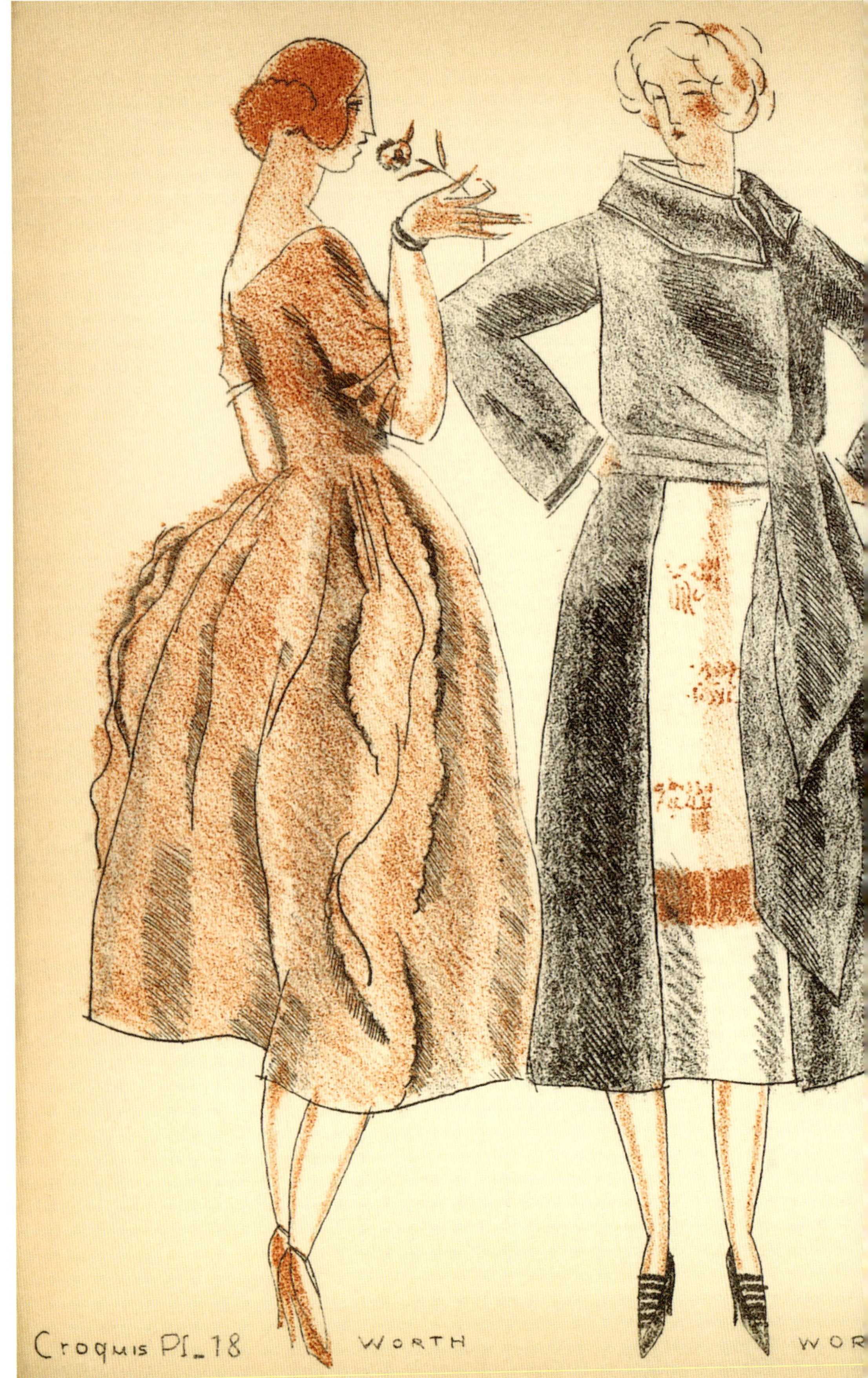
Croquis Pl_18
WORTH
WOR

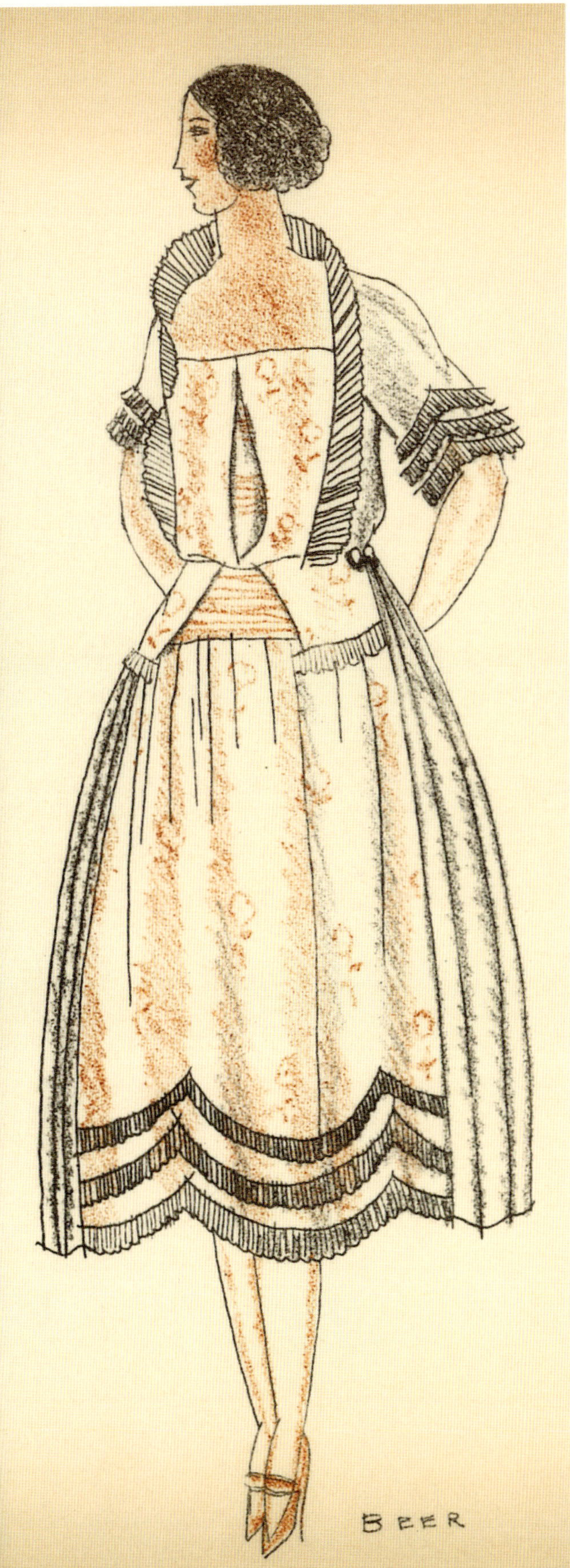

Left
Two silhouettes by Worth and one by Beer. These drawings were presented as 'Croquis', quick sketchy drawings of live models and are very different and more fluid than the Bon Ton's more formal fashion plates. *Gazette du Bon Ton*, 1920

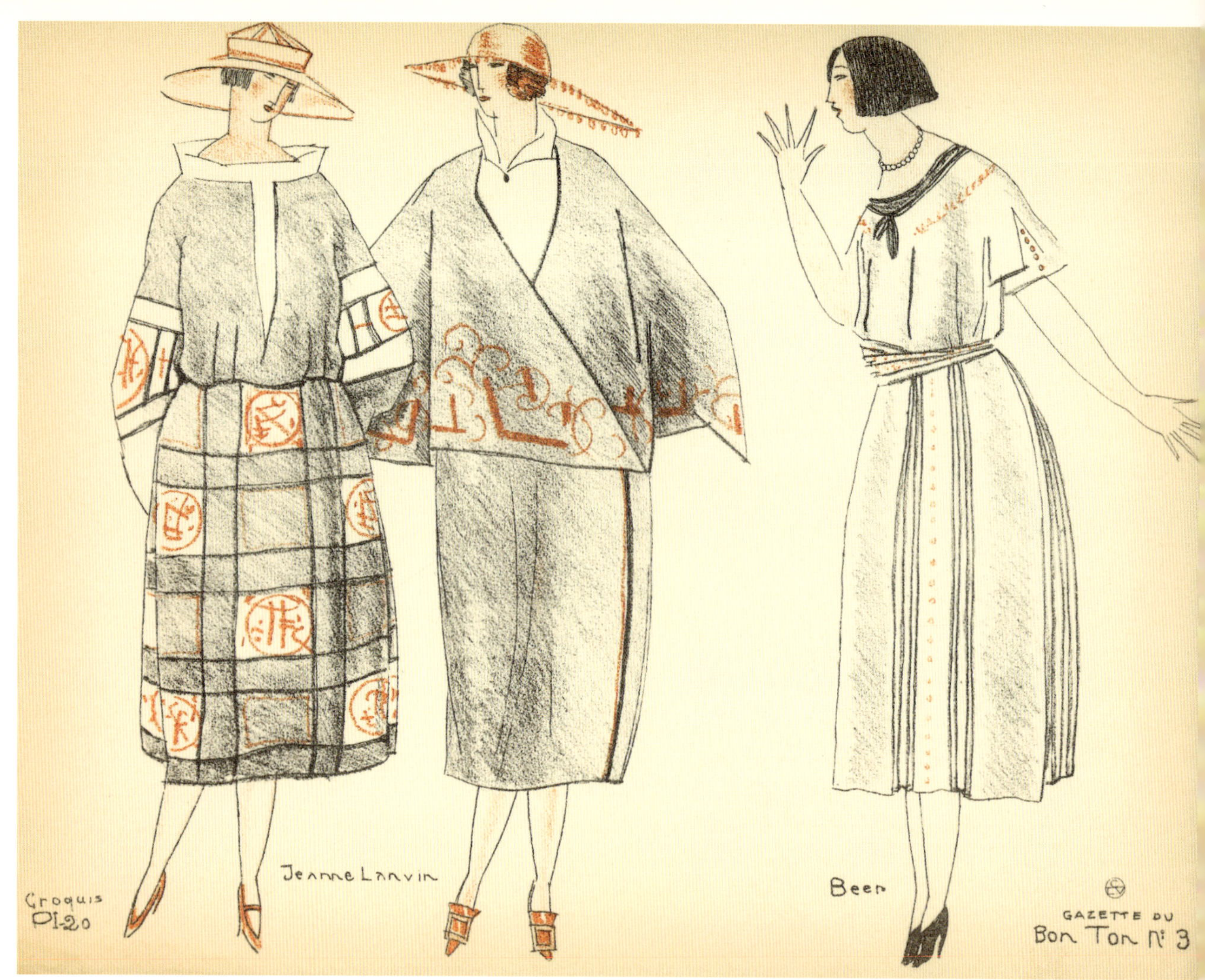

Above

Two silhouettes by Jeanne Lanvin and one by Beer. The Oriental influences of the Lanvin silhouettes are mirrored in the models' depiction and styling. *Gazette du Bon Ton*, c.1920

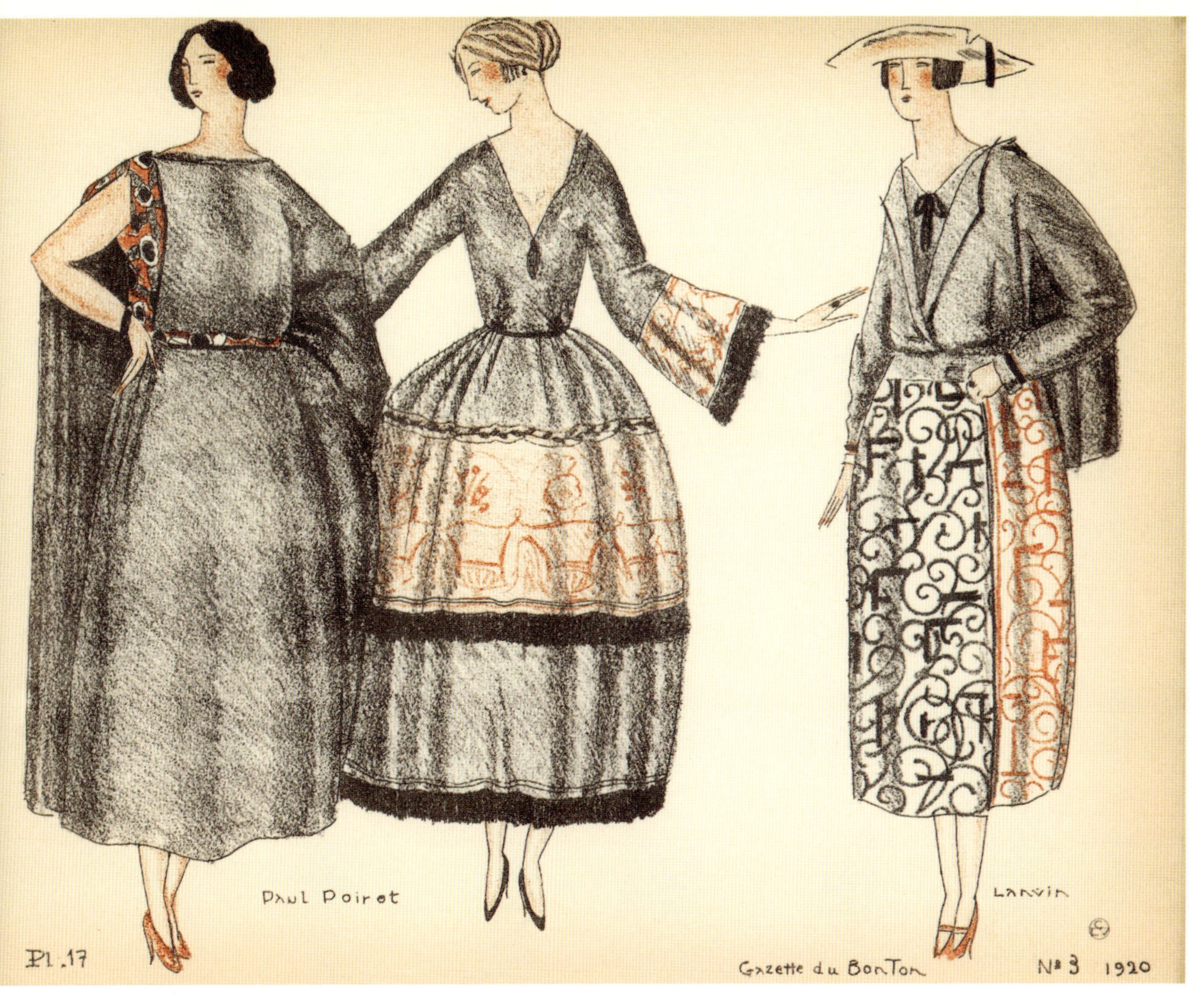

Above
Two evening dresses by Paul Poiret and a day ensemble by Jeanne Lanvin. The Poiret dresses present a contemporary use of historic influences: the dress on the left is a stylised modern version of a Greek chiton, and the dress on the right takes inspiration both for the silhouette and the decorated skirt panel from 18th century pannier dresses. The Lanvin model draws inspiration from the 19th century sailor suit. *Gazette du Bon Ton*, 1920

Right
Evening ensemble by Worth. *L'Illustration des Modes*, 1920

Next page
"Une Fête de Venise" (Venice Festival) – black evening dress with green scarf by Worth, pink silk dress by Poiret, silver and diamante dress by Beer, yellow dress with green motifs by Martial et Armand, and evening ensemble with satin and fur coat by Doeuillet. *L'Illustration des Modes*, 1920

Première Année. — N° 2. REVUE BI-MENSUELLE Jeudi 4 Novembre 1920.

L'ILLUSTRATION DES MODES

Lucien Vogel Directeur

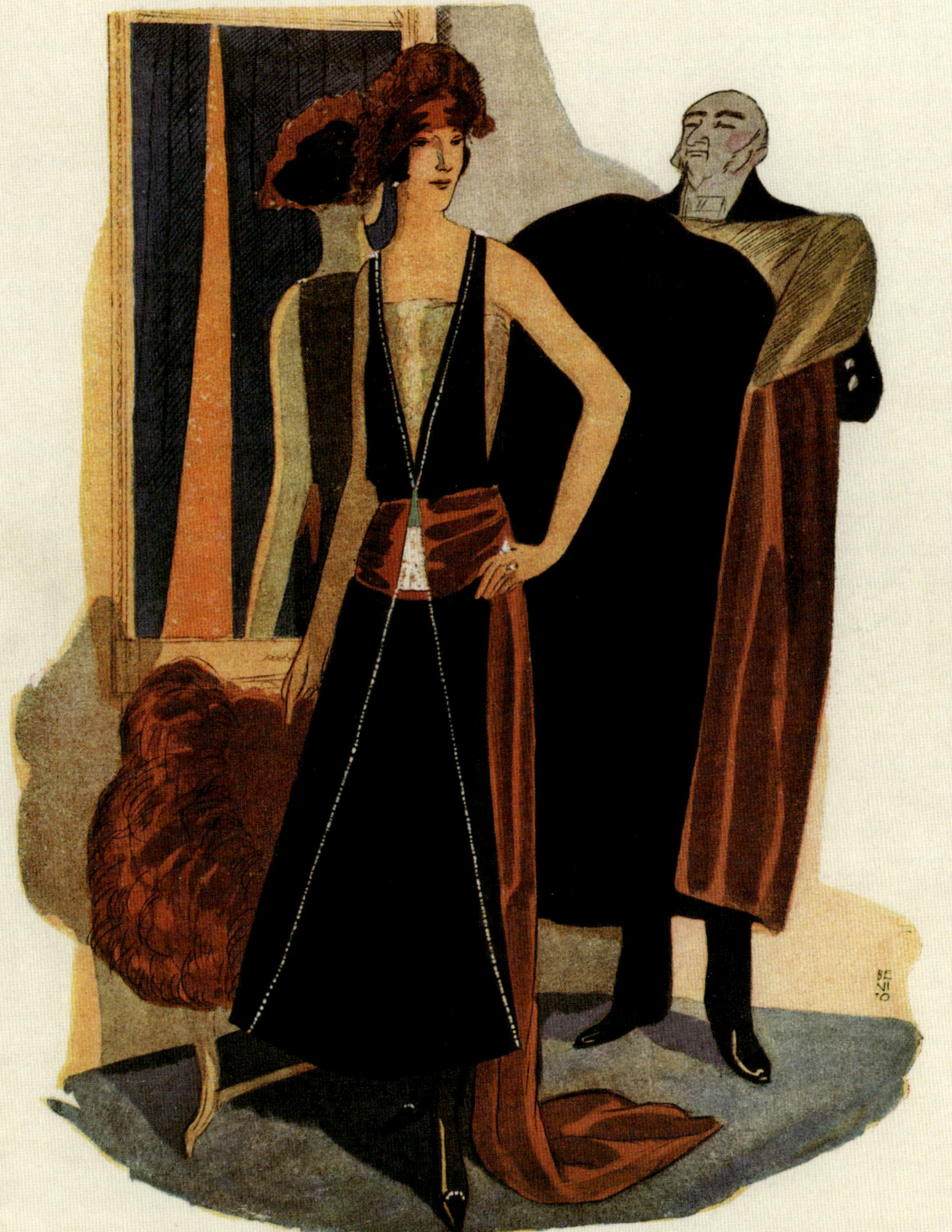

"MON MANTEAU..." ou LE DÉPART DES INVITÉS

Un Ensemble pour le Soir, de Worth (11)

Prix du Numéro : 2 fr. 50. 13, Rue St-Georges, Paris.

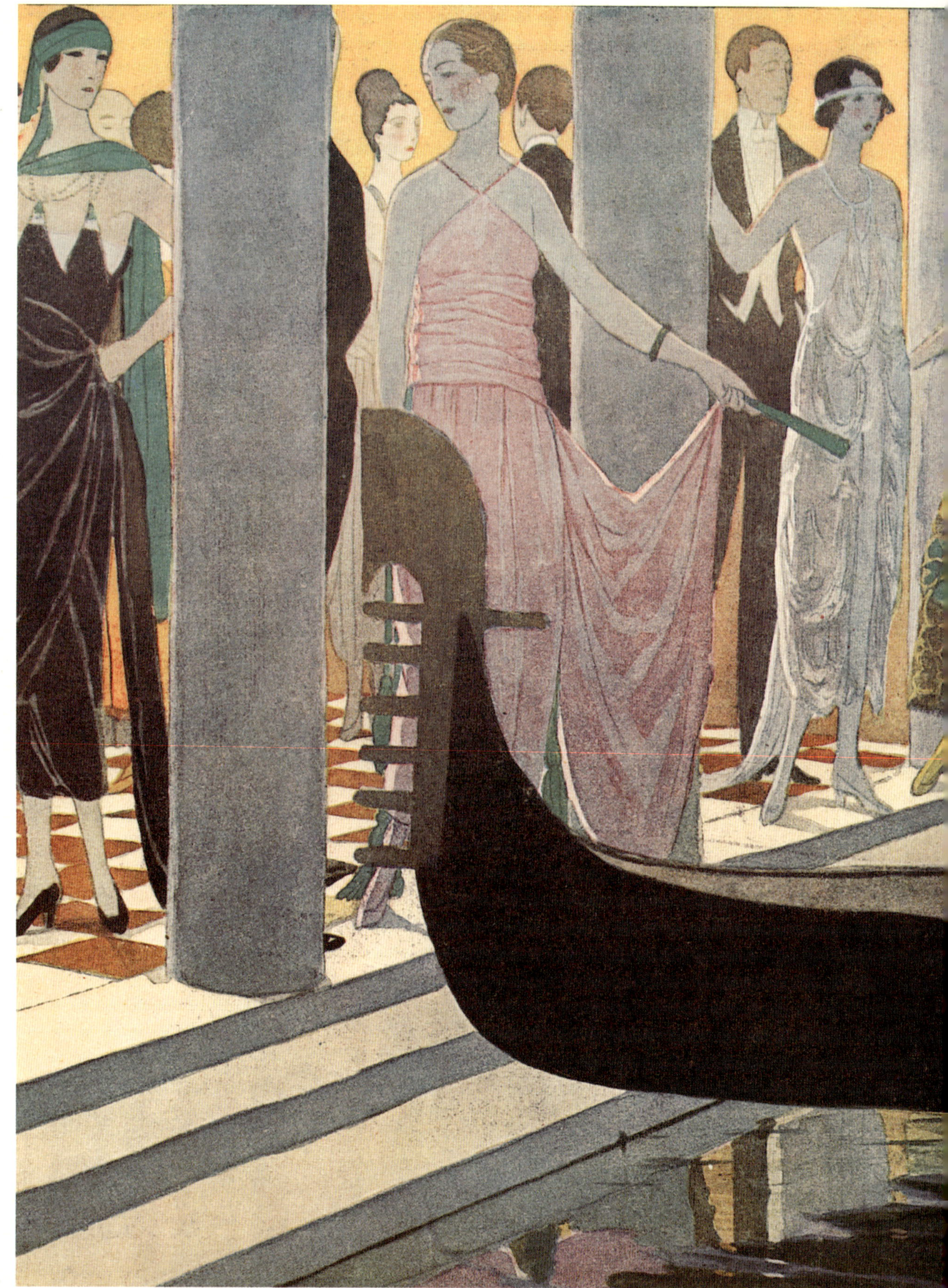

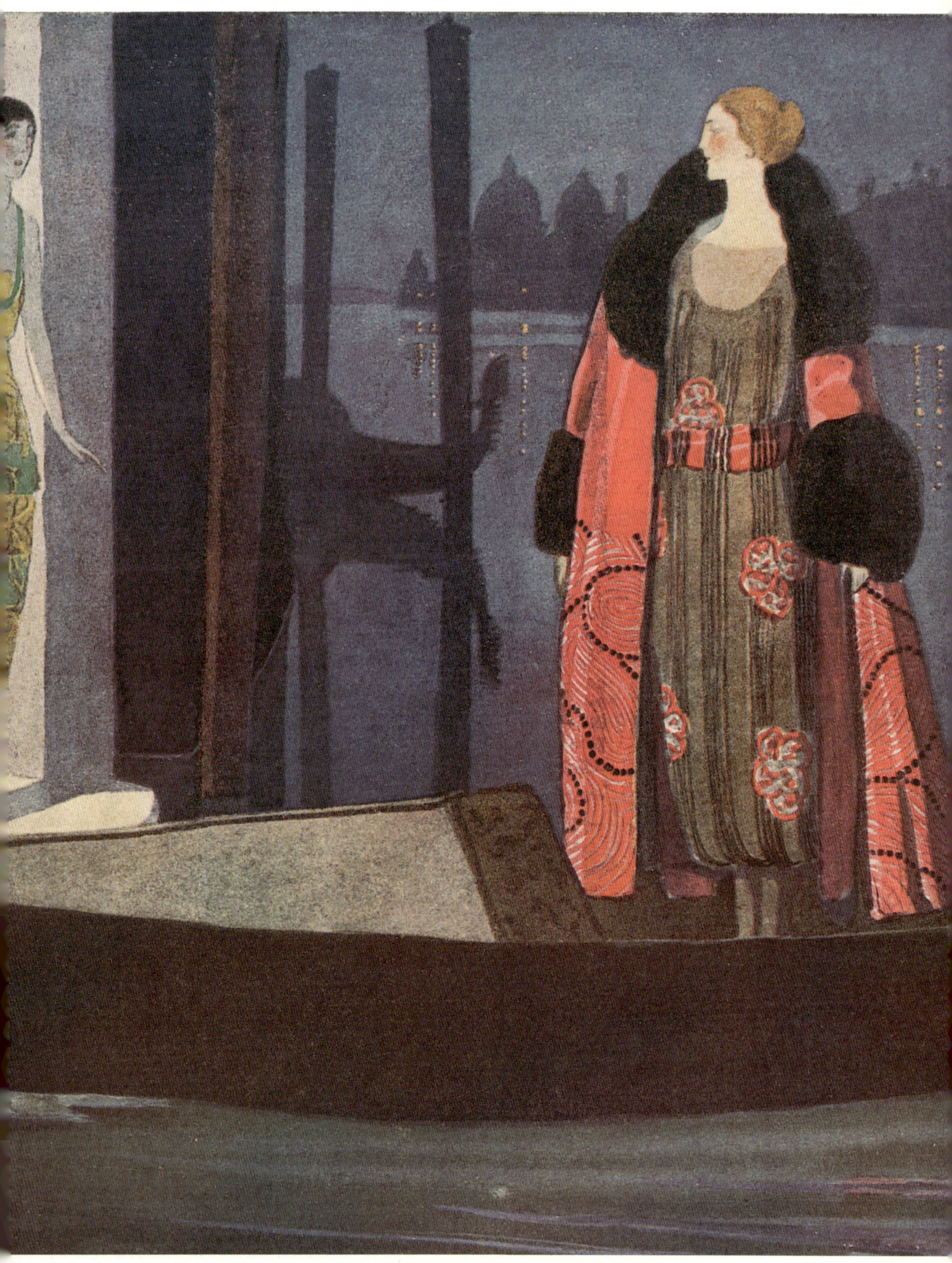

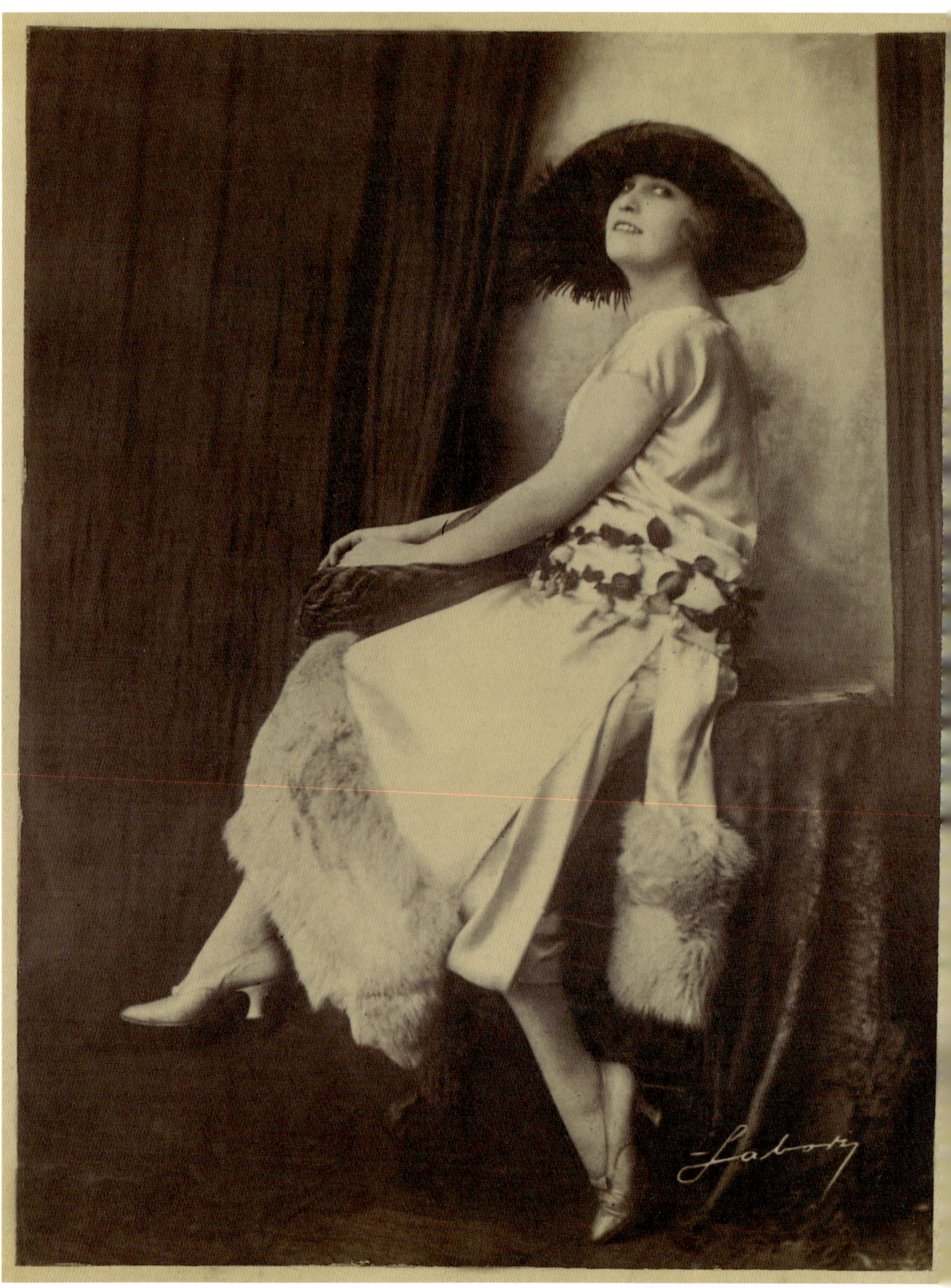

Above
A woman wearing a fur-trimmed tunic worn over a skirt and belted with a band of fabric embellished with artificial leaves, c.1923

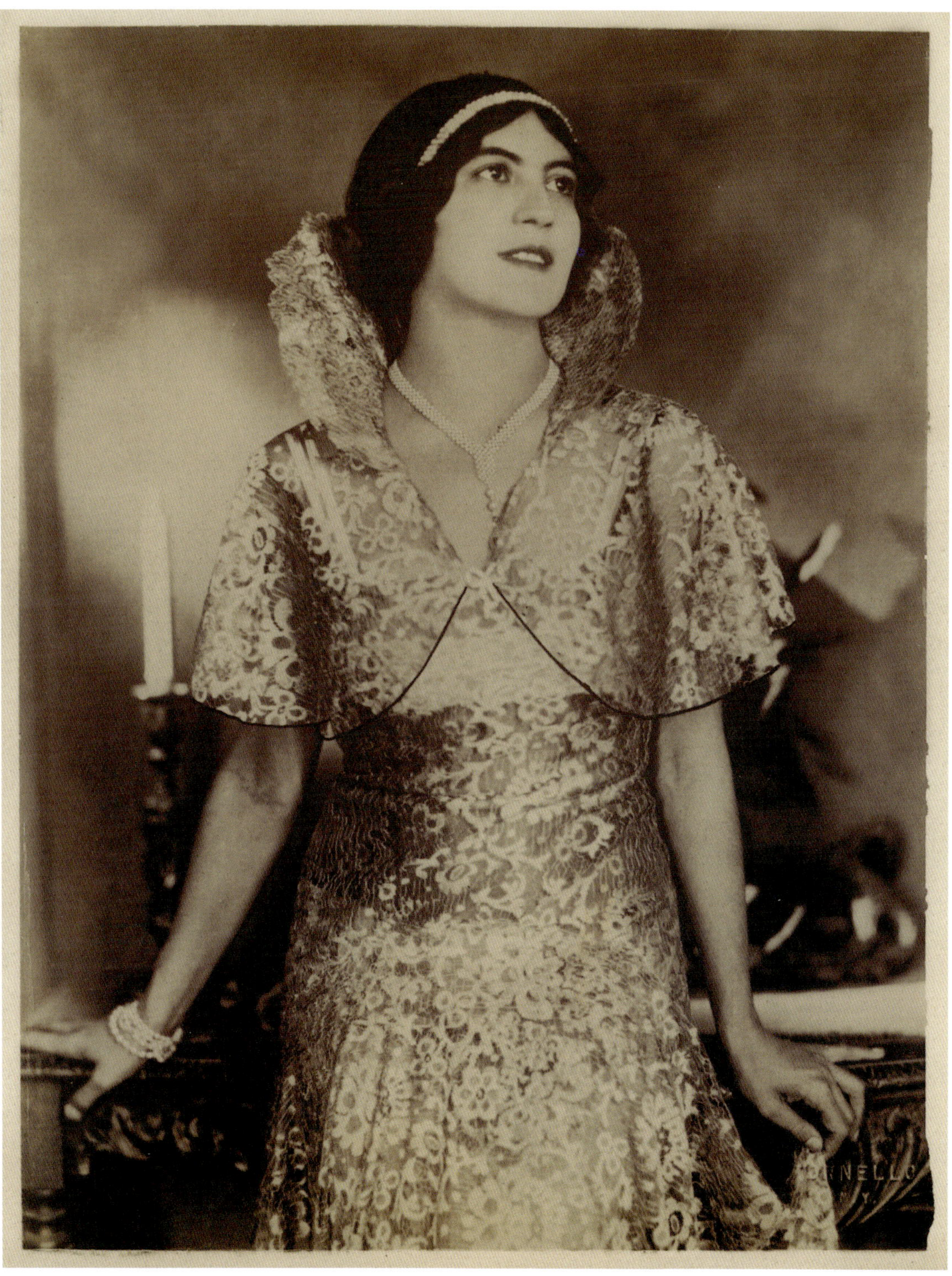

Above
American designer Marion Stehlik wearing one of her own creations made of lace with an Elizabethan-style collar, c.1927

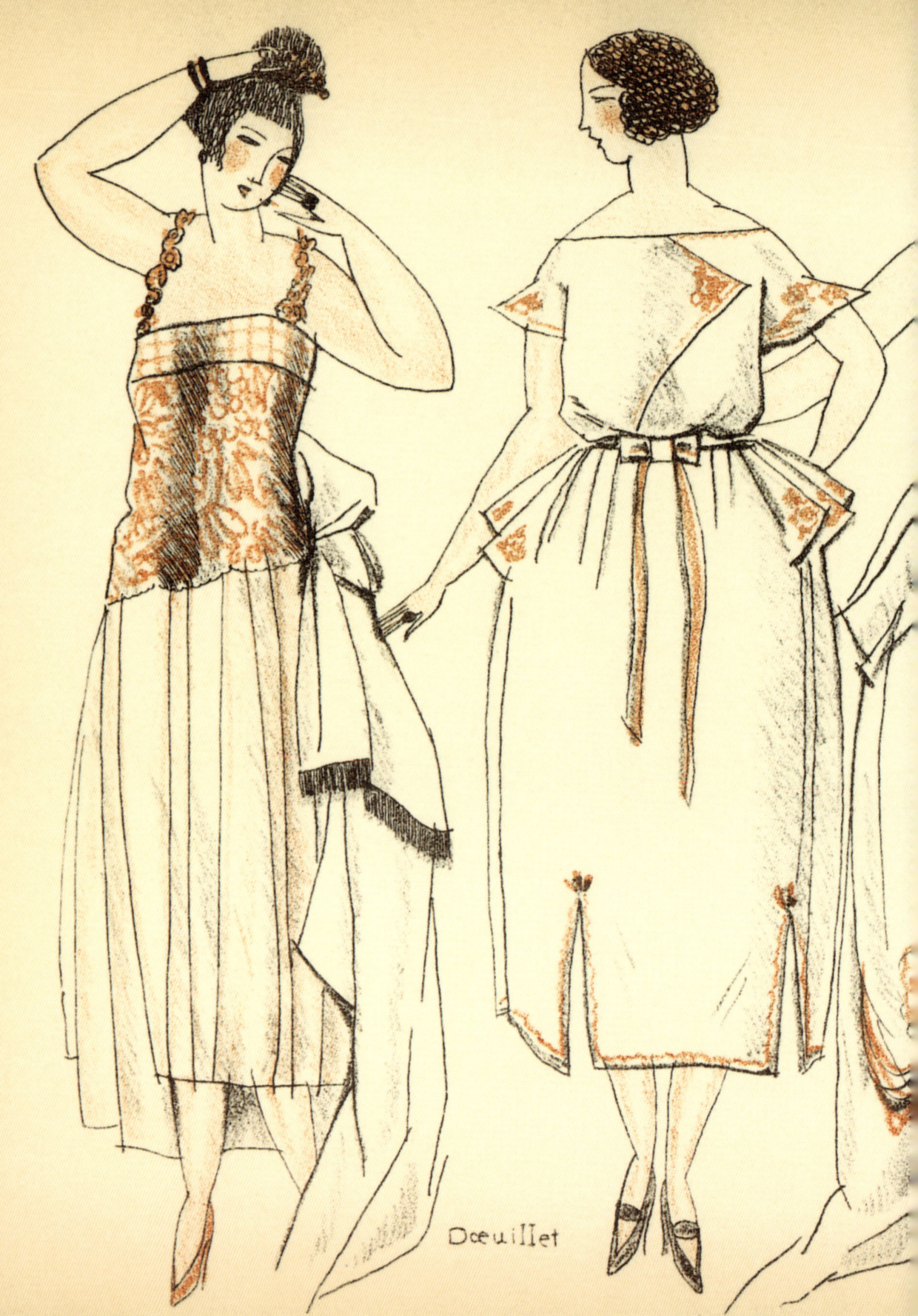
Pl 19
Dœuillet

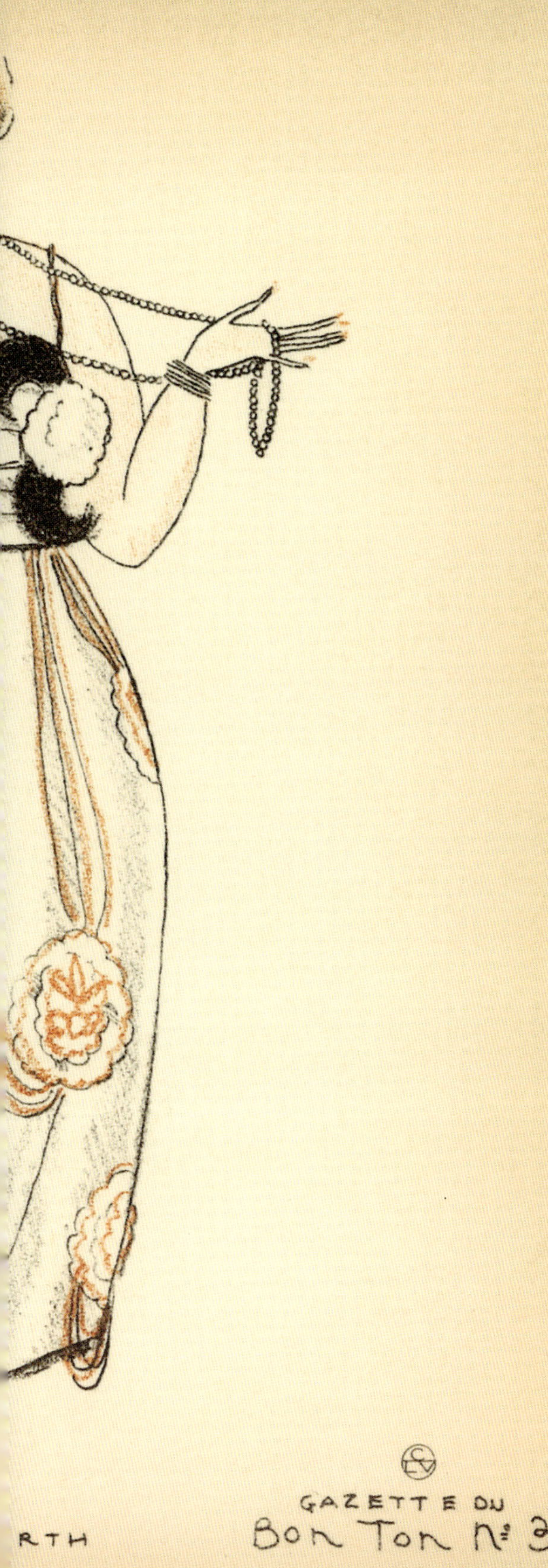

Left
Two evening gowns by Doeuillet and one by Worth. The models' nonchalant poses are typical of the way women were represented in graphic design, including fashion illustration in the first half of the 1920s. *Gazette du Bon Ton*, 1920

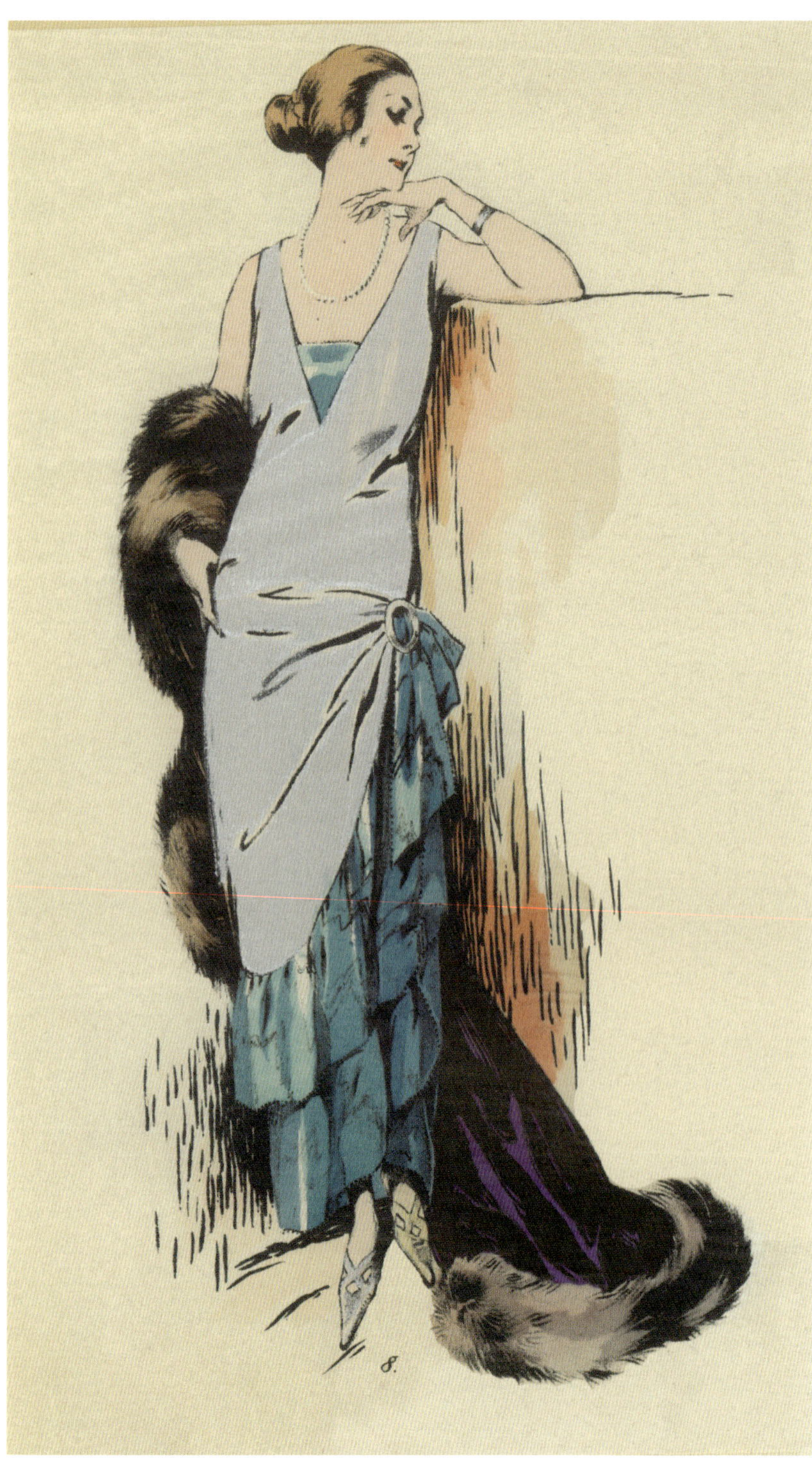

Above
A silver lamé and green moiré evening dress with skirt flounces. *Dernières Créations*, c.1923

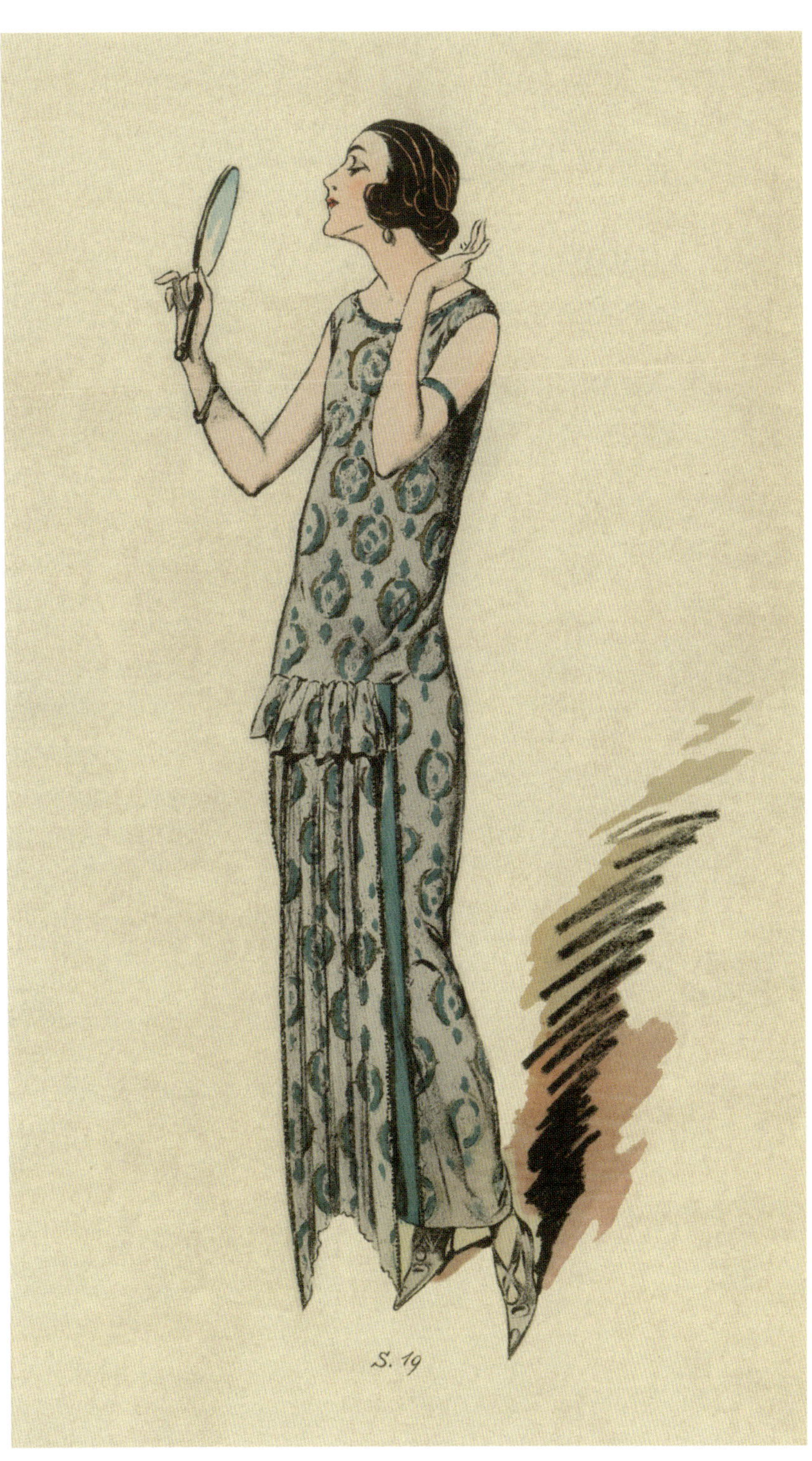

Above
A silk damask grey and light green evening dress with a gathered tablier.
Dernières Créations, c.1923

Right
Hollywood actress Pauline Frederick wearing a brocade satin evening gown with crystal trimmings, accessorised with a large marabou fan, a gold leaf headband and satin shoes, c.1922

Next page
Seven evening dresses by Atelier Bachroitz. *Chic Parisien Beaux-Arts des Modes*, c.1926. The dresses show the wide variety of fashionable styles on offer, from tiered romantic lace dresses, to fur-trimmed sash dresses, richly embellished sack dresses and black evening dresses in lace or with low-cut backs.

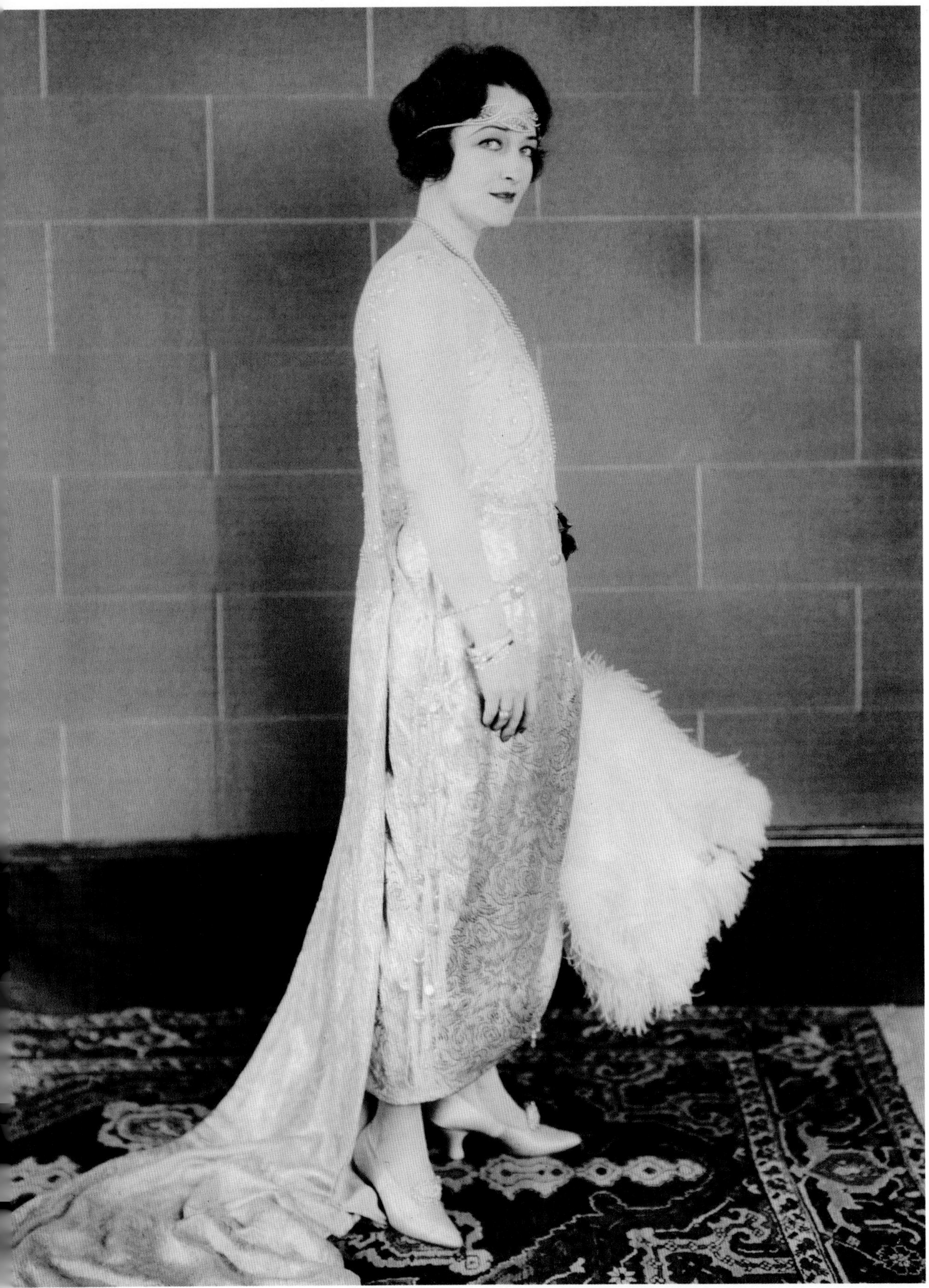

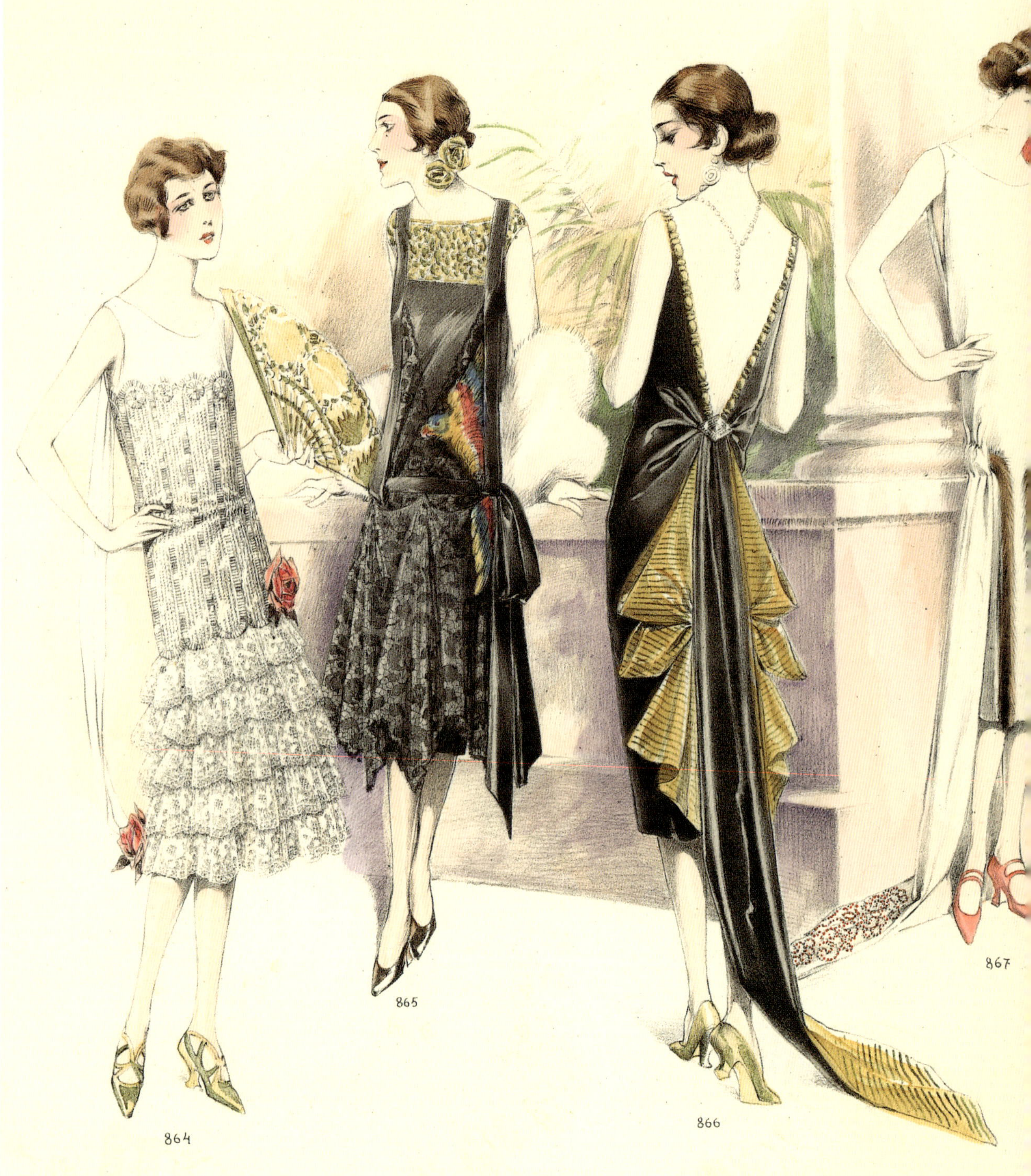
865
867
864
866

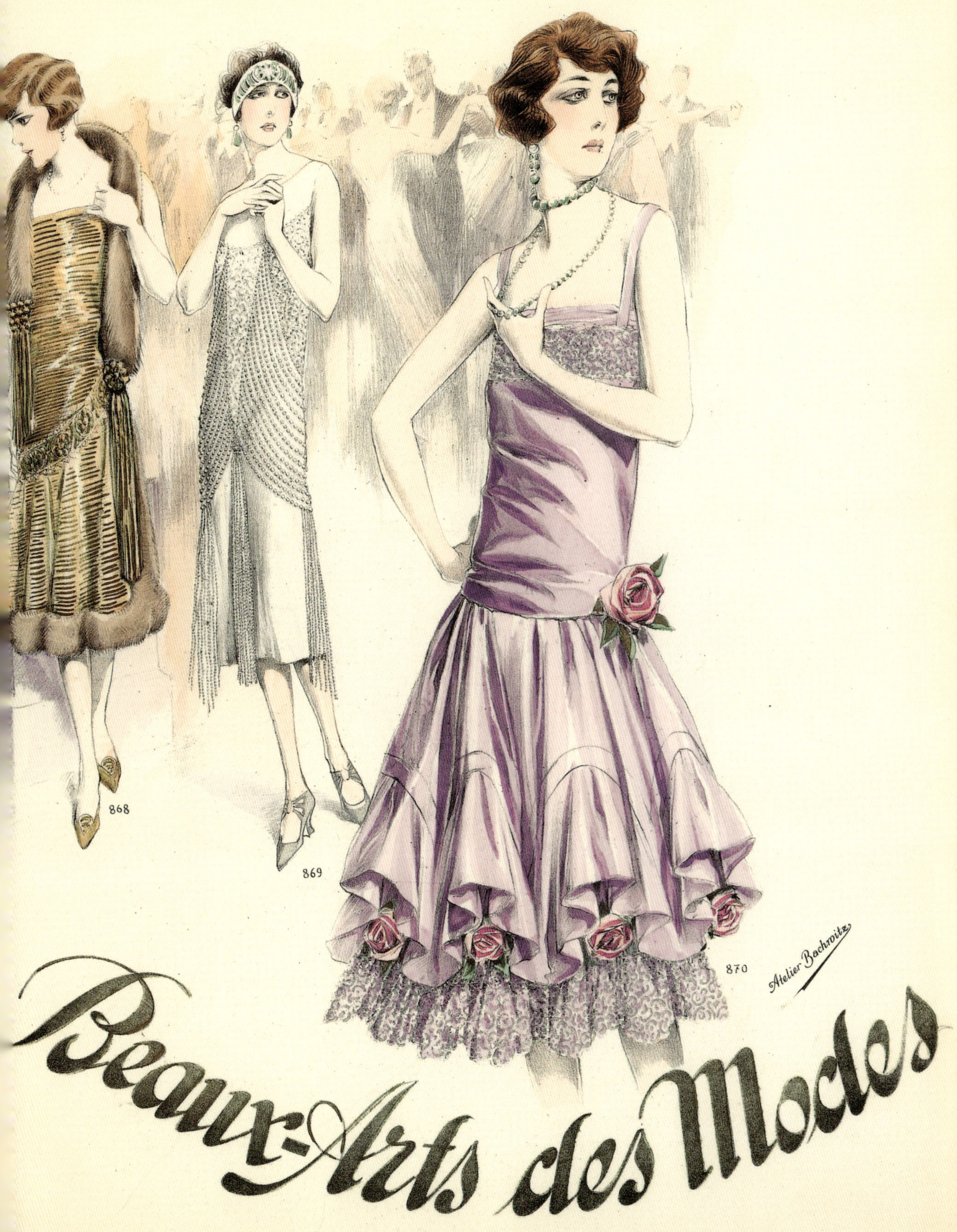
868
869
870
Atelier Bachwitz
Beaux-Arts des Modes

Right
A gold brocade evening coat with a large multicoloured collar and a pink and grey dancing dress. *Paris Élégant*, c.1925

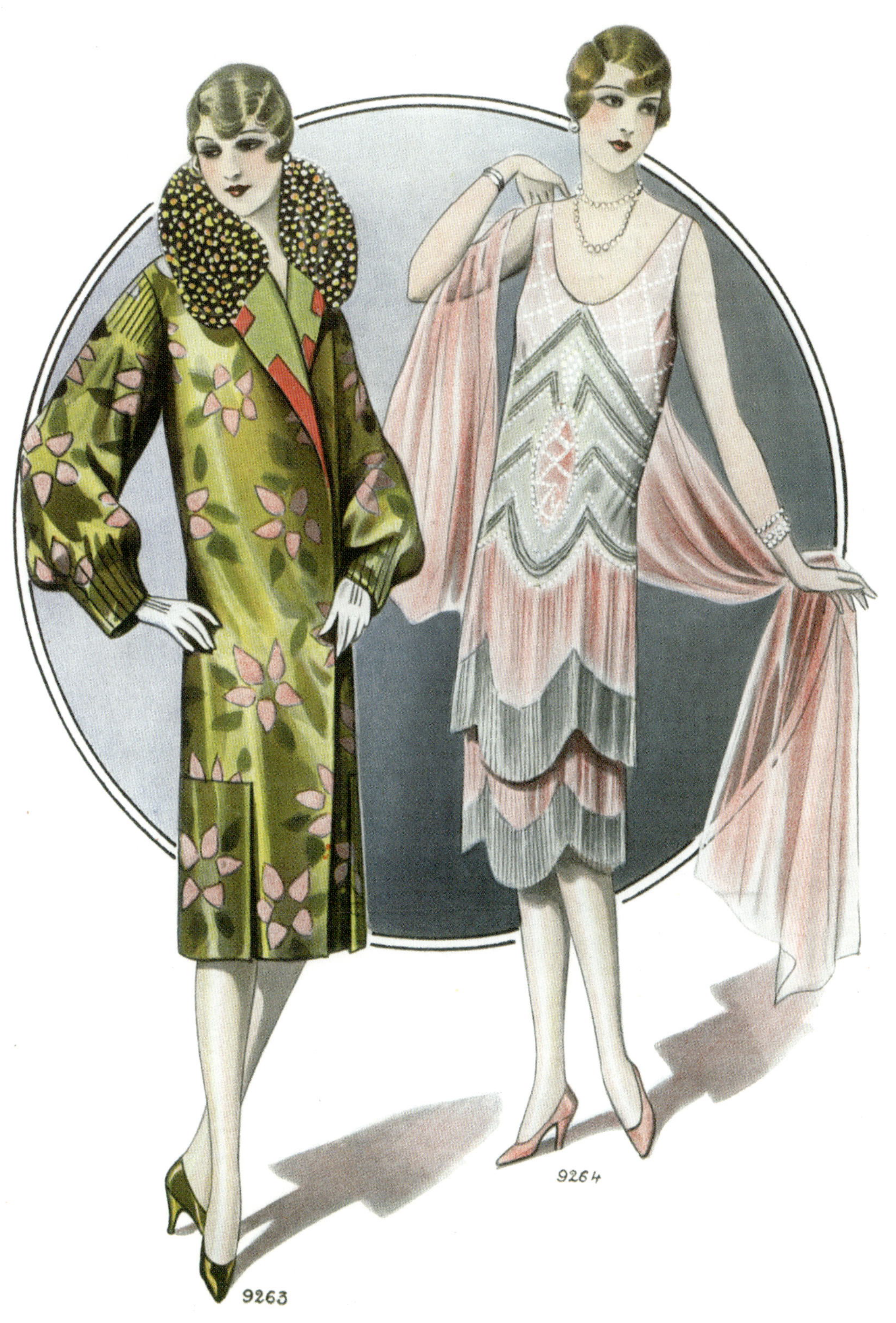

Très élégant ensemble pour le soir créé par Mariette Pognot.

GASTON DROUET, Éditeur - Gérant
29, rue de la Sourdière,
PARIS (1er)

PARIS-ÉLÉGANT
Supplément au N° 230. — Pl. 565

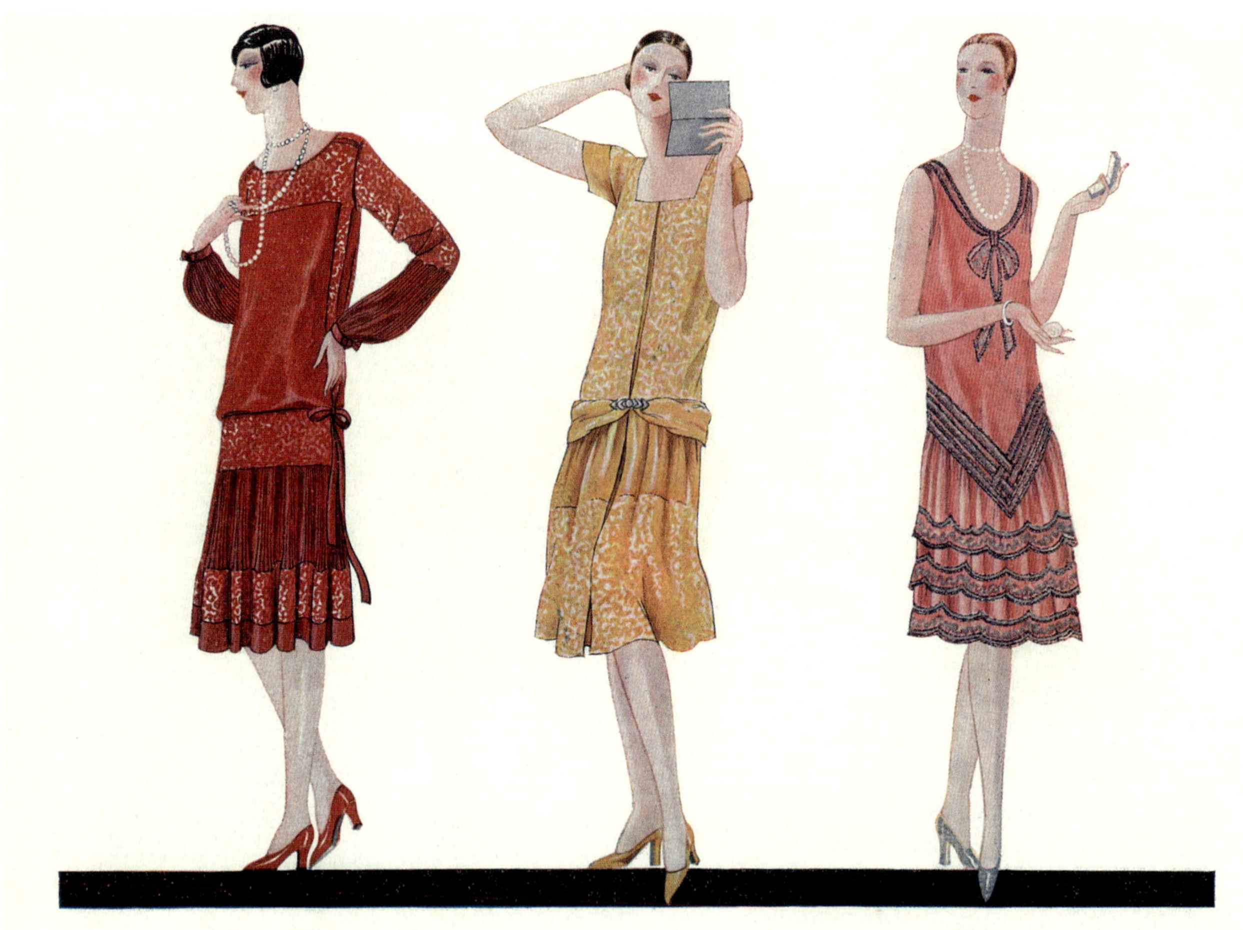

Above and right

Three evening dresses by Maison Gerda. Maison Gerda Catalogue, c.1925

Design for a turban headdress. *Les Chapeaux du "Trés Parisien"*, 1923-1924

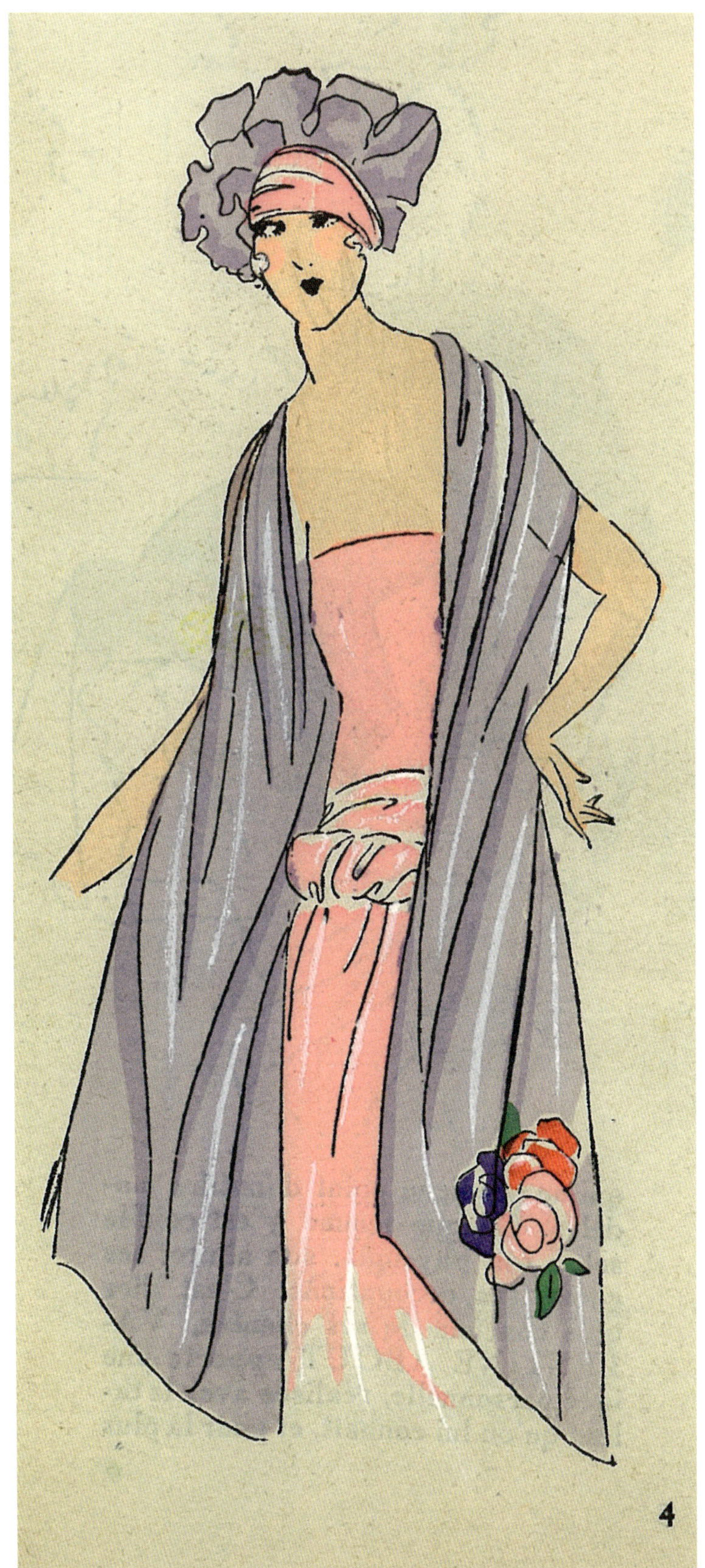
4

Below

A ball gown of gold lace worn over a gold lamé slip dress with a matching fringed scarf, and a ball dress of crepe de Chine with richly beaded embroidery by Atelier Bachroitz. *Chic Parisien Beaux-arts des Modes*, 1925

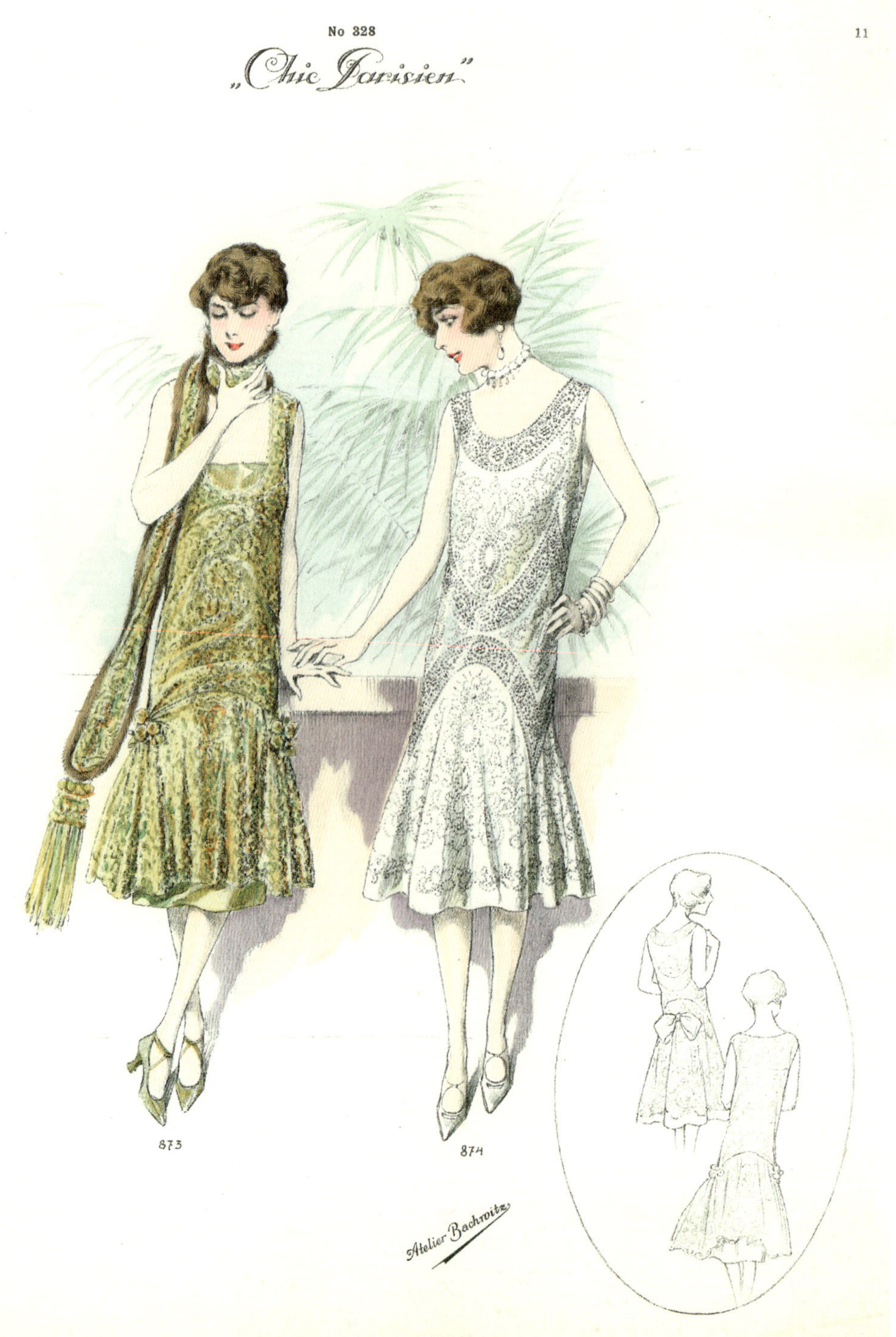

Below
Georgette evening dress embroidered with multicoloured tinsels, and an informal satin evening robe embroidered with a flower border on the left and back by Atelier Bachroitz. *Chic Parisien Beaux-Arts des Modes*, 1927

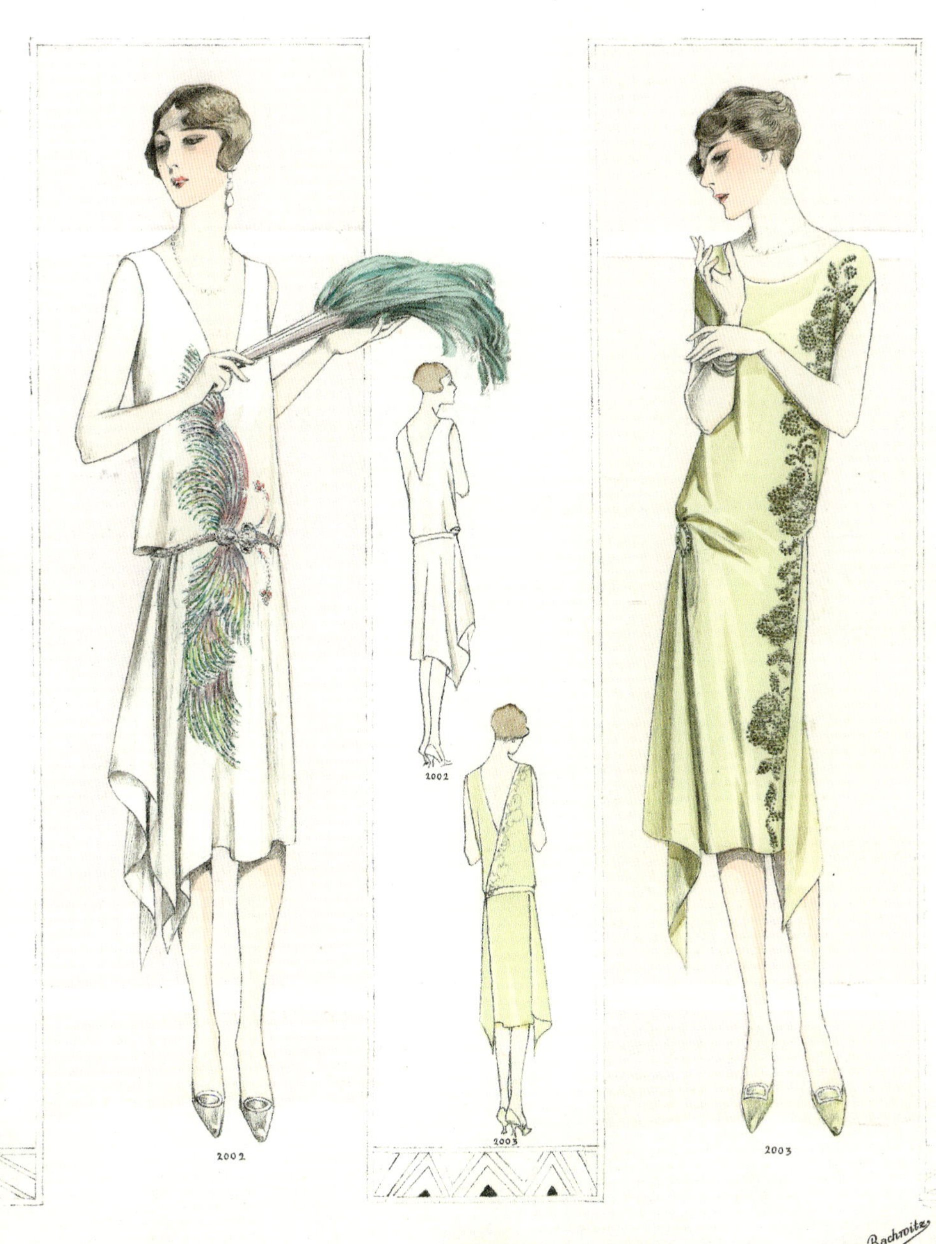

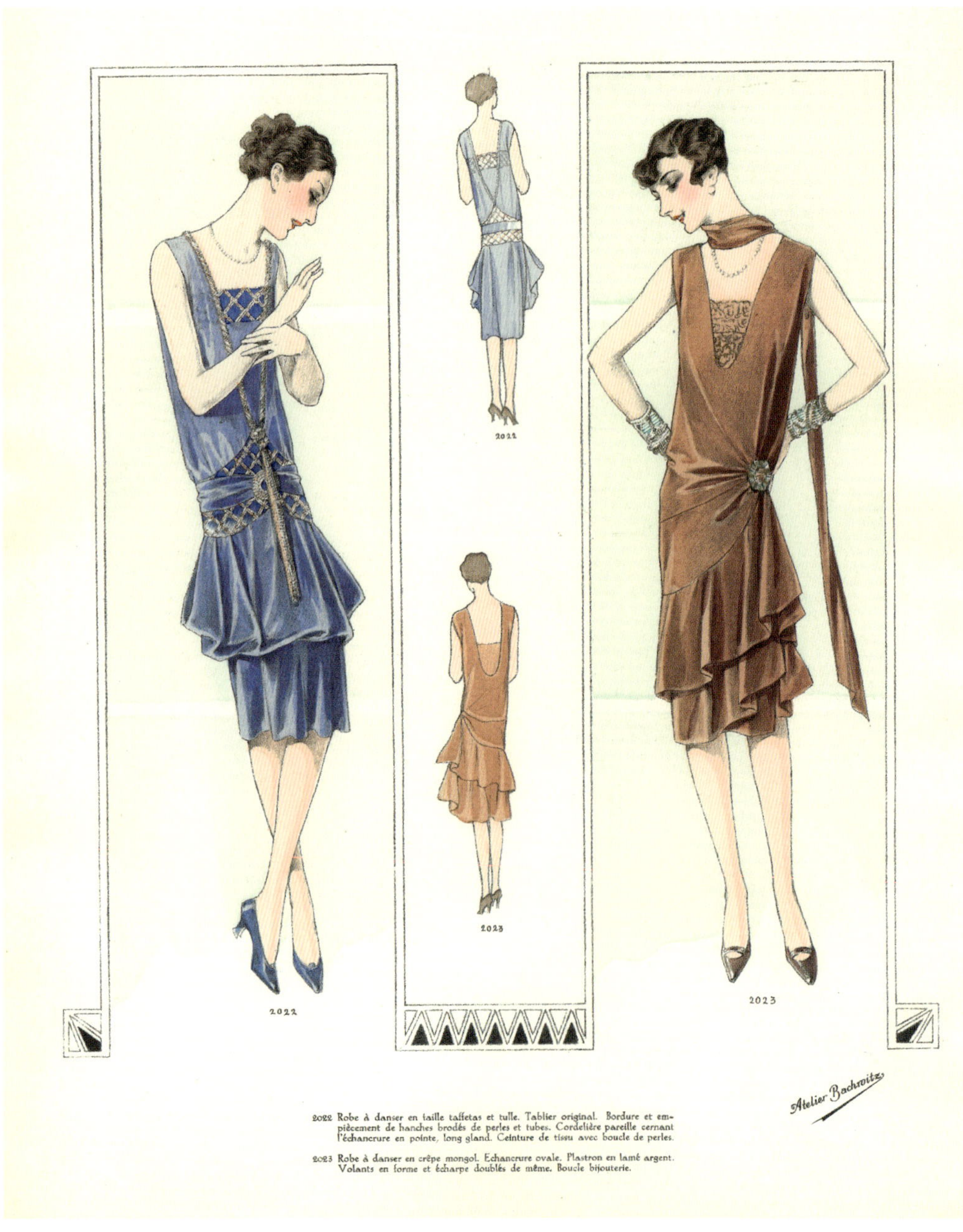

Above

Faille and tulle dancing frock with tasseled and embroidered detailing, and a crepe dancing dress with bell shaped flounces by Atelier Bachroitz. *Chic Parisien Beaux-Arts des Modes*, 1927

Right

Satin evening dress with a bolero shaped top flaring out below on the right as a circular yoke and a lace lower part, and a dancing frock in metal lace on a satin slip by Atelier Bachroitz. *Chic Parisien Beaux-Arts des Modes*, 1927

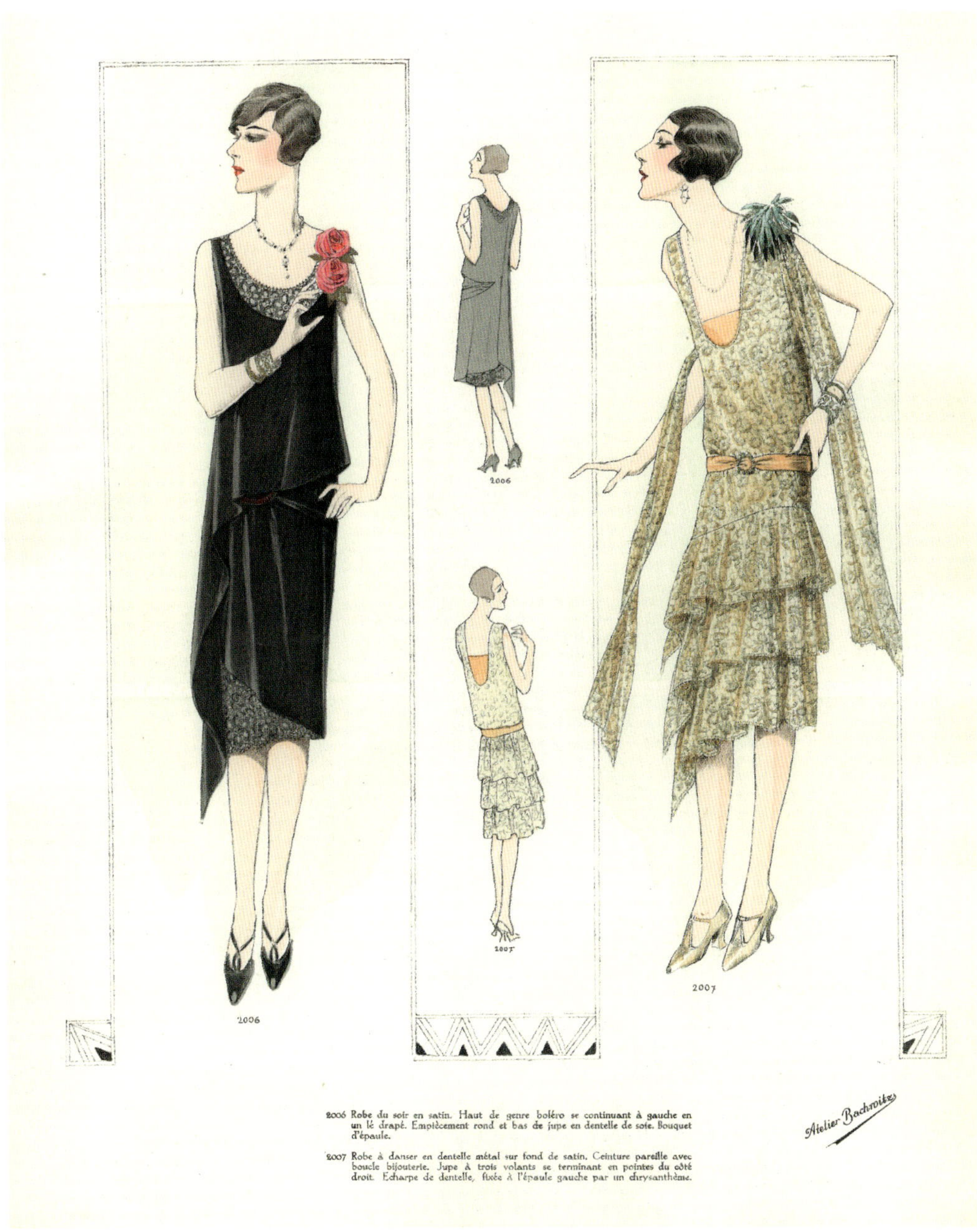

Next page
"Dresses in all styles", black evening gown with loops of pearls and sequinned pink evening gown by Eugénie et Juliette; fur-trimmed ensemble, black day dress and maroon ensemble by Alice Bernard; yellow evening gown with artificial roses and black velvet and pink satin evening gown by Alice Bernard.
La Femme Chic, 1926

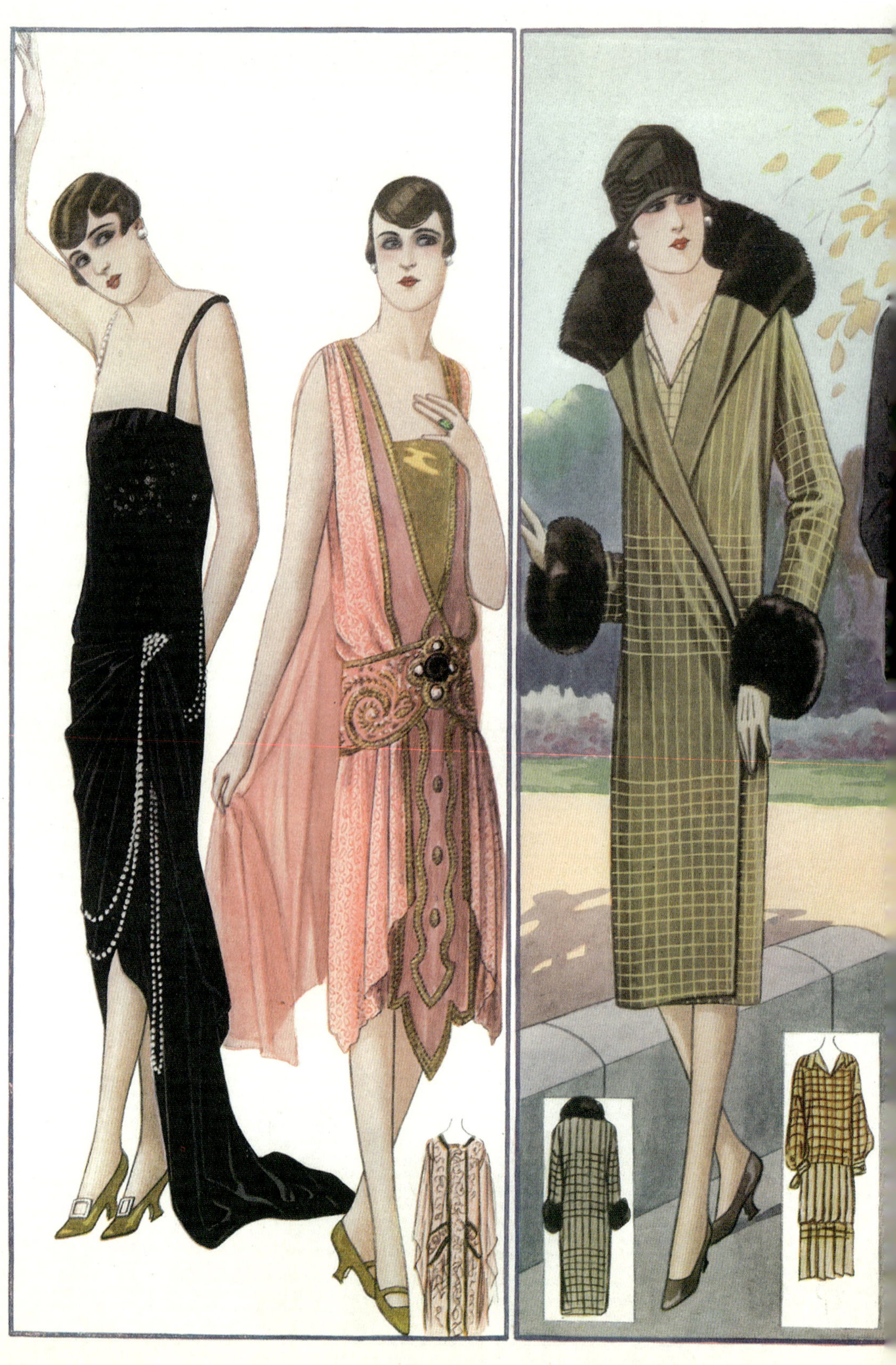

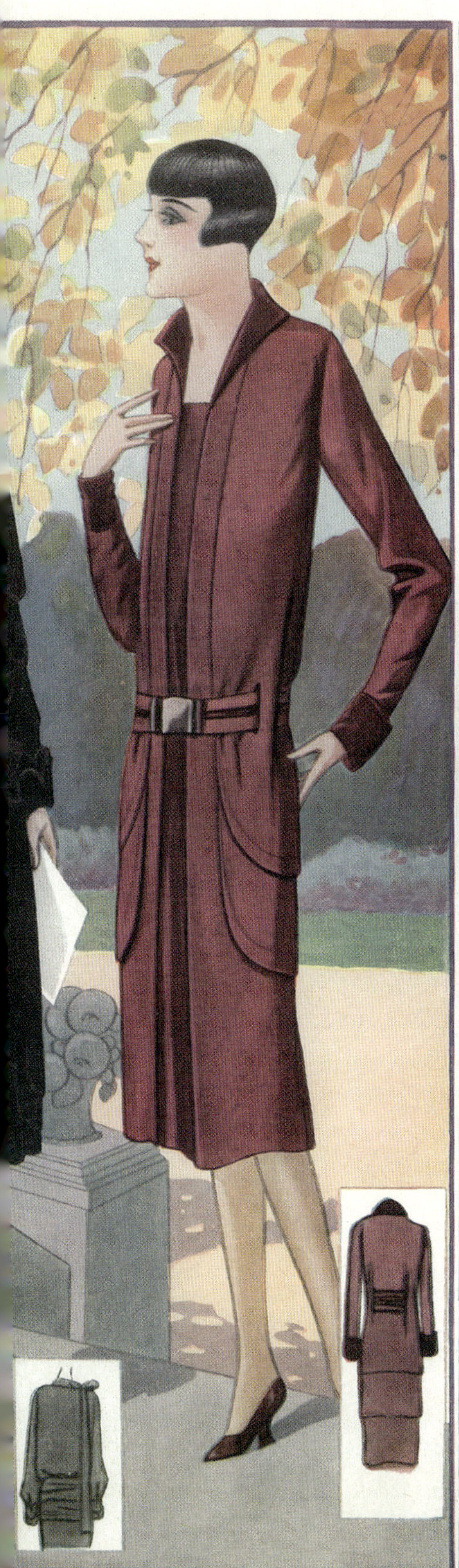

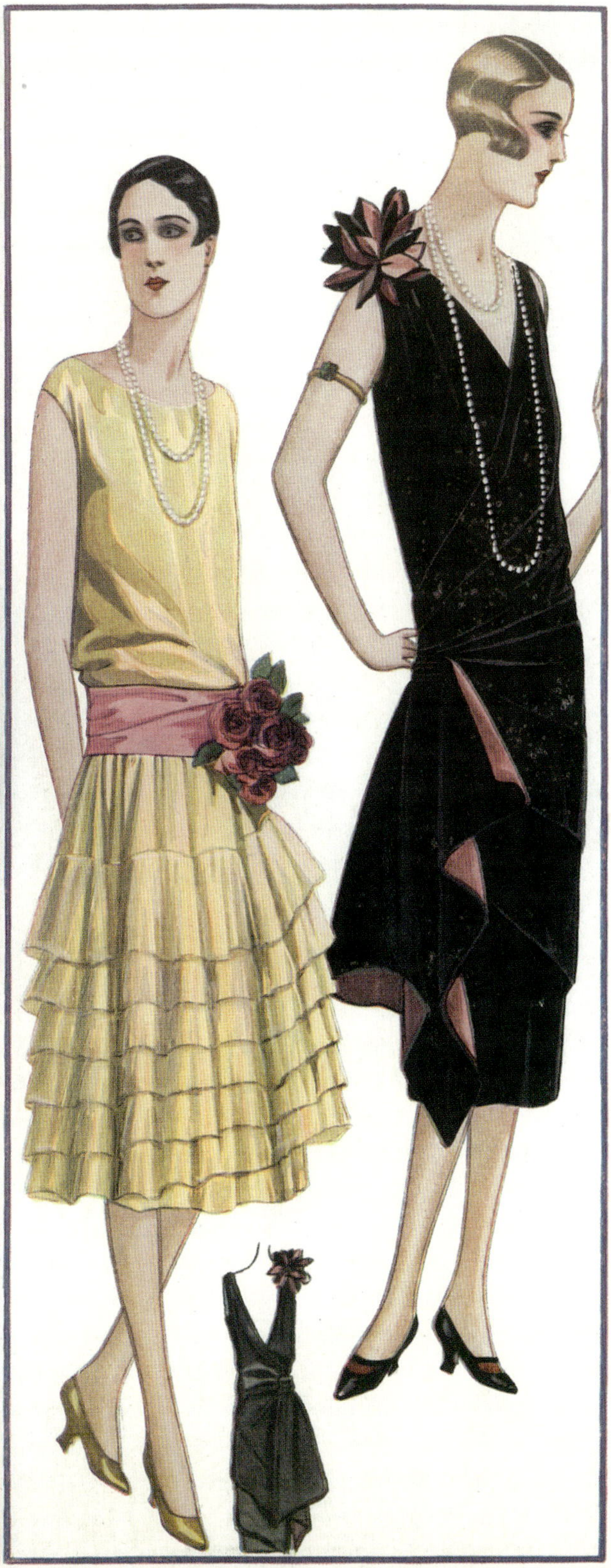

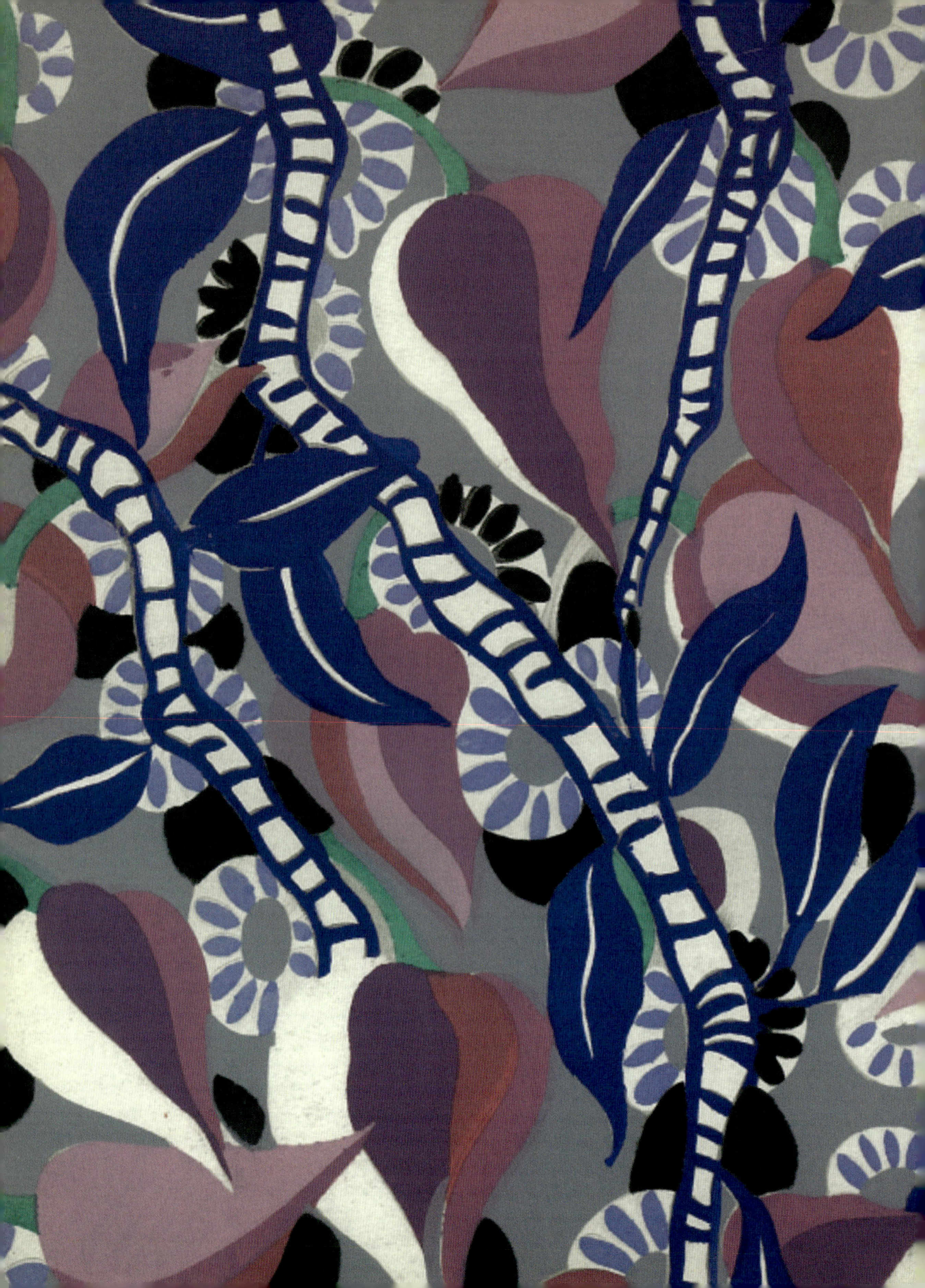

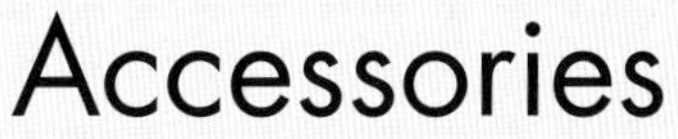

Accessories

Below left and right

A spring hat made of picet-straw with a flat crown of rose-colored satin and finished off with a small diamante buckle, c.1924

A navy blue hat made of corded ribbon in a close fitting cloche shape with a large beige velvet flower and an eye veil, c.1925. The vogue for of wearing multiple strands of pearls is accredited to Coco Chanel.

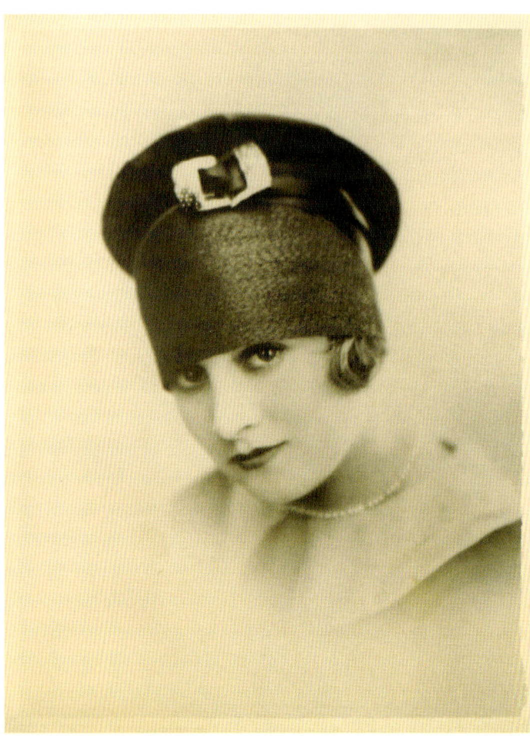

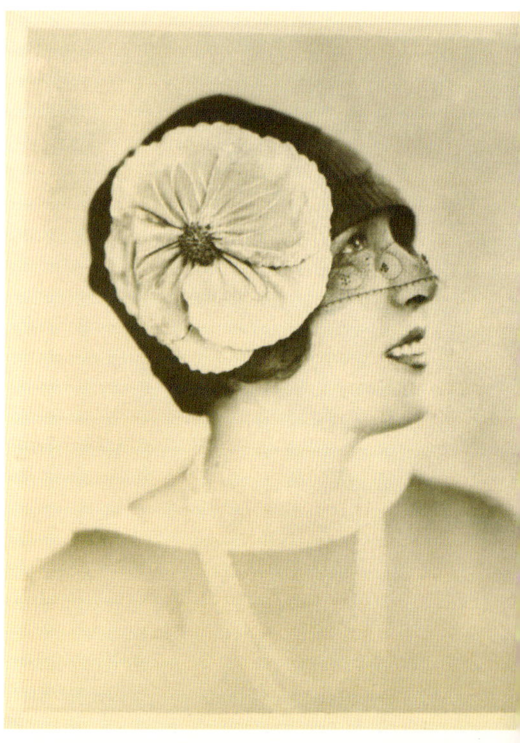

Below left and right

A large brimmed hat in pale green crepe de Chine with a bunch of artificial flowers worn on the brim, c.1925

A wide-brimmed hat of champagne-coloured straw, piped with a ribbon in a darker shade to match the satin crown, which is elaborately trimmed with embroidered gold brocade, c.1924. The image is very similar to the popular actresses postcards of the time and shows that whilst the cloche hat became the preferred choice of headgear in the 1920s, more romantic styles were equally popular.

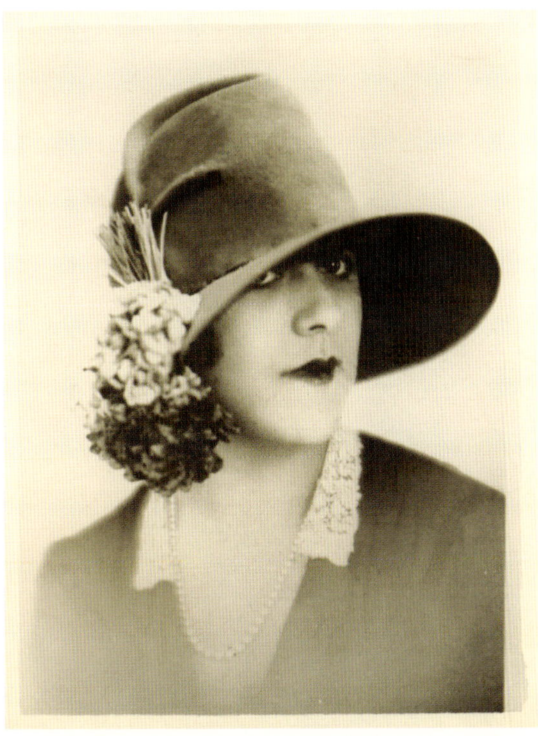

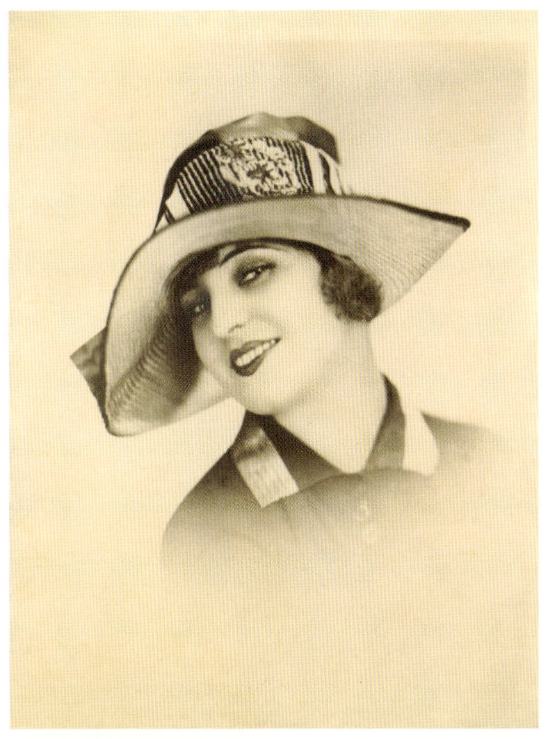

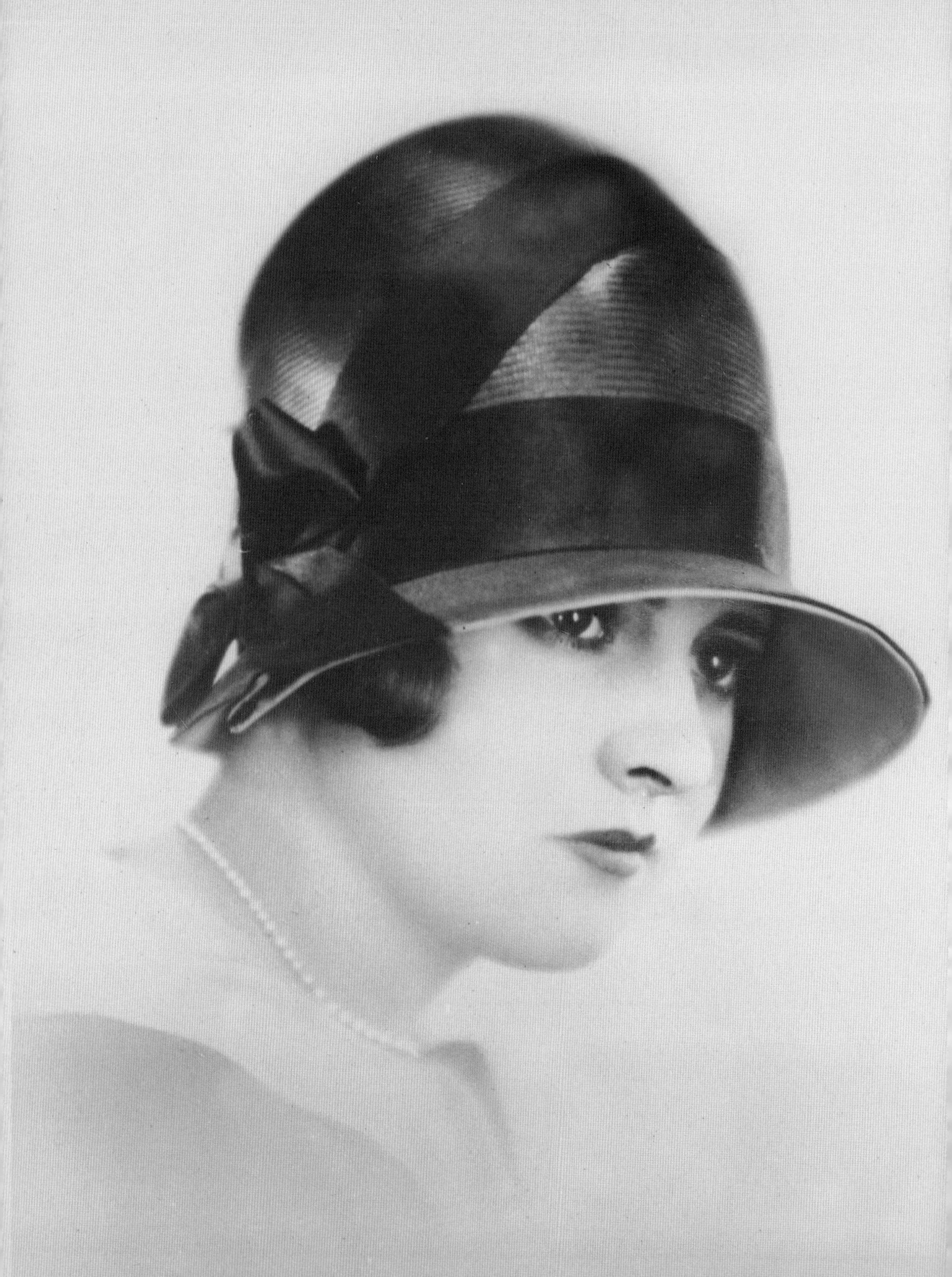

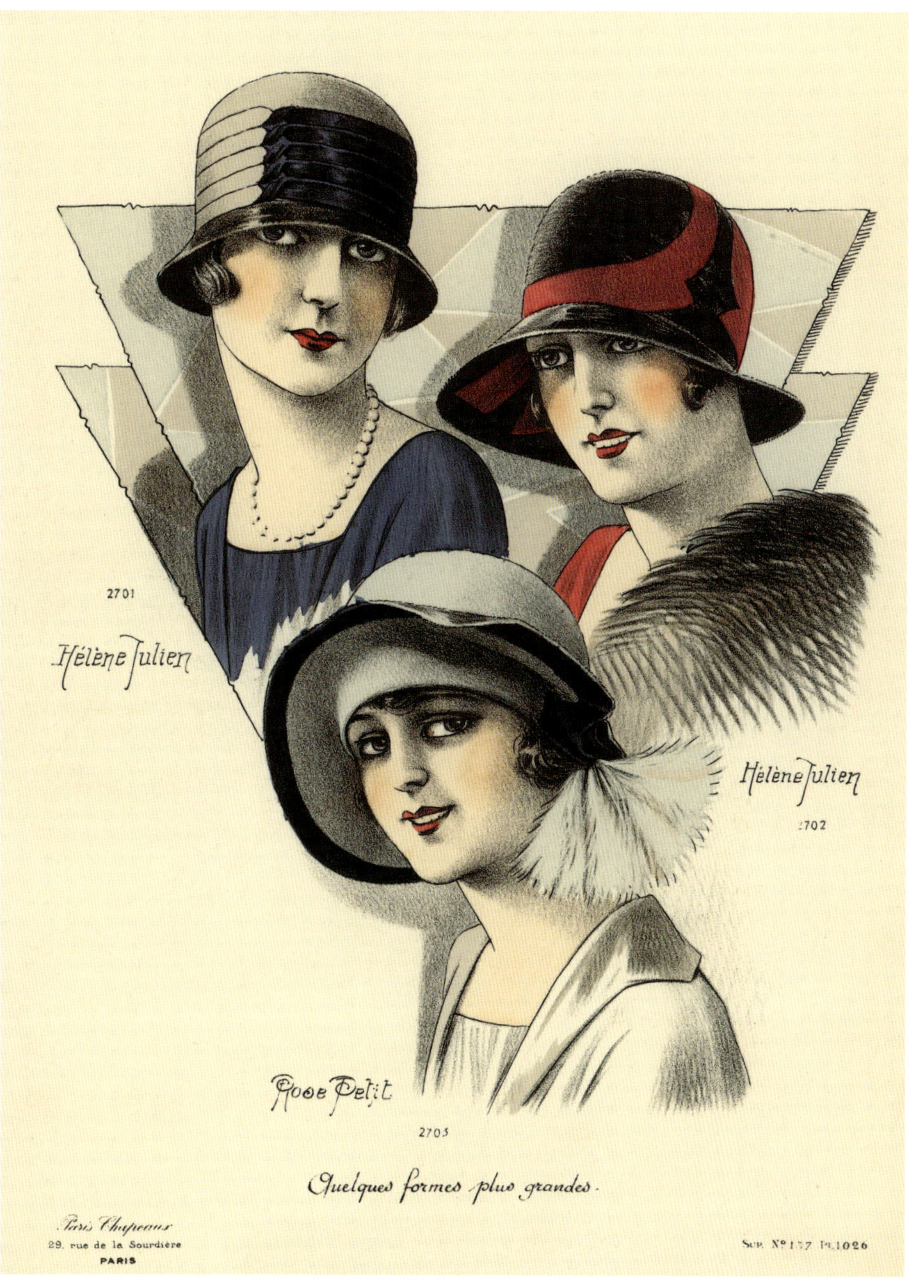

Left and above

A Parisian spring hat made of "Bangkok Straw" and trimmed with ruby-coloured velvet with a brim lined to match the ribbon, c.1925

Three cloche hat designs by Hélène Julien and Rose Petit. *Paris-Chapeaux*, c.1926

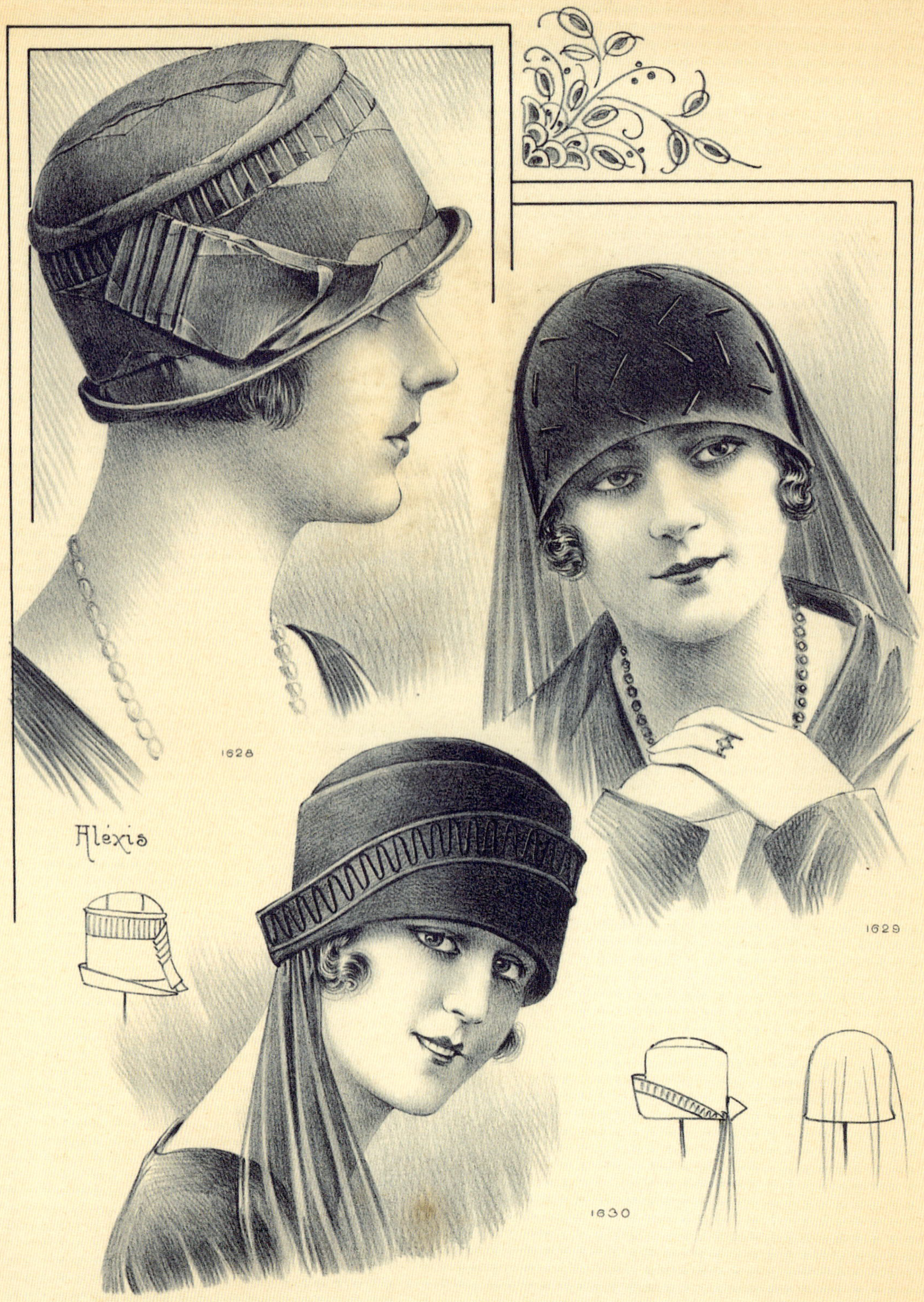

Paris-Chapeaux

Les chapeaux de deuil et leurs sobres garnitures

29, Rue de la Sourdière
PARIS (1er arrt)

Supplément
N° 132 – PL. 654

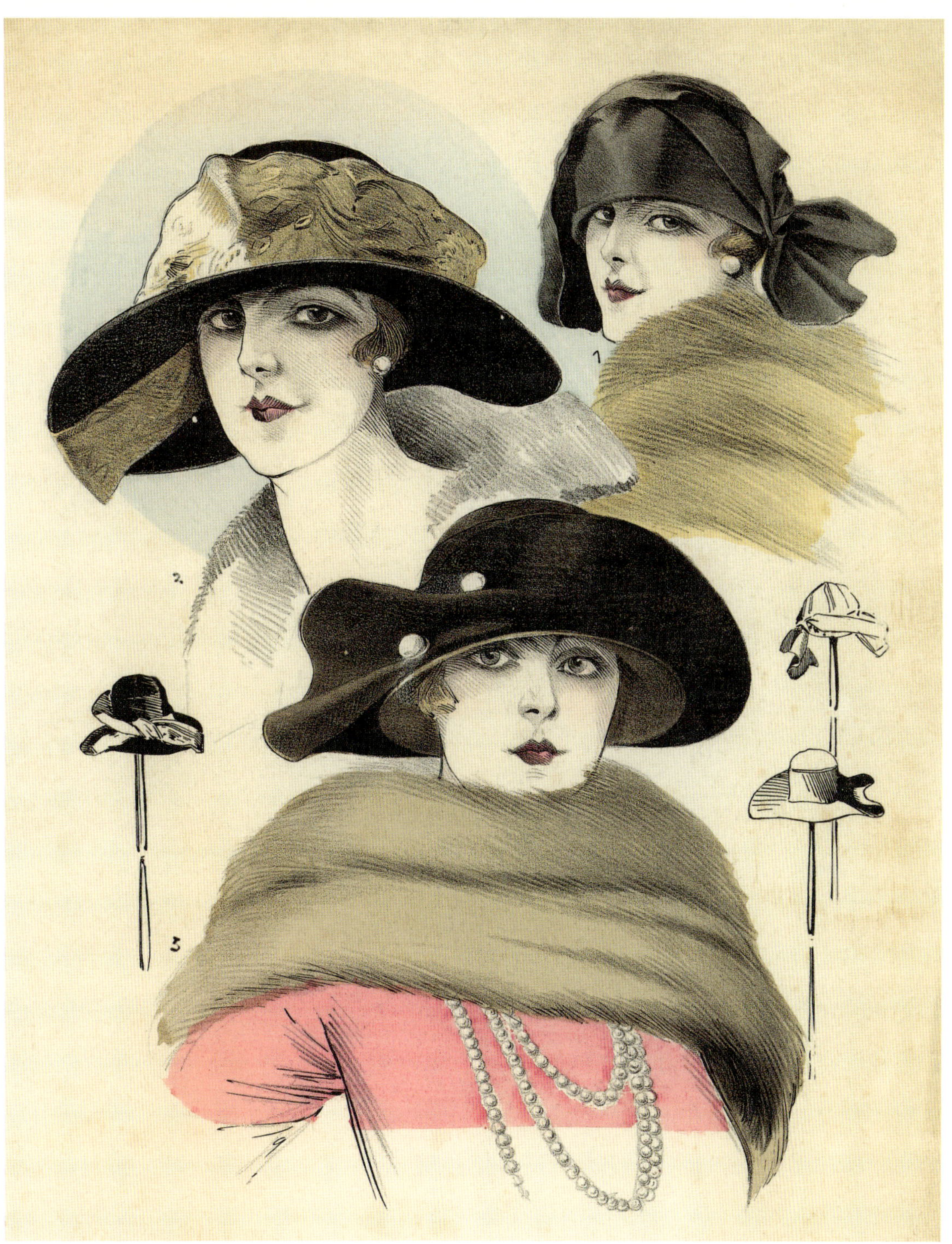

Left and above

Three Parisian mourning hats, *Paris-Chapeaux* c.1924. The designs of the hats are very fashionable and it is only the long black veils that single them out as mourning attire.

Three creations by Parisian milliner Amicy Boinard. *Les Chapeaux de La Femme Chic*, c.1924

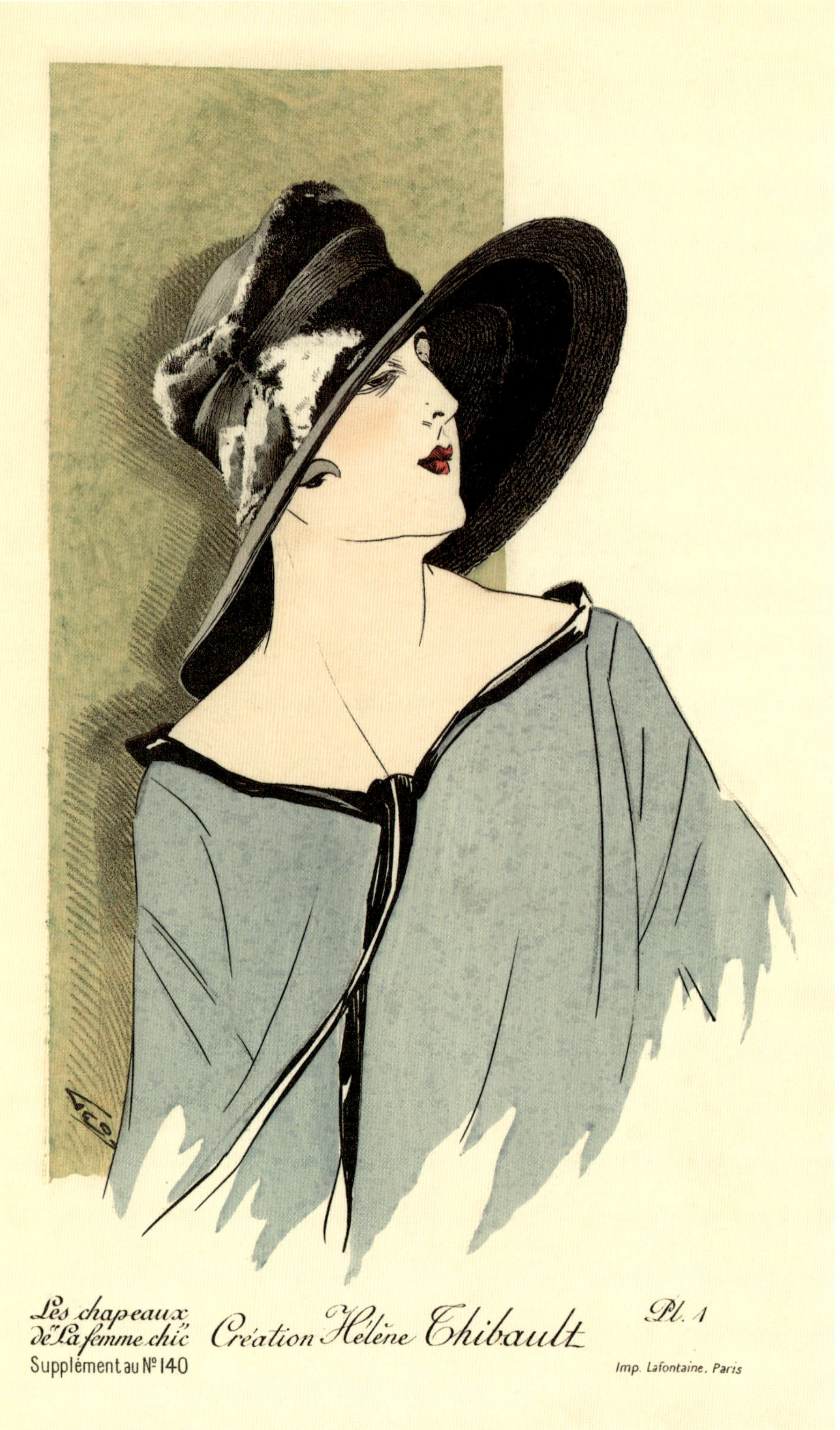

Above
Black straw and fur hat by Hélène Thibault, Les Chapeaux de "*La Femme Chic*", 1927

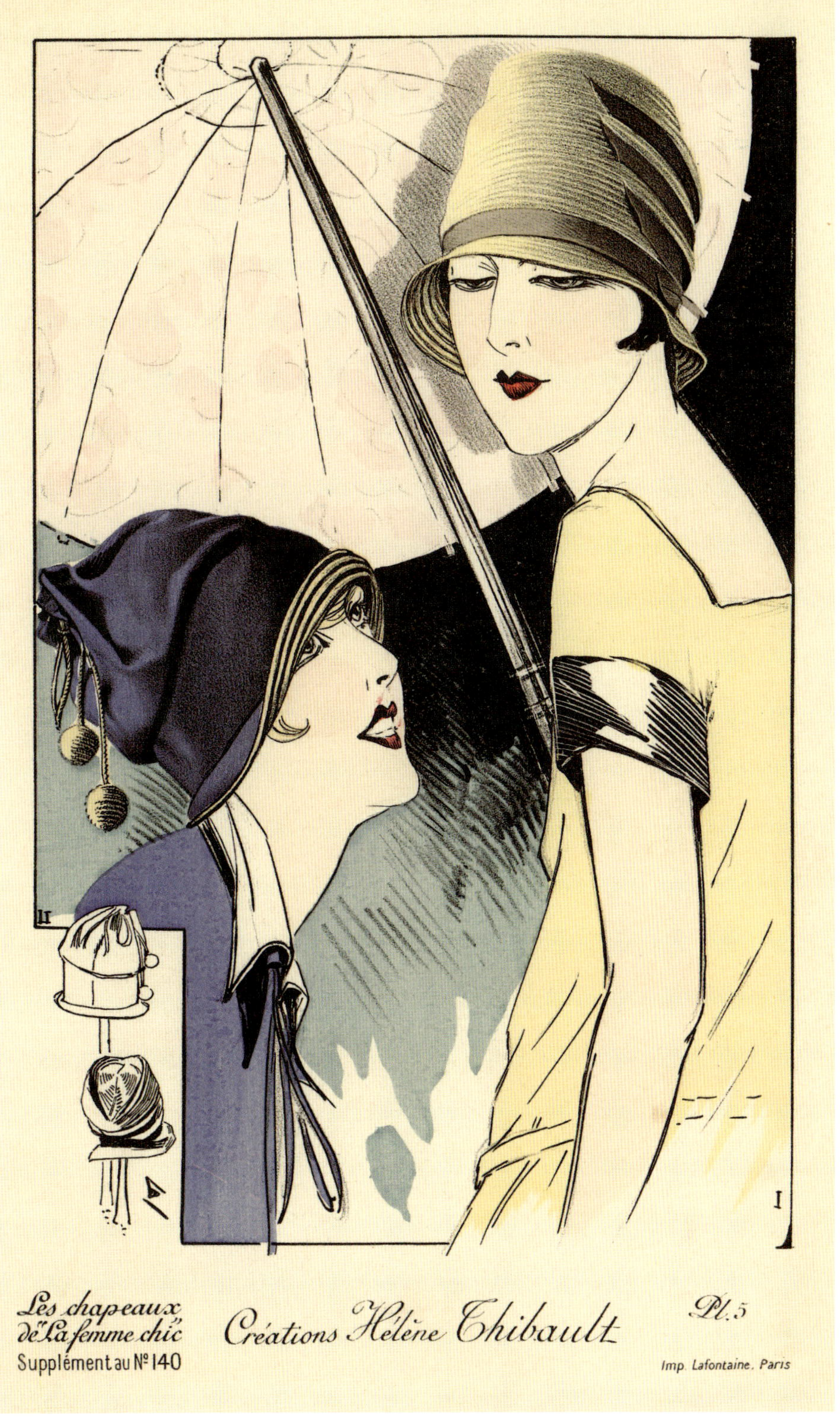

Above
Two cloche hats by Hélène Thibault, *Les Chapeaux de "La Femme Chic"*, 1927

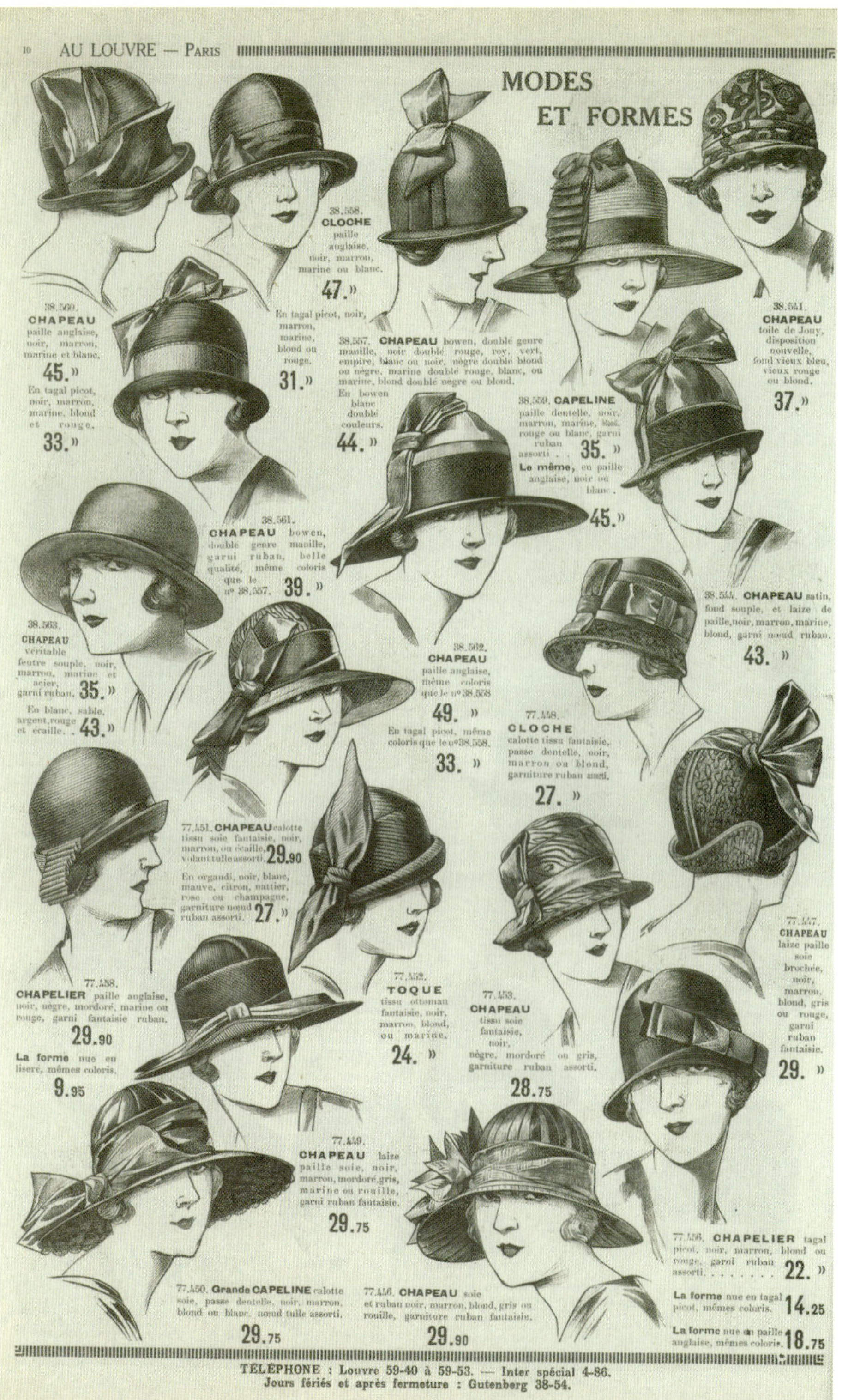

Above
Selection of day hats.
Au Louvre catalogue, 1925

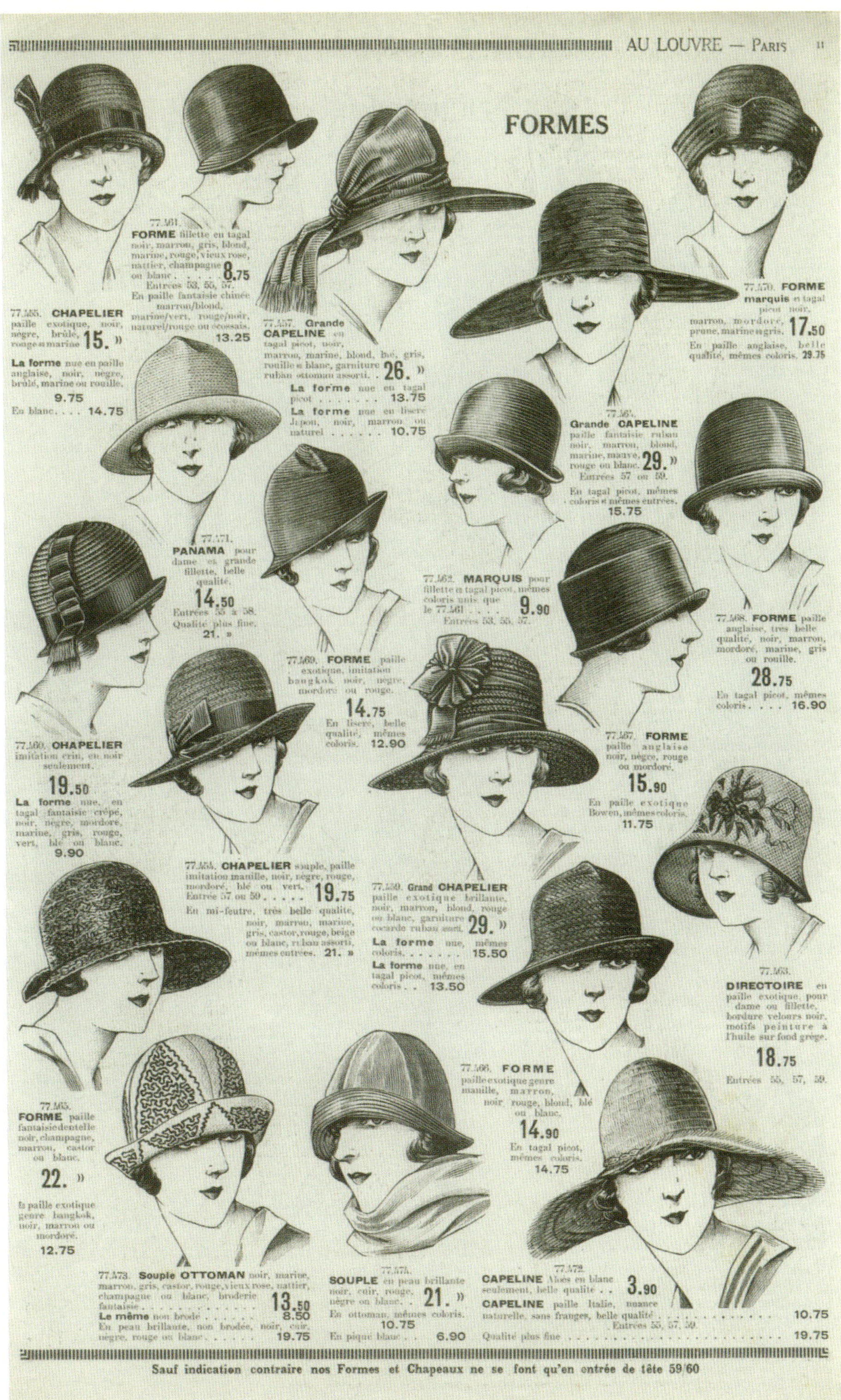

AU LOUVRE — PARIS 11

FORMES

77.455. **CHAPELIER** paille exotique, noir, nègre, brûlé, rouge ou marine 15. »
La forme nue en paille anglaise, noir, nègre, brûlé, marine ou rouille. 9.75
En blanc. . . . 14.75

77.461. **FORME** fillette en tagal noir, marron, gris, blond, marine, rouge, vieux rose, nattier, champagne ou blanc 8.75
Entrées 53, 55, 57.
En paille fantaisie chinée marron/blond, marine/vert, rouge/noir, naturel/rouge ou écossais. 13.25

77.457. **Grande CAPELINE** en tagal picot, noir, marron, marine, blond, blé, gris, rouille et blanc, garniture ruban ottoman assorti. . 26. »
La forme nue en tagal picot 13.75
La forme nue en liseré Japon, noir, marron ou naturel 10.75

77.470. **FORME marquis** en tagal picot noir, marron, mordoré, prune, marine et gris. 17.50
En paille anglaise, belle qualité, mêmes coloris. 29.75

77.464. **Grande CAPELINE** paille fantaisie ruban noir, marron, blond, marine, mauve, rouge ou blanc. 29. »
Entrées 57 ou 59.
En tagal picot, mêmes coloris et mêmes entrées. 15.75

77.471. **PANAMA** pour dame et grande fillette, belle qualité. 14.50
Entrées 55 à 58.
Qualité plus fine. 21. »

77.462. **MARQUIS** pour fillette en tagal picot, mêmes coloris unis que le 77.461 . . . . 9.90
Entrées 53, 55, 57.

77.468. **FORME** paille anglaise, très belle qualité, noir, marron, mordoré, marine, gris ou rouille. 28.75
En tagal picot, mêmes coloris. . . . 16.90

77.469. **FORME** paille exotique, imitation bangkok noir, nègre, mordoré ou rouge. 14.75
En liseré, belle qualité, mêmes coloris. 12.90

77.460. **CHAPELIER** imitation crin, en noir seulement. 19.50
La forme nue, en tagal fantaisie crêpé, noir, nègre, mordoré, marine, gris, rouge, vert, blé ou blanc. 9.90

77.467. **FORME** paille anglaise noir, nègre, rouge ou mordoré. 15.90
En paille exotique Bowen, mêmes coloris. 11.75

77.454. **CHAPELIER** souple, paille imitation manille, noir, nègre, rouge, mordoré, blé ou vert. Entrée 57 ou 59 . . . . . 19.75
En mi-feutre, très belle qualité, noir, marron, marine, gris, castor, rouge, beige ou blanc, ruban assorti, mêmes entrées. 21. »

77.459. **Grand CHAPELIER** paille exotique brillante, noir, marron, blond, rouge ou blanc, garniture cocarde ruban assorti. 29. »
La forme nue, mêmes coloris. 15.50
La forme nue, en tagal picot, mêmes coloris . . 13.50

77.463. **DIRECTOIRE** en paille exotique, pour dame ou fillette, bordure velours noir, motifs peinture à l'huile sur fond grège. 18.75
Entrées 55, 57, 59.

77.465. **FORME** paille fantaisie dentelle noir, champagne, marron, castor ou blanc. 22. »
En paille exotique genre bangkok, noir, marron ou mordoré. 12.75

77.466. **FORME** paille exotique genre manille, marron, noir, rouge, blond, blé ou blanc. 14.90
En tagal picot, mêmes coloris. 14.75

77.473. **Souple OTTOMAN** noir, marine, marron, gris, castor, rouge, vieux rose, nattier, champagne ou blanc, broderie fantaisie 13.50
Le même non brodé 8.50
En peau brillante, non brodée, noir, cuir, nègre, rouge ou blanc 19.75

77.474. **SOUPLE** en peau brillante noir, cuir, rouge, nègre ou blanc. . 21. »
En ottoman, mêmes coloris. 10.75
En piqué blanc . . 6.90

77.472. **CAPELINE** Aloès en blanc seulement, belle qualité . . 3.90
CAPELINE paille Italie, nuance naturelle, sans franges, belle qualité 10.75
Entrées 55, 57, 59.
Qualité plus fine 19.75

Sauf indication contraire nos Formes et Chapeaux ne se font qu'en entrée de tête 59/60

Above
Selection of day hats.
Au Louvre catalogue, 1925

Below and right

Three travelling hats by Parisian milliner Jane Blanchot. *Les Chapeaux du "Trés Parisien"*, 1923

Hat designs by Marcelle Dumay. *Les Chapeaux du "Trés Parisien"*, 1923-1924

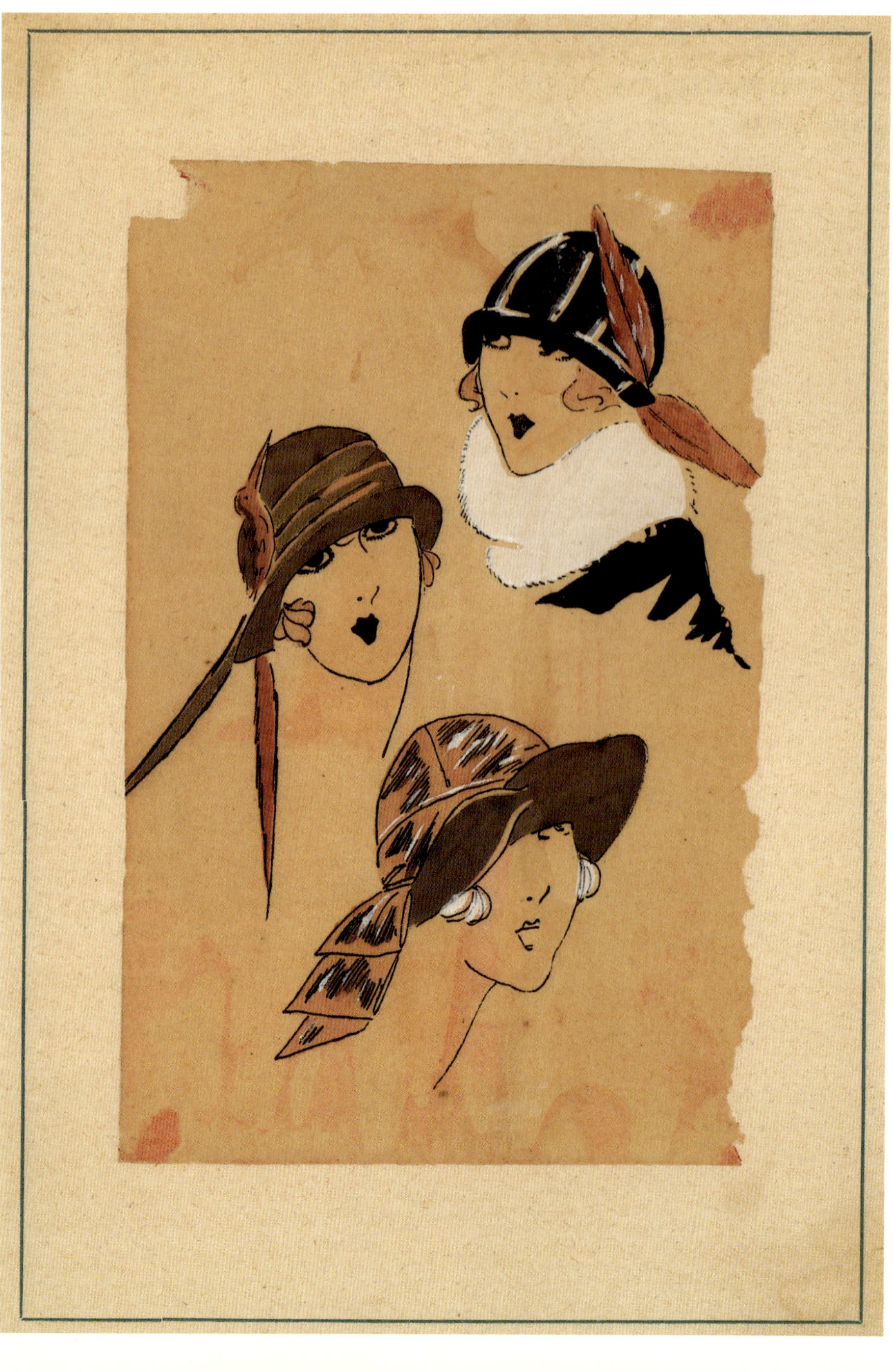

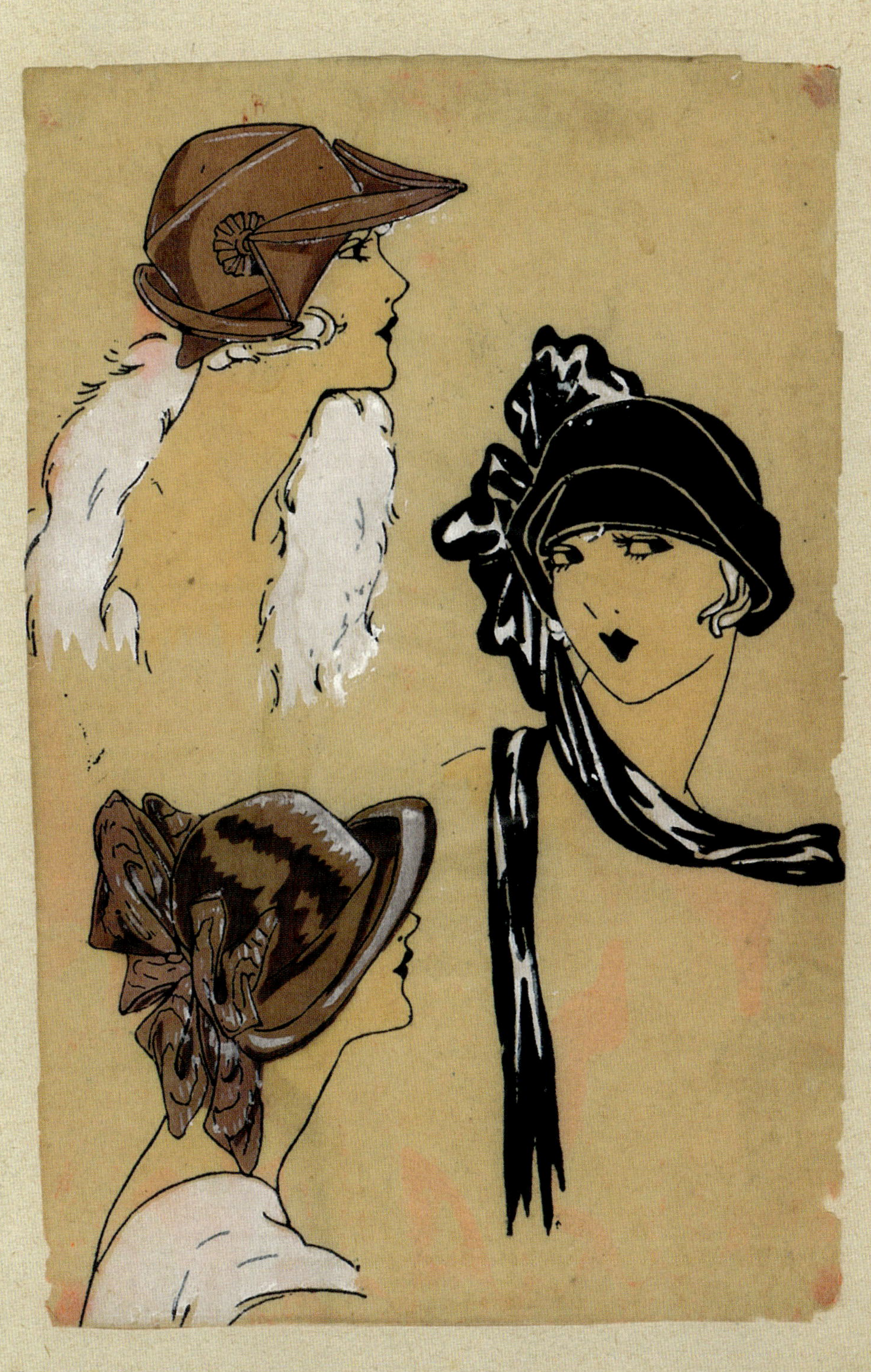

Below and right

Woman wearing a black single-breasted jacket over a white blouse and cloche hat. *Nouvelle Mode*, 1926

Silent film actress Mary Anderson in a blue and grey woven day dress and a blue and white hat with a large pearl hatpin, c.1921

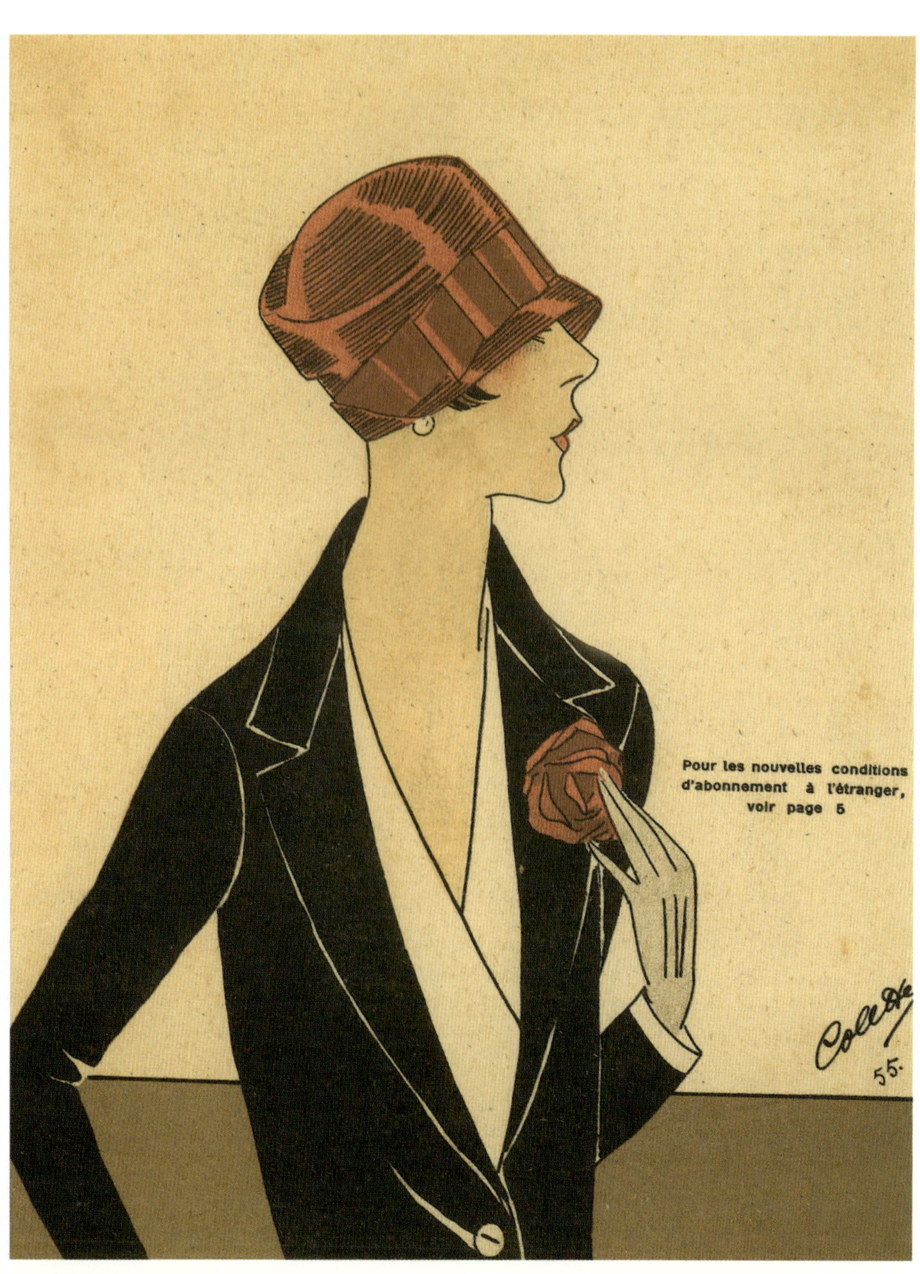

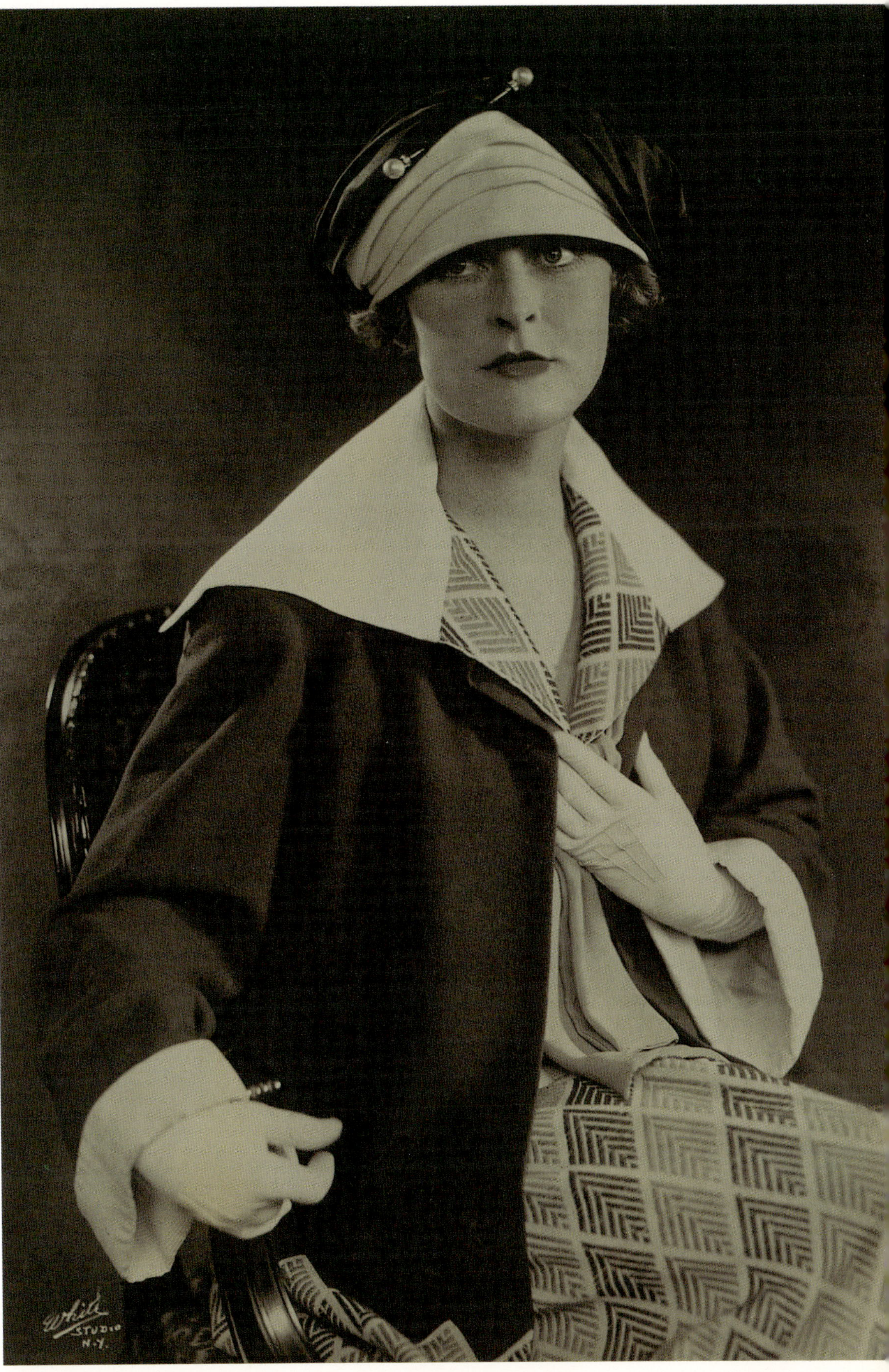
White
STUDIO
N.Y.

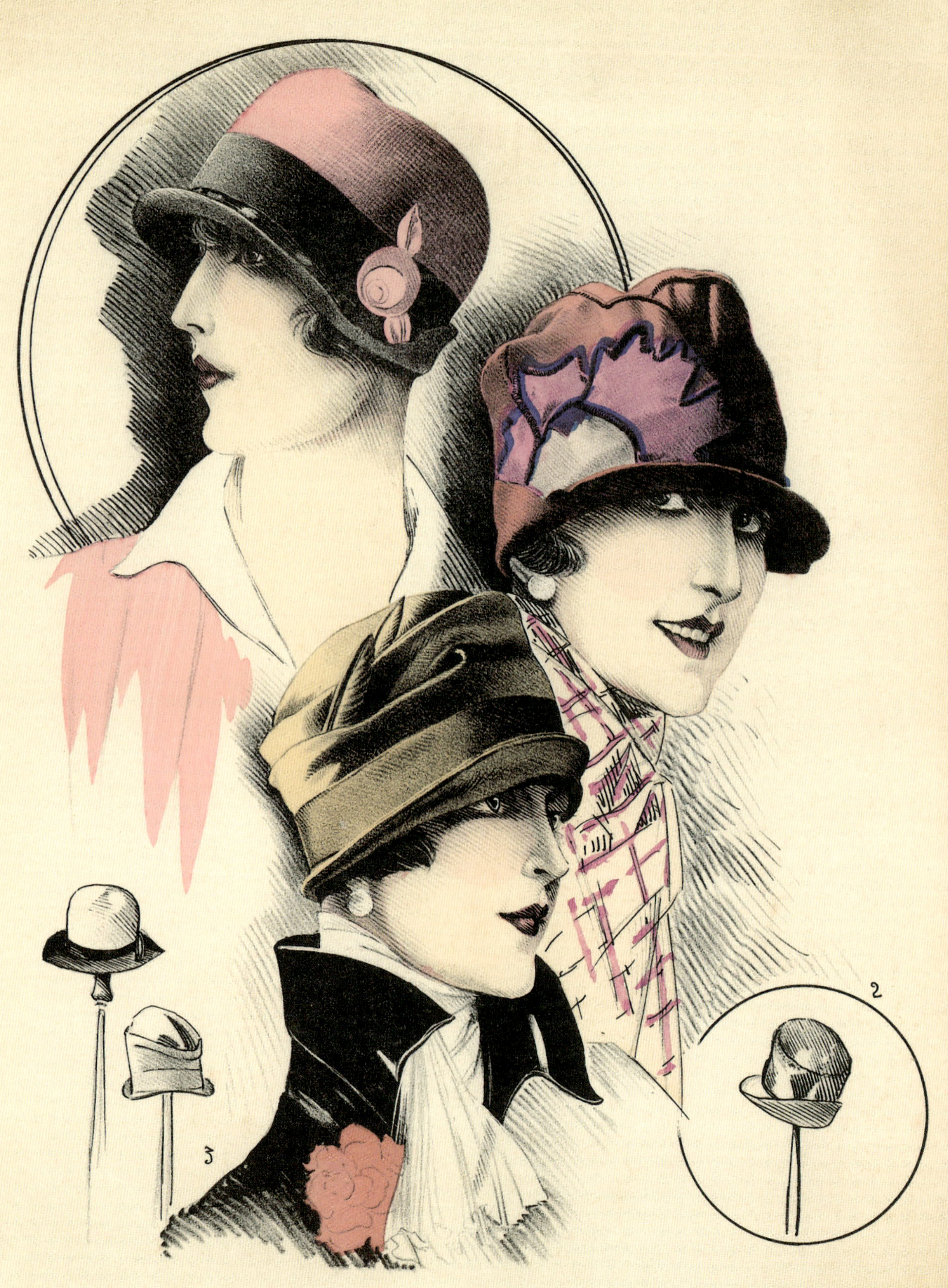
2
3

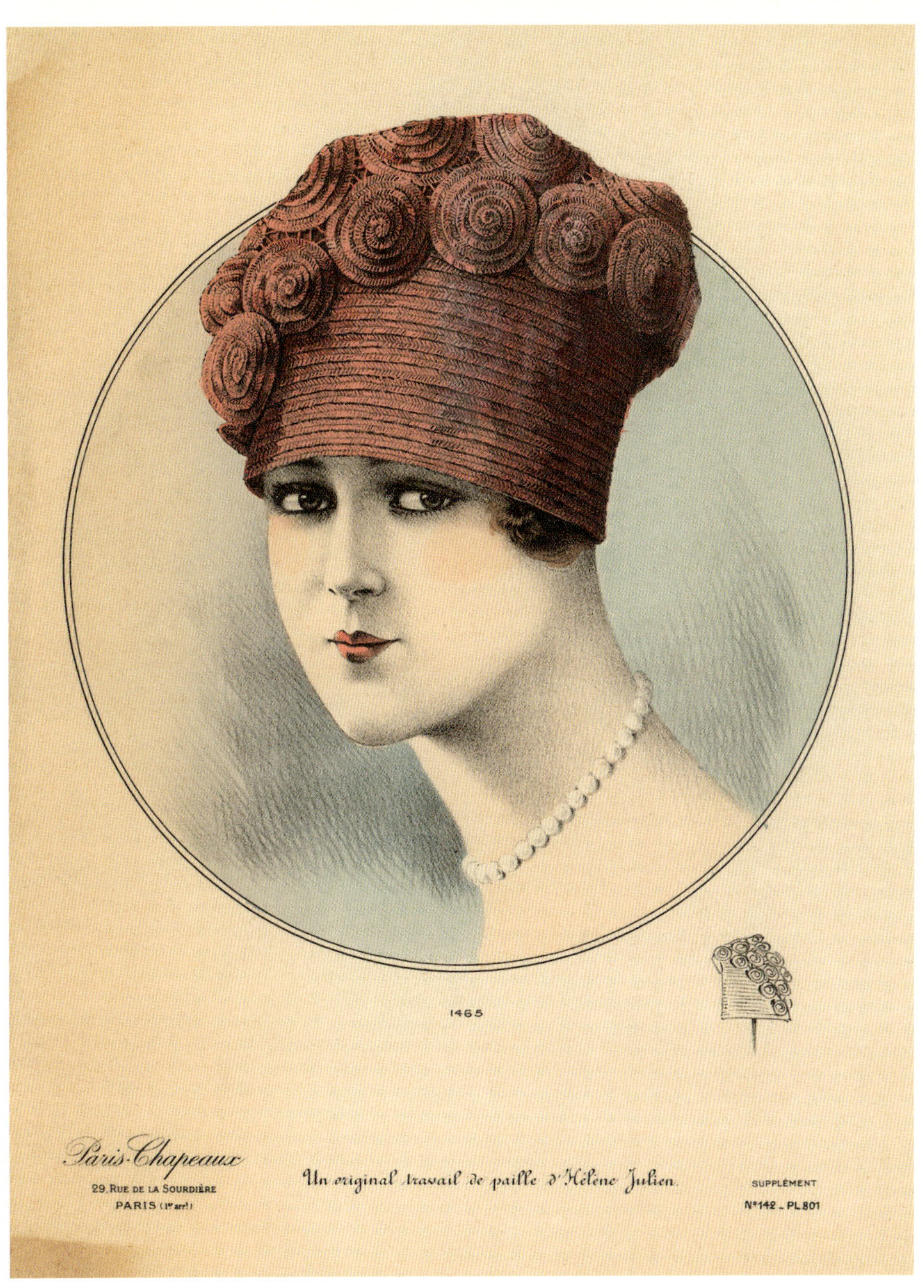

Left and above

Three creations by Parisian milliner Jane Blanchot. *Les Chapeaux de La Femme Chic*, c.1923

An original hat model constructed out of burgundy straw by Parisian milliner Hélène Julien, *Paris-Chapeaux*, c.1923. Note the model's rouged cheeks and red lipstick.

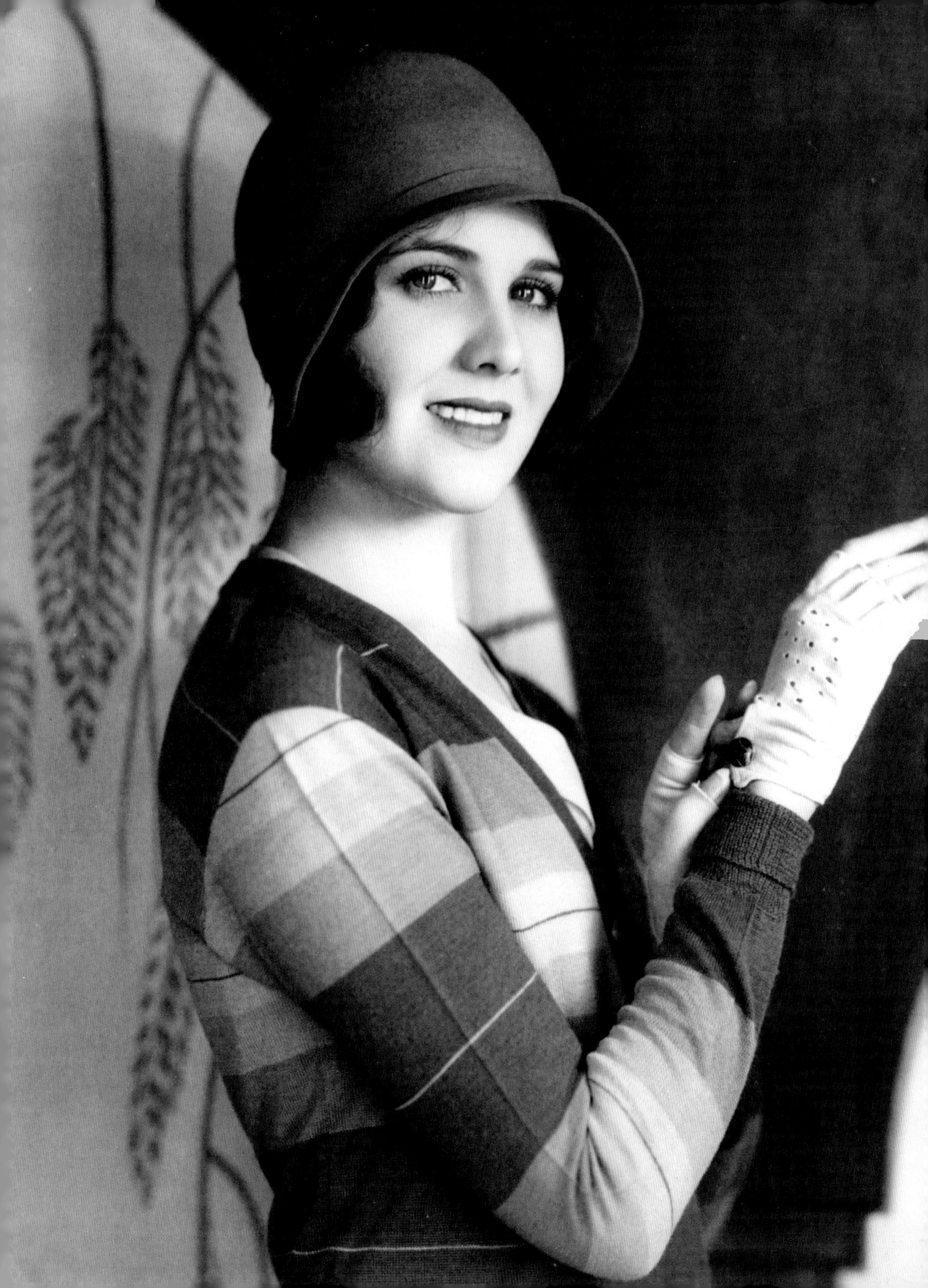

Left and below
Actress Mary Brian wearing a cloche hat, a sports sweater and leather fingerless golfing gloves, c.1925

Actress Betty Bronson in the movie "Paradise" wearing close-fitting hat with ribbon banding, 1926

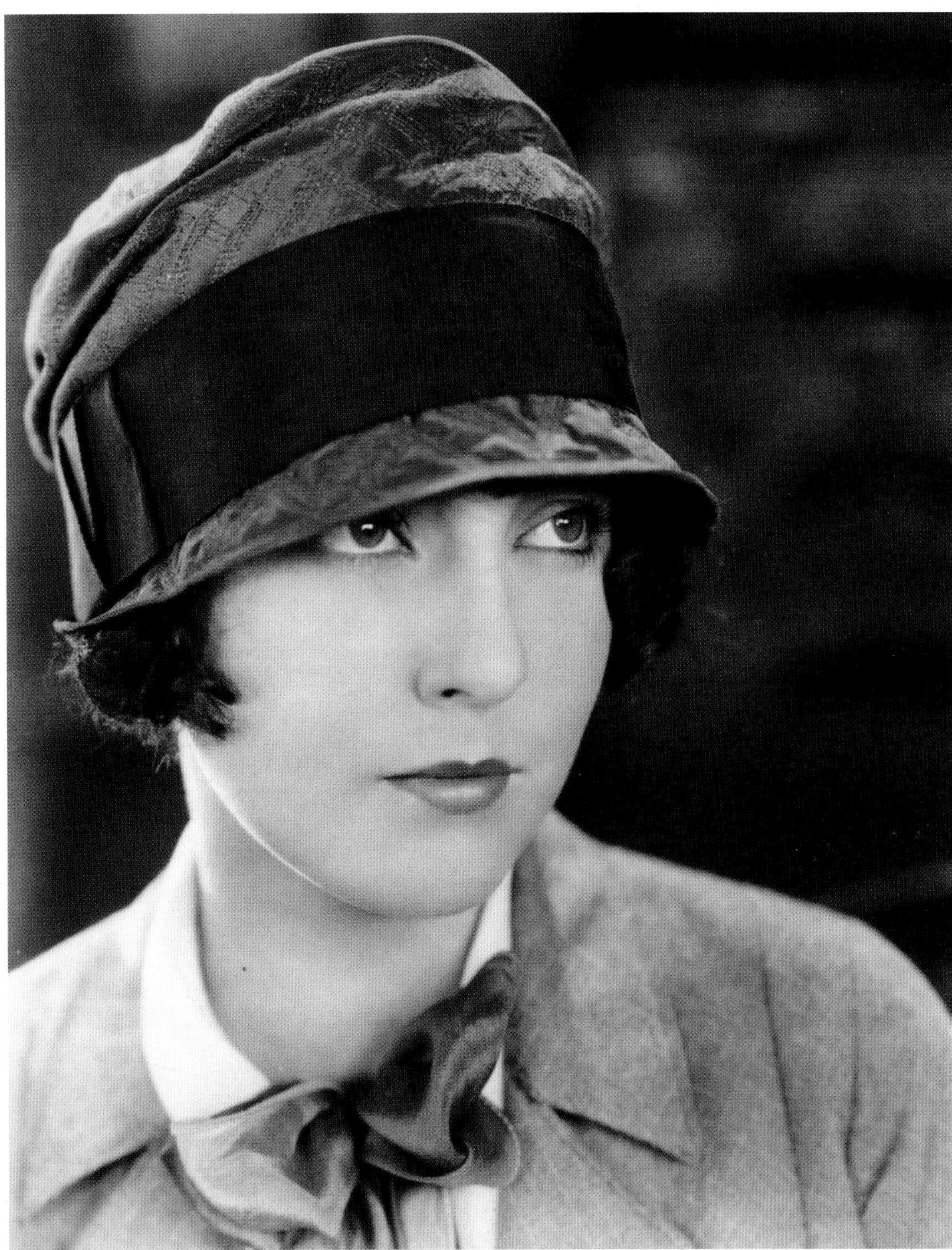

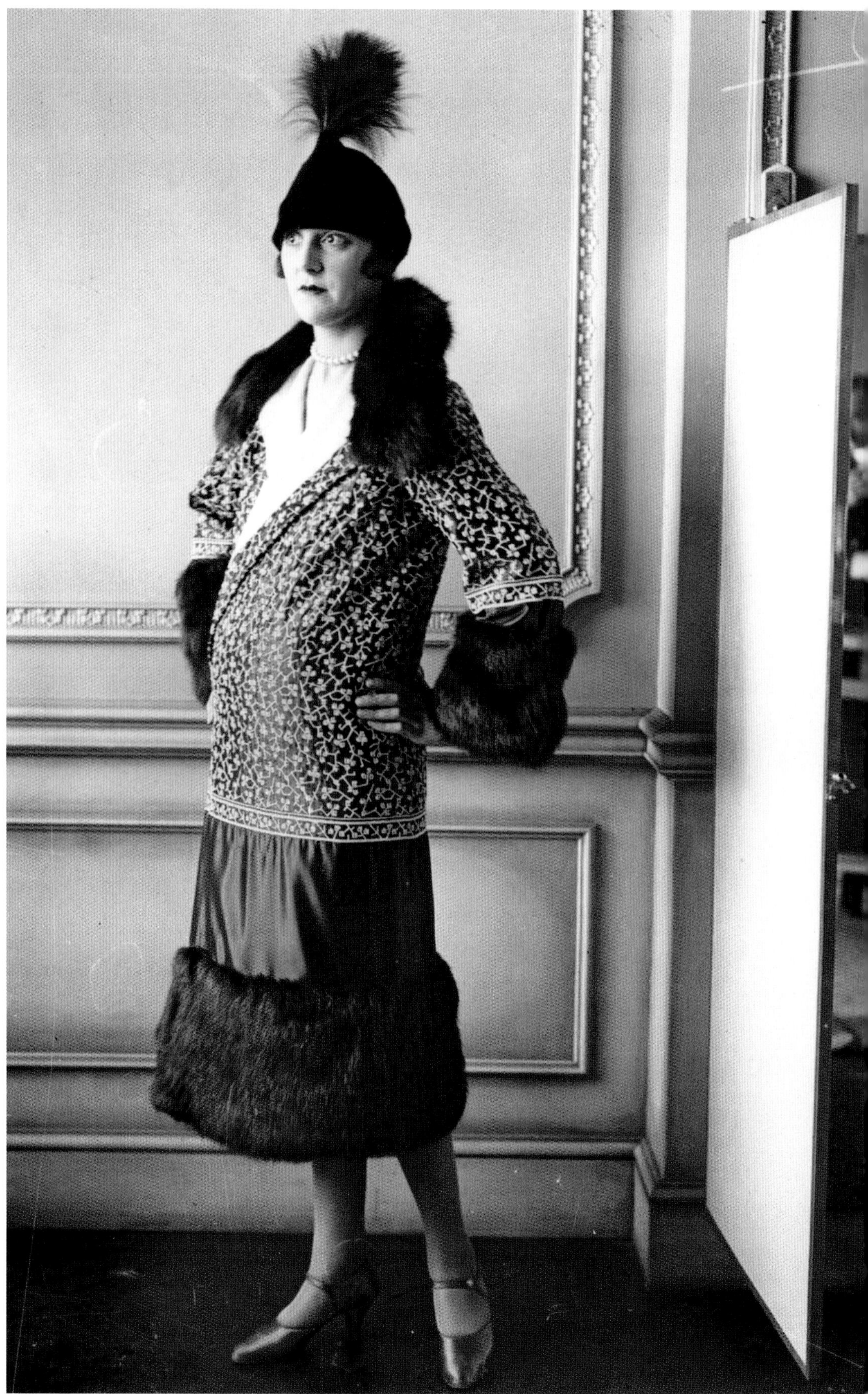

Left and below
A black satin afternoon coat studded with white beads and trimmed with a black fox collar and cuffs and worn with a tight-fitting hat with plumes. Central News photograph, c.1923

A winter hat of dark straw trimmed at the side with an ornament of ostrich feathers. London, c.1924

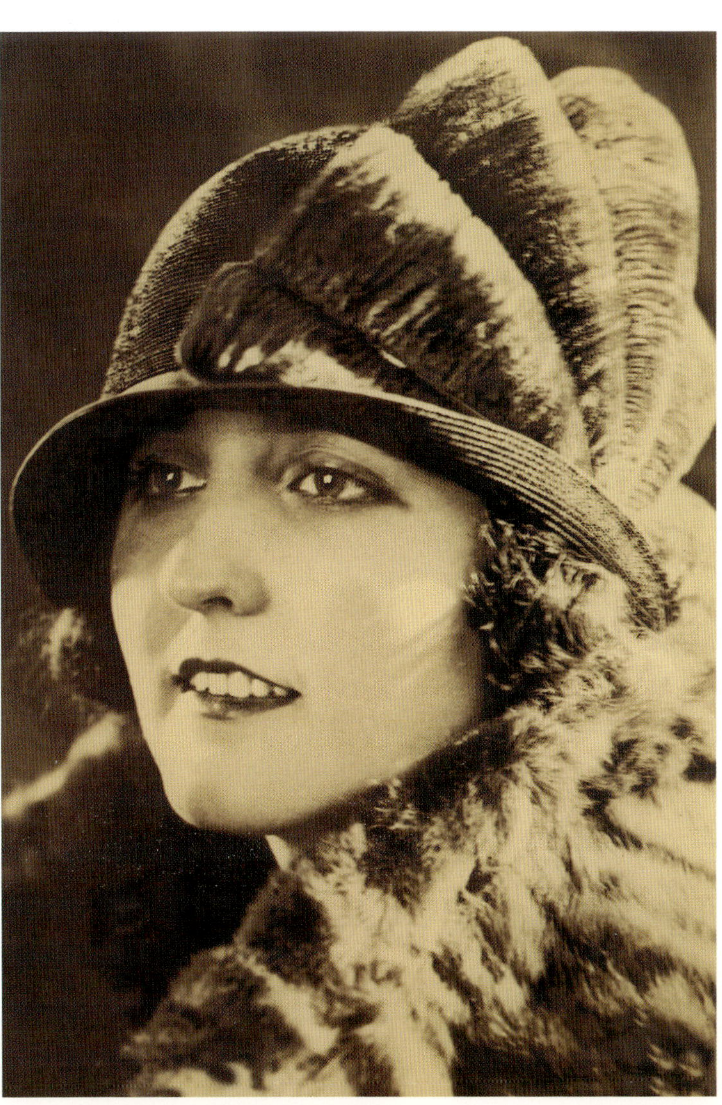

Right
"Le Madras Jaune" (The Yellow Madras), headdress: a silk evening turban. Illustration by Charles Martin. *Gazette du Bon Ton*, 1920

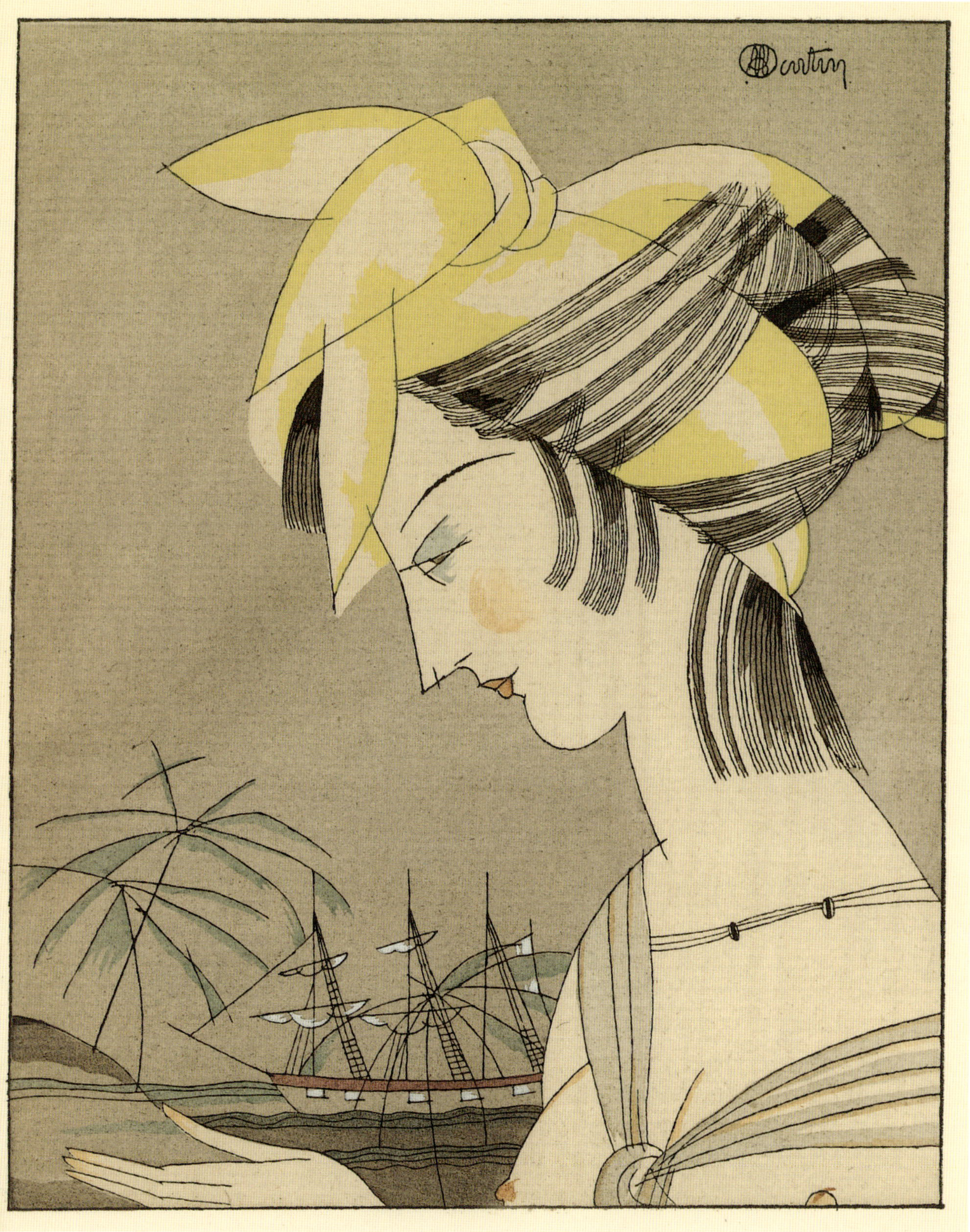

Below
Selection of fashionable hats including cloches, berets and tight-fitting skull caps. *The New Silhouette from Paris*, Hamilton Garment Co. New York catalogue, c.1929

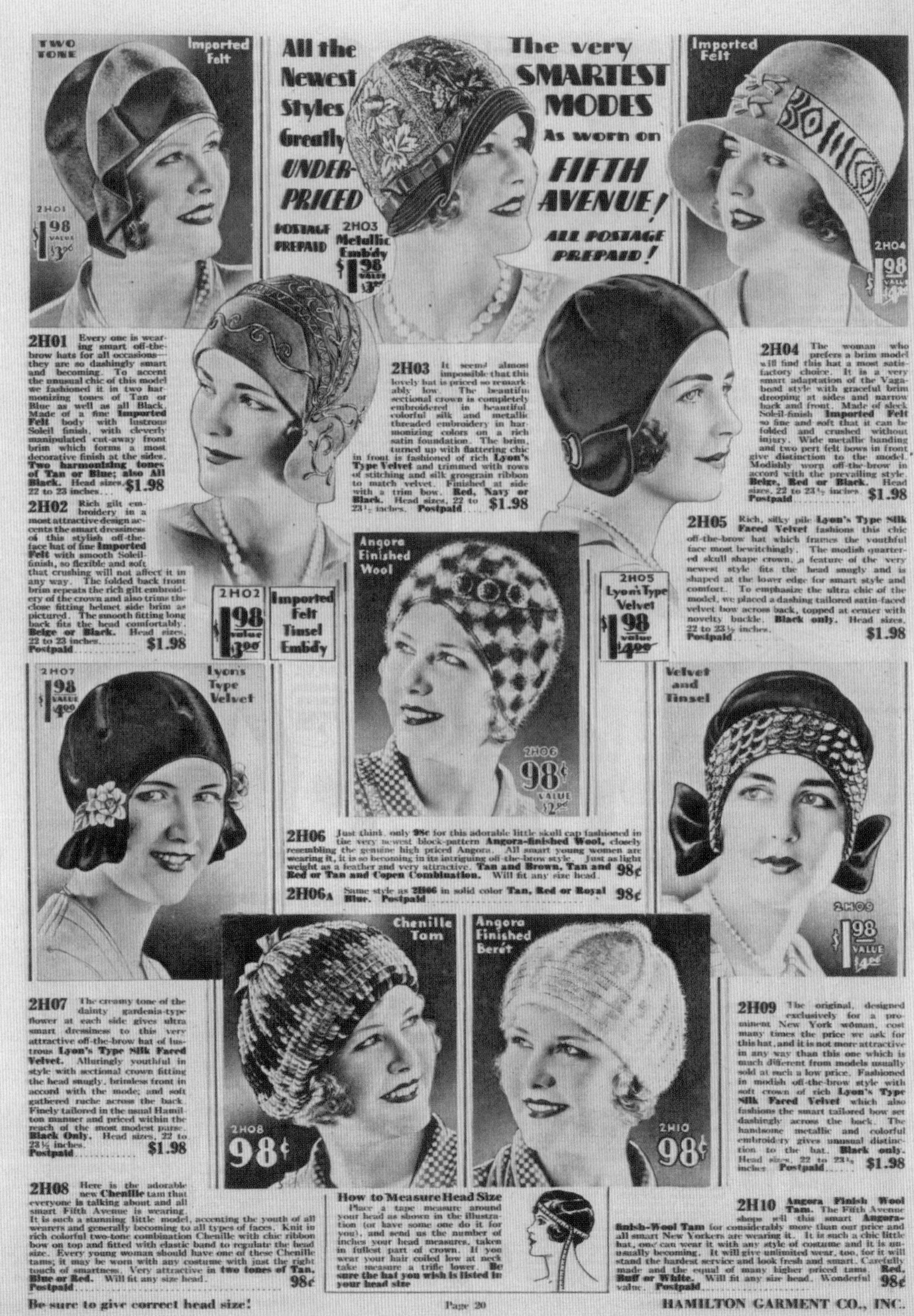

TWO TONE
Imported Felt
2H01 $1.98 VALUE $3.00

All the Newest Styles Greatly UNDER-PRICED
POSTAGE PREPAID
2H03 Metallic Emb'dy $1.98 VALUE $3.00

The very SMARTEST MODES As worn on FIFTH AVENUE!
ALL POSTAGE PREPAID!

Imported Felt
2H04 $1.98 VALUE

2H01 Every one is wearing smart off-the-brow hats for all occasions—they are so dashingly smart and becoming. To accent the unusual chic of this model we fashioned it in two harmonizing tones of Tan or Blue as well as all Black. Made of a fine **Imported Felt** body with lustrous Soleil finish, with cleverly manipulated cut-away front brim which forms a most decorative finish at the sides. **Two harmonizing tones of Tan or Blue; also All Black.** Head sizes 22 to 23 inches... **$1.98**

2H02 Rich gilt embroidery in a most attractive design accents the smart dressiness of this stylish off-the-face hat of fine **Imported Felt** with smooth Soleil-finish, so flexible and soft that crushing will not affect it in any way. The folded back front brim repeats the rich gilt embroidery of the crown and also trims the close fitting helmet side brim as pictured. The smooth fitting long back fits the head comfortably. **Beige or Black.** Head sizes, 22 to 23 inches........ **Postpaid** **$1.98**

2H02 $1.98 value $3.00
Imported Felt Tinsel Emb'dy

2H03 It seems almost impossible that this lovely hat is priced so remarkably low. The beautiful sectional crown is completely embroidered in beautiful colorful silk and metallic threaded embroidery in harmonizing colors on a rich satin foundation. The brim, turned up with flattering chic in front is fashioned of rich **Lyon's Type Velvet** and trimmed with rows of stitching and silk grosgrain ribbon to match velvet. Finished at side with a trim bow. **Red, Navy or Black.** Head sizes, 22 to 23½ inches. **Postpaid** **$1.98**

2H04 The woman who prefers a brim model will find this hat a most satisfactory choice. It is a very smart adaptation of the Vagabond style with graceful brim drooping at sides and narrow back and front. Made of sleek Soleil-finish **Imported Felt** so fine and soft that it can be folded and crushed without injury. Wide metallic banding and two pert felt bows in front give distinction to the model. Modishly worn off-the-brow in accord with the prevailing style. **Beige, Red or Black.** Head sizes, 22 to 23½ inches. **Postpaid** **$1.98**

2H05 Rich, silky pile **Lyon's Type Silk Faced Velvet** fashions this chic off-the-brow hat which frames the youthful face most bewitchingly. The modish quartered skull shape crown, a feature of the very newest style fits the head snugly and is shaped at the lower edge for smart style and comfort. To emphasize the ultra chic of the model, we placed a dashing tailored satin-faced velvet bow across back, topped at center with novelty buckle. **Black only.** Head sizes, 22 to 23½ inches. **Postpaid**. **$1.98**

2H05 Lyon's Type Velvet $1.98 value $4.00

Angora Finished Wool
2H06 98¢ VALUE $2.00

2H07 $1.98 VALUE $4.00
Lyons Type Velvet

Velvet and Tinsel
2H09 $1.98 VALUE $4.00

2H06 Just think, only **98¢** for this adorable little skull cap fashioned in the very newest block-pattern **Angora-finished Wool,** closely resembling the genuine high priced Angora. All smart young women are wearing it, it is so becoming in its intriguing off-the-brow style. Just as light weight as a feather and very attractive. **Tan and Brown, Tan and Red or Tan and Copen Combination.** Will fit any size head. **98¢**

2H06A Same style as **2H06** in solid color **Tan, Red or Royal Blue. Postpaid** .... **98¢**

Chenille Tam
2H08 98¢

Angora Finished Berét
2H10 98¢

2H07 The creamy tone of the dainty gardenia-type flower at each side gives ultra smart dressiness to this very attractive off-the-brow hat of lustrous **Lyon's Type Silk Faced Velvet.** Alluringly youthful in style with sectional crown fitting the head snugly, brimless front in accord with the mode; and soft gathered ruche across the back. Finely tailored in the usual Hamilton manner and priced within the reach of the most modest purse. **Black Only.** Head sizes, 22 to 23½ inches. **Postpaid** **$1.98**

2H09 The original, designed exclusively for a prominent New York woman, cost many times the price we ask for this hat, and it is not more attractive in any way than this one which is much different from models usually sold at such a low price. Fashioned in modish off-the-brow style with soft crown of rich **Lyon's Type Silk Faced Velvet** which also fashions the smart tailored bow set dashingly across the back. The handsome metallic and colorful embroidery gives unusual distinction to the hat. **Black only.** Head sizes, 22 to 23½ inches **Postpaid** **$1.98**

2H08 Here is the adorable new **Chenille** tam that everyone is talking about and all smart Fifth Avenue is wearing. It is such a stunning little model, accenting the youth of all wearers and generally becoming to all types of faces. Knit in rich colorful two-tone combination Chenille with chic ribbon bow on top and fitted with elastic band to regulate the head size. Every young woman should have one of these Chenille tams; it may be worn with any costume with just the right touch of smartness. Very attractive in **two tones of Tan, Blue or Red.** Will fit any size head. **Postpaid** .... **98¢**

How to Measure Head Size
Place a tape measure around your head as shown in the illustration (or have some one do it for you), and send us the number of inches your head measures, taken in fullest part of crown. If you wear your hair coiled low at neck take measure a trifle lower. **Be sure the hat you wish is listed in your head size**

2H10 Angora Finish Wool Tam. The Fifth Avenue shops sell this smart **Angora-finish-Wool Tam** for considerably more than our price and all smart New Yorkers are wearing it. It is such a chic little hat, one can wear it with any style of costume and it is unusually becoming. It will give unlimited wear, too, for it will stand the hardest service and look fresh and smart. Carefully made and the equal of many higher priced tams. **Red, Buff or White.** Will fit any size head. Wonderful value. **Postpaid** .... **98¢**

Be sure to give correct head size! Page 20 **HAMILTON GARMENT CO., INC.**

Below
Selection of fashionable cloche hats. *The New Silhouette from Paris*, Hamilton Garment Co. New York catalogue, c.1929

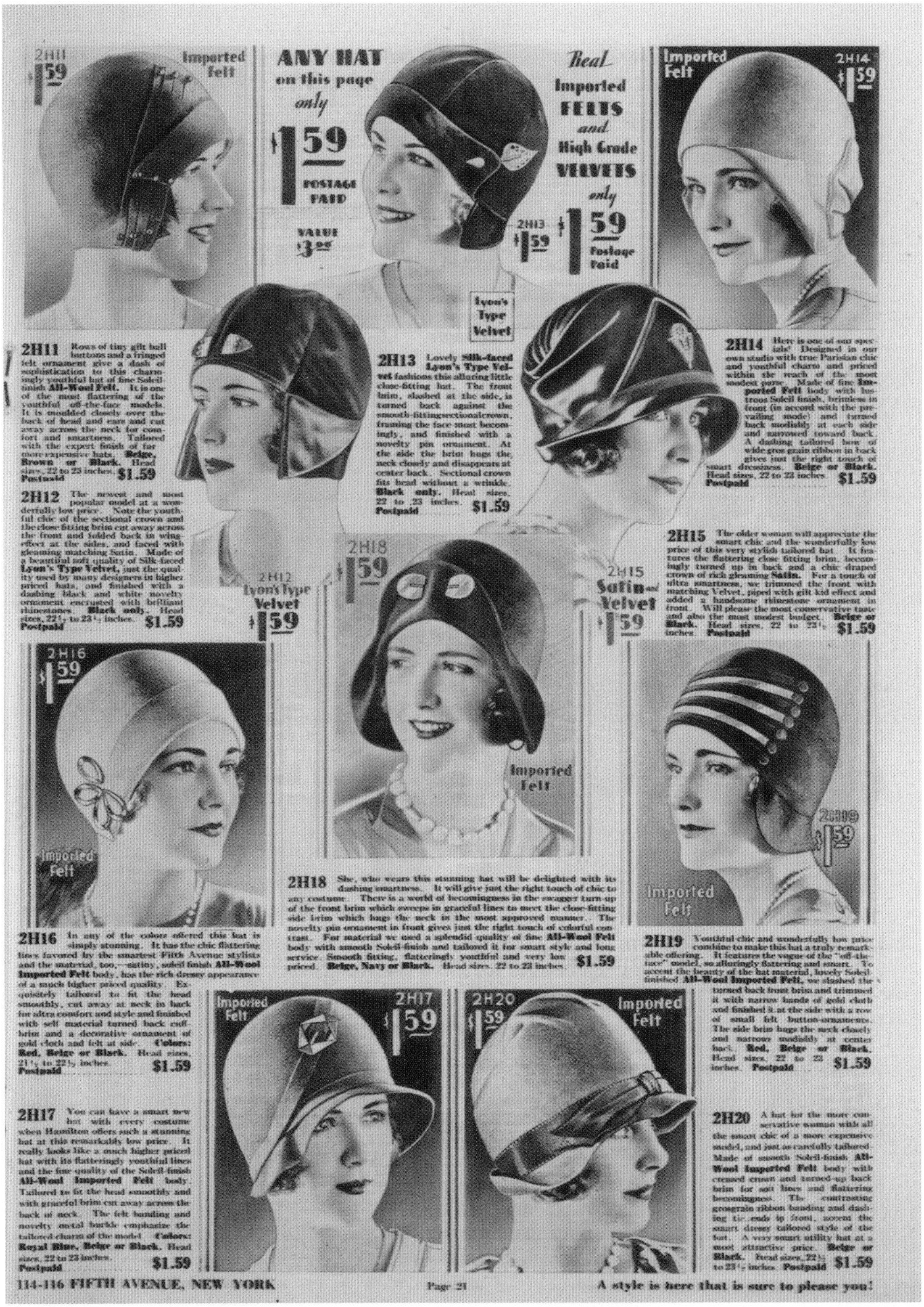

2H11 $1.59 Imported Felt

ANY HAT on this page *only* **$1.59 POSTAGE PAID** VALUE $3.00

Real **Imported FELTS** *and* **High Grade VELVETS** *only* **$1.59 Postage Paid** 2H13 $1.59

Imported Felt 2H14 $1.59

Lyon's Type Velvet

2H11 Rows of tiny gilt ball buttons and a fringed felt ornament give a dash of sophistication to this charmingly youthful hat of fine Soleil-finish **All-Wool Felt.** It is one of the most flattering of the youthful off-the-face models. It is moulded closely over the back of head and ears and cut away across the neck for comfort and smartness. Tailored with the expert finish of far more expensive hats. **Beige, Brown or Black.** Head sizes, 22 to 23 inches. **Postpaid** **$1.59**

2H12 The newest and most popular model at a wonderfully low price. Note the youthful chic of the sectional crown and the close fitting brim cut away across the front and folded back in wing-effect at the sides, and faced with gleaming matching Satin. Made of a beautiful soft quality of Silk-faced **Lyon's Type Velvet,** just the quality used by many designers in higher priced hats, and finished with a dashing black and white novelty ornament encrusted with brilliant rhinestones. **Black only.** Head sizes, 22½ to 23½ inches. **Postpaid** **$1.59**

2H13 Lovely **Silk-faced Lyon's Type Velvet** fashions this alluring little close-fitting hat. The front brim, slashed at the side, is turned back against the smooth-fitting sectional crown, framing the face most becomingly, and finished with a novelty pin ornament. At the side the brim hugs the neck closely and disappears at center back. Sectional crown fits head without a wrinkle. **Black only.** Head sizes, 22 to 23 inches. **Postpaid** **$1.59**

2H14 Here is one of our specials! Designed in our own studio with true Parisian chic and youthful charm and priced within the reach of the most modest purse. Made of fine **Imported Felt** body with lustrous Soleil finish, brimless in front (in accord with the prevailing mode) and turned back modishly at each side and narrowed toward back. A dashing tailored bow of wide gros grain ribbon in back gives just the right touch of smart dressiness. **Beige or Black.** Head sizes, 22 to 23 inches. **Postpaid** **$1.59**

2H12 Lyon's Type Velvet $1.59

2H18 $1.59

2H15 Satin and Velvet $1.59

2H15 The older woman will appreciate the smart chic and the wonderfully low price of this very stylish tailored hat. It features the flattering close fitting brim, becomingly turned up in back and a chic draped crown of rich gleaming **Satin.** For a touch of ultra smartness, we trimmed the front with matching Velvet, piped with gilt kid effect and added a handsome rhinestone ornament in front. Will please the most conservative taste and also the most modest budget. **Beige or Black.** Head sizes, 22 to 23½ inches. **Postpaid** **$1.59**

2H16 $1.59 Imported Felt

Imported Felt

2H19 $1.59 Imported Felt

2H16 In any of the colors offered this hat is simply stunning. It has the chic flattering lines favored by the smartest Fifth Avenue stylists and the material, too,—satiny, soleil finish **All-Wool Imported Felt** body, has the rich dressy appearance of a much higher priced quality. Exquisitely tailored to fit the head smoothly, cut away at neck in back for ultra comfort and style and finished with self material turned back cuff-brim and a decorative ornament of gold cloth and felt at side. **Colors: Red, Beige or Black.** Head sizes, 21½ to 22½ inches. **Postpaid** **$1.59**

2H18 She, who wears this stunning hat will be delighted with its dashing smartness. It will give just the right touch of chic to any costume. There is a world of becomingness in the swagger turn-up of the front brim which sweeps in graceful lines to meet the close-fitting side brim which hugs the neck in the most approved manner. The novelty pin ornament in front gives just the right touch of colorful contrast. For material we used a splendid quality of fine **All-Wool Felt** body with smooth Soleil-finish and tailored it for smart style and long service. **Smooth fitting,** flatteringly youthful and very low priced. **Beige, Navy or Black.** Head sizes, 22 to 23 inches. **$1.59**

2H19 Youthful chic and wonderfully low price combine to make this hat a truly remarkable offering. It features the vogue of the "off-the-face" model, so alluringly flattering and smart. To accent the beauty of the hat material, lovely Soleil-finished **All-Wool Imported Felt,** we slashed the turned back front brim and trimmed it with narrow bands of gold cloth and finished it at the side with a row of small felt button-ornaments. The side brim hugs the neck closely and narrows modishly at center back. **Red, Beige or Black.** Head sizes, 22 to 23 inches. **Postpaid** **$1.59**

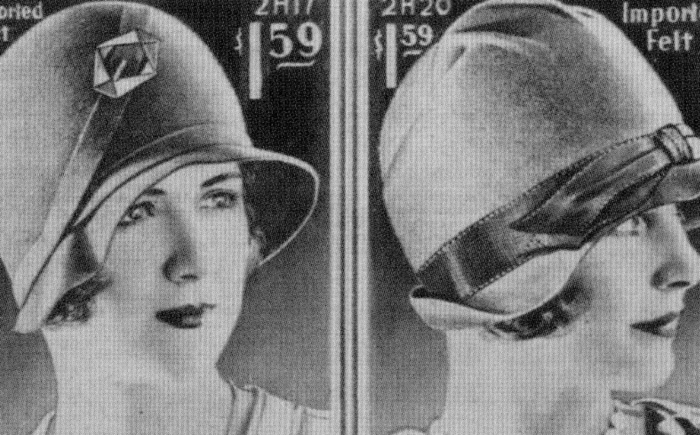

2H17 You can have a smart new hat with every costume when Hamilton offers such a stunning hat at this remarkably low price. It really looks like a much higher priced hat with its flatteringly youthful lines and the fine quality of the Soleil-finish **All-Wool Imported Felt** body. Tailored to fit the head smoothly and with graceful brim cut away across the back of neck. The felt banding and novelty metal buckle emphasize the tailored charm of the model. **Colors: Royal Blue, Beige or Black.** Head sizes, 22 to 23 inches. **Postpaid** **$1.59**

2H20 A hat for the more conservative woman with all the smart chic of a more expensive model, and just as carefully tailored. Made of smooth Soleil-finish **All-Wool Imported Felt** body with creased crown and turned-up back brim for soft lines and flattering becomingness. The contrasting grosgrain ribbon banding and dashing tie-ends in front, accent the smart dressy tailored style of the hat. A very smart utility hat at a most attractive price. **Beige or Black.** Head sizes, 22½ to 23½ inches. **Postpaid** **$1.59**

114-116 FIFTH AVENUE, NEW YORK Page 21 **A style is here that is sure to please you!**

Right
A selection of hats illustrating the wide variety of fashionable styles in the early 1920s. *The Delineator*, 1922

FABRICS HEAD THE HAT LIST

Many Hats of Crêpe Silks and Satin Mingle with Spring Straws and Horsehair

Photographs from Underwood & Underwood

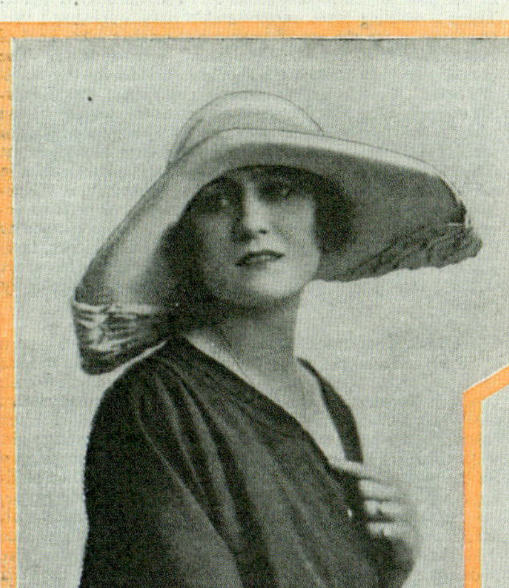

The collarless dress has brought into vogue a type of hat that frames the neck as well as the face, or that partially fills the hiatus between head and shoulders with a cascade of ribbon or lace or the softening influence of a draped veil. From Berthe Desbois

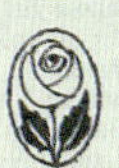

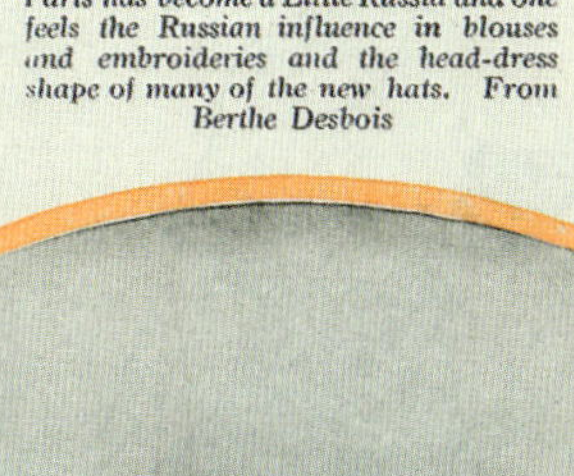

Paris has become a Little Russia and one feels the Russian influence in blouses and embroideries and the head-dress shape of many of the new hats. From Berthe Desbois

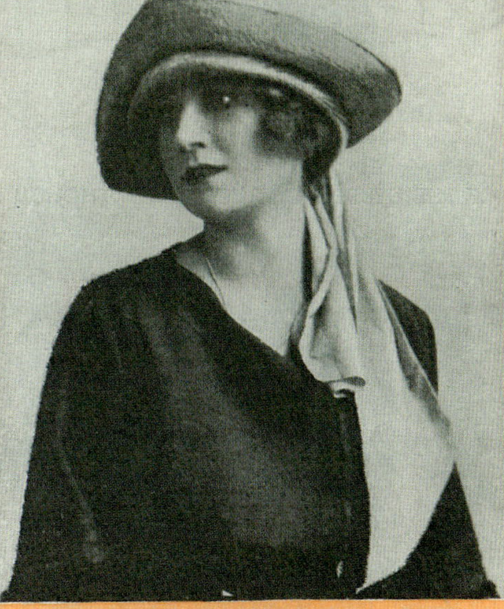

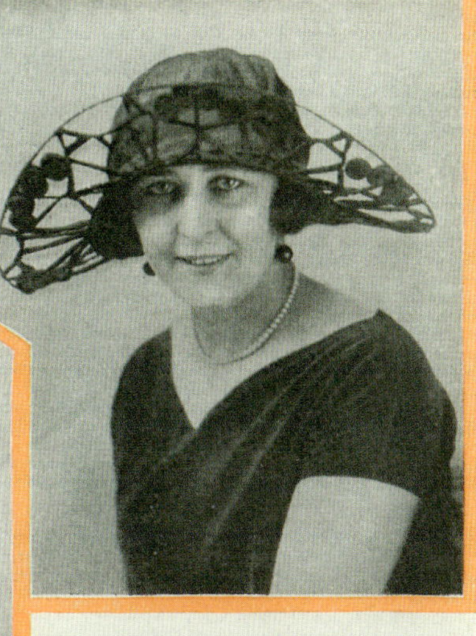

An afternoon hat of crêpe silk sees the light through its wide brim of lattice-work and fabric flowers. Many hats are made of fabric, satin, taffeta and the crêpe silks, and for afternoon they are usually large and very lightly trimmed. From Simone et Gaby

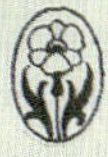

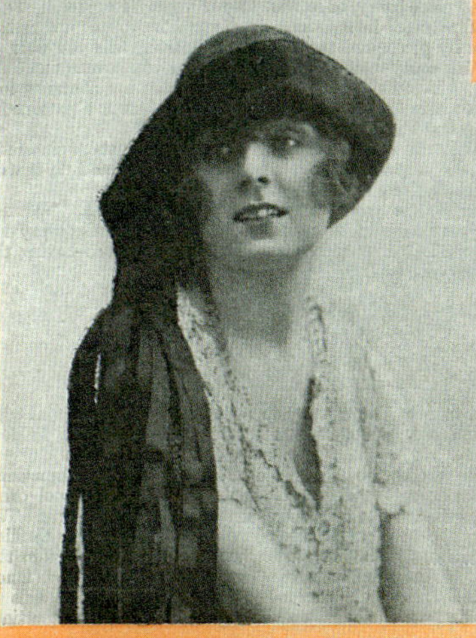

"Keep to the right" is the rule for trimming, whether it is a many-ended fall of ribbons, a feather, a cluster of flowers or an ornament of fantastic shape. Ends of ribbon are new and very smart. From Lewis

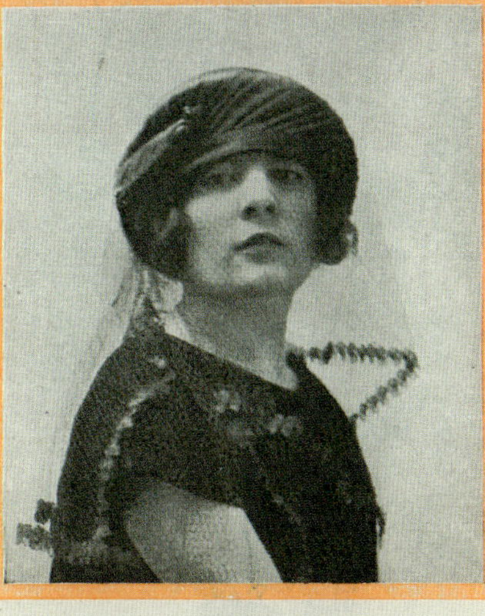

A small hat has many uses. It is at home in any society with a silk or satin frock, and it can also be worn with a tailored suit for shopping, the morning promenade or for a voyage by boat or rail. From Lewis

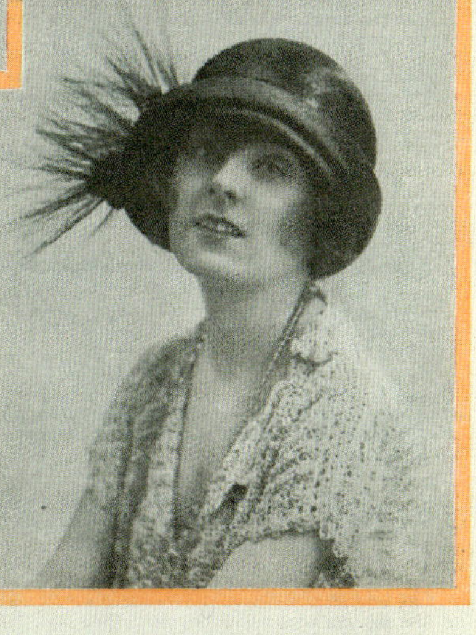

The present style of hat, whether large or small, is the hatpinless type that fits the head snugly and is worn to the eyebrows, a fashion that suits both bobbed hair and the close-to-the-head style of hair-dressing. From Lewis

Below and right

Woman at the races in floral crepe dress with pleated skirt, a dark blue coat and an envelope bag. *Nouvelle Mode*, 1926

"Latest Fashions" in hats. The pyramid-like hats were derived from traditional festive Russian kokoshnik headdresses and reflect the impact of Russian émigré designers on Parisian fashions. *La Nouveauté Francaise*, 1921.

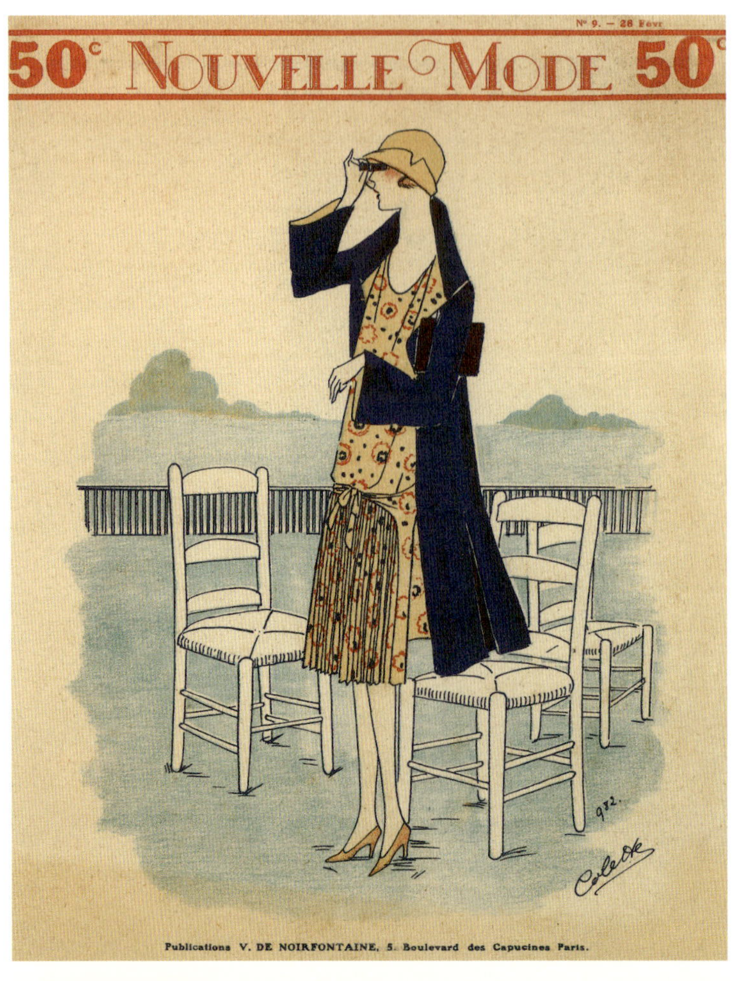

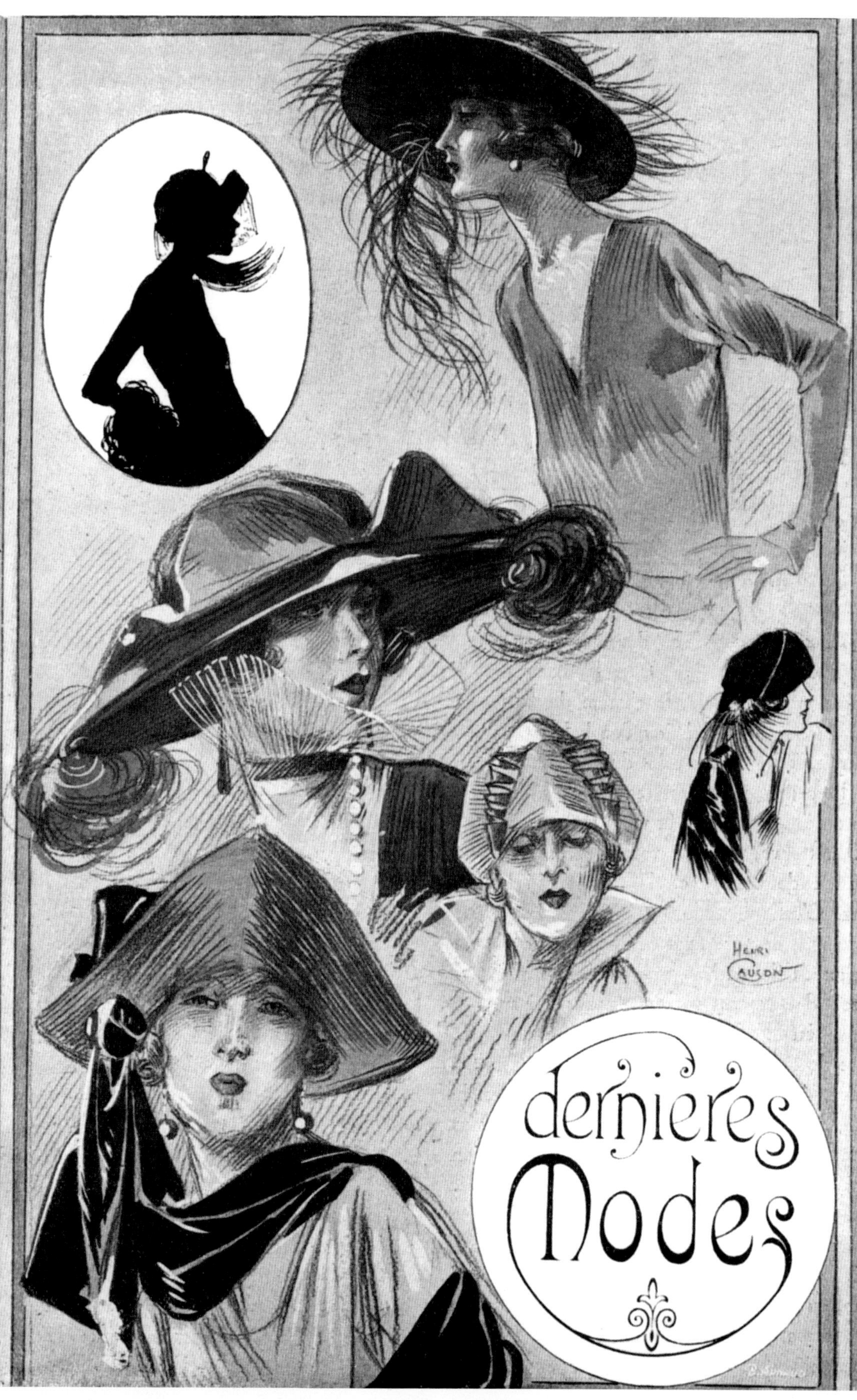
HENRI CAUSON
dernieres
Modes

Right
Cover of *La Femme Chic à Paris*, July 1926

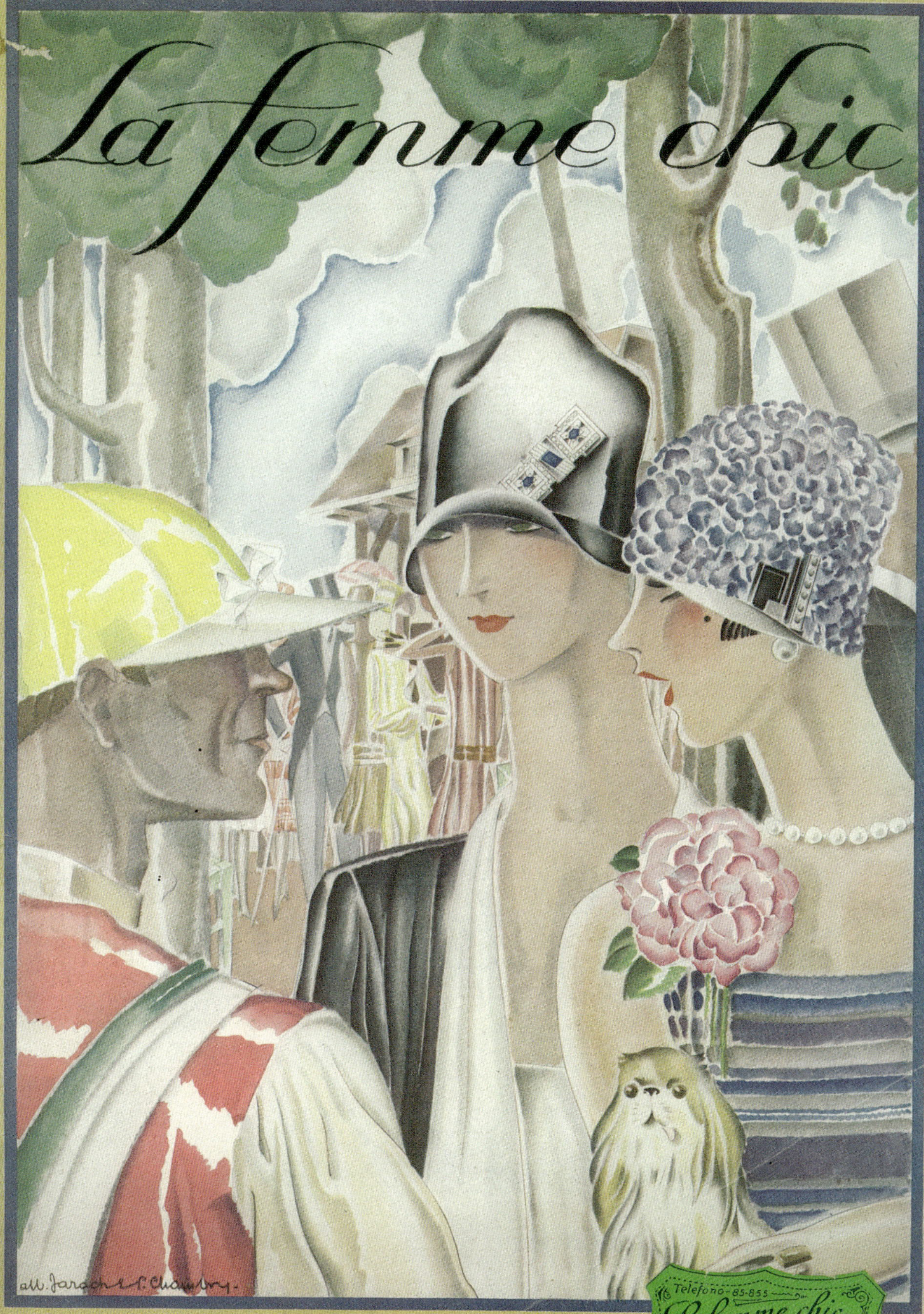
La femme chic
Telefono-85-855
La femme chic

Right
A creation by Reville of Hanover Square, London – a close-fitting almond green jumper matched with motoring gauntlets, c.1928

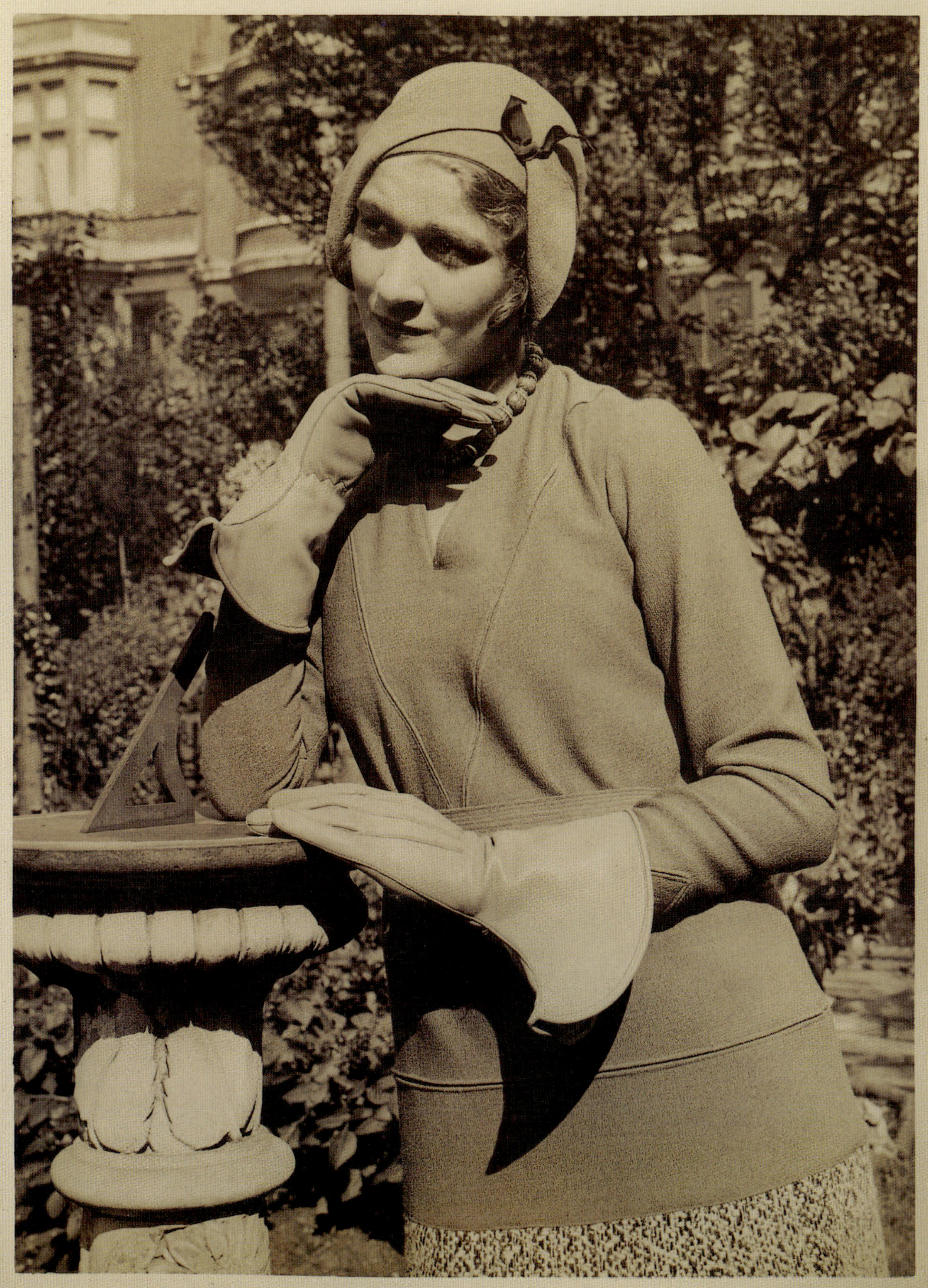

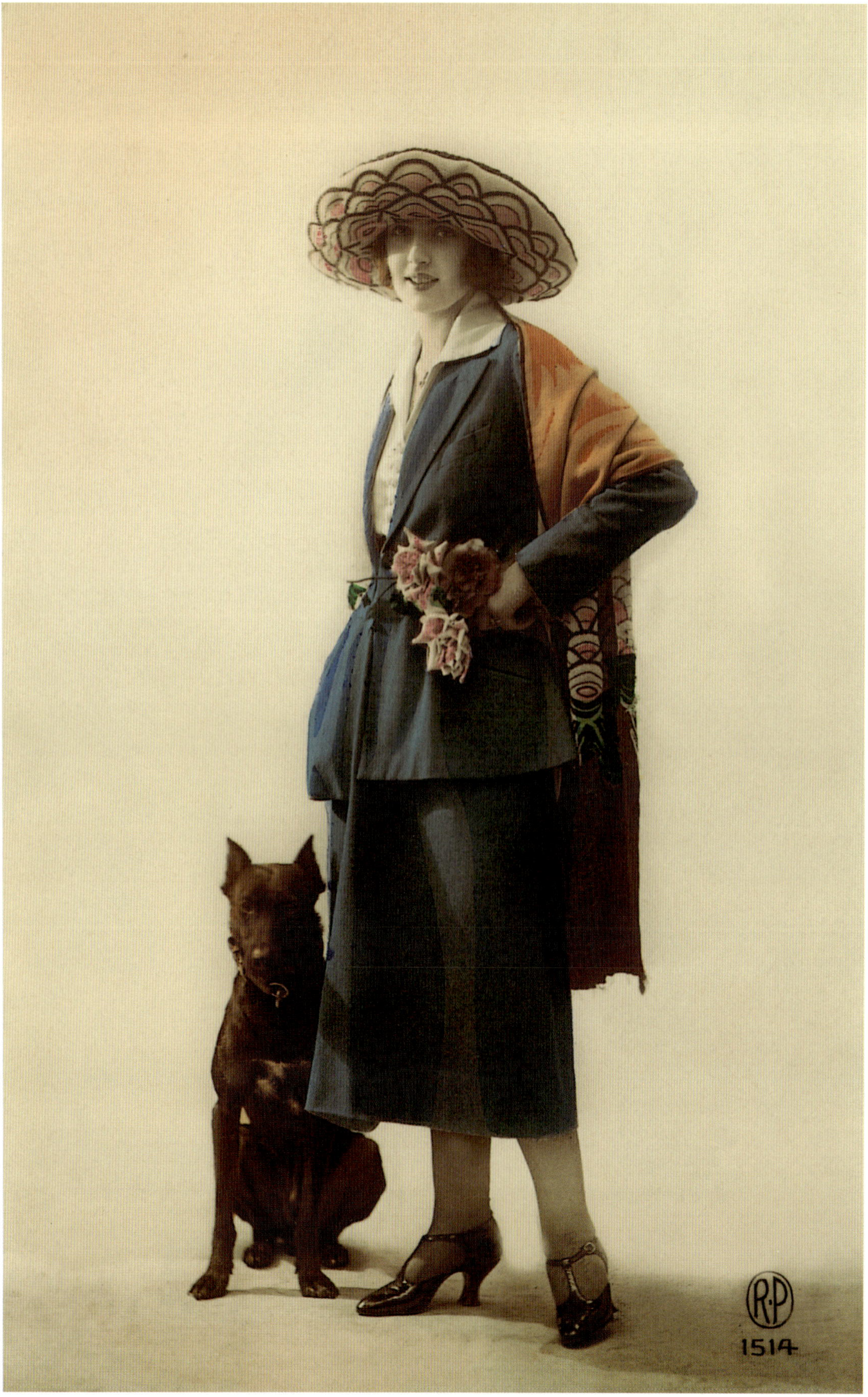

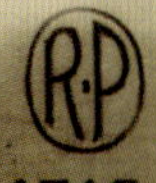
R·P
1514

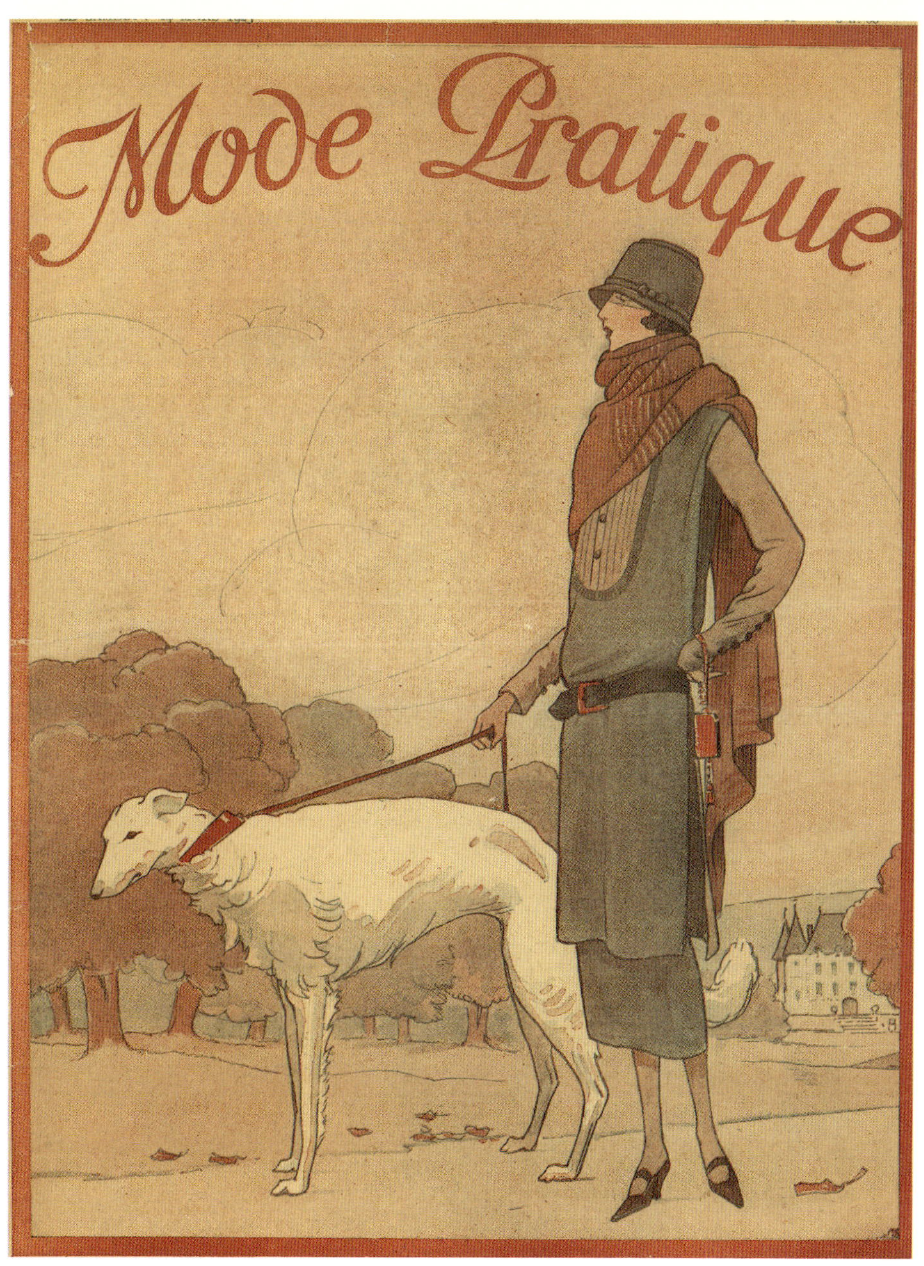

Left and above

Postcard of a woman in a blue ensemble with an exotic scarf, 1922

Woman in a fashionable knitted tunic suit, with matching hat and Bakelite handbag. *Mode Pratique*, 1925

Right
Photograph of two fashionable women, with the model on the left wearing a velvet cape coat with a wide ruffled collar, while the one on the right wears a luxurious fur stole, c.1923

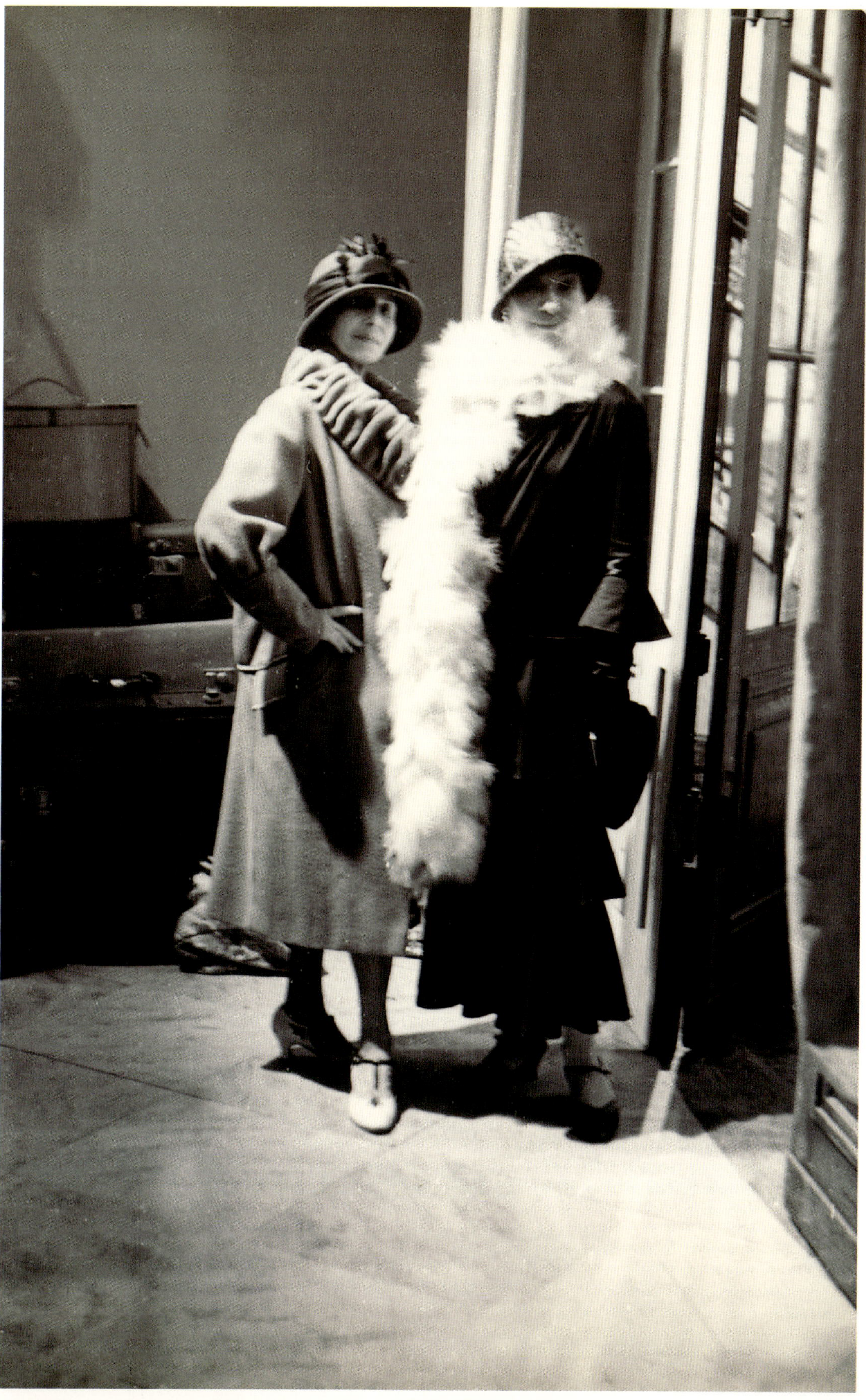

Right
Woman in a blue sweater dress with matching scarf and toque in multicoloured design. *Nouvelle Mode*, 1924

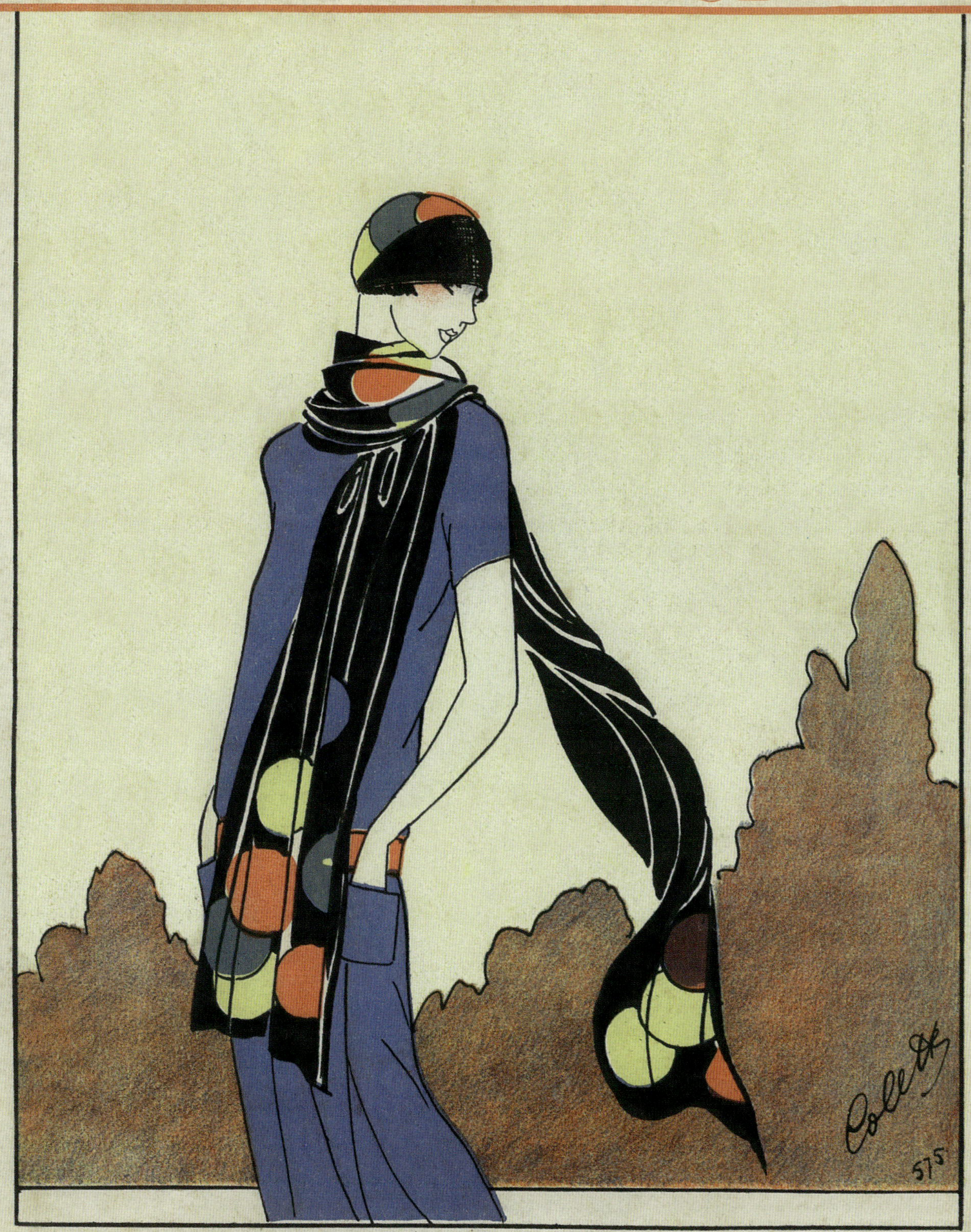
Nº 20. — 18 Mai 1924
NOUVELLE MODE
Colette
575
Publications V. DE NOIRFONTAINE, 5. Boulevard des Capucines Paris.

Below and right

Design for a wide brimmed hat. *Les Chapeaux du "Trés Parisien"*, 1923-1924

Woman wearing a black opera coat with a fur collar, accessorised with a matching fur turban-style hat and muff. *La Mode*, 1920

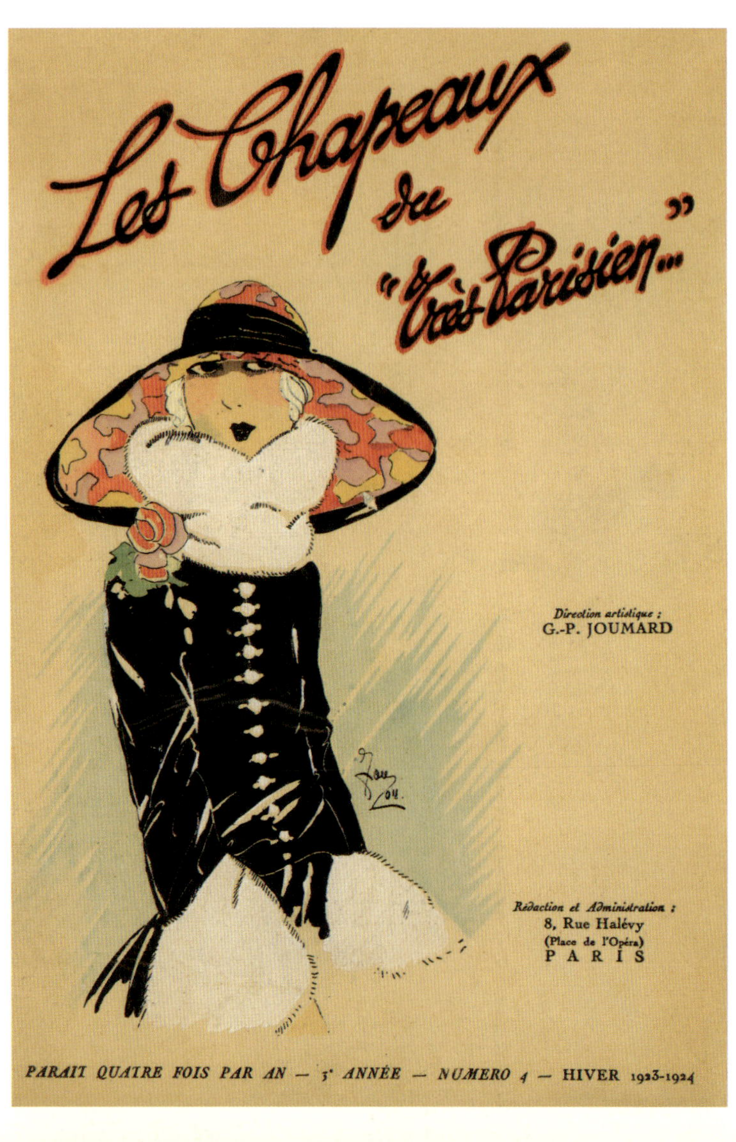

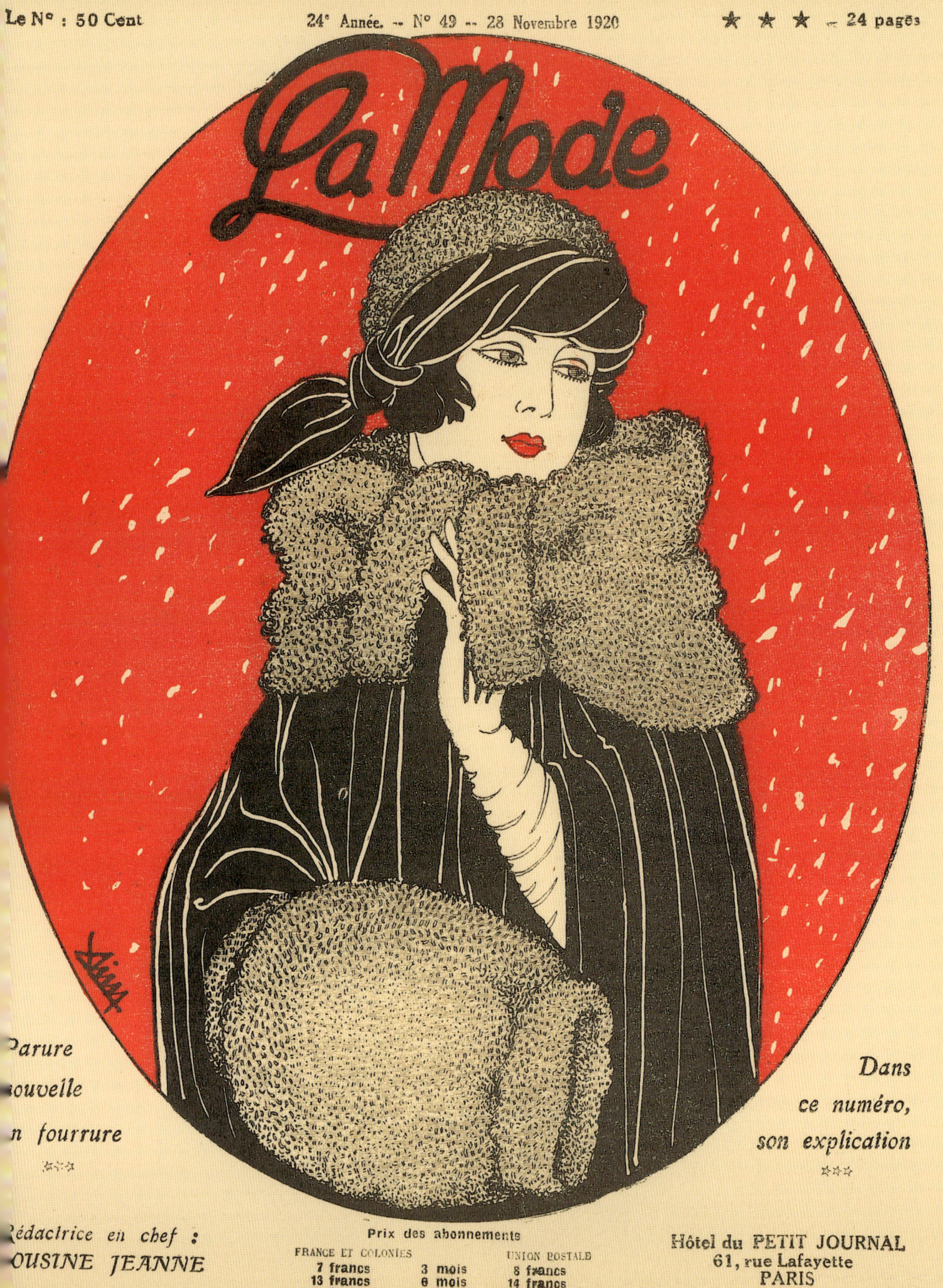

Le N° : 50 Cent — 24e Année. -- N° 49 -- 28 Novembre 1920 — ★ ★ ★ -- 24 pages

La Mode

Parure
ouvelle
n fourrure

Dans
ce numéro,
son explication

Rédactrice en chef :
OUSINE JEANNE

Prix des abonnements

FRANCE ET COLONIES		UNION POSTALE
7 francs	3 mois	8 francs
13 francs	6 mois	14 francs
25 francs	Un an	27 francs

Hôtel du PETIT JOURNAL
61, rue Lafayette
PARIS

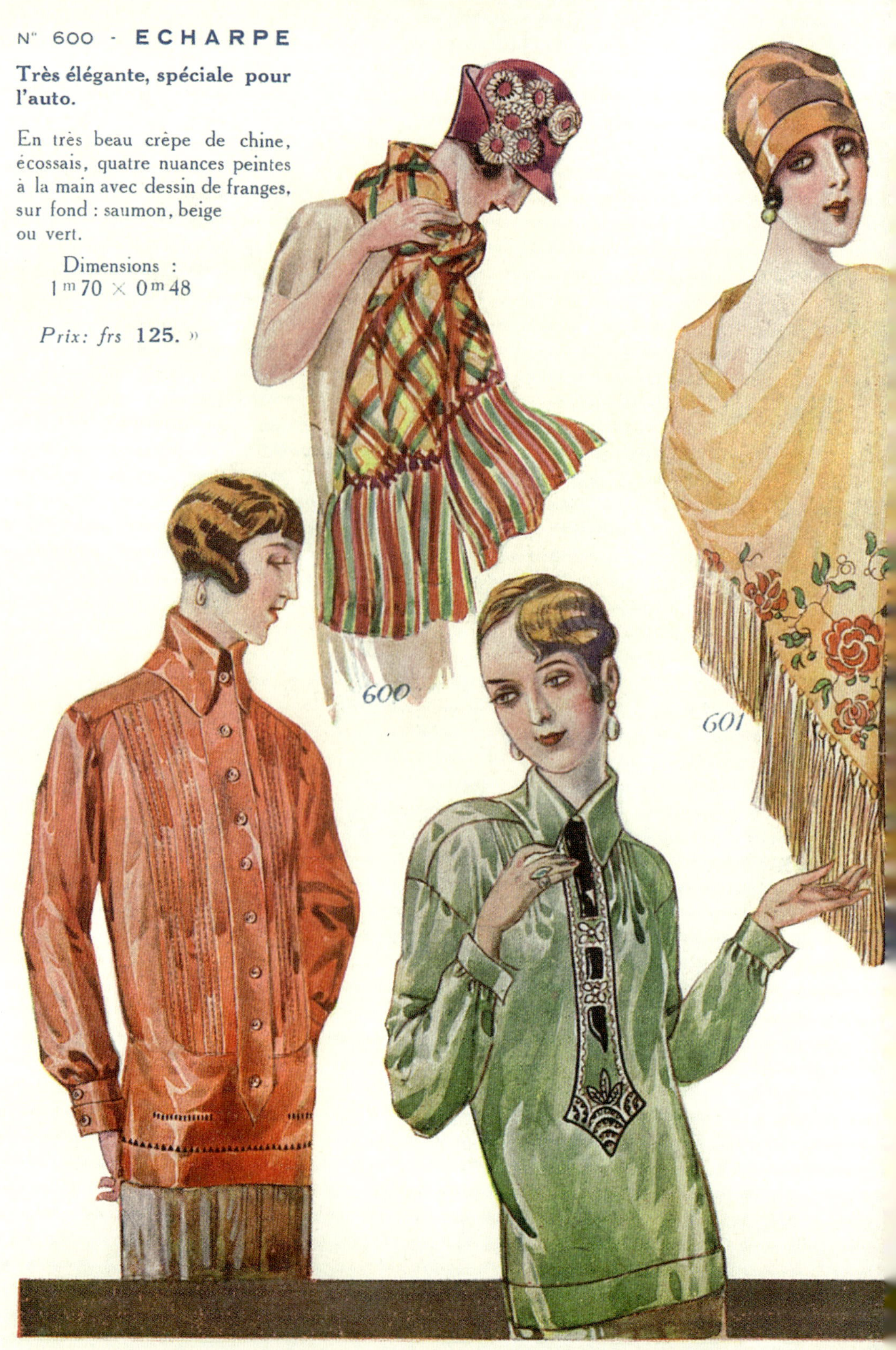

"GERDA" 20 boul^d M

N° 600 - **ECHARPE**

Très élégante, spéciale pour l'auto.

En très beau crêpe de chine, écossais, quatre nuances peintes à la main avec dessin de franges, sur fond : saumon, beige ou vert.

Dimensions :
1 m 70 × 0 m 48

Prix: frs **125.** »

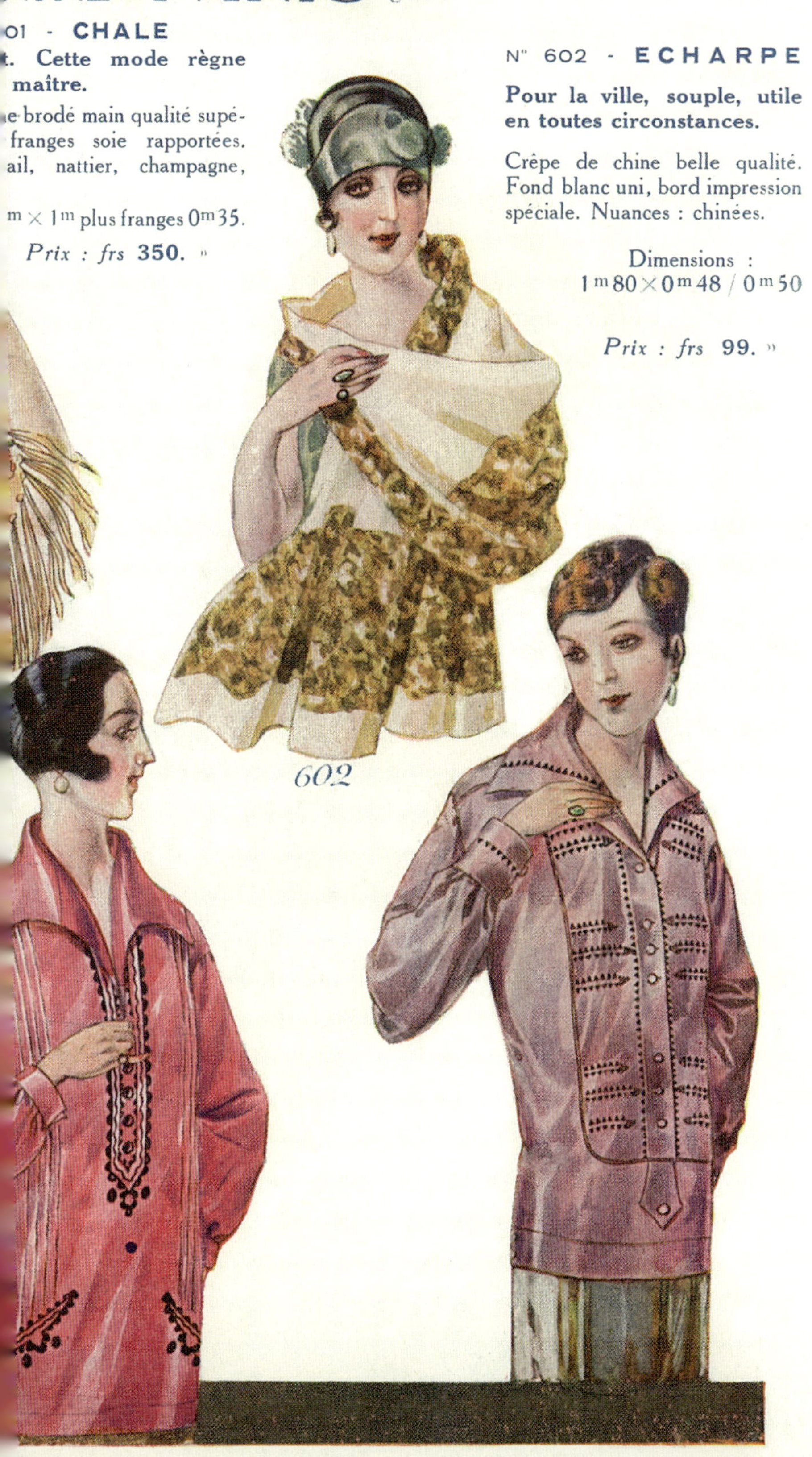

RTRE PARIS

01 - CHALE

t. Cette mode règne maître.

e brodé main qualité supé- franges soie rapportées. ail, nattier, champagne,

m × 1 m plus franges 0 m 35.

Prix : frs **350.** »

N° 602 - ECHARPE

Pour la ville, souple, utile en toutes circonstances.

Crêpe de chine belle qualité. Fond blanc uni, bord impression spéciale. Nuances : chinées.

Dimensions : 1 m 80 × 0 m 48 / 0 m 50

Prix : frs **99.** »

602

Previous page

Blouses and shawls by Maison Gerda. Maison Gerda catalogue, c.1925

Below and right

Four summer dresses in crepe, embroidered in a variety of designs and colours. *The Ladies' Home Journal*, 1922 – with a prerequisite parasol

Crocheted and knitted fashions and accessories. *Woman's Home Companion*, 1922

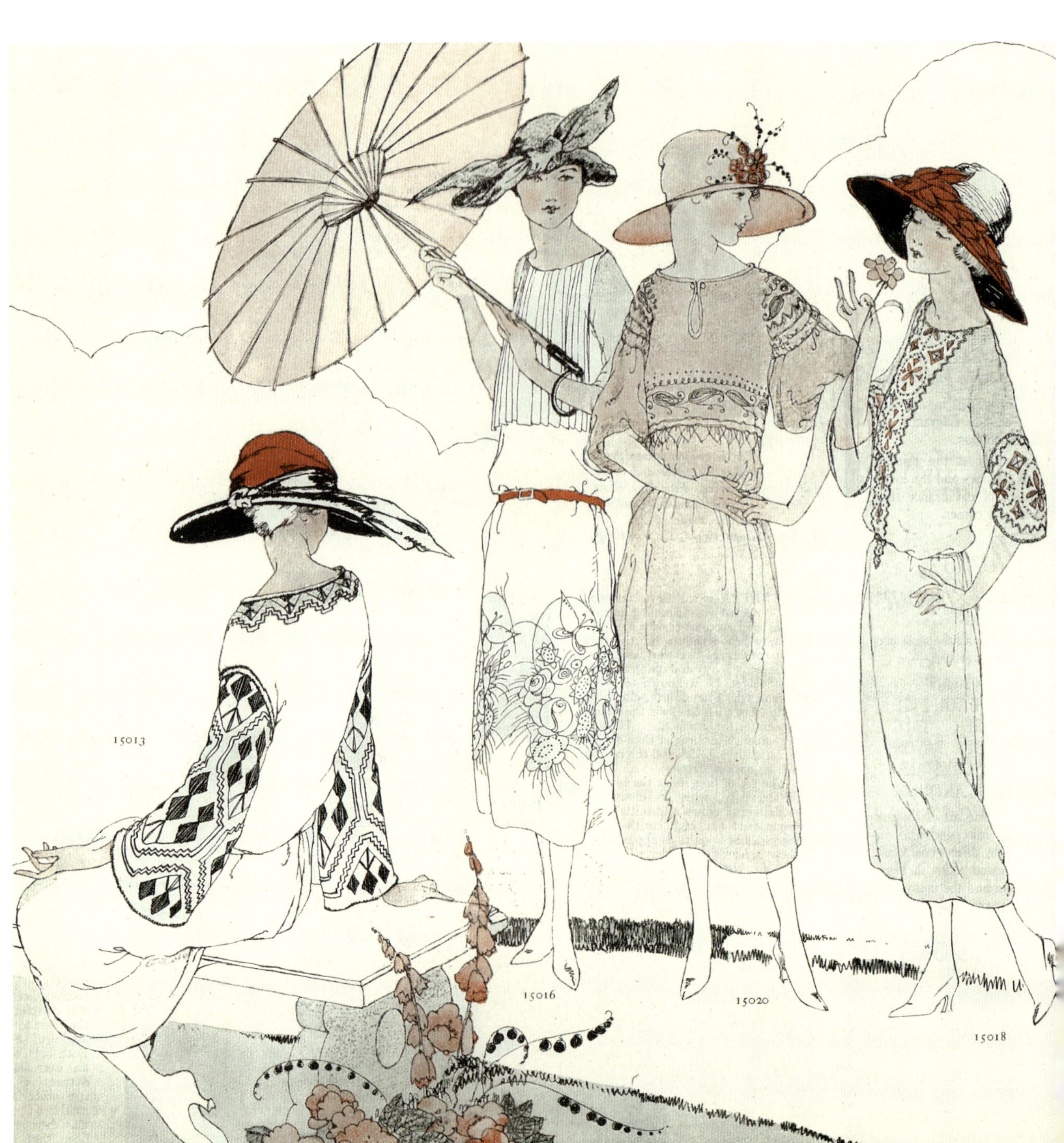

Spring Smartness Phrased in Wool

Cleverly knit and crocheted for sports and street wear

Designed by HELEN MARVIN

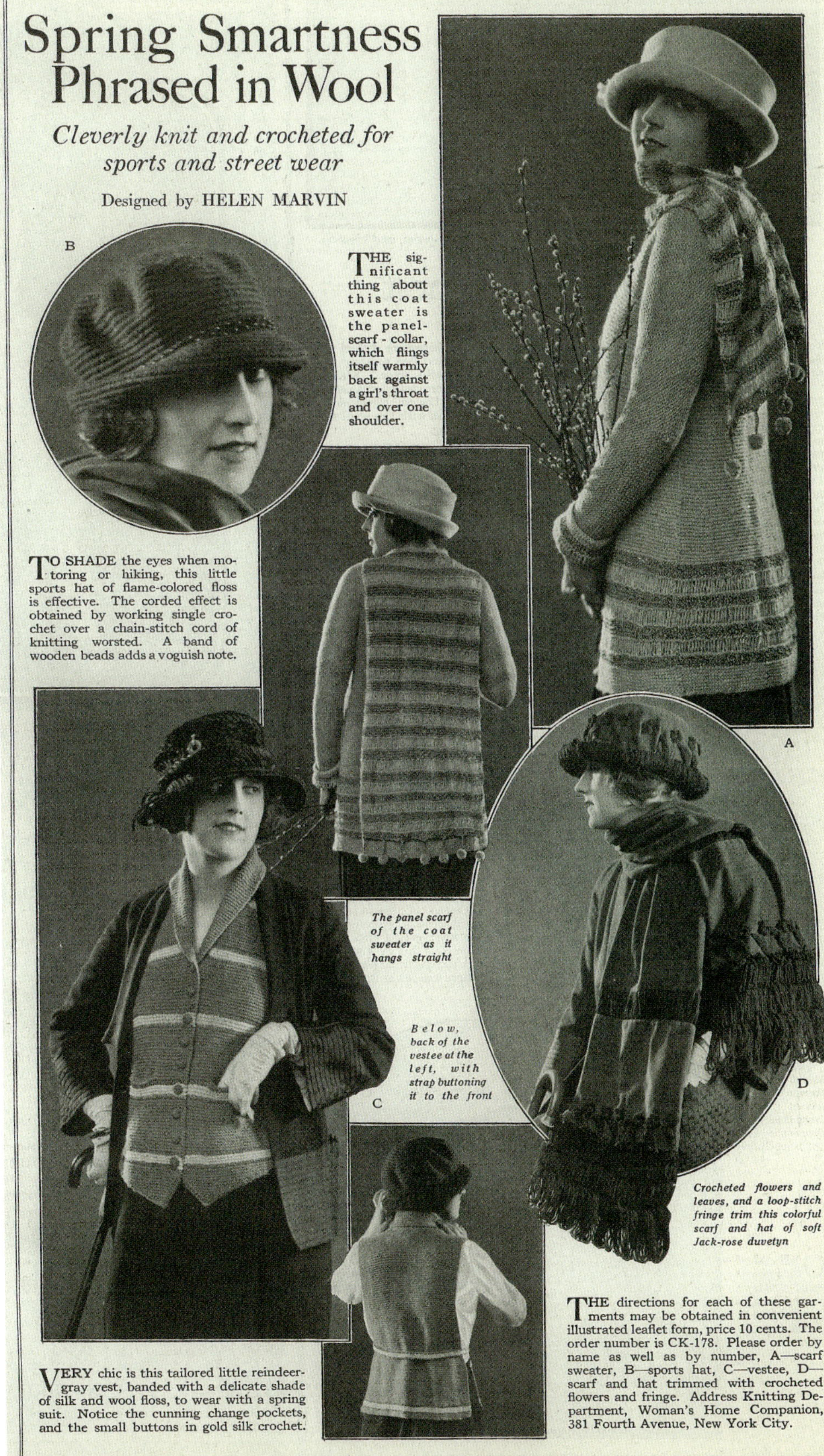

THE significant thing about this coat sweater is the panel-scarf-collar, which flings itself warmly back against a girl's throat and over one shoulder.

TO SHADE the eyes when motoring or hiking, this little sports hat of flame-colored floss is effective. The corded effect is obtained by working single crochet over a chain-stitch cord of knitting worsted. A band of wooden beads adds a voguish note.

The panel scarf of the coat sweater as it hangs straight

Below, back of the vestee at the left, with strap buttoning it to the front

Crocheted flowers and leaves, and a loop-stitch fringe trim this colorful scarf and hat of soft Jack-rose duvetyn

VERY chic is this tailored little reindeer-gray vest, banded with a delicate shade of silk and wool floss, to wear with a spring suit. Notice the cunning change pockets, and the small buttons in gold silk crochet.

THE directions for each of these garments may be obtained in convenient illustrated leaflet form, price 10 cents. The order number is CK-178. Please order by name as well as by number, A—scarf sweater, B—sports hat, C—vestee, D—scarf and hat trimmed with crocheted flowers and fringe. Address Knitting Department, Woman's Home Companion, 381 Fourth Avenue, New York City.

LA MODE DES VOILETTES

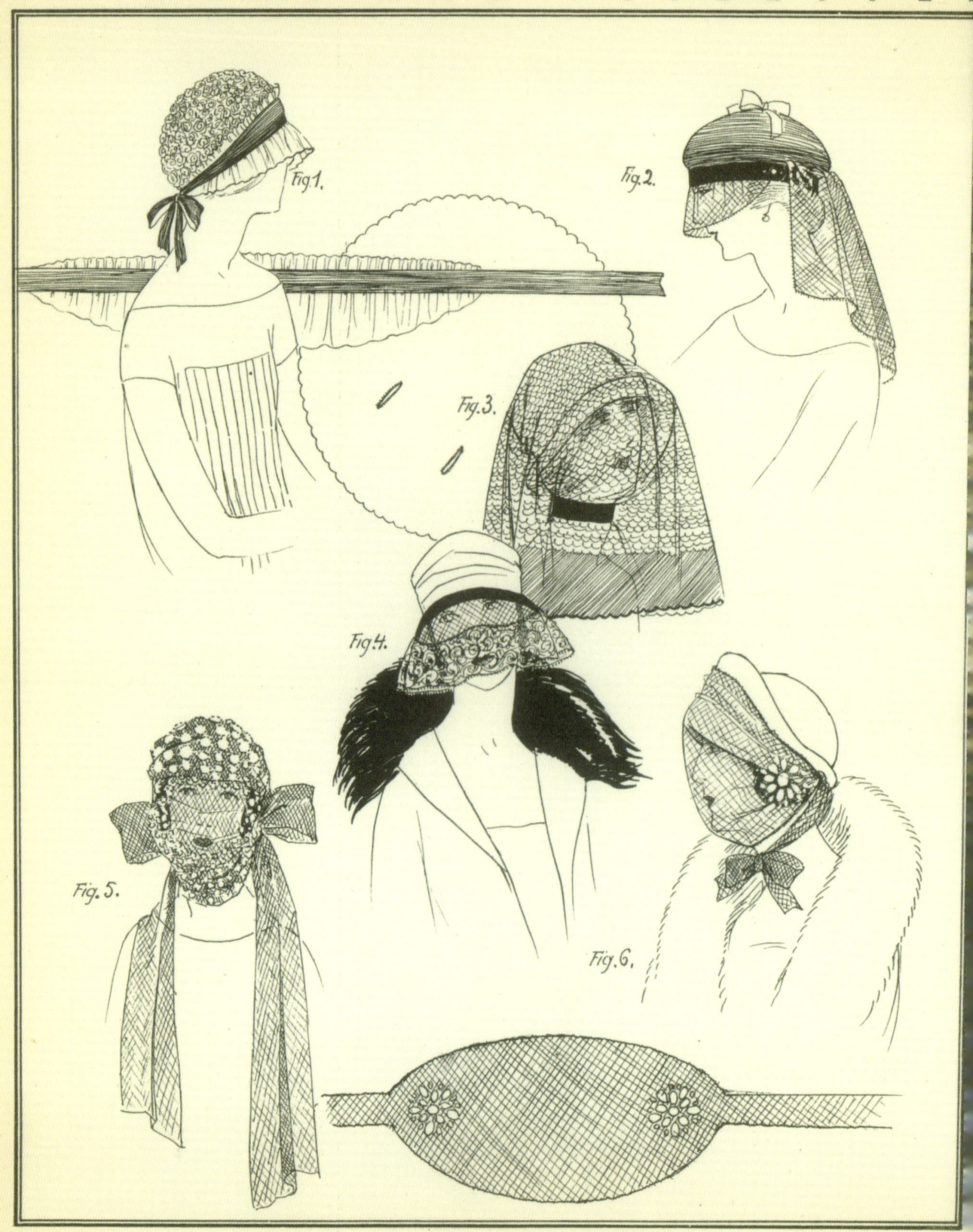

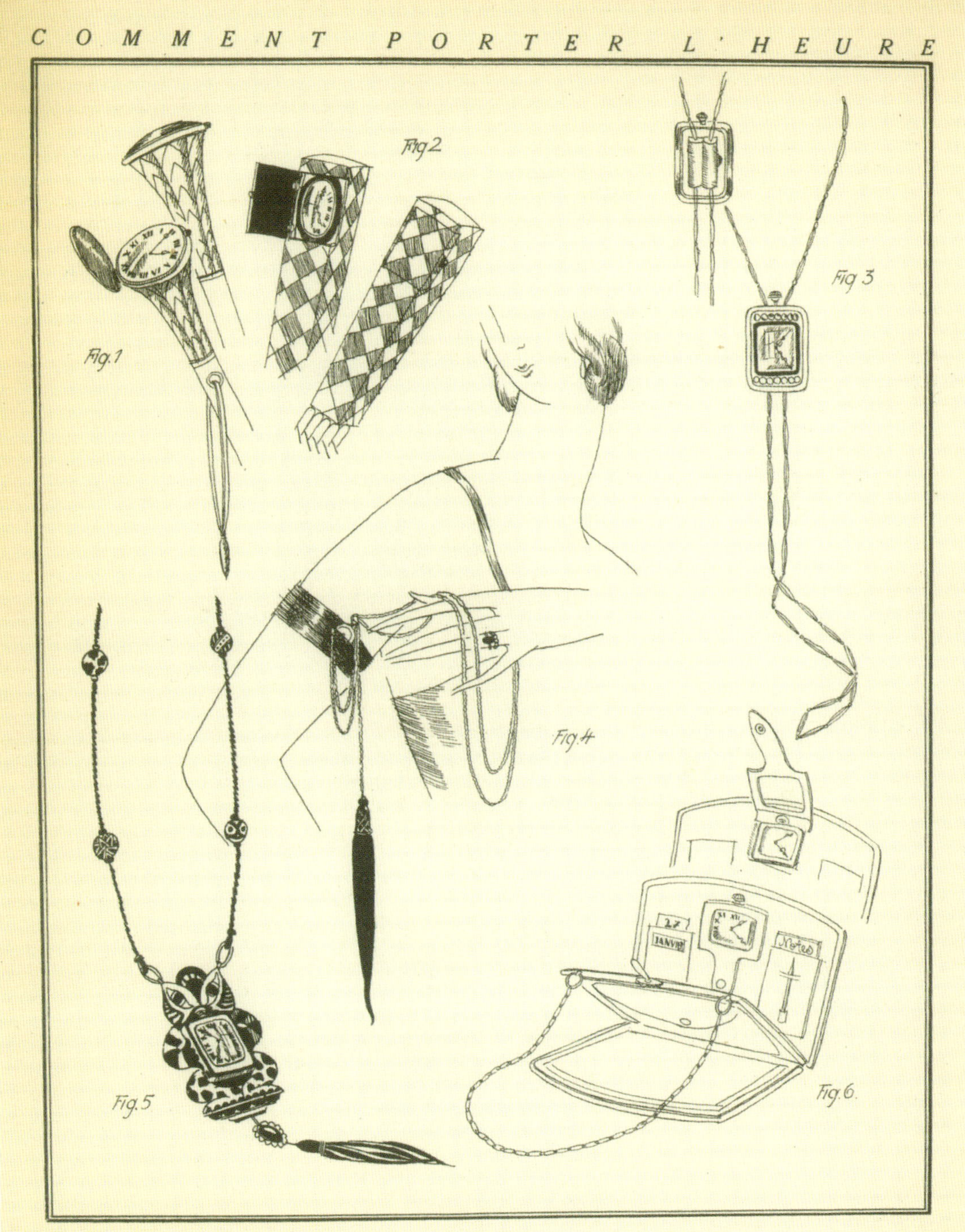

Left and above

Selection of fashionable veils.
Gazette du Bon Ton, 1922

Illustration of upmarket novelty watches. *Gazette du Bon Ton*, 1922

Right
Woman in a white summer dress with a bold rose motif, pleated panels and bell sleeves carrying a parasol.
Nouvelle Mode, 1926

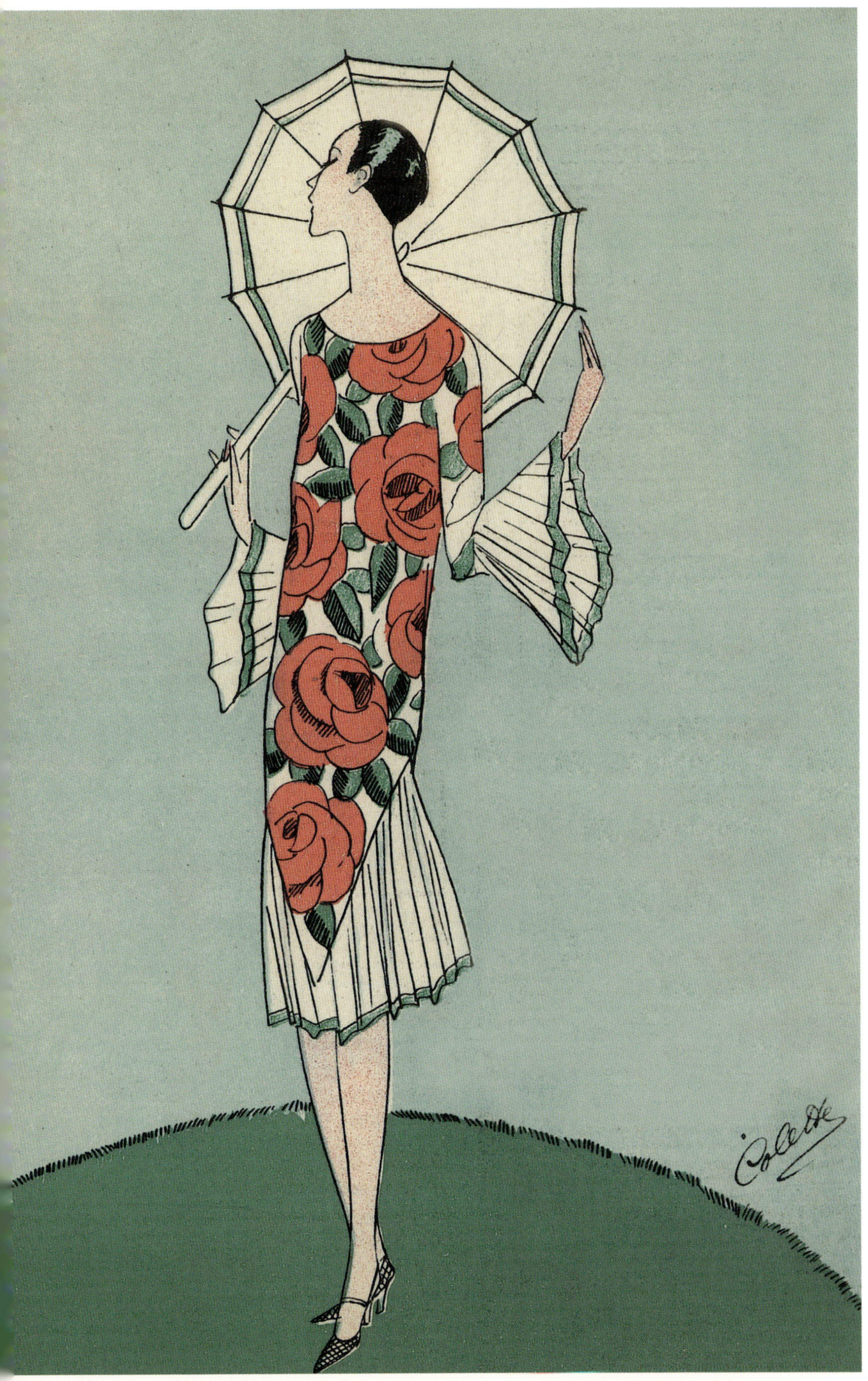

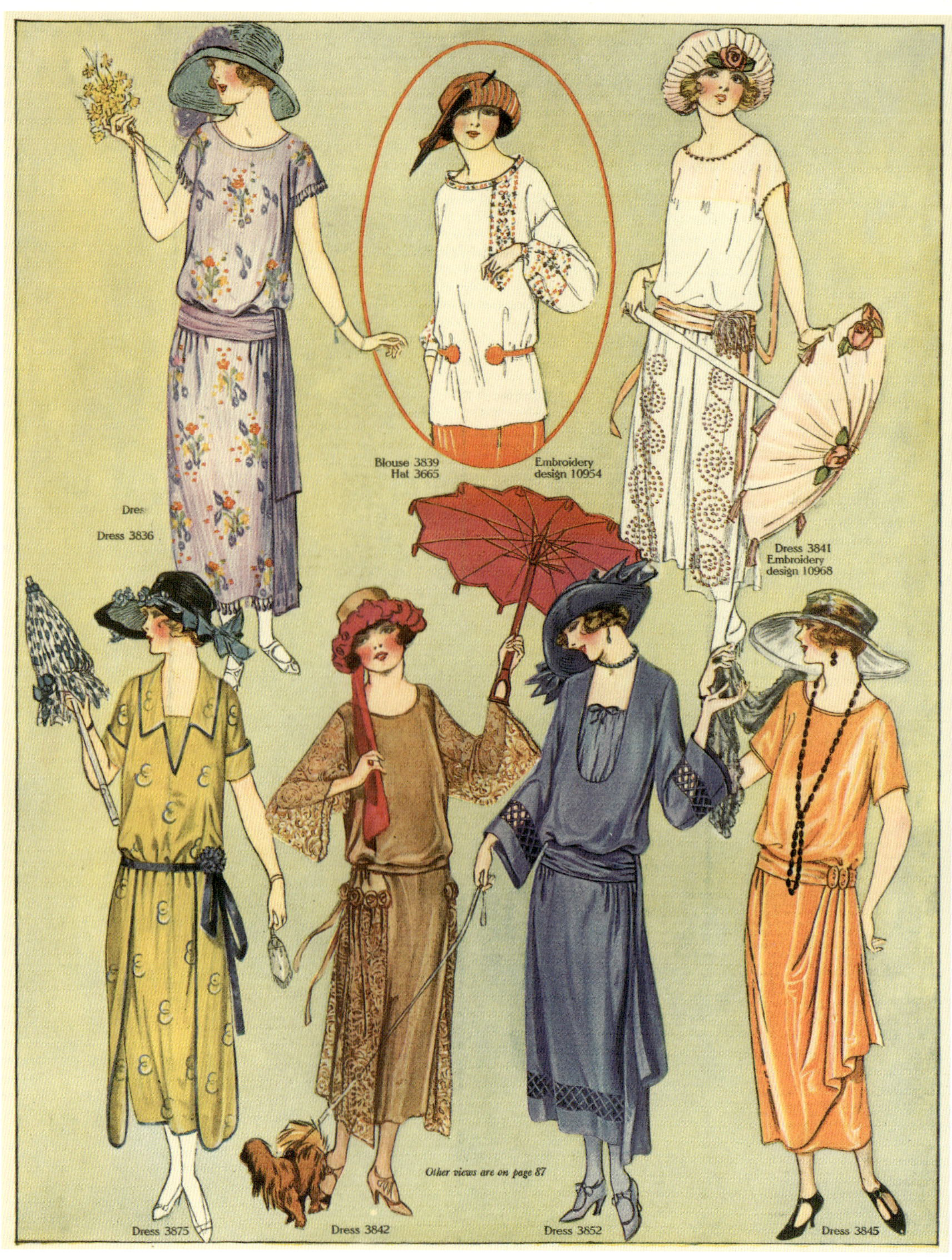

Above
Designs for summer dresses accompanied by a variety of accessories. *The Delineator*, 1922

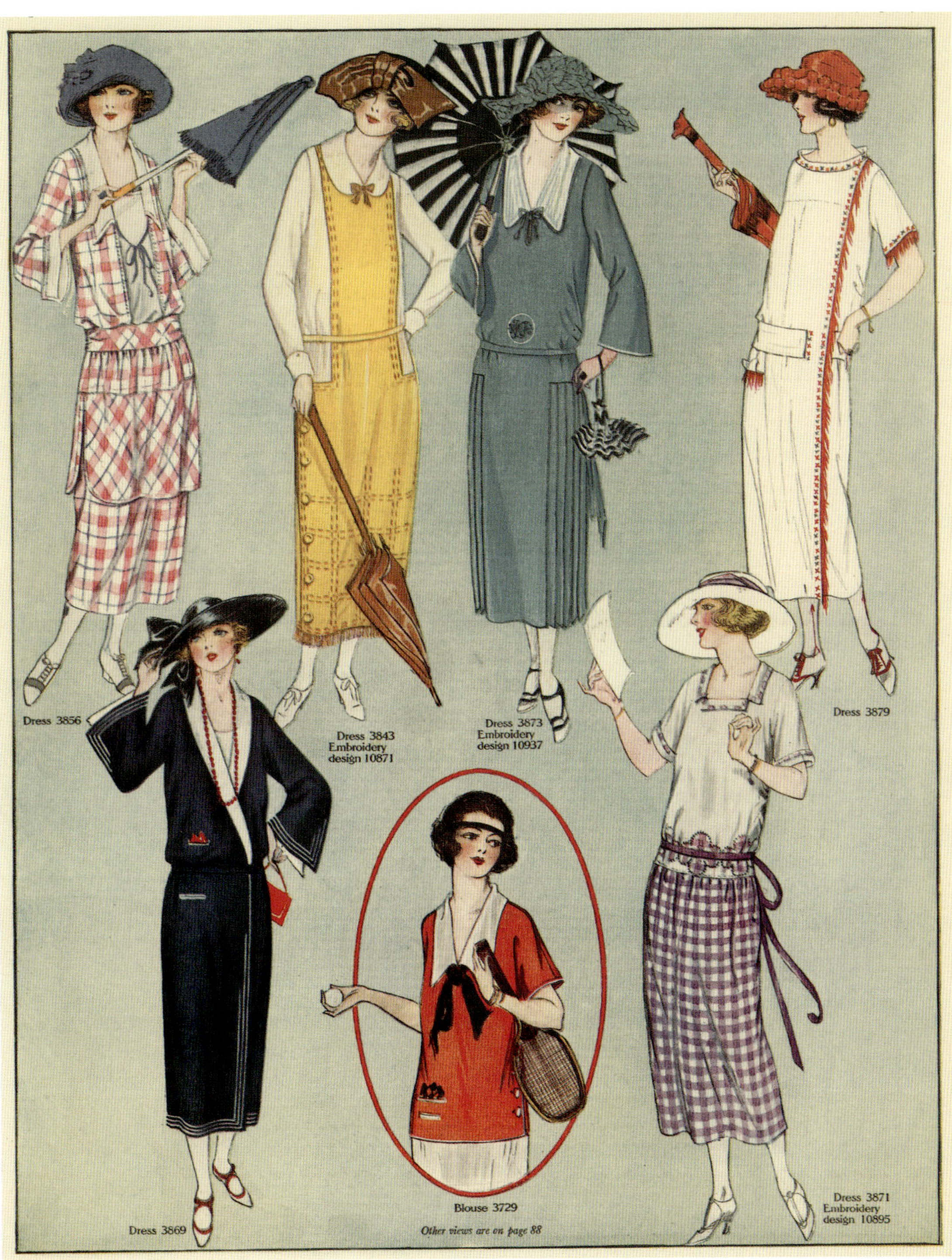

Above

Designs for summer dresses accompanied by a variety of accessories. *The Delineator*, 1922

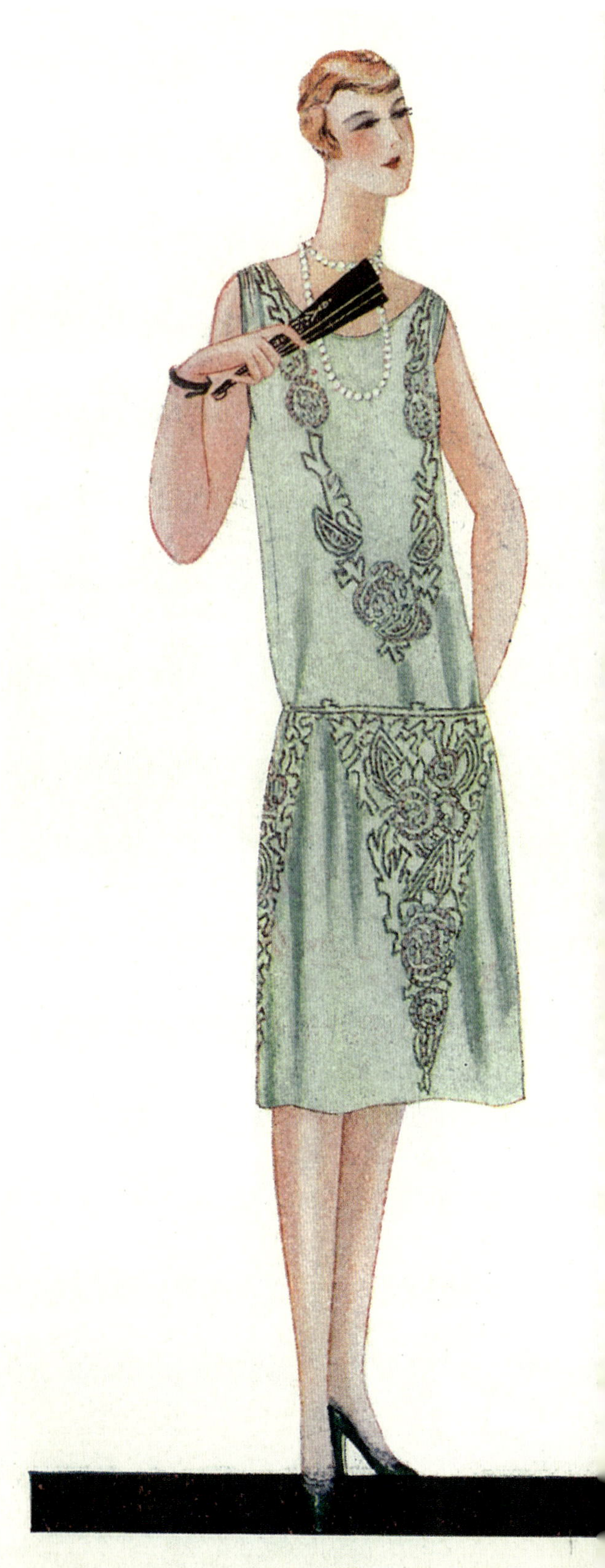

Right
Three evening dresses by Maison Gerda. Maison Gerda Catalogue, c.1925 – with fans including one made from ostrich feathers

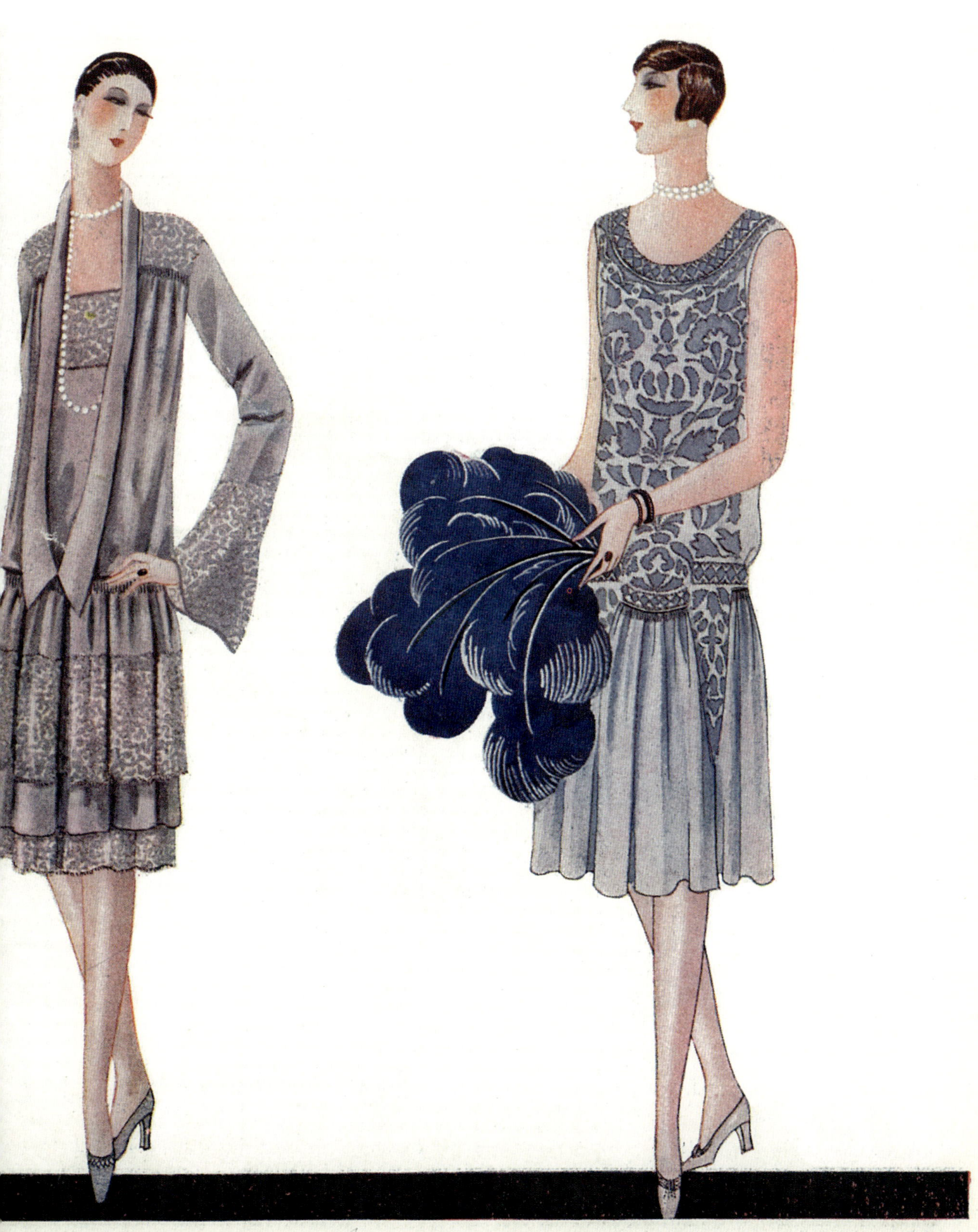

Right
A luxurious evening gown in diaphanous material cut into an upwards v-shape at the front and trimmed with panels of metallic fabric. The top half of the dress is made from the same material. The style is finished off with a floral fabric corsage and an ostrich feather fan. London, c.1926

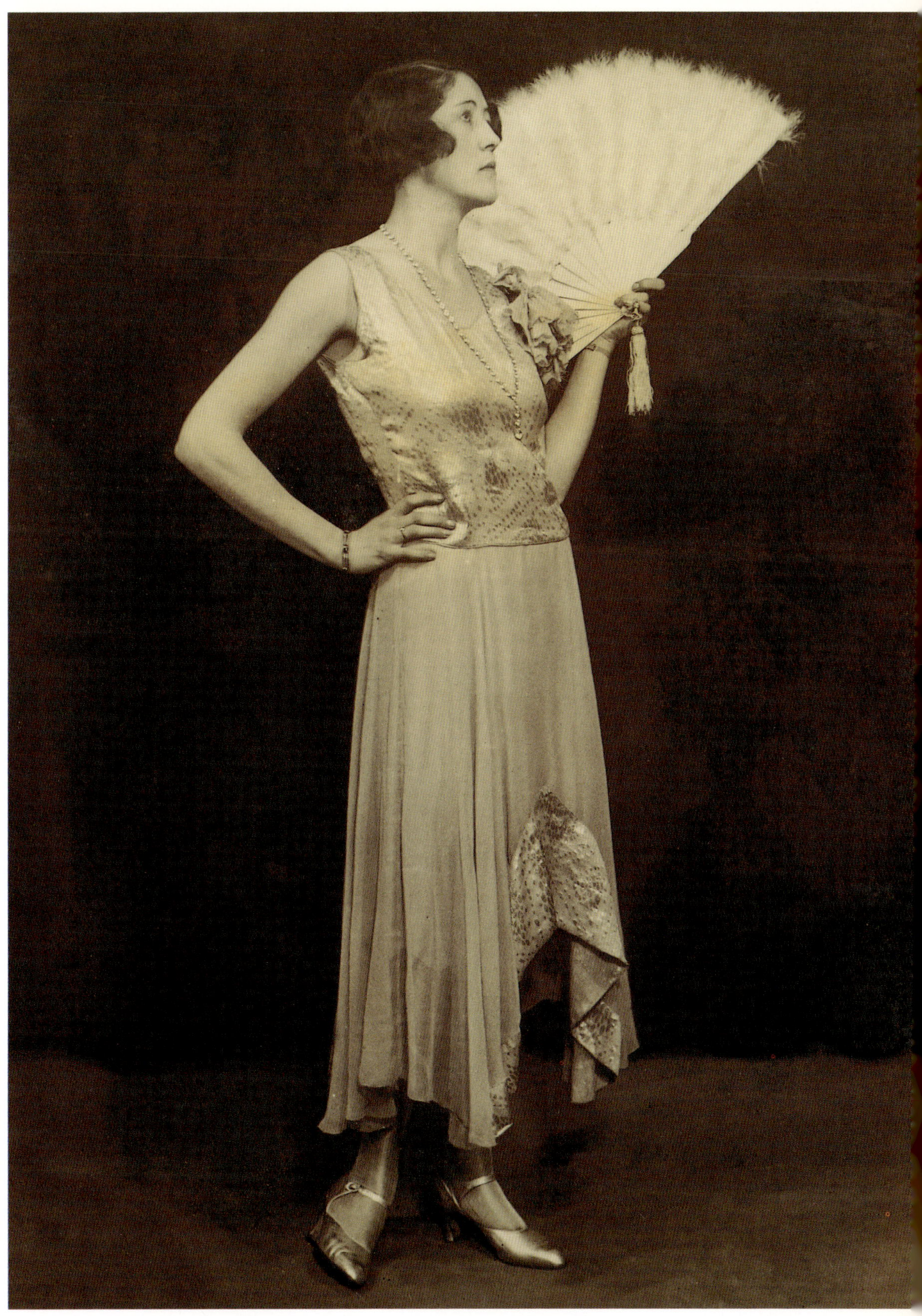

Below
Over-the-knee decorative jersey spatter dashers worn over leather heels. 'Spats' had traditionally been made of leather and were mostly worn by men to protect their shoes and trousers although they did have a decorative function. In the 1920s they became a purely decorative ladies fashion. USA, c.1925

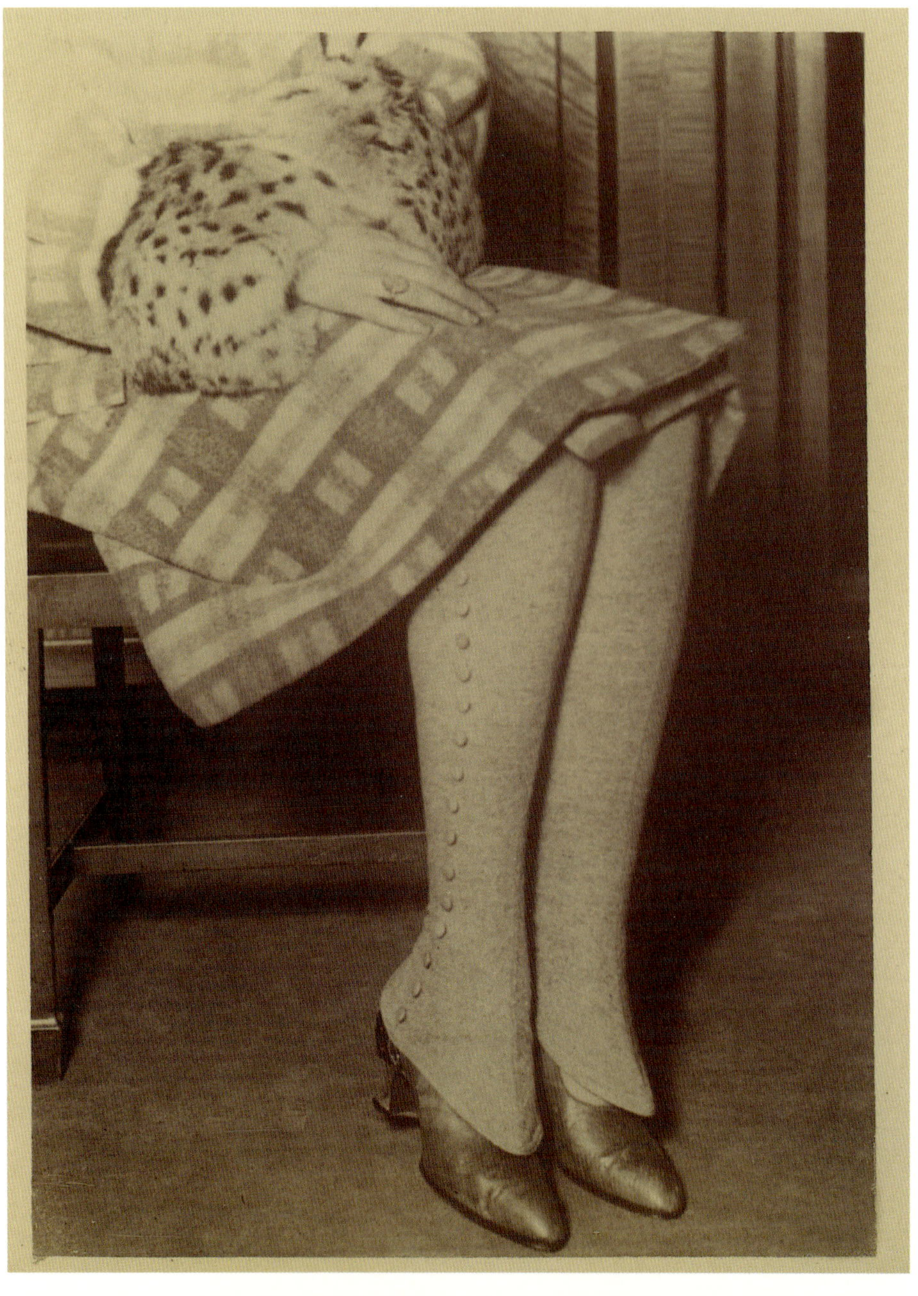

Below
Anklets or decorative ankle bands worn over a nude shade of patterned stockings and with decorated leather strappy heels. USA, c.1925

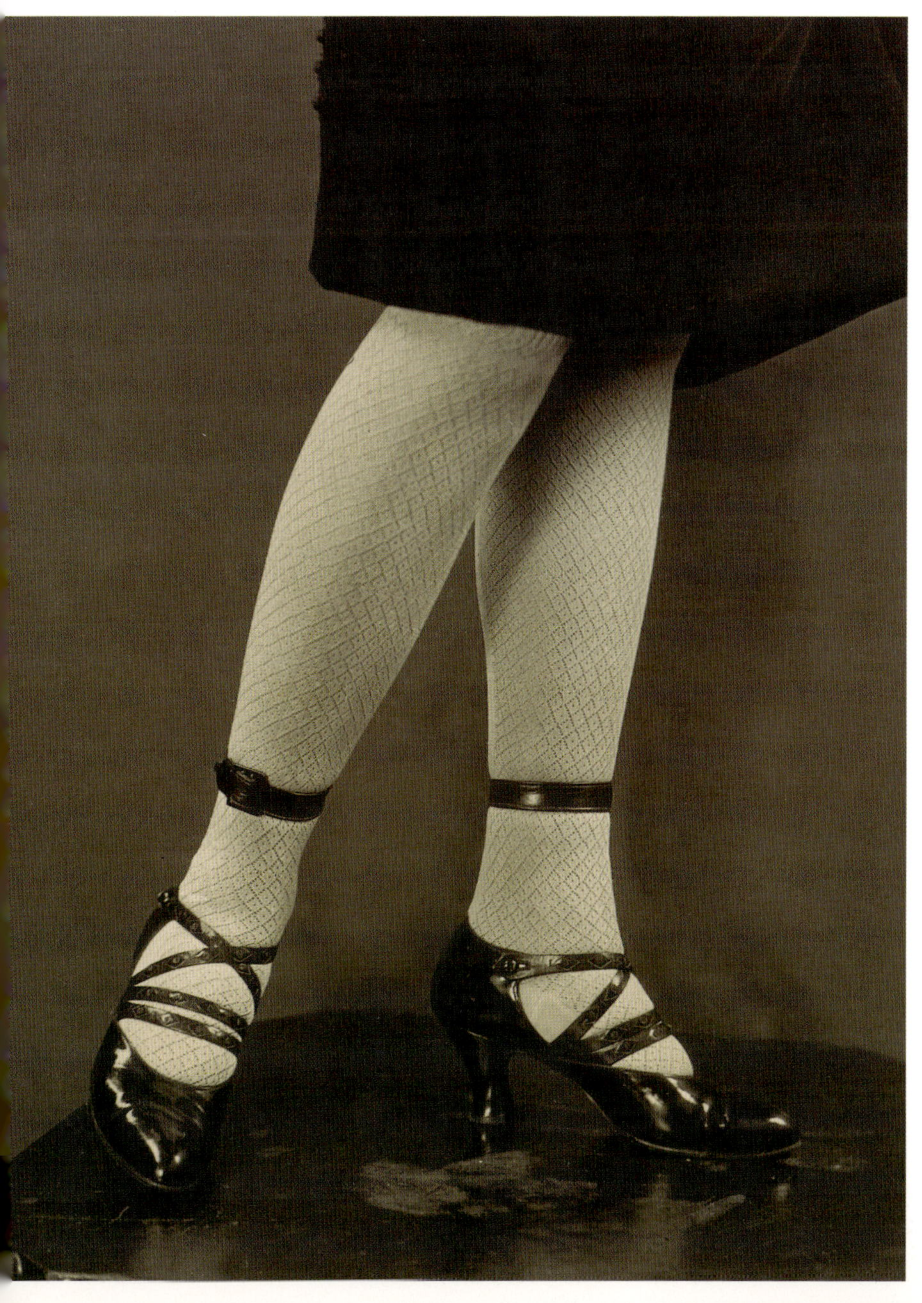

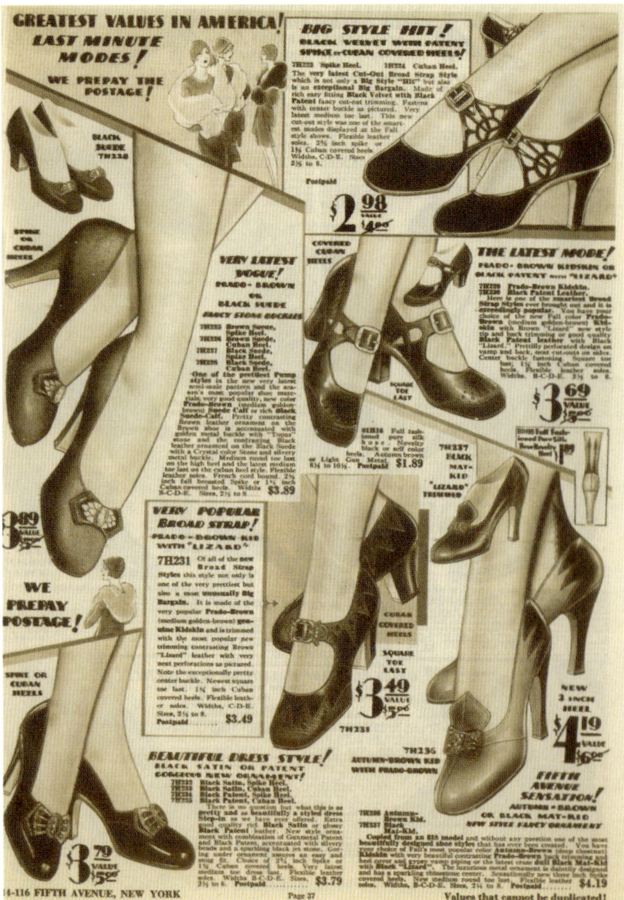

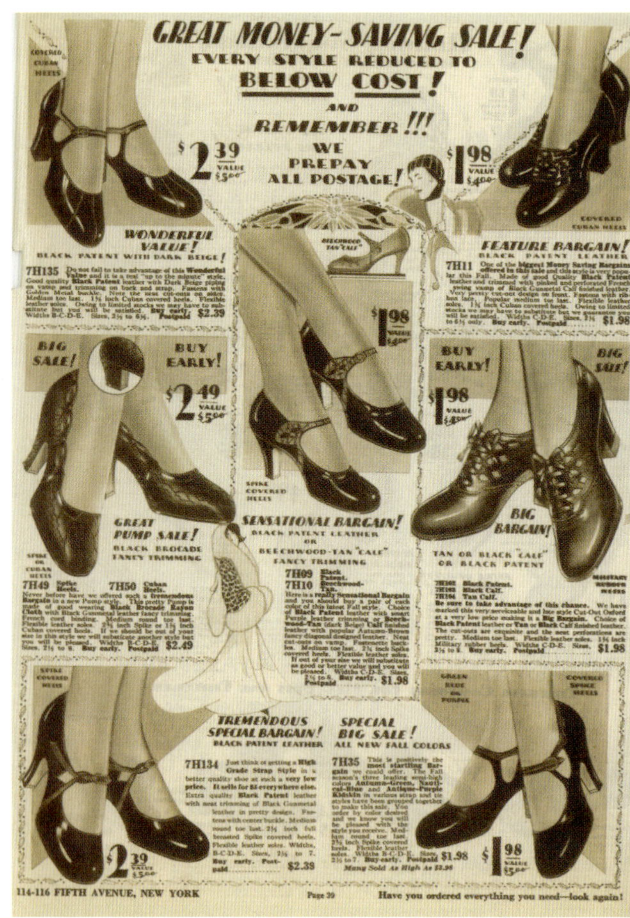

All Above
Selection of fashionable shoes.
The New Silhouette from Paris,
Hamilton Garment Co. New York
catalogue, c.1929

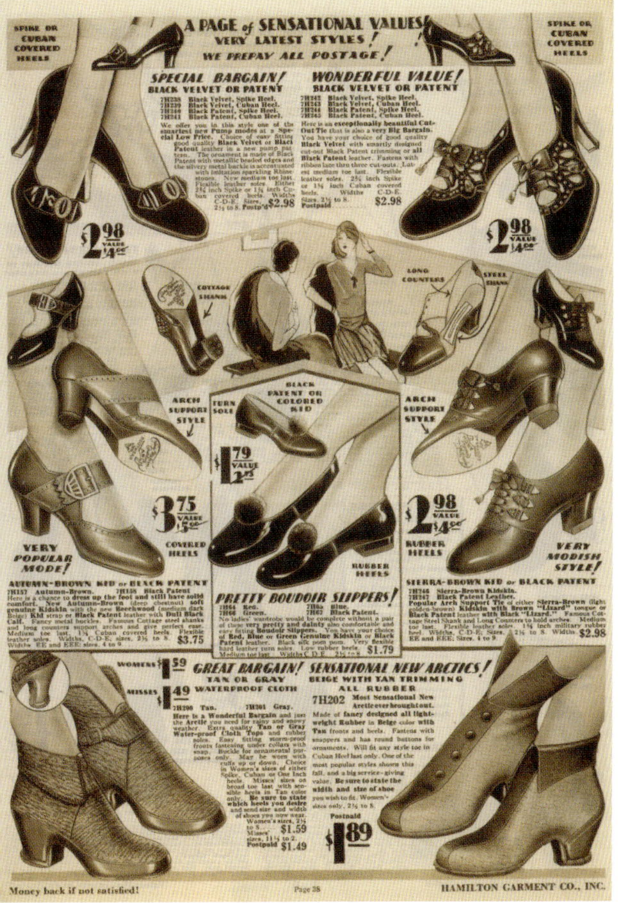

A PAGE of SENSATIONAL VALUES!
VERY LATEST STYLES!
WE PREPAY ALL POSTAGE!
SPECIAL BARGAIN!
WONDERFUL VALUE!
VERY POPULAR MODE!
PRETTY BOUDOIR SLIPPERS!
VERY MODISH STYLE!
GREAT BARGAIN!
SENSATIONAL NEW ARCTICS!
Money back if not satisfied!
HAMILTON GARMENT CO., INC.

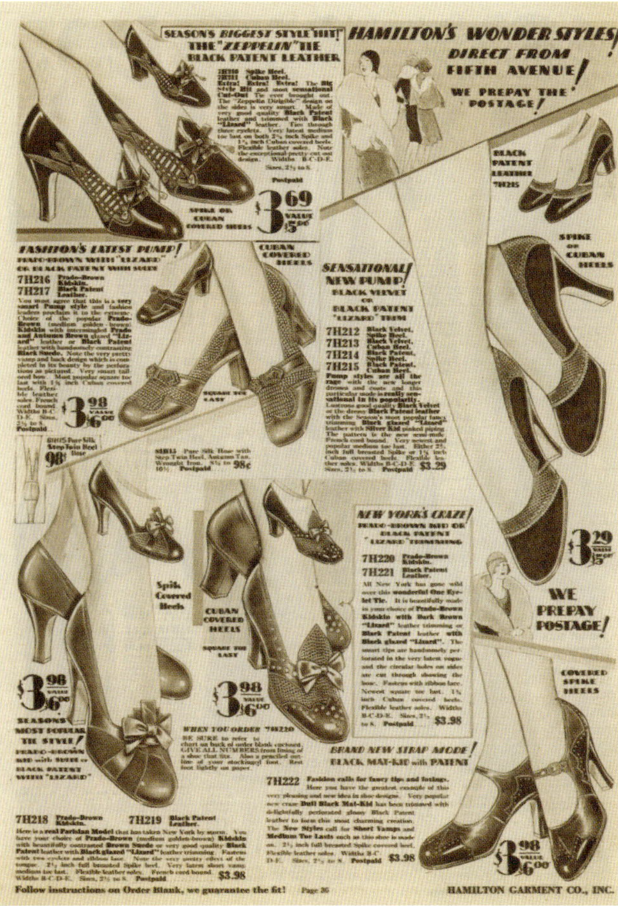

SEASONS BIGGEST STYLE HIT!
THE "ZEPPELIN" TIE
BLACK PATENT LEATHER
HAMILTON'S WONDER STYLES!
DIRECT FROM FIFTH AVENUE!
WE PREPAY THE POSTAGE!
FASHION'S LATEST PUMP!
SENSATIONAL! NEW PUMP!
NEW YORK'S CRAZE!
WE PREPAY POSTAGE!
BRAND NEW STRAP MODE!
Follow instructions on Order Blank, we guarantee the fit!
HAMILTON GARMENT CO., INC.

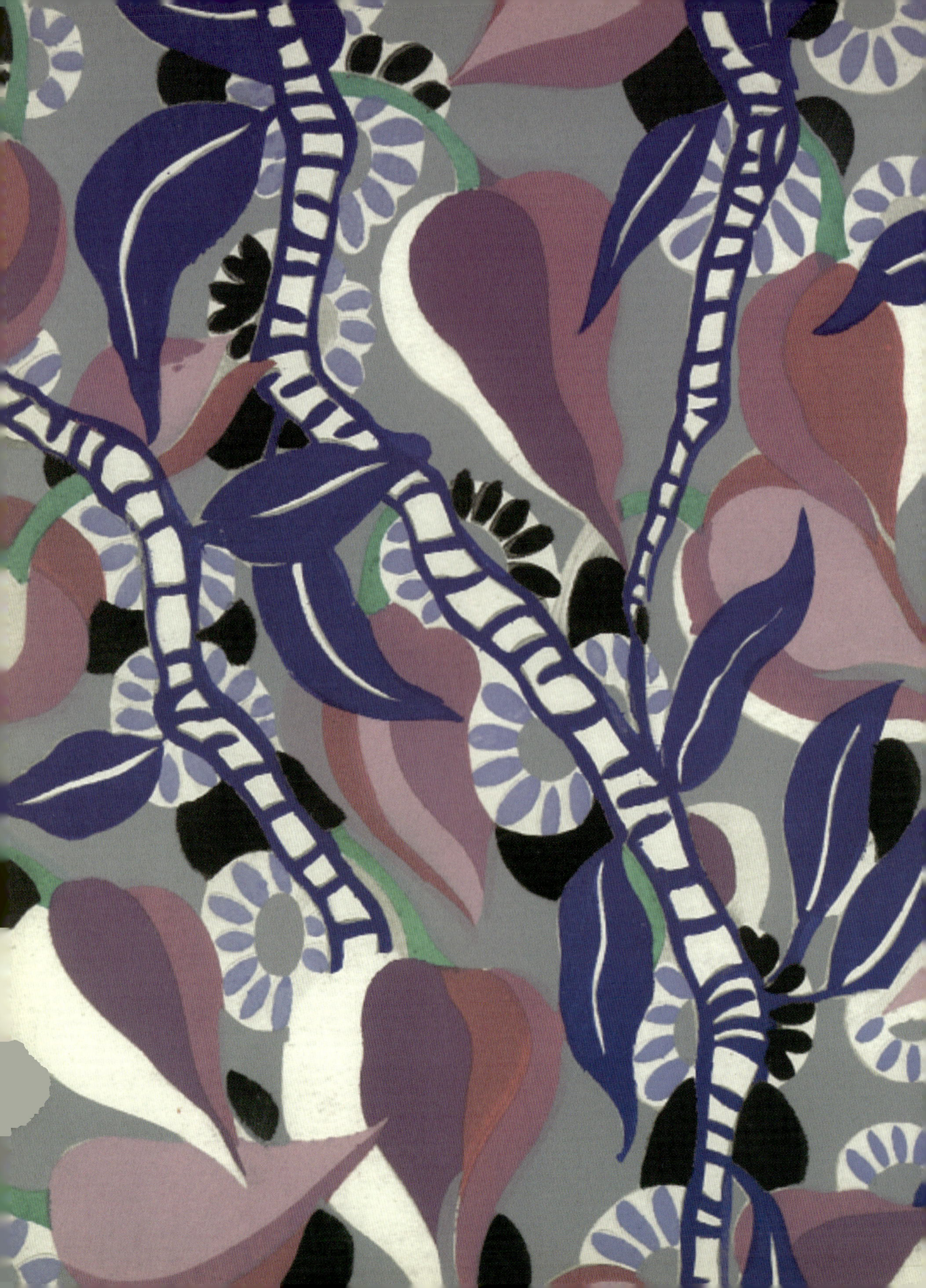

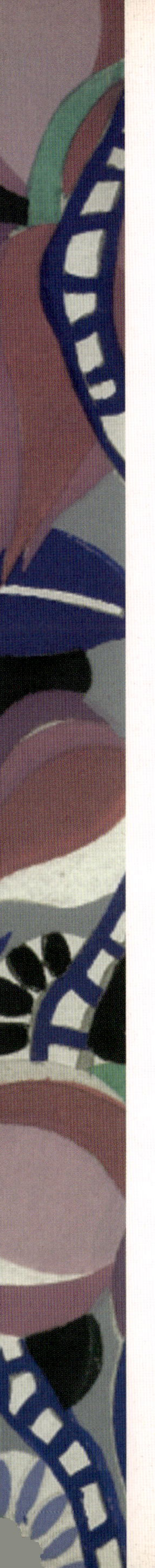

Other

Below and right
Four French negligee designs with luxurious lace, ribbon and flower detailing. The Twenties saw a shift to all-in-one undergarments. The model on the right is wearing a lace bed cap. *Paris-Blouses*, 1920

Four chemises with embroidery or openwork detailing. *Paris-Blouses*, 1920

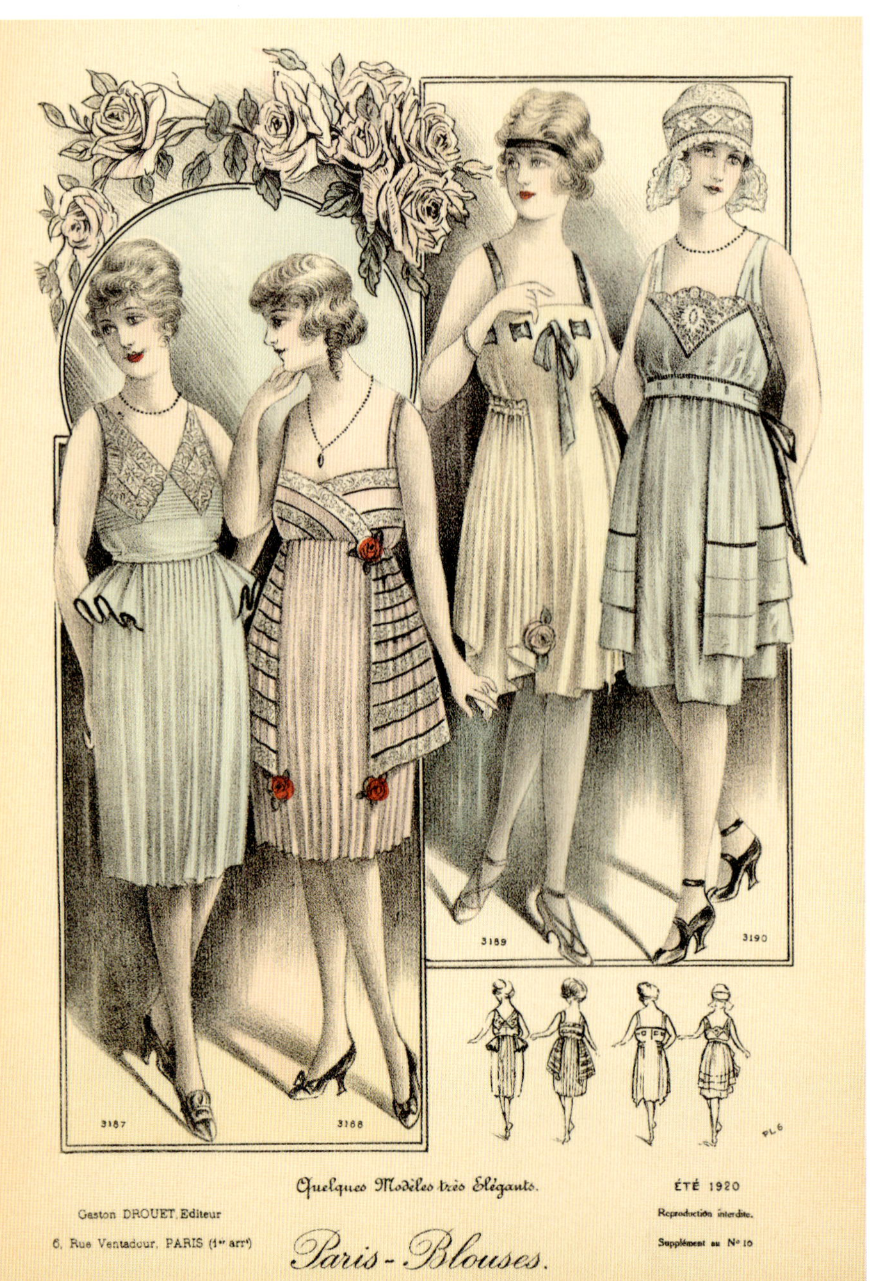

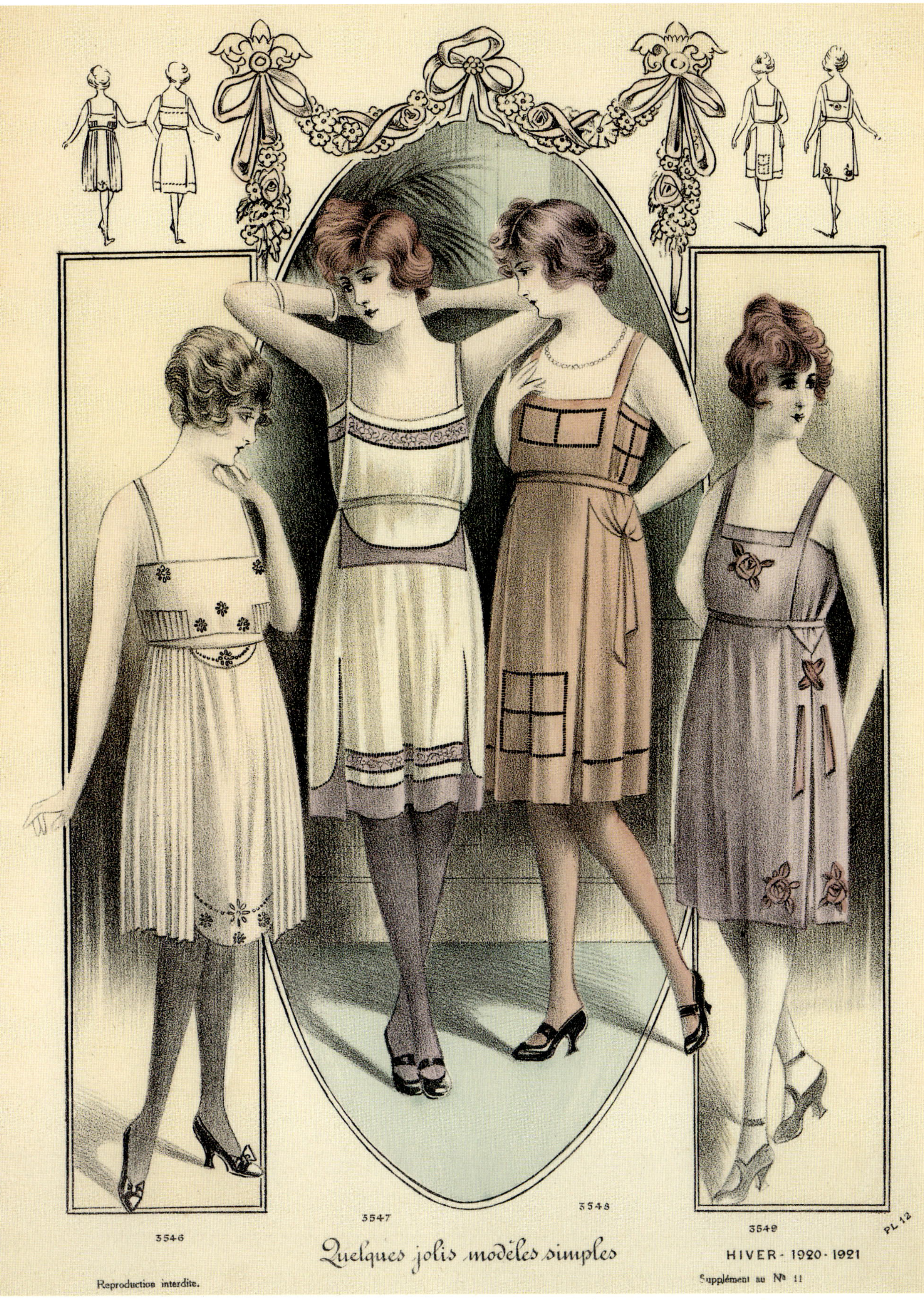

3546
3547
3548
3549
PL 12
Quelques jolis modèles simples
HIVER - 1920 - 1921
Reproduction interdite.
Supplément au N° 11

Right
Advertisement for the supple and discreet "Le Select" corset. *L'Illustration des Modes*, 1920

"LE SELECT"
corset parisien par excellence

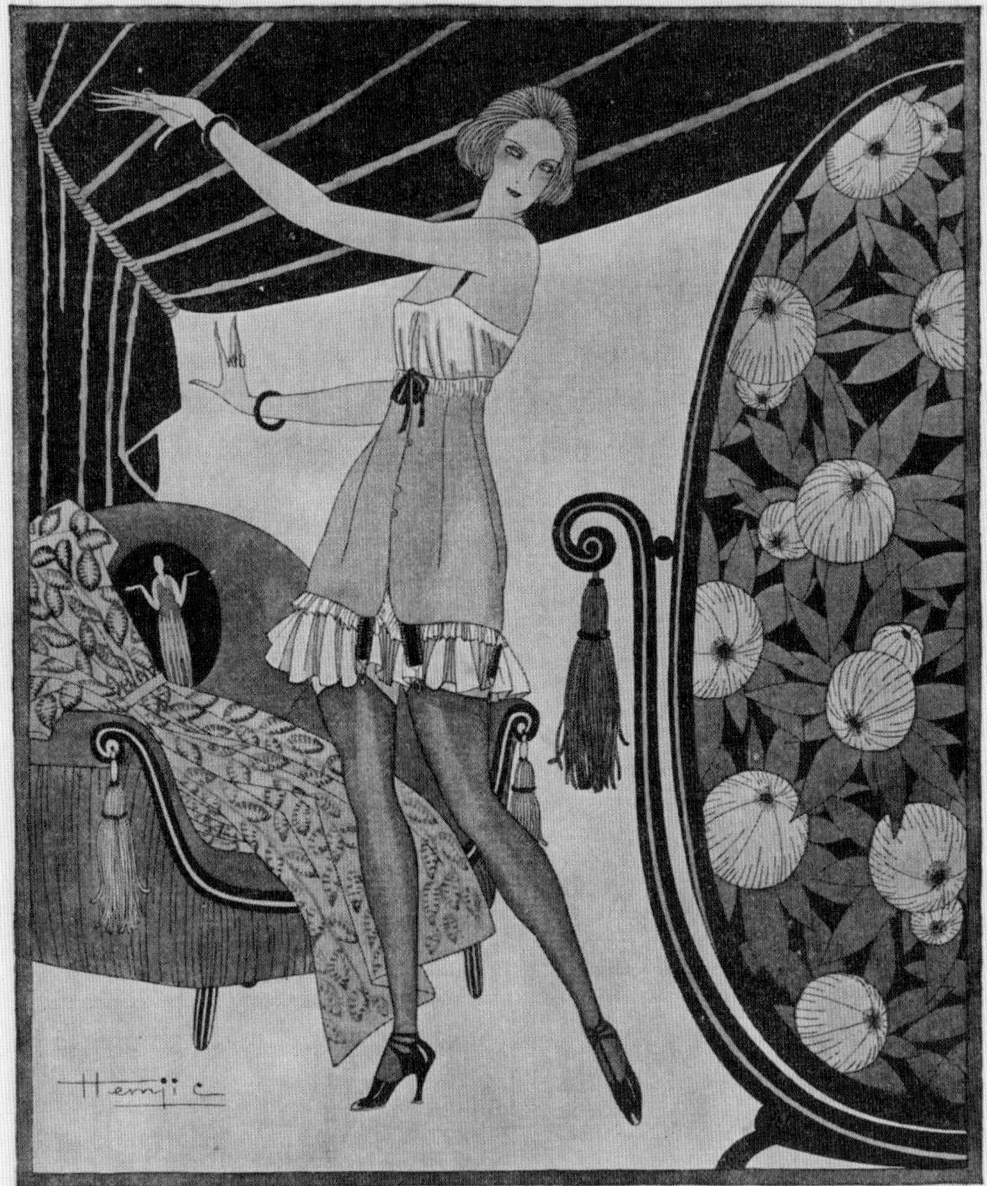

"Le Select" n'est plus le rigide corset
c'est un gracieux soutien souple et discret

en vente à paris dans les grands magasins du louvre et du printemps
et en province dans toutes les bonnes maisons

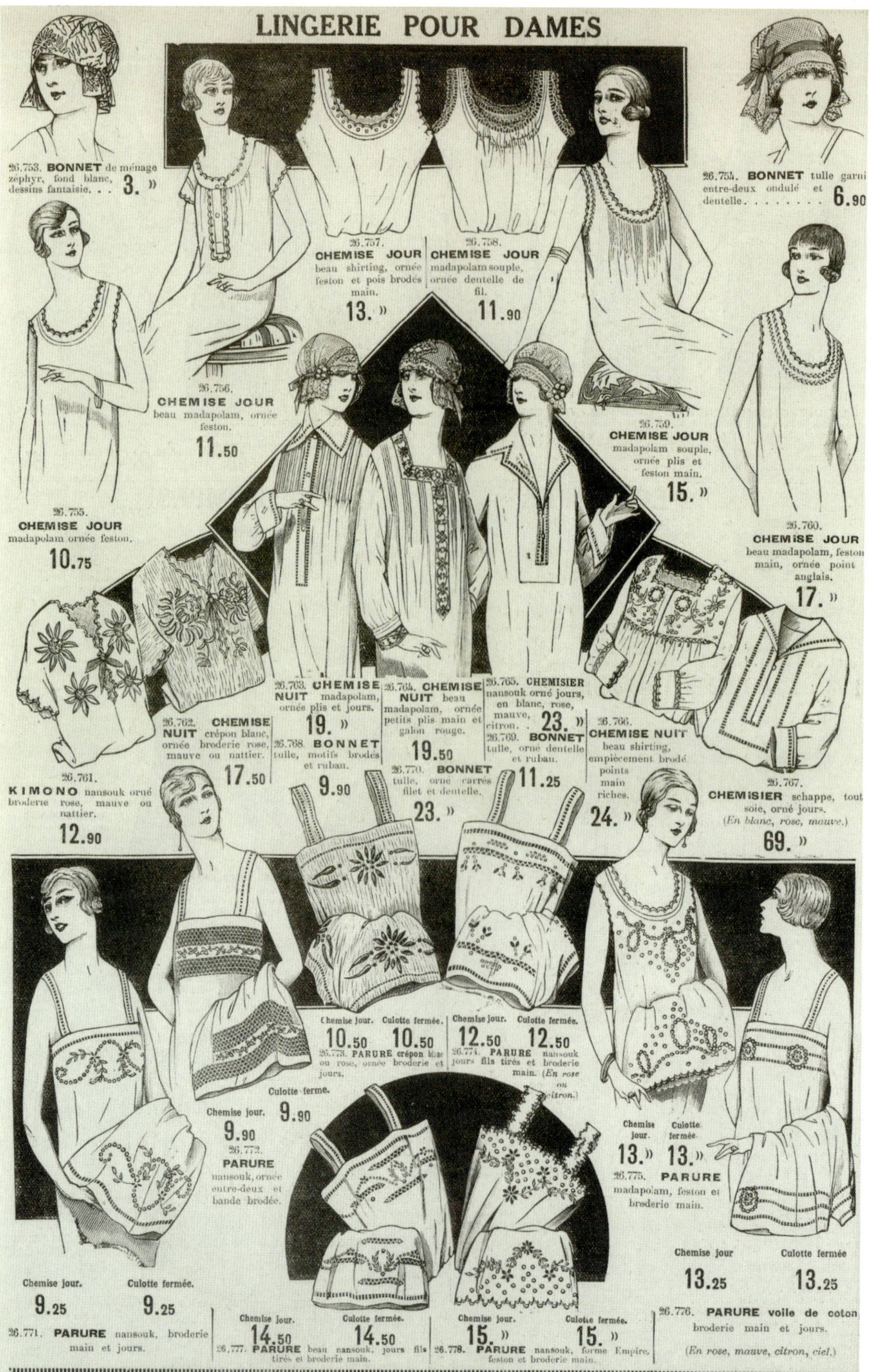

LINGERIE POUR DAMES
26.753. BONNET de ménage zéphyr, fond blanc, dessins fantaisie. . . 3. »
26.757. CHEMISE JOUR beau shirting, ornée feston et pois brodés main. 13. »
26.758. CHEMISE JOUR madapolam souple, ornée dentelle de fil. 11.90
26.754. BONNET tulle garni entre-deux ondulé et dentelle. 6.90
26.756. CHEMISE JOUR beau madapolam, ornée feston. 11.50
26.759. CHEMISE JOUR madapolam souple, ornée plis et feston main. 15. »
26.755. CHEMISE JOUR madapolam ornée feston. 10.75
26.760. CHEMISE JOUR beau madapolam, feston main, ornée point anglais. 17. »
26.763. CHEMISE NUIT madapolam, ornée plis et jours. 19. »
26.764. CHEMISE NUIT beau madapolam, ornée petits plis main et galon rouge. 19.50
26.765. CHEMISIER nansouk orné jours, en blanc, rose, mauve, citron. 23. »
26.762. CHEMISE NUIT crépon blanc, ornée broderie rose, mauve ou nattier. 17.50
26.768. BONNET tulle, motifs brodés et ruban. 9.90
26.770. BONNET tulle, orné carrés filet et dentelle. 23. »
26.769. BONNET tulle, orné dentelle et ruban. 11.25
26.766. CHEMISE NUIT beau shirting, empiècement brodé points main riches. 24. »
26.761. KIMONO nansouk orné broderie rose, mauve ou nattier. 12.90
26.767. CHEMISIER schappe, tout soie, orné jours. (En blanc, rose, mauve.) 69. »
Chemise jour. 10.50 Culotte fermée. 10.50
26.773. PARURE crépon blanc ou rose, ornée broderie et jours.
Chemise jour. 12.50 Culotte fermée. 12.50
26.774. PARURE nansouk jours fils tirés et broderie main. (En rose ou citron.)
Culotte fermée. 9.90
Chemise jour. 9.90
26.772. PARURE nansouk, ornée entre-deux et bande brodée.
Chemise jour. 13.» Culotte fermée. 13.»
26.775. PARURE madapolam, feston et broderie main.
Chemise jour 13.25 Culotte fermée 13.25
Chemise jour. 9.25 Culotte fermée. 9.25
26.771. PARURE nansouk, broderie main et jours.
Chemise jour. 14.50 Culotte fermée. 14.50
26.777. PARURE beau nansouk, jours fils tirés et broderie main.
Chemise jour. 15. » Culotte fermée. 15. »
26.778. PARURE nansouk, forme Empire, feston et broderie main.
26.776. PARURE voile de coton, broderie main et jours. (En rose, mauve, citron, ciel.)
La lingerie du LOUVRE se recommande par sa qualité et le soin mis à son exécution.

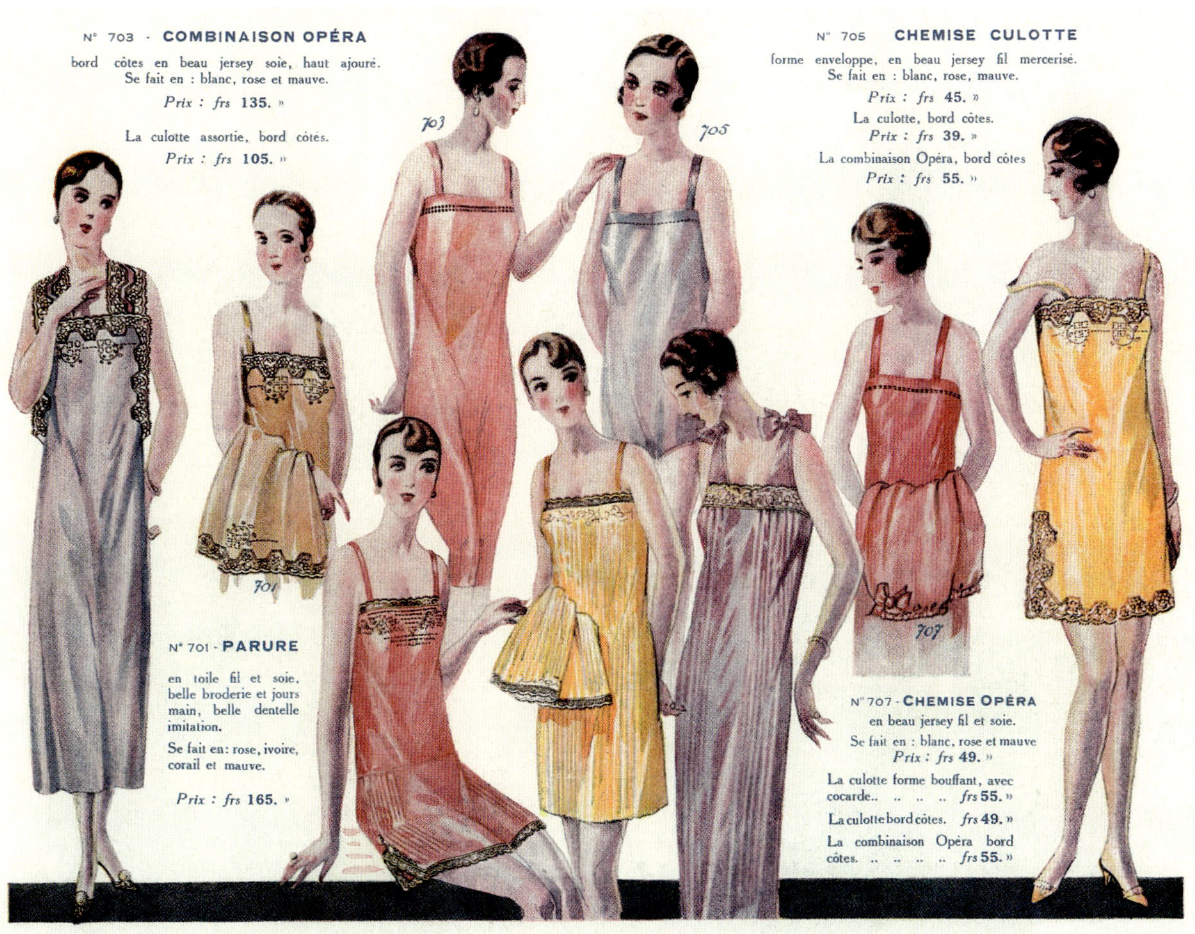

Left and above

Selection of lingerie. Au Louvre catalogue, 1925

Selection of lingerie by Maison Gerda. Maison Gerda catalogue, c.1925

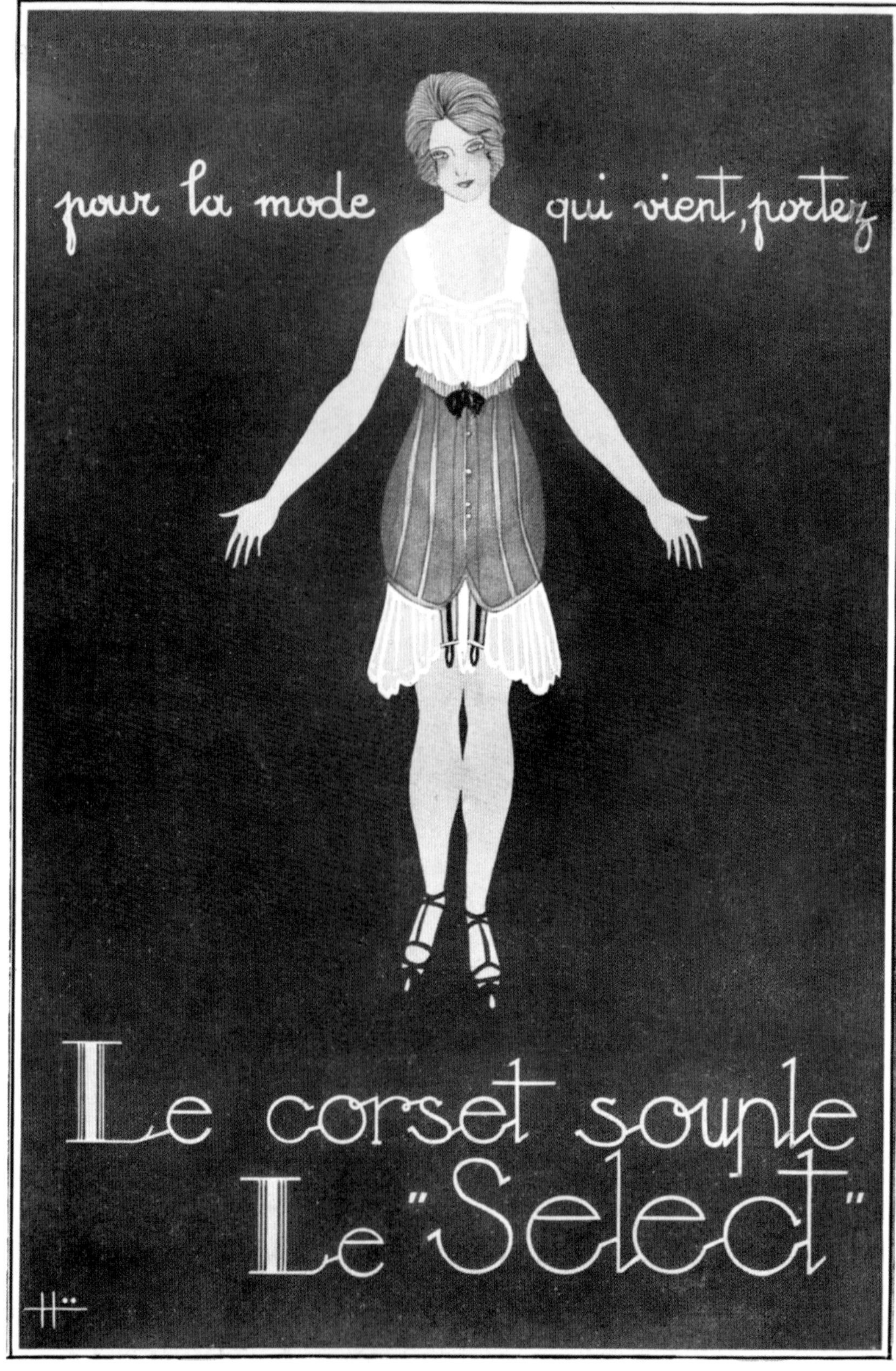

LIBRON & Cie, Manufacture de Corsets, 54, Avenue de Clichy, PARIS

Left
Corset advert "for fashions to come, wear the supple Le Select corset". This elasticated corselet flattened curves in order to provide the fashionable silhouette of the era. It was worn over a thin negligee and had suspender clips attached for stockings which had become increasingly popular owing to rising hemlines. *La Nouveauté Française*, 1921

Below
Selection of lingerie.
La Nouveauté Française, 1921

La Nouveauté Française

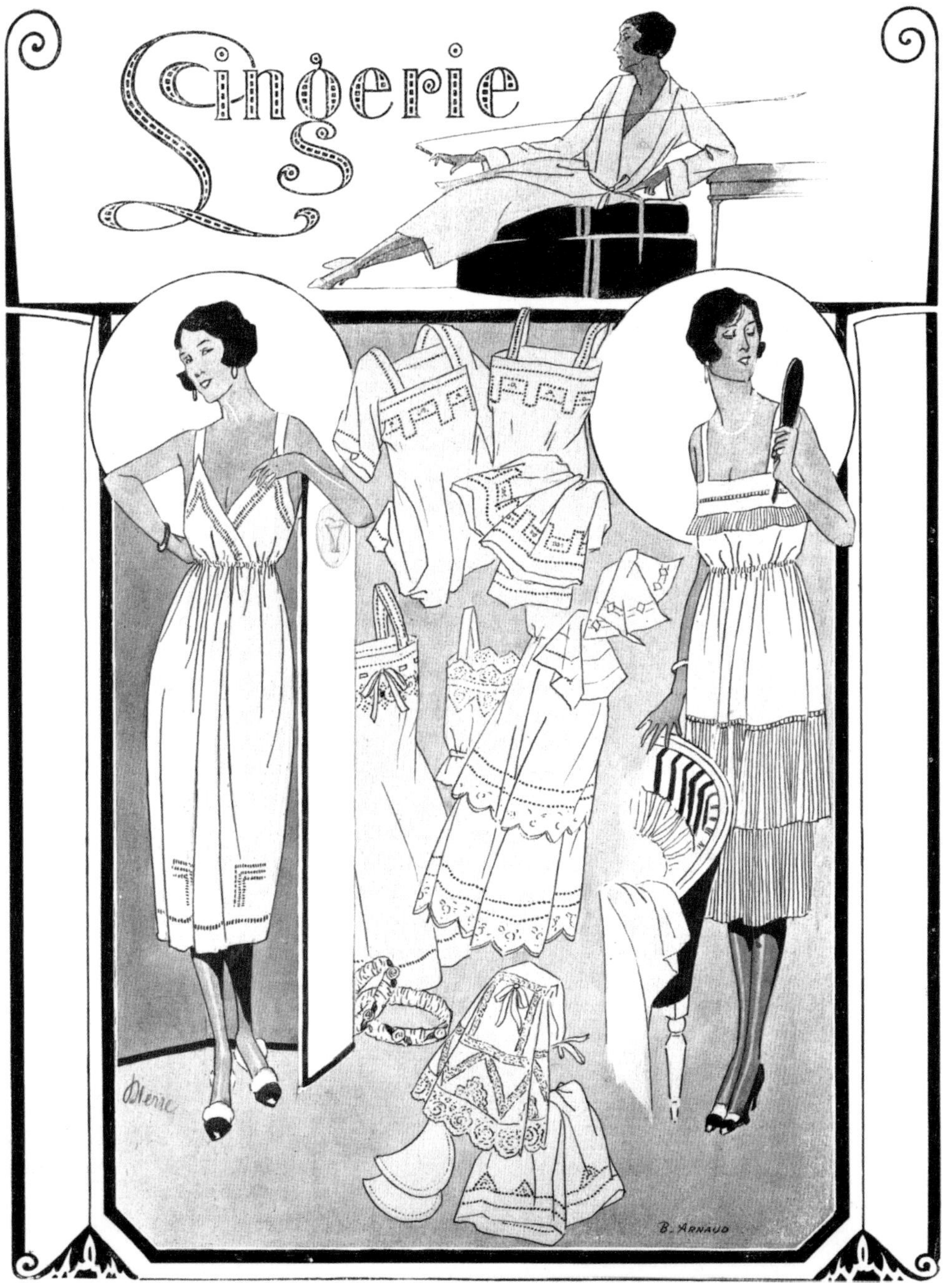

Right
A bride's nightgown in white Georgette and bedroom wrap of chiffon velvet lined with marabou by Sonia Bloor of Brook Street, London, c.1922

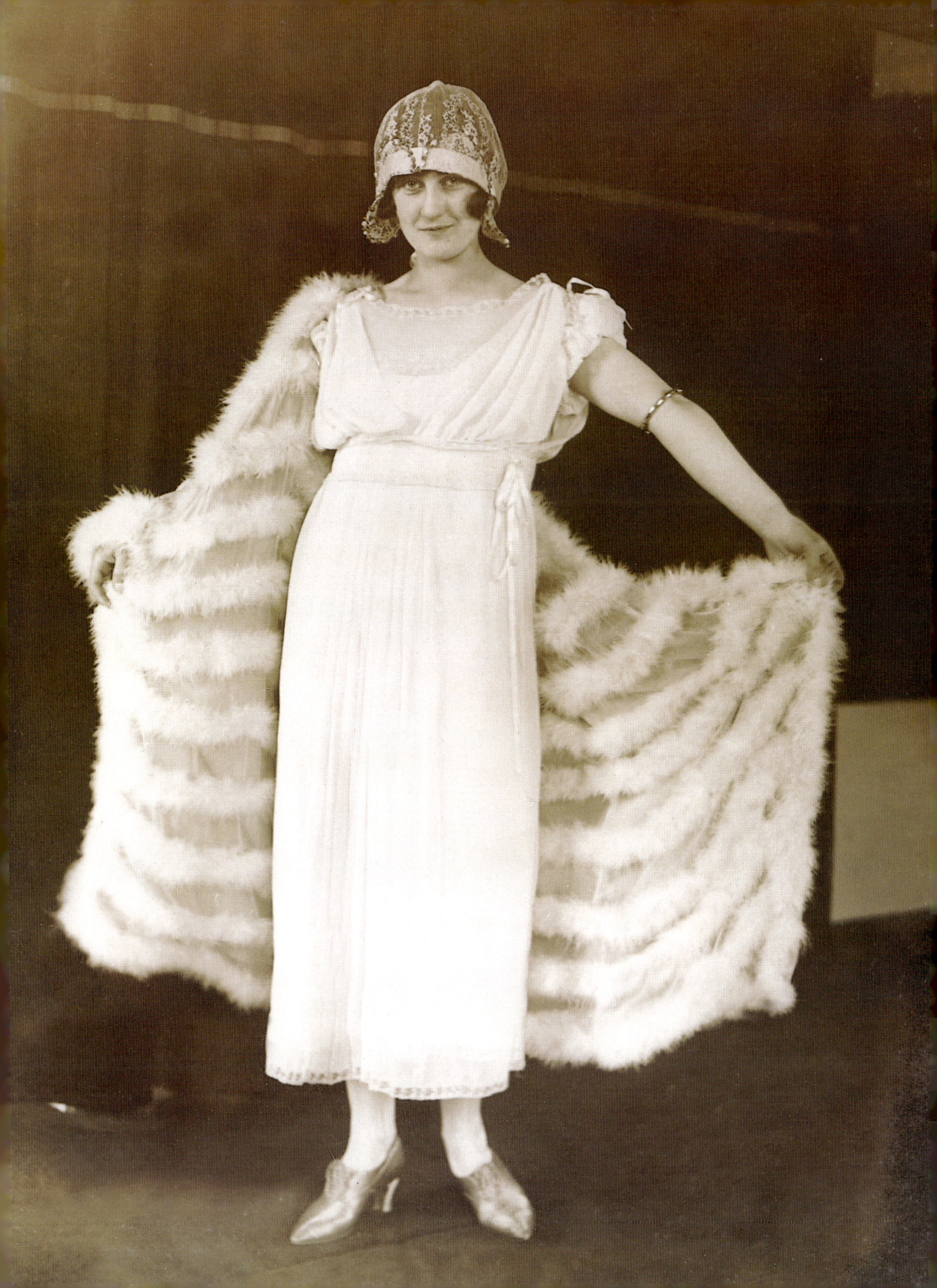

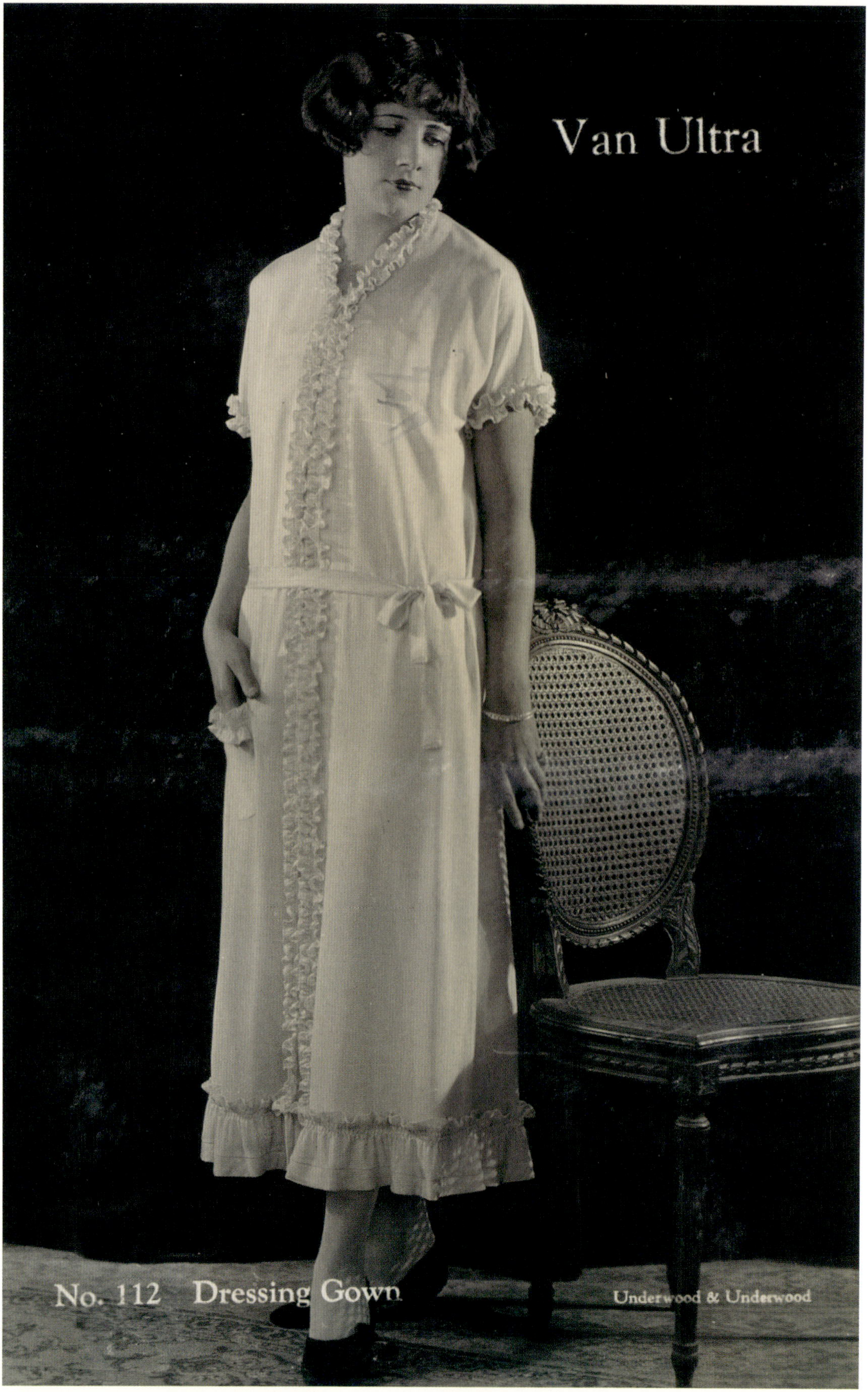

Van Ultra

No. 112 Dressing Gown

Underwood & Underwood

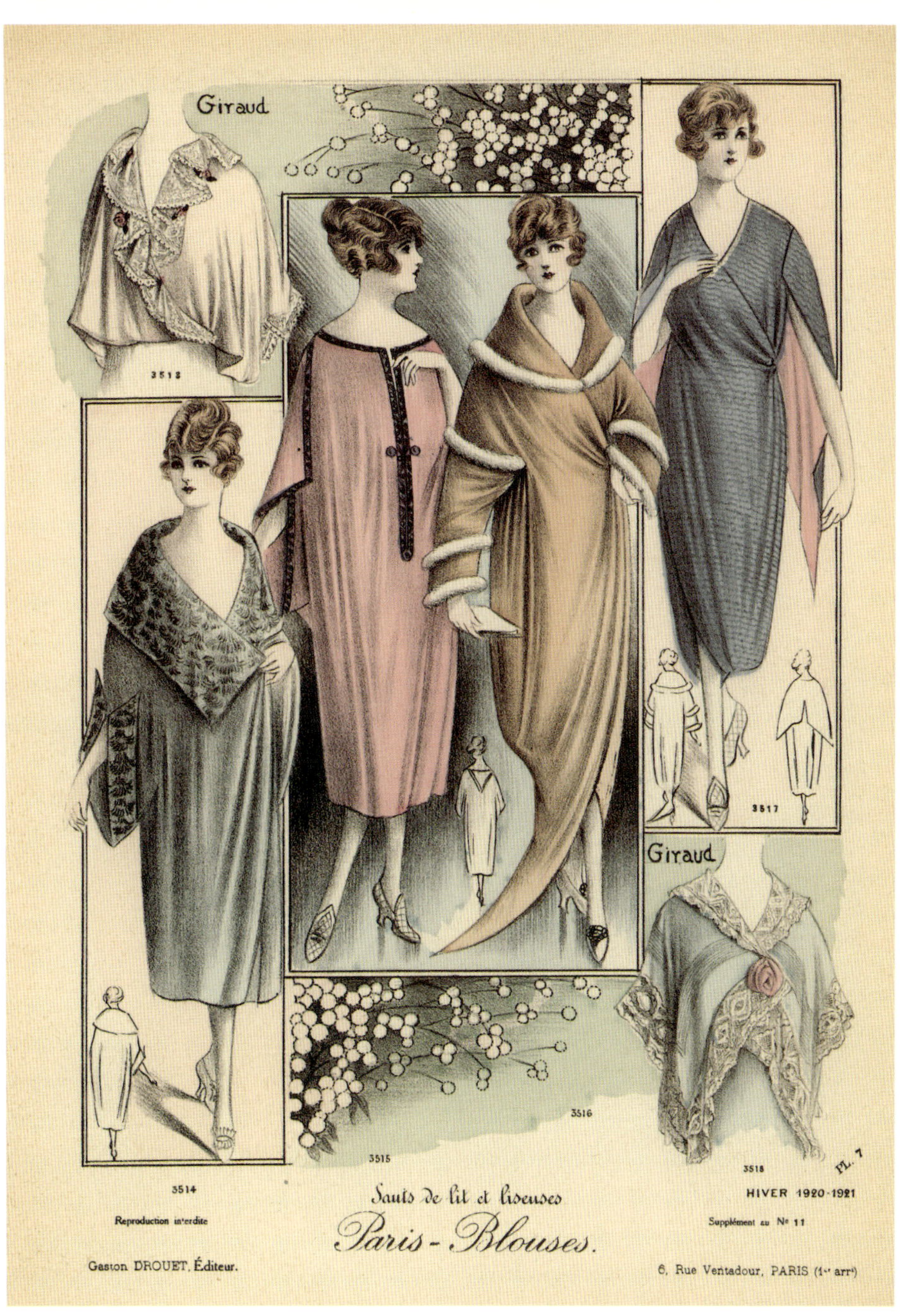

Left and above

A dressing gown with ruffling trimming by Van Ultra. Underwood and Underwood, c.1923

Selection of morning dresses, bed jackets and housecoats. *Paris-Blouses*, 1920

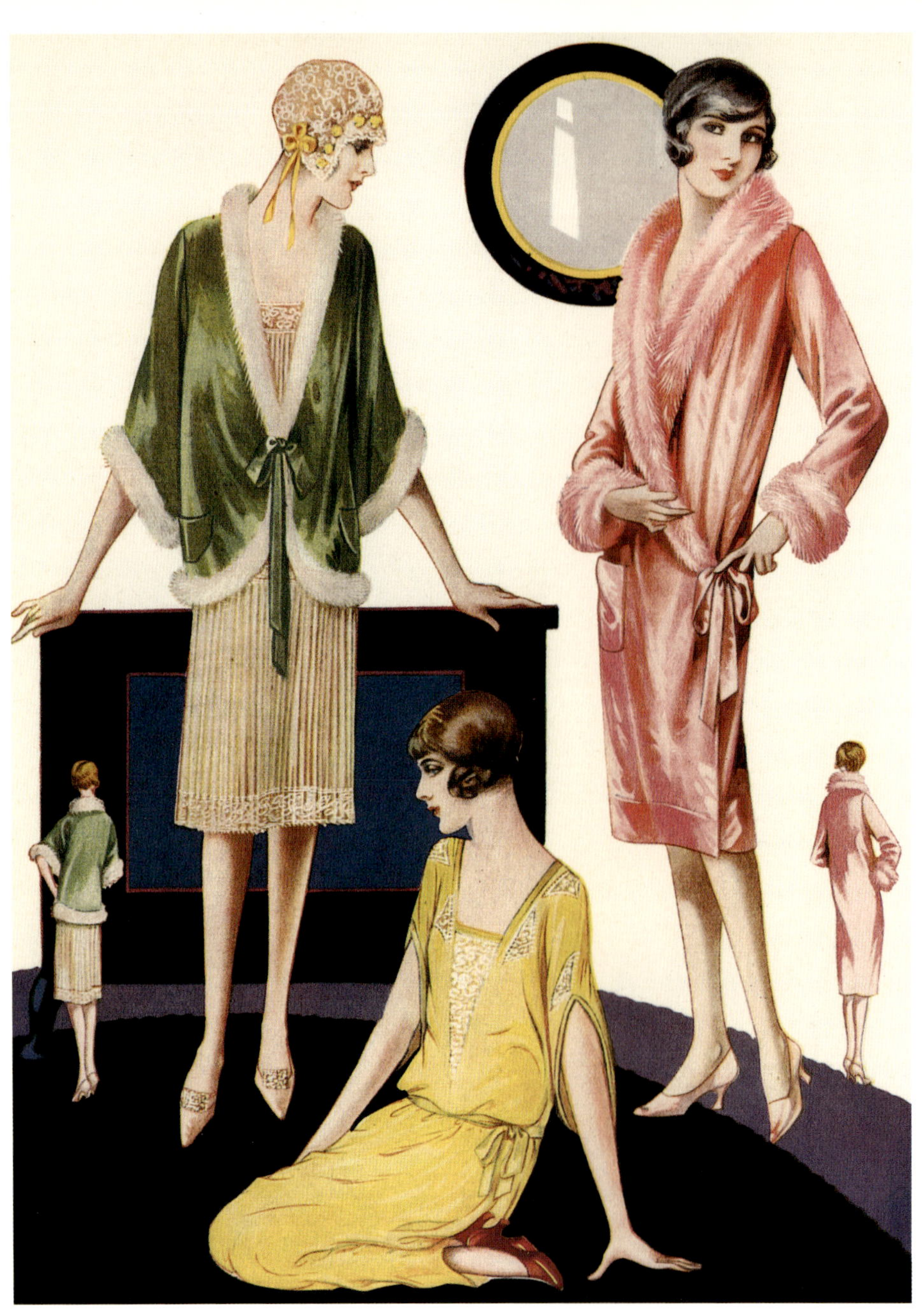

Above
Satin boudoir jacket trimmed with swansdown, nightdress and negligee trimmed with marabou. *Fashions for All*, 1927

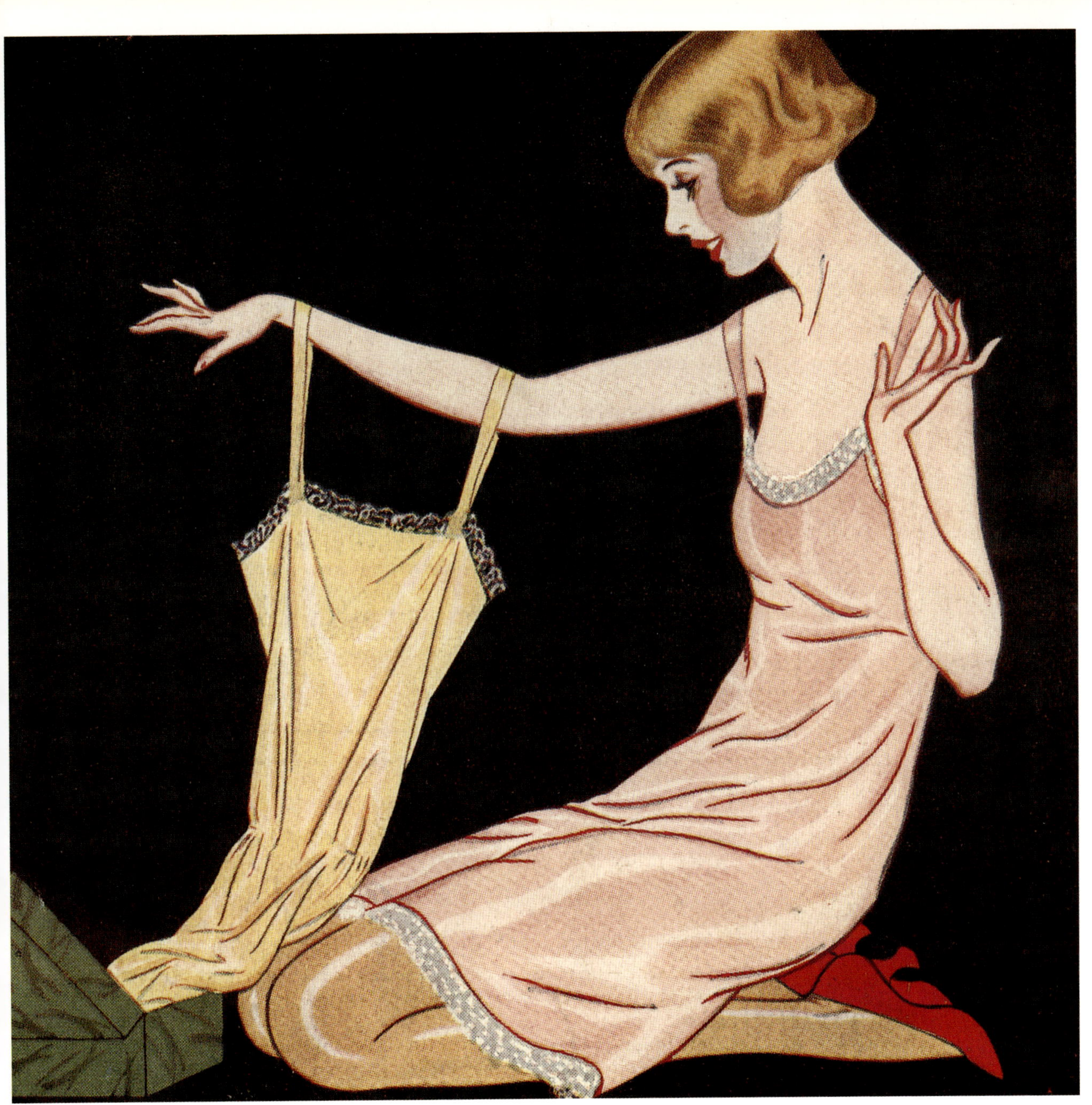

Above
British Celanese Limited advertisement for artificial silk underwear, 1926

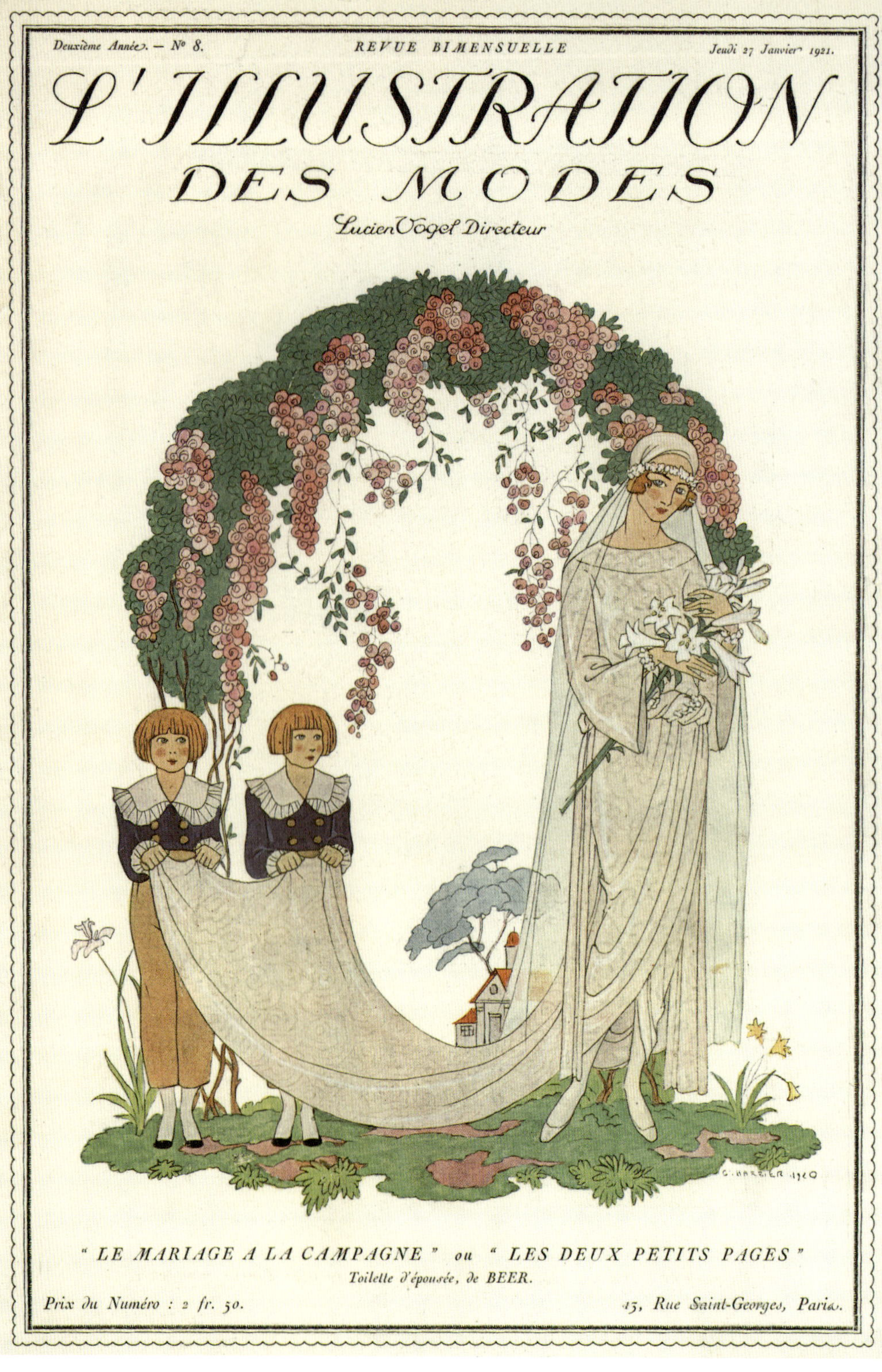
Deuxième Année. — Nº 8. REVUE BIMENSUELLE Jeudi 27 Janvier 1921.

L'ILLUSTRATION DES MODES

Lucien Vogel Directeur

G. BARBIER 1920

" LE MARIAGE A LA CAMPAGNE " ou " LES DEUX PETITS PAGES "

Toilette d'épousée, de BEER.

Prix du Numéro : 2 fr. 50. 13, Rue Saint-Georges, Paris.

Above

Cover of *L'Illustration des Modes* showing bridal gown for a countryside wedding by Beer, 1921

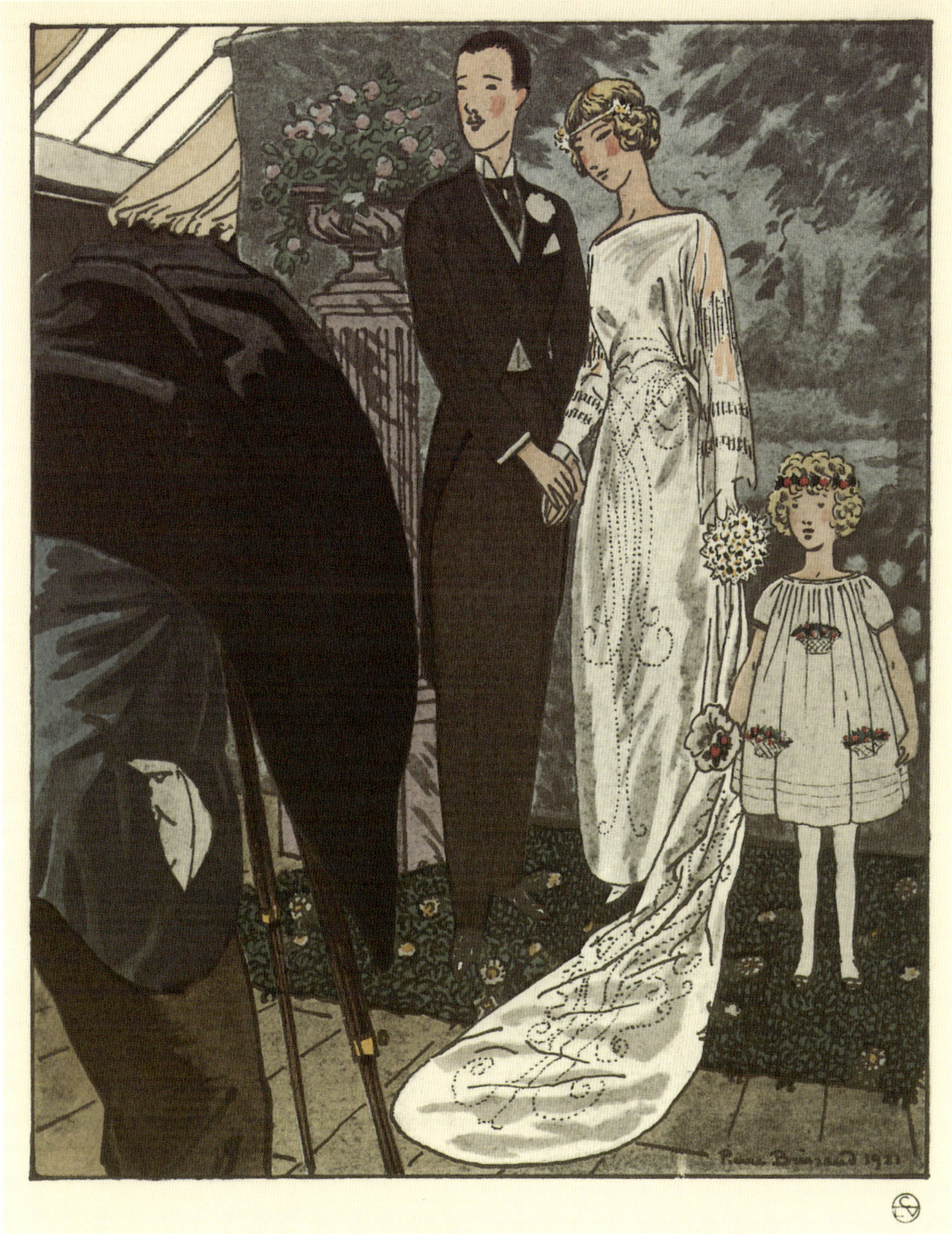

Above
"A la ville voisine" (To the neighboring town), wedding dress by Jeanne Lanvin. Illustration by Pierre Brissaud. *Gazette du Bon Ton*, 1921

Right

Actress Betty Bronson wearing a bridal gown, 1928. Betty Bronson starred in the silent movie "The Compassionate Marriage" which was retitled in Britain, "The Jazz Bride".

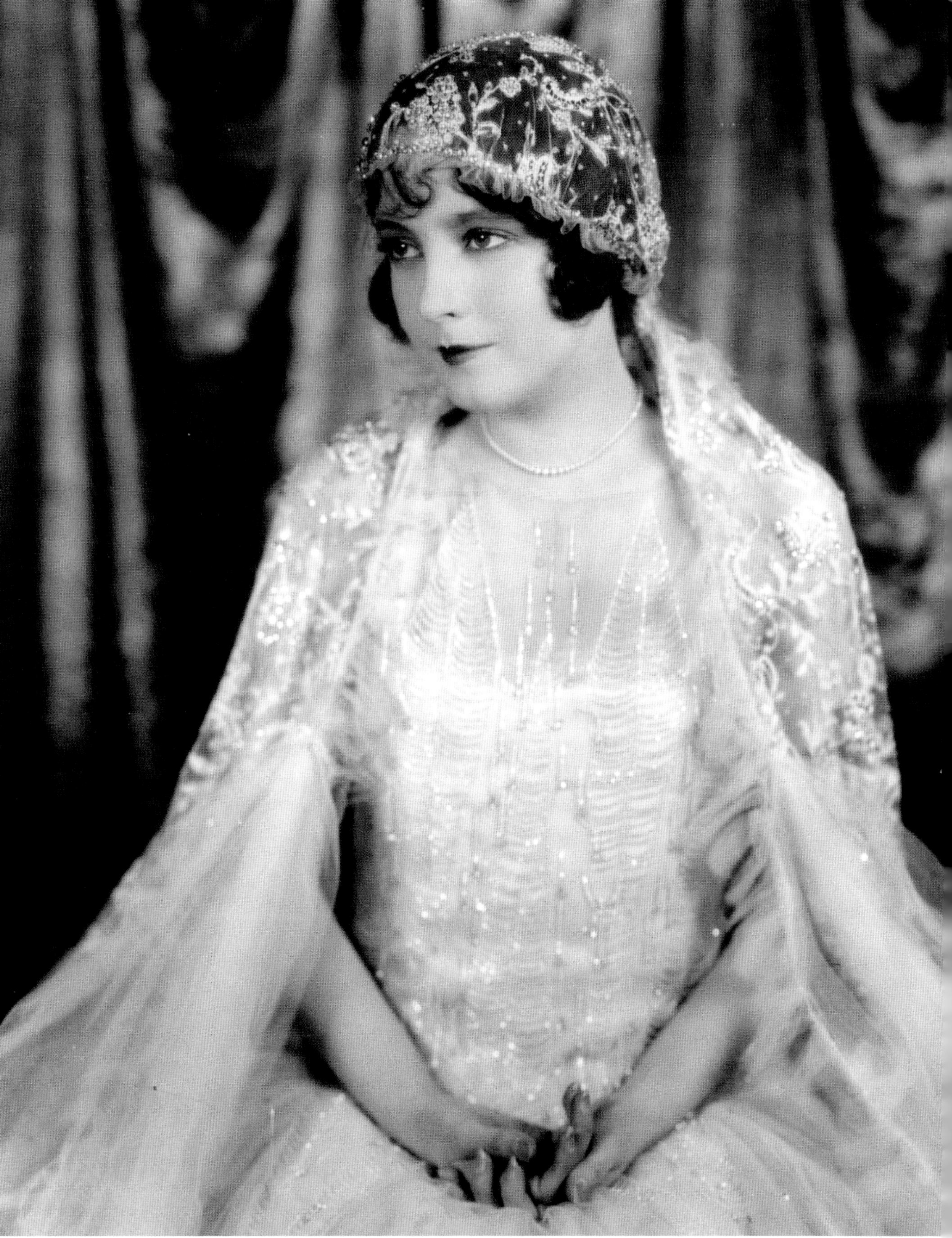

Right
A white wedding dress with a cross-over bodice and gathered side sash with a pearl headdress and long veil, and a formal black dress with lace flounce and cuffs.
La Femme Chic, c.1924

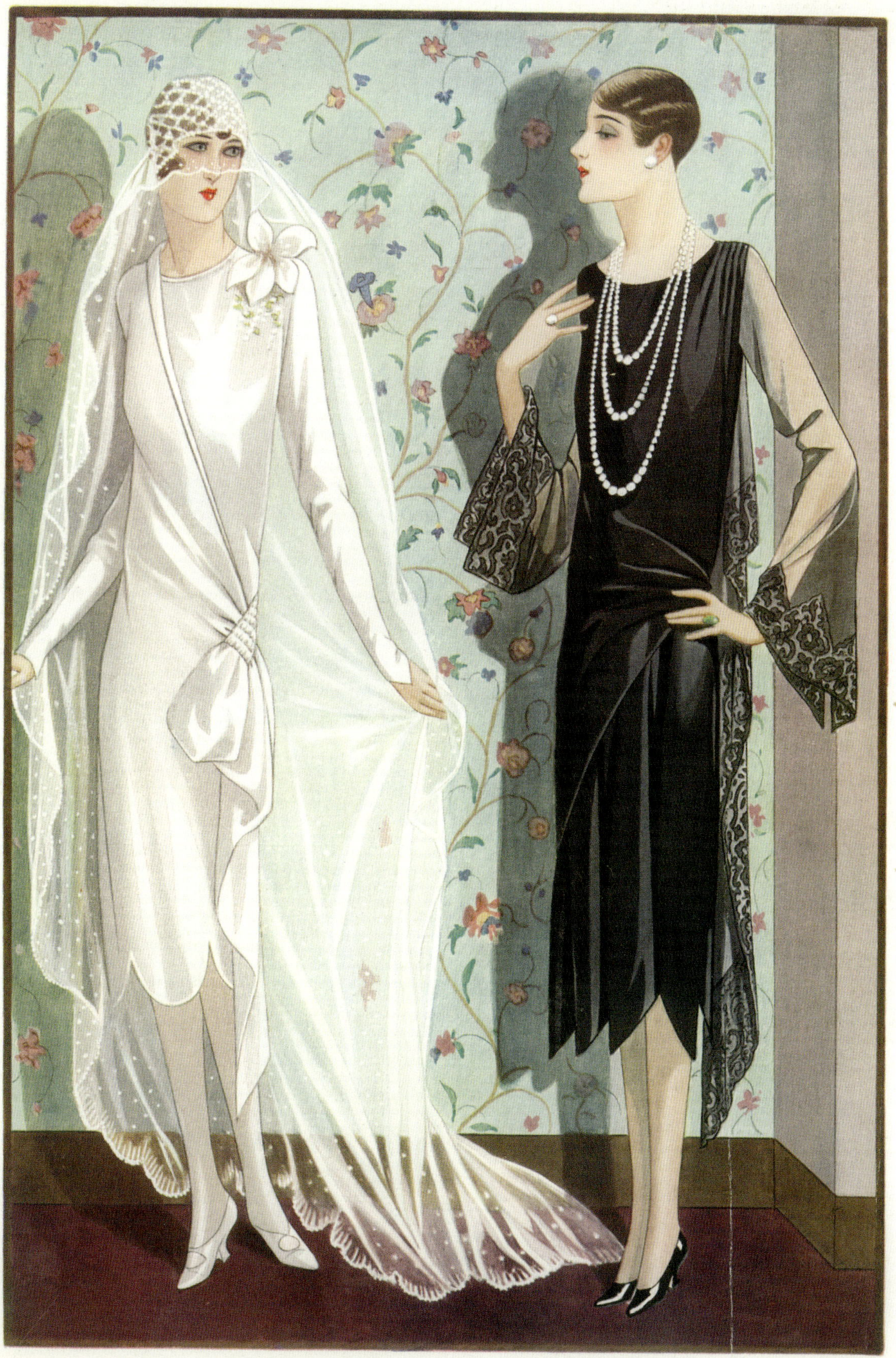

Below and right

A lace wedding dress with a long train and veil. *Mode Pratique*, 1926

Four elaborate wedding dresses with lace and net veils. *The Delineator*, 1922

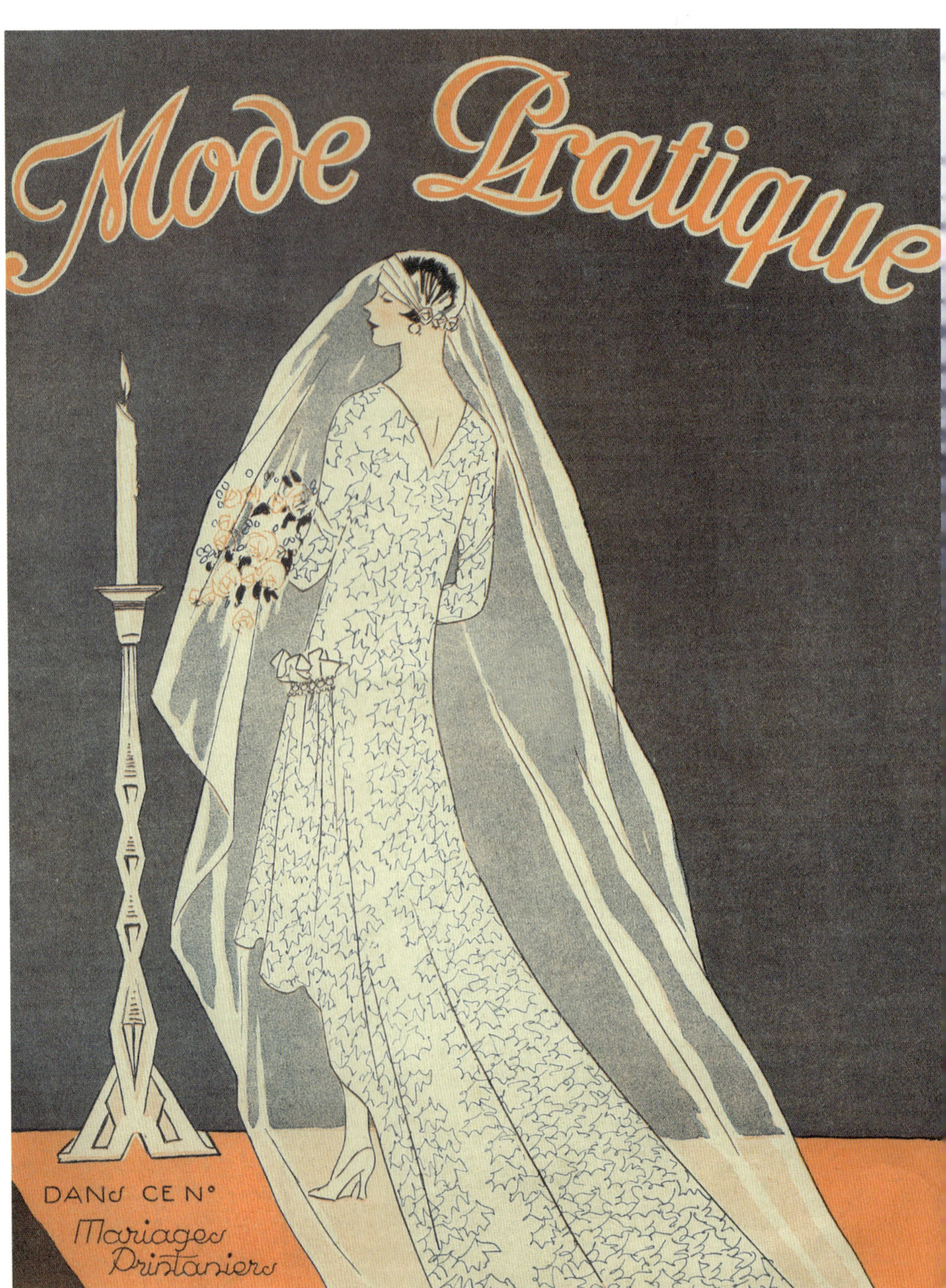

IN THE CRYSTAL'S ROSE-MISTED FUTURE, EVERY MAID SEES HERSELF A RADIANT BRIDE IN WEDDING GOWN AND MAGIC VEIL

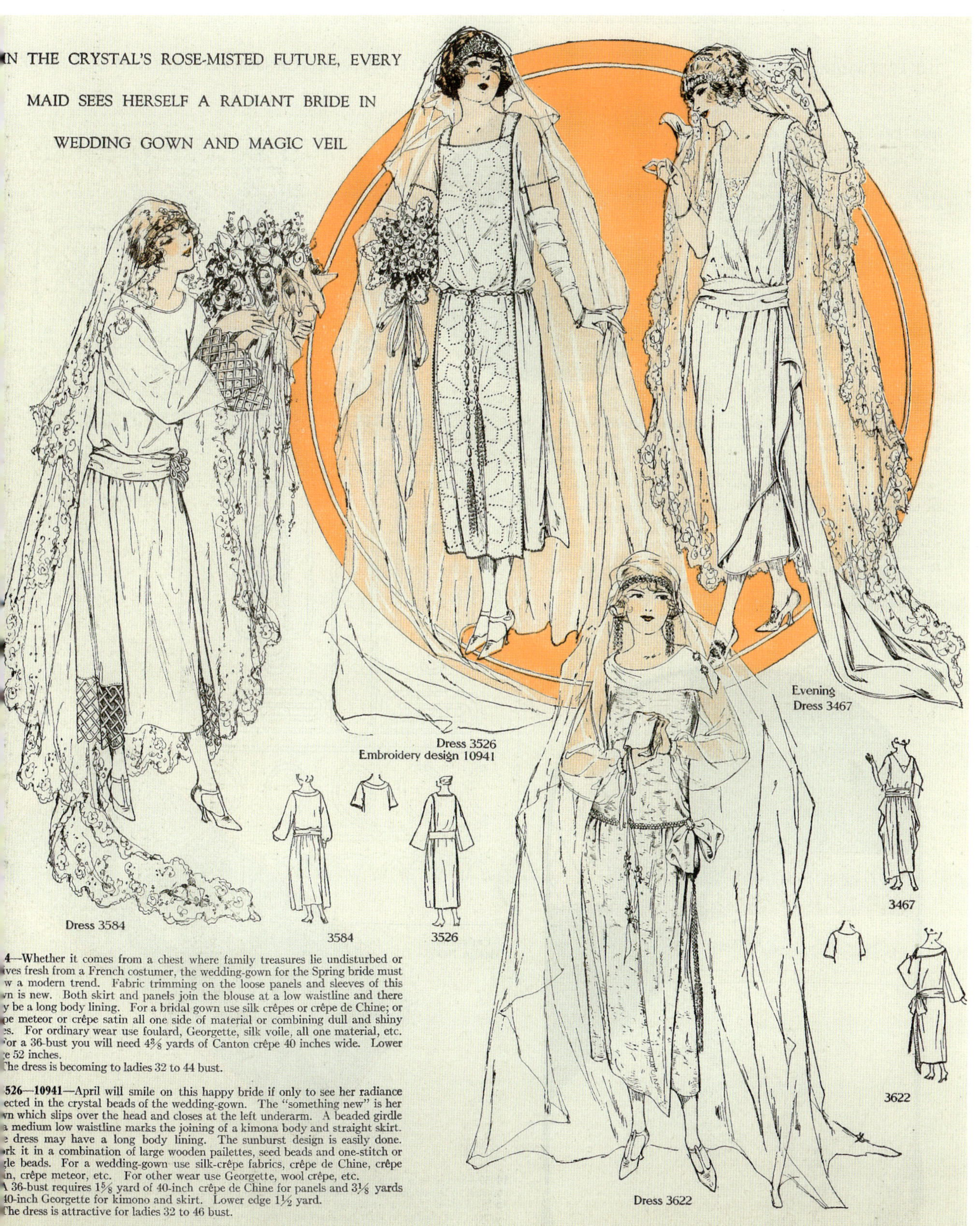

Dress 3584

3584

3526

Dress 3526
Embroidery design 10941

Evening Dress 3467

3467

3622

Dress 3622

4—Whether it comes from a chest where family treasures lie undisturbed or ives fresh from a French costumer, the wedding-gown for the Spring bride must w a modern trend. Fabric trimming on the loose panels and sleeves of this vn is new. Both skirt and panels join the blouse at a low waistline and there y be a long body lining. For a bridal gown use silk crêpes or crêpe de Chine; or pe meteor or crêpe satin all one side of material or combining dull and shiny es. For ordinary wear use foulard, Georgette, silk voile, all one material, etc. 'or a 36-bust you will need $4\frac{3}{8}$ yards of Canton crêpe 40 inches wide. Lower e 52 inches.

The dress is becoming to ladies 32 to 44 bust.

526—10941—April will smile on this happy bride if only to see her radiance ected in the crystal beads of the wedding-gown. The "something new" is her vn which slips over the head and closes at the left underarm. A beaded girdle a medium low waistline marks the joining of a kimona body and straight skirt. e dress may have a long body lining. The sunburst design is easily done. rk it in a combination of large wooden pailettes, seed beads and one-stitch or gle beads. For a wedding-gown use silk-crêpe fabrics, crêpe de Chine, crêpe in, crêpe meteor, etc. For other wear use Georgette, wool crêpe, etc.

A 36-bust requires $1\frac{5}{8}$ yard of 40-inch crêpe de Chine for panels and $3\frac{1}{8}$ yards 40-inch Georgette for kimono and skirt. Lower edge $1\frac{1}{2}$ yard.

The dress is attractive for ladies 32 to 46 bust.

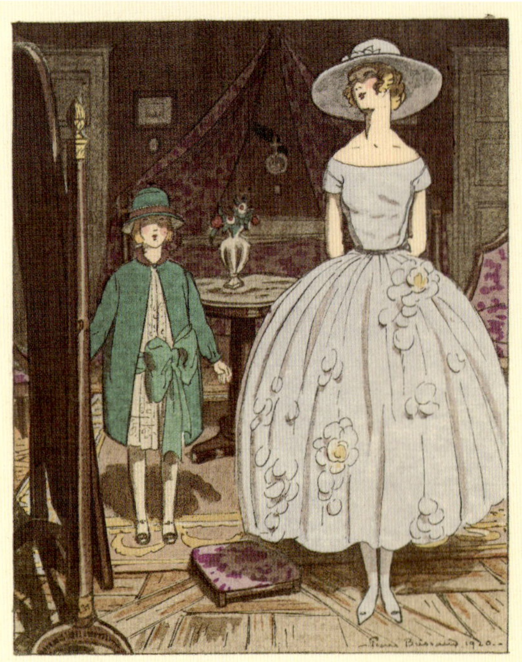

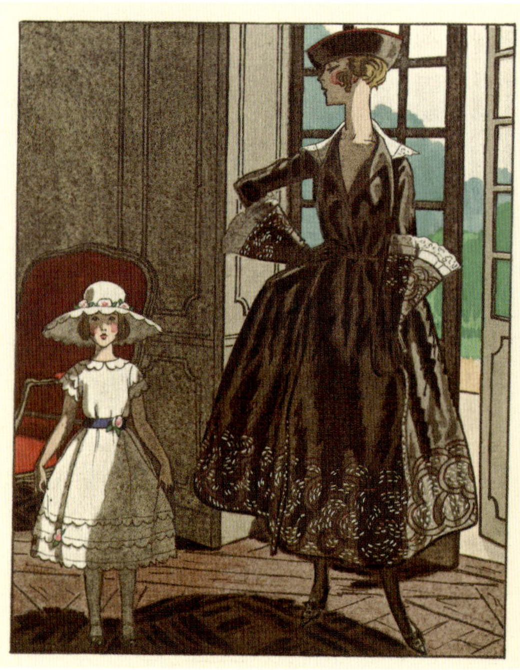

Above left and right

"On t'attend!" (We are waiting for you!) – crinoline dress and child's coat by Jeanne Lanvin. Illustration by Pierre Brissaud. *Gazette du Bon Ton*, 1920

"Voyons cette Révérence" (Let's see that curtsey) – afternoon dress and child's dress by Jeanne Lanvin. Illustration by Pierre Brissaud. *Gazette du Bon Ton*, 1920

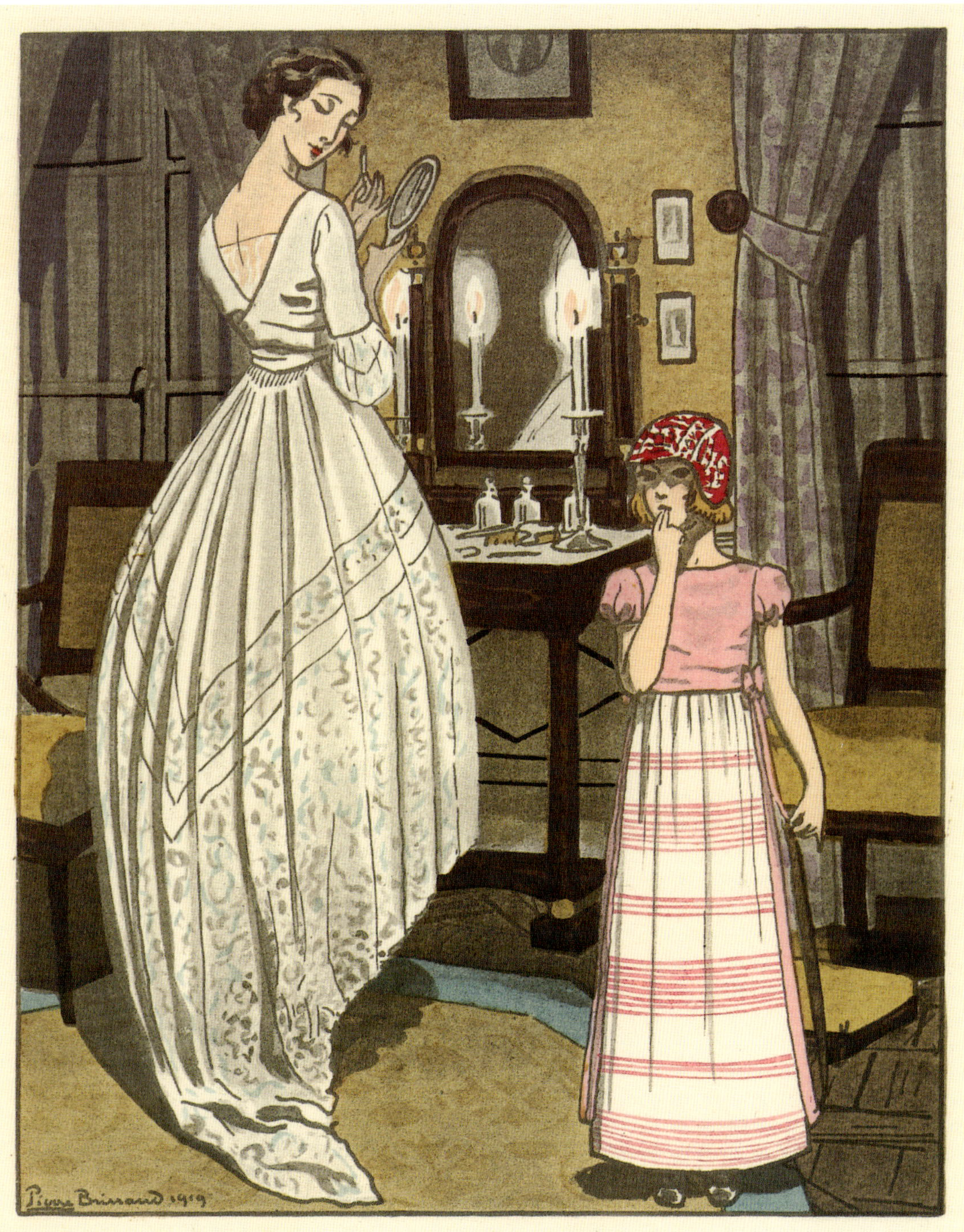

Above
"As-tu ete Sage?" (Have you been Good?), evening gown and child's dress by Jeanne Lanvin. Illustration by Pierre Brissaud. *Gazette du Bon Ton*, 1920

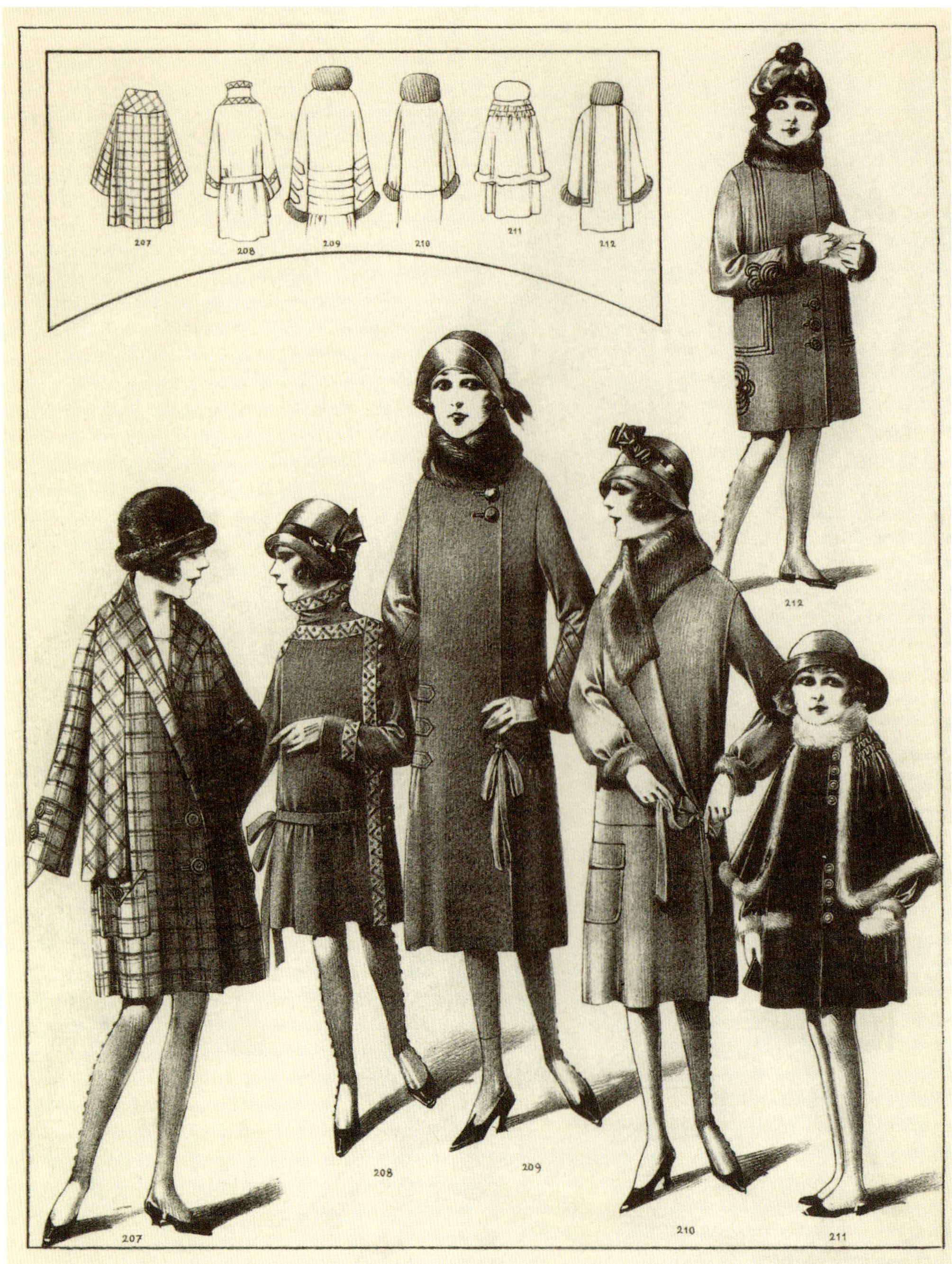

Above and right
Selection of coats for children
by Atelier Bachroitz, c.1924

Practical children's clothes.
Paris Élegant, 1921

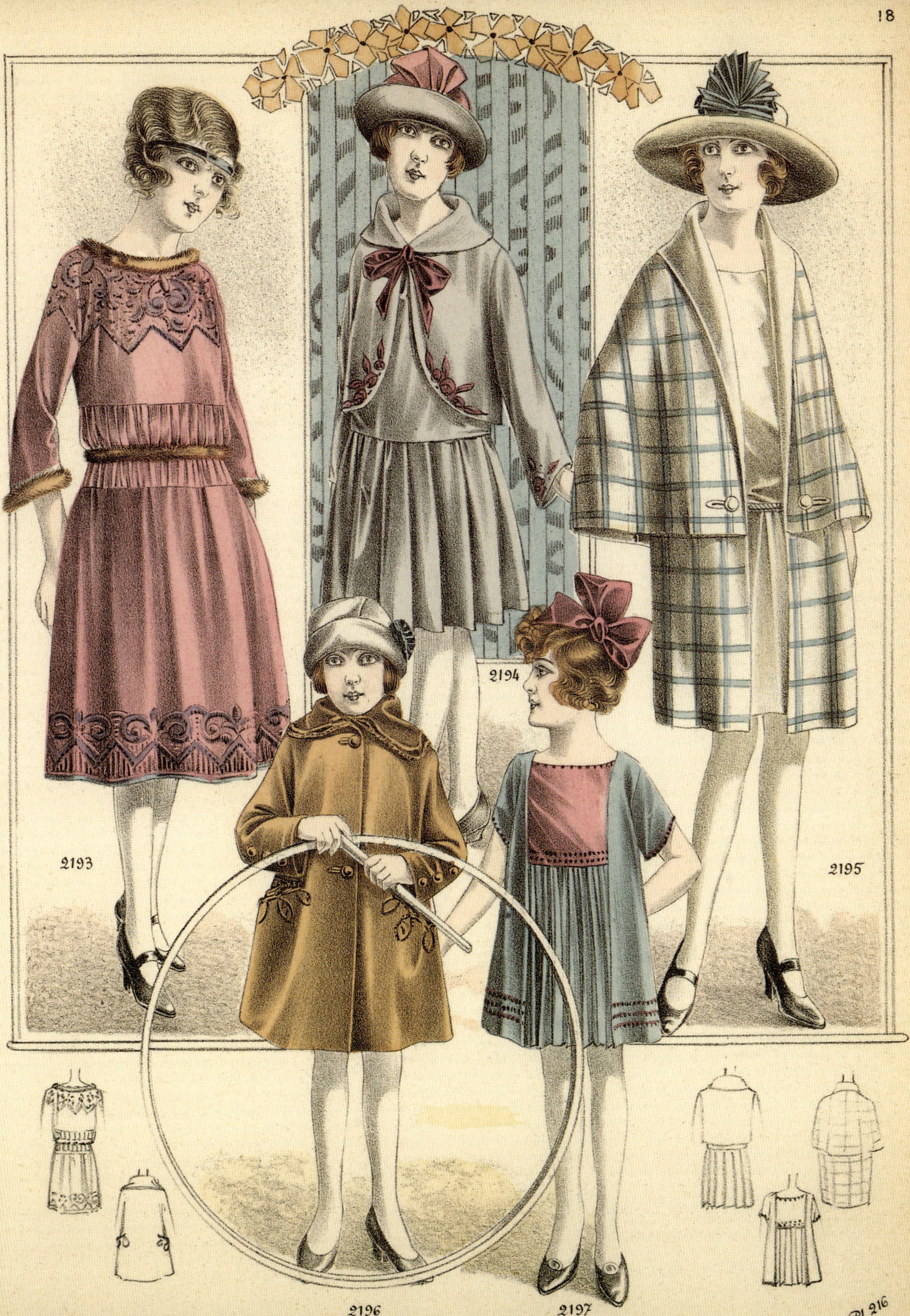

2194

2193

2195

2196

2197

Pl. 216

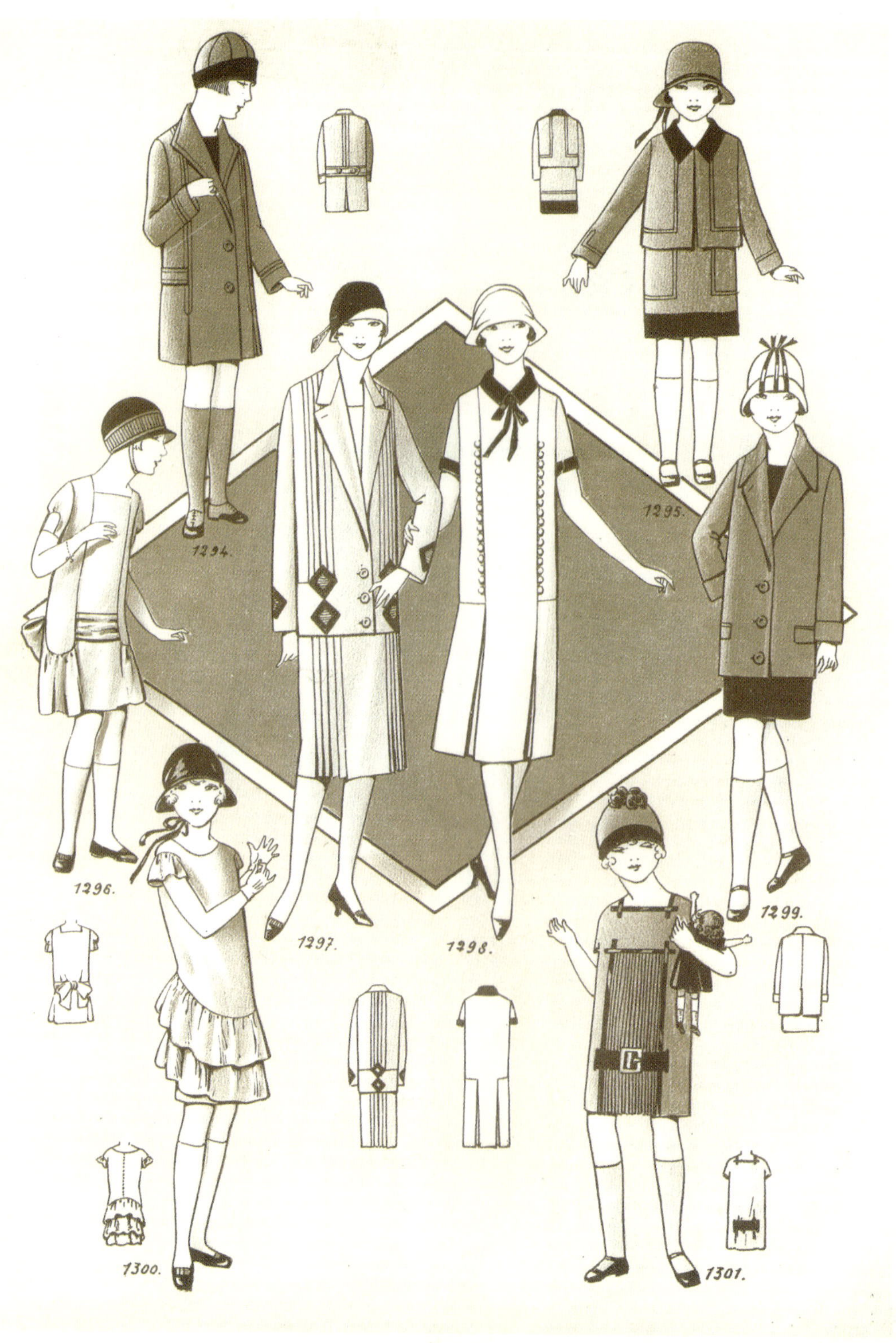

Above

A selection of children's and young girls' outfits. *La Femme Élégante à Paris*, 1926

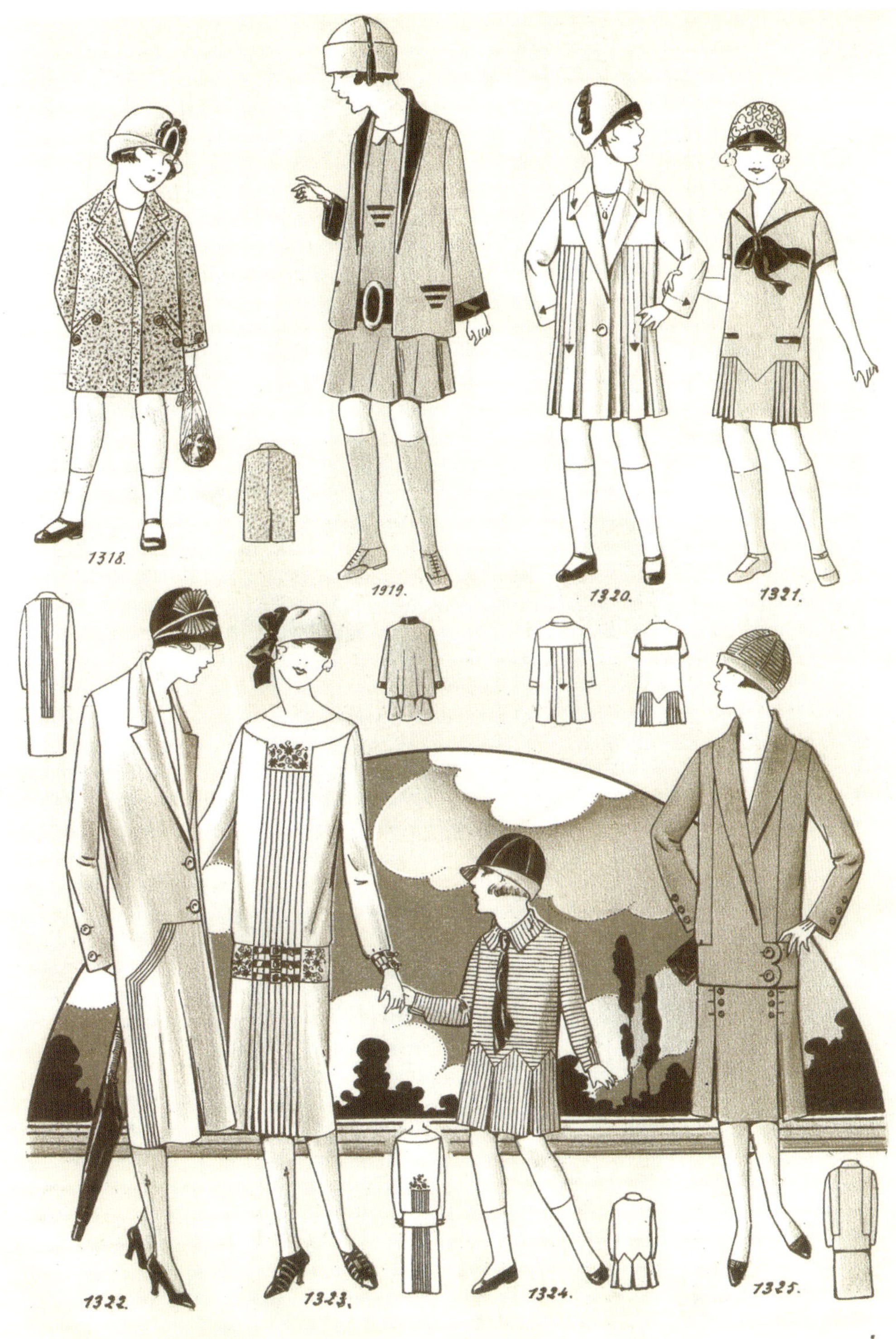

Above
A selection of children's and young girls' outfits. *La Femme Élégante à Paris*, 1926

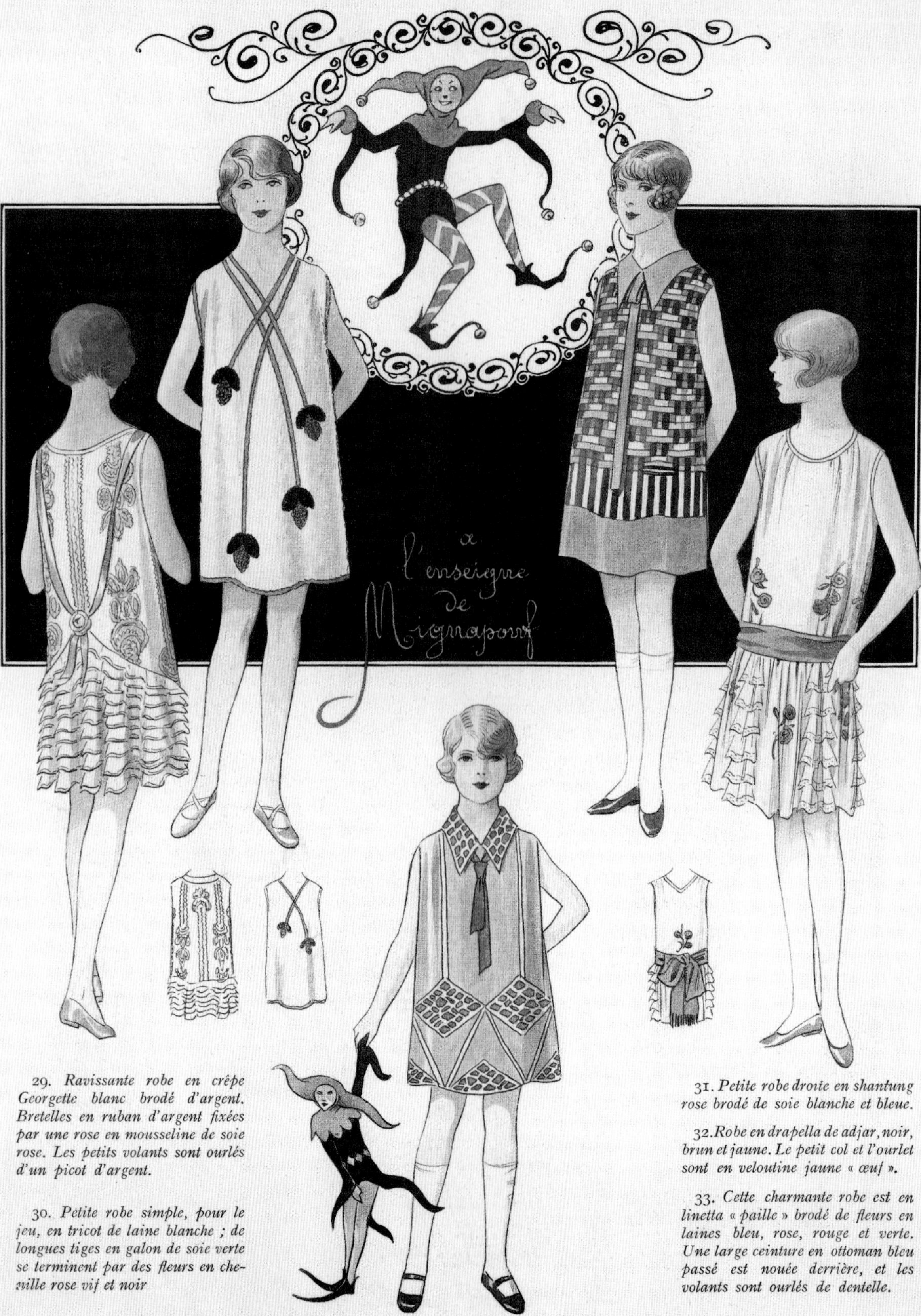

29. *Ravissante robe en crêpe Georgette blanc brodé d'argent. Bretelles en ruban d'argent fixées par une rose en mousseline de soie rose. Les petits volants sont ourlés d'un picot d'argent.*

30. *Petite robe simple, pour le jeu, en tricot de laine blanche ; de longues tiges en galon de soie verte se terminent par des fleurs en chenille rose vif et noir.*

31. *Petite robe droite en shantung rose brodé de soie blanche et bleue.*

32. *Robe en drapella de adjar, noir, brun et jaune. Le petit col et l'ourlet sont en veloutine jaune « œuf ».*

33. *Cette charmante robe est en linetta « paille » brodé de fleurs en laines bleu, rose, rouge et verte. Une large ceinture en ottoman bleu passé est nouée derrière, et les volants sont ourlés de dentelle.*

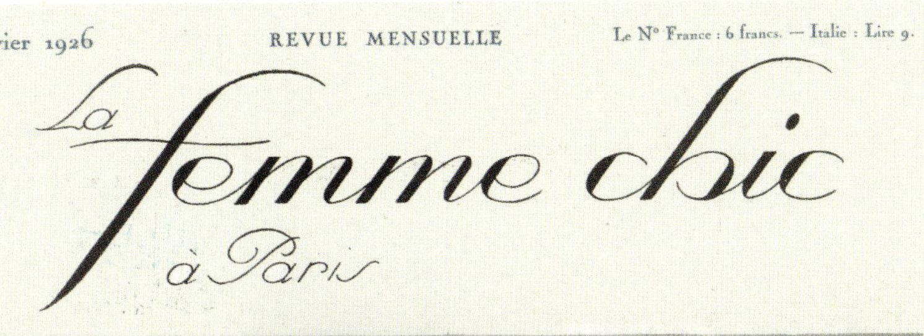

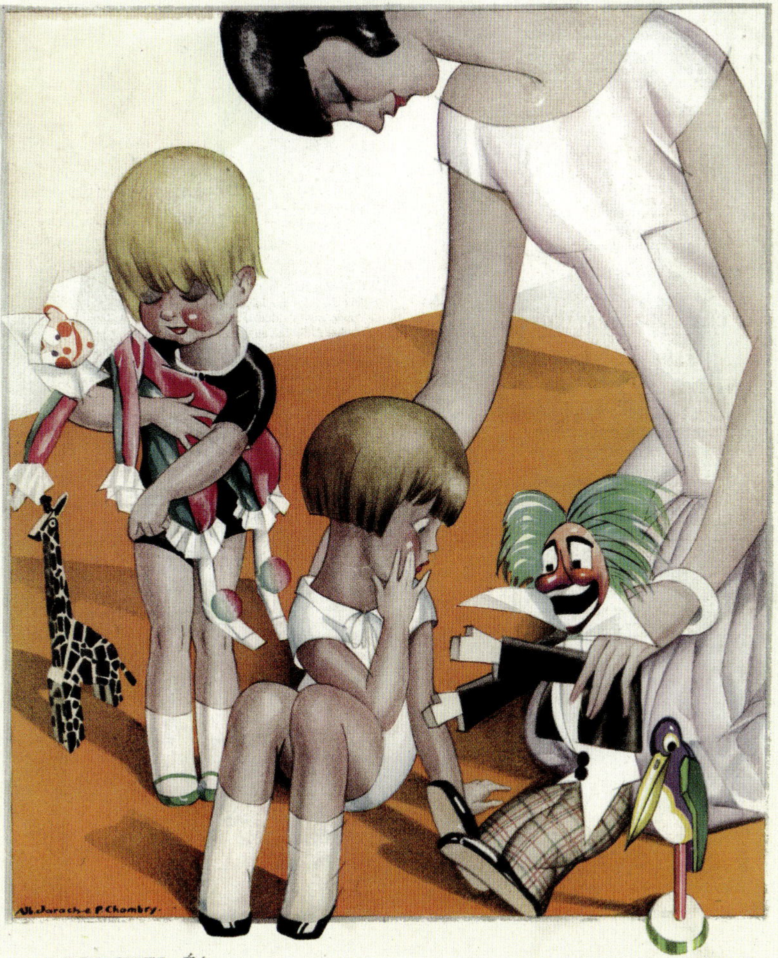

Left and above

Various children's dresses by Mignapouf. *La Femme Chic*, 1926

Cover of *La Femme Chic* à Paris, January 1926 – showing children's fashion

Right
"Laisse-le moi prendre" (Let me hold him), dresses by Jeanne Lanvin. Illustration By André Edouard Marty. *Gazette du Bon Ton*, 1922

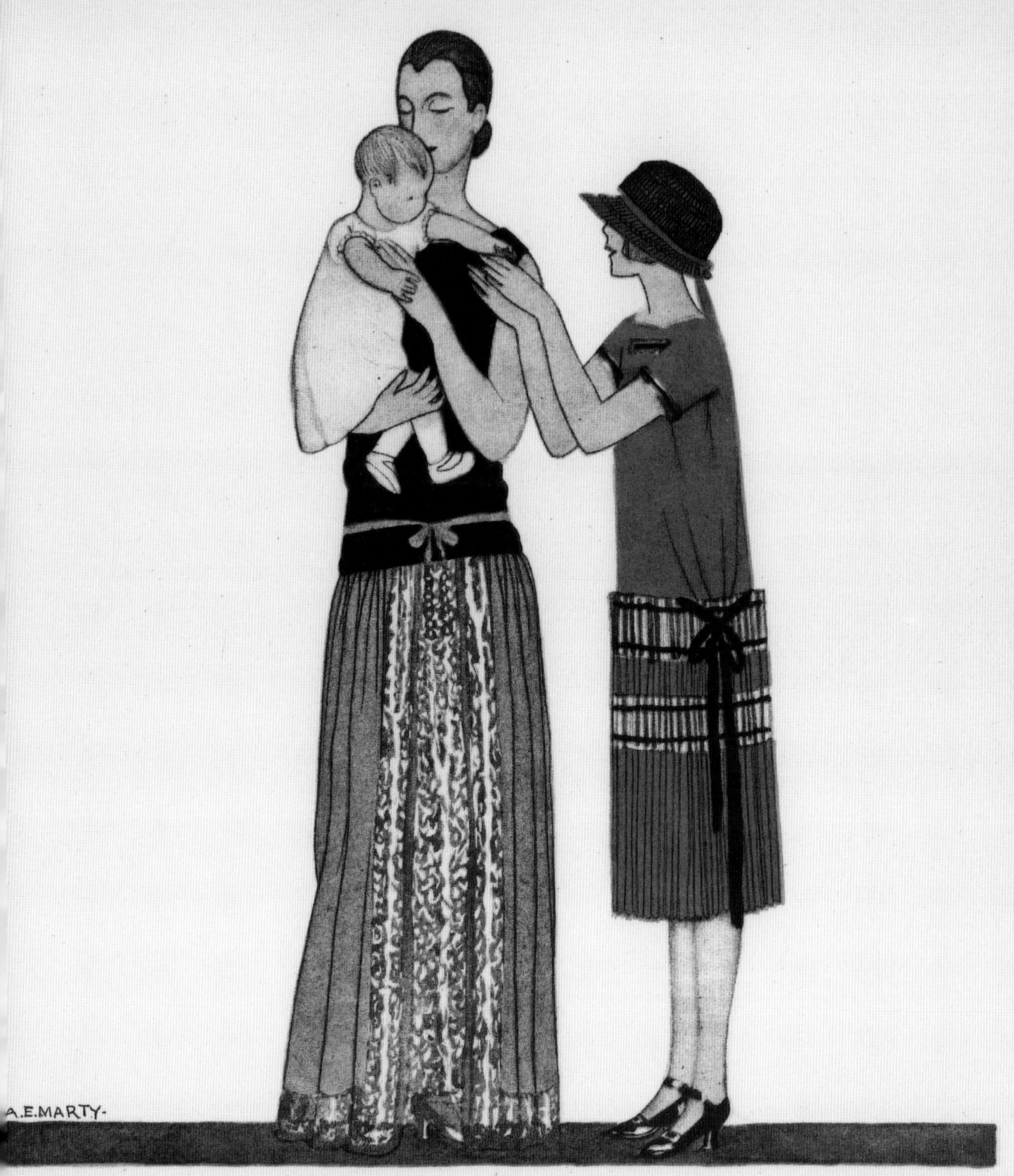

"LAISSE-LE MOI PRENDRE..."

ROBES, DE JEANNE LANVIN

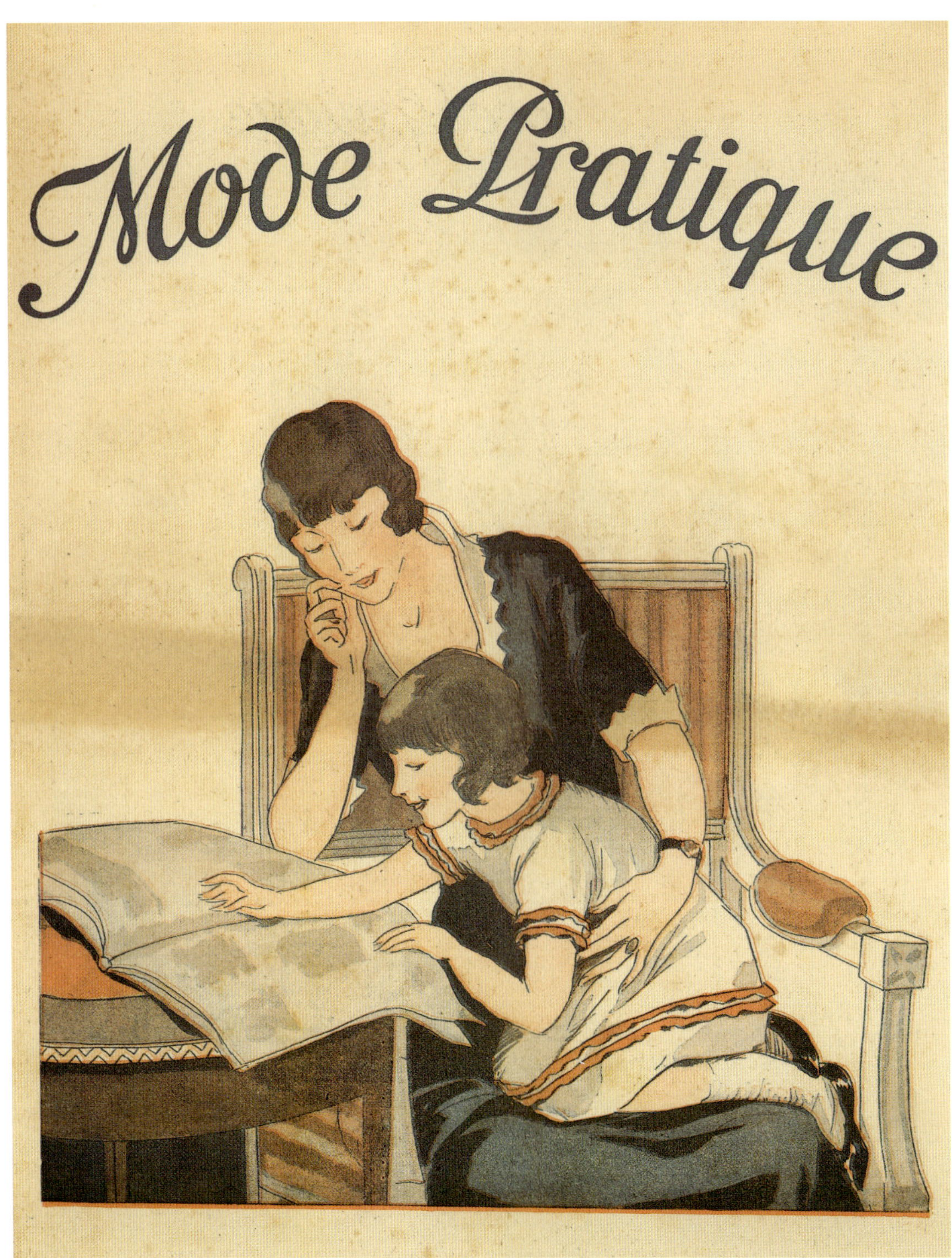

Above
Cover of *Mode Pratique*, 1924
– with young girl wearing a simple dress with ruffled details

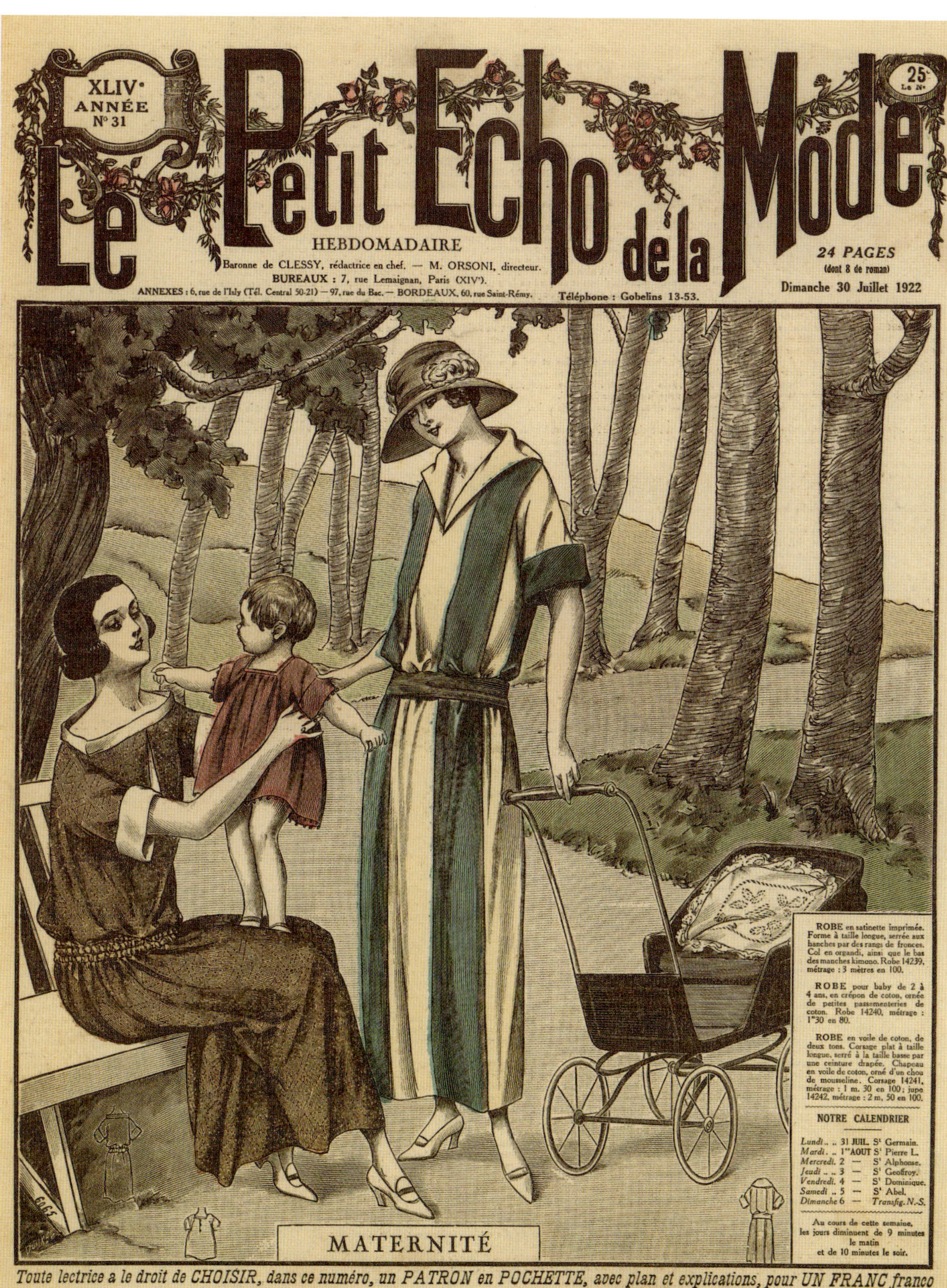

XLIV[e] ANNÉE N° 31

25[c] Le N°

Le Petit Echo de la Mode

HEBDOMADAIRE

Baronne de CLESSY, rédactrice en chef. — M. ORSONI, directeur.
BUREAUX : 7, rue Lemaignan, Paris (XIV[e]).
ANNEXES : 6, rue de l'Isly (Tél. Central 50-21) — 97, rue du Bac. — BORDEAUX, 60, rue Saint-Rémy.

Téléphone : Gobelins 13-53.

24 PAGES
(dont 8 de roman)
Dimanche 30 Juillet 1922

ROBE en satinette imprimée. Forme à taille longue, serrée aux hanches par des rangs de fronces. Col en organdi, ainsi que le bas des manches kimono. Robe 14239, métrage : 3 mètres en 100.

ROBE pour baby de 2 à 4 ans, en crépon de coton, ornée de petites passementeries de coton. Robe 14240, métrage : 1[m]30 en 80.

ROBE en voile de coton, de deux tons. Corsage plat à taille longue, serré à la taille basse par une ceinture drapée. Chapeau en voile de coton, orné d'un chou de mousseline. Corsage 14241, métrage : 1 m. 30 en 100 ; jupe 14242, métrage : 2 m, 50 en 100.

NOTRE CALENDRIER

Lundi .. .. 31 JUIL. St Germain.
Mardi . .. 1er AOUT St Pierre L.
Mercredi. 2 — St Alphonse.
Jeudi .. .. 3 — St Geoffroy.
Vendredi. 4 — St Dominique.
Samedi .. 5 — St Abel.
Dimanche 6 — *Transfig. N.-S.*

Au cours de cette semaine, les jours diminuent de 9 minutes le matin et de 10 minutes le soir.

MATERNITÉ

Toute lectrice a le droit de CHOISIR, dans ce numéro, un PATRON en POCHETTE, avec plan et explications, pour UN FRANC franco

Above

Two women in walking dresses. *Le Petit Echo de la Mode*, 1922 – with toddler in square-necked dress

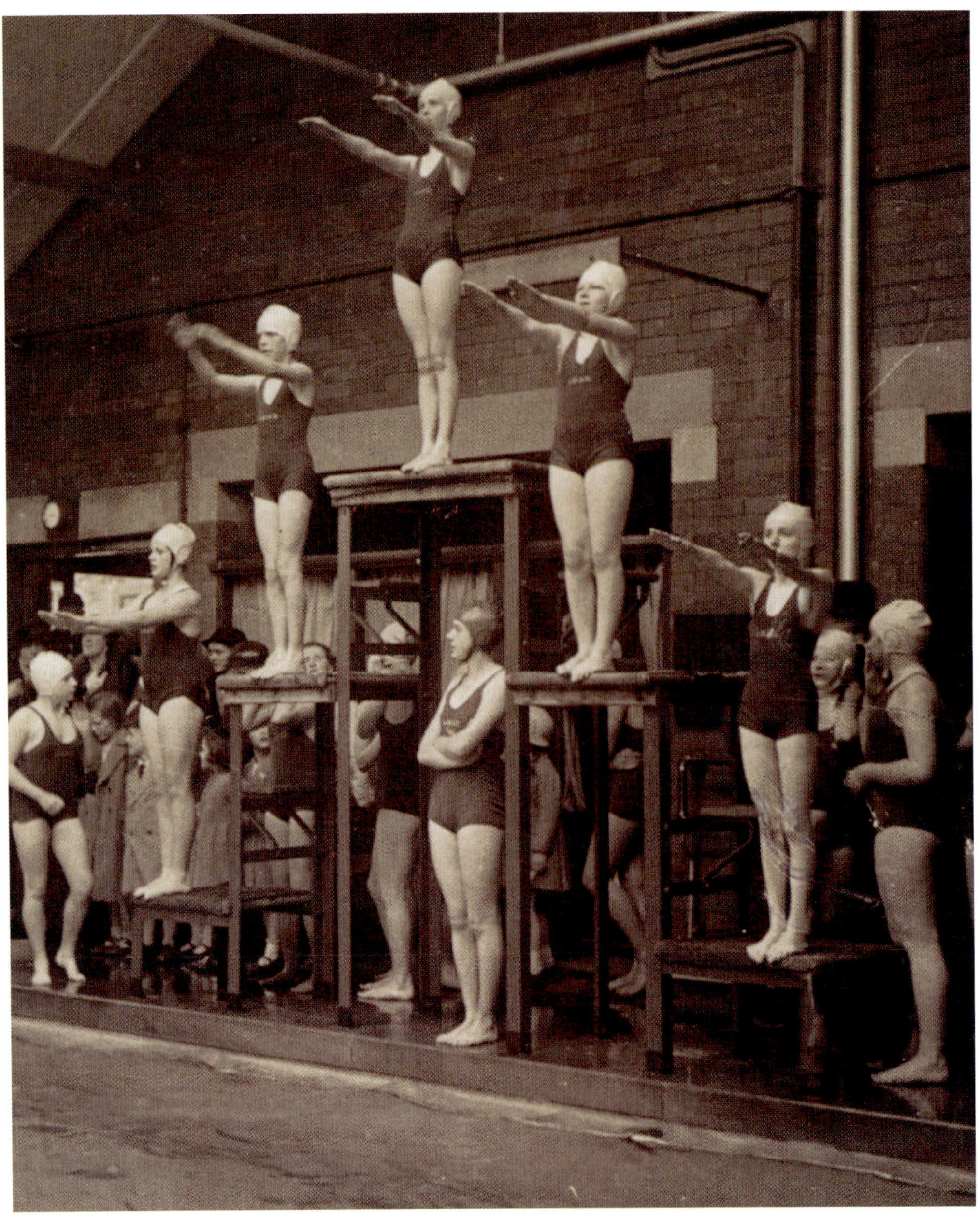

Above and right

Photograph taken at a public swimming pool in Sheffield, England, c.1925

A 'Leyland Bathing Cap' advertisement, c.1927

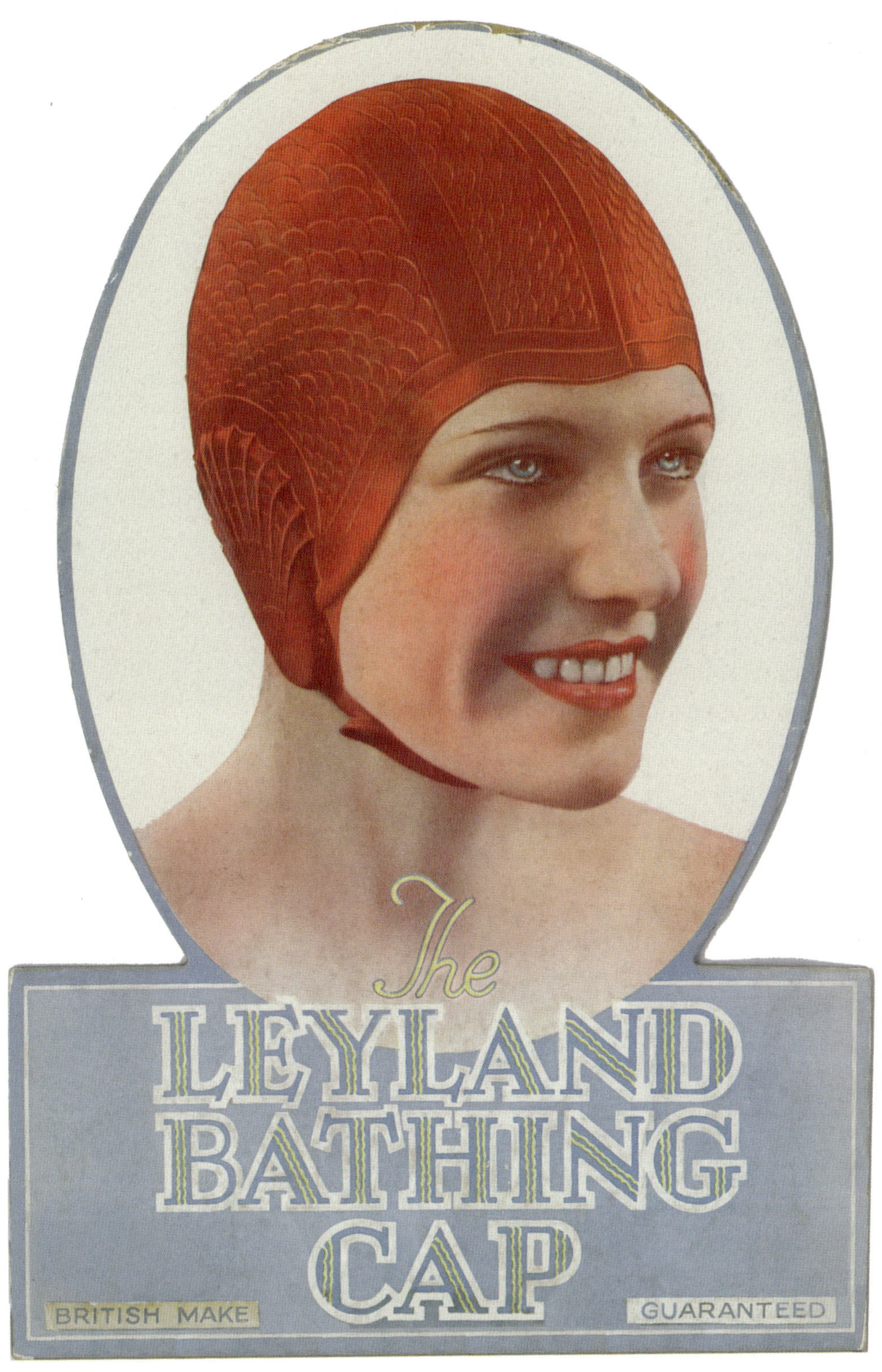
The
LEYLAND
BATHING
CAP
BRITISH MAKE
GUARANTEED

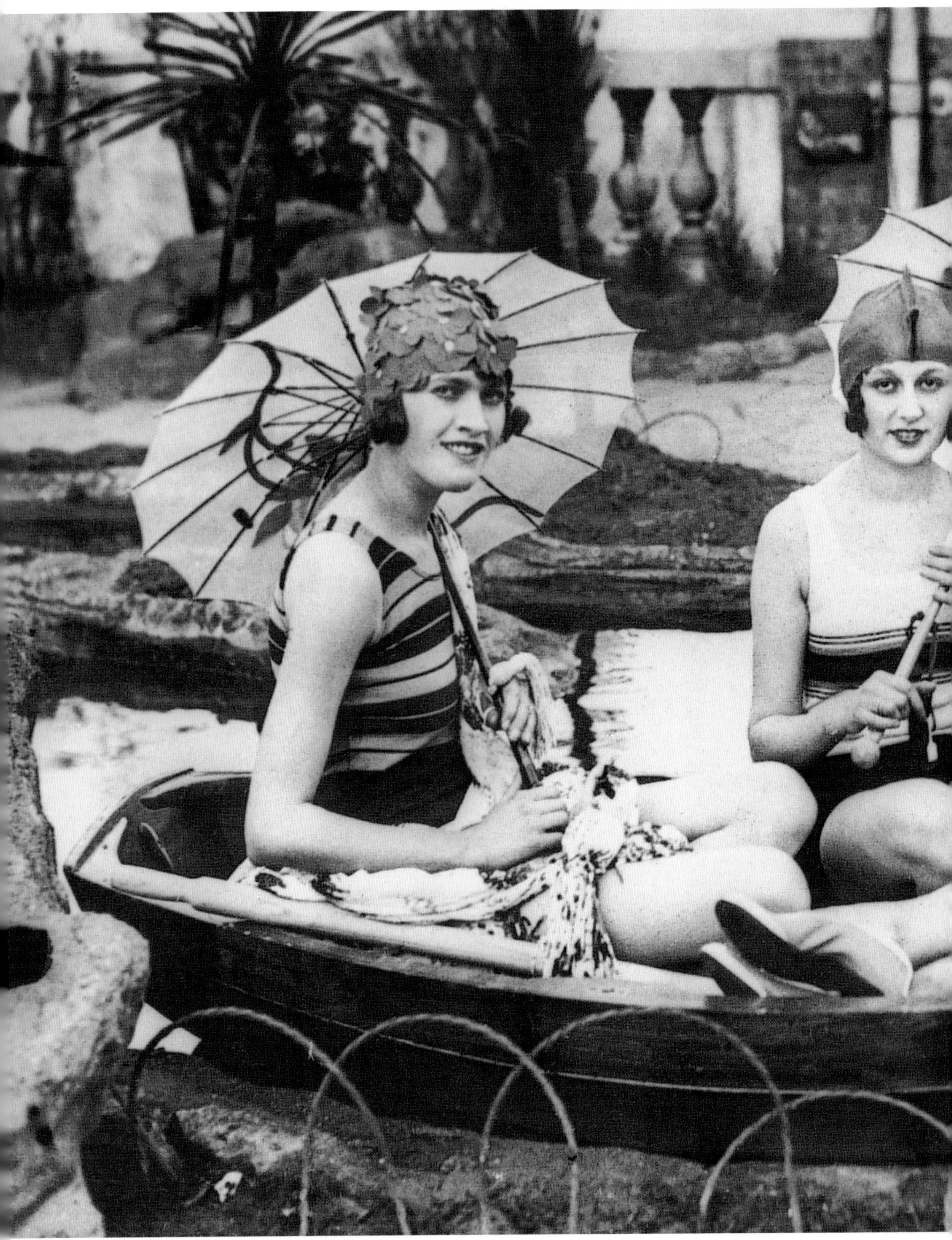

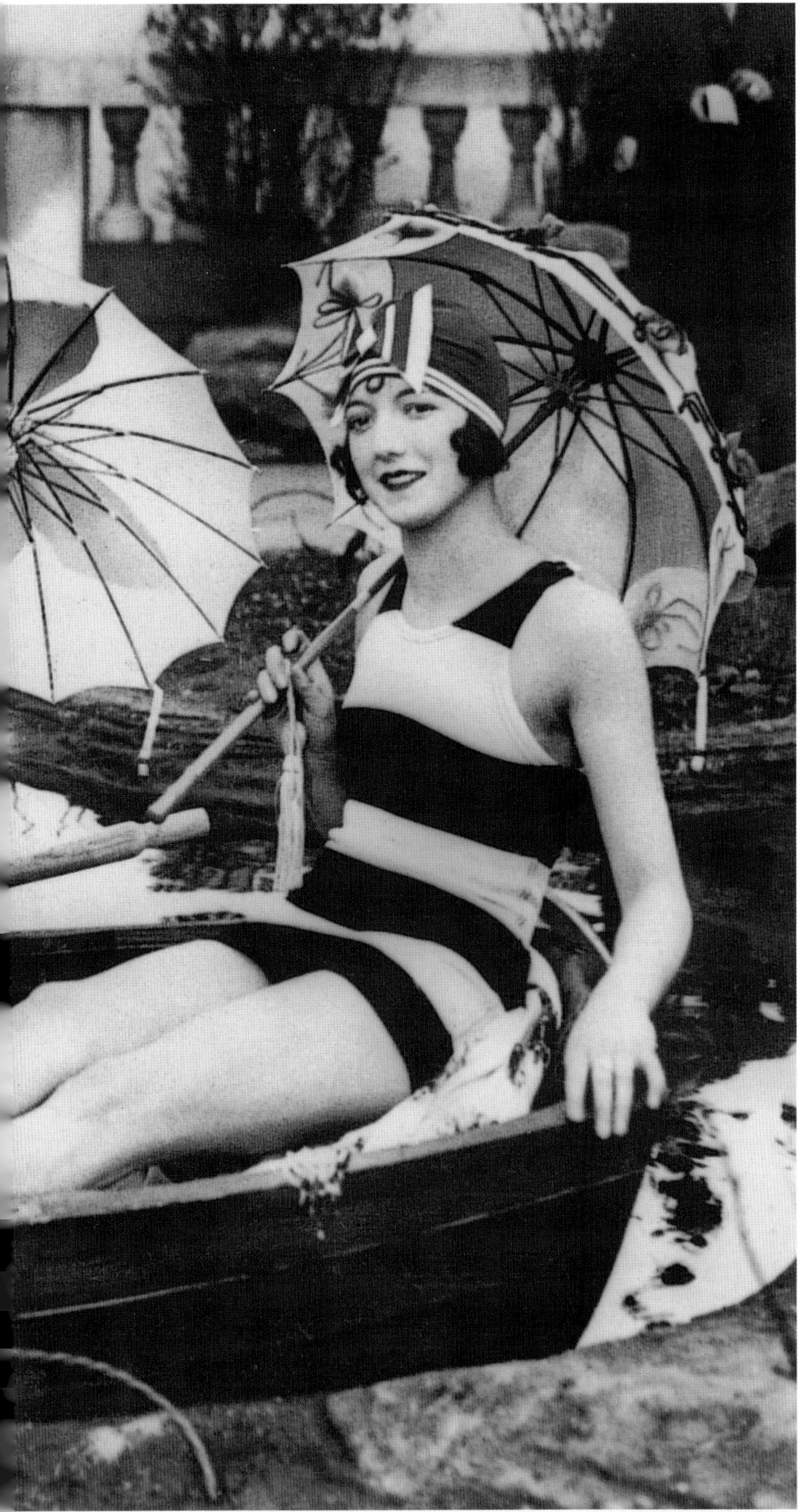

Previous page and right
Three models posing in a shop window in London's West End, whilst showing off the latest fashions in swimwear and beach accessories, c.1924

Hollywood actress Shirley Mason dressed in a satin one piece swimming costume and matching cap, accessorised with a large tassled Spanish shawl with a batik print. International newsreel photograph, c.1924

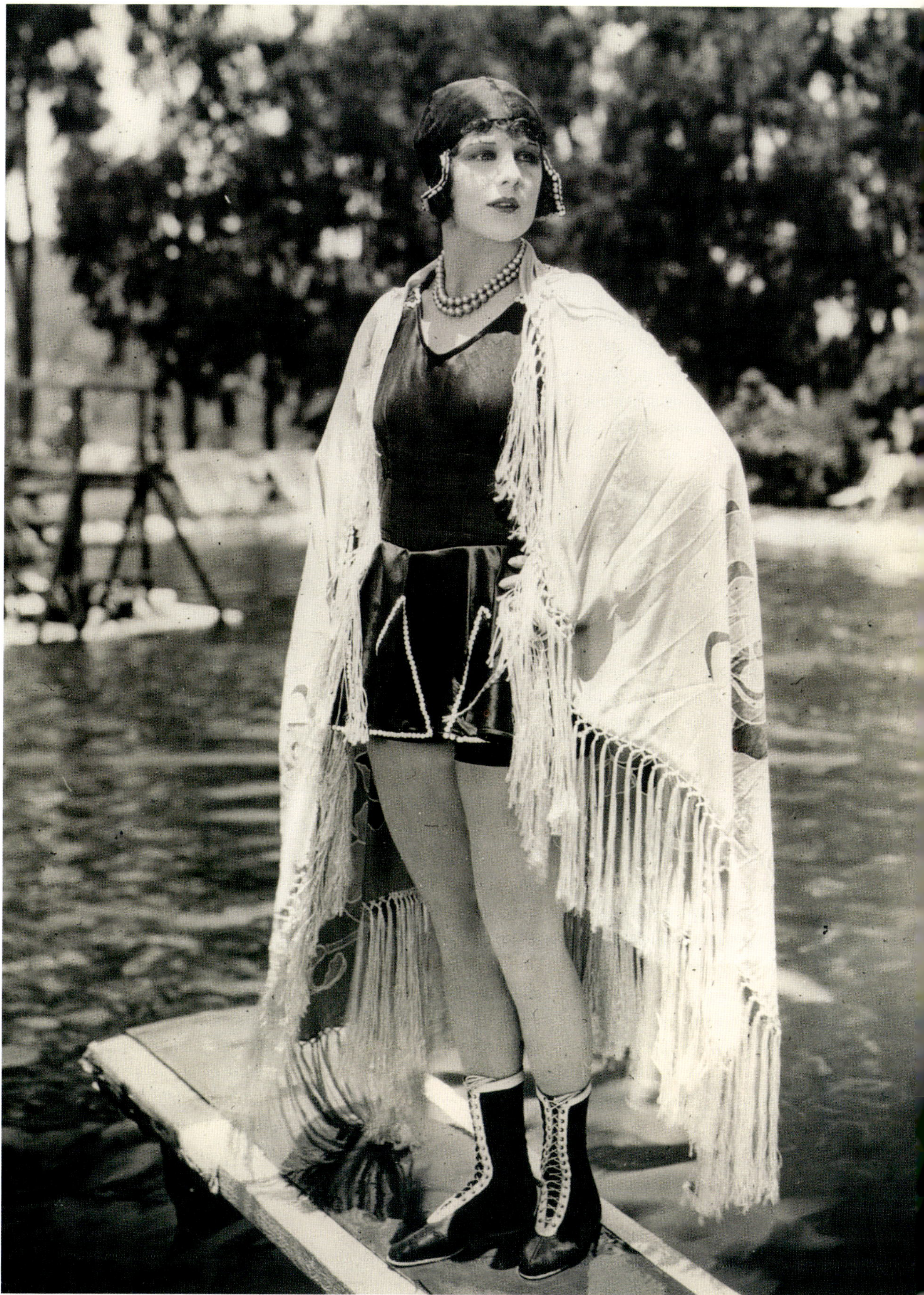

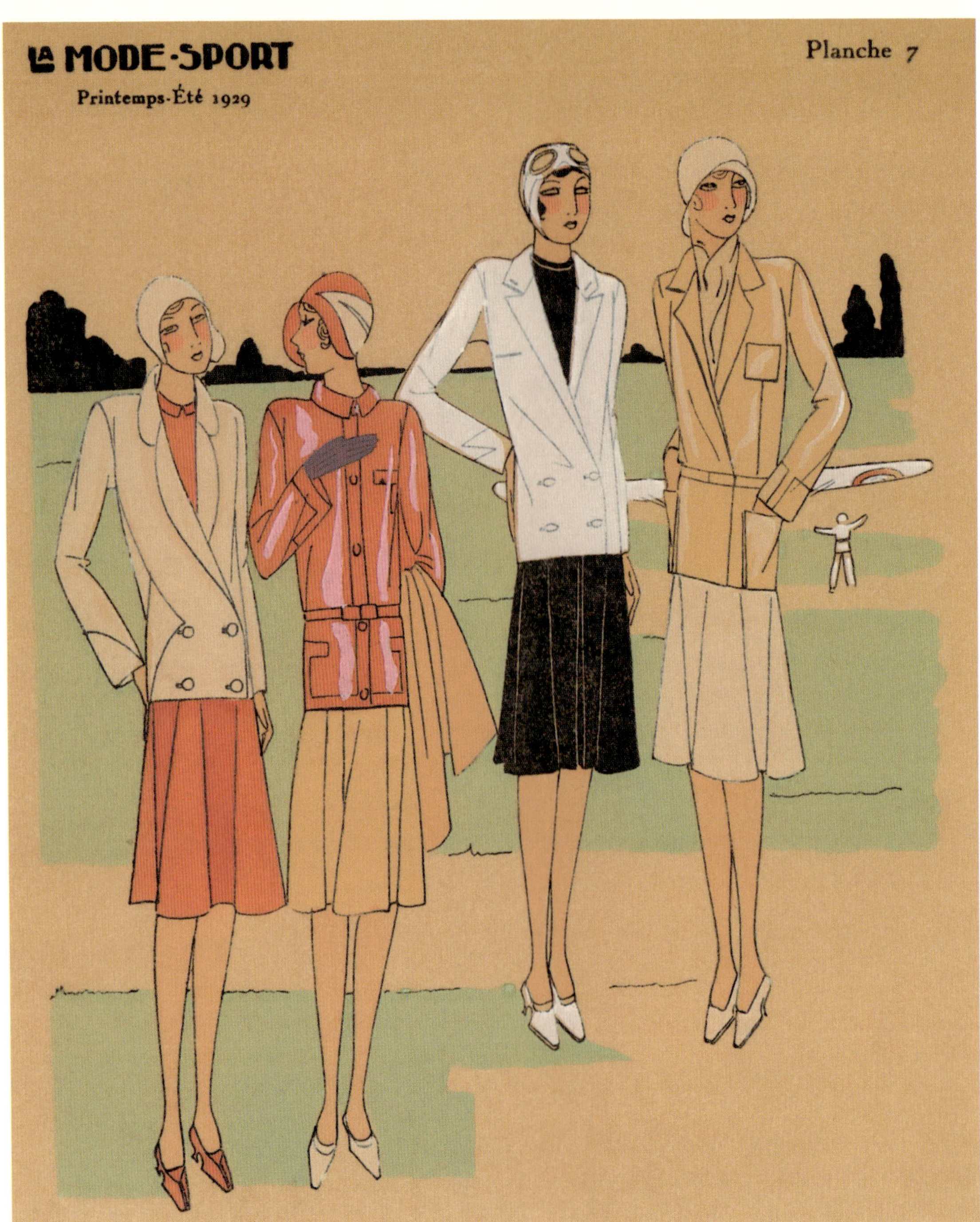

Above and right

Four sports skirt and leather jacket ensembles for motoring and flying. *La Mode-Sport*, 1929

Three beach outfits by Jenny. *La Mode-Sport*, 1929 – a beige Kasha embroidered dress, a blue and white jersey jumper with a red cravat detail and paired with a blue crepe de Chine pleated skirt, and a back-pleated dress worn with a green and orange jersey jumper.

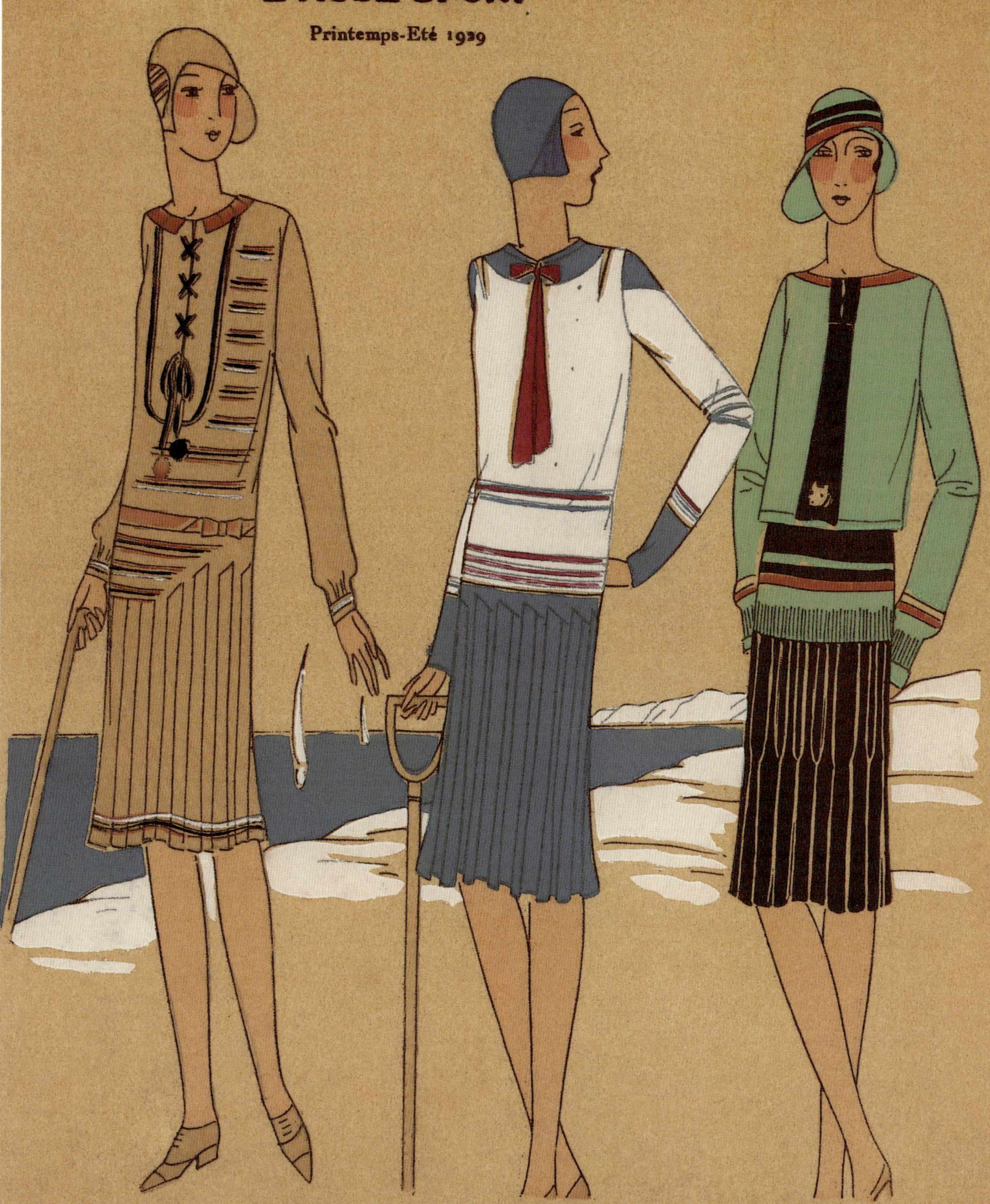

Créations Jenny

Pour la plage, une jolie robe en kasha beige brodée de lignes de soie marron, orange, beige et blanc, effet de plastron lacé, col de gros-grain orangé. — Deux-pièces en jersey blanc tissé de rouge et bleu garni de bleu uni pour le pull-over, la jupe plissée est en crêpe de Chine bleu. — Cette jupe de marocain noir d'un effet très chic se porte avec un sweater en jersey vert et orangé réappliqué de marocain noir.

LA MODE-SPORT

Printemps-Été 1929

Planche 11

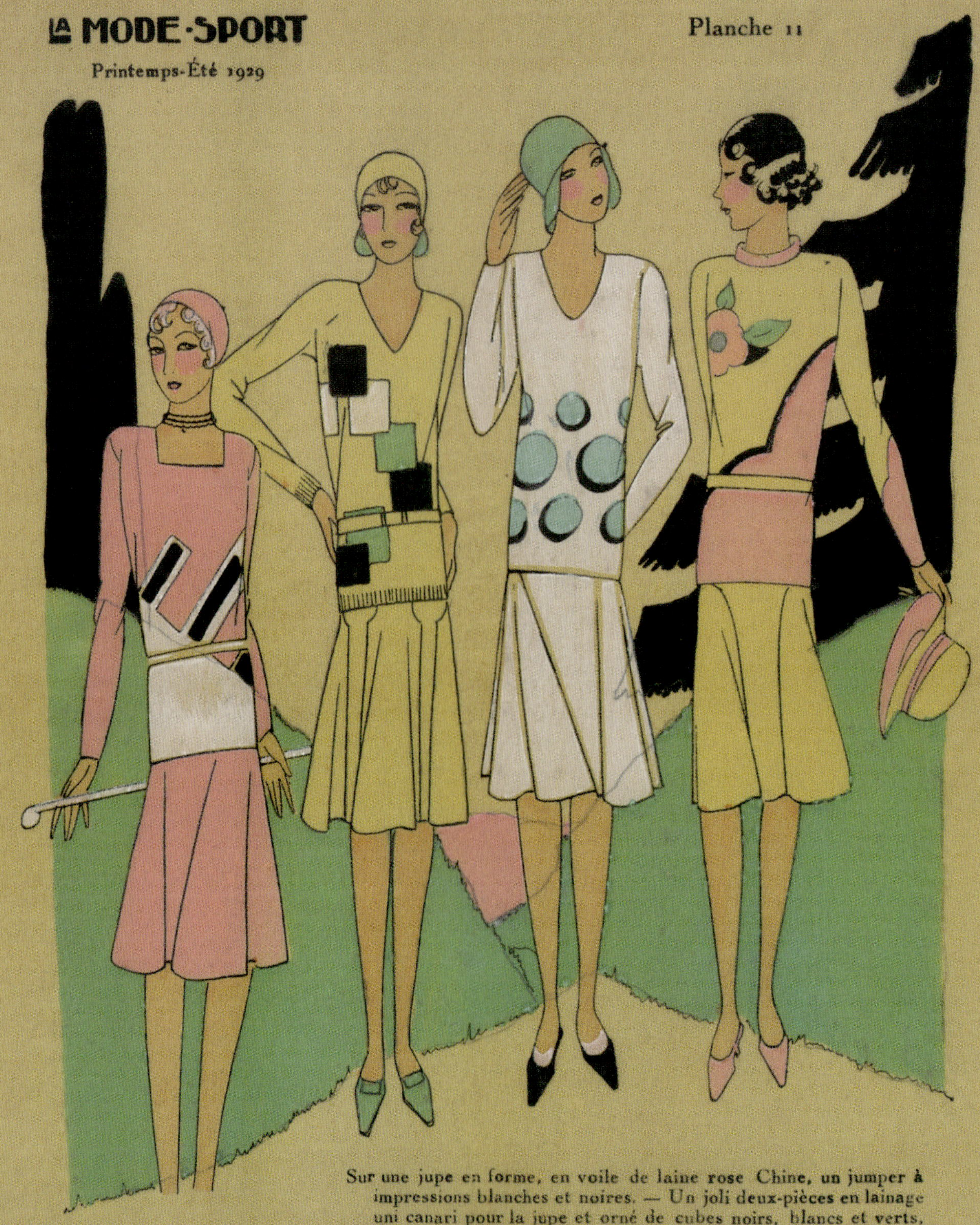

Sur une jupe en forme, en voile de laine rose Chine, un jumper à impressions blanches et noires. — Un joli deux-pièces en lainage uni canari pour la jupe et orné de cubes noirs, blancs et verts, sur un côté du sweater. — Un ensemble de forme droite en lainage angora blanc, imprimé sur le jumper de gros pois de faille dégradée verts cerclés de noir. — D'une allure juvénile, ce deux-pièces jaune est en marocain de laine se colorant sur le pull-over de rose cerné de noir et d'une fleur rose, verte et noire.

Modèles des Tissus d'Art

8, rue de Lévis

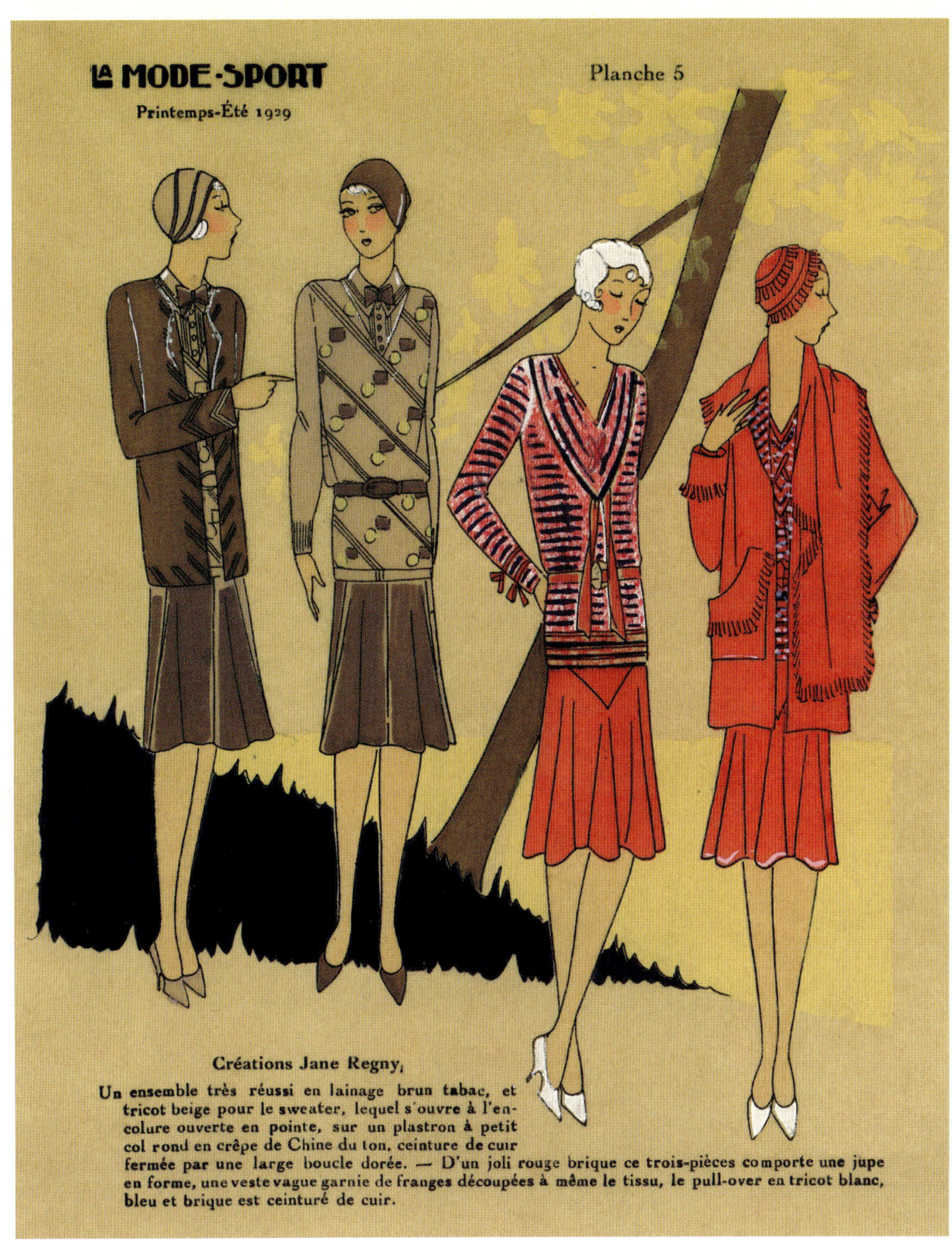

Left and above

Four sportswear outfits of dresses and sweater-and-skirt ensembles. *La Mode-Sport*, 1929

Four sportswear ensembles by Jane Regny. *La Mode-Sport*, 1929

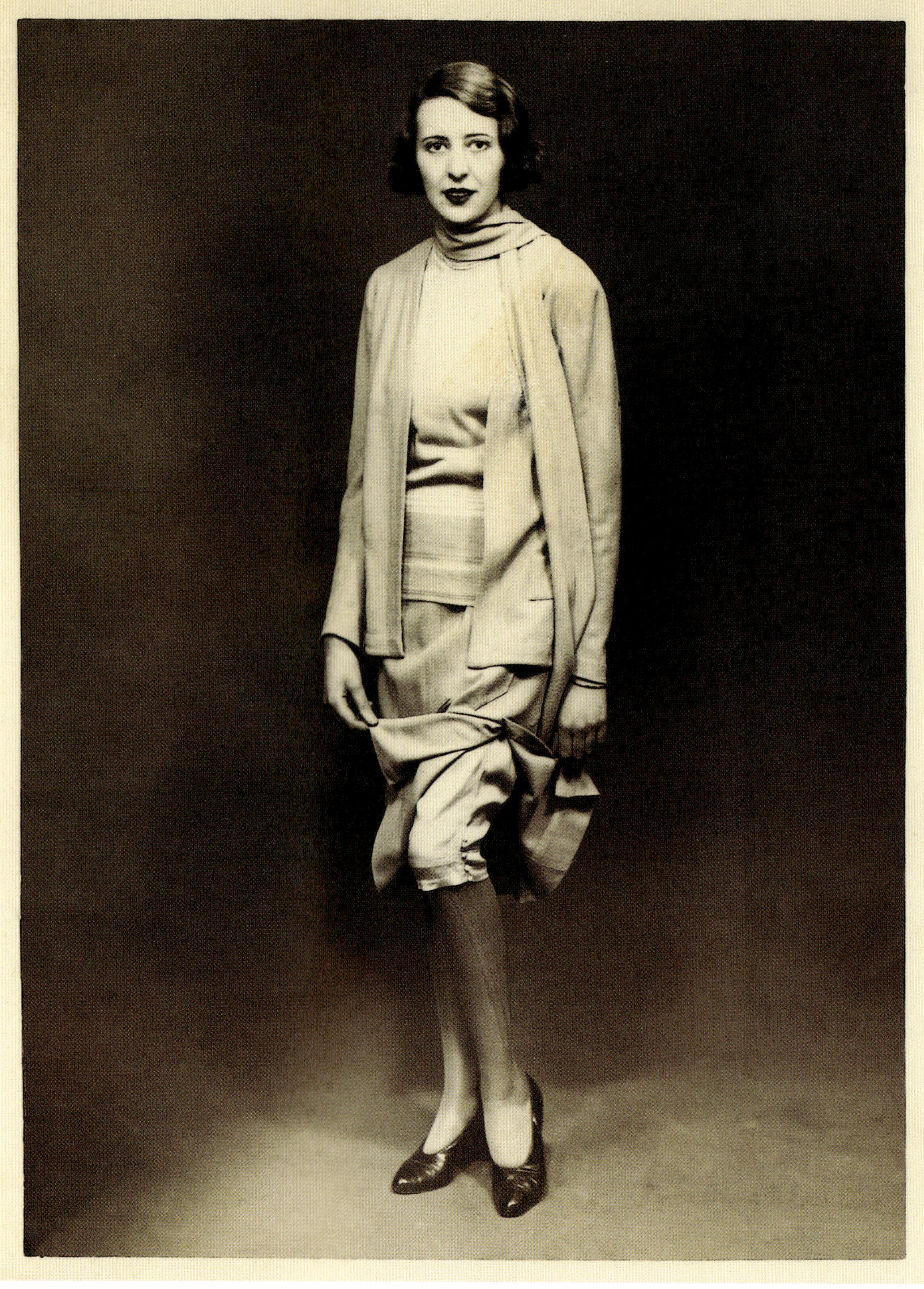

Above
A skating suit with crepe de Chine breeches, c.1924

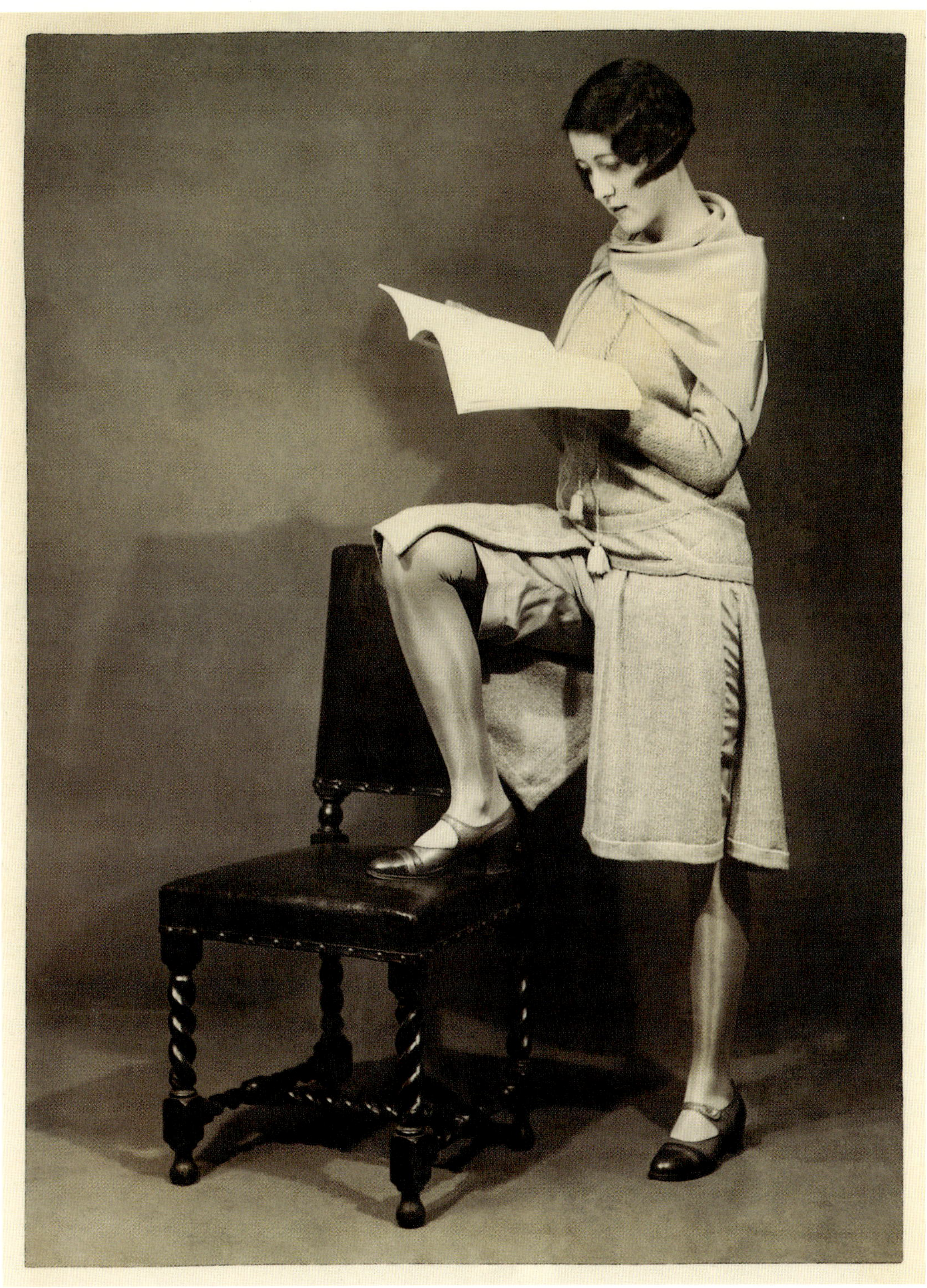

Above

A sport suit, possibly a skating or walking outfit, made up of breeches and a wool jumper dress with split details, c.1924

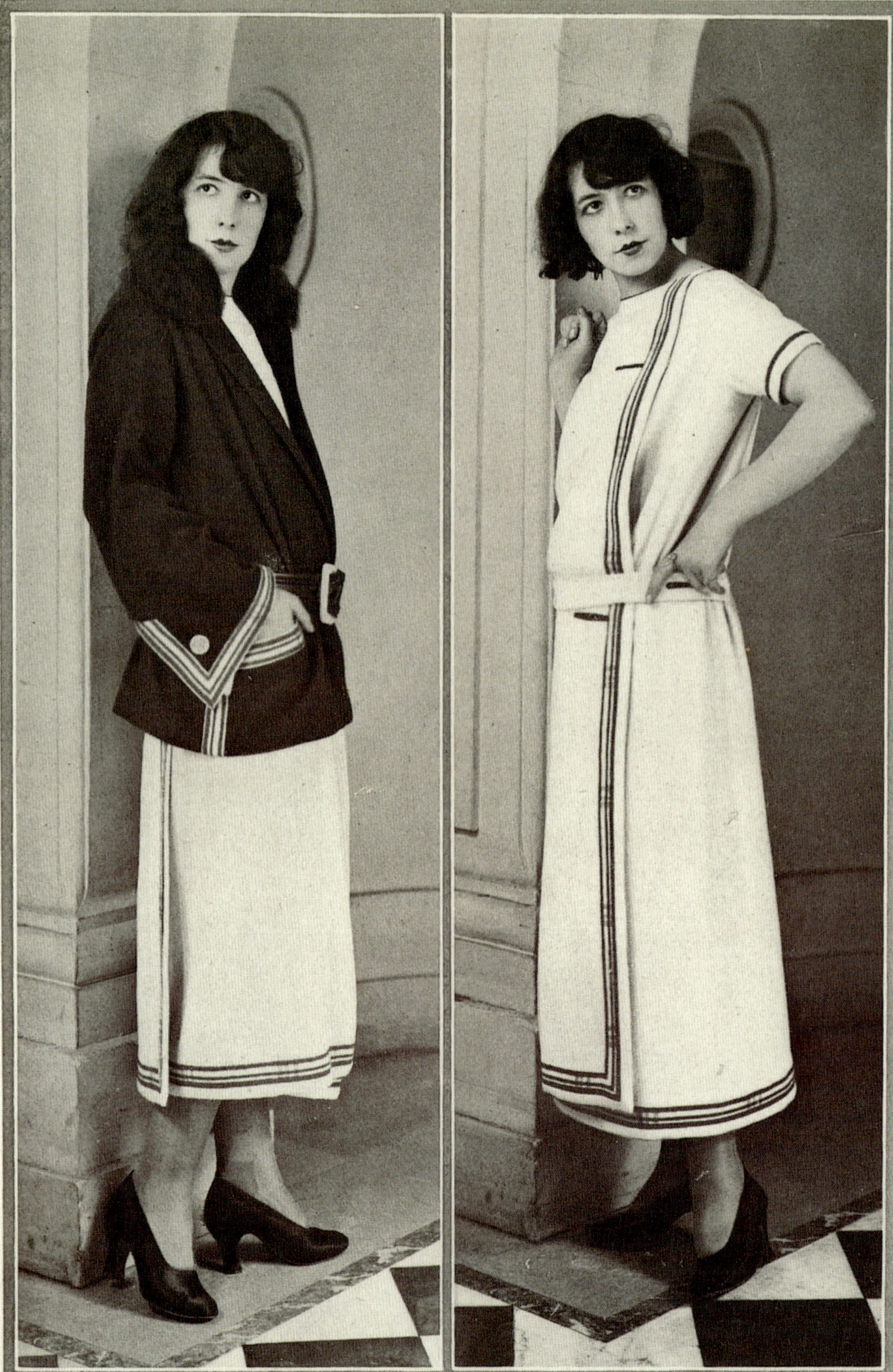

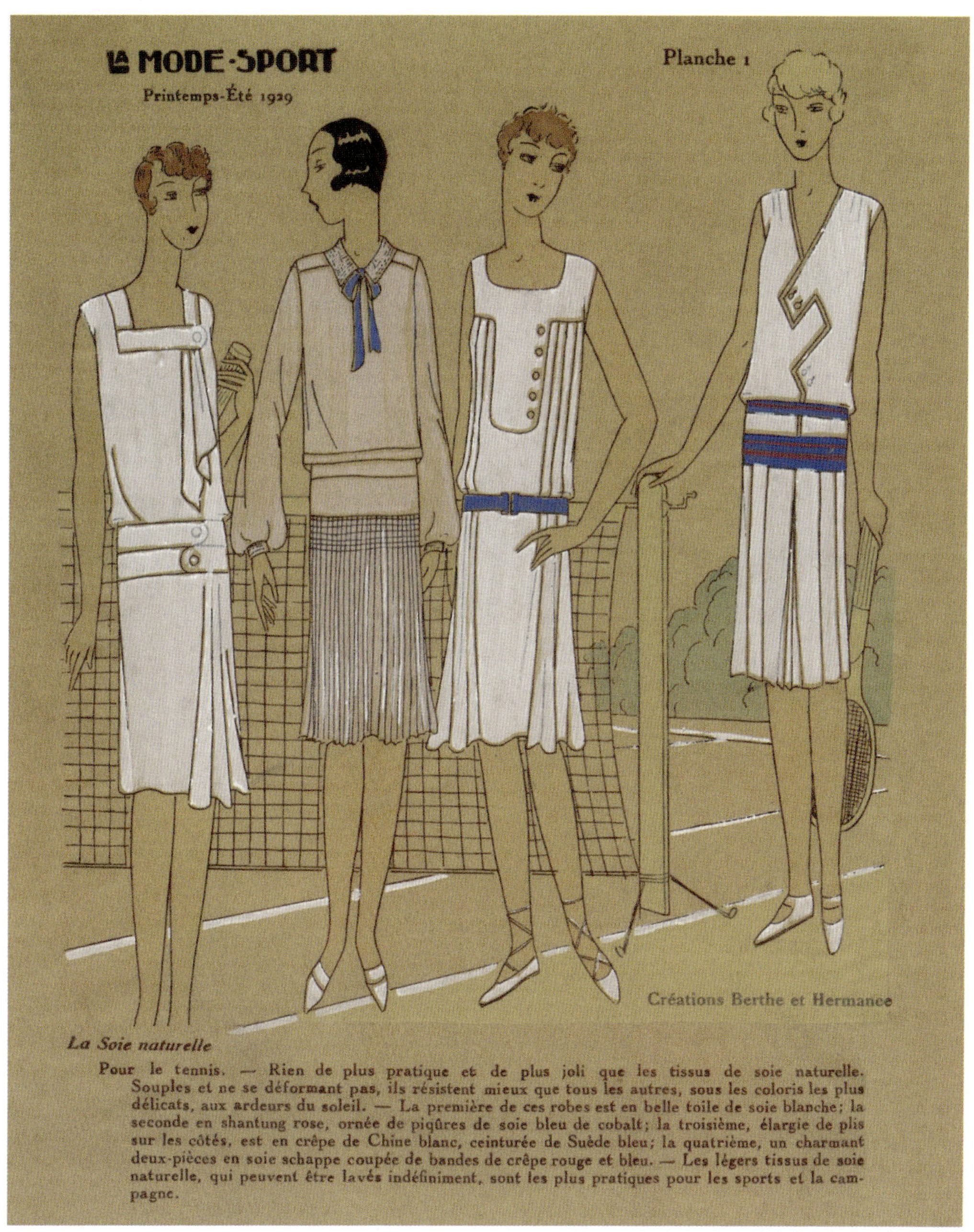

Left and above

Advertisement for two ensembles for the beach or golfing by Jean Patou. *L'Illustration des Modes*, 1922

Four tennis outfits in silk by Berthe et Hermance. *La Mode-Sport*, 1929

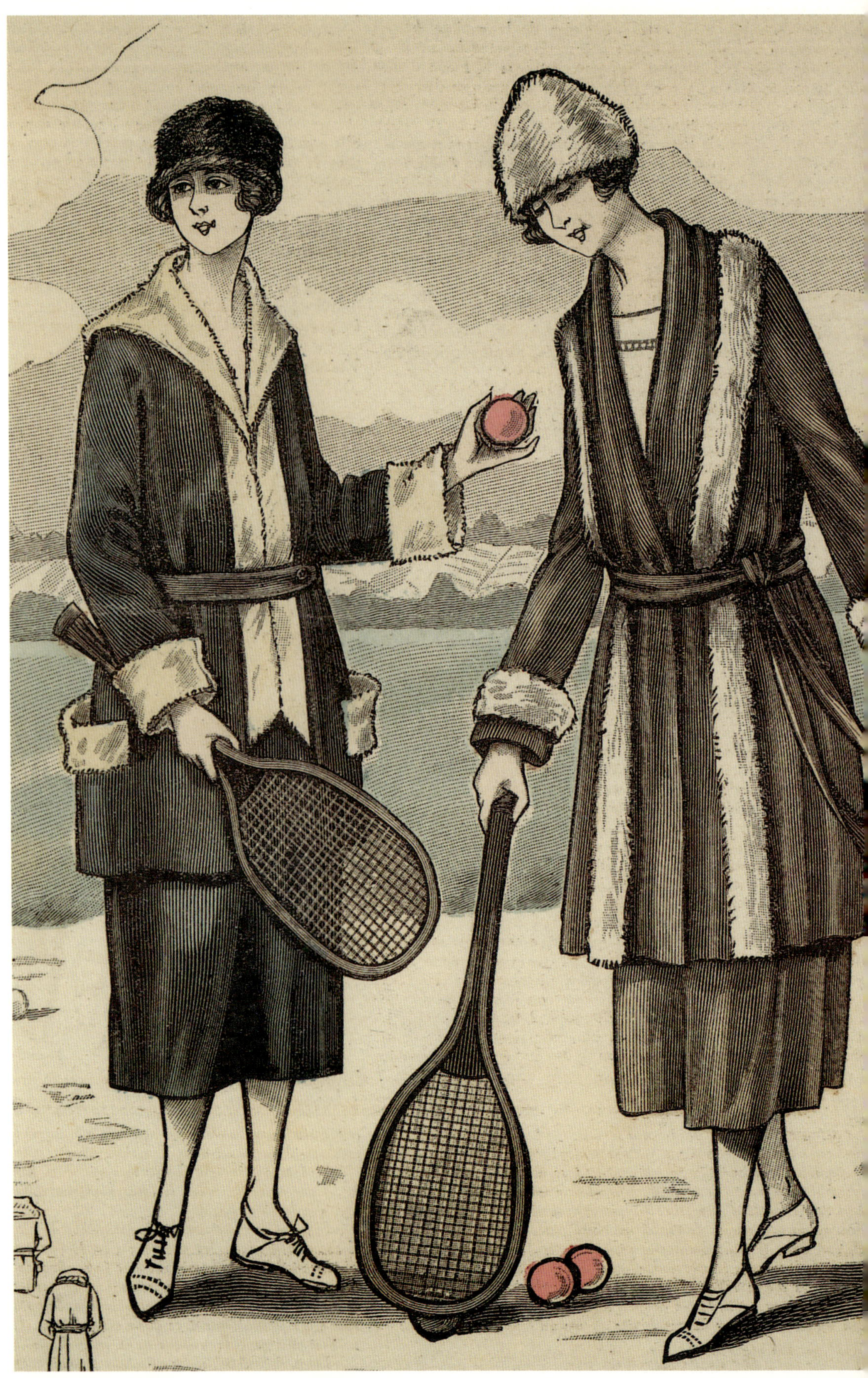

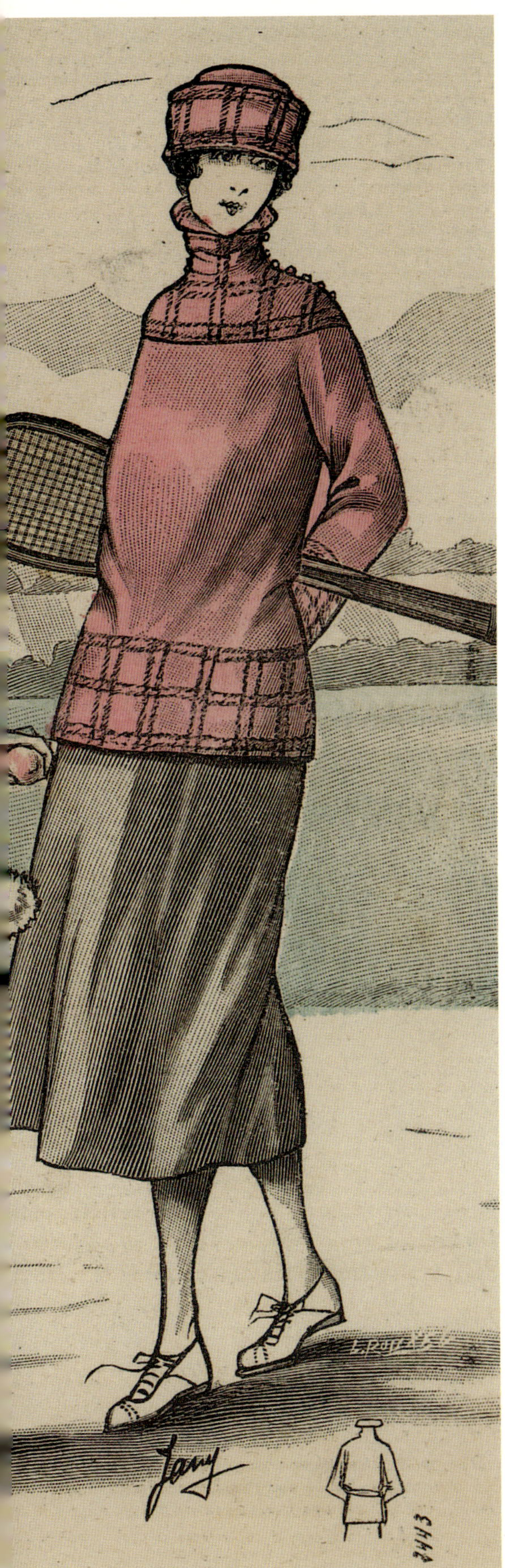

Left
Three women in tennis outfits.
Le Petit Echo de la Mode, 1921

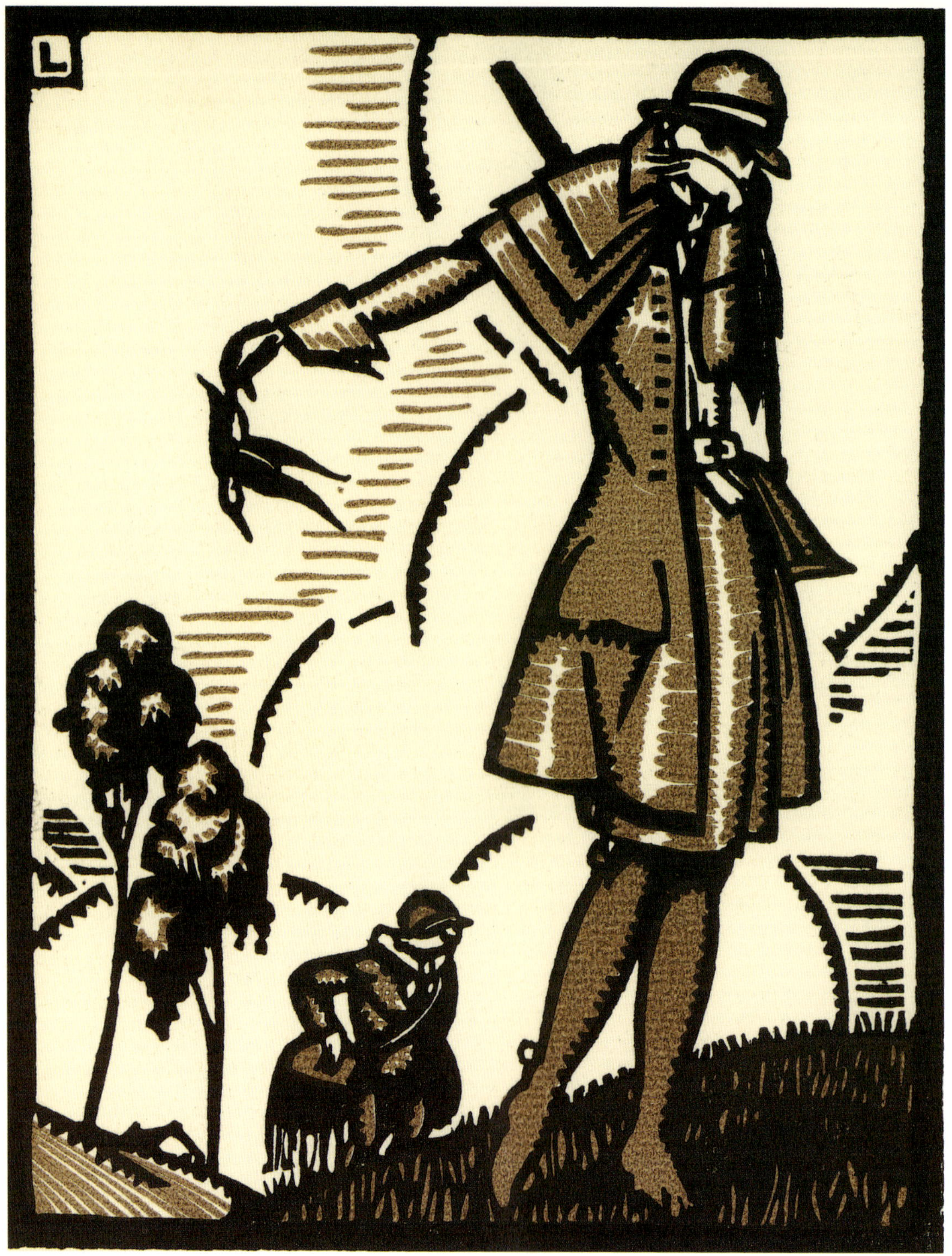

Above

"Remords" (Remorse), hunting outfit. Illustration by Maurice Leroy. *Gazette du Bon Ton*, 1920

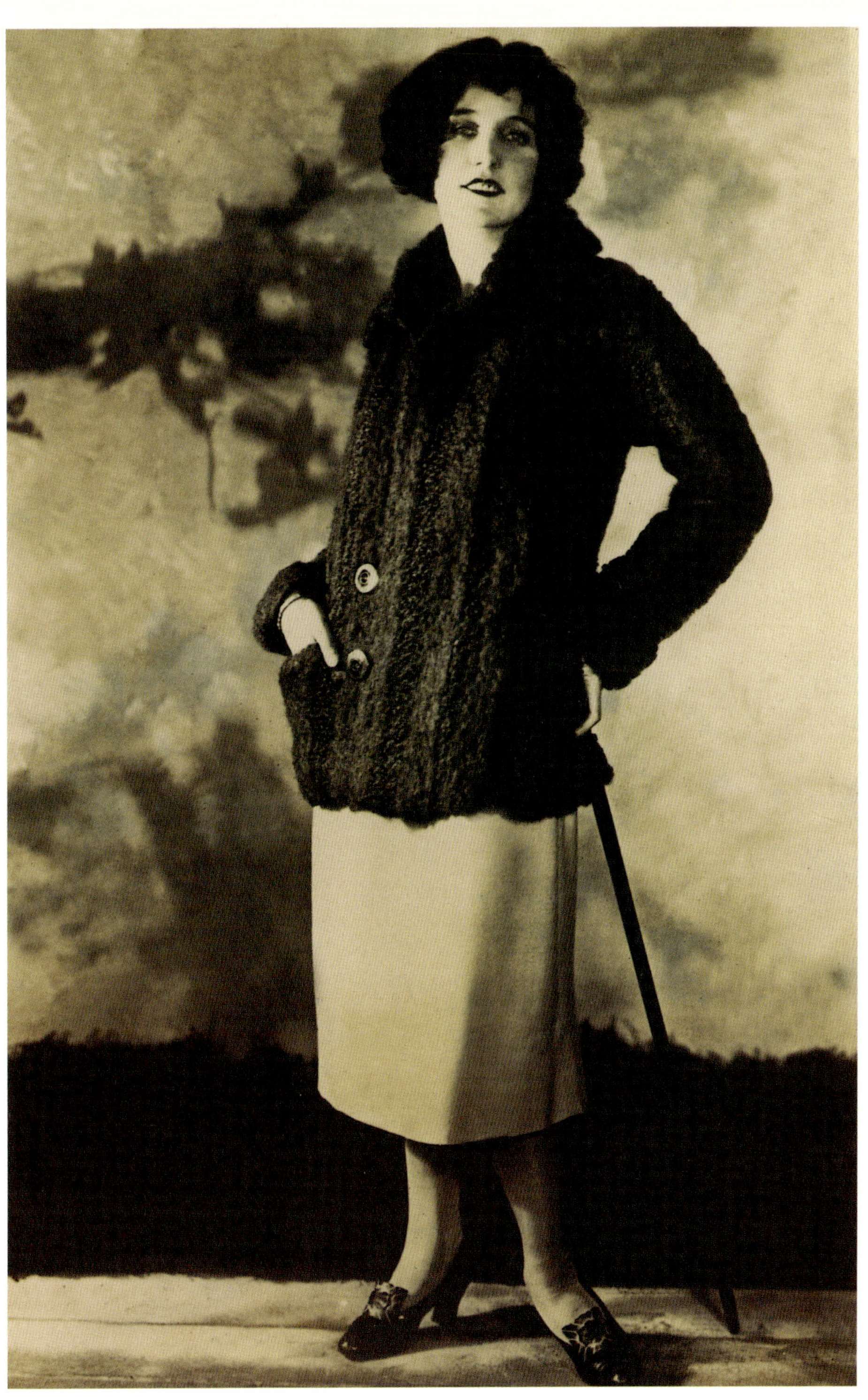

Above
A model in a knitted sports coat worked in a knit to resemble Astrakhan fur in flaming orange worn with a kasha coloured jersey skirt, c.1924

Right
A fashionable skiing ensemble with knee socks, a buttoned cravat fastening and matching fur hat and scarf, c.1926

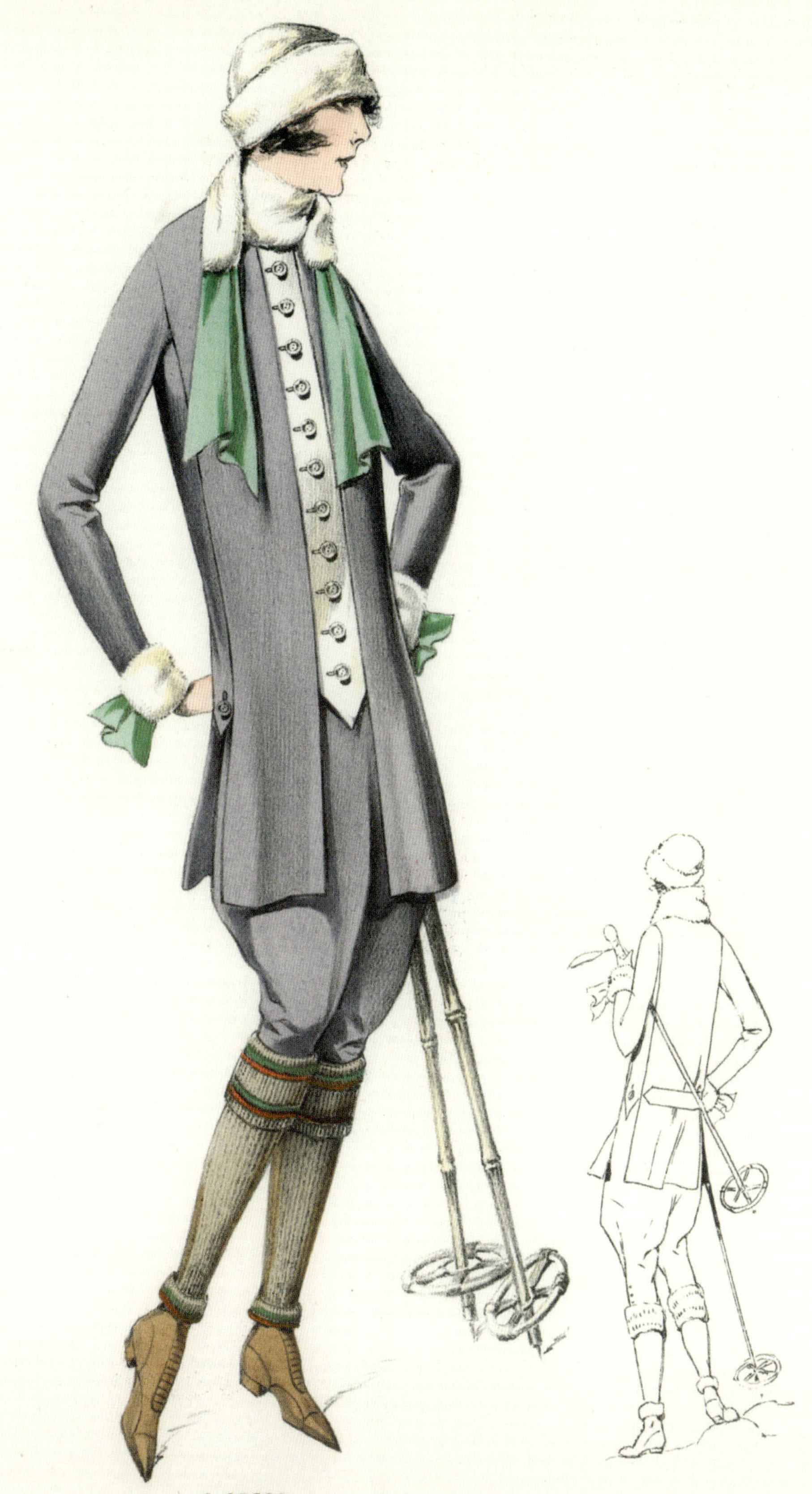

A 25069

Selected Biographies

Beer
Parisian Couture House
1905 – 1929

The German designer Gustav Beer moved to Paris in 1905 to found Maison Beer, which specialised in conservative feminine daywear and evening wear and was particularly known for its lingerie collections. Gustav Beer was the first designer to open on the Place Vendôme. He would visit big luxurious hotels to sell his collections to tourists and as his popularity grew he opened couture salons in Nizza, Italy and in Monte Carlo. In 1931 the fashion house merged with Agnes-Drecoll, although Beer dresses continued to be made until 1953. Located at 7 Place Vendôme, Paris.

Alice Bernard
Parisian Couture House
c.1916 – c.1926

Little is known about the Maison of Alice Bernard although its designs featured in several publications throughout the first half of the 1920s. A reference appears in the French press when in 1923 the fashion house's seamstresses went on strike over pay. Located at 40 Rue François, Paris.

Bernard et Cie
Parisian Couture House
Active 1920s and 1930s

Bernard et Cie was originally founded as a tailoring company in 1905 by M. Bernard in partnership with M. Jourda and M. Hirsch. The firm produced tailor-made costumes, afternoon dresses, evening gowns, coats and furs. Their garments were notable for their elegant slender silhouettes and elaborate detailing. In 1915, the New York Times stated, "Bernard, who is always an American favorite, has a collection of more than 100 modes". Certainly the famous American department store, Bonwit Teller carried many Bernard et Cie models, with prices as high as $550. The firm's heyday was during the 1910s and 1920s, however, it continued operating until the mid-1930s. Located 33 Avenue de l'Opera, Paris.

Jane Blanchot
Parisian Millinery Company
c.1921 – c.1949

Jane Blanchot was a sculptoress and continued to devote herself to her vocation, whilst also pursuing a career as milliner, which began in 1910 with the opening of an atelier in Paris. Until the 1960s, she designed hats, exploring sculptural forms and innovative structures. Her passion for sculpture also found an outlet in her creation of jewelry. After the war, as honorary President of the Chambre Syndicale de la Couture, she struggled to safeguard artisan perfectionism within the fashion profession. Located at 11 Faubourg St-Honore, Paris.

Doeuillet
Parisian Couture House
1900 – 1939

Georges Doeuillet was born in France in 1875. He started out as a silk merchant, and later trained with the Soeurs Callots as their business manager. He subsequently established his own eponymous fashion house in 1900, and the same year exhibited at the Paris Exhibition. He became the first designer to make *robe-de-styles*, what we now call cocktail dress. The house was best known for its detailed dresses and elaborate designs, and for parading live mannequins at the beginning of each season's showings. In 1915, he included in his collection, a black velvet and taffeta dress with the newly popular tiered handkerchief hem, and two years later introduced the barrel-line silhouette. In 1919, one of his gowns was a white satin brocade chemise with the new straight look and short skirt, which anticipated the look of the 20s. In 1926, he was fashionable up-to-date with his very short-skirted black satin dress, brocaded with flowers, with an uneven butterfly hem. Doeuillet had an exclusivity contract with *Gazette du Bon Ton* to promote his fashions. He took over from Doucet when the former died in 1929 and continued designing for both houses for nearly another decade. The house closed in 1937. Located at 24 Place Vendôme, Paris.

Drecoll
Viennese and Parisian Couture House
1900/02 – 1929

A Belgian baron, Christophe von Drecoll originally founded the House of Drecoll in Vienna in 1896. The house designed Belle Époque fashions for the Imperial family of Austria. In 1902 the Couture house Drecoll opened in Paris and was run by Monsieur and Madame Besançon de Wagner who had bought the business and the right to the name. In 1929 their daughter-in-law, the designer Maggie Rouff took over the business. In 1931 the firm merged again this time with Maison Agnès. Maison Agnès-Drecoll eventually closed in 1963. The maison was known for two distinct styles. In the Belle Époque period Drecoll specialised in fussy and luxuriously trimmed promenade gowns, tea gowns and evening dresses with boned bodices and full skirts. In the 1920s, however, the house was known for short, simple and elegant dresses. Located 130 Avenues des Champs-Elysées and 4, Place de l'Opéra, and later at 24 Place Vendôme, Paris.

Groult
Parisian Couture House
1912 – early 1960s

The sister of Paul Poiret, Pauline Marie Poiret (1887 – 1966) initially trained at her brother's house before setting up her own maison as Nicole Groult. She was married to the French decorator and furniture designer, André Groult (1884 – 1966) hence the house name. She was known for two styles in particular – simple black dresses with coloured detailing and colourful tea dresses. Located at 29 Rue d'Anjou, Pairs.

Heim
Parisian Haute Couture House
1899 – 1967
Maison Heim
1930 – 1969

Jacques Heim started his career as the manager of Isadore and Jeanne Heim's fur fashion house. Around 1925 he set up a couture department for coats, suits, and gowns and in 1930 he opened his own couture house. Heim never allied himself to a particular look or style, which is the main reason why he is not remembered as a fashion innovator. Instead his fashions moved easily with the times, which was the key to the house's longevity. Heim was president of the Chambre Syndicale de la Couture Parisienne from 1958 to 1962. Located at 48 Rue Laffitte, Paris.

Jenny
Parisian Couture House
1908 – 1938

The House of Jenny was known for its simple and comfortable sports fashions and leisurewear. In 1927 Jenny designed the wardrobe for Miss France. In 1938, Jeanne Bernard merged her firm with the house of Lucile Paray. It finally closed in 1940 when the Germans occupied Paris. Madame Bernard died in 1961 at the age of 89. Located at 70 Avenue des Champs-Elysées, Paris.

Jeanne Lanvin
Parisian Couturier
1867 – 1946
Maison Lanvin
1909 – present

Jeanne Lanvin trained as a milliner at Madame Félix and as a dressmaker at Talbot. She later became a member of the Syndicale de la Couture in 1909. Lanvin started making children's clothes after being asked for copies of the dresses she had made for her daughter. Soon she was also dressing their mothers and coordinated mother and daughter outfits became a mainstay of her work. Lanvin was famed for her exquisite "robes de style" – dresses inspired by historic styles characterised by full skirts sometimes supported with petticoats or panniers. In the 1920s Lanvin opened shops devoted to home interiors and lingerie. Lanvin also opened a menswear boutique in 1926 and was responsible for the decoration of the Pavilion d'Elegance at the 1925 "Exposition Internationale des Arts Décoratifs et Industriels Modernes". After her death the House of Lanvin was passed down to her daughter Marguerite di Pietro and is still in operation today having changed hands several times. Located at 22 Rue du Faubourg Saint-Honoré, Paris.

Jeanne Margaine-Lacroix
Parisian Couture Designer
c.1889 – c.1929

Jeanne Margaine-Lacroix rose to fame during the Belle Époque period. Margaine-Lacroix won a gold medal for corsetry at the 1899 Paris exhibition She is credited with creating the Sheath dress and slashed skirts (1912) and the Sylphide corset and sinuously curved Sylphide dress. In 1908, three models wearing her tight empire style gowns were arrested at the Longchamp racecourse for their own safety as their garments were considered too shocking (it is suggested they were so tight they split at the sides when the models bent down). During WWI she collaborated with artist Albert Marque and commissioned him to create a hundred fashion dolls, which she clothed in French historic outfits and regional costumes. Louis Sue of Sue & Mare designed the shop's interior. Located at 19 Boulevard Haussman and later at 29 Avenue du Marigny.

Martial et Armand
Parisian Couture House
Active 1920s – 1940s

There are references to Martial et Armand of Paris as far back as 1830 but it is unclear what the firm was producing at this point or if this was indeed the same firm as the couture house. The house is mentioned often in 1920s fashion magazines as specialising in couture dresses, furs and lingerie. The house launched its own perfume around 1924, while the designer Pauline Trigere trained at the house in the 1930s. Located at 10 Place Vendome and 13 Rue de la Paix, Paris.

Below
Five designs for the first days of spring – a black dress by Welly Soeurs, a red dress by Jean Patou, a black coat by Heim, a fur trimmed jumper suit by Jean Patou and a brown crepe dress with a patterned sash. *Le Femme Chic*, c.1925

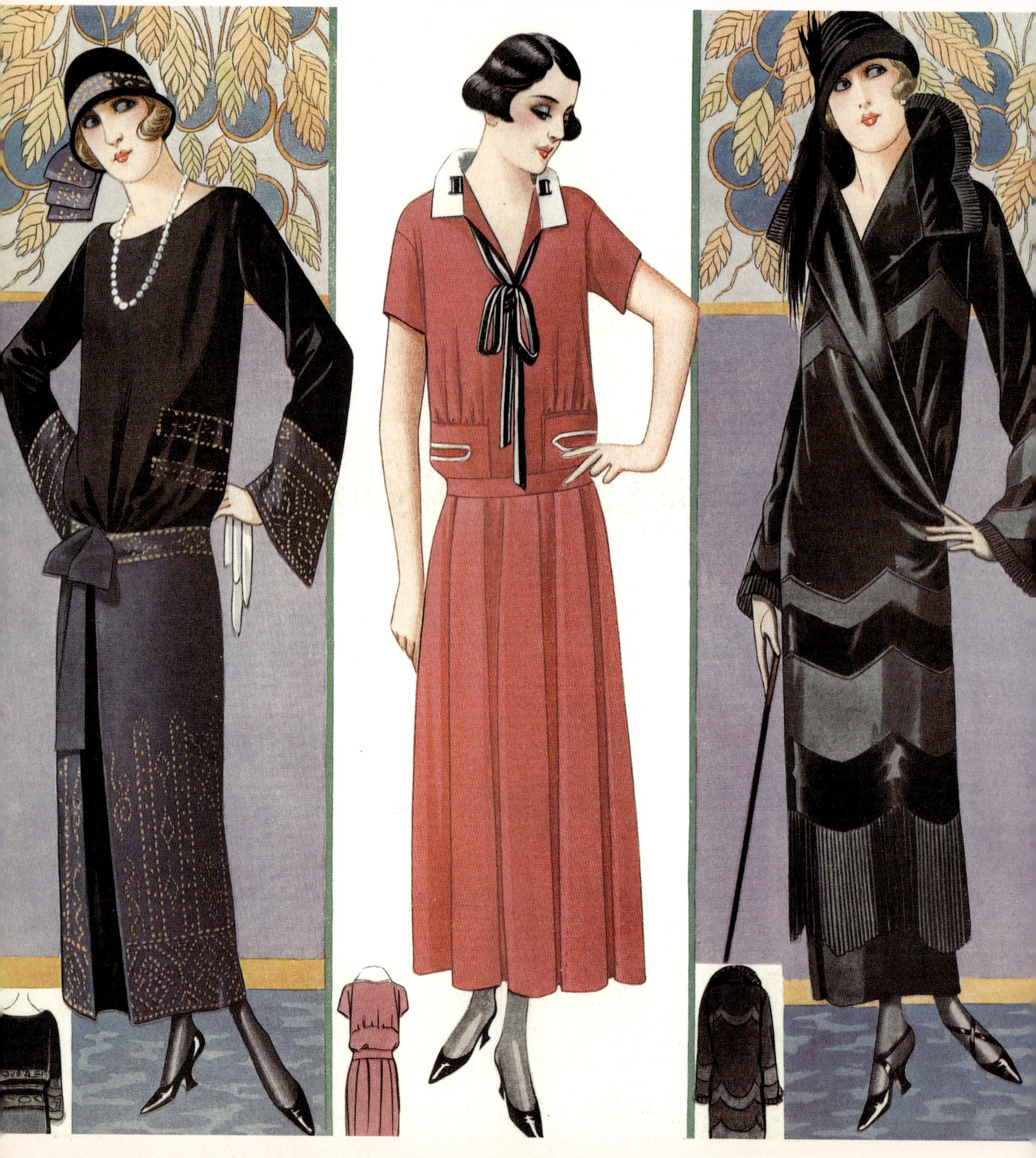

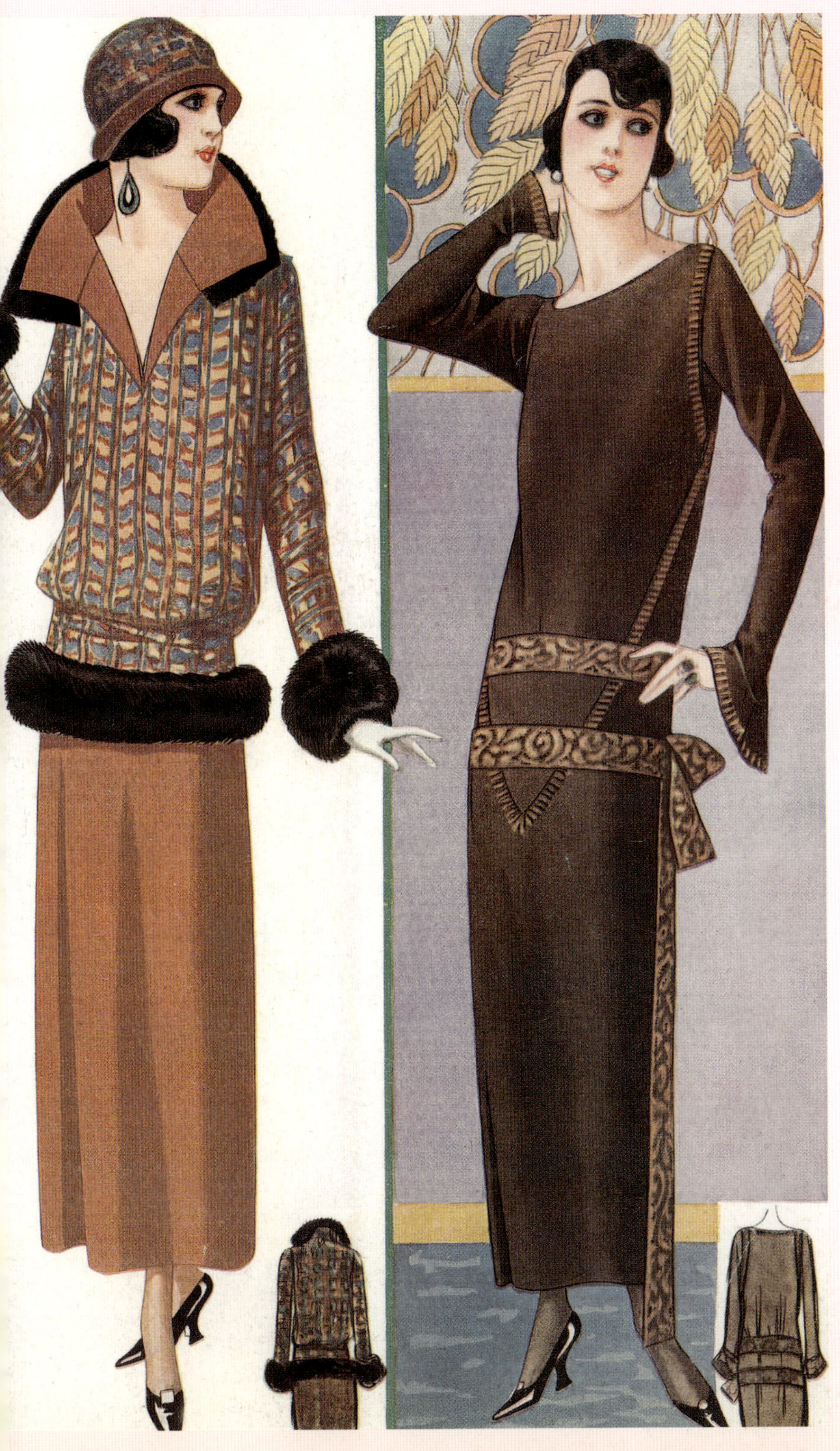

Selected Biographies

Mignapouf
Active 1920s & 1930s
Parisian Couture House of Exclusive Children's Clothing

Established by Cécile Welly, Mignapouf was the premier fashion house to specialise in the creation of stylish children's clothes and garments for young adolescent girls. Often these clothes cost as much as their adult haute couture equivalents. Mignapouf also designed patterns for McCall's in 1927 and 1928. Located at 12 Rue Bloissies Anglais & 130 Boulevard Haussmann, Paris.

Patou
Parisian Couture House
1919 – present

Jean Patou (1880 – 1936) opened the small dressmaking shop called Maison Parry in 1912. After serving in WWI he returned to Paris and reopened his business under his own name. Patou was best known for his sportswear and sports fashions. He dressed tennis legend Suzanne Lenglen both on and off the court. In 1925 he opened a Parisian boutique named Le Coin des Sports (The Sports Corner), a shop with a series of rooms each devoted to a different sport. Outfits and accessories for aviation, riding, swimming, tennis, golf and several others were stocked and met with great success. Patou capitalised on the leisure industry and opened salons in the upmarket resorts of Deauville and Biarritz selling his trademark casual chic fashions.
He was the first designer to embellish his sweaters and sportswear with his initials and he launched the first designer sun lotion 'Huile de Caldée' in 1928. The house has stopped producing fashion collections but remains open as a perfume house Located at 7 Rue Saint-Florentin, Paris.

Élise Poret
Parisian Couturier
Active 1910s – 1920s

Little is known about the Parisian fashion designer, Élise Poret other than she created elegant Belle Époque dresses during the 1910s. She also designed lingerie and nightwear. During the 1920s she also designed Grecian-inspired ensembles. Located at 20 Rue des Capucines

Paul Poiret
Parisian Haute Couturier
1879 – 1944
Maison Poiret
1903 – 1929

Poiret began his design career by selling sketches to Madeleine Chéruit. In 1896 he was hired by the fashion designer Jacques Doucet, and later moved to the House of Worth in 1901. He established his own fashion house in 1903, and made his name with the kimono coat. Mostly remembered for his straight silhouettes, his hobble skirts, harem pantaloons, lampshade tunics and for liberating women from the s-bend corset and petticoats.
He equally had a shrewd instinct for marketing and branding, promoting the total designer lifestyle and established the perfume company, Rosine and the interior decorating company, Atelier Martine. His influence on modern fashion both in terms of design and business achievements is formidable. He was one of the first courtiers to introduce perfume into his product line. By 1920s, however, his luxurious Oriental fashions were being supplanted by more functional and rational styles. Poiret took part in the "Exposition Internationale des Arts Décoratifs et Industriels Modernes" of 1925, where he showed his creations in barges along the River Seine, however, such an expensive display appears to have been a financial disaster and the house was eventually forced to close in 1929. Located at 1 Rond-Point des Champs-Elysées, Paris.

Premet
Parisian Couture House
1911 – 1931

Madame Charlotte, often referred to as the most beautiful woman in Paris and easily recognisable with her pale mauve hair, succeeded Mme. Lefranc as head-designer for Maison Premet in 1918. The house is best known for its 1923 'La Garçonne' model, a simple black dress with white collar and cuffs. Over a million copies of the dress are said to have sold in the USA alone. Premet is credited with introducing the 1920s "gamine look" by raising hemlines, pioneering low cut backs and the use of light and floaty materials. In 1923 Germaine Krebs, (later known as Alix and then Madame Grès) trained with the house for several months. In 1928 Premet collaborated with watchmakers Elgin to produce an exclusive design for the American market. Located at 8 Place Vendôme, Paris.

Redfern
Parisian & London Couture House
est. 1881 – 1940

Charles Poynter Redfern (1850 – 1929) was the son of English designer John Redfern, who had been the dressmaker to Queen Victoria and various members of the British aristocracy. In 1881 Charles Poynter Redfern established his own fashion house in Paris, which became known for his elegant blue ladies' suits as well as for the elaborate costumes that he created for actress Sarah Bernhardt. He also employed extremely attractive sales assistants to promote his fashions and they became known as the "Redferns Bunnies". His tailoring section was directed to the market generated by the famous Cowes week held every August. While his son, Ernest, managed the London branch of the business, Redfern himself looked after the company's Paris branch. Other branches were also opened in Cowes, London, Edinburgh, Manchester, Paris, Nice, Aix-les-Bains, Cannes, New York, Chicago and Newport, Rhode Island. In 1892, John Redfern & Sons was formally incorporated and so began its development from the most successful ladies' tailoring business to an international couture enterprise equal of Worth. The company's aggressive advertising in the most important fashion journals in Britain and the cultivation of royal patrons made a 'Redfern' the desired dress of women around the world. By 1885, Maison Redfern was producing yachting, riding, and travelling suits and was not only the officially appointed dressmaker to Queen Victoria, but also counted the Empress of Russia as another client. In 1916 Redfern designed the first women's uniform for the Red Cross. In 1911 he declared that "the cultured American lady is the best-dressed lady in the world" and he continued to create elegant if somewhat sombre fashions during the 1920s. The Redfern fashion houses closed in 1932, briefly reopened in 1936, and closed again in 1940. Located 242 Rue de Rivoli, Paris & 27, Old Bond Street, London.

Jane Regny
Parisian Couture House
Active 1920s & 1930s

A keen golfer and tennis player, Jane Regny was sports editor of the *Annuaire des Golfs* and specialised in sports fashions. During the 20s and 30s, she was as well known and successful as Chanel and Patou for her comfortable and stylish creations. Located at 11 Rue de la Boetie, Paris.

Reville
London Couture House
1906 – 1949

Mr William Wallace Terry Reville and Miss Rossiter, who had both previously worked as buyers for Jay's department store, founded Reville in 1906. During its existence the company operated under several names and was the court dressmaker to Queen Mary, designing her coronation robe in 1911. William Wallace Terry Reville worked as the house's designer, while Rossiter was in charge of running the business. It gained a royal warrant in 1910, which ensured it subsequently became patronised by the leading members of London society. By the 1920s Reville's garments seemed rather outdated, as they did not seamlessly adapt to the newer modern styles like some of their competitors, and the firm eventually merged with the London branch of Worth during the late 1930s. Located at 15 – 17 Hanover Square, London.

Suzanne Talbot
Parisian Modiste and Couture Milliner
c.1914 – c.1947

Suzanne Talbot's real name was Madame Mathieu Levy and she is considered one of the most important modistes of the 20th century. Lanvin was apprenticed with Talbot and she was an early patron of Eileen Gray and commissioned her to design her stylish apartment in Rue de Lota, Paris in 1919. Located at 10 Rue Royale, Paris.

Welly Soeurs
Parisian Couture House
Active 1920s – 1930s

Specialising in couture clothes and sportswear, the Welly Soeurs fashion house was founded by Cécile Welly and her sister. The former was also responsible for founding the children's couture house, Mignapouf. Located at 21 Faubourg Saint Honore, Paris.

Worth
Parisian Couture House
1858 – 1956

Charles Frederick Worth (1825 – 1895) established the first haute couture house in Paris in 1858, offering bespoke garments chosen by clients from a seasonal portfolio. Maison Worth had the royal patronage of Empress Eugénie and Princess Pauline von Metternich. The fashion house was known for its exquisite designs and execution. It was also one of the first couture houses to extend its name to luxury perfume in 1924. After Worth's death, his sons Gaston-Lucien and Jean-Phillipe took over the business which merged with Paquin only two years short of its centenary in 1956. Located at 7 Rue de la Paix, Paris.

Below
Illustration of various winter outfits.
La Mode, 1920

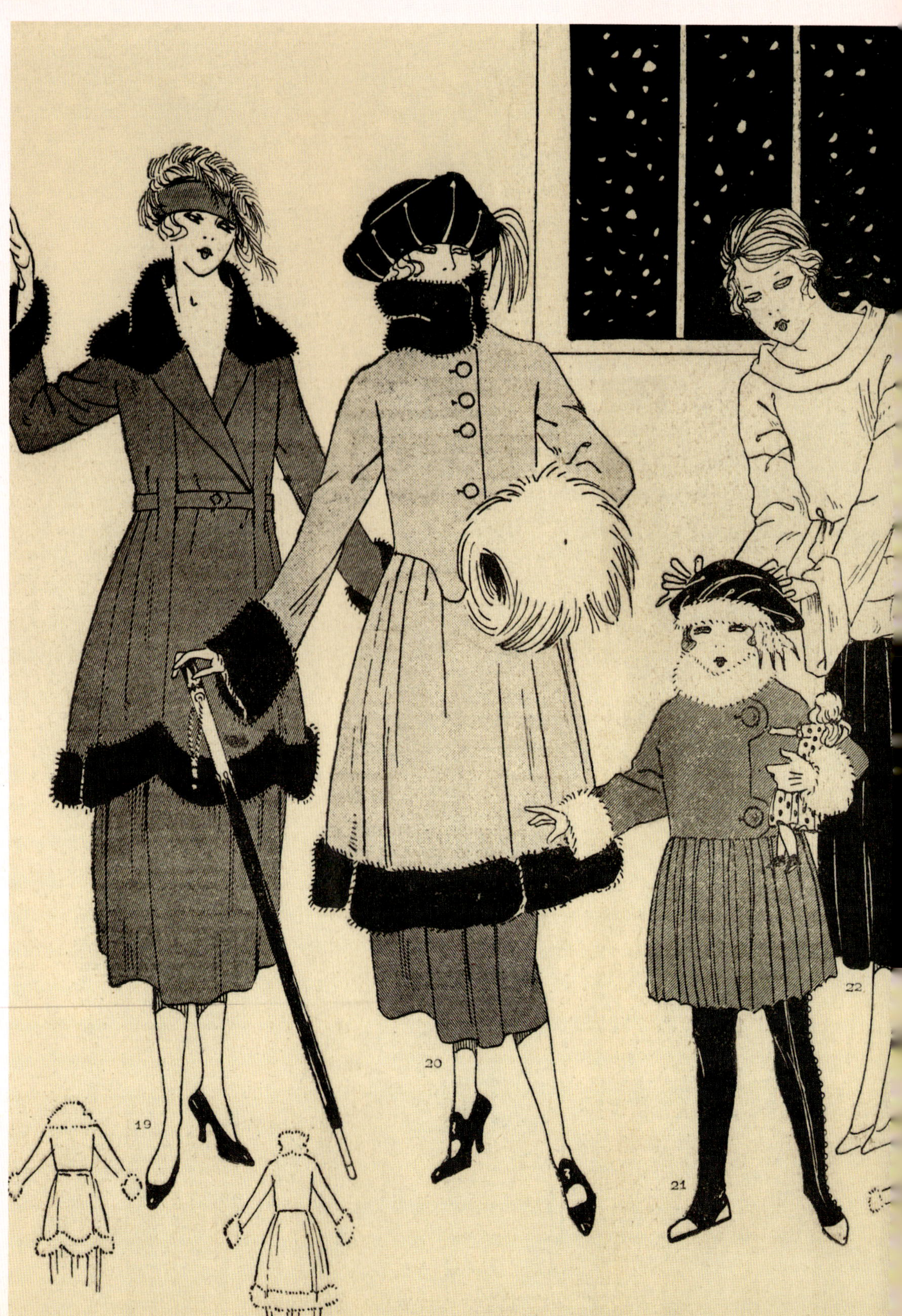

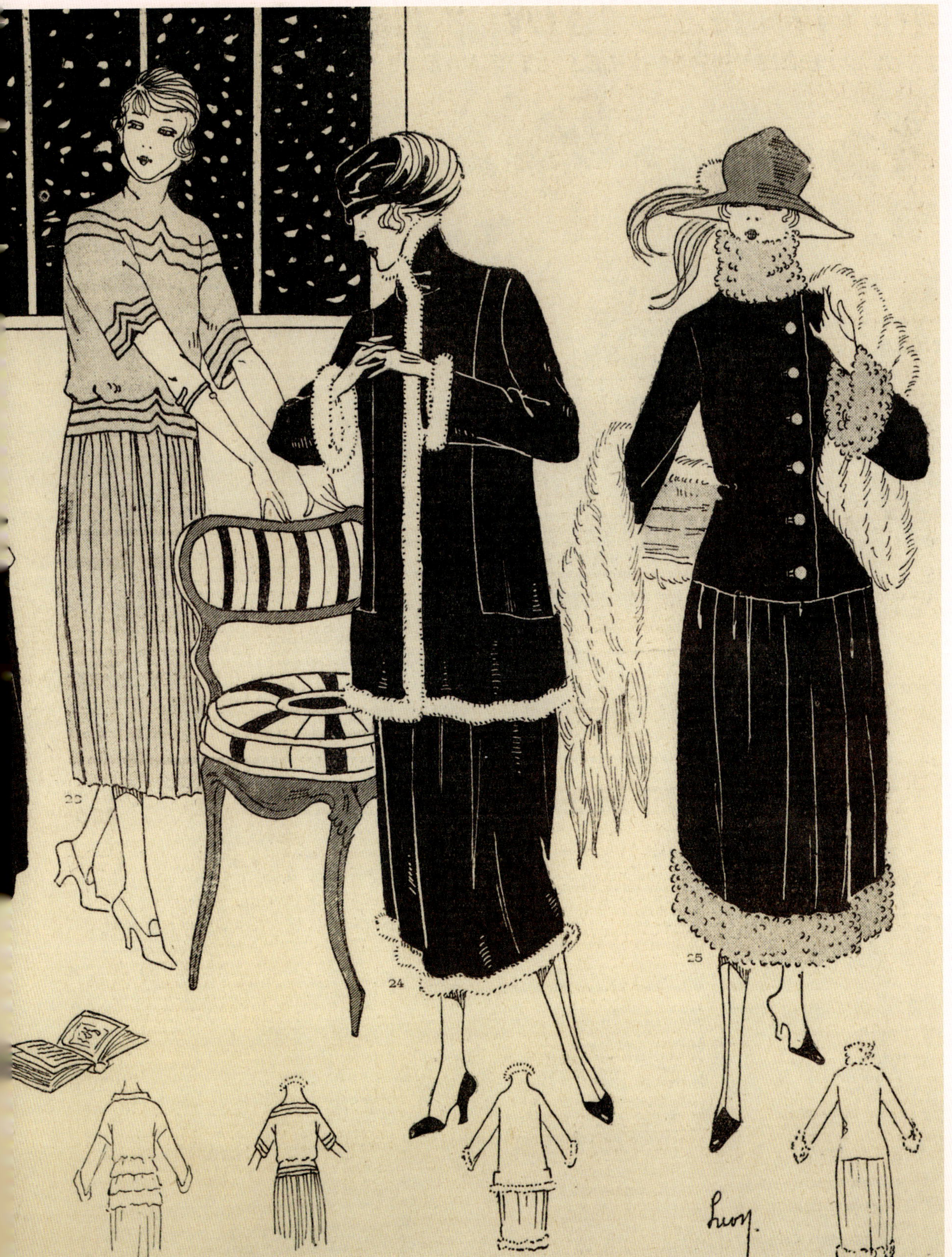

Index

Bibliographies

1920s Fashions from B.Altman and Company, Dover Publications, 1999

Baudot, F., *A Century of Fashion*, Thames & Hudson, 1999

Blackman, C., *20th Century Fashion: the 20s and 30s Flappers and Vamps* Heinemann Library

Blum, S. *Everyday Fashions of the 20's* (Dover Books on Costume), Dover Publications, 1999

Chadwick, W., *The Modern Woman Revisited: Paris between the Wars*, Rutgers University Press, 2003

Chahine, N., Beauty: *The 20th Century*, Universe, 2000

Chenoune, F., *Hidden Femininity: 20th Century Lingerie*, Assouline, 1999

Entwistle, J., *The Fashioned Body: Fashion, Dress and Modern Social Theory*, Polity Press, 2000

Gaines, J. & Herzog, C., *Fabrications: Costume and the Female Body*, Routledge, 1990

Herald, J., *Fashions of a Decade: 1920s*, Facts of File Inc., 2006

Hollander, A., *Seeing Through Clothes*, University of California Press, 1993

Horwood, C., *Keeping Up Appearances: Fashion and Class Between the Wars*, The History Press, 2011

Kirke, B., *Madeleine Vionnet*, Chronicle Books, 1998

Langley, S. & Dowling, J., *Roaring '20s Fashions*: Deco, Schiffer Publishing, 2005

Lehmann, U., *Tigersprung: Fashion in Modernity*, MIT Press, 2000

Lehnert, G., *A History of Fashion in the 20th Century*, Konemann, 2000

Mackrell, A., *Coco Chanel*, Holmes & Meier, 1992

Martin, R., *Cubism and Fashion*, Metropolitan Museum of Art, 1998

Martin, R. & Koda, H., *Orientalism: Visions of the East in Western Dress*, Metropolitan Museum of Art, 1994

Mendes, V. & de la Haye, A., *20th Century Fashion*, Thames & Hudson, 1999

Muller, F., *Art & Fashion*, Thames & Hudson, 2000

Pattison, A & Cawthorne, N., *A Century of Shoes: Icons of Style in the Twentieth Century*, Chartwell Books, 1997

Rasche, A., *STYL: The Early 1920s German Fashion Magazine: Das Modejournal der frühen 1920er Jahre*, Arnoldsche, 2009

Richards, M., *Chanel: Key Collections*, Hamlyn, 2000

Steele, V., *Paris Fashion: A Cultural History*, Berg, 1988

Stewart, M., *Dressing Modern Frenchwomen: Marketing Haute Couture, 1919–1939*, The John Hopkins University Press, 2008

Vassiliev, A., *Beauty in Exile: the Artists, Models and Nobility who fled the Russian Revolution and influenced the World of Fashion*, Abrams, 2000

Watson, L., "*Vogue*" *Twentieth Century Fashion: 100 Years of Style by Decade and Designer*, Carlton, 1999

Wigley, M., *White Walls, Designer Dresses: the Fashioning of Modern Architecture*, MIT Press, 1995

Wilson, E. & Taylor, L., *Through the Looking Glass: a History of Dress from 1860 to the Present Day*, BBC Books, 1989

Wilson, E., *Adorned in Dreams: Fashion and Modernity*, Virago, 1987

Wollen, P., *Addressing the Century: 100 years of Art and Fashion*, Hayward Gallery Publishing, 1998

Credits & Acknowledgments

This project has been a wonderful learning experience as well as a fascinating trip into the world of fashion history. Firstly I would like to offer my immense gratitude to Emmanuelle Dirix for her good-natured perseverance and infectious passion, as well as for her insightful introduction and skillful captioning. I would also like to thank my daughter, Clementine for her help with picture sourcing and Guy Jackson for his work on the graphic design side of things, especially his tireless enthusiasm for getting the layout absolutely right. Thanks must also go to Zoë Fawcett for her help with the production of this title and to Rosanna Negrotti for her painstaking copy-editing. And lastly, an acknowledgement of gratitude to Isabel Wilkinson and her forensic checking of captions. A big thank you to everyone!

We regret that in some cases it has not been possible to trace the original copyright holders of early publicity photographs or images from earlier publications. We have, however, endeavoured to respect the right of third parties and if any such rights have been overlooked in individual cases, the mistake will be correspondingly amended where possible.

The all images used in this publication were sourced from the Fiell Archive, London, with the exception of:

Emmanuelle Dirix: Breakspread, 20, 204, 205, 494, 495, 546, 547

TopFoto (TopFoto.co.uk): 208 – 209